THE GOTHIC

Literary Sources and Interpretations through Eight Centuries

The Gothic

Literary Sources and Interpretations through Eight Centuries

BY PAUL FRANKL

PRINCETON, NEW JERSEY
PRINCETON UNIVERSITY PRESS
1960

L. C. CARD 57-5471

Publication of this book has been supported in part by a generous grant from the Institute for Advanced Study, Princeton, New Jersey.

Printed in the United States of America

By Princeton University Press, Princeton, New Jersey

Foreword

In this book have been assembled comments and commentaries on Gothic which have to do with its basic principles. It is not a bibliography nor a collection of historical data relating to the individual buildings, but is concerned with the question of what has been thought and written about the phenomena of Gothic as a whole since Suger.

This at least was to have been the subject when I began the work nineteen years ago. In the course of time, however, a number of special problems closely connected with the general theme have cropped up, which, while they have deepened the scope of the book, have also added considerably to its size.

Many authors, particularly among those writing after 1850, have been purposely omitted. Earlier writers whom I have overlooked may be tracked down by other scholars who are interested in the history of art history. Undoubtedly, however, since the collection of sources and authors assembled here is already very large, the attention of critics will be focused mainly upon the interpretations which I have attempted.

It was originally planned to close the book with the year 1944, the eight hundredth anniversary of Suger's document, but since that time several publications have appeared which cannot be ignored. A chapter written on the recent historians of Gothic was finally excluded because the basic approach of Dehio, Lasteyrie, Bond, Porter, etc. is simply a reflection of that of other scholars. They are of value chiefly because they present the facts which had been so far established, or supposedly established. The theories of these scholars, insofar as they are their own, are discussed independently.

The center of gravity of the book lies in the actual quotations. In the text they have almost all been translated into English, while in the footnotes, for purposes of reference, many of them are given in the original language. Some texts are contained in the appendices.

The illustrations are intended in some instances to clarify certain points for the reader, as for example, the drawings of Christopher Wren and of Viollet-le-Duc; in others, they are provided for his amusement, as in the case of the illustration used by James Hall to demonstrate his theory of Gothic.

A foreword is the place to thank publicly those who have assisted the author. I think with gratitude of many librarians who consider not only the finished books and the catalogues, but also the living authors. A long list of acknowledgments to all those of my colleagues who have drawn my attention to obscure sources could be added, but I mention only Dr. Erwin Panofsky of Princeton, who checked over almost all of the translations of the Latin texts, and Dr. Josepha Weitzmann-Fiedler of Princeton, who helped me in many ways including the reading of the proofs.

In another sense, I express my gratitude to the Institute for Advanced Study in Princeton, for providing me, since my departure from Germany, with the material support which has enabled me to continue my work as an art historian. I give my thanks to Dr. Frank Aydelotte, to his successor, Dr. Robert Oppenheimer, and to the Trustees.

The text was written in German and was originally intended for a German publisher, who, however, withdrew because of the rising cost of publication. The very accurate English translation I owe to Mrs. Priscilla Silz of Princeton.

Princeton, New Jersey
January 1959

CONTENTS

ILLUSTRATIONS

PLATES

(Following Index)

TEXT FIGURES

ERRATA

For text:

Page 316, line 6, for Fig. 44 read Fig. 45
Page 391, line 19, for Fig. 55 read Fig. 53

For illustrations:

Captions for Figures 20-22, 27, 34-36, 38-39, 42, 52, and 57 should read as in the List of Illustrations above.

I. SOURCES FROM THE GOTHIC PERIOD

1. Abbot Suger of St.-Denis

The church of St.-Denis in the city of the same name is situated north of the gates of Paris. It was, in a certain sense, more distinguished than all the cathedrals of the Isle-de-France and of the surrounding principalities which comprise modern France; for here is buried, together with his two companions St. Rusticus and St. Eleutherius, the leading missionary of Gaul, St. Dionysius. According to legend he was a native of Athens, was sent to Gaul after the year 240, and suffered martyrdom about 250.[1] One version of the legend relates that after he was beheaded on the *mons martyrum* in Paris he picked up his head and carried it five miles to the place where he wished to be buried. His grave occasioned the building of a church, though probably not until 475, through the efforts of Ste. Geneviève. Beginning with the death of King Dagobert I in 638, St.-Denis became the burial place of the French kings and therefore, according to secular rank, the foremost church in the land.

As a result the abbots of St.-Denis were close to the royal house. However, not all the abbots managed to derive full benefit for their abbey from these friendly relations. Abbot Adam I (1099-1122) had secured certain privileges for his abbey but at his death the monastery was badly disrupted, both the religious discipline of the monks and the economic production of the monastery lands.

When Suger (1081-1151) was appointed Adam's successor in 1122, he faced a difficult task and the way in which he accomplished it would in itself create respect for his character and his administrative gifts, but it would not have connected his name with the history of art. This ensued only when the abbey revenues had been placed on a sound basis and had permitted him to renew the dilapidated and inadequate church. By this reconstruction he gained a lasting place in the history of Gothic architecture. But Suger was also a writer; he devoted three treatises to an account of the building and consecration of his work, and that assures him of a lasting place in the literature of art as well.[2]

1 Sumner McKnight Crosby, *The Abbey of St. Denis,* New Haven, 1942, pp. 24-40. From the same author: *L'Abbaye Royale de Saint-Denis*, Paris, 1953, p. 5.

2 Richard Albert Lecoy de la Marche. *Œuvres complêtes de Suger*, Paris, 1876. Julius von Schlosser, *Quellenbuch zur Kunstgeschichte des abendländischen Mittelalters* (*Quellenschriften für Kunstgeschichte*, N.F., VII, Vienna, 1896, pp. 268ff.), gives only excerpts. Everything that concerns the historian of art can now be found in the original text, together with an English translation and commentary, in Erwin Panofsky, *Abbot Suger on the Abbey Church of St.-Denis and Its Art Treasures*, Princeton, 1946. For particulars about the manuscripts see p. 145; for

Suger appears to have been born in St.-Denis. His parents, people of humble estate, sent him to the monastery school of St.-Denis, where he became the friend of Prince Louis, the son of King Philip I (1060-1108). Since Prince Louis, later King Louis VI, the Fat (1108-1137), was of the same age as Suger (both were born in 1081) and was also a pupil of the abbey school, the boys became classmates.[3]

Philip I himself showed such great confidence in the young Suger that he sent him as his diplomatic representative to the Roman Curia. From that time on Suger was constantly in intimate contact with the great political events in Europe. The strongest forces with which the French kings had to reckon were the popes, the German emperors, the English kings, and the principal monastic orders, that is to say, the Cluniacs and the Cistercians. The latter were at that time represented by no less a personage than St. Bernard (1090-1153), who criticized the monastic life of St.-Denis and was not satisfied with Suger until he had reformed his abbey according to the Rule of Cluny. St. Bernard preached against all luxury in church construction and from his ascetic point of view also objected to Suger's building enterprises.[4] That was only partially justified for the cause of the new work was originally not a desire for regal luxury but the dilapidation of the old church and the narrowness of its entrance, about which Suger has reported.

Of Suger's three treatises that deal with St.-Denis, the *Ordinatio*, written in 1140 or 1141, is the earliest. It contains regulations for the intramural life of the abbey, for festivities and banquets, for the care of the sick, and so on, and ends with a description of the consecration of the new westwork.

The second treatise: *Libellus alter de Consecratione Ecclesiae Dionysii*, aside from minor addenda, was written in 1144, immediately after the consecration of the choir. It is called "alter," the "second" little book on the consecration, because Suger here again refers to the consecration of the westwork, repeating verbally the section of the *Ordinatio* in question. But he enlarged his theme in two directions, recapitulating and continuing to the consecration of the choir.

Sugerii Abbatis Sancti Dionysii Liber de Rebus in Administratione

---

the dating of the three treatises see p. 144. Panofsky published supplements and emendations of his book: "Postlogium Sugerianum," *Art Bulletin*, XXIX, 1947, pp. 119 and 287.

Before Panofsky's English translation there appeared a French one: Dom Jean Leclercq, O. S. B., *Suger, Comment fut construit Saint Denis, Traduction et Introduction*, Paris, 1945.

[3] Otto Cartellieri, *Abt Suger von Saint-Denis*, Berlin, 1898 (*Historische Studien*, XI, ed. by E. Ebering).

[4] *Ibid.*, p. 21; Panofsky, *op.cit.*, pp. 10ff.

Sua Gestis, the third treatise, was composed probably between 1144 and 1149. It is divided into thirty-four chapters, of which the first twenty-three concern the administration, the rest the reconstruction of the church. This treatise contains important supplements, particularly about the portals, the stained glass, and church furniture.

Since Suger has incorporated in his second treatise the description of the consecration of the narthex contained in his first, the *Ordinatio*, and since, moreover, the description of this festivity, although interesting in itself, contributes nothing of importance to our main topic, we can restrict ourselves to the second and third treatises.

Suger relates in *De Consecratione* and in more detail in *De Administratione* that as a young man he witnessed highly dangerous crowding at the west entrance as well as in the choir of the old Carolingian structure of St.-Denis and that those conditions, which almost ended in fatalities, aroused in him the wish to rebuild the west entrance and the east choir. The crowds resulted from the belief that St.-Denis possessed the crown of thorns and a nail from Christ's cross, which were offered to the faithful on certain holy days to kiss.[5] Apparently the crowds were later so regulated that mortal danger to monks as well as laity was obviated because we hear nothing of the persistence of these incidents. Nevertheless Suger, from about 1130 on, was already preparing the new section, began it perhaps even before 1137 on the westwork and continued it with the choir from 1140 to 1144. It was the solemnity of the consecration of the westwork and later of the choir with the participation of many high church dignitaries that impelled Suger to take up his pen, for this son of simple folk was at least as proud of his social connections as of his reconstruction.[6]

The treatise *De Consecratione*, since it is the older one, may be considered first, and we shall observe the sequence of topics that Suger chose.

The introductory sentences affirm that his gratitude for all the divine mercies that he has experienced has caused him to put down in writing for posterity an account of the consecration of the choir. For modern readers it is important to dwell constantly on Suger's piety and to take his faith seriously, even though today interest is directed more toward the plenitude of dates concerning the history of the structure. Whoever

[5] Lecoy, *op.cit.*, p. 216; Panofsky, *op.cit.*, p. 86.

[6] Lecoy, *op.cit.*, p. 112, "de stercore erigens pauperem" (from the *Vita Ludovici*); or Panofsky, *op.cit.*, p. 48, "Quis enim ego sum, aut quae domus patris mei." There are numerous analogous sentences.

wishes to judge mediaeval texts correctly must learn to understand the complete interpenetration of the two realms of thought.

After he has sufficiently evidenced his devotion to God, Suger turns to the old church. Here he commits an error which is pardonable for his times. He used the *Gesta Dagoberti* of about 832 and in places copied them word for word; in so doing he overlooked the fact that the church about which he was writing was no longer identical with that of the seventh century but was that of the Abbot Fulrad, begun after 750 by Pippin and consecrated in 775 in the presence of Charlemagne.[7] There is now a monograph on this Carolingian structure by Crosby which permits a reconstruction of considerable authority, based on modern excavations. Although the exact dimensions of the western access do not appear from the excavated foundations and it remains unclear whether any or how many entrances existed in the old aisles, the inadequacy of a single portal on the west side is evident from Crosby's reconstructed ground plan.[8] In the east the apse was attached directly to the transept, according to early Christian custom. About 1137 Suger's architect was given the task of constructing three new portals in the west,[9] and in 1140 a second architect was commissioned to enlarge the choir, that is, to push back the apse far to the east and to provide it with an ambulatory.[10]

Suger goes on to say that for a long time before beginning the construction he had been searching for a quarry which could deliver stone that would match the marble columns of the old Carolingian basilica. From that we conclude that he had then no intention at all of tearing down the nave itself. He was afraid that the columns would have to be brought from Rome, from the Baths of Diocletian or other thermae, by sea and up the Seine to Paris. Perhaps the columns of the nave were

[7] Suger's error was probably first noticed by M. de Guilhermy, *Monographie de l'église royale de Saint-Denis*, Paris, 1848, p. 8. L. Leville discussed it more fully in *Bulletin monumentale,* 1907, p. 193, whence this correction was presumably taken over by E. Gall in *Die Gotische Baukunst in Frankreich und Deutschland*, Leipzig, 1925, I, p. 101.

[8] Even the most recent excavation gives no absolutely certain clue to the location of the west portal or west portals, etc. Sumner McKnight Crosby, "Excavations in the Abbey Church of St. Denis, 1948, The Façade of Fulrad's Church," *Proceedings of the American Philosophical Society*, XCIII, 1949, p. 347. According to Crosby's interpretation the reason for the crowding could be easily understood, for he assumes that between the northwest tower and Pippin's polygonal apse there was an entrance that afforded a passage of only two meters. But the interpretation given by Crosby is, according to himself, probably not yet the final one.

[9] The date of the beginning of the construction is usually given as 1137, but it might be assumed to be several years earlier.

[10] As is well known, it was a two-aisled ambulatory. Probably the press of the faithful was the reason why the architect did away with the partition walls of the chapels, thereby creating more space for the circulation of visitors and monks.

antique. Suger would not have hesitated to plunder Roman buildings, but he had been in Rome and could calculate the costs of such a long haul. Finally he found what he wanted quite near Paris in Pontoise. This quarry had previously been utilized only for millstones, and the pious abbot, inclined to interpret everything that pertained to his church as a miracle, says that the quarry had preserved its treasures for the house of God. But that was not miracle enough. "Whenever the columns (*columnae*) were hauled from the bottom of the slope with knotted ropes, both our own people and the pious neighbors, nobles and common folk alike, would tie their arms, chests, and shoulders to the ropes and, acting as draft animals, draw the columns up; and on the declivity in the middle of the town the diverse craftsmen laid aside the tools of their trade and came out to meet them, offering their own strength against the difficulty of the road, doing homage as much as they could to God and the Holy Martyrs."[11]

This is the earliest mention of a behavior similar to the so-called cult of the carts. Yet the help given in Pontoise was not a cult. By *columnae* are meant monolithic pieces. The jamb columns of the west portals were not so heavy that their transport would have caused difficulties; so it may be assumed that it is here a question of the link between the new narthex and Bishop Fulrad's Carolingian structure of the year 775. The new narthex was about ten meters distant from the west wall of the old nave. When the old west façade, together with the narthex behind it, was torn down, the distance was increased to about sixteen meters, necessitating the placing of three columns to the right and three to the left. It was these that were to be matched to the original series of columns. Usually the beginning of the cart cult is connected with the reconstruction of the narthex of Chartres in the year 1145; but, according to Suger's account, which refers to events of the period before 1140, St.-Denis had priority.

If Suger was unexpectedly helped by others in the transportation of the columns, he was obliged to help himself when the narthex was to be roofed over and twelve beams of the necessary length seemed hard to come by. The carpenters and woodsmen declared that all the large trees in the abbey forests had been depleted by the erection of defensive

[11] Lecoy, *op.cit.*, p. 219; in Panofsky, *op.cit.*, pp. 92, 93, "Quotiens autem columnae ab imo declivo funibus innodatis extrahebantur, tam nostrates quam loci affines bene devoti, nobiles et innobiles, bracchiis, pectoribus et lacertis, funibus adstricti vice trahentium animalium educebant; et per medium castri declivium diversi officiales, relictis officiorum suorum instrumentis, vires proprias itineris difficultati, offerentes obviabant, quanta poterant ope Deo sanctisque Martyribus obsequentes."

towers and bulwarks. But he went himself into the woods with his men and in a single day found the twelve trunks that his architect required. In that he again recognizes a divine miracle.[12]

After the porch had been completed and consecrated, as well as the *camera* above it, Suger postponed until a later time the erection of the upper stories of the towers and turned to the building of the choir. To understand the procedure in this part of the work, one must correctly distinguish Suger's choir from the present structure. This is possible with the help of Crosby's plans, but we shall not anticipate his investigations here.

The chief hindrance to a proper comprehension of the building process lay in the textual obscurities which have now been removed by Panofsky's translation and interpretation.[13] The relevant passage in his version is as follows: "Deliberating under God's inspiration, we choose—in view of that blessing which, by the testimony of venerable writings, Divine action had bestowed upon the ancient consecration of the church by the extension of [Christ's] own hand—to respect the very stones, sacred as they are, as though they were relics; [and] to endeavor to ennoble the new addition, which was to be begun under the pressure of so great a need, with the beauty of length and width. Upon consideration, then, it was decided to remove that vault, unequal to the higher one, which, overhead, closed the apse containing the bodies of our Patron Saints, all the way [down] to the upper surface of the crypt to which it adhered; so that this crypt might offer its top as a pavement to those approaching by either of the two stairs, and might present the chasses of the Saints, adorned with gold and precious gems, to the visitors' glances in a more elevated place. Moreover, it was cunningly provided that—through the upper columns and central arches which were to be placed upon the lower ones built in the crypt—the central nave of the old nave should be equalized, by means of geometrical and arithmetical instruments, with the central nave of the new addition; and, likewise, that the dimensions of the old side aisles should be equalized with the dimensions of the new side aisles, except for that elegant and praiseworthy extension, in [the form of] a circular string of chapels, by virtue of which the whole [church] would shine with

[12] Lecoy, *op.cit.*, pp. 221, 222; Panofsky, *op.cit.*, pp. 94, 96.

[13] For all details regarding problems of the translation (and the errors in the earlier attempts at translation by Levillain. Porter, and Gall) cf. the article by Erwin Panofsky, "Note on a Controversial Passage in Suger's De Consecratione Ecclesiae Sancti Dionysii," *Gazette des Beaux-Arts*, Sixth Series, XXVI, 1944.

the wonderful and uninterrupted light of most sacred windows, pervading the interior beauty."[14]

From these sentences we learn that Suger wished to preserve the nave and beautify the choir by greater length and width (Fig. 1). The Carolingian structure, which was completed in 775, had an annular crypt beneath the apse; some forty years later, Abbot Hilduin (814-841) built behind the apse a chapel whose floor corresponded to the level of the old annular crypt but the top of whose barrel vaulting extended higher than the vault of the old crypt. Suger, who, from a sense of piety, did not wish to destroy these parts, took the top of Hilduin's chapel as the floor level of his new choir. The difference between the ridge of the vault in the lower annular crypt and this new level was equalized by filling in. This increased the difference in level between the nave and the new choir, which was advantageous as far as the displaying of the relics was concerned. Since stairs led up to the choir from both sides, the visitors ascending them could get a good view of the treasures. The old apse of the Carolingian structure was torn down to the floor of this new choir, and on this level the new, that is, Gothic choir piers could be erected after the new Gothic crypt beneath them had been finished.[15]

Suger emphasizes the fact that the axis of Hilduin's chapel did not form a continuation of the nave axis. Such irregularities occur frequently in mediaeval buildings. The explanation is that the "orientation," that is, the facing east, was determined by the sunrise and depended entirely on what day this sighting was undertaken. Suger, on the other hand, wanted the new choir to continue exactly the direction of the central nave. His express mention of the success of this measuring is understandable if we visualize the situation. Probably the apse was left standing as long as possible, in order to continue services there. The architect began to set the first piers of the new crypt, back of the apse and back of Hilduin's chapel; in so doing, he was not able to sight directly along the inner axis of the central nave. He could mark the end point of this axis on the exterior of the apse, but here Hilduin's chapel was in the way. He had to use indirect measurement, which was not easy with the instruments of that day. Any mistake, from the

[14] Lecoy, *op.cit.*, p. 224; and Panofsky, *op.cit.*, p. 98. For this cf. also Crosby, *op.cit.*, p. 113. Panofsky, *op.cit.*, p. 220, interpreted the passage in the text correctly. My attempt at a reconstruction, there reproduced, has been partially superseded by Crosby's subsequent studies. Cf. Latin text, Appendix 1a.

[15] Cf. Crosby, *op.cit.*, p. 147 and fig. 86; also Panofsky, *op.cit.*, p. 220, the commentary to p. 100.

very first stone on, would be glaringly revealed when the apse was torn down and choir and nave were supposed to meet. The success of this filled Suger with such great admiration for his architect that he mentions it particularly, without naming the architect.

Only in exceptional cases do Gothic churches have a crypt. The reason for the building of a subterranean room beneath the choir in early Christian times is to be found in the cult of the burial place and relics of saints and martyrs. The form of the annular crypt developed when the tomb of an especially venerated saint was placed in the middle of the apse beneath the main altar and a semicircular passageway constructed along the wall of the apse, so that the worshipers reaching the center of the ambulatory could see or even touch the sarcophagus through an opening in the wall. This annular form of crypt was later enlarged, and there evolved the type of hall crypt with small apses, so that services might be held in the immediate vicinity of the tomb or the enshrined relics. It was a consequence of the rich elaboration of the crypts that the upper church was provided with a choir which also had a circular passage and chapels; but when such an elaboration of the choir grew to be the primary concern of the builder, the converse became necessary, namely, to give the crypt a corresponding form, even though the relics were brought up into the upper church and, liturgically speaking, there was no longer any real reason to retain the crypt. In St.-Denis we see a transitional case. Suger needed an elevated stage for the display of his precious relics; although we may well believe that his piety forbade him to lay hands on the two old crypts, it may be surmised also that these crypts served him very handily as a raised platform. The rest of the crypt no longer had any immediately obvious liturgical importance, and, therefore, in the case of new construction of Gothic churches the crypt is usually eliminated entirely, unless differences in terrain made it imperative, as for example, in Bourges or in Erfurt. The abandonment of the crypt in Gothic has been explained by the removal of the relic cult to the upper church, and the verse from the *Younger Titurel* cited, where we read that in the church of the Holy Grail there were no crypts to be seen, for one should "not proclaim Christianity in the crevices of the earth but in radiant space." It should not be forgotten that the German monks of Hirsau had abandoned crypts even in Romanesque time and that they were connected with the Cluniacs, so that perhaps through them the relinquishment of the crypt passed over to the Cistercians. Suger, therefore, would have had at his disposal a host of precedents for the suppression of the crypt. The bringing up of the relics into the upper church cannot be interpreted as specifically Gothic, any more than the retention of the crypt as specifically Romanesque. Whether a crypt is to be called Romanesque or Gothic is decided today according to the forms of each individual case. About that Suger has not said a word.

It is all the more important to see with what deep appreciation he speaks of the effect of the stained glass, even though this finds mention only in a subordinate clause. The glazing of windows goes back to Roman times and the staining of the panes perhaps to the ninth century of the Christian era. It is not known whether the Carolingian church of St.-Denis already possessed stained glass. Perhaps it did not even have glazing everywhere, for otherwise Suger could hardly say that the monks often fled into the open through the windows to escape the press of the laity (per fenestras cum reliquiis multoties effugerunt), unless one assumes movable casements. There is nothing extant of the earliest stained glass of the ninth and tenth centuries (except the small piece of Sery-Les-Mezières), the existence of which is indicated by written tradition. Until recently the figures of the prophets in the cathedral at Augsburg, which were supposed to be from 1065, were considered to be the earliest stained glass preserved to us; they are now attributed to a considerably later time.[16] In France there was probably stained glass at this period. For the Romanesque cathedral of Chartres, the predecessor of the present structure, there are donations for stained glass documented in the archives from at least 1097, but the glass itself has vanished. Further donations of stained glass followed in Chartres, of which the *Vierge de la belle Verrière* has been preserved. The accounts allow us to assume an already highly developed tradition, which Suger continued. What was new in his choir, however, was the *lux continua* the "continuity" of the stained-glass windows with their mysterious light, which gave to the whole choir a hitherto unknown effulgence, easily visible even from the nave, so that Suger could speak of their effect for the whole church. It was only this spatial continuity in the arrangement of the stained glass that produced the specific Gothic light, and, beginning with St.-Denis, stained glass remained an integral element of Gothic, even though its style itself remained for a time Romanesque.[17] With the expression *lux con-*

16 Albert Boeckler, *Zeitschrift des deutschen Vereins für Kunstwissenschaft,* x, 1943, p. 153.

17 Josef Ludwig Fischer, *Handbuch der Glasmalerei*, Leipzig, 1937, p. 5. The earliest historically documented stained glass was probably in the colored glass windows that Pope Benedict III (855-858) had installed in Santa Maria in Trastevere, if we are justified in assuming, as Fischer does, that these were really paintings on glass. It is, however, not very probable that

tinua Suger uttered the decisive principle. He writes thoroughly about the representations in the stained glass. How far the iconography can be called Gothic is an open question.

Suger's remarks just quoted are formulated as though the construction were still a project or only in its early stages, and even the comment on the stained glass can be understood to refer to the time when it was being ordered, although he is describing the impression that it made on him in 1145 after the completion and consecration of the choir. For Suger continues, apparently chronologically, to speak of the laying of the foundation stone of the choir and the arrangements for the building funds. Then only does the description of the choir begin, as it appeared in its completed state: "The *midst* of the edifice, however, was suddenly raised aloft by columns representing the number of the Twelve Apostles and, secondarily, by as many columns in the side aisles signifying the number of the [minor] Prophets, according to the Apostle who buildeth spiritually. *Now therefore ye are no more strangers and foreigners*, says he, *but fellow citizens with the saints and of the household of God; and are built upon the foundation of the apostles and prophets, Jesus Christ Himself being the chief cornerstone* which joins one wall to the other; *in Whom all the building*—whether spiritual or material—*groweth unto one holy temple in the Lord*."[18] If the choir were not preserved, no reliable reconstruction could be made from this indication of the number of the columns, for we do not learn how the columns were distributed in the space. Suger, however, was not writing for modern investigators. The important thing for him was the exegesis of the columns as symbols of the twelve apostles and twelve prophets, with reference to the Biblical quotation from Paul, *Ephesians* 2:19.

If one thinks in terms of the Christian scale of values with which Suger was so deeply imbued and of his primary interest in the cult, then it is no wonder that he does not attempt to say anything further about the architecture. To him it could only be the frame for the religious exercises. It is also understandable that he now turns to the detailed description of the chasses and their embellishment with gold and precious stones, then to the description of the enclosing structure which was to protect these chasses when they had been placed together in the

---

this technique originated in Rome, since stained glass is not subsequently found in Italy until 1250 in the west choir of the upper church in Assisi, and we must, in addition, recognize that it was produced by German glass painters.

[18] Lecoy, *op.cit.*, p. 227; Panofsky, *op.cit.*, p. 104. Cf. Latin text, Appendix 1b.

choir, and next to that of the frontal tablet, adorned equally richly with panels of gilded copper. Finally he tells of the altar, his new donation, in front of the "bodies of the Saints" where there had hitherto been none, and of the antependium which was decorated with especial magnificence, thanks to the gifts of the king and other princes. These furnishings were naturally more important for Suger than the architectural style, about which he maintains silence.

But he does, after all, return once more to the building, and relates how the vault of the choir was in danger of collapsing in the midst of a storm. He mentioned this event, of course, because he recognized another miracle in the fortunate escape from disaster, which in this case was to be attributed to the relic of St. Simeon. But for us this passage is of uncommon value, because he touches on a technical question which has been much debated in recent times.

The storm took place on January 19, 1143. The roof of the choir was already in place and the vaulting was being constructed beneath it. ". . . When the work on the new addition [the new east choir] with its capitals and upper arches was being carried forward to the peak of its height, but the main arches (*principales arcus*)—vaulted independently (*singulariter voluti*)—were not yet held together, as it were, by the bulk of the vaults, there suddenly arose a terrible and almost unbearable storm with an obfuscation of clouds, an inundation of rain, and a most violent rush of wind. So mighty did this [storm] become that it blew down, not only well-built houses but even stone towers and wooden bulwarks. At this time, on a certain day (the anniversary of the glorious King Dagobert), when the venerable Bishop of Chartres, Geoffroy, was solemnly celebrating at the main altar a conventual Mass for the former's soul, such a force of contrary gales hurled itself against the aforesaid arches (*praefatos arcus*), not supported by any scaffolding (*podium*) nor resting on any props (*suffragiis*), that they threatened baneful ruin at any moment, miserably trembling and, as it were, swaying hither and thither. The Bishop, alarmed by the strong vibration of these [arches] and the roofing, frequently extended his blessing hand in the direction of that part and urgently held out toward it, while making the sign of the cross, the arm of the aged St. Simeon; so that he escaped disaster, manifestly not through his own strength of mind but by the grace of God and the merit of the Saints. Thus [the tempest], while it brought calamitous ruin in many places to buildings thought to be firm, was unable to damage these isolated and newly made arches, tottering in mid-air, because it was repulsed by the power of God."[19]

The point to be determined is what is meant by *principales arcus* and how the words *podium* and *suffragia* are to be interpreted. In his book on Suger, Panofsky corrected most of the mistakes of earlier translators but realized only after his work was published that the former reading "principales arcus singulariter veluti voltarum cumulo cohaererunt" would have to be changed and the word *voluti* supplied for *veluti*. This change has been made in the translated passage just quoted. *Singulariter voluti* means "vaulted independently" and the *principales arcus* can then be only the transverse arches and, as a matter of fact, the ribs of the choir. The wall arches had already been raised up together with the wall; they are here designated as *arcus superiores*. That they existed is to be deduced from the fact that the roof was finished and it, of course, rests on the wall arches and the upper wall as a whole. The *voltarum cumulus* Panofsky has recognized as the upper part of the vault severies. The only point which still needs proper elucidation has reference to the scaffolding, already dismantled, for centering the ribs and transverse arches.

Panofsky has translated the word *podium* by scaffolding and *suffragia* by props; in his commentary he says: "Props here in all probability in the specific sense of centering." *Suffragia* are accordingly the wooden centerings for the stone arches, no matter whether it is a question of the transverse arches or the ribs. That is correct, and Panofsky's whole argument on pages 224 and 225 is convincing, but it fails to explain why the *podium* was removed before the masonry of the severies was completed. What does *podium* or scaffolding mean in this case? What scaffolding is it and what did it look like? Was it a horizontal board platform or a staging rising from the floor of the choir? One can only understand the word *podium* if one knows what a mediaeval scaffolding for a ribbed vault really looked like. The probability that one could have been preserved intact was very slight, but, nevertheless, by a mysterious chance, such a centering scaffolding is still intact today. This unique object is to be found on the island of Gotland in Sweden. The church in Lärbro has a tower with a vault fitted into its top story under the roof. Here almost the whole of the centering scaffolding was left standing (Fig. 2), just in one small place have the sheathing boards been removed from one of the severies. The work can only have been broken off for a very urgent reason: war, stoppage of the workmen's

[19] Cf. Latin text, Appendix 1c.

pay, or the death of the contractor? One can let fancy have free rein. Since no one had any business in the upper story of the tower, the centering structure, once abandoned, was preserved through the centuries and forgotten until modern investigators recognized its archaeological value.[20]

Whereas the centering in common use today is constructed of boards that are sawed to fit the particular curve desired, we see here round timbers, small in diameter, which have been simply bent.[21] This curvature is obtained by bracing other round timbers of the same kind, set aslant, against them. Some stand on horizontal beams which are laid diagonally through the center and the corner points of the octagonal space and some on boards underneath these beams. The church seems to date from the fourteenth century, around 1330; the scaffolding for the centering is, accordingly, from a much later time than the scaffolding which Suger mentions, but it can hardly be doubted that this method of curving round timbers was in use from the eleventh century on, and originated perhaps in Normandy, making the assumption undeniable that it was carried over directly from shipbuilding. The same carpenters who were given the task of preparing for the first ribbed vaults in Durham or some other Norman or English city used automatically their accustomed method of constructing the ribs of a boat or ship, and there was no reason to substitute a better one for it. If it was still being used in the fourteenth century in Sweden, it is all the more probable that in St.-Denis it was the exclusive method, when the construction of masonry ribs was only two generations old.[22]

A glance at the scaffolding in Lärbro proves that by *suffragia* are to be understood the curved timbers that lie under the ribs, that is to say, the centerings themselves, but that *podium* is to be taken as the whole

[20] Sigurd Curman and Johnny Roosval, *Sveriges Kyrkor*, II, Gotland, 1935, p. 93, figs. 150, 152. In 1933 during the meeting of historians of art in Stockholm, Mr. Roosval drove Messrs. Hamann, Conant, Hahnloser, and me to this church. Mr. Hahnloser took several photographs, which he has allowed me to publish and for which I wish to express my gratitude here.

[21] In the Middle Ages there were no mechanical saws. Boards were hewn with an axe in such a way that each trunk produced only one board.

[22] However plausible the suggestion of the analogy to the ribs of a ship may be, the masons and stonemasons of the Roman, Byzantine, Carolingian, and Romanesque buildings, before cross ribs were constructed, must have had a method of erecting true semicircles, or segments of arches, as centerings for arcades and archivolts. Whether that could have been carried out exactly with round timbers is doubtful. One can make hypotheses, but for the time they will probably remain merely hypotheses. Perhaps miniatures showing scaffoldings will afford further help. In his review of Panofsky's book on Suger, Kenneth John Conant identifies the "principal arches" with "the range of clerestory windows" (*Speculum*, 1953, p. 604). This interpretation is connected with that of the whole scaffolding, but there seems to be no relation of the *podium* and the *suffragia* to the arches of the clerestory windows.

centering scaffolding beneath them, although not a scaffolding below, if such be used, on which the horizontal crossed beams might lie. In Lärbro these are probably let into apertures in the wall or supported on consoles (the exact detail has escaped my memory); in all circumstances scaffoldings were erected very thriftily, even where wood was abundant, as in Sweden. The work was kept to a minimum since scaffoldings are only temporary aids. Suger, who saw during the building such a centering scaffolding poised at the level of the springings, does not use *podium* and *suffragia* pleonastically but is referring to two different parts of the whole scaffolding, DuCange, in his *Lexicon of Mediaeval Latin*, cites this passage from Suger. In the abridged edition, the editor (W. H. Maigne D'Armis or perhaps the chief editor Migne) writes: "Podium—Res quaevis, cui innitimur . . . et généralement tout ce qui sert à soutenir. . . ." Thus by *podium* is understood not so much the layer of crossed horizontal beams, although this can be included in the concept, but the round timbers, standing some vertically, some obliquely, which serve to brace the curved timbers. On the day of the storm, then, these standing round timbers that make up the *podium* had been removed, and, consequently, also the *suffragia*, since they rest on this *podium*; and they had been removed because otherwise it would not have been possible to fill in the masonry of the severies with the forest of round timbers preventing any free movement of the masons. It is, on the other hand, quite possible that the horizontal layer of beams had not been taken away, because on that could be laid a plank floor such as the masons would need later. The Bishop of Chartres could very probably look up through these beams and see the roof and the ribs standing free in space and the severies so far as they were finished. The visitor today to that centering scaffolding in Lärbro mounts to the loft on a ladder going up among the beams; the spaces are large enough for that, and in St.-Denis they must have been far greater.

This is probably a sufficient interpretation of the passage. The text says nothing about the method of constructing the masonry of the severies, whether on sheathing boards, as in Lärbro, or freehand; it gives no indication of whether Suger believed that the rib carries or, as a new theory would have us believe, does not carry. He was interested only in the miracle which rendered the storm harmless when the relic of St. Simeon was stretched forth. It is scarcely necessary today to wage a campaign of enlightenment against such miracles, but it may perhaps be said legitimately that the stability of the ribs, even without the staying masonry of the severies, is not such an astonishing miracle. The force of the wind struck the roof probably from one side only, in spite of Suger's expression "oppositorum ventorum impetus." The roof must have been so constructed in itself as to withstand the pressure of the wind. That it shook does not necessarily mean that it affected the upper walls strongly enough for the arches, both the transverse arches as well as the diagonal ribs, to be in danger of collapsing. At any rate, the transverse arches would be then the more seriously threatened, for the diagonal ribs braced each other reciprocally. But we need not doubt that the whole system of roof and isolated arches swayed, and that this looked exceedingly ominous, because the usual assumption is that such constructions should not move at all.

Suger concludes his *Libellus* with the detailed description of the final consecration of the choir on June 11, 1144.

His third treatise, *De Administratione*, was probably written after 1144 and completed before 1149. As we have said above, this work, from Chapter xxiv on, deals with the building of the abbey church. It offers, in part, supplements to what has already been said in *De Consecratione.*

Here belong the details of the façade in Chapter xxvii. Bronze casters and sculptors, brought to St.-Denis especially for this work, made the doors of the middle portal (*valvae principales*). These were adorned with scenes from the Passion, Resurrection, and Ascension and were gilded. "Also we set up others, new ones on the right side and the old ones on the left beneath the mosaic which, though contrary to modern custom, we ordered to be executed there and to be affixed to the tympanum of the portal."[23] Suger was so interested in the cast doors that he forgot to say anything about the equally important stone sculpture of the portals. On the other hand, he stresses the fact that in one of the portals he re-used the old bronze doors, obviously those of the former Carolingian main portal, and that in the tympanum above them he had a mosaic executed, which was perhaps a substitute for an older one, also Carolingian, but which was in any case a continuation of Early Christian tradition. If Suger's veneration for the old church is clearly revealed in all this, his insistence on having a new mosaic executed goes far beyond mere piety. Mosaics were scarcely reconcilable with the

[23] Lecoy, *op.cit.*, p. 188; Panofsky, *op.cit.*, p. 46: "Valvas siquidem principales, accitis fusoribus et electis sculptoribus, in quibus passio Salvatoris et resurrectio vel ascensio continetur, multis expensis, multo sumptu in earum deauratione, ut nobili porticui conveniebat, ereximus; necnon et alias in dextera parte novas, in sinistra vero antiquas sub musivo, quod et novum contra usum hic fieri et in arcu portae imprimi elaboravimus. Turrim etiam et superiora frontis propugnacula, tam ad ecclesiae decorem quam et utilitatem, si opportunitas exigeret, variari condiximus; . . ."

plastic character of Gothic style. There could occasionally be found in Italy the union of flat mosaic with strongly three-dimensional members of a Gothic structure, where Gothic supplanted the older habits only slowly; but to insist on the application of the mosaic technique in the Isle-de-France was a confession of loyalty to a bygone stylistic trend. From this passage can be detected the fact that Suger had grave difficulty in getting his wish carried out by the architect, who certainly was not pleased by this mosaic next to the sculptured archivolts of the portal. Its optical splendor contradicted what the architect intended by his decidedly plastic articulation, but Suger doubtless looked on the mosaic as a glittering ornament and had an especial fondness for anything connected with effects of light. He had a deep understanding for the significance of stained glass and probably did not comprehend why mosaics should have become old-fashioned since they, too, consisted of colored glass. In the light of our modern concepts we should say that a stained glass occurs in the midst of the wall-thickness and the whole relief of the architectural members is "read" outward from this plane toward the front; a mosaic, on the other hand, lies on the surface of the wall and, to our way of feeling, takes its place: mosaics are antiplastic and antistatic. Certainly the architect presented no such argumentation, but presumably he felt the difference between mosaic and stained glass much as we do.

Of the façade Suger mentions also the crenelations which he ordered "both for the beauty of the church and, should circumstances require it, for practical purposes." The present battlements are said to date from the fourteenth century.[24] As is well known, this appurtenance of fortified structures is not to be considered a normal feature of Gothic churches, although perhaps many cathedrals were once crowned with battlements which later vanished; Reims, for example, originally had them.[25] Possibly it was not so much the Abbot Suger, who was concerned for the defense of his church, as the king, who knew his Parisians and thought that during popular uprisings the tombs of saints might be safe but not those of royalty. It is even more probable that the battlements served to defend the *camera* of this westwork, which was perhaps a treasure room.

Suger then speaks of this upper *camera* and the erection of the upper stories of the towers,[26] but says very little about the nave. The reason

[24] Gall, *op.cit.*, p. 103 n. 1.

[25] According to the drawing and the text of Villard de Honnecourt; cf. below p. 47.

[26] Lecoy, *op.cit.*, p. 188; and Panofsky, *op.cit.*, p. 48. The façade today makes a rather

ought to have been made clear from other passages of the text already cited, namely, that he did not intend to tear down the Carolingian nave. Crosby's excavations have proved that the construction of a new nave was not undertaken during the time of Suger's administration, aside from the connection with the westwork by two piers.[27] The Carolingian nave remained standing until the erection of the High Gothic structure by Pierre de Montereau in 1231.

We learn nothing more about the architecture than what was contained in the earlier treatise. On the other hand, Suger writes again in great detail about the golden jeweled "crest" that embellished the tomb of St. Dionysius and about the golden crucifix with its equally rich adornment of precious stones. Here follows a passage in the text which must be quoted in entirety because it has been applied by Kingsley Porter to Gothic as a whole.[28] "*Every precious stone was thy covering, the sardius, the topaz, and the jasper, the chrysolite, and the onyx, and the beryl, the sapphire, and the carbuncle, and the emerald.* To those who know the properties of precious stones it becomes evident, to their utter astonishment, that none is absent from the number of these (with the only exception of the carbuncle), but that they abound most copiously." Suger begins the next sentence with the word "unde," and draws, therefore, from this connoisseurship, which he naturally claims for himself, the following inference: "Thus, when—out of my delight in the beauty of the house of God—the loveliness of the many-colored gems has called me away from external cares, and worthy meditation has induced me to reflect, transferring that which is material to that which is immaterial, on the diversity of the sacred virtues: then it seems to me that I see myself dwelling, as it were, in some strange region of the universe which neither exists entirely in the slime of the earth nor entirely in the purity of Heaven; and that, by the grace of God, I can be transported from this inferior to that higher world in an anagogical manner. I used to converse with travelers from Jerusalem and, to my great delight, to learn from those to whom the treasures of Constantinople and the ornaments of Hagia Sophia had been accessible, whether the things

---

flattened impression, and especially the portals create an effect of proportion not Gothic; the reason is that the terrain was considerably filled in to a height of 1.80 m, during the course of street improvements in the nineteenth century.

[27] According to Crosby, *op.cit.*, p. 3. Crosby's volume II will give more exact information on this point. The investigations in St.-Denis are not yet ended and constantly show surprising results. See Crosby's volume quoted above.

[28] Cf. Latin text, Appendix 2, according to Lecoy, *op.cit.*, p. 198; and Panofsky, *op.cit.*, p. 62. This passage begins with the quotation from Ezek. 28:13.

here could claim some value in comparison with those there. When they acknowledged that these here were the more important ones, it occurred to us that those marvels of which we had heard before might have been put away, as a matter of precaution, for fear of the Franks, lest through the rash rapacity of a stupid few the partisans of the Greeks and Latins, called upon the scene, might suddenly be moved to sedition and warlike hostilities. . . ."

Kingsley Porter has said of this passage: "These words of Suger, written in the middle of the twelfth century, when Gothic architecture had not yet emerged from the mists of the early morning twilight, express more happily the peculiar qualities of this art, than any modern criticism that has ever been spoken. . . . In all the long centuries that have rolled by since the days of Suger, who has stood beneath the soaring vaults of a Gothic cathedral, without, however unconsciously, repeating to himself this time-worn but ever new thought of the abbot of St.-Denis? It is this peculiar quality which for lack of a better term we may call emotional power, that separates Gothic from all other architectures and raises it to the supreme height."[29] Granted that Suger's words give excellent expression to our feelings at the sight of Gothic cathedrals, nevertheless, Porter commits an error; for though Gothic architecture may affect us with mystical emotion, Suger is not talking of architecture at all: he is speaking of the precious stones, the sardius, the topaz, and the rest, which many admirers of Gothic cannot identify and which do not induce in them the same spiritual rapture that Suger experienced or that Gothic induces in Porter. It should not be considered inconceivable that Suger could have experienced or actually did experience, through absorption in Gothic architecture with its ribbed vaults, pointed arches, and so forth, the same mystical rapture as Porter, but he did not say so.

One should also be careful, therefore, not to misunderstand the comparison with Hagia Sophia. More recent literature on this church never wearies of repeating that Justinian exclaimed at its consecration: "Praise be to God, through whose grace I have fulfilled this work; I have surpassed thee, Solomon!"[30] The modern reader of Suger may be tempted

[29] Arthur Kingsley Porter, *Mediaeval Architecture*, New Haven, 1915, II, p. 252.

[30] The oldest source for this anecdote that we possess today seems to be Georgios Kodinos, who did not live earlier than toward the end of the fifteenth century. The text can be found in Ducange, *Historia byzantina*, Paris, 1680, liber III, paragraph v, p. 9; also in Migne, *Patr. Gr.*, 157, col. 628, and in the edition of Immanuel Bekker, *Georgii Codini Excerpta de Antiquitate Constantinopolitanis*, Bonn, 1843, p. 143: "He drove in his chariot from the royal doorway to the ambo and, with hands outstretched, he uttered the following words, Praise be to God, through whose grace I was deemed worthy to fulfill such a work. I have surpassed thee,

to insinuate that he meant to say: Justinian surpassed Solomon, I have surpassed Justinian. But it is highly improbable that Suger knew the anecdote of Justinian's exclamation given by Georgios Kodinos; furthermore, he definitely had at his disposal no clear description, far less depiction, of Hagia Sophia. Above all, however, he is again not speaking of the architecture but of the church treasures. The pilgrims tell him that the *treasures* of St.-Denis are greater and more valuable than those in Hagia Sophia. Because the treasures in Constantinople are kept under lock and key, Suger concludes that it must be the result of fear of the rapacious Franks, and he is proud that in St.-Denis such things can be publicly displayed. Here there was not as much need for this fear.

With these remarks everything of importance for our topic has probably been extracted from Suger's writings. Do these passages contain anything about Suger's personal conception of Gothic? It would seem at first glance that the reply to this question must be negative. For the modern critic Gothic means either the evocation of a sense of infinity and mystical transcendentalism, as Porter indicates, or, for more matter-of-fact critics, the attenuation of the wall as a consequence of ribbed construction, and so on—we shall meet all variations. Suger seems to have nothing specific at all to say of Gothic in this sense. Yet he talks about it. He was no aesthetician, no historian of art, no architect. He was most certainly not the designer and draftsman of the architectonic composition and its details. Rather was he a cultured and gifted monk, the abbot of his monastery; and the abbey's sacred relics, which it was his duty to guard but also to make accessible to the people, were the core of his existence. He believed in the miraculous power of all these unusually distinguished relics, which had to do, not with a saint of inferior grade, but with the missionaries of Gaul and Christ himself. For the sake of these relics he undertakes the reconstruction; it is they that by their cultic or religious power of attraction provide the financial means, the building materials, and the decorations, together with those

Solomon." The excerpts of Kodinos go back to several older works. The treatise, *Patria,* that Kodinos used chiefly, dates even from 995 (under Basilios II), according to Karl Krumbacher, *Geschichte der Byzantinischen Literatur*, Munich, 1897 (2nd ed.), p. 423. Krumbacher (*loc.cit.*) indicates the sources of the *Patria.* The section on Hagia Sophia, however, goes back to a special treatise that is perhaps even older than the other sources of the *Patria.* It is, therefore, quite possible that the anecdote, which is always cited unquestioningly in modern times, was transmitted by a contemporary of Justinian and a witness to his exclamation. From all this it appears that Suger could have known the story, but we cannot say with certainty that he did. If the anecdote used to be told to the pilgrims in Constantinople (which we do not know), Suger could have learned it in this way. But that is pure fancy.

precious gems and noble metals. For him the Christian faith is shot through with miracles, mysticism, magic, and superstition, deeply believed. His metaphysics of light, the mystical, or, as he says, wonderful (*mirabilis*) light of the stained-glass windows, the sparkle of jewels open to him the way to God. In conscious opposition to St. Bernard he says that the adornment of his church cannot be costly enough to match the costliness of the relics.[31] Art and splendor are for him a part of the worship of God. His most sublime symbol for God was certainly that light which God created on the first day, even before he created the sun. This light, not identical with physical light, may well have had for him the meaning of the words at the beginning of the Gospel according to St. John. Architecture is not only formed stone and formed space, it is also formed light. Suger speaks neither of the style of the stone forms nor of that of the space forms, but he does speak all the more eloquently of that of the light in the chapels of the choir, of that specifically Gothic light which has a material origin but which is such a significant symbol of that spiritual world never very far from Suger's thoughts.

But the use of jewels, stained glass, or symbolism is in itself not Gothic. The magical power of gems is an ancient belief of humanity; it is as old as the habit of symbolism; and the art of staining glass was practiced even in Carolingian time. A formulation can be most easily found for the latter: that the specifically Gothic character in St.-Denis lay in the completeness with which all the windows of the choir chapels were filled with colored light. Of symbolism, as it was represented in Suger's comparison of the columns to the apostles, it can only be said that it was especially cultivated and systematized in the Gothic era. Of the mysticism and magic of gems it may be roundly asserted that they are not characteristics of Gothic but can be associated with any style. To this complex of questions we shall return.

An evaluation of the so-called cult of the carts leads to another difficulty. This cult was unquestionably new and contemporaneous with the beginnings of Early Gothic in St.-Denis. But that does not make it "Gothic." The fact that nobles and common folk alike harnessed themselves to the carts had no influence on the style of the churches; and, conversely, it was surely a matter of complete indifference to those ascetics, whether the stone blocks that they dragged had a Romanesque or a Gothic profile. But the cult of the carts is rooted in a religious enthusiasm which also colored other facets of contemporary culture.

31 Lecoy, *op.cit.*, p. 229; Panofsky, *op.cit.*, p. 106.

The politics of the age is dominated by the stimulating idea of the Crusades and by an intensified hope of establishing the *civitas dei* on earth. Metaphysics of light, symbolism, the cult of the carts, and crusades do not explain Gothic, any more than Gothic could explain those phenomena. They all, however, have their common roots in the heightened religious fervor of that generation. Gothic architecture expressed in its language what was taking place in those other intellectual fields. For art is form as the expression or, more precisely, the symbol of the spiritual content inherent in this form. Just as Suger was filled with the ideas of his generation, so must the architect have been who worked for him; he must have been inspired by the same religious enthusiasm. But, beyond that, he had to have the gift of making the form strongly expressive of that spirit that linked him with the ideas of his generation, and, furthermore, he had to have the sobriety that distinguishes the true artist from the amateur: he had to be master of his craft. Suger expressed precisely what united him with his architect; on the factual side of the building program he touches upon everything that had to do with the liturgy, but he was silent about the style of the architecture. In this way he put his finger on that which constitutes the intellectual foundation of Gothic; he spoke only of one of its two factors, that is, of its deeper *meaning*, without having the ability to say anything of the other factor, its stylistic *form*, which lends expression to that deeper meaning. Suger is, therefore, a literary source only for the one side of Gothic, but for this he is an exceedingly rich one.

Suger's architect, or rather his two architects, since it must be assumed that another man is responsible for the choir than for the westwork, are in their determining qualities as specialists dependent on the evolution which had begun in Durham with the appearance of the ribbed cross vault. To discuss this evolution is not the purpose of this book, but however it may be reconstructed, Suger himself must have been in some degree affected by it. He traveled widely; not only was he in the Rhineland and in Rome but he studied from 1104 to 1106 in Burgundy, probably in St.-Benoît-sur-Loire, and was from 1107 to 1112 *praepositus* in Berneval-le-Grand and in Toury in Normandy.[32] From his twenty-sixth to his thirty-first year, at an age when a man is still receptive to the new aims of his generation, he was, then, in the midst of a region where the early experiments with the new ribbed construction were being carried out. In 1130, at the age of forty-nine, he was in Cluny, where the new porch was in process of building. It

32 Cartellieri, *op.cit.*, p. 126.

belongs to the history of Gothic architecture as the history of the monuments themselves to discuss whether he could have learned something for his church in Normandy, for example, in Rouen, or in Burgundy, that is to say, in the porch of Cluny, or whether he could have obtained his architects from Normandy or Burgundy. The main thing is that he picked an architect who was trained in Gothic. It becomes evident that this was not so absolutely a routine matter, if one realizes that at that time, in the decade from 1130 to 1140, the Romanesque style reached its peak of maturity. One would like to assume that when he was faced by the choice of building his reconstruction in the old or in the new style—for neither was there a name—he must have reflected on the difference. That he says nothing about that, proves ultimately only that he did not yet possess the necessary concepts and, therefore, the necessary technical terms for a stylistic comparison; it does not prove that he did not recognize the difference. He most certainly recognized it and he decided in favor of the new style so far as Gothic was already in existence in buildings of transitional style, as in St.-Étienne in Beauvais or the porch in Cluny.[33]

2. Gervase of Canterbury

WHAT we miss in Suger we find half a century later in Gervase of Canterbury (ca. 1141-ca. 1210), his successor in the literature on Gothic. He speaks in detail of the architecture itself and emphasizes its specifically Gothic characteristics, using the old and the new choir of Canterbury as examples in a stylistic comparison that remained unrivaled for many centuries.

Stubbs,[1] the editor of Gervase's works, has tried to reconstruct the biography of the man from his writings. From them it may be presumed that he was born around 1141 in the county of Kent. Nothing is known about his family. In 1163 he became a monk in Canterbury and there witnessed the strife of Henry II and Thomas à Becket, Archbishop of Canterbury. The king demanded that the clergy should submit to the jurisdiction of the state. An irritated, perhaps not seriously intended remark of the king caused four knights to proceed to Canter-

[33] This chapter was written before 1947. Marcel Aubert's book about Suger, published in 1950, is excellent in its complete survey of all sides of Suger's life and personality, but it does not enter into the problems which had to be discussed in the present investigation.

[1] William Stubbs, *The Historical Works of Gervase of Canterbury*, I, London, 1879, Preface.

bury in 1170 and strike down the Archbishop before the altar of the cathedral. Gervase does not seem to have been an eye-witness of this murder, but he attended the funeral on the following day. Not active in politics himself, he observed with a keen eye the struggle for domestic power in England and Europe, siding with the church, though privately, in his voluminous chronicles.

Of all these works, which fill two stout volumes, only the short "treatise on the fire and the rebuilding of the cathedral of Canterbury" is fruitful for our subject.[2] The conflagration occurred on September 5, 1174. Since the chronicle ends with the enthronement of Archbishop Baldwin in May 1185, Stubbs was of the opinion that Gervase did not begin his history until after that date, and his literary activity in general is thought not to have started before this. But the description of the fire is so lively as to permit the assumption that the monk made notes about events of interest immediately and merely needed to put them together at a later date. One is inclined to explain in this way the transposing of a spatial description of the cathedral into a chronological sequence of structural processes; of course, one might prefer to credit Gervase with conscious employment of this Homeric means of genetic exposition to lend immediacy and vividness to his account, or one could see in it simply an imitation of the usual method of chronicles in stringing annals together.

The fire broke out in houses surrounding the old church, built in 1070. While efforts were being made to extinguish the flames there, it passed unnoticed that the wind had carried sparks onto the choir roof and that the choir was also beginning to burn. It was already too late when people saw it. The monks attempted to save the relics, curtains, and robes; selfish lay persons made use of the confusion to commit theft. Not only was the choir destroyed but also the infirmary and the Lady Chapel. But the nave was preserved, as the fire stopped at the wall of the tower over the crossing and the arms of the transept. Here a new altar was erected until the choir could be restored. Then architects were summoned from England and France to make their proposals, but for

[2] *Ibid. Chronica Gervasii, pars prima, Incipit tractatus de combustione et reparatione Cantuarensis ecclesiae.* This tractate was partially translated by W. Woolnoth, *A Graphical Illustration of the Cathedral of Canterbury . . .* , London, 1816, pp. 16ff.; he omitted what he did not properly understand, but also made mistakes where he thought he understood. Robert Willis, on the other hand, *The Architectural History of Canterbury Cathedral*, London, 1845, made a perfect English translation, providing also very good explanations for the technical expressions. His translation is the basis of the one given here, likewise his analyses of the structural history, which are for their time extraordinary in their clarity and correctness. Cf. also what Carl Schnaase, cited below in note 8, has written about Gervase.

a long time no decision was reached because some declared that the piers could be retained, while others advised tearing everything down. Finally the choice fell upon Master William of Sens, Gervase calls him "vir admodum strenuus," an energetic artificer (*artifex*) in wood and stone. All the other architects were dismissed, and he was engaged "because of the liveliness of his spirit and his good reputation." He convinced the monks that all of the old choir that was still standing would have to be torn down to ensure the new structure the necessary durability. Then he prepared the machines for the transport of the building materials and gave the masons the wooden models for the profiles: "Formas quoque ad lapides formandos his qui convenerant sculptoribus tradidit . . ." (page 7). With these preparations and the clearing of the building-site the first year came to an end.[3]

Here Gervase interrupts his history of the reconstruction and turns to the story of the three preceding phases in the growth of the cathedral. Only brief accounts of the oldest structures have been preserved.[4] A later edifice was described in detail by Edmer, a writer of the eleventh century,[5] and Gervase quotes this rather long text verbatim. In a history of architectural description this specimen would certainly receive a distinguished place. Here it may merely be remarked that Edmer says the church was "Romanorum opere facta." That was the contemporary designation for the style that we call today Early Christian or, as the case may be, Carolingian. This structure, erected in the time of Archbishop Odo (942-959), was completely destroyed by fire in 1067.

Archbishop Lanfranc (1070-1089) built a new church in the relatively short period of seven years. The ground plan of this stage in the building was determined quite accurately by excavations in 1895; it shows that Lanfranc adhered closely to Norman models, the abbey church of Jumiège being perhaps the prototype.[6] The latter had been finished in 1067 and was certainly known to Lanfranc because he had been educated in Normandy in the monastery of Bec, later became Prior there, and then in 1067 Prior of the monastery in Caen in Normandy founded by William the Conqueror (1066-1087), the Abbaye-aux-hommes.

[3] In this tractate Gervase reckons his years from the anniversary of the fire, September 5.

[4] A first, legendary church dated from Roman time. Bishop Augustine, the Apostle of the English, replaced this edifice in 597.

[5] Augustine's church was extensively renewed in 942; it is this edifice that Edmer describes.

[6] Willis' reconstruction of the ground plan was drawn before 1845, long before the excavations; *op.cit.*, p. 38.

Lanfranc's choir in Canterbury, however, proved to be too small even after only two decades. Prior Ernulph (1096-1107) began a reconstruction of the choir on a grand scale, preserving Lanfranc's old nave. This new choir was finished by Prior Conrad (1108-1126) and therefore goes by his name, although it was not consecrated until 1130. It was Conrad's choir that was destroyed by fire in 1174 and that Gervase described. Corresponding to these chapters in the history of the church, Gervase's whole interpolation consists of four parts: first, the description of the Carolingian structure according to Edmer; second, of Lanfranc's nave, which was preserved and which Gervase, therefore, had before him; third, of Lanfranc's choir, which he had never seen, so that he apologizes for having to be so brief in regard to it; and fourth, of Conrad's choir, which he describes in much detail. Of this latter section it may be remarked that he emphasizes the thickness of the walls and the smallness of the windows, without criticizing, but yet with his thoughts presumably on the Gothic reconstruction that must have seemed to him far to surpass the Romanesque choir. He speaks further of the triforium of this Romanesque choir: ". . . Above this wall was a passage, which is called triforium, and the upper windows." This technical expression does not occur here for the first time; it is found around 1170, thus only a few years before Gervase was writing, in the romance *Floir et Blancheflor*, verse 555. Gervase certainly did not mean here a gallery (tribune), for he speaks of a way or passage in the wall itself.

After his excursus Gervase returns to the account of Master William's work. Schnaase called this the most important document in the history of mediaeval building and he has incorporated many of Gervase's statements in his own discussion.[7] Here the whole passage must be quoted, closely following the original text (Fig. 15).

["William] . . . began to prepare everything that was necessary for the new construction and to tear down the old. With that the first year of the building was over [1175]. In the following year, after the Feast of St. Bertin [after September 5, 1175], before winter set in, he erected four piers, that is, two on each side; when winter was over he added two more, so that three stood in a row on each side. Above these and above the outside wall of the aisles he erected appropriate arches and vaulting, namely, three vaulted compartments (*claves*) on each side. I use the word keystone (*clavis*) for the whole quadripartite vault (*ciborium*), because the keystone, placed in the mid-

[7] Carl Schnaase, *Geschichte der bildenden Künste im Mittelalter*, III, Düsseldorf, 1872 (2nd ed.), p. 179. (Unchanged reprint of the first edition.)

dle, locks and unites the parts coming from each side. The second year of building ended with these works [1176].

"In the third year he set two piers on each side, adorning the two outermost ones [farthest to the east] with engaged columns of marble and making them main piers, since in them crossing (chorus) and arms of the transept were to meet. After he had set upon these the quadripartite ribbed vaults (*claves*) with the [complete] vaulting, he supplied the lower triforium from the principal tower[8] to the above mentioned piers of the crossing, that is, to the transept,[9] with many marble columns. Over this triforium he placed another of different material, and the upper windows. Furthermore [he built] the three ribbed vaults of the great vault,[10] namely, from the [old] tower over the crossing to the [new eastern] transept. All of this seemed to us and to all who saw it incomparable and worthy of the highest praise. Joyful, therefore, at this glorious beginning and hopeful of its future completion, we were solicitous to hasten the accomplishment of the work, our hearts full of fervent longing. With that the third year was ended and the fourth begun.

"In that summer [1178] he erected ten piers, starting from the transept (*crux*), five on a side. The first two of these he decorated with marble engaged columns and constituted piers of the crossing like the two other [western] ones. Above these he set ten arches and the vaults. But after the two triforia and the upper windows on both sides were completed and he had prepared the machines (*machinas*) for vaulting the great vault in the beginning of the fifth year [September 1178], he suddenly plunged to the ground, as beams gave way under his feet, stones and timbers falling with him, from the height of the capitals of the upper vault, namely, fifty feet. Painfully injured by the impact of the stones and timbers, he had become of no use to himself or the work, but no one else was in any way hurt. Against the master alone raged the vengeance of God or the malice of the devil.

"The master, thus injured, although he lay long in bed under care of doctors in the hope of recovering his health, was disappointed in his expectation and could not recover. Since, however, the winter [1178] was approaching and it was necessary that the upper vault be completed, he delegated the finishing of the work to an industrious and gifted monk, who had supervised the masons; whence much envy and intrigue resulted, because the monk, though younger, seemed wiser than others, richer and more powerful. The master, however, gave orders from his bed as to what should be done first and what later. Thus the vault between the four main piers was completed;[11] in the keystone of this quadripartite ribbed vault (*ciborii*) the choir and the arms of the transept seem, as it were, to convene (*convenire*).

[8] What is meant is the old tower over the crossing in Lanfranc's edifice.
[9] What is meant is the new western transept.
[10] Supply: of the nave of the choir.
[11] Here is meant the vault of the eastern crossing.

Two quadripartite ribbed vaults were also constructed on each side before winter [1178]. Heavy continuous rains did not permit of more work. With that the fourth year was concluded and the fifth begun [September 5, 1178]. In the same year, the fourth [1178], there occurred an eclipse of the sun [September 13, 1178] at the sixth hour before the master's fall.[12] Since the master knew that no art or diligence of the physicians could enable him to recover, he gave up the work and returned home across the sea to France.[13] He was followed, however, in the charge of the work by another of the name of William, of English descent, small in stature, but very wise and skilled in various kinds of work. In the summer of the fifth year [1179] he completed both arms of the transept, the southern and the northern, and constructed the vault over the great altar, the completion of which had been prevented by the heavy rains of the preceding year in spite of all the preparations.[14] Beside this, he laid the foundation for the extension of the church to the east, since there the chapel of St. Thomas [Becket] was to be built. This place, then, was destined for him, namely, the chapel of the Holy Trinity, where he had celebrated his first mass, where he was wont to prostrate himself with tears and prayers, under whose crypt he had lain buried for so many years, where God through his merits performed so many miracles, where rich and poor, kings and princes had revered him, from whence the sound of his praise had gone forth to all the lands of the earth.

"Thus Master William began to dig up the cemetery of the monks, because of the new foundation, and was compelled to exhume the bones of many holy monks. These were carefully collected and buried in a great pit in the corner between the chapel and the infirmary on the south. After he had made the foundation of the exterior wall of the strongest stone and

12 Stubbs explained the confusion of dates with regard to the master's fall as a corruption of the text. But one can accept the text as it is, if one does not identify the words "in anni quinti innitio" exactly with September 5, 1178, but takes "the beginning of the year" to mean the first days. The eclipse of the sun on September 13, 1178, was a partial one and visible in Canterbury between approximately ten and twelve o'clock. The fall occurred, then, about five o'clock in the afternoon of this same day. Thus, actually the fifth year is meant, beginning with September 5, 1178. Since Gervase says that the master had prepared the machines (scaffoldings?) for vaulting the great vault at the beginning of the fifth year, that refers to the first week of the fifth year of his reckoning. It might be interpreted that the master fell from the scaffolding just erected in the crossing. There is confusion in the words "in istis annus quartus completus est." In the course of the autumn after the fall the master's substitute completed the vault of the eastern transept, then the work was interrupted by rain, and winter began. "Annus quartus" can be here only the *calendar* year, that ends after winter begins, that is, the year 1178. This consideration may seem to be superfluous for the subject of Gothic, but for an appraisal of Gervase's reliability it is not. The date of the solar eclipse is found in T. von Opholzer, *Canon der Finsternisse,* Vienna, 1887.

13 That is, the charge of the work.

14 In the Middle Ages, as well as later and even today, it was customary to construct vaults only after the roof had been put in place. Suger's account of the storm that made the roof sway above the vaults in process of construction is an apposite illustration. Thus, in Canterbury the rain presumably prevented the completion of the roof and so, indirectly, of the vaulting.

cement, he also erected the wall of the crypt as far as the bases of the windows. Thus the fifth year came to an end and the sixth began [autumn 1179].

"As now the spring of this same sixth year after the fire approached and the time for the building was imminent, the monks wished with heartfelt longing to take up the work of the choir, so that they might enter it at the next Easter festival. When the master realized the monks' desire, he urged the work on manfully, to satisfy the wish of the convent. Therefore he carried up the wall that surrounds the choir and the presbytery with the greatest speed, and erected also the three altars of the presbytery. He carefully prepared the resting place of St. Dunstan and St. Elfege. A wooden wall to ward off the weather from the east was built across between the two next to the last piers on each side and it was provided with three glass windows. Thus they intended to enter the choir for the Easter Vigil [April nineteenth] with the Easter Fire, although the edifice, in spite of the most diligent efforts and the greatest speed, was scarcely ready. But since on that holy day of the Sabbath they could not do everything connected with the sacred festivities as it should be done, it was necessary to transfer the holy fathers, our patrons, St. Dunstan and St. Elfege, exiled with the monks, to the new choir beforehand."[15]

This latter was done and is painstakingly described by Gervase. The monks blame the Prior for the secrecy of the transfer, but the quarrel is settled and there ensues the entrance of the monks into the choir and its consecration on April 29, 1180. Gervase then discusses the position of the new altars, the start of the work on the chapel of Thomas, and the exhumation of Lanfranc.

Before he takes up the work of the seventh year, he interpolates the following observation, which contains for us the most important matter of the entire treatise:

"It was said above, that after the fire practically all the old parts of the choir were torn down and transformed into a new edifice of noble form (Fig. 3). But now it must be stated in what the difference of the two works consists. The form of the old and new piers is the same and also their thickness is the same, but their length is different. That is to say, the new piers were increased in their length by about twelve feet. In the old capitals the work was plane; in the new ones the chisel work is subtle. There, twenty-two piers stood in the passage around the choir; here, on the other hand, are twenty-eight. There, the arches and everything else had been made flat [in relief], as though done with an axe and not with a chisel; here, there is suitable chisel work on almost all things. No marble columns were to be found there, but here there are innumerable ones. There, in the passage

[15] Stubbs, *op.cit.*, p. 19. Cf. Latin text, Appendix 3a.

around the choir, there were quadripartite groined vaults (*fornices planae*); here, they are provided with ribs (*arcuatae*) and keystones (*clavatae*). There, a wall, built above the piers, divided the arms of the transept from the choir, but here, not separated from the crossing, they seem to meet in the one keystone in the middle of the great vault that rests on the four main piers. There was a wooden ceiling there, adorned with excellent painting; here, there is a vault, gracefully wrought of stone and light tufa. There is only one triforium; here, there are two in the nave of the choir and a third in the aisle. All this, if one wishes to understand it, will be revealed more clearly by the sight of the church than by words. In any case, this must be known, that the new work is as much higher than the old as the upper windows, both those of the nave (*corporis chori*) and those of the aisles of the choir, are raised by the marble intermediate story. But lest anyone in future times be doubtful as to why the great width of the choir next to the tower should be so much contracted at its head at the end of the church, I did not consider it superfluous to give the reasons."[16]

The reasons lie in the retention of the two towers that flanked the passage around Conrad's choir on both sides and that had withstood the fire. Gervase then continues his narrative. In the seventh year the crypt was finished. In the eighth there were constructed eight piers at the end of the choir, in addition, the vaults and the windows in the ambulatory, and the tower of the east crossing as high as the ledges of the windows under the vault. In the ninth year a pause ensued for lack of funds; in the tenth, the tower over the crossing was completed. From the last statements about the work on this tower and on the arms of the transept it is evident that, by exception, the roofs were constructed only after completion of the vaults. The treatise ends with the account of Archbishop Baldwin's election (1184).

In comparison with Suger's complicated manner of expression, Gervase's Latin is clear and unambiguous; only his technical terms are not immediately intelligible, and the translation of them given here requires justification.

The word *triforium* has already been discussed. It means what we mean by it, including the passages in front of the windows in the nave and the aisles of the choir.

The word *crux* does not mean in Gervase the whole transept, but each of the individual crossarms; thus, already in the description of Lanfranc's choir, he speaks of the *crux australis* and the *crux aquilonalis*,[17] and correspondingly in the description of the new eastern tran-

[16] *Ibid.* p. 27. Cf. Latin text, Appendix 3b.
[17] Stubbs, *op.cit.*, p. 19.

sept. *Chorus* he uses in a double sense: now for the crossing and now for the arm of the choir, sometimes even for the entire new addition. When he says, for example, that the last pier of the construction of 1177 was adorned with engaged marble columns, *chorus* means the crossing ("quia in eis chorus et cruces convenire debuerunt"), just as in the important passage where he says that the arms of the transept were separated from the *chorus* in the Romanesque edifice but, in contrast, in the Gothic seem to meet in the keystone of the *chorus*. On the other hand, *chorus* even means the whole reconstruction in the description of the entrance of the monks at Easter 1180; in other cases it is only the eastern arm of the choir. What Gervase means is always immediately evident upon a comparison of the text with the church itself; but as long as a language applies the same word to two or more different things it is not yet mature enough for unambiguous description.

For this reason Gervase's efforts to create technical terms for different vault forms are especially interesting. The word for vault in general, without distinction of species, is *fornix*. The quadripartite vault he calls *ciborium* and differentiates clearly quadripartite groined vaults from quadripartite ribbed vaults. The former he calls *fornices planae*, the latter *fornices arcuatae et clavatae* (Stubbs, page 27). Schnaase translated *fornices planae* by barrel vaults,[18] but in a note offered the alternative "groined vaults." R. Willis translates unsatisfactorily here, when he says: "the vaults were plane." If one looks at the ground plan of Conrad's choir, one will be convinced that it had quadripartite groined vaults and not barrel vaults.[19] Willis drew in quadripartite groined vaults in his reconstruction of the transverse section of Conrad's choir. The word *arcuatus* can be considered a development of the terminology of Suger, who, in the account of the storm, makes no distinction and calls the ribs *arcus* along with the rest of the arches of the vaults. *Fornices arcuatae* are accordingly vaults provided with arches and, since the *fornices planae* also have four arches on their edges, it is not these frontal transverse arches that are meant here, but the diagonal ribs. However, to prevent any misunderstanding, he designates the ribbed

18 Schnaase, *op.cit.*, p. 182 n. 2.

19 Alfred William Clapham, *English Romanesque Architecture before the Conquest*, Oxford, 1930, p. 86, lists the few examples of barrel vaults in the still preserved Romanesque buildings in England. None of these offers an analogy to Conrad's choir. The most significant example is St. John's Chapel in the Tower of London, ca. 1080. It may be added here that a suggestion, made in discussion, to translate "fornices arcuatae" by "domed vaults" is not acceptable, because the vaults of which Gervase speaks are not domed.

vaults further as *clavatae*. This word is derived from *clavis*, about which he previously remarked: ". . . clavem pro toto pono ciborio." He uses "keystone" as *pars pro toto* because it locks and makes firm the parts that meet in the middle. The manner in which he expresses himself permits the supposition that he invented this term himself because there did not yet exist a suitable, particular word for the new Gothic vault form, and he needed one for his description. In the comparison of styles he reverts once more to the ribbed vault, saying that it consists of stone and tufa. Here again it is clear how important it was for Gervase to make a distinction between the ribs constructed of stone and the vault severies made of light tufa.

In emphasizing the difference between Romanesque and Gothic vaults Gervase already foreshadows modern concepts, but it is much more astonishing that he attempts a comparison of stylistic principles at all and that he carries it out in his examples by means of the criteria of proportion, relief and profiling, dissolution of the wall, and spatial fusion. Only when one substitutes these modern words does it become clear what he really wanted to say and did say in his still undeveloped vocabulary.

Naturally he was not blind to the difference of proportions; he stresses the fact that the piers are considerably higher than in the Romanesque structure, that, in addition, the intermediate story changes the total proportion.

The capitals and arches of the Romanesque cathedral were shallow, as though hewn into shape with an axe. Only the archivolts, which lie in one plane, can be formed with an axe, but not the semicircularly curved intrados of the arches; however, Gervase doubtless means the whole rectangular profile of the arch. When he remarks that in the Romanesque church not only the arches but everything else is flat, as though shaped with an axe, he means to indicate the shallow profiling of all structural members, so extremely characteristic of the Romanesque style, without being capable of saying expressly that in the Romanesque profiles the right angle dominates. In the Gothic capitals he calls the sculpture subtle (*subtilis*). By that can only be meant that the sculpture here was not shallow, as in the Romanesque capitals, but cut deeply with a chisel. And the same thing is stated of the Gothic arches, vaguely and inadequately, in the words: "hic in omnibus fere sculptura idonea." "Omnibus" must be completed by "arcubus," but perhaps Gervase is referring here to the entire preceding clause: ". . . the arches and everything else. . . ." By "sculptura" are meant the Norman ornaments that are applied to the arches in Canterbury, but the implication is that the arches in their total profile are no longer carved rectangularly but are just as patterned over with hollows and shadows as the capitals. In this connection belongs the statement about the "flat" Romanesque vaults and the Gothic vaults which have lost that flatness because of their ribs. It looks as though Gervase had put his finger on the decisive spot, that is, on the importance of the rib for the relief effect of Gothic vaults in its perfect congruity with the profiling of the other structural members, of which he spoke in an immediately preceding passage.

What we call today the attenuation of the wall was implied by Gervase when he stressed the wealth of triforia and passageways at the windows. It is debatable how clear he was about this, but it cannot be denied that he emphasized the means even though he had no word ready for their effect.

Finally, he must have felt, in a similarly primitive way, that Romanesque architecture aims at a decided separation of the various spatial units of the interior from each other, while Gothic, on the other hand, tends to fuse them; for he stresses especially the fact that in the old building the arms of the transept were separated from the crossing by a wall placed above the arches, but that in the Gothic structure the arms of the transept seem to push into the crossing from both sides so that, as we might interpret it, they extend to the middle and meet in the keystone of the crossing.

All this has by no means been read into the text; it is merely easier to formulate with the aid of our modern concepts what is suggested in it. Therewith the place of the monk Gervase in the history of the literature of art is fixed. It took seven centuries, as far as we can conclude from written record, until the conceptual development of architectural theory advanced enough to comprehend Gothic in its form as profoundly as Gervase did, so that it could create clear formulations and terminology for his meanings and, therefore, appreciate him fully, progressing in his direction. Schnaase has already conjectured that Gervase exchanged ideas actively with the two architects of the cathedral. But even if one is willing to grant this, it does not diminish Gervase's merits. The architect has his own wordless language in the forms he gives to the spatial units and structural members; he works with tangible shapes, not with intellectual concepts and words. His interest is to produce the building itself and let it make its own effect, but not to describe it. Literature on art, however, depends entirely on the creation of such descriptive concepts and words as are capable of giving expression to that which is implicit in the style of the structural forms. And in this Gervase was amazingly far ahead of his time.

3. Villard de Honnecourt and Magister 3

SCHNAASE's conjecture that Gervase gained his clearest insight into Gothic from conversations with the two architects of Canterbury Cathedral (Fig. 4) makes one desirous of reading firsthand comments of Gothic architects. Chance has preserved a manuscript that can satisfy this desire, the Lodge Book of Villard de Honnecourt.[1]

The manuscript seems to have remained at first in the lodge where Villard had worked, since two other masters of a not much later time made additions to the text. They are anonymous and are designated now as Magister 2 and 3. Later the manuscript must have come to Chartres, for in 1666 it was in the possession of André Félibien who mentions it approvingly in one of his books.[2] Félibien, historiographer at the court of Louis XIV and confirmed classicist, scarcely had the right perspective to appreciate Villard's book fully, but he praises him as a draftsman, which is a greater tribute than any of us today could pay.[3] Through one of Félibien's two sons, either Dom Michel (d. 1719), who composed a history of the Abbey of St.-Denis, or the architect Jean François (d. 1733), the manuscript passed to the monastery of St.-Germain-des-Près in Paris and from there, during the Revolution, to the Bibliothèque Nationale.

An approximate biography of Villard can be reconstructed from the text, though much remains hypothetical. He was probably born in Honnecourt, a small place near Cambrai in Picardy. The year of his birth can be taken as about 1195; thus, in round numbers, he is half a century younger than Gervase and represents for the literature of art the generation of the French High Gothic. He probably received the first impulse toward his profession in the nearby Cistercian monastery

[1] Hans Hahnloser, *Villard de Honnecourt, Kritische Gesamtausgabe des Bauhüttenbuches ms fr 19093 der Pariser Nationalbibliothek*, Vienna, 1935. Hahnloser has worked through all the older literature on the subject and has made such thorough investigations that this chapter can concentrate on a few problems.

[2] F. Ed. Schneegans, "Über die Sprache des Skizzenbuchs von Villard de Honnecourt," *Zeitschrift für romanische Philologie*, 1901, p. 45. Cf. Hahnloser, *op.cit.*, pp. 194ff.

[3] *Entretiens sur les vies et les ouvrages des plus excellents peintres anciens et modernes*, Paris, 1666 (2nd ed., 1696), p. 528: "Il y a quantité de figures de la plume qui font connoistre, le gout de desegner estoit alors aussi bon que celuy d'Italie l'estoit du temps de Cimabue."

of Vaucelles, a ground plan of the choir of which he sketched into his book.[4] Together with another architect, Pierre de Corbie, he designed a choir for a particularly opulent Cistercian church with a double ambulatory.[5] What he himself built is not quite certain but it is probable that he drew the plans for the Collegiate Church of St.-Quentin, which was being constructed from 1225 to 1257. In his book he entered also the ground plan and the elevation of Cambrai Cathedral (1227 to after 1240)—the elevations to which the text refers have been cut out—but here although he was not the responsible architect he must have had personal contact with this lodge for otherwise he would not have been able to make use of plans at that time not yet executed.[6] Since St. Elisabeth of Hungary, Landgravine of Thuringia, established an endowment for Cambrai in 1231 shortly before her death, it can be assumed that Villard's mission to Hungary came about through this princess. At the same time Villard's connection with the Cistercians may have played a part, as this order was then expanding in Hungary. This journey, which Villard mentions several times with considerable pride, must have taken place around 1235. What he was to build in Hungary is not known. Probably he put together his sketchbook with the intention of having some architectural models at hand in Hungary and he may have utilized some older drawings of his own for this purpose in addition to making new ones. The sketches concern—besides Vaucelles and Cambrai—Meaux, Laon, Reims, Chartres, Lausanne, thus partly indicating his itinerary. In Hungary he copied for himself the pattern of a floor covering and after his return wrote the comment: "I was once in Hungary where I spent many days. There I saw in a church a floor covering of such a kind."[7] But the book may have included many other sketches of buildings in Hungary, France, and elsewhere, because it originally contained fifty leaves (one hundred pages), seventeen of which have been cut out.

After his return, in 1242 at the latest (when the Tartars invaded Hungary), Villard gradually filled the pages and portions of pages in his book that were still empty, but his purpose had changed. He might still collect models for eventual commissions of his own, but now, as a mature and experienced master, he became the teacher of the younger generation, and the book of samples developed into a textbook encompassing everything that a Gothic architect needed to learn. In a certain

[4] Hahnloser, *op.cit.*, p. 78 and pl. 33; cf. Marcel Aubert, *L'Architecture cistercienne en France*, Paris, 1943, I, p. 225.

[5] *Ibid.*, pp. 69ff. and pl. 29. [6] *Ibid.*, p. 67 and pl. 28. [7] *Ibid.*, p. 73 and pl. 30.

sense Villard may be considered for Gothic as similar to Vitruvius for the classical period, the Renaissance, and subsequent times. The comparison, of course, merely indicates that both acted from the same practical necessity of offering the novice, beset by so many demands, the collected experience of the art as developed up to that time. Villard, the "Gothic Vitruvius," gives, therefore, an insight into the principal subjects studied by a French architect of the High Gothic.

A first impression on leafing through the sixty-six pages that have been preserved is confusing; they seem to be a planless juxtaposition of notes, ideas, and copies, as chance gave rise to them. But a draftsman of the thirteenth century picked out for his finer drawings the better, smoother parchment leaves of his notebook and saved the coarser ones for sketches, where delicacy of line was not so important. Hahnloser pointed out that the drawings of animals are so scattered through the entire manuscript that they may be recognized as the final thing that Villard considered necessary to complete his treatise. Hahnloser's careful analysis shows that Villard treated six main topics in all: 1) Architectural drawings. 2) Interior furnishings of buildings. 3) *Maconerie* and geometry. 4) *Carpenterie* and *engiens*. 5) The human figure. 6) Animals.

In this list some of Villard's expressions have been left untranslated and in his orthography, because one must first consider what they mean. We should also look in vain in this book for a definition or general characterization of Gothic, because the Gothic style as such was for Villard the language of forms most natural to him and in which he had been reared. But through him we learn something of far greater importance, though he made no conscious attempt to formulate it, that is, what a man of the Gothic age had to learn in order to become a competent architect.

In the thirteenth century Gothic was not considered historically; history, or rather the history of art, was itself being made. Modern authors in their consideration of the date of Villard's journey to Hungary have found fault with him for having included in his book around 1235 such outdated examples as the tower of Laon or the west rose window of Chartres, but just that showed freedom from historical prejudices. Moreover, Hahnloser was able to prove that Villard, consciously or unconsciously, modernized all the older examples, including the west rose of Lausanne.[8] Scholarly method in the sense of historical fidelity was foreign to his nature. As a productive artist he criticized and corrected

[8] *Ibid.*, pp. 76 and 77.

older works of Gothic from the standpoint of his generation and his personal taste.

This latter he betrayed especially strongly twice: with regard to the tower of Laon and the window of Reims. The text accompanying his drawing of the tower reads, following Hahnloser's German translation of the Old French: "I have been in many countries, as you can judge from this book; [but] nowhere have I ever seen such a tower as that in Laon. . . . And consider it well: for if you want to make a good tower, you must choose buttresses (*pilers forkies*) that are of sufficient depth. Pay good heed to your work, thus will you do what is worthy of a wise and noble man."[9] However the last words of the text, "si feres que sages et cortois," are translated,[10] there can be detected in them a strong and proud consciousness of social position. Villard regarded the master of Laon as the model of a wise and "courtly" man. Perhaps he knew him personally and revered him.

The statement about the window in Reims is even more personal: "Behold here one of the windows of Reims, of the bays of the nave, such as stand between two piers. I was commissioned [to go] to the land of Hungary when I drew it, because I liked it best (*por co l'amai io miex*)." Hahnloser calls this "the most personal artist's judgment of the high Middle Ages."[11] The Reims window, probably designed as early as 1211, was about the year 1235 still almost the most modern solution; it had been superseded in 1231 by Pierre de Montereaux in the windows of his new construction in St.-Denis. The drawing of a "form" in the lodge, however, did not in those days make it a matter of public knowledge; often years passed before it was carried out and in that state could be seen by everyone.

The drawings in the lodges were, of course, available to an architect. Thus, for example, Villard was able to make the sketches of Cambrai Cathedral in his notebook only from plans in the lodge, as the building had scarcely progressed in 1230 beyond the foundations. With reference to the drawing of Reims,[12] Villard once more emphasizes the importance of the elevations of that cathedral as a model for Cambrai: "Of just such a kind must those [chapels] of Cambrai be, if one is to do them justice." Reims was for Villard *the* classical structure, down to the last detail, for example, in the joining of a shaft with its pier and in the profiles of all its important structural members. He drew these

[9] *Ibid.*, p. 50. The long description of the tower is here omitted.
[10] Hahnloser translates *courtois* by the German word *grosszügig*.
[11] *Ibid.*, pp. 56 and 57.
[12] *Ibid.*, p. 162 and pl. 60.

profiles side by side and commented: "Behold the profiles of the chapels on the preceding page, of the window arches and the tracery, of the diagonal ribs and the transverse arches and wall arches above them."[13]

Molles are the carved wooden models of the profiles that Gervase calls *formae*. For Villard, on the other hand, the word *formes* signifies, according to Hahnloser, "the Gothic window-form *par excellence*." The word *ogive* for rib occurs here for the first time. It is still the common term today in France and is usually derived from the Latin *augere*, to augment.[14] The word *sorvol* is found only here; as appears from the profile and because all the other arches have already been named, it must mean the wall arches.

If one adds the expression *piler forkie* for buttress from the passage about the tower in Laon, Villard had a complete vocabulary for the specifically Gothic structural members developed at that time; only the pointed arch has no name of its own.[15] In order to talk or write about an architecture one needs, as we saw in the case of Gervase, not only terms for its structural members—the membrological vocabulary—but also another terminology for its specifically aesthetic, stylistic, and artistic properties, which are, to be exact, three distinct things. This latter vocabulary was in Villard's time almost nonexistent. He uses the word *bon* where he wishes to praise, and when he considers something beautiful, he says that he likes it most. The aesthetic judgment is still entirely dependent upon subjective taste; however, inasmuch as generally acknowledged beauty is meant, only that word *bon* is available that indicates ethical quality as well. Architectural analysis still had a long way to go.

What can be reconstructed as Villard's second chapter, treating of interior furnishings, comprises the drawings of the clock-case (12),[16] the lectern (13), the sepulchral monument of a "heathen" (11), by which is meant one of classical times, the side pieces for choir stalls (54, 57), and the labyrinths (14, 17). Perhaps to them should be added the wheel of fortune (42), although it belongs at the same time to *portraiture*; also, in a sense, the single crucifix (4), and the group of the crucifixion with Mary and John the Evangelist (15). Of the lectern Villard remarks: ". . . behold the best kind that I know."

13 *Ibid.*, p. 170."Ves ci les molles des chapieles de cela pagne la devant, des formes [et] des verrieres, des ogives [et] des doubliaus [et] des sorvols p[a]r deseur."

14 See below p. 155.

15 Villard calls every arch "arc." For the theory of the construction of the pointed arch with constant compass span cf. Hahnloser, pl. 41 h with the textual addition of Magister 2.

16 These numbers in parentheses refer to the plates in Hahnloser.

We are inclined to assume that woodworkers who carved the choir stalls and metalworkers who wrought the lecterns also invented the drawings for these things. According to Villard's conception it belonged to the duties of a universally talented architect to provide the producing artists with sketches for all their works. In the case of the sides for the choir stalls, moreover, he does not seem to have presented an original sketch but one by some other architect. He copied it faithfully and did not transform the semicircular arches beneath the seat into pointed ones.[17]

Much more astonishing than Villard's ability to draw foliage as deftly as he did in the side pieces for the choir stalls is his mastery of the human and animal figure. Hahnloser enumerates 163 human and 62 (or 67) animal figures. Iconographically the list of human figures is very rich: Christ, Mary, the Apostles, symbolical figures such as Ecclesia, Humilitas, Superbia; then priests, monks, nuns, kings, knights, jugglers, hangman's helpers, ladies of fashion, female dancers, and others. To these are added such individual scenes as the Flagellation of Christ, the Crucifixion, Descent from the Cross. Also there are some from profane life, such as gamblers, wrestlers, the pair of lovers, lion fights and lion taming. Finally Villard even included in his collection drawings of nudes from classical models or, as the case might be, Byzantine models based on the classical.

Stylistically, these drawings are at the stage of the sculptures in Chartres of the period from 1225 to 1230. They make use of the so-called "hollow style."[18] The many and sometimes uncommonly lively animal figures were important for Gothic architecture because of their symbolical as well as their decorative significance.

Villard has always been admired as a draftsman. Vitztum ascribed to him a missal from Noyon. Whether one agrees with this or not, it decidedly suggests the theory that Villard was as much painter as architect. And this theory can be extended. The crucifix, which is very advanced for the period around 1235,[19] and the Ecclesia (8) should not be looked upon merely as works of graphic art: they betray the sculptor. We are accustomed to imagine every *mediaeval* craftsman and artist as restricted by the limits of his guild. Is that true around 1235? Villard gives us the right to answer in the negative.

17 Cf. the retention of the round arch in other places as well as on plates 12, 27, 30, 40, and 42.

18 The German name is *Muldenstil*, Hahnloser, *op.cit.*, p. 216.

19 For the importance of crucifixes in the history of style, cf. the remarks by Hahnloser on pp. 19 and 40.

We are less surprised that Villard was interested in *maconerie* and geometry, as well as *carpenterie* and *engiens*. It will be assumed at first that these words meant simply masonry, geometry, carpentry, and machinery. At least the translation of the word *carpenterie* is correct, for it includes types of roof framing (34) and the drawing (45c) that teaches a method of building a tower or house when the available beams are too short. Probably among the drawings that were removed were still others that belonged to carpentry in the modern sense.

For Villard, however, the dividing line between *carpenterie* and *engiens* is not sharp; he even writes *engiens de carpenterie*, which refers to the many wooden machines that he demonstrates for the pupil, unless one is to think of carpenters' machinery. One can distinguish four categories: machines such as the water-driven saw (44a) and the *perpetuum mobile* (9), the earliest one documented; actual building machinery such as that for hoisting loads (44d); engines of war like the crossbow (44b) or the great catapult (59); and finally, marvels. The latter yield considerable information about Gothic. An example is the clockwork that causes an angel on top of a spire to point an arm constantly toward the sun—the earliest clockwork for which there is literary evidence;[20] another instance is the eagle that always turns his head toward the deacon when he reads the Gospel (44e); Villard also constructs a dove that is enabled by a concealed mechanism to drink up a bowl of water. What we shall later meet in the epics is here technically verified.

There are now left two groups of drawings: the one is comprised of those human and animal figures that are drawn in sketchy outlines and provided with all sorts of geometrical auxiliary lines, triangles, quadrangles, and so on; the other consists of examples of mensuration. The terms that cause difficulty are "iometrie, maconerie, portraiture." We meet them at once in the title of the treatise that Villard entered on the second page; it reads, using Hahnloser's reading of the Old French: "Villard de Honnecourt gives you greeting and beseeches all who will work by the aids that are found in this book to pray for his soul and bear him in remembrance. For in this book one can obtain good advice on the grand art of *maconerie* and the *engiens de carpenterie*, and you will find in it the art of drawing (*le force de la portraiture*), the principal features (*les trais*), as the discipline of geometry (*li ars de iometrie*) requires and teaches them."

The word *iometrie* means, of course, the same thing as our word

[20] Hahnloser, *op.cit.*, p. 135.

geometry, but whether *li ars* is properly rendered by "discipline" may be questioned. Certainly geometry is the comprehensive scientific method that is a prerequisite for the practice both of *maconerie* and *portraiture*, but *ars* here means perhaps not the science of geometry in its whole compass or, as Hahnloser puts it, the discipline as a whole but merely applied or practical geometry: *ars* does not mean "art" in the Middle Ages but the "practice" of an art.

The word *trais* means, following Hahnloser, principal features, and is contained in the word *portraiture*, which word must not be taken in the sense of the modern "portrait" that has been formed from it.[21] *Portraiture* is for the rest probably always identical with "drawing," but *force de portraiture* is here not simply the same as the "art of drawing." We must try to derive the correct interpretation of the expression from a proper understanding of the drawings themselves. Which ones are meant appears from three notations. On page 35 we read: "Here begins the matter of *portraiture*." On this page is drawn a man's head of the type of Peter, which was already there when Villard added the other, quite different little sketches. The word *portraiture* refers only to these latter, for they continue on page 36 with twelve examples, and here the title of the chapter is repeated in a simple, more informative variation: "Here begins *li force des trais de portraiture* as *li ars de iometrie* teaches them, *por legierment ovrer*. On the other sheet are those of *maconerie*." (Villard writes *maconerie* without the cedilla.) Fourteen more examples of the method of *portraiture* follow on page 37 without any notation; on page 38 are six further instances and here the conclusion is reached: "On these four sheets are figures *de l'art de iometrie*. But he who would know what work each one is to serve must pay heed that he may understand."

What *portraiture* is appears from these four pages but not, however, what purpose it really serves. Villard's last comment should be a warning against overhasty judgments. Much has been written about these figures, and up to the present they have only been taken in the sense that the words "por legierment ovrer" mean "in order to work [that is, draw] easily." Some of these figures will now be discussed as far as is helpful to an understanding of the whole series. For this purpose two groups of drawings within *portraiture* must be differentiated: in the one a definite frame of proportions is fundamental and the figure

21 Hahnloser, *Ibid.*, p. 16, has brought together in detail everything that is known about the word portraiture from the philological point of view. I believe that my interpretation does not contradict this, especially as Villard "tried three times," had then no current term at his disposal, and thus chose the quite general one. Cf. on "portrait," *ibid.*, p. 32.

is subsequently sketched into this framework; in the other, conversely, the human or animal form is primary and on it are drawn in all sorts of geometrical figures that fit the given contour. Besides these there are other possibilities that may be touched upon later, but that were not employed by Villard.

The frontal face (38c) can be taken above all as an example of the *first* group (Fig. 8). The quadratic net is based on the length of the nose as its unit. The face is divided into three equal heights: from the point of the chin to the tip of the nose, from there to the root of the nose, from there to the hairline. The quadratic net also determines the height of the crown of the head and the most important widths. Villard also partially drew in on the individual quadrangles the diagonals that must likewise have had a definite significance for him and his pupils.

Another example of this group (37g) is the drawing of a man in frontal position (Fig. 9). At first one imagines that the lines form a strangely distorted pentagram; but Hahnloser is doubtless correct when he completes this geometrical figure as a rectangle with its diagonals and a triangle constructed above the base of the rectangle with the middle of the upper side of the rectangle as its apex.[22] Then it appears that the height of the head is the principal unit of measure. The breadth of the shoulders equals two such lengths, the body from the feet to the shoulders six. This scheme is also adaptable to the drawing of figures in motion, as Villard shows in the twisting shoulder on plate 35d and e.

The examples of the *second* group vary greatly among themselves: on the stag (35c) are drawn a rectangle for the body and two intersecting triangles for the neck and head (Fig. 10); for frontal faces one is not necessarily restricted to the quadratic frame, but can also utilize an equilateral triangle (36g) or the pentagram (36f) (Fig. 7). In this connection it should be noted that the two faces drawn by Villard for these two different constructions are exactly similar in type. He probably drew the one with the pentagram first and then made the other one smaller, as it looks narrower and longer. Villard perhaps wanted to demonstrate to his pupils that one can freely evolve a type of head from any preconceived proportion and then invent a suitable geometric figure for it. This is shown even more strikingly in two heads in profile, absolutely dissimilar in subject, one of a man (36e) and the other of a horse (36b): for both the same equilateral triangle is used

22 *Ibid.* fig. 127 (after the plates).

with one side lying along the profile of the face and the opposite point behind the ear (Fig. 7). If the four figures just discussed are taken together, it appears that Villard intended the quite logical formulation: you can use for two almost similar heads two quite dissimilar geometrical figures and, conversely, one and the same figure for two dissimilar heads; or, the human or other figure that is your real objective and your geometrical auxiliary figure are independent variables. Now the question arises as to the purpose served by this method, if it is indeed what Villard calls *portraiture.* He himself gave the answer: "por legierment ovrer." Does that mean: so that the beginner can draw more easily? Villard, as far as we can see, nowhere uses in the drawings he made himself such auxiliary or, as Hahnloser calls them, "guiding" lines. One might say that he was no longer a beginner. But, even though such crutches are unquestionably helpful to an untalented draftsman, are we to believe that such a variable method was devised for the training of the Gothic architect?

Here it must be remembered that the Egyptians had already evolved a definite canon for standardizing the proportions of the human form, the function of which was two-fold: first, to determine commensurable intervals for the distance between the most important points of articulation; and second, to have—at the same time—a method of reproducing a drawing on any desired scale.[23] The quadratic net is suitable for the latter purpose, though it does not fulfill the first function. Moreover, it is a neutral system of coordinates, completely alien to the object, such as has been frequently used, especially in modern times, in mural painting, to transfer a design to a wall. Villard seems not to have known or not to have desired this rational application of the quadratic net. But all his examples of *portraiture*, whether they are intended to standardize definite proportions or not, can be used for transfer on any desired scale. The quadratic net seemed to him perhaps less commendable for this purpose because it is too minute; such a net must be built up from many lines, whereas his own proposals are confined to a few boldly outlined geometrical figures. If, however, this method is chiefly for the purpose of transferring small drawings from the parchment to the sculptor's stone block, the mural painter's wall, or the glass designer's table, then Villard's statement is more correctly understood by referring *ovrer* to this sort of "working" and not to drawing in general. *Portraiture*, in that case, does not serve to

[23] Erwin Panofsky, "Die Entwicklung der Porportionslehre als Abbild der Stilentwickelung," *Monatshefte für Kunstwissenschaft,* XIV, Leipzig, 1921, p. 188.

provide the beginner in an easy way with proportions for his sketches so that he can produce something tolerable, still less to hold him to quite definite norms of "beautiful" proportions, but rather to assist the productive craftsman in the execution of a small sketch on a large scale. *Portraiture* is therefore exactly what Villard said of it on the second page of his notebook: "this is the power of *portraiture* [to place] the lines as applied geometry demands and teaches."[24] That this interpretation is more correct than the previous one, which always adhered too rigidly to the idea that proportions are only to serve to standardize a kind of beauty, will be evident from a series of further investigations of the sources.

We need only to turn to Villard's *maconerie* to make further progress. He wrote on page 36: ". . . and on the other sheet are those of *maconerie*," meaning the page after *portraiture*. But Magister 2 erased that completely and in place of his teacher's drawings entered a series of geometrical constructions. For us, then, the information about *maconerie* begins instead on page 40 and extends to page 41. Here it is entirely a question of methods of mensuration, for instance, the measurement of the height of a tower from below (40l). The ground plan of a chapter hall with a sort of rib vault resting on a central column seems also to be intended as an example of mensuration (41a).[25] Magister 2 explained the next drawing (41b) by a note without which we should be baffled, since even with its aid we must still puzzle a while: "In this fashion one places an egg under a pear in such a way that the pear falls down onto the egg." Hahnloser explains the significance of the three measuring rods (page 123) and pronounces the whole to be a metaphor of the vertical projection of a point. It is indeed nothing more. In all the literature of geometry there has probably never been so charming an illustration of this prosaic problem as Villard's pear tree with its ornamental curves (Fig. 11). This problem of the projection of a point in space down to the ground is found just beside the ground plan of the chapter hall, about which Magister 2 comments: "In this fashion a chapter hall of eight columns [eight engaged wall shafts] is gathered together on a single one; it is by no means so complicated; that is good *maconerie*." Whether this design has a connection with the device of projecting a point downward (or upward?) is not clear. Nor is it known how Villard wanted to form the severies in the interstices between the ribs, respective-

24 ". . . le force de la portraiture, les trais, ensi come li ars de iometrie le commande et ensaigne."

25 Hahnloser, *op.cit.*, p. 122 and pl. 41.

ly between the ribs and the walls. None of the existing explanations or interpretations of this design is convincing.

All the other instances of *maconerie* are to be regarded as problems of measurement, for example, the adjusting of two capitals to the same level (40l), and so on. The shaping of the stone blocks for the pendant vault (*vosure pendant*) (40i) falls in this category, though it includes at the same time a problem in mechanics. The translation of the word *maconerie* by masonry is correct in itself, but it appears from all these drawings that it is not a question of all sorts of masonry, including building in brick, but exclusively the art of the stonemason. The word *maconerie* directs our thoughts to *maçon* (stonemason), and to the disputed problems of the secrets of the masons and their lodges. Villard's warning on page 38, referring to *portraiture*, can be extended to *maconerie*: ". . . but he who wants to know for which [kind of] work each figure ought to be used, has to be careful to make no mistake."[26] Applied geometry serves both *portraiture* and *maconerie*; there were measuring methods that were specially used to enlarge sketches for the work of the sculptors and painters, and others that were intended for the stonemasons. Magister 2 went more deeply into the latter and therefore must be discussed by himself. Here we shall take up Magister 3, though he is later in time, because he does not depart so far from Villard.

According to Hahnloser, the so-called Magister 3 is scarcely much younger than Magister 2. To arrive at an approximate dating one must try to determine the hypothetical date of Villard's death. If he was in Hungary between 1235 and about 1240 and afterward worked one or two decades in St.-Quentin, he might well have presided over the lodge as a man of forty-five to sixty-five years of age, and Magister 2 could have succeeded him in office perhaps around 1260, supplementing the inherited book before it passed into the hands of Magister 3, whose period would in this way be fixed as the decade after 1280.

Magister 3 is responsible for relatively few additions. The most interesting one is his repetition of what Villard himself wrote on page 63 as an explanation of page 62, where he drew the system of elevations of Reims Cathedral, interior and exterior, side by side. Magister 3 now wrote the same thing once again in his own words on page 62, probably so that it would be on the page to which it properly belongs. For purposes of comparison both sets of comments are printed here in parallel columns:

26 ". . . mais al conoistre covient avoir grant esgart ki savoir velt de que cascune doit ovrer."

Villard (page 63)	Magister 3 (page 62)
Behold the drawings of the elevation of the church of Reims [and] of the wall inside and outside. The first story of the aisles must form a battlemented parapet so that a passage can lead around in front of the roof.	Heed well these drawings of the elevation. In front of the roof of the aisles there must be a passage.
Against this roof on the inside are [built] passageways, and, where these passages are vaulted in and paved, there the passages lead outside, so that one can walk past along the sills of the windows.	Above the story and above the roof of the aisles in front of the windows there must likewise be a way and low battlements, as you see it in the view before you. And on the upper end of your piers there must be angels and in front of them flying buttresses.
And the topmost story must have battlements so that one can go around the roof.	In front of the great roof there must again be passages and battlements on the story, so that one can get up there in case of fire, and there must be gargoyles on the story to throw off the water.
Behold here the manner and method of the whole elevation.	As to the chapels, I told you.

Villard was especially impressed by the wall passages in Reims because they were not developed to such a degree in his homeland of Picardy. He says merely that they are there so that one can walk past the windows and up along the foot of the roof. Magister 3 adds that they are there to help in extinguishing fires. Today we are inclined to see in the wall passages exclusively, or at least chiefly, a stylistic means of dissolving the wall, of splitting it apart into layers, and Magister 3 would be laughed to scorn as an antiquated old fogey of the materialistic nineteenth century. But this epigonus of French High Gothic wrote down what he thought and what he had perhaps heard from Magister 2, even possibly from Villard himself. It is fitting that he speaks of the gargoyles as though they had no decorative function at all but only a practical one. The whole way in which he partly abbreviates and partly extends Villard's text, however, is for us a vivid example of development in this almost completely vanished literature of the lodge books. Villard was certainly one of the really productive thinkers in this branch of literature, but already, as we can guess from certain stereotyped turns of phrase, he had his predecessors. Later, in the fourteenth century, there again arose theorists, who developed the inherited tradition into rigid rules. The entries of Magister 2 and Magister 3 are for us links with the almost legendary "Squires of Prague"; they were in this matter not really independent minds and their service was not so much to spin the thread further as to keep the doctrine alive.

Villard's book, originally a collection of samples for the journey to Hungary, then a textbook for his students, then a lodge book in which his successors entered their improvements, is a fragment of a long chain. The book itself has come down to us only as a fragment and it is only a fraction of the total sum of Villard's importance. Whether he drew the plan of St. Quentin remains uncertain; whatever he may have created as painter, as sculptor, as architect is unknown; his plan for a Cistercian church is theoretical.[27] He must have executed a large commission in Hungary and helped to transplant to the East the High culture of the France of that day; but the invasion of the Tartars, it is assumed, destroyed it all. As in the case of many another creative spirit there is something tragic about the life work of this man. Humanity certainly lost more by this than Villard. For he lost only posthumous fame; the joy of creation remained his. Only his drawings have been preserved to us, together with the instructive, painstaking notes which were no more to him than means to an end. He never dreamed that they would make his name immortal.

4. Magister 2 and the Secret of the Lodges

THE French annotations of Magister 2 show him to have been a native of Picardy like Villard himself. It is a natural assumption to recognize in him Villard's immediate successor in St.-Quentin or in a neighboring lodge. This master wrote a considerable portion of his notes in Latin, but it need not necessarily be concluded that he belonged therefore to the clergy. Any architect was surely conversant with Latin from the monastic school.

[27] Hahnloser, *op.cit.*, p. 65 and pl. 28. On this point recently: Marcel Aubert, *L'Architecture cistercienne en France*, Paris, 1943, p. 195. According to this, there was a very similar edifice in Fontainejean (Loiret), of which very little has been preserved. Ground plan reconstructed in Aubert, p. 194.

Of his additions[1] the most important is that on page 39, at the end of which is the explanation: "All these figures are taken from geometry." Part of these eighteen figures, together with the accompanying text, is unintelligible. Hahnloser, therefore, sees in Magister 2 a man who copied from a book on geometry things he did not himself understand. But one should be cautious in such accusations, and perhaps the fault lies in us for not having discovered the right interpretation for all these drawings.

Those of the figures that can be understood without great difficulty all have to do with problems of mensuration. They are, then, examples of the "practice of geometry" and are, naturally, closely connected with the scientific geometry of that day, but the difference between the two geometries is that the science poses and solves problems from a purely theoretical interest without consideration of any practical applicability, whereas the sister subject is entirely oriented toward methods of mensuration that the stonemason uses every day. For example, in renovating an engaged wall shaft the latter has to insert a new block; he needs to know the curvature of the horizontal section of this shaft, that is, the length of the radius. How does one find this when the center of the circle lies inaccessible in the interior of the column? The first figure on the page (39a) shows the solution of this very simple geometrical problem and the second figure beside it (39b) gives the appropriate construction. A young mason simply had to learn this. Another easy task seems to have nothing to do with the masons' building site: the measurement of the width of a river from one bank (39l); this is a problem for a bridge builder. But corresponding measurements could be necessary on the building site, and dividing line between architect and engineer was not sharp. The next problem goes back to the field of architecture: the measurement of the width of a window that is at a distance (39m); of course, the object did not always need to be a window.

Probably all eighteen figures, including those not previously understood, can be thought of as problems in practical measurement. This supposition was confirmed only a short time ago when, at least for some of the figures, a meaning was found.[2] Ueberwasser interpreted four of them, but it will suffice to discuss only two of these here.

[1] Brought together in Hahnloser, *Villard de Honnecourt*, p. 195.

[2] Walter Ueberwasser, "Nach rechtem Masz," *Jahrbuch der preussischen Kunstsammlungen*, LVI, Berlin, 1935.

The one problem (39o) has the annotation: "Par chu partis om one pirre que les II moities sont quareis." Hahnloser renders it: "In this way one divides a stone so that both halves are quadratic." The solution is to draw in a square lying diagonally with its corners coinciding with the midpoints of the sides of the first square (Fig. 13). It will be easily seen that the sum of the four corner triangles thus created is equal to the area of the diagonally placed middle square, and that thus the main square has been divided into two equal halves. Hahnloser made a correct but probably too literal translation of Magister 2's note. That is, in order to create two squares in this way, one must saw off the four corner triangles of the stone and put them together to form a square. If that were the intention, one might ask if such a problem would ever arise in practical building. Since the answer is no, one can only conclude that Magister 2 is also interested in purely theoretical problems, although it would be strange, then, that he should speak of a stone. The clarification of these obscurities lies in the fact that this figure reappears in later sources where its significance for mensuration becomes clear. At any rate, we can translate the word *partis* simply by "reduce" instead of "divide" or "cut." The stone is to be geometrically "reduced," not mechanically divided, and in such a way as to create two halves equal in area. Up to this point everything is now clear. The rest is awkwardly expressed by Magister 2. What he probably meant, can be guessed from the other figure.

This problem (39k) has the notation: "In this way one lays out a cloister, both with regard to the passages and to the garden." The drawing shows a quadratic cloister (Fig. 12). In actual practice the question arose as to how wide the ambulatories should be made without causing difficulties in measurement. To understand this latter concern one must visualize what a modern Gothicist of the nineteenth or twentieth century does when he wants to lay out a cloister in square form. He draws a ground plan on a scale of perhaps 1:50, on which he enters the width of the ambulatories according to partly practical and partly aesthetic considerations. He can decide this dimension as he wishes because, however it is expressed in numbers, the builder, or whoever stakes out the plan in its actual size on the site, always has the same assignment: either to read off the dimensions, if they are figured, or to work them out by means of a compass or pocket rule according to the scale, which must be indicated, so that the dimensions thus obtained can be marked off in their true size with the usual measuring apparatus, whether it be the same pocket rule, or measuring tape, or the like; and then to hammer in his stakes or lay his stones.

A Gothic architect of the thirteenth century could not proceed in this way because he had no pocket rule; or if he did have one, he could not count on the fact that his foremen, masons, carpenters, and other artisans would have similar ones. Nor were standards of measure uniform in the different countries, territories, or even in the various cities of the same territory. The architect, therefore, placed no value at all on plotting his drawings in a determined scale. That does not mean that he could get along without them entirely. He had at least to indicate the length in feet for the first measure that he prescribed, and it was then, so to speak, the preordained fate of the building whether a foot in that locality was, for example, 29 cm or 30 cm long. But for the further course of his work it was not important to be able to express every distance between two points of the structure in arithmetical quantities; he had only to determine the interval geometrically. Of course, he had to see to it that his geometrical figures could be enlarged to any desired size by a purely geometrical method, and this method is, in general terms, that of the transfer of proportions and angles. The angles remain the same in the transfer and likewise the proportions. The length is what changes. But then a method must be found for determining all the lengths without numerical measurement once an initial dimension of length has been adopted. Here we return to the question above: what width is to be indicated for the wings of the cloister, or, in general, the dimensions of all the various parts of the structure, without creating difficulties when the staking-out on the site is done in actual size? One could not choose any desired dimensions, but was restricted to those that could easily be transferred by the aid of simple geometrical figures. For this purpose Magister 2 chooses the same figure that was previously discussed, the square with the inscribed diagonal square, only that he now turns the latter parallel to the large square. He confines himself in his drawing to a few lines that exactly correspond to what the builder actually has to do on the site.

The builder, that is, marks off the outer square first, for example, a side length of seventy feet, describes at the end points right angles, and marks off from there the seventy foot sides. Then he runs two strings along the diagonals, first, to test the right angles and second, to determine at the same time the center. Next he divides one of the sides of the square into two equal halves, connects the center of this side with the center of the square by means of a string, and marks off this length on the diagonal from the center out. The point so obtained is one of the corner points of the "garden," that is, the open court. He finds the other three points by the same simple method and can now connect these four points by strings. Thus the mason or stonemason is enabled to begin setting the stones.

It is clear that through this method the area of the four wings is equal to that of the "garden," but that is an incidental outcome of the whole exercise, not its real objective. That is understood only when one recognizes this example of mensuration on the site as the beginning of a process that can be and is continued in the same way. For a Gothic cloister requires that next the piers be determined, that the details of the piers, the dimensions of the bases, of the shafts, of the capitals, the dimensions of the vaulting members, of the tracery, and so on, be read off and transferred over and over, all without the use of a pocket rule. That can all be done with this one figure 390, if all the details are given only such dimensions as can be derived from that figure.

Here the difference between *portraiture* and *maconerie* is clear. In *portraiture* it is a question merely of a process of transference from the small drawing to the block or wall surface, and Villard shows how one must invent that geometrical figure that approaches the contour or indicates important points of articulation; but anything further is unnecessary, because the sculptor or painter does not transfer blindly but works according to his feeling, once the main proportions are determined. On the other hand, it is necessary for the mason to measure all the stones that he chisels individually to size in the lodge so that they will afterward fit together exactly. Magister 2's method makes that possible, starting as it does with one single dimensional unit and from that one obtaining all the other dimensions by the help of the key figure of the square with the inscribed diagonal square. Looked at geometrically, the example of the monastery courtyard is, as a matter of fact, the same figure as that in the example of the stone that is to be "reduced" into two equal squares. In the cloister court there are actually two quadratic figures represented, an outer and an inner one, the latter consisting of half of the former. The other half, that is, the ambulatories, is not itself a square, but is quadratic in shape, and this probably was what Magister 2 had in mind, although he expressed himself in language as clumsy and inexact as that commonly used by workmen who have not had very much education. Magister 2 would doubtless reject this censure with indignation and point out that after all he, too, had studied Latin. But we have seen that the Latin of Suger and of Gervase differed in clarity, and Magister 2 must certainly be ranked lower than they.

There still remains the question of why Magister 2 says that one should "reduce" a *stone.* Why not simply a *square* in a purely theoretical, ideal sense; why not a square on parchment? The answer is that the key figure could be traced immediately onto the stone. Roriczer, who will be discussed later, plots his key figure on paper, before he gives it to his stonemason, but the mason himself marks his square on the stone block of the plinth and when he has finished this plinth of a pinnacle, he can indicate directly on its square upper surface with a few quick motions the lines on which the next, narrower block shall be placed.

In view of the many gaps in written tradition it can be regarded as a miracle that we probably have here an insight into this method of mensuration in its Gothic codification, if not in its historical beginnings. Ueberwasser tried to prove that Villard used the key figure of the square in the drawing of the ground plan of the tower of Laon. He is probably right. At any rate, Villard knew it already, for we find it in his treatment of *portraiture* in the drawing of two wrestlers (37h). The hypothesis can be made that up to the time of the High Gothic this quadratic figure was known, but not yet recognized in all its manifold applicability; that at the end of the High Gothic period Magister 2 began to lay emphasis on it; and that only at a later time was it raised to the position of the almost supreme key figure, because it was so simple to construct and gave exact results. From the examples Magister 2 gives it is not clear whether he already knew that this quadratic figure is also useful for ascertaining fractions of the total length of the side of a square. Perhaps it sufficed to divide the side into halves, quarters, and eighths. The knowledge that a division into three, five, seven, and nine equal parts can very easily be performed by the drawing in of a few auxiliary lines does not seem to be documented for the Middle Ages.[3]

Arithmetically we know that given a, the length of the side of a square, the length of the diagonal d equals $a\sqrt{2}$; or conversely, a equals $d\frac{1}{\sqrt{2}}$. The relation of the two quantities is irrational. That was of no importance for the above method, because it was purely a question of

[3] Johann Knauth, "Das Strassburger Münster und die Cheopspyramide, Rätsel der Baukunst," *Illustrierte elsässische Rundschau*, IX, 1907, pp. 21ff.

geometrical constructability. The stonemason needed to know only about the latter; he had to be able to draw the construction readily and exactly in order to be able to carry out the drawings given him, though these were not drawn with exact dimensions and he had no pocket rule. As an apprentice he had to be initiated into this method without which it was impossible to work as a stonemason. Anyone outside the guild did not need this knowledge, and, moreover, was not supposed to learn the key figure, lest he should be able to compete with the guild. If there was anything kept secret, it must have been this key figure and its practical application. It was believed that the secret of the lodges must have been a rule for proportions that in some mysterious fashion automatically assured the "beauty" of the Gothic cathedrals. Written tradition has preserved the key figure, which, not so long ago, we learned at last to understand. There is no written evidence that this key figure contains the main secret of the lodges; but all the considerations of this point make it seem probable, and, in agreement with the investigations of Ueberwasser and others, we are compelled to decide that the method of mensuration inserted in Villard's *maconerie* by Magister 2 must be declared to be the secret of the Gothic freemasons. Its origin did not lie in a desire for beautiful proportions, but no one is prevented from recognizing *one* source of secret harmony in the regularity resulting from the constant dependence of all dimensions on one basic dimension derived from the building itself. It was not the sole source. This can be taken in a double sense: in addition to the method of the square, which later received the name quadratura, there was also that of the triangle, or triangulation; moreover, it should not be forgotten that an architecture does not consist merely of proportions, although within the architecture everything must be in proportion.

We cannot make Magister 2 the inventor of quadrature; he may have been a relatively insignificant head of a lodge, but for us he is the oldest source for the secret of the Gothic lodges. The study of Vitruvius and classical architecture convinces us that not only was this secret known to Vitruvius but that it was also an ancient open secret of practical building, as ancient, perhaps, as the art of monumental building itself. We shall return more than once to these problems.

5. The Chronicle of Burchard von Hall

THE sources mentioned up to this point come from France and England; Burchard von Hall's *Chronicle* (ca. 1280), a brief treatise on the monastery of St. Peter in Wimpfen-in-the-Vale, takes us to Germany. Among other things Burchard gives an account of the new construction, begun in 1269, of the Wimpfen Church. The work went on until about 1300, but the choir and transept are said to have been completed by 1274; Burchard's information can accordingly be applied to the decade from 1270 to 1280, even if the writing of the chronicle might have been done somewhat later. Burchard died in the year 1300.[1]

The passage that has gained a certain fame reads: "Richard . . . caused the basilica to be constructed in the French style by a very experienced architect who had recently come from the city of Paris." What has been translated here somewhat freely by "French style" is in the original "opus francigenum."[2] The German chronicler had no doubt that the style of the Wimpfen church was "born in France" or "of French descent," just as Gervase knew that the Gothic of Canterbury Cathedral derived from Sens in France. Burchard mentions especially the statues of the saints in the interior and on the exterior of the church, the windows, and the piers, and says finally that the crowds streaming in from all directions admired the edifice, praised the architect, and revered Richard, the servant of God. The text shows on the whole that Gothic architecture in the vicinity of Wimpfen around 1280 was no everyday affair. This seems strange, because Gothic appeared on German soil if not as early as 1209 in the lower part of the choir of the cathedral at Magdeburg, at least in its gallery 1225. In the following decades Gothic edifices arose in other German cities, for example, in Gelnhausen, Limburg on the Lahn, Marburg, Treves, and,

[1] August Pothast, *Wegweiser durch die Geschichtswerke des europäischen Mittelalters bis 1500*, Berlin, 1896, I, p. 177.

[2] *Joannis Friderici Schannat Vindemiae literariae Collectio secunda*, Fuldae et Lipsiae, 1724, p. 59. *Burchardi de Hallis Chronicon ecclesiae Collegiatae S. Petri Winpiensis.*

Richardus (de Villa Ditensheim trans Renum) [sic] . . . Monasterium a Reverendo Patre Crudolfo praefato constructum, prae nimia vetustate ruinosum, ita ut jam in proximo Ruinam minari putaretur, diruit, accitóque peritissimo Architectoriae artis Latomo, qui tunc noviter de villa Parisiensi è partibus venerat Franciae, opere Francigeno Basilicam ex sectis Lapidibus construi jubet; idem vero artifex, mirabilis Architecturae Basilicam yconis sanctorum intus et exterius ornatissime distinctam, Fenestras et Columnas ad instar anglici operis multo sudore et sumptuosis fecerat expensis, sicut usque hodie in praesens humano Visui apparet: Populis itaque undique advenientibus, mirantur tam opus egregium, Laudant artificem, venerantur DEI servum Richardum, gaudent se eum vidisse, nomenque ejus Longe Latèque portatur, et à quibus non agnoscitur saepius nominatur.

above all, Cologne and Strasbourg. One can only grant that peasants and townspeople of the region around Wimpfen had not traveled far afield. Abbot Richard may be assumed to have known what was, for his time, modern. Burchard stood, perhaps, between the two poles. The more one reflects on his wording, the more one has the impression that although Gothic was felt to be an innovation, it was familiar to the writer and he used the words *opus francigenum* as a current term. What we call "Gothic" today was at that time "French" or "Frankish." It was known that this new style had been already developed in France long before it was learned by German architects and brought to Germany.

The architect who came from Paris was by no means himself a Frenchman but one of the many Germans who made their way to France to study. He was a finished master who felt the need of increasing his knowledge at the source, certainly not an itinerant journeyman. His schooling as a journeyman lay behind him in Strasbourg. In spite of his studies in Paris, however, he was not quite on the level of the Parisian architects of his day. Dehio has unmercifully reckoned up all his faults or weaknesses according to the standard of the classical style of Paris.[3]

In his chief work Dehio mentions Burchard von Hall only in a note.[4] He says: "If the French origin of the Gothic style were not verified on other grounds, one could scarcely prove it from this passage. By *opus francigenum* the chronicler hardly meant what we mean by 'style,' but certain structural or technical characteristics. But which? cf. the controversy between H. Graf: Opus francigenum, *Studien zur Frage nach dem Ursprung der Gothik*, 1878, and Reimers: 'Scema novum' in the *Zeitschrift für bildende Kunst*, 1887." Dehio seems to issue a warning here against putting the modern concept of style in the mouth of the chronicler of the thirteenth century, but at the same time he is thinking of structural and technical characteristics from the point of view of his conception of Gothic, and is, therefore, himself attributing modern theories of style to Burchard. How can one believe that the contemporaries of Gothic architecture failed to see its "Gothic" quality and only noticed its structural and technical side? No, they looked upon Gothic as Gothic, even though they wrote or could write no monographs about it. Gervase is a witness for the comprehension of Gothic as "style."

3 Georg Dehio, *Handbuch der deutschen Kunstdenkmäler*, IV, Berlin, 1926, p. 368.

4 *Idem, Die kirchliche Baukunst . . .*, II, p. 38.

When, after centuries of contempt, Gothic began to be appreciated again, in Germany and England as well, its origin in France had fallen into oblivion, and with national pride both England and Germany put forward the claim to be the motherland of the style. For the German patriots the reference to Burchard von Hall was most uncomfortable; but they said that this solitary designation of Gothic as *opus francigenum* proved nothing. The dispute had lost all significance ever since we possessed an incontestable chronology of Gothic. Even if one does not consider French Gothic to have begun until St.-Denis in 1137, it has priority over Canterbury in 1174, and certainly over Magdeburg in 1209.[5] But although the question of origin no longer arouses nationalistic excitement in anyone, it may be of interest that Philibert de l'Orme even in 1567 writes that his workmen call Gothic "la mode Françoise."[6] At that time the Italians called it the German style, "la maniera tedesca." In France they called it French, and it is quite possible to recognize in this the survival of the meaning that was intended by *opus francigenum.* Burchard perhaps only used the expression because he was repeating what his architect from Paris employed as a technical term.

6. The Expertises of Chartres, Milan, and Gerona

THE coherence of the development of mediaeval architecture presupposes that the architects traveled about even after their years as wandering journeymen were over. We know from individual cases that the patrons, that is, the higher clergy or the city officials, ordered the architects to inspect a building that they considered in some respect instructive or worthy of imitation. These patrons traveled themselves for various reasons. What was said above about the immobility of the rural population of Wimpfen does not hold for the clergy, nobility, or gentry. Among the eternal wanderers belong also the architects and stonemasons, who moved on when a building was completed or when work

[5] Anyone is privileged to date the earliest Gothic architecture in England before Canterbury, or in Germany before Magdeburg, if he can find evidence to prove it; but he will find in Germany hardly anything earlier than St.-Denis in France except the introduction of single rib vaults since 1120 in Alsace and elsewhere. We shall return to a detailed discussion of the question of the earliest ribbed vaults.

[6] Philibert de l'Orme, *Architecture*, Paris, 1567, 2nd ed., 1648; cf. below p. 297.

was interrupted for financial, political, or other reasons. Porter has shown the importance of the Pilgrimage Roads for the period of the Romanesque style; in Gothic times the goals are no longer the sites of the most venerated shrines but of the leading lodges. If the local architects had become uncertain about measurements and so on, and if a professional judgment was needed, they turned to these centers. Such expert opinions must have been obtained far more frequently than we know so far, for Mortet says that a series of documents dealing with French expertises from the fourteenth and fifteenth centuries is as yet unpublished. He mentions briefly documents of this sort from the year 1393 concerning the rebuilding of the spire of Notre-Dame-des-Tables in Montpellier, but they do not seem to be particularly fruitful.[1] We must wait to see what the still unpublished documents will teach us. Those already printed are uncommonly informative about a number of questions.

Of the three expertises published, the earliest is that of Chartres (1316), edited anew by Mortet in 1901 since an older edition was not satisfactory from a philological point of view.[2] The text is difficult and for it Mortet's notes should be consulted. But, however valuable Mortet's monograph is, the text is not translated into a language spoken today and the content of the expertise is not interpreted exactly. Here only a few of the obscure passages that bear on our main topic will be discussed. A translation of the text reads:[3]

"In the year 1316 on the Tuesday after the festival of the birth of the blessed Mary, the Holy Virgin, the report on the defects of the church, made by those who were commissioned to investigate those defects, was written down by the chapter in the following wise:

"Sirs, we say to you that [each of] the four arches that help to carry the vaults is good and strong, and the piers that carry the arches good, and the keystone that carries the keystone good and strong; and it will not be fitting to take down more than half of your vault, to the point where it will be seen what is to be done. And we have seen to it that the scaffolding will be moved above the *enmerllement* of the stained glass windows; and this scaffolding will serve to protect your rood-loft and the people who will pass beneath the scaffolding, and it will serve the other scaffoldings to be made in the vault, that one will recognize as fitting to be done and [what] job [there] will be.

"Here is the damage of the church of Notre-Dame of Chartres, viewed

[1] Victor Mortet, "L'expertise de la Cathédrale de Chartres en 1316," *Congrès Archéol. de France*, 67th session, Paris, 1901, p. 323.

[2] Ad. Lecocque, *La Cathédrale de Chartres et ses maîtres de l'œuvre*, Chartres, 1876.

[3] According to Mortet, *op.cit.*, p. 312. See Appendix 4.

by Master Pierre Chielle, master of the work of Paris, by Master Nicolas de Chaumes, master of the works of our Lord the King, and Master Jaques de Lonc-Jumel, master carpenter and sworn officer of Paris, in the presence of master Jean de Reate [Rieti, near Perugia], canon of Chartres, native of Italy, master Simon Daguon, master of the work [of Chartres], master Simon, the carpenter, and master Berthaust, sworn officers of the aforesaid work, answerable to the dean [of the chapter of the cathedral].

"Firstly, we have seen the vault of the crossing: it assuredly demands repairs, and [if] one will not make them at once there could be great danger.

"Further we have examined the flying buttresses that support the vaults; the joints are sadly in need of sealing and of reinvestigation [repair] and if one will not do it at once there may well be great damage. . . ."

[After a number of other defects have been listed or discussed, the report comes back again to the vault first mentioned:]

"Further, we have seen to it, for the advantage of the church, that the first scaffolding will be moved above the *enmerllement* of the stained glass windows in order to construct the vault of the crossing."

Mortet has brought together all that is known about the three experts from Paris;[4] they give their judgment in the presence of four men of Chartres, one of whom is likewise a carpenter, because obviously the scaffoldings were also to be discussed in detail. The second man from Chartres is the architect in charge, and the third, Berthaust, seems to have been the legal representative of the chapter.[5] Jean de Reate, finally, is the chapter's building authority, himself a member of the clergy and, as is expressly emphasized, an Italian.

Four points in the report itself must be explained.

First of all, we must consider what is meant by "IIII arcs." The expression is usually taken to refer to the ribs; but by the four arches could also be meant the transverse and wall arches, which in every quadripartite vault of Chartres give the number four. One can also refer the words "qui aident à porter les voutes" to these four peripheral arches just as well as to the ribs. This interpretation of the "IIII arcs" as peripheral arches is strengthened by the reflection that the ribs of a four-celled quadripartite vault consists of only two arches; for an arch, of course, rises from one end point to its crown and descends to its other end. But one may object that the individual rib extending from the springer to the keystone is, geometrically speaking,

[4] *Ibid.*, p. 320. For the revision of the translation I thank Mr. John French, Jr., Princeton.

[5] He is mentioned in the report in connection with the repair of a statue of the Magdalen, but Mortet doubts that he was himself a sculptor (p. 322).

also an arch. A decision in favor of the interpretation of peripheral arches results from the evidence of the second doubtful passage in the text.

This consists of the words "la clef qui porte la clef." Since the keystone cannot carry itself, the word must be used here in a double sense. The solution lies in Gervase's statement: "clavem pro toto pono ciborio." Obviously, the experts inherited this terminology, but it had changed somewhat in the period from 1186 to 1316, for the passage undoubtedly means: the ribs that carry the keystone. Although Villard already possessed the word *ogive*, the word *clef* (clavis) seems to have been commonly used as well. Our interpretation relies not only on Gervase but also on the fact that first mention was made of the "IIII arcs," which, therefore, definitely do not refer to the ribs, as otherwise the text would be uselessly saying the same thing over again after a brief interval. The passage becomes logical, if one renders the sense of it in a free translation as follows: "Good are the four piers, the four arches that carry the vault [that is, the two transverse and the two longitudinal arches], and the ribs that carry the keystone. The severies of the vault, on the other hand, are not good, but they will not have to be dismantled completely; it will suffice to take down a part, and just how much is necessary, will be seen as the work goes on."

The third thing that must be of particular interest to us in this experts' report is its contribution to our knowledge of the ideas held by Gothic architects concerning the statics of their buildings. In recent times it has become an acute question how far the nineteenth century view that all the structural members of Gothic are to be interpreted as "functional" can be justified. Since even today this problem has not been solved as completely as one might wish, it would be rather helpful to know at least what the masters of Gothic themselves thought about it. Assuming that the interpretation of the text given above is correct, this expertise proves only that the four peripheral arches carry the whole vault, while the ribs, on the other hand, carry the keystone. Whether it was believed that the ribs also carry the masonry of the severies cannot be judged from the text. However, it does offer proof that it was a matter of firm conviction that the vaults were supported by the flying buttresses, the statical necessity of which has been likewise disputed in recent times.

The fourth thing of interest is the repeated discussion of the scaffolding. Mention is made of a first scaffolding that has the double function of protecting the rood-loft and the people below and perhaps also the stained glass windows above. One is forced to think of the latter, since the text speaks of the famous stained glass, one of the greatest treasures of the entire art of the Middle Ages. But the more one reflects, the more improbable does this interpretation seem. The scaffolding was intended for the vault over the crossing. At first no precise indication is given as to which vault the expertise means, but then the choir screen is mentioned, restricting the possibilities to the vault over the crossing and the first vault of the arm of the choir, and finally the experts return to the same problem and say: "nous avons veu la vouste de la croez" (Mortet, p. 314). It is, therefore, certain that the crossing is meant (Fig. 6). But the crossing of Chartres has no windows at all and thus no stained glass to be protected. If, in spite of this, one wishes to keep the theory that there was fear of damaging stained glass, one can argue that falling debris from the dismantlement of the vault might have hit the windows of the adjacent bays. Certainly, the higher the floor of the scaffolding was raised, the smaller this danger would be. It was, therefore, advantageous for the protection of the stained glass that only the uppermost part of the vault was defective. But even though there had been no stained glass windows, the plank floor would have been laid as high as possible for reasons of economy because, whatever one imagines the form of the scaffolding to have been, it would in that case require less lumber and labor. But it was also more convenient for the construction to take up the first scaffolding, "le premier eschaufaut," as high as possible, since it was then easier to erect the upper, second one. But if the text says nowhere that the scaffolding is to protect anything other than the people and the choir screen, why then does it mention the stained glass windows at all?

The windows of Chartres have as yet no tracery. In each bay is a pair of long windows with pointed heads and an oculus above them. The tops of the former extend to a height of 10 meters above the springings of the vault over the transept. The height of the oculus is 6 meters. For all concerned, including the master carpenter Simon, it was, of course, the easiest thing to say, instead of giving numerical measurements: Place the lower plank floor of the scaffolding above the *enmerllement* and this mysterious word is thus to be interpreted as the line of demarcation above the lower pairs of windows; in other words: Lay the plank floor approximately above the heads of the paired windows.

This explanation, however, granted its correctness, is only a preliminary to what really interests us: what was the upper scaffolding to look like? On that point nothing is said, at least not directly. Obviously that was left to Simon, the master carpenter. But from the whole expertise it is clearly evident that this upper scaffolding did not serve to construct the masonry of the ribs, for they were not to be torn down; they were good: "la clef qui porte la clef." Therefore, the second or upper scaffolding can only have served for the filling in of the severies of the vault. And now comes the main question: was this a wooden sheathing above which the masons stood and on which they laid stone after stone at their feet, or was it only a matter of a trestled framework on which the workers stood, reaching up from there to set the stones above their heads or at hip height, perhaps working with the help of a curved rule, perhaps completely freehand and by eye? Of late this question has been raised for the whole period of Gothic generally, and it would have been some gain if a document were to give an authoritative answer, at least for a single Gothic vault—but in this matter, unfortunately, the expertise affords no help. It may be added that when the work was done, the entire vault over the crossing, together with the ribs, was taken down and built afresh; that can be seen from the profiles of the ribs. The severies have been domed, and, therefore, are completely new as of 1316. Whether the flying buttresses of the choir were also completely rebuilt in 1316 has not yet been finally determined; at any rate, they are no longer those of the first period of construction.

On the whole, this expertise is valuable because, in spite of its obscurities, it casts light on building practices. It belongs in the same category, therefore, as certain parts of Villard de Honnecourt's book.

That can also be said, to some extent, about the expertises of Milan (1391-1400), only in them the main interest is directed toward the problem of proportions as aids to measurement, bearing some relation therefore to Magister 2. There is a whole series of reports dealing with the edifice at Milan and a partial review of the structural history of the cathedral is unavoidable.[6]

[6] The main source for the events in Milan of the period from 1386 to 1400 is the *Annali della fabbrica del Duomo di Milano dall' origine al presente*, pubblicati a cura della sua amministrazione, I, Milan, 1877. Even before the documents were published an account of the quarrels was given by Fr. W. Unger, "Die deutschen Dombaumeister in Prag und Mailand." *Zeitschrift für bildende Kunst*, VI, Leipzig, 1871, pp. 99 and 125. There the older literature is listed on p. 125. The chief work on The Milan Cathedral is by Camillo Boito, *Il duomo di Milano e i disegni per la sua facciata*, Milan, 1889. Guiseppe Merzerio, *I Maestri Comacini*, Milan, 1893, devoted a whole chapter to it, I, 305ff. Georg Dehio, *Die kirchliche Baukunst des Abendlandes*, Stuttgart, 1901, II, p. 534 gave a brief description of the disputes. After the completion of my manuscript, I came upon the book by Herbert Siebenhühner, *Deutsche Künstler am Mailänder Dom*, Munich, 1944. It is in many respects supplementary, but does not touch the main problems.

Milan Cathedral was founded in 1386. We do not know who made the first plan; it may be that the name of this master is contained in the long list transmitted to us of masters who were connected with the building. There existed from the very beginning a model of the structure, to which the builders by and large adhered. In 1388 a commission already had to be called together because a mistake in measurement had shown up: the wall of the transept had been made too wide at one point and had partly to be torn down. But that was only the prelude.

Already by 1389 the authorities seem to have lost confidence in their own architects and they called Nicolas de Bonaventure from Paris, who settled the form for the horizontal section of the piers and for the profiles of the bases. The height of the piers was already determined by the model, but that was not reached all at once. The exterior walls of the choir and transept and those of the beginning of the nave were being built up simultaneously. For these parts Bonaventure designed the profiles of the windows and doors. One year later the master fled, having belied his name by getting into financial difficulties.

What was at that time partly executed and partly intended is revealed to us in a survey sketch (Fig. 14). Antonio di Vicenzo, the *capo maestro* of S. Petronio in Bologna, was sent to Milan by the Bolognese to study the cathedral. It is, at first glance, difficult to understand what benefit this study could have been to him since both edifices are so different in every respect. But for us this sketch is *per se* priceless. Unless a bad mistake was made, it reveals to us the original intention of building three bays in each of the arms of the transept instead of the existing two bays. Naturally it was not drawn to a definite scale; but, in addition to the ground plan of the eastern part (obviously taken from the model), it also gives a transverse section of the nave, on which the dimensions are indicated in (Milanese) braccia or feet. The total dimension of the height of the nave, including the vault, is not given, but that of the piers is; and by drawing in a normal quadripartite vault, one arrives at the conclusion that this height was to be equal to the total width of the nave and four aisles (measured in the clear). Thus the whole transverse section was inscribed in a square. It is that which, in this connection, is called *ad quadratum*. Antonio presumably did not enter the measurements of elevation because for him they resulted automatically from the ground plan.

By 1391 the structure had risen to the point where the height of the piers and, therefore, that of the exterior walls as well had to be finally determined. But now doubts arose as to whether the height prescribed by the original model really ought to be carried out. We do not learn whether these doubts were of an economic, statical, or aesthetic nature or perhaps a combination of these. The authorities wanted an expert opinion, and Master Giovanni di Fernach was sent to Cologne to persuade the master there to make the journey to Milan or possibly only to give his advice on the basis of drawings brought from Milan.[7] It is not quite clear who presided over the Cologne lodge at that date. If it was still the same Master Michael who is mentioned for the first time in 1353, it is not surprising that he declined an arduous journey of several weeks. And it was probably this aged master whose opinion was sought, for we hear of no other name there until 1395, when Master Andreas von Everdingen appears in Cologne and officiates until 1412, without being approached by the Milanese. When Giovanni di Fernach returned alone, they decided to apply to Ulrich von Ensingen in Ulm; but he, too, refused.[8]

After this interlude, which illustrates for us the connections of the Gothic lodges, the Milanese wrote to a mathematician in Piacenza, Stornaloco (Fig. 15). Why to a mathematician? Are mathematicians especially competent as regards beauty of proportions? Hardly. But if the Milanese were not thinking of beauty when they turned to Stornaloco, they were thinking of it just as little when they turned to the Cologne master and to Ulrich von Ensingen. For everything that now ensues we have the right perspective if we remember what we learned from the geometrical figures of Magister 2. The problem was how to determine the height of the cathedral, so that this dimension could be conveniently used on the building site.

Stornaloco came to Milan, worked for ten days, went back, and presently sent on his advice. This proposal was at first adopted by the authorities and a new model constructed by a carpenter from Piacenza. But very soon a chorus of dissatisfaction was heard. The result was that the model was first locked up in a private house and then, since even there it was not safe from critical glances, in a shed near the campanile of the old cathedral.[9] Exposed to the hostility of the

[7] According to Thieme-Becker, *Allgemeines Lexikon der bildenden Künstler*, XI, p. 406, Fernach is a place near Freiburg i. Br. Hans von Fernach was, then, a German. He made the design for the door of the southern sacristy of the cathedral, simplified in 1393 by the commission. It may be that Hans von Fernach was the same person as Giovanni da Firimburg, which means Freiburg. Yet more probably these are two different persons.

[8] Ulrich von Ensingen had gone to Milan in November 1394, and was back in Germany by March 1395.

[9] This campanile had collapsed in 1385, but a remnant was still standing in 1391.

citizens by this situation, the building authorities again hoped for a decision based on an expertise. They approached Heinrich Parler of Ulm. It is not known whether this choice was influenced by a recommendation from Ulrich von Ensingen, who sent him, as it were, as his representative. Heinrich belongs to the Parler family who dominated the German lodges in the fourteenth century. Their genealogy is not absolutely clear; in this case, it is probably the so-called Heinrich III of Ulm, a member of the South German branch of the Parlers.[10] Boito confused this Heinrich Parler with Heinrich I Parler of Prague (born about 1300), father of Peter Parler (1330-1399), the most prominent representative of the family. Heinrich von Gmünd or, as he is called in the Milan archives, Heinrich von Ulm arrived in Milan on November 27, 1391, and after fourteen days was appointed for three months. During this period Parler seems to have urged a return to the first plan *ad quadratum*. After three months had passed there was just as great indecision as before. The Italians not only did not want to go back to the square but they even wished to reduce Stornaloco's measures still further.

Why the German preferred the slender and the Italians the lower transverse section seems easy to answer: it was a matter of the difference in taste of the two peoples. But we cannot be satisfied to talk only of steeper and shallower proportions when obviously the dispute was about quite exact measurements. Why, for example, did they reduce the height of Stornaloco's springers on the inner aisles from 42 to 40 braccia and not to 41 or 39? Why did they reduce the part above the capitals of the piers of the nave from 56 to 52 braccia and not to 51 or 53?

To aid in a real understanding of the measurements we have the minutes of May 1, 1392, and various drawings. Boito used the drawing by Luca Beltrami that, in a very telling way, joins half of Stornaloco's transverse section to half of the transverse section that corresponds to the minutes of 1392. It is a question of understanding that the measurements entered on the drawing are in complete accord with the text of the minutes of May 1, 1392. In agreement with Boito we distinguish four stages in all.

The first stage corresponds to the model that was the standard at the beginning of the construction and the chief dimensions of which have been preserved by Vicenzo's drawing. It was *ad quadratum*, that is, the height of the nave amounted to the same dimension as the clear width of the nave and four aisles, 96 braccia.

[10] Cf. Thieme-Becker, s.v. Parler.

The second stage is Stornaloco's drawing. It is *ad triangulum,* that is, an equilateral triangle is the basis for all the important points of elevation. In Beltrami's drawing a height of 84 braccia is entered for the nave. That means a sharp reduction as against the 96 braccia of the plan *ad quadratum.*

The third stage is that of the minutes of May 1, 1392. From Beltrami's drawing it is apparent that the height of the nave was now reduced to 76 braccia.

The fourth stage is the actual execution, which differs from the minutes of May 1, 1392, only in that all measurements of elevation are lower by a half braccio.

At a first glance neither the drawing, the minutes, nor the last reduction by a half braccio is intelligible. In order to arrive at an interpretation, it is best to start with Stornaloco's drawing. Curiously enough, no one except Boito seems to have noticed that in it the measurements do not correspond to the drawing. Beltrami and even Boito entered expressly the angle of 60 degrees to show that the triangle was equilateral. But if an equilateral triangle has as its base 6 x 16 = 96 braccia, then its height cannot be 84 braccia; that can be seen without much calculation, because the height of an equilateral triangle cannot be expressed in whole numbers if the base is in whole numbers (and correspondingly the converse is true). Actually, given a base of 96 braccia, the height is only 82.5 braccia. Why did Stornaloco, the mathematician, write in 84 braccia instead?

To understand this, reference must be made to the fact brought out by Kossmann's investigations that in the Middle Ages a "great basic measure" was used in measuring.[11] It was not possible, namely, to measure high elevations exactly by means of strings, because the latter stretched differently depending on how tightly they were drawn. Therefore wooden rods were used for measurement and these had to be of a handy dimension that was neither too large nor too small. It will soon become clear that this basic measure was in dispute.

In Stornaloco's drawing there are entered on the middle line the numbers 14, 28, 42, 56, 70, 84, that is, the arithmetical progression of 14 braccia. It is easy to guess that the great basic measure was not 14 but half of it, 7. On the nave, 32 braccia in width, Stornaloco drew in the equilateral triangle and adjusted the mathematically exact dimen-

[11] B. Kossmann, *Einstens massgebende Gesetze bei der Grundrissgestaltung von Kirchenbauten,* Strasbourg, 1925.

sion of elevation from 27.68 to 28 braccia, because it was more convenient to use whole numbers for the great basic measure.[12]

In the session of May 1, 1392, Heinrich Parler wanted to raise the great basic measure from 7 to 8 braccia, which, then, would have been identical with the great basic measure of the ground plan (this is not reported but we can deduce it from the evidence). The short designation *ad quadratum* revealed to the initiated that for both ground plan and elevation the same great basic measure was to be employed. Stornaloco set the great basic measure of the elevation at only 7 braccia. The other Italians on the commission wanted to reduce the great basic measure to 6 braccia, and this was to be decisive from the level of the capitals of the nave piers upward. Their choice is understandable as soon as one observes the triangle that now results from a base of 32 braccia, the width of the nave, and an elevation of 12. It can be divided by a bisecting line into two right-angled triangles with the catheti 16:12 braccia, or, in general terms, with the proportion 4:3. This is, as Beltrami has already recognized,[13] the Pythagorean triangle (Fig. 16). This triangle, known and popular since ancient times, has the advantage of facilitating the marking of the right angle by means of sides in terms of whole numbers. For with the catheti 4 and 3 units long, the hypotenuse will be 5 units long. If the horizontal line is marked off on the scaffolding with a string from the upper edge of one capital to that of the opposite capital, it is relatively easy to plot out exactly the height desired, because the hypotenuse of 5 units can be used as a control dimension. Realization of this fact makes the dimensions above the capitals of the nave piers intelligible.

It remains to be explained why, when the work was carried out, all the dimensions were made a half braccio lower. This change began in the piers of the aisles. Stornaloco, as we saw, adjusted the actual height of the equilateral triangle with a base of 32 braccia, that is, a height of 27.68 braccia, to 28 braccia. That was an adjustment *upward*. The architects in charge, however, chose instead of 27.68 braccia only 27.50 braccia for the height of the piers in the outer aisles. They therefore went down half a braccio below Stornaloco's 28 braccia. They adjusted *downward*, and the reason for this was that in so doing they approached more closely the real measure of elevation of the equilateral triangle. The reduction by half a braccio (that is, by a foot) can have

12 A supplement to this statement is contained in my article, "The Secret of the Mediaeval Masons," *Art Bulletin*, 1945, pp. 46ff.

13 Quoted in Boito, *op.cit.*, p. 122.

been neither for statical nor economic nor aesthetic reasons. Practically, the procedure was that first the height of the piers of the outer aisles was determined by raising up the great basic measure of 7 braccia by four lengths, thus reaching a height of 28 braccia, and then going down half a braccio from that point. Above this level they employed the newly chosen great basic measure of only 6 braccia; in connection with the dimension of the width of the nave, that means that they employed the Pythagorean triangle. Rods 8 braccia long are 4.76 meters in length and thus still quite manageable. On them could be marked off the eight individual lengths of one braccio each and then the same type of rods used both for the dimensions of the ground plan and those of the elevation (below and above the capitals of the piers); or rods 7 braccia long could be specially cut for the superstructure. The employment of a "great basic measure," as it was deduced by Kossmann, is no mere hypothetical assumption, but is testified to by the passages in Stornaloco's letter where he speaks of the *unitas*. It is, moreover, a compelling conclusion from the whole train of thought of the negotiations of 1392.

After we understand the drawing, we can turn to the text. Of the questions in the minutes, eleven in all, numbers three, four, and five are for us the decisive ones. They read in translation:

"Question 3. Whether the church itself, that is, not counting the tower over the crossing, is to be raised according to the square or according to the triangle?

Answer 3. They declared that the church itself is to be raised up to the triangle or to the triangular figure and not above it.

Question 4. How many braccia are the piers that serve the nave to have?

Answer 4. They declared that the piers themselves, including their bases and capitals, should have 40 braccia and no more.

Question 5. How many braccia are the middle shafts to be that are on the wall above the great piers themselves up to the vaults or arches over them, and how many braccia are the vaults over them to be made?

Answer 5. They resolved and declared that the middle shafts should be 12 braccia high and the vault of the nave should rise according to the triangle, that is, 24 braccia."

What was meant in the third question by *ad quadratum* and *ad triangulum* is perfectly clear. But the answer brings the variation: "ad triangulum sive ad figuram triangularem et non ultra." According to the analysis of the drawing that must mean: "up to the Pythagorean triangle or up to the equilateral triangle and not above it." The words *et non ultra* refer to the decision not to adjust upward but downward. It looks as though the men who formulated question 3 had thought only of the equilateral triangle in contrast to the square, while the men who gave the *answer* were now talking about two different triangles. In this answer, then, the word *triangulum* means the Pythagorean triangle; on the other hand, *figura triangularis* is the equilateral one,[14] because only for the latter does the addition *et non ultra* make sense.

The Pythagorean triangle is fixed as to dimensions in answer 5, where the height of "the middle shafts" (that is, the wall shafts over the nave shafts) is set at 12 braccia. The word *triangulum*, however, is there connected with the vault. Without the foregoing analysis one would have to assume that here simply that triangle is meant that results from the width of the nave and the height of the vault, in other words, the triangle with a base of 32 braccia and a height of 24 braccia. This triangle is neither Pythagorean nor equilateral. But from the drawing it follows that here two triangles are drawn in, one above the other, each of which consists of two symmetrical Pythagorean triangles. Thus we may conclude that by *triangulum* here again was meant the Pythagorean triangle.[15]

The inference is that in the session of May 1, 1392, the height of the piers in the outer aisles was set at 27.50 braccia. If this is correct, then there is a contradiction in the individual answers. Question 4 reads: "How many braccia are the piers that serve the nave to have?" The answer that they were to be 40 braccia high overlooks the fact that all the upper measurements were to be reduced by half a braccio on

14 That had already been understood correctly by G. Dehio, *Die Kirchliche Baukunst des Abendlandes*, II, p. 564. This I overlooked when I wrote my article of 1945.

15 Boito introduced into the discussion still a third triangle, the so-called Egyptian triangle with a base of four units and a height of two and a half. This triangle was nowhere used in the cross section of Milan Cathedral; to bring it into the discussion only creates confusion with regard to these problems, which are in any case none too simple. Moreover, it is a false assumption that the masters of 1400 knew anything about this so-called Egyptian triangle, which is supposed to have determined the cross section of the Pyramid of Cheops. In the interpretation of the passage it can each time be a question only of the Pythagorean and the equilateral triangles. A detailed discussion of the "Egyptian triangle" was given by Daniel Ramée, *Histoire générale de l'achitecture*, I, Paris, 1860, p. 161. He refers to M. Jomard, *Description de l'Égypte*, Paris, 1809-1822, p. 718. Viollet-le-Duc took over from these sources what he had to say about this Egyptian triangle in the *Entretiens sur l'architecture*, Paris, 1863, I, p. 394, and in the *Dictionnaire raisonné de l'architecture*, Paris, 1864, VII, p. 534, s.v. "Proportion." From Rameé he also took the quotation from Plutarch, *Traité sur Isis et Osiris* (d'-Amyot, trans.) on the Pythagorean triangle, which is there called, following Plato's *Republic*, "une figure nuptiale." (The first edition of Ramée, *Manuel de l'histoire générale de l'architecture*, Paris, 1843, does not contain anything about these triangles in the corresponding chapter, p. 269.)

the basis of answer three: *et non ultra.* Boito is, therefore, right in differentiating between the decision of 1392 and the actual execution, especially if one deduces that there was still some vacillation in the meeting or that the contradiction between answers three and four became apparent only afterward during the exact working out of the measurements.

What we gain from this whole interpretation of the drawings and the text is the confirmation of what we learned from Magister 2 in Villard's Lodge Book: that in the Gothic period one measured according to proportions, and that this method did not aim at mysterious calculations of beauty but rather had the purely practical purpose of measuring without modern pocket rulers. But this applies only to the dimensions in their absolute exactitude. The aesthetic tendency that would make a transverse section more sharply sloped or more flattened is superior to or, more properly, anterior to this method of mensuration. Heinrich Parler, who wanted to return to the square, meant the exact square and not one braccio or a fraction of a braccio more or less, because according to that he set the great basic measure at 8 braccia for ground plan *and* elevation. The method of measuring either *ad quadratum* or *ad triangulum* or *ad figuram triangularem* exists, therefore, to determine the dimensions *exactly, within* the limits of a *previously* decided tendency toward a general proportion which has been chosen for *aesthetic* reasons. The secret of the lodges does not relate to "beauty" itself but to the exact measurements of that which was considered at the time beautiful.

The report of the proceedings on May 1, 1392, is chronologically the next source after Magister 2 to give us a glimpse of the secret of the lodges. It is not merely a confirmation of what we know from his drawings and annotations but also an invaluable supplement. That earlier source explains only what the method *ad quadratum* was; the second one explains also what that *ad triangulum* was. We can judge from Heinrich Parler's attitude that in his circles, that is, among the Squires of Prague, the method *ad quadratum* had become the central theory of the geometry of workshop or building site, whereas in Italy *ad triangulum* was preferred, though it ran into the difficulties revealed in Stornaloco's letter. That the latter, a mathematician, was called in, is evidence that no practical method had as yet been found to operate with the triangle in such a way as to render harmless the irrationality of the measure of elevation. If that is so, we gain in unexpected fashion and despite the paucity of sources an insight into the genesis both of the method *ad quadratum* and that *ad triangulum*.

Heinrich Parler with his predilection for steep proportions stood alone against the united front of the Italians. Only one of them, Simone da Orsenigo, yielded on one question; it was, whether the outer aisles should be cut up into chapels by means of transverse walls. Simone decided for the latter because he hoped thereby to improve the statics of the edifice, but on other points he voted against the German. Thus Heinrich had become superfluous and was to go back to Germany. From then on he struggled only to obtain his salary for the period subsequent to March 11 and money for the return journey. On July 7 he received an indemnification and his dismissal. A German interpreter translated the document setting forth the verdict, which contained the harsh words that he had served the *fabrica* badly by his misdeeds (*malegestis*) and had done great harm. Parler returned no answer and left. This dispute of May 1, 1392, may have been very unpleasant for the participants, but for us it is an invaluable source for the working procedure of Gothic architects.

The building now progressed fairly smoothly. We can pass over the episode of Ulrich von Füssingen "de Ulma" in the year 1395.[16] Not until 1399 did the old problem become acute once more. They seem to have completed most of the piers up to the beginning of the vaults and were not of one mind about the latter. Two architects were called in from outside. Both of them, Masters Giovanni Mignoto from Paris and Giacomo Cova of Bruges, arrived simultaneously in Milan on August 7. In the first entries in the annals they were called *pittori*. Of Cova nothing more is heard, but all the more of Mignot, who was obviously by chief profession an architect and not a painter. Actually Mignot was to be consulted about the vaults, but he informed the Duke that the whole edifice threatened to collapse. That naturally created in the responsible circles great excitement and hostility against the stranger. On Sunday, December 28, it was resolved to have the wooden model completed by Giovanni de' Grassi, and at the same time Mignot was requested to hand in by Wednesday, December 31, a list of the damage together with proposals for its repair. Mignot made a list of fifty-four points. On January 11, 1400, this list was discussed. The masters answered only the first twenty-five points and declared that the building would never be finished if Mignot's list was considered

[16] Boito, *op.cit.*, p. 128.

further. As a matter of fact, the criticisms subsequent to point 25 are uncommonly petty; for example, he objected to mistakes in measurement from one to three fingers wide. Today Mignot, on the basis of his own words, seems to us a *Beckmesser*, a pedantic and pompous person, who considered himself infallible, called everything poor that had been done by others, and wanted to change, tear down, and make as many additions as possible, both because he could not see beyond his Paris tradition and because he wished to collect money and fame. On the other hand, the Italians, with the architect in charge, Marco da Carona, at their head, may have been touchy, unteachable, and prejudiced against the foreigner. One will always be inclined to smile off this whole dispute as a psychologically interesting document of human weaknesses, but it does reveal, like that of 1392, something as well of the way in which professional experts of Gothic criticized their own and others' works.

Of course, the whole dispute cannot be discussed here point by point. Our interest is directed in some places toward Mignot's accusations and in others toward the Italians' defense. The passages to be stressed are points 1, 3, 7, 9, 14, 15, and 16.

Mignot started with the east end and objected first of all that the piers between the windows of the choir were too weak. Here, above all, he presumably expected the collapse. The Italians replied that the foundations were excellent (reportedly fourteen braccia, going down approximately eight meters to bed rock), that the stone in them was strong (*sarizzo*)[17] that the blocks were well fastened with iron clamps, and that it was intended to install in the church above the capitals great iron tie-rods (*strictores ferri magnos*)—and later this was done. But then comes the statement that they expected to construct pointed arches and that pointed arches exerted no thrust on the buttresses ("dicunt quod archi spiguti non dant impulzam contrafortibus"), and, therefore, all the buttresses were strong enough. This is historical testimony as to what was thought in Milan in the year 1400 about the statics of pointed arches.

In points 3 and 7 Mignot criticizes the proportions of the window profiles and their figures, also the fact that the canopies hover too high above the figures. This criticism has nothing to do with statics; it has exclusive reference to aesthetics, or, more precisely, to personal taste. The Italians retort to point 3 that with other proportions the figures would be less visible; their counterargument is, therefore, rational. In

[17] The word *sarizzo* seems to be a local expression for a kind of stone.

point 7 Mignot says that the arches and jambs of the windows of the sacristy do not have their reasonable ratio (*suam rationem*) so that figures could be set into them, and the Italians simply contradict: "they stand well according to their ratio (et archi bene stant secundum suam rationem)." One sees that behind these statements lie aesthetic judgments, but that neither of the parties was capable of grasping them conceptually.

Point 15 tempts us to see in Mignot a strict classicist of Gothic. He mainly objects to the lack of engaged wall shafts as carriers of the ribs (*croxeriae*) in the inner corners of the sacristies, and adds that thereby the church is made weaker than it should be. The Italians counter this apparently *aesthetic* or stylistic thesis by the assertion that the engaged shafts are not *statically* necessary. We shall presently realize that Mignot, too, means only statics in this point and not aesthetics.

In point 14 Mignot demands that the gargoyles of the sacristy should be raised by five braccia, according to their *ratio* ("minus bassae quam requirunt rationes illarum"), without indicating the *rationes*. Obviously he wanted to move them closer to the gutter. But the Italians answer that the water flows off better in their present location; they would like to place them even lower down, for when the wind blows, it drives the water against the windows. If it were possible to conduct the water down completely inside the buttresses, they would do it, but that is impossible. This argumentation of the Italians is strikingly rational, and Viollet-le-Duc would certainly have been their enthusiastic ally in this one point.

In point 9 Mignot speaks of the piers of the nave. The passage is not absolutely clear. It will therefore be translated literally first and then interpreted.

"Item quod capitelli pilonorum positi in opera supra ipsis pilonis non sunt positi ad rationem suam, quia pedes ipsorum pilonorum sunt brachiorum duorum pro quolibet in longitudine, et capitelli sunt br. x pro quolibet ipsorum in longitudine, debent esse ipsi capitelli tantae longitudinis quantae sunt pedes ipsorum pilonorum.

"Dicunt et respondent quod pedes

Further, that the capitals of the piers, placed in the work above the piers themselves, are not set reasonably, because the bases of these piers are each two braccia in length and the capitals each ten braccia; these same capitals ought to be of such a length as the length of the bases of their piers.

They say and answer that feet or bases of the piers, if the capitals have

sive bassae pilonorum si sunt brachiorum II capitelli debent esse brachium unum, ipsis rationibus dicunt bassam pilonorum et pes dicitur pes hominis et capitellum dicitur caput piloni, ita caput hominis dicitur a capitello. Ita quod pes est quarta pars capitis hominis et per istam rationem naturalem deberet esse brachia VIII et si essent facti de br. x essent propter ad ornamentum pilonorum per ponere figuras."

two braccia, must be one braccio high; according to reason they call them the base of the piers and foot means the foot of a man and capital means the head of the pier, just as the head of a man is said from capital. Now the foot is the fourth part of the head of a man and by this natural ratio it ought to have eight braccia, and if they have been made 10 braccia, they were made for the adornment of the piers in order to place figures.

From the drawing by Beltrami and Boito it is clear that Mignot meant the head-pieces of the piers including the capitals; their length is actually ten braccia. For Mignot, as for anyone used to French Gothic, these decorated tops were an irritation, and he declared ill-naturedly that according to the rule a capital had to be just as high as the foot of the pier. The Italians answer in his own tone: if one wants to stick to rules, then it is a rule that a capital must be twice as high as a base, but these terms refer to the human members of head and foot and therefore human proportions are authoritative. According to Vitruvius (who is not actually mentioned here) the length of the head ought to equal four times the height of the foot (naturally not the length of the foot); therefore, the capital would have to be eight braccia; that it is ten braccia, is explained by the decoration.

If this explanation of the text is correct, then it shows that the rule of proportions was different in Milan and Paris, and—what is more interesting—that the Milanese, following Vitruvius, were already playing with analogies to the human figure even before there was a Renaissance architecture. Brunelleschi's first building with classical proportions, the Ospedale degli Innocenti in Florence, was not begun until 1419, and in Milan the Renaissance did not get under way until 1455.[18] It is clear that Mignot was still entirely grounded in Gothic theory while the Milanese were already orienting themselves by that of antiquity. Both sides disputed dogmatically about preconceived principles that were intended to be purely aesthetic and had nothing directly to do with the secret measuring method of the lodges.

18 That was the branch bank of the Medici, a gift of the Sforza to the Medici, but, in spite of that, not in Milanese style; it was designed by Michelozzo and was, thus, purely Florentine.

These differing trends of taste are distinctly apparent in point 16: Mignot objects that the buttresses of the sacristies have no set-offs, "which is bad, a fault that cannot be made good." The Italians answer that the two buttresses of the sacristy are well built and just like the others and if they were receding, they would make the work ugly and they would stand badly, if some were tapered and the others not, because the weight of the piers ought to follow its own reason in a vertical direction (*per rectam lineam*). Again it is striking how meager the concepts of this generation still were. Mignot says: "quod male est," and the Italians answer: "sunt bene fabricati." Here the judgments really seem to be meant aesthetically, yet the Italians talk in the same breath of statics: "quia onus. . . ." But to derive from statics the theory that the piers ought to follow the vertical line undoubtedly called forth only scornful laughter on Mignot's part. He obviously knew that the vault, at that time not yet begun, would exercise a side thrust.

Mignot was not satisfied by the replies to the twenty-five of his fifty-four objections in the form presented. He again demanded an examination of the construction of the edifice and this led to the sharpest opposition of the two parties' convictions. This time everything is brought together under three headings.

First of all, Mignot says that all the buttresses around the church are too weak, because they ought to be three times as strong as each individual pier of the nave. He reverts, therefore, to point 16 of the previous session.

To that the Italians now reply that all the buttresses are strong enough to carry their load and more than that for many reasons, because a cube of one braccio of their marble and *sarizius* is as strong as a cube of two braccia in France or in the French church that Mignot cites as an example. Since each buttress in the Milan Cathedral has the strength of one and one half piers, it is *ad suam rationem*, that is, reasonable; and if the buttresses were larger, they would darken the church by their obstruction as in the case of the church of Paris, the buttresses of which are of the kind recommended by Mignot. Thus the Italians do not hesitate to tell the Parisian that Notre Dame is gloomy. But we learn from this whole reply that they measured the resistance of different types of stone or weighed one against another ($1^3:2^3 = 1:8$).

The second paragraph of the minutes of January 25, 1400, must again be translated literally first, because of its linguistic difficulties:

"Furthermore, he [Mignot] says that four towers for the support of the *tiburio* of the aforesaid church have been begun and there are no piers nor any other foundation capable of supporting these same towers, so that if the church were suddenly to be made with the said towers quite [complete], it would infallibly collapse; furthermore, [he says] that they [the towers] were surely made according to their own ideas by some ignoramuses who maintain that vaults with pointed arches are stronger and of a lesser weight than those with round arches, and, furthermore, it is a proposition [project] more according to personal opinion than good rules; and thereto [to this accusation] that the work was so bad, it is replied (by those Italian ignoramuses) that the theory (*scientia*) of geometry plays no part in this matter, because theory is one thing and practice (*ars*) another. The said Magister Johannes says that practice without theory is nothing and that the vaults, whether pointed or round, are worthless if they have no foundation, and aside from that they have a very great weight, even though they are pointed.

"Furthermore, they [the Italians] say that they want to construct the towers of which they have spoken [they say] with various points of view and reasons, to wit, first, in order to bring into harmony the aforesaid church and the crossing, because they both correspond to the square according to the order of geometry; the second reason relates in truth to the strength and beauty of the *tiburio*, that is, as it were, as an example: in Paradise sits God the Lord on a throne, around the throne are the four Evangelists according to the Apocalypse; and these are the reasons why they were begun. And although the two piers in front of each sacristy have no foundations, beginning above ground, nevertheless the church is strong enough for the following reasons, because there are *reprexae*, on which the aforesaid piers rest, and these said *reprexae* consist of large stones and are joined with iron clamps, as was mentioned in the other chapters, and the weight of the aforesaid three towers rests everywhere on their squares, and they will be built straight and strong; what is straight, however, cannot fall; therefore, they say that they are strong and thus will they give strength to the *tiburio*, because it is enclosed in the midst of those towers, wherefore the aforesaid church is sufficiently strong." (See Appendix, p. 873, for Latin text.)

The clerk wrote unusually bad Latin; it may be that he himself did not clearly understand what it was all about. By analogy with the other minutes in the annals, the whole first paragraph is devoted to Mignot's thesis. The sense of it is as follows: the *tiburio* (the tower over the crossing, called *tiburio* in Milan and Lombardy) must collapse because there is no foundation or, more properly, no abutment. To be sure, the Italians say that the vault of the *tiburio*, which they intend to construct with pointed arches, needs no abutment, because pointed arches exercise no thrust (in contrast to round arches). But when

Mignot preaches to them that an abutment *is* necessary, these ignoramuses reply that it is here a question of practice, not of theory. But Mignot teaches: "ars sine scientia nihil est," and if foundations (abutments) are lacking, any vault will collapse, be its arches pointed or round.

The second paragraph conveys the Italian answer, that is, the presumptive rebuttal to Mignot's objection. The four corner towers of the *tiburio* are necessary. As the first reason is given "pro rectificando praedictam ecclesiam et croxeriam quod respondet ad quadrangulum secundum ordinem geometriae." This is probably to be interpreted that the Italians intend to say: the *tiburio* is a consequence of the whole concept of the ground plan and, as a matter of fact, is according to the rules of geometry *ad quadratum*. This sounds as though they want to make the point: we know as well as Magister Mignot what the *scientia geometriae* demands, but we naturally recognize it only where it belongs. The second reason is the reference to the four Evangelists about the throne of God. That this has to do with "strength and beauty" throws light upon the faith of those Gothic architects. But then, all of a sudden, there are mentioned two piers of each sacristy. A glance at the plan helps us to guess that Mignot put it to the Italians that the vaulting of the crossing would exercise a diagonal thrust corresponding to the direction of the ribs of the dome or quadripartite vault over the crossing, that, therefore, the weight would have to be borne by those corner piers of the sacristies, for which reason they should be strengthened by those engaged shafts that he had already demanded in the previous list. In the Latin text it looks as though the discussion were about foundations, but the addition "incipiende super terram" makes it clear that no subterranean foundations are meant, but that the piers themselves in their whole extent above ground are to be understood as abutments. Toward the west the situation is different; there, even in Mignot's opinion, the system of buttresses suffices. That is why suddenly only three towers are mentioned: they are the *tiburio* itself and its two eastern corner towers, as they were then planned. Thus, from this passage, it is evident that Mignot on January 11, 1400, in point 15 of his list did not object to the lack of engaged shafts in the corners of the sacristies out of hostility to Late Gothic practices but simply because he foresaw that this would surely bring about the collapse of the vaulting over the crossing. One now understands belatedly why the Italian masters then replied expressly that these corner piers were of great strength for "the whole church." Now they come back to them and say that the *reprexae* are sufficient, because they consist of good stone and are well anchored. The word *reprexae* is found in Du Cange. It may be derived from *reprimere* and means, as the context shows, the actual foundations of the piers. The Italians think to invalidate Mignot's warnings by asserting that the *tiburio* will not exercise a diagonal thrust, since they will construct the vault with pointed arches and pointed arches, in their opinion, do not exercise a thrust. The weight of the vault over the crossing will be transmitted vertically through the piers of the crossing. That is in principle the same belief that they had expressed in connection with the discussion of the buttresses. This dispute is our main source for the actual ideas of Italian Gothic architects on statics. Mignot called them ignoramuses; obviously, the French masters of Gothic had a better knowledge of the subject.

In the third section of the minutes Mignot demands that they call in experts from Germany or France or England. He meant to say: all the professionals of Gothic think as I do in this matter, only you Milanese are ignoramuses. He therefore advises that work on the *triburio* be stopped until those experts can be heard.

Thereupon follows the Italian answer, which the secretary did not understand and which we, too, can scarcely interpret fully. The literal translation runs as follows: "Furthermore, they [the Italians] say and answer in the same chapter, that where he says (*ubi dicit*) that the science of geometry shall play no part in this matter, to that those listed above say that according to his own testimony, that is, according to the rule of geometry, Aristotle said that the movements of men are either movements from place to place, which we call locomotion, or straight motion (*rectus*) or circular or a mixture of these. Furthermore, the latter said in another connection that every body is perfect in the trinity and [likewise] in its motion, and now the aforesaid church is being erected according to the triangle, as was already explained by other engineers, therefore they say that everything is constructed according to the straight line or the circle, therefore it is concluded that what has been done has been done according to geometry and to practice, because he himself says that theory is nothing without practice; of practice there has already been a discussion in other chapters."

First of all, it seems unclear in this puzzling section *who* is meant when the secretary writes: "ubi dicit quod scientia geometriae non debet in iis locum habere." Mignot could hardly have said that, rather he reproached the *Italians* for having talked such nonsense. One must, therefore, assume that they dictated to the secretary: "ubi dicit quod diximus . . . ," that is, "where he says that we said. . . ."

The second thing that demands explanation as a matter of principle is the frequent recurrence of the words *scientia* and *ars*. The modern reader is inclined to translate *ars* by art and thus to read into the text what we understand by art today, especially its emotional, irrational or antirational elements. Correspondingly, one is inclined to declare *scientia* to be exact science. Boito, therefore, gathered from this passage that the Italians are and were in all ages untrammeled artists who follow their inspiration, whereas the French were always cold intellectuals, and that this contrast found its ultimate, classic formulation in the dispute of 1400. This interpretation is untenable. The last sentence of the minutes makes it clear that *ars* is meant as a synonym for *practica*. By *scientia*, on the other hand, is generally meant theory as opposed to practice; *scientia* can therefore be taken as a synonym for geometry and this in the special sense of the lodge secret of proportional measurement. But it can also be referred to the theory of statics and that is the case here.[19] One can, then, summarize the principal stages in the whole controversy by the following formulations:

The Italians say: "Scientia est unum et ars est aliud." That is, theory is *one* thing and practice is *another*. By that is also implied: we have no exact theory of statics and so we build on the basis of our experience within the domain of practice.

Mignot retorts: "Ars sine scientia nihil est." That is, practice, too, requires theory, namely, knowledge of the laws of statics. This latter Mignot could not express clearly, since he had very little idea of the laws of statics.

The Italians reply to this, in a rearguard action: Practice is indeed nothing without theory, but we have the theory of statics and dynamics of Aristotle on our side; thus, the cathedral of Milan is in order in every respect: in practice *and* in theory. Aristotle was the only textbook of mechanics to which they could resort. The passage from his *Physics* was later also cited by Alberti, who understood it perhaps more clearly. In the printed edition of the Milanese documents we read the word *reclusus*, which does not make sense. Panofsky suggested in discussion that *rectus* be substituted; a false reading may have crept in because in the manuscript the word appeared as *rect'*, which perhaps looked like *recl'*. Boito spoke quite correctly of three

[19] Compare with this the pair of words *fabrica* and *ratiocinatio* in Vitruvius, I, I.

movements, the straight, curved, and that made up of these two. In Aristotle's text the word is likewise "straight" (εὐθεία).

Mignot's demand that new experts should be called in, was satisfied, except that they brought in Italians. Bertolino da Novarra and Bernardo da Venezia made their report on May 8. They proposed a strengthening of the supports on the inner side, that is, they returned to Simone da Orsenigo's suggestion of separating the outer aisles into chapels by means of transverse walls; further, they sided with Mignot by advocating chapels in the ambulatory at the east end as abutments for the vaults of the ambulatory. Thus Mignot seemed to have prospects of carrying his point. For the time he remained in office.

On May 15, 1401, a fourteen-man commission held a new hearing. Seven questions were put before them. Since among the members there were four nonprofessionals, only the ten architects were obliged to answer—and we can study seventy statements by Gothic architects. That, however, does not need to be carried through here. It will suffice to give the sense of the questions and, as a sample, the ten answers to one of the questions, also in abridged form.[20] The questions are:

1. Are the vaults and ribs (*croxiere*) begun by Mignot stable?

2. Is the work beautiful and praiseworthy?

3. Was the work more beautiful and more solid, as it was originally begun, or is Mignot's work more beautiful and more solid?

4. Which of the two sorts is cheaper and is the difference in costs great?

5. Can one use for Mignot's project stones of the same size and quality as for the preceding project?

6. How many stones must be taken down? (It was a question of an arch that had been begun at both ends and was not yet closed; it is not clear which arch it was.)

7. Does Mignot's project change only the height of the church, or the width as well, or does it change the edifice in its substantial form?

On the whole the questions show that there was concern about the extent of the proposed changes, about stability, beauty, and expense. Mignot had begun the vaults, and his enemies suspected that he was not keeping to the dimensions long since agreed upon, therefore the seventh question.

A modern architect would know least what to do with the second question, since today no one can guess what the difference is between *bello* and *lodevole*. Fortunately the answer of the architect Lorenzo

[20] See Appendix 5.

Donato clarifies this for us. He says that a change in elevation is, to be sure, actually present "ma questa variazione è lodevole poichè segue la ragione geometrica del triangolo." Praiseworthy and beautiful are, therefore, two utterly different criteria. Beauty has reference to Milanese taste, about which there could obviously be a disagreement, as the answers shortly to be listed proved, but praise—to put it briefly—relates to the secret of the lodges, to *maconerie*, thus, to the mensurability on the building site. The ten answers to this second question run (abridged):

1. Mignot's work is beautiful, but not praiseworthy.
2. Likewise.
3. Beautiful, but would be even more so if there were mosaics in the vaults.
4. Neither beautiful nor praiseworthy.
5. More beautiful than the original plan.
6. Very beautiful and very praiseworthy.
7. Cannot be made more beautiful or more praiseworthy.
8. Beautiful and praiseworthy.
9. Solid, beautiful, and praiseworthy.
10. Very beautiful and praiseworthy.

If, after all that has appeared from the texts already discussed, anyone were still doubtful whether geometrical rules or secret rules might not have something to do with beauty—meaning by beauty either individual taste or an absolute—this must convince him that such was not the case; for the first two answers show that something can, in fact, be beautiful without being praiseworthy, that is, well adapted to practical building. The ninth answer implies that stability could likewise be judged independently of the rules of geometry; it is clear that something can be stable without being beautiful, and so, too, something may be stable without satisfying the needs of mediaeval building practice for it to be executable without exact dimensions. But from other textual passages it appears that in spite of this there existed an inner connection between statics and *maconerie*.

Of course, one can learn all sorts of things from the other sixty answers, as just now we came across an architect who wanted to provide the vaults with mosaics, a suggestion which would have rejoiced the heart of Abbot Suger; but all these details may be left to future investigations. Here only the final act of Mignot's tragedy must be related. They accused him of extravagance, demanded on September

4, 1401, that a capital already in place should be made lower, and it seems that the Italians were especially gleeful at being able to prove a mistake in measurement on the part of the foreign pedant and critic who always knew better. The Duke intervened once more in Mignot's favor, but on October 22, 1401, he was dismissed. The document is couched in extraordinarily harsh language. His last report, which has not been preserved (perhaps they destroyed it because they were afterwards ashamed), is characterized as neither good, nor suitable, nor true, nor sufficient, nor acceptable, and he is discharged "because of continual arrogance and insubordination, especially as shown in the present session." The damage that he caused "is enormous and insupportable"; he is accused of ignorance and malice.

Here is testimony that the history of Gothic cathedrals reveals a tissue of human frailty and enmity, of which we suspect nothing when, with a piety like that of Suger before his jewels, we contemplate the edifices. If he thought that he was in a place that belonged neither quite to the purity of heaven nor quite to the slime of the earth, the annals of Milan Cathedral, at least in part, give us more insight into the latter than into the former.

But, after all, the dispute sprang not merely from contentiousness but also from the desire to make the house of the Lord as beautiful and enduring as possible. Unquestionably, personal quarrels were not conducted in all cathedral building with as much acerbity as in Milan, but we may assume that they often occurred, simply because even the best experts had at their command neither a workable theory of beauty nor a satisfactory theory of statics, and therefore had to rely on their personal taste, or, in other words, on their experience of life.

Modern architects can hardly think of themselves in the situation of their mediaeval colleagues. In the Romanesque period problems of statics were relatively simple, as long as the nave was not vaulted. With the decision to extend to the naves the knowledge of the technique of vaulting gained on a smaller scale from crypts, upper stories of towers, and aisles, entirely new difficulties had to be faced. The history of ecclesiastical architecture in developed Romanesque and, above all, in Early Gothic is at the same time a history of technology. Every step forward demanded the greatest courage on the part of architects and builders, because they could not calculate in advance and learned only through mistakes. We can read between the lines of the Milanese annals that Mignot was partly clear about the thrust of the vault. If he acted arrogant, he probably had a certain justification.

He called the Italians ignoramuses because they thought the pointed arches exercised no thrust and because they constructed the buttresses without set-offs. The latter were justified only because they corresponded to the line of pressure and so saved material. But even Mignot knew nothing of "lines of pressure." Whether he knew and used the principle of the parallelogram of forces is more than doubtful. Mach has not stated clearly whether Jordanus de Nemora, a mathematician of the thirteenth century who is regarded as Leonardo's predecessor, taught that principle in his treatise. He reports that Stevin used it at the end of the sixteenth century and that it was formulated simultaneously by Newton and Varignon only in 1686.[21] But Mignot had the practical experience that vaults exercise a thrust. We know today that the round arch thrusts more than the pointed and that the thrust of the latter diminishes according to the degree of pointedness. The first 30 degrees of the arch are today by mechanical calculation attributed to the pier itself. A lancet arch, such as was frequently used in early English Gothic and which consists of two halves of 30 degrees each, really exercises no side thrust at all. But the vaults in Milan span a considerably greater arc and therefore must exercise a side thrust. Thus Mignot was right.

The Italians also asserted that round arches are lighter than pointed arches. Perhaps they meant the actual weight if the individual weights of the stones are added. Naturally, a pointed arch is in that case heavier than a round arch over the same span. But that is true for the sum of the stones only as long as they are being carted. Once in place, vertical and horizontal components work together and it is this fact that was not clearly recognized in those days.[22]

21 Ernst Mach, *Die Mechanik in ihrer Entwicklung*, Leipzig, 1912, 7th ed. p. 36. (First edition, 1883.)

22 I wrote a treatise upon the expertises of Milan in 1943; recently there appeared an article on this subject by James S. Ackerman, "'Ars sine scientia nihil est.' Gothic Theory of Architecture at the Cathedral of Milan." *Art Bulletin*, XXXI, 1949, pp. 84ff. I call the reader's attention to this valuable supplement, but do not feel it necessary to change my presentation. Ackerman rejects my explanation for the reduction of Stornaloco's measure by a half braccio (p. 93 n. 39): "This explanation unfortunately does not work." Perhaps my argument in the article in the *Art Bulletin* was not clear enough; in my earlier explanation, which appears for the first time here, I state expressly that a contradiction exists, but interpret it as having been noticed only after the session. Ackerman also assumes that the chief reason for the reduction was the preference of the Milanese for proportions that were not too slender, but my explanation goes beyond that: the adjustment of the measure downward (*et non ultra*) approaches more closely the desired triangle. I hold that this explanation fortunately works. But if two separately undertaken investigations differ in nothing more than this, one can be satisfied. Ackerman did not go into the distinction between *bello* and *lodevole*. The account of the session of May 15, 1401, could be discussed far more fully than either Ackerman or I have done.

That in architectural circles they were, in principle, clear about the existence of a side thrust in the case of ribbed vaults can be seen definitely from Boffyi's expertise with regard to GERONA (1417) in Spain.[23]

Before the Arab invasion there had been a cathedral in Gerona that was transformed into a mosque by the Mohammedans. After the Arabs were driven out, the edifice was restored and in 1038 reconsecrated. The old choir of this church was replaced by a new one in High Gothic style during the years from 1312 to 1346, and the old nave was to be rebuilt in 1416 (Fig. 5). Boffyi, the architect in charge, began this nave as an unaisled space equal to the full width of the chancel and two aisles of the Gothic choir. Although there were enough precedents for this arrangement as such, doubts arose on account of the unusually great span of the vaults, for the nave was to have a width of seventy-three feet, more than any other church of the Middle Ages.[24] Therefore eleven other architects were consulted and were asked three questions:[25]

1. Whether the unaisled body of the cathedral in question, as originally begun, could be continued with the certainty that it would remain stable and safe.

2. Granted that it is not possible to continue this work safely without aisles, or that it would not be stable, will it then be appropriate, fit, and such as deserves continuation; or should it be given up and changed; and in this case, up to what elevation would it be right to continue what was already begun, and to form the whole so that a mistake would be avoided?

3. What sort of construction of the aforesaid work would be most compatible and in good proportion to the choir of the church, which has already been begun, built, and completed?

To the first question the masters give a unanimous answer in the affirmative; the reconstruction can be made unaisled, it will not collapse, and it will also be safe against earthquakes and storms, if the remainder is continued in the way in which Boffyi had begun the nave.

The answers to the second question are also fairly similar. The proposal was made to make the first bay of the choir nave higher in

[23] George Edmund Street, *Some Account of Gothic Architecture in Spain*, London, 1865, p. 318. Cf. text, Appendix 6.

[24] For purposes of comparison Street gives the clear widths of several other churches: the cathedral of Toulouse, 63 feet; Albi, 58 feet; Chartres, 50 feet, etc. Street, *op.cit.*, p. 502.

[25] Street, *op.cit.*, p. 502, gives the text in English translation. Cf. Spanish text, Appendix 6. On Gerona see also Pierre Lavedan, *L'Architecture gothique religieuse en Catalogne, Valence, et Baléares*, Paris, 1935, pp. 198ff.

order to introduce into its east wall a round window. This idea seems to have been simply adopted from the arrangement already carried out by Boffyi for this wall, which now rises considerably above the old choir at the place where the new nave began.

With regard to the third question the answers vary. Seven architects recommend the continuation of the nave and aisles of the choir. The four others, however, give their vote with great warmth for Boffyi's unaisled project. Antonius Canet maintains also that the unaisled edifice would be cheaper and not merely more impressive. Guillermus Sagrera asserts that the building was conceived from the very beginning with one single broad nave of this sort, which, for the period of the construction of the choir, 1316, is very interesting. Joannes de Guinguamps denies that the old choir would look small beside the wide nave, which had obviously been maintained by unknown opponents. This proves that the architects in Gerona knew that there were such things as "relative proportions."

After these masters had given their statements, Boffyi himself was finally questioned in the same way, obviously after long hesitation (March 8, 1417). To the first question he replies that the unaisled plan can very well be carried out, because the foundations and buttresses, as he has already begun them, are more than sufficient; their breadth is a third more than necessary. Whether by *anchura* the breadth or the depth of the buttresses is meant can hardly be determined. The buttresses of the cathedral in Gerona are magnificently monumental, both in breadth and in projection, and from the text can be judged, in any case, that Boffyi knew a definite rule that prescribed a minimum measurement, as otherwise he would not have been able to say that the dimensions chosen by him were a third larger than necessary.

In the answer to the third question Boffyi, like some of the other architects, stresses the fact that the light will be particularly favorable, since his plan permits the opening of circular windows in the east wall of the nave.

If we consider the three expertises of Chartres, Milan, and Gerona as a whole, they are astonishingly informative about two problems that always beset every practicing master of Gothic: the method of mensuration and the subject of statics.

Of the latter we learn that the architects had definite empirical rules that they could not prove theoretically and that were different in different schools but nevertheless sufficed for their purposes. Milan Cathedral, in spite of Mignot's prophecies, has not collapsed, and the cathedral in Gerona is also still standing today, as all the experts concerned said it would. The experts of Chartres knew that the structural members of Gothic carry in actuality, not merely in appearance—if we may generalize from their remarks—and so did Mignot and the Spanish architects in Gerona, his contemporaries.

In conclusion it must be pointed out that Boffyi's statement that the buttresses were a third stronger than necessary shows, taken exactly, that the statically determined measures were correlated with those found necessary for general measurements such as could be carried out on the building site, that is, with triangulation and quadrature. Otherwise he could not have made use of whole proportional numbers, namely 2:3.[26]

7. Architectural Theory and Aesthetics in the Middle Ages

THE studies of Magister 2 and the expertises of Chartres, Milan, and Gerona make it advisable to insert at this point a chapter on the theory of architecture in the Middle Ages.

The oldest book we have which treats the whole subject of architecture systematically is by M. VITRUVIUS POLLIO[1] who lived in the first century before Christ.[2] In the service of Julius Caesar he built military engines;[3] in addition, he tells us, he erected the basilica for the tribunal

26 Postscript on bibliography: Two further expertises must be noted, that of the cathedral of Zaragoza, 1500, and that of the cathedral of Salamanca, 1512; cf. George Edmund Street, *op.cit.*, pp. 370-484. The text of the expertise of Salamanca has been published by Street in an English translation.

1 The earliest printing (without place and year) was that of Giovanni Sulpicius in Italy about 1486. The subsequent editions and translations were listed almost completely and described by G. K. Lukomski, *I Maestri della architettura classica*, Milan, 1933, p. 65. He cites 62 editions. To these should be added the editions of Krohn, Leipzig, 1912, and of M. H. Morgan, Cambridge (Mass.), 1914. Most convenient to use is the edition of Valentin Rose, *Vitruvii de architectura libri decem*, Leipzig, 1899 (Teubner), or that of Krohn. My chapter on Vitruvius, etc. was concluded in 1946. When I was in Berlin in 1947, Herbert Koch (Halle) sent me his manuscript "Das Nachleben des Vitruv"; this article, which extends to Winckelmann, Goethe, and Schopenhauer, has been published in *Deutsche Beiträge für Altertumswissenschaft*, 1, Baden-Baden, 1951. See also Otto Stein, *Die Architekturtheoretiker der italienischen Renaissance*, Karlsruhe, 1913, p. 1.

2 For his biography cf. Francesco Pellati, *Vitruvio*, Rome, 1938, p. 31. Pellati also cites special studies in periodicals, so that by the help of this source one can find all the relevant literature.

3 Vitruvius 1, *Prooemium*, 2.

in Fano;[4] and from a writer about a century later we learn that he was also occupied in the construction of Roman aqueducts.[5] He composed his book toward the end of his life and there are good reasons to fix the time of its presentation to the Emperor Augustus after the year 27 B.C.[6] Since Vitruvius refers to the recommendation of Octavia, the Emperor's sister, he must be imagined as a man of the upper classes. He traveled widely in the Roman Empire, probably making a long sojourn in Greece and perhaps attending the schools of Athens. He quotes almost exclusively from Greek technical literature and clings conservatively to the Greek tradition of building; he says nothing about the combination of the Greek columnar orders with arcuated construction, so characteristically Roman, and only occasionally mentions vaults. After the end of the Civil Wars in 31 B.C. Rome rose anew as a "city of marble," rich in public buildings, so that the architects could find use for an encyclopaedia such as Vitruvius offered. He says himself that he wanted to unite the scattered individual Greek treatises into a whole.[7] He was not the first Latin author to write on architecture[8] but certainly one of the earliest, and so it was natural that he should compile Greek writings. For us Vitruvius is both the unique source of this rich and vanished Greek technical literature and the sole important representative of the Latin.[9] For the following centuries his work became the recognized textbook on architecture, at first, in the Middle Ages, the only one to our knowledge and then, after Alberti, the model for all subsequent manuals down to the nineteenth century, insofar as architecture remained classicistic in trend. Curiously enough, Alberti, though otherwise such an engaging character, judged Vitruvius with the most extreme severity and ingratitude.[10] He says that

4 *Ibid.*, V. I. 6. Cf. Jakob Prestel, *Des Marcus Vitruvius Pollio Basilika zu Fanum Fortunae*, Strasbourg, 1901.

5 *Frontinus de aquaeductu urbis Romae*, ed. Krohn, Leipzig, 1922. Sextus Julius Frontinus (A.D. 40-103) wrote at the time of the Emperor Nerva, who ruled from 96 to 98.

6 Octavian was granted the title of Augustus by the senate in the year 27. Vitruvius does not yet address him by this title; he does, however, mention the *aedes Augusti* in V. I. 7. (The year 28 B.C. is certainly a *terminus post* because the temple of Apollo in Rome, mentioned by Vitruvius, was dedicated in that year.) Cf. H. Degering, "Wann schrieb Vitruv sein Buch de Architectura," *Berliner Philologische Wochenschrift*, 1907, pp. 43ff.; and W. Dietrich, "*Quaestionum Vitruvii specimen*," Diss. Leipzig, 1907.

7 *Vitruvius* VII. 10ff.

8 He cites as technical writers Futicius, Terentius Varro, and P. Septimius; about the latter we know nothing further.

9 The few Latin treatises after Vitruvius, such as that of Frontinus, can be disregarded here.

10 Leon Bapt. Alberti, *De re aedificatoria libri decem*. Alberti's manuscript was completed in 1452; the publication was in 1485, after his death (1472). The passage cited is from VI. I.

the Romans considered him a Greek and the Greeks a Roman; "It would be as well to have written nothing at all, as to write what we cannot understand." Nevertheless, Alberti made much use of Vitruvius and thus had some comprehension of him after all. But it cannot be denied that Vitruvius is not entirely clear. Anyone who resorts to different translations soon sees with despair that each author translates the difficult passages differently.[11] If that is the case, one must ask what the mediaeval reader could have understood of Vitruvius. Once Brunelleschi had made exact measurements of classical buildings and details in Rome, there existed the possibility of making reconstructive drawings for Vitruvius' text; the mediaeval readers had only the text.[12] But this they actually did have. The tale that the Humanist Poggio rediscovered a manuscript of Vitruvius may be true as far as this discovery relates to Poggio himself,[13] but it does not prove that Vitruvius was unknown and forgotten throughout the entire Middle Ages.

Mentioned by Pliny, highly praised by Sidonius Apollinaris in the fifth century, and so on,[14] Vitruvius was read all through the mediaeval period after the ninth century. Proof of this is that we still possess fifty-five manuscripts.[15] Einhart, Charlemagne's learned minister, owned a Vitruvius;[16] so did the monasteries of Reichenau and Fulda. The oldest manuscript preserved is Carolingian;[17] the next oldest dates from the tenth century;[18] and the rest vary from the eleventh to the fifteenth.[19] Thus, just during the evolution of Romanesque and Gothic

11 German translation by Reber, 1865, French by Choisy, 1909, English by Frank Granger, 1931; in addition an older Italian translation by Galliani, 1790, and a French by Perrault, 1673, etc. The most recent German translation by Prestel, 1912, leaves much to be desired, but his notes are valuable nevertheless, at least in part.

12 W. Sackur, *Vitruv und die Poliorketiker*, Berlin, 1925, p. 12, discusses the question as to whether the original text of Vitruvius was illustrated, and assumes that it contained geometrical figures only where special attention is called to them; there are only ten such places. Cf. the whole informative chapter in Sackur. An investigation of this subject will be published by Mrs. J. Weitzmann-Fiedler. (The word *Poliorketiker* means the authors who wrote about fortifications of cities and connected topics. See Pauly-Wissowa, *Real-Encyclopädie* Halbband 240, Stuttgart, 1952, column 1381.)

13 Gian Francesco Poggio Bracciollini (1380-1459) attended the Council of Constance as secretary of the Curia, afterward visited the Swiss libraries, and in 1414 found a manuscript of Vitruvius in St. Gall.

14 On the various mentions of Vitruvius, also in Johannes Tzetzes (12th Century), etc., cf. Pellati, *op.cit.*, pp. 46ff.; in addition, more recently, the essay by Herbert Koch cited in note 1 above.

15 Completely enumerated in Lukomski, *op.cit.*, p. 62.

16 He attempted to imitate Roman masonry in Steinbach i. O. in 821; Schlosser, *Schriftquellen zur Geschichte der Karolingischen Kunst*, No. 16, Vienna, 1892.

17 Harleianus, Brit. Mus. 2767 (ninth century).

18 Gudeianus, Wolfenbüttel 69.

19 According to Choisy, *Vitruvius* II, I, twelve manuscripts date from the twelfth century, the rest from the thirteenth to the fifteenth, down to the first printing around 1486.

architecture Vitruvius was copied again and again, obviously because he was used in monastic schools and certainly later in the lodges. Vincent de Beauvais quotes his theory of proportions verbatim.[20]

Since Vitruvius is so difficult to understand and since Gothic architecture could have had nothing at all to do with his columnar orders and structural types of ancient temples, theaters, and baths, what were the men of the Gothic age able to learn from him? According to the general view, nothing. But that is surely wrong. Unquestionably Vitruvius contains an infinite number of technical hints that must have interested any mediaeval architect. But that is not all.

In his first chapter Vitruvius differentiates between *fabrica* and *ratiocinatio*, which corresponds to our concepts of manual labor and mental work, or practice and theory;[21] he who has only practice never attains to authority, that is, he remains only a subordinate workman, carrying out the orders given him and unable to give other workers directions; on the other hand, he who possesses theory alone seems to be following the shadow instead of the thing itself. To become an architect one must combine the two. Then comes a very theoretical passage. In all things, especially in architecture, there are contained the following two (factors) "quod significatur et quod significat" (that which is signified and that which signifies), thus probably: the purpose signified (fulfilled) by the architecture and the language that signifies (expresses) the same thing by means of the "demonstratio rationibus doctrinarum explicata," that is, by means of the "demonstration developed [explained] according to the arguments of the doctrines." Therefore, he who sets up as an architect must be trained in both parts: he must have talent (*ingeniosum oportet esse*) and he must be responsive to the teaching of science (*et ad disciplinam docilem*). "Neque enim ingenium sine disciplina aut disciplina sine ingenio perfectum artificem potest efficere" (neither talent without schooling nor schooling without talent can produce a perfect artist).

"Talent" in this last sentence means, according to the context, approximately the artisan's talent for the practical fulfillment of the

[20] Vincent de Beauvais, *Speculum naturale* I. XXVIII. 2, in the edition of Douai, 1624, I, 1994; quoted according to Julius Schlosser, *Lorenzo Ghibertis Denkwürdigkeiten*, Berlin, 1912, II, p. 33. It is a question of the proportions of the human figure. Likewise Hildegard of Bingen, 1098-1179, knew Vitruvius' theory of the proportions of the human figure, cf. Ildefons von Heerwegen, "Ein mittelalterlicher Kanon des menschlichen Körpers," *Repertorium für Kunstwissenschaft,* XXII, 1909, p. 445. If a scholastic and a mystic read Vitruvius, then surely many an architect studied him.

[21] Granger translates: craftsmanship and technology, but the meaning of *ratiocinatio* is much broader than that of technology.

purpose as opposed to *disciplina*, schooling in the sciences. Anyone who knows the Milanese records of 1400 must recall here Mignot's words: "Ars sine scientia nihil est" and the proud justification of the Milanese architects that they combine the two—one might add: "as Vitruvius requires."

What Vitruvius means by *disciplina* or scientific schooling he enumerates at once in the next sentence: literary training heads the list, because the architect must be capable of expressing himself in writing, second comes drawing, then geometry, knowledge of history, philosophy, music, some medicine, some law, and astronomy (*astrologiam*) as well. For all these requirements Vitruvius gives detailed reasons that fill seven pages and are amusing to read. The architect needs philosophy primarily to learn ethics and thus himself to become ethical, law to be able to make contracts that will harm neither the owner nor himself, music because in many military catapults the tension of the ropes is designated by tones, and so on.

After these preparatory remarks Vitruvius turns to the theory of architecture itself, which can be reduced to six main concepts:

1. ordinatio (taxis)
2. dispositio (diathesis)
3. eurythmia
4. symmetria
5. decor (thematismos)
6. distributio (oeconomia)

In four instances Vitruvius does not trust his translation of the Greek technical terms and adds the Greek words;[22] in two cases he does not attempt a translation at all. He defined and explained all six concepts, but that does not mean that every reader has the same understanding of them. A part of them offers no difficulty; the difficult part, however, appears in a new light if one has read and interpreted the mediaeval sources.[23]

"Ordinatio est modica membrorum operis commoditas separatim universaeque proportionis ad symmetriam comparatio.

Ordinatio is the proper measure of the members of the edifice [considered] separately and the relation of the total proportion to *symmetria*.

[22] For the word *thematismos*, in addition to the translation by *decor*, is also used the word *statio*. I. XI. 5, "is [auctoritas] perficitur statione, quod graece thematismos dicitur, . . ."

[23] For the translation of Vitruvius' six definitions cf. André Jolles, *Vitruvs Aesthetik*, Freiburg i. B., 1905. In the following much, but not all, has been taken from Jolles.

haec componitur ex quantitate, quae graece posotes dicitur.	This [*ordinatio*] consists of the *quantitas* which in Greek is called *posotes.*
quantitas autem est modulorum ex ipsius operis (membris) sumptio e singulisque membrorum partibus universi operis conveniens effectus."	*Quantitas,* however, is the extraction of modules from the (members of the) building itself and the consistent effect (resulting) from the single parts of the members of the total building.

This definition is at first completely unintelligible to modern readers, because they apply modern meanings to *ordinatio* and *quantitas. Quantitas* is not quantity in that abstract sense in which the word is used in modern physics or chemistry. A quantity of any given material is for us today the amount of the material which can be measured. *Quantitas,* is for Vitruvius the concrete measure itself with which one can measure anything. But this statement does not suffice.

One may orient oneself by thinking of the work of the sculptor who wishes to create a human figure, for example, an Apollo. He can make it as large as his living model, but also as much larger or as much smaller as he wishes. If he measures the living model according to foot lengths—the foot length of this particular model—and if he adopts for his Apollo figure another foot length, as large or small as convenient, then, once this first choice has been made, he can express all dimensions of his statue by means of these foot measures, by constantly measuring the lengths on the model in feet and substituting for the natural foot length the chosen foot length of his statue. This is exactly what Vitruvius implies for the field of architecture but with this difference, that here no natural model is "imitated." One may ask: why then use the same method? The answer is evident when one has analysed Vitruvius' definition completely.

Quantitas, the measure with which one measures, is to be taken from the structure itself (as the foot measure from the man). The unit of measure is called module (*modulus*). In consequence, the putting together of these modules forms the measuring device or rule. *Ordinatio* is therefore the rule. It is misleading to think of modern yardsticks which are conventional and at the same time neutral with regard to the object to be produced. Vitruvius' *ordinatio* or "yardstick" is conceived together with the given object. The measuring rule (the device of measurement) is connected with it closely and individually not only because the unit of measure has been taken (*sumptio*) from one of the members of this work (*opus*) and therefore "is proportionate to the members of the building individually" but also because it has been taken equally from the total building. This last provision is defined most clearly if we say: the module (the unit of measure) and the *ordinatio* (the measuring device or rule) shall make possible rational measures not only for the three dimensions of the structural members themselves but also for the spaces between them, that is, for the building as a whole, measured by diameters of columns and intervals between columns. Vitruvius is thinking of this when he speaks of *conveniens effectus* in the last words of his definition. If the intervals are expressible in whole modules or rational fractions of modules, then it is possible to measure in modules also the members of the entablature above the columns, the triglyphs and metopes, the dentils, consoles, and so on. Hence, one can measure the building stones in the lodge exactly without possessing a neutral measuring rod, and hence one can also put them together on the site in such a way that everywhere they correspond to the distances between the axes (centers) that are drawn in on the sketch. The architect must make his drawings with modules and then the workmen can execute the design, exactly as the sculptor uses the foot measures of the living model to create the likeness. This explains what purpose the method serves. Even in the case of the sculptor it has nothing to do with the very problematical concept of the imitation of nature, but it is in both cases a process of transference: in the case of the sculptor from the natural object to the statue, in that of the architect from the plan to reality. *Ordinatio* is therefore identical with *regula* and the measuring device is "rule" in an etymological sense, but rule in this connection does not mean regularity or "order" and it would be wrong to translate *ordinatio* by the word "order." The best word would be "coordination," for it is here a question of the method by which the measuring device is brought into strict coordination with the structure.

In this first definition Vitruvius already uses the fourth concept, symmetry. He doubtless assumed that his readers already knew what he meant by that. One can, however, grasp the concept of *ordinatio* even before one understands its connection with symmetry.

"Dispositio autem est rerum apta conlocatio elegansque e compositionibus effectus operis cum qualitate.	*Dispositio* however is the fitting arrangement of things (*rerum*) in space and the elegant effect of the work [resulting] from putting them together, combined with *qualitas*.

Species dispositionis, quae graece dicitur ideai, sunt hae, ichnographia, orthographia scaenographia. . . .	The kinds of *dispositio,* which are called in Greek *ideai,* are ground plan, elevation, and perspective drawing for the stage. . . .
Hae nascuntur ex cogitatione et inventione.	These originate from cogitation and invention.
Cogitatio est cura, studii plena et industriae vigilantiaeque, effectus propositi cum voluptate.	Cogitation is concern, full of effort, industry and vigilance, for the accomplishment of the purpose, accompanied by delight.[24]
Inventio autem est quaestionum obscurarum explicatio ratioque novae rei vigore mobili reperta.	Invention, however, is the explication of obscure questions and the reason [or understanding] of a new thing discovered by means of a mobile vivacity.
Hae sunt terminationes dispositionum."	These are the definitions of the dispositions.

Having relied upon *quantitas* for his first concept, Vitruvius here in his second speaks of *qualitas* and the elegant effect. The reference to ground plan, elevation, and perspective shows that he is now talking of the arrangement of things (*rerum*), which we must take to mean spaces as well as the corporeal structural members. The concept of *quantitas, ordinatio,* or measuring rod is anticipated, because the architect must constantly lay out all his dispositions in accordance with the standard of measurement. But *quantitas* alone is not sufficient; for each new building project the suitable (rational) solution must be sought. For this are needed cogitation as to purpose and agreeableness (*propositum cum voluptate*) and invention in the face of the new requirements of the project. These are theoretical considerations, general enough to have been applicable in all ages, in the Gothic as well as in the Greek and Roman. They went without saying, perhaps, but Vitruvius demands that the architect should be fully conscious of what he is doing, and so this passage may have been read and understood also by the men of the Gothic period. One often has, indeed, to "learn" in school what one has long since known.

The definition of the third concept is far harder to explain:

[24] Reber referred the words *cum voluptate* to the emotion of the working architect. Choisy simply made the literal appendage *avec volupté,* leaving the translation just as ambiguous as Vitruvius' text. Frank Granger related *voluptas* to the structure itself: "imagination rests upon the attention diverted with minute and observant favor to the charming effect proposed." Granger construes *effectus* as a genitive and relates *propositi* to it as a modifier.

"Eurythmia est venusta species commodusque in compositionibus membrorum aspectus.

Haec efficitur cum membra operis convenientis sunt altitudinis ad latitudinem, latitudinis ad longitudinem et ad summam omnia respondent suae symmetriae."

Eurythmy is beautiful appearance and proper aspect in the compositions of the members.

This [eurythmy] is attained when the members of the building correspond in their height to their width and in their width to their length, and everything corresponds to the whole of its [the structure's] symmetry.

Eurythmy, the good, pleasing appearance, is unquestionably intended to be a purely aesthetic quality and means, briefly, *venustas* (beauty). Vitruvius says *venusta species* and traces it back to proportions. We can also judge from the text that he is not thinking here of the beauty of a single line—an eighteenth century problem—but of that of whole structural members. He sets up requirements: first, the height shall correspond to the width, second, the width to the length, which can here be only the third dimension, and third, both shall correspond to the symmetry of the whole. Again he mentions a connection with the concept of symmetry, as yet undefined, and again we must first make an interpretation independently of it.

First of all it seems that Vitruvius meant: height and width are indeed to be different and thus form rectangles (and not squares)[25] but they are to be neither too tall nor too broad; they are to be balanced in themselves (corresponding to the Greek concept of μέσον) which would be tantamount to the Golden Section. That is by no means the rule in a Greek or Roman building, but certainly their proportions do not have the slenderness of some Gothic or the massive heaviness of some Romanesque. Analogously, the relief (perhaps of the metopes and triglyphs, of the cornices, and so on), which ought to be neither too delicate nor too crude, can be thought of with reference to the beautiful ratio of width to depth. Did Vitruvius mean a proportion beautiful in itself? If that were the case, he would doubtless have indicated it as the one and only norm of beauty.

But if the particular proportion in the buildings is different each time, Vitruvius presumably could not have meant the Golden Section or some other definite proportion, but rather perhaps quite generally the harmonizing of the proportions of various structural members. This would lead to the interpretation that he implied that law of

25 The metopes are, moreover, sometimes squares or almost square.

"similar figures" which August Thiersch rediscovered and also demonstrated in classical buildings.[26] According to this the architect may choose for an individual structural member any proportion whatsoever but, once having chosen it, he is bound to it for the proportion of other members; it sets the tone, as it were. However, if Vitruvius intended to say this he would have had to express himself somewhat more clearly. In that case the text ought to read: . . . This eurythmy is attained when structural members are of *different* size and yet of the *same* ratio of height to width. In any case, the reference to the symmetry of the whole signifies that Vitruvius demanded the harmonizing of each structural member both with every other one and with the whole structure, an end reached mathematically by similar figures, that is, constant proportions. From all the literature of antiquity on proportions it appears that builders did not work vaguely and emotionally but with deliberate and regular measures.

Would it be easier to interpret Vitruvius' definition of eurythmia if we knew at least what he means by rhythm itself, a word that has received countless definitions? The concepts of rhythm and symmetry occur also in Xenocrates, "the father of the history of art."[27] Schweitzer explains symmetry in Xenocrates as "the relationship of the smaller part to the larger and of all parts to the whole" which does not correspond to Vitruvius' symmetry, but to eurythmy; rhythm, on the other hand, "belongs in Xenocrates' sense to the realm of the organic world and to invention including the organic. It means form, inspired and molded by a unifying trait, arousing conceptions of movement." Thus, for many aestheticians of antiquity as well, eurythmy can be related to the anthropomorphic element in the columnar orders, as indeed Vitruvius, too, stresses the analogy to the proportions of the human body. But Vitruvius mentions this in connection with symmetry, not eurythmy; obviously these words and concepts underwent a slow semantic change. One should not deduce from this a general relativism but rather merely that it is the duty of the historian to understand and date precisely all the stages in the change.

When I wrote this I was not aware of the existence of such a study, a book by Schlikker,[28] that makes an important contribution to the

[26] August Thiersch, "Die Proportionen in der Architektur," *Handbuch der Architektur*, Part IV, Vol. 1, Stuttgart, 1883.

[27] Bernhard Schweitzer, *Xenokrates von Athen* (*Schriften der Königsberger Geisteswissenschaftlichen Gesellschaft*, Klasse 9), Halle a. S., 1932, p. 11.

[28] Friedrich Wilhelm Schlikker, *Hellenistische Vorstellungen von der Schönheit des Bauwerks nach Vitruv* (*Schriften zur Kunst des Altertums, herausgegeben vom Archäologischen Institut*

literature on Vitruvius. According to Schlikker the word eurythmy originated in the 5th century B.C. and meant at first a "beautiful rhythm." "*Rhythmos* meant measured movement, dance time, dance figures, and was then transferred from the dancer's movement to a kinetic attitude in the representation of a human being. . . . In pre-Hellenistic times the word eurythmy was not applied at all to the representational arts; like rhythm it was probably first related to the motif of motion in sculpture. In Vitruvius it is identical with the phenomenon of grace. How did this semantic change come about? The sole logically intelligible link is the conception of grace as beauty of motion. Thus did Schiller also define grace, following a suggestion from antiquity."

For Schlikker, therefore, eurythmy signifies the same quality as grace, and the latter he here defines as beauty of motion or "the pose between a back and forth movement" (p. 83). But on page 77 Schlikker wrote: "Grace or eurythmy is, then, attained by avoiding on the one hand what is swollen and on the other what is weakly." If by that can be understood the same thing that I believe I have proved about the Golden Section,[29] then eurythmy would be identical with this harmonious proportion and would consequently mean harmonious motion, the harmonious pose of something mobile, or, as the case may be, harmony of the motionless proportions of architecture.

Schlikker's dating of the several concepts employed by Vitruvius as though they had all originated at the same time is certainly a forward step, but his remarks on the concept of eurythmy cannot be taken as the last word on the subject. Grace and beauty are for us today not tautological words. Something can be beautiful without possessing grace. Were the words *eurythmia* and *venustas* tautological for Vitruvius? Schlikker translates Vitruvius' definition as follows: "Eurythmy is grace, beautiful appearance (*venusta species*), and pleasing aspect in the forms of the structural members. It is attained when the structural members have a height balanced by the width and a width balanced by the length, and all [members] generally correspond to their symmetry." Granted that further investigation may succeed in establishing incontestably what Vitruvius meant by eurythmy and other

des deutschen Reichs, Berlin, 1940). Only a few copies of the book are in existence, as the edition was burned in a bombing attack and the copies that had already been distributed were destroyed in their libraries.

29 Paul Frankl, *Das System der Kunstwissenschaft*, Brno, 1938, p. 149. The majority of the edition of this book also was destroyed.

concepts, the question still remains: what did the men of the Gothic age think when they read these definitions? If eurythmy is identical with beauty and the latter with harmony, that is, the harmonious proportion of the Golden Section, then the Gothic architects must have told themselves that it was of no use to them.

The same would have been true had eurythmy meant the visual impression of proportion. This has been suggested by Kalkmann.[30] "The eye deceives itself," he writes, quoting Philon (Mechan. Synt. IV.4), "in regard to the parts of buildings which seem to be different but have in reality equal dimensions, because it [the eye] is not always at the same distance from them. As a result of many experiments one has learned that it is necessary to subtract or to add in order to create a pleasant impression for the eye (ὁμόλογα τῇ ὁράσει καὶ εὔρυθμα φαινόμενα)." This is precisely what Adolf Hildebrand, the sculptor, meant by the words *Daseinsform* and *Wirkungsform*, form as it is and form as it seems to be.[31] Both Hildebrand's book and Kalkmann's article appeared in 1893. The difference between them is that Kalkmann associates form as it seems with the word eurythmy—quoting its use by Philon—while Hildebrand speaks of making corrections in order to create the right impression of proportion but does not use the term eurythmy. Even supposing that Vitruvius had in mind this problem of subtle corrections when he wrote his definition of eurythmy and that the word had the same meaning for the Gothic architects as it has for Philon, nevertheless it held no practical significance for them because they never made such corrections.[32] Finally Kalkmann himself, on page 5 of his introduction, gives a different definition of eurythmy: "The word ῥυθμός signifies a beautiful, pleasant harmony, both static and moving." Therefore the word rhythm at least is basically independent of the differentiation contained in the terms *Daseinsform* and *Wirkungsform*.

The investigation of what the term eurythmy meant to authors other than Vitruvius obviously contributes nothing to our understanding of his definition. Though the Gothic architects may have wondered why Vitruvius should have used the term *venusta species* rather than merely *venustas*, they probably encountered no difficulty in accepting the following sentence which simply discusses the pro-

[30] August Kalkmann, *Die Proportionen des Gesichtes in der griechischen Kunst* (Winckelmannsprogramm, 53.) Berlin 1893. p. 38 n. 2.

[31] About Hildebrand see below page 615, n. 18.

[32] See below page 730.

portions of the parts and their correspondence to the proportions of the whole.

With regard to the fourth concept one should not think of the modern meaning of the word symmetry in the sense of mirrored likeness but:

"Item symmetria est ex ipsius operis membris conveniens consensus ex partibusque separatis ad universae figurae speciem ratae partis responsus."

Symmetry is the concord resulting from the members of the work itself and the conformity of the mensural units derived from the separate parts to the appearance of the whole figure.

To this is appended the explanatory comparison of the architectural proportions with the canon of the human figure:

"Uti in hominis corpore e cubito pede palmo digito ceterisque particulis symmetros est eurythmiae qualitas, sic est in operum perfectionibus."

Just as in the human body from forearm, foot, hand, finger, and the other little parts *symmetros* is the quality of eurythmy, so it is in the completion of buildings.

Vitruvius goes on to say that in all works the *ratiocinatio symmetriarum*, the theory of symmetries, is obtained from the members: as in temples from the diameter of the columns, from the triglyph, or also from the *embater*, so likewise in ballistae, and in shipbuilding from the distances between the oars.

Embater, according to Schlikker, is the fractional measure of the module; thus, for example, the diameter of the lower part of the column was chosen as the module and the latter was divided into thirty parts. This thirtieth part was then the *embater*. In the principal sentence of the definition Schlikker explained the words *rata pars* as identical with *embater*. His rendering of this sentence is: "Symmetry is the accord resulting from the members of the structure itself, that is, the constancy of the *embater* (*rata pars*) from the individual parts down to the appearance of the form as a whole." (p. 70)

Literally translated into Latin *symmetria* is *commensura, sym* becoming *con* and *metron* equal to *mensura.* Symmetry is what we call commensurability, the quality of having a common measure. The purpose of commensurability in the classical orders is to express the distances between columns in terms of diameters of columns, so that above in the entabulature the subdivision by triglyphs and metopes, or that of the denticulation, of consoles, and so on, can be carried out easily, because their measures, being rational fractions of the unit of measure from center of column to center of column, divide without a remainder (except at the corners of the Doric order).

Let us return—just as Vitruvius does here—to the sculptor's measurements. He finds that in nature the foot length corresponds only approximately to the length of the forearm or the width of the *palma* (the outstretched fingers). Objective (anthropological) mensuration has the difficulty of determining the initial point of each measurement, that of the sculptor—if we now regard the problem, mentioned earlier, of the transference to desired sizes as settled—the added difficulty of choosing rational measures, thus, to fix upon one foot length for the height of the head even though in the model it is seen to be somewhat more or less, and finally to adapt the transferable length to the ideal of beauty as well.

The Greek architect had exactly the same problem. *Ordinatio* gave him the method of transference, eurythmy, as it were, the method of beauty, and finally symmetry was necessary in order to measure rationally the beautiful proportions by the *ordinatio* (rule), thus, to be able to transfer.

Here we face in principle the same difficulty in the case of the Greeks and Romans as in that of the mediaeval masters. It remains possible, indeed probable that the former laid out their ground plans, and so on, with a definite (neutral) measuring standard, but even then they needed a method by which to transfer these measurements without a neutral measuring rod.

It is not necessary to go further into these problems, for what has been said suffices to show that the monastic schools and the lodges could learn from Vitruvius exactly what they needed practically. It is, therefore, quite probable that they understood these passages referring to symmetry, which the modern reader has always found obscure, because at that time the practical application of this theory lived on; it was lost only when every workman carried his standard measure in his pocket and had no further need of modules and symmetry.

The fifth concept relates to the structure as a work of art in the strictest sense of the word.

"Decor autem est emendatus operis aspectus probatis rebus compositi cum auctoritate.

Decor is the faultless appearance of the structure, composed of approved [recognized] things, combined with authority.

"Is perficitur statione, quod graece Θεματισμὸς dicitur, seu consuetudine aut natura."

This [authority] is attained by establishment which the Greeks call thematism, either through custom or through nature.

The sense of these statements is evident from the explanatory examples: for Zeus, Sol, Luna one should build hypaethral temples (so that heaven, or the divinities themselves can look down into the temple); for Minerva, Mars, Hercules one should choose the Doric order; for Venus, Flora, Proserpina, the nymphs, the Corinthian; for Juno, Diana, Liber, the Ionic. That means, in generalized terms: choose the form that will express the character of the spiritual center of your work of art. The second element of *decor, consuetudo*, Vitruvius illustrates by the following example: if a building is splendid inside it should also have a splendid vestibule; thus, in general, the interior and exterior of a building should agree in character. But *consuetudo* also means in Vitruvius' sense custom: one should not place an Ionic entablature over Doric columns. He states this pedantically, but the real meaning is that the orders, as they have been transmitted, *are* of a unified nature and therefore not interchangeable in their members. The third element, *natura*, is quite trivial: bedrooms and library rooms should face east, picture galleries north, and so on. A textbook should not be afraid to state the obvious, for in the last analysis all the correct things are obvious.

Decor, then, means suitability. The Greek term signifies that the form is to be derived from the "theme." Modern readers will understand this idea most easily if they think of the significance of functionalism in architecture, except that thematism is meant in a far more spiritual sense: not as the expression of a banal purpose or of structural mechanics, but as the representation of a most profound idea through comprehension of its specific character (Venus as delicate and graceful) and reproduction of this character by the form of the columnar order (thus, not Venus herself but her delicacy and grace). The word *auctoritas* also suggests suitability, but that which is generally acknowledged because it is inherently reasonable. Perhaps this is Vitruvius' addition to the Greek theories or a combination of various Greek doctrines.

Of course, the fundamental idea of *decor* existed consciously or unconsciously wherever art was created. In mediaeval times Vitruvius' theoretical idea were connected with "symbolism" and externalized:

one should remember Suger's comparison of the columns of the choir to the apostles and prophets. The specific idea that the edifice should characterize the individual god, was not pertinent for mediaeval men, inasmuch as they thought monotheistically, all churches representing the one God. The dedication of the edifices to definite principal patrons, Mary, Peter, Catherine, and so on, never led to such sharp differentiations in suitable architecture as, for example, in the case of Jupiter, Juno, or Proserpina. But the change in the conception about Jesus himself, Mary, and the saints is, of course, reflected in the changing phases of architectural style. And this change in the symbolization of fundamental conceptions through expressive form is in all styles the essential, always constant, *artistic* requirement. Art is form as the symbol of that meaning which is inherent in the form.[33]

The sixth concept offers no difficulty:

"Distributio autem est copiarum locique commoda dispensatio parcaque in operibus sumptus cum ratione temperatio."	*Distributio* is fitting disposal of the building materials and of the site and thrifty moderation of expense in the structures, with rational calculation.

It is a matter of superintending the work from the economic point of view.

We can easily guess that Greek theorists of architecture before Vitruvius had pondered on these six concepts through the centuries and that the sequence of their treatment was also adopted by Vitruvius from older writings. First of all a measuring scale must be chosen, then the sketch of ground plan and elevation is evolved according to the project in hand, next the architect tries to make the whole conception eurythmic, that is, aesthetically beautiful or harmonious, then he corrects all the proportions by precise observation of the *quantitas*, that is, he makes everything commensurable, and finally, as an additional factor, the *decor* must be taken into consideration. Expressed in modern terms, the first four concepts relate in part to the serviceable method of producing the plan (*ordinatio* and *dispositio*) and in part to the aesthetic element in a formal sense (*eurythmia* and *symmetria*); then one must think of the essential character of the underlying meaning of the whole structure and choose the *aesthetic* form that will also be *artistic*, that is, express the meaning. Only after the plan has been completed in this way does the concern for materials, site, money,

[33] Cf. my book cited above in note 29 and Willi Drost, "Form als Symbol," *Zeitschrift für Aesthetik und allgemeine Kunstwissenschaft*, Stuttgart, 1927, p. 254.

and—let us add—workmen, in Vitruvius' time slaves, begin. All of this is very logically conceived and there can be no doubt that the masters of Gothic studied these few pages with the deepest interest and tried to penetrate their meaning. Were they able to?

We can say—however paradoxical it may sound—that the secret of the Gothic lodges was derived from the *ordinatio* and *symmetria* of Vitruvius, only it appears that the Gothic builders from the time of Magister 2 on specialized in the method of the square with the inscribed diagonal square. Surprisingly, however, this construction is also found in Vitruvius.[34] He ascribes the solution of the problem of doubling a square to Plato and explains that a square with a side ten feet long contains one hundred square feet and therefore one double that size would contain two hundred square feet: "For that (that is, for the length of the side belonging to this latter square) no one can find a number;[35] for if one takes fourteen that will give one hundred ninety-six when multiplied by itself; if one takes fifteen, there will be two hundred and twenty-five. . . ." Vitruvius means to say that although no one can extract the square root of two hundred *arithmetically*, Plato solved the problem *geometrically*. Like Magister 2, Vitruvius does not indicate what purpose this halving (or doubling) of the square serves.

Once one has found the right clue it is no longer very surprising that Vitruvius should discuss the construction of the Pythagorean triangle 3:4:5 immediately after this problem. Without a doubt Vitruvius was read by Magister 2, by Stornaloco, by Mignot; surely many Milanese architects knew him, likewise the German architects, above all the Parlers who advocated quadrature. To adopt a smaller measure instead of the original basic measure of eight braccia meant to Heinrich Parler perhaps the abandonment of "eurythmy," if not of "symmetria" as well.

Did Villard de Honnecourt know Vitruvius? Or was he at least indirectly dependent on him? After concluding his definitions and explanations, Vitruvius starts afresh to survey the whole field of architecture.[36] "Partes ipsius architecturae sunt tres, aedificatio, gnomonia, machinatio." Architecture has three parts: erection of buildings, clock making, machinery. What does Villard's Lodge Book concern? Buildings, clocks, machines. Presumably that goes back to Vitruvius'

[34] "Vitruvius" IX, second paragraph. Rose's ed., p. 210.

[35] A whole, rational number is meant, for irrational numbers do not exist for Vitruvius.

[36] *Op.cit.*, I. 3.

Greek predecessors. Vitruvius also demands that the architect should know something of medicine. However one interprets it, the fact remains that Villard's Lodge Book contains a remedy for healing wounds.[37] Even if he took it from older lodge books, these, his hypothetical intermediaries, would point back to Vitruvius. Villard gives his theory of *portraiture* and in that connection treats of proportions. The division of the face into three equal parts is found in Vitruvius. Is it a better hypothesis to suppose that Villard got all this at second hand, or is it simpler to assume that he read Vitruvius himself? He surely understood Latin.

In accordance with the tripartite division of his matter Vitruvius divided the types of buildings into three groups: buildings for defense, religion, and public use (such as harbors, forums, baths) and then he sets up three further concepts as requirements for all buildings: *firmitas, utilitas, venustas* (firmness, utility, beauty).

In this triad firmness or stability appears as a new concept, since the other two are already contained in the six definitions. But Vitruvius has little to say about *firmitas*.[38] A specific chapter on structural mechanics is lacking, and Gothic likewise had only very approximate rules of mechanics. We have seen how confused the ideas of the Milanese were on the thrust of vaults. The Byzantine architects have also left no treatises on structural mechanics. In this matter the men of the Gothic age had to rely entirely on their own thinking, and the lack of this subject was, one might say, a negative inheritance from antiquity, that is, from Vitruvius. The positive inheritance was what he had to say about *venustas*.

If then one asks about *the* book on the aesthetics of architecture in Gothic times the paradoxical answer must be: Vitruvius.

It is strange that histories of aesthetics have scarcely recognized Vitruvius,[39] although his role since Alberti's time is familiar to everyone. That, however, is connected with the history of aesthetics itself.

[37] Hahnloser, *op.cit.*, pp. 173-175.

[38] He defines it: "firmitas erit habita ratio, cum fuerit fundamentorum ad solidum depressio et quaque e materia copiarum sine avaritia diligens electio." In Rose's edition, p. 14.

[39] The older histories of aesthetics—E. Müller, *Geschichte der Theorie der Kunst bei den Alten*, 1834; R. Zimmermann, *Geschichte der Aesthetik*, Vienna, 1858; Max Schasler, *Kritische Geschichte der Aesthetik*, Berlin, 1872; Bernard Bosanquet, *A History of Aesthetic*, London, 1892—do not mention him at all. Julius Walter, *Die Geschichte der Aesthetik im Altertum*, Leipzig, 1893, mentioned him first, but he picked out only the passage on *decor*, insofar as an interpretation of the three columnar orders can be made from it. Even in the most recent history of aesthetics: Katherine Everett Gilbert and Helmut Kuhn, *A History of Aesthetics*, New York, 1939, Vitruvius is barely touched upon.

Its beginnings are sought in Pythagoras, the mathematician, and in spite of the many theorists of architecture listed by Vitruvius[40] the important stages can be named quickly: Socrates, Plato, Aristotle, and perhaps Cicero. Plotinus occupies an intermediate position,[41] but he already belongs more to the Middle Ages, if one follows Kalkmann's broad distinctions. This archaeologist characterized with a few lapidary phrases the development of aesthetics in classical times,[42] finding it distinguished by its formal character. On the other hand, there occurs, as he says, simultaneously with the beginnings of Christianity a transformation of the old classical ideas: "From now on sublimity transcends thought; and inward power and grandeur, form." Unquestionably this transformation is the reason for the alienation of interest from art, the work of man, and the exclusive preoccupation with God and with the world only as the work of God.

It is not within the province of this book to insert here a complete history of mediaeval aesthetics. The reason, however, is not so much the usual excuse of lack of space as that investigation of this field is still in its infancy. The leading names, up to now, seem to be: Plotinus, Augustine, Dionysius the Pseudo-Areopagite, Albertus Magnus, Ulrich Engelbert, Thomas Aquinas, Bonaventura, and perhaps also Dionysius Ryckel the Carthusian (the latter in the late fifteenth century).[43] What we learn about them, though it does not provide an insight into the gradual development, does give us an understanding of its character.

We can restrict ourselves here to the chief period of scholasticism, the thirteenth century, and to the theories of Thomas and Ulrich. Both are contemporaries of Villard de Honnecourt, and of Master Erwin, whom Ulrich surely knew since he lived in Strasbourg.[44]

About 1260 Thomas Aquinas (1225-1274) wrote: "Everywhere the

[40] In the *Prooemium* of the seventh book.

[41] Plotinus *Enneades* I. 6.

[42] August Kalkmann, *op.cit.*, pp. 6 and 7.

[43] On Plotinus, W. R. Inge, *The Philosophy of Plotinus*, London, 1918. On Augustine, K. Swoboda, *L'ésthetique de St. Augustin et ses sources*, Brno, 1933.

[44] On Ulrich, Martin Grabmann, *Des Ulrich Engelberti von Strassburg O.Pr. (1277) Abhandlung de pulchro*, Sitzungsberichte der Bayr. Akademie der Wissenschaften, Philos. philol. Klasse, Munich, 1926. This gives the best survey of the studies concerning the aesthetics of scholasticism that have been in progress only for a few decades. On Thomas cf. Adolf Dyroff, "Über die Entwicklung und den Wert der Aesthetik des Thomas von Aquino," *Archiv für systematische Philosophie und Soziologie*, N.F. XXXII, Berlin, 1929. Cf. also Josef Koch's corrections of this, "Zur Aesthetik des Thomas von Aquino," *Zeitschrift für Aesthetik und allgemeine Kunstwissenschaft*, Stuttgart, 1931, p. 266. The few brief studies of Bonaventura are cited by Grabmann, *op.cit.*, p. 9, n. 1. Cf. *ibid.*, p. 19, for Dionysius the Carthusian. Bosanquet, *History of Aesthetic*, Ch. VII, attempted to make a survey of the history of the subject; also recently Gilbert and Kuhn, *op.cit.*, Ch. V.

perfect and good is to be found in a certain *commensuratio*, the greater the distance from the proper *commensuratio*, the greater will the bad [evil] be, just as health consists of the proper *commensuratio* of the limbs; truth, however, consists of the *commensuratio* of the intellect or speech to the object."[45]

In a later work he glosses the sentence from Dionysius, "Beauty is the cause of consonance and clarity in all things," as follows: "Thus we call a human being beautiful because of the proper proportion (*propter decentem proportionem*) of the limbs in their *quantitas* and location and because he has a clear and fresh color (*nitidus color*). Wherefore, correspondingly, it can also be assumed in other connections that each thing will be called beautiful because it has clarity of its kind (*claritatem sui generis*), whether spiritual or physical, and, correspondingly, because it is constructed in proper proportion."

We meet again the classical concepts of *proportio, quantitas, commensuratio*, but they do not serve exclusively, as in Vitruvius, to explain the beauty of a building or of the human body; rather, they have been intellectualized and generalized. *Quantitas, commensuratio, proportio*, and similar concepts are now applied to good and evil, health and sickness, truth and error. But in this scholasticism is not wholly new. The identification of the good with the beautiful goes back at least to Socrates and Plato. To a certain degree it may be understandable when spiritual balance, the ideal of virtuous life, is compared to the beauty of a Doric temple, for example, and an ethical human being called beautiful because of his virtue. However the words *virtus* and ἀρετή mean more than "virtue." But to us it seems incomprehensible when a philosopher, be he ever so great, identifies the two, as though one could, conversely, call a Doric temple virtuous or ethical. Actually, no scholastic would ever have called even the most beautiful Venus virtuous on account of her beauty. But this confusion persisted and was firmly established in the scholastic era by the argument that the most beautiful of all existing things must be God.

This thought also, in itself, had its inception before the age of scholasticism. But if one reads about it in Ulrich ENGELBERTI,[46] one can in a few minutes comprehend the aesthetics that predominated when the Gothic cathedrals were rising, however ancient the roots of these aesthetic ideas may be. "God alone is the true Light, which lighteth

[45] Thomas' writings that develop his theories of aesthetics were composed between 1254 and 1272; Ulrich's *Summa*, containing the chapter *de pulchro*, was written between 1262 and 1272; see Dyroff or Grabmann.

[46] Dyroff, *op.cit.*, p. 159.

every man that cometh into the world (John 1:9). God is this true light by his nature, which is light in the fullness of divine cognition and which sheds light on the *suppositum*, on the bearer of the divine nature, diffusing radiance. . . ." (God is *suppositum*, that is, bearer of the light by which he is himself irradiated.) The light is "not merely *in consonantia*, in perfect harmony, with the divine nature, but is intrinsically identical with this nature." Thus the Three Persons of the Trinity are related to each other *in consonantia*. "God is not only flawlessly beautiful in his essence and existence, the absolute zenith of beauty, he is also the efficient cause, the formal cause, and the final cause of all created beauty."

But Ulrich speaks also of formal laws of beauty in corporeal things. Proportion is necessary, that is, a harmony between matter and form. In the realm of the corporeal this proportion is found in a fourfold *consonantia*: 1) in the proportion and harmony between the disposition of matter and form; 2) in an agreement in the quantity of matter and form, because, according to a statement of Aristotle, there is in all natural creations a limit of size and growth, determined by this relationship; 3) with animate organisms, in the concord, the proper relationship, of the number of potentialities springing from the form; 4) in the proper proportions of the sizes of the parts to each other and to the whole body.

To such passages must be added others if one is to be acquainted with the basic tenets of scholastic aesthetics. An example is the statement, going back to Augustine and antiquity, that the beauty of a human being is based on the proportion of his limbs combined with a suitable clarity of color (*cum quadam debiti coloris claritate*);[47] another is the identification of love and beauty, and so on.[48] But since the complete system of scholastic aesthetics is no more our purpose than the history of its development, the passages already cited may suffice for a comprehension of its character.

They illustrate the survival of certain definite concepts of classical aesthetics. For example, in Vitruvius we found *taxis* (order) and *symmetria* in a distinct sense applicable to measurable buildings; both concepts are found in an abstract sense, for instance, even in Aristotle as factors of beauty;[49] symmetry by itself already in Plato, and both

47 Thomas, *Summa Th.* 211 qu. 145 a, 2, quoted in Grabmann, *op.cit.*, p. 49. See also Plotinus *Enneades* I. 6.

48 Dyroff, *op.cit.*, pp. 180ff.

49 Aristotle *Metaphysics* XIII (1078 a 36): "*τάξις καὶ συμμετρία καὶ τὸ ὡριζμένον*" (quoted by Grabmann, p. 31).

together again in the scholastics. Scholasticism laid great emphasis on three concepts, as though they were decisive: *claritas, integritas, consonantia,* but there are many others; in Thomas and others the element of what is *decens* plays a part, now approaching Vitruvius' *decor,* now the *honestum* of Stoic ethics. All these concepts are transformed in the course of centuries, as the atmosphere in which they continue to exist changes. They usually retain something of a common identity, but it is almost more important to notice what it is in them that varies. Thus, though we might understand correctly what Vitruvius intended by his terms, that is no guarantee for the understanding of the same terms as used by Plato and Aristotle and on down to Ulrich, Thomas, Bonaventura, and so on. And then the question arises as to what the Gothic architects thought, or what Erwin "von Steinbach" in Strasbourg may have thought, if he was in fact acquainted with Ulrich's aesthetics. We may assume that Vitruvius offered him even more than Ulrich.

Let there be no misunderstanding and, above all, no underestimation of this problem as such. It is not indeed that Erwin had nothing at all in common with Ulrich. But between the cathedral at Strasbourg and Ulrich's *Summa* there exists no immediate causal relationship. The common factor does not lie, for example, in the somewhat superficial analogy of the "system" of cathedrals and the system of the scholastic *Summae*; not only scholastics built systems, so did Aristotle and Kant, who both have surely no kinship with Gothic. The common factor is to be found in the subject, that is, neither in the cathedral nor in the philosophy but in God as the goal of life, God according to the Christian concept of the divine in the thirteenth century.

Nevertheless formal aesthetics or, more specifically, the art theory of Vitruvius had more to offer a Gothic architect than the aesthetics of scholasticism. As a reason for this may be cited the abstractness of the latter, its lack of concrete reference to the accomplishments of Gothic architecture. It is astonishing that the scholastics, all of them clerics or monks, themselves witnesses of the growth of the cathedrals, who celebrated mass in them, heard confession, preached, who had a voice in the plans, superintended the building activity, managed the finances, who philosophized on the "beautiful" and wrote treatises, never refer to Gothic by a single word and do not mention a single cathedral. Suger and Gervase do not belong to the school of scholasticism and are not themselves aestheticians. Besides them there are numberless mediaeval historians to whose statements we owe our ability to date particular edifices in whole or in part, but they, too, never think of wasting a word on the Gothic element of Gothic architecture or its "beauty." How can this be explained?

There are two reasons for it. The first is that architecture did not belong to the system of the arts, either in the sense of *ars* in the Middle Ages or in that of "art" in modern usage. Only a trained and industrious philologist could really explain the semantic changes of the Greek word *techne* as well as the Latin words *ars* and *scientia.* Here it must only be remembered that Vitruvius calls the theory of architecture in the first sentence of the first book *scientia,* opposed to the *other artibus, ars* otherwise being seldom mentioned by him;[50] that, on the contrary, *ars* in the Middle Ages means approximately science: the *septem artes liberales*; and that to these seven "arts" were added, from the twelfth century on, seven *scientiae,* which were called *mechanicae* and less highly esteemed. To them belongs architecture. The *artes liberales* are the concern of free men who are not obliged to earn their bread by working and thus have time to philosophize; the *scientiae* are tasks for subordinates. Since antiquity something of the social position of the workman clung to the artist.[51] Vitruvius says that the illiterate can have no authority as architect and he would scarcely have stressed so heavily the necessity of comprehensive education if he had not suffered from a lack of social recognition. Proud, conscious of his culture, he fought for his colleagues. In the Middle Ages the situation seems to have been similar. The architect felt that on the site and in the lodge he was a king, but his field could not receive the same recognition as the church qua temporal institution and the university. For this reason architecture fell entirely outside the scholastics' range of vision whenever they reflected on the beautiful, for it was no *ars liberalis* but merely a *scientia mechanica.* The passage

50 Vitruvius I. I. I: "Architecti est scientia pluribus disciplinis et variis eruditionibus ornata, cuius iudicio probantur omnia quae ab ceteris artibus perficiuntur opera." Reber translates this: "Die Bildung des Baumeisters ist mit mehreren Wissenschaftszweigen und mannigfachen Elementarkenntnissen verbunden, da durch sein Urtheil alle von den übrigen Künsten geleisteten Werke erst ihre Billigung finden müssen." Vitruvius does actually speak here of the "other *artes*" and so the *scientia architecti* must be an *ars.* Others may blaze a trail through this jungle. On *ars* cf. H. Nohl, *Index Vitruvianus,* Leipzig, 1876, p. 12.

51 Albert Dresdner, *Die Entwicklung der Kunstkritik* (Part I on *Die Kunstkritik* . . . ; the sequel has not appeared), Munich, 1915. The excellent first chapter, "Das Altertum und die Kunstkritik," discusses the changing evaluation of the artist, and not only in his own estimation; but Dresdner talks entirely about painters and sculptors. Only a few pages, 58-66, treat the Middle Ages. One may summarize that the appreciation of the artist in Plato was negative, became more positive in Isocrates (436-338 B.C), rose in Plotinus A.D. 204-270), and again declined, if it did not actually disappear, until at least the Carolingian period. Vitruvius is thus a link between Isocrates and Plotinus.

from the Milanese records must be understood this way: *ars sine scientia nihil est* means practice (of architecture) without (the) science (of geometry) leads nowhere. The architect had to have command of both things. The scholastics were not interested in practice or *ars mechanica*, but in all *artes liberales* including the science of geometry.

Trier has pointed out that the German and French languages had no word for what we call art today.[52] He has given evidence for this at least for Middle High German. *Kunst* and *List* mean in the Middle Ages "the same thing that is usually admired in the engineer, in the constructer of ingenious military machines and fortifications, not free creative accomplishment and the energy behind it." The word *List* hints at uncanny magical powers, also at the daemonic aliveness of automatons, which were regarded as a kind of *homunculi*, indeed, half as an impious crime. *Kunst* and *List* mean skills that are based on knowledge and ability gained through training. This "knowledge" is also called "art" and here also belong rhetoric and music, which are part of the *artes liberales*. Arts (*Künste*) and skills (*Liste*) were distinguished from each other, though not always consistently. The two *artes* rhetoric and music are arts (*Künste* in the modern sense) and everything else, including architecture, belongs to the *Liste*, that is, to all skills that have no theoretical-dialectical foundation.

The second reason for the silence of the scholastics is more profound: no one in the Middle Ages was capable of talking (writing) on art and, specifically, architecture because there was no vocabulary developed to formulate aesthetic judgments, draw fine distinctions, and suit different types of styles. There were certain stylistic designations such as *mos Romanorum* (for Carolingian) or the solitary *opus francigenum*, but even though they might serve to characterize larger categories, any further shades of meaning were lacking. In any case the old concepts from the time of Aristotle to Vitruvius and then to Thomas afforded no help. As far as unfinished structures were concerned and such as combined various styles, *integritas* and *consonantia* mean nothing; whether they were fruitful for works completed in almost homogeneous style like Reims, and Amiens, no scholastic ever asked. Such general concepts could indeed express only the common, never the individual quality of the structures.

This brings us to one of the most important problems, the history of which we shall have to trace in later chapters: how did literature

52 I. Trier, "Architekturphantasien in der mittelalterlichen Dichtung," *Germanisch-Romanische Monatsschrift*, 1929, p. 12.

gradually develop the technical language, and specifically, the language of aesthetics?

8. Masons' Guilds and Stonemasons' Lodges

WHAT we have learned in the preceding chapter is, from the modern point of view, partly too vague and too far removed from the tangible reality of Gothic buildings and partly, in contrast to this, so closely connected with the technique of measurement that it does not fathom the specifically Gothic essence of these buildings. Yet both types of literary tradition help to supplement our personal relationship to the structures; understanding of the method of mensuration has lifted the veil from the lodge secret and this in turn arouses our interest in the "lodges." Their literary remains can be divided into two groups: the lodge ordinances, that is, the statutes of these societies; and the lodge books, preserved from the latter days of Gothic, descended from Villard's Lodge Book.

To this literature may be appended a sketch of the terminology of Gothic. This whole chapter is directed toward the sociological side of Gothic architecture, for technical language forms a part of sociology inasmuch as it starts from the division of society into groups that because of their calling constitute a unit. The terminology of Gothic is the language of the masons' guilds and the lodges.

Janner says quite properly that there must have been lodges since the time of Cheops and Solomon,[1] that is, ephemeral structures beside the monumental ones, where the draftsmen worked, where the drawings and tools were kept, and where conferences of all kinds could be held. We know that there were in Roman times *collegia*, guilds of architects; but there existed at that time no necessity for guilds of masons and stonemasons since such work was done by slaves for whom, being without rights, no legal regulations whatsoever were possible. The slaves' revolts were not able to achieve any permanent liberation of these unhappy masses of human beings. Of course there were Romans who treated their slaves humanely, but against the usual cruelties and degradations there was no defense. The principles that today we call

[1] Ferdinand Janner, *Die Bauhütten des deutschen Mittelalters*, Leipzig, 1876, as a supplement cf. the more popular treatment by Sartell Prentice, *The Voices of the Cathedral*, New York, 1938, pp. 131ff.

the rights of man and the whole fundamental ideology of modern democracy were given to Europe only by Christianity, which preached the equality of all human beings as children of the one God.

This doctrine undermined the institution of slavery, as it was practiced in classical times, and cut its very root. Simultaneously it created a revolution in the estimation of work. Whereas work had been far beneath the dignity of a free Roman and despised by those impoverished free citizens who had to follow a trade for their livelihood, now the idea took hold that work, though it might not yet ennoble, at least no longer degraded. But the process of eliminating slavery in Europe was very slow, lasting into the tenth century. The freedom of the individual was, moreover, not immediately and for everyone the freedom of modern man in democratic countries; for slavery was followed by serfdom, the juridical attachment of the peasant to the soil, and by the binding tie of the townsman to the city.[2] Only some callings afforded freedom to move from place to place, among them that of the stonemasons, who very early freed themselves from city jurisdiction in order to wander freely to places where ecclesiastical construction attracted experienced workmen. From their associations developed the firmly knit organizations that we call in a narrower sense mediaeval lodges.

The masons' guilds occupy a position in time between the Roman *collegia* and the lodges. The historical course of their development is as yet rather obscure despite the fact that much has been written on the subject.[3] From the first millennium references to the *magistri comacini* are almost the only available sources. They are to be found in the laws promulgated by the Lombard king Rothari (636-652) in the year 643.

Two of the laws mention the *comacini*. Article 143 decrees that the *magister comacinus*, together with his colleagues, is responsible for fatal accidents at the site of the building if he has hired the individual in question; the owner is not responsible. Article 144 adds that even if a *comacinus* is killed or injured at the work the owner is not liable;

[2] George Clune, *The Medieval Gild System*, Dublin, 1943, gives in his introduction the main stages of the development.

[3] Friedrich Heldmann, *Die drey aeltesten geschichtlichen Denkmale der teutschen Freymaurerbrüdernschaft sammt Grundzügen zu einer Geschichte der Freymaurerey*, Aarau, 1819. On pp. 57ff. Heldmann gives a history of the Roman *collegia* since King Numa, referring to Karl Christian Friedrich Krause, *Die drei ältesten Kunsturkunden der Freimaurerbrüderschaft;* as far as he quotes texts no objections can be made; it is only questionable whether the mediaeval *collegia* of workmen, especially those in the monasteries, had any historical connection with these precursors.

however, if an outsider (*extraneus*) is killed or injured by a beam or stone then not the master is liable for damages but the owner who engaged (*conducit*) him (the master).[4]

There are various derivations for the name *comacinus*. The obvious connection with Como or the island Comacina in Lake Como must be rejected on philological grounds because the adjective from Como (Latin *comum*) is *comensis* or *comanus*. Du Cange linked the word with *macio* (French maçon).[5] A *comacinus* is a mason or stonemason who is associated with other men of the same calling. That is Thompson's explanation.[6]

We learn from these two laws that there was a masons' guild in Lombardy in 643, that it consisted of a chief master and his colleagues, and that the chief master hired workmen. More exact information on the inner organization of the guild cannot be obtained from this source; it only defines the responsibility of the chief master for fatal accidents. That this Lombard guild was descended from the Roman *collegia* is possible but has not been proved, and indeed almost everything that has been written further on the *comacini* lacks historical evidence.[7] The interest shown by the "Freemasons" in the history of the "freemasons" and the literature resulting therefrom make the study of this confused subject difficult.

For the history of the guilds as well as the lodges the most important word in these laws of Rothari seems to be *extraneus*. Since the master's liability for an accident only applies to the case of guild members, there must have been conditions and certificates of membership, but that is all that can be said. If records of masons' guilds in the era of the Romanesque style have been preserved, no one has as yet published or worked on them. Dehio mentions as the earliest recorded guild organization of masons in the Gothic period that of Paris in the year 1258, "but at that time Gothic church construction had passed the peak of its most intense activity. One is probably justified in considering the

[4] Muratori, *Edicta Regum Langobardorum*, Turin, 1755, p. 38. Cf. text and translation, Appendix 7.

[5] For other proposals (*machina, Macigno*) cf. Thieme-Becker, s.v. *Comacini*. Ugo Grozia derived it from the German word *Gemach* according to a statement of Giuseppe Merzario, *I Maestri Comacini*, Milan, 1893, p. 43.

[6] A. Hamilton Thompson in an appendix to the English translation of Rivoira, *Lombardic Architecture*, Oxford, 1933, I, p. 127 (G. McN. Rushforth, trans.).

[7] Especially uncritical is the work by Leader Scott (pseudonym for Mrs. Lucy E. Baxter), *The Cathedral Builders, the Story of the Great Masonic Guild*, New York, 1899. In the extension of the concept, she follows Merzario, *op.cit.*

origin of the masons' guilds to be older than this documented date."[8]

The great gap between 643 and 1258 raises many questions.[9] Even if we were able to discover further records of masons' guilds in Romanesque times, they would scarcely have for us the same importance as those from the Gothic period. Janner confined his account to the *German* lodges and here recognized that the stylistic similarity of the churches of the Hirsau Order reflects the connection of all of them with *one* "lodge." The word lodge already has here that metaphorical meaning of an intellectual center and is not merely a wooden shed or half-timbered structure. The plans may have been worked out in detail each time in the local lodges and adapted to the particular requirements of the locality, so that the change of style was also influenced from that direction. The central importance of *one* lodge must have resided rather in its function of administering justice, and probably decisions about plans were made there only rarely. This observation goes beyond Janner; his book can otherwise be consulted for what we know about the building practices of the monasteries of that time, which created permanent troops for the erection of all necessary buildings by instituting the *conversi*, that is, *oblati* (or *barbati*), and *servi* (or *famuli*). The *conversi* ate their meals together but apart from the monks in order that the latter might carry out their clerical duties undisturbed. But the *conversi* were bound to attend divine services; occasionally they had a special chaplain. The bishops or other clergymen in the Romanesque period doubtless always gave an opinion of the plans, as every patron has done in all ages. But that only the clergy drew the plans is an exaggeration originating in the nineteenth century when an attempt was made to explain the difference between the Romanesque and Gothic styles by the fact that the building supervision passed from the control of conservative clerics to that of more gifted and daring laymen. This hypothesis of Ramée, represented especially by Vitet, Viollet-le-Duc, and Schnaase, is not a sufficient explanation of the actual course of events, however convenient it may be. This or that cleric may have made a rough sketch of a ground plan, but the exact dimensions of even a relatively simple Hirsaugien-

[8] Dehio, *Die Kirchliche Baukunst des Abendlandes*, Stuttgart, 1901, II, p. 2. Literature on ordinances of every sort of guild is indicated by Hans Huth, *Künstler und Werkstatt in der Spätgotik*, Augsburg, 1923, p. 87, n. 7. In his text Huth discusses only sculpture and painting.

[9] Heldmann, *op.cit.*, p. 94, published a York constitution of 926 that Georg Franz Burkhard Kloss, *Die Freimaurerei in ihrer wahren Bedeutung*, Leipzig, 1846, declared to be a forgery. (Kloss lived from 1787 to 1854).

sian church, together with the elevation and the drawings for the capitals, portals, and so forth, undoubtedly were drafted every time by a trained professional, were he cleric or lay, the *magister operis.*[10] As long as the *conversi* worked in close contact with the monasteries or cathedral chapters their organization could be loose; disputes among masters or questions regarding the moral conduct of masters, journeymen, apprentices, and laborers were settled as a matter of course by the clergy. Jurisdiction of their own could only have become desirable when the stonemasons had detached themselves from the clergy, especially the monasteries, and were threatened with subjection to temporal justice with its dubious understanding and partiality, for groups that were not attached to a particular sovereignty could easily be regarded as foreigners and judged with animosity. The detachment from the monasteries, therefore, was presumably connected with the development of the secular architecture of the cities. Thus the distinction between the "lodges" and the city masons' guilds seems to depend entirely on the word freedom, in the sense of freedom to move from place to place as opposed to the local restriction of the guilds, and out of this developed autonomous government and administration of justice. But that is hypothetical as long as all these problems have not been investigated more thoroughly than heretofore by experienced legal historians. Of documents there is no lack.[11]

Another factor beside the juridical doubtless played an equally important part: the increasing necessity for specialized skills in building processes and techniques. For Romanesque structures trained stonemasons had also been needed but the introduction of the ribbed vaults and the development of complicated individual forms, such as tracery after 1210, demanded of the stonemasons competence of a particular kind. The Romanesque workman of course was primarily a stonemason,

[10] In the Romanesque period there were clerics of whom it is expressly said that they designed buildings, for example, Benno von Osnabrück. Cf. Ilse Hindenberg, *Benno II, Bischof von Osnabrück als Architekt*, Strasbourg, 1921.

[11] An overwhelming wealth of details is contained in Douglas Knoop and G. P. Jones, *The Mediaeval Mason*, Manchester, 1933. Beside the books already mentioned by Janner, Clune (with bibliography), and Leader Scott, there should be noted Edgcumbe Staley, *The Guilds of Florence*, London, 1906. The last takes the legend of the *Comacini* seriously again, but offers much information that awaits critical treatment. Newer literature not used in this chapter, which was written many years ago, includes L. F. Salzman, *Building in England down to 1540*, Oxford, 1952; Pierre du Columbier, *Les Chantiers des Cathédrales*, Paris, 1953. Older literature: *Sarsena oder der vollkommene Baumeister*, 7th ed., Leipzig, 1859; J. Winzer, *Die deutschen Bruderschaften des Mittelalters, insbesondere der Bund der deutschen Steinmetzen und dessen Umwandlung zum Freimaurerbund*, Giessen, 1859; Friedrich Albert Fallou, *Die Mysterien der Freimaurer, sowie ihr einzig wahrer Grund und Ursprung*, Leipzig, 1859.

unless one thinks of him as the sculptor who created the capitals with their foliage and figures. The Gothic stonemason, on the other hand, was always more or less a sculptor as well; moreover, he had to be familiar with the transference of complicated drawings to the scale of the execution. The lodge statutes breathe a spirit of self-respect, originating here as always in the consciousness of the difficulty of replacing trained ability. Gothic culture in its essential Christianity required of the individual master or journeyman modesty and anonymity, but this requirement did not apply to the fraternity of masons or stonemasons as a whole. As a member of a lodge every stonemason had a right to hold his head high.

This train of thought may answer, though hypothetically, the question why lodge statutes came into existence only at a late period. They presuppose the fact that Gothic had progressed to complicated forms and that the cities had consolidated their guild jurisdictions. The Parisian organization that Dehio characterized as a late phenomenon was a masons' guild of the city, not a lodge for stonemasons with freedom of movement. There must have been masons' guilds early, that is, long before 1258, not only in Paris. But "Gothic lodges"?

Naturally these were found wherever great churches were being constructed, but in the sense described by Janner. What we mean by lodge is something quite specific, a close-knit organization growing out of the relations of the various local lodges to each other. In France and England each local lodge seems to have been organized only to a degree necessary for its own functions. Evidence for this is offered by what little information Durand[12] has compiled about Amiens from records and bills. No statute proves the existence of the organization but it is indicated by the combination of official designations appearing in the archives at various times. Some mentions go back to the thirteenth century, not, indeed, to the first period of the work on the cathedral (1220), although the *procurator fabrice* is documented for the year 1234.

In Amiens the *fabrica* or administration was identical with the chapter, which delegated authority to a canon and a *maître de la fabrique*. The latter had under him a *clerc*, a *varlet de l'œuvre*, a *maître maçon*, a *maître charpentier*, a *couvreur* (master roofer), "and other" master artisans. This group worked with the *maître des ouvrages*, a citizen chosen annually as representative of the citizenry, who for

[12] Georges Durand, *Monographie de l'Église Nôtre-Dame, Cathédrale d'Amiens*, Amiens and Paris, 1901, p. 103. Mr. Louis Grodecki (Paris) drew my attention to this chapter.

his part had a *clerc des ouvrages* as assistant. The *maître de la fabrique* is mentioned in 1375, but Durand assumes that this whole organization goes back to the time of the first construction in 1220. A lodge in the later sense (French *loge*, Latin *logia*) was included in the *fabrica*; it is evidenced by the *maître maçon*. But Durand says (page 111) that to this lodge belonged also the glaziers, roofers, thatchers, slaters, rope-makers, and smiths. The term lodge (*Hütte*), used in German literature where reference is made to lodge organizations, applies only to stonemasons; it is in contrast to the term guild (*Zunft* or *Gilde*) which was used, for example, for the craft of the masons. Lodge and guild were in Germany two separate corporations and in the fifteenth century we find exact provisions for their mutual relations, since it happened that an apprentice mason would change over to the trade of stonemason during his term of apprenticeship; or journeymen stonemasons, lacking work, would bind themselves to master masons. It is certain that the masons' statutes were earlier than the lodge statutes.

The ordinance of Paris[13] can serve us as a substitute for many lost guild statutes of masons and so forth. It begins: "He who will can become a mason in Paris, provided he knows (*sache*) his trade and works according to the custom and habits of the trade, which are: No one can have in his workshop (*mestier*) more than one apprentice, and if he has an apprentice he cannot take him for less than six years of service, otherwise he must pay a fine of twenty Parisian *sous*; but for more years of service [that is, longer] he can well take [some] for money, if he can have it. . . ." After the course of five years he can engage a second apprentice. The number of *aides et vallés* is unlimited provided they are all trained. The regulations include under this Article 48 the masons, stonemasons, plasterers, and mortarers, but individual provisions are limiting for certain of these crafts. All must swear by the saints (no specific ones are named) that they will do their work well and honestly (*loyal*) according to custom and usage. After termination of the period of apprenticeship the master testifies before the chief master that the apprentice (*aprentis*) has served faithfully, whereupon the latter swears to observe the usage and custom of the trade. Working hours are limited, exceptions for finishing certain kinds of work after vespers are listed (closing an arch, finishing an

[13] George Bernhard Depping, *Règlemens sur les arts et métiers de Paris, Rédigés au XIII siècle et connus sous le nom du Livre des Métiers d'Etienne Boileau*, Paris, 1837, pp. 107ff. (Collection de Documents inédits . . . , First Series, XXXI). Cf. text, Appendix 8.

entrance, and so on). Infringements are punishable by a fine. The chief master of the guild has jurisdiction by royal authorization. Like all citizens of Paris the masons and plasterers are obliged to serve on the guard and pay taxes, "but the mortarers have been released from guard duty, likewise the stonemasons, ever since the time of Charles Martel, as the wise men have heard it said from father to son." Also the chief master is exempt from guard duty. (Each of the one hundred articles contains provisions for guard service and taxes.)

The period of apprenticeship lasted in Paris at that time six years,[14] later in Germany it was reduced to five and even four. If the apprentice presumably began his training at the age of fourteen he would then become a journeyman at twenty or nineteen or eighteen. The actual point in dispute is never stated, but we can deduce that the difficulty of the trade required a long apprenticeship but that the masters, on the other hand, did not want to be burdened any longer than necessary with the support of an apprentice, especially with the prospect of being able to engage a second when the first had served the greater part of his time. The disputes on the length of the apprenticeship arising later in Germany are easily understandable if one realizes that a lodge with a shorter time of apprenticeship gave its journeymen a head start, which naturally called forth protests from the journeymen of other lodges; it was both a question of economics and one of "seniority." But such competition could only develop among wandering journeymen going from lodge to lodge in search of work. The question is: when were these lodges organized?

The beginnings are very obscure.[15] According to Janner a lodge with autonomous jurisdiction was founded in 1275 at Strasbourg and confirmed in that year by Emperor Rudolf I of Habsburg. But the passage in the text, which he cites according to Heldmann from the Constitution Book of the Archimedes Lodge in Altenberg, states explicitly that a "freed masonry" was founded "according to the English fashion," thus showing that such things existed earlier in England. The chief personage at the founding ceremonies is said to have been

[14] In 1356 in York seven years, see below, p. 121.

[15] For the literature (Kreuser, Krause, Heldmann, etc.) and the relevant passages of text cf. Janner, *op.cit.*, pp. 39ff. In Joshua Toulmin Smith, *English Gilds, the Original Ordinances of More Than One Hundred Early English Gilds*, London, 1868 (Early English Text Society, XL), we read, p. CXXVI: "Whenever [the wardens] held a court, it was under special forms and solemnities: thus, for instance, in 1275 the chief warden of the Masons building Strassburg Cathedral held court sitting under a canopy." Cf. also pages CXXVII, CXXXIV. The book treats all the craft guilds, contains a wealth of material as well as enumeration of the entire older literature on the subject, but offers little that applies to the problems under discussion here.

Erwin "von Steinbach," who assembled "the most illustrious masters of the works and artificers from Germany, and from Italy, to which latter the Pope had given permission by a Bull, and from England as well." Evidence for the Papal Bull has never been found and everything else that has been reported of this stage in lodge history is uncertain. Nevertheless, it is very probable that these statements are essentially correct, that is, with regard to the derivation from Italy and England, the foundation of the Strasbourg Lodge in the year 1275 and its elevation to the rank of master lodge for Germany in 1277.

On the basis of a document of 926 England lays claim to the creation of "free masonry," from which "freemasonry" was derived.[16] However, the validity of this document is in dispute.

On the other hand, we possess an Italian document reputedly of 1292, thus only seventeen years after the likewise reputed founding of the Strasbourg Lodge and here we discover for the first time a substantial basis for judging the lodge organization. The document in question is the ordinance of the lodge in Siena. Della Valle published the text in 1782[17] and Hagen called attention to it in 1818;[18] since then it seems to have been forgotten. Hagen gave its date as 1292. This date is actually to be found in one of della Valle's notes, strangely enough after the second paragraph, as though it referred to that alone (or to the first and second paragraphs alone) and not to the following paragraphs. This note reads in translation: "Tizio says of the year 1292 that at that time the statutes were published in the mother tongue in order to do away with ambiguities"; della Valle continues: "Probably these were not published, because practically all sculptors, who were also painters, governed themselves according to the statutes of the painters, being satisfied with some small supplement to them." That is contradictory: Tizio says reputedly "furono volgarizzati" and della Valle "non furono volgarizzati."[19] Granted that an Italian translation was published in 1292, which would have been remarkably early, it must be concluded that the Latin version originated *before* 1292, since misunderstandings had already arisen. This would bring us even

16 J. T. Smith, *ibid.*, p. 44, according to Müller's article in Ersch and Gruber's *Encyclopädie.*

17 Guglielmo della Valle, *Lettere senesi . . . sopra le belle arti*, I, Venice, 1782, p. 280. (della Valle's dates are ca.1740-ca.1794) Cf. text, Appendix 9.

18 Friedrich Heinrich von der Hagen, *Briefe in die Heimat*, Breslau, 1818, II, p. 258.

19 Luise Maria Richter, *Siena* (Berühmte Kunststätten), Leipzig, 1915, p. 182. Also Paolo Piccolomini, *Una lettera inedita* (Archivio Storico Italiano, Fifth Series, XXVII, 1901) p. 306. The autograph manuscript of the *Historiae Senenses* is in Rome. It belongs to the Codices Chigiani and is now preserved in the Vatican, GI 31-39. The second volume, GI 32, contains the year 1292.

closer to the date of the Strasbourg lodge. The work on the cathedral at Siena had already begun in the first half of the thirteenth century, and thus our imagination is stimulated to take the ordinance of the Sienese lodge even further back than that of Strasbourg. Giovanni Pisano was *capomaestro* in Siena from about 1287 to 1296. At that time the façade was erected; the east end and the nave had been completed. All through the preceding decades stonemasons had been constantly in demand and one can say that an unusually large number of them was needed for the façade, so rich in figures. In fact, the document mentions sixty-one stonemasons, a number which scarcely included Pisano himself.

But the connection of the statutes published by della Valle with the year 1292 must probably be abandoned completely. Sigismondo Tizio lived from 1448 to 1528 and wrote a history of Siena in ten volumes, none of which has been published. Della Valle may be otherwise reliable; in this case, the investigation must presumably be undertaken anew. As far as our knowledge, or the lack of it, is concerned today, the classification of the Sienese statutes as earlier than the London Regulation of 1356 remains provisional.[20]

The document begins solemnly: "In the name of the Lord, amen. To the honor of God and the Blessed Virgin Mary and to the power of the people and the Twenty-Four of Siena and to the honor and prosperity of the Sienese master stonemasons and their future rulers." This preamble indicates the religious and political background of which mention was made earlier. The provisions themselves run: every six months three *rectores*, a *camerlengus*, and thirteen *conciliarii* are to be elected; the election always takes place one month before expiration of the term of office; substitutes are only admissible in cases of illness or if the person in question is sojourning outside Siena. No one may be reelected in the following three years. *Rectores* and *camerlengus* may make expenditures only with the consent of all or a majority of the masters. Disputes among the masters are to be brought before

[20] On fol. 147 of the manuscript in Rome there is a report of a commission of nine and after that of a revision of city statutes and prerogatives of several churches, but nothing about a lodge ordinance or an ordinance of a masons' guild. On fol. 148r there is mention of the *lingua volgare*, the exact wording of which Dr. Friedrich Wilhelm Deichmann most kindly copied out for me. From all that he tells me it appears that della Valle partly misunderstood the text and partly connected it with the undated guild ordinance for no visible reason. I am grateful to Dr. Deichmann for his trouble in consulting and deciphering the apparently very difficult script. It may be added that two *copies* are in existence, one in the Biblioteca Communale in Siena, the other in the Biblioteca Nazionale in Florence. Perhaps these may be helpful in further investigations.

the *rectores* and the *camerlengus*; the disputants may bring judges, notaries, and advocates with them. Foreign masters must become members of the lodge. Fifteen days before expiration of his term of office the *camerlengus* must submit his accounts and divide any surplus among all the masters.

These provisions sound like those of other corporations. Striking is their democratic spirit, expressed in the brevity of the terms of office and the coordination of all, especially the *rectores* and the *camerlengus*, since the limitation on reelections gives every member the prospect of occupying an executive position within a very short time. Democratic, even reminiscent of modern cooperatives, is the equable distribution of the surpluses. It remains uncertain whether the *capomaestro*, in this case Giovanni Pisano, was the superior of the biennially changing *rectores* and *camerlengus*, but one can hardly assume otherwise since he doubtless also drew a special salary. The provision that foreigners must become members of the guild should be interpreted not so much as a sign of liberal-mindedness as a legal *conditio sine qua non* for permission to work, valid for any stonemason regardless of his origin.

This Sienese ordinance contains nothing about journeymen and apprentices; it concerns only the coordinated masters and gives no hint as to the law of their court or possible penalties inflicted.

Provisions regarding these details were already contained in the Parisian ordinance of the city masons and they reappear in the London Regulation of 1356.[21] It was a question of disputes between "mason hewers" and "mason layers and setters." According to Knoop and Jones the former are the stonemasons who shape the blocks, the latter those who put them in their ultimate places. Their wages were different.[22] At that time (1356) there appeared before the "aldermen and sheriffs" six masters for each group (among them Henry de Yeevelee). The provisions relate 1) to the requirement of completed training; 2) to penalties—if the requirement is not properly observed or if a stone has been cut badly, the first time one mark, the second time two marks, the third time the guilty party is to be expelled forever; 3) stonemasons must bring guarantors (of their guild) to testify that they are capable of completing the work undertaken; 4) apprentices and journeymen shall work only in the presence of the master until they

21 Knoop and Jones, *op.cit.*, p. 249. According to these authors the guild of masons in Lincoln, founded in 1313, was only a religious fraternity and not a "craft guild"; that is, there were common religious interests and church attendance but no regulations that applied to the building trades.

22 *Ibid.*, p. 83.

have been fully trained—infringements of this rule are punishable by fines; 5) the period of apprenticeship lasts *seven* years; 6) the master is responsible for the work of his day laborers; 7) disobedient members are to be handed over to the burgomaster for punishment (prison or otherwise); 8) no master shall engage the apprentice or journeyman of another master before their time of service has expired—here, too, fines are imposed for infringements.

How severely the stonemasons in the service of the English king were treated is revealed by two edicts of Edward III (1327-1377). Whoever does not remain at work on the site will be imprisoned. But these two edicts of 1359 and 1361[23] from London have to do with the building of Windsor Castle and, therefore, according to what has been said above, must be evaluated differently from lodge ordinances of the "free masons" who worked for cathedral chapters.

An ordinance of the latter kind is that of York from the year 1370.[24] It stipulates when the stonemasons are obliged to work—the hours of the day depending on the season of the year—when they shall pause for meals, when they may drink after twelve o'clock, or sleep in the lodge, and, further, that a bell must indicate the different times of the daily routine. Each new member shall do one week's work on trial before he is engaged on the unanimous vote of the master, the keeper of the work, and the master mason. Then he shall swear on the book. It is not quite clear whether the Bible is meant or the Lodge Book containing the constitution.[25] He may then leave the work only with the permission of the masters.

This ordinance of York gives one a sense of being transported to the building place. Gothic York Cathedral, one of the most important in England, was at that time largely completed; the transept was under construction from 1230 to 1260, the nave from 1291 to 1324, the choir from 1361 to 1370, thus it had just been completed.[26] But work was still proceeding on the west front and the tower over the crossing. Discipline was strict. We get the impression that a part of the stonemasons slept in the "lodge," so that it must have been a fairly large

[23] *Ibid.*, p. 244.

[24] *Ibid.*, p. 248. Cf. text, Appendix 10.

[25] In the German ordinances discussed by Janner "book" does not mean the Bible but the Lodge Book, containing special laws and doubtless also calculations of wages that have not been transmitted to us.

[26] According to Konrad Escher, *Englische Kathedralen*, Munich and Berlin, 1927, p. 113. The choir 1361-1405; also Findlay Muirhead, *Great Britain* (The Blue Guides), London, 1930, p. 328. Different dates in H. Felton and John Harvey, *The English Cathedrals*, London, 1950, p. 87.

and solid structure.[27] It is not expressly stated that the members of the guild had to attend divine services because it is self-evident. The ecclesiastical background is sharply revealed at the end of the ordinance by the threat that anyone who disobeys may be cursed by God and St. Peter.

The next ordinance extant is that of Treves from the year 1397.[28] It was enacted for the stonemasons by the presiding alderman and the other aldermen of the city of Treves for the advantage of the citizens as well as of the stonemasons themselves. The latter, for the glory of God, the Blessed Virgin, and all the saints, also for the honor, profit, and business (*gemach*) of their office, have formed a good and honorable fraternity, which from now on shall be held inviolate by them and by all those brothers of this trade coming after them. Approximately ten provisions follow: the fraternity is to be obedient to the presiding alderman, the other aldermen, and the council; the members are to furnish good work; they shall pass the fraternity, that is, probably, pass an examination, which is, however, not more precisely described; whoever is the child of a brother (of this fraternity) need pay only half the fee for entrance; foreign masters or journeymen shall pay nothing as long as they are in the service of the city; whoever undertakes to work for a brother need pay nothing for fourteen days, but if he stays longer he must pay the membership fee, and if he stays over a year then he must pay again; no brother shall forbid another to do a particular piece of work, nor shall he issue any order in the fraternity other than what is prescribed. There follow regulations for burials, for the annual election of the presiding master of the fraternity, and for the transfer of office from the outgoing to the incoming master. Finally, the master, together with the aldermen, shall take steps against foreign masters, journeymen, or apprentices who do not want to enter the fraternity, and shall likewise proceed against any disobedience.

For most of these regulations the fines for infringements are indicated and, as a matter of fact, by quantities of wine and wax. In cases of disobedience wine is also to be paid to the *Rymeler* (treasurer) and to the master of the fraternity: "die zwene Seister Wins des besten als vorgeschriewen steit—usgeschieden alle arglist und geverde,"[29] (two

[27] In many lodge ordinances the workmaster had the privilege of sleeping in the lodge after the midday meal.

[28] The text has been published in full by August Reichensperger, *Vermischte Schriften*, 1845, pp. 164-167.

[29] The Middle High German *geverde* is derived from *gawarida* (see Schade, *Altdeutsches Wörterbuch*, Halle, 1882). It means deceit; *on geverde* means without deceit or, expressed posi-

sesters of wine of the best sort, as is prescribed—without any trickery or deceit).

The Treves ordinance is, as Hasak has already realized, an ordinance for a guild and not a lodge.[30] It belongs therefore to the same group of documents as the Paris ordinance of 1258. Both types of ordinances are equally interesting as sources for the history of Gothic. However, the difference in the statutes of the two categories—guilds and lodges—is not absolutely clear. They were alike in many respects. The difference between the two corporations lay above all in their practice. The lodges sought to preserve their complete independence and that was justifiable, inasmuch as a citizen, a councilor or city judge, who had not learned the stonemasons' trade, could not have a proper opinion in disputes that concerned the form of stone blocks and their placement. In other trades also one had to acquire skills, in baking, butchering, tailoring, and so on, but nowhere was geometrical exactitude so important as in Gothic architecture and it ennobled its adepts, or at least set them apart in the realm of the *artes technicae* as an upper stratum of educated men. The *lodges* not only had to safeguard discipline on the building site and watch over the technical side of the building but they also had to preserve discipline themselves, to the fullest extent, in the personal lives of their members. The *guilds* left the judging of moral or, as the case might be, juridical behavior to the city courts, presumably only because, as we have said, no disputes difficult to settle were to be expected in their affairs, deriving from their professional work (for example, glovemaking).

The professional knowledge of the stonemasons' trade was, from this point of view, the source of the autonomous jurisdiction of the lodges, but the difficulty of divorcing the professional from the personal in disputed questions was the deeper reason for the claim to dispense justice generally to all members of the lodge, in every case of disagreement or misdemeanor or crime. The imputation is that this trend must have had a gradual development, the extension of the jurisdiction taking place stage by stage. Such widening responsibility for human behavior should, accordingly, be viewed in connection with the jurisdiction of the guilds, in town and empire, thus, with the entire development of law in Gothic times in mind. The historian

tively, with sincerity; see Franz Jelinek, *Mittelhochdeutsches Wörterbuch*, Heidelberg, 1911, p. 307.

[30] Max Hasak, "Die romanische und gotische Baukunst," *Handbuch der Architektur*, ed. Josef Durm, 2nd series, IV, 3, Stuttgart, 1902, p. 268.

of art, therefore, must leave it to the historian of law to settle this question.

Gurlitt, who did work on the lodge ordinances, probably on the basis of Janner's book, came across a hitherto unknown ordinance in Erfurt from the year 1423. He published it together with other Erfurt documents and made a rough interpretation.[31]

He says himself (page 338) that the Erfurt "lodge" was a *city* guild with no connection with other lodges. The word "master" is here replaced by that of "guardian" (*Vormund*). The officers consist of two "guardians" and four "Kumpane" (*Paliere?*) chosen annually (one is reminded of the other, but similar, organization of Siena). The guild includes both masons and stonemasons. The innumerable details cannot be discussed here. Every city developed individual paragraphs, and a unification of the ordinances only became necessary where there was a question of wandering journeymen and resulting claims of competence. We must, therefore, assume that there was on the one hand a broadening of the claim to jurisdiction within the individual guild or lodge and on the other a problematical situation with regard to competence outside it.

Gurlitt cites examples for these legal problems from a somewhat later period. A Master Hans in Passau—Gurlitt cannot decide which of the many individuals of that name it was—summoned an Erfurt Master Hans to appear before him (between 1471 and 1481), but the Erfurt council did not consent to let one of its citizens stand trial in Passau, and wanted to pass judgment itself. In another case, a dispute between Hans Olmützer and Conrad Pflüger, the former in Vienna and the latter in Passau, the council of Görlitz (Silesia) made inquiries in Passau as to whether Olmützer was a stonemason (that is, recognized by the lodge) and whether he would be given work there. One can see how complicated the situation was, even after the meeting in Regensburg in 1459.

In the main the contents of the Erfurt ordinance have been dealt with by Gurlitt; the subject matter relates to the period of apprenticeship, to regulations for journeymen and masters, to business manage-

[31] Cornelius Gurlitt, *Kunst und Künstler am Vorabend der Reformation*, Halle, 1890 (Schriften des Vereins für Reformationsgeschichte, XXIX, p. 42); by the same author, *Erfurter Steinmetzenordnungen des 15. und 16. Jahrhunderts* (Repertorium für Kunstwissenschaft, XV), Berlin, 1892, p. 332. The texts of 1423, 1502, then the undated ordinance of the beginning of the sixteenth century, the ordinance on the penny levies, and the guild ordinance of 1588 are all published in full on pp. 340ff.

ment, proper personal behavior, taxes, and fines. Article 15 is probably the most interesting for the topic of "Gothic":

"Also no one shall be accepted into the guild unless the guild acknowledges that he can guarantee his work to everyone, a brick layer as a bricklayer, a mason as a mason, a workmaster as a workmaster, each one according to his status." "Gothic," if one may personify this style, did not suffer impostors gladly.[32]

The next stonemasons' ordinance to have been preserved is that of Siena from the year 1441. It remains doubtful whether the one of 1292 (?), which was discussed above, had already been revised in the interim or whether revision had only now become necessary after almost a century and a half. This ordinance was published by Milanesi;[33] Leader Scott mentioned it briefly;[34] whether it has been treated in more recent literature I do not know.

Of the forty-six chapters two are repeated almost word for word (chapter 45 duplicates 31, and 44 duplicates 14). Furthermore, chapter 43 states that chapters 42 and 43 are abrogated because they are to be considered as replaced by the more detailed version of the copy of 1447. These passages concern the codification of the rights of carpenters and stonemasons. But chapter 39 already delimits the rights of the carpenters: "We establish and ordain, in order to prevent all disputes and disagreements, that in the future no master carpenter may make anything other than roofs, floors, and scaffoldings as balconies. . . ."[35] From the sequence of the chapters one receives the impression that this lodge ordinance came into being gradually; confirmation of this would seem to be offered by the fact that in chapter 40 provision is made for emendations for each half year, these then to be voted upon

[32] The original text runs thus: "Ouch sal man nymanden in dy czunft nehmen eyn hantwergk erkenne dann, das her eyme iclichen syne arbeit kan bewaren, eyn murer also eyn murer, eyn steynhower also eyn steynhower, eyn wergkmeister also eyn wergkmeister, einen iclichen nach synen state." (Translated in modern German: Man soll auch niemanden in die Zunft aufnehmen, es sei denn, die Gilde anerkennt, dass er seine Arbeit jedem garantieren kann, ein Maurer als ein Maurer, ein Steinmetz als ein Steinmetz, ein Werkmeister als ein Werkmeister, einen jeglichen nach seinem Stand. The word: bewaren means: gewährleisten. The word eyme is the dative. The accusative einen iclichen at the end seems to be related to the word nymanden at the beginning of the sentence.)

[33] Gaetano Milanesi, *Documenti per la storia dell'arte senese*, Siena, 1854. I, p. 105.

[34] Leader Scott, *op.cit.*, p. 286.

[35] Cap. XXXIX, "Che niuno maestro di legname possa fare di pietra. Anco statuimo et ordiniamo, per fuggire ogni lite et differenza, che per l'avenire niuno maestro di legname possa fare altro che tetti, palchi, et armadure di ballatoi: a pena di soldi dieci per chi darà opera in altro che di legname." By "armadure di ballatoi" are probably meant the ordinary scaffoldings that are erected like balconies against the interior and exterior sides of the walls.

in the main meeting. The original of the text has been lost. Milanesi used a seventeenth century copy, and it is therefore not possible to draw any conclusions about additions from the characteristics of the script.

The rich content can only be suggested here. The first chapter forbids cursing under pain of a fine of twenty-five lire, if two or more witnesses testify to the offense. The second requires an oath of loyalty to the Signoria of Siena. Then follow provisions for the election of three *rectores* and a *camerlengho*, showing that the organization had not changed substantially since 1292 (?). Particular regulations were introduced, however, on the administration of justice (chapter 5), disobedience (chapter 6), and other matters. The provision that no member of the lodge (*nissuno sottoposto*) might take over a work already undertaken by another either under contract, or at his own risk, or for daily wages is also found in German lodge ordinances. Contracts with apprentices are to be handed over to the *camerlengho* (chapter 12). Foreign masters must take the oath like the natives; they must pay four lire for admission within a month, and if they do not, no one may work with them (chapters 14 and 44).

Chapter 13 gives directions for the celebration of the festival of the Four Crowned Ones; chapter 18 for other festivals. All the forty-four holidays are enumerated; three days are allotted for Easter. Among the ecclesiastical regulations are those concerning funerals (chapter 22); the *rectores* and the *camerlengho* are required to be present at the burials of lodge members and those of their fathers, mothers, wives, and children, and to escort the bereaved to their homes after the ceremonies.

Chapter 31 shows the tendency of the lodge to include in its jurisdiction other trades belonging to the building enterprise.

There is much in this Sienese lodge ordinance of 1441 that is reminiscent of the ordinance of the masons' guild in Treves of 1397. An exact comparison of all the ordinances cannot be made here; it should only be pointed out that many similarities resulted from the nature of the subject, and conclusions as to reciprocal influences should not be drawn too hastily. The variations that evolved from local customs and traditions may well reveal the peculiarities of the Italians, English, Germans, and French.

The Regensburg stonemasons' ordinance of 1459 is more full of matter than the preceding ones. Meetings in Speyer and Strasbourg had taken place immediately before. The Saxon lodges were not represented; they joined afterward, but the ordinance of Torgau, established a few years later (1462), deviates from that of Regensburg in many respects. Subsequently, also, the Saxons were disinclined to take a subordinate position to Strasbourg.

The Regensburg ordinance was first published by Heldmann,[36] who used a late copy of the chief lodge in Strasbourg that was destroyed by fire in the bombardment of 1870.

The study of this ordinance is complicated by the destruction of the original. The text that is best known, because Janner reprinted it in 1876, is that published by Heldmann in 1819.[37] In 1888 Neuwirth published the Klagenfurt ordinance of 1628,[38] thinking that it corresponded to the original version. A few years later (1894) Luschin reproduced the Admont lodge ordinance of 1480;[39] two years afterward Neuwirth proved that manuscript 14898 in the Vienese Hofbibliothek represented the Tirolese lodge ordinance of 1460.[40] A preparatory session of Tirolese stonemasons took place in Sterzing on February 5, 1460, followed by a meeting in Hall near Innsbruck on February 23, 1460, which was much better attended. Neuwirth was of the opinion that this version, which stands closest in time to the session in Regensburg on April 25, 1459, has the best claim to be considered a copy of the ordinance decided upon in Regensburg. But all of these "copies" differ from each other. They coincide in many statements and the innumerable variants in wording, not to say in orthography, do not

36 Heldmann, *Drei älteste geschichtliche Denkmale der deutschen Freimaurerbrüderschaft*, Aarau, 1819, pp. 203ff. Reprinted by Karl Christian Krause (with the same title), III, pp. 269ff., and then by Carl Heideloff, *Die Bauhütte des Mittelalters in Deutschland*, Nuremberg, 1844.

37 Heldmann, *op.cit.*, p. 50, says that he himself owns the three documents that he is printing. However, on pp. 200ff. he relates how he tried in vain in Strasbourg in 1818 to see the ordinance of 1459, which was kept under triple locks, but that he obtained from two other freemasons in Switzerland copies that had been made at the time of the French Revolution. What has since become of the original of the ordinance of 1459 does not seem to be reported anywhere; cf. later in the text Neuwirth's conjecture. Heldmann's text was reprinted by Krause (1819) and by Heideloff (1844), and again by Janner. The Strasbourg text that Heldmann was able to establish by means of two similar copies has never been under suspicion and arouses no doubts of any sort. Heldmann did not name his authorities, who were both freemasons as he was, but he had their permission to call upon them. He also cites *in extenso* Goethe's remark on the lodge ordinance, *Über Kunst und Altertum in den Rhein- und Maingegenden*, No. 18, p. 191. Goethe had obtained a text through Boisserée in 1815. It is possible that it was a Cologne copy of the Strasbourg ordinance.

38 Joseph Neuwirth, *Die Satzungen des Regensburger Steinmetzentages im Jahre 1459 auf Grund der Klagenfurter Steinmetzen- und Maurerordnung von 1628*, Vienna, 1888.

39 Arnold Luschin von Ebengreuth, "Das Admonter Hüttenbuch und die Regensburger Steinmetzordnung vom Jahre 1459," *Mitteilungen der Zentralkommission*, N.F. XX, 1894, p. 168.

40 Joseph Neuwirth, "Das Tiroler Hüttenbuch," *Zeitschrift für Bauwesen*, 1896, p. 175.

matter to us as long as the sense is the same. The confusing thing is that the sequence of the articles is different each time, making comparison difficult because one must hunt for corresponding statements. Luschin made a master list for four "copies," but this would have to be supplemented by a fifth rubric for the Hall ordinance, discovered by Neuwirth. It is also disturbing that the designations of all these ordinances show variations. The Regensburg ordinance is named thus because it was decided upon in that city, but it is also called the Strasbourg ordinance because it was previously discussed in Strasbourg. Thus, the Hall ordinance of 1460 (the Vienna manuscript) is also called the Tirolese ordinance and shares this title with the Tirolese ordinance of 1480. When compared with the other "copies" the deviations of the Torgau ordinance of 1462, mentioned above, prove to be no exception. The investigations made hitherto, including those of Hasak,[41] cannot be considered exhaustive. A separate book would be needed to do justice to the subject in all its ramifications. Luschin's tabulation is useful for a quick orientation in the subject matter of the articles. In the following I shall confine myself to the version published by Janner. As has been said, it goes back to a manuscript that was burned, according to Neuwirth's conjecture, during the bombardment of Strasbourg in 1870. One might well suppose the situation to have been that the wording debated in Speyer and Strasbourg was discussed once more in Regensburg and finally resolved upon, but that the document with the signatures was taken back to Strasbourg, since it had been acknowledged as having the highest rank of all the lodges. Though Kloss, Heideloff, Janner, and Hasak probably considered the text of this manuscript, meanwhile destroyed by fire, to be the original because it was kept in Strasbourg, the sequence of the articles under discussion arouses doubts, since it is more logical in the Tirolese ordinance of 1460 printed by Neuwirth. However, one cannot insist on this argument because all "copies" are doubtful in this respect, and it must be admitted that a strictly logical arrangement was difficult. Though the ordinance as a whole was divided into three parts, that is, regulations first for masters, second for journeymen, and third for servants (apprentices), there were provisions that were supposed to apply to a reciprocal relationship or to two categories, and so on; thus, no great value was probably placed on a logical order for the articles. This, however, still does not explain why the sequence varies each time.

[41] Max Hasak, *Der Kirchenbau des Mittelalters*, Stuttgart, 1913 (2nd ed.), pp. 279ff.

As is well known, only the lodges in the German language area strove toward an over-all organization; it is lacking in other countries. The initiative came from Strasbourg, which meant from Master Jodokus Dotzinger. Correspondingly, Neuwirth has shown the likelihood that the union of the Tirolese stonemasons and their adherence to the Regensburg-Strasbourg ordinance could be attributed to the personal efforts of two men, Master Hans Sewer of Hall and Master Hans Reichharttinger from Innsbruck. In spite of all their determination to create a centralized organization, the various lodges remained individual in the drafting of their statutes, a phenomenon which one might easily be inclined to call typically German. But why then was a strict centralization lacking in centralized France or England? Were the peoples of these countries more intensely individual than those of German stock? However that may be, this peculiar blending of the desire for centralization and the demand for autonomous decision may be the reason why all the "copies" begin with the same preamble, which states that the ordinance was discussed in Speyer and Strasbourg and that the promise had been given in Regensburg "to preserve it faithfully for us and all our descendants," although what was promised was formulated somewhat differently in each lodge.

This preamble has a solemn beginning: "In the name of the Father, the Son, and the Holy Ghost, and of the venerable Mother Mary, and likewise to the everlasting memory of her beloved servants, the holy Four Crowned Ones." The Four Crowned Ones are the Quattro Coronati of Rome, stonemasons who refused to create heathen images and who suffered martyrdom on November 8, 303, during the persecutions of the Christians under Diocletian.[42] They were considered the patron saints of the lodges. The preamble defines as its chief purpose that owners, including also municipalities wishing to have churches or other great structures built, should be well served and that at the same time masters and journeymen should be able to carry on their trade without dissension. Janner divided the ordinance, which is written without a break, into fifty-three articles, printed it in the appendix of his book (page 251), and interpreted it in detail in the text. It is thus permissible to discuss here only a few aspects of this unusually manifold complex.

[42] According to one version these four saints are Severus, Severianus, Carpophoros, and Victorinus; according to another they are Castor, Sempronianus, Nicostratus, and Claudius; cf. J. P. Kirsch, "Die Passio der hl. Vier Gekrönten in Rom," *Historisches Jahrbuch der Görresgesellschaft*, 1917, p. 72. Also D. Knoop, G. P. Jones and D. Hamer, *The Two Earliest Masonic Manuscripts*, Manchester, 1938, p. 44.

The first article envisages the possibility of subsequent aggravations or mitigations;[43] the development prior to this could probably be judged according to these points of view, if we knew more.

The organization of the individual lodges is based on the distinction of six grades. *Three* of them represent the well-known stages in training: apprentice (*Diener*), journeyman, master. Between journeyman and master is a *fourth* category, that of the foreman (*Parlier*), who is really a journeyman assigned to special duties. Above the masters in rank is, in certain cases, the *fifth* category of the workmaster. One might think that this title was given to the man having the chief authority where several masters, with their journeymen, were working together on one building; but Article 9 prescribes: "es sollent auch nit zwey Meister ein Werk oder einen Gebeue gemein miteinander haben, Es wer den, dass es ein kleiner Gebeuwe were, dere in Jorsfryst ein ende näme ungeverlich; den mag man wol gemeyn haben mit dem, der ein mytbruder ist" (two masters shall not undertake a work or a building in common, unless it be a small building that can be finished without question in a year's time. Such a one may be undertaken in common with him who is a fellow brother). Thus, workmaster seems to be a title only given to a master who is executing a large work.[44] The *sixth* category, finally, is that of the servants of art (*kunstdiener*). These, according to Janner, are journeymen "who desired to serve the master for an extra period of time in order to get further training in various matters, in artistic skills such as designing, art secrets, sculpture, and so forth."[45]

This organization can also be used as a guide to the education of the stonemason. At that time the apprentice usually was about fourteen years old when he began his training, though the ordinance says nothing on that point; he then served five years and was thereafter solemnly pronounced free. How much time had to elapse before a journeyman could become a master is here not stated definitely. We know from other trades that the grade of master was reached in the guilds at about the age of twenty-five. But the journeyman who became master had to be married, since, according to Janner, his apprentice was to live with him. It is more probable that the church

43 In the Tirolese ordinance of 1480 this article is no. 8.

44 Janner, *op.cit.*, p. 109, assumes, however, that in the larger lodges several masters were engaged as *Untermeister* under one *Obermeister*. These terms have been taken by Janner from modern usage; they do not originate in the mediaeval period.

45 Janner, *op.cit.*, p. 152.

insisted upon marriage. Article 17 says: "Es soll auch kein Werkmann noch Meister nit öffentlich über Steinwerk zu der Unee sitzen. . . ." (Nor shall any workman or master working on stone publicly live in concubinage.)[46]

The journeyman *could* wander; but he *had* to wander, and for at least a year, if he wanted to become a foreman (*Parlier*). The duties of the foreman as representative of the master and mediator between him and those who work on the site are well known.[47] In spite of the detailedness of the Regensburg ordinance for stonemasons much remains unclear. It would seem that the workmaster drafted and calculated within the lodge in his special spot for working; the foreman, on the other hand, carried his commands to the various workmen and supervised their execution.

Janner's book should be consulted by anyone who wishes to inform himself about wages, management of funds, and minor fines, the latter inflicted for infringements of ordinary discipline. Equally, one may gather from the innumerable scattered notes of the book what the situation was with regard to morality and religious duties. Whoever did not receive the sacraments each year or keep to the Christian way of life was held to be dishonorable. Monogamy was a requirement that was a matter of course, and therefore every apprentice had to produce paternal testimonial to his legitimate birth.

Hempel made an excellent arrangement of the statutes, dividing them according to the grades of lodge master, foreman, journeyman, and apprentice (also mason and lodge helper). By this means there has been created a substitute, if one wants to look at it that way, for the lost original version of the Strasbourg-Regensburg ordinance. It is only questionable whether such an amalgamation of all the lodge ordinances that have been preserved gives the proper picture. Hempel has everywhere indicated in parentheses from which ordinance the individual statute has been taken, and so one can perhaps brush aside this objection as too severe and accept the reconstruction gratefully.[48]

Personal relationships were regulated in every respect by conventions and the formulas of proverbial wisdom. In the preamble is the admirable statement, "Friendship, concord, and obedience are the foundations of all good," but from the mass of superficial formulas

46 However, *Unehe* (*Unee*) probably means the unmarried state and not simply concubinage, although it might well arouse a suspicion of the latter.

47 Janner, *op.cit.*, pp. 119ff.

48 Otto Schmitt, *Reallexikon zur Deutschen Kunstgeschichte*, II, p. 27.

we must conclude that "friendship and concord" had to be artificially sustained. Of disputes there seems to have been an abundance.

Janner has collected all the essential facts about lodge jurisdiction and also about the various courts, from the courts of the local lodges to the regional court and the supreme court in the four chief lodges of Strasbourg, Cologne, Vienna, and Berne.[49] Strasbourg had the highest rank and was the court of last appeal. Presumably it was mostly a question of matters pertaining to building and not to personal or moral behavior. We have no record of any such judicial process, but can think back to the expertises of Milan. Problems of design, that is, of measures and statics, may have been brought before the highest court in Strasbourg, if it were a question of a German lodge, and likewise that already mentioned stabilization of the period of apprenticeship, in order to apply the same law to all.

The journeymen exercised a private justice among themselves whenever one of them had spoiled a stone block. The stone was laid upon a stretcher and carried to a pit called the "charnel house"; the guilty one walked behind the "corpse" as the chief mourner and all the others followed. Afterward the guilty one was *gebrütscht*, that is, given a mock beating which was probably not always gentle. This justice is an excellent example of the common sense of responsibility for good work with no loss of material, of the humor of the cathedral builders, and of the seriousness of the geometrical tasks that they faced. Apprentices could probably make their mistakes without fear of reprisals. However, these mock beatings were placed under the supervision of the workmaster so that they would not get out of hand.

This brings us back to the question of the course of the Gothic architect's education. Modern literature offers no basic information; the following answer has been gleaned from the context of the lodge ordinances.

Stonemasons had to be able to read and write. The apprentice who entered the craft at the age of fourteen must have had an adequate education such as the monasteries of the day afforded. Up to 1300 instruction was given chiefly in Latin. During the years of apprenticeship the stonemason learned to use his tools; he undoubtedly had to turn his hand to everything, even to lowly tasks like carrying water and building materials; he made the practical acquaintance of every process of the building, including the erection of scaffolding, although the

[49] *Op.cit.*, pp. 182ff.

carpenters were responsible for that. But he worked himself on the scaffoldings and therefore had a personal interest in learning to judge their utility and safety. Above all, the maturing apprentice had to learn the "lodge secret," that is, the use of quadrature and triangulation, as well as the Great Basic Measure (Stornaloco's *unitas*); thus, he had to learn as much geometry as he would later need. His teacher in these professional secrets was the master of the lodge.

These two courses of study, that of the lower school up to the fourteenth year and the practical-theoretical training up to the nineteenth, were followed by the years as a journeyman with their travels that broadened a young man's horizon whether he stayed in Germany or went to France, Italy, or other countries, afoot or on horseback. On the way he worked in other lodges, saw what old buildings were still standing and what new ones were rising, became acquainted with the problems of the day and the different opinions of different masters. When the time came to settle down, he chose a wife, married, became a master, and took an apprentice whom he now instructed.

But where did one learn Gothic architecture? Undoubtedly from a workmaster. Probably the class of foremen (*Parliere*) were selected talents; and though some of them seemed to be more gifted for building supervision, others inclined to designing. These must have been the *servants of art* (*kunstdiener*). Janner has little to say about them. Servants of art were "servants" like the apprentices, who were also called servants, that is, pupils who learned their trade through service. The servant of art, however, already knew his *trade* and what he now learned was *art*; he became an apprentice again, a pupil, but on a higher level. If this interpretation is admissible, we should translate the words "servant of art" in our modern terminology by "student of architecture." The servant of art, under the tutelage of his master or workmaster, learned to solve the higher problems of designing. The architectural designs that have been preserved from the Gothic period—from Strasbourg, Ulm, Vienna, Cologne, for example—were, according to this assumption, drawn by men who had completed a course in drafting, lasting one or more years, as servants of art. One might hazard the hypothesis that only journeymen or masters who had been servants of art could become workmasters; only after such schooling could one design a Gothic cathedral or continue one already begun by creating the detailed drawings as yet incomplete. According to this view, a master would be a master stonemason, but a workmaster would be an architect, and every workmaster would have gone through all the lower stages of the stonemasons' calling. If this interpretation is tenable, then the phrase "servant of art" is evidence of the semantic change of the word art to that which we mean by it today.

The Regensburg lodge ordinance was formulated by such *architects.* Janner has listed them, following Heldmann. We know that some of them were really architects in the modern sense of the word. Jost Dotzinger was cathedral architect in Strasbourg from 1452 until 1472; the cathedral was completed at that time, but the maintenance of the structure required a trained architect. Hans von Landshut is the son of the well-known Bavarian architect, Hans von Burghausen; Hans von Esslingen is Hans Böblinger, who built the tower of the Frauenkirche in Esslingen; Steffan Hurder of Berne is the successor of Matthäus Ensinger at the cathedral in Berne.[50]

Gurlitt pointed out that Jodokus Dotzinger and Hans von Burghausen had been childhood friends,[51] and that Ensingers and Böblingers were friends. "There was a veritable web of friendship and cousinship connecting several leading clans in Regensburg, which centered around the cathedral at Strasbourg and sought to gain control of the most important lodges. The chief families in Suabia succeeded in this to such a degree that hardly a master outside of their membership ever attained to a position of effectual control of any larger works. However, decentralization was necessary, and Strasbourg did not come to recognize it fully until 1563 when the age of Gothic was past."[52] That the lodge ordinance of 1459 was, as Gurlitt thought, the product of an oligarchy is possible, and undoubtedly this view of the

50 Many of those who signed the Regensburg ordinance are, as a matter of fact, not even mentioned in Thieme-Becker's *Lexikon.* Hans von Landshut is referred to in a contract regarding the delivery of an altar in 1453 as painter, stonemason, and workmaster, cf. Huth, *op.cit.*, p. 83. The father Hans von Burghausen by mistake has been called Stettheimer in modern times.

51 Gurlitt made a mistake (on page 45) in identifying Hans von Landshut with the architect of the Laurentius portal of Strasbourg Cathedral; Hans von Burghausen the Younger was born around 1400 and the portal was constructed in 1494. Moreover, this architect's name was Jakob von Landshut.

52 Gurlitt, in the *Repertorium für Kunstwissenschaft*, 1892, p. 335: "Strassburg sucht 1459 alle nicht von Cöln, Wien und Bern abhängigen Hütten Deutschlands an sich zu bringen, 1498 hat es diesen Wunsch hinsichtlich des Nordostens aufgegeben, seit 1516 beginnt durch die Magdeburger Hütte ein neuer Einigungsversuch, den die Sachsen ablehnen. Diese wieder schliessen sich hinsichtlich der Büchsenpfennige an die Erfurter an. Erst 1563 vollzieht sich die Einigung ganz Deutschlands unter der Strassburger Hütte. Dort wird die fünfjährige Lehrzeit nun auch von den Erfurtern und Sachsen zugestanden. Es bestand also die vielgerühmte Hüttengemeinschaft nicht während der gothischen Periode, sondern kam erst zustande, seit die Renaissance dem Steinmetzengewerbe seine hohe Bedeutung genommen hatte."

matter is important for judging Gothic as the artistic expression of particular social circles. This conception would lead us to think of these workmasters not as simple master stonemasons but as an exclusive group, very conscious of its worth; they were, socially speaking also, really what we call architects.

There is a very instructive monograph by Pevsner on the use of the term architect in the Middle Ages.[53] The word remained alive because of Paul, I Corinthians 3:10: "According to the grace of God which is given unto me, as a wise architect, I have laid the foundation, and another buildeth thereon."[54] Two of the many passages collected by Pevsner are extremely interesting for the problem under consideration here. Thomas Aquinas says that a philosopher is a man who knows how things are to be ordered in their own order and how, therefore, the purposes of other secondary sciences are to be defined. Subjects of such a superior nature as philosophy must, accordingly, be called architectonic, as it were, fundamental sciences, "architectonicae . . . quasi principales artes," he continues surprisingly, the artists who are called architects arrogate to themselves the name of sages: "artifices qui architectones vocantur nomen sibi vindicant sapientium." Pevsner shows that this statement, which to our way of thinking turns things topsy-turvy, goes back not only to the passage in Paul but also to Aristotle's *Metaphysics* I. I. 17 and *Politics* III. 2. 11, works that became accessible in a complete translation by Moerbecke in 1260. Moerbecke, like Thomas, was a Dominican; it is known that there was a connection between the two men, and Thomas was composing the *Summa contra Gentiles*, which contains the statement quoted, just in the period from about 1259 to 1264. The thesis that the philosopher should by rights bear the name of architect and that the architect has usurped it by a dubious claim does not support the modern thesis that scholasticism and Gothic are related, for Thomas can just as well have been thinking of Romanesque or Early Christian architecture familiar to him from buildings in Italy. On the other hand, it does support the thesis that around 1260 the workmaster or architect was looked upon as a man who had duties on the building site comparable to those of the philosopher in the university lecture hall. It is said that men of those generations were incapable of appreciating fully the inventive

[53] Nikolaus Pevsner, "The Term 'Architect' in the Middle Ages," *Speculum*, Cambridge, Mass., 1942, p. 549.

[54] "Secundum gratiam Dei, quae data est mihi, ut sapiens architectus (*ὡς σοφὸς ἀρχιτέκτων*) fundamentum posui, alius autem superaedificat."

genius and the intellectual productivity of Gothic architects; that may be, but obviously they were quite sensible of the organizing ability that placed every stone in its proper position until the miraculous edifices stood completed.

The other passage is even more important.[55] In precise terms, there are actually two passages: one comes from a sermon by the Dominican NICOLAS DE BIARD, delivered in 1261, that is, approximately at the same time that Thomas was writing his remarks; the other is found in a treatise, *Distinctiones*, ascribed to this same monk, Biard.

The first reads: "The masters of the masons, holding in their hands [measuring] rod and gloves, say to the others, 'Cut it [the stone] in this fashion,' and they do not work; yet they receive greater pay than many experienced men do."

The second reads: "Some work only with words. Note well: In these great buildings it is the custom to have a chief master who only directs things by word, seldom or never lays hand to the work himself, and yet draws larger stipends than the others, and so forth."[56]

At that time Villard de Honnecourt was perhaps still alive; certainly Magister 2 and Magister 3 were. We must, then, picture them and their colleagues of like rank as distinguished gentry with rod and gloves, issuing orders.[57] Rod (*virga*) can also mean measuring-rod, as in the passage cited earlier from the period of the cult of the carts.[58] But these men were no philosophers, no theologians with a university

[55] It was published by Victor Mortet and Paul Deschamps, *Recueil de Textes . . .*, Paris, 1929, p. 291, and before that by Mortet in the *Bulletin Monumentale*, 1906, p. 263, "La Maitrise d'œuvre. . . ." Cf. on this Helen Rosenau, *Design and Medieval Architecture*, London, 1934, p. 28.

[56] "Magistri cementariorum, virgam et cyrothecas in manibus habentes aliis dicunt: 'Par ci me le taille,' et nihil laborant; et tamen majorem mercedem accipiunt, quod faciunt multi moderni prelati." *Cyrothecae* are according to Du Cange *chirotecae*; the word *prelati* doubtless has here the sense of *probatus* (also according to Du Cange) and not that of prelates of the church; rather does it have the censorious meaning of "those who have arrived," "upstarts." "Operantur aliqui solo verbo. Nota: In istis magnis aedificiis solet esse unus magister principalis qui solum ordinat ipsa verbo, raro aut unquam apponit manum, et tamen accipit majora stipendia aliis, etc." Evidence for workmen with gloves is found in a miniature of the Univ. Libr. Cambridge, Ee 3. 59, vol. 1, Mid 13. cent. (D. H. and M. M. Elliot, *Life and Work of the People of England*, London, 1931, pl. 18) and in the stained glass of window XLII in Chartres Cathedral. (Y. Delaporte, *Les Vitreaux de la Cathédrale de Chartres*, Chartres, 1926, p. 337, pl. 123). I owe these references to Mrs. J. Weitzmann-Fiedler.

[57] Heldmann says, *op.cit.*, p. 44, that the Templars wore gloves and that in later times the Catholic clergy suspected the freemasons of being followers of the Templars and of wanting to avenge the latter's former condemnation. To disprove this he points out that the stonemasons wore leather gloves at their work in order to avoid injury. Heldmann does not say from what source he knows this. In any case, this would explain Biard's saying that the master held gloves in his hand, that is, did not have them on.

[58] See above pp. 7 and 27.

background; they rose to success through the practice of the building site and the theory of the lodge.

Stein wrote a special book on Gothic architects,[59] collecting a number of details on the payment of the *maitres de l'œuvre* and otherwise discovering many useful facts about them. The contract of appointment of Martin de Louay in St.-Gilles en Languedoc is, for example, very interesting. He receives 100 *sous tournois* a year for clothing, two sous a day for his work, if he begins before noon; every day of the year he has a right to food for himself and his horse; he sits at the abbot's table or can, if he desires, take his meal outside, except on fast-days when he eats in the kitchen, receiving, however, one and a half times the portion given to a monk. He lives in Vauvert, near St.-Gilles, and only in summer is he obliged to be in St.-Gilles, although he must always come over at once if there is need of him. Stein's book contains information about 220 architects, chiefly of the thirteenth to the fifteenth centuries. A portrait of one of them has been handed down to us, if one can call a memorial tablet of 1263 a portrait. It is that of Hugue Libergier, the architect of the church of Saint-Nicaise in Reims, begun in 1231 and destroyed in 1793. Libergier died in 1263, two years after Biard had preached against the superior airs of architects. In this representation we see, indeed, a very aristocratic man, and for Biard's word *virga* we have here an illustration almost from the same year. It is more like a long scepter of office than a measuring-rod and yet the rod must have functioned at the same time as an instrument for measuring. In the *Itinerarium* of *William of Worcester*, which we shall discuss later, the measurements of the buildings are indicated in *virgis*. That is two hundred years later, but it is probably a point in the argument nevertheless. The memorial inscription to Pierre de Montreuil, who died in 1266 (three years after Libergier), runs: "Flos plenus morum, vivens doctor latomorum."[60] Probably the word doctor is used because geometry is indispensable for High Gothic designs.

Many more names of English architects have been collected from archives by John Harvey in the second of his works in note 59 but most of them remain names only, some could be revived, for

[59] Henri Stein, *Les Architectes des cathedrales gothiques*, Paris, 1909. For English architects see John Harvey, *Gothic England*, New York and London, 1947; and *idem, English Mediaeval Architects, A Biographical Dictionary down to 1550*, London, 1954. Harvey, *The Gothic World*, London, 1950, gives on page 157 a list of 470 names of architects of mediaeval times covering all Europe.

[60] Ernst Gall, *Die gotische Baukunst . . .*, Leipzig, 1925, p. 11, n. 3.

example, Henry Yevelee (1353-1400) and William Orchard (1468-1504).

In recent times Paatz interpreted in detail a document concerning Giotto that had already been published in 1839 but had subsequently failed to receive proper consideration.[61] Giotto, although in our eyes exclusively a painter, became in 1334 the chief director of all the public building enterprises in Florence. He not only designed the campanile of the cathedral but continued the work on the cathedral itself and had the supervision of the city fortifications. Paatz stresses especially the passage where Giotto's "scientia et doctrina" is mentioned; he collates several other texts and comes to the conclusion that even in 1334, two generations before Mignot in Milan, intellectual work was more highly valued than handicraft. To see Giotto placed against this background is especially illuminating because in his frescoes we meet so many architectures and must assume that his architectural sketches intended for execution, in spite of their similarity of style, must have been different with regard to the method of the transference of dimensions. In the inscription on the pulpit of Nicola Pisano, 1260, geometric design is presumably also meant by the words *docta manus* (with learned hand).[62] As the development of Gothic progressed, scholarly circles must have felt an ever-increasing respect for the intellectual abilities of the architect-designers and recognized them as equal in gentility to themselves. We recall the amusing anecdote about Giotto, related by Boccaccio in the *Decameron*, in which he borrows a shabby cloak of a peasant during a rainstorm and his companion asks him whether anyone could now detect his importance in that guise.[63]

In the memorial tablet mentioned above, Libergier carries no gloves, but he holds a model in his right hand. We know many representations of donors of churches who are characterized as such by a model which they offer. Here, on the other hand, it is the attribute of the *architectus.* A comprehensive study of models of buildings from mediaeval

[61] Walter Paatz, "Die Gestalt Giottos im Spiegel einer zeitgenössischen Urkunde," *Festschrift für C. G. Heise,* Berlin, 1950, p. 85. The Latin text printed on p. 102 according to Giovanni Gaye, *Carteggio inedito degli artisti,* I, 1839, p. 481.

[62] The passage on Bishop Benno von Osnabrück (1090-1100), quoted by Paatz, is not clear: "quam tamen non usui constat eum didicisse, sed arte"; Paatz interprets *usus* as relating to the crafts, or bound by custom. According to that it is understandable that he explains *ars* as "spiritual or intellectual values in the realm of the representative arts." Does *ars* not mean *practice* as well? Or did the meaning of the word change only in the thirteenth century? Obviously in that text of about the year 1100 *usus* and *ars* are intended as opposites, so that Paatz would seem to be right for the 11th century only.

[63] Giovanni Boccaccio, *Decamerone,* VI, 5.

and, specifically, Gothic times is still lacking; such a study should be related to a corpus of the architectural drawings that have been preserved.[64] In the Milanese records, for example, mention is made again and again of the original model; it is probable that in many cases the architects of the Gothic period made models (cf. S. Petronio in Bologna). This Regensburg ordinance of 1514 speaks of a *visierung* of loam and clay, that is, a model, three-dimensional, and in that instance probably in actual size; this will be discussed later.

If it is true that the architects of Gothic, whom we think of as the creators of the long series of *designs* that are the documents of the inner history of the style, were the products of the sphere of the lodges, then the idea of the lodge secret may become even more comprehensible. In that article on Stornaloco's drawing for Milan,[65] attention was drawn to the age of two factors in the system of measurement. Kossmann's "great unit," Stornaloco's "unitas," occurs as early as ca. 597 B.C. in Ezekiel (40:3 and 5); the halving or doubling of the square is found in Plato's *Meno*, written between 394 and 390 B.C., and the equilateral triangle functions as the fundamental figure of world creation in his *Timaeus* (55D-56C); the right-angled triangle 3:4:5 can be traced back to Pythagoras in the sixth century B.C. In Vitruvius we found quadrature and the Pythagorean triangle presented one after the other. The utilization of all these figures for the transference of a sketch to "true size" without using a standard measure was the secret of the lodges that is meant in Article 13 of the Regensburg ordinance.[66] On renewed reflection I believe that this was the part of the secret that was divulged to every apprentice, because otherwise he could not work at all. But there must have been further "secrets," that is, geometrical methods, which made it possible to draw designs as complicated as those that were necessary for Gothic and certainly for Late Gothic. On this point we possess two late pieces of evidence, one from 1514 and the other from 1588, that permit us to draw some conclusions.

The first, namely the Regensburg "Stainmotzen [*sic*] mauern und deckern Ordnung de anno 1514" (Stonemasons', masons', and roofers' ordinance of the year 1514), is presumably a new version of that of 1440, which was still used by C. T. Gemeiner for his history of

[64] Helen Rosenau, *Design and Medieval Architecture*, London, 1934, pp. 18ff.

[65] P. Frankl, "The Secret of the Mediaeval Masons," *Art Bulletin*, 1945, p. 46.

[66] Janner, *op.cit.*, p. 225. Art. 13: "Es sol auch kein Werkmann noch Meister noch Parlierer noch Geselle, niemans, wie der genennd sige, der nit unsers Hantwerks ist, us keinem uszuge unterwisen, us dem Grunde zu nemen: der sich Steynwerks sin tage nit gebrucht hat."

Regensburg but which has since been lost.[67] The extant version of 1514 is the ordinance of the city guild, here called "Hanns," a word identical with "Hansa" and meaning about the same thing as company or corporation. Thus the preceding ordinance must have been related to a city, and, without rejecting Schuegraf's hypothesis of Roriczer's jealousy of Dotzinger, we can find a more probable reason for the lack of Roriczer's signature on the Regensburg ordinance in the assumption that the "lodge" of Regensburg was not a *genuine* lodge but merely a city guild. The opening words say that at once: the ordinance has been promulgated by the chief treasurer, and the council together with the *Hanns* of the city of Regensburg. The details of this ordinance are especially numerous and could only be given exhaustive treatment in a book that would make the complete interpretation of all the ordinances, touched upon here, its central and sole objective.

This Regensburg guild ordinance of 1514 prescribes in Article 18 that a "servant" who has studied for three years with a stonemason and who wishes to settle in Regensburg as a stonemason (it does not say as master) shall be assigned by the "four masters (*viermaystern*)" to the company (*Hanns*) for instruction. "Auch mögen die in der Hanns sunst auch vnnterricht empfachen wo Sy gut gedunckt vnd wie Sy die Hanndlung fünden, sollen dy entschaiden vnd dabey beleyben." (Also those otherwise in the company may also receive instruction when they shall see fit, and as they find the matter they shall decide and stand by their decision.)

The following article lists the six masterworks that the journeyman must make in order to become master.

"1. ain Schlechts Creutzgewelb (a simple quadripartite vault)

2. ain schelche tür von stucken (a . . . doorway of pieces)

3. ain schlechts thor (a simple gateway)

4. ain ansladung [*sic*]

5. das er grund uber haimlich gemach kund machenn vund wo ain ortmaur oder Egkh an ainem haimlichen gemach Schadhafft wirt, die zu uergründen vnd der wissenn ze hellffenn. (that he can make foundation walls for a home and where a wall or a corner in such a one has become damaged to rebuild the wall and know how to help.)

6. das ainer soll wissen nach der Höch aine itlichn maur wie dick die sein sol, darnach wissen grund machen. (that he shall know from

[67] J. Rudolf Schuegraf, *Nachträge zur Geschichte des Domes von Regensburg* (Verhandlungen des historischen Vereins der Oberpfalz, XVI), Regensburg, 1855, p. 100 (N.F. VIII).

the height of any wall how thick it should be and know how to make the foundation accordingly.)"[68]

What *schelche* is I cannot say with certainty.[69] *Heimlich Gemach* means the same as *Heim* in modern German. *Ansladung* is surely a misprint for *Ausladung*, projection (as in a cornice), a profile.

Article 20 adds that if he fails partially in these masterworks, the candidate must make a *Visier* of clay or *Visierung* (*tägl*). Here, it is clear that *Visierung* is not a drawing but a model. The words "das paw darczu nit Hyett" seem to mean that it was not always practical to execute certain masterworks, which could be said, for example, of the instance of the damaged corner of a cellar and the renewal of its foundations; in such cases a model is to be made.[70] One should not always think, therefore, only of models for new buildings.

The second piece of evidence is even later, from 1588. Gurlitt cites it word for word in the above-mentioned article on the *Erfurt* guild ordinances (page 348). It requires that every stonemason wishing to become a master must submit as masterpieces: "Firstly, a twisted spiral or hollow spiral central support for a staircase, with support for the casing and a handrail along the edge of the stair well, with full moldings and delicate projections, and the stairs shall not be cramped or constricted as it rises, and should one or more faults be found then it shall not be accepted as a master's testimony, but rejected, until such time as he who is to make it shall learn how he shall properly accomplish this skilled work. . . ."[71] The candidate is then allowed six months to make a new drawing and if it again fails to be accepted, he receives a further extension of a whole year but must pay a fine of four gulden, two to the "most wise council," two to the "guardians."

68 In the original we read "with regard to the first . . . , to the second . . . ," etc. I have cited only the most important parts.

69 The Dictionary of the Brothers Grimm among others gives no real help on this point.

70 Gurlitt, *op.cit.*, p. 348: "Doch vorbehalten, wo also ainer mayster werden wolt vund ettlich obgemellte Stuck, das paw darczu nit Hyett, dadurch Er der maysterschafft verhindert sollt werden, so soll es dermassen gehalten werden, wie hernach volgt: So soll derselb ain visier machenn von ledtenn oder aus tägl, das den sachenn ain gestallt geb, daraus die vier mayster sein maysterschafft mügenn erkennen, ob er beym weg belegt vund gennogsam sey. Soll also in der Hanns angezaygt werdenn vund aldo des geschyds gewarttenn." According to Grimm, *Wörterbuch*, XI, p. 231, "letten oder tägel" means clay and loam.

71 "Erstlich ein gewundener holer schnecken- oder Wendelstein, in der schellunge mit einem wiederleger, und in der Zarge mit einer handthaben, voll versimbst und zierlich ausgeladen und soll sich dem steigen nach nicht krumpfe oder würgen, und so sich der Mengel einer oder ander mehr befinden wurden, so soll das als Meisterstücke nicht auffgenommen, sondern verworfen sein, bis solange das der, so das Meisterstück bedarf, recht erfahre, wie ehr das kunstliche wergk verrichten soll. . . ."

For the second master's *Meisterstuck* a flat ceiling adorned with ribs and keystones is required.[72] Paragraph 3 reads: "For the third of these masterworks there shall be an overlaid and sloping facing. The overlaid part shall be well and delicately corniced, the sloping shall be done in the usual way but also somewhat corniced so that one can at once notice and observe the mastery of it. In addition he shall sketch by hand something of the five columns and distinguish them according to their proper order and arrange them in the work with the right disposition."[73] Probably "eine uberworffene und schroege schellunge" means the gable of an aedicula that is to be furnished with columns from one of the five orders (according to Rivius or even Vignola). This task may refer to a corresponding one in Gothic times: the designing of a decorative gable over a door or window, and so on. The fourth masterwork is the practical performance of laying a foundation.

The ordinance prescribes for *masons* four other master's testimonies that relate to quadripartite vaults and scaffoldings for their centerings; these scaffoldings are called here *vorbogen* or also *bogengestelle.* There are also regulations given for work done on doors, windows, and so on, by bricklayers and stonemasons in common. A complete interpretation of the many difficult passages in the text is still lacking.

In none of the older lodge ordinances is there any mention of tests or master's testimonies; the value of the Regensburg ordinance of 1514 and this Erfurt ordinance of 1588 lies in the fact that they suggest the much earlier existence of such examinations for the position of master. Were these only from the Gothic period on? We need only ask: did the master of the cathedral in Speyer have to pass a test? He had to be a professional to lay foundations; he had to know how to draft the ground plan and elevation, how to construct the groined vaults in the aisles; and he had to build the centerings for them. But as Gothic progressed, a master had to learn more and more. The Erfurt tests correspond to the very last of the Late Gothic and already include the "*funff Seuln.*" It is left to our imagination to reconstruct the tests that Villard de Honnecourt himself had to pass and later may

72 We shall return to this point because of the terminology, see p. 155.

73 "Zum dritten soll das dieses Meisterstücke sein als eine uberworffene und schroege schellunge. Die uberworffene schellunge soll woll und zierlich vorsimbst sein, die schroege aber soll nach gemeinem lauff, doch auch etwas vorsimbst werden, damit man gleichwoll das meisterstücke daran spuren und mercken kan. Dazu soll ehr auch von den funff Seulen etwas mit seinen Henden reissen und abtheilen nach derselbigen abtheilunge und gerechtigkeit, und dasselbige auch mit der rechten austheilunge ins werk richten."

have assigned to his pupil Magister 2, or that Peter Parler in the fourteenth century gave to his journeymen, and in the same way every supervising master gave in his own lodge.

The stonemasons' ordinance of 1563 mentions in Article 59 the "marks of honor" (*ehren zeichen*),[74] and from the context it appears that the stonemasons' mark was given to the apprentice when he was promoted to journeyman. Janner occasionally speaks of "journeyman-pieces" by analogy to masterwork. We know nothing more specific about them; however, it seems credible that journeyman-pieces were not particular theoretical drawings but shaped blocks that were to be actually used in a building.

There is an enormous modern literature on the stonemasons' marks. The explanation of them as producers' or originators' marks is, in that general sense, probably still correct.[75] Friederich has given a brief and clear account of their connection with the rising money economy and their function as a control of work done when wages were being calculated under the piece-work system.[76] In this book one also finds an expert selection of stonemasons' marks in chronological sequence. The rejection of Ržiha's theories is fully justified.[77] Friederich calls the networks that Ržiha constructed torturer's racks, but beds of Procrustes would be an even more fitting designation, for the real stonemasons' marks simply do not agree at all with the networks that Ržiha invented in order to reduce these marks to "mother figures" corresponding to the four chief lodges. The marks, aside from the fact that they are free of all reticular constructions, go back to centuries before 1459, the year of the division according to four chief lodges.

The next in time after the Regensburg ordinance of 1459 and the Tirolese of 1460 is the Torgau ordinance of 1462, which was discovered in a copy of 1486 in Rochlitz and is therefore called the Rochlitz ordinance. The Saxons now joined the central organization, but in this case the preamble is worded quite differently and only mentions that "divers workmasters in the South have had two diets at Regensburg and at Strasbourg . . . so have they tirelessly sent out a book of regulation and guidance to this land and exhort us in it."

74 Printed in Janner, *op.cit.*, pp. 272ff.

75 C. G. Homeyer, *Die Haus- und Hofmarken*, Berlin, 1870, p. 277.

76 Karl Friederich, *Die Steinbearbeitung in ihrer Entwicklung vom 11. bis zum 18. Jahrhundert*, Augsburg, 1932, pp. 13-25. The examples on pp. 93-103 are all taken from the monograph by J. Knauth, *Die Steinmetzzeichen des Strassburger Münsters*, Strassburger Münsterblatt, III, 1906. Other literature cited fully in Friederich.

77 Ržiha, *Studien über Steinmetzzeichen*, Mitteilungen der Central Commission, N.F., Vienna, 1881, pp. 26ff.

This ordinance, published by Janner (page 294), is very rewarding if studied for itself, as it contains a number of provisions regarding management and customs that are not even touched upon in the one from Regensburg. Anything new in principle, however, we do not learn from it.

In 1473 a new ordinance was promulgated in Siena, or, more correctly, the old one of 1441 was enlarged, as the words "come dice il nostro statuto" indicate. It is a matter of placing the rights and duties of the Lombard masters on an equal footing with those of the Sienese. Suddenly two *camerlenghi* appear; one should always be a Sienese, the other a Lombard. From the signatures it follows that there were twenty Lombards to nineteen Sienese. One of the specific provisions says that the *camerlengho lombardo* is obligated in exactly the same way as the *camerlengho cittadino*.[78]

A new settlement followed in 1491,[79] but the dissension could not be healed and in 1512 the Lombards seceded "in grave danno e vergogna della nostra citta."[80]

An ordinance of the London masons of 1481 has been preserved.[81] In 1498 the Regensburg ordinance was confirmed by Emperor Maximilian I. Janner and Gurlitt give information about later documents.[82] The reports of the decline of the lodges make an important contribution to the understanding of Gothic inasmuch as they show how the incoming Renaissance and Reformation were bound to change the whole social structure of these organizations. From the ordinance of 1563 Janner has extracted everything that relates to the transformation from Catholicism to Protestantism. But the lodges remained in existence because the Gothic edifices had to be maintained by professionally trained men. Instruction in architecture, however, passed from the lodges to the academies.

The few remains of the lodge books, the descendants of the Lodge Book of Villard de Honnecourt, testify to the lodge instruction in Gothic. The lodge ordinances often mention books, but these seem to have been lists of personnel and wages, as well as collections of regu-

78 Gaetano Milanesi, *Documenti* . . . , I, p. 126.

79 *Ibid.*, p. 129.

80 *Ibid.*, p. 130.

81 Knoop and Jones, *op.cit.*, pp. 251-256. Here the guild is called "Craft mistere or science of masons." Although this ordinance contains many interesting details, it is not necessary to discuss them here.

82 Janner, *op.cit.*, pp. 68ff.; the ordinance of 1563 on p. 272ff., further, Gurlitt, above p. 124, n. 31, *op.cit.* Confirmation of the Erfurt ordinance by Cardinal Raimund von Gurk in 1502. The undated Erfurt ordinance from the beginning of the sixteenth century, etc.

lations such as are found so abundantly in the Torgau ordinance. Villard's book is quite different in character, and we must assume that in the chief lodges piles of designs by leading masters accumulated and formed the basis of study for future generations, for much remained unexecuted and required reworking to make it correspond to the progress in the stylistic development. Beside these architectural drawings there must have been those books on geometry that, like the relevant parts of Villard's book, were derived from earlier texts. Of this branch of lodge literature there have been preserved:

1. the Viennese *Sketch Book* (*Musterbuch*) of about 1450
2. the *Geometria deutsch* by Hans Hösch, perhaps 1472
3. the *Rectitude of Pinnacles* (*Der Fialen Gerechtigkeit*) by Matthias Roriczer, 1486
4. the *Geometrie* by Schmuttermeyer, probably after 1486
5. the *Instruction* (*Unterweisung*) by Lorenz Lacher, 1516

The Viennese *Sketch Book* has, as far as I know, not been published, and only a summary of the contents was given by Rathe.[83] He reports that it consists of three parts different in subject matter. The first and third contain architectural drawings, the middle one forms a treatise on structural techniques "or, more properly, a loose sequence of lodge rules." The drawings give typical models for almost all details of Gothic ecclesiastical architecture; here and there they also include secular buildings: bridges, a construction for a dam, defensive towers, but these structures could very well have been needed in connection with the church. Rathe enumerates: ground plans of choirs and chapels, sketches of keystones, pillars, arches, Gothic gables, pinnacles, gateways, towers, and spiral staircases. "The schematic constructions of structural and ornamental forms complete in themselves are varied in a far more extensive mass of patterns, the demonstrational method of which is unique among contemporary stonemasons' books: in order to illustrate, for example, the rib system of quadripartite, fan, and stellar vaults, or the tracery of the parapets of a gallery, a cut-out method, reminiscent of a lace pattern, is chosen, revealing the configuration of the lines all the more vividly because all intermediary members have been omitted. Unless one wishes to assume—but obviously without sufficient reason—that not the originator but merely a late-born owner wielded the scissors, we see here those portions of the Viennese *Sketch Book* that demonstrate

[83] Kurt Rathe, "Ein Architektur-Musterbuch der Spätgotik mit graphischen Einklebungen," *Festschrift der Nationalbibliothek in Wien*, 1926, p. 667.

with equal effectiveness the playful characteristics of the latest Gothic in both means and purpose of representation." Rathe's description is not illuminating enough to give a clear idea of this "cut-out method." Further, the justification of speaking of "playful characteristics of the latest Gothic" is more than dubious; today we are inclined to take these "whimsies of formal fancy" just as seriously as they were certainly taken at the time of their conception. Everything that Rathe says only makes us wish that some expert may soon publish a complete reproduction of the manuscript.

Such publication is particularly urgent because the volume is also said to contain drawings of centerings and their scaffoldings, which would presumably throw light on the method actually used in Gothic times to construct the vaulting. We possess simply the evidence of Lärbro (see above page 14) and otherwise can only indulge in hypotheses; perhaps one single page of the Viennese *Sketch Book* would upset all the theories and reveal the historical facts—if indeed it did not create new problems.

Rathe has at least reprinted the first sentence of the manuscript.[84] The sense of it is: "Whoever wishes to make a pilaster, let him make it one shoe long and equally wide; such pilasters belong on the choir." Rathe thinks that the author intended to evolve a system of proportions beginning with the choir; but the next paragraph deals with the foundations for a well and it is, therefore, unlikely that, starting with the measurements of the choir pillars, other measurements were to be found. One could perhaps relate the information about the foundation for a well to that of the pilaster for the choir, since both represent more or less the same problem. But such a rather far-fetched interpretation is scarcely justified in view of the aphoristic nature of the whole book. That the intention was to create a reference book for the workmaster (architect) or the servant of art (student of architecture) is clearly revealed by the engravings of ornaments that have been pasted in and that are all probably unique examples;[85] they are reminiscent of Villard's ornamental drawings, only replaced by engravings in conformity with the time. The interspersal of domestic remedies, for instance one against loss of hair, confirms the impression

84 "1) It[e]m wer ein pfeyler mach will der in de[r] maur sten solt, der nach sol in ainem schuech fur die maur als preit, als er ist czwysen als langk sol er sein und die pfeyl[er] gehören an den kor."

85 According to P. Jessen, *Der Ornamentstich*, Berlin, 1920, p. 10, only twenty Late Gothic architectural engravings are known. Is that still correct? Are those of the Viennese *Sketch Book* included in this number?

of prescriptions intended for the initiated who knew the correct application, practically and intellectually, of all these *disjecta membra.* They are *collectanea* for a textbook, exactly as in the case of Villard's Lodge Book. In contrast to what Thomas Aquinas says about the architectonic spirit within philosophy, no Gothic architect seems to have had the ability or the wish to reduce his prescriptions to a logical system. The Viennese *Sketch Book* also offers no support to the widely spread attempt to link Gothic and scholasticism. The statement that the scholastics were Gothic can be allowed to pass as a metaphor, but the Gothic architects were no scholastics, no systematizers, and composed no *Summae* of Gothic.

In spite of this reflection, the Viennese *Sketch Book,* on the mere evidence of its table of contents, belongs with Villard's Lodge Book to the few remnants of the *higher* type of lodge literature. Hösch's little book, on the other hand, acquaints us with remnants of the *lower* type of this category.

The *Geometria deutsch* is not dated.[86] Panofsky once set its date as "before 1490" and another time as "around 1500." Schnaase wrote "*Geometria deutsch,* allegedly by HANS HÖSCH of Gmünd in 1472."[87] Where he got this date he does not say but obviously he mistrusted his source. The reason that I place it chronologically before the treatises of Roriczer and Schmuttermeyer is not so much its primitiveness as the fact that Hösch does not yet reveal anything of the secret of the lodges. The construction of the tilting helmet would then occur for the first time here—within the mass of extant treatises—but the quadratic frame that is stipulated for the construction or for its transference to scale is already found in Villard, although in another connection.[88]

Hösch was not writing for mathematicians but for artisans, and, as appears from the drawing of the tilting helmet, not only masons and stonemasons' apprentices were intended to be his readers. The whole "book" gives instruction on nine points. It begins with the construction of the right angle. For that there are of course various methods. Hösch teaches it using the angle at the circumference of a

[86] Hans Hösch, *Geometria deutsch.* Already published in Heideloff's book, *Die Bauhütte des Mittelalters,* Nuremberg, 1844, pp. 95-113, and then once more, with no knowledge of this first publication, by Sigmund Günther, "Zur Geschichte des mathematischen Unterrichts im deutschen Mittelalter," *Zeitschrift für Mathematik und Physik, Historisch-literarische Abteilung,* xx, 1875, p. 1.

[87] Erwin Panofsky, *Dürers Kunsttheorie,* Berlin, 1915, p. 50, or *Albrecht Dürer,* Princeton, 1943, I, p. 242. Carl Schnaase, *Geschichte der bild. Künste,* IV (1874), p. 228.

[88] See above p. 43 and Hahnloser, *op.cit.,* p. 100.

semicircle, a method that could easily be adapted on the site to the staking out of walls at right angles to each other. Above all, the right angle is necessary for the construction of the square by which the stonemason can obtain his chief measurements, but this is not mentioned here. Then follow the constructions of a regular pentagon and octagon, necessary, for example, for tracery of a certain sort, but also for other things such as choirs. The fifth rule illustrates the unwinding of the circumference of a circle into a straight line by a rough, but practically useful approximation. The sixth shows how one finds the correct center for a portion of an arc—perhaps an inheritance from Magister 3; the seventh demonstrates how one finds a triangle equal in area to a given square (the solution is only approximately correct); the eighth concerns the tilting helmet already mentioned; the ninth relates to the construction of an escutcheon using compass and ruler.

The reason that Hösch says nothing about the regular triangle and hexagon is that both are contained in the seventh rule. The purpose of the fifth rule and of the seventh is not clear; it is possible that here one must think of quite different handicrafts as in the case of the helmet.

RORICZER's book, which is dated 1486, brings us to a somewhat higher level of Gothic instruction. It was adorned with the coat of arms of the Eichstätt Prince-Bishop Wilhelm von Reichenau, who had the book printed in Regensburg and to whom it is dedicated.[89] He ruled from 1464 to 1496. Matthäus Roriczer is the son of Konrad Roriczer who was cathedral architect of Regensburg at the time of his death in 1475. Matthäus became his father's successor and died some time after 1492 (before 1495). He is called cathedral architect, "Tummaister," and printer, having written the treatise as architect and set it as printer. His career as a stonemason took him to Esslingen where he spent his year as traveling journeyman with Hans Böblinger. Since Böblinger went to the Frauenkirche in Esslingen as foreman (*parlier*) in 1439 and was definitely engaged as workmaster there in 1440, one can assume tentatively that Roriczer worked under him at that time and thus must have been born about 1420. In 1459 at the time of the meeting in Regensburg he would then have been twenty-nine years old. From 1462 to 1466 Roriczer was in Nuremberg where his father

[89] Matthäus Roriczer, *Puechlein der Fialen Gerechtigkeit*, Regensburg, 1486. The text was printed by Heideloff, *op.cit.* Previously August Reichensperger had published a translation into New High German, Trier, 1823. Karl Schottenloher made a facsimile edition, Regensburg, 1923. Cf. also August Reichensperger, *Vermischte Schriften über christliche Kunst*, Leipzig, 1856, p. 55.

Konrad had begun the choir of the church of St. Laurentius in 1445. In 1466 Matthias was back in Regensburg and in 1473 he was in Eichstätt where he received an invitation to deliver an expertise on the Frauenkirche in Munich. From these few facts can be gathered that in 1486 Roriczer possessed a varied experience of the South German forms of Late Gothic. As against that his treatise seems very primitive. We have here a textbook for apprentices, written by a master who had doubtless instructed many pupils and learned in so doing to suit his presentation to the beginner's comprehension.

The text begins: "If you want to draw a ground plan according to the stonemasons' method and the right geometry, then begin by drawing a square and designating it by the letters a,b,c,d. . . ." Roriczer then draws, like Magister 2, the diagonally placed square of half the length of the diagonal of the first square, and so on, and then step by step produces the ground plan of the pinnacle (Fig. 19). Then he gives instruction for drawing the center line of the elevation and describes each further step so precisely that the pupil has no chance either to hesitate or to invent anything new. Since we know that not all pinnacles are alike but rather that every master was perfectly free to vary the schematic construction, we realize that Roriczer was only giving an example from which could be learned the secret procedure for transferring the drawing to true size. The pupil who understood that had perfect "freedom" only within the limits of this method. The abundance of Late Gothic forms that have been preserved proves that these limits did not restrict imagination. That should be clear to anyone who has followed what was said above about the *symmetria* of Vitruvius. However, a study of historically existing pinnacles is still a *desideratum*. As for the rest, the pinnacle itself was, as it were, a side issue; it was only *one* means of teaching and learning the proper method of measuring "nach stainmeczischer art" (according to the stonemasons' way). From this example the principle could be learned.

At the end of the little book is the sentence: "Accordingly the figure is called a correct pinnacle, the elevation derived from the ground plan, for which an illustration is given beside the text, the ground plan and the elevation." As a matter of fact, the text is accompanied by as many figures as are necessary to make each separate step of the construction comprehensible. Only quite at the end does the title of the book occur: *Puechlein von der Fialen gerechtigkeit* (*Little Book about the Rectitude of Pinnacles*). Once more "rectitude" is stressed, of course not in the sense of *justitia* but of "rightness." A drawing is only right when the stonemason can utilize it, that is, transfer it without standard measurements and without a yardstick.[90]

Roriczer said modestly that he was not the inventor of this method but that it originated with the Squires of Prague. The same thing is said in SCHMUTTERMEYER's treatise of which one single copy, kept in the Germanic Museum in Nuremberg, has been preserved. This "book" is only eight pages long; the text has been published in entirety, the first page in facsimile as well.[91] The editor, Essenwein, attributes the type to the printer G. Stuchs who worked in Nuremberg after 1484. He was still using the same type blocks in 1489 but since by that time they were somewhat worn, it may be assumed that the book was published a few years earlier. Essenwein proposed 1486. It is difficult to decide whether Schmuttermeyer or Roriczer has priority. Of the former we know nothing except that he published this treatise. Since Roriczer was in Nuremberg from 1462 to 1466 and Schmuttermeyer published his work there, one might suppose that the two men were acquainted. Fancy would have entirely too much play if both treatises did not appear until twenty years later. But it is hardly important to come to a decision as to whether Schmuttermeyer's book appeared before or after Roriczer's; they are alike in method, adopted from older tradition. However, Schmuttermeyer is somewhat more detailed. His first sentence which is grammatically very complicated and fills the whole first page is translated here in several sentences: "By the grace of God have I, Hans Schmuttermeyer of Nuremberg, written this book. It concerns the noble and free art of geometry and serves to instruct masters and journeymen. I wrote it to further not my own glory but the fame of the ancient inventors of this noble art of building, which has its true basis in water poise, protractor, triangle, compass, and ruler. Therefore I shall describe both the old and the new way of drawing correctly square, circle, pinnacles, gables, piers, and everything pertaining thereto. Not I invented it but the Squires of Prague, Masters Ruger and Niklas of Strasbourg, and many others."

In spite of some uncertainty the Squires of Prague are today generally taken to be the Parlers.[92] Essenwein connected the name Ruger

90 From books such as Janner's, it is generally known that the stonemason's had various secrets, the handclasp, for example, and certain formulas used in applying for work, etc. Apart from these trivialities, the triangulation and quadrature must be considered "the" secret. It does not go back merely to Roriczer, but to Magister 2 about 1260.

91 August Essenwein, "Hans Schmuttermeyers Fialenbüchlein," *Anzeiger für Kunde der deutschen Vorzeit*, Nuremberg, 1881, XXVIII, Sp. 65.

92 On these see the long article by Otto Schmitt in Thieme-Becker, XIX, 1927, also Otto Kletzl, *Die Junker von Prag in Strassburg*, Frankfurt a.M., 1936. Here the relations between

with the master of the church of St. Reinhold in Dortmund, the choir of which was under construction from 1421 to 1450.[93] Niklas of Strasbourg is said to be Nicolaus Dotzinger, who was present at the Regensburg meeting as a journeyman. He should not be confused with Jodocus Dotzinger, the first signer of the lodge ordinance; he may perhaps have been the son of Jodocus. It is not unlikely that Schmuttermeyer meant Niklas Dotzinger, who during his lifetime occupied a particularly high position because of the elevation of the Strasbourg lodge to supreme authority in the land. It remains in doubt, however, whether Masters Ruger and Niklas Dotzinger added anything new to the old doctrine. Even the Parlers cannot be of too great importance for this theory, since it can be traced back to Magister 2. The repetition of the diagonal square was perhaps new.

Schmuttermeyer begins his text as Roriczer does: "In the name of Our Lord. If you want to draw a pinnacle and a Gothic gable, first make a square of any desired size. . . ." The side of the square he calls "an old shoe (*ein alt schuch*)." By means of the diagonally placed square of half the length of the diagonal of the first square he obtains "a new shoe." Then he continues this procedure and creates a half old "shoe," then a half new "shoe." He repeats this until he has eight units of measure, enough for the construction of the pinnacle and the gable.

Kletzl suggested that Schuttermeyer's treatise has not been completely preserved. If that is so, the question arises as to what beyond Roriczer he could have taught. Unfortunately, that must remain an open question, but we have the impression that there were lower and higher courses. The Viennese *Sketch Book* seems to be an example of a course for advanced students, as was also, in an earlier stage of the development of Gothic, Villard's versatile book. The *Instruction* (*Unterweisung*) of Lorenz LACHER takes us back to a similar higher level. It is dated 1516 and thus comes from a period when the very

Schmuttermeyer and Roriczer are treated in more detail (p. 51). Kletzl assumes that Schmuttermeyer's *Büchlein* appeared immediately after Roriczer's book. For this whole group of problems cf. by the same author *Planfragmente aus der deutschen Dombauhütte von Prag in Stuttgart und Ulm*, Stuttgart, 1939, and Kletzl's article on the *Parlers* in Thieme-Becker, *Allgemeines Künstler-Lexikon*, XXVI, Leipzig, 1932 (thus written before the two other studies).

93 On this Roger cf. the brief notice in Thieme-Becker, XXIX, Leipzig, 1935, where he is discussed under the name of Roseir; the name was also written Rosier and Roseer, and he was perhaps of Flemish origin. Far more detailed is the investigation in Kletzl's book mentioned in the previous note, *Die Junker von Prag in Strassburg*, p. 54. *Ibid.*, p. 55, for a discussion of Niklas von Strassburg. In the present connection it is unnecessary to go into all these problems.

last of the Late Gothic was already being threatened by the onsurging Renaissance. Although the lodge secret on the more elementary level had already been made accessible to everyone through the printed works of Roriczer and Schmuttermeyer, Lacher enjoins his son Moritz to keep everything secret even from his brothers, if they do not become stonemasons.

The text has been published in full, but it has not been nearly so thoroughly investigated as Villard's.[94] Lacher calls himself architect and gunsmith, and is, therefore, a specialist in firearms. We are reminded of the drawing of the tilting helmet in Hösch's book, and elsewhere. The architects of that period combined architecture and engineering in their work.

In the introduction Lacher states his aim as the giving of examples of how one should work *maassgerecht*, with correct measures. By that is meant exactly what we know from the other lodge books.[95]

The actual text begins with the construction of a choir, just as in the Viennese *Sketch Book*. Lacher uses absolute measurements. They are expressed in *Schuh* or shoe, that is, the same thing as "foot," the length of a human foot or about thirty centimeters. Schmuttermeyer used old and new "shoe" in a different sense.

Only a few details of the very interesting contents can be discussed here. Several times Lacher mentions boards that are to be cut out as models for profiles, for example: If you want to obtain the [model] board for the diagonal arch, divide the thickness of the wall into six parts and take one of them for the length, this is the [model] board of the diagonal arch, and half of it for the width it [that is the model board] ought to be. This is the great diagonal arch that our forefathers used. . . .[96]

The treatise, like that of Villard, is unsystematic. The most diverse structural parts follow each other indiscriminately: canopies, orientation of the choir by means of a compass,[97] tower (strength of the wall and of the foundation), pile-work, tracery (that he calls *Zipernwerkh*, p. 142), pinnacles of various heights, and gables. Here is found the

[94] August Reichensperger, "Des Meisters Lorenz Lacher Unterweisung, *Vermischte Schriften über christliche Kunst*, Leipzig, 1856, pp. 122, 155.

[95] ". . . darumben so will ich Erstlic Anfangen und weissen, wie du khantz Massgerechtigkeit von Anfang biss zu endt auss dem viel Andern gepey Iren grundt vnd Mass habendt, auch ich will von Andern Peyen, mancher Handtmuster Anzaigt."

[96] *Op.cit.*, p. 136: "Item wen du das Chreutz bogen bredt gewinnen wilst, so teil die maur dicke in sechs teill vnd nimb derselben teill eines, dass ist das Creutzbogen bredt, vnd alss lang das Chreutzbogen bredt ist, halb so breith soll es sein, dises ist der grosskreutzbogen, den unsere Altvetter haben gebraucht."

[97] The compass served to read off angles and to determine the east line. Compass was also used in the sense of *Zirkel* (compasses).

statement: "If you want to design a ground plan yourself, then follow this rule with your squares; whether the work be large or small you can take the square for the pinnacle from the upper body [of this pinnacle] . . . as you will take the whole elevation from the ground plan, corresponding to the figure drawn in beside this. As soon as an elevation is finished you must renew [*vergingen*] the square; do that over and over."[98]

The word *vergingen* does not mean "*verjüngen*." For "*Verjüngung*" i.e. to make an upper part narrower, Lacher says pp. 140 and 145 "ab-kleitung"; *vergingen* means to make new, that is, one must continually fit the ground plan to the new structural part about to be undertaken. In many places Lacher advises his son to measure by eye, for instance, in the matter of moldings on pillars. Much in Lacher's *Instruction* is obscure (for example, *op.cit.*, page 149). Undoubtedly these obscurities were unintentional and not the result of an affected mysteriousness. A distinction must be drawn between a secret and an esoteric doctrine. The dogmas of the Catholic church are "secrets," in the sense of mysteries, but Catholic dogmatics is not an esoteric doctrine, whereas the "secret of the lodges" was not a secret in the sense of a mystery, but was, on the contrary, an esoteric doctrine, intended for the protection of the lodge. The doctrine of the "right measure," finally, cannot be considered as specifically Gothic, since its roots go back at least to Vitruvius, but the refinement of the method to aid in the evolution of more and more complicated drawings was Gothic. The scanty remains of this surely once abundant literature with its different levels of instruction are important evidence for Gothic; we can picture the apprentice on the site, proud of his poor little lodge secret, the studious servant of art, the knowing foreman, and the workmaster with gloves and measuring-rod, conscious of his gifts.

These youths and men made drawings, used a chisel, and sometimes even wrote, but far more important than their writing was the fact that they talked among themselves. Their vocabulary of technical terms was still fluid and new forms demanded new designations. The extant sources, taken in their full compass, that is, far more completely than they were examined here, offer us a surprisingly long list of words, from those used by Suger down to the cryptic terminology of

[98] "Item wan du einem grundt von dier selber wilt fissiren oder anlegen so halt dich dieser meinung mit dein firungen, das werkh sey khlein oder gross, du magst auch mit dem figallen dein firung nemen von dem Obern leib . . . wie du den ganzen ausszug auss dem grundt nemen solst wie du den angezeichets findts in der figur, alss Offt ein ausszug ein Endt hat, als Offt muestu die firung vergingen, dass du für und für" (p. 145).

the Erfurt ordinance of 1588. For some of these we are acquainted with the concepts behind them, for some of them we are not. This "language of Gothic" still awaits its philologically trained lexicographer; here the subject can be discussed only cursorily.

The entertaining glossary of Johannes de GARLANDIA (Jean de Garlande, ca. 1195-ca. 1272) was formerly dated about 1080 or 1098,[99] but recently another work of the same author, *Morale scolarium*, has been assigned to the year 1241. If the *Dictionnaire* is really his work also, then it too belongs to the High Gothic period and to Paris. But in the brief chapter that begins with the words "In aula mea haec architectari feci: trapetas, solivas, etc." we meet, as far as the words can be interpreted, only terms for the art of building in wood. For ceilings Garlandia has the words *lacunaria* and *laquearia.* Vaults and arches are not mentioned. Not particularly Gothic is the phrase: columns whose parts are base, shaft, architrave (*columpnas quarum partes sunt: basis, stilus, epistilium*), in which *epistilium* might perhaps be translated by "capital." Of the tools listed the expression *latomega* or *lathusmega* should be noted. Gerard translated it by *grande règle*,[100] and one thinks immediately of Stornaloco's *unitas.*

Rita Schlaepfer has worked out a glossary of expressions used by Villard as an appendix to Hahnloser's edition. We need a complete dictionary; but an alphabetical index of this kind ought to be placed at the end of a work that would be arranged systematically according to concepts. One could perhaps begin with the history of the designation of what we today call *rib, Rippe, ogive.*

Suger, if my interpretation is tenable, calls the wall ribs—perhaps also the transverse arches—*arcus superiores* (to distinguish them from the arcades and the arches of the triforia and windows); he calls the diagonal ribs *arcus principales.* Gervase talks of *fornices arcuatae*, of vaults provided with arches. In the German sources we shall find the word *Schwibbogen*, and Lacher said *Kreuzbogen.* In all these designations the rib is looked upon as an *arch* (*Bogen*), in other words, considered in its *spatial* form. Villard, on the contrary, uses for the

99 The editions of the *Dictionarius* are cited by Charles Homer Haskins, *Studies in Mediaeval Culture*, Oxford, 1929, p. 81 n. 2. The Dictionarius of John de Garlande has been published by Joseph Mayer, *Volume of Vocabularies*, as vol. 1 of A Library of National Antiquities, London, 1857, p. 120. This volume contains several other vocabularies, beginning with Alfric's Colloquy of the Tenth Century. I owe these references to Mrs. J. Weitzmann-Fiedler.

100 Hercule Geraud in *Documents inedits sur l'histoire de France*, p. 610. (In Geraud the article is numbered 77, in Scheler's edition 79; the readings vary somewhat.)

first time *ogive*, which recurs several times in French sources in an enlarged form as *croi augivère* (1347), *crouzées des ogives* (1386), *croix d'augives* (1468),[101] and so on. The word is derived from the Latin *augere*, to strengthen; thus it refers to the *dynamic* form, that is, to the static or dynamic function of the rib. Proposals that *ogive* is derived from other sources, from the Arabian *algibe*,[102] from the German *Auge*,[103] or from the word *ogis*,[104] only one single occurrence of which can be proved, do not make sense. In the Milanese records mention is made of *croxiere*, thus emphasizing again the spatial form, and not so much the arches themselves as the fact of their crossing.

I cannot answer the question as to how the terminology for the ribbed vault developed in England in the period after Gervase and when the word *Rippe* came into use in Germany or "rib" in England. In the Erfurt guild ordinance of 1588 there is required as the second master's testimony: "ein gewundene, und scheitrechte Reüppn, welche aus vier Ecken, aus jeder vier schenkel aus des anfangk haben soll, welche im Mittelpunkten zusammen schleifen sollen. Und in solcher Rüppen sollen auch vier Klebschlossteine sein und durch die andern vier gewundene und scheitrechte schleife . . ." (a twisted and horizontal rib, which shall have its beginning from four corners, from each of four sides that shall loop together in the center. And in such a rib there shall be also four attached keystones and through the other four twisted and horizontal loops). Certainly the word rib is older than this;[105] it is a happy combination of the ideas of spatial *and* dynamic form, arousing at the same time the conception of the skeleton as the firm structure on which the muscles, or vault severies, are stretched.

The development of the Spanish terminology does not seem to have been studied enough. From Kubler's essay we learn the names of

101 Marcel Aubert cites many textual passages at the end of his article, "Les plus anciennes croisées d'ogives . . . ," *Bulletin Monumental*, XCIII, Paris, 1934, p. 235.

102 G. S. Colin, "Origine arabe du mot français ogive," *Romania*, LXIII, Paris, 1937, p. 377.

103 L. Hatzfeld and A. Darmstetter, *Dictionnaire général de la langue française*, Paris, 1900ff. In French *auge* means manger or trough.

104 I know of this proposal only by hearsay. Reference is made to Ducange s.v. *Ogis*: Nicolaus de Braje in *Ludovico VIII Reg. Franc.*, p. 290, "Rex regum mundi venerabilis ille Philippus, Catholicae fidei calidus defensor et ogis." The word *ogive* is not found in Ducange. He did not translate or paraphrase *ogis*. It is said to be identical with *aegis*, meaning shield, which would fit well in the verse. Cf. the derivation from ἀίσσω and ἄιξ in Pauly-Wissowa, *Real-Encyclopädie*, I, p. 971. Shield has nothing to do with ribs. One would then have to speak of *Schildrippen*!

105 The word *Rippe* does not appear in Lacher, he says, "Chreutz-bogen" pp. 136, 147, 151, etc. I do not know what the expressions are in the Viennese *Sketch Book*.

the arches of Late Gothic vaults around 1538. The transverse arch is called *arco pripiaño*, the diagonal rib *diagonal ó cruzero*, the wall rib *forma*, the tierceron *rampante ó tercelete.*[106]

For the Late Gothic period we possess a kind of glossary for the parts of the profile in the book by WILLIAM OF WORCESTER, of which occasional mention has already been made.[107] The real name of the author was William Botoner. He was a monk, visited numerous buildings in England, and diligently noted what he saw. In this latter activity the measurements were of importance to him, and here we find the word *virga* as the designation for the unit of measure. On page 79 we read: "50 virgas, id est 150 pedes," a *virga* was, then, three feet long. On page 220 Nasmith has simply written down without any order the various expressions used by William for parts of the profile: *cors wythout, casement, bowtelle, felet*, and so on. We could not make much of them if Willis had not published the drawing belonging to them, the profile of the portal of St. Stephan's church in Bristol,[108] a drawing which has proved to be so accurate that Willis assumes it was drawn for William of Worcester by a professional. That may be a correct assumption, for anyone who has tried to sketch such profiles himself knows how difficult it is. But one can draw the further conclusion that William was told the names of the details of the profile by that same architect or stonemason. Willis pointed out that even before him Willson had attempted to list the names of the parts of Gothic structures.[109] After Willis several authors published alphabetical lists of technical terms connected with architecture, most of them not restricted to Gothic. Willis' book contains 333 terms, of which about one hundred can be understood without explanation; it is obvious that the remaining 233 cannot be discussed here.

It is not without interest that Willis used in the case of the words for the profile the handwritten marginal notes entered by INIGO JONES in his copy of Palladio,[110] although the meaning of the terms is clearly

106 Gazette des Beaux-Arts, 1947, p. 139. An explanation of the word *tierceron* is given in my article: "The 'Crazy' Vaults of Lincoln Cathedral," *Art Bulletin*, XXXV, 1953, p. 100.

107 *Itineraria Symonis Simeonis et Wilhelmi de Worcester*, Cambridge (England), 1781, ed. by Jacobus Nasmith. The title of the second *Itinerarium* runs: *Wilhelmi Botoner Itinerarium sive liber rerum memorabilium*, Cod. autog. autoris in biblitheca Coll. Corp. Christi, Cambridge, No. 210.

108 Robert Willis, *Architectural Nomenclature of the Middle Ages*, Cambridge (England), 1844.

109 Edward James Willson, "Glossary of Technical Terms Descriptive of Gothic Architecture." This glossary appeared as an appendix to A. Pugin's book, *The Specimens of Gothic Architecture*, II, London, 1822.

110 These marginal notations have been published in Giacomo Leoni's third edition of Palladio, *The Architecture of Palladio in four books . . .*, 1742.

apparent from the drawing. Jones (1573-1652) himself had been reared in the Gothic tradition; as a young painter in Italy from 1596 to 1604 he was occupied in scenography. Only after his second Italian sojourn (1613-1614) did his architectural activities begin in England, and thus the beginning of English Renaissance architecture falls in the last years of Shakespeare's life. But Inigo Jones remained half Gothic at heart. In the year 1616 he built simultaneously the Queen's villa in Greenwich in Palladian style and the new chapel of Lincoln's Inn in Tudor Gothic. He translated *torus*, for example, by "a great bowtell," *astragalus* by "a small beat or bowtell." He lacks only the word *ressant*, which according to Willis, or William of Worcester, corresponds to the German word *Kielbogen*, the English "ogee arch," and the French *arc en accolade*. The word ogee is supposed to be connected with the older word ogive. In Palladio such ogee arches simply do not occur.

As a second example of Gothic terminology may be cited the designations for the parts of a rectilinear window. They are found in records of accounts and it is natural that graphic words were desired in such statements for glaziers and glass-painters. Willis sketches a window in six compartments, over the lower division of which two arches issuing from the middle axis form, together with their marginal arches, a grouping of the lower halves into three axes each. Since what date the modern expression "axis" has been used for axis of symmetry I do not know. The English mediaeval term for the lower six axes was "lights," as it still is today. For the upper division no word exists to describe the whole field, though there are designations for the compartments: the latter are called *batements* and the halves remaining at the corners *angells* (from angle, the corner); the larger rectangles immediately above with two concave and two convex sides are called *katurs* (*cater* = *quater*), but presumably referring to the rectangular form as such) and the smaller concave-convex rectangles *quarelles*. The center topmost field itself consists of compartments that are all called *oylements*, or *oylets*, a term connected according to Willis with the French *yeux* (*oeil*, eye).

Willis' work is still a model of the proper treatment of this subject. In readily comprehensible tables he entered the expressions of Vitruvius and Alberti in the left-hand column, and then made five further columns on the right hand for the translations into Italian, French, Dutch, English, and German. Here, too, the Spanish terminology is missing. As an example may be cited: Vitruvius' expressions *sima*, *unda* and Alberti's *undula, gugula* are rendered in Italian *gola, scima, onda,* in French *doulcine, ogive, gueule, cime, talon,* in Dutch, *odiif, odyf, keel, keeltjen, Scima, kim,* in English *ressant, ogee, gula, throat, Sima, Cyma,* in German *Schlangenlini* (Dürer), *Glockenleisten, Kehlleisten.* A revision should examine all these words; in this instance it seems doubtful whether Vitruvius' *sima* can be equated with *ogive.* Certainly Willis' tendency to make the alphabetical listing an appendix only for reference and to consider in the text as a unit what belongs together is the correct one.

Reflection upon these matters leads one to treat as the first group the expressions referring to the church building as a whole—*ecclesia,* and so on—together with its spatial divisions, for example, *chorus.* (That the latter can have various meanings was seen in Gervase's text.) The terms for the members—*arcus,* and so on—the second group, are in the foreground in Willis. A third group would be composed of aesthetic and stylistic designations, such as were discussed above (p. 33). Words with a sociological color, like *architectus, magister,* and so on, make a fourth group. Extensive preliminary work has been done for all four groups, but there is no presentation of the material that is both philologically reliable and as complete as possible, while penetrating deeply into problems of semantics and semantic changes. Unquestionably this latter requirement is already being satisfied by numerous specialized studies, but a synthesis is needed. That this can hardly be restricted to a single stylistic epoch like Gothic is shown by Willis' work.

The subject would swell to discouraging proportions if the terminology of secular building, especially that of defensive structures, were included, thus placing the chivalric side of Gothic in a sociological sequence with the lodges and the universities. This chivalric culture will be indirectly touched upon when we now turn to the mediaeval epics in order to search in them for mentions or descriptions of Gothic structures. Here we find what we missed in the scholastics; the tone of this poetic literature is characteristically different from that of the lodge literature.[111]

111 Postscript on bibliography: George Gordon Coulton's book, *Art and Reformation,* Oxford, 1928, 2nd ed. Cambridge, 1953, contains many additional details, as does also the excellent book by L. F. Salzman, *Building in England down to 1540,* Oxford, 1952, which I discovered too late. A saw, managed by two men, is to be seen in a miniature of the 15th century, reproduced in Salzman, *op.cit.,* pl. 19. But the beam which they are sawing seems to have been prepared with the axe. I owe this reference to Mrs. J. Weitzmann-Fiedler.

As regards the centering for the construction of Gothic vaults, particularly in the early period,

9. The Architectural Fantasies of Mediaeval Poets

THE value of architectural descriptions intended to serve scientific or practical purposes lies in the exactness with which ground plan, section, and elevation can be drawn from them. To expect descriptions of this kind from the poets of the Middle Ages would be a mistake; they not only leave many details uncertain and conjure up instead impressions of splendor and material expense, but they also envelop the arrangement as a whole in a dreamy haze. At first we turn to these passages of text to see whether they apply to Gothic structures and whether they can inform us about the poets' attitude toward Gothic, but soon our interest widens almost immeasurably, for these architectural fantasies, whether Gothic or not, reveal what types of ecclesiastical, secular, or sepulchral architecture the poets and their readers regarded as desirable. Many used in part impressions gained from the architecture of their own times; many persisted rather in the tradition of their particular field of art and enlarged upon accounts of imaginary structures or sometimes also reminiscences of actual buildings such as they found in their literary predecessors.

The following survey is based on the extensive literature concerning mediaeval poetry in France, Germany, and England; the passages describing architectural fantasies have been brought together in the main by Söhring for France and Lichtenberg for Germany. There would be no purpose in referring to the innumerable texts that are often only variations of a type already formulated. Although we shall be obliged to extend our investigations temporally far beyond the beginnings of Gothic, we shall start with the *Pèlerinage de Charle-*

---

these books also fail to mention any illustrations in miniature.

Concerning the question as to how planks were produced, cf. Villard, pl. 44. Du Colombier includes a reproduction of a miniature of 1023 which shows two workmen sawing a block of marble into thin slabs, *op.cit.*, plate I. In a miniature in the British Museum a wooden beam is being sawed into planks; cf. Dorothy Hartley and Margaret M. Elliot, *Life and Work of the People of England*, London 1928, plate 27,c.

For the sources on the constitution of the freemasons see Douglas Knoop, G. P. Jones, and Douglas Hamer, *The Two Earliest Masonic MSS.*, Manchester, 1938. Concerning the continuance of the Strasbourg lodge, cf. François Pariset "Étude sur l'Atelier de la Cathédrale de Strasbourg," *Archives Alsaciennes*, VIII, 1929, p. 169; particularly on Boisserée, p. 202.

The most complete information concerning the architects of the Middle Ages may be found in Martin Briggs, *The Architect in History*, Oxford, 1927, 52ff. with a bibliography p. 129. Middle High German expressions for Gothic details are also found in a poem describing a Gothic Throne; see Julius von Schlosser, *Quellenbuch zur Kunstgeschichte . . .* (*Quellenschriften . . .*, N.F. VII) 1896, p. 298.

magne,[1] which has recently been dated about 1150. With this work we go back to the time of Suger. For the dating of the Old French epics Olschki should be consulted.[2]

The *Pèlerinage de Charlemagne* is a mixture of the serious and the comic. Gaston Paris remarked: ". . . le Charlemagne de notre chanson a un pied dans le sublime et l'autre dans le ridicul."[3] Koschwitz considered the entire poem a travesty of the contemporary gleemen's poetry, but Paris refuted this idea. In any case, when we come to the description of the reception hall in the imperial palace in Constantinople it is important to know that the whole story was not intended to be taken altogether seriously.

Charlemagne, arrayed in crown and sword, strides up and down before his barons in (Carolingian) St.-Denis, then stops in front of his spouse, and asks: "Lady, think you that there is a man under Heaven who can wear crown and sword better than I?" The unexpected answer comes: "Sire, one should not be too overweening. I know an even more impressive and amiable king." Charlemagne is shamed and angry, and resolves to seek out his rival at once; if the empress is proved wrong she shall be beheaded. Finally, upon Charlemagne's insistence, she names the rival king: the emperor of Greece and Constantinople.

Of all that follows in the romance only the sights that Charlemagne sees in Constantinople are important to us, but we must interpolate that Gaston Paris calls attention to other situations very similar to this prelude. There is a story about Harun-al-Rashid, who asks a question as vain as Charlemagne's; here a vizier refers to a gentleman in Bassora, whereupon the unfortunate official is thrown into prison and the caliph journeys to Bassora with his knights. Gaston Paris adds that the motif presumably derives from India; he also points out a second example from the *Edda.* This beginning of the *Pèlerinage de Charlemagne* has, indeed, no real bearing on the subsequent depiction of the palace in Byzantium, but for the literary relationships of the descriptions of fantastic edifices this reference to Arabia, India, and the North is a significant warning not to declare everything Gothic simply because it was written in the Gothic age.

1 Text edited by M. Koschwitz, Heilbronn, 1880 (*Altfranzösische Bibliothek*, II).

2 Leonardo Olschki, *Die Romanischen Literaturen des Mittelalters*, Wildpark-Potsdam, 1928 (Handbuch der Literaturgeschichte).

3 Gaston Paris, "Le chanson du Pèlerinage de Charlemagne," *Romania*, IX, Paris, 1880, p. 1. A new and convincing interpretation is given by Alfred Adler, "The Pèlerinage de Charlemagne in New Light on Saint-Denis," *Speculum*, XXII, 1947, p. 550.

Charlemagne journeys with his paladins through Burgundy, Lorraine, Bavaria, Italy, and Greece to Jerusalem where the Patriarch receives him with honor and bestows upon him most valuable relics, among them the Crown of Thorns, a nail from the Holy Cross, the handkerchief of St. Veronica, the chemise or veil of the Virgin, and the arm of St. Simeon who carried the child Jesus. That was the legendary "first" Crusade, in the historical truth of which the Crusaders of 1196 firmly believed. The relics are in part familiar to us from St.-Denis, where the arm of St. Simeon assuaged the storm there on January 19, 1144. The Virgin's garment, however, was preserved in Chartres. For readers of the period around 1150 when St.-Denis and Chartres were being rebuilt these relics were realities that assured the credibility of the *Pèlerinage de Charlemagne.* Probably this part of the romance was originally a self-contained entity that was later connected with Charlemagne's journey from Jerusalem to Byzantium.

There the fictitious King Hugo receives him in the great hall of his palace. Gaston Paris comments on this passage: "The richness is astounding. In the domed hall all the furniture is of gold. The walls, finished with an azure blue border, are covered with paintings of all the animals of the earth, all the birds of the air, and all the fishes and reptiles of the waters. The vault is supported by one pier adorned with niello work on silver. Along the wall are a hundred pilasters of marble with gold inlays. In front of each of them stand two bronze figures of children with ivory horns at their lips. They seem to be alive. When a breeze blows from the sea the hall revolves, the bronze children look at each other and smile, their horns sound sweetly, the one high, the other low. One imagines that he hears the angels in Paradise singing." However, proud Charlemagne with all his knights falls down in fright, covers his face, and whimpers: "Sire, cela ne va-t-il pas bientot finir?"

Gaston Paris believed that the prototype of this hall, since it had to be sought in any case in the imperial palace at Constantinople, could be recognized in the *chrysotriclinium,* as it was described in the Book of Ceremonies.[4] According to this it most probably was an octagonal domed structure similar to SS. Sergius and Bacchus in the same city. Excavations made heretofore have shown nothing that could be connected with the *chrysotriclinium,* and it is in any case out of the question that such a heavy domed edifice could be made to revolve.[5]

[4] Gaston Paris, *op.cit.,* p. 11.

[5] Alfons Maria Schneider, *Byzanz . . . ,* Berlin, 1936, pl. 10, where the results of the

Söhring therefore rejects the *chrysotriclinium* and proposes the reconstruction of a circular structure the floor of which revolved "perhaps by means of a horse capstan operated by horses or donkeys in the cellar." This created "an impression of motion in the opposite direction owing to a very simple optical illusion."[6] If one wanted to take the revolving hall seriously one could say in reply to Söhring that a circular floor might also be built into an octagonal space. It would be tempting to brush aside his explanations on the theory that fairy tales should not be tested according to the principles of mathematics and mechanics, but *one* such revolving structure did actually once exist, not, to be sure, in Byzantium, as far as we know, but in Rome, in Nero's *casa aurea.* That is a further clue for us.

The subject of the romance obliged the French poet to use the locale of Byzantium and not Rome. He acquaints us with a second hall of the imperial palace where Charlemagne and his paladins retire after an abundant meal and even more abundant drink. Again it is a vaulted room, and since twelve beds are grouped around the thirteenth one can imagine it to be circular in shape. The beds are of bronze and so heavy that twenty oxen are needed to move them; Charlemagne's has silver legs. The rest of the furnishings are described and we hear of luxury and splendor instead of architecture, an inheritance from older literature and a requisite of all subsequent architectural fantasies. Much of this was actually to be found in the palace of Byzantium, also gilded trees and automatically singing birds, and the like, in part not created until the ninth century.

It would have contradicted fact if this contemporary of Suger had described the Byzantine palace as a work in the Gothic style, for neither in Byzantine nor in Gothic structures could he have found around 1150 a dome that rested on a central column. He wanted to present something extraordinary, and astounded his readers with marvelous automata. It is possible that others, returning from their pilgrimages, related what marvels were to be found in foreign parts, but also that many a man who had never left his native place saw in

---

excavations are entered on the plan of the present Turkish buildings. The reconstruction by Charles Jules Labarte, *Le Palais impérial de Constantinople . . .* , Paris, 1861, is based on a kind of scientific fantasy. In the text pp. 75, 161. Cf. his own remarks in the preface. Further: Jean Ebersolt, *Le grand palais de Constantinople et le livre des cérémonies*, Paris, 1910, p. 77. The miniature of Skylitzes (quoted by Ebersolt, p. 78, reproduced by de Beylié, *L'Habitation byzantine*, Paris, 1902, p. 122) is, for our topic, disappointing.

[6] Otto Söhring, "Werke bildender Kunst in Altfranzösischen Epen," *Romanische Forschungen*, XII, Erlangen, 1900.

his vivid imagination far greater wonders than they. One is inclined to the latter view if one has read Scheludko's essay.[7] Today one can build automata and revolving stages of which the poet of 1150 merely dreamed, if one has the taste for that sort of thing. The deranged King Ludwig II of Bavaria had a table constructed in his palace in Munich that could be let down through the floor and up again so that he could be alone in his dining room. This "marvel" actually existed.[8] The parallel is not intended to imply that the Oriental kings and emperors were mentally ill but that the French for which the epics were written and the cathedrals built had a predilection for the marvelous and a large share of naïveté as well.

Although no revolving domed halls existed in Constantinople, there was an actual model for the two figures that announce the approaching storm: the imperial palace had such sounding figures above its gateway. This gateway is mentioned in 1071 by William, Bishop of Tyre (1030-1090), who was at that time sojourning in Constantinople with Amalric I, King of Jerusalem (1062-1074). Later, around 1500, it was described by Georgius Codinus: the tower was hollow and "whenever the south or north wind blew more strongly and drove the water of the sea against the wall, the wind, forced inward, rose to the opening of the trumpets and made a harmony wonderful to hear, like that of the sirens." A second tower echoed the sound. The two figures, apparently on the first tower, were of bronze, as in the *Pèlerinage de Charlemagne.* One naturally thinks of the statue of Memnon in Egypt, but it is superfluous to cite further examples, since every visitor to Constantinople must have been acquainted with the gateway of the imperial palace.

In the article by M. Schlauch passages from Byzantine romances have also been collected that contain descriptions of palaces with splendidly furnished halls, automata, and so on.[9] I shall revert to this.

Around 1160, about a decade after the *Pèlerinage de Charlemagne*, the *Roman de Troie* was composed by the poet Benoît de Saint-Maure near Tours.[10] It contains three descriptions of buildings.

The *chambre de beauté* is a room in the four corners of which on pillars—each one of amber, jasper, onyx, and gagaret—figures

[7] D. Scheludko, "Orientalisches in der altfranzösischen Dichtung," *Zeitschrift für französische Sprache und Literatur,* LI, Jena and Leipzig, 1928, p. 255.

[8] In the top story of the northwest corner tower of the Munich palace, where I saw it before 1921. It was destroyed in the Second World War.

[9] Margaret Schlauch "The Palace of Hugon de Constantinople," *Speculum* VII, 1932, p. 500.

[10] Aristide Joly, *Benoît de Saint-Maure et le Roman de Troie*, Paris, 1870.

stand, two maidens and two youths. The first maiden holds a mirror. The second, however, "performs on her pedestal the most difficult feats of dancing and leaping." One youth plays on twelve musical instruments, which are all enumerated, better than King David. The real result of his playing, however, is that one can exchange secrets in the room without their being overheard by any eavesdropper outside the door. This youth can do still more: he strews the floor with fresh flowers, and so on. He, in turn, is far surpassed by the second youth, for the latter gives each person present in the room quite particular advice as to how he shall conduct himself.[11]

Söhring comments: "In all probability a kernel of truth can also be found in this description of marvels." He is of the opinion that granted only a fraction of them existed, we must nevertheless admire the goldsmiths and technicians of that time, "even though we have to think in this case of the Orient and not of the countries of the West." If a philologist of the year 1900 had so much faith we may assume that the readers of the *Roman de Troie* around 1160 had no doubts at all. In any case Söhring could have found a supporter in Villard de Honnecourt who, although he wrote seventy-five years later, must certainly have had predecessors; Villard, as we know, constructed automata.

The *Roman de Troie* also contains the descriptions of two tombs, in which more emphasis is put upon the architectural element than in the case of the *chambre de beauté*. The poet Benoît himself calls Hector's tomb[12] a tabernacle: ". . . tabernacle preciox / Rich et estrange et merveillox." (verse 16607) We may anticipate and mention the most impressive feature at once: Hector's embalmed corpse, unsheathed sword in hand, sits on a throne in the upper story of the tabernacle. The lower story has a domed vault which rests on four statues that are, in turn, carried by four lions. The upper story has a wall of varicolored marble and is also vaulted, but whether with a dome or in some other form is not stated. The material of its keystone,

[11] Söhring, *op.cit.*, pp. 592ff. The *Chambre de Beauté* was depicted by a painter around 1400 in the Manuscript of the Bibliothèque Nationale, Fds. fr. 301, folio 94r. It is a charming picture. Hector is receiving the Host from a priest, and lies ill in a bed that fills the whole width of the room, so that there is hardly space for the other persons. But in the four corners stand the four figures, in this case three maidens and only one youth, set up on Gothic engaged piers. One of the maidens scatters golden flowers. The two little flying angels are perhaps intended to furnish the picture with the motion that is mentioned in the text. The miniature was reproduced by Louis Petit de Julleville, *Histoire de la langue et la litérature française*, I, Paris, 1896, p. 192.

[12] Söhring, *op.cit.*, p. 540.

however, is described; it is enamel work of gold and pulverized jewels. For the rest of the precious materials Söhring should be consulted. Joly,[13] the editor of the text of the Trojan war, says: "La sépulture d'Hector représente très exactment la disposition du *ciborium* dans les églises du moyen-âge. . . ." This statement directs the search for models toward minor architecture, but it does not at all follow that the ciboria, tabernacles, and so forth, that were the prototypes must have been Gothic.

The third description of a building in the *Roman de Troie* is that of Achilles' tomb. Here unquestionably is meant a larger architectural work that has in form nothing to do with minor architecture. A base-like substructure contains several rooms but its door is walled shut; above this rises the statue of Polyxena, the beloved of Achilles. Sadly she holds in her hands the urn in which Achilles' ashes are preserved. Söhring says quite properly that this composition, however unclear it may remain in its details, is imbued with a thoroughly classical feeling. It is un-Gothic. In this negative statement lies the implication that in France around 1160 Gothic did not yet dominate the imagination of the public as absolutely as one might suppose from a consideration solely of the history of architecture. At that time St.-Denis was already standing, together with Sens and a part of Noyon.

Approximately at the same time as this reworking of Homer there existed one of Vergil. The name of the poet of the *Eneas* has not come down to us; from his dialect he must have been a Norman.[14] This epic also offers two descriptions of tombs.

For the tomb of Camilla, princess of the Amazons, a quadripartite ribbed vault is described very clearly. This mention of a Gothic vault is therefore presumably older than that of Gervase. The passage runs

"de desus ot deus ars asis,
en croiz esteient vols amont,
a aguilles taillé reont;
dreit en furent asenblé,
par maistrie furent soldé." (verse 7542)

This reads in translation: "Seated above them [above four springers in the shape of lions] the vault was carried aloft with two arches in the form of a cross, cut round with an instrument like a needle; exactly in the middle they were joined, and made firm in masterly fashion."

13 Aristide Joly, *op.cit.*

14 Jacque Salverda de Grave, *Eneas*, *Text critique*, Halle, 1891.

The words *a aguilles* may mean approximately "as exactly as though they were chiseled with a needle." They are perhaps to be taken analogously to Gervase's comment that the Romanesque arches seem to be hewn to shape with an axe and not with a chisel (*cum scisello*), whereas he says of the Gothic: "hic in omnibus [arcubus] fere sculptura idonea."

Above the keystone of this quadripartite ribbed vault stands a marble pillar (*piler*) seven fathoms high (about fourteen meters). Its base and capital are richly adorned with sculptures, flowers, hinds, and birds. This pillar supports the next, circular story. The passage is commonly understood to mean that this story is really supposed to balance on the single pillar. It is possible that the poet, who by no means tells us everything that would be necessary for the reconstruction of this tomb, did not expressly mention the round exterior wall of this second story because he took it for granted; but since we find something similar in the *Letter of Prester John*, which we shall soon discuss, we need not give up the idea of the one pillar. On it, then, rests the third story, twenty feet in diameter and twenty feet high. Here the exterior wall is described: it is decorated with little pilasters (*pilerez*, in verse 7568) and arches, but is windowless. Above the projecting cornice follows the fourth story, circular and broader than the third but of the same height. Above that, again projecting, is the fifth story, thirty feet high, the actual tomb chamber containing the sarcophagus of the Amazon princess with another whole collection of minerals. The mortar consists of pulverized stones mixed with the blood of snakes, so that the gruesome side of existence is also not forgotten. Above the roof, which was probably conical, is attached a mirror. It is justifiable to assume that a ciborium was the prototype of this tomb also, that is, to think of gold or another metal and of a work on a small scale. The projections of the upper stories are a common motif in wooden structures, at least in later times. The fantastic element lies then mainly in the assertion that all this was carried out in stone and on a large scale. For the poet and certainly for the reader as well the chief attraction was to be found precisely in this fantasticality. If anyone should ask whether this tomb was Byzantine, Romanesque, or Gothic, he could only be told that it was none of them, but is in the style of a fairy tale.

Once a quadripartite ribbed vault has been documented for Camilla's tomb, at least in its bottom story, it is permissible also in the description of Pallas' tomb to deduce from the text, following Söhring, a quadripartite vault, though it is here an open question whether a ribbed or a groined vault was meant. The passage reads:

> "La volte sist en poi de leu [peu de lieu]
> dedenze fu peinte a or museu,
> tot environ ot pilerez
> a tabernacles et archez
> et altres uevres en peintures
> et molt buenes entailleures." (verse 6437)

The first line may be translated: the vault rests on but few points (or on small bases). Presumably there should be a period after *leu* since the gold mosaics were probably on the walls and not on the quadripartite vault. The contrary can, however, be defended. There also exist quadripartite vaults with mosaics and, on the other hand, the walls are already provided with the little columns or pillars. This forces us to recognize again that the description does not tend to create an unambiguous picture.

A few years earlier than the Norman *Eneas* is the epic *Eracle* of the year 1164.[15] It contains a description of the throne of "Cosdroe," which the Emperor Heraclius had destroyed after the defeat of Chosroes. This throne has been described several times, each time differently. According to this source it was a tabernacle with a domed vault. The vault represented the starry firmament, and in it was fastened the Holy Cross, which Chosroes had robbed from Jerusalem. Beneath this sky the ruler sat enthroned and caused himself to be worshiped as God. The king could produce lightning, thunder, and rain, that is, the throne was equipped with the appropriate machinery. Here, too, there can be no question of Gothic architecture; rather, the whole conception rests on a romantic admiration for the exotic and already long since vanished splendor of Oriental architecture. The throne of Chosroes was, of course, in Persia. This imaginative creation must be mentioned because it has points in common with Albrecht's description of the temple of the Grail.

If the dates of literary history are reliable, *Eracle* is followed by the *Letter of Prester John* of 1165. This letter, addressed to Emperor Emanuel Komnenos, Emperor Friedrich Barbarossa, and Pope Alexander is a hoax, inasmuch as there never was a presbyter in India named John who was, at the same time, king over seventy-two kings. The unknown author of the letter made use of the historical fact, already

[15] Söhring, *op.cit.*, p. 525.

become legend, that an Indian priest of a Nestorian community had come to Byzantium in 1122, had there related fabulous things about India, and had been taken to Rome by ambassadors of Pope Calixtus II who were then present in the city. This letter of 1165 is at one and the same time the description of a wonderland or Land of Cocaigne and a Utopia improvised from ancient stories about India. In that land could be found all sorts of creatures, among them the phoenix, all sorts of plants, also medicinal herbs with miraculous powers, stones that gave knowledge, human beings of all kinds, including Amazons, satyrs, cyclops, people without heads and with mouths on their breasts. In this realm there was no private property and hence no theft, lying, nor like evils. Olschki has shown in an excellent analysis that the hoax and the Utopia are only artistic means of making the letter interesting.[16] Actually it had a political and didactic purpose: it held up to the West as an example an empire of peace and Christian toleration, the theocratic model government of a priest and king to whom all secular rulers voluntarily submitted;[17] in other words, it was the opposite of the confused political conditions of a Europe suffering under the rivalry of the Pope and the Byzantine and German emperors. Pope Alexander credulously answered John's letter, but not until the year 1177 after he himself had attained political security.

The letter aroused enormous interest; it was disseminated in many copies and translations, much read, and doubted by no one. Zarncke reproduced the original text and published with it the later interpolations and the Middle High German translations.[18] It is very entertaining.

Naturally the priest-king also has a costly palace. Unfortunately its external appearance is not made very clear. The author speaks almost exclusively of the precious materials that all have practical significance in addition to their aesthetic values. Curiously enough, the description begins with the roof. It is of cedar and covered with "incombustible" ivory. On the point of the roof is placed a carbuncle that shines by night—a detail that recurs in many stories. The doors are made of sardonyx and horn: these materials prevent the entry of anyone bearing poison. This is all that we learn of the architecture. Then follow some

16 Leonardo Olschki, "Der Brief des Priesters Johannes," *Historische Zeitschrift*, CXLI, 1931, p. 1.

17 Wilhelm Weber left a note to the effect that this could be a reminiscence of King Asoka of India (3rd century B.C.).

18 Friedrich Zarncke, "Der Priester Johannes," *Abhandlungen der phil. hist. Classe der kgl. Sächsischen Gesellschaft der Wissenschaften*, Leipzig, 1878, VII, p. 825; cf. also V and VIII.

details of the interior furnishings. The tables have ivory tops and the legs are partly of gold and partly of amethysts. The illumination comes entirely from lamps burning balsam. The bed is of sapphire "because of the virtue of chastity." Here the description goes off on a tangent; we are told that the priest-king has handsome wives (*speciosissimas*), who are distinguished by chastity: ". . . they approach us four times a year only for the procreation of sons and, blessed by us as Bathsheba was by David, each one returns to her dwelling place." In front of the palace is an arena, the floor of which is of onyx so that the courage of the fighters may grow by virtue of the stone (*ex virtute lapidis*).

Beside the arena is set up a mirror of extraordinary size, approached by one hundred and twenty-five steps of alabaster, serpentine, and so on. The mirror rests on a grandiose structure. At the bottom is a single column, it carries two columns, above these on a new base are four columns, then follow eight, and so each story continues with twice as many columns as the preceding one until sixty-four are reached. Then comes another story with sixty-four columns, followed by one with thirty-two, and so on, decreasing until one single column stands at the top. It carries the mirror, which reveals all dangers that may threaten the ruler.[19] It appears that these columns all stand in a vertical plane and thus do not form rotundas, as in the case of Camilla's tomb. But the fantastic element and the playing with improbable statics are akin to both structures. The author of Prester John's letter could scarcely have known and utilized the *Eneas*, only one year older if the dates are correct, and it remains for the literary historians to search for a common older source. The literature on India, of course, goes back to the literature on Alexander the Great whose campaign stimulated men's imaginations down to the Middle Ages.[20]

Probably a quadripartite ribbed vault is also described in the *Roman d'Alexandre* by Lambert li Tors and Alexandre de Bernay, which was

[19] On the origin of the mirror motif cf. Heinrich Lichtenberg, *Die Architekturdarstellungen in der mittelhochdeutschen Dichtung*, Münster i.W., 1931, p. 104. Recently a new investigation by Charles E. Nowell, "The Historical Prester John," *Speculum*, XXVIII, 1953, p. 435 comes to the conclusion that the letter was written by an European, the name John taken from Zan, meaning King or majesty, as title of the rulers of Ethiopia, and that the man was Yeh-lü Ta-shih, who in 1141 won an overwhelming victory over Sanjar, the ruler of the Sel-juk Turkish empire. Supposing all this to be correct, it is clear that the European writer could have had no intention of making the Prester John dwell in a Gothic palace.

[20] The extant classical literature on Alexander can be traced back to the lost account of Callisthenes (d. 327 B.C.). In the history of Alexander by Q. Curtius Rufus, 8:32, is to be found a brief description of an Indian palace: the columns are of gold and are entwined with silver vines, in which birds perch. This still very modest passage was elaborated, or it may be that other ancient sources were more extravagant.

completed after 1170.[21] Verse 444,3, referring to the tomb of the Emir of Babylon, reads: "a IIII ars par dedens qui tout cou [coup] sostenoient" (with four arches on the inside, which support every thrust [every weight]). The passage is very problematical because by the four arches could be meant not ribs but wall arches. However, if one takes the four arches to be ribs, one must ask whether the number indicates that the poet was thinking of the four half arches or possibly of two diagonal ribs and two ridge ribs. Hardly anyone will care to insist on the latter for the year 1170; nor will anyone probably want to use this passage as proof that the ribs actually carry or that the contemporaries of Gothic believed this; and, since we are dealing here with pure poetry, it is to be hoped that no one will quote these lines to show that the rib vault originated in the Orient.[22]

The romance also contains a description of Alexander's tomb.[23] A foundation story has a vault, which is described no more precisely and which is supported by a central pillar of iron. Above four ivory statues is built a story with one hundred windows filled with transparent snakeskin. On this rests a pyramid the keystone of which is the sarcophagus, crowned with the statue of Alexander himself. It is left to the individual judgment to reconstruct this edifice with classical or Gothic forms. The concept of the form as a whole is in either case equally monumental.

The romance of *Floire et Blancheflor*, after 1170,[24] combines the Occidental and the Oriental, for the tale of the heathen prince and his Christian lady love is partly laid in Baghdad. The tomb of the reputedly deceased Blancheflor rises in the shade of a tree before a cathedral. Above a richly decorated base of marble stand the statues of the two lovers. Of the base it is said: "Si fut entaille environ / De la trifoire Salemon." (verse 555) There is also mention of a triforium in the *Eneas* (verse 7571): "de fors esteit tote trifoir," referring to the fourth story of Camilla's tomb. According to Söhring the expression *œuvre Salemon* is tautological for triforium.[25] It probably means quite vaguely merely "in the fashion of Solomon's temple." We met the word triforium also in Gervase, about sixteen years after the composition of the romance of *Floire et Blancheflor*. The etymological deriva-

21 The text published by Henri Victor Michelant, Stuttgart, 1846.

22 For the rest cf. Söhring, *op.cit.*, p. 535.

23 *Ibid.*, p. 531.

24 *Manuscript A, Floire et Blancheflor*, published by Du Mesnil, Paris, 1856; cf. Söhring, *op.cit.* p. 529.

25 Söhring, *op.cit.* p. 538.

tion from *tres* and *fores* in the sense of "three openings" is not certain. It is also unclear whether or not the base with the triforium is to be thought of as Gothic in form.

Probably far more important for the poet and his readers than the question of style were the golden figures above the base. Floire bears on his head a carbuncle that shines in the night for many miles around. But even more wonderful is the fact that every breeze sets the lovers in motion. Then they embrace and kiss one another, and Floire says to Blancheflor: "Baisiez moi bele, par amor," and Blancheflor kisses him and replies: "Je vous aim plus que riens vivant." One should not mockingly assume that the poet intended to imply that he loved automata more than nature. Such was not his intention; on the contrary, he was merely continuing the tradition of the *Pèlerinage de Charlemagne* with even greater boldness. We do not need to go into the question here of how far the facts of the development of mechanical techniques in Byzantium corroborate the existence of automatic figures. It is only of interest to us that poetic imagination in the Gothic era, which was unable to construct such automata (in spite of all Villard's skills) was certainly more inspired by them than our sophisticated times. The poets simply expressed the wishes of the Gothic public of the day; but one cannot call our modern technology Gothic, though it fulfills such wishes; one can, however, in this round-about way come to see that in it is to be found essentially the fantasticality of our own age.

In Version B of the romance the sculptured group is even more complicated. The lovers stand apart from each other, Floire on a higher level, and a third figure in the costume of a messenger moves back and forth on a chain. Each time the messenger changes the balance, the other of the two chief figures rises. It is like a pair of scales that oscillate around a central point. In this case, then, the poet himself seems to have considered the matter from a rational point of view. It was indeed a miraculous work, but nevertheless everything had a perfectly natural cause. Whenever this kind of mechanical explanation is found, one may assume an especially sophisticated taste. In a certain sense the readers of these romances probably looked up at the Gothic vaults with the same credulous astonishment. These were marvels that they could not explain to themselves and yet they had to assume that the architects operated with perfectly rational procedures, as far as structural mechanics was concerned. Söhring collected the passages where the poet has the edifices that he invents built by magicians instead of architects, and in this connection it should not be forgotten that there are plenty of mediaeval legends about architects who are supposed to have carried out their works in league with the Devil.

The reworking of the *Eneas* by the Flemish Heinrich von Veldeke, whose *Eneit* has come down to us in the Thuringian dialect, testifies to the spread of ideas from France to Germany. Ehrismann assigns the completion of the work to the years between 1184 and 1188.[26] Veldeke greatly simplified Camilla's tomb. The marble structure is also circular and, like its prototype, twenty feet in diameter; it has in this case a floor of jasper. Although the ground plan is a circle, Veldeke, too, indicates a quadripartite ribbed vault:

"dâ lach in vier sinnen	There lay in the four corners
vier steine wale gehouwen	four well-hewn stones
die man gerne mochte skouwen.	goodly to see.
dat seget man ons ongelogen.	This is told us truly.
drop stonden twêne swibogen.[27]	On them stood two (rib) arches.
der wîse man Geometras	The wise man Geometras,
der des werkes meister was	who was the master of the work,
he worchte sî met moete.[28]	he built them with care.
sî wârn hô twentich foete.	They were twenty feet high.
des konde er wale gerâmen,	This he could well arrange
dâ sî tesamene quâmen	because they came together
in krûcewîs bovene."	crosswise above.

A quadripartite ribbed vault does not consist merely of ribs. Trier expressed surprise that the poet did not mention the severies of the vault,[29] and the Norman model, the *Roman d'Eneas*, also says nothing of severies. On the other hand, one should not conclude that the poets imagined ribs without severies, nor should one underestimate the significance of the fact that they did not, conversely, mention the severies and keep silence about the ribs. It seems after all that the generation of this poet knew the rib was an important structural member. It is mentioned for the first time by Suger, 1144, where he gives the account of the storm, next about 1160 in the romance of *Eneas*, subsequently

26 Gustav Ehrismann, *Geschichte der deutschen Literatur bis zum Ausgang des Mittelalters*, II, Part I, Munich, 1927, p. 82.

27 In other cases also written *swibbogen*. The etymological derivation from *schweben* is regarded as false in the *Deutsches Wörterbuch* of the Grimm brothers, Leipzig, 1854ff.

28 Otto Behaghel, *Heinrich von Veldeckes Eneide*, Heilbronn, 1882, p. 379. (Other editions: Ludwig Ettmüller, Leipzig, 1852, etc.)

29 Jost Trier, "Architekturphantasien in der mittelalterlichen Dichtung," *Germanisch-Romanische Monatsschrift*, XVII, Heidelberg, 1929, p. 17.

in the passage in Veldeke's *Eneit*, ca. 1184, and then around 1186 by Gervase.

These lines from Veldeke have been frequently cited by those recent authors who have concerned themselves with the problems of Gothic proportions, and indeed the significance of geometry for Gothic architecture is thrown into sharp relief when Veldeke calls his architect the wise man, Geometras. Even if one interprets the text cautiously it cannot be denied that Veldeke alludes to the rib and geometry in the same breath, and thus singles out two central features of Gothic.

Gottfried von Strassburg's *Tristan*, completed about 1210,[30] takes us into a very different atmosphere. The central theme is *Minne*, the blissful and destructive passion of love. Gottfried transferred the story, which already had been treated in another epic, into the realm of the psychological. For our subject the grotto of love is significant.[31] Tristan and Isolde betake themselves thither after their banishment by King Mark. If one merely reads this uncommonly delightful chapter for the sake of an architectural description one will be disappointed, for very little can be learned about the architecture itself. The grotto is a round chamber with a dome, hewn into the cliffs in the midst of a forest wilderness. The floor is of green marble, the walls are white, the dome is studded with gems. There is a detailed description of the bed that stands in the center of the room; it is carved from crystal, beautiful and clear, with an inscription around it to the effect that it has been dedicated to the goddess of love. The chamber has small windows through which King Mark later observes the sleeping pair from his vantage point in a tree.

To this account of the grotto is appended an allegorical interpretation such as was customary in the case of an ecclesiastical structure. The curvature of the chamber typifies the single-mindedness of love: there are no corners because they signify betrayal and treachery. The breadth of the room is the power of love, its height high-spiritedness, and so on. The bed is of crystal because love should be transparent and pure. The arrangement for locking the door is also described in detail, and all the details are allegorically explained; for example, on the inside two bolts are inclined toward each other, the one of cedar wood signifying

[30] Ehrismann, *op.cit.* p. 300; cf. also A. Baumstark, *Geschichte der syrischen Literatur*, 1922.

[31] In the edition by Reinhold Bechstein, *Gottfried von Strassburgs Tristan*, Leipzig, 1891, II, pp. 218ff., in the modern German translation by Wilhelm Herz, *Tristan und Isolde*, Stuttgart and Berlin, 1911, pp. 362ff. This translation is neither complete nor literal; it is adapted for modern readers and in that respect very valuable. As long as there are no literal translations of Middle High German literature, it remains a closed book to all but a small scholarly group.

wisdom and forethought, the other of ivory symbolizing chastity and purity, and so forth. The three windows are interpreted as humility, kindness, and decorum.

To the description and the interpretation in the traditional manner is added a third element. Gottfried declares quite unexpectedly that he very well knows what he is talking about with regard to the grotto of love because he has himself been in it (verse 17104). He has been acquainted with it from his eleventh year, although he was never in Cornwall. All at once the whole passage acquires a crass sexual significance, and when one turns back and rereads the circumstantial description of the door of the grotto and the method of opening it, one is amazed and must consider whether it is not almost improperly suggestive. The whole poem revolves about passion, sensuality, and adultery, so that this allegory is not inconsistent with the rest. The forbidden love of Tristan and Isolde is not their fault; the tragedy comes from the love potion, which had been intended for Isolde and Mark. What was sin from the point of view of the church thus appeared as the consequence of enchantment. Whether sensual love was considered as sin or enchantment, the Gothic age produced not merely ascetic monks and priests who at least preached asceticism, but also the secular militant caste of chivalry. Gottfried was himself of the middle class, but his poem glorifies the tragedy that was played out at a royal court and that is as a human conflict almost timeless, although its outer trappings may be called Gothic. In any case this architectural fantasy of the utterly non-Gothic grotto of love confirms our interpretation of the whole group of poetic examples: they are all shot through with vagueness and ambiguity.[32]

32 Ehrismann, *op.cit.*, pp. 314 and 324, discusses this symbolism. Friedrich Ranke offers the most detailed discussion of the grotto of love, "Die Allegorie der Minnegrotte . . . ," *Schriften der Königsberger Gelehrten Gesellschaft*, Geisteswissenschaftl. Klasse, 2. Jahr, Berlin, 1925; see also Lichtenberg, *op.cit.*, p. 36, and Julius Schwietering, *Die deutsche Dichtung des Mittelalters*, Potsdam, pp. 183ff. Since none of these authors mentions the suggestiveness of the passage, I turned to Mr. Schwietering, who called my attention to an article by Gottfried Weber, just about to appear, and said that it had never been considered whether the text gave rise to sexual conceptions, but that according to Weber's new interpretation this idea was not absolutely impossible. The article by Gottfried Weber, "Prolegomena zur Wesenserkenntnis von Gottfrieds Tristan," *Zeitschrift für deutsches Altertum und deutsche Literatur*, Berlin, 1950, p. 335, deals with the problems of the Tristan motif in fascinating fullness, so that those historians of art who see a close connection between *Minne* and Gothic will have a much broader basis for their investigations than heretofore. The reason that I present this thesis of sexual symbolism so tentatively is that these ideas do appear, but then they vanish almost immediately; in any case they are difficult to reconcile with the idea of the real architecture of the *fossiure*, the grotto. Presumably psychoanalysts would at once interpret the poem in this direction, as

The allegorical method became, in a somewhat dry fashion, the ruling principle in Guillaume de Loris's *Roman de la Rose*, composed between 1225 and 1250, that is, in the time of Villard de Honnecourt.[33] Here is described a castle that Viollet-le-Duc took to be the Louvre in Paris.[34] If this were correct, we should have a third description of a historical edifice to place beside those of Suger and Gervase. However, it is all in general terms: moats, thickness of the walls, towers at intervals that are easy to defend, donjon, and four gates. The castle has the name *Jalousie*; the gates are called *Dangier, Honte, Paor* (*Peur*), and *Male-Bouche*. The Louvre, constructed from 1190 to 1202, was at that time still a comparatively modern structure, and one may for that reason assume that the romance alludes to the same type of building. But Viollet-le-Duc was wrong in supposing that the Louvre had four gates. The excavations of 1866 resulted in a definite knowledge of the ground plan, and a miniature provides information about the elevation.[35] The Louvre had only two gates, one toward the east and the other toward the south and the bank of the Seine. Even two portals are unusually many for a Gothic castle. The portal toward the Seine was allegedly intended as an emergency exit if the Parisians should attack their king. At that time the Louvre lay outside the city walls of Paris. Viollet-le-Duc discusses also some other descriptions of castles.[36]

Before we come to the temple of the Grail we must say a word about the *Capella vitrea*, which a scribe of the *Letter of Prester John* inserted into his manuscript around 1250, the so-called *Interpolation D*.[37] The designation "chapel of glass" makes one think first of all of a structure like the more or less contemporaneous Ste.-Chapelle in Paris. But in this case it is a matter of glass that can stretch to any extent. If three people enter the building the chapel is full and all have room; if ten enter it is full and all have room; and so it continues to

Sterba does in the article to be cited later on p. 748. But I find this type of interpretation abstruse. What we detect in Gottfried is a second layer of symbolism behind the usual religious symbols. Weber's article is so profound because he sheds light on the conflicts of earthly love with Christian salvation; he stresses the daemonic and anti-Christian elements in Gottfried's views, as well as the heretical influence of Catharism. (Since this was written, G. Weber has published *Tristan* by Gottfried von Strassburg, Stuttgart, 1953.)

33 Olschki, *op.cit.*, pp. 180ff.

34 Viollet-le-Duc, *Dictionnaire raisonné de l'architecture . . .* , III, Paris, 1859, pp. 122ff.

35 M. F. Hofbauer, *Paris à travers les ages*, Paris, 1885, I, in the chapter "Histoire du Louvre," pp. 6ff. The ground plan of the original arrangement was marked by different kinds of pavement in the courtyard of the present Louvre. In the Salle des Caryatides a piece of the wall is still preserved. That fifteenth century miniature is also reproduced by Hofbauer. Further, see L. Hautecoeur, *Histoire du Louvre*, Paris, p. 1 and fig. 7.

36 Viollet-le-Duc, *op.cit.* p. 128. From the *Roman du Renart*, verses, 8463ff.

37 Zarncke, *op.cit.*, p. 922.

infinity. But when the people leave, the chapel contracts again correspondingly until the lowest limit of three persons is reached, a number vaguely connected with the idea of the Trinity. Perhaps the whole passage has an obscure symbolical meaning that awaits a correct explanation.

Finally we come to the acknowledged showpiece of this series, the temple of the Grail in the *Younger Titurel.*

It appears that Büsching was the first to draw attention to this passage.[38] Sulpiz Boisserée writes that he has been occupied with the epic since 1810, probably inspired by Büsching, who published the first summary of its contents and a kind of translation of the description of the Grail temple. Boisserée procured various manuscripts of *Titurel* and in 1835 after long preparation published the results of his investigations.[39] The poem had been considered to be the work of Wolfram von Eschenbach, since the poet introduces himself in the first strophes by this name. But in other places he calls himself Albrecht. In 1810 Docen identified this Albrecht with the poet Albrecht von Scharfenberg, and Boisserée believed that he had found convincing proof of this; thus the epic often goes by this name even today. However, Spiller disproved this attribution;[40] we must, accordingly, be satisfied with the simple Christian name Albrecht.

The epic of Titurel belongs to the great cycle of mediaeval legends about the Holy Grail. According to Golther the Old French epic *Conte del Graal,*[41] written by Chrestien de Troyes around 1180,[42] is not only the earliest source of the *Parsifal* saga that is known to us but also really the oldest in fact, whereas the legend of the *Grail* is far older in origin. But even the story of Parsifal is not a completely independent invention. It is related to Celtic sagas, to innumerable adventure stories of young heroes, and to the fairy tale of the unpromising brother, which exists in many variations. The actual story of the Grail was related about 1200 (thus later than Chrestien's epic) by the French poet Robert de Boron in the epic *Joseph of Arimathea.*[43] Its main theme was

[38] J. G. Büsching, "Der heilige Graal und seine Hüter," *Museum für altdeutsche Literatur und Kunst,* I, Berlin, 1810, p. 491.

[39] Sulpiz Boisserée, "Beschreibung des Tempels des heiligen Grales," *Abhandlungen der philos. philol. Klasse der K. Bayerischen Akademie der Wissenschaften,* Munich, I, 1835.

[40] Reinhold Spiller, "Albrecht von Scharfenberg und der Dichter des Jüngeren Titurel," *Zeitschrift für deutsches Altertum,* XXVII, p. 158, who refers to Docen.

[41] Wolfgang Golther, *Parzival und der Gral in der Dichtung des Mittelalters und der Neuzeit,* Stuttgart, 1925.

[42] For Chrestien cf., in addition to Golther, Ehrismann, *op.cit.,* pp. 246ff. with extensive bibliography.

[43] Golther, *op.cit., passim.*

that when Christ was removed from the cross, Joseph collected his blood in the same chalice in which Jesus had transformed the wine during the Last Supper; after imprisonment, miraculous liberation, and so on, Joseph made the chalice the center of a cult in the oldest Christian community, founding the table of the Grail in memory of the table of the Last Supper; later he made his way with the Grail to Britain (Glastonbury).[43a] After his death other chosen ones enter the service of the Grail and the office of king of the Grail eventually becomes hereditary in one single family, the same one to which Parsifal belongs; in this way both stories are brought together. This is, however, a great simplification, for these themes were also connected with the Arthurian legends and their circle. Golther follows the individual threads of this confusing web all through the Old French and Middle High German epics: the anonymous continuation of about 1210 (the adventures of Gawain), the works of Heinrich von Türlin (about 1210), Wauchier (1220-1230), Manessier, and others. Meanwhile in 1205, there appeared in Middle High German the first six books of Wolfram von Eschenbach's *Parzival*; up to about 1214, the other eight. Wolfram cites as his source a poet named Kyot, a Provençal, who in turn was supposed to have taken his story from an Arabic manuscript. Golther declared Kyot to be pure invention on Wolfram's part, believing that he thereby also showed the connection with Arabic to be fictitious;[44] Ehrismann is less decided on this question;[45] and Olschki identifies Kyot with Guiot of Provins.[46] This is of interest here only in connection with the question of the extent to which Oriental tradition can be detected in the poetry of the Grail and indirectly also in the imaginary structure of the temple of the Grail.

The studies of Iselin should be consulted for basic information about the whole subject of the Grail.[47] This literary historian differentiates two versions of the legend, which, however, frequently impinge upon each other. According to the one version the Grail is a sacred vessel, according to the other a stone from which that vessel was made. This stone comes from heaven. Its history goes back to the time before the

[43a] Mrs. J. Weitzmann-Fiedler has called my attention to a modest reconstruction in Thomas Hearne, *The History and Antiquities of Glastonbury*, Oxford, 1722, p. 8, of the first chapel, built by Joseph of Arimathea in the first century A.D.: a small rectangular building, the walls constructed like primitive palisades, the roof with thatch, the windows covered with pointed arches.

[44] *Ibid.*, p. 136.

[45] Ehrismann, *op.cit.*, pp. 234ff.

[46] Olschki, *op.cit.* p. 109.

[47] Ludwig Emil Iselin, *Der morgenländische Ursprung der Grallegende*, Halle a.S., 1909.

creation of the world when some of the angels rebelled against God and crowned Lucifer as their leader. When St. Michael thrust the latter out of heaven into hell, he struck the crown with his lance and a stone fell down into Paradise, which apparently was also already in existence. Adam found the stone and when he had to leave Paradise he took it with him. He preserved it in the cave which he inhabited with Eve and which became the eventual burial place of the pair. This "treasure cave" is the center of a cycle of sagas that are connected on the one hand with the cycle of sagas concerning Paradise and on the other with the legends about Adam. Since Adam's grave was thought to be in the exact center of the earth's surface and this was the spot where Christ was crucified, that is, Golgotha, there is then also a connection with the legend of the cross (the Helena legend). The blood of Christ that dripped down at the crucifixion fell upon Adam, baptized him, and redeemed him from sin. At this point the other version enters, for the blood was collected in the vessel from the Last Supper, the property of Joseph of Arimathea. The joining of the two cycles of ideas results in the identification of the chalice of the Grail with the stone mentioned above, and this is in turn brought into connection with all the stones to which there is a reference in the Bible. It is always the same stone: the one used to seal the tomb that belonged to Joseph of Arimathea and that once had been destined for Joshua (Joshua and Jesus are the same name), the altar table or the table of the Last Supper, Jesus himself as the cornerstone (Eph. 2:20). The stone performs miracles: it can, for example, preserve human life, provide food and drink, reveal the future.[48]

In 1938 a fresh contribution was made to the study of the Grail by the posthumous book by *Burdach*.[49] Here many of the legends mentioned above are discarded; the principal personality becomes the blind Longinus and the principal object the bleeding lance of the Parsifal story. The blood miracle has its origin in the words of Christ at the Last Supper and in the changing interpretations of theologians since Origines: Tertullian, Pseudo-Origines, Cyprian, and Kyrill of Jerusalem. In connection with these attempts to understand the meaning of wine and bread, as well as that of the blood and water which issued from the wound in Christ's side made by the lance thrust of Longinus,

[48] Golther, *op.cit.*, pp. 199ff., discusses Wolfram's knowledge of the East. In this place something is said also about the connections of the stone of the Grail with the Kaaba in Mecca, the philosophers' stone, etc.

[49] Konrad Burdach, *Der Gral, Forschungen über seinen Ursprung . . .* , Stuttgart, 1938.

Burdach investigates the symbolism of the Greek mass, adding the Greek sources to those from Syrian and from farther to the east. The mystical quality of the Greek sources and their "dramatization" of Christ's passion in the treatment of the words relating to wine and bread are of the utmost importance to the understanding of the epics of Chrestien de Troyes, Robert de Borron, and Wolfram von Eschenbach. Moreover Burdach, drawing upon his prodigious knowledge of the Greek and Latin theological literature of the first century A.D., gives an account of the representations of the crucifixion up to the thirteenth century which is the best to date, though it is not altogether complete.

However the unfinished book ends with Wolfram's epic and does not therefore enter into the problems presented by the description of the temple of the Grail in Albrecht's poem. Burdach's investigations prove that the legend of the Grail is Oriental in its basic elements.

In this case Oriental means approximately Syrian. The book about the treasure cave has come down to us in the Syrian language.[50] But by the Orient can also be understood everything that lies farther to the east: that is, Persia and India as well. Görres believed that the name Parsifal was Persian and meant "the pure fool," a theory that is considered untenable.[51] The temple of the Grail was itself connected with the Indian scene only at a late date: in the *Titurel* epic, the whole temple was finally transported to India by angels.[52] Thus we must be content to associate the Grail legend only with the Near East. This is hardly of much consequence for the architecture of the temple of the Grail unless we were to go back to the temple of Solomon, about which very little is known. What do we know about this temple of the Grail?

According to Ehrismann the *Younger Titurel* of Albrecht was written around 1270.[53] The designation "younger" does not refer to Titurel's age. Wolfram had begun an epic about Sigune and related characters that was called *Titurel* because in its beginning this hero appears. The "younger" Titurel is already fifty years old when he is made king of the Grail and well over four hundred when he begins the construction

[50] G. Bezold, *Die Schatzhöhle, nach syrischen Texten nebst einer arabischen Version herausgegeben*, Leipzig, 1888. The same author had already published a German translation of the Syrian text in 1883.

[51] Joseph Görres, *Lohengrin*, Heidelberg, 1813, Introduction.

[52] For Wolfram's borrowings from the *Letter of Prester John* cf. Golther, *op.cit.*, p. 212.

[53] Ehrismann, *op.cit.*, II, Final Part, Munich, 1935, p. 70. The best edition of the text was made by Friedrich Zarncke, *Der Graltempel, Vorstudie, zu einer Ausgabe des jüngeren Titurel*, Abhandlungen der kgl. sächsischen Akademie der Wissenschaften, XVII, Leipzig, 1879, p. 373.

of the temple. He is the grandson of Senabor, who here takes the place of Joseph of Arimathea, and his great age is explained, aside from the fact that the Grail preserves the youth of its guardians, by poetic necessity: he was to be a contemporary of King Arthur, and Albrecht knew from Geoffrey of Monmouth's *Historia* that Arthur died in 542. If one were to take this dating of the temple seriously and assign it in consequence to about the year 530, it would be of the same age as Hagia Sophia. But Albrecht did not intend to write a historical novel. If the temple does not necessarily have to be considered Byzantine, may one assume that it was meant to be Gothic?

There is no literal translation of the *Titurel.* Aside from the summary by Büsching that has already been mentioned, van den Berghe's French version approaches the text most closely;[54] this is confined to the 112 four-line strophes that are of interest for our subject. Golther also tries to give a summary, attempting to suggest something of the linguistic character and the poetry of the work as well. The account that follows intends only to select what is necessary for a visualization of the chief features of the architecture.

The mountain Monserrat near Barcelona (Fig. 19) that was singled out to bear the temple of the Grail is said to be a cliff of onyx. Titurel had the weeds and a layer of earth a fathom deep cleared away and the onyx polished so that it shone like the moon. On this surface, more than one hundred fathoms in diameter, he finds one day that a ground plan has been drawn: a circle with seventy-two choirs on its periphery and a choir on the east twice as wide as the others. It is dedicated to the Holy Ghost, the patron of the church. Around this central edifice runs a ring-shaped platform reached by circular steps. In the middle is a tower, which must also have been drawn in on the ground plan. Three portals lead into the interior from north, west, and south. To the south are the adjoining quarters of the knights of the Grail, palace and dormitory.

The external effect of the structure is like that of a gigantic crown, for over each of two chapels rises an octagonal tower of six stories, each with three windows. The roof of the main building is of gold but overlaid with enamel so that it will not be dazzling in the sun. Likewise the roofs of the thirty-six towers and of the doubly high central tower are covered with red gold. On the steeples of the peripheral towers are knobs of intensely glowing rubies. They carry crosses of

[54] Oswald van den Berghe, "Le Temple du Gral," *Annales archéologiques*, Paris, 1857, pp. 217 and 285.

crystal on each of which hovers a golden eagle. From a distance the crosses are invisible and the eagles appear to hover in the air. Above the golden roof of the central tower gleams a carbuncle, the light of which guides the Templars, should they lose their way at night in the enormous forest of "Monsalvaesche." In the same tower hangs a bell with a golden clapper, and a similar one is in the monastery; they summon the knights of the Grail to divine worship, to meals, and to the daily military exercises.

The portals have five archivolts of different sorts of precious stones, their doors are of gold. All wall surfaces are richly adorned; reliefs depict the glorious deeds of the knights of the Grail. The corners of the choirs have twisted columns adorned with figures of dwarfs and strange creatures of the sea.

In the interior, ribbed vaults are carried on bronze columns. The ribs are embellished with pearls and coral and the surfaces of the vaults covered with blue sapphires among which carbuncles shine like stars, illuminating the edifice by night. In the middle vault, that is, in the tower over the crossing, the ribbed vaulting has a keystone decorated with a lamb holding a cross. On the pillars are sculptured figures of the Evangelists, the Apostles, prophets, and saints. The walls are covered with mosaics, not a hand's breadth of surface has been left without adornment. The greatest richness is employed in the seventy-two choirs. Along the partition walls of these choirs are stalls of aloe wood. Above them the wall is set with emeralds and, in addition, provided with a blind gallery of columns and arches. These arches are decorated with golden grapevines, covered with verdure, that extend upward from the capitals of the columns, meet in the center of the arches, and then hang down free over the choir stalls. In the vines sit birds and angels; on the capitals are red roses and white lilies. In each choir an altar of sapphire, which has the power to cleanse men of sin, stands facing the east. Above each altar is a ciborium provided with a mechanism by means of which a dove brings an angel down from the vault during Mass and afterward bears him aloft again. The angel brings the Host (strophes 24 and 25). Each choir is separated from the central portion of the gigantic church by a screen with an altar in the middle facing the central space. Two doors lead through the screens into the choirs. The main choir of the Holy Ghost (*der vrone*, strophe 79) is similarly furnished. An elaborate clock with a gold sun and a silver moon announces the seven canonical hours. In the middle of the space the Grail stands in a tabernacle that is a small model of the whole temple.

The floor is a crystal sea. As though through a thin layer of ice one sees the waves passing and in them fish and marine wonders darting to and fro. Here there was no crypt.

When a wind stirs, the leaves of the golden trees and the golden vines move and it sounds as though a thousand falcons with their little gold bells were winging upward. Over the western portal in the interior an organ was constructed. It has the form of a golden tree in whose branches sit birds that sing, each in its own way, when they are operated by invisible bellows. Likewise the angel figures of the choirs are operated by bellows and can say a prayer and beat their breasts. The sound of any voice raised in the temple is magnified by the breadth and height of the space like an echo in the forest "that in May returns the greetings of the little birds."

The light is mystic. The windows all have jewels instead of glass. These shone so brightly that they had to be softened by painting. This light would hardly be really necessary for the illumination of the interior, for the other jewels give out light spontaneously night and day. In addition there are innumerable chandeliers, borne by hovering angels, larger than life, and on or over the altars many lamps filled with balsam.

This very much abbreviated summary probably gives a more lucid picture than the original, which presents the details in a different sequence: ground plan, vaults, piers, sculptures, altars with their machines, windows, roof, windows again, clockwork, statues of the Evangelists, external wall of the choirs, towers, and so on. It is not very probable that the strophes might have been jumbled when the poem was copied; one must assume rather that the desultoriness of the description, treating now the exterior, now the interior, is intentional, and must grant that it stimulates the imagination. It creates a far deeper impression of the incomprehensibleness of this structure than a systematic description would do. But however clear the sequence is made, much remains unclear. A considerable number of scholars have tried to clarify the obscurities of the text.

The first to struggle with this problem was Boisserée.[55] Since he worked out unique drawings for a reconstruction of the ground plan, transverse section, and elevation of the exterior we know down to the

[55] See above note 39. Further, cf. Josef Ponten, *Architektur, die nicht gebaut wurde*, Stuttgart, 1924, page 16, and vol. II, pp. 2, 3.

last detail exactly how he saw the temple of the Grail in his imagination (Fig. 23). But do we thereby know also how Albrecht saw it? It was only Boisserée's imagination that ordained two naves crossing at right angles and towering over the rest of the structure like basilicas. Was he concerned about the lighting by day? The middle portions of the interior are very far away from the windows of the peripheral chapels, but Albrecht was untroubled by such petty worries since, of course, his carbuncles, candles, and balsam lamps created everywhere a bright radiance. The two naves in Boisserée's plan form four quadrants in which he distributes piers. He is forced to decide on some solution, but it remains purely arbitrary. His disposition of the main choir has been very properly rejected and the arrangement of towers on every second chapel does not conform to Albrecht's idea of one tower on each two chapels. Just how Albrecht imagined that, remains, as a matter of fact, completely vague. But if the text contains such ambiguities is it not an absurd ambition to want to make an exact reconstruction from which the structure could be built today? A longer discussion of Boisserée's drawings would be unfruitful. They can be further evaluated as an interesting document of German Romanticism and we can be grateful for the trouble that Boisserée took, for thereby the vagueness of the text has been disclosed.

But Boisserée's reconstruction has also revealed with particular clarity how problematical is the question of the architectural style. Boisserée had assumed that the poem was begun in 1310 and completed in 1347. Therefore he reconstructed the temple of the Grail with High Gothic forms reminiscent of the tower of Freiburg Cathedral or of Cologne Cathedral with which he was so familiar. But if the epic had already been written around 1270, the tower of Freiburg Cathedral could not have been a model, and it is even questionable whether one may use the choir of Cologne Cathedral, begun in 1248, as a guide, since it was built very slowly and the vaults of the choir were not completed until 1320. One must, therefore, choose as prototypes churches of an earlier origin, and the Liebfrauenkirche in Treves, constructed from 1227 to 1244, would be a possibility. This edifice was declared to have been Albrecht's real model very early in modern literature on the subject.[56] It is a Gothic church of central type with

[56] Ernst Droysen, *Der Tempel des Heiligen Gral . . .*, Bromberg, 1872, says on p. 51 that Pastor G. Weber first maintained this (in 1868 or possibly 1865) in a work entitled *Der Dom des heiligen Gral*, Quedlinburg, 1868.

a high middle tower and chapels on its periphery, though four and not seventy-two. Boisserée concluded that Albrecht's temple was intended to be Gothic from several indications, of which the most important are: ribbed vaults with keystones, polygonal chapels, painted windows, and towers pierced with many windows and with interior spiral staircases.

The first three of these are indisputable. Twice there is mention of the ribbed vaults. In strophe 15 we read:

> "da sich diu gewelbe reifent nach der swibogen krumbe von siulen übersweifent, vil manic spaehiu liste daran alumbe wart ergraben . . ."
> (as the vaults bend toward the curve of the ogives rising above the columns, there was carving on them round about with skillful art . . .)

and in strophe 96:

> "Die cleinen und di grozen gewelb war unverdrozzen mit swibogen under stozen je von vier ecken über sich geslozzen."
> (The small and the great vaults were carefully supported by ogives, each one rising from four corners locked above.)

The keystone is mentioned in strophe 97. There is a reference to the corners of the choirs in strophes 55 and 57, but there is no justification for simply taking these corners to be buttresses, to which there is nowhere an allusion. That the window surfaces, which were made of jewels, were painted is explicitly stated in strophe 28. On the other hand, the fourth of Boisserée's indications, the spiral staircases, is not tenable. It is based on a mistaken translation of strophe 60.[57]

Droysen, however, has seen further proof of the Gothic style of the temple in the absence of a crypt.[58] Albrecht considers the worship of God in these dark, subterranean chambers "wrong," and says that one should proclaim the Christian faith in radiant space. On this point much has been written.

Here we may refer to what was said earlier in connection with the crypt of St.-Denis, adding that Albrecht seems to be the only source that expressly indicates a reason for relinquishing the crypt. It remains an open question, however, whether this explanation re-

[57] Cf. Zarncke, *op.cit.*, p. 487, and Blanca Röthlisberger, *Die Architektur des Graltempels im jüngeren Titurel*, Berne, 1917, p. 25. The passage has never been interpreted satisfactorily.

[58] Ernst Droysen, *op.cit.*, p. 36.

flects the official conviction of the ecclesiastical authorities or merely the private opinion of the poet.[59]

Zarncke did not express his views on this matter of style in a connected essay but one can divine what they were from his various notes.[60] The chief one refers to strophe 96: "This passage likewise does not necessarily indicate the Gothic style, since the Romanesque vault also can have diagonal ribs and indeed even rosettes in the middle of the vaults." As authority for this he cites Caumont, even in 1879.

Röthlisberger has taken a far more vigorous stand.[61] She believes that everything that was adduced as an argument for the Gothic style was already present in the Romanesque: stained glass, octagonal choirs, diagonal ribs with keystones, and so on. To be sure, she no longer relies on Caumont (1802-1873), but she is still uncertain about stylistic evolution. From Dehio's differentiation of active and passive transitional styles she could, even in 1917, have obtained more light. For us today a quadripartite ribbed vault is always Gothic; however, despite the presence of such a vault, we do not call the whole structure Gothic if it is in its other features still Romanesque, but we say that it is Transitional—active in England and France from 1093, passive in Germany from about 1120—because at that time the rib and other Gothic structural members were introduced from France. We cannot enter into a discussion here of the errors of older critical literature, but it should at least be mentioned in passing that Röthlisberger's reference to the polygonal choirs in the cathedrals at Bamberg and Worms is equally misleading. The earliest instances of a polygonal choir in French Early Gothic were perhaps the two site choirs of the transept and the upper part of the east choir of Laon Cathedral, the latter in its first (no longer extant) form, dating from about 1160.[62] Everyone knows that polygonal choirs were to be found even in Early Christian and Byzantine times. But in the architecture of the twelfth century the breaching of the hitherto round choirs is a result of the whole development of Gothic, corresponding to its tendency toward "diagonality," which was inaugurated with the diagonal rib.[63] Even if all the

[59] In the original the passage reads:
ob si da haeten grüfte? nein, herre got enwelle,
daz under erden slüfte reine diet sich immer valsch geselle,
als entwenne in grüften wirt gesammet!
man soll an liehter wite kristen glouben künden und Kristes ammet.

[60] Zarncke, *op.cit.*, p. 57 n. 2, p. 96 n. 2, p. 97 n. 1.

[61] Röthlisberger, *op.cit.*, p. 55.

[62] Hanna Adenauer, *Die Kathedrale von Laon*, Düsseldorf, 1934, pp. 19-21.

[63] The polygonal choirs of Gothic probably arose as a result of the requirements of stained

rest of the structure were Romanesque, which cannot be asserted of either Bamberg or Worms Cathedrals, the polygonal character of the choir is Gothic. All buildings in Transitional style have in part remnants of Romanesque and in part presages of Gothic structural members, and it is just this juxtaposition in the same edifice that we characterize by the word Transitional.

Röthlisberger noted that there was no mention of flying buttresses, gablets, pinnacles, crockets, and finials in *Titurel* and this strengthened her in her rejection of the Gothic style for the temple of the Grail. She thought that Albrecht had not yet been able to make full use of the architectural ideas of Gothic because at that time the great Gothic cathedrals were only in their beginnings. Here one can call to mind the somewhat earlier *Chronicle* of Burchard von Hall (about 1280). As a matter of fact the South German Albrecht could have been acquainted with Strasbourg Cathedral, the nave of which, begun before 1250, was then far advanced, but nothing hinders us from letting him journey on from Strasbourg to Paris, where he perhaps met his countryman who later (after 1259) built Wimpfen. As the latter made sketches, so Albrecht could have entered in his travel diary architectural notes on Ste.-Chapelle, and so on. The more clearly we picture him as a traveling historian of art the more pointless does the whole question of particular influences on the style of the temple of the Grail become.

Schwietering tried to find a way out of this impasse.[64] He called the attempts of Boisserée, Droysen, and especially Röthlisberger, to treat the temple as a real entity, rationalistic. Zarncke had already pointed out the importance of the magical effects of light and the echoing of the voices, and these, according to Schwietering, are the true means employed by the poet to arouse in the reader the mood of the vast church, its specifically Gothic element. What results when the covering of the walls and vaults with jewels is actually carried out can be seen in the chapel of Castle Karlstein in Bohemia, and in the chapel of St. Wenceslaus in Prague Cathedral,[65] where at the behest of Charles IV Albrecht's idea "was translated into the everyday language of reality

glass, that extends over plane surfaces and was, therefore, difficult to reconcile with circular choirs. When tracery was introduced (1210), the polygonal form was even more necessary. The early instances of polygonal upper stories on bases that are still semicircular begin exactly at the sills of the windows, e.g. Soissons.

64 J. Schwietering, "Der Graltempel im Jüngeren Titurel," *Zeitschrift für deutsches Altertum und deutsche Literatur,* LX, Berlin, 1923, p. 118.

65 Droysen, *op.cit.* p. 40, where in a long note older literature on both structures is also mentioned.

with no understanding of its symbolical content." Real jewels do not glow without light; therefore we miss the 14,000 candles that in Charles IV's day shone here.[66] The costly walls with their material splendor seem to us simply barbaric.

Schwietering shows effectively how Albrecht's purely poetic light is intended quite in the sense of innumerable texts of the mystics: as supernatural. Light is without question a "technical term of religious mysticism. . . . God is light and his illumination pure Grace; light is also the human soul whose mystical union with God is revealed and experienced in light." But Schwietering's assertion that Albrecht anticipated architectural development with his ideal of a mystical light is an error that is hard to understand, if he means by this the light in the cathedrals. Gothic light in its highest perfection had already been achieved in Chartres around 1220, also, for example, in Ste-Chapelle in Paris at a later date (1243). Where Albrecht himself saw such Gothic light remains unknown. (Perhaps in Strasbourg Cathedral?) Nevertheless, Schwietering is right in saying that Albrecht had in mind the dematerializing and spiritualizing effect of Gothic and was able to communicate these qualities to his readers by the means of poetry and mysticism. When Schwietering refers in this connection to the *capella vitrea* in *Interpolation D* of the *Letter of Prester John* (about 1250), we must reject his suggestion because this infinitely expansible chapel of glass has nothing to do with Gothic light—although it certainly has something in common with mysticism.

Curiously enough, Schwietering regresses to the older stage of critical investigation, considering the Liebfrauenkirche in Treves the stimulating factor in Albrecht's fantasy. He concludes his argument with the statement that "the poet experienced the spirit of Gothic not as a practicing artist or advisory cleric but as a layman, and indeed quite in the sense of recreative romanticism and modern scientific investigation of art." We must cling to Schwietering's thesis that Albrecht was inspired by a "mystical primary experience" (p. 126), which is expressed both in Gothic architecture and in the writings of the mystics as a colored light that does not seem to be of this world. Mechthild von Magdeburg (about 1210 to 1285) was Albrecht's contemporary.[67]

[66] The number of candles seems likewise to be based on poetic license. One cannot imagine how enough servants could crowd into the small chapels to light all the candles at once, or where there would be room for the candles themselves.

[67] Mechthild von Magdeburg, *Das fliessende Licht der Gottheit*, ed. Johannes Escherich, Berlin, 1909. The text, however, as far as I can see, does not revert to the idea expressed in the title.

Mystical light is not Albrecht's only means of removing the temple from everyday reality to a sphere of impenetrable mysteries. The jewels with which the structure is studded have mystical powers, and the many mechanical figures and devices stand midway between rational technology and the higher world of wonders. For both, Albrecht could rely on an old literary tradition with which we have already become somewhat acquainted.[68] The most precious and most mystical of all precious stones is the Grail itself. We know what value Suger placed on his jewels in St.-Denis. He was undoubtedly a connoisseur, and not everyone had an adequate knowledge of this subject. Albrecht says, therefore, that before every portal of the temple all the kinds of stones used in it were displayed, each sample being provided with an explanation of its mysterious powers. To us this seems as prosaic as a mineralogical museum, but to a certain degree at least mysticism could be inculcated like mineralogy.

Whoever understands this will likewise be able to appreciate properly the mechanical contrivances and especially the musical instruments of the temple of the Grail. The sound of an organ can be mystical, and in a church with golden trees in all its chapels a golden tree whose golden denizens really sing can arouse no particular astonishment. It may be, moreover, that organs of similar construction did actually exist, though hardly made of gold.[69]

To the mechanical wonders belongs also the clock that is presumably to be imagined in the main choir. Its case has a vault adorned with carbuncles just like all the other vaults. These, of course, are intended as stars. But the clock had also a sun and moon. In this connection Röthlisberger called attention to a passage in the *Kaiserchronik*, composed about 1150.[70] In the chapter on Emperor Heraclius there is an account of the destruction of the throne of Chosroes, in the course of which the throne is described as follows: a bronze sky over the land,

[68] To Söhring's collection of examples from Old French literature should be added what Zarncke cites from Middle High German literature in the notes to strophes 5ff. He mentions briefly ancient authors as well: Herodotus 7. 27, Xenophon, etc. On the jewels see also J. G. Büsching, "Die Kräfte der Edelsteine nach dem Glauben des Mittelalters," *Museum für altdeutsche Literatur und Kunst,* II, Berlin, 1811, p. 52.

[69] X. Barbier de Montault, "Orgue en forme d'arbre," *Annales archéologique*, XVIII, Paris, 1858, p. 91. There the reproduction from a manuscript of the Abbaye de St.-Blaise. He also calls attention to a statement by Simeon Logothetes to the effect that Emperor Theophilus ordered such an organ in the tenth century, and to the *Chronique d'Alberic* with the description of the throne of Constantine Porphyrogenetos (also tenth century), where golden lions roared beside the throne and birds sang—perhaps not simultaneously.

[70] Röthlisberger, *op.cit.*, p. 43. Cf. also Hans Ferdinand Massmann, *Kaiserchronik*, Quedlinburg and Leipzig, 1894, p. 133.

in the vault of which sun and moon were painted [*sic*] of carbuncles; the clouds were of lead, the stars of carbuncles; Chosroes could make rain fall from this sky. Line 11162 says: "viel gerne wolde er got sin" (right well did he wish to be God). The passage already mentioned from the French *Eracle* relates similar things.[71] However, it was felt to be obligatory to go back to the older sources.

We owe a comprehensive investigation of this subject to Herzfeld.[72] Chosroes II reigned from A.D. 590 to 628 and was one of the last kings of the Sassanid dynasty before the conquest of Persia by the Arabs (633 and 637). His throne seems to have been described for the first time in a manuscript of Theophanes in the second half of the eighth century. Then other descriptions follow.[73] From these sources and with the help of representations in works of art from different lands and times, Herzfeld formulated the theory that it was not a question of a throne at all but of a clockwork. Saxl contradicts this,[74] insisting that the famous work of art was a throne, though, to be sure, connected with a clockwork. The stars are to be understood as the zodiac; in conjunction with moon and sun the clockwork served to cast horoscopes. If one adds to this practical significance of the clock the continually recurring accounts of the machines that create lightning, thunder, and rain, then it becomes clear that this throne represented the universe.

The dating of the throne is uncertain. According to Firdausi it was not originally created by Chosroes but he merely caused it to be repaired, from which may be concluded that it was already very old. Firdausi relates that Chosroes commissioned 1,120 masters for the repairs and that each of them had thirty journeymen; this would result in the fantastic total of 33,600 persons. They worked for two years. This exaggeration can be pruned at will, but it appears, nevertheless, that there was a surviving memory of a very complicated work that was solidly constructed and that lasted for many centuries before it needed repairs. The throne can therefore date from the time of the *Apocalypse*, written at the end of the second, or in the third century

[71] See above p. 167.

[72] Ernst Herzfeld, "Der Thron des Khosrô," *Jahrbuch der preuszischen Kunstsammlungen*, Berlin, 1920, pp. 1, 103.

[73] Herzfeld discusses: Nikephoros of 827, Ado of Vienne, about 870 (p. 22), Firdausi in Shahnama, 1011, finally Theophanes and Georgios Kodinos (p. 17). Theophanes wrote in the second half of the eighth century, Kodrenos in 1057.

[74] Fritz Saxl, "Frühes Christentum und spätes Heidentum in ihren künstlerischen Ausdrucksformen," *Wiener Jahrbuch für Kunstgeschichte*, II (XVI), 1923.

after Christ. Here the throne of God is described (Rev. 4:2-6) in terms that make one feel that he has reached the source of all these fantasies: "... and, behold, a throne was set up in heaven, and one sat on the throne. And he that sat was to look upon like a jasper and a sardine stone: and there was a rainbow round about the throne, in sight like unto an emerald. And round about the throne were four and twenty seats: and upon the seats I saw four and twenty elders sitting, clothed in white raiment; and they had on their heads crowns of gold. And out of the throne proceeded lightnings and thunderings and voices: and there were seven lamps of fire burning before the throne, which are the seven spirits of God. And before the throne there was a sea of glass like unto crystal...."

As far as I know, it cannot be decided whether this passage was influenced by the throne of Chosroes, that is, by the one created by his ancestors, or whether the converse is true. It is, however, certain that Albrecht knew the *Apocalypse*, and probably he also knew descriptions of the throne of Chosroes from German or French literature. From the manuscript illustrations of the *Apocalypse* we are accustomed to imagine the twenty-four thrones arranged in a semicircle. Perhaps Albrecht took the sentence more literally. The twenty-four thrones stand in a complete circle round about the throne of God. Here then would be a source for the idea of a church of circular form, the seventy-two choirs of the temple of the Grail corresponding to the twenty-four thrones. That the number in the *Apocalypse* is multiplied by three can be connected with the symbolism of numbers dominating the whole structure of the temple. But even should this analogy of the circular form be disputed, there are enough details left that no one would deny: the jewels, God in the *Apocalypse* even being compared to them, lightning, thunder, as well as the sea of glass. The seven lamps of fire or Spirits of God are, finally, somehow analogous to the seven canonical hours of the liturgy.[75]

These verses from the *Apocalypse* have recently been related to Early Christian apses according to an interpretation of the basilica that sees it as the Heavenly Jerusalem in meaning and as an imperial Roman city in form.[76] Essentially this theory suggests that the façade

75 Several German poems of the eleventh and twelfth centuries were influenced by the Apocalypse; cf. the informative dissertation of Elisabeth Peters, *Quellen und Charakter der Paradiesvorstellungen in der deutschen Dichtung vom 9. bis zum 12. Jahrhundert*, Breslau, 1915 (Germanistische Abhandlungen, No. 48), especially the Introduction and Chapter II; also p. 87 on the Heavenly Jerusalem and pp. 101ff. on *das himilrîche*.

76 Lothar Kitschelt, *Die Frühchristliche Basilika als Darstellung des Himmlischen Jerusalem*,

of the basilica corresponds to the city gate, the nave and aisles to the street of market halls, the windows of the clerestory to the upper stories of the walls of the houses, the roof to the sky, the presbytery to the throne room of the ruler. The passages collected by Kitschelt, as well as his other arguments, are so overwhelming that one is sorely tempted to abandon all the older derivations of the Early Christian basilica and adopt this new hypothesis. But in spite of its convincingness there is still something else to be said. The program of an ecclesiastic—build me a Heavenly Jerusalem on earth with a street like that described by John—demanded an architectural "translation" of the text by an architect of great imagination. For even though it is reported that the main street of the city with its side halls was occasionally roofed over with fabrics, the city, as far as its streets went, remained essentially an *exterior* space, formed by houses and palaces with *interiors*. In the basilica all this has been merged, the interior of the throne room fused with the street of market halls, now become an interior, and possibly also with the transept (as *cardo* and *decumanus*). Thus the chief thesis that Kitschelt sets forth at the very beginning of his book, namely, that in the Early Christian basilica the Heavenly Jerusalem has been *realistically* not merely *symbolically* represented, is not correct. The basilica *is* no city, it *signifies* one; and it composes its interior from parts that existed as *membra* of the city. These *membra* have been given a fresh interpretation, both as to meaning and form. Those individual features of the basilica that the architects invented, the forms of the aisles, the clerestory (with mosaics), the transept, and the presbytery, breathe an atmosphere characterized by the word heavenly, whereas by Jerusalem itself is meant merely the city, the earthly, Roman city, to which traces of the material world still cling.

Kitschelt restricted his evidence to the period down to 500. Sedlmayr's attempt to extend the idea of the Heavenly Jerusalem as a church in the form of a city to subsequent centuries, including those of the Gothic period, is not convincing. In particular, Albrecht's architectural fantasy in the *Younger Titurel* is not a splendid street but simply a throne room, the latter being, however, as we have said, not a mere apse but a whole church of central type; it is not a city, though it does represent more than any real architecture could do the

Munich, 1938. It is understandable that the author exaggerates his thesis; one must recognize, however, that older theories also contained some truth. See also Hans Sedlmayer's essay, *Die Dichterische Wurzel der Kathedrale*, Mitteilungen des Österreichischen Instituts für Geschichtsforschung, XIV, Innsbruck, 1939.

Heavenly Jerusalem of Rev. 21:9ff. The lamb "with the seven horns that are the seven Spirits of God" that plays such a central role in the *Apocalypse* and stands in the midst of the throne of God, the four beasts (the Evangelists), and the four and twenty elders, has been moved by Albrecht to the keystone of the middle vault, where it was a decoration characteristic of Gothic structures. Despite all arguments to the contrary Gothic cathedrals were Albrecht's actual prototypes and the idea of the Heavenly Jerusalem was only a metaphor; the throne room of God, however, as the *Apocalypse* depicts it, is conceived as an infinite space, the door that was opened notwithstanding—it is the prototype that could be seen only by the eyes of the *spirit.* In addition other conceptions, like the throne of Chosroes, may have had some influence on the poet.

In a speech to the knights of the Grail, Albrecht put into the mouth of Titurel his own interpretation; it remains entirely in the traditional pattern of mediaeval symbolism. Zarncke also published these fifty-nine strophes.[77] The ten balsam lamps in each choir represent the ten commandments; the two doors to the choirs signify the two paths to blessedness, that of innocence and that of remorse and penitence; the three portals are faith, hope, and charity, and so on. But almost at the beginning the poet says that the *temple of the Grail* is a copy of the *Heavenly Jerusalem,* and with that we have it on Albrecht's authority at least that this architectural fantasy is meant to represent the spiritual universe of the Christian religion, thus not India, which was merely seen by the poetic imagination as a sort of fairy-tale background.

But if not India, then perhaps Persia, and Persia not merely as a poetic background, but as the real source. Ringbom tries to persuade us that this is the case.[78] But his interpretation of the poetic fantasy of Albrecht turns out to be a scholarly fantasy. He reduces the seventy-two chapels to twenty-two, because this is the number given in one manuscript of Albrecht's poem, and he identifies his own reconstruction of the Grail temple with that of St.-Gereon in Cologne as it was in the fourth century, despite the fact that it had not twenty-two chapels but only ten.[79] Twenty-two arcades, not chapels, can be discerned in the ornamentation of a Persian bronze bowl in the Museum at Berlin, attributed vaguely to the time of Chosroes II (590-628). In the small

[77] Zarncke, *op.cit.,* p. 497.

[78] Lars-Ivar Ringbom, *Graltempel und Paradies: Beziehungen zwischen Iran und Europa im Mittelalter,* Kungl. Vitterhets Historie och Antikvitets, Del. 73, Stockholm, 1951.

[79] Gertie Gretz und Otto Koch, *St. Gereon zu Köln,* Bonn, 1939.

central circle stands a building which, according to Ringbom, is a fire temple of the Parsis. One has only to put this building behind the circle of arcades and to fill out the central circle with water to see that the drawing on the bowl represents the sanctuary of Siz near Azerbeidjan in Persia where Zoroaster was born either in 660 B.C. or several centuries earlier. Since there is a tree in each arcade, the sanctuary is identified with Paradise. While it is gratifying to hear that Paradise still exists and can be fixed geographically, the unfortunate fact is that the four reconstructions of St.-Gereon, the bowl at Berlin, the sanctuary of the Persian Paradise, and the temple of the Grail do not have enough in common to corroborate Ringbom's theory. Fortunately for us, his other hypotheses and theories have so little connection with our problem that we need not discuss them. Suffice it to say that the temple of the Grail is not Persian.

We owe to Zarncke also the publication of the so-called *Marienlob* (*Praise of Mary*) that follows immediately upon the description of the temple of the Grail. These forty-two strophes are to be found only in one particular group of manuscripts. If they are the interpolation of a scribe, as seems probable, they are presumably not older than the fourteenth century. One can characterize them as a mannered exaggeration of the previous description.

The poet expresses the wish to build a temple to Mary. This was to be "a mile in diameter and correspondingly high; the temple of the Grail would occupy in relation to it only the space of an annexed choir, five hundred of which were to surround Mary's temple. Obviously the author imagines his church as a rotunda like the temple of the Grail. The interior was to be provided with an abundance of sculptures representing the foretelling of Mary and manifold symbolical allusions to her, as well as to the passion of her son . . . hospitals and monasteries were to be founded in conjunction with the temple and administered by an archbishop; ten choirs were to be placed one over the other, and provision was to be made for choral and church music."

If the mile is reckoned according to modern standards as 1609.3 meters the diameter of this circular church would be about twelve times the length of Cologne Cathedral. Correspondingly, the structure would have been twelve times as high as Cologne Cathedral, that is 522 meters. (Towers are very prudently not mentioned; using Cologne as the scale again, a main tower would have had to be 1,920 meters high. The Empire State Building in New York is only 330 meters.)

Whether architectural fantasies of a later date are related to these two from the *Younger Titurel* is not known.

Chaucer's poem, the *House of Fame*, can be assigned with considerable certainty to the year 1381[80] and is therefore more than a century younger than Albrecht's epic. The description of the temple of Venus is only fourteen lines long. It is approximately as follows: "As I slept it seemed to me that I was in a temple of glass. In it there were many images of gold standing in sundry stages and rich tabernacles with pinnacles of precious stone and many strange pictures of old work . . . here was portrayed the figure of Venus naked, floating on the sea." We have no ground for assuming that Chaucer knew Albrecht's poem, which was not translated into English;[81] on the contrary, it is highly probable that he never read the German epics. With the *Letter of Prester John* he was perhaps acquainted; the *Capella vitrea*, however, could hardly be the forerunner of the temple of Venus.

The mountain of the Grail was also identified with the Venusberg in the late Middle Ages. This seems to be first documented for the year 1410.[82] But, even if Chaucer's "Venusberg" were connected with the temple of Venus near Pozzuoli (in the vicinity of the Cumaean sybil and the grave of Vergil, the old magician) that would still be no proof of any relationship to Albrecht's temple of the Grail, which had an entirely Christian significance.

The last mediaeval architectural fantasy to be mentioned here is Lydgate's *Temple of Glass*. Schick, the editor of the text, gives a summary of the relevant part in modern English.[83] It runs approximately as follows: "Restless for a long while, I finally fell into a deep sleep in which I was carried in spirit to a temple of glass far in the wilderness on a rugged hill, frozen like ice. As I drew near it seemed to me that the temple shone clear as a crystal in the sun; the light dazzled me so that I could perceive nothing, until finally some dark clouds moved before the face of the sun and I could see about me. This place was circular, round in shape. After I had sought for a long time I found an opening and quickly entered. I turned my eyes to every side and I saw pictures of various lovers painted on the wall. Some sat, some

80 The most recent edition of Chaucer is that by F. N. Robinson, *The Complete Works of Geoffrey Chaucer*, London, 1933.

81 For the English poem *Sir Perceval* of about 1350 cf. Golther, *op.cit.*, p. 118. It does not contain a temple of the Grail.

82 Golther, *Parzival und der Gral . . .* , p. 252.

83 Joseph Schick, *Lydgate's Temple of Glass*, London, 1891 (Early English Text Society, Extra Series, No. LX), p. 1.

stood, many knelt with papers in their hands containing complaints intended to be brought before Venus. First I saw Dido of Carthage. . . ."

The poem is a learned enumeration of famous pairs of lovers. This subject is, to be sure, not monkish, but the monk Lydgate had so little of Tannhäuser's temperament that the reading of his poem leaves our morals unendangered. The vision of the temple of Venus is obviously influenced by Chaucer with whom Lydgate, in his youth, was personally acquainted. Whether there is any connection with Albrecht's temple of the Grail is hard to say, since we do not know whether Lydgate was able to read that epic. One can, of course, assume that someone told him about the temple of the Grail. The poem itself reveals surprising parallels: the circular form, the blinding radiance, the location in a wilderness on top of a hill like ice, the representation of tales on all the walls. But these representations, which in the case of the temple of the Grail are presumably on the exterior, are here on the interior walls. That their subject matter is different would not, of course, militate against a borrowing of the idea in general.

More important than the question of possible borrowing is the problem of how far this temple of glass can be called Gothic. It is tempting to imagine a stone church of central type, the window surfaces of which so predominate over the piers that the expression "temple of glass" appears justified. In that case all the pairs of lovers should be regarded as works of glass painting. But Lydgate says that he saw the paintings on the walls and we have no right to assume that by walls he means the windows, however much a modern historian of art might incline to such a mode of expression.

Again the natural question is: if these two imagined architectures are not Gothic, what then are they? And the answer is equally natural: they are temples of Venus, therefore they are Renaissance. This answer would be, from the point of view of architectural history, entirely wrong. Chaucer's poem of 1381, Lydgate's of about 1410 were conceived before Brunelleschi's appearance on the scene; in the structural members of their architecture they are certainly entirely free of any hint of classical forms, of columns with an entablature and classical gables, and so on. But perhaps it may be thought by some that this is not decisive, that it is a matter of the spirit of the whole, and that a temple of Venus must be Renaissance even though it has individual features of the Gothic and not the classical style. In this case the temple of Venus with its talking statue of the goddess in the city of Chrysa, as it appears in Heinrich von Neustadt's poem, would be Renaissance.

The date of this work was indicated vaguely by Lichtenberg (page 117) as the second half of the thirteenth century. Those who can discern at that time a return to the classical in sculpture also, may use this to their advantage, but Heinrich von Neustadt and Lydgate knew nothing of these questions and would have been astounded and helpless had anyone asked them whether they imagined the details of the temple of Venus to have been more like the Parthenon or Cologne Cathedral.[83a]

The *Hypnerotomachia* of Francesco Colonna from the year 1467 must be considered as a continuation of this series of architectural fantasies and as a transition to the spirit of the Renaissance.[84] Polifilo comes first to an enormous monument with a square basement and stepped pyramids, crowned by an obelisk. Splendidly furnished inside, it is unfortunately inhabited by a dragon, so that the hero flees, blundering into a labyrinth from which he is rescued by prayer. Across a meadow and a bridge, he comes to a spring-house with a domed chamber on eight columns where he bathes with nymphs. After crossing a courtyard the nymphs lead him to the palace of Venus, who offers him hospitality. He strolls through gardens—one is of glass, the other of silk, and so on. Finally his beloved, Polia, appears in the distance and with her he reaches a circular temple crowned by a dome with a lantern. Later he discovers the ruins of a temple where the unhappy lovers of previous ages are buried. After crossing to Cythera, Polifilo visits yet another magnificent garden, which is laid out according to a circular plan. Even this cursory summary of the contents gives an indication of how much has been borrowed from older models, but also how many forms of Renaissance architecture have been employed as the dominating features of a huge castle and park arrangement. The whole conception has been transformed from Gothic to Renaissance.

Chaucer mentioned one single structural member of Gothic, the tabernacle. To be sure, tabernacles need not always be in the Gothic style, but it is improbable that the poet would have imagined classical forms for this feature. Lydgate likewise would hardly have thought of the Ionic columns of classical antiquity, even had he read in his

[83a] There was certainly a continuation of antique traditions; see Richard Hamann-MacLean, *Antikenstudium in der Kunst des Mittelalters, Marburger Jahrbuch für kunstwissenschaft*, xv, Marburg, Lahn, 1949, p. 157, but whether the temples of Venus in the poems were meant to be Ionic or Gothic is another question.

[84] Otto Stein, *Die Architecturtheoretiker der italienischen Renaissance*, p. 71. Francesco Colonna (1433-1527) was a Dominican. His epic was not published until 1499. The beloved, Polia, "grey old age," signifies antiquity.

Vitruvius that temples of Venus were to be built in the Ionic style. Is then a "Gothic temple of Venus" a *contradictio in adjecto*? Christianity banned the cult of the goddess Aphrodite-Venus and banished her to the world of myth and fairy tale, but she did not die, at least not with respect to what she had formerly symbolized. Venus and Cupid are as old as humanity inasmuch as they signify love. Venus wears the girdle of charm; the desire for adornment as the symbol of the heightened worth of its wearer or possessor is also just as old as the human race. The series of architectural fantasies from the *Pèlerinage de Charlemagne* to the *Temple of Glass* is for the Gothic age the literary expression of the demand for the highest attainable splendor to distinguish persons of highest degree.

Earlier than Gothic, that is, between the passage in the *Apocalypse* (Rev. 4:2-6) and the *Pèlerinage de Charlemagne*, there are intermediate links to be found in Byzantine literature. They have been discussed in an article by M. Schlauch.[85] She has not adhered to the chronology of these Byzantine romances, almost all of which have been dated approximately by Krumbacher. The story of *Basilios Digenis Akritas* is perhaps the oldest in this series; it takes place in the tenth century, which is the only reason for attributing its composition to the eleventh.[86] Here marble, gold, jewels, and sculptures are mentioned in the descriptions. In *Charistes and Drosilla* from the second half of the twelfth century there are statues that stand in a circle about a spring. From the same period comes *Hysmine and Hysminias* where four statues representing virtues occur. These modest things, however, are far surpassed by the poet of *Kallimachos and Chrysorrhea* from the thirteenth century. The castle of the dragon is completely of gold and jewels, more brilliant than the sun; in it there is a bathroom with flowers of gold, with red lychnite stone, and pearls, while another room has a golden ceiling showing the course of the planets. The dragon approaches with lightning, thunder, and storms, so that one is reminded of Chosroes. The epic *Belthandros and Chrysatra* is also attributed to the thirteenth century. Belthandros, cast out by his father, comes "to a splendid castle built of sardonyx, from which gushes forth a stream of fire (that he had previously seen from a distance); golden heads of lions and dragons look down from the battlements. On a diamond door he discovers an inscription that tells him that he is standing

85 Margaret Schlauch, "The Palace of Hugon de Constantinople," *Speculum*, VII, 1932, p. 500.

86 Karl Krumbacher, *Geschichte der byzantinischen Literatur*, Munich, 1897, p. 827.

before the *Erotokastron*."[87] In the interior of this "castle of love" he finds a griffin and a peacock from whose eyes and tail the stream of fire emerges. He is then conducted to the king of love, and the extravagant use of precious materials continues. In *Lybistros and Rhodamne* from the fourteenth century there is a castle of silver, gleaming like the sun; in it are pictures of the months, the virtues, and love, and in addition sounding figures above the gate. The latest Byzantine romance of this sort, *Sophrosyne*, by Meliteniotes, which has the most parallels to the *Pèlerinage de Charlemagne*, is presumed to be from the fourteenth century, thus long after the latter romance and dependent on French poetry. Here there is a rotating hall, and other similar features.

If one attempts to arrange these later Greek fantasies in a chronological series which includes the French and German epics, one must assume reciprocal influences, the study of which must be left to the philologists.

As a background to all these fantastic structures in which the expenditure of gold, silver, jewels, and sculptures costs nothing, there was an actual palace, that imperial palace in Byzantium of which we have already spoken above.[88] It consisted of a group of buildings stretching out between the Hagia Sophia and SS. Sergios and Bacchos toward the sea and to the east. Probably remains from the time of Constantine were preserved for centuries and built into later structures. Probably Justinian had already changed older portions and added new ones; it is certain that he renewed the interior furnishings in the fashion of his time. Everything that originated in that period was ostentatious, but even this seems to have been surpassed by the new buildings of the Emperor Theophilos (829-842). In the period after Charlemagne—so that the *hero* of the *Pèlerinage de Charlemagne* could not have known these additions—Theophilos built the *Trikonchos* between the older buildings (Justinian's ?) of the *Daphne* and the *Chrysotriclinium*; the *poet* of the *Pèlerinage de Charlemagne*, however, could have heard of them. This *Trikonchos* was a throne room with walls encrusted with colored marbles, columns of Phrygian marble, and a golden ceiling. In one of the side rooms, the "triclinium of the pearl," the walls were adorned with mosaics, representing, however, only animals since this was still the age of the iconoclasts. In another apartment there were gold mosaics depicting figures picking fruit. In the

87 *Ibid.*, p. 327.

88 Gerard Brett, W. J. Macauley, Robert B. K. Stevenson, *The Great Palace of the Byzantine Emperors*, London, 1947.

hall called Magnaura, where the solemn receptions took place, a plane tree of gold shaded the throne; on its branches sat golden birds. At the foot of the throne crouched lions, at its sides were griffins. The birds sang, the lions arose, waved their tails, and roared.[89]

One can scarcely doubt that many details of the mediaeval epics, certainly also the golden trees and singing birds in the epic about the Grail, go back to these historical realities in Byzantium. But what should be concluded from this? Diehl traces the splendor in the palace of Theophilos to prototypes in Baghdad, to buildings of Harun-al-Rashid (766-809), a contemporary of Charlemagne.[90] Recently Bargebuhr translated a Hebrew poem of *Jbn Gabirol*, which he interprets as a poetic description of the Alhambra in Granada. He believes, therefore, that the Alhambra has to be dated in the eleventh century A.D. Certainly the poem belongs in the realm of the architectural fantasies of mediaeval times. Although the theory of Bargebuhr is very important in itself, it does not solve the problem at hand.[91] We have already asked whether the Grail were Gothic. Shall we now ask whether it is Byzantine or perhaps Arabic? Were the knights of Monsalvasch, who trained themselves in arms in order to fight the Mohammedans, perhaps stimulated by Mohammedan fantasies that go back to Harun-al-Rashid's architects, or to those of the Alhambra?

It becomes ever clearer that we must separate the poetical embellishments that are conceived in the imagination from the style of the architectural forms. For even though the embellishments remain constant, the resulting effect takes its character from the particular poetical style in terms of which the fantasy is conceived. King Solomon had made for himself a throne of gold and ivory with lions at the sides and on the six steps six lions on either end (I Kings 18:12). But the form of the throne was undoubtedly one that was peculiar to his time and his land. Similarly, all these splendors existed both in Islamic forms and in quite different Byzantine forms. From the remains of these cultures and their buildings we can picture to ourselves the character of the palaces in Baghdad and Byzantium, vaguely, but nevertheless as Arabic on the one hand and Byzantine on the other. The ideas of splendor qua ideas, on the contrary, are passed down through the centuries from people to people and from potentate to potentate. They, too, are trans-

89 Charles Diehl, *Manuel de l'art byzantin*, Paris, 1925, I, p. 367.

90 *Ibid.*, p. 369.

91 Frederick P. Bargebuhr, "The Alhambra Palace of the Eleventh Century," *Journal of the Warburg and Courtauld Institutes*, XIX, 1956, nos. 3 and 4. Jbn Gabirol lived c. 1021-1058 (or c. 1070).

formed, and above all the spiritual background is transformed. The latter, or rather its character, can be gathered from the Arabic as well as from the Byzantine stylistic forms; we understand what is apparently the same thought—the lions, golden trees, etc.—differently each time. And so the iconoclastic philosophy of life does not belong to the temple of the Grail, far less the Mohammedan. How is it with that of the Apocalypse?

Are we not acquainted with corresponding imaginary architectural splendors from the time even before the *Apocalypse*, aside from the splendor of Solomon? M. Schlauch has called attention to Ovid's *Metamorphoses*.[92] Phaëton seeks out his father to receive confirmation of the fact that he really is the son of this god. He finds him in a palace, the description of which sounds like a prelude to everything that we have come to know about fairy-tale mansions: a columnar structure illuminated by a *pyropus* or tinsel, the ceiling of ivory, the doors shining with silver. *Materiam superabat opus*, the execution surpassed the material, for here Mulciber (Vulcan) had depicted the ocean with Triton and Proteus, Aegaeon with the whale, Doris and her daughters, human beings and cities, forests and wild beasts, rivers, nymphs, and satyrs. Above this was an image of heaven, the zodiac, six signs on the right and six on the left. Phoebus sits on a throne of shining emeralds. Here stood to the right and left day, month, and year, Chronos and the Horae at equal intervals, and here stood the four seasons.

The *Metamorphoses* had already been composed when Ovid was obliged to go into exile in the year 9 B.C. Up to the time of his death (A.D. 17), he remained in contact with his Roman friends by letter; his poetic works continued to be favorites of the reading public. Nero (37-64) was certainly acquainted with them since he was interested in poetry, whatever the reason may have been. One may assume without further argument that he was especially familiar with Ovid's account of Phaëton, for we know that he had himself represented as the sun god in the portico before his palace. When this idea seized him, he changed his style of hairdressing so that the hair stood up like a wreath of flames around his forehead.[93] His palace on the eastern slope of the Palatine Hill had several dining apartments with flat ceilings of ivory, and perfumes were sprinkled about through a system of pipes. One of these dining rooms, the most important, was circular, completely

92 Ovid's *Metamorphoses* II, I.

93 H. P. L'Orange, *Apotheosis in Ancient Portraiture*, Instituttet for Sammenignende Kulturforskning, Serie B: Skrifter XLIV, Oslo, 1947, pp. 57ff.

gilded, and turned "day and night like the world." In this rotating hall (or did only the ceiling or dome revolve?) Nero had himself venerated as the sun emperor. The account of Suetonius cannot be doubted, although he could not well have seen the hall himself, if it is correct that he was born in 69, when Vespasian became emperor. The latter, for political reasons, soon had Nero's palace, which had been erected at an unheard-of cost, torn down. What is still standing today, or what has been incompletely excavated, no longer contains anything that could be considered remains of that rotating hall.

The information that the rotation of the golden hall was accomplished by horses that pulled a horse capstan beneath the floor is only indirect; Ado reports that for the throne or the throne room of Chosroes.[94] Saxl saw in the throne of Chosroes a representation of the universe; just as God is enthroned in the universe, so the Oriental despot is in his small copy of it. He is himself God's image and representative and he demands a divinity's worship from his subjects. In recent times L'Orange published a study on the *casa aurea*, assembling everything that written tradition can contribute to an understanding of the matter.[95] According to this work, the avenue of access, the portico with the statue of the ruler as god, and all the furnishings of the official apartments were "not a unique phenomenon, the caprice of imperial delusions, but rather the continuation of a tradition or the intimation of the existence of one." He looks for antecedents in Hellenistic-Oriental courts and goes back to similar arrangements in the palace of Nebuchadnezzar (604-561 B.C.) in Babylon, where a forecourt was connected with the throne room in such a way that one could see the king from outside and file past according to a set ritual. Something of the same sort is said to have existed in Persepolis. The *domus aurea* is "more than an emperor's residence: it is the dwelling of the sun-emperor and the expression of a definite monarchical-theocratic idea." Alexander the Great also learned the principle of self-deification in the Orient. Its political meaning is very clear: it is a question of the authority of a usurper, conqueror, tyrant, which does not seem to be sufficiently ensured by force and terror but needs accreditation by the grace of God. The principle of the divine right of kings has been in all ages a misuse of religion in favor of political autocracy. Prester

94 Ado is quoted exactly in Lehmann's essay. With regard to the horses cf. the *Passionale* (second half of the thirteenth century), where a "heaven" in the form of a tower is shaken by a horse-drawn machine that at the same time produces thunder. Lichtenberg, *op.cit.*, p. 57.

95 H. P. L'Orange, *Domus Aurea, der Sonnenpalast*, Serta Eitremiana, Oslo, 1942, p. 68.

John said explicitly that he did not let himself be worshiped like God, and this statement was clearly directed against the Byzantine emperors.

This survival and constant reemergence of the theocratic principle is connected with a series of representations of heaven, which Lehmann has reconstructed as decorations of flat and vaulted ceilings.[96] However, these are not mere decorations but have a profound meaning of their own. Moreover, the religious idea of heaven was not only represented on ceilings as "the universe" but the attempt was also made to give it visible reality by means of whole structures. In this connection we should not only think of the significance of the Heavenly Jerusalem for the Early Christian basilica. We know that the Gothic cathedrals sought through the iconographic programs of their sculptures and stained glass to illustrate that fundamental idea of the universe more and more vividly, comprehensively, and systematically. The church was to be the dwelling place and throne of God, not only as a spiritual and ecclesiastical institution for salvation but also as a tangible edifice of stone, and therefore the image of the universe.

Schlauch has called attention to an Irish poem, composed before the twelfth century, perhaps before the *Pèlerinage de Charlemagne*; it belongs to the general cycle of architectural fantasies and may, as the philologist implies, be related to prehistoric Nordic conceptions, which would then take us back to the time before Ovid, perhaps even to the period of Nebuchadnezzar.[97] But casting our net as widely as possible, in order to ascertain everywhere the constant fundamental idea of all architectural fantasies, leads to the contrary effect. For the fundamental idea underwent transformations, and with the recognition of this fact we arrive at what is probably the correct appraisal.

The experts in this matter can discover all the more subtle transformations, but in general it is clear that Oriental autocracy with its identification of emperor and God is opposed to the Christian idea that placed the pope between the two. Neither emperor nor pope are deified human beings; they only wish to be representatives of the god-man. Nero appeared as the incarnation of the sun god, and for the Middle Ages Jesus was the unique incarnation of the absolute God, the *logos* become flesh. Conceptually, also, the symbol of the universe had become in the Middle Ages different from what it was in Oriental and Roman antiquity, and by a fluid process the sociological expression of these changed ideas appeared among clergy and laity side

96 Karl Lehmann, "The Dome of Heaven," *Art Bulletin*, XXVII, 1945, p. 1.

97 Margaret Schlauch, *op.cit.*, p. 510.

by side with the attempts to clarify and stabilize the relationship of emperor and pope.

There were two ways to God: the asceticism of monasticism and the conventionalized sinfulness of chivalry. Monasticism emulated Jesus in humility and poverty, chivalry sublimated its robust love of battle by the fiction that it had to defend Christianity against Islamic heathendom. Islam was exactly as convinced that it had discovered the truth; it likewise developed a heroic caste of warriors that wanted to conquer the world for its ideas; and the world of these heroes was on both sides equally secular in spite of all the religious embroidery. One must not assume, of course, that all monks were pure saints, but monasticism chose the tendency toward a saintly way of life as its ruling principle far more consistently than chivalry, which remained worldly in the sense that it succumbed to the delusions of earthly power. All knights and soldiers desire to be admired and feared, like Chosroes, who seems to us childish but who simply acted in the same way as all who have played the role of hero. With this in mind one can understand without the need for further argument that there are two trends in mediaeval architecture, the ascetic and the secular-chivalric. The cathedrals of the knightly bishops are imbued with that worldliness. St. Bernard of Clairvaux would have declared the fantasy of the temple of the Grail to be a work of the devil. Everything that is more characteristic of a pasha than a monk in Albrecht's temple, everything regal, luxurious, or extravagant stems from the worldliness of courtly knighthood that cannot only worship God as though he were the supreme feudal lord standing one stage higher than the pope, the emperors of the West, and the caliphs of the East.

The knight of the Gothic age is an adventurer. The word adventure (*Abenteuer, aventiure*) had at that time the same force as the classical *moira*, only the Greek confronted *moira*, this fate decreed by the gods, in an essentially more fatalistic spirit than the Gothic knight his *aventiure*. The latter seeks out adventure; he is more active, more voluntaristic. Parsifal is the representative of this type. Ehrismann says of Wolfram's epic: "Thus is revealed the moral biography of the hero in his deeds and convictions from unsophisticated, natural childhood to maturity of mind and spirit; and the fundamental idea of this inner development is that of the soul struggling from error to clarity, from the unconscious to the conscious, from the nature to intellect." This can be applied to chivalric culture as a whole: its ideal way is that through amorous adventure (not only Tristan), through battle, dangers, and sin to redemption. This way leads into the distances, to the unknown. Like a magnet the Grail attracts the noble man who is given the grace to follow. To a high degree this is a romantic attitude toward life, and it is stylistically fitting that a nursery wonderland should appear as the background of these religious ideas, transforming the distant Orient into a paradise. In the *Younger Titurel*, as we have seen, the entire temple of the Grail was transported by angels to the place where it really seems to belong, to India.

Only on the basis of these considerations is it possible to answer the question of the architectural style of the temple of the Grail. Its Gothic members, diagonal ribs, keystones, and the like, no one will fail to appreciate; they are definite borrowings from the buildings that Albrecht saw rising during his lifetime. Nevertheless, they by no means make the whole structure Gothic. But there is just as little justification for speaking of a transitional style; the temple of the Grail is not a Romanesque church with a few Gothic features. It is a cathedral from a fairy tale, overwhelmed by all the wealth of this world; its style is Oriental, though not as the Orient was then or ever, but as the poet fancied and desired it in his romanticism. From this point of view the fantasy of the temple of the Grail can be called *Gothic*. It reveals what lay behind the fantasticality of actual Gothic. Gothic is steeped in the Christian faith but it is at the same time a great adventure. This is what we can so easily overlook in the cathedrals of stone and what Albrecht's temple teaches us.

We must add that not every adventure is Gothic. What then is the "Gothic" element in the "Gothic" epics? Perhaps we are seeking for something that never existed. The mediaeval poets had no intention of describing *Gothic* architectural fantasies; in their fantastic romances they wanted no buildings that could be seen everywhere every day; it had to be something quite exotic, something unheard of, thus, something *un-Gothic*. Or could it be that they were unable to escape from the spirit of their age, so that against their will and subconsciously even their most un-Gothic architectural imaginings became in essence Gothic? If we want to assume this we are obliged to define that Gothic element that remains Gothic even when it shows no or only few characteristics of regular Gothic. Is there any point in attempting to discover, so to speak, Gothic "Un-Gothic"?

This lengthy investigation of architectural fantasies of the Middle Ages would have been unavoidable even though the results were negative. But we may anticipate at this point and say that Albrecht's temple of the Grail *is* Gothic, and not only because it has ribs. The problem cannot be settled from the standpoint of poetry and architecture alone, nor from that of the Apocalypse or Bible alone, nor from that of chivalric culture alone. It is only soluble when one surveys the entire range of "Gothic" culture and seeks to discover what of it is "Gothic."[98]

10. The Culture of the Gothic Age

In the age of Gothic itself no one spoke of "Gothic culture." There surely existed at that time, however, what we today understand by the term. It is only doubtful if we are justified in applying to scholasticism and to whatever else is usually cited in this connection the adjective Gothic in the same sense that it is applied to architecture.

First of all, the fact is that in our study of the sources that give an account of Gothic architecture we have encountered a considerable number of other cultural fields without intentionally seeking them out: for example, the belief in miracles, the cults of relics, the cult of the carts, and the like. If we consider these somewhat more thoroughly and comprehensively we may perhaps by their aid determine whether there was a real connection between such phenomena of culture and Gothic.

The emphasis on these cultural areas is a heritage from those nineteenth century historians of art who prefaced their studies of monuments by an introduction dealing with cultural history, thus providing

[98] Postscript on bibliography: See further as regards the architectural phantasies: Julius von Schlosser, *Quellenbuch zur Kunstgeschichte des abendländischen Mittelalters*, Vienna, 1896, pp. 342ff. In the letter of Prester John it is written that the palace corresponds to that which the Apostle Thomas designed for King Gundoforus in India. Schlosser quotes (p. 343) the apocryphal text according to Odericus Vitalis, *Historia ecclesiastica*. The description purports to be connected with plans from late antiquity which derived from illustrations of Homeric palaces. For Prester John, cf. Charles E. Nowell, "The Historical Prester John," *Speculum*, XXVIII, 1953, p. 435, which is a fusion of the various older theories. Further, Elain Sanceau, *The Land of Prester John*, New York, 1944, which describes the effect upon the Portuguese navigators of the fifteenth century. For the discussion on page 203 above see Elena Eberwein, *Zur Deutung mittelalterlicher Existenz*, Bonn, 1933 (Kölner Romanistische Arbeiten, ed. by Leo Spitzer), where the concept of *Aventure* is discussed. See also Urban T. Holmes, *A New Interpretation of Chrêtien's Conte Del Graal*, Studies in the Romance Languages and Literature, 8, Chapel Hill, 1948; and Sister Amelia Klenke, O.P., *Liturgy and Allegory in Chrêtien's Parceval*, *ibid.*, 14, 1951. Although these interpretations are fundamentally different from the older ones, they contribute nothing to the problem of this chapter. All these references, from Schlosser through Klenke, I owe to Mrs. J. Weitzmann-Fiedler.

a lively, colorful, historical background so that the cathedrals do not stand in a vacuum. Many scholars consider this scene painting futile, however much it may be valued for its own sake, for to them the cathedrals remain isolated nevertheless and they do not grant that this method may reveal the sought-for clues. They demand, on the contrary, that the architecture should be understood on the basis of its own characteristics alone. Up to now the whole problem has been in dispute, but it cannot be simply ignored here because it is still unresolved and difficult.

The previous chapter on the poetry of the Gothic age was a contribution to this study. The result was largely negative, that is, it seemed as though many of the architectural fantasies were not intended to be Gothic at all, while others had Gothic details that gave the impression, however, of merely external characteristics. The real problem, whether the epics in their subject matter and its treatment (even when they utilize themes of antiquity) are Gothic according to their deeper meaning and their form, was barely suggested. In the following survey of a selected number of cultural areas or cultural phenomena, much must also be answered in the negative simply as a clarification of the problem before it becomes possible to approach a positive solution. The reader, therefore, should not allow himself to be confused by the many negatives.

For modern readers the belief in miracles in Suger's account of St.-Denis appears hard to understand. Since the existence of a natural science that has discovered natural laws, it seems illogical still to believe in miracles. One may argue that it is for God a more fitting state of affairs to make laws once and for all, rather than to abrogate them from time to time in favor of some pious human being or other. The old conception, however, was exactly the opposite, namely, that it is more fitting for God to rescind as well as promulgate laws in perfect freedom; this view was held to be a matter of course during the entire period of Gothic. But it did not originate with Gothic. Belief in miracles is as old as the human race. All mythologies and religions testify to it, and for the Christians who knew the Old Testament and regarded it as the necessary preface to the New the history of miracles began at least with those of Moses and his deeds in Egypt, if not in fact with the miracle of creation itself. The urge toward the miraculous did not die out even after the discoveries of Galileo, Copernicus, and Newton. People today with an insufficient scientific education explain in the most superficial way everything that seems to them "miraculous" by talk of "rays" that are as yet unknown but soon to be discovered. This is the modern, self-nullifying, belief in miracles. The ancient Greeks believed in oracles and mysteries against the background—or as the background—of their sculpturally determined Olympian divinities. The Catholic church still adheres firmly to faith in miracles.[1] The New Testament is a series of miracles, and faith in them is a consequence of Christian spiritualism. Suger's uncritical belief in miracles is specifically Christian in that its intention is purely spiritual; but it is likewise completely personal: God continually intervenes in Suger's personal affairs. The latter seems to have been inclined to consider the fulfillment of any wish a miracle. Correspondingly, the Middle Ages regarded the nonfulfillment of wishes or even undeserved misfortune as an intervention of the devil. Sometimes, as a matter of fact, the case was not entirely clear. So Gervase, for example, was uncertain whether Master William's fall should be attributed to divine retribution or the malice of the devil. Suger could actually have explained the pushing crowd around the relics as devil's work—or equally well as God's hint that the church should be rebuilt. He wisely avoided the question or, more probably, it never even occurred to him. Whether we like to grant it or not, even what we can explain today by physical, chemical, or biological means can still have and retain for us the character of a miracle.

If we try to understand the mediaeval Christian belief in miracles—"to become as little children"—then only does the question that concerns us here arise. Is Suger's faith in miracles Gothic, that is, just as Gothic, or as Early Gothic as the St.-Denis which his architect had just built? With this question we have defined the type of formulation that we shall encounter in ever new variations as we proceed. In this case the answer is certainly no. That Suger found the suitable quarry and the necessary twelve trees may be called a miracle, but it was by no means a "Gothic" miracle, even though a Gothic church rose from the stones and the wooden beams. If the architect had erected a Romanesque structure the miracle would have been just as miraculous, though also not at all "Romanesque." Faith in miracles is therefore *still* alive in Gothic but it is not specifically Gothic.

There is, however, a body of texts that can be cited as testimony of the association of miracles with the erection of Gothic churches. These concern the so-called "cult of the carts," that is, the dragging

[1] Cf., for example, the essay by Schanz in Wetzer und Welte, *Kirchenlexikon*, Freiburg i.B., XII, 1901, cols. 1811ff., or that by Driscoll in the *Catholic Encyclopedia*, New York, X, 1911, p. 338. Further, *Encyclopedia Britannica*, 1911, XVII, p. 570.

of building materials by human beings as an expression of devotion and, at the same time, as a penance, in short, as "service of God."

These texts agree in stating that the cult of the carts originated in Chartres in 1144. If one takes Suger's word for it, then St.-Denis had the priority—this point has already been discussed in connection with the interpretation of Suger's text.[2] It may be that in St.-Denis "nobles and common folk alike" simply lent a hand with the hauling of the *columnae* quite spontaneously, in order to assist in the passing of a difficult spot in the rough road and with no thought of whether the columns were intended for a church or not, or, on the contrary, because they knew that the rebuilding of St.-Denis was involved; but in either case this assistance could have been rendered without its being explicitly accompanied by the idea of personal penance. The beginning of the cult of the carts as a conscious "cult" may have come about quite independently only later in Chartres.

Abbot Haymo gave the most detailed account of these occurrences.[3] He described how more than one thousand men and women of all ages and conditions harnessed themselves to each heavily laden cart and silently pulled it over the rough terrain. During the pauses for rest they listened to sermons, lamented their sins, and praised God. Upon arrival at the old cathedral of Chartres, at that time still standing, they bared the upper parts of their bodies, threw themselves on the ground, wept, and begged the priests to scourge them, which the latter—though with tears—did. The crowd prayed for the healing of the sick, and the hoped-for miracles occurred. From Chartres this new custom was brought to Normandy, and Haymo says that it spread over the whole countryside, wherever churches were consecrated to the mother of God. This again points to Chartres as the place of origin, since Mary was especially venerated in that cathedral.

The letter of Hugo, Bishop of Rouen, to Archbishop Thierry of Amiens,[4] also written in 1145, says even more definitely that the pilgrims who went to Chartres for the sake of the relic of the Virgin Mary brought back the cult of the carts from there to Rouen, and that it then spread over Normandy. One might only participate in the rites

[2] See Panofsky, *Abbot Suger . . .*, p. 214; there was something similar earlier in Montecassino, in 1066.

[3] Letter of Haymo, Abbot of St.-Pierre-sur-Dives, to the monks of Tutbury, England, written in 1148, published by Delisle, *Bibliothèque des Chartes*, XXI, pp. 120ff.

[4] Migne, *Patr. Lat.* CXCII, col. 1133. Also in Porter, II, p. 156 (Latin and English). Further, in Bouquet, XIV, p. 319. A partial German translation in Dehio's *Kirchl. Baukunst . . .*, II, p. 23.

of the cult after one had confessed, experienced remorse, and forgiven one's enemies; *humilitas* and *obedientia* were demanded according to the concept of Christian discipline, that is, the mortification of the individual will. Thereupon many miracles ensued, especially cures of the sick. But let it be said: the Gothic churches were not the miracle.

Kingsley Porter has already pointed out that these occurrences were exclusively concerned with the salvation of the penitents and had absolutely nothing to do with the architectural style. What mattered was the degree of remorse, the difficulty of the work, not the Gothic form of the stones that were dragged. Porter assumed that this wave of religious enthusiasm scarcely lasted beyond the period about 1145. He very properly shows that a third account, which is usually cited by everyone and which mentions Gothic, that of Robert du Mont,[5] does refer to 1144 and to Chartres but was not written until 1184, and that Robert expresses himself like someone who can only rely on documents (that is, the letter of Bishop Hugo of Rouen) and not on personal experience. This impression is strengthened by what we read about the enthusiasm that broke out, when in 1194, after the destruction by fire of the old cathedral of Chartres, the relic of Mary's veil, which had been given up for lost, was rediscovered. The relic saved itself, as it were, and in addition the lives of several monks, who were found in the crypt along with it, after having been buried alive for a number of days. This enthusiasm, as is well known, brought about the construction of the present cathedral, but in this case the cult of the cart could not be revived.[6]

Nevertheless, Porter has limited the period of the cult too severely. We still have an account of 1164 about some building operations in Boulogne-sur-mer, where the work concerned only a churchyard wall but where we hear of the same participation by the laity. In this instance the situation deviated from the pattern in that the abbot and his workmen were threatened by an ill-disposed neighbor; since the workmen allowed themselves to be intimidated, the abbot caused monks and laymen to harness themselves together to the carts, even monks together with women.[7] Finally there is one more account con-

5 Robertus de Monte, *Epistola ad abbatem Beccensum anno 1182*, Migne, *Patr. Lat.*, CCII, col. 1507.

6 Marcel Joseph Bulteau, *Monographie de la Cathédrale de Chartres*, Chartres, 1887, I, p. 100. Here the account of Guillaume le Breton (1165-1226), "Histoires des gestes de Philippe Auguste" (for the year 1194), and the poem "Miracles" are to be found. (The events differ somewhat from the earlier ones.)

7 On this occasion he measured the stones with a yardstick; the passage can therefore be considered in connection with the problems of building-site geometry.

cerning Châlons-sur-Marne from about the year 1165.[8] Perhaps one may call the voluntary, completely unselfish intervention in St.-Denis around 1140 the prelude and the forced labor in Boulogne-sur-mer the dying reverberation, with the climax of the cult of the carts lying between them—geographically restricted to St.-Denis, Chartres, and Normandy. It would then have lasted hardly a generation. Porter, moreover, has yielded too much to the pressure of modern enlightenment when he accuses the monks, themselves enlightened, of exploiting the people's faith in miracles for the advantage of the churches.[9] The monks were surely not "enlightened" but firmly believed in miracles. Whether they were crafty is another question, which we can leave unanswered. It also contributes nothing to historical understanding when one explains these mass actions as hysterical psychoses;[9a] that can be left to the psychiatrists. As a historian of art one prefers to ask whether one can detect anything Gothic in them, and the answer to this question must be that the miraculous cures were not Gothic, and neither was the hysteria, if this diagnosis is correct, specifically Gothic in the same sense.

Let us proceed undismayed: Suger ascribed the miracles that made his church possible and furthered the work to the relics owned by his monastery. The belief in their healing effect brought the gifts by means of which he financed the construction. But the Christian cult of relics, itself a continuation of that of antiquity,[10] was then already a thousand years old; it is said to have begun in the second century when the remains of the martyred Bishop Polycarp were collected in Smyrna and people were convinced that possession of the relics assured community of mind and spirit with the deceased. In the beginning the church opposed this sort of cult, but in vain; it was obliged to recognize it. Cyril of Jerusalem (315-386) extended the cult also to objects that the martyrs had used or touched in life; according to his doctrine these also had received supernatural power. The cult of relics thus took its place as a link in the chain of concepts of the supernatural that, like the belief in miracles, are as old as man.[11] But can an Early Christian, a Carolingian, Romanesque, or Gothic

[8] Letter of Guido de Bazoches to his sister in Chateau-Porcion, cf. Wattenbach, *Neues Archiv der Geschichte für ältere deutsche Geschichtskunde*, 1891, pp. 75ff.

[9] Kingsley Porter, *op.cit.*, II, p. 154.

[9a] *ibid.*, p. 160.

[10] Friedrich Pfister, *Der Reliquienkult im Altertum*, *Religionsgeschichtliche Versuche und Vorarbeiten*, v, Giessen, 1909 and 1912.

[11] Ernst Lucius, *Die Anfänge des Heiligenkults in der christlichen Kirche*, Tübingen, 1904.

cult of relics be differentiated? In other words, can a stylistic history of the cult be written as it can be for architecture? Up to the present no one has remarked on such stylistic differences or even looked for them, and yet it would be a prerequisite for extending the concept of Gothic to this aspect of culture. The only thing that can at present be said with certainty is that the relics increased quantitatively. The collecting mania had even by the year 1071 assembled 683 relics in Eichstätt, and when the Reformation began, Wittenberg had 19,013, Halle actually 21,483. The Reformation abandoned this cult but Catholicism retained it; it is, however, hardly likely that anyone has succeeded in discovering in the Catholic cult of relics per se a trend toward Renaissance, Baroque, or later styles. Naturally the containers or other settings of the relics changed with the changing styles, but scarcely the spirit with which they were venerated.

This spirit is in part connected with that of symbolism. The relic, whether one member or the whole body of a saint, the instrument of his martyrdom, or the like, is always *pars pro toto*, that is, the representative of the saint himself as a whole personality, especially with respect to his religious existence, which because of his holy life had been close to God. In this sense the relic is a symbol of holiness.

But again it must be said that symbolism is older than Gothic. When Suger relates the double sets of twelve columns to the Apostles and prophets and calls Jesus the cornerstone, he is moving in completely traditional patterns of ecclesiastical phraseology stemming from the Bible, that itself goes back to a far older tradition. Everything that is truly mystical and genuinely occult, the ultimate secrets of religious experience, cannot be described; from the beginning of time man has substituted symbols for them. In all ages some may have erroneously taken the symbol, that is, what symbolizes, for the thing symbolized. This confusion can make a fetish of a relic, an idol of the image of Mary; it can, therefore, lead to iconoclasm, when the spirituality of the faithful is intensified in one direction only, or, on the other hand, it can become for skeptics an argument against faith in the very thing to be symbolized. But symbolism in its "legal" form remains indispensable for religious life. It therefore has a history, and again we ask: does it have a stylistic history?

To know the vocabulary, as it were, and the history of Christian symbolism is a requisite for the understanding of the iconography of Christian representational art; it is not sufficient to give the right name to a sculptured or painted figure or scene, but one must also know what the figure or scene really meant to the mediaeval Christian. But what is obvious for Gothic stained glass, panel paintings, and sculptures becomes questionable with regard to the churches, which also had their systematic symbolism. To be sure, it is convincing when St. Paul regards the virtuous man as a temple of God,[12] but it is no longer so in the same degree when a mediaeval theologian equates the mediaeval man with the individual building stone of the church. This comparison, however, is at least still intelligible: that is, as the stone is a member of the structure of the church, so the individual is a member of the Kingdom of God. But these ideas were elaborated. Durandus says:[13] "The binding material of the stones is the mortar, which by its composition of lime, sand, and water typifies Christian love. The seething lime is love, which unites with sand, that is, the earthly element, because true love never relaxes its care for the earthly concerns of the poor and needy. But so that love and good works may contribute to the durability of the wall, the water of the Holy Ghost must still be added."[14] Josef Sauer points out that Augustine had already called *caritas* the binding matter of the living stones (*lapides vivi*).[15] To modern readers this comparison seems mannered. However, if we abstain from all unfruitful criticism and ask whether the stones thereby achieve a Gothic style, we must answer in the negative. The entire method of these comparisons is mediaeval spirit and thus one is confronted by an infinite ambiguity. One example may stand in place of many: "The exterior roof received varying interpretations: now it represents concern for the heavenly, that is, the *vita contemplativa*; now it is the body of man, now the tabernacle of the Old Testament and the obscurity of the Holy Book; now, on the other hand, because it does not strive upward like the walls, in which the *vita contemplativa* is typified, it is, in contrast to them, also the *vita activa*, which leans more toward the earth than toward heaven."[16] Thus one and the same roof was for Hrabanus Maurus the *vita contemplativa* and for Hugo de St. Victor the *vita activa*. Obviously there is no value placed on consistency here. The essential is that for this conception

[12] Paul, Cor. 1: 3, 16: "Nescitis quia templum domini estis et spiritus Dei habitat in vobis?" and Cor. 2: 6, 16: "Vos estis templum divi dei."

[13] A translation of the first book of the *Rationale divinorum officiorum* of William Durandus de Mende was published by John Mason Neal and Benjamin Webb in their book, *The Symbolism of the Church Ornament*, for the Camden Society, 1842. A reprint appeared in London in 1906, proof that interest in this type of pious fancy was still alive.

[14] Quoted according to Joseph Sauer, *Symbolik des Kirchengebäudes* . . . Freiburg i.B., 1902, p. 114. Sauer cites Durandus 1, 1 and 10, according to the edition of 1509.

[15] *Ibid.*, note 2.

[16] *Ibid.*, p. 118.

every part of the church is seen as two: first, as what it *is* in the tangible foreground, so to speak, and second, as that which it ideally or religiously *means*. For the believer, that is, it always means a background, thus, more than it materially is, and it is not important to define precisely the specific background meaning once and for all, or rather to show clearly the path into that actually unfathomable background of all things. Symbolism is a directional arrow of spiritual thought, a signpost to the realm of the invisible and the eternal.

In painting and sculpture the symbolical meaning of the representations was usually already present from the beginning; in architecture, on the other hand, it was often read into the work afterward, for the architects would scarcely on their own account have set the number of columns at twelve so that they could signify the Apostles. Moreover, if the number had been larger, the very highly developed symbolism of numbers would have offered as many other interpretations as desired.[17] But even in these interpretations *post festum* the theorists of symbolism never paid any attention to stylistic differences. They interpret the stones, the mortar, the walls, the ceiling, the roof, the cornices and battlements, the portal, the windows, the screens, floors; but when, for example, the portal means Christ, because Christ is the way to the Father,[18] it is unquestionably entirely independent of whether the actual portal is Early Christian, Carolingian, Romanesque, or Gothic. One can adduce any number of such examples, all proving that the symbolists were never concerned with style. Never did they make a symbolical interpretation of Romanesque as Romanesque or Gothic as Gothic.

What is called the symbolism of the church edifice refers always to *concepts*. Sauer says: "A symbol is nothing but an image representing a thought or a fact that does not necessarily and immediately result from the concept of that image."[19] Art is also a symbol, but artistic symbolism has reference to *forms*. Art is—to use Sauer's words—an "image" representing a thought, but one which, in contrast to conceptual symbols, is directly intelligible from the form. Conceptual symbols can, or must be, learned. The form symbols of art can only be felt and must be understood intuitively, just as the expressions and gestures of one's fellow men are understood. The form symbolizes not so much the content itself as the idea on the background of this content. Gothic, correspondingly, does not so much symbolize the Apostles

[17] Sauer, *op.cit.*, p. 134.
[18] John 14:6; Sauer, *op.cit.*, p. 119.
[19] Sauer, *op.cit.*, p. 2.

as pillars (or vice versa) as the changing idea that people had of the Apostles. This is just as true of the prophets and all the persons and incidents taken from the Bible, legend, and history, and, above all, of God the Father, Christ, and Mary. If we conceive of the forms of the sculptured Apostles, for example, as visible, transparent foreground and, looking through these forms from the aesthetic point of view, understand the spiritual background, there is opened to us an understanding of the spiritual background of the whole age. In the same sense we are able also to recognize that spiritual background through the forms of architecture as through a transparency. But that is a modern, one might say, strictly a present-day theory. One cannot equate the symbolism of the Middle Ages with a modern theory. The former remained conceptual symbolism and was not even conscious form symbolism, although art was surely in all ages form symbol. What went on, then, in the minds of those men who explained architecture "symbolically"? According to their own words they did not go beyond the method of conceptual symbolism. Whether they understood the symbolism of form they have never revealed. We must assume that the architects at least felt and understood what they were creating, and we may also assume that likewise the theologians, philosophers, symbolists of the Middle Ages had a correct understanding of the language of form, just as we do, even though they had as yet no possibility of expressing their comprehension. In practice Gothic was unconsciously a form symbol; in theory, on the contrary, only a conceptual symbol.

But even if one assumes this, that the men of the Middle Ages felt Gothic exactly as we do—and this is disputable—there remains the difference that for them there was that conceptual symbolism added to the formal. Thus, if we want to look at Gothic through the eyes of the educated mediaeval public, we must study the symbolism of that time. Its method was, in fact, especially well developed during the Gothic age. The chief sources are:

Honorius Augustodunensis, who was active in the first half of the twelfth century, and was thus a contemporary of Suger,

Sicardus, in the second half of the twelfth century, and thus a contemporary of Gervase,

Vincent de Beauvais, who died in 1264, a contemporary of Villard de Honnecourt,

Durandus de Mende (1230-1296), a contemporary of Dante. Sauer says: "To go beyond Durandus is no longer fruitful, for with the fourteenth century a different intellectual current makes itself felt, as a result of which new thoughts and new perceptions came into being."[20] Later symbolists were dependent on Durandus. According to this view one can apparently limit the flowering of symbolism chronologically to the twelfth and thirteenth centuries, that is, to the period of Early and High Gothic; and yet here, too, a clear relationship to the *style* of Gothic is lacking. Why? Sauer gave the answer quite indirectly when he gave an account of the highly interesting symbolism of candles (also of the Easter candle) and then remarked that no author paid any heed to the form of the candlesticks. "Here, where art was allowed to have a free hand, in forms that were, as is always emphasized today, not merely artistic but also full of profound content, the symbolist is silent and thus shows most clearly that he wants to concern himself only with a symbolism hallowed by unbroken tradition and above all inspired by the liturgy, and not at all with more independent, individual conceptions."[21]

This explains much. Our surprise that the symbolists make no attempt to interpret Gothic stylistically vanishes when we comprehend that this style was considered by them only as a "more independent, individual conception" of a historically limited period. Today we rank the form symbol higher than the literary symbol of meaning or the theoretical conceptual one. The age of Gothic had created its form symbol in the style of its architecture, but this was esteemed less highly than that which the individual part of the structure, for example, the portal as such, signified in a religious or conceptual sense, independently of the transitory stylistic form.

One can measure the value of this insight when one turns to the so-called metaphysics of light. The comparison of God the Father or of Christ with light or the sun as the source of all light accompanies the Christian writings, beginning with the New Testament.[22] It goes back to the ancient nature religions, in which God and light were identical. In Christianity, on the other hand, the light is only a symbol for God, and from this comparison there resulted a number of speculations, greatly varied in form and of a metaphysical, ontological, physical, as well as an ethical and aesthetic nature. Therefore the term "metaphysics of light" is too narrow. Bäumker traced these variations of an essentially simple idea in his study of Witelo (ca. 1225-ca. 1270).[23]

[20] *Ibid.*, (2nd ed.), p. 191. His *Rationale Divinorum* was written in 1286.

[21] *Ibid.*, (first edition), p. 191. [22] *Ibid.*, p. 186.

[23] Clemens Bäumker, *Witelo, ein Philosoph und Naturforscher des XIII. Jahrhunderts*, Münster, 1908, pp. 358ff. (Beiträge zur Geschichte der Philosophie des Mittelalters, III, No. 2); by the same author: *Der Platonismus im Mittelalter*, Akademische Rede, Munich, 1916.

This excursion gives an insight into the habit of thought of the most highly educated men of the Gothic age, but here, too, one learns nothing about the relation of these philosophers and theologians to Gothic. The few passages already cited from Suger and Gervase are exceptional; again Suger seems to be of uncommon importance because he speaks of light in connection with his Gothic church.

Panofsky has recently clarified why Suger was so deeply concerned about the ideas of the metaphysics of light. The most important representatives of this theory, rooted in the Neoplatonism of Plotinus (204-270), were Proclus and Pseudo-Dionysius, who was dependent on him, both writing in Greek.[24] In them were combined the Platonic tradition and the religious mysticism of the Near East. The connecting link between Pseudo-Dionysius and Suger was Johannes Scotus Eriugena (ca. 800-ca. 877). From his double name it would seem that this Johannes was born in Ireland, the son of Scottish parents. In the course of his life he visited Greece and acquired the ability to translate works in Greek. When he was called to Paris by Charles the Bald to the then flourishing *schola palatina*, he translated the Greek book of Pseudo-Dionysius the Areopagite into Latin. In 827 Emperor Michael the Stammerer had presented a copy of the latter's works to King Louis the Pious, who gave it immediately to the abbey of St.-Denis. Hilduin, then abbot, reestablished the thesis that the Areopagite was identical with the martyred Dionysius of Paris. Thus, since Eriugena's day the abbey of St.-Denis had owned both the Greek text and the Latin translation of the Areopagite. Since monastic libraries of that time were not very extensive it is very likely that Suger read, in addition to the Bible, all the books in his library often and thoroughly, and so Panofsky explains the surprisingly strong emphasis on the metaphysics of light in his works as the heritage of the doctrines of Pseudo-Dionysius, or Plotinus. It is not necessary to dwell here on the differences in the theories of all these philosophers,[25] since in this field, too, it would be fruitless to ask whether the metaphysics of light had undergone stylistic transformations parallel to those of architecture, or, in other words, whether Suger's particular—and, moreover, unoriginal—conception was Early Gothic. Yet the thought persists that behind all these negative results something positive must lie hidden.

24 Erwin Panofsky, *Abbot Suger*, p. 18. Plotinus was introduced to the Latin world by Gaius M. Victorinus, the teacher of Augustine. See also Otto v. Simson, *The Gothic Cathedral*.

25 For the differences between the Neoplatonic conception and that of Eriugena cf. Hermann Dörries, *Zur Geschichte der Mystik, Eriugena und der Neuplatonismus*, Tübingen, 1925, especially pp. 106ff.

Suger extended his veneration for phenomena of light as messengers of God, so to speak, to precious stones, and here, too, he was following an old tradition. There was a literature on stones, the rudimentary stage of modern mineralogy. It can be traced back to works of classical times, above all to a lost book by Aristotle.[26] Aristotle's genuine book on stones had undoubtedly been based predominantly on empirical knowledge. This can be concluded from the character of the mineralogy of Theophrastus, Aristotle's pupil. The connection of stones with magical powers goes back to Egyptian and Babylonian popular medicine and further than that to prehistoric times. Suger's knowledge of precious stones, however, derives from some sentences of the Bible, perhaps he knew the *Naturalis Historia* by Pliny the Elder (ca. A.D. 23-79) and other books of the enormous literature upon this subject. During his lifetime St. Hildegard (1098-1179) wrote a book *Physika*, full of fantastic statements about stones. In the thirteenth century follow dissertations on stones by Gervasius from Tilbury (around 1200), Vincent from Beauvais (d. 1264), Arnoldus Saxo, Albertus Magnus (d. 1280) etc. This literature is partly influenced by Arabic authors as early as the ninth century.[27] German Romanticism showed an interest in this literature,[27a] attracted by the mixture of knowledge and imagination; it still remains a fascinating subject for close study, but it seems impossible to identify the beliefs of those primitive forerunners of modern mineralogy with Gothic or any other style of the Middle Ages.

In the passage cited previously from Suger his complete absorption in the radiance of the jewels must be called mysticism, because it carries him away to supernatural realms. Metaphysics of light and mysticism of light are two different things, even though they are closely related and interconnected spiritual experiences. True mysticism does not seek knowledge of earthly or other visible objects or of their real or imagined qualities but elevation to the immediate proximity of God. Thus the precious stones do not have in the mysticism of jewels the function of symbols. For the Christian metaphysics of light in mediaeval times the thesis is characteristic, for example, that the light is

[26] The texts referring to stones in the extant works can be found in Herrmann Bonitz, *Index Aristotelicus*, s.v. λίθος, in *Aristotelis Opera edidit Academia Borussica*, v, Berlin, 1870, p. 431.

[27] The best survey is given in Philipp Schmidt, S.J., *Edelsteine, Ihr Wesen und ihr Wert bei den Kulturvölkern*, Bonn, 1948. Furthermore, see Julius Ruska, *Untersuchungen über das Steinbuch des Aristoteles*, Heidelberg, 1911; about Johannitius (d. 873), see *Encyclopaedia Britannica*, XVIII, 45.

[27a] J. A. Büsching, *Die Kräfte der Edelgesteine . . .*, Museum für altdeutsche Literatur and Kunst, II, Berlin, 1811, p. 52.

the origin of the world. In the early thirteenth century Robert Grosseteste (1175-1253), Bishop of Lincoln, started out in his metaphysics of light with the sentence: "I assume that light is the primal corporeal form that many call corporeality."[28] This of course is related to the first chapter of Genesis. On the first day God created the light and the sun only on the fourth day. According to Grosseteste (who cites the *Hexameron* of Basilius) the light of the first day means light per se, the substance of light itself, whereas the sun is the bearer of light.[29] These are speculations concerned with the subtle analysis of concepts as a means of arriving at unambiguous knowledge. Suger, on the contrary, has been lifted up above the slime of the earth, not to heaven itself, but still close to it, in an "anagogical" manner (an expression borrowed from Eriugena and supposed to go back to Parmenides). He does not seek knowledge but a spiritual state, which for its part affords something that might be called "knowledge" of God, not, however, really knowledge in the philosophical or scientific sense but rather simply immediate religious experience. Just as one experiences light—without being obliged to have philosophical or scientific cognition of it—so one can experience God immediately, without any other consequences than enrichment through the certainty of being a creature of the ultimate basis of the world, his child. To speak of mysticism to people who have themselves never had any mystical experience is as difficult as to talk of color to the blind. In the age of Gothic men were predisposed to mysticism by tradition, and prepared for it by example and precept. It is, therefore, hardly possible to separate the scholars of the time into scholastics and mystics. They were always both at once, some inclined more strongly toward scholasticism, others toward mysticism.

As we have seen, mysticism does not take things as symbols. But art, thus also architecture, since it is itself a form symbol, can by its form symbolize the mystic. Therefore it is correct to say that Gothic symbolizes mysticism, but Gothic itself is not identical with mysticism; it *is* not a personal state of mind, though it *symbolizes* one and can induce one. It arouses a definite conception of a particular kind of other world, just as a sculptured *crucifixus* symbolizes a particular conception of Christ, one specific one by means of Romanesque form,

28 Ludwig Bauer, *Die philosophischen Werke des Robert Grosseteste, Bischof von Lincoln*, Münster, 1912 (Beiträge zur Geschichte der Philosophie des Mittelalters, IX), p. 15 of the text: "Formam primam corporalem, quam quidam corporalitatem vocant, lucem arbitror."

29 Inconsistently Grosseteste also calls light the finest body.

another by means of Gothic. The Romanesque *crucifixus* can be broadly characterized as the expression of the words: "Thy will be done," the Gothic, correspondingly, as: "My God, why hast Thou forsaken me," as the expression of suffering and immediate longing for God. Both states can also be expressed by architectural forms. Neither, however, is mysticism or symbol of mysticism. What Albrecht intended in his temple of the Grail, on the other hand, *is* mysticism.

Here we enter for the first time a field that is immediately connected with Gothic. But one should not succumb to the temptation of characterizing mysticism at the time of Gothic as likewise Gothic. Mysticism is fundamentally a very simple, indeed the simplest and most immediate, if also the strangest experience and in all ages and in all cultures the same, even though individual peoples and schools of mysticism have different methods of contemplation and attain, or differentiate, different stages.[30] It is true that there is an Indian, Oriental, and a European mysticism, but when any one refers to each individual type, he means the outer coloring, the trappings, not the inner essence. So one can also speak of Gothic mysticism, if one means the Gothic coloring: for example, the veneration of Mary for men, of Christ for women (*Gottesminne*). Actually, however, the expression "Gothic mysticism" ought to refer to something Gothic in mysticism itself, not merely to a connection with religious ideas typical of the time.

"Gothic mysticism" found the Gothic light of stained glass one of the most convincing form symbols. In the chapter on Suger there has already been a discussion of it. Stained glass existed before Gothic but the new style reveals a reciprocal effect: the more people became aware of the effect of the light, which "falls dimly through painted panes," the larger they made the windows, and the larger the window surfaces became, the more possibilities there were for the glass painters to carry out their experiments in color and to revel in the effects. Gothic stained glass belonged to Gothic as an integrating, mystical building material, so to speak, just as much as stone or brick.

The history of stained glass shows that the degree of brightness, or of dimness, was not the same in all generations, but rather that a lightening of its scale was already begun in the fourteenth century and that at times toward the end of Late Gothic a brightness was reached that displeased conservative souls. For this there is a curious

[30] Rudolf Otto, *West-Östliche Mystik*, Gotha, 1926.

piece of evidence in a chronicle of Chemnitz, printed in 1716,[31] in which the author quotes the Humanist and monk NIAVIS (Schneevogel), who had still seen the old church of Annaberg and who wrote of it as follows: "that it was a strongly built but old-fashioned building and not light, because people formerly thought that it encouraged religious fervor when a church was not too light" (fit enim saepe in saeculo, ubi ecclesias habent prorsus lucidas, ut dediti homines libidini, quum inspiciunt amantes, plus cupidini operam dant quam orationibus).[32] In any case, his chief aim seemed to be to recommend the mystic light of ancient tradition. As soon as one becomes acquainted with the entire context of this passage, which describes "the old mountain monastery and present castle," one is inclined to question the advisability of mentioning it at all when mysticism is being discussed. For Niavis begins with a description of the monastery beer and with the admission that it tastes better to him than that of Kempten; then we hear of the pleasure garden with sweet smelling and medicinal herbs; further, of a crucifix with a crooked or distorted mouth ("Maul" in the German); then comes the sentence about light, after which the description turns to the fishpond, the forests in which the abbot goes hunting, the bathroom where the monks bathe every fortnight, the stables and their animals, the plants that are grown for their efficacy against vermin, the many hens, because the monks ate chiefly eggs, and so on. Niavis' "mystical" note is thus embedded in an account of cheerful, everyday affairs and the enjoyment of life; perhaps it is well to remind modern scholars who are hunting for analogies to Gothic that even the monks who knew how to appreciate Gothic light did not live by it alone, and that the task of proving a parallelism to Gothic in the styles of agriculture might be difficult.

The situation with respect to the favorite comparison of Gothic with scholasticism is similar to that regarding mysticism. Dehio summed up the usual points of comparison well: in both there was a high intellectual accomplishment and an artistic composition, "common to both is the enthusiasm in the work, common also the method of thought; both have the same combination of boldness and sobriety, the same strictly rational development of arbitrary premises, the same

[31] Cornelius Gurlitt, in *Kunst und Künstler* . . . (cited above, p. 124n, called attention to this source; it comes from A. D. Richter, *Chronik der Stadt Chemnitz*, Annaberg, 1753, or 1767; it is reprinted *in extenso* in Appendix 11.

[32] ". . . for it often happens in the secular world where there are utterly well-lighted churches that people given to libidinousness, when looking at lovers, pay more attention to lewdness than to the sermons."

heady enjoyment of logical formalism. . . . As scholasticism begins its doctrinal structure at the top, as it were, from whence it derives everything else deductively, so in Gothic everything is the result of a particular system of vaulting. As scholasticism proves the unprovable with the help of the authority of revelation lying outside thought, so Gothic produces the miracle of its vaulted halls resting on incredibly weak supports with the help of the system of buttresses lying outside the building itself."[33] Though such comparisons are beguiling on a first reading they do not stand the test of more serious consideration. The Doric temples were also built with enthusiasm for the work, intelligence, artistic composition. The Eiffel Tower is also bold and sober; every vaulted structure, even the un-Gothic Pantheon in Rome, is begun with the consideration of the top, that is, with the vault. The comparison of the buttresses with revelation we would read with friendly sympathy in Durandus, but not in a modern historian of architecture. Dehio says in conclusion: "When scholasticism tries to solve the riddle of existence by such means it does not convince us; the symbolical solution by Gothic still has power over our spirits."[34] If Gothic convinces us and at the same time is supposed to be the expression of scholasticism, why then does not scholasticism convince us? It is because Gothic architecture is not the expression of scholasticism at all. Both are contemporaneous states of two different spheres of activity and intellect.

Insofar as scholasticism is natural science, dependent on or independent of Aristotle and the Arabs, it is just as rational in its tendency as it is irrational in its metaphysical quality, but not more so. It did not gain complete freedom to trust to native reason and to question nature methodically by experiment in order to arrive at general principles. But there was a preliminary stage of modern natural science in the Middle Ages that reveals a greater variety within the limits defined by the Church than the popular conception of the "dark Middle Ages" would lead one to suspect.[35] Geometry and natural science, with mechanics at their head, resulted from practical work. Both, geometry and mechanics, we have met—geometry on the building site and mechanics in the Lodge Book of Villard de Honnecourt, in the Milanese records, and so on. One can perhaps clarify the general question as to Gothic culture most easily if one turns it into the specific question

33 Georg Dehio, *Die kirchliche Baukunst* . . . , II, p. 15.

34 *Ibid.*, p. 15.

35 Charles Homer Haskins, *Studies in the History of Mediaeval Science* (Harvard University Historical Studies, XXVII), Cambridge, Mass., 1924.

as to whether there is a Gothic geometry. There was, of course, a "Gothic" structural geometry if one means by that a method of building measurement practiced at the time of Gothic, such as we learned especially from the Milanese expertises. But no one can call the half diagonal of the square as such Gothic. The method served indeed to measure the Gothic churches but the mensuration itself is not Gothic.

Even in the case of the automata the description "Gothic automata" is questionable. When Villard caused the figure of an angel to turn in such a way that it always points toward the sun, the idea was presumably connected with the metaphysics of light, but this, as we have seen, is not Gothic, any more than the wheel-work itself that was described by Villard. The angel, which he did not draw, would doubtless have been just as Gothic a sculpture as the angels of Reims Cathedral, but that is again form symbolism, in other words, art, and the works within the automaton, the wheels that were never intended to be seen, had no sort of form symbolism. If one were to argue that the automata really represented wonders, that is, miracles, then the answer would be that miracles are not per se Gothic.

As long as one asks whether the individual cultural spheres have a direct effect on one another, the answers received are always in the negative. Architecture has no effect on scholasticism, and vice versa. The corresponding is true of the other spheres. On the other hand, sculpture and painting influence each other, which, however, cannot surprise us since they are both fundamentally the same, that is, are representation, be it of an idea or of a real model, and differ only in the number of dimensions. In the Middle Ages they are also dependent on architecture, from which result again direct and even reciprocal influences. Moreover, sculpture, painting, and architecture are *arts*, they all speak the same language of form symbolism. If now the other spheres as well—theology, metaphysics in all its variations, and so on—are connected with art, the explanation lies in the fact that they are all held together by a common center. One can distribute the various subjects, such as economics, technology, politics, science, philosophy, art, as individual points on a circle and then observe that the periphery connects them only slightly or superficially. On the other hand, all these points are firmly united with each other across the center. In this case one can, for example, say that architecture in Point A is connected across the Center M with the other Points B, C, D, and so on. This Center M is man. In him is united everything that we have touched upon and that could still be added in a long series. In him everything finds its unity, because every individual has a tendency toward harmony or at least toward the assimilation of his experiences. Man has an astounding ability to unite in himself disparate elements as well, but then he often feels inwardly torn. He seeks the harmony of all spheres of life and constantly destroys it himself by forwarding the continual evolution of each sphere individually, a contradiction that reveals itself to be almost the root of all historical happenings.[36]

The statement that man forms the center of all the areas of culture is, of course, a generalization, inasmuch as it is entirely a matter of utterly different individuals, an intellectual stratum within a broad, anonymous, and relatively unintellectual mass. In this culture-bearing stratum each is influenced by each. All are united by a common tradition of education, the co-workers in each individual field of activity being especially close to each other. It is the "subject" that has its own inner logic and of itself urges the specialists on to a common goal. Architecture, once having entered upon a particular tendency, for example, Gothic, demands of the architects a continued development in liturgical, technical, aesthetic, and specifically stylistic fields; theology, once having taken the direction of so-called scholasticism, demands of its scholars likewise that the way adopted be continued as a result of the "subject"—that is, of its specific subject matter. In every intellectual field of endeavor there is a similar *immanent* logic of evolution, which is in turn always *extramanent* for all the other fields. From this it would seem to follow that all fields will develop with no reference to each other and under certain circumstances will even develop divergently. But these fields do not hover isolated in the air but are all united in Man. When specialized fields diverge, it is man, or rather society, that forces them to converge again. One can visualize this process by returning to the figure used above and imagining man in his intellectual development not as the center M of a circle but as an ascending line, that is, as the axis of a cylinder. In man and his desire to form

[36] Wilhelm Weber commented on this passage: "In the case of such universal minds as Albertus Magnus and Thomas Aquinas the effect of the center M is obviously much stronger than the theory indicates. Should we not imagine that the architects of the same age, who invented and executed such daring structures, felt, thought, planned, and acted just as universally?" Weber's question is justified, but we know too little about the great architects of Gothic to be able to attribute to them the same universality as to an Albertus Magnus or a Thomas. In the case of philosophers of such powers, we may say, using that geometrical figure, that the whole circle, i.e. its periphery, is included in the personalities themselves, but that in the case of the architects the majority of the periphery lies outside them. However, this objection of mine cannot be proved; even with regard to Villard de Honnecourt it is not known how extensive his knowledge was of all areas of life lying outside his art. That is a subject for a longer investigation.

a unity, harmonious in itself, would reside the power of attraction by means of which the diverging evolutionary lines of the specialized fields, ascending on the periphery and standing, as it were, on the peak of a cone, would be forced together, so that they do not separate toward the outside but remain parallel as on the surface of a cylinder. Object and person are mutually affected. The "person" is inclined to believe that he has full mastery over the "object," and often does not notice how much he is dominated by the latter. One can see this in its crassest form in our present situation where the development of physics with its immanent logic has arrived at results that threaten the existence of all the other fields, which were thought to be able to progress independently in their own way and are now forced to a revision and assimilation; so that all these diverging lines of economics, politics, military science, and the like, are compelled to adopt a parallel course in order to allow "the" human being his harmony. Such has been the case, however, to a greater or lesser degree, in all ages, and very often there has occurred, as today, a radical change in the fundamental attitude of an entire culture. One should, however, not take this geometrical figure of the evolution of culture in the sense of dead mechanics but substitute, for "the" human being universal spirits like Albertus and Thomas.

To the all pervading basic ideas of the Middle Ages belong those of Christianity, in the stage which it reached in the course of the development of the twelfth century. The inclination to carry out in real life the doctrines of the New Testament was inhibited by definite inclinations of society in a secular direction. The papacy, the church, monasticism, and the knights of the militant orders were opposed by the secular empire and feudalism, in the later Middle Ages by the citizen class as well. In the early part of the period the church Christianized the laity; in the latter half of the Middle Ages the ideas of the laity secularized the church. In the former case the solution of all problems was sought in the so-called other world, that is, in our own spirituality, in a redemption from sinfulness and worldliness. As long as this ideal dominated, natural science was not permitted to develop freely, but the authority of the Bible and the tradition of recognized authors was in the ascendancy. Through the influence of Petrarch, classical philology and, even more important, the Humanistic idea were strengthened in the fourteenth century. With the resurgence of the classical spirit men slowly became free to investigate the world and prepare the way for modern natural science. In all this the spirit of Christianity itself was not lost; it merely slowly changed its relationship to the "world." Thus it was classical philology as a particular, limited, specialized field that offered to comprehensive minds the means of changing gradually the predominantly Christian basic idea of culture, and that, therefore, as a transformed "object" transformed the "person."

The picture of culture and its development that has been sketched here really becomes alive only when one studies the great personalities of the Middle Ages. In the case of Suger it is extraordinary how much of what filled the minds of the men of his age is apparent in his writings. He is both particular and universal. The more universal men are the more they are representatives of their time and even include in themselves all the fields about which they are silent. It is their universality that also connects them with Gothic, although they may have written nothing about it, as in the case of Albertus Magnus and Thomas Aquinas.

This becomes clear by pointing to DANTE Alighieri (1265-1321). Nowhere in his work do we find anything said about Gothic, yet it would be leaving an unpardonable gap to discuss Gothic and not think of Dante. It would be false to try to consider his *Divine Comedy* as architecture; it has no place in a chapter on architectural fantasies. His hell, with its funnel shape, is to be compared to a classical arena or the Colosseum rather than to a Gothic cathedral. But the *Divine Comedy* is Gothic in the sense we mean when we talk of Gothic culture.

Understanding of Dante is a touchstone for the understanding of Gothic. Anyone who despises Dante and who nevertheless maintains that he loves the Gothic cathedrals probably has not understood the cathedrals—at least not in the way that they were intended in their time. Of course, much of Dante is strange to us, but this is equally true of the cathedrals. They are just as fearful, just as purifying, just as paradisiacal as the three parts of the *Divine Comedy*. They are just as unbourgeois, extravagant, magnificent, adventurous, fantastic, ambiguous, obscure, and at the same time irradiated and suffused with unaccustomed light. Dante was the universal spirit of his time, very much of his earthbound world with all his hatred, bitterness, defiance, ambition as a Florentine nobleman, delivered into the power of fellow citizens who shared his vices without having his greatness, his inexhaustible force and freedom of imagination, or his stringency of form. But these countrymen did share with Dante scholastic education, mysticism of the Franciscan provenience, knowledge of classical literature, and the Christian metaphysics of the age; there were specialists in all these fields, but Dante comprised them all, because he was, we may say, a "specialist for poetry." Dante is hard to understand; one must work at him if one does not merely wish to be carried away by the melody of his speech; and likewise one must first seek the way to the cathedrals. One of these ways is through Dante's poem.

In his many-sidedness Dante also wrote theoretical treatises on politics, poetics, and so on, but these prose works are today read by only a small group of specialists. The poem, in spite of its difficulties, with or without commentaries, is open to everyone—as the cathedrals are. Here we do not stand before two disparate intellectual fields. Both are works of *art*. Even though mediaeval aesthetic theory had not yet recognized the fact, architecture and poetry were analogously constructed: art or *form symbols* expressed in different media. We have traced the mediaeval epics from the Grail to Chaucer and Lydgate on the basis of points of external resemblance between the temple of the Grail and the temple of glass. Chronologically the description of the temple of the Grail of about 1270 is followed by the *Divine Comedy* around 1300.[37] It is the next religious epic, thoroughly imbued with the spirit of the age, with the Christian doctrine of salvation and Christian ethics, with Christian belief in the spirit and the other world, with classical mythology, with astrology and astronomy, with metaphysics of light, scholastic and mystic, with politics, physics and magic of stones, with history, contemporary reporting, and autobiography. An incalculable mass of persons appears on this infinite stage of the world. Dante's journey through Hell, his ascent of the mountain of Purgatory to the spheres of the planets and up to the highest heaven is a spiritual and, on the whole, mystical progress, attributed indeed to one individual and inwardly experienced by that individual but representative, nevertheless, of humanity's purification and redemption through mystical experience. At first Dante submits himself to the guidance of his friend Vergil, then to that of Beatrice, the perfect beloved, in whom Dante's Christian love is merged with the personal. Only through her does he attain the highest level and the ultimate vision.

In the *Divine Comedy* Dante mentioned Giotto. The latter was also active in architecture and built the Gothic campanile of the Cathedral of Florence, but Dante speaks of him only as a painter (Purg. XI, 95).

37 There is no evidence as to when Dante began the *Divine Comedy*; the various views are brought together by Friedrich Schneider-Jena, *Dante*, Weimar, 1947 (4th ed.), pp. 124ff. Dante had already begun the *Inferno* before his banishment in the year 1302. The work was perhaps completed by 1317. The best introduction to the study of Dante is Karl Vossler's, *Die göttliche Komödie, Entwicklungsgeschichte und Erklärung*, Heidelberg, 1907 to 1910; 2nd ed., 1925.

He was in Padua in 1306 when Giotto was painting in the chapel of the Arena. There he immortalized Dante in a portrait in the *Last Judgment.* Those are direct links between Dante and the painting of High Gothic, and this illustrates what was said above about the connection of all fields of culture.

If one were to compare the *Divine Comedy* with the cathedral of Florence one would find the task insoluble, and in connection with this unreasonable demand one would be somewhat taken aback that an Italian poet should be recognized as the representative of Gothic when, after all, Italian Gothic is not taken quite seriously by admirers of French Gothic. And yet that is justified. Dante is a "European," his horizon embraces the whole Catholic world of his day, including France and the domains of the Roman emperors of the German nation.

These remarks ought to have made it clear that all poetic and scientific literature of that time can be considered a source of Gothic, the important thing being, of course, to interpret it correctly. On no account should one deprive historical reality of its richness, its irrationality, its incalculable and unpredictable freedom, because of a preconceived idea that all contemporaneous intellectual movements must also automatically tend in the same direction. Its preestablished harmony and, as it were, preestablished disharmony have their origin in the profound mystery of the life process, itself rooted in the mystery of the spiritual.

What has been discussed here must be understood in relation to what was said in the chapter on the architectural fantasies. We comprehend the spiritual entity of Gothic itself all the more deeply the more we are acquainted with the entire literature of the time, but the form of Gothic must be grasped as an architectural problem. If we succeed in the latter effort, something essential is then reflected from this knowledge back to the understanding of the literature and "culture" of the age of Gothic.

Dante has been taken here as *one* example. Many others can be mentioned; and the more of them one learns to know, the more vivid does the outline sketched above become. Master ECKHART (1260?-1327) is, because of his linguistic power, as great in the German field as Dante, his contemporary, in the Italian. He is a preacher, not a poet, and as a mystic he is more profound than Dante. His best interpreter, Rudolf Otto, called him a "Gothic man par excellence" and immediately thereafter referred to Worringer.[38] But, when we spoke above of "the" hu-

[38] Rudolf Otto, *op.cit.* On Worringer cf. below p. 669. Cf. also Georg Weise, "Das Schlagwort vom gotischen Menschen," *Neue Jahrbücher für Wissenschaft und Jugendbildung,* VII, Leipzig and Berlin, 1931, p. 404.

man being, it was not done in order to support the generalization of the "Gothic man." We may well speak, however, of Gothic society, or of the Gothic stratum which created and fostered the culture that is called Gothic.

Because the word Gothic, originally introduced only for architecture,[39] was extended not only to sculpture and painting but also to all spheres of culture developing simultaneously with Gothic architecture, the problem arose as to how far these had something in common, that is, something Gothic. As is well known, Gothic architecture developed step by step and so also did, for example, mediaeval metaphysics. Even as early as the lifetime of Dante and Eckhart, the dispute between *realism* and *nominalism* came to a head. It seems as though even today it has not been completely laid to rest. By realism was meant the thesis that reality should be ascribed to general concepts; from the universal ideas individuals were supposed to be derived, and the problem was to explain the *principium individuationis* by which from the idea "horse" the individual horses eventuated. The theory of nominalism declared, on the contrary, that the general concepts were only *nomina*, empty sound; only the individuals were real. To speak, however, of the "Gothic man" is realism (in the sense of the scholastic use of the term). If, however, we speak of Giotto, Dante, Eckhart, Occam, we mean, in the sense of nominalism, the real and living individuals, to whom we apply the adjective "Gothic" after we have created a general concept that is intended to include the most diverse phenomena, for example, even two such different theses as those of scholastic realism and scholastic nominalism; both are for us "Gothic."

Gothic society consisted of innumerable individuals living in their cultural atmosphere that was common to all of them; they themselves created the continuously changing web. In modern terms culture is a "configuration," "Gestalt," but a dynamic, labile, fluid configuration. It has been very convincingly proven that just that fundamental contrast between realism and nominalism can be demonstrated in sculpture, painting and in the poetry of the Middle Ages as well and the conversion to subjectivism discovered everywhere.[40] Recently the rise of perspective, or of its forerunner, the oblique parallel projection, in Duccio and Giotto has also been brought under the general heading of subjectivism, and the same thing has been claimed for the interior aspect

[39] The history of the word Gothic will be discussed later.

[40] Georg Weise, *Die geistige Welt der Gotik und ihre Bedeutung für Italien*, Halle a.S., 1939.

of Late Gothic churches.[41] It is here, however, more a question of the method of the cultural historians and their enlargement of the concept of Gothic, than of the details.

The web of intellectual connections among contemporaries, their exposure to the patterns of thought of the particular past and present, can be spun out three-dimensionally and the comprehensive minds seen as large, thick knots in the web, their function being to receive the threads in tangled form and spin them out in their own spirit as a particular clue. The more they comprehend of the fields of contemporary life and gather productively into a personally colored unity, the more they appear to us as representatives of their age.

Yet despite all this, it remains astonishing that the word Gothic, which has prevailed for architecture only since the seventeenth century, was chosen to designate the "common denominator." We should be content that such a term has become adopted and as Neo-nominalists not demand more of it than it has to give. Above all, one should cease to exaggerate analogies or indeed to insist on them where they are not present. Our task is rather to define precisely the extended concept Gothic, and for that, as will be seen, we do not need at all this hunt for analogies.

The field that lies closest to church architecture is that of the liturgy. The architectural program is conditioned by the purposes and needs of the liturgy; and when the latter changes, the architect must adapt himself to the innovations. The best general account of this subject is still the chapter that Dehio wrote on the architectural program in Gothic.[42] He describes in detail seven components of the church building: the enlargement of the choirs; the transference of the relics to the upper church and in connection with that the abandonment of crypts; the introduction of the rood loft and choir screens in order to protect the clergy from disturbances during their seven daily canonical offices; the increase in the number of masses and therefore in both altars and chapels; the increase in the number of towers, or their abolition among the puritanical Cistercians and the mendicant orders; the increasing significance of the sermon, especially in the parish churches, combined with the latter's ambition to vie in externals with the cathedrals; and, finally, the relationship of the church proper to its adjuncts, the chapter houses and cloisters. Much has been written about the in-

[41] Erwin Panofsky, *Gothic Architecture and Scholasticism*, Latrobe, 1951.

[42] Georg Dehio, *Die kirchliche Baukunst des Abendlandes*, Stuttgart, 1901, II, p. 24.

fluence of the architectural program in the case of the Cistercians and the mendicant orders. To Dehio's list might be appended the question what was the liturgical significance of the transept, which was sometimes left out and sometimes, on the other hand, doubled (in Cluny and England), if it had any liturgical significance at all.[43]

Since Dehio only Mayer has, as far as I know, treated this subject of the liturgy.[44] Although he is influenced by Dehio, he tries to penetrate to a deeper level, that of history of ideas. From the great mass of relevant literature he took the suggestion of the subjectivity of the emotional life that also extended to the piety of the time. He finds in representational art and poetry, the tendency toward multiplication of forms, intensification of means of expression, the realistic urge to grasp concrete details (realism here in the sense of modern usage), particularization, and he discerns analogies in the cumulation of masses and prayers, sees a multiplication in the rosary, also in the increase in the number of the saints, and finally, he stresses the humanization of Joseph, the foster father, St. Anne, and even Jesus. In this category belongs also the rise of the worship of the heart of Jesus. Of interest is what he says about the elevation of the host: it was to be seen by all.

Presumably much more can still be explored from this point of view; we feel, however, that the question of style cannot be exhausted in such digging for intellectual roots. Dehio's concrete observations are in themselves correct, but it suffices to reflect in the case of the first of his seven programmatic points, the arithmetically calculable enlargement of the choirs (he gives ratios of the choirs to transept and nave), that Strasbourg Cathedral is Gothic in spite of its apse preserved from Romanesque time. To be sure, this is an exception that does not essentially change anything in Dehio's thesis, especially since Strasbourg had a rood loft, acquired two chapels—and yet, more important than the size of the choir, for example, that of Cologne Cathedral, are its specifically Gothic structural forms. The forms of the piers, arches, and so on, are the real problem, whether the choir be large or small.

Perhaps from here we can find the key to this whole problem that troubles us so much today. In Gothic architecture the spatial form,

43 Since this was written the article of George H. Forsyth, Jr., has been published: "The Transept of Old St. Peter's at Rome" (in *Late Classical and Mediaeval Studies in Honor of Albert Mathias Friend*, Princeton, 1955, p. 56) showing convincingly that the transept was first created in St. Peter's in Rome about 340 to permit pilgrims as part of the liturgy to pass around the tomb of the Apostle. In later churches the copy of the transept was independent of pilgrimage, keeping only the aesthetic function that it already had in its first appearance.

44 Anton L. Mayer, "Die Liturgie und der Geist der Gotik," *Jahrbuch der Liturgiewissenschaft*, VI, Münster i.W., 1926, p. 68.

looked at *roughly*, is often explained by the architectural program, and if this is derived from a changed conception of the liturgy, there is here revealed *one* thread leading directly to *one* of the many spheres of life. This analysis—one might almost say anatomy of the intellectual system—is indicative of the method to be followed for all similar inquiries. But what one means by "Gothic" in the history of culture as well as art is something deeper; it is the common root from which spring the changes in the liturgy and those in the architectural forms, even if these are not themselves simply determined by the liturgy.

We know that there are today adherents of the materialistic conception of history, which seeks to derive and explain all intellectual processes by way of economic requirements. Literature on economics during the period of Gothic is sparse. Dehio said very little on the subject; above all, he stresses the fact that in the first period of the Middle Ages an agrarian economy prevailed, while in the second the system of money economy began in the second half of the twelfth century, that is, contemporaneously with Gothic.[45] It would be interesting to read the paradoxical proof of how Gothic poetry, and so on, can be derived from the system of money economy in strictly materialistic fashion. But anyone who does not believe this theory dogmatically knows that economics are always a factor, but never explain everything. Thus it would be hopeless to try to explain Gothic from *this* root alone, and we may add that the root we seek is itself complicated and branching. Following his casual remark on money economy, Dehio said that economy of materials and therefore of cost of transportation was to many a patron "more interesting than any questions of style." What was saved on materials and transportation, however, was expended on more elaborate stone masons' work, high towers, and so on. Thus Dehio's statement has no real basis. Moreover, we should not forget that, not only for Suger, relics and later indulgences also represented a most important source of income. Money flowed in rivers—sometimes, only drop by drop—as soon as the spiritual attraction was there. Economics always is based on "spirit." In this case the spirit was "Gothic." But this by no means implies that money economy is simply and always Gothic.

To approach a real insight even more closely, a last example may

[45] Dehio, *op.cit.*, II, p. 19; cf. more recently Heinrich Bechtel, *Wirtschaftsstil des deutschen Spätmittelalters*, Munich and Leipzig, 1930; to the older investigations belong those of Stephan Beissel, S.J., *Die Bauführung des Mittelalters, Studie über die Kirche des hl. Victor in Xanten*, Freiburg i.b., 1889, and Josef Neuwirth, *Die Wochenrechnungen und der Betrieb des Prager Dombaus in den Jahren 1372-1378*, Prague, 1890.

be adduced: that of the Crusades.[46] They originated as armed pilgrimages and were then idealized as "holy wars," for pacifistic ears a contradiction in terms. What they actually were is well known: the interplay of political forces from about 1096 to 1291. The chief protagonists were the popes with their religiously colored rallying-cries—war on the "infidels," more properly, those of other faiths, the freeing of the Holy Sepulcher—and with the princes of Europe, as military leaders, each with his own personal claim to power, the emperors of Byzantium, the many Mohammedan potentates in Asia Minor, Syria, Egypt, the commercial city-states of Genoa, Pisa, Venice, that possessed the indispensable fleets but put them at the disposal of the Crusades only when the undertaking spelled profits. This drama of two hundred years in length is, from the psychological point of view, a paradigm of all human frailty and inner contradictions. On the whole it was a failure, at least with respect to the original goal, but in widening geographical horizons, fostering an upsurge of commerce and the prosperity of cities, and making European Christianity receptive to new ideas it was enormously successful. The Crusades are politically the most important factor in the first two centuries of Gothic. They gave birth to the militant orders that accomplished the miracle of fusing the ideals of monasticism with the chivalric values of heroism, forcefulness, and soldierly honor. These orders functioned as patrons, and the Teutonic Order, like the Cistercians and the mendicant orders, evolved its own architectural characters within the later stages of Gothic. For the early period of Gothic, however, it has been assumed that there was direct influence from local specimens of architecture in the East, and the spread of the pointed arch in France has been attributed to the Dome of the Rock in Jerusalem. The First Crusade ended on July 15, 1099, with the storming of Jerusalem, and after a senseless and brutal massacre in the streets, the blood-spattered noble lords met in the church of the Holy Sepulcher for a service of thanksgiving and a few days later in the Dome of the Rock for a council. It is a very romantic idea to mingle the fundamental idea of the Crusades, namely, mass murder in the name of Christ, with the pointed arches of the Dome of the Rock, and in this way to see the birth of Gothic as a divine reward. Of course, this has never been so explicitly expressed, but it can be read between the lines in Wren's theory

46 Eduard Heyck, *Die Kreuzzüge und das heilige Land* (Monographien zur Weltgeschichte, XII), Bielefeld und Leipzig, 1900. Further, Ernest Barker's article in the *Encyclopaedia Britannica*, s.v. Crusades, where further literature is given.

of the derivation of Gothic from the Saracens.[47] Today we are of the opinion that the quadripartite ribbed vaults were more important for the initial development of Gothic than the pointed arches, and we know that the former were already introduced some years before the First Crusade. Gothic and the Crusades run on parallel courses, they are connected by some threads, and in that fact, if anywhere, must be sought their common root.

It was natural that the Franks who founded kingdoms in the Levant and in Cyprus should transplant their Gothic architecture to the Orient and that, conversely, borrowings and reminiscences of the Orient should be demonstrable in the West. Before the knights and their vassals left the homeland, they dedicated themselves to their holy mission in *Gothic* churches, at least from the Second Crusade on (Suger's period). Many never reached the Holy Land; many remained there and died in exile; many returned home, most of them disillusioned and skeptical. A whole literature arose seeking to explain the failures. Gothic, on the other hand, had no failures. It built at home places of divine worship for the same God who let the Crusades be wrecked, who allowed even the initial successes to be lost in personal jealousies. The Crusades are the real world, real humanity, real history; Gothic is also absolute reality, but it is the realization of that ideal or, more properly ideated, intended, dreamed of world, humanity, and history. Albrecht's temple of the Grail is as poetry, in addition to all else, liberated from any cares of practice, procurement of materials, costs, statics; it is Gothic, if we call that *dream* which impelled the knights and the armed pilgrims to take the cross Gothic. This dream is the root for which we are seeking.

But is this not true of every epoch of cultural history? Certainly. What we mean from the point of view of history of ideas, the dream, the imaginative conception, which society in its generations creates by common intellectual effort, is always a wish image that occupies the mind as much as wishing and desiring. It is now clear that the root of culture is not *one* of its threads but always and from the very beginning a many-colored, loose tissue composed of all. In this colorfulness there is a dominant shade. We have met it over and over again in the case of the culture of the Gothic age. Spirituality, the idea of the other world, the concern for the forgiveness of sins, all accompany the cult of the carts and the Crusades. Crimes and violations of the laws promulgated by the state, sins and transgressions against divine commandments: redemption

[47] For this thesis see below p. 364.

from sin is the religious as well as ethical basic conception, and within its confines the change to nominalism, to subjectivism, to this-worldliness could and did occur, without loss of the spiritual, mystic fundamental attitude.

The architecture of Gothic symbolized through its forms that which was the great theme in all the individual areas of contemporary culture. This may perhaps only be expressed with complete clarity at the end of this book, but it can already be seen at this point that the literary sources for Gothic go far beyond the texts quoted and that the answer to the question of how the contemporaries of Gothic felt about this style will only then be full and resonant when we include the scholasticism and mysticism of the period, the fantastic Crusades, the poetry of Albrecht and Dante, not as a beautiful background but as the Fata Morgana that hovered before men's minds and gave direction to their lives, their deeds, their writings, their sculpture and paintings, and thus also to their buildings, secular as well as sacral. If we want to express it in the style of that age we may say that the idea of Gothic was the pillar of fire, showing the way to the pious amid the wilderness of the reality of human passions.

The cult of relics was in itself not Gothic, the same is true of the belief in miracles, of the magic of precious stones, of symbolism, of the metaphysics of light, or of the entertaining automata, but they all, as parts of the total culture, as a new "configuration," acquired a common hue: everything is miracle, even the automata share in it, everything is Grace, for man alone is frail. We have seen how many names of architects have come down to us from the age of Gothic, but the men behind these names are for us almost without exception pale shades. Even today the great cathedrals seem to us like miracles. He who sees them as such, despite all his knowledge of their statics and rationality, sees Gothic architecture with the eyes of the Gothic.

Yet, if scholars insist on getting at the root of Gothic culture, comprising scholasticism, mysticism, liturgy, crusades, cult of relics, asceticism, poetry, and all the other components, then the answer has to be that the root of all roots is Jesus from Nazareth. In the language of symbolism he could be identified with the pillar of fire in the desert of life, himself not "Gothic." The ideal of following his teaching generated different styles before Gothic and afterwards. The common root feeds different blossoms; they are alike Christian, only in different degrees and according to other interpretation. Gothic culture seems to be the purest and most intensive realization of the spirit contained in the New Testament.

II. THE PERIOD OF REACTION AGAINST GOTHIC

1. Early Humanism

THE historians of our generation have been slow to learn to distinguish between Humanism and Renaissance. They sought the beginnings of the Renaissance and arrived at Humanism;[1] they tried to define the boundary between mediaeval and modern, many ultimately abandoning the idea of drawing a dividing line at all.[2] Indeed, they thought it could be shown that the classicism of antiquity, at least in Italy, had never come to an end. To a certain extent this is true. All during the "Middle Ages," although this period supposedly did not exist, the Latin authors, Cicero, Virgil, Vitruvius, and so on, were copied; Latin was spoken, it was the official language of the chancelleries, the language of divine worship, of theological and other scientific literature; it was also the epistolary medium. The belief in Rome as a world power persisted. Both the Papacy and the Empire were bound to Rome and ideologically inseparable from the concept of the supremacy of the Roman Empire. Even the pagan Roman religion survived in many folk customs and superstitions, and so one can continue the prolongation of antiquity. But this thesis inevitably leads to its opposite, namely, that these were only externals. Intensely realistic struggles for power were masked by an ideology that sought to prove its right on the basis of classical tradition, yet was thoroughly mediaeval. Mediaeval Latin was spoken, but only as a means of communication within the Holy Roman Empire; and the copies of ancient authors served merely as schoolbooks in the monasteries and as grammars for the study of the language of the Empire.

The new element in the attitude of PETRARCH (1304-1374) toward Cicero and Virgil was his delight in the perfection of Latin poetry and literary prose. From about 1325 on he appears as a writer of letters that were intended for the public, though they were sent to specific individuals. His laborious life centered about the idea that his own time—the mediaeval—was ugly, classical antiquity was beautiful, and with his "elegant," that is, classical Latin he was called to stamp out the barbaric (literary) crimes of a "dark" age.[3] He declared that Scholasticism should be repudiated and that one should go back to Plato, not Aristotle.[4] He could not read the Greek Plato that he owned, but he knew

[1] A standard work on early Humanism is still Georg Voigt's book, *Wiederbelebung des klassischen Altertums oder das erste Jahrhundert des Humanismus*, Berlin, 1859 (2nd rev. ed., 1880; 3rd ed., 1893).

[2] Fedor Schneider, *Rom und Romgedanke im Mittelalter*, Munich, 1926.

[3] H. W. Eppelsheimer, *Petrarca*, Bonn, 1926, p. 37.

[4] *Ibid.*, p. 61.

certain dialogues in Latin translation and tried to obtain guidance from those Latin authors whose mode of thought was Platonic. Aristotle, of course, was also a philosopher of *antiquity*, but for Petrarch he was identified with scholasticism and the gloomy spirit of the Middle Ages. Petrarch scorned natural science, too, as a matter of fact, in its scholastic form. In short, he painted for himself a picture of the two epochs in which the one was represented by all the bright colors, the other by all the dark. To carry this out consistently was not easy. For later Humanists the criterion was *ratio*, inner harmony, and intellectual clarity, but for Petrarch this was not yet significant. In any case, his admiration for ancient Rome is thoroughly emotional, poetic, and irrational, and so, too, his contempt for the barbarians is an emotional patriotism with respect to his ideal world that he localized in Rome. It was difficult for him to be reconciled to the person of Emperor Charles IV, who was on the one hand the *Roman* emperor, hence the glorious successor of Caesar and Augustus, but on the other hand merely a *German*.[5] This dilemma prevented him from being, in political matters, specifically anti-German; instead he saw as the real opponents of his intellectual world the French and the Greeks, meaning, of course, the modern Greeks or Byzantines.[6]

Contradictory as all human beings are, Petrarch nevertheless praised Cologne Cathedral. In 1333 he was in Cologne and wrote: "In the middle of the city I saw an uncommonly beautiful temple, which, though still incomplete, can be called with good reason the most magnificent (*summum*)."[7]

By Humanism was formerly understood simply the reawakening of interest in ancient languages and literatures. These, however, were only the indispensable means of approaching the spirit of antiquity. Viewed less superficially, Humanism was concerned with comprehending the characteristic values of antiquity, its universally human, transcendental values—if one goes back to the word *humanitas*—and consequently with admiring them and making them the absolute standard of all critical judgment.[8] This new evaluation of antiquity meant a revalua-

[5] *Ibid.*, p. 97.

[6] *Ibid.*, p. 149.

[7] Petrarca, *Epist. famil.*, ep. IV (quoted from P. Clemen, *Der Dom zu Köln*, Düsseldorf, 1937, p. 59).

[8] Eppelsheimer, *op.cit.*, p. 45. It is not my intention here to go deeply into this problem. Attention may be called to Werner Jaeger, *Antike und Humanismus*, 1925, and *Paideia*, Berlin, 1933; further, to J. Huizinga, "Das Problem der Renaissance," *Italien, Monatsschrift für Kultur, Kunst und Literatur*, Heidelberg, 1927, p. 327.

tion of contemporary mediaeval ideals and a division of history into two epochs: antiquity and the Middle Ages.

Art was also affected by this division. In his will of 1370 Petrarch says of a panel painting by Giotto in his possession that the ignorant do not understand its beauty but the masters of art are astonished.[9] One may assume that by masters of art are actually meant artists, but it is clear that Petrarch included himself as an expert of art, and indeed all humanistically trained men seem to have been considered by him as *cognoscenti*, or, as we should say today, *connoisseurs.* With the new differentiation of historical periods according to humanistic values, the history of art was also divided into two epochs: a brilliant age of good art and a gloomy one of poor art. Good art was understood to mean ancient Greek and ancient Roman, bad art was on the one hand mediaeval Greek, that is Byzantine (*maniera greca*), and on the other French and German, that is, Gothic. Good art descended from Petrarch's (ostensible) forefathers, the Romans, poor art from barbarians.

Petrarch does not seem to have expressed this theory of the barbaric origin of Gothic so explicitly and pointedly, but it has its root in his nationalistic construction of history. Even today it is not dead. Not only in Romance countries is there a kind of unspoken agreement that German art is barbaric, but also in Germany many half-educated persons identify art with "beauty" and this beauty with Greek and Roman sculpture. In this view the artist is really a man who has first of all good taste, thus enabling him to discover in nature what is beautiful, and who is then skillful enough to imitate this given "nature" exactly and compellingly. As is well known, this aesthetic theory underwent great refinement in the course of centuries, the conception of beauty itself also being subjected to many transformations, but the essence survived. Only in modern times did a counter-movement arise that dethroned beauty and the imitation of nature, retaining the theory of barbaric origin but changing the indices of values: anti-naturalism and character were again esteemed and became the prerogative of a few chosen nations, among them the German. But the development of the older theory of imitation—itself inherited from antiquity—was an essential factor in the contempt for Gothic. This contempt was later to become a humanistic dogma. It began as a critique of the representational arts and was then inevitably applied to architecture. Therefore we must consider these early manifestations in their general outlines.

9 Lionello Venturi, "La Critica d'arte in Italia . . . ," *L'Arte*, xx, 1917, p. 306.

Dante Alighieri had emphasized two contemporary painters in the *Divine Comedy*, Cimabue and Giotto. He said merely that Cimabue had formerly been highly valued but was now surpassed by Giotto.[10] The commentators, however, drew all possible conclusions from this remark. Above all, they had to ask themselves what could be meant by saying that Giotto had progressed beyond Cimabue. Dante had not indicated what the nature of this progress was. BOCCACCIO (1313-1375), who was himself one of the early commentators on Dante, gave the first decisive answer. In his *Decameron*, which appeared in 1353, he recorded his interpretation of Dante's comment on Giotto: "Giotto was able to paint all natural and artificial objects in a completely lifelike manner, so that many persons considered them to be real. In this way *he brought to light again the art* that had been buried for centuries through the fault of many painters who painted to please the ignorant, rather than the *cognoscenti*."[11] Similarity to nature, a main prop of ancient aesthetics, is here stressed as a characteristic of Giotto's paintings in the service of a reawakening of ancient art, and with it is mingled, as in Petrarch, the vanity of humanistic literati, who felt that they formed a higher aristocratic class of experts and connoisseurs. The fame of the great artist is here considered to be dependent on the writer who praises him.

By his remarks Boccaccio made Giotto the reviver of naturalism and "in consequence" of antiquity. With this implicit "in consequence" he unwittingly left to posterity the task of freeing itself of an error as an initial step in acquiring a better insight, but at first his immediate successors adopted the error, in order to elaborate rather than eliminate it.

Filippo VILLANI (about 1404) was the first to follow in Boccaccio's footsteps. He wrote biographies of famous men of his native city, including Giotto also in his collection. Artists were thereby recognized for the first time as of equal importance with politicians and scholars; they became, as it were, socially acceptable. Villani says in the introduction to Giotto's biography: "Let me be permitted at this point—I might say, to quiet the mockers—to mention the excellent Florentine painters who have revived the bloodless and almost extinct art. Among them Johannes, called Cimabue, was the first who began with skill and understanding to recall to naturalness the antiquated art of painting, which, thanks to the painters' ignorance, had childishly lapsed from fidelity to nature and was for a long time, as it were, playfully roaming

[10] Purgatorio, XI, 95.

[11] Cf. text, Appendix 12.

in uncertainties. It is a fact that before this [painter] Greek and Latin painting had lain prostrate in its execution because of many centuries of coarse work, as the figures and pictures that are to be seen on panels and walls adorning the churches of the saints clearly demonstrate."[12] This definitely goes back to Boccaccio's words: "avendo egli quella arte ritornata al luce." Later the concept was defined by the word *rinascita*—Renaissance, Revival. Villani contends that Cimabue was the first to lead the old art of painting back toward similarity to nature which, out of the ignorance of the painters, deviated from that similarity to nature. Whether Villani is justified in claiming for Cimabue in particular the virtue of fidelity to nature does not need to be discussed here. What he means seems to be clear, yet the interpretation is not quite so simple.

In general it amounts to the following thesis: what existed prior to Cimabue was without imitation of nature, and what he contributed was just this imitation; the former is bad art, the latter good art *or* rebirth of antiquity, since, as was well known, the decisive factor of good art, according to the ancient authors, was always its verisimilitude, when, for example, grapes were painted the birds would peck at them. Therefore Villani considered that Cimabue began the "Renaissance."

But what do *we* understand by Renaissance? In sculpture it begins in Florence about 1408 with Nanni di Banco's group of the *Quattro Coronati* for Or San Michele, in architecture with the Ospedale degli Innocenti in 1419, and in painting not until 1421 with Masaccio's frescoes for the chapel of the Brancacci. Villani, however, died before all this, in 1404. His biographies are even supposed to have been composed by 1382, and he had no experience at all of what *we* call Renaissance. What he meant by it, namely, the works of Cimabue and Giotto, *we* call *Gothic*.

As can be seen, it is entirely a question of what is understood at various times by Gothic or by Renaissance. If one were to identify Renaissance merely with naturalism, then it would begin with the earliest cave paintings of the Stone Age. But one can then also call Renaissance what was naturalistic in Gothic or what seemed to be so in the opinion of the time. If, on the other hand, by Renaissance is understood only the imitation of antiquity, thus a quite specific stylization and idealization within naturalism, then the Renaissance began with Niccolo Pisano. Today, naturalism is no longer considered a suf-

[12] Cf. text, Appendix 13.

ficient sign of Renaissance,[13] and Giotto, insofar as the concept of Gothic is extended from architecture to painting, is attributed to Gothic in its Italian modification.

Krautheimer, therefore, has tried to interpret Villani differently from Schlosser. He relates the division of epochs that Villani had in mind to the temporal boundary between the *maniera greca* and Gothic, as represented by Cimabue.[14] Objectively, that is, as far as history itself is concerned, Krautheimer is right. But if Villani were to rise from the dead he would have to reply: I know nothing of Gothic, nothing of Renaissance; I am talking (in all naïveté) only of a rebirth of that kind of imitation of nature which, in the opinion of us Humanists, characterizes antiquity.

Just this is the result of the confusion caused by Boccaccio. The Humanists emulating him damned the Middle Ages, but they saved Cimabue and Giotto from this hell, partly because *Dante* had mentioned them, partly because these two artists had turned away from Byzantine idealism and become more lifelike in their work. Thus Villani created a new system of epochs.

St. Jerome divided history into four periods, according to Daniel 2:40. The fourth period he assigned to the Roman Empire. This fourth period was declared by Orosius to be perpetual until the coming reign of Antichrist. In this way, the empire was prolonged down through papal rule to the Holy Roman Empire, so that antiquity and the Middle Ages merged into each other.[15] Petrarch distinguished subdivisions of the history of the world within this fourth period, as it were, IV a Antiquity, and IV b the Middle Ages. Villani added a third epoch IV c: modern times, intended to begin with Cimabue and Giotto. *This* concept of *modern times* is not identical with *our* concept of *Renaissance*. Thus the paradox arises that Cimabue and Giotto, called by us *Gothic*, were declared by Boccaccio and Villani, with ostentatious contempt for

13 Johan Huizinga, "Renaissance und Realismus," in *Wege zur Kulturgeschichte*, Munich, 1930, p. 140. It may be said, moreover, that the naturalism of cave art, of Gothic, and so on, is different each time.

14 Richard Krautheimer, "Die Anfänge der Kunstgeschichtsschreibung in Italien," *Repertorium für Kunstwissenschaft*, Berlin and Leipzig, 1929, vol. 50, p. 49.

15 On this matter of historical epochs cf. Wallace K. Ferguson, "The Humanist View of the Renaissance," *American Historical Review*, January 1940. Orosius divides the history of the world into seven eras: 1) the creation to the division of Alexander's empire, 2) to the conquest of Rome by the Gauls, 3) to the division of Alexander's empire, 4) to the destruction of Carthage, 5) to the first Civil War, 6) to the birth of Christ, 7) to 417, the year in which Orosius was writing. This latter date, however, does not mean the end of an epoch, for Orosius did not consider his work epochal. He died a year later, in 418. The mere enumeration of his divisions reveals much about his conception of history.

Gothic, to be creators of the *Renaissance* that they did not yet know —insofar as our concept is meant. Rebirth or revival is indeed a very vague expression, unless one indicates each time exactly what is actually reborn or revived. The real solution to the problem doubtless lies in the fact that the criterion of historical division for the Humanists was *value*, and their judgment of value was oriented toward the similarity to nature and to antiquity, once the latter had become their idol. The fallacy in logic was that they wanted to divide historical epochs according to the values of antiquity although each epoch has, after all, its own specific values; and the difference between epochs must accordingly be sought elsewhere. Dante, with his verses about Cimabue and Giotto, was the highest authority. If he praised Cimabue and, even more, Giotto, they both became unquestionably valuable. But since the Middle Ages were not considered to be of value, it followed that these artists could no longer belong to the Middle Ages and were, therefore, both to be recognized as something new, or, really, as something very old, for in them antiquity lived again. In this sequence of ideas the possibility that a thing could be both good *and* Gothic was completely overlooked, since this was incompatible with the fundamental conception of Humanism. The most astonishing aspect of this circular argument is that Dante himself was considered "good" and was nevertheless by no means a Renaissance author, but the greatest poet of "Gothic"—at least according to our modern view.

The interrelation of the concepts of imitation of nature, beauty, and antiquity has been very well clarified by Landsberger.[16] After a discussion of many passages he makes this statement: "Imitation of nature is now no longer the imitation of individual objects or even of parts of objects, but imitation of its supreme formative law. Only now do we understand why the imitation of nature could also be obligatory for architecture." The word "now" refers to the fifteenth century, the time of Alberti's aesthetics and artistic theory. Landsberger thus bridges the gap between the aesthetics of imitation in painting and sculpture and the new form of architecture. He believes that the contradiction between the rejection of the artists' imitation of older paintings and statues and the tendency to "imitate" classical architecture none the less, was not recognized because in the latter field the process was free and independent, more "a creating *like* antiquity than *after* antiquity (p. 3)." Whether or not Landsberger succeeded in being more precise about this "like," he here put his finger on the essential point. We sense a

[16] Franz Landsberger, *Die künstlerischen Probleme der Renaissance*, Halle, a.S., 1922.

principle of Humanism as yet to be discovered that finally—really only finally—called forth the Renaissance in art. But the Humanists needed, by no means, to have foreseen the conclusions that the artists did not reach until after Brunelleschi. Indeed, we have evidence showing that the appreciation of Gothic lingered even after the full development of the Renaissance; this is to be found in passages from the writing of Aeneas Silvius and Jakob Wimpheling.

Aeneas Silvius de PICCOLOMINI (1405-1464), born in Corsignano near Siena, grew up in poverty. He became a Humanist after his training in the school of Siena and later with Filelfo in Florence, but for the most part he was self-taught. His talent inclined him toward poetry; his poverty forced him to earn his bread as the secretary of cardinals. His dependence on these employers, whom he changed upon occasion, brought him into close contact with the political intrigues within the church—the Council of Basel and Pope Eugene IV—as well as with those between this pope and Sigmund, the German king, who aspired to and attained the imperial coronation. Silvius was in Basel from 1431 to 1435, traveled to England and Scotland as ambassador, became secretary to the Anti-Pope, Felix V, in 1438, and was in Frankfort on the Main in 1442, becoming there private secretary to Frederick III and living for a long time in Vienna in this capacity. In 1447 he entered the priesthood and soon became Bishop of Trieste; shortly thereafter he was appointed Bishop of Siena by Pope Nicholas V. After he had arranged the concordat with Frederick III, he was made a cardinal in 1456, and in 1458, after the death of Calixtus III, he was elected pope, taking the name of Pius II, with reference, it is said, to Virgil's words "pius Aeneas." The character of this man is in dispute. As pope he not only turned away from the notorious poetry of his youth, as far as it was in the frivolous style of the *Decameron*, but he also changed diametrically in his attitude toward church councils. One may be reminded of the proverb, "un ministre radical n'est plus un radical ministre." Modern historians call him an opportunist and adventurer, but the adventurer was several times undaunted by mortal danger, and his opportunism, his frequent changes of front, might be more justly regarded as a courageous acknowledgment of the various stages of his intellectual development. The more one learns of this man who rose from a dissolute student through many vicissitudes to the papal throne, the more his innermost being, his Faustian striving, his industry, his elegant Latin style, his comprehensive knowledge triumph; one gradually forgets the fairy-tale pattern, the unrecognized Cinderella passing from the depths to the heights—whether this pattern is interpreted as the result of native energy or of grace—and one takes pleasure in the frank, clear gaze of an Italian who could look at the Europe of his day so objectively, so realistically, and at the same time so subjectively from the standpoint of his personal advantages.[17]

The purpose of this brief sketch is to provide a background for the understanding of Silvius' descriptions of cities. He was a geographer and a historian. In 1457 he wrote a little book on Germany, three passages from which shall be cited. Of Frankfort on the Main he says: "In Franconia on the River Main lies Frankfordia, a place of commerce between Lower and Upper Germans (*Teutones*), and though it is for the most part built of wood, nevertheless one sees it adorned with palaces of stone, in which kings might not unworthily be received, churches (*templa*) truly sacred to God and exceedingly proud with cut stone."[18] Then he mentions also the long stone bridge and the *Praetorium nobile* where the imperial elections take place.

A second description concerns Nuremberg. "What a countenance has this city, what splendor, what pleasantness, what delight, what cultivation (*cultus*), what a form of government, what more than this could anyone ask for a commonalty [city] perfect in all its parts! What a sight (*panorama*) of this city for those who approach from Lower Franconia and behold it from nearby; what majesty, what adornment for those seeing it from outside, what beauty (*nitor*) of the squares within, what neatness of the houses! What is there more impressive than the church of St. Sebaldus, what is more resplendent than the church of St. Laurentius! What is prouder or better fortified than the Royal Castle, what more famous than the moats and city walls! How worthy of kings is the City Hall here! The most excellent kings of the Scots would wish to dwell like the lesser citizens of Nuremberg."[19]

When Silvius wrote that, St. Sebaldus already had its hall choir (built 1361-1377), that of St. Laurentius, on the other hand, was still in the initial stages (begun 1439, not finished until 1477). These sentences are rhetorical; but the Humanist had seen the city silhouette and appreciated it as much as the squares and houses. In those days the architecture was still entirely Gothic, nowhere was there any of that Nuremberg Renaissance that later filled the city with questionable revivals of the

[17] Anton Weiss, *Aeneas Sylvius Piccolomini als Papst Pius II*, Graz, 1897; William Boulting, *Aeneas Silvius, Orator, Man of Letters, Statesman, and Pope*, London, 1908; Thea Buyken, *Enea Silvio Piccolomini, sein Leben und Werden bis zum Episkopat*, Bonn, 1931.

[18] Friedrich Heininger, *Aeneas Silvius Germanica*, Leipzig, 1926.

[19] Cf. text, Appendix 14.

antique. The northern Gothic of the city charmed the Italian Humanist as a work of aggregate arts; he had no prejudice against Gothic.[20]

The third description is of Strasbourg. Here Aeneas Silvius felt reminded of Venice because of the canals that then still traversed the city, but in Venice, he says, the waters are salty and of a bad odor, whereas in Strasbourg the contrary is true. Then he speaks of the cathedral: "The episcopal church, called the minster, built most magnificently of cut stone, rises as a very extensive edifice, adorned with two towers, of which the one that is completed, an admirable work, hides its head in the clouds."[21] "Caput inter nubila condit" may also be called a rhetorical phrase, but Silvius did not criticize or reject the tower of Strasbourg Cathedral, but called it a "mirabile opus." We shall see that here is to be found the root of Goethe's panegyric of 1772. Silvius' laudatory, even enthusiastic remarks in favor of Gothic testify to the fact that the Humanists themselves had not yet drawn for architecture the ultimate inferences of their own change of conviction.

After Silvius had become Pope he built the Palazzo Piccolomini in his native city, Corsignano, that from now on was called Pienza, and he also built the Palazzo Vescovile, Palazzo Communale, and the cathedral. The latter he described himself in detail, an important example for the Early Renaissance in the series of extant architectural descriptions. In our connection the following passage should be stressed: "Three naves (as they say) make up the edifice, the central one broader, all of equal height: thus Pius commanded it, who had seen this type among the Germans in Austria. This thing [arrangement] is more beautiful (*venustius*) and makes the church lighter."[22] By this his own direction to build a hall-church, Silvius gave proof in deeds of his sympathy for Gothic. The architect in charge, Rosselino, who had never seen German hall-churches, as far as we know, seems to have worked from the Pope's sketch. He employed the new forms of Brunelleschi's and Alberti's school wherever he could or was allowed, but he covered the tripartite hall-church with Gothic ribbed vaults and filled the large

20 How different was Mozart's reaction to Nuremberg. In a letter from Frankfurt a.M. of September 28, 1790, he writes to his wife about the journey from Vienna: "In Regensburg we dined splendidly, with divine music, angelic service, and an excellent Mosel wine. We breakfasted in Nuremberg—an ugly city. In Würzburg, a beautiful, magnificent city, we strengthened our precious stomach with coffee—the food was tolerable everywhere—only two and a half posts from here, in Aschaffenburg mine host took it upon himself to cheat us abominably." From Ludwig Schiedermair, *Die Briefe W. A. Mozarts*, II, Munich and Leipzig, 1914, p. 317.

21 Cf. text, Appendix 14.

22 Ludwig Heinrich Heydenreich, "Pius II als Bauherr von Pienza," *Zeitschrift für Kunstgeschichte*, VI, 1937, p. 105. Here the original text is printed on p. 110.

pointed arched windows with Gothic tracery. Silvius stresses the windows in his description: " . . . when the sun shines they let in so much light that the churchgoers imagine themselves in a house of glass, not of stone." Here one is reminded of the *capella vitrea,* and also of Niavis. The brightness is now that of the Renaissance, it belongs together with the columns, round arches, portals and aediculae of the façade, with their gables and all the profiles. This brightness without stained glass is the new style's form of light, and Silvius seems to have been quite clear about the difference between Gothic illumination and the modern one. His pride in the "house of glass" has reference to the daylight.

Little can be added to Heydenreich's study. He has tried to define the visual contrast to the buildings of Hans von Burghausen (erroneously called Stettheimer), those prototypes of the Pienza Cathedral, by the words "spatial totality" and "spatial aspect." The former expression refers to the "Late Gothic space that extended dynamically in all directions," the latter to the "Renaissance space that had a static-scenographical direction." I believe that Heydenreich means precisely what I tried to define for the form of light by the words *vielbildig* (in Gothic) and *ein-bildig* (in Renaissance),[23] except that he includes in addition the form of the forces, that is, the contrast between the dynamic and the static. This brings us back to what was probably in Landsberger's mind when he wrote that the Renaissance created *like* antiquity, not *after* it. This "like" can be expressed by precise concepts; Silvius, however, did not yet have such means of argumentation at his command, but we nevertheless deduce from his words that he possessed that peculiar understanding both for Late Gothic and for Early Renaissance which permitted the erection of such a charming structure as a mixture not only of two temporal styles but also, at the same time, of two national styles.

At this stage we can revert to the question of the principle of Humanism that was raised earlier. The Middle Ages and, in the highest degree, the intellectual culture of the Late Gothic period do not take Man as their point of departure but God, the universe; the Humanistic principle, on the other hand, means shifting the focus, seeing from

[23] A verbal translation of these terms would be "unispect" and "multispect"; it means that Renaissance tries to give the impression that one could grasp the whole building from one point and at the same time to get the idea of the total form from each point, whereas Late Gothic aims to many different aspects, each one individual and surprising. Comparing Early Renaissance and Late Gothic Heydenreich says that the space of S. Spirito in Florence is "im Vergleich zu dem dynamisch allseitig sich ausdehnenden Totalraum der Spätgotik ein statisch-skenographisch gerichteter Ansichtsraum."

man's point of view, and, to this extent, it is the discovery of personality in Michelet's and Burckhardt's sense. With this in mind, Renaissance realism and naturalism can be understood, as well as the necessity for replacing Gothic with something expressive of the new man, the new humanity, the new way of "being man." To create *like* antiquity means precisely to be "humane" in that implied sense that we do not need to analyze further. The difference in the concepts of Humanism and Renaissance that is meant here can be defined as that between notion and perception. Humanism stayed in the realm of notions; in matters of the spirit, it remained literary. The Renaissance introduced that fundamental concept of seeing from the human point of view into the world of sensuous perception. The expression "seeing" is metaphorical, just as the "viewing" of the world is in the German expression *Weltanschauung*; what the Humanists "saw" in their minds was visibly expressed in the Renaissance.

Aeneas Silvius lived on in the memory of following generations through his literary works, which acquired a belated authority because of the ultimate ecclesiastical eminence that their Humanistic author had attained. Thus it is understandable that another Humanist, Wimpheling, should refer to him.

Jacob WIMPHELING (1450-1528) born in Schlettstadt, studied in Freiburg and Erfurt, spent the years from 1469 to 1483 in Heidelberg, and was preacher at the cathedral in Speyer until 1498. He returned to Heidelberg for three years, but then passed the remainder of his life, 1501-1528, in Strasbourg.[24] He never left South Germany and though he doubtless observed much German architecture open-eyed, he was not familiar with a single *Italian* Renaissance structure. There was no German Renaissance architecture before 1509, when the Fugger chapel, which Wimpheling did not see, was built in Augsburg. We can say that when he wrote his *Germania* in 1501 and then his *Epitome rerum Germanicarum* a year later, this Humanist was acquainted only with Romanesque, Gothic, and Late Gothic architecture.

His *Germania* has been published in a new High German translation.[25] The first part of the book is a polemic against the claim that Alsace is French; the second, a moral discourse forming a frame for Wimpheling's recommendation that a *Gymnasium* be founded in Strasbourg, that is, a Latin school where boys should learn Latin "in-

24 Joseph Knepper, *Jakob Wimfeling (1450-1528). Sein Leben und seine Werke, usw.*, Freiburg, 1902. (The spelling of the name Wimpheling varies.)

25 E. Martin, *Wimphelings Germania*, Strasbourg and Tübingen, 1885.

stead of letting themselves be debauched, corrupted, and ruined by hawking, revels, idleness, gambling, hair curling, and bad company of both sexes." As a matter of fact, the lodges were also afraid of such dangers for their apprentices and journeymen. Wimpheling, however, was no longer interested in the building of cathedrals but rather in Latin and classical literature, and incidentally, as he says, in the idea that the boys could learn about architecture from Vitruvius. Murner prevented the execution of his plan at first by highly unfair, though amusing polemics,[26] and not until 1538 did Wimpheling's pupil, Johannes Sturm, succeed in establishing such a Latin school, from which Strasbourg University eventually developed, where Goethe, very much later, spent a semester. If Wimpheling may be called the intellectual father of Strasbourg University, Goethe is connected with him by an invisible, historical bond, as well as by his pronouncement on Strasbourg Cathedral.

This is to be found in Wimpheling's history of the German people, his *Epitome rerum Germanicarum*, of 1502. The first sixty-three of the seventy-two chapters discuss the history of the Germanic people subsequent to Caesar's time, then that of the German kings from Charlemagne to Maximilian I, and finally the particular merits of the Germans. Chapter 64 praises the invention of *Bombarda*, that is, gunpowder, chapter 65 that of printing (chapter 66 is missing in the edition I used).[27] Chapter 67 concerns the architecture of the Germans, and here the statement occurs: "In architecture the Germans are the most distinguished. Aeneas Silvius writes that he was able to admire their buildings but not explain them. In my opinion, so he says, the Germans are wonderful mathematicians and surpass all peoples in architecture. An Italian asserts this of the Germans, and he has not said anything untrue, as is abundantly proved by the cathedral in Strasbourg and the tower connected with it, even if one ignores the other buildings that have been erected on a most magnificent scale everywhere in Germany. I assume that nothing on earth is more rare, more excellent than this one edifice. Who can admire enough or praise enough the Strasbourgers' tower, which easily surpasses all the buildings in Europe in its carved ornamental work, statues and sculptures of manifold objects, and which has a height of more than 415 ells? It is a miracle that one

[26] Waldemar Kawerau, *Thomas Murner und die deutsche Reformation* (Schriften des Vereins für Reformationsgeschichte, VIII), parts 30-32, Halle a.S., 1890.

[27] *Epitome Germanicarum Rerum*, in Simon Schard: Rerum Germanicarum Scriptores varii, ed. Thoma, Giessen, 1673, pp. 229-238; cf. also A. Horawitz, "Kunstgeschichtliche Miscellen aus deutschen Historikern," *Zeitschrift für bildende Kunst*, Leipzig, 1873, I, p. 26.

could raise anything to such a height. If Scopas, Phidias, Ctesiphon, and Archimedes, artists highly praised by highly praised authors, should ever rise from the dead, they would declare or openly admit themselves vanquished by what has been accomplished by our masters in architecture, and would prefer this work to the temple of Diana in Ephesus and the Egyptian pyramids and all [works] that are included in the seven wonders of the world."[28]

For a Humanist there was no higher praise. The allusion to the seven wonders later crystallized into the thesis that the tower of Strasbourg Cathedral was the eighth wonder of the world. Such is the designation given to it in 1548 on Konrat Monrat's engraving, and in 1617 the expression occurs again in Schadäus. This praise was handed down in its literary form, and persuaded one generation after another to believe in the excellence of Strasbourg Cathedral. *Saxa loquuntur*—but for many, words speak far more intelligibly than stones.

In the passage just quoted, a differentiation must be made between what goes back to Aeneas Silvius and what stems from Wimpheling's own rhetoric. Aeneas Silvius had written: ". . . in my opinion the Germans are wonderful mathematicians and in architecture they surpass all peoples."[29] For him the concepts of mathematics and architecture are almost identical; in German architecture he admires the mathematical, that is to say, the geometrical method. Wimpheling also admires the mechanical achievement of raising the stones to the height of the Strasbourg tower. The sentence that Wimpheling quotes verbally from Silvius does not refer to Strasbourg directly, but Wimpheling used it nevertheless as the introduction to his own panegyric.

The brief chapter on the contributions of the Germans to architecture is followed by one on the fame of their painting and sculpture. He mentions Israel Alemanus (Israel of Meckenem), Martin Schon of Colmar (Schongauer), Albertus Dürer, and Johannes Hirtz of Strasbourg. In the case of Israel of Meckenem he refers to the fact that his works are in demand everywhere in Europe and are in the highest degree esteemed by other painters. Of Schongauer's works he mentions among others the Virgin in the Rose Arbor from the Martinskirche in Colmar. Dürer, "his pupil," is the most distinguished of all; he paints the "most absolute" pictures in Nuremberg; and the merchants carry them to Italy, where they are as highly valued by the most experienced painters

[28] Cf. text, Appendix 15a.

[29] Aeneas Silvius, *Epistolae*, CLXVII, p. 740: ". . . sunt meo judicio Theutonici mirabiles mathematici omnesque gentes in architectura superant."

as "Parrhasii aut Apellis tabulae." Hirtz, who died in 1463, he mentions from a sense of local patriotism.[30]

The few sentences on sculpture are surprising. He commends the earthenware vases and other vessels for daily use, adding that Corebus of Athens, the inventor of pottery, could admire and praise them. Perhaps he was thinking of vases with figured reliefs. In his description of the cathedral he had mentioned sculpture; that he forgets it here, shows his uncertainty in the field of art theory. (Cf. Appendix 15b.)

Wimpheling's judgment was not very profound, but at least the citation of the four masters, Meckenem, Schongauer, Dürer, and Hirtz, as equals of the architects of Strasbourg Cathedral shows how contemporary art was reflected in the mind of a German Humanist. It is clear that the graphic arts predominated in his knowledge, and that he ignored or forgot stained glass. He lived in the Abbey of St. Wilhelm, which had an abundance of excellent stained glass of the period around 1470, about a quarter of which was designed by Peter Hemmel, who died in Strasbourg after 1501 when Wimpheling returned there. He does not mention Hemmel.[31]

Wimpheling belonged to the circle of Strasbourg Humanists—Johannes Geiler (1445-1510), Sebastian Brant (1457-1521), Thomas Murner (1475-1537)—and he had connections with Erasmus. He is famous as a pedagogue, as *praeceptor Germaniae*, who fought against flogging in the schools. His *Epitome* is the first attempt at a history of the German people; some condemn it as chauvinistic and nationalistic, but some also emphasize the fact that it takes the step from mediaeval to modern historical writing.

While Wimpheling was studying the works of Aeneas Silvius and writing his *Germania*, the Libreria was being added to the cathedral in Siena by Silvius' nephew, Francesco Piccolomini. Pinturicchio completed the ceiling paintings in 1503. Thus, when Wimpheling was working at his *Epitome*, Pinturicchio was painting the wall frescoes with scenes from the most important events in the life of Pope Pius II. It is enough to suggest here that the frescoes and their architectural backgrounds should be compared with what Wimpheling wrote. It should also not be forgotten that in 1504 the ground plan for the rebuilding of St. Peter's was being decided in Rome. Wimpheling was a Humanist, still without knowledge of Renaissance art at a time when

30 About Hans Hirtz see Lilli Fischel, *Die Karlsruher Passion und ihr Meister*, Karlsruhe, 1952.

31 P. Frankl, *Peter Hemmel, Glasmaler von Andlau*, Berlin, 1957.

Renaissance was already entering upon the classic stage of its development. We must now turn our attention to Renaissance itself, which necessarily completed the turning away from Gothic.

2. The Judgments of the Early Renaissance

WHILE the word Renaissance was for a long time applied to everything that could be explained as a rebirth either of antiquity or the religious feeling of the Middle Ages (Burdach) or whatever it might be, Humanism could also be called Renaissance. Conversely, however, Italian *art* of the period from 1410 to 1520 was not also called Humanism, but always *solely* Renaissance. The word Humanism was reserved for the philological, literary, and philosophical studies that were oriented toward antiquity. This lack of precision is partially responsible for the difficulty of determining the "concept" of Renaissance. Behind the "word" stretches out a whole series of different, but partly identical "concepts." It is not necessary here to penetrate this thicket, it will be sufficient to say that in what follows Renaissance is to be understood only as Italian *art* from 1410 to 1520.[1]

The first Renaissance artist after Villani to write a few lines on the history of art was Lorenzo GHIBERTI (1378-1455).[2] Schlosser thought that he was not familiar with Villani's book, but Villani still lived to see the competition for the second door of the Baptistry in Florence and it is quite probable that he was personally acquainted with the circle of young artists in his native city. It would seem to be practically

[1] Probably the best appraisal of the various theories about the Renaissance is to be found in H. W. Eppelsheimer, "Das Renaissance-Problem," *Deutsche Vierteljahresschrift*, 1933, XI, p. 477. He divides the leading authors into two groups: that of the classicists—Stendahl, J. Michelet, J. Burckhardt, H. Wölfflin; and that of the romanticists—H. Thode, E. Gebhard, C. Neumann, K. Burdach. A third, most recent trend is represented by J. Huizinga and by Eppelsheimer himself. Mention of these names by no means exhausts the bibliography on the subject of the true nature of Renaissance; it is merely a clue to the rest of the literature. For the titles of books, as well as further information, Adolf Philippi, *Der Begriff der Renaissance*, Leipzig, 1912, will also be found valuable in addition to Eppelsheimer's essay. The article by Fergusson, cited above, offers some supplements. For the specific subject of the rebirth of the arts cf. the fine collection of sources in the article by Herbert Weisinger, "Renaissance Theories of the Revival of the Fine Arts," *Italica*, XX, No. 4, 1943, pp. 163ff. He cites Villani, Gyraldus, Lorenzo Valla, Erasmus, Palladio, Cosimo Bartoli, Leonardo da Vinci, and Vasari.

[2] For Ghiberti and the literature on him cf. Thieme-Becker, *Allgemeines Lexikon der bildenden Künste*, XIII, Leipzig, 1920, p. 541. Further, the works by Julius von Schlosser mentioned in Appendix 13, and his studies on Ghiberti: *Lorenzo Ghibertis Denkwürdigkeiten . . .*, Berlin, 1912, and *Leben und Meinungen des Florentiner Bildners Lorenzo Ghiberti*, Basel, 1941. Richard Krautheimer, *Lorenzo Ghiberti*, Princeton, 1956, I have not yet read.

certain that his conception of the history of art was known to everyone in the coterie of Florentine artists, and thus to Ghiberti as well.

Toward the end of his life Ghiberti began to write a book that bears the title *Commentarii.* It combines discussions on the history and theory of art with a series of biographies of artists. The latter fill the second volume of the *Commentarii*, and the biography of Giotto is preceded by a brief general survey of the history of art,[3] the contents of which can best be indicated by listing the epochs. Ghiberti distinguishes five periods:

1. Antiquity to the triumph of Christianity in 312.
2. The age of the decline of art, from 312 to around 1000.
3. The age of the crude *maniera greca*, down to about 1160.
4. Here a gap occurs, the age about which Ghiberti can find nothing to say. It has been interpreted as the (later so-called) Greek Renaissance in the Tuscan mosaics, and so on.
5. "comincio l'arte della pictura a s'ammontare in Etruria . . . ," that is, from the birth of Giotto in 1266 (or 1276) to the time at which Ghiberti wrote, thus to about 1450.

This division into epochs is intended to serve a specifically artistic orientation, but in its essentials it is based only on Italian political history; moreover, Ghiberti's geographical horizon is merely Florence, Siena, Rome, and Naples. His system of epochs is also based on value judgments. He writes as an artist for artists—in part probably for pupils or, possibly, successors of his own artistic bent. He is very independent in his judgments. Although he naturally misunderstands and criticizes adversely the *maniera greca*, he esteems not only Cimabue, as would be expected on Dante's authority, but also Duccio, whom Dante did not mention. His ideas are in part very vague and even barren. What he calls "decline" comprises without differentiation the art of the West from Constantine to Charlemagne, the Byzantine art of the East, the *maniera greca* of the West, Romanesque, and Gothic. His fifth period extends from Giotto to and including Ghiberti himself. There is lacking here, then, the distinction that *we* make between Gothic and Renaissance, just as it is in the case of Villani, although Ghiberti not only experienced the Renaissance, but helped to create it. One would like to assume that he must have known that his sculpture was different from that of the *trecento* in that field, although the transition was not so abrupt because of the works of Niccolò Pisano and Andrea Pisano.

[3] Cf. text, Appendix 16.

The question whether the contemporaries of a new style are as conscious of it as we should expect today arises here just as it did with Suger. There, a generation later, this consciousness was fully awakened in Gervase, and the corresponding is true of Alberti's generation.

The most casual comparison of Ghiberti's *Commentaries* with the fragments of the Lodge Books reveals the changed atmosphere. However meager Ghiberti's survey of the history of art before Giotto may be, his biographies of artists since Giotto are correspondingly rich, though the adjective is relative. In the literature of the lodges, which was very sparsely preserved, only the reference to the Squires of Prague can be adduced in this connection, and that owes its origin not to historical thinking but to the need to rely on authorities.

Ghiberti's book is exclusively based upon painting and sculpture. It inevitably aroused the desire for a corresponding division of architectural history into epochs. Here the objects spoke much more distinctly. Brunelleschi's buildings were a break with Gothic tradition. It is, then, quite consistent that the next step of criticism is to be found in the biography of Brunelleschi by Antonio di Tuccio MANETTI (1423-1491).[4]

Manetti is, moreover, the first author to attempt a more detailed survey of architectural history. After a consideration of primitive architecture in wood, stone, and brick (with reminiscences of Vitruvius), he takes up the pyramids of Egypt, the temples of the Greeks, the buildings of the Romans, and, strangely enough, those of the Tatars (with reference to the writings of Marco Polo). With the decline of the Roman Empire "architecture and architects declined also, and when the Vandals, Goths, Langobards, Huns, and others came, they brought with them architects and built in their native fashion in the lands that they ruled for centuries. But since the nations that came from afar had no gift for such things, they took the architects and masons that they found in the vicinity. . . ." He does not find a reflection of the splendor of the old Roman buildings until he comes to those built by Charlemagne in Florence, "in San Pierro Scheraggio et in Sant'

[4] The ascription of the biography to Manetti is not absolutely certain, but it goes by his name today. The text was published several times: in 1812 by Moreni, by H. Holz in *Filippo Brunellesco di Antonio Tuccio Manetti*, Stuttgart, 1887, and simultaneously by K. Frey in the *Sammlung ausgewählter Biographien Le Vite di Fil. Brunellesco*, Berlin, 1887. In the latter edition cf. pp. 78ff., and especially pp. 81 and 82. A more detailed summary of the contents than can be given here, together with an attempt to interpret the obscurities of the text, can be found in Julius Schlosser: *Lorenzo Ghibertis Denkwürdigkeiten*, Kunstgeschichtliches Jahrbuch der k.k. Zentralkommission, Vienna, 1910, p. 63 (not to be confused with Schlosser's edition of the text, of the year 1912). Cf. also Julius Schlosser, *Die Kunstliteratur*, p. 192.

Apostolo," for which Charlemagne had brought along his own architects. (It is well known that these structures are not Carolingian.) This kind of "Renaissance," however, did not last long, but was followed by another decline and "the empire passed into the hands of the Germans over the greater part of the world, and they grew strong and revived the German methods of building that endured down to our century, the age of Filippo [Brunellesco]."

Manetti's division results in four epochs from the conclusion of antiquity:

1. Decline from the end of the Roman Empire to the destruction of the Langobardic kingdom by Charlemagne, approximately 476-774. (One should perhaps add: the period of the barbarians between the last Roman and the first Holy Roman emperor;[5] Charlemagne, like Charles IV for Petrarch, is not an absolute barbarian, for his barbarianism was modified by the imperial Roman crown—which he received, only in the year 800.)
2. The Carolingian Renaissance, 774-?.
3. Renewed decline (despite all the Roman emperors), ?-1419.
4. The epoch of Brunellesco.

From this it appears that Manetti was the first to recognize in the Renaissance a new epoch in our sense, letting it begin for architectural history with Brunelleschi. On the other hand, he seems either not to have realized or considered important the difference between Romanesque and Gothic, since both fall under the common heading of barbarism. Manetti is even more limited to a local patriotism than Ghiberti, for he lists only buildings in Florence.

Manetti's treatise must have been written soon after Ghiberti's death (1455) and shortly before 1465, which would make it approximately contemporary with the treatise also completed in 1464 by Antonio FILARETE (ca. 1400-ca. 1469). The two men, therefore, certainly produced their work independently of each other, but it is probable that writers on architecture of the same nationality were acquainted and shared the same general views.

On the whole, Filarete's treatise does not rank too high,[6] as, indeed, his work as architect and sculptor does not belong to the best of his

[5] Note by W. Weber: "None of the last Roman emperors were of Roman origin; many were barbarians, inasmuch as this term means simply an approximation of 'foreign,' 'alien.'" Manetti, however, was surely not referring to the origins of the emperors, but to Mediterranean culture in contrast to that of the Nordic peoples of the Migrations.

[6] Wolfgang von Oettingen, *Antonio Averlino Filaretes Traktat über die Baukunst . . .*, Vienna, 1890 (Quellenschriften für Kunstgeschichte . . ., N.F., III).

generation. The contrast between ancient and "modern" architecture —modern being for Filarete the mediaeval styles—is drawn with the intention of businesslike self-advertising. He recommends himself to his eventual patron as the learned expert in classical architecture, and never tires of disparaging Gothic. In what has been published of the treatise the word *rinascere* occurs only once.[7] Immediately following this passage is a discussion of the reasons for the decline of ancient architecture "until about fifty or perhaps sixty years ago" (that would be about 1400). He says that the decline and coarsening (*grossezza*) came about through the wars of the barbarians. Italy became impoverished, could no longer engage in much building, and thus lost its practical skill. Therefore, those who wanted to build something, turned to the goldsmiths and painters. "The goldsmiths make tabernacles [monstrances?] and censers, and modern [Gothic] forms seem beautiful for these. Such forms were then carried over to architecture. And this application and fashion were derived, as has been said, from the people who dwell north of the Alps (*transmontani*) that is, the Germans and French."[8] It is not clear whether Filarete knew that Gothic originated in France. He makes the French responsible together with the Germans in order to remove the onus from Italy. But what he says about Gothic minor arts is a strange concession on the part of such a despiser of Gothic. It indicates to some extent a divided opinion, such as we have already met in Ghiberti. Why does Filarete half appreciate the Gothic minor arts? Presumably he found monumental architecture petty, from the point of view of the classical orders, because (as we shall presently hear) it piles so many forms on top of each other. And this judgment may have led him to the hypothesis that the architecture of the cathedrals was evolved from the work of goldsmiths and painters. Probably he had never seen the great cathedrals of France and Germany. This goldsmith theory of Gothic, however, exercised no influence, doubtless because Filarete's treatise was at that time not printed. Only in the eighteenth century does a similar idea occur as an isolated phenomenon (in Goethe).

Filarete once more expressed his views on "Gothic and Renaissance,"

[7] *Ibid.*, p. 428, ". . . a me pare uedere di quegli degni hedificij, ch'erano a Roma antichamente e di quegli che si leggie, che in Egipto erano. Mi pare *rinascere* a uedere questi così degni hedificij, et a me ancora paiono molto begli." In translation approximately: ". . . it seems good to me to regard those worthy edifices that stood in Rome in ancient times and those that were, we read, in Egypt. It is like being born again to see these worthy buildings, and to me they still appear very beautiful."

[8] Cf. text, Appendix 17.

as we should say today, in a letter. "Therefore I beseech everyone to give up this modern [Gothic] habit, and do not let yourself be advised by those masters who make use of this botchery. Cursed be he who introduced it. I believe it was none other than barbarians who brought it to Italy."[9]

More important than these remarks of Manetti and Filarete would be an expression of opinion on the part of Leone Batt. ALBERTI (1404-1472), the intellectual leader of the generation of architects in Florence following Brunelleschi. He, however, was eloquently silent on the Middle Ages. Manetti's sentence on mediaeval architecture is also not much more than silence. Alberti quite certainly had his own thoughts on Gothic, for he, after all, was commissioned to rebuild a *Gothic* church of the Mendicant Order in Rimini in 1447 (S. Francesco), just as his much venerated predecessor, Brunelleschi, had had to complete the *Gothic* cathedral in Florence. Furthermore, Alberti continued the Gothic church of Santa Maria Novella in Florence and used Gothic forms in part for the façade, etc. In his writings he is far too dignified to combat Gothic architecture or even to recognize Gothic architects as rivals, and much too tactful to curse an already defeated opponent. In conversation, however, he might have been less reticent.

Krautheimer tried to reconstruct Alberti's whole conception of the history of architecture and gain a deeper understanding of it.[10] He is probably right in assuming that only two styles existed for Alberti, the good, antique style, to which belongs also its imitation since the time of Brunelleschi, and, on the other hand, everything else without discrimination, that is, poor architecture, into which category Gothic tacitly falls. Certainly this division according to values was also in his case connected with the nationalistic prejudice that good architecture was a symptom, or also a necessary consequence, of the higher degree of value among Greeks, Romans, and Italians, as compared with the lower one among the barbarians, that is, the Germans and French.

One single passage in Alberti's *De re ædificatoria* betrays, perhaps, a secret sympathy for the darkness of mediaeval churches. He writes: "The window openings in temples [that is, churches] ought to be modest [of moderate size] and placed high: whereby one could see

[9] Gaye, *Carteggio*, I (1839), p. 205: "Siche priegho a ciaschuno che lassi andare questa usanza moderna, e non vi lassate consigliare a questi maestri che usano questa praticuccia; che maladetto sia chi la trasse, credo che non fusse se non gente barbara, che la reco in Italia." MS 372 of the Bibliotheca Palatina in Florence. J. Burckhardt translated *praticuccia* by *Pfuscherei* (bungling) *Geschichte der Renaissance in Italien*, Stuttgart, 1868, p. 29).

[10] R. Krautheimer, (quoted above p. 242, n. 14), p. 58.

nothing but the sky, and both those who offer the sacrifice [that is, say mass] and the worshipers may not be distracted in spirit from the sacred act by anything whatsoever. The horror that is excited by shadow increases by its nature religious fervor in the souls of men, and severity is in large measure united with majesty."[11] In his early youth Alberti became acquainted with Venice and Padua, he studied in Bologna, and came to Florence about 1428 (after the sentence of banishment against the family was revoked). In the following years, until 1432, he traveled to France, Belgium, and Germany, where, as far as we know, only the skaters and the enormous stoves impressed him. One cannot doubt, however, that in those Italian cities, as well as in foreign lands, he viewed Gothic churches with thoughtful eyes.

True, the continuation of the passage cited above can be regarded as somewhat of a recantation of the sympathy for darkness in sacred edifices that he had just betrayed. At first he is of the opinion that too much brightness would make the candlelight of the altars grow pale, and then follows a proposal for the shading from light to dark: "However, I like it when the entrance to the church is perfectly light and also when the interior is as little dim as possible. But the place where the altar is erected can have more majesty than charm."

One should not read too much into remarks of this kind, and yet one cannot deny that Alberti wanted to see something of the Gothic mystic light retained for the choir, strangely combined with the desire for a clearly lighted nave. The Latin text, presumably begun in 1451, the seventh book being written about 1466, appeared posthumously in 1485. Although there is not the slightest connection between the two, it may be noted as a curiosity that in that same year 1485

[11] Leone Baptista Alberti, *De re aedificatoria,* VII, 12: "Apertiones fenestrarum in templis esse oportet modicas et sublimes: unde nihil praeter caelum spectes: unde et qui sacrum faciunt, qui ue supplicant, nequicquam ab re diuina mentibus distrahantur. Horror qui ex umbra excitatur natura sui auget in animis uenerationem: et coniuncta quidem multa ex parte maiestati est austeritas. Adde, quod ignes qui templis debentur, quibus nihil ad cultum religionis ornamentumque diuinius habeas, nimia in luce languescunt. Veteres ea nimirum re sola plerumque apertione hostii contenti erant. Sed mihi quidem probabitur: ubi aditus in templum omnino erit illustris: interiorque ambulatio minime erit tristis. Ubi autem ara statuta sit: maiestatem praese ferat locus uelim magisque uenustatem." (The Latin edition is not paginated.) Cf. the German translation by Max Theurer, Vienna, 1912, p. 386. An approximate dating of Book VII results from the studies of Otto Stein, *Die Architekturtheoretiker der italienischen Renaissance,* Karlsruhe, 1914, p. 82. Books I and II were completed about 1452, likewise Book X, which was originally an independent treatise and was only joined to the other nine books after Alberti's death. He seems to have worked on Book V in 1452, and seems not to have begun the sixth until 1455. Chapter 2 of Book VIII can be dated around 1463, but chapter 3 was not yet finished in 1467. If Alberti wrote the chapters in order, the seventh book was then composed approximately in 1466.

Paulus Niavis penned his justification of the gloom of sacred places. Do we need written testimony to the fact that around 1485 people reacted just as aesthetically to light and darkness as we do now? Anyone who doubts the immutability of human nature in this respect will perhaps be critical of both texts as insufficient evidence.

In the period of Early Renaissance we should not expect to find the *term* "Gothic" used in our present sense, considering the paucity of knowledge of the field of architectural history and the inability of the time to distinguish successive styles and define them chronologically, as well as to make a general geographical survey of architectural schools. The word is lacking as long as the concept is lacking. Yet the adjective appears twice in Italy during the fifteenth century, first in Alberti, in 1435, then around 1440 in Valla.

Alberti discusses the requirement that all the members of a piece of sculpture should be determined according to their particular iconographical significance: ". . . it would be absurd if the hands of a Helena or an Iphigenia were aged and Gothic, . . ." The Italian text reads: "mani . . . vecchizze et gotiche," which Janitschek translated as "withered and rough."[12] It is, however, not certain whether the original text was Italian or Latin; the Latin translation, printed in 1450, reads "seniles et rusticanae." Alberti wrote in his dedication to Brunelleschi: ". . . it would make me happy to have you peruse this little work of mine that has been made for your name [dedicated to you] in the Tuscan language."[13] Thus the word may have been originally "Gothic" after all, but its value as evidence in the tracing of the first occurrence of the term is diminished by the fact that Alberti himself translated it as *rusticanae*. Gothic, then, actually meant for him "rustic," boorish, coarse, and this meaning can be extended to the entire Middle Ages after the destruction of Rome by the Goths under Alaric in the year 410. Gothic is a term of contempt that could be taken here as equivalent to Byzantine; in this passage it does not mean what it stood for later, but actually "uncultivated," just as the Visigoths were. We know that the damage done during Alaric's capture of Rome was relatively small; nevertheless, the memory of the desecration of Rome by these barbarians remained alive. Gothic became synonymous with inferior, and when opinion crystallized that mediaeval architecture was inferior with

[12] Leone Battista Alberti, *Della pittura libri tre*; in Hubert Janitschek, *L. B. Albertis kleine kunsthistorische Schriften*, Vienna, 1877 (Quellenschriften für Kunstgeschichte . . . , XI), pp. 114 and 115.

[13] *Ibid.*, p. 48.

respect to classical Roman, the first step was taken on the path that led to our term Gothic.

In book III, chapter 13, Alberti enumerates the different kinds of arches. The round arch he calls *arcus rectus*, the segmental arch *arcus comminutus*, the pointed arch *arcus compositus* or *arcus angularis*, composed of two segmental arches. Instead of condemning the pointed arch, he simply says: "Pointed arches did not exist in antiquity," which is sufficient to exclude it from good architecture. "Some people," he continues, "believe that they have to be used in the apertures of towers in order to split the weight above, as in the forepart of a ship, although these composite arches are strengthened rather than weakened by the pressure of the weight above them."[14] Although Alberti was obviously aware that the pointed arch needs to have such a weight above it, he declares the round arch to be the best from the point of view of mechanics.

In the following chapter he discusses the different kinds of vaults and mentions *ossa* which Theurer translated as ribs. Alberti, however, is speaking not of *Gothic* ribs, but rather of those invisible ribs of the cupola in the cathedral of Florence and of the cryptoribs of ancient vaults, such as are to be found in Sette Bassi, which he describes very accurately.

The second occurrence of the word is of far less significance. Laurentius VALLA (1406-1457) wrote in 1440 on "Codices gothice scriptos," meaning Gothic letters as opposed to Roman. But the adoption of Gothic script is characterized in this connection as pernicious.[15] Everything Gothic is bad, and everything bad is Gothic.

Thus, in this chorus of croaking voices Filarete was, one might say, a half-white raven, since he at least accepted the Gothic of the goldsmiths.

[14] "Compositi arcus apud ueteres non uisuntur. Sunt qui turrium appertionibus inducendos putent: quo nimia superposita pondera quasi prora obiecta diffidant. Tam etsi compositi arcus istiusmodi ponderibus confirmentur supradiectis magis quam opprimantur." Writing about pointed arches in towers he probably thought of the campanile in Florence.

[15] Paul Hoffmann, *Studien zu Leon Battista Albertis zehn Büchern* . . . , Leipzig diss., Frankenberg i.S., 1883, pp. pp. 33 and 34. He quotes Valla, *Praef. ad lib. III*: "argumento sunt codices Gothice scripti, quae magna multitudo est, quae gens si scripturam Romanam depravare potuerit quid de lingua praesertim relicta subole putandum est?" Hoffmann is cited in Jakob Burckhardt's *Geschichte der Renaissance in Italien*, beginning with the third edition, in chapter III, par. 22: *Der spätere Hass gegen das Gotische*; this paragraph contains some further evidence which I have omitted. A new English translation of Alberti's work has been published by Joseph Rykwert, *Ten Books on Architecture*, London, 1955, containing a good bibliography on page viii.

3. The Attitude of the High Renaissance

STYLISTICALLY only those works of BRAMANTE (1444-1514) that fall in his seventh decade (1504-1514) belong to what is called High Renaissance.[1] His expert opinion on the *tiburio* of Milan Cathedral—if it is his at all—is certainly earlier than this period, but Bramante's intellectual individuality seems to us so much a representative of the class that the assignment of his opinion to "High Renaissance" will hardly be disputed. Leonardo's case is similar, for his life, as it seems, was never divided into an Early and a High Renaissance phase. Francesco di Giorgio cannot be separated from the subject of this chapter, and it remains an open question how much of his personality and his art still belongs to the "Early Renaissance."

What brought these three *ingegneri* into contact with Gothic was concern for the *tiburio* (the tower over the crossing) of Milan Cathedral. By 1419 the edifice was finished except for this part. The crossing was provided with a temporary roof. After many attempts, a model by Antonio di Firenze was accepted in 1452 and stones were quarried and shaped. There can be no doubt that this model was still Gothic, but for reasons not known to us the work came to a standstill. Gian Galeazzo Sforza wrote to Strasbourg in 1481 and asked that an architect be sent him. In 1482 Master Johannes Niessenberger of Graz (Nexemperger) arrived with fifteen workmen. He was given a festive reception, but when cracks appeared in the walls, he left the city by stealth in 1486, and the work that had been started had to be torn down at once. Again there is no doubt that the Strasbourg master intended to build a *Gothic tiburio*. Several other appointments followed, about which Boito reports.[2] He assigns Bramante's expertise to the last years of the fifteenth century.[3] Geymüller had discussed the date of this undated document even earlier; it has no signature and is not in Bramante's own hand. The ascription rests on the title: *Bramanti opinio supra domicilium seu templum magnum*. In this expertise Bramante mentions models by Leguto, Pietro da Gorgonzola, Amadeo, Pandino, and Molteno. Of these, Amadeo is well known as a sculptor and architect, the others are unknown persons that are not even to be found in Thieme-Becker's *Allgemeines Künstlerlexikon*. Boito says that Antonio da

[1] The court of S. Maria della Pace in Rome was completed in 1504; one may, thus, to be exact, even go back to the preceding years. Bramante had left Milan in 1499.

[2] Boito, *Il Duomo di Milano*, Milan, 1889, p. 228.

[3] *Ibid.*, p. 230.

Pandino was a priest.[4] In 1490 a model constructed by Amadeo together with Dolcebuono was judged in a final session, to which we shall return later. It is quite improbable that another competition took place after 1490. Moreover, it is said that Bramante himself submitted a model in 1488, and it is psychologically unlikely that the authorities would first have rejected it and then subsequently asked his opinion about competitors. Things must have happened the other way around: first the expertise was given, and then Bramante received the commission to show how he thought the *tiburio* should be built. Since it is assumed that the commission was already given in 1487 at the same time as that to Leonardo, the expertise must have been written even before 1487.

The text is difficult to understand in places. Mongeri, who was the first to publish it,[5] interpreted the most obscure words. Geymüller, who printed the document once again,[6] did not translate it, but in his discussion of the contents undoubtedly gave a correct commentary on all the essentials.

Bramante divides his judgment according to four concepts: *forteza, conformita con il resto del edificio, legiereza*, and *bellezza*. What is meant by these concepts would not be entirely clear without the explanation that follows them.

In the case of *forteza* it is a matter of the thesis that a square *tiburio* is safer than an octagonal one; an octagonal one could, however, be built if the foundations are good and if, furthermore, as in Pietro da Gorgonzola's model, discharging arches are constructed above the main arches. Then follows the sentence: "With respect to the main arch I say that for many reasons it is better round than pointed."[7] He praises Amadeo's model because in it eight arches issue from the eight piers (of the nave, aisles, and transept) that are next to the piers of the crossing. This would benefit the stability of the *tiburio*, but it is also good for the conformity. (The latter is not clear to me.)

In the section on conformity Bramante analyzes the cathedral into its various parts, nave, aisles, and bays, in order to demonstrate that the *tiburio* is only possible over the crossing. Why that needed so many

[4] *Ibid.*, p. 231, but on p. 227 and p. 313 he calls him *ingegnere*.

[5] G. Mongeri, *Bramante e il Duomo*, Archivio Storico Lombardo, Milan, 1878, p. 538.

[6] Heinrich Adolph von Geymüller, *Die ursprünglichen Entwürfe für S. Peter in Rom*, Paris and Vienna, 1875, p. 116. This work appeared in parts, thus the apparent discrepancy of the dates; Geymüller even cites Mongeri from 1878.

[7] "Circa larcho maestro dico star meglio tondo ch'acuto per molte ragioni." (Mongeri, *op.cit.*, p. 542) Compare with this the passage from the dispute of 1400 in Milan that was quoted above on p. 72 "archi spiguti non dant impulsam."

words is not evident. It is, however, easy to understand the demand that buttresses should be built for the *tiburio* so that it will be adapted to the rest of the cathedral. Once more Bramante recommends the square because then the buttresses (flying buttresses, *contraforti*) would stand in right angle to the wall like the others on the edifice. "But since you disrupt the order of the edifice to make it [the *tiburio*] octagonal, the order of the buttresses must be disrupted, so that they may be conformable to the *tiburio*."[8] Even more contrary to the "order" would be a circular *tiburio* without a buttress system. The word *ordine* has *here* approximately the meaning of "style."

The concept of lightness is mentioned briefly. Again Amadeo is praised, except that his *tiburio* is too high.

This height is discussed in connection with the concept of *bellezza*. The vault over the crossing being agreed upon at an elevation of eighty braccia, the *tiburio* should consequently be forty braccia high. True, the higher one makes it the more beautiful it will be, as long as there is no infraction of the *ordine*, which is fixed dogmatically at 2:1. If the *tiburio* is too low, one would have to stand a mile away in order to see it above the roof (he means from the west) and the flying buttresses will hide it (which is taken into account on one of the models). Again Amadeo is praised because he has given proper consideration to all this. "With regard to the ornaments, such as flights of stairs [outside?], galleries, windows, gargoyles, piers (*pileri*), and pinnacles (*lanterne*), one should for the most part observe what was done above the sacristy or, even better, one should consult several drawings that can be found in the *fabrica* (cathedral lodge) and that were made at the time that the cathedral was being built; it does not seem to me necessary to go further."[9]

In conclusion Bramante thinks that if all the competitors came together, one could settle in less than an hour on a new model that would unite the advantages of all the others.

The reason for Bramante's singling out Amadeo's model so favorably may be connected with the fact that both men had already worked on it jointly. Perhaps he praised certain features of this model because they were based on his own suggestions. Bramante, born in

[8] "Ma siccome voi rompete l'ordine de lo edificio per volerlo fare in octavo, cosi si conviene rompere l'ordine del directo de contraforti, per confarli al tiburio." (Mongeri, *op.cit.*, p. 543)

[9] "Quanto a li ornamenti come sono scale corridoi: finestre, mascherie, pileri e lanterne, quello che, é facto sopra la sagrestia bona parte ne da intendere, e meglio se intende anchora per alchuni desegni che ne la fabrica se trouano facti in quelo tempo, che questo Domo fu edificato: si che più oltra non me pare, in questo, neccessità de extendere." (Mongeri, *op.cit.*, p. 543)

1444, was originally a painter. He did not begin his activity as an architect of ecclesiastical buildings until 1479 with Sta. Maria presso S. Satiro in Milan, when he was thirty-five years old. In the seven years up to 1486, the time of the expertise (if the date we have proposed is accurate), he perhaps had commissions for secular buildings. The sacristy of Sta. Maria presso S. Satiro was begun only in 1488; it is octagonal and so planned from the very beginning, so that Bramante's preference for the square form is only to be related to the connection with the cathedral. Yet, as a matter of principle, the Renaissance architect is opposed to the diagonal position of the flying buttresses resulting from the octagon, since this "diagonality" was truly Gothic. In other things, however, he is not only tolerant but even conservative; like a trained historian of art, he wants to go back to the original plan.

Geymüller already called attention to the representation of a quadratic *tiburio* in Cesariano's translation of Vitruvius (1521), without drawing the obvious inference that we have here, if not an exact depiction of Bramante's model, at least a reminiscence of it. We can ascribe this lost model to approximately the year 1487, the same time that Leonardo started his.

Like Bramante, LEONARDO DA VINCI (1452-1519) was convinced that the *tiburio* could only be designed with Gothic forms. In his famous letter of about the autumn of 1482, in which he recommends himself to Ludovico il Moro and lists his universal abilities, he calls himself architect as well.[10] There is, however, no structure known that he might have designed or built before this date, during his stay in Florence. Ground plans of Sta. Maria degli Angeli, S. Spirito, and the exterior front elevation of S. Lorenzo in Florence are proof of his interest in architecture by Brunelleschi.[11] He moved to Milan in 1483, and here found his painter colleague, Bramante of Urbino, seven years his senior, already active as an architect. He mentioned Bramante twice in his writings, and considering Leonardo's sociable nature that knew or needed no jealousy, it can only be assumed that the two men were friends and exchanged ideas and information about architecture. Which of the two had at that time more to offer in this field we do not know.

[10] *Il Codice atlantico di Leonardo da Vinci . . .* , Milan, 1894, IV, p. 1295. Point 10 of the letter reads: "In tempo di pace credo satisfare benissimo a paragone de onni altro in architectura, in composizione di edifici e pubblici e privati, e in conducer agua da uno loco ad un altro."

[11] Jean Paul Richter, *The Literary Works of Leonardo da Vinci*, London, New York, and Toronto, II, 1939 (2nd ed.), pp. 31 and 40, pl. XCIV.

Several sketches give us an approximate idea of Leonardo's model for the *tiburio*. They represent different versions, and show that Leonardo was still feeling his way; perhaps his model looked quite unlike them. It is certain, however, that the forms were Gothic, an octagonal dome accompanied by a system of flying buttresses and very slender pinnacles (Fig. 22). On one of the designs (Fig. 21) is the note: "The inverted arch is better than the ordinary kind for buttressing, because the former has a wall beneath it that opposes its weakness, while the latter finds nothing but air under its weak part."[12] Such concave flying buttresses were widespread in Late Gothic north of the Alps. Orthodox Gothicists reject them because they are statically less good than the classical type that is concave on its under side; Leonardo maintains the contrary. In one of the sketches (Fig. 21) these concave flying buttresses are drawn frontally, that is, in the directions of the nave and transepts, so that each two (of eight) are at right angles to each other, as though the *tiburio* were square, but the dome is clearly intended to be circular.[13] Immediately beside this sketch the interior is depicted as octagonal.

Whereas our subject places the emphasis on the stylistic question, the chief concern of the building administration was for statics, hence for the construction of the parts between vault and roof that are not at all visible in the completed state, and finally for technique, that is, the process of construction with scaffoldings, and so on. The matter of cost was certainly a factor, but was not predominant. Are the four piers of the crossing strong enough for the enormous weight of the *tiburio*? Are their foundations sufficient? Those were the most urgent questions of the men responsible, namely, the Duke, the Archbishop, and the *Deputati*. They could rely for answers neither on Leonardo nor on Bramante, not to mention the others such as even Amadeo; they needed a practical architect who had built many buildings. In this emergency they summoned Francesco DI GIORGIO MARTINI (1439-1501) from Siena.

The events of the dramatic weeks from the end of May to July 7, 1490, during which this expertise ran its course, can be traced in a series of documents. On April 17 Gian Galeazzo Sforza wrote to the Signoria in Siena asking that they permit their illustrious architect

[12] *Ibid.*, pl. 99 and p. 47: ". . . larcho rivescio è migliore per far isspalla che l'ordinario, perchè il rivescio trova sotto sé muro resistente alla sua deboleza ellordinario non trova nel suo debole se non aria."

[13] *Ibid.*, pl. XCIX, I.

Francesco di Giorgio to come to Milan. On May 15 the affirmative answer arrived, very friendly in tone. After May 20 Francesco reached Milan; the Milanese provided good lodgings and inquired eagerly whether he was satisfied; Francesco was not only satisfied with their hospitality but highly pleased. By June 10 the model was already under construction, and it appears that *at that time* Leonardo withdrew his, though surely not because he was offended. The Duke was informed in writing that Leonardo will always be ready to assist. On June 21 the work was interrupted, or the cabinetmakers worked on at the model alone, while Francesco and Leonardo, accompanied by a suite of servants, rode out together to Pavia to deliver their common expertise on the intended dome. Only two years after the beginning of construction, there could not have been very much of the work actually to be seen. Probably here, too, it was a matter of judging the wooden model and the architectural drawings.[14] The two men returned on June 22 to Milan. On the 27th a solemn session took place with Ludovico il Moro presiding, those present being the Signoria, the *Consiglio segreto*, the *Fabricieri*, and many *ingegneri*. The result was the appointment of Francesco di Giorgio, together with Amadeo and Dolcebuono, as chief superintendents of the work with the duty of making all decisions, so that the *tiburio* might be beautiful, worthy of honor, and eternal, "se le cose del mondo possano fare eterne." The minutes contain twelve regulations. The one most important for our subject runs: ". . . to make the decoration, the drum, the foliage conform to the order of the structure and the rest of the church."[15] The other provisions concern the construction and stipulate the principal dimensions. The very first one reminds us of Bramante's opinion; it states that round arches of marble should be raised above the pointed arches of the crossing. The minutes are characterized by absolute clarity, so that Papini was able to make

[14] According to whose design the cathedral of Pavia was built, is not clear. It was begun in 1487 or 1488. Probably the design was indeed Bramante's. Cristoforo de Rocchi (died in 1497) presumably only constructed the model. Cf. Adolfo Venturi, *Storia dell' arte italiana*, VIII, Part II, Milan, 1924, pp. 710ff. (14 illustrations); further, Constantino Baroni, *Bramante*, Bergamo, 1944, pp. 27ff. and the brief note on p. 51. According to Baroni the first design was by Rocchi and Amadeo in 1487, and Bramante came to Pavia several times in 1488. However, Amadeo had already worked together with Bramante on S. Maria near S. Satiro, so that the latter perhaps exerted an influence on Amadeo from the very beginning.

[15] Allen Stuart Weller, *Francesco di Giorgio*, Chicago, 1943, p. 371: "Item; de' fare li ornamenti, lanterna, et fiorimenti conformi a l'ordine de lo hedificio et resto de la Chiesa." Printed again by Roberto Papini, *Francesco di Giorgio architetto*, Florence, 1946, p. 288. By *ordo* is meant here style. On the cover of his book Papini has reproduced Francesco's drawing with the division of a straight line into seven parts; I cannot indicate where he refers to this in the text. It may in any case be remarked that this division is mathematically inexact, though sufficient for practical purposes.

1. Francesco di Giorgio Martini, Reconstruction of His Proposal to Secure the Tiburio (From Roberto Papini, *Francesco di Giorgio architetto*, Florence, 1946, p. 26)

from them a precise drawing of what Francesco proposed (text fig. 1);[16] without question the latter dictated these minutes, as he was the decisive authority. On July 4 his honorarium was fixed, and on July 7 he returned to Siena.

The four discharging arches of the crossing were constructed. Whether everything else was built exactly as the minutes prescribed cannot be determined from the considerable literature on Milan Cathedral. Francesco did not oversee the execution of the work, nor did Amadeo and Dolcebuono, who soon undertook the construction of

[16] Papini, *op.cit.*, p. 263.

the Certosa near Pavia. Bramante had begun the small yard of the chapter there in 1490. It appears that all these men worked together peaceably, and the determination of each one's share is therefore highly difficult. Leonardo, when he withdrew his model, doubtless did so in the knowledge that Francesco's proposal was incomparably simpler than, for example, his highly complicated method of constructing the dome with all the stones notched into each other (Fig. 20).[17] It is a question whether his sketches of structures of the central type did not originate only after he had talked for days to Francesco. The latter's role in the history of Italian Renaissance art did not become clear until relatively recent times. Born in 1439, he was five years older than Bramante and thirteen years older than Leonardo. Like them, he was at first a painter; afterward he had a very productive artistic career as a sculptor and architect. He did the chief work on the palace at Urbino, and thus returned to the position that was his by rights, in place of Luciano Laurana. He had a flair for theory and wrote a treatise on architecture,[18] in which can also be found very finely drawn sketches for buildings of the central type,[19] as well as basilical types connected with central arrangements as choirs.[20] Leonardo read Francesco's treatise; on one page of the manuscript there is a note in his handwriting. Part of the work is said to have been written in Urbino in 1482.[21] Some of Leonardo's sketches that relate to the *tiburio* must derive from Francesco's idea of strengthening the tower over the crossing by iron anchors.[22]

Today, Francesco di Giorgio seems to have provided the inspiration. His buildings show no trace of Gothic; only in the case of the cathedral at Milan did he demand a continuation of the original style, just as his

17 J. P. Richter, *op.cit.*, pl. 100, fig. 1. Papini connects Leonardo's opinion that Francesco had solved the problem of the *tiburio* with a passage from a letter, which is preserved only in a first draft. There he speaks of the physician, who must know the nature and origin of disease, and adds: "The same thing is necessary for the ill cathedral, namely, an architectural physician, etc." According to this argument the physician was Francesco di Giorgio (Papini, *op.cit.*, p. 219). The text has been printed in full with an English translation (J. P. Richter, *op.cit.*, II, p. 330). There we read that the same comparison of architect and physician was used also by Francesco di Giorgio in lib. IV, cap. 4, by Filarete in lib. XV, and by Alberti in lib. X.

18 *Trattato di architettura civile e militare di Francesco di Giorgio Martini* . . . , published by Cesare Saluzzo, Turin, 1841. See Weller, *op.cit.*, pp. 268ff.

19 Papini, *op.cit.*, pl. 288.

20 *Ibid.*, pl. 286.

21 Weller, *op.cit.*, p. 268.

22 J. P. Richter, *op.cit.*, pl. 100, figs. 2 and 3; cf. also Luca Beltrami, *Il Codice di Leonardo da Vinci nella Biblioteca del Principe Trivulzio*, pl. 13, more complete than in Richter; further, pls. 17, 27, 37, 40. The profile head on pl. 68a drawn by Leonardo looks like the portrait of Francesco in his biography by Vasari.

colleagues did.[23] On the other hand, there is a drawing by Leonardo containing eight designs inscribed in squares, which can hardly be interpreted as anything other than Late Gothic vaults.[24] They are partly very complicated; the "whirling vault" (Ueberwasser's expression is *wirbelndes Gewölbe*) could only be carried out on a domed surface; the seventh variation is crossed out, perhaps because Leonardo himself had doubts as to its practicability.

At the top of this sheet are the words: "la ragion d'una volta quadra civé del diamitro della sua . . . del tedesco in domo." The gap does not seem to have been deciphered as yet, and the sense of the sentence is not clear; it is also not certain that this note refers to the eight vaults. Richter explains the *tedesco* as identical with Brother J. Mayr of Hustorf. This is Hans Mayr, son of the carpenter, Andreas Mayr, who had gone to Milan in 1483 with Niessenberger and was the only one of his fifteen companions to remain there and become a monk. Boito reports that he was indeed called *venerabile,* but that he did not possess the humility and unpretentiousness of a preaching friar. He, too, submitted a model, and demanded money, until finally the *Deputati* lost patience and declared that they needed neither him nor his model. The mention of this *tedesco* is, however, an inestimable clue to the problem of where Leonardo got his inspiration for these vault configurations. If one leafs through his manuscripts, one is continually astonished at the range of his interests, his powers of comprehension and creative power, and his incredible industry. It would seem that a slight suggestion from Mayr, or whoever else it was, sufficed to stimulate his imagination to independent experiments. On the bottom of this same sheet is a casual sketch for the plan of a Late Gothic reticular vault with *Principal* arches. Leonardo had the same objectivity toward these Late Gothic forms as toward works of nature; he does not express an opinion on them, he merely notes their existence and considers the variability of the scheme.

Who determined the details of the *tiburio's* exterior, or, first of all, of its drum, is not known. The dome and the octagonal drum were completed during the years following 1490. The *guglia,* that is, the

[23] However, in 1484 he continued in Renaissance style the Palazzo degli Anziani in Ancona, which had been begun in 1447 in Gothic, allowing the pointed arches of the portico to stand and furnishing its piers with new colonnettes at the corners, in conformity with his own style; Papini, pl. 238.

[24] J. P. Richter, *op.cit.*, pl. CIII and the relevant text on p. 82. Ueberwasser reproduced this sheet and interpreted it in the opposite sense, *Jahrbuch der Preussischen Kunstsammlungen*, Berlin, 1935, p. 268.

pyramidal roof with the middle pinnacle, was not carried out, and in an engraving by an unknown artist of 1735 we can still see the building in this state.[25] A number of intermediary stages remained on paper: in 1537 Vincenzo Soregni, in 1590 Martino Bassi, in 1652 Lorenzo Bernini. In 1750 a model was made by Francesco Croce and Merlo, and this was then carried out. It is decidedly "Late Gothic" in the middle of the eighteenth century. Whether its concave flying buttresses are an echo of Leonardo's drawings is not certain; the latter were placed against the drum (not over it), and how he envisioned the *guglia* can hardly be told from his fleeting little sketches. The cathedral that had been begun in 1386 was not really completed until the gilded figure of the Virgin was placed atop the *guglia* in 1774; its style is that of 1774.[26] Large portions of the side exterior elevations, and other addition were not added until the nineteenth century.[27]

With reference to the subject of Bramante and Leonardo one more observation on Sta. Maria delle Grazie in Milan must finally be interpolated here, although it does not belong to the theme of literary sources. The church was begun in 1464 by the Dominican Order and finished in 1482. It is a building typical of the Italian Mendicant Orders of the time. The nave and two aisles in seven bays, with chapels on the aisles, have Gothic ribbed vaults throughout.[28] What the choir looked like has been revealed, according to Beltrami's assertion, by a modern investigation (before 1914); he does not say whether the ground plan of the choir was published; it was certainly Gothic. In 1492 this choir was torn down and replaced by the domed choir attributed to Bramante. In a copy of Vasari's *Lives* there was found a marginal note in an unknown hand ("perhaps that of Sebastiano Resta") to the effect that the dome was erected by Leonardo. Richter, who reports this, accompanies it by a representation of the profile of the choir edifice that Leonardo drew in connection with sketches for the Last Supper.[29] Julius Baum tried to distinguish what was completed by Bramante before his departure for Rome in 1499.[30] It must

25 Reproduced in Boito, *op.cit.*, pl. 143.

26 Good reproduction in Giorgio Nicodemi, *Il Duomo di Milano*, Turin, 1938, ill. 312.

27 The façade cannot be discussed here, although it is an interesting blending of Gothic and Baroque, cf. Boito, *op.cit.*, pp. 257ff. and plates 43 and 85. These attempts should be treated together with the dispute about the façade in Bologna, as well as with the designs for Florence. For the latter cf. Vera Daddi Giovanozzi in *L'Arte*, 1936, p. 33.

28 The details cannot be discussed here; cf. Luca Beltrami, *La Chiesa di Maria delle Grazie in Milano*, 1914, in *L'Italia monumentale*, no. 12.

29 J. P. Richter, *op.cit.*, II, p. 48.

30 In Thieme-Becker, *Allg. Künstlerlexikon.*

be remembered that Bramante wanted to make the *tiburio* square, whereas the drum in Sta. Maria delle Grazie is a figure of sixteen sides. However, we need not solve this riddle here, but merely point out that the choir arch, opening toward the square of the choir, is higher than the Gothic vaults of the nave. A solution had therefore to be found for the joining of the two parts. It consisted of leaving in place in the last bay (counting from west to east) the ribs that branched from the west side to the crown, and breaking off their continuation. Three cells were allowed to stand, the eastward cell is raised to meet the semicircular arch, whether Bramante's or Leonardo's. Thus two ribs rise to the crown and are continued as groins! Such a meeting of ribs and groins in the crown of a vault is probably unique in this form.[31] For modern questions as to whether the rib carries, the statics of this vault surely deserves some consideration. For those who are interested in stylistic problems it may be said that the raised portion of the vault, which joins the Renaissance structure, is not particularly exciting; rather, it is surprising that half the Gothic ribs were allowed to remain. The visual effect is actually such that one hardly notices the transition. This fact is a strange supplement to the remarks quoted above about the necessity of making the *tiburio* conform to the rest of the building. In Sta. Maria delle Grazie a continuation in Gothic forms was rejected, but in the critical place an unusually delicate compromise between Gothic and Renaissance was achieved. Quadripartite vaults became more and more rare, only groined vaults were still tolerated—unlike the attitude of Aeneas Silvius in Pienza.

It would be pleasant to be able to add to these testimonials one from Raphael also, but the letter or official report that went by his name for more than two hundred years has very properly been shown to be a false ascription.[32] The author is not known, though he is still called

[31] A longitudinal section is shown in Banister Fletcher, *A History of Architecture . . .*, New York, 1946 (13th ed.), p. 620. Although the whole drawing is very good, the draftsman has forgotten to indicate just the groin that is so interesting; it rises from the old Gothic springer.

[32] The letter was found among the papers of Count Castiglione, whose portrait was painted by Raphael, and was therefore at first attributed to the author of the *Cortegiano* and published together with his other letters: *Opere volgare e latine del Conte Baldassare Castiglione*, ed. Pierantonio Serassi, 1769. Not until 1799 did Francesconi declare the document to be a report of Raphael to Pope Leo X. This was for many reasons plausible, as Raphael was also active as an architect and in the last years of his life had been commissioned by the Pope to make a survey of the antiquities of Rome. For specific literature cf. Julius Schlosser, *Die Kunstliteratur*, Vienna, 1924, pp. 175ff. Here most recent works are listed, also a letter from Christian Huelsen to Schlosser, in which this authority on Rome expresses his doubts of Bramante's authorship and points to Peruzzi.

PSEUDO-RAPHAEL instead of simply "anonymous." Since the latter designation is very common, however, it may be more practical to continue to use the already established name of Pseudo-Raphael.

The letter consists in the main of three parts:

1. Ancient Rome still exists and is splendid. Love for the forefathers and the fatherland enjoins its preservation. But it has been much destroyed: by the influences of the time, the ruthless fury of the barbarians, and the encroachments of the ignorants, who utilize the masterpieces of the ancients as stone quarries. Even popes have misused ancient works.

However, the unnamed pope, to whom the document is addressed, knows how to appreciate the value of antiquity. He has commissioned the author of this report to make drawings of the old Rome. A complete reconstruction of all its ancient buildings is intended.

2. Any doubt as to whether the ancient works can be distinguished from later ones is refuted in detail by the author, who gives a survey of architectural history.

3. After it has been determined which buildings are to be depicted, the author describes his method of reading off angles by the aid of the constant meridian line, using an instrument that is essentially a compass.

Of these three parts the second is the fruitful one for the attitude toward Gothic. The author divides the buildings of Rome into three groups, and adds to them the modern structures (modern here in the sense of contemporary). He thus distinguishes four types in all, which represent at the same time styles:

the first period lasts from Augustus to the destruction of Rome in 410;

the second until a century after the collapse of the Ostrogothic rule (through Narses in 555), therefore, until 655; the third from then "until our day," which can only mean until the beginning of the Renaissance in Rome under Bramante, for, with the author's preoccupation with Rome, he does not think here of Florence and Brunelleschi;

the fourth period is the modern one, that of the author, from about 1500 on.

After this general division the anonymous author goes into more detail. He notes a decline of the arts even in the first period. Architecture kept its standards the longest, for example, the Arch of Constantine, which is in itself still good, though its sculptured decoration belongs in part already to the decline, or, correspondingly, the (no longer extant) paintings in the Baths of Diocletian. The real decline, however, does not come until after the invasion of the Goths under Alaric in 410: ". . . and it appears that this frightful and cruel storm of war and destruction broke not only over Italy but also spread across Greece," where formerly such great masters lived. From there came the poor Byzantine style: ". . . onde anchor la nacche una maniera di pictura et di scultura et architectura pessima, et di niune valore." This sentence is followed abruptly by: "Cominciossi di poi quasi per tutto a surgere la maniera dell' architectura tedescha . . . la maniera delli quali in molti luochi anchor dura. . . ." If we relate this to the main division, it means that the decline in Italy and Greece (Early Christian and Byzantine styles) lasts until 655. Then the German style begins, which is still alive in many regions (we are here about in the time of Wimpheling). At this point the author transcends his Roman local interests and describes the *maniera tedescha* as practiced in Germany and elsewhere, that is, Gothic in our sense, although there was in Rome no great danger that the architect making the survey of ancient buildings could confuse antique with Gothic, there being in Rome practically no Gothic (except Sta. Maria sopra Minerva, 1280).

We are, however, grateful for his digression. The characterization of Gothic reads as follows: "The Germans use as ornaments for a console to carry a beam [either] a crouching, poorly executed, and even more poorly understood little figure and [or] other strange animals and figures and leaves beyond natural reason (*fuori d'ogni ragione naturale*). This architecture did make some sense, however, as it was derived from trees, not yet cut down, whose branches were bent over and made to form pointed arches when tied together. And although this origin is not wholly to be despised, it is nevertheless weak; for huts made from fitted beams arranged as columns, with gables and a covering roof, as Vitruvius describes with respect to the origin of the Doric order, would be stronger than the pointed arches with two centers. For indeed, according to the law of mathematics, a semicircular arch, with each part of its line related only to one center, can carry much more. And beside this weakness, the pointed arch does not have the same grace to our eye, for the perfection of the circle is pleasing, and one sees that Nature seeks almost no other form." In conclusion he then reverts to the idea that antiquity and the Middle Ages are really not apt to be confused, for the buildings of the Imperial Age were built with good reason—"forno sempre edificati con buona ragione di architectura"—and can, therefore, easily be distinguished from those of the period of the Goths and many years thereafter, because these are, as it were, *two extreme opposites*: "che *furono al tempo delli* gotti et anchora molti anni da poi, perche furono questi quasi *dui extremi direttamente oppositi.*"

With this last assertion Pseudo-Raphael seems to stand on most modern ground, inasmuch as we today regard antiquity, as it is represented in the Parthenon, and Gothic, for example, in Cologne Cathedral, as polar, stylistic opposites. But one should not read into this sentence the subtleties of the most recent stylistic analyses, for it is clear that it was still questionable in those days whether the two styles could be differentiated at all. In any case, Pseudo-Raphael himself was beyond this stage, though it is uncertain what buildings he had in mind when he tried to characterize Gothic. Even if he knew nothing but Italian Gothic, for instance, Milan, Florence, Siena, Orvieto, and Sta. Maria sopra Minerva in Rome, it is incomprehensible why he mentions in censure of Gothic sculpture little figures that carry a beam (wooden beams used in secular architecture or architraves in stone). The solution to this riddle probably lies in the fact that the discussion of the pointed arch constantly reminds us of the style that we today call Gothic. Pseudo-Raphael, however, understood by Gothic all the architectural styles from 410 to 1500. In the case of the little figures that he finds objectionable he was obviously thinking of Romanesque decorative sculpture. That he should criticize these works adversely is natural from the point of view of Renaissance aesthetics.

What he has to say about the pointed arch is far more interesting: it is indeed not completely bad, but certainly poorer than the absolutely perfect semicircular arch. The pointed arch is saved by the fact of its originating in nature. For a Renaissance aesthetician anything that originates in nature cannot be wholly reprehensible. The Doric order was distantly derived from nature (Vitruvius) and the pointed arch from the German forests. But the writer did not trust his own argument entirely. The imitation of nature does not seem to him a sufficient justification, and therefore he appends the criticism that the pointed arch does not carry as well as the semicircle. His reasoning shows that he imagined the mechanical forces in the case of the semicircular arch to be all directed toward the center of the curve, and, correspondingly, toward two centers in the case of the pointed arch. Why the latter, even if it were so, should be less favorable is not clear. We are not interested in that here; we know that the forces are distributed in a curve in the inner third of the arch, and that the pointed arch is statically more stable than the semicircular form. The only really cogent justification of the semicircle is that it is more pleasing: "oltre la debolezza, un terzo acuto non ha quella grazia all occhio nostro, al quale piace la perfezione del circolo. . . ." The Renaissance artist could not imagine that to a Gothicist the pointed arch was more pleasing. He would have had to ask himself why the barbarians, even though they found the form of the pointed arch suggested in their forest huts, nevertheless preferred the pointed arch, if *everyone* likes the semicircle better. Or did he mean merely: everyone in the South? When the author says in conclusion: "onde vedersi che la natura non cerca quasi altra forma," one is surprised, for he has just been deriving the pointed arch from this very nature, even though changed by man.

The forest theory is connected with the naturalistic aesthetics that was an effective force from the time of Petrarch on. Good art means a good nation, bad art, a bad one. In Italy all building had been bad for a thousand years—from the invasion of the Goths in 410 to Brunelleschi's Ospedale degli Innocenti—or even for eleven hundred years, if one wants to reckon the time to Bramante (in Rome). A scapegoat was needed, and one was found in the Germans, who were, if not the descendants, at least the unspiritual spiritual heirs of the bad Goths. But since the Germans had at that time a culture that was after all respectable (the anonymous author wrote before the *sacco di Roma,* that free variation on the theme of Alaric), a secondary scapegoat was needed and was, accordingly, discovered in the almost prehistoric ancestors of the Goths, people who vegetated in the forests and perhaps did not even have axes with which to fell trees. Thus the forest myth of the origin of Gothic is related to Roman patriotism of about 1510, a romantic thesis in the service of classic Renaissance. The forest theory is a poetic theory, though this is a contradiction in terms. Ineradicable as a weed, it has stayed alive for centuries and in many places still persists in popular teaching of the history of art even today. It was still publicly advocated by Huysmans in 1898 and by Lempertz in 1926.

With all its nonsense, the forest theory contains a grain of truth if one takes it not as a theory, but as poetry, namely, as a metaphor. Presumably the inventor of the "theory" had the idea that Gothic looks "like" a forest, that in Gothic cathedrals we sense elasticity and living growth, something of a plantlike nature, and that this is the "extreme opposite" of the classical style with its weightiness that tends downward to the earth, its coherence, and its eternal repose. As a description of an aesthetic impression this was correct, but historically neither the rib nor the pointed arch is derived from the time when the Germans were living in forests.

Pseudo-Raphael does not say that he invented the forest theory himself. It is much more probable that some one put it forward in conversation, with no more feeling of responsibility than for a clever idea, and that it was then transmitted orally until it received a place in literature in this document, and was thus attributed to Pseudo-Raphael. This attribution could not satisfy scholars permanently, and attempts were made to give the anonymous author his right name. Since he is recognizably a professional architect, it cannot have been Castiglione. Raphael was not only a painter but also an architect, and could certainly take the measurements of buildings—no very difficult feat—but J. Vogel has proved convincingly that he must be eliminated.[33] For where the anonymous author accuses the popes of having destroyed classical works, he also mentions the tearing down of the *meta* in the year 1499. Was this an ancient tomb in the form of a pyramid,[34] similar to the still extant Pyramid of Cestius in Rome? It appeared that this monument would block the pilgrims' path to St. Peter's during the Holy Year of 1500, and so Pope Alexander VI (Borgia) added to his many other sins that of commanding its removal. Since the author of the letter states that he was an eyewitness of this destruction in the course of the eleven years that he passed in Rome, the letter can have been written at the latest in 1510, and in 1503, after the accession of Julius II at the earliest, for the writer makes no attempt to interest Alexander VI. Raphael did not see the tearing down of the *meta*, as he did not come to Rome until 1508.

According to Vogel's conclusions the letter was written in 1510.[35] A second, slightly different version of this letter he dates 1511. He suspects Bramante to have been the author. The fact that the latter actually betook himself to Rome in 1499 after the capture of Milan by the French, and remained there until his death in 1514 is in favor of this idea. There is a tradition that he immediately began to make drawings of ancient ruins. But what architect of the day did not do that in Rome? In connection with the expressed preference for the semicircular arch, Vogel pointed to Bramante's opinion on the *tiburio* of Milan Cathedral, the

[33] Julius Vogel, *Bramante und Raffael*, Leipzig, 1910.

[34] The *meta* was the pillar in the Circus around which and up to which the races were run. The *meta* that is meant here was not mentioned by Huelsen in his topography of Rome. Was it a *meta* or a tomb? See Pauly-Wissowa, *Real-Encycl.*, Meta.

[35] Vogel, *op.cit.*, p. 72.

statement quoted above: ". . . as main arch the semicircle is to be preferred to the pointed arch for many reasons."[36] Again one may ask: what Italian architect did not at that time prefer the round arch for many reasons?

Bramante mentioned no grounds for his preference in this matter. Ought one to believe that he, like Pseudo-Raphael, committed the error of considering the semicircular arch as statically more favorable? In Milan he had an opportunity to reflect on the subject and discuss this point with German architects; he is said to have written on Gothic himself.[37] Whether Leonardo da Vinci, with whom Bramante was closely acquainted in Milan, had a very clear conception of the statics of arches is hard to tell. Perhaps the theoretical principles of mechanics were distorted even for such an objective thinker as he because of enthusiasm for the unbroken line of the circle and its sanction in antiquity. Whether or not this was the case is a matter of indifference, as he has nowhere expounded his mechanical theory of the arch.[38] Thus one may ascribe to the great Bramante an imperfect understanding of the distribution of forces in the two arch forms, but must one then conclude that he could also have taken the forest theory seriously?

Peruzzi was proposed as author, instead of Bramante. True, he did not move to Rome until 1503, thus four years after the destruction of the *meta*, but since not much is known about his life, a little imagination would let him journey to Rome for the Holy Year like so many other unknown pilgrims, or, if necessary, even a little earlier. Christian Huelsen, an advocate of Peruzzi's authorship, argued that he employed the method of measuring by compass.[39] This is not at all convincing: the compass was for any architect a common instrument of the building site.[40] We must, then, for the present content ourselves with the name Pseudo-Raphael, unless one would prefer to say Pseudo-Bramante or Pseudo-Peruzzi.

More important than the identification of the author is the appraisal of the document itself. The previously mentioned evidence from Leonardo, Bramante, and Francesco di Giorgio can be summed up briefly in the formula that they tolerated Gothic under certain circumstances. Pseudo-Raphael, however, asked the question: what is Gothic? In his

36 See above p. 262, n. 7.

37 Vogel, *op.cit.*, p. 65. "Ha poi fatto [Bramante] un Trattato del Lavoro Tedescho . . ."

38 J. P. Richter, *op.cit.*, II, p. 86.

39 In the letter to Julius Schlosser mentioned above, p. 271, n. 32.

40 Lacher also refers to the compass in the year 1516, but there the word probably means a pair of compasses.

answer the hardly calculable richness of Gothic was reduced to two elements: the pointed arch and bad—presumably unnaturalistic—sculpture. This simplification persisted for a long time. If the criticism of the sculpture were dropped, when architecture alone was under discussion, the equations then resulted: Gothic is construction with pointed arches, and construction with pointed arches is Gothic. Only with this statement does one understand fully how reassuring it was to have an explanation for the origin of the pointed arch. The further history of the theory of Gothic clung to this question, and discovered or invented new hypotheses.

Scholars who have written about RAPHAEL's (1483-1520) own attitude toward architecture thought him to be an exclusive devotee of High Renaissance. This is, of course, borne out in all the edifices erected according to his designs, and in much of the architecture in his paintings, e.g. the interiors in the predella of the *Coronation of the Virgin*, 1503, in the Vatican in Rome, or the exterior view of the "temple" in the Sposalizio, 1504, in the Brera in Milan. Yet in his youth Raphael also painted architecture of a mediaeval character.

One of his earliest works, the *Dream of Scipio* (ca. 1500) in the National Gallery in London (Fig. 28), shows in the background behind *Virtus* her castle on a steep mountain and behind *Voluptas* a bridge leading to a palace with a tower.[41] The style of the latter as well as that of the bridge and the building at the entrance of this bridge is indeterminate; that of the castle on the mountain is clearly Gothic. The high tower with turrets at the corners of the spire even suggests a monastery, which would be quite appropriate for Virtus, though less so for Scipio.

Whether the city of Hell in the background of the St. Michael in the Louvre (also about 1500) is Gothic, is difficult to determine, but in any case it is neither antique nor Renaissance (Fig. 25). While the monsters are reminiscent of Hieronymus Bosch, the architecture shows no similarity with that which appears in the work of this master.

The most surprising architecture to be found in Raphael's painting is that which we see in the background of the *Holy Family with the Lamb* (Fig. 27) in the Prado, Madrid, dated 1507. It is considered today to be a copy made by Raphael himself of a picture which he painted in 1504 when he came to Florence.[42] In both pictures the archi-

[41] Erwin Panofsky, *Herkules am Scheidewege*, Leipzig, Berlin, 1930, especially p. 79.

[42] Viscount Lee of Fareham, "A New Version of Raphaels Holy Family with the Lamb," *Burlington Magazine*, LXIV, 1934, p. 3.

tecture is almost identical, consisting of a chapel with a round apse and of a tower of circular shape behind it. The east wall of the chapel is seen from the left side and the west wall from the right side, giving the impression that they would converge instead of being parallel. The two windows on the south side of this chapel—seen in the picture frontally—have Gothic tracery beneath round arches, at least this is so in the second version of 1507, while in the older version the windows are divided into a lower and upper opening. On the roof there is a turret of Gothic character, also with tracery. The tower looks as if it belongs to the wall of a town rather than to a church. Its gables and oriel are Late Gothic and the domelike roof with the lantern bears a resemblance to similar structures in northern Gothic architecture. The group as a whole is very surprising from an architectural standpoint, and not merely because it is the work of Raphael.

A similar tower appears in the background of the *Madonna Tempi* in Munich, ca. 1505. There are two towers in the picture of St. George in Washington (ca. 1504 or 1505), one with a thin Gothic spire, the other either ruined or under construction. The village behind the *Madonna al verde* (Fig. 29) in Vienna is an unprepossessing group of buildings; still simpler are those behind the St. Catherine in London (National Gallery) of ca. 1507. Some pictures show cities or monasteries of mixed style, perhaps "portraits" sketched on the way from Urbino to Florence, e.g. the background of the *Terranuova Madonna* (Fig. 30) in Berlin or the Canigiani *Madonna* (Fig. 31) in Munich, both painted about 1505 and the *Belle Jardinière* (Fig. 26) in Paris of about 1505-1507. Here the big central part and the tower have Gothic details.

In the same period, in the *Madonna del Cardellino*, Raphael painted a Renaissance church of circular (?) shape, domed and enriched with semicircular chapels suggesting that he might have been acquainted with certain sketches of Leonardo.

All this leads one to the conclusion that in his youth Raphael was very tolerant of mediaeval architecture, that he appreciated the picturesque silhouettes and irregularities of such villages on the bank of a river or of castles at the foot or on the top of a mountain. Some scholars have suggested that these may be traced to northern models such as can be found in the works of Memling, Schongauer or Dürer. It is not necessary, however, to seek for "influences" from the north, since structures of this sort appear in Italian panel paintings and frescoes through the centuries down to Perugino. In any case, these examples from Raphael's works provide further evidence that he is not the author of the report written about 1510. Even as late as 1511 an irregular group of buildings in the *Madonna di Foligno*, almost at the center of the picture, represents "bad architecture" and the fact should not be overlooked that in the altarpiece of 1515 of the Saint Cecilia in the museum in Bologna the pedum of St. Augustine is Gothic.

The term Gothic as used here applies to the form. Just as the genuine Raphael can be distinguished from Pseudo-Raphael, so also this form can be readily differentiated from antique and Renaissance forms. No such clear-cut distinctions can be made, if the term is identified with a certain sentiment. To say that there was much that was Gothic in Raphael's soul, meaning that he was a pious man, is to venture upon very uncertain ground, for it is misleading to identify all religious feeling with Gothic. It may be admitted that certain figures in Raphael's work are taken from Roger van der Weyden, as, for instance, the kneeling woman in the *Expulsion of Heliodorus* which is very much like that in the *Entombment* in the Uffizi.[43] Nevertheless one cannot but be struck by the difference. Fischel devotes his entire chapter on "Raphael and Gothic" to painting and to this vague "sentiment." The fact that there was Gothic architecture in the background of the *Holy Family with the Lamb* does not make Raphael's work Gothic. In his mature works, painted in Rome, he achieves a uniformity of style in the architecture, figures, and the composition as a whole. Only in the fresco of the *Fire of the Borgo* do we see Gothic tracery in the façade of the old St. Peter's, but this is because he had to give a true representation of this building. These Gothic details are heavily overbalanced by the rest of the picture.[44]

It remains our duty simply to list all of the little Gothic details in Raphael's works without overestimating their importance. To call Raphael Gothic would be just as mistaken as to call Schongauer or even Roger Renaissance, although the latter was affected by the new style.

The translation of Vitruvius by Cesare CESARIANO (1483-1543) brings us back to problems similar to those in Bramante, Leonardo, and Francesco di Giorgio. Cesariano surrounded every bit of his translation

43 Oskar Fischel, *Raphael*, London, 1948, II, figs. 230 and 231. It is hardly necessary to say that Fischel combined scholarship with intimate connoisseurship and that his attempt to penetrate to what he called Gothic in Raphael is an important development in the understanding and appraisal of this master.

44 The architecture in the Battle of Ostia is probably a reproduction of a real building. The fresco is by Giulio Romano, not by Raphael.

with an extensive commentary, and in it he reverts to the subject of the Milan Cathedral.

The book appeared in 1521,[45] thus (according to the usual chronology) one year after the end of the High Renaissance and in the first of Mannerism. The beautiful type face of the book belongs to the High Renaissance. However, it is doubtful whether Manneristic types can be distinguished from those of the High Renaissance, and whether in this field also the change can be dated as exactly as 1521. Since Cesariano composed his treatise before 1520, it belongs in content to the technical literature of the High Renaissance. His style is, if not indeed "Manneristic," at least extraordinarily mannered and without the clarity that one expects after Alberti; Boito said on occasion that Cesariano wrote "in linguaccio maccheronico."[46] Thus it is difficult to read this diffuse commentary and only a few scholars seem to have had the time, desire, and energy to peruse it sentence by sentence. It may be questioned, however, how many of the obscurities are Cesariano's fault.

This painter, architect, engineer, and learned archaeologist was born in Milan in 1483, and was, accordingly, of the same age as Raphael and Martin Luther. In 1498, at only fifteen, he was working under Bramante and at the same time painting in Leonardo's atelier. But that same year he had to flee from Milan because his stepmother tried to poison him in order to obtain possession of his paternal inheritance. He wandered from city to city, finally settling in Ferrara, where he painted scenery at the d'Este court and also studied at the university. Probably he discovered Vitruvius there. From 1512 on he was back in Milan—the stepmother had died—and Duke Massimiliano Sforza engaged him as an engineer. He began the translation of Vitruvius after 1515. When the book was printed in Como in 1521, it came out that the revisers had altered the text without consulting him. Cesariano protested angrily, was thereupon thrown into prison in Como, and robbed of his manuscripts and drawings. The lawsuit that followed was not decided in his favor until 1529. From then on he worked as constructer of fortifications, and died in 1543.

How much of the obscurity of this commentary must be attributed to the revisers, who thought that they could do the work better, could be determined exactly, since Cesariano's own copy with his own margin-

[45] Cesare Cesariano, *Di Lucio Vitruvio Pollione de architectura libri decem, traducti de latino in vulgare, affigurati, commentati et con mirando ordine insigniti*, Como, 1521.
[46] *Op.cit.*, p. 237.

al notes is still extant in the Biblioteca Melziana in Milan. I assume that the woodcuts, which are of primary interest to us, were not touched by the falsifiers, even though the man who cut the blocks perhaps made mistakes. Thus, the most important thing for us is first, that Cesariano chose the Gothic cathedral of his native city to illustrate what Vitruvius says about proportion, and second, that he for his part committed the presumably unconscious falsification of determining its proportions according to the scheme of the equilateral triangle, *secundum Germanicam Symmetriam*,[47] instead of adhering to the dimensions as actually carried out. His woodcut, adorned with all sorts of auxiliary lines beyond those of Stornaloco, led many later adepts of the secret of the lodges astray (Fig. 32). The mantle of Vitruvius' authority passed to Cesariano, and the result was that Vitruvius, the architect of Caesar and Augustus, now became the star witness to the beauty of Milan Cathedral, or, rather, the other way around, the cathedral in Milan was to prove that Vitruvius was right. True, Cesariano has nowhere said this so pointedly, but that must have been the impression gained by many who leafed through his book. Whether this glorification was in part due to local patriotism we do not know, nor would it change the essentials of the matter.

Cesariano depicted Milan Cathedral on three sheets. First he offers the ground plan, and although he leaves out the transverse arches everywhere and only draws in the diagonal ribs, in the crossing he indicated the transverse arches, revealing clearly that he wanted to have the *tiburio* square, as his teacher Bramante formerly had.[48] If the attribution to Bramante of that opinion discussed above needed proof, it would be found in Cesariano's loyal adherence to this wish of his. The diagonals of the crossing show a simple quadripartite vault, such as appears on Sheet xv. Here, the transverse section of the nave and the four aisles is given, and with it the exterior view of the *tiburio*. On the following page, xv verso, is drawn the transverse section of the interior of the *tiburio*—if I understand it rightly—and, in addition, the exterior of the *guglia*, as well as the exterior of the transept, seen from the west. The *guglia* differs in the two representations. On Sheet xv, beside the *tiburio* as it ought to have been according to Cesariano-Bramante, there

[47] These words are found in the title of the illustration of Milan Cathedral, p. xv; cf. also p. xiii v (line 19 from the bottom) ". . . la regula che usato hano li Germanici Architecti in la Sacra Aede Baricephala de Milano." *Baricephala*, means top-heavy, and probably refers to the tops of the piers.

[48] Boito says that he speaks of himself again as Bramante's pupil; one passage is to be found on p. iv v: "si como fece il mio praeceptore Donato Cognominato Bramante urbinate." (line 46)

is drawn in an exterior view of the octagonal *tiburio* in a sort of perspective, as it ought *not* to be (Fig. 32). Cesariano wrote the description—in the version of the wood engraver—"Idea octogonae Hecubae phalae. et pyramidatae sipercumbere eam super columnas quatuor pariquadrati volumus totam extra solidum invenietur quod contra mentem sapientum architectorum si maximi oneris perpetuitatem obtinere velit."[49] The word Hecuba in this connection is a philological riddle; its meaning is made clear by two passages in the text,[50] and remains unchanged even though one were to make the emendation *phalatae* or *tholatae* for *phalae*. The period must be placed after *pyramidatae*, not after *phalae*, and then the preceding words form the title of the following sentence, which becomes perfectly clear if one restores *si supercumbere* for *sipercumbere*. Then the whole note can be translated: "Elevation of the octagonal, centrally arranged *tiburio*, surmounted by a spire. If we want to place it (*eam*) on the four piers of the crossing, it will be entirely outside the solid parts, which is contrary to the intelligence of wise architects, if this [intelligence] intends to attain the permanence of the very heavy load."[51]

Boito says (page 237) that in 1521 the *tiburio* was already well under way. If that is so, it is difficult to understand Cesariano's harking back to Bramante and the opposition to the octagon because it would hang in the air. His drawing of the *tiburio* conforms largely to the structure that had been then carried out or was being carried out. The drawings of the *guglia* are in both cases relatively similar to each other; the buttresses are upward sloping counterforts, not real flying buttresses, but rather walls pierced by a series of arches; in the Bramantean sketch (if we may call it so), these arches are semicircles. But the great windows of the quadratic vault over the crossing are filled with tracery, and the walls between the pillars have bar tracery with ogee arches. which does not exactly connote Bramante. It should also be mentioned that the square tower over the crossing has no flying buttresses, the same being true of the octagonal one in Cesariano's drawing (and also of

49 The words are all lettered in Roman majuscules.

50 Cesariano, p. XIII, line 12 from the bottom: "la quadrata Hecuba Tholata et Pyramidata," and the words ". . . La Hecubale seu Tholata Pinacola Piramidale . . . ," which Boito, *op.cit.*, p. 237, cites without indicating where the sentence is to be found; I have not discovered it. The first passage means: the quadratic *hecuba*, of central type and provided with a pyramid (tent roof or *Guglia*); the second: the *hecubale* or centrally arranged, pyramidal crown of the building. Even if *hecubale* in the second phrase is taken as an adjective, its meaning is made clear by the *seu*: it is simply the *tiburio*. According to Ducange *phalae* are *turres rotundae in ovi speciem*. One of the seven columns of the *spina* in the ancient Circus was called *phala* or *fala*.

51 The word *pariquadratum* means literally a "rectangle" with equal sides.

the one actually built); the counterforts come only afterward above it as support for the *guglia*. The work as built in the eighteenth century did not adhere to Cesariano's octagonal drawing that obviously depicts what was intended in his time.

The title of Sheet xv contains in the phrase "*secundum Germanicam symmetriam*" a variant for the vocabulary that can be documented for the concept of Gothic. More important than word or concept is the objectivity of Cesariano's attitude toward Gothic, and his indifference to the interpolation of genuine (Italian) Gothic into his translation of Vitruvius. One might almost say that just as an architect of the High Renaissance unhesitatingly combined Gothic with the classical, the Gothic architects could also couple Vitruvius with the Middle Ages.

Of the five men discussed here, Francesco di Giorgio, Leonardo, Bramante, and Cesariano can be associated insofar as they are relatively tolerant toward Gothic. Pseudo-Raphael is opposed to them as the intransigent who continues the series of condemnatory judgments on Gothic. His situation, however, was a very different one, inasmuch as he did not have to give an opinion on the continuation of a Gothic structure. Nevertheless, a consideration of the two camps leads one to decline to ascribe the report for Julius II to Bramante. Peruzzi must be eliminated for the same reasons; whoever speaks of Gothic as Pseudo-Raphael does, would scarcely have made Peruzzi's design for S. Petronio in Bologna, to which we shall return in the following chapter. To identify the anonymous author remains a task for the future.[52]

4. France, Italy, and Spain (1530-1600)

IN *Pantagruel* by François RABELAIS (ca. 1490-1553), published in 1533, Gargantua writes in a letter to his son in Paris about the cultural ignorance that reigned during his own youth: "The age was still dark and affected by the misfortune and misery of the Goths, who had de-

[52] In a recent book of Otto H. Förster, *Bramante*, Vienna and Munich, 1956, pp. 161ff., the report of Pseudo-Raphael is again emphatically attributed to Bramante. It remains difficult to believe that the glorified Bramante, familiar with the cathedral of Milan, could have taken seriously the silly theory expounded by Pseudo-Raphael. Förster's book also treats S. Maria delle Grazie in Milan, pp. 112ff., and refers to his older article, "Bramante's Pläne . . . " in *Festschrift Heinrich Wölfflin*, Dresden, 1935, pp. 1ff. (especially p. 22). The cancelling of the ribs is mentioned superficially on p. 26; it is important that he proves that the proportions were changed by the unknown architect who executed Bramante's designs. The transverse arch at the entrance to the crossing was heightened and this made an adjustment of the eastern vault of the nave necessary. This alteration, therefore, cannot be attributed to Bramante.

stroyed all good literature; but by divine grace, light and dignity were restored to literature in my time, and I see such progress that I would now scarcely be accepted as a pupil in the lowest class (with such a knowledge as those had) who, in the years of my maturity, were not unjustly considered as the greatest scholars of that century."[1]

The Goths are here made responsible not for the decline of good architecture but of good literature. One can perhaps include Rabelais as a satirist under the generalized concept of "Mannerism," but this single sentence could hardly be given much weight within the chaos of ideas that he has spread out in his books for the entertainment of the astonished reader. In any case, this passage is meant seriously in the midst of a stream of humor. Rabelais is speaking of his own school days. Later he became a Franciscan monk, then a Benedictine, an anatomist, a doctor, and a writer; he was certainly a representative of the culture of his generation. His thrust at the Goths reflected the general opinion of the educated class in France; it remains doubtful whether he thought even remotely of Gothic architecture when he was writing that sentence. One senses, however, that he and his like around 1530 felt themselves far superior, because of their classical education, to everything that was mediaeval. Rabelais speaks of the lowest classes in school: the logical inference is, and no doubt always was, that buildings like Nôtre-Dame in Paris were assigned to the mental level of schoolchildren, or to that of simple people who lived out their lives without a knowledge of Cicero and Virgil. Still other passages from Rabelais' works have been connected with this problem, but they can be ignored here.[2]

This humanistic arrogance began to have its social effects. A striking example of the social evaluation of Gothic is offered by Sebastiano SERLIO (1475-1554). His textbook (1551) begins with elementary planimetry, thereby betraying his debt to the tradition of the literature of the lodges, back to the time of Villard de Honnecourt. Even quadrature and triangulation live on here, but without any useful application, as though their meaning had been lost. Quadrature, the doubling

[1] *Œuvres* de François Rabelais, *Pantagruel*, I, chap. 8, ed. Abel Lefranc *et al.*, III, Paris, 1922, p. 102. Cf. text, Appendix 18.

[2] Jakob Burckhardt, *Geschichte der Renaissance*, Stuttgart, 1891, p. 30 (3rd ed.), refers to *Pantagruel*, Prologue to Book V; he obviously means the sentence: "Fat est un vocable de Languegoth et signifie non sallé, sans sel, insipide, fade. . . ." The form "Languegoth" instead of "Languedoc" has a humorous effect, however, only on the assumption that "goth" is something ridiculous. Here are again meant Alaric's Goths or, by extension, the barbarians in general; moreover, the reference is to language, not to architecture. De Beer cites another passage in his article, "Gothic: Origin and Diffusion of the Term," *Journal of Warburg and Courtauld Institutes*, XI, 1948, p. 144; this is from *Gargantua*, where "escripre Gottiquement" is intended in the same sense as earlier in Valla, namely, as Gothic type in contrast to Roman.

of the square with the help of the diagonals, equilateral triangle, and circle belong to the rudiments of planimetry; and the composition of segments of arcs (the so-called curve thrust) is employed in order to plot the shape of vases from classical models by means of compasses. The second book is an introduction to the now indispensable subject of perspective; it is, one might say, after planimetry a (visual) stereometry. Everything that follows, the treatise on classical buildings, the five columnar orders, and the like, typical of the thinking, the methods, and the architecture of the sixteenth century, contains nothing about Gothic, with one exception to which we shall return. But that second book ends with a *Trattato sopra le scene* where, to be sure, the word Gothic itself does not occur, although the designation *opera moderna* does, by which Gothic is meant; and this style appears, as it were, in person in one of the interesting scenes.

Serlio gives examples of three stage settings: for the *Scena Comica*, the *Scena Tragica*, and the *Scena Satirica.* The buildings for comedy (Fig. 34) "ought to be such as belong to private persons, for instance, citizens, advocates, merchants, parasites, and others like them. Above all the house of the procuress must not be omitted; there ought also to be an inn, and a church is here very necessary. . . ."[3] The house of the procuress stands in the right foreground; on the ground floor it is of wooden construction in front, above are two splendid windows with Gothic ogee arches. Serlio provides this house with a humorous coat-of-arms.[4] Behind it is a noble palace in Renaissance style with a loggia in the second upper story, then comes a smaller house, also Renaissance. Each of the three houses juts out into the middle street, so that the square is narrowed toward the back; at its end is seen the simple façade of the church with a high tower at the rear, which has the pointed arched Gothic windows together with the horizontal divisions of the stories characteristic of Renaissance. Its upper end is in ruins, overgrown with bushes. This is not early romanticism of ruins,

[3] The first edition of Serlio's first book lies before me (the orthography of this, not of the second edition, I follow in quoting), *Il Primo Libro d'architettura di M. Sebastiano Serlio Bolognese*, 1551. The title page is framed by a developed Manneristic cartouche with scrollwork and glyphs, in the lower part of which, however, are compasses, ruler, right angle, tetrahedron, and a cube in frontal position; on the latter's front surface is drawn Roriczer's quadrature with three squares overlapping, together with their appropriate circles. The passage on the scenery for a comedy is as follows: "Questa prima sarà la Comica, i casamenti della quale vogliono essere di personagi priuati, come saria di cittadini, auocati, mercanti, parassiti, et altri simili persone. Ma sopra il tutto che non vi manchi la casa della Rufiana, ne sia senza hostaria, et uno tempio vi e molto necessario. . . ."

[4] ". . . L'insegna della quale sono li rampini, o vogliano dire hami; . . ." Perhaps snares or fishing hooks are meant, in order to catch men, or perhaps something else.

but mockery at neglect. At the left, again beginning with the foreground: "poggiuli, altri gli dicono pergoli, altri Ringhiere." Here again there are pointed arches. The house in back, in the same row, is Renaissance, provided with a balcony; then comes the inn, emerging at right angles. Below, it has a shop with an overhanging roof, in the main story is a large Gothic window surmounted by a Medici coat-of-arms with a cardinal's hat (!); then comes a story with rectangular windows and this projects on wooden beams on the side toward the church. The inn has the sign of the moon and as decoration a scorpion.[5]

"The *Scena Tragica* is intended for the presentation of tragedies (Fig. 35). The buildings for this [*scena*] ought to be those of exalted personages, because here love stories and surprising events, violent and cruel deaths (as one reads in antic and modern tragedies) take place inside the houses of nobles, dukes, great princes, and even the king, and because for that reason (as I have said) one will not construct in such settings (*apparati*) any building that does not have something noble about it, as the following figure shows, where I (because it is small) could not make these large (magnificent) buildings of a royal and lordly fashion that could be constructed in a spacious place."[6] Here there is in the left corner a triumphal arch; back of it are astonishingly modest houses, which is why Serlio has to apologize. In the background in the middle of the street is another triumphal arch in the form of a church façade, and back of this a kind of pyramid of Cestius and an obelisk (instead of the tower in the first setting). In the right foreground are two palaces, the first with a loggia, but now with round arches resting on rustica pillars, and so on. Serlio had worked together with Peruzzi, and inherited the drawings that he left; both these settings go back to a single drawing by Peruzzi.[7]

[5] This woodcut appears in later editions reversed from left to right.

[6] *Ibid.*, p. 29: "La Scena Tragica sarà per rappresentare tragedie. Li casamenti d'essa vogliono essere di grandi personagi: percioche gli accidenti amorosi, et casi inopinati, morti violenti et crudeli (per quanto si lege nelle tragedie antiche, et ancho nelle moderne) sono sempre interuenute dentro le case di signore, duchi, ò gran principi, imo, di Re, et perho (come ho detto) in cotali apparati non si fara edificio che non habbia del nobile: si come se dimostra nella seguente figura, entro la quale (per esser cosa piccola) non ho potuto dimostrare quei grandi edificij Regii, et signorili: che in vn lugo spatioso si potrebbono fare. . . ."

[7] After the completion of this manuscript I discovered an article by Richard Krautheimer, "The Tragic and the Comic Scene of the Renaissance," *Gazette des Beaux-Arts*, New York, 1948, p. 327. The explanation there advanced of the panels in Urbino and Baltimore as the earliest known scene paintings of the Renaissance, designed in connection with the passage from Vitruvius, is completely convincing. They are shown to be preliminaries to Peruzzi and Serlio, and at the same time connecting links with even earlier stages in the reliefs of Ghiberti and the theory of Alberti. The complete lack of figures in the two panels, which gives a strange effect, is now explained by the fact that the actors were to be imagined against the

"The *Scena Satyrica* serves to represent satires, in which all those who live undisciplined and bad lives are ridiculed (indeed even discredited), those who in the classical *satyri* were ruthlessly held up to the finger of scorn, as it were, as persons leading vicious and evil lives. In any case, such freedom is understood to be allowed with regard to persons who speak in a disrespectful (ill-mannered) way, such as, one might say, peasants: wherefore Vitruvius, in his discussion of theatrical scenes, demands that they should be adorned with trees, cliffs, hills, mountains, plants, flowers, and springs; he also desires a few cottages of a rustic nature, as are here shown. . . ."[8] This drawing represents a forest path leading into the background, low cottages stand to the right and left of it, half hidden among high trees (Fig. 36).

The place in Vitruvius to which Serlio refers (v. 6. 9) reads: "There are three kinds of stage scenery, one called the tragic, a second the comic, and a third the satiric. The scene paintings of these are, however, among themselves dissimilar and unequal, because the tragic stages are adorned with columns, gables, statues, and other objects suited to kings, while the comic offers a view of private buildings and oriel-like fronts and various views through the windows, in imitation of ordinary buildings; and the satiric stages, finally, are decorated with trees, caves, mountains, and other rural things, grouped into a landscape picture." Serlio adhered closely to Vitruvius, and there arose for the third setting a discrepancy as regards the classical concept of the satire.

Serlio speaks of *gente rustica* and *capane alla rustica.* One immediately thinks of peasants and peasant cottages, but in Serlio's day there were no peasant plays, but only pastoral plays, descended from Sannazaro's novel, *Aminta* (or even further back, from the *Eclogues* of Theocritus).[8a] The Greek satyr play formed an epilogue to the trilogy. Vitruvius took his enumeration of the three scenic backgrounds from Greek sources, but in his time there was said to have been a kind of descendant of the satyr plays in Rome also, so that he may even have been justified in adding to his list the third type of Greek stage setting.

---

backgrounds. For the rest, Krautheimer goes into many matters not touched upon here, as they lie outside the subject of Gothic.

[8] Serlio, *op.cit.*, p. 30: "La scena Satyrica e per rappresentar satyre, nelle quali se riprendono (anzi vero se mordeno) tutti coloro che licentiosamente viuono, et senza rispetto nelle satyre antiche erano quasi mostrati a dito gli huomini viciosi et mal viuenti. Perho tal licentia si puo comprendere che fusse concessa a personaggi che senza rispetto parlassero, come saria a dire gente rustica, percioche Vitruvio trattando delle scene, vuole che questa sia ornata di arbori, sassi, colli, montagne, herbe, fiori, et fontane, vuole anchora che vi siano alcune capanne alla rustica, come qui appresso se dimostra. . . ."

[8a] Alois Nagler, *Sources of Theatrical History*, New York, 1952, pp. 73ff.

Serlio, however, connected this scenery with pastoral plays, although shepherds with their beasts probably would prefer open meadows. This lack of distinctions is characteristic of his dependence on Vitruvius.

Serlio's three settings differentiate three distinct social classes: shepherds, middle-class citizens, noblemen, and, corresponding to these, artless nature, Gothic, Renaissance. Granted that the *Scena Comica* is scarcely fifty percent Gothic, nevertheless the old-fashioned style is here the form symbol of the *cittadini*, which can be translated by "bourgeois" or "Philistines" in a derogatory sense. For Rabelais, everything Gothic was fit for the level of schoolboys; for Serlio, it is fit for the average citizen of the middle class, and though there also appeared on this stage *auocati*, supposed to have humanistic education, they were, after all, figures ridiculed as pedants. Classic art, cool and aristocratic, is reserved for kings and nobles. Although Serlio admitted Gothic to his stage setting for comedy only with great moderation, something of that snugness, human warmth, and friendliness radiates from it that every mediaeval street still in existence, from England to Italy, offers to the receptive spirit. Perhaps Serlio was secretly susceptible to these charms, but he was working for *grandi personaggi*, whose architecture creates the aloofness that corresponds to the social cleavage.

Serlio showed in Chapter 62 of Book 7, the second place where Gothic occurs in his work, how one ought to restore old Gothic houses.[9] As an example he cites a remodeling—without naming the place, architect, or even owner—and relates a moralizing story. The owner had been born in this large house built by his grandfather "in quei tempi che la buona Architettura era ancora sepolta." The owner, who was very rich, but miserly and who felt quite comfortable in his dwelling, did not want to change anything, but the *Principe* insisted that the façade should be rebuilt. In the interior only one room of the ground floor had to be altered in order to move the portal into the middle of the front. Serlio censures avarice severely and so appeals to Christian virtue in order to commend good architecture, which in this façade can hardly be characterized as "antique." How important morality was for him is illustrated by the end of the story; here it is expressly stated that the niches on either side of the main portal and of the Palladian pergola were intended for statues of the *quattro virtù morali*. In this edifying anecdote the role of the dictatorial *Principe* is that of the very

[9] This is at hand in the edition of 1600; here the passage is on p. 156.

progressively minded man to whom a Gothic house façade is an annoyance; it is a disgrace to the whole city.

Another example is given on page 170. Two neighboring houses, one jutting out of line with the other and extending obliquely as well, were the property of one and the same gentleman. The remodeling leaves on the façade no more trace of its former Gothic.

Even more important than these passages from Serlio are VASARI's recurring hostile judgments on Gothic. The chief one is in the *Introduzione alle tre arti del disegno cioè architettura, scultura e pittura.* In the first chapter he discusses the different sorts of stone (porphyry, serpentine, and so on), in the second he explains the significance of ashlar, that is, hewn stone either with rectangular surfaces (*quadro*) or with ornamental profiles (*opera di quadro intagliata*, p. 128). "Of this sort of squared or chiseled stone all the kinds of orders are built: Rusticated, Doric, Ionic, Corinthian, and Composite; and so German work was made at the time of the Goths."[10] But even this is not the most important passage: he says in this chapter only that in any architectural construction of hewn stone, including the "German" from the time of the Goths, a larger block (in Italian *bozzo*, in German *Bosse*) must always first be finished (the "bossage") before the profile or the ornament is chiseled out. By "German work" is meant not merely Gothic, but the architecture of the entire Middle Ages.[11] The third chapter discusses the five orders, and then *il lavoro tedesco.* This is the place where Gothic receives its literary *coup de grâce.*

"There are works of another sort that are called German, which differ greatly in ornament and proportion from the antique and the modern. Today they are not employed by distinguished architects but are avoided by them as monstrous and barbarous, since they ignore every familiar idea of order (*ogni lor cosa di ordine*); which one can rather call confusion and disorder, for in their buildings, of which there are so many that they have contaminated the whole world, they made portals adorned with thin columns twisted in corkscrew fashion (vine tendrils), which do not have the strength to support a burden, however light. And so, above all their façades (*facce*) and their other decorative parts, they built one cursed tabernacle on top of the other, with so many pyramids [pinnacles] and points (*punte*) and leaves that they do not stand, as it appears, not to mention their being able to hold

[10] Giorgio Vasari, *Le Vite . . .* , ed. Gaetano Milanesi, Florence, 1878, I, p. 128. "Di questa sorte opra di quadro e d'intaglio si fanno tutte le sorti Ordini: rustico, dorico, ionico, corinto e composto; e così se ne fece al tempo de' Goti il lavoro tedesco."

[11] This is not correctly recognized in the article by E. S. de Beer, "Gothic: Origin and Diffusion of the Term," *Journal of the Warburg and Courtauld Institutes*, XI, 1948, p. 148.

themselves up, and they have more the quality of seeming to have been made of paper, than of stone or marble. And in these works they made so many projections (*risalti*), openings (*rotture*), little consoles, and twining vines (*viticci*) that they threw the works that they built out of proportion; and often they reached such a height, by placing one thing on top of another, that the end of a door touched its roof. This manner was invented by the Goths, who, after the destruction of the ancient buildings and the dying out of architects because of the wars, afterwards built—those who survived —edifices in this manner: these men fashioned the vaults (*girarono le volte*) with pointed arches of quarter circles (*quarti acuti*), and filled all Italy with these damnable buildings, so that their whole method has been given up, in order not to let any more be built. God preserve every land from the invasion of such ideas and [such] an order of works [structures]; since they are so unlike the beauty of our buildings, they deserve no more than that to be said about them. And therefore let us proceed to vaults."[12]

Much in this hostile, even malicious criticism has been well observed and equally well understood and formulated. The rebuke of *confusione e disordine* probably means that Vasari missed the *classical* orders, and thus *order* in general, for there was for him no other sort. The classical orders and, correspondingly, those of the Renaissance, really do bring "order" into a building; they offer clear, intelligible proportions; compared with them, Gothic is—we should say—"free." For Vasari its order is no "order" at all, but confusion, and he at once refers to statics. The twisted columns annoyed him especially; we must, however, assume that he made little distinction between what we call the style of the Cosmati and what we call Romanesque and Gothic. The works of the Cosmati, especially, teem with twisted columns. Where he mentions the cursed tabernacles and the Gothic gables, "che la fine d'una porta toccava loro il tetto," and where he speaks of pointed arches, of pinnacles and leaves (finials and crockets), there he means Gothic in our modern sense, and asserts of it as well that the *Goths* invented this *maniera*.

In his own way he formulates for the first time much that was correctly observed and has, therefore, continued to be accepted down to our own day: the dematerialization of the stone (*fatte di carta*), the web of decoration thrown over all the surfaces, the significance of the tabernacle form as a kind of setpiece, and verticalism, which is un-

[12] Cf. text, Appendix 19. *Quarto acuto* means a pointed arch having as centers the points dividing the diameter into four parts; *terzo acuto* those dividing into three parts.

doubtedly what he means when he says "di proporzione molto differenti degli antichi e dai moderni."

Vasari calls this bad architecture *maniera tedesca.* Several times he reverts to this German manner, but he never calls it Gothic, either as adjective or noun. The adjective Gothic we met in Alberti and Valla, in the former with the extended meaning "ugly," as is everything *architectural* for which the Middle Ages could be held responsible. Vasari surely knew that buildings like the cathedral in Florence had nothing to do with the Goths; what he meant was that the mediaeval manner was the fault of the destruction of classical tradition through Alaric and his Goths. To this ugly manner belongs, among others or as its historical conclusion, that German manner he describes. In consequence of Vasari's text the term Gothic seems to have evolved by slow oral stages, and the use of the word in the *modern* sense is, as far as we now can tell, not found until 1610.[13] Scribanius writes of the Bourse in Antwerp: "Hic columnis triformes insistunt arcus opere Gotico. . . ." (Here trefoil arches rest on columns in Gothic work. . . .) One should, however, never forget that the word was at that time occasionally used of the epoch that we call Gothic, but that other authors extended it again to cover the concept of mediaeval. When, for example, Palladio mentions St. Mark's in Venice also among the buildings in the *maniera tedesca* (he does not say *gotica*), it does not mean that this architect, who was certainly capable of judging and who was at home in Venice, considered the church "Gothic" (for example, because of the superimposed ogee arches of the façade), but that he explained all the mediaeval styles in contrast to "good architecture" as the result of the migrations, that is, as the fault of the Germans, and thought of them all together under one heading. The exclamation marks, that many modern authors have put in brackets after Palladio's word, expressing thereby their disapproval as well as their superior knowledge, reveal a misunderstanding of the old terminology.

Vasari, who showed such intolerance, uttered his death sentence so relentlessly, and cursed the pointed arch, drew a pointed arch in an unguarded moment as the stylistically appropriate frame for a drawing in his collection considered by him to be a work of Cimabue. The

[13] de Beer, *op.cit.*, p. 150. C. Scribanius, a Jesuit priest, described on p. 51 of the *Antverpia* the second building for the Bourse, erected in 1531 by Dominicus Waghemakere (1460-1542). This Late Gothic structure burned down in 1858 and was rebuilt in similar form from 1868 to 1872. The translation of *triformes arcus* by trefoil arches is justified by a depiction that was preserved of the building in its original state; cf. Richard Graul, *Altflandern*, Munich, 1918, p. 18.

frame corresponds more or less to the style of Arnolfo di Cambio. The significance of this sparse, inglorious Renaissance of Gothic (or should we say Gothic of the Renaissance?) was recognized and psychologically interpreted by Panofsky. In his essay[14] one reads that the drawing in question has nothing to do with Cimabue, that the Gothic of the frame is not particularly correct, and so on, but that Vasari's feeling for purity of style, together with a mistaken attribution, led him to the paradox of making an exception and, though a despiser of Gothic, of producing bad Gothic. His attitude in this instance is like that of Leonardo and Bramante, for whom it was perfectly natural to complete a Gothic work in Gothic style, though in good Gothic.

Three other passages where Vasari touches on this subject have been cited by de Beer,[15] but they add nothing essential. Often quoted also is the sentence where Vasari inveighs against buildings by his contemporaries in the words: ". . . hanno a'tempi nostri certi architetti plebei, prosontuosi e senza disegno, fatto quasi a caso, senza servar decoro, arte ò ordine nessuno, tutte le cose loro mostruose, e peggio che le tedesche."[16]

How Vasari looked at the history of Italian architecture after the downfall of the Roman Empire can be learned in the *Proemio delle Vite* that follows the *Introduzione*.[17] He has more extensive knowledge than Ghiberti and Manetti had previously. Strangely enough, he praises the palaces of Theodoric in Ravenna, Pavia, and Modena, built "indeed in the barbarian manner, but still rich and grand, well planned, or of good architecture."[18] In Florence he praises Santi Apostoli as the model for Brunelleschi's two basilicas, and S. Miniato al monte. He appreciates also the Byzantine edifices in Ravenna, the cathedral in Pisa, S. Martino in Lucca. Because of the fact that he dates some things wrongly, he occasionally includes quite unintentionally something Gothic in his praise, but otherwise his historical survey breaks off rather obviously just before Gothic.

In the *Lives* themselves he does, however, occasionally mention Gothic; for example, in the *Vita* of Arnolfo di Lapo he speaks of the cathedral in Florence, without, however, saying anything of importance

14 Erwin Panofsky, "Das erste Blatt aus dem 'Libro' Giorgio Vasaris," *Städel-Jahrbuch*, Berlin and Frankfurt a.M., 1930, p. 25.

15 de Beer, *op.cit.*, p. 148.

16 Vasari, *Le Vite* . . . , ed Milanese, Florence, 1878, I, p. 136.

17 *Ibid.*, pp. 228ff.

18 *Ibid.*, p. 233. ". . . pur di maniera barbara, e piuttosto ricchi e grandi, che bene intesi o di buona architettura."

about it. In this biography can be found in almost perfect form the stylistic designation that was to become the future norm. He says of a piece of sculpture that it is "*alla maniera de' Goti*" (page 272), and shortly afterward occurs the sentence: "Buono . . . fece l'abitazione vecchia dei signori d'Arezzo [1232]; cioè un palazzo della maniera de' Goti . . . il quale edificio che di quella maniera era ragionevole, fu gettato in terra . . . l'anno 1553 . . ." Vasari was born in Arezzo and was thus inclined to be indulgent toward his dead fellow countryman.

It is probable that MICHELANGELO Buonarotti (1475-1564) shared Vasari's opinion of Gothic. The evidence for this is a remark, which we know, however, only through Vasari. In the biography of Antonio da Sangallo we read that as architect of St. Peter's he made a new ground plan and had his design carried out in a model by Antonio d'Abaco.[19] Vasari praises this work in the highest terms, but then he reports that, to Michelangelo and many others who beheld it, the model and the beginning of the execution seemed trifling. In the sentences that follow it is not clear to what extent they reproduce Michelangelo's words or how far they derive from Vasari himself. He writes that the whole thing is trifling because of the *Risalite*, the little structural members, the columns, "archi sopra archi, e cornici sopra cornici." The two towers, the four small apses (*tribune*), and the garlands are not pleasing; also unsatisfactory are "the many pyramids that in the aforesaid model imitate rather the German manner and work than the classical and good, which today all the better architects observe [practice]."[20] The model is still in existence.[21] The criticism of multiplicity is understandable, but no one today would be reminded of Gothic pinnacles by the *aguglie*, the pyramids. From the standpoint of Michelangelo's later work in St. Peter's, this criticism is very characteristic of the man. If it can be said that he himself called the many little obelisks *maniera tedesca*, then he did not mean this literally but more as a means of giving a universally intelligible and vigorous expression to his rejection. Since Michelangelo had the incomparably greater genius, which Vasari venerated, one might assume that everything the latter says is only a reflection of Michelangelo's opinions. But such an insinuation against Vasari is not necessary; his criticism of Gothic is not original enough. It formulates what was *communis opinio* in the artistic circles of the

[19] *Ibid.*, v, p. 467.

[20] Vasari, *op.cit.*, v, p. 467 ". . . e parimente non piacevano molto e non piacciono quelle tante aguglie che vi sono per finimento, parendo che in ciò detto modello immitti più la maniera ed opera tedesca, che l'antica e buona che oggi osservano gli architetti migliori."

[21] G. K. Loukomski, *Les Sangallo*, Paris, 1934, pl. 93.

an opinion shared by Michelangelo also, though he did not create 'he salient point of the criticism directed against Sangallo lies not ıuch in the comparison with Gothic as in his treatment of Renais-e forms themselves and, without its being expressly stated, in his ıre to "compose" the stories by means of the "grand order." In this matter a Gothicist would have been naturally superior—but rding to his own way.

ichelangelo's own opinion of Sangallo's model has come down to ı a letter to Amanati from the year 1555, thus after the appearance 'asari's *Lives*. Here there is no word either of the many obelisks or ;othic.[22]

ıe second edition of Vasari's biographies appeared in 1568; in the : year there appeared in Paris *Architecture*, by Philibert DE L'ORME 1512-1570), an enlarged reprint of the edition of 1567.[23] Here the ıde toward Gothic is quite different, in any case, free of contempt.[24] : L'Orme, born in Lyons, was descended from a family of crafts-, or perhaps one should say artists; the father, Jean de L'Orme, was *ıître maçon*. Under his tutelage Philibert grew up to be a practical ler. From 1533 to 1536 he was in Rome, studying classical struc-, Vitruvius, Alberti, and Serlio diligently; the latter he probably v personally. In 1561 he published a book entitled *Nouvelles inven-· pour bien bastir et à petit frais*, in which he presents construction 'ood that far exceeded in span what was usual at the time.[25] His s were for the most part not carried out, his buildings have almost erished. He was one of the most important of the second generation .enaissance architects in France. His book became for his native a kind of new Vitruvius. As in the case of the latter, his work re-; a man who had complete mastery of his craft together with the larship that differentiates an architect from a *maître maçon*. Serlio been accused of being a dilettante writing for dilettanti, and one ders whether de L'Orme judged him so. In 1547 he succeeded in the work on the castle at Fontainebleau. It is not clear whether ıpplanted him unfairly; more probably Serlio really failed to meet :ompetition of an expert with practical training.

Ienry Thode, *Michelangelo, Kritische Untersuchungen seiner Werke*, II, Berlin, 1908, .

.e *Premier Tome de l'architecture de Philibert de l'Orme . . .*, Paris, 1567.

:f. text, Appendix 19.

Ienri Clouzot, *Philibert de l'Orme*, Paris, 1910, shows on plate XIV "la Grande Basilique," gn that looks like a railroad station of the nineteenth century. Further, cf. Reginald .eld, *Studies in Architecture*, London, 1905, pp. 135-190, in particular p. 178 on Philibert rme.

Two observations must be made to characterize his beautifully printed volume. The first is expressed in an anecdote, perhaps apocryphal: during the printing of the edition of 1648, in which every chapter commences with a handsome initial, the printer used up the vignettes for *J*, and was obliged to change the beginnings, all of which started with *Je*. The second is the wealth of woodcuts and, more important, the inclusion of complicated drawings of what was later called descriptive geometry, that is, ground plan and section in combination. Of course, these woodcuts had a tradition; Late Gothic vaults with their complicated shapes for the stone blocks presuppose the same method, and one feels that de L'Orme was influenced by these works as a constructer and technician. Whereas Cesariano included a Gothic cathedral in his book because of its proportions and Serlio classified Gothic houses under the heading of comic, de L'Orme devoted three short chapters to Gothic vaults, discussing Gothic seriously, and accompanying the text with illustrations, as one would expect in a textbook. It is astonishing that these chapters are part of a work that otherwise treats only of classical and Renaissance buildings.

In Book IV, Chapter VIII, he speaks of "voûtes modernes, que les maistres maçons ont accoutoumé de faire aux Eglises, et logis des grands Seigneurs." By *voûtes modernes* he means Gothic ribbed vaults: *croisées d'ogives*. "Many make use of *liernes, formerets*, and *tiercerons*, with their *doubleaux*, and other sorts of branching ribs . . . these types of vaults were considered very beautiful, and one sees well-constructed ones employed in various places in the kingdom and especially in this city of Paris, as also in many others. Today those who have any knowledge at all of true architecture do not follow this fashion of vaults, called by the workmen *la mode Françoise*; nor in truth do I mean to despise them, but will rather confess that very good and difficult designs have been planned and carried out. But inasmuch as this method requires great buttresses, that is, great support to serve as a counterthrust, and flying buttresses to hold the work together, as one sees in large churches, for that reason I shall at the end of this chapter. . . ." He defines *croisée d'ogives* as diagonal arches. Then follow on page 107 precise definitions of *lierne*,[25a] *tierceron* or *tiercerct* (a rib springing from the corner point and leading to the *lierne* but not to the intersection of the diagonal ribs), *formerets* (wall ribs), *tas de charge* (the

[25a] Today this word has different meanings in English and French. (See Russell Sturgis, *A Dictionary of Architecture*, II, New York, 1901, p. 762.)

mass of the vault above the springing line, holding itself in equilibrium).

A marginal note contains in a few words, compared with the prolixity of the text, what interests us: "The author approves of the Gothic method of vaulting but without, however, desiring to use it."[26] Thus his attitude toward Gothic is positive only insofar as it has been employed by others. One may recall in this connection that his father, Jean de L'Orme, who died in 1538, was undoubtedly still trained exclusively in the Gothic *maniera*. Perhaps Philibert's tolerance must be accounted for by filial piety. In the description of how Late Gothic vaults are to be constructed he evades the issue and says that one should have recourse to architects or *maistres maçons* who are in charge of such work. It is noteworthy that he makes a distinction here between architect and master mason, for he means either architects *or* masons (page 108).

In the following Chapter IX he discusses the stellar vault of a choir with an octagonal end. In the drawing he indicates the individual arches both on the ground plan and in their true form (fold-over technique).

The tenth chapter treats of a quadripartite ribbed vault with a pendant keystone; the word clef should really be translated "keywood" in this place, because de L'Orme refers to a drawing taken from his preceding work on wood construction. In the text, however, he discusses stone vaults as well, mentioning on page 110 verso pendant keystones that were richly adorned and which "were considered very beautiful at the time that such kinds of vaults were made that were then called by the workmen (as we have already said) vaults *à la mode Françoise.*" At the end of the chapter he repeats again: "voûtes modernes, appellées ainsi, que nous avon dict, voûtes de la mode et façon Françoise."

The word then (*lors*) means the time before de L'Orme and at the earliest, insofar as it applies to the decorated pendent keystones in France, the fifteenth century. If we thus date the term *mode Françoise* about 1400, which is pure hypothesis, we are still more than a century removed from Burchard von Hall (1280). We can follow the effort to comprehend conceptually and, therefore, terminologically as well the architecture that arose between antiquity and Renaissance. This process was begun in Italy by Petrarch. Alberti spoke of Gothic hands, *mani gotiche*. Vasari understood the style (in his fashion) but called it *ma-*

[26] Clouzot, *op.cit.*, p. 107: "L'Autheur approuver [*sic*] la façon moderne de voutes [*sic*], toutefois ne s'en vouloir ayder."

niera tedesca, also *maniera de' Goti*. In de L'Orme what was call Italy *German* is called *French*; in Germany, however, the source silent on this point, and we are inclined to assume that a parti word was superfluous there, because construction could mean not other than Gothic construction, just as in the preceding period struction meant only Romanesque construction. The passage Burchard von Hall is understandable for Germany at a time there was still a strong feeling that the former native style had changed by the French. Anyone who wants to get to the botto this matter must go back to the time when people first spoke of *Romanum*.

Two more points must be made with regard to de L'Orme. Fir Chapter XI he speaks of spherical vaults and now turns his bac Gothic. He says that the new vaults are longer lasting (how cou know that, as they had only stood for a short time compared to much older Gothic ones?); furthermore, they are, he says, che because they require no buttresses; they exercise less sideways th He is thus much more polite than Vasari, but in the end the res the same.

Second, attention should be called to the drawing on page 23 is a section of a Renaissance church, constructed *ad quadratum* an entrance door "according to the right measure," that is, the w of the door is used for the drawing of a square, and the diagona this square give the height for the door. That is the proportio Roriczer's quadrature. It is amusing to see the secret of the lo combined with a Renaissance domed church. De L'Orme had cert no intention of bringing in anything "Gothic"; he was simply fol ing, without much reflection, his father's tradition, thus presum the teaching of his own days of apprenticeship. The introductio this alternative between a doorway of Gothic proportion and one t from antiquity was perhaps not even noticed by his readers.

These readers, all architects who had no longer any desire to c new Gothic buildings, may well have been astonished at the t chapters dealing with Gothic. Their inclusion belongs to the pic that one must make of Philibert de L'Orme. His perpetual talk a himself betrays a strong consciousness of personal worth, but it not repel us, and the whole textbook, compared to others, is full of It is perhaps permissible to deduce from his whole work that to mobile spirit, who invented new constructions, built French ca d was a fully trained Humanist, Gothic was interesting, perhaps even rious, but certainly not a matter of indifference.

The voices of Rabelais, Vasari, Serlio, and de L'Orme may appear to ve no connection, but beneath the visible surface they are related each other like islands beneath the surface of the sea. That also may applied retroactively to the judgments of Humanism and the Early d High Renaissance. Vasari was probably unfamiliar with the letter Pseudo-Raphael, at that time not yet printed, as otherwise he would ve alluded to the forest theory; but the tendency is everywhere the ne, and the inner connection of all the literary documents as the ult of widespread oral discussion becomes completely clear when we n to the dispute between the Gothicists and Classicists that excited whole city of Bologna and could be heard as far as Rome and nice because of the participation of Giulio Romano, Vignola, and ladio.

n 1388, two years after the foundation stone of Milan Cathedral was l, the building of S. Petronio in Bologna was decided upon, and in o it was begun. The ambition of the Bolognese to surpass in size rything done up to that time was apparently greater than their ans. Only the nave was completed; of the transept there are only innings; and the central part of the nave ends immediately in an e, as was formerly true of Early Christian churches—in this case a l temporary measure. But this abandonment of a transept with a ne over the crossing and the eastern choir did not result from a of funds, for these, as well as building material, were at one time nother actually held in readiness; the abandonment was caused by ility to make the workmen and the leading nobility agree to com- e in Gothic style what had been begun in Gothic.

he first architect, Antonio di Vincenzo (ca. 1350-1402) who had sent to Florence and Milan to study the cathedral buildings there, le in 1390 a model of brick and plaster on an enormous scale.[27] Its th was 18.71 meters; one could walk into it, and it seemed at the that later generations would have no difficulties if they only ad- d to this model. In addition, Antonio's design for the façade was esented *al fresco* on the Palazzo Communale. But the model, which finally an encumbrance in the Palazzo Pepoli, was dismantled in , and in 1423 the Palazzo Communale was burned to the ground. 1401 the nave chapels, at least, were in use; Jacopo della Quercia

'or Antonio's biography cf. (in addition to Thieme-Becker) the account of Ludwig , *San Petronio in Bologna*, 1904, pp. 69ff.

faced the lower part of the façade and provided reliefs for the main portal, but death cut short his work in 1438. A provisional flat ceiling was constructed over the nave in 1440. The work lagged, and it may be that even then, in the time of Brunelleschi (1446) and Alberti, it was doubtful whether the building should be continued in forms that had suddenly become suspect. It took until 1656 for the edifice to reach the stage in which we now see it as a grandiose fragment. Two and a half centuries were occupied in the construction, but the disputes that interest us here took place essentially in the eighty years from 1521 to 1600.

This quarrel has been described and expounded in detail several times, above all by Springer,[28] Weber,[29] Panofsky,[30] and Zucchini,[31] and recently by Bernheimer.[32] Here we shall give the briefest possible survey, in the course of which we shall have to discuss the designs for the façade, although this would seem to transcend the frame of "literary" evidence about Gothic. These designs were, however, partly the result of the dispute and at the same time partly its object.

The oldest design extant is the wooden model from 1514 of Arduino di Domenico degli ARIGUZZI (ca. 1482-ca. 1517), which is still preserved in the sacristy of S. Petronio. How much it differed from the lost one of Antonio di Vincenzo we do not know.[33] The façade is pronouncedly Gothic, of course in the sense of Italian Gothic. The predominant forms are the five rising gables and the ornamental gablets of the portals. The three windows of the nave and the two aisles are oculi.

Zucchini puts the undated proposal of Domenico VARIGNANA (died in 1539) at the head of all the extant drawings. It probably originated in the second decade of the sixteenth century. The buttresses, continuing the already accomplished division of the ground floor, produce the rhythm $\beta\ b\ a\ b\ \beta$; the five axes are graduated by means of separate gables, the inner *b* axes having Late Gothic gables with ogee arches, the other gables being 45 degree triangles. The Gothic and the Renaissance parts are fairly well harmonized by an incrustation of rectangular

[28] Anton Springer, *Bilder aus der neueren Kunstgeschichte*, Bonn, 1867, pp. 147ff.

[29] Ludwig Weber, *op.cit.*

[30] Erwin Panofsky, "Das erste Blatt . . . ," *op.cit.*, chiefly pp. 42-64.

[31] Guido Zucchini, *Disegni antichi e moderni per la faciata di S. Petronio di Bologna*, Bologna, 1933. Here all the designs for the façade are reproduced; drawings concerning other parts of S. Petronio will be published separately by Zucchini.

[32] Richard Bernheimer, "Gothic Survival and Revival in Bologna," *Art Bulletin*, XXXVI, 1954, had access to my manuscript.

[33] The model is reproduced in Ludwig Weber's book, *Bologna* (Berühmte Kunststätten), Leipzig, 1902, p. 42; also in Pierre de Bouchaud's *Bologna* (Les Villes d'Art célèbres), Paris, 1909, ill. on p. 32.

panels, which were presumably intended to have some differentiation through color. On the whole one could scarcely have found a better way out. The buttresses end in Gothic tabernacles, but the two styles blend with each other unobtrusively, unexcitingly; if one wanted to criticize, one might say that such a façade causes no offense, but is boring, squat, sprawling.

The contrary may be said of one of the sketches by PERUZZI (1481-1536). On request he submitted four sketches in 1521. The third one (Fig. 38), fully worked out, divides the middle portion (*a* in Varignana's design) according to the rhythm *b a b* by means of overslender pilaster or column orders, and continues the jambs of the main portal, already built, vertically. For the side parts he has two proposals; on the right he sketches the clustered shafts in such a way that here the rhythm *a b′* results; over the side axis *a* he places a Gothic ogee arch, while the other gables are triangular. On the left half, however, the façade is varied by ending it with an octagonal tower. This has four main stories, the lowest one divided into two levels; the roof is a sharp, eight-sided pyramid surrounded by eight slender, triangular gables. Between the Corinthianized piers in the antique style that are chosen to divide the axes are Gothic windows with tracery, many of them with twisted columns like those found in the side windows of S. Petronio, so that Vasari later doubtless shook his head gravely to think that an important architect of Bramante's school could have been capable of such aberrations.

Peruzzi's preliminary sketches contain even more "aberrations" of this sort (Fig. 39), especially rotating *vesicae piscis* in the middle oculus, and for the aisle axes and portals a choice of four different kinds of Late Gothic forms such as were popular in related variations in the frames for Sienese and Florentine paintings of the fourteenth century. One could almost imagine that he intended to demonstrate how not to do it. But that would surely be a wrong assumption. Peruzzi tried seriously to mate incompatibles, no doubt enjoying these half-breed results; moreover, one cannot help calling the design with the corner tower ingenious.

The fourth design has disappeared since its publication by Geymüller.[34] As far as can be judged from the reproduction, it must be

[34] Reproduced several times, first in Carl von Stegmann and Heinrich von Geymüller, *Die Architektur der Renaissance in Toscana*, VII, Munich, 1885-1908, Baldassare Peruzzi, p. 3; then by William Winthrop Kent, *The Life and Works of Baldassare Peruzzi*, New York, 1925, pl. 4, corresponding text on p. 34; also by Zucker in Hans Willich and Paul Zucker, *Die Baukunst der Renaissance in Italien*, Wildpark-Potsdam, n.d., p. 204.

recognized as a variation of the third design—the first discussed l It offers only the middle section *b a b*, somewhat altered as to prc tions, and overloaded with sculptured decoration. The middle above the main portal, as well as the broad-side rectangles the side portals, have been interpreted by several writers as mosa possibility that can hardly be proved; they might equally well been intended for frescoes or reliefs. With regard to the treatmen the side portals, Geymüller called attention to Peruzzi's decoratior the interior of the apse in the cathedral at Siena.[35] This consists of s circular niches with (painted?) ribs in their vaults. The three g of this middle section are correspondingly filled with sculptured ures.

To what extent these designs reveal Manneristic traits must be undiscussed here; in any case, they fall under the heading of ming of styles, a concept not identical with Mannerism. It would, howeve wrong to talk of "historicism," because Peruzzi was obliged to pres as much as possible of the already completed ground story of the faç

Peruzzi also made stage designs. One of them (Fig. 37) was publi by Geymüller in the work on Tuscany,[36] and depicts a varied collec of Renaissance buildings, combined with the upper story of the C seum rising in the background and beside it the so-called tower of N Surprisingly, we find here as the third building on the left a h with a shop on the ground floor, above which is an overhanging it has in the first of the upper floors a Gothic pointed arched win of two lights with an oculus; in the next story are rectangular winc with lunettes surmounting them, and toward the central street a lo projecting on large consoles. It is easy to recognize the fact that S knew this design and evolved from it his *Scena Comica*—as well a *Scena Tragica.*

Peruzzi was a pupil of Bramante's and, however paradoxical it sound, it was from that source that he derived his lack of preju against Gothic. In Bologna, however, all his designs were ignore not actually rejected, while the authorities waited for something better. The then architect of S. Petronio at the time, Ercole SECCADE (died in 1540), who redesigned and erected the side portals in p of those that had been constructed after Varignana's drawing,[3

[35] Stegmann-Geymüller, *op.cit.*, p. 2 (design) and vol. 1 (execution).

[36] Stegmann-Geymüller, *op.cit.*, x, text, p. 16; ill., vol. 2. The original is in the Uffiz lection in Florence, no. 291 (Catalogue p. 119). It is reproduced, reversed, in the bo Zucker on p. 218.

[37] Angelo Gatti, *La Basilica petroniana*, Bologna, 1913, p. 74 and *passim*, ill. 31.

ed perhaps against the execution of Peruzzi's ideas. After the er's death, Giacomo RANNUCCI (d. 1549) became his successor. first sight this architect's plan is shockingly amateurish, but on tion it becomes interesting, above all because of the complete nciation of Gothic[38] and its proportion. None of the other designs the effect of being spread so wide, although it is planned for a it of 104 feet. This is the result of the high entablature of the : order, and the very flat gable in the middle axis. In the present e this gable would cut across the middle window, but at that time calculated on a vaulting height of 96 feet (without the roof), eas the work as carried out in 1648 came to 120 feet. The dominant ession is created by the Venetian semicircular gables of the inner s; the terminal volutes of the outer b axes seem like flourishes, the arrangement of a central pillar above the portal, creating in quence a double axis, and the long windows, again Venetian, clear Ranuzzi's origin in the Venetian school. The attribution of ccaria that runs through the literature on the subject is, however, idless. No definite prototype can be proved; with all its weaknesses ketch is original. The Bolognese doubtless thought: something like can be built in Venice, but not here.

-Bolognese and this time with reminiscences of Milan was Cristo-LOMBARDO's sketch.[39] He placed Gothic windows in a grand Corin- order embracing two stories. The design did not please.

ore dangerous to Ranuzzi as a rival than Cristoforo was Giulio NO (1492-1546), who was the next to be summoned to help in the gency. One of his sketches is dated January 23, 1546. He died on mber 1 of that same year, only forty-seven years old. His two hes are in their clearly Corinthian orders anti-Gothic. His con-n to Gothic lies in the wheel windows, the gables, and pinnacles, the case may be, tabernacles. The second design (Fig. 39) seems correction, because the gable over the portal is transferred into one above the entablature of the lower order. Here, too, the co-tion of sculpture (or painting) in the individual fields has been doned, so that the latter seem like empty coffers, but in both de- Giulio placed Gothic tabernacles with figures on the front sur- of the Corinthian pilasters, quite a demand on the toleration of

acchini, *Disegni, antichi* . . . , pl. 14. In spite of the signature "Di Jacopo Ranuzzi a" the authorship is in doubt. Ranuzzi died in 1549.
id., pl. 4.

worshipers of the antique.[40] This transplanting is certainly the purest Mannerism.

Ranuzzi, who doubtless felt somewhat relieved by Giulio's premature death, soon saw a new competitor in Giacomo Barozzi VIGNOLA (1507-1573). His two designs differ only slightly from each other. He goes back almost to Peruzzi's rhythm, *β a, b a b, a β*, follows Giulio's second sketch, but replaces the side oculi with long tracery windows (Fig. 41). The heights of Giulio's stories are altered in order to accommodate three superposed orders; the pilasters end in Gothic pinnacles of which the inner ones cut through the main gable and tower over it. In this gable a smaller gable stands above the field *a*, so that there results a sort of broad frame, already the case in Peruzzi's design.[41] Vignola filled these strips with Flamboyant tracery, which hardly appears anywhere else in monumental architecture in this form. Something similar may be found in Late Gothic furniture. The six wavy lines that partly cross and partly touch each other are reminiscent of Irish and Lombard interlaced ornamentation. It is justifiable to mention them here particularly, because this ornament dominates the façade through its size and position, and because it is not Renaissance; if, however, it is Gothic, it is misunderstood Gothic.

Ranuzzi sent in a critique; it has not been preserved but we have Vignola's defense that refutes Ranuzzi's fourteen objections point by point.[42] Nothing is said of the gable ornament. A modern critic would certainly object to very different things, but would also approve of much, for, after all, Vignola had to let stand the three portals and the base of the façade. Ranuzzi's Beckmesserishness is somewhat reminiscent of Mignot at the time of the dispute in Milan; this time, however, the matter relates to mistakes against Renaissance style, so that we do not need to go into it. But one of Vignola's sentences is repeatedly quoted: ". . . with regard to this point I believe that if the first founder were alive one could quite easily persuade him to recognize and confess the mistakes that he made through the fault (*causa*) of that time and not through his own, because at that time good architecture had

[40] I do not need to discuss the proposal for the transformation of the side fronts, Zucchini, *op.cit.*, pl. 9, and the design for the façade attributed to Giulio, pl. 11, which looks more like a reworking of his other designs, with changed window forms and pinnacles, and the omission of the figured tabernacles on the pilasters. On the other hand, the outer fields that were already in existence have been retained.

[41] Zucchini, *op.cit.*, pl. 11.

[42] Vignola's letter to the *Ufiziali di San Petronio* has been published in full by Giovanni Gaye, *Carteggio inedito d'artisti* . . . , II, Florence, 1840, pp. 358-363.

not yet been brought to light again, as in our centuries."[43] However interesting it is that Vignola reverts to the phrase, by now often repeated, of the rebirth of good architecture, one should not forget the first part of the sentence. It refers to Point 7 of Ranuzzi's critique, namely, that Vignola had substituted long windows (*finestre*) for oculi (*occhi*), and conversely, both contrary to the intention of the first founder. Vignola answers that this was necessary to achieve good proportions, "come ricercha la bona architettura"; a long window above in the middle would pierce the entablature of the upper order. This latter is the real point. For Vignola, the continuity of the entablature is an almost sacred norm. He says quite openly at the end of the document that one can see how little intelligence Ranuzzi has. However, we must doubt whether Vignola could have convinced Antonio di Vincenzo as easily as he thought. Vignola sketched Gothic tracery windows, and in the middle a Gothic wheel window; on the gables of the outer axes, that correspond to the rows of chapels, he actually set Gothic blind windows; and he drew pinnacles, even some at an angle of 45 degrees. Vincenzo, however, would have commented with wrinkled brow that these details are not, indeed, good but will do; but what is the idea of these orders with these entablatures? Is not the structure of the interior Gothic?

The debate of the living turned into an argument with long dead minds, and that was the real crux of the matter. It was not important whether Ranuzzi was wrong, but that Antonio di Vincenzo—even though through no fault of his own—was wrong. "Gothic" itself was the problem. Men had to try to come to an understanding with it, and they realized that it could not be done.

Vignola's letter is dated February 1, 1547. We may assume that Ranuzzi seethed with rage and hatred. Two years later he died. Vignola went to Rome where he found other commissions that demanded no mingling of styles; and the authorities of San Petronio were at their wits' end, and for the time did nothing again.

When Francesco Morandi il TERRIBILIA, who did not die until 1603, was appointed master of San Petronio in 1568, the game was played over again with different players and somewhat different cards. First of all, the new master had the experience of seeing Domenico TIBALDI (1541-1583) submit a design (Fig. 42) that must indeed be charac-

[43] *Ibid.*, p. 361: ". . . pertanto io creddo s'esso primo fondatore fosse in vita, con manco fatica se li farebbe conoscer et confessar li errori, che per causa di quel tempo ha comesso, e non di lui, perciò che in quel tempo non era ancora riformata la buona architettura in luce come alli nostri secoli."

terized as very Gothic, especially because of the tall pinnacles, bu adopts for the central gable, as well as the gables above the three forms that would be suitable for framing an altar of the fourt century, but scarcely for monumental architecture. Anyone in Bo who sympathized with Gothic was probably repelled by *this* G and the others who thought that one should build something temporary instead of compromising or even creating inferior G doubtless said: you see, after all neither will do. This latter opinio represented by the upper stratum of city society, the nobles with manistic training. Thus the population of Bologna split into two c What Serlio had represented side by side in two separate thea sets, was here mingled in one *Scena Tragicomica*, and the title (piece was: the dispute between intellectual nobility and humdrum dle class, or, Renaissance versus Gothic.

Two aristocrats, Fabio and Giovanni Pepoli, arranged for A PALLADIO (1518-1580) to be invited to give an opinion, and in 15 came to Bologna, reporting a few months later in writing wh thought would be a good solution. He writes among other th "With respect to the plans of these two worthy men I say that both and I for my part could wish for nothing else; it is, how correct that I would remove some facings and also some of those mids that would be very expensive and would be very likely to down. . . ."[44] One of the *valenthuomini* is either Vignola or Terrib and the other probably Tibaldi. Palladio says, really, in one br nothing needs to be changed, aside from the existing marble f of the ground story and the pinnacles, that is, nothing needs changed except everything that is there and that was projected by o To call structural parts that one dislikes expensive and dangero an old trick; it is only surprising that Palladio can have believed he could persuade anyone that pinnacles are accustomed to coll What he really meant is shown by his four sketches. They are un promisingly purest Palladian,[46] aside from the inconsistency of

[44] Giovanni Gaye, *Carteggio* . . . , III, Florence, 1840, p. 323: "Quanto poi alli diseg da questi due valenthuomini, dico che tutti doi mi piaccino, nè io per me li saprei de cosa alcuna; egli è bene vero chio levarei alcuni intagli et anco alquanti di quelle piran quali avriano gran spese e sono molto pericolose di cascar. . . ."

[45] One would like to assume that he means Terribilia, with whom he was dealir Terribilia's design, according to Zucchini, was not drawn until 1580, the year of Palladio's One may suppose, however, that at that time, in 1572, there was a sketch by him that been preserved.

[46] Reproduced in, among others Gurlitt, *Andrea Palladio*, Turin, 1921, plates 10 (from woodcuts in Palladio's *Quattro Libri*); also in Zucchini, *op.cit.*, pls. 16ff.

on each corner of one design, which he worked out in common Terribilia, not pinnacles but three obelisks set close together. His ate proposal was a portico,[47] such as Michelangelo intended for eter's in Rome in 1546 and Palladio himself had introduced into ar architecture in 1550 on the Villa Rotonda in Vicenza—a final quence of High Renaissance in already Manneristic form. Palla- espected certain Gothic buildings, as he explains in his first report; list of good Italian Gothic he mentions also the Palazzo del Com- in Padua, "il quali si dice esser il maggio vaso che sia in tutta pa," but he had so surrounded its exterior with his splendid halls from that aspect there was little Gothic left to see. The portico of troni was, naturally, also intended to serve purely practical pur- , namely, to minimize the noise from the market place! In 1577 anni Pepoli was obliged to write to Palladio that influential per- were objecting to his designs because they were not adapted to was already in existence. Palladio, up until now so diplomatic, be- blunt and said (in a document of more than five printed pages, January 11, 1578): "the *maniera tedesca* can be called confusion, rchitecture."[48] Words came to his pen that he must have read in ri. Two years later, in 1580, he died. Terribilia again stepped into inence. His design of 1580 is once more Gothic. In spite of Vi- 's arguments against a long window over the main portal, a large ic traceried window is here drawn in, the mullions with twisted . Together with the ornamental gable of the portal beneath it he gable above it this window is the dominant form. The design ot be called satisfactory, but it would have been a noteworthy lement to the facing of the ground story, to a certain degree stic, and harmonious in itself.[49] Palladio's last design, the one with ortico before 1577 (Zucchini, plate 21), is the work of an older and a mature masterpiece, but it is not suited to S. Petronio. It is ssible to weigh the values of one design against the other, for this d mean playing off the values of Gothic against Renaissance (or

cchini suggests as a hypothesis that the double design, pl. 21, represents in its left half co, which would have consisted, according to this view, of four columns. I believe that es not need to call this a hypothesis.

Gaye, *Carteggio* . . . , III, p. 398. This letter, moreover, indicates what he understood ythmy: "that the body shall have a harmonious proportion to the members, and that his, accordingly, will result the beauty which was called by the ancient Greeks *mia*."

e facts in Thieme-Becker, *Allg. Künstlerlexikon* (under Morandi, XXV, p. 120), do not ith those of the most recent authorities. There, two designs are mentioned, the first from r 1572, the second around 1600. Zucchini speaks only of one, "esguito nel 1580."

possibly against Mannerism), and that, from our point of view of objective history, is senseless. The insolubility of the question, the inner conflict of the situation, caused the tragedy of S. Petronio.

The façade remained as it was, a victim of the tragedy. Even today its upper part is still a rough brick wall, neither Gothic nor Renaissance, not "art" at all, and a mockery of the doctrine that functionalism alone is enough to produce beautiful architecture. The church front has become a *symbol* of *renunciation* in the face of three possibilities: Gothic, Renaissance, or compromise between the two.

This intellectual struggle for purity of style, above all, for the recognition of what purity of style is and how far it is justifiable when times change, has been made the subject of an investigation of fundamental principles by Panofsky in the article on the drawing from Vasari's *Libro*, an investigation that penetrates especially into Vasari's conception of the history of art. The essential result of this study can be summarized in the statement that Vasari was caught in an inner conflict between his idea of perfection in art and the (moral) demand for justice toward its historical preliminary stages. We see here fully unfolding the process that had begun with Petrarch and Boccaccio, the unresolved problems of which became most troublesomely apparent in an intensified degree now that the Renaissance had reached its maturity—for Vasari, in the works of Michelangelo. Vasari steered his course this way and that, in order to "save" Arnolfo di Cambio's work, for example, and the authorities were helpless before the question of what should be done with the façade of S. Petronio. In his critical opinion Palladio leans on Vasari, who, for his part, leaned on his predecessors.[50] Gothic was condemned, but while many of its judges acted with cold hearts and no twinges of conscience, others felt that something like a judicial murder had taken place. Subsequent developments in criticism down to our own day are fundamentally concerned with the discovery of the right judgment, one that should be *just* from the sense of artistic *evaluation* and at the same time *correct* from the point of view of objective historical *knowledge*.

Panofsky has also shown in detail how Vasari, on the basis of his philosophy of art, combined with the likes and dislikes peculiar to him and to his age, arrived at the division of the history of art into three phases corresponding to the biological course of human life: childhood, youth, maturity. Of the fourth stage, old age, Vasari spoke only vaguely:

[50] Vignola's design was drawn before Vasari's *Vite* appeared, but his views parallel those of Vasari.

he merely mentions a phase of completion, in which "art has risen so high that one may fear its decline rather than anticipate a further achievement."[51] The process has occurred twice, according to Vasari, once in antiquity and again in the Renaissance down to Michelangelo, who surpassed the ancients. Vasari can imagine nothing beyond this. What lies between the two epochs is a catastrophe, and one suspects that Vasari pessimistically expected a new catastrophe. It is as though one were to say: human beings experience the stages of childhood, youth, and maturity, and then there comes just at the right point a murderer, an accident, or a disease to spare them the troubles of age. Other attempts to categorize by periods were mentioned above. Panofsky cites, in addition, L. Annaeus Florus, whose *Epitome Rerum Romanorum*, which appeared in 1546 in an Italian translation, differentiated four eras in Roman history, thus an epoch of old age as well. A *conditio sine qua non* of any division of the history of art into phases was the proper understanding of art itself, and it is this that we see these thinkers of the sixteenth century struggling to attain; they seek for the right "theory of art" in order to be able to write the right "history of art." Failure to solve the complex of problems in artistic *theory* led to uncertainty of critical opinion on artistic *history*.

But while Vasari labored with theories of art and the question of writing artistic history, the *living history* of art continued to evolve of itself, actuated by artists who adhered now to this and now to that theory. In Bologna, Gothic, which had been pronounced dead, achieved a victory over Palladio. Pellegrino de PELLEGRINI gave an opinion in 1582 in which he said that he personally would prefer a design "a forma di architettura antica," but that if the authorities wished to retain Gothic, "he would like to see the rules of this architecture observed, which are in truth more reasonable than others think, without mingling the one *ordo* with the other, as has been done."[52] In this statement Gothic is recognized, in opposition to Palladio, both as architecture and as an "order." The main point is the declaration of the principle of stylistic purity: if Gothic after all, then at least pure Gothic! With Terribilia's design (Fig. 43) Gothic triumphed—on paper.[53]

The second act of the drama can be seen as a parallel to this. Since

[51] Panofsky, "Das erste Blatt . . . ," p. 59; Vasari, *Le Vite* . . . , II, p. 96.

[52] Gaye, *op.cit.*, III, p. 447: ". . . a me piaceria osservare più che si pùo li precetti di essa architettura che pur sono più ragionevoli di quello che altri pensa, senza compore uno ordine con l'altro, come altri fano."

[53] The later designs are, however, by no means all Gothic, cf. those of Rainaldi, 1626, and Carlo Francesco Dotti, 1752; the others down to the year 1887 are "Gothic," namely that of the nineteenth century.

1440 the middle part of the nave had had its provisional flat ce
There were people who wanted to place on the piers a classic
tablature, in order, as I understand it, to raise above it a perm
flat ceiling. That idea, however, was rejected; purity of style dem
Gothic quadripartite ribbed vaults, and since 1587 Terribilia had
constructing the eastern bay. The debate that now ensued was
cerned with the proper proportion; the latter required that the h
should be measured according to the equilateral triangle. Carlo CA
called Cremona, led the attack against Terribilia. He was a tailo
a professional architect; nevertheless he knew and defended one
doctrines of the lodge secret against Terribilia, the architect.

In 1840 Gaye did not print the two epistles by Carazzi, g
as his reason that they seemed to him absurd; in 1904 they were
lished by L. Weber.[54] We can now judge for ourselves. Spring
not take Carazzi seriously although, it seems, without having
known his writings.

The first document is undated, but presumably it is from the
1598 or somewhat earlier—obviously after the bay, vaulted by Terr
had been completed, cleared of scaffoldings, and opened to the p
Carazzi found it too low. He starts with the premise that bea
what is required and that this is the result of harmony of the pr
tions. Harmony here means, however: S. Petronio was begun i
maniera tedesca, and thus the structure must be finished in the
maniera. This thesis is an echo of the dispute about the faça
terms of the vaulting this same requirement means for Carazz
the height must be determined according to the equilateral tri
Terribilia had not only taken off seven feet, but had also mad
crown of the vault itself too shallow. Earthquakes had caused s
churches and towers of private palaces in Bologna to collapse. C
and his adherents had on their side, then, statics as well as aes
arguments, because they knew that a steeper vault was more s
But Terribilia concluded as a result of the same fear of earthq
that one ought not to build too high. Carazzi, the tailor, whon
would not suspect of any higher Humanistic education, calls to w
Euclid, Aristoxenos, Vitruvius, Alberti, and Cesariano. It may be
he wanted to show how learned he was, but "educated" men wer
never loath to exhibit their reading. From Cesariano's drawing o
cathedral in Milan Carazzi deduced that all three-aisled Gothic

54 Ludwig Weber, *op.cit.* Both letters are to be found here, pp. 76-89, in the origi
without translation.

tures, or such as had series of chapels like S. Petronio, should be triangulated. He did not know that even Milan diverges from this theoretical pattern, but his opponents knew it even less.

Recourse was had to Rome, and a letter of Cardinal Montalto of June 17, 1589, which refers to the written opinion of "maestro Carlo Cremona, sartore," advises caution and unity; he recommends a jury of professional experts in Rome "presente sempre il Terribilia et maestro Carlo." The invitation was repeated on July 8, but the disputants remained in Bologna; Weber supposes that Terribilia felt it beneath his dignity to appear before a jury together with a tailor. A third communication, preserved only in a copy and without a signature, came from Rome, presumably still in 1589, to the effect that Terribilia's vault was good; to raise the springers and the vault itself would be dangerous. A fourth letter from Rome asserts finally that the *regola del triangolo equilatero* is worthy of nothing but praise, however, only in churches that are really arranged in all their parts according to triangulation; but this *regola* is not absolutely necessary and has also not been followed in all noble and admired edifices (*tanti nobili et laudati edifitii*)—a statement recognizing Gothic, written in Rome in 1589—for example, San Petronio was not so begun; as far as the height within the vaulting itself is concerned it is a matter of adjusting to the strength (bearing power) of the parts already completed.[55]

The next document is Terribilia's rebuttal.[56] He promises to be as brief as is consistent with making himself properly understood; however, seven printed pages seemed to him necessary. He, too, is convinced that the vault should be built *dordine tedesco*, which obviously refers, however, to the form of the quadripartite ribbed vault, not to the matter of triangulation. Weber remarked of this defense of Terribilia's that it was "not honest, either from a literary or a human point of view." It is not clear what the difference is here between literary and human, but the reproach of dishonesty must be allowed to stand. Terribilia deliberately misunderstands Cremona and then refutes the errors he has foisted upon him. He cleverly mixes these unjustified accusations with arguments against individual theses of Cremona that really have nothing at all to do with the main point at issue; thus, for example, he says: "parlo del bello dell' architettura e non de' filosofi e musici." (Cremona had referred to Vitruvius' statements on the many-sidedness of the architect.) What Terribilia finally says about the equilateral

[55] These four letters from Rome are printed in Gaye, *op.cit.*, III, pp. 485-490.
[56] *Ibid.*, pp. 490-507.

triangle, a little treatise in itself, is exceedingly obscure, and the whole overlong account gives the impression that Terribilia himself had no real faith in the vault he had constructed. One does not like to acknowledge mistakes when they are difficult to correct.

Carazzi's final answer is all the clearer. He refutes Terribilia's arguments point by point, reveals his eristic tactics and his lack of logic, and states the dimensions that are necessary for the vault.

Even before Ludwig Weber published Carazzi's two documents in 1904, there appeared in 1895 an article by Dehio with a reproduction of an engraving by Floriano Ambrosino, dated 1592. This depicts in the foreground Carazzi's proposal with the equilateral triangles drawn in, and immediately adjacent in the background Terribilia's vault.[57] The elevation here proposed differs essentially from the work as later carried out, for above the lateral arches an entablature was projected with a balustrade, strongly emphasizing the horizontal; above this was a double window with a small oculus. The eventual execution conformed in elevation to what Terribilia had built. Neither of the disputants lived to see it. Girolamo RAINALDI (1611-1691), the well-known Roman architect of Baroque, gave an opinion in 1625, in which the height of the vaults was calculated at 114 feet. Step by step, or, as Weber says, foot by foot, the Bolognese forced him to increase this, until a height of 120 feet was reached. In 1648 Francesco MARTINI (ca. 1626-ca. 1659) vaulted the first bay, then the following ones, and in 1656 he dismantled Terribilia's vault and reconstructed it to correspond to the others. With this was reached the stage that we see in Bologna today. It may be remarked that at the same time of Baroque the Gothic ribbed vaults were being built in the nave of St.-Germain-des-Près in Paris—apparently without dispute. The quarrel in Bologna, as well as the earlier one in Milan, warn us against imagining the course of Gothic architecture as a series of blissful hours of dreamy artists. Humanly speaking, the history of Gothic is in the main to be thought of as an inferno, where each one hated the other, though this applies not only to the history of Gothic. One is amazed at how much excellent work was accomplished nevertheless.

In this whole drama in Bologna there was in addition to the Gothicists and the Classicists a third party, as it were, that should not be

[57] Georg Dehio, "Zur Frage nach der Triangulatur in der mittelalterlichen Baukunst," *Repertorium für Kunstwissenschaft*, 1895, pp. 105ff. Again reproduced in his chief work, *Die Kirchliche Baukunst* . . . , II, p. 528. Cf. further L. Weber's account of a letter by Lorenzo Pisanelli. Long before Dehio, Seroux d'Agincourt had published the engraving, see below p. 514.

forgotten: the *Delegati* or *Operai di San Petronio.* Not one of their voices has penetrated to our ears. They are, perhaps, the saddest figures of all, for they could not come to a decision. Just this, however, was a novel attitude; it was certainly quite different when Gothic had as yet no competitor and when the ecclesiastical officials not only decided, with all the force of their authority, what should be done but also knew what was appropriate to the times. In Milan it was the *Principe* who had always to decide and who was really helpless; in Bologna it was a body of citizens—we do not know to what extent the clergy were represented in it, although Cardinal Montalto's letters prove that they had a voice in the matter.

One other problem, finally, is posed by this chapter on Rabelais, Serlio, de L'Orme, Vasari, Peruzzi, Romano, Vignola, Palladio, Terribilia, and Carazzi. It is the *age* of Mannerism; is it also the spirit of Mannerism that speaks to us here? In the appendix to that frequently cited essay on *Das erste Blatt* . . . Panofsky raised the question of whether it was necessary to insert in the architectural history of Italy a phase of Mannerism between Renaissance and Baroque, as had been found necessary for sculpture. The decision which he reached at that time, as well as the subsequent attitudes of other writers, I shall not discuss;[58] the matter is still in flux, and its treatment does not belong to the subject of this book.[59] However, if today we speak of Mannerism in architecture and slowly grope toward a comprehension of this phenomenon, is it then unreasonable to ask whether the intellectual battle for and against Gothic, together with the indecisiveness of the struggle, does not belong as a purely intellectual phenomenon to that Mannerism which we are still trying to define? The problem is new but the subject itself is very old. History of art with an attempt at division into phases begins, as we have seen, with the Humanists; Vasari, himself a "Mannerist," was in a quandary between historical justice, that relativistically pays impartial homage to all generations, and artistic justice, that differentiates levels of value and administers praise and blame. Even for us Mannerism has become a problem of the history of art, as regards the division into phases; the intellectual situation of the undecided ones,

[58] The following should be mentioned: the article by Rudolf Wittkower, "Michelangelo's Bibliotheca Laurenziana," *Art Bulletin*, XVI, 1934, pp. 123ff., particularly p. 201; Ernst Michalski, "Das Problem des Manierismus in der italienischen Architektur," *Zeitschrift für Kunstgeschichte*, II, 1933, p. 88; further, Hans Hoffmann, *Hochrenaissance, Manierismus, Frühbarock*, Zurich and Leipzig, 1938; N. Pevsner, *The Architecture of Mannerism*, 1946; finally, Richard Zürcher, *Stilprobleme der italienischen Baukunst des Cinquecento*, Basel, 1947.

[59] In the meantime I returned to the general phenomenon in: "The 'Crazy' Vaults of Lincoln Cathedral," *Art Bulletin*, XXXV, 1953, p. 105.

like Peruzzi, Giulio Romano, and, most characteristically, the *Operai di S. Petronio*, was an inner split, a spuriousness, a lack of directness. These words give a clue; they cannot in the least exhaust the problem. Mingling of styles as such is by no means Mannerism, and Mannerism is very often free of any such mingling. But the human beings themselves that stand behind the works are divided in their souls, even though they may have taken up the cudgels with perfect one-sidedness either for Renaissance, like Palladio, or for Gothic, like Carlo Carazzi. Palladio's design was appropriate to his age, not to S. Petronio; conversely, Carazzi's demands were appropriate to S. Petronio but not to his age. But how then are the judgments of Humanism and Renaissance to be differentiated from Mannerism? Let us leave the answer to the next generation.

Only once more in Italy was there a flicker of objective interest in Gothic: in Vincenzo SCAMOZZI (1562-1616). This does not mean, however, that he acknowledged Gothic as having equal rights with the antique. In his extensive textbook on architecture he also wrote the obligatory chapter on the decline of good, classical architecture, but it is broader and more substantial than anything that had hitherto been assembled on this subject.[60] He demonstrates the mistakes of Gothic by means of specific examples: the cathedral of Milan, Notre-Dame in Paris, the Palace of the Doges in Venice; obviously he has studied these buildings closely. But he went even further. On his travels he made detailed notes of Gothic edifices and sketches of "façades, sections, and interiors," which have been preserved. There is a prospect that these will be published.[61] It would even be interesting just to know what buildings attracted his attention.

Franco Barbieri has recently given some valuable information in an article on Scamozzi.[62] On his journey to Paris the latter sketched three Gothic churches, St.-Denis, the cathedral of Châlons-sur-Marne, and St.-Etienne in Toul. Barbieri reproduced the drawings of St.-Denis and Toul. In both cases Scamozzi noted the ground plan, transverse section, and west façade. The façade of St.-Denis is inexact in the top story of the north tower compared to the etching of Chapuy (this

[60] Vincenzo Scamozzi, *Dell' idea dell' architectura universale*, Venice, 1615, cap. XVIII (ed. of 1694, p. 57).

[61] Cf. the article in Thieme-Becker, *op.cit.*, XXIX, Leipzig, 1935, p. 526. The Manuscript *Sommario del viaggio . . .* of 1600 is in the Museum in Vicenza. An edition of it is to be prepared by Achille Bertini Calosso.

[62] Franco Barbieri, "Vincenzo Scamozzi, studioso ed artista," *La critica d'arte*, Florence, 1949, pp. 222 and 300. The drawings are reproduced on pl. 170, the text referring to them is on p. 229 n. 20.

tower was removed in the nineteenth century). The choir apse of the cathedral in Toul is drawn round instead of polygonal. On the whole, however, the sketches are very careful and bear witness to Scamozzi's intense interest and understanding.

From then on all interest in Gothic ceases in Italy—except Guarino Guarini—until the time of the Risorgimento in the nineteenth century and the construction of the façade of the cathedral in Florence by de Fabris in 1867.[63]

As Spanish judgments on Gothic are rare, the few sentences of the historian José de SIGÜENZA (1554-1606) may be mentioned.[64] He talks about the cloister of the Hieronymites in Granada, which was begun 1515. "The architect presented to the Spaniards a manner of building better than that which the Goths, Moors, and other barbaric nations had possessed." He adds "that with their arrival all good art was abolished in Spain for more than a thousand years."[65] Obviously Sigüenza repeats what he had read elsewhere—probably in Vasari.

5. Germany in the Sixteenth Century

WHEN Renaissance style was introduced in Florence by Brunelleschi in 1419, Gothic did not stop all at once, even in Italy. Decades passed before the new style was established in Venice, Milan, and Rome, and almost a century before it crossed the Alps to Germany. One should not forget Wimpheling's remarks on the tower of Strasbourg Cathedral; they must be assigned to Gothic in spite of their date, 1502.

The triumph of Renaissance in Germany is personified by Albrecht DÜRER (1471-1528). He has left us no detailed literary formulation of his judgment on Gothic and Renaissance, but it can be reconstructed both from statements here and there in his writings and from the silent testimony of his works. The following chronological survey does not intend to take cognizance of everything in Dürer's works that relates

[63] The beginning of work on the façade in Florence in 1875, according to the design of 1867. Thieme-Becker, IX.

[64] José de Sigüenza, *Historia de la Orden de San Jeronimo*, Madrid, ca. 1600. I quote from the second edition. I owe this information to Mr. Amerigo Castro (Princeton).

[65] *Ibid.*, II, Madrid, 1909, 2nd ed., p. 43. "Lenantose un claustro grande, y de los bien entendidos de la Arquitectura de aquel tiempo, que yua ya abiendo los ojos a mejores trazas, dando en rostro a los Españoles lo que les anian dexado Godos y Moros, y otras naciones Barbaras que arruinaron, por decirlo ansi, con sus anemidas todas las buenas artes, y en España las ahogaron casi de todo punto, por mas de mil años."

to architecture; it leaves out cases that belong entirely to Renaissance or to what is called German Renaissance. Our interest is focused primarily on the Gothic element.

From the artist's early period—undated—is a plan of a crucifix with Mary and John (or of a monstrance), a design for a goldsmith, definitely Late Gothic and clearly employing quadrature (Fig. 44).[1]

The *Crowning with the Thorns*, a woodcut of 1494,[2] and the *Rejection of Joachim's Sacrifice* (from the *Life of Mary*), approximately from 1502 to 1505,[3] still have Gothic quadripartite ribbed vaults, but the *Holy Family* of 1500 to 1505 is shown in a Renaissance setting with barrel vaults of wood, and a double arch on the middle column in the rear wall with an oculus (blind) over the column. The framing arch is correspondingly semicircular and in its spandrels are figures reminiscent of classical prototypes.[4]

Dürer became acquainted with Italian Renaissance on his first journey in 1494. From this period comes a sketch, L.13 (Fig. 44) containing the façade of a Late Gothic palace, below it a perspective view of a Renaissance setting, further, an anchor with two links of chain, and, on the far right, a pinnacle drawn unmistakably after Roriczer or Schmuttermayer, with the addition of the halving of the square, and the eight-point as a star-shaped figure (made by the intersection of two equal squares).[5] The very pleasing Gothic façade, with its two symmetrical entrances of a Late Gothic character, the continuous loggia in the upper story, and the central tower with its oriel, creates a Tyrolean effect. According to Winkler,[6] however, the Palazzo is similar to a building in Venice that is represented on Barbari's plan.

In the *Apocalypse* of 1498 interlacing ogee arches appear in several sheets, for example, on the polygonal altar in the upper part of the *Battle of the Angels*—B.69 (Rev. 9:13). Here the ogee arches are like branches with leaves, as in Hemmel's glass-paintings. The altar in the next sheet, B.70, has very flattened, interlacing ogee arches, carried on twisted colonnettes. One of the buildings in the "Heavenly Jerusalem,"

[1] Hans and Elisabeth Tietze, *Kritisches Verzeichnis der Werke Dürers*, I, Augsburg, 1928, No. 38.

[2] Friedrich Winkler, *Dürer* (*Klassiker der Kunst*), Berlin, 1928, p. 186.

[3] *Ibid.*, p. 260.

[4] *Ibid.*, p. 238. Related spandrel figures are found as early as around 1425 in the stained glass of the Besserer Chapel in Ulm. (The latter perhaps dependent on the triumphal arch of Septimius Severus in Rome.)

[5] Friedrich Lippmann, *Zeichnungen Albrecht Dürers . . .*, Berlin, 1883-1929; further, Friedrich Winkler, *Die Zeichnungen Albrecht Dürers*, I, Berlin, 1936, fig. 93.

[6] Winkler, *op.cit.*, I, p. 68.

B.75, also has interlacing ogee arches, but behind the great gate tower at the left edge one glimpses an almost hidden dome, doubtless a reminiscence of Italy. This very German Jerusalem does not correspond to the text of Rev. 21:10ff. It is not even clear whether the ring of the city wall is complete; it is, however, certain that the city is not square in plan, as the text in Rev. 21:16 indicates. Dürer could not use such a severe form in his linear pattern.

The lower sketch of L.13 is apparently unfinished. It is a hall-like structure—the two stories have piers and a horizontal entablature; in the upper story the parapet is extended across to form the base of the piers order in a very High Renaissance fashion. The façade of the narrow side has a simple classical gable; at the corners, between the corner pier and its neighbor, arches are introduced in the upper story, while below, the intercolumniation has been left empty. The whole middle distance is empty, and could not be so carried out in stone (hardly in wood).[7] The impression of a market hall is strengthened by about four steps that run along the two sides; people were to be able to enter the interior of the building from any point. The structure is indistinct on the left side; it can only be seen that it is round.[8]

The date of the front side of the sheet, L.12, can be determined by the sketch of a badger, of which only the front part has been preserved.[9] Dürer used it in the *Life of Mary* in the *Annunciation*, B.83, where it is represented with exactly the same elongated head.[10] A badger appears once more in the *Little Passion* on wood, as a matter of fact in the *Fall of Man*;[11] here it looks quite different, long-legged and almost like a wild boar. Dürer's utilization of the badger in 1503 dates the reverse side of the sheet as well, unless one assumes that he filled in blank spaces later, as Villard de Honnecourt did. The Tietzes date both sides of the sheet 1510. However understandable their doubts are, only the

[7] It is improbable that a solid wall is meant.

[8] In the reduced size reproduction in H. and E. Tietze, *Kritisches Verzeichnis der Werke Dürers*, II, Basel and Leipzig, 1937, No. 403, this part is more distinct than in Lippmann, *op.cit.*, I, 13, but still can scarcely be made out. Cf. Winckler, *op.cit.*, I, p. 93.

[9] There is a hind foot visible; when the sheet was cut, the right edge was taken off, that is on the reverse side, the left edge, where the pinnacle is incomplete.

[10] Ill. in Winkler's *Dürer*, p. 266, in H. and E. Tietze, *op.cit.*, I, p. 189. The dating is Panofsky's, cf. his *Dürer*, II, p. 139 (No. 1470), and for the reverse side p. 157 (No. 1680). The Tietzes discuss the sheet twice, *op.cit.*, I, under A 34 and A 35, dating the lower structure here because of its High Renaissance character as 1510, and in II (1937), p. 52 under Nos. 402 and 403. Winkler (*Zeichnungen* . . . , I, p. 65) discusses the sheet and inclines toward an early date, 1494 to 1495 (according to Elfried Bock).

[11] Ill. in Winkler, p. 286, in Tietze in *op.cit.*, I, p. 405. Cf. Panofsky's explanation of the badger, *Dürer*, I, p. 143 (the badger represents the phlegmatic temperament).

parapet of the upper story reveals a High Renaissance character; everything else is possible even around 1490. If the attribution to Francesco di Giorgio of the panel painting of an ideal city in the Museum at Urbino is correct, it must have been painted before 1502, the year of his death. Here we see in the second upper story of a building a gallery with its piers on a continuous parapet. One may doubt whether anything of such an advanced character was actually constructed before 1510, but Dürer may have noted the background of a painting or an intarsia, or the like. From all that we now know about Luciano Laurana, Piero della Francesca, and Francesco di Giorgio, this form is already conceivable in the decade from 1480 to 1490. To be exact, only the parapets are classical, the other details not at all.[12] The *Annunciation* of 1501, which was mentioned above because of the little badger under the steps at the left, is free of Gothic reminiscences, and is thus, so to speak, Renaissance.

A Late Gothic star vault—a year later—covers the space of the *Flagellation of Christ* in the drawing in Coburg.[13] The front and rear transverse arches are semicircular, while the wall arch visible at the right is pointed, but it rests as a tympanum on a horizontal cornice supported by a center column that has in its lower portion the candelabra form of Renaissance. The date 1502 is fitting for this mixture of styles with a preponderance of Gothic.

From the first, or, more probably, the second Italian journey comes the survey sketch, now in the British Museum, of a house in Venice (Fig. 46). Because of the exact details given for all the interior rooms it has been argued that this was the house in which Dürer lived. All the plans of the five stories are drawn individually, and in addition the front and side views, which are perfectly typical of Venetian Renaissance. But strangely enough, the house has a character symbolical of Dürer's own duality. All the rooms on the ground floor are vaulted, apparently with groined vaults, for in the entrance hall Dürer draws an irregular stellar vault with double lines in order to indicate that here there are ribs.[14] If Conway is right in supposing that Dürer lived here, the date of the sketch is 1506. The Venetian house had a Renais-

[12] For Francesco's architectural paintings cf. in R. Papini, *op.cit.*, II, plates 75 and 79. The problem is complicated; attention should be called to Fiske Kimball, "Luciano da Laurana and the High Renaissance," *Art Bulletin*, x, 1928, pp. 125ff.; further, to A. S. Weller, *op.cit.*, pp. 186ff., and R. Papini, p. 105. The latter has made a reconstruction of the buildings in the paintings in orthogonal projection, pl. IV.

[13] Tietze, *op.cit.*, I, No. 201; Winkler, *Zeichnungen* . . . , I, 185, text on p. 127.

[14] William Martin Conway, *Literary Remains of Albrecht Dürer*, Cambridge (England), 1889, plate facing p. 45, text on p. 219.

sance exterior, but whoever penetrated into its interior saw that love for Gothic had not yet quite vanished, just as in the case of Dürer himself. It is like a confirmation of this that he drew on the back of the sketch twenty-four squares with various star vaults, reminding us of similar sketches by Leonardo (Fig. 47).[15] On this sheet there is sketched a Renaissance capital very like the one used in the *Little Passion* on copper of 1512 in the engraving *Christ before Pilate.* Similar Renaissance columns occur also in the *Little Passion* on wood of 1509 to 1511.

The *Last Supper* of the *Great Passion* of 1510 has a groined vault (thus no Gothic ribs); the room with its massive walls and relatively low proportion makes a quite un-Gothic impression.

The drawing of three ground plans (Fig. 48),[16] probably belongs also to the period from 1500 to 1510. The upper plan, drawn on a large scale, is an octagon with equal sides but alternatingly unequal angles. The very small central space is bounded in circular form by four sturdy piers, from which arches lead to the four principal corners. The connection of these piers with the intermediary corners is brought about by setting in other piers from which one arch is extended to the outer corner and two to the inner, principal piers. The latter fields are, accordingly, triangular, the others being irregular quadrangles. The combination of this Late Gothic ambulatory with a round central space is perhaps unique. The structure is thought of as being not on the ground level but as an ornamental top. Since, however, stairs are lacking, it undoubtedly represents some sort of minor architecture, thus, a baldachin, a sounding board, a monstrance, or the like. A connection with the *tiburio* in Milan has been suggested, but that is improbable.

Below this ground plan is drawn on the left, on a smaller scale, a rectangle with narrow arms and even narrower apses, a model of pure spatial addition in the style of Brunelleschi and Leonardo; beside this is an octagon with a concentric ambulatory, each field having quadripartite vaults. It is as though Dürer had wanted by this means to make clear to himself the contrast of Gothic and Renaissance; from this point of view one can place this sketch side by side with the one already discussed, L.13,[17] but it is hazardous to impute to Dürer modern stylistic confrontations in such conspicuous form. However, one should not

[15] Front and reverse sides reproduced in Tietze, *op.cit.*, II, p. 189. The reverse side also in Conway, *op.cit.*, p. 221.

[16] Ms. Sloane 5229 fol. 171r in the British Museum. Published by Erwin Panofsky, *The Codex Huyghens . . .* , London, 1940, pl. 109, text on p. 114 n. 2.

[17] Panofsky sees in this a parallel to Dürer's contrasting a Nuremberg housewife and a Venetian *gentildonna* (L.87).

doubt that he was conscious of the fact that it was here a question of two "polar" styles, though he did not put it into words, and that he juxtaposed them without siding with one or the other.

The *Triumphal Gate* for Emperor Maximilian I, B.135, follows chronologically in 1515. "The woodcut monster of a triumphal gate has always been a very indigestible morsel for admirers of Dürer," says Wölfflin,[18] to whose further analysis attention should be called. The design was not Dürer's but that of Jörg Kölderer, court painter and architect of Innsbruck; the programme for the learned details was determined by Stabius. Attempts have been made to discriminate between what goes back to Dürer and what was designed by others. One may say by way of excuse for Dürer that he could not dissociate himself from this unsuccessful undertaking of the imperial court. The decisive fact for our subject is that in his intermediate position between the old Gothic and the new classicism he could, indeed, have greatly improved the total composition qualitatively, but even so could not have given it stylistic unity. Kölderer had emancipated himself from the strict discipline of the lodges without understanding the Renaissance. Dürer may have inwardly comprehended both, yet he remained—in architecture—undecided. It would be difficult to assign the *Triumphal Gate* to any of the usual stylistic concepts, unless it were the designation "German Renaissance" which involves the thought that not antiquity alone was recalled to life, but much that was German as well. These were two components that resulted in a mixture, not an organic unity.

This duality also characterizes Dürer's book on instruction in measurement. It has long been properly classified as a continuation of the Lodge Books and at the same time recognized as a significant broadening and intensification of their scientific *niveau*. Dürer admired Vitruvius, he owned a copy of Euclid that he had purchased in Venice, he had a considerable knowledge of theorems of Archimedes, Hero, and others,[19] and he seems to have known Alberti's writings, perhaps also much of Francesco di Giorgio and Leonardo.[20]

Often quoted is his statement that no writer on architecture is the equal of Vitruvius, for which reason he believes that one should follow his teaching above all. But he continues: "When I now undertake to teach the construction of one or two columns so that young journeymen may obtain practice in this, I am mindful of the German character, for usually all who want to build something new would like to have for it

[18] Heinrich Wölfflin, *Die Kunst Albrecht Dürers*, Munich, 1905, p. 233.

[19] Panofsky, *Dürer*, p. 254.

[20] *Ibid.*, p. 257.

a new fashion that has never been seen before. Therefore I intend to make something different, from which each one can take what pleases him, and make it according to his own desire."[21] Dürer claims for the Germans what Tacitus said of the Gauls, that they were *novarum rerum cupidi.* This passage of Dürer's text is illustrated by ground plans of piers that are partly Gothic and partly Late Gothic; he preserved his freedom of imagination vis-à-vis Vitruvius and in so doing went back with his "new" columnar order to the old Gothic in which he had been reared. Schmuttermayer's *Büchlein* appeared about 1486 in Nuremberg when Dürer was still a journeyman. It is not too bold a hypothesis to think that he bought the slim book and was thereby inspired to plunge into theoretical problems.

His book, *Instruction in Measurement,* contains yet another Gothic reminiscence, a Late Gothic stellar vault almost identical with one of the twenty-four vault plans on the Venetian sketch of 1506 (in the second row from the bottom, the second one from the right). This he annotated as follows: "Four piers of the same size may be set opposite each other, each one having its particular ornamental form (*zyrd*) in the ground plan; when these are raised and a vault is sprung from the upper members of these piers, it looks very queer; but whoever has a liking for equal things let him use them according to his pleasure. However since there are many who are very fond of unusual arrangements of ribs in building vaults, for the sake of good appearance, I will sketch one below; if anyone likes it, he may make use of it. I will also make some ground plans for the piers and draw them."[22]

In his article Ueberwasser reproduced the whole page on a reduced scale showing the text and the ground plans of the vault; he explained the words "von wolstandes wegen" as "to make a show with unexpectedly miraculous (*wunderbaren*) vaults." The Latin translation of 1532 (by Camerarius?) reads "propter venustatem," which is more accurate. At any rate, in the year 1525 Dürer still did not consider an idea of 1506 outdated. According to Ueberwasser the very complicated ground plan was constructed by means of triangles and oblique

21 Dürer, *Unterweisung der Messung,* not paginated.

22 *Ibid.* "Es mügen vier pfeyler gegen einander gesetzt werden einer gröss, vnd ein ytlicher sein sunder zyrd im Grundt haben, so die aufgezogen vnd auss der pfeyler teyl ein gewelb geschlossen wirdt, sieht gar wunderlich, wer aber lieb zü gleychen dingen hat der gebrauch sich der seins gefallens. Nach dem aber vil sind die grosse lieb haven zü selzamen reychungen in den gewelben zu schliessen, von wohlstandes wegen, so will ich vnden eine aufreisesn, ob die ymant gefelt der mag sich ier gebrauchen. Auch will jch etlich grund zü den pfeileren machen und aufreysen."

squares.[23] The vault can be carried out as a spherical vault with four lateral penetrating severies, and with all the ribs on the spherical surface, that is, of equal radius.[24]

In contradiction to such relapses into Gothic an expert opinion of Dürer's on roof construction can be considered as having an anti-Gothic tendency.[25] On one sheet, or double sheet, are drawn three different roofs in all. At the top of the left sheet (Fig. 17) is shown in section a roof with one-quarter of the width to the height, at the bottom is shown, one with one-third of the width. To the latter belongs the middle drawing illustrating the stiffening of the timber supports (*Dachstuhl*) by means of diagonal struts and the tying of the horizontal roof beams at their joints; here can also be seen clearly that diagonal boards come from the pier, as a sort of capital to carry the board on which the beam rests. At the top of the right sheet (Fig. 18) there is drawn in section a steep Gothic saddle roof with seven sets of timber supports, or chairs,[26] one above the other; below it is its exterior view, and to the right of it Dürer's counterproposal: a roof with only two sets of timber supports and the slight pitch of Greek temples. Below this is the exterior view in two variations: a saddle roof hipped on the narrow sides, and a pyramidal roof of equally slight pitch. Underneath are other sketches: at the right, one for the center posts of the roof with their struts, at the left, a detail of the joint for the beams (the bond) and a variation of the system of struts. Finally, there is at the bottom of the sheet a ground plan of a three-aisled, pillared hall of five bays with buttresses on the exterior and with the entrance to the choir equal in width to the center aisle. Dürer calls this building a church.[27] Dürer's tendency to keep all three roofs low could be interpreted without more ado as a protest against Gothic and a preference for Renaissance, if he himself had not given quite different reasons, at least for the third roof: less wind pressure, less weight of snow (about which opinions may be divided), advantages in making repairs and in case of fire, in which connection he refers to Vitruvius. A low roof would also be cheaper, he says, as one could construct it, for the most part, with the still well-preserved timber of the former framework. Villard de Honnecourt was motivated by ex-

23 Walter Ueberwasser, *Nach rechtem Masz . . .* , p. 266.

24 The ground plan appears in similar form yet a third time in the drawing in Dresden, Tietze, II, No. 513, below at the left.

25 W. M. Conway, *op.cit.*, the double plate to p. 218, where Dürer's many descriptive titles are translated into English.

26 Conway translates the German word *Dachstuhl* (in Dürer's orthography *stull*), with Chair, p. 218. The usual term seems to be: truss of the roof.

27 For the German text, see Conway, *op.cit.*, p. 226.

actly as sober considerations when he recommended his triforia that would be useful in case of fire. One sees that fire and water are as helpful in the justification of Renaissance as of Gothic. In all ages architects have thought of such material things as safety and costs, not merely of the Heavenly Jerusalem. Today we think we can detect behind the mask of such reasoning the *Kunstwollen.*

That the descriptions of the drawings are in Dürer's hand is beyond doubt; the sketches themselves are drawn in part with a ruler (in the one of the steep roof there are *pentimenti*) and what was added freehand does not have Dürer's sure touch, so that they may be considered products of his workshop. As a matter of fact, the plan of the house in Venice that he drew himself (1506) shows irregularity of stroke, probably because he held the sheet in his hand without a stiff enough pad beneath it as he went from room to room. In the opinion on the roofs his judgment is as authoritative as though he were a master of the carpenter's craft, but in this field he is decidedly in favor of Italian Renaissance roofs. Perhaps it can be concluded from this that the expertise dates from one of his last years.

To 1526 belongs the drawing of the *Annunciation* (Fig. 33),[28] "which has a spaciousness and generosity of design hitherto not seen in Dürer. . . . One of the happiest creations of his late period. . . . With mature serenity the master evolves a splendid, imaginative spectacle that combines liveliness and dynamic simplicity. The angel in his quite new, easy movement with its powerful, noble sweep, the precious, attractive furnishings, the delicate and simple coloration . . . all contribute charmingly to the intensification of the mood of solemn seriousness." It may seem petty to add to this appreciation, which is so completely in keeping with the drawing, that in the upper right corner, hardly noticeable, there is the beginning of a quadripartite ribbed vault; but this detail in a sheet of such pronouncedly High Renaissance design is simply a vestige of an earlier, youthful memory that has crept into the older artist's mature style.

Reminiscences of the opinions expressed by the Humanists (Villani, Boccaccio, Ghiberti) appear in Dürer's writings. In the dedication to his *Unterweisung der Messung* he said that painting had been held in high esteem in the time of the Greeks and Romans "although it [the art] afterwards was lost and for a thousand years hidden and only two

[28] Winkler, *op.cit.* (*Zeichnungen*), IV, p. 73, No. 894. The drawing is in the Musée Condé, Chantilly.

hundred years ago brought to light by the Italians."[29] Here in the printed book from 1526 he obviously thinks of Giotto. In a preparation to this text, dated 1523 (by Lange and Fuhse) he wrote: "As Rome was weakened, art perished with it. And these arts were almost extinguished, until they came to light again one hundred and fifty years ago."[29a] Here he probably thought of the time of Brunelleschi. (Both calculations are inexact.)

This series of remarks does not exhaust everything that Dürer's works have to offer on the subject of Gothic and Renaissance, not to mention architecture in general,[30] but it will suffice to show that Dürer never formally renounced the impressions gained from his early training and became, as it were, an enemy of Gothic. There can be no question here of adding anything new to what we already know of Dürer as a personality, but simply of assigning him his place in the history of the judgments on Gothic. Wölfflin concludes the section on Late Gothic and Renaissance with the following observation: "Late Gothic is an intoxicating style; the concept 'picturesque' does not suffice. . . . The Renaissance, on the other hand, is a reflective and clarifying force. The Germans could not quite understand the vital content of life which called forth the Renaissance in Italy as its outward form of expression . . . but it was represented by an art of clear perception and as such alone must . . . have been welcome to that rational generation." This is Wölfflin. But it does fit Dürer. The rational element in Gothic and Late Gothic was concealed behind what Wölfflin calls intoxicating; Dürer developed in a direction away from Gothic with his glance directed toward the new *ratio*, and that left him the power to remain benevolently disposed when he looked back at the art of his youth with its mixture of the rational and the irrational.

To turn to Walter RIVIUS (c.1500-c.1550) after Dürer is to revert to the mediocre. His real name was Walter Ryff, but he Latinized it as being all too German for a Humanist. The first of his two books contains a geometry on the basis of Dürer's book and those of the Italian teach-

[29] Konrad Lange und Franz Louis Fuhse, *Dürers Schriftlicher Nachlass* . . . , Halle a.S. 1893, pp. 181, 338-339. "Der Mangel der Meister ist bei uns gross. Dann uns ist in tausend Johren Nichts von Kunst zukummen. Dann do Rom geschwächt ward, do gingen diese Kunst all unter. Und diese Künst ist schier gar erloschen gewest, dann was sie anderthalb hundert Johren wieder ins Licht ist kummen."

[29a] *Op.cit.*, p. 181, "Wiewol sie nachfolgend gar verloren und ob tausend Jahren verborgen gewest und erst in zweihundert Jahren wieder durch die Walchen an Tag gebracht ist worden."

[30] Cf., for example, the drawing in London, Tietze, II, 1, No. 428 (p. 210). In addition, attention should be called to the very early drawing "The Presentation in the Temple," reproduced in Winkler, *Zeichnungen* . . . , I, 21, "Maria standing in the Niche with the Stellar Vault" of 1512, the "Great Table-fountain" of about 1500, *ibid.*, pls. 150 and 233.

ers of perspective,[31] further, the theory of the columnar orders according to Vitruvius, as well as a treatise on weapons and fortifications, the latter a branch of architecture with which Dürer had concerned himself earlier.[32] Like Lacher, Rivius combined in his own person the skills of the engineer and the architect. That was an old tradition since the days of Villard de Honnecourt, indeed, it remained quite common during the Renaissance in Italy. Even though Leonardo comes to mind in this connection, no one would fail to note a difference, for Rivius was not an independent thinker. He must, however, have had considerable importance as a disseminator of knowledge in Germany, since now many things that Dürer had not touched upon could be read about in the German language.

His second book is the *Vitruvius Teutsch* of 1548.[33] In the title and at the end of the dedication to the "Learned, Prudent, Honorable, and Wise Lords, the Burgomasters and Council of the City of Nuremberg, my Respected and Gracious Masters" he calls himself "Medicus et Mathematicus, etc." On the title page can be read furthermore: "A Rendering of which into the German Tongue has not previously been attempted by anyone but has been considered an Impossibility." The work is actually a translation of Vitruvius and at the same time one of Cesariano's commentary. Here and there Rivius becomes even more involved than Cesariano. Anyone who wishes may compare the definitions of Vitruvius that were discussed above with those of Rivius' translation, also the difficult description for the octagonal *tiburio* (which is omitted in the illustration) that reads as though the final decision on the structure had still been pending in 1548.[34]

As a title for the transverse section of Milan Cathedral he writes: "An ingenious sketch of the Orthography or Drawing of the above-mentioned plan, or Ichnography according to the German Stonemasons on the basis of the Triangle, measured with particular care." He says (on page 27) the purpose of his teaching is that everyone shall be able to apply such "measurement" and be able to "enlarge or reduce or renew

[31] Walter Rivius, *Der fürnembsten, notwendigen gantzen Architectur angehörige Mathematischen Kunst, eigentlicher Bericht . . .* , Nuremberg, 1547.

[32] Wilhelm Waetzoldt, *Dürers Befestigungslehre*, Berlin, 1916.

[33] Gualtherus Rivius, *Vitruvius Teutsch*, Nuremberg, 1548.

[34] P. XXIX: "Hie merck das zu disem trefflichen baw ein acht eckiger oben hoch auffgespitzter thurn verordnet gewesen, auff das quadrat der vier mitlern Seulen zu setzen, wo aber solchs beschehen wer, befindet sich das solcher last allenthalben auff keiner feste sondern ganz bloss sten musste, mit etlichen ecken, welches wider alle erfarne Bawmeister, wo man gedenckt ein schweren last der massen zusetzen, das er lange zeit besteen müge." From this it must be concluded that Rivius was never in Milan.

it (*sie ergrössern oder verkleinern und verjüngen*)."[35] These words would not be intelligible without a knowledge of Lacher's manuscript. If the structural dimensions are determined according to the theory of the stonemasons by the measures resulting from square and triangle, any architectural drawing can be enlarged or reduced at will. The meaning of the word *verjüngen* in this connection is certainly debatable. According to Lacher it refers to definite changes of the measures whenever the stonemason proceeds to another structural member that has the same form, but is smaller, or, as the case may be, larger; for *verjüngen* seems to mean "renew," "make anew."

On page five Rivius mentions as his sources Luca Paccioli, Cesariano, Jovius, Maurus, Alberti, Guilielmus Philander, Serlio, Petrus Nonnus, Orontius, Fineus, Nicolaus Tartaleus, etc.

The woodcuts, as far as they reproduce those of Cesariano, are on a reduced scale; some of the illustrations have been taken from other works. All were drawn and cut by Peter Flötner (ca. 1485-1546).[36]

That Rivius should have used Milan Cathedral at all as an example only goes to prove his slavish dependence on Cesariano, and not a genuine adherence to Gothic. At the most one may deduce that he was not hostile toward the older style.

Whatever else Germany produced in the sixteenth century in the way of architectural theories is completely devoted to the principles of the columnar orders. The only energetic advocacy of the accomplishments of German architecture seems to be a passage in the preface to the *Treatise on Fortifications* of 1589 by Daniel SPECKLIN (1536-1589). I do not know the book,[37] and quote following Stange:[38] ". . . he would like to answer the Italians back, who attack us Germans with great contempt and consider no one good enough, as though we were completely without sense or brains and to be deemed children, and who maintain that they have never yet seen or heard of anything we have done that we did not steal from them, and that we have never yet in-

[35] *Ibid.*, p. 27. "So wir unsers beduncken nach genugsam erkleret, wie ein baw erstlichen in grundt zu legen . . . beduncket uns nit allein allen kunstliebhabern nutz vnd fürderlich zu sein sondern auch den anfahenden schulern hoch von nöten, das wir solche kirchen . . . solcher gestalt auff das eigentlichst nach rechter Symmetrie abgemessen, mit jrer Bezeichnung auffzureissen, damit ein yeder solcher messung nachtrachten, und die selbig ergrössern oder verkleinern und verjüngen mag, mit aller zugehör."

[36] Heinrich Röttinger, *Die Holzschnitte zur Architektur und zum Vitruvius Teutsch des Walter Rivius*, Strasbourg, 1914; cf. the article by F. F. Leitschuh on Flötner in Thieme-Becker, *op.cit.*, XII, 1916, especially p. 113. He rejects Röttinger's attribution to Vergil Solis.

[37] Daniel Specklin, *Architectura von Vestungen*, Strasbourg, 1584.

[38] Alfred Stange, "Die Gotik in der deutschen Baukunst um 1600," *Repertorium für Kunstwissenschaft*, Berlin and Leipzig, 1928, p. 281.

vented anything original." According to Stange's article the reference here is to Gothic; Specklin thus points to it as an achievement equal to Renaissance. From this it would seem that he believed the Germans invented Gothic. Its defense is colored by wounded national pride, and there comes to the forefront the bitter feeling of not having received proper recognition that accompanied Wimpheling's earlier partisanship of Gothic and Goethe's much later. Specklin was surrounded by the same atmosphere as they, for he was born in Strasbourg (in 1536) and after travels and sojourns in Austria, Hungary, Poland, Prussia, and Scandinavia finally settled in his native city in 1564, contributing to the fame of his homeland by depictions of Strasbourg Cathedral,[39] as well as a map of Alsace. He was an architect of fortifications, and the citizens of Strasbourg created the post of city architect for him. He collected materials for a sort of architectural chronicle of Strasbourg, probably the first attempt at a history of municipal architecture in Germany. It undoubtedly contained a section on the cathedral together with a declaration in favor of Gothic. The collection perished by fire in 1870 during the bombardment of the city.

These three names, Dürer, Rivius, and Specklin, exhaust the number of German judgments on Gothic in the sixteenth century that have been preserved. However, as a sort of terminal flourish, they may be supplemented by mention of some pages in *Architecture* by Wendel DIETTERLIN (1550-1599).[40] Sheets 196 and 197 employ Late Gothic forms of altar tabernacles with interlacing ogee arches twisted three-dimensionally; equally "Late Gothic" are plates 202 (Fig. 49) and 203, also the monstrance on plate 206. In the architectural examples the style of the structural frame is so-called Late Renaissance with Gothic as an overlay with wide meshes and feelers that clamber up and stretch thin tendrils into the air in the greatest contrast to the weightiness of the actual architectural masses. In places roots hang down free, and similar use of vegetal elements was made by Dietterlin more than once (for instance, on plate 52). The portal on plate 24 with all its creatures is a most promising and horrible prelude to the subject of romanticism of ruins (Fig. 50); Gothic it is certainly not, though it may perhaps be

[39] A view drawn by him was cut by B. Jobin in 1566; another one of the cathedral and one of the whole city appeared as copperplate engravings. Cf. Thieme-Becker, *op.cit.*

[40] Wendel Dietterlin, *Architectvra und Ausstheilung der V Seüln*, 1593; *Architectvra von Portalen vnnd Thürgerichten, Das Annder Buch . . .*, Strasbourg, 1594; then the chief edition, *Architectvra Von Ausstheilung, Symmetria vnd Proportion der Fünff Seulen*, Nuremberg, 1598; a reprint, *ibid.*, 1655. An exhaustive treatment of him is given by Margot Pirr (Mrs. Schmoll Eisenwert), *Die Architectura des Wendel Dietterlin 1598*, Gräfenhainichen, n.d.

Manneristic, depending on what one understands by the term. Undoubtedly it is a product of that state of mind that Wölfflin meant when he contrasted the intoxicating quality of Late Gothic with the reflectiveness of Italian Renaissance. Here it is a question of one single component, derived from a dark sphere of the Satanic and destructive, and revealing, side by side with Dietterlin's exuberant fancies, something of the interplay of creative and annihilating forces that lie hidden in the depths both of nature and the human spirit. It would be too strong to call this fantasy a portal to Hell, but it is surely no entrance to a Heavenly Jerusalem. Pirr explains the sheet as follows: ". . . the first human pair [reclining on the gable, freely rendered according to Michelangelo] and the animals of the wilderness on the unhewn pieces of rock symbolize an architectonic primeval state of unsapped energies, as it were, a myth of the origin of architecture itself. . . ." This may be accepted and one then will find it easier to realize why, should a stylistic classification be attempted, this sheet that contains no trace of Gothic members is far more likely to be placed in the vicinity of Late Gothic than in that of Renaissance or even Baroque.

Dietterlin's last sheets combine Late Gothic and Renaissance motifs in a fashion unlike Dürer's, but their incompatibility is obvious in both cases. In the history of the changing estimation of Gothic these minglings are significant, for they tell us what was nowhere expressed clearly in words, namely, that in Germany it was thought that a compromise was possible: do the new but do not neglect the old. An illustration of this is the ground plan that is appended to the well on plate 34: Roriczer's quadrature still lives on! Also Gothic is the geometrical net for a doorway on plate 23, immediately preceding that primeval portal. It is only a question of how far the real meaning of quadrature was still intelligible to Dietterlin. He no longer needed any quadrature, kept only approximately to the proportions of Vitruvius, and gave his fancy free rein. This freedom from strict restraint was a main factor in German Renaissance: Dürer sought the guiding, clarifying *ratio* without submitting to it entirely; Rivius remained a theorist without a firm conviction on the subject; Specklin defended "German" Gothic and would nevertheless have undoubtedly felt at home with the Italian Gothic tailor of Bologna; Dietterlin teaches rules and invents fantastic variations on a theme that is almost lost in these very variations.

6. Germany in the Seventeenth Century

IF one calls to mind the continued existence of Gothic building practice in Germany in the seventeenth century, the attitudes of Uffenbach, Schad, and Crombach become far less astonishing. Italian standards cannot yet be applied to the first half of the century.

Philipp UFFENBACH (1566-1636) was chiefly a painter, but he also took an interest in architecture, for he redrew the original plans for the finished cathedral tower in Frankfort on the Main on a larger scale. The drawings themselves have not been preserved; we know of them only through a mention in an official document. What purpose they served is not certain. In his paintings Uffenbach also showed Gothic architectural details and it is therefore possible that he made these drawings as studies. Schönberger, who called attention to the documentary note, believes that they were intended to create interest in the completion of the Gothic tower.[1] If this assumption is correct, there must have been in the Frankfort of that day circles which still cherished a completely positive attitude toward the Gothic tradition.

To discuss posthumous Gothic is not within the scope of this book. The case in question belongs here only if the correctness of the above interpretation is granted, and it can be assumed that Gothic continued vigorously alive. One could then speak neither of posthumous Gothic nor of historicism. Basically it is a question of the same problem that remained unsolved in Bologna: the stylistically proper continuation for an uncompleted edifice of the Gothic period. Uffenbach's drawings were from the year 1611; our information about them should be considered in connection with what we learn from the following two sources.

The first is the guide to Strasbourg Cathedral by M. O. SCHAD (1586-1626), who, like Rivius, wrote in German but, also like him, Latinized his German name to Schadaeus. He was a deacon of Old St. Peter's in Strasbourg. His slim little volume of pocket size was undoubtedly a welcome guidebook for many natives and strangers. Handy and certainly not expensive, it was written in a popular style, and by means of pompous praise stirred to admiration readers who understood little of architecture. It could possibly be considered the original ancestor of the later mass of small printed church guides.

The long, characteristically Baroque title promises a description of

[1] Guido Schönberger, *Der Frankfurter Dom St. Bartholomäus*, I, *Das Bauwerk*, Koblenz, 1929, p. 26.

the edifice and beautiful illustrations, betraying at the same time the author's patriotism.[2] Strictly speaking, there is no description given at all, and to call the copper engravings beautiful is a great exaggeration. These six engravings represent the exterior view seen diagonally from the south side, the pulpit, an altar ("Isaac Brun Argentino sculptor Ao 1617"), the clock, three equestrian statues (on the façade) representing "Clodovaeus, Dagobert Magnus, Rudolphus Hapsb. Romanus," and, finally, the south portal of the transept. A ground plan is omitted. On the other hand, in the place where the Early Christian basilica is mentioned, which is said to have existed earlier even than the predecessor of the present cathedral, there is sketched a curious ground plan that reveals to the reader what Schadaeus' idea of a basilican church was. The significant thing about the other engravings is that for the first time a Gothic work was given the honor of more detailed, scientifically intended illustration. There had been reproductions of classical and Renaissance works before this, de L'Orme's book was accompanied by examples of Gothic vaults, and so on, but to insert a reproduction into a historical text on an existing *Gothic* structure, scarcely to be compared to Villard, was completely new. In this respect Schad is the forerunner of Dugdale and Hollar.

The engravings are a substitute for the missing description. It may be that Schad did not even notice that he had failed to describe the cathedral, for he says that it must be recognized as one of the seven wonders of the world, or as the eighth. Thereupon he describes the seven wonders! Of the eighth he says: "At which all beholders must marvel in the highest degree, not alone because of its size and height, but also, and indeed much more, because of the ingenious work that the architects and builders have displayed and shewn forth in it, with all diligence; to such an end that not a few or undistinguished persons have numbered it among the greatest and most excellent architectural

[2] M. Oseas Schadaeus, *Summum Argoratensium Templum, Das ist Auszführliche und Eigendtliche Beschreibung des viel künstlichen, sehr kostbaren, und in aller Welt berühmten Münsters zu Strassburg: Auch alles dessen, so An und In demselben Denckwürdiges zu sehen: Mit schönen Figuren und beigefügten underschiedlichen Kupferstücken gezieret: Jetztmahls zum Ersten, seinem vielgeliebten Vaterland und Teutscher Nation zu Ehren in Truck verfertigt,* Strasbourg, 1617. Cf. also Georg Heinrich Behr, *Strassburger Münster- und Thurnbüchlein* [*sic*] *oder Kurtzer Begriff Der merkwürdigsten Sachen, so im Münster und dasigen Thurn zu finden* . . . , Strasbourg, 1746. Behr calls himself "Hochfürstl. Hohenloischen Rath und Leib-Arzt, wie auch der Kayserlichen Academie deren Naturwissenschafter Mitglied. . . ." This rare book is occasionally cited, but one should not expect anything unusual of it: it is a new edition of Schadaeus. Alfred Neumeyer cited a Strasbourg *Turmbüchlein* of 1739 in his essay in the *Repertorium für Kunstwissenschaft*, Berlin, 1928; probably this is an older edition; an anonymous description of the cathedral of 1737 may well be the first reprint of Schadaeus.

wonders of the world, and still number it so today, if they do not even far prefer it to most of these. And in truth if we were to draw a *comparatio* and parallel between the cathedral here in Strasbourg and the seven wonders of the world, and examine such *secundum quatuor causarum genera*, and illustrate them, all persons of a right understanding could not but agree with those who either prefer it to the majority of the seven wonders, or at least deem it to be the eighth one of the same." Conrad Morant had already designated the tower of Strasbourg Cathedral as the eighth wonder of the world on an engraving in 1548 (Fig. 55); rhetorical formulations of this kind, whether in criticism or praise, are inherited from generation to generation as ready-made judgments.[2a]

Schadaeus' structural history of the cathedral is good, and based on sufficient knowledge. At least he gives the chief stages, including one which is mythical and prehistoric, but there is, of course, no structural analysis. Of individual details he discusses the bells, sepulchral monuments, altars, the pulpit, and the famous astronomical clock; he gives the chief dimensions of the cathedral and conscientiously puts down side by side the varying figures of measurement given by different authors for the height of the tower.

In addition to all this there is, finally, the patriotic note. He quotes Wimpheling *in extenso*, and is as proud of the cathedral as he, because it is the glory of his native land.[3] The contempt of the Humanists and Classicists never prevented Alsatian patriotism from esteeming its Gothic minster.

The minster had been partly restored in the seventeenth century. Johann Heckler restored small damages of the tower after it had been damaged by lightning, also the two chapels of St. John and St. Andrew (1633, 1634). His son Hans Georg Heckler removed the lectern and the chapel of the Virgin, both works of Master Erwin. He proposed the erection of a second tower similar to the existing one, and it seems clear that it was intended that, like its model, it should be Late Gothic.[4]

A year after the little Schadaeus book had appeared in praise of Strasbourg and its Gothic, there occurred the famous "Defenestration" of Prague, and the resulting war completely changed German culture.

2a Hans Rott, *Quellen und Forschungen zur Südwestdeutschen und Schweizerischen Kunstgeschichte . . .*, III. Oberrhein, Stuttgart, 1936, (Quellen I) p. 223. Morant, called Schweblin, is mentioned from 1546 to 1556. He was a painter and a citizen in Strasbourg. I am indebted to Mr. Charles Henri Arnhold in Colmar for the permission to reproduce his rare original woodcut.

3 See above, p. 249.

4 Thieme-Becker, *op.cit.* Furthermore Johannes Ficker, *Das Strassburger Münster als Symbol*, Halle a.S. 1924, p. 14.

The central problem of the struggle, the spiritual claims of the adherents of the Reformation against the Roman Catholic church, lost all meaning when it became apparent that neither of the conflicting parties could bring about the destruction of the other. The Counter Reformation, supported by the Jesuit Order, mingled the mediaeval ideas of the Christian church with those of the modern philosophy of life that had evolved since Humanism. In Italy the Jesuits were the mainstay of the Baroque style, while in other countries they simultaneously fostered posthumous Gothic. Nevertheless, when in 1648 the war came to an end in Germany, the way was opened for the importation of Roman Baroque by Italian architects coming from the south. We might, therefore, assume that from then on hostility to Gothic, as it was preached in Vasari's much read book, dominated Germany as well. But it should not be forgotten that the men who had survived the Thirty Years' War could still view Gothic, going back to the days of their youth, without hatred and, indeed, even with love.

Hermann CROMBACH (1598-1680) belonged to this group. He was born in Cologne in 1598, and in 1617 entered the Jesuit Order. In 1618 the Jesuits began the construction of their church, The Ascension of Mary, in Cologne. In its essentials it is still a Gothic building, one of the most beautiful examples of posthumous Gothic in Germany.[5] Crombach's taste developed in this atmosphere, for, aside from travels (surely to Rome) for which there is no documentation, he seems to have remained in Cologne. One may suppose that he was no less concerned for the fame of Cologne Cathedral than *Schad* for that of Strasbourg. But whereas *Schad* contented himself with a little church guide, intended for unassuming patriots, Crombach wrote a fat folio volume for learned Catholics. Since the days of Friedrich Barbarossa the relics of the Three Kings have been preserved in the cathedral at Cologne. Crombach had no doubts as to their authenticity, and wrote this long book in Latin about the three saints.[6]

We shall pass over the first 798 pages; on the next page is to be found the chapter title: Descriptio memphitici templi metropolitani Coloniensis iuxta ideam primam, quale iam est et futurum erit, si coronis operi aliquando imponatur (Description of the Memphitic Cathedral as it is now and as it will be upon completion).[7] Crombach believed in

[5] Destroyed in World War II, but now rebuilt.

[6] Hermann Crombach, *Primitiae Gentium sive Historia et Encomium SS. Trium Magorum*, Cologne, 1653-1654. (A copy from which the two engravings are missing can be found in the Divinity School, Harvard University, Cambridge, Mass.)

[7] The meaning of the word *memphiticus* in this connection is unintelligible. Cf. the lexica

the possibility of a continuation of the work. That took courage in the year 1654. But he went even further: he believed in its completion in Gothic style according to the still extant mediaeval designs.

If this is interesting in itself, his description compels our even greater respect when we have fully appreciated its objectivity and abundance.

Characteristically, the first sentence of this chapter refers to the linguistic difficulty: "In this chapter I shall make use of the technical terms employed by Vitruvius, which I shall endeavor to fit to the Gothic construction." He then begins with the information that the stone came from the Drachenfels, a cliff in the Siebengebirge near Bonn, and goes on to say that it is ash gray, very hard, and durable. "The *Symmetria partium*, that is, the disposition of the whole, does not follow the Ionic, Corinthian, or Composite Orders, but the Gothic. However, this does not mean that it is for that reason bad, but the work is more substantial and at times seems more beautiful, particularly in the exterior aspect, which presents its elegance (*elegantia*) everywhere to the eye, more clearly than the interior. This is to be seen on all sides: from below up to the gable and the enormous bell tower, which is strengthened by fourteen paired buttresses, everything furnished with suitable ornaments, moldings and blind tracery (*fenestris caecis*), statues, and pyramids. The columns are provided with capitals that have recurved leaves and stems . . . most of the upper ornaments on the buttresses (*pleraque costarum ornamenta summa*) cannot be seen with mortal eyes because of their height, unless one observes them from the three passageways (*tribus ex ambulacris*). He who considers them for this reason to be superfluous forgets that the work has been constructed not merely for the admiration of men, but for God. No costs should be spared for His glory. . . ." Then follow dimensions, a description of the cruciform ground plan, further, the information that the structure was completed, to the stage reached in those days, in seventy-four years. "The main choir of St. Peter has costly, many-colored stained-glass windows. Vault and roof of the choir are carried on piers . . . between them is a wall for the protection of the choir stalls." Then he discusses the organ, main altar, tabernacle, and aisles of the choir, the chapels, including that of the Three Kings, their shrine (*hierotheca*), tombs, the Romanesque crucifix (*crux prodigiosa*), and so on; further, the arms of the transept, the screens, and the crossing. Of the latter he says that in it an enormous mausoleum was to be erected to house the shrine

of Georges, du Cange, and Pauly-Wissowa. Did Crombach think that the Three Kings came from Egypt?

of the Three Kings (which never came to pass). But the assertion met with in the literature on the subject that Crombach proposed a dome for the crossing is not accurate. He says that up until now the crossing has had no vault, but that an eventual vault should be made the same height as those of the choir and of the arms of the transept.[8]

Then follows the description of the nave, very detailed and extremely factual, but it is not necessary to discuss it, as the samples already given will suffice.

Crombach provided for his book two copperplates, one representing the ground plan, the other the old design for the west façade.[9] It is reported that he had the engravings made at his own expense and presented them to the City Council of Cologne as an encouragement to continue the work on the cathedral.[10] However excellent the whole description is for a period when a descriptive technique like our modern one had not yet been evolved, it is nevertheless surprising that Crombach, with all his exactitude, fails to make any mention of what is today regarded as the most important member of Gothic: the rib. Although on page 801 he says of the part completed at that time: "undique fornicatum," he does not describe these vaults, as though all vaults in the world were alike. The word *costa* occurs twice, but always in conjunction with descriptions of the exterior; it means there a riblike traverse wall, that is, a buttress. In spite of overlooking the rib, Crombach had an understanding of Cologne Cathedral and of Gothic that the Italians of the day had lost, if, indeed, they had ever had it to that degree. Whether Cologne Cathedral is considered as German or French Gothic plays no part in this matter.

In 1611 Uffenbach (presumably) proposed the continuation of the

8 *Op.cit.*, p. 801: "Quos inter choros in meditullio . . . mausoleum ingens altitudine, specie, et arte visendum dignumque tantis Regibus Deo propitio restat aedificandum: nam totum hoc transuersum crucis spacium cum naui templi chori S. Petri altitudinem adaequabit, ideoque nunc adhuc fornicibus caret; depressa ad aequam proportionem et operis totius symmetriam alarum utrarumque concameratione." A somewhat later sentence on p. 802 reads: ". . . columnae . . . ob oneris gravitatem: in alis octorum pedum sunt ob testudinem depressiorem: sicut in templi et crucis meditullio quatuor columnae quae maximum pondus crucis mediae vel cupulae forte supra chorum trium Regum erigendae sustinebuntur, ad 12 pedes esse crassae videntur." It is improbable that the *cupula* of this passage means a dome in our sense of the word. A dome would have surpassed the height of the vaults of the choir and the arms of the transept, whereas Crombach previously stated expressly that the vault over the crossing should be of the same height as the neighboring vaults. Boisserée, *op.cit.*, p. 54 (2nd ed.), says that Crombach's supposition that a dome was intended is "quite incorrect." He adds that the domes in Florence and Milan were a step backward; he believed, rather, that in Cologne there had been plans for a tower over the crossing (p. 31).

9 The plates are reproduced in the book by Helen Rosenau, *Der Kölner Dom*, Cologne, 1931, figs. 64 and 65.

10 Cf. the short biography of Crombach in the *Allgemeine Deutsche Biographie.*

cathedral tower in Frankfort in Gothic style, in 1653 Crombach made the same proposal for the towers of Cologne Cathedral, and in 1665 Johann Georg Heckler, an architect, urged that the second tower be added to the cathedral in Strasbourg. This evidence all goes to prove that in Germany there were still convinced adherents of Gothic, although its conclusive force is somewhat weakened by the failure, perhaps because of post-war impoverishment, to execute these towers in the seventeenth century.

The sands had now run out for Gothic in Germany as well as elsewhere. Joachim von SANDRART (1606-1688) made out its death certificate. In his *Teutsche Akademie* he took Vasari and Scamozzi as his models.[11] After discussing the five columnar orders, he lists the *Gothica* as the sixth, which is in itself nonsense, as Gothic is not a columnar order; this mistake, however, he adopted from Vasari. Then he goes on to say, in a free rendering of Vasari, that it is not a "proper order, proportion, and measure" and is now too heavy and now too delicate. The reproach that Gothic drapes the columns (by which are meant piers) with vine leaves and tendrils, "now so thick and numerous as though a whole vineyard were planted on them, now, however, so delicate, tenuous, and sparse, as though they were little cut-out pieces of cards," is also copied from Vasari. All the Gothic buildings that are still standing today can be searched in vain for the actual structure with vine leaves that could have been the cause of this criticism.

Sandrart's appraisal of Gothic is all the more destructive because of its brevity, for his few remarks are embedded in a work of two thick folio volumes. The conclusion of his condemnation is a warming over of the judgments of Manetti, Pseudo-Raphael, Filarete, and Vasari: "The Goths brought this monstrosity to Italy: for after they had devastated and destroyed Rome, and almost all Roman artists had perished in these same wars, they subsequently introduced this vile fashion of building, whereby they brought upon themselves and called down upon their heads more than a thousand million curses, throughout all Italy." Filarete, a man of the affable Early Renaissance, contented himself with one single curse; Sandrart, the man of Baroque, employs more than a thousand million.[12]

The sequence—Rivius, Crombach, Sandrart—is symptomatic of the

[11] Joachim Sandrart, *Teutsche Akademie*, Nuremberg, 1675-1679, I, p. 17.

[12] Note, however, what Sandrart wrote on Mathis G. Nithard (Grünewald) and on Rembrandt; it does not belong directly to my subject, but indirectly it sheds light on the problem of whether or not Nithard is entirely or predominantly Gothic, and to what extent the familiar (modern) comparison between Gothic and Baroque is tenable.

cultural development in Germany. Rivius writes a muddled and prolix German, he still follows the tradition of the lodge secrets, and he aspires to give his German readers a sense of perspective and system through his translation of Vitruvius and Cesariano. Crombach is a polished Jesuit, who writes Latin and has a clear well-trained intellect; his humanism is at the service of his childlike faith in the Three Kings and their relics, but he has a warm spot in his heart for Gothic. Sandrart, finally, the compiler, writes a vigorous, Baroque German, and despises and curses Gothic. With him, Germany happily—according to the opinion of the age—caught up with Italy's cultural lead, at least with respect to the judgment of Gothic.

7. France, Italy, and Spain in the Seventeenth Century

ALTHOUGH the prevailing French opinion in the seventeenth century was hostile to Gothic,[1] there are also isolated favorable judgments. In 1605 Pierre BONFONS calls the St.-Chapelle in Paris admirable, with the reservation that the columns of the lower church seem too weak to carry the upper church.[2] These columns, of course, support only the floor of the upper church; Bonfons is thus not really commenting on Gothic, but on statics, a matter he misjudges.

André DUCHESNE (1584-1640), in 1609, mentions Nôtre-Dame in Paris with high esteem: "... a church that far surpasses all other churches in Christendom, in discipline as well as grandeur; so was it built of parts artistically joined in the artistry of its being, and so many were the dignities required to clothe it, and which are as it were the key to its perfection, royally and ambitiously created in this work in order to render it full of the perfection of beauty: a work that has since risen to the noon of honor, where it stands, and this honor in the last line, at the ultimate and highest point of its ascendant."[3]

[1] For the subject of this chapter cf. J. Corblet, "L'Architecture du moyen-age, jugée par les écrivains des deux dernières siècles," *Revue de l'Art Chrétien*, III, 1860, p. 68.

[2] Pierre Bonfons, *Les fastes, antiquitez et choses les plus remarquables de Paris, labeur de curieuse et diligente recherche*, Paris, 1605, p. 132 (Corblet, p. 35).

[3] André Duchesne, *Les antiquités et recherches des villes, châteaux et places les plus remarquables de toute la France*, Paris, 1609, p. 73 (quoted from Corblet): "... église qui en discipline comme en grandeur va bien loin devant toutes autres églises de la chrétienté; tant elle fut bastie de pièces artistement ralliées en son estre artificiel, et tant les dignités requises pour la vestir et qui sont connue la clef de sa perfection, furent royalement et ambitieusement

In the same year, 1609, Sébastien ROUILLARD (ca. 1568-1639) surpasses the praise of Duchesne in his description of the cathedral in Chartres: "It is magnificently built on a mount in the highest part of the city, its fabric of very hard, cut stone, raised on high and supported by flying buttresses of many stories, enriched with double galleries, both high and low, so that one may walk around it on the outside, and provided with massive towers, partly round, partly rectangular, platforms, pyramids, columns, tabernacles, niches, and images of such exquisite and distinguished sculpture that at the mere sight of them all the Polyclituses of old would throw away their chisels and all the Vitruviuses of the past would wish to take this masterpiece as the model of their architecture. . . ."[4] As far as the "Vitruviuses" are concerned this was too optimistic. The phraseology is the same as that used by Wimpheling, obviously a common rhetorical convention.

Somewhat later than Paris and Chartres, Amiens also found an enthusiastic interpreter. In 1627 Adrien de la MORLIÈRE (ca. 1600-ca. 1650) wrote: "In truth, one could hardly find a masterpiece with a greater spirit of enterprise, nor one more difficult to represent than this church. . . ." One would have to have drawings at hand "to show the towers and the flights of stairs, the portals and roses, the flying buttresses and the pinnacles, and all the many others of its members and individual beauties. . . ."[5] In short, one must see for oneself. "Marvel of the beholders!"

---

créés en cet ouvrage, afin de le rendre du tout accomply en perfection de beauté: ouvrage qui depuis s'est haussé au midy de l'honneur, où il est, et cet honneur à la dernière ligne, au dernier et plus haut point de son ascendent." Wilhelm Weber left the following note on this passage: "The bombastic, turgid, almost unintelligible language of the last sentence can only be understood when one realizes that the author was playing with concepts, images, and terms derived from *astrology*. For this is perfectly clear from the expressions 'ascendant' (the rising point or degree of the ecliptic) and 'noon of honor' (the degree of the ecliptic that stands, at the decisive moment, in the middle of the visible heavens, in *medium caelum*). Thus in this passage a kind of horoscope is cast for Notre Dame, or, expressed more precisely, the introductory sentence about the pre-eminence of this church above all others in Christendom is made to depend on the aspect of its stars. Actually, the '*honores*' in *medium caelum* are, by the aid of current Renaissance astrology, the dates of the founding, and those of the dedication of Notre Dame, interpreted further to become the basis for the church's 'horoscope' and its rank in the world."

[4] Sébastien Rouillard, *Parthenie, Histoire de la très auguste église de Chartres*, Paris, 1609, p. 132 (Corblet, p. 37): ". . . elle est magnifiquement bastie, sur une montagne, au plus haut endroit de la ville, sa structure de pierre de taille très dure, hault eslevée et soutenue d'arcs boutants à plusiers étages, enrichie de doubles galleries haute et basses, pour aller en dehor tout autour, revêtue de grosses tours, parties rondes, parties carrées, plate-formes, pyramides, coulomnes, tabernacles, niches et images de si esquise et insigne sculpture qu'au seul aspect d'icelles, tous les Polyclètes du jadis jetteroient là leur ciseau et tous les Vitruves du passé voudroient prendre ce chef-d'œuvre pour le modelle de leur architecture."

[5] Adrien de la Morlière, *Histoire et choses les plus remarquables de la ville d'Amiens*, Paris, 1627, p. 91 (Corblet, p. 36): "De vray, l'on ne scaurait rencontrer chef-d'œuvre de plus haute

LA MOTHE le Vayer (1588-1672) confesses in 1660 "that one never wearies of admiring the beautiful church of St.-Ouen [in Rouen]."[6]

These panegyrics, however, can by no means simply be extended to apply to Gothic in general. They are cases of more monographic interests, where local patriotism plays a part, just as in the case of *Schad* in Strasbourg. The need to increase the stature of one's hero brings about a closer examination of *things*, and yet what these men had to offer is still very superficial.

Jean MABILLON (1632-1707), the great scholar, apparently said nothing about Gothic although he lived in St.-Denis from 1663 on.

Bernard de MONTFAUCON (1655-1741), no less famous than Mabillon, regarded the statues of the portals of St.-Denis and Chartres as portraits of Merovingian kings, and dated them accordingly as of the sixth century. Incidentally, the publication that presents this view is not earlier than the eighteenth century, but Montfaucon still belongs in tradition and education entirely to the seventeenth.[6a]

Whether any remarks on Gothic can be found in the works of Dom U. PLANCHERS (1667-1750) I do not know.

The great poet Jean Baptiste MOLIÈRE (1622-1673) had a completely negative attitude toward this subject. He was a close friend of Pierre Mignard (1610-1695), who, in 1658, adorned the dome of Val-de-Grâce in Paris with frescoes. In 1669 Molière wrote a long poem of three hundred and sixty-six verses, *La Gloire du Val-de-Grâce*, celebrating Colbert, the edifice, and the frescoes.[7] Several lines are devoted to Gothic:

> "Tout s'y voyant tiré d'un vaste fonds d'esprit,
> Assaisonné du sel de nos grâces antiques
> Et non du fade goût des ornements gothiques,
> Ces monstres odieux des siècles ignorants,
> Que de la barbarie ont produit les torrents,
> Quand leur cours, inondant presque toute la terre,
> Fit à la politesse une mortelle guerre,
> Et, de la grande Rome abattant les remparts,
> Vint, avec son empire, étouffer les beaux-arts."

entre-prise ni plus difficile à representer que cette église . . . pour montrer les tours et le montées, les porteaux et les roses, les arcs boutants et les espis et tout tant d'autres de ses membres et beautez à parcelles. . . . Merveille des regardants!"

[6] La Mothe le Vayer, *Œuvres*, Paris, 1662, *Traité de l'envie*, p. 434. A biography of him has been written by Florence L. Wickelgreen: *La Mothe le Vayer, sa vie et son œuvre*, Paris, 1934.

[6a] *Monuments de la monarchie française*, Paris, 1729, I, 57ff.

[7] *Œuvres complètes de Molière*, Nouvelle Edition par Eugène Despois et Paul Mesnard, IX, Paris, 1886, p. 541.

A second passage from the same poem reads:

"Et toi, qui fus jadis la maîtresse du monde,
Docte et fameuse école en raretés féconde,
Où les arts déterrés ont, par un digne effort,
Réparé les dégâts des barbares du Nord;
Source des beaux débris des siècles mémorables,
O Rome! qu'à tes soins nous sommes redevables
De nous avoir rendu, façonné de ta main,
Ce grand homme, chez toi devenu tout Romain.
Dont le pinceau célèbre, avec magnificence,
De ces riches travaux vient parer notre France,
Et dans un noble lustre . . . ."[8]

The editors of Molière's works have pointed out that he drew inspiration from the Latin poem, *De Arte graphica*, by DUFRESNOY, Mignard's colleague.[9] In this can be found analogies to both the passages quoted from Molière. Both poems are concentrated on painting, but "fade goût des ornements gothiques" and "monstres odieux des siècles ignorants" surely apply not merely to painting, while the same is true of the second passage crediting Rome with the restoration of the damage done by the barbarians of the North.

Shortly after Molière had expressed his scorn in verse, a priest in Chartres, Vincent SABLON (1619-1693), wrote an enthusiastic encomium of his cathedral—also in poetic form, and interspersed with many proofs of his acquaintance with classical mythology.[10] This poem of one hundred verses forms the third chapter of a guide to the cathedral of Chartres, an attractive little book of duodecimo size in the manner of Schadaeus, and is devoted to a description of the exterior of the edifice. It begins:

"Au centre de la Ville entre huit avenuës,
Ce saint Temple s'élève à la hauteur des nuës,
Et sa base s'enfonce autant dans les Enfers
Que son faîte orgueilleux s'élève dans les airs.
Dans le vast Vnivers il n'est pas une [*sic*] roche
Dont la pointe superbe à sa hauteur approche."

[8] *Ibid.*, p. 554, verses 227ff.

[9] *Ibid.*, p. 219. Charles Dufresnoy, 1611-1688, is also said to have been active as an architect. The Latin poem in question appeared shortly after Dufresnoy's death, and attained great renown; it was translated into several languages.

[10] Vincent Sablon, *Histoire de l'auguste et venerable église de Chartres, dédiée par les anciens Druides à une vierge qui devoit enfanter*, Chartres, 1671. I quote from the second edition of 1683.

Line 20:

"Ce Temple est merveilleux en son Architecture,
Merveilleux en son art, non moins qu'en sa structure,
Merveilleux au dedans, merveilleux au dehors,
Et merveilleux enfin en tout son vaste corps.
Il est immense et vaste, et de structure antiqué [*sic*],
L'ordre gottique l'orne avec le Mosaïque,
Et par leur ornement et leur antiquité
Ils le font venerable à la postérité.
Des entrailles d'un mont sa masse composée,
D'un Art ingenieux en croix est divisée.
Son superbe lambris en arcade ployé
Sur cent fermes piliers a son faix appuyé,
Et cent forts arc-boutans faits à plusiers êtages [*sic*]
Le deffendent par tout des vents et des orages,
D'ouvrages si divers l'edifice assorty,
Par un maître sçavant artistement bâty,
Ne se voit point orné de marbre ou de porphire,
Ny de ses ornemens que le vulgaire admire,
Mais l'habile Architecte a voulu faire voir
Qu'il n'est rien qui ne cede à son rare sçavoir."

Sablon then turns his attention to the sculpture, and does not fail to remark that nature has been imitated perfectly and that one finds portraits everywhere; he mentions *platte-formes, balcons* (triforia?, or passageways on the exterior), where the inhabitants of Chartres often frisk about in innocent fashion; he speaks of the thrice three portals and their sculptures (verse 77ff.):

"Toute la cour Celeste y semble historiée,
Il semble qu'elle y soit toute petrifiée. . . ."

The description of the interior is written in prose; it gives a general survey of the spatial parts of the cathedral (nave, aisles, transept, choir, chapels), and then goes into details of accessories such as choir screens and stained-glass windows, the latter of which can be recognized as old because the glass is as thick as a finger. Subsequent chapters concern the altars, the chapel of St. Piat and St. Jerome, the crypt, the towers[11] and bells, and the trusses of the roof. Besides these descrip-

[11] In describing the towers, Sablon once more adopts poetic form (p. 66): "Le Clocher parle." The tower itself relates how it was struck by lightning and burned in 1508, was rebuilt in stone, and so on.

tive chapters there are some of a purely historical nature—on the bishops and canons—and others on the relics, ceremonies, and the like. The work is thus a monograph, containing much dry learning shot through with enthusiastic poetry. In the history of mediaevalism Sablon's uncompromising verses are important because they are so clearly on the defensive against the classicistic party. His defensive attitude is combined with the offensive where he says that Chartres is not embellished with the marble and porphyry admired by the crowd, and he employs the jargon of the academicians when, in opposition to the Classicists, he calls the Gothic stonemasons *savants*, because they constructed flying buttresses and achieved proper symmetry. Thus one cannot maintain that Sablon was not acquainted with the current point of view of the educated class in Italy and France. He lived in Chartres and his heart went out to this masterpiece of Gothic.

The leading French theorist on architecture, Nicolas François BLONDEL (1617-1686), on the other hand, thought like Molière; he, too, had fallen under the influence of the Italian fashion for damning Gothic. In his big folio volume he gives all the rules that an architect of his day needed to enable him to work in the classical orders. He had no reason to make any mention of Gothic style; nevertheless, he was impelled to proclaim his antipathy. In the Introduction, on page 4, he wrote:

"Thus it is very probable that the Romans added much to the inventions of the Greeks, especially in those times when they, the rulers of the universe, were at pains to dedicate their memory to eternity by the majesty of their buildings, and to leave to posterity sublime tokens of the magnitude of their power and their spirit.

"But when the barbaric peoples had overrun the Roman Empire, they not only cast down its might and authority, but even attempted to efface its memory; its superb buildings were demolished, and Architecture found a monument in the ruin of those very works by means of which it had thought to be able to attain immortality.

"It remained buried for a span of thirteen centuries, allowing that outrageous and insupportable fashion of building to reign in its stead, of which our fathers long made use under the name of Gothic Architecture that had been given to it by the Goths, its first Authors. . . ."

Here, then, the theory of the barbaric origin of Gothic crystallizes in the thesis that the Goths themselves had already called Gothic "Gothic."[12]

[12] François Blondel, *Cours d'architecture*, Paris, 1675, p. 4: "Mais lors que les nations barbares s'estant débordées dans l'Empire Romain, eurent non seulement abattut sa puissance et son autorité, mais mesme tâché d'en deffaciner la mémoire; Ces superbes bâtiments furent

The same book, however, contains a surprising inconsistency when Blondel reaches the point of discussing the façade of Milan Cathedral.[13] He writes: "Here is an example that cannot be disputed; it is the façade of the Cathedral Church of Milan, which is regarded as the most beautiful specimen of Gothic architecture in the world, and which I never beheld without being moved by a feeling of veneration and pleasure. Its proportions have been described, confusedly enough, in the Italian translation of Vitruvius by Cesare Cesariano, a Milanese and Professor of Architecture, that was printed in the reign of King François I, King of France and Duke of Milan, in the city of Como in the year 1521." Blondel here succumbs to literary tradition, and is suddenly touched by awe and delight (*plaisir*). He believed that the painstaking determination of proportions in the case of Milan Cathedral was prompted by the desire to achieve beauty, indeed, even to guarantee it. He was used to this idea from the doctrine of the classical orders, but he, too, failed to notice that the proportions of the completed façade did not agree with the scheme of regular triangles reproduced in Cesariano. It would even seem that it was Blondel who introduced this error into the literature on the subject, for subsequent writers and theoreticians saw in him the infallible authority. The illustration of the façade of the cathedral in Milan that he published on page 777 is, nevertheless, historically important; it shows the state of the work in 1675 and 1698 (second edition).

Blondel's inconsistency in calling Gothic a "façon énorme et insupportable" and at the same time pronouncing beautiful an edifice of *Italian* Gothic, of all things, can be instructive with regard to the judging of nationalistic conceptions of history. Blondel rejected the architecture of his fathers, which is for many Frenchmen the strongest expression of the French spirit; he advocated the art of the Romans, in

renversés, et l'Architecture trouva son monument dans la ruine des ouvrages de qui elle avoit cru pouvoir attendre l'immortalité.

"Elle y demeura ensevelie dans l'espace de treize siècles laissant règner à sa place cette façon de bâtir enorme et insupportable, et dont nos Pères se sont longtemps servis sous le nom d'Architecture Gotique, que les Gots qui en estoient les premiers Auteurs lui avoient donné. . . ."]

[13] *Ibid.*: "En voici un example que l'on ne peut contester; C'est la façade de l'Eglise Cathédrale de Milan, qui passe pour le plus bel Ouvrage qui soit au monde en Architecture Gothique, et que je n'ay jamais regardé sans me sentir touché d'un sentiment de vénération et de plaisir. Ses proportions sont décrites assez confusement dans le Vitruve traduit en Italien par Cesare Cesariano Milanois et Professeur en Architecture, et Imprimé sous le règne du Roy François Premier Roy de France et Duc de Milan, en la Ville de Come en l'année 1521." For Blondel cf. Mauciaire and C. Vigoureux, *Nicolas François Blondel*, Paris, 1938; and Thieme-Becker, *Allgemeines Künstlerlexikon*.

the form, of course, of the Italian Renaissance. However, instead of rejecting *Italian* Gothic as well, like the nationalists of his country, he felt himself drawn to it, though we cannot calculate to what extent he was merely obeying literary tradition, or to what extent he saw in the more moderate, that is, less steep, less Gothic proportions in Milan a greater approximation to antiquity.

One can perhaps differentiate a more Italian trend in the appraisal of Gothic in this period from a more French one. The former is represented by the *Vocabulary* by Filippo BALDINUCCI (ca. 1624-1696),[14] and is almost radically condemnatory; the latter, on the other hand, conceded some value to many things in Gothic, with a certain respectful indulgence. The most important representative of this willingness to compromise is Jean François Félibien des Avaux the son of the royal historiographer, ANDRÉ FÉLIBIEN des Avaux (1619-1695). During his years in Rome the father was a close friend of Poussin; after his return to France he was appointed by Colbert director of the newly founded Académie de l'Architecture. One of his works contains a casual mention of Gothic,[15] for it includes an extensive "Dictionnaire des termes propres" to all three arts, in which the word *Ogive* is listed: under the concept *Voûtes* can be found a short note on "Voûtes d'Ogive, autrement à la Gothique ou moderne." *Ogives, ou Augives* he defines as arches that extend diagonally from one corner to the other. According to what he says in the section on vaults, he seems to call all ribs that do not pass through diagonally *Nerfs d'ogives.* No stand either for or against Gothic can be discerned here.

André's son, Jean François FÉLIBIEN des Avaux (1658-1733), succeeded to the office of royal historiographer; his more friendly attitude toward Gothic may be interpreted as mild opposition to his father.

In his biographies of great architects he speaks of "Gothic" in the preface of 1687.[16] He says, though no author has made known its rules

14 Filippo Baldinucci, *Vocabulario toscano dall'arte del disegno*, Florence, 1681, p. 113: "Ordine Gottico: Dicesi quel modo di lauorare, tenuto nel tempo de' Goti, di maniera Tedesca, di proporzione in niuna cosa simile a' cinque buoni Ordini d'Architettura antichi; ma di fazzione in tutto barbara, con sottilissime colonne, e smisuratamente lunghe, auuolte, e in più modi sneruate. . . ." "Gothic Order. This name is given to the manner of working in the time of the Goths, the German manner, of a proportion in no way similar to the five good orders of ancient architecture but of totally barbarian execution with very thin and immensely long columns, twisted, and in more [many] ways enfeebled. . . ." What follows repeats literally what Vasari had written in the preface of *Le Vite.*

15 André Félibien des Avaux, *Des Principes de l'architecture, de la sculpture, de la peinture, et des autres arts qui en dependent. Avec un dictionnaire des termes propres à chacun de ces arts*, Paris, 1676.

16 Jean François Félibien, *Recueil historique de la vie et des ouvrages des plus célèbres archi-*

(as Vitruvius did those of ancient architecture), one can differentiate two sorts. The older is only remarkable for solidity and size; the "modern" contrasts with the older Gothic buildings because of its *délicatesse.* In Félibien's terminology "Gothic" means approximately "mediaeval"; the older epoch is thus the period of Early Christian style down to and including Romanesque, while the younger or modern corresponds to that which we call Gothic. He distributes the buildings according to their (aesthetic) weight, as it were, to the right and left of the harmonious middle of ancient structures: some are too heavy, others too light. In spite of this appraisal he discusses in subsequent chapters the great architects of Gothic: Robert de Lusarch (Amiens), Thomas de Corment, Renault, Hugue Libergier (Reims), Jean de Chelles (Paris), Pierre de Montereau (Paris), Erwin von Steinbach (Strasbourg), and praises their works.

About Strasbourg he says: "L'on ne voit guère d'édifices gothiques plus grands ni mieux construits . . . la tour . . . ce qui ne peut sans doute passer que pour merveilleux, sur tout lors qu'on en connois la délicatesse." Delicacy, from what he said in his preface, cannot be construed as unconditional praise—but in any case he does praise. The description that follows is factual and dry. He does not fail to mention "Jean Hilts" [*sic*], who continued the tower. It was completed "par un Architecte Suabe dont on ne sait point le nom."[17]

Eleven years later he wrote more fully that modern Gothic was still employed for a long time in Italy, because through the centuries people had become accustomed to this manner "which made the edifices appear light, delicate, and of an astonishing daring of structure. Among a considerable number of great churches constructed in this manner in various parts of Europe there are ancient ones that lacked neither solidity nor beauty." This is no mere repetition of what he had already said, for *beauté* is a far greater concession. He goes on to say that the state of preservation of these churches is also admired by the architects, not only because of good construction, but also "because of some main proportions (*proportions générales*) that can be found in them." And now comes the inevitable remark: they are opposed to Nature; "some [the Romanesque] have retained something of the rustic crudeness (*rusticité*) of the dens and caverns that the Northern peoples once inhabited,

tectes, Paris, 1687. There is confusion about the authorship because later editions of this work appeared together with the book of the father, André, *Entretiens sur les vies . . . des Peintres*, and the Christian names were omitted.

[17] The tower octagon of Strasbourg was erected by Ulrich von Ensingen (1399-1419), the spire by Johannes Hültz (1420-1439).

and the others [the Gothic] share in the lightness of the foliage of the trees that one finds in the woods or that the inhabitants of temperate climes create [plant?] themselves in order to provide shade in open country."[18] Here, by analogy to the forest theory of Gothic, a troglodyte theory of Romanesque has been invented, and the forest theory itself enlarged by a derivation from deforested regions.

After so much imagination, Félibien's understanding of the statics of vaults is all the more surprising: "The use of stilted arches and of ribs served to diminish the thrust of the vaults, and also was a cause of substantially reducing their weight and thickness."[19] In the literature on the subject this seems to be the first proof of a proper comprehension of the mechanical side of Gothic. Immediately thereafter, the author relapses into the prevailing opinion of the day, saying that the Gothic architects justified their principles on grounds that no one could refute because in that ignorant period Vitruvius had not yet been rediscovered.

Félibien concludes his remarks with a judgment on Late Gothic that blocked the way to an understanding of it for centuries to come. He declares that Gothic destroyed itself. Its good principles were overwhelmed "in the confused amassing of an infinite multitude of ornaments, and in an unrestrained daring of execution."[20] Its last works became *filigree*; they completely lost "la simplicité, l'ordonnance," and even "la solidité." From this it must be concluded that in Félibien's opinion Gothic, "dans la meilleur manière du goût," had both simplicity and order, qualities that were otherwise only conceded to antiquity. But it is certain that he did not intend to say this. It was only that High Gothic (though he did not yet have the term), compared with the

[18] Jean François Félibien, *Les Plans et les Description de deux des plus belles maisons de campagne de Pline le consul, avec des remarques sur tous ces bâtiments et une dissertation touchant l'architecture antique et l'architecture gothique*, Paris, 1699. In the edition at hand, London, 1707, pp. 116ff.: "qui faisoit paroitre les édifices legers, délicats, et d'une hardiesse de travail capable de donner de l'étonnement. Entre un nombre considerable de grandes Églises construites de cette manière en divers endroits de l'Europe, il y en a d'anciennes qui ne manquent ni de solidité ni de beauté. On en voit qui se sont conservées jusqu'à nos jours aussi entières que si l'on achevoit de les bâtir: et ces mêmes Églises sont encore souvent admirées des plus habiles Architectes, non seulement par leur bonne construction, mais aussi par quelque proportions générales qui s'y trouvent. . . . Les uns [the Romanesque] ont retenue quelque chose de la rusticité des antres et des cavernes, que des peuples septentrionaux habitoient autrefois; et les autres [the Gothic] participent de la legerté de ces feuillées d'arbres qu'on rencontre dans les bois, ou que des habitants des climats temperez font eux-mêmes, pour se donner de-l'ombre en rase campagne."

[19] *Ibid.*, p. 119: "L'usage des arcs surhaussez et des ogives servoit à diminuer la poussée des voûtes et donnait lieu aussi d'en diminuer beaucoup la charge et l'épaisseur."

[20] *Ibid.*: "dans l'amas confus d'une multitude infinie d'ornements et dans une hardiesse de travail démesurée."

rather intricate Late Gothic, seemed to him simpler and more ordered, and in that respect he was quite right.

Félibien was undoubtedly much read. It was a favorable circumstance that his relatively positive judgments on Gothic were interspersed in books that treated questions of classical archaeology with great learning.

Thus a remark of the traveler DUMONT (ca. 1650-1726),[21] on Strasbourg Cathedral may be an echo of Félibien's praise of this structure: "I believe that I am not mistaken when I say that this tower does not have its equal in all the world. The inhabitants of Strasbourg call it also without more ado the wonder of the world *par excellence*. . . . It is a pyramidal edifice of such a skillfully ordered height that one might say its top is lost in the clouds. It is built entirely of cut stone, of which there are scarcely any blocks that are not worked in Gothic relief. It is open-work (*ouvrage à jour*) of such a sort that the eyes can see through it, which, together with the other remarks, produces a wonderful effect." Here are verbal reminiscences both of Aeneas Silvius and of Schad. LE COMTE (d. 1712), a sculptor and painter repeated in his "Cabinet" of 1669 Félibiens differentiation of two kinds of Gothic buildings (1687), the older ones are remarkable only by their size and solidity, the "modern" ones on the contrary exceed in delicacy. Yet he adds two other kinds of buildings, "la manière de bâtir des Sarazin ou Arabes" e.g. in Granada, Seville, and Toledo in Spain, and "la manière qui fut celle des derniers Grecs" a mixture of "goût Antique" and "goût Arabesque," e.g. San Marco in Venice. Le Comte enumerates then through fourteen pages mediaeval buildings from Julian the Apostate until François I. Since it may be the first sketch of the history of French architecture, the errors and lacunes are as interesting as the amount of knowledge.[22]

The influence of J. F. Félibien is even clearer in the case of his brother, DOM MICHEL FÉLIBIEN (1666-1719), who wrote a history of the Abbey of St.-Denis.

The folio volume contains among other things a detailed bi-

[21] Jean Dumont, *Voyages en France, en Italie, en Allemagne . . .*, The Hague, 1699, p. 50: "Quand je dirais que sa tour n'a point de pareille au monde, je crois que je me tromprais pas. Aussi les habitants de Strassbourg la nomment-ils sans façon la merveille du monde par excellence. . . . C'est un édifice pyramidal d'une hauteur si bien entendue que l'on dirait que la pointe s'en perd dans les nues. Elle est toute fabriquée de pierre de taille, dont il n'y en a guères qui ne soient travaillées en relief à la gotique. C'est un ouvrage à jour de manière que les yeux pénêtreant au travers, ce que, joint avec les différentes remarques, fait un effet merveilleux."

[22] Florent Le Comte, *Cabinet des singularitez d'Architecture, Peinture, Sculpture et Graveure ou Introduction a la Connoissance des plus beaux Arts, figurés sous les Tableaux, les Statues, et les Estampes*, Paris 1699, I, at the beginning (pages are not numbered).

ography of Suger, a description of the abbey church, and a good ground plan, drawn by Alexandre le Blond. "The whole work is, nevertheless, Gothic; but one of those beautiful Gothic structures that have been rightly compared to those delicate works called filigree, or to the foliage of trees that one sees in the woods."[23] He develops the comparison with trees in more detail, and cites his brother's dissertation. Then he remarks on the interior light: "Although the church is pierced on all sides with surprising boldness, painting and the thickness of the glass temper the full daylight in such a way that one always finds there a certain somberness which seems to invite that composure of mind so suitable to a holy place. . . . The boldness and the beauty of the workmanship make this structure one of the most important that there are in this genre."[24] This is followed by a description of the nave and choir in very general terms.

Michel Félibien with his favorable, unprejudiced attitude is at the same stage as Sablon, though he is to be taken more seriously as a scholar. It can be said of most of the French authors of the seventeenth century who expressed themselves on Gothic that they thought themselves cultured and learned, but were actually ignorant to a shocking degree. Michel Félibien confined himself to the architecture that was familiar to him; he has not revealed how much he overlooked, even of the history of architecture in France itself. It is not particularly significant that his book appeared in the eighteenth century, for then, too, in the field of architectural history knowledge still remained for a long time at the same stage as in the preceding period. Corblet gives several examples of the inaccuracy of this knowledge.[25] In 1673 Pierre LOUVET (1617-ca. 1680) wrote in a history of the city of Beauvais that the Basœuvre was once a pagan temple, and heathen images could still be seen on its west portal; the Bas-œuvre, however, dates from A.D. 996. Jacques LEVASSEUR (1571-1638) wrote in 1633 that the cathedral of Noyon had been built by St. Médard, and its nave by Charlemagne; the facts are that St. Médard built the first cathedral about the year 532, but this had been destroyed by fire in 676; in the new church that rose in its

[23] Dom Michel Félibien, *Histoire de l'abbaye royale de Saint Denis en France*, Paris, 1706, p. 529: "Tout l'ouvrage néanmoins est gothique; mais l'un de ces beaux gothiques qu'on a eu raison de comparer à ces ouvrages délicats qu'on nomme filigranne ou à ces feuillées d'arbres que l'on voit dans les bois. . . ."

[24] *Loc. cit.*: "Quoique l'église soit percée de tous costez avec une hardiesse surprenante, la peinture et l'épaisseur du verre tempèrent le grand jour de telle sorte, qu'on y trouve toûjours un certain sombre qui semble inviter au recueillement si convenable au lieu saint . . . . La hardiesse et la beauté du travail rendent cet ouvrage l'un des plus considérables qu'il y ait en ce genre."

[25] Corblet, *op. cit.*, p. 6.

place Charlemagne (if the account is correct) was crowned king; the present choir, however, was begun after 1145.[26] Levasseur held to the written chronicles and referred them blindly to the church that was standing in his day. This error is not the exclusive property of the seventeenth century; it persisted down into the nineteenth, and our own knowledge of many non-European fields is still as vague as French information at that time was for France itself.

This fact makes us wonder how such "ignorance" was ever overcome. The answer serves as a kind of correction of the picture shown us by the texts on Gothic. The learned world in France was by no means uninterested in the Middle Ages as such. In the brief "Conclusion" of his long book Edelman has emphasized the fact that the Middle Ages continued to exist.[27] It was a survival in many fields: chivalric culture was admired and idealized; national heroes and heroines were honored, for example, Clovis and Clotilde, the founders of the French monarchy, Roland, Godfrey of Bouillon, Louis IX, as well as Jeanne d'Arc, who was even then considered a saint; the poetry of the troubadors, the *Roman de la Rose*, and the other epics were also esteemed highly; research was carried on in archives, histories of the Middle Ages were written, and its genealogies studied. We shall become acquainted with the forerunners and sources of Romanticism and Mediaevalism in England, but France, too, had a corresponding group of learned and, also important, of unlearned men as well, who never ceased to cling to the old tradition.

This can be seen most clearly in cases where Gothic structures were restored in Gothic style. The chief example for France is the cathedral in Orléans, which was destroyed by the Huguenots in 1568 and rebuilt in the seventeenth century. To go into the history of the construction of this work of posthumous Gothic would transcend the subject of this book. It may, however, be pointed out that here also proposals of a modern tendency were in conflict with those of Gothic style. When it came to the renovation of the transept in 1626, it was recorded: "Father MARTELLANGE appeared before the board and promised to make a design *à la Gothique* for the transept of Ste-Croix."[28]

[26] For the further history of the church cf. Charles Seymour, *Nôtre-Dame of Noyon*, New Haven, 1939.

[27] *Attitudes of Seventeenth-Century France toward the Middle Ages* by Nathan Edelman, New York, 1946, although it contains an immense amount of information on the subject in general, does not offer anything on the question that concerns us here. On the last page, however, Edelman speaks of a forthcoming book that will treat this theme.

[28] Georges Chenesseau, *Sainte-Croix d'Orléans*, Paris, 1921, p. 83: "Le père Martellange

In comparison to this abundance of French comment upon Gothic, Italy is nearly silent. Scamozzi's book of 1615 has been mentioned above. There seems to be silence up to Guarino GUARINI (1624-1683). He points out that Vitruvius recommends a deviation from the right proportions and the "*symmetria*" if the situation (*locorum natura*) demands it. This, he observes, has been practiced by Roman architects, and he continues: "This can also be acknowledged in Gothic architecture, which surely must have been liked at that time, nevertheless today is not at all esteemed, even ridiculed, although those really ingenious men made in this manner artistic buildings, which seen with proper judgment [occhio], even they are not exact in symmetry, cannot be called other than marvelous and worthy of much praise."[29] Guarino Guarini in his works used ribs in most complicated arrangements. He was influenced by late Gothic examples, which he saw in his travels in Spain, and by Mohammedan works like the Mihrab of the mosque at Cordova.

The Spanish attitude to Gothic in the seventeenth century seems as yet hardly to have been investigated. Only one text has come to my attention, and this speaks admiringly of the Gothic cathedral in Seville, though in somewhat empty, rhetorical phrases. This book by Fernando della Torre FARFAN (1608-1671) is, however, accompanied by engravings which show the ground plan, the eastern and southern exterior views, as well as the west front.[30] They are all from the year 1671, thus chronologically somewhat later than the work of Dugdale and Dodsworth, which we shall presently discuss.

The Portuguese literature seems to be without any reference to Gothic, if we can assume that the article of Figuerido is trustworthy.[31]

---

s'est présenté au bureau et a promis de faire ung desseing à la Gotique pour la croisée de Ste-Croix." Etienne Martellange lived 1569-1641.

29 Guarino Guarini, *Architettura civile*, Turin, published 1737 by Bernardo Vittone, p. 7: "Si può anche questo conoscere, e nell'Architettura Gotica, la quale doveva pur piacere a que'tempi, e pur al giorno d'oggi non ê punto stimata, anzi derisa, benchè quelli Uomini veramente ingegnosi abbiano in essa erette Fabriche si artifiziose, che chi con giust' occhio le considera, sebbene non così esatte in Simmetria, non lasciano però di essere meravigliose, e degne di molta lode."

30 Fernando de la Torre Farfan, *Fiestas de la S. Iglesia metropolitana y patriarcal de Sevilla al nuevo culto del senor Reys Fernando el tercero de Castilla y Leon, Seville*, 1671. Cf. text, Appendix 21.

31 Fidelino de Figuerido, "Do Gothico e das Cathedraes na litteratura portuguesa: Apontamentos criticos," *Estudios eruditos in Memoriam de Adolfo Bonilla y San Martín*, II, Madrid, 1930, pp. 583-599. The essay treats Herder, Goethe, Chateaubriand, and several Portuguese authors of the nineteenth century.

8. England in the Seventeenth Century

HUMANISM acknowledges Petrarch as its progenitor. It is tempting to preface Mediaevalism also with the name of a poet, and indeed of an even greater one: Shakespeare. The analogy, however, is only valid with limitations. One does think of Shakespeare's *Hamlet, King Lear*, the Nordic fairy world of the *Midsummer Night's Dream*, and, if one wants to extol him as a poet of mediaeval subjects, above all of the chronicle plays; but he wrote *Julius Caesar, Anthony and Cleopatra*, and *Troilus and Cressida* as well. Shakespeare did not regard himself as the harbinger of a return to the better times of the medieval era, like Petrarch to the better age of antiquity. He stands between the epochs, still with a feeling for Gothic, but yet already responsive to Renaissance. For literary historians, however, his period marks the beginning of the so-called pre-Romanticism of the eighteenth century. Spenser, Shakespeare's contemporary, wrote the *Faerie Queene* in the years from 1590 to 1596, and with this work the poets of the eighteenth century felt a sense of kinship.[1]

But poetry was only one of the roots of Humanism; the second was philology, and here there is a striking analogy to Mediaevalism, of course with the difference that for the Humanism of the fourteenth century the root was Latin philology, while for the Mediaevalism of the seventeenth it was Anglo-Saxon. From the very beginning Humanism adopted a pagan attitude, Mediaevalism a Christian and churchly one. The whole Mediaevalistic movement can be traced to the juridical interests of the clergy as they fought sometimes for and sometimes against the crown. Legal claims could be based only on ancient records, and documents were accordingly collected from all the ecclesiastical archives. Since the language of these was Anglo-Saxon, glossaries had to be composed for Anglo-Saxon, grammars rewritten, and the documents examined as to their authenticity. Francis Junius (born in Heidelberg) came in 1621 to Thomas Howard, earl of Arundel, and founded at Oxford the first Saxonist school, collaborating with Marshall. The charm of quiet, scholarly, philological research with its patient attention to minutiae attracted other men to take part in the work. In the course of some three generations, this group of so-called English Scholars produced a mountain of folios, publications of documents, and chronicles of English history. Once diligently studied by the European learned

[1] Reinhard Haferkorn, *Gotik und Ruine*, Leipzig, 1924, p. 51.

world, this literature was later forgotten completely until it was rediscovered by Douglas in recent times and made accessible by means of an excellent book.[2] Douglas' work is as significant for the understanding of Mediaevalism as Georg Voigt's book is for that of Early Humanism. There would be no point in mentioning by name the long series of scholars of the seventeenth century, even less in listing the titles of their works—almost all these men were gifted with an overwhelming productivity; they come alive only when one learns from biographies of their often all too human characters and sometimes tragic fates. It must suffice to say that back of this deciphering of ancient manuscripts loomed the whole historical past, of course transfigured. Antiquaries read the inscriptions on tombstones and dreamed of noble, knightly spirits, or studied the history of the monasteries and sensed the divine peace of the monks who were such ardent scribes. From the excitement of disputed issues and the aridity of legal processes the way led by gradual stages through linguistics to a fondness for the atmosphere of the Middle Ages. It was not the first and not the last time that a path had a different end from that originally intended or assumed.

Spelman, one of the earliest Mediaevalists, was eighty years old when he acquainted the still youthful Sir William DUGDALE (1605-1686) with Roger DODSWORTH (1585-1654). It appears that Spelman had conceived the idea of the *Monasticon Anglicanum*, but he was too old to carry out himself his plan of a history of the English monasteries in a series of monographs. Dodsworth seemed to be the suitable man for this project, for he had discovered the greater part of the documents and was doing philological work on them. What he lacked was the ability to organize the enormous mass of material. Here Dugdale took a hand, to such an extent that in spite of this division of labor, the ensuing work is still known for the most part by the name of Dugdale alone. The first two volumes appeared under both names, the third was published by Dugdale after the death of his colleague (1654), simply under his own name. To steal a whole folio volume is a record achievement that could, however, not remain unnoticed, and consequently Dugdale is known in the history of scholarship as the greatest plagiarizer.[3]

These volumes were of fundamental importance for subsequent generations of English historians. Every scholar knew them, studied them, and referred to them. Today these folios are also forgotten; there is no

[2] David Charles Douglas, *English Scholars*, London, 1939.

[3] *Ibid.*, the whole second chapter: The Grand Plagiary.

specific work on them from which one could learn whether or not they contain any expression of opinion on Gothic. A superficial examination reveals that the authors concentrated on editing records connected with endowments, privileges, and other, narrower interests of the monasteries. Neither Dodsworth nor Dugdale seem to have been capable of describing the buildings themselves, not to mention judging and analyzing them from the point of view of stylistic history. Yet they must have had an interest in them, for engravings were to supply what they could not say in words. Thus, the *Monasticon Anglicanum* became the first illustrated architectural history of a mediaeval style, although the text dealing with its purely artistic side still remained to be written. In this connection one should remember the illustrations for *Schad's* guide to Strasbourg Cathedral and Crombach's engravings of Cologne Cathedral, the latter having appeared only the year before. But the novelty of the *Monasticon* was that almost all the important mediaeval monasteries and cathedrals of a whole country were presented as a collection in several volumes, and thus scholars were enabled to compare the buildings with each other. There is no doubt that architects had always had this desire. Initial attempts can be noted as early as in Villard de Honnecourt's Sketch Book, and presumably every architect had his private collection of traveller's sketches made by him and perhaps also by others. The *Monasticon* is new in offering not models for construction, but historical illustrations.

The reproductions in the first volume, made by the engraver Daniel King, are crude and even amateurish, but occasionally valuable nevertheless, because they show the state of the buildings in the period around 1655. From the second volume on, the services of Wenzel Hollar were obtained for the enterprise.

All branches of Gothic painting, from about 1250, including frescoes, miniatures, panel painting, and engraving, offer an almost inexhaustible wealth of representations of Gothic architecture, both sacral and profane; only a negligibly small number of them are of real objects. The architectural portrait, if one may call it so, developed as a result of topographical interests. The woodcuts of Michael Wolgemut (1434-1519) may be mentioned here as an example. A survey of this development is still wanting.

Not until the age of Mannerism did the architectural picture free itself of its role as background accompanying the scene of a Biblical or other event, and become independent to such a degree that figures and stories were reduced to mere accessories.

Architectural painting reached its peak in the seventeenth century in Holland. The work done by Jantzen makes it possible simply to refer to the long series of painters he lists, from Hendryck Steenwyck the Elder to Samuel de Witte, a series that extends down through the whole century.[4] We cannot tell from the pictures what theories their painters held about Gothic—probably they had none at all—but their relationship to it was very positive. As painters they were interested in the effects of light and shade created by Gothic interiors and in the silhouettelike exteriors of Gothic buildings. In addition one can assume a historical interest and, in many cases, one of local patriotism. The painters may well have counted on finding purchasers for such pictures because there were citizens who felt they had personal ties connecting them with these churches; many a picture of this sort may have been especially commissioned.

Side by side with interest in the homeland there must also have been a very lively curiosity about foreign parts, for engraving seized upon this field, thus presupposing that people who wished souvenirs of their journeys or who wanted to see what the world looked like without undergoing the vicissitudes of traveling were a good source of income. The best example of such a business enterprise is offered by the German family of painters called MERIAN.[5] The topographical interest dominates to such an extent that, though most of the German and other churches of Gothic are depicted in the numerous volumes that successively comb one countryside after the other for picturesque views of cities, the scale is so small that they seem only like excrescences on the silhouettes of the cities. Large-scale representations of individual Gothic structures, such as that of the cathedral in Strasbourg (Fig. 57), or of the cathedral in Regensburg (the exterior view) or that of the marketplace in Munich with the towers of the church of Our Lady in the background, are rare in Merian's work.

Wenzel HOLLAR (1607-1677), a Czech Protestant, who left Prague after the battle on the White Hill (1620) and went to Frankfort on the Main, worked for Merian for a time. In 1627 he became connected with Matthias Merian, and from 1629 to 1630 he lived in Strasbourg. From 1636 on, he was in the service of Thomas Howard, earl of Arundel, accompanying him on his travels and finally to England, which be-

[4] Hans Jantzen, *Das Niederländische Architekturbild*, Leipzig, 1910. The chief masters are the two Steenwycks, the Neefs, Jouriaensz von Baden, Saenredam, Berckheyde, Nickels, Houckgert, Cornelisz de Vliet, and Emanuel de Witte.

[5] Matthäus Merian the Elder, 1593-1650, and his sons, Matthäus the Younger, 1621-1687, and Kaspar, 1627-1686.

came his second home. Thus this uncommonly gifted engraver, exiled by the religious war, became a traveler through many regions, everywhere occupied in depicting on small-sized sheets landscapes, figures, often in native costume, and important buildings. The number of Gothic structures that captured his attention is surprisingly large. Among his drawings[6] are sketches of the cathedrals of Antwerp, Cologne, Strasbourg, and Vienna, of Westminster Abbey in London, the cathedral in Mainz, and the marketplace in Brussels. The cathedral of Strasbourg he engraved in 1630 (Fig. 51). When he was entrusted by Dugdale about 1660 with the task of producing the engravings for the *Monasticon Anglicanum*, two souls with kindred tendencies joined forces.

Dugdale could scarcely have found a man better suited to his purposes. The engravings represent almost entirely the exteriors of the buildings. Hollar then proceeded to add the ground plans, the measurements of which he had taken himself, and, here and there, interior views, for example, in the case of Lincoln Cathedral, where the piers are not detailed on the ground plan (he draws the outlines of the bases) and where the vaults of the choir are shown in proper perspective, in spite of their complexity.

A selection of names of buildings discussed may give some idea of the contents of these volumes: in the first are the cathedrals of Canterbury, Rochester, Winchester, Durham, Malmesbury, Westminster, Peterborough, Ely, Gloucester, Beverley, Rippon, Oxford, St. Alban, Bath, Wells, Chester, Exeter, Selby, Norwich, and so on. In the second volume are less important, smaller monasteries. The third contains Chichester, York, Herford, Lichfield, St. Paul's in London, Salisbury, Southwell, Windsor, Eton, Lincoln. Not one important example of English Gothic is missing. The despised style began to be an object of research just as much as Roman antiquity.

The value placed upon this work by the learned world can be seen from the fact that two supplementary volumes appeared in 1722, and an elaborate revised edition was prepared in the nineteenth century, in the course of which the work with its supplements swelled to eight volumes.[7]

Dugdale published the monograph on St. Paul's in London separately

[6] Franz Sprinzels, *Hollar, Handzeichnungen*, Vienna, 1938; also Alexander Hirschhoff, *Wenzel Hollar, Strassburger Ansichten und Trachtenbilder* . . . , Frankfurt a.M., 1931.

[7] London, 1817-1830.

in 1658.[8] On the title page is shown his portrait, engraved by Hollar. Hollar's detailed drawings of Old St. Paul's, ground plan, longitudinal section, and so on, are especially valuable because this chief example of English Gothic was destroyed in the Great Fire in 1666. Dugdale begins the architectural history of the cathedral with a survey of the entire history of architecture, starting, characteristically enough, not with the Greek temples, but like the free masons with Adam, who, even in the short time that it was given him to live in Paradise, erected an altar for the worship of God (how did Dugdale know this?), and later provided that his sons should have one to use for their sacrifices. Dugdale next jumps to the Tabernacle, then to King David and Solomon's Temple, after which he speaks of synagogues in general. This forms the transition to Christian architecture, since Jesus taught in synagogues and the Apostles preached in them. Then comes another jump to the first Christian missions to England and the churches that must have preceded the Gothic cathedral of St. Paul's in London. In this survey all antiquity would be left out, were it not for the fortunate fact that the question had to be discussed as to whether there had been a temple of Diana on the site of St. Paul's in Roman times.

This Mediaevalistic history of architecture is the opposite of what the Humanists from Manetti to Scamozzi and his successors had understood by the term: it is the Bible versus Vitruvius. The conception is in itself, of course, not new; it was the normal arrangement of material in mediaeval historical writing. But introduced as it was here into the history of art, it must have had the effect of a protest against pagan Humanism, even of a first revival of Gothic, at least in scholarship. Humanists would have had a right to ask: why then did Dugdale make no attempt at description anywhere? He indicates the chief dimensions, but says nothing at all about the forms, not even about the rough spatial arrangements, such as how many aisles the structure has, whether it has a transept or two transepts, whether the transverse section is basilical, and so on. It is as though he lacked the entire vocabulary for such matters, whereas the Humanists, thanks to Vitruvius, could describe their objects. One should, however, think back to Gervase and, much closer in time, to Crombach.

In spite of all imperfections, these volumes of Dodsworth and Dugdale had a lasting effect. If, in view of the lack of discrimination in dating buildings on the part of French writers (Louvet in 1613, Levasseur

[8] William Dugdale, *The History of St. Paul's Cathedral in London from its Foundation until these Times . . .*, London, 1658.

in 1633), we had to ask how it was possible to overcome such ignorance, we find the answer here: by monographic treatment.

Dugdale's works, including his *Antiquities of Warwickshire*, stimulated other Englishmen to view their native land through the eyes of the archaeologist and with the heart of the Romanticist who savors the melancholy of ruins as a personal *memento mori* and at the same time also protests vigorously against all unintelligent destruction. Beverly Sprague Allen has drawn a lively portrait of such a personality: Anthony à WOOD (1632-1695) of Oxford.[9] He deprecated the neglect of old city walls, rejoiced that traces of frescoes were still visible on the wall of the choir in Dorchester, and criticized the removal of stained-glass windows from Merton College (in 1693). He visited and admired the ruins of Eynesham (1657) and of Malmesbury (1678); he spoke of Westminster Abbey with "awe and astonishment," and called Henry the Seventh's Chapel "a nice piece of embroidery work." All this reveals no particular expert knowledge, but rather an interest that can be regarded as a first step toward future research. The number of such amateurs of native antiquities increased and led to the founding of Societies of Antiquarians in the eighteenth century. In these circles the volumes of Dugdale and Dodsworth must have formed the basis for the attainment of an extensive knowledge of English Gothic through comparisons of the engravings. Since there were sufficient books and engravings dealing with the architecture of antiquity and the Italian Renaissance, the comparison of these buildings with those of Gothic, long since recommended by the Classicists, now became more of a concrete reality. There gradually arose a phalanx of scholars and laymen who opposed the promulgators of classical proportion and harmony, clinging to the tradition of their fathers from a sense of respect or habit, or perhaps also of patriotism. Many of these no doubt became involved in inner conflicts and either began, like Evelyn, by esteeming Gothic to some degree, only to abjure it violently later on, or, like Wren, had as objective thinkers an understanding of both styles, though with a stronger inclination in the direction of Renaissance.

John EVELYN (1620-1706) of Sayes Court, born at Wotton House near Dorking in Surrey a younger contemporary of Dugdale, cannot be counted among the Mediaevalists. He represents in a far more comprehensive way the type of the cultivated Englishman of the aristocracy, whose social and economic status afforded him the opportunity

[9] Beverly Sprague Allen, *Tides in English Taste (1619-1800), a Background for the Study of Literature*, Cambridge, Mass., 1937, II, pp. 48ff.

of skimming the cream off life in every respect. When he was twenty he began his European tour, visiting Holland, Belgium, France, and Italy. His diary is a reflection of his innumerable relationships with people, beginning with the King of England, his attitude toward problems of the time, and his personal interests, for example, his taste for all works of the fine arts, architecture, including landscape architecture and horticulture, as well as his love for music.[10]

The word Gothic occurs relatively often in his descriptions of things seen on his travels, but it is most important, perhaps, that he nowhere uses it in conjunction with a negative appraisal. The scantiness of his judgments is, however, disappointing. A few examples will prove this. In 1641, at the age of twenty-one, he arrives in Haarlem, and writes: "Haarlem is a very delicate town, and hath one of the fairest churches of the Gothic design I had ever seen. There hang in the steeple, which is very high, two silver bells, said to have been brought from Damietta, in Egypt, by an earl of Holland, in memory of whose success they are rung out every evening."[11] He continues in this sexton-like style. But how could such a very young man know much about Gothic? In Antwerp he says this about the cathedral: ". . . it is a very venerable fabric, built after the Gothic manner, especially the tower, which I ascended, the better to take a view of the country adjacent. . . ."[12] He goes on to discuss the unusually fine October weather, the bright sunlight, and his conviction that the moon must be of some such substance as the earth. Of the cathedral in Brussels, Sainte Gudule, he remarks only that one must mount steep steps.[13] More interesting is the entry on Abbéville: "The principal church is a very handsome piece of Gothic architecture, and the ports and ramparts sweetly planted for defence and ornament. In the morning, they brought us choice of guns and pistols to sell at reasonable rates. . . ."[14] It is uncommonly interesting that Evelyn calls a Late Gothic structure "a very handsome piece of Gothic architecture." It is in keeping with his uniform evaluation of everything he sees and experiences that he comments on churches, ports, pistols, all in the same breath.

Of St.-Denis he writes that the church was built by King Dagobert, but later much enlarged, being then 390 feet long, 100 wide, and 80 high, without the roof. It has a high stone tower and doors of brass. He speaks in detail of the royal tombs and of the church treasure,

[10] Austin Dobson, *The Diary of John Evelyn*, 3 vols., London and New York, 1906.
[11] *Ibid.*, I, p. 40. [12] *Ibid.*, p. 50. [13] *Ibid.*, p. 54.
[14] *Ibid.*, p. 65.

which was in those days very rich. The relics are mentioned with gentle mockery, but he is scornful of the vases of beryl and agate that he was permitted to measure: one has a representation of a Bacchanalia and a sacrifice to Priapus, "a very holy thing truly, and fit for a cloister!"[15]

It does not seem necessary to quote further from all the passages where he writes of Gothic, but it must not be forgotten that for him Gothic still had the extended meaning that we found in Palladio's writings, for he says of St. Mark's in Venice, "the church is also Gothic." The Lateran Church in Rome is likewise Gothic: ". . . the church is Gothic, and hath a stately tribunal; the paintings are of Pietro Pisano."[16] This terminology, however, was not that in general use. Henry WOTTON, in a book of the year 1624, expressly attributed the invention of the pointed arch to the Goths or the Lombards,[17] thus representing and propagating in England the theory that had originated in Italy. Evelyn presumably did not know this book.

In September of 1677 Evelyn notes a visit to St. Edmundsbury, writing that he had seen "this ancient town, and the remains of that famous monastery and abbey. There is little standing entire, save the gatehouse; it has been a vast and magnificent Gothic structure. . . ." It appears that subsequently he underwent a change of opinion, though it is not clear just when it occurred or by what circumstances it was caused. This turning away from Gothic led to a study of the literature on the columnar orders, and Evelyn resolved "for the benefit of builders" to translate FRÉART's treatise from French into English.[18] This was a work that compared the theories of Palladio, Scamozzi, Serlio, Vignola, Daniele Barbaro, Cataneo, L. B. Alberti, Bullant, and de L'Orme with each other. To this treatise, which was accompanied by handsome engravings, Evelyn appended a work of his own, *Account of Architects and Architecture*, with a detailed explanation of the terminology of the classical orders. In the introduction to this account he indulges in invective against Gothic that combines and surpasses all that had hitherto been said against it.

[15] *Ibid.*, pp. 66 and 67.

[16] *Ibid.*, p. 190. Who is Pietro Pisano?

[17] Henry Wotton, *Elements of Architecture*, 1624, pp. 42 and 44; in the more readily accessible reprint, London, 1903, p. 40.

[18] Rolland Fréart de Chambray, *Parallele de l'architecture antique et de la moderne. . . .* The original text appeared in Paris in 1650. The first edition of Evelyn's translation, *Parallel of the Ancient Architecture with the Modern . . .*, appeared in London in 1664, the second edition, a year after his death, in 1707; a third edition including Henry Wotton's *Elements of Architecture* (1624) came out in London in 1723.

This passage, however, is not found in the first edition of 1664. At that time Evelyn had simply sided with modern architecture, that is, Renaissance, but for the second edition of 1707, which appeared posthumously, he added the explicit condemnation of Gothic. He says that he intends to treat exclusively works of ancient Greek and Roman architecture that would still be standing today, had not the Goths, Vandals, and other barbarous nations demolished them "introducing in their stead a certain Fantastical and Licentious Manner of building, which we have since called *Modern* (or *Gothic* rather), Congestions of Heavy, Dark, Melancholy, and Monkish Piles, without any just Proportion, Use, or Beauty, compar'd with the truly Antient . . ." (page 9). There follows a criticism of their "lamentable Imagry," and so on.

After writing these lines, which were freely adapted from Vasari and which we believe are to be applied to Gothic, he continues: "It was after the Irruption, and Swarmes of those Truculent Peoples from the North; the Moors and Arabs from the South and East, over-running the Civiliz'd World; that wherever they fixed themselves, they soon began to debauch this Noble and Useful Art. . . ." Then follows a list of some of the mistakes of Gothic: the slenderness and wretchedness of the piers or clustered shafts (bundles of staves), the lack of entablatures, and so on. "For Proof of this (without Travelling far abroad) I dare Report myself to any Man of Judgment, and that has the least Taste of Order and Magnificence: If after he has looked a while upon King Henry the VII's chapel at Westminster; Gaz'd on its sharp Angles, Jetties, Narrow Lights, lame Statues, Lace and other Cut-work and Crinkle Crankle; and shall then turn his Eyes on the Banqueting-House built at Whitehall by Inigo Jones, after the Antient manner; or on what his Majesty's present Surveyor, Sir Christopher Wren, has lately advanc'd at St. Paul's. [There follows a list of other buildings by Wren.] I say, let him well consider, and compare them judiciously, without Partiality and Prejudice; and then Pronounce, which of the two Manners strikes the Understanding as well as the eye with the more Majesty, and solemn Greatness. . . ." We do not need to read further, for it is clear what the decision must be. But Evelyn is still not satisfied. Once more he begins to blame Gothic, and this time he really means Gothic, with its sharp pointed arches, and pinnacles, thickly set with monkeys and chimeras. He enumerates the buildings that are "not worthy of the name of architecture"—one hears again an echo of Vasari—beginning in England with Westminster, Canterbury, Salisbury, and all the great cathedrals, including Lincoln and

Durham, but continuing with Utrecht, Haarlem, Antwerp, Strasbourg, Basel, then Amiens, Paris, Rouen, Tours, Lyons, Milan, Venice, Florence, "nay Rome herself," Burgos, Seville, the Alhambra in Granada; next, to our astonishment, come S. Sophia in Constantinople and the Temple of the Sepulcher in Jerusalem. After these he becomes even more inclusive and mentions the palace of the Zerif in Morocco and the gloomy cells (monasteries) built in all these places by Christians, Greeks, Latins, Armenians, and Moors; finally, the long rhetorical sequence of thought ends with the words: "and compare them (almost numberless as they are) with One St. Peter's at Rome only," though he goes on nevertheless to point to Naples, Florence, the Escorial, Paris, Amsterdam, and to "Bramante, Raphael, Michelangelo, Palladio (Bernini), and other Heroes and Masters of our Parallel." Evelyn shows here that he knows the world, that he has had a classical education, and that he is, therefore, justified in judging. It is incidentally worth noting that he puts the name of Bernini in parentheses, presumably because he is not mentioned in Fréart's *Parallel*. These heroes "Recover'd and even Raised this Art to Life again . . . after so tedious and dismal a Night of Ignorance and Superstition, in which Architecture had lain buried in Rubbish. . . ." It was not merely a matter of strength, he says, for the Gothic buildings stand fast, also not one of mere utility, but a matter of proportion, order, and beauty.[19]

Evelyn does not actually say anything new, but he turned with the old calumny to a new public, to English readers, that is, to those English readers who still remained faithful to Gothic; he contributed to an intensification of the differences between the two camps. Those who were cultivated enough to read Evelyn's book concurred in his judgment; on the other hand, those who were not accustomed to consult theoretical books on columnar orders remained true to the Gothic tradition of their fathers. There can also be seen here clearly the gulf between social classes that we found in Serlio and then in Bologna in the sixteenth century. The difference is that now there began to be also a scholarly comprehension of Gothic.

Ten years before he published his treatise on architecture, in 1654, Evelyn became acquainted with Christopher WREN (1632-1723), then twenty-two years old. "After dinner, I visited that miracle of a youth, Mr. Christopher Wren, nephew to the Bishop of Ely."[20] Much later, they both inspected the dilapidated cathedral of London, St. Paul's, in the company of a commission of experts, and concurred in their judg-

[19] Cf. text, Appendix 22.

[20] Evelyn, *op.cit.*, II, p. 77.

ments. Contrary to the opinion that deviations from the verticality of the walls had been intentional, they both declared that it was a question of the settling of the foundations. They also found the tower over the crossing to be badly decayed, and proposed that a cupola be substituted for it, "a form of church-building not as yet known in England, but of wonderful grace."[21] What was then still standing after the removal of the upper part (in the year 1651) Evelyn calls "very mean." This inspection took place on August 27, 1666; on September 2 the Great Fire broke out in the city, destroying St. Paul's also in its course.

Wren was a distinguished spirit, of unusual versatility and productivity, esteemed by everyone. He was an important mathematician, an expert in contemporary theories in the natural sciences, and a scholar who had original results to contribute in almost all fields of research. In accordance with his comprehensive education and as an adherent of the church, being also a clergyman's son, he had grown up in the atmosphere of the Mediaevalists, as far as his interests in political and intellectual history were concerned. He belongs to the younger generation of Mediaevalists, and is approximately one generation younger than Dugdale. What we learn from his writings is undoubtedly the fruit of his own thought; it became the dogma of his social circles, that is, the uppermost level of educated men in England. Wren was also a Member of Parliament.

As a Mediaevalist he was not entirely hostile to Gothic. He rebuilt Gothic churches in their original style, and after the Great Fire in 1666 followed mediaeval tradition to some extent in many London buildings. But he preferred to build in the "modern" manner, and became the chief exponent of English Baroque, in so far as this stylistic designation is applicable to English architecture. His buildings are not to be discussed here, only his writings on the subject of architecture.

Three of Wren's professional reports have been preserved that concern the conservation of monuments: one on Old St. Paul's in London from the year 1666, one on the cathedral in Salisbury from 1668, and finally one on Westminster Abbey from 1713. All are characterized by clarity and expert knowledge. In addition, there has also been preserved an unfinished essay on the aesthetics of architecture.[22]

21 *Ibid.*, p. 251: "When we came to the steeple, it was deliberated whether it were not well enough to repair it only on its old foundation, with reservation to the four pillars; this Mr. Chicheley and Mr. Pratt were also for, but we totally rejected it, and persisted that it required a new foundation, not only in regard of the necessity, but for that the shape of what stood was very mean, and we had a mind to build it with a noble cupola, a form of church-building not as yet known in England, but of wonderful grace."

22 All these rather long texts can be found in James Elmes, *Memoires of the Life of Sir*

The report of 1666 on the state of St. Paul's proposes that the greater portion of the Gothic structure then still standing should be rebuilt "after a good Roman manner," without following "the Gothic rudeness of the old design." However, in the same report he wrote: ". . . to deviate from the whole form would be to run into a disagreeable mixture, which no person of good taste could relish."[23] These words refer to his design for the restoration of the tower over the crossing. That he at least enunciated this principle of conservation with regard to ancient monuments is a tribute to his objectivity; like Bramante and Leonardo, he is a forerunner of the historically-minded conservationists of the nineteenth century. When the Gothic church of St. Paul was destroyed in the Great Fire shortly after the report of 1666 had been made, Wren was given a free hand. He no longer needed to restore, but could build afresh on new foundations, realizing his idea of a modern domed structure "after a good Roman manner."[24]

His report on the state of Salisbury Cathedral, written in 1668, begins by praising: "The whole pile is large and magnificent, and may be justly accounted one of the best patterns of architecture in the age wherein it was built."[25] Then there is a good description emphasizing the fact that the flying buttresses are concealed under the roof of the aisles. This roof rises almost as sharply as the angle of an equilateral triangle. "The whole church is vaulted with chalk between arches and cross springers only, after the ancienter manner, without orbs and tracery. . . ."[26] The upper part of the tower over the crossing he recognizes as the work of a later master. Then he speaks of the arcades, the proportions of which he finds good; he also praises the absence of tracery in the windows, "which was the ill fashion of the next following age: our artist knew better, that nothing could add beauty to light. . . ."

Of the slender engaged shafts that can bear nothing he remarks that they "are only added for ornament," a statement that can easily be un-

---

Christopher Wren, London, 1823, p. 255, and appendix, p. 104. The essay on aesthetics of architecture is reprinted there in the appendix, p. 118.

23 *Op.cit.*, p. 188.

24 There are, as a matter of fact, connections between St. Paul's in London and Val-de-Grâce in Paris, begun by Fr. Mansart in 1645 and finished in 1666, exactly when Old St. Paul was destroyed.

25 The complete text is reprinted in Elmes, *op.cit.*, p. 255. For parts of it cf. Appendix 23.

26 According to *Webster's Dictionary* (1934), the word orb cannot be explained with absolute certainty, but it probably means a member of a blind arcade, or blind tracery. In the following sentence Wren applies the word tracery to figured vaults; "orbs and tracery" in Salisbury is an obvious reference to the lack of both tracery and ridge ribs, tiercerons, etc. in the vaults.

derstood, although such shafts are not ornaments or decoration in the same sense as, for instance, the foliage of a capital. This terminology is, however, still common even today. Wren then criticizes some faults: first of all, the foundations; and second, that the floor was not raised above the level of inundations. There are matters of statics that he discusses very intelligently, for example, the use of metal braces, and the buttressing throughout. Wren restored the edifice, and it is probably owing to him alone that the steep spire of the tower over the crossing has lasted so long.

The third report, *On the State of Westminster Abbey*, addressed to the Bishop of Rochester in 1713,[27] is even more important. Like a modern historian of art, Wren gives a complete history of the building, the details of which it is not our concern here to correct. He declined to believe that an ancient temple of Apollo once stood on the site, because not one single ancient fragment had been turned up, though he had renewed all the foundations. He declares it a fable that after the alleged destruction of this temple by an earthquake King Lucius built a small church in A.D. 170. Not until Sebert, King of the East Saxons, does the real history begin. He built a monastery in 605, which was destroyed by the Danes and restored by King Edgar (944-975). Examples of this type of architecture are still to be found, Wren says, and from them can be judged what the ancient monastery was like.

This all sounds like modern critical scholarship, and Wren cannot be blamed for the fact that mistakes crept in. This tendency toward strict accuracy can be explained only on the basis of the historical-philological research, which then was new. It is quite like an official record when, in the case of the restoration or possible complete rebuilding under King Edgar, he cites a publication in which the mediaeval account could be found: a work by Camden in 1606. He gives the actual text in Latin and then in English translation. Dugdale had already called attention to Camden, but Wren was the first to examine the text critically.

Then he takes up the new Westminster Abbey of 1220,[28] and here his theory of Gothic is introduced: "This we now call the Gothic manner of architecture (so the Italians called what was not after the Roman style), though the Goths were rather destroyers than builders; I think it should with more reason be called the Saracen style, for these people

[27] Elmes, *op.cit.*, the Report on Westminster Abbey, appendix, p. 104 (from *Parentalia*, 1750, p. 296, the work of Wren's grandson, Christopher Wren the younger).

[28] The exact date is 1245, see W. R. Lethaby. *Westminster Abbey, Re-examined*, London, 1925, p. 38.

wanted neither arts nor learning: and after we in the west lost both, we borrowed again from them, out of their Arabic books, what they with great diligence had translated from the Greeks."[29] We do not need to discuss Wren's subsequent characterization of Islamic architecture. He then continues: "The crusado [*sic*] gave us an idea of this form, after which King Henry built his church, but not by model well digested at first; for, I think, the chapels without the aisles were an afterthought. . . ."[30] This is followed by an analysis of the fabric of Westminster Abbey according to the phases of Gothic style! He continues: "The Saracen mode of building, seen in the East, soon spread over Europe, and particularly in France, the fashions of which nation we affected to imitate in all ages, even when we were at enmity with it. Nothing was thought magnificent that was not high beyond measure, with the flutter of arch-buttresses, so we call the sloping arches that poise the higher vaulting of the nave."[31] He criticizes the flying buttresses: "The Romans always concealed their butments, whereas the Normans thought them ornamental."[32] This is to be understood from the point of view of the Italian dogma, but it expresses in 1713 what was asserted anew in 1899 and then in 1928. This, too, must be qualified, for Wren says that the flying buttresses were exposed to the weather and their corrosion resulted in the collapse of the vaults. Thus, he did not mean that the flying buttresses were *merely ornamental*; they were both "ornamental" and *statically necessary*.

For the problems of the nineteenth and twentieth centuries the following statement of Wren's is interesting: "Pinnacles are of no use and as little ornament. The pride of a very high roof raised above reasonable pitch is not for duration, for the lead is apt to slip. . . ."[33] From the further context a few more important passages may be cited: "I have yet said nothing of the King Henry the Seventh's Chapel, a nice embroidered work. . . ."[34] Thus, seventeen years after Evelyn's verdict and seven years after Félibien's, he shows appreciation of later Gothic. "I have made a design which will not be very expensive, but light, and still in the Gothic form, and of a style with the rest of the structure, which I would strictly adhere to throughout the whole intention: to deviate from the whole form would be to run into a disagreeable mixture, which no person of a good taste could relish."[35] Here he repeats what he had said in his report of 1666.[35a] Still a third

[29] Elmes, *op.cit.*, p. 107.
[30] *Ibid.*, p. 108.
[31] *Ibid.*, p. 110.
[32] *Ibid.*, p. 110.
[33] *Ibid.*, p. 110.
[34] *Ibid.*, p. 112.
[35] *Ibid.*, p. 116.
[35a] Cf. note 23 above.

passage that may be cited is interesting, not to say amusing, because of its rationalism: "The angles of pyramids in the Gothic architecture were usually enriched with the flower the botanists call *calceolus*, which is a proper form to help workmen to ascend on the outside to amend any defects, without raising large scaffolds upon every slight occasion: I have done the same, being of so good use, as well as agreeable ornament."[36] One can almost hear Viollet-Le-Duc! Ornament is only justified when it has a practical purpose.

Evelyn had referred to the Saracens, that is, the Moors and Arabs. Wren knew this treatise, for it was dedicated to him: "to my most honoured friend, Sir Christopher Wren, K^{t}." Since Wren introduces his theory as though it were his own creation, it may be assumed that he had discussed the problem orally with his older friend, Evelyn, before 1707. We must try to understand this Saracen theory of Gothic, which seems to be founded on nothing at all. From now on it takes its place beside the old barbarian and forest theories. It might be supposed that a derivation from the treeless deserts of Arabia would eliminate the forest theory, but both ideas lived on in peaceful juxtaposition, sometimes even in combination.

Evelyn had alluded to Granada and "the Temple of the Sepulchre in Jerusalem"; perhaps he did not mean the Church of the Holy Sepulcher but the Dome of the Rock, which has pointed arches. My assumption that he had in mind at the time Wren's oral remarks leads to the further idea that the conversation must have turned on the question of the origin of Gothic. Because the pointed arch was regarded as Gothic's most flagrant sin, ever since the appearance of Renaissance on the scene, the question of the origin of Gothic was merged with that of the origin of the pointed arch. Increasing knowledge of architectures, including those outside the Christian orbit, inevitably led to the discovery that the Mohammedans had employed the pointed arch even before the French. The conclusion was thus not far to seek that the Frankish knights must have seen pointed arches in Jerusalem in 1099 and now wanted to see them constructed at home also. This interpretation of Wren's Saracen theory reveals as a motivating factor the demand for historical continuity. Wren's contemporary, Newton, made the statement: "Hypotheses non fingo." Wren perhaps knew that his thesis was only a hypothesis, but he may well have thought that it followed inevitably from the facts.

Our present estimate of the pointed arch as the characteristic feature

36 *Ibid.*, p. 116.

of Gothic is a different one, especially with regard to the early stages of this style in Normandy and England. It seems to us that the decisive step was the introduction of the rib into the quadripartite vault, even before the latter was combined with pointed arches, and the earliest authenticated ribbed vaults in Durham precede the First Crusade by three years. Wren, however, did not ask about the derivation of ribs, but about the origin of the pointed arch, because to him this seemed the distinguishing basic form of Gothic. Our modern knowledge, on the other hand, has made it clear that the pointed arch was not combined with the ribbed vault until some two generations after the First Crusade. A more detailed critique of Wren's thesis, together with an exposition of the chronology of ribs and pointed arches, can be omitted here, as it was when the same subject was touched upon in the chapter on Gothic culture.

Wren, of course, was not entirely immune to the prejudice of his age against Gothic. In his expertise of Old St. Paul's in 1666 he criticizes Gothic not merely because of poor statics, but because of poor proportions as well: the nave is too long and too high. Anyone who tries to explain the concept of "*Kunstwollen*" by that of volition can derive support from the judgments of all these enemies of Gothic. On the basis of their own artistic will, that of Gothic was completely unintelligible. They judged Gothic cathedrals according to the norm of the Greek temple or the standard of Palladian churches. They acted as though the mediaeval architects really *should* have and *would* have built Greek temples had it not been that they were unfortunately *unable* to do so before Vitruvius was rediscovered.[37] Thus all such condemnations of Gothic suffer from this fundamentally false prejudice, together with the inability to recognize the artistic will of Gothic as justified in itself; Wren's was no exception, however much he strove to comprehend Gothic.

Although he was infected by the common prejudice, he remained surprisingly objective. In his capacity as architect and physicist he was interested in the statics of Gothic buildings, and for this reason he outlined for himself a theory on the statics of Gothic piers with accompanying diagram (text fig. 2). The passage reads: "Let ABC be an arch resting at C against an immovable wall KM, but at A upon a pillar AD, so small as to be unable to be a sufficient butment to the pressure of the arch [that is, of half the arch] AB: what is then to be

[37] However, in my opinion Riegl meant something else by his concept of *Kunstwollen*; cf. below p. 628ff.

done? I cannot add [an abutment against the nave] FG to it to make it a butment, but I build up E so high, as by addition of weight, to establish it so firm as if I had FG to it to make it a butment: it need not be inquired how much E must be, since it cannot exceed, provided AD be sufficient to bear the weight imposed upon it; and this is the reason why, in all Gothick fabricks of this form, the architects were wont to build towers or steeples in the middle, not only for ornament, but to confirm the middle pillars against the thrust of the several rows of arches, which force against them every way."[38]

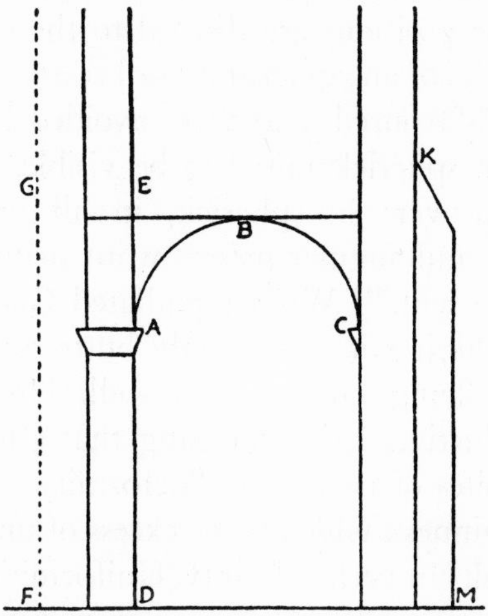

2. Wren's Diagram for the Statics of Gothic Piers (From Elmes, *Memoires of the Life of Sir Christopher Wren*, appendix)

This theory, that a pillar gains in stability if it is vertically weighted, occurs again later in Viollet-Le-Duc. Whether he adopted it from Wren or whether there existed a continuous tradition in the literature on mechanics, particularly on structural mechanics, has still to be investigated.

The fragment that has been preserved of Wren's architectural aesthetics is in many respects unusually interesting,[39] but we shall discuss here only the passages relating to Gothic.

One begins with the thesis that geometrical figures are more beautiful than irregular ones: "in this all consent as to a law of Nature." [The use of the word geometrical as a synonym for "regular"

[38] Elmes, *op.cit.*, p. 115 (of the appendix).
[39] *Ibid.*, p. 119ff. (of the appendix).

is of frequent occurrence.] The square and the circle are the most beautiful of geometrical figures; next come the rectangle and the oval ["oval," that is, the line of the egg, for "ellipse" is still common today in inexact language]. Straight lines are more beautiful than curved; and next to straight lines, regular and geometrical curves; an object that rises in the middle is more beautiful than one that sinks.

This is a series of classicistic axioms. In the same sense Wren continues: "Position is necessary for perfecting beauty. There are only two beautiful positions of straight lines, perpendicular and horizontal: this is from Nature, and consequently, necessity; no other than upright being firm. Oblique positions are discord to the eye, unless answered in pairs, as in the sides of an equicrural [*sic*] triangle; therefore Gothick buttresses are all ill-favoured, and were avoided by the ancients, and no roofs almost but spherick raised to be visible, except in the front, where the lines answer: in spherick, in all proportions, the ribs answer. Cones and multangular prisms want neither beauty nor firmness, but are not ancient."[40] Wren repudiated Gothic's vital principle, diagonality, exemplifying it in the ugly buttresses, a word that here doubtless includes flying buttresses as well. His aesthetic theory is normative and deductive. It is surprising that after these remarks he says that the opposites of beauty are "deformity, or a defect [lack] of uniformity, and plainness, which is the excess of uniformity." A variety of uniformities results in perfect beauty. Uniformities are best tempered by being repeated alternately, like rhyme in poetry, or sometimes with more variety, as in stanzas. Wren did not notice that the dogma of unity in variety can also be applied to Gothic, for he excluded this style *a priori* from the category of the beautiful by his condemnation of oblique lines.

In the second, also unfinished, chapter Wren speaks of the columnar orders. At the very beginning is the remark that their proportions have been too pedantically reduced to definite ratios. It would thus seem that Evelyn's translation of Fréart's book had opened men's eyes to the differences to be found in the various ancient remains and, on the other hand, in the various modern adaptations. Wren does not dwell on the matter of proportions, but seeks to explain the origin of colonnades: at first temples were built as little *cellae* with an open door through which the image of the god could be seen while the priest offered the sacrifice. The people remained outside, and trees were planted around the *cella*, not only to shade the worshipers in the

[40] *Ibid.*, appendix, p. 120.

southern climate, but also to create by means of darkness a sense of awe and devout contemplation. But the trees died in time, or grew irregularly, or had no room, and, when the temples were brought into the cities, were replaced by stone piers that supported the shadowing roof. This origin can still be detected in the capitals and elsewhere.[41] The same derivation is also employed for the halls of the fora. Wren accounts for the differences of eustyle, systyle, pycnostyle, and the like by the substitution of stone architraves for the original wooden ones (cf. Vitruvius 3. 3).

He reproaches his predecessors with having concerned themselves too one-sidedly with these questions of proportions and ornaments, and of having neglected the "geometrical" problems that are the essential part of architecture. "For instance, can an arch stand without butment sufficient? If the butment be more than enough, 'tis an idle expense of material; if too little, it will fall; and so for any vaulting; and yet no author hath given a true and universal rule for this, nor hath considered the various forms of arches."[42] In the following paragraphs that have to do with the statics of vaults and the drawing of figures to demonstrate the various strengths of abutments, Wren also discusses *Gothic* vaults. Whereas iron hoops were used in the dome of St. Peter's in Rome, the "free-masons" were not much concerned about such ties, because they used buttresses on the exterior of their buildings, as well as pinnacles that could be made any desired height. After a discussion of Roman vaults he comes to the Gothic: "The moderns [here, the Gothic architects], whose arches were not circular, but made of sections of circles, used commonly another sort, where the spandrils resting upon the pillars, sprang every way round as their arch rose. It is not easy to give a geometrical definition, but by calling it a circular inverted cone, resting upon its apex; the middle they filled up with tracery work, for which this way gave them great opportunity of divers variations, which I need not insist on."[43] If I understand this passage correctly, Wren first refers to quadripartite vaults and then to fan vaults.

After some observations on domes (S. Sophia and St. Peter's in Rome) he reverts to the subject of quadripartite ribbed vaults. In spite of the accompanying figures his remarks are not absolutely clear to me; it must be left to the specialists to find the right interpretation. It should only be said, with regard to the theme of this book, that Wren was

[41] Elmes, *op.cit.*, appendix, p. 126.
[42] *Ibid.*, appendix, p. 128.
[43] *Ibid.*, appendix, p. 130.

striving for a theory applicable to all the types of vaults known to him, not excluding a single one out of stylistic narrow-mindedness. He maintains again and again that the dome is in every respect the best form of vaulting, and that he employed it for that reason in St. Paul's in London.

In the work of Philibert de L'Orme, Wren had a precedent for his short essay on Gothic vaults that breaks off in mid sentence. Probably he felt the lack of a theory of vaults in Vitruvius, whom he knew well. From Vitruvius' history of the origins of all building, sketched in the preface to his second book, he may also have gained the courage to deduce the classical columnar orders from sacred groves. Wren was an impressive human being, incredibly productive as an architect, and he may well be pardoned for having derived classical architecture from groves, and Gothic from the Orient (or Spain?).

9. Popular Views of the Eighteenth Century

One result of Humanism was the gradual liberation of men's minds from the tutelage of the church. People began again to think independently, almost like the ancient philosophers—although these, too, had had to suffer persecution from conservatives and reactionaries; men no longer felt bound to every word of the Bible; and thus one may say that there was a consistent increase of Rationalism from Petrarch to Galileo, Descartes, and Newton. After the long period of darkness this augmentation of intellectual light was given the name of Enlightenment. It brought to suffering humanity at least release from the Inquisition of the church and the madness of the trials for witchcraft, each of which had its roots in both sadism and the conviction that the souls of the fallen had to be saved. It freed philosophy from scholasticism, and opened the way for a natural religion. Men believed finally in supreme reason and were yet so unreasonable as to believe that all religion was an invention of sinister priests and still more dubious monks. The road seemed to be clear for infinite progress in the understanding of nature and the attainment of human happiness. In the opinion of the age, Humanism, archaeology, academicism, Classicism, paganism, and atheism formed a single ascending line of development.

While, however, Rationalism, this branch of Humanism, continued its splendid growth, there cropped out Romanticism, following the law of antithetical undercurrents. In their endeavor to prove the rationality of the world the philosophers met a stumbling block in the irrationalities of the psyche and of history, and consequently drew closer to the movement for the revival of the Middle Ages that had been initiated in England.[1]

This interaction of Classicism and Romanticism is exceedingly complicated. The course of the Gothic Revival, which had begun with the linguistic study of Anglo-Saxon, ran from the seventeenth-century writers of English history to the English poets of the eighteenth century, to the English fashion in Germany after 1750, to the culmination of German and French Romanticism in the early 1800's, and finally to the really scientific history of the nineteenth century. There is a considerable literature that treats of this process.[2] Our task here can only be to reveal the various stages in its development, leaving out of our discussion an overwhelmingly large mass of uncommonly fascinating material. Every historian of this movement has his difficulties, because he is often tossed back and forth between two extremes. On the one hand, most of the material reflects such childlike enthusiasm that one is inclined to turn away in embarrassment, as though from memories of similar aberrations of one's own long forgotten youth, or is undecided whether to be touched, amused, or moved by feelings of sympathetic condescension. On the other hand, however, one recognizes that it is a case of embryonic states of a subject that we ourselves are today trying to master: true knowledge of Gothic and its history—but again we vacillate between interest in the transitional character of anything

1 Friedrich Überweg, *Grundriss der Geschichte der Philosophie*, 12th ed., Berlin, 1924, III, pp. 350ff., where this duality of reason and emotion is traced in various philosophers.

2 We owe the first scholarly work in this field to Charles L. Eastlake, *A History of the Gothic Revival*, London and New York, 1872. After a long interval there followed two works by Hans Tietze: "Wiener Gotik im 18. Jahrhundert," *Kunstgeschichtliches Jahrbuch der K. K. Zentralkommission . . .* , Vienna, 1909, pp. 162ff., and "Das Fortleben der Gotik durch die Neuzeit," *Mitteilungen der K. K. Zentralkommission für Denkmalpflege*, XIII, third series, Vienna, 1914, pp. 197ff. An account in popular style (without indication of sources) and marred by nationalistic feeling was given by Hermann Schmitz: *Die Gotik im Deutschen Kunst- und Geistesleben*, Berlin, 1921. Reinhard Haferkorn's *Gotik und Ruine in der englischen Dichtung des 18. Jahrhundert*, Leipzig, 1924, is a basic work. A parallel investigation is the book by Lotte Kandler, *Die deutsche Ruinenpoesie des 18. Jahrhunderts bis in die Anfänge des 19. Jahrhunderts*, Wertheim a.M., 1933. H. H. Stoldt's *Geschichte der Ruinenpoesie in der Romantik*, Kiel, 1924, treats specifically the nineteenth century. Obligatory for anyone who wishes to penetrate further into this development of Gothic is the reading of Kenneth Clark's *The Gothic Revival*, London, 1928, 2nd ed. 1950. Supplementary for Germany: Alfred Neumayer, "Die Erweckung der Gotik in der deutschen Kunst des späten 18. Jahrhunderts. Ein Beitrag zur Vorgeschichte der Romantik," *Repertorium für Kunstwissenschaft*, Berlin, 1928. Supplementary for England: Agnes Addison, *Romanticism and the Gothic Revival*, New York, 1938.

embryonic, and the admission that what appears to us childlike and purely transitional continues to survive perpetually in humanity as the effective force of longing for the irrational. We need not pass over ridiculous elements in silence, but it is also our duty not to ignore the positive side of this development.

In England the movement had, of course, a specifically English character, and in France a specifically French one, but in the eighteenth century it was, nevertheless, essentially European, so that it is justifiable to arrange the sources in this chapter chronologically, leaving national differences out of consideration.

The determination of the beginning of the literary movement that led to the Gothic Revival is to a certain extent arbitrary. Haferkorn is of the opinion that it can be found in the poem by William HARRISON (1685-1713) on the subject of the touching Woodstock legend. In 1706 the poet could still see the remains of the "labyrinth" built by Henry II (1154-1189) to protect Fair Rosamund from Eleanor, his jealous queen. Harrison calls this ruin "a romantick dome," and is the first writer to characterize a ruin by the word romantic.[3] In this case it was probably only a *Norman* ruin, which he termed Gothic because all mediaeval architecture subsequent to the destruction of Rome by the Goths was given that designation. In the poem Gothic is associated with ideas that persisted throughout the whole century: legend, tragedy, transitoriness, melancholy.

Haferkorn was especially interested in literary texts showing enthusiasm for ruins of *Gothic* architecture. One ought rather to consider the discovery of the specific beauty of Gothic ruins in connection with the interest exhibited in the *ancient* ruins in Rome, for it is a matter of transference. Brunelleschi and Donatello, who were the first to study Roman ruins, made their measurements with the practical end in view of utilizing these studies in their own works. Recognition of ancient ruins as a "picturesque" decoration of the landscape is seen in painting even in the sixteenth century and continues through the whole of the next century. The representation of ruined buildings of a nonclassical character was demanded by many subjects (for instance, the birth of Christ), but later acquired an independent value. Haferkorn's establishment of the first mention of a mediaeval ruin in English literature

[3] After Haferkorn, *op.cit.*, p. 56. The word romantic itself is older, appearing as early as 1659; cf. Logan Pearsall Smith, *Four Words, Romantic, Originality, Creative, Genius* (Society for Pure English, Tract 17), Oxford, 1924, p. 3.

must, therefore, be seen against the background of this whole trend.[4] The positive appraisal of both ruins and Gothic was a presupposition for the admiration of *Gothic ruins*, and this admiration was necessary, in turn, for the development of the idea of building artificial Gothic ruins as a garden decoration.

That advocates of Gothic and those of Classicism or Renaissance existed side by side can be proved from literary sources. In the year 1708 Edward HATTON called King Henry VII's Chapel in London "an unparall'd Edifice," "a Pattern of Ingenuity," "the Admiration of all Travellers," and he marveled at "the Incomparable Roof" (meaning by that the vaulting).[5] This was written a year after Evelyn's attack on the "Crinkle Crankle" of the same chapel, and it may be that Hatton's praise was intended as a concealed polemic against Evelyn (though the latter had already died in 1706).

Haferkorn considers that the earliest objective appraisal of Gothic is an observation of HUGHES, who in 1715 brought out a new edition of Spenser's *Faerie Queene* and wrote in the introduction: "To compare it [The Faerie Queene] therefore with the models of Antiquity would be like drawing a parellel between the Roman and the *Gothic* architecture. In the first there is doubtless a more natural Grandeur and Simplicity; in the latter we find great mixtures of Beauty and Barbarisme, yet assisted by the invention of a Vanity of inferior Ornaments; and though the former is more majestic in the whole, the latter may be very surprising and agreeable in its parts."[6]

In France, George Louis Lerouge seems to have been an isolated positive voice. He admired Nôtre-Dame in Paris, and declared the Ste-Chapelle to be one of the most beautiful buildings in Europe (1716);[7]

[4] R. Michéa, "La poésie des ruines au 18e siècle et la contribution de l'Italie à la sensibilité préromantique," *Études italiennes*, Paris, 1935 (N.S. v). Here only ancient ruins are discussed, together with their representations, for example, by Hubert Robert, Giov. B. Piranesi and his son Francesco.

[5] *A New View of London*, 1708, quoted from B. Sprague Allen, *Tides in English Taste (1619-1800), A Background for the Study of Literature*, Cambridge, Mass., 1937, II, p. 60. The whole fourteenth chapter is uncommonly fruitful for the relation to Gothic, pp. 43ff.; also the fifteenth chapter, which treats the Classicists' criticisms of "Gothic Taste," pp. 87ff.

[6] Richard Haferkorn, *Gotik und Ruine* . . . , Leipzig, 1924, p. 49.

[7] M. L. R., *Les Curiositez de Paris, de Versailles, de Marly, de Vincennes, de S. Cloud, et des Environs* . . . , Paris, Chez Saugrain l'aîné Libraire Juré de l'Université . . . , 1716; II, 1723. For later editions see the Catalogue of the Bibliothèque Nationale. Corblet repeated the mistake of his predecessors in attributing the book to Claude Marin Saugrain, who was the editor. The initials M.L.R. are a pseudonym for George Louis Le Rouge (or Lerouge). Neither for Saugrain nor for Lerouge do the dates of birth and death seem to be transmitted. The original text in I, p. 8, about the Nôtre-Dame in Paris runs as follows: "Son Architecture, bâtie l'an 1150, quoique gothique, a quelche chose de si singulier et de si délicat, qu'elle a toujours passé pour

later, in his travel diary, he praised almost all the great edifices of France, occasionally apologizing because they were Gothic.[8]

These and many other remarks yet to be quoted give the impression, when torn from their context, of being casual ideas of individual writers. It is, therefore, well to know that there existed in London a Society of Antiquaries, newly formed in 1707 after an older one had been dissolved (in 1685?). After 1717 it was strictly organized, holding weekly meetings under the leadership of its secretary, William STUCKELEY (1687-1765). Its field of activity was research in the antiquities of England before the reign of King James I (1578-1625).[9] Stuckeley was a physician, and pursued his antiquarian studies merely as an avocation. Even at the age of seventeen, when he began to study at Cambridge, he admired King's College Chapel. Sprague Allen gives an account of his pilgrimages to Gothic ruins, his love for old stained glass, and his sadness at the destruction of so much of it because the ministers wanted more light, only afterward to be obliged to resort to curtains.[10]

The founding of the London Society of Antiquaries in 1707 was followed by that of Spalding, in Lincolnshire, and others in Peterborough, Stamford, Lincoln, Worcester, and so on.

Stuckeley remained secretary of the London organization until 1726, took holy orders in 1729, and in 1740 wrote about Stonehenge. His personality is important for our conception of how the study of mediaeval culture was extended, for he is representative of a gradually increasing group of men of all professions who took the time to visit cathedrals, castles, and ruins in their native land and delve into the history of these monuments. Stuckeley's description of his tour to Northamptonshire with the sister of one of his friends is a rare piece of evidence regarding the way in which interest in the history of art was echoed among the women of the time. This excursion took place

---

la plus belle Eglise du Royaume. Sa grandeur et sa hauteur ont de quoi vous étonner."

I, p. 26, about Ste-Chapelle: "c'est un Ouvrage des plus hardi et des plus admirables de l'Europe. Il semble n'être fondé que sur de foible colonnes n'étant soutenu d'anciens piliers dans oeuvre, quoiqu' il y ait deux Eglise, l'une sur l'autre; ce qui en fait la beauté et la délicatesse. Le dedans n'est pas moins admirable. Les Vitres peintes de toutes couleurs sont d'une excellente beauté. Le Trésor . . ."

Interesting is the illustration of Nôtre-Dame on page 9, showing the place before the façade as it was in 1716.

8 *Nouveau Voyage de France*, 1720. I quote here from René Lanson, *Le Goût du Moyen Age en France au 18e Siècle*, Paris and Brussels, 1926, p. 32. The original text is not available to me.

9 Allen, *op.cit.*, II, p. 53; and Nichols, *Literary Anecdotes*, VI, pp. 4-5, and 136-162. See also Joan Evans, *A History of the Society of Antiquaries*, Oxford, 1956, which I saw only after this chapter was in proof.

10 Allen, *op.cit.*, II, p. 58.

in 1709, when Stuckeley was only twenty-two years old. If, during the following decades, he continued able to win converts to Gothic, those scattered literary observations collected by Haferkorn must be interpreted as evidence of an increasing inclination in that direction.

In this period England is the country that provides us with the most comments on Gothic. Contrary to the opinion that it was a matter of a "revival," Allen thought to prove that it was rather one of a survival of Gothic. There is little sense in quibbling about words; both designations contain some of the truth. What Allen calls survival, however, is no longer genuine Gothic at all, but an attempt to preserve respect for "fallen grandeur" in the face of the more and more exclusive domination of Renaissance and the Baroque style descended from it, or to restore such respect, insofar as it had been destroyed. The texts show a continual taking sides, and it is hardly important to collect them all. A derogatory opinion, even from such a high dignitary of the church as Fénelon, could be passed over, if it did not contain an interesting version of the Saracen theory.

François de Salignac de la Motte FÉNELON (1651-1715), archbishop of Cambrai, was appointed in 1689 tutor to Prince Louis de Bourgogne (the oldest son of Louis XIV), for whom he wrote *Télémaque*, the best known work of his astonishingly productive literary career. In his *Lettre sur les occupations de l'Académie Française* he turns to a comparison of ancient and modern poetry,[11] in the course of which he weighs the desire and the hope of surpassing antiquity. This leads to the following reflection: "The inventers of the architecture that is called Gothic and that is, so they say, a product of the Arabs doubtless thought that they had surpassed the Greek architects. A Greek edifice has no sort of ornament which only serves to adorn the work; the parts necessary for support and shelter, such as the columns and the entablature, appeal to us because of their proportion; everything is simple, everything is measured, everything is intended only for use, one sees neither boldness nor caprice that could impress the eye; the proportions are so just, that nothing seems very large, although the whole may be large; everything is restricted to satisfying true reason. In contrast to this, the Gothic architect raises on very slender piers an enormous vault that ascends to the clouds; one expects that it will all collapse, but it endures for many centuries; it is all full of windows, roses, and pinnacles; the stone seems to have been cut out like cardboard, everything is in light, everything is in the air. Is it not natural

[11] *Œuvres de Fénelon*, Paris, XXI, 1824, p. 259. Cf. text, Appendix 24a.

that the first Gothic architects flattered themselves that they had surpassed Greek simplicity by their vain refinements?" He goes on to say that so also did Lucian think to have surpassed Virgil, or Tasso, Homer. Fénelon's tirade is interesting not only for the persistence of Vasari's statements but also for such striking characterizations as "tout est à jour, tout est en l'air,"—which can be placed on a par with Jantzen's "diaphanous structure." But how could Fénelon imagine that the first Gothic architects intended to surpass the ancient temples?

The *Dialogue on Eloquence* was written during the last years of his life, and was not published until after his death.[12] Here Fénelon inveighs against antitheses and plays on words, demanding simplicity; he attacks the rhetoric of Isocrates. Antitheses are permissible if they are natural, but "to express one's meaning circuitously in order to use a battery of words is childish. At first it will dazzle persons with poor taste, but in the end such affectations are wearisome." At this point Fénelon, the speaker *A* in the dialogue, jumps to architecture: "Are you acquainted with the architecture of our old churches, which is called Gothic?" *B* answers that he knows it; one finds it everywhere. *A* then continues, saying, although the analogy is not made clear, that the roses, pinnacles, small ornaments, and so on, are in architecture the same thing as the antitheses and "the other plays on words" in eloquence. After some words in praise of Greek architecture comes this passage: "This architecture, which we call Gothic, came down to us from the Arabs; their type of mind, very lively and unrestrained by rules or culture, could not do otherwise than plunge into false subtleties. Thence comes poor taste in all things."[13]

Where did the well-read, highly educated archbishop pick up this theory? We know that it originated with Christopher Wren in 1666. Evelyn, who wrote his attack on Gothic at about the same time as Fénelon, if the latter's undated treatise may be assigned to the year of Evelyn's death (1706), accused first the Goths and Vandals coming from the North, and then also the Moors and Arabs from the South and East. It is, however, improbable that Fénelon studied the English translation of Fréart, when he could read the French original, where there is no mention either of Gothic or of Saracens. Whatever was the bridge from Wren to Fénelon, the adoption of the theory by the latter undoubtedly contributed greatly to its dissemination in France.

[12] *Dialogue sur l'Eloquence en général et sur celle de la chaire en particulier*, Paris, 1718, pp. 156ff. In the collected edition of his works, Versailles, 1824, XXI, p. 77.

[13] Cf. text, Appendix 24b.

Countless members of the clergy read Fénelon's dialogue and accepted this dogma, which in its reference to the *esprit arabe* seems to be, in spite of all its mistakes, a first step in the direction of history of ideas. If one considers the matter from the point of view of modern developments in this field of history, one becomes somewhat sobered in the face of the Saracen theory of Wren, Evelyn, and Fénelon, and must ask whether the word *esprit* is not out of place here.

This question will be answered according to individual taste. In addition to the foregoing texts, the preface to the great work by Johann Bernhard Fischer VON ERLACH (1656-1723) should also be taken into consideration:[14] ". . . to those other reasonable and well-intentioned judges, who do not need to increase their own stature by belittling others, and who, therefore, are more intent on improvement than on censure; to them it will at once be clear: that by sundry examples of all sorts of architectures we had in mind to delight the eye of the amateur and stimulate the artists to inventions, rather than to instruct the learned. Although the latter also cannot deny that we have endeavored to observe the truth (which in all representations deserves the highest praise), as far as time, our own expenses, and the nature of the evidence have permitted."

The *Entwurf* has many purposes: "Although those who practice drawing will gain the opportunity of comparing the tastes of the various countries (which, as they are dissimilar in food, are so also in costume and in building), and of choosing the best, and, moreover, of recognizing that in architecture there is in truth something to be said for custom not bound by rules (as, for example, in the minor ornamental carving of Gothic, and in the pointed arches, in the towers,

[14] *Entwurff Einer Historischen Architectur in Abbildung unterschiedener berühmter Gebäude, des Altertums und fremder Völcker, umb aus den Geschichtbüchern, Gedächtnüssmünzen, Ruinen und eingeholten wahrhafften Abrissen, vor Augen zu stellen.*

In dem Erstern Buche, Die von der Zeit vergrabene Bauarten der Jüden, Egyptier, Syrer, Perser und Griechen. In dem Andren Alte unbekannte Römische.

In dem Dritten, Einige fremde in- und ausser- Europäische, als der Araber und Türcken, etc. auch neue Persianische, Siamitische, und Japonische Gebäude.

In dem Vierten Einige Gebäude von des Autors Erfindung und Zeichnung.

*Alles mit grosser Mühe gezeichnet und auf eigene Unkosten herausgegeben, von S*er *Kaiserl. Maj. Ober- Bau Inspektoren Johann Bernhard Fischers, von Erlachen. Auch kurtzen Teutschen und Französischer Beschreibungen*, Leipzig, MDCCXXV.

The work is also the first architectural geography. Plate 5 shows a map, drawn from Southern Italy to the Caspian Sea, the Persian Gulf, and the Red Sea, on which the chief buildings of the ancient world are indicated by little pictures. However inclusive the drawings are, beginning with the fantastic reconstruction of Solomon's Temple and the Pharos in Alexandria, and continuing down through representations of Hagia Sophia, mosques, etc. to Fischer von Erlach's own buildings, there is not a single Gothic structure deemed worthy of reproduction. Gothic is mentioned only in the one passage quoted.

and the like, or in the series of Indian dragons, and twisted dragons [*in den Indianischen Drachen-Zügen, und krummen Drachen*]), in which one can as little deny a people its opinion as its taste; nevertheless, there are in architecture, in spite of all variation, certain general principles that cannot be ignored without obvious ill effect. Such are symmetry. . . ."

There is one edition of this book with the French text only; the first edition had had the German and French texts side by side. Anyone having only the French edition at hand would wonder what was meant by the reference to *toits à l'Indienne*, since there are no Indian roofs to be found in the whole work. The passage reads: "Enfin ils y reconnaitront, qu'à la vérité l'usage peut authoriser certaines bisarreries dans l'art de bâtir, comme sont les ornements à jour du Gothique, les Voutes d'Ogive en tiers point; les tours d'Eglise; les ornements et les toits à l'Indienne. . . ." The translator confused the word *Drachen* with the typographically similar German word *Daecher*. From this can be concluded that Fischer von Erlach did not verify the translation, or did he not know French? The translation is inaccurate in other respects, for example, *voûtes d'ogive* for "pointed arches."[14a]

At first glance, Fischer's tolerant attitude toward all tastes, including even Gothic, seems to be extremely liberal for a man of 1721. The great architect of Austrian Baroque continues, however, in a restrictive and academic vein: in spite of all variation there are certain general rules and principles; thus his broad-mindedness is only a refined gesture. He feels at heart that he belongs to the elite who know what good architecture really is. Nevertheless, he did attempt to give in his folio an illustrated history of the architectures of the world, providing most interesting reconstructions, for example, that of Solomon's Temple, of Nero's *casa aurea*, and so on. He also sketches Chinese buildings (as a result of the great wave of interest in *chinoiserie*), the Imperial Palace in Peking, the Pagoda in Nanking, and the like—but no Indian objects at all.

Contemporaneous with Fischer's work (1725) is a remark of Alexander POPE (1688-1744) in the preface to his edition of Shakespeare: "I will conclude by saying that Shakespeare, with all his faults and

[14a] The original text is in some respects very different: ". . . anbey zu erkennen, dass im Bauen zwar etwas auf eine Regel-lose Gewohnheit ankomme, (als etwan in dem Gothischen kleinen Schnitz-Werk, und in den oben zugespitzten Bogen, in den Thürmen ec. oder in den Indianischen Drachen-Zügen, und krummen Drachen) wo man einem jeden Volke sein Gutdunken so wenig abstreiten kann, als den Geschmack. . . ." Cf. also Georg Kunoth, *Die Historische Architektur Fischers von Erlach*, Düsseldorf, 1956, p. 10.

with all the irregularity of his drama . . . one may look upon his works, in comparison of those that are more finished and regular, as upon an ancient, majestic piece of *Gothic* architecture, compared with a modern building: the latter is more elegant and more glaring, but the former is more strong and more solemn."[15] Here we have evidence showing that in 1725 Shakespeare was really considered "Gothic," even though such parallels did not then have the same meaning that they have in the twentieth century. Antiquity has "grandeur and simplicity"—a phrase that appears again later in Winckelmann's "noble simplicity and quiet grandeur"—but Gothic, like Spenser (1552-1599) and Shakespeare, has its own, quite different beauty, and Hughes and Pope try to characterize it in words: "surprising and agreeable in its parts," "more strong and more solemn," "majestic." The last expression is in direct contrast to Vasari's description.

Such solitary voices can be found among authors whose works are so voluminous that remarks like these are hardly noticeable, whereas, in the case of men who were not so used to writing, corresponding ideas were perhaps far more apt to represent a vital interest. Daniel DEFOE (1659-1751) wrote in the years from 1724 to 1727 a description of "the Whole Island of Great Britain,"[16] in which he praised Lichfield more than all the other cathedrals not only of England, but also of Europe! One has the impression that the interior was somewhat of a problem to him, for his enthusiasm manifested itself "especially for the Outside," where he admired the towers, and the portal with its "carv'd Work and Imagery." No spot is left bare where ornament could be applied. Finally he abandons his attempt at description, saying that it is not an easy task to picture in words the beauty of the west front, the towers of which are terminated by pyramidal spires, alike in height, breadth, and craftsmanship, but so beautiful that no pen can describe them. Defoe also mentioned other cathedrals, for example, Gloucester and York. His approbation is expressed in varying degrees, and it can be viewed as progress that he tries to distinguish individual qualities within Gothic, however subjective his judgments may be.

It is not necessary to cite all the evidence that Allen has collected. Some of it reminds us that in all ages tastes have differed, even when

[15] Alexander Pope, Last paragraph of the Preface to the edition of the Works of Shakespeare, I.

[16] Daniel Defoe, *A Tour through the Whole Island of Great Britain*, London, 1724-1727; quoted from Allen, *op.cit.*, II, p. 60. (Defoe is the author of *Robinson Crusoe*, 1719.)

sharing a common tendency. In the Chapterhouse at York Defoe read the inscription: "Ut rosa flos florum, sic est domus ista domorum" and remarked that this was an exaggeration. A few years later, however, Thomas GENT (1693-1778), in a book on the city and cathedral of York (1730), describes with relish the "antick Postures, both of Men and Beasts."[17] Although the word "antick" is somewhat surprising in this connection—presumably it means simply "ancient"—Gent is, nevertheless, the first writer to judge the much criticized grotesques with humor and approval.

Neither Fischer nor the English authors were interested in making an exact stylistic analysis. For the latter, Gothic was, rather, a kind of movable scenery to the poetry of their day, which, in order to be properly poetic, sought refuge in a world of dreams, in the uncertainties of legend (the Woodstock legend), in the rural scene that brought forgetfulness of the clamor of the world and the disappointments of life (*Lady of Winchelsea*), or in the nocturnal land of faerie. Gothic buildings were appropriate to this atmosphere as witnesses of the past, and ruins as uncanny, gloomy reminders of the transitoriness of all things.

Gothic, therefore, fell, on the one hand, into the role of evocative background for a sunny and beautiful English park landscape, and, on the other hand, into the company of the owls crying eerily in the darkness of night and the ghosts that rise up from graves, while it sometimes became an accessory to the melancholy, magically sweet stillness of the moon.[18] This latter Gothic is more northern and demonic than Christian. When the Enlightenment with its sober clarity thought it had driven everything mediaeval from the field, and was victoriously attacking the church, religion, and God with the principles of pure reason, hard-pressed faith fled into the hide-and-seek of poetry, living on there as superstition under the guise of Gothic.

From this castle of refuge Gothic soon dared to sally forth again cautiously into reality. In 1735 Samuel BOYSE (1708-1749) sang of the ruin of the Palace of Falkland, and provided his poetic verses with two very prosaic explanatory notes. In one he says that those noble persons responsible for the care of royal palaces and other ancient buildings, both sacred and profane, should expend more effort, either by order or in the way of duty, on the conservation of these venerable

[17] Thomas Gent, *Ancient and Modern History of the Famous City of York, and in a particular Manner of its Magnificent Cathedral*, 1730; from Allen, *op.cit.*, II, p. 62.

[18] I. Huizinga, "Themen der Romantik," *Wege der Kulturgeschichte*, Munich, 1930, p. 378, especially the amusing list of themes on p. 384.

remains of the past, in order to preserve them as carefully as possible for posterity. The other states that King James V repaired and beautified this palace, and built that of Linlithgow, both of which testify to the fine taste of that time and are superior to many a modern building celebrated today.[19] Thus the poet demands conservation of mediaeval structures, just as Pseudo-Raphael had done with respect to those of antiquity, and now, even though with reservations, he ranks Gothic buildings higher than "many" modern ones, as Pseudo-Raphael had, conversely, ranked antiquity and the Renaissance above actually the whole Middle Ages. It is important that Boyse speaks of both sacred and profane buildings.

He is followed in his esteem for Gothic secular buildings by an anonymous writer of 1739. This author looks at the subject from the point of view of landscape gardening, that peaceful, bucolic, elegiac component of English pre-Romanticism, and criticizes the architecture of the country estates of the English nobility. He admits that taste is indeed a subjective matter, but goes on to say that architecture in Egypt, Greece, and Italy was not just merely a matter of taste, but surprisingly enough, rather a question of climate. Only when Italian villas are imitated in England does architecture become a matter of taste. "Methinks there was something Respectable in those old hospitable Gothic Halls, hung round with Helmets, Breast-Plates and Swords of our Ancestors, I entered them with a Constitutional Sort of Reverence and look'd upon those Armes with Gratitude as a Terror of former Ministers and the Check of Kings. . . . Our old Gothic Constitution had a noble Strength and Simplicity in it, which was well enough represented by the bold Arches and the solid Pillars of the Edifices of those days. And I have not observed that the modern Refinements in either have in the least added to their Strength and Solidity."[20] This bellicose unknown is obviously more familiar with the secular than with the ecclesiastical works of Gothic.

Amadée François FRÉZIER (1682-1773), in his textbook on construction and practice, written in 1739, devoted a few pages to Gothic vaults, which he calls "Voûtes d'arêtes Gothique," and observes that they are no longer employed, but a knowledge of them is necessary in restorations.[21] After listing the names of all the types of arches in

[19] Haferkorn, *op.cit.*, p. 81. Linlithgow is in Scotland; King James V ruled from 1512 to 1542.

[20] *The Gentleman's Magazine*, ed. by Sylvanus Urban, London, 1739, p. 641.

[21] Amadée François Frézier, *La Théorie et la pratique de la coupe de pierre et des bois pour la construction des voûtes . . .*, Strasbourg, 1737-1739, III, p. 25.

ribbed vaults, he demonstrates the construction of the arches in their vertical, orthogonal aspect. "One can observe an admirable variety of these compartments in the old churches and Gothic cloisters; the most beautiful and best executed that I have seen are in the Monastery of Bethlehem near Lisbon in Portugal, both in the church and in the cloister, where the majority of the ribs are of marble."[22] He rejects pendent keystones as artificial (*situations forcées*) and none too durable. As advantages of Gothic vaults he mentions the ease of their execution, the saving of material, easier transport of the individual stones, and savings in working hours. We know that a pointed arch has the tendency to bend inward about in the middle of the haunch, and that it needs a weight on the point. The pendent keystones originally performed this static function, so that Frézier's criticism of them is unjust. It betrays, however, that his real motive for casting suspicion on them as being unstable was aesthetic aversion.

Frézier's admiration for Portuguese Late Gothic has apparently been overlooked by those who characterized the astonishment of Thomas GRAY (1716-1771) at French and Italian Gothic as an unusually early awakening to the merits of the style. Gray was thirty-four years younger than Frézier when he set forth his opinions in the same year as the latter. In 1739, then twenty-three years old, he traveled through Europe with the somewhat younger Horace WALPOLE (1717-1797); it was the usual educational grand tour of the day, made by sons of aristocratic and wealthy parents.[23] The letters written by the pair were later published. From them can be seen the interest the two young men took in Gothic cathedrals. In 1739 Gray described Reims to his mother as "a vast building of surprising beauty and lightness all covered with a profusion of little statues and other ornaments."[24] Amiens he calls "a huge Gothic building, beset on the outside with thousands of small statues and within adorned with beautiful painted windows, and number of chapels dressed out in all the finery of altarpieces, embroidery, gilding and marble."[25] He writes of Siena: "What it has

[22] *Ibid.*, p. 28: "On peut remarquer dans les anciennes Églises et Cloîtres Gothiques, une variété admirable de ces compartimens; ce que j'ai vu de plus beau et de mieux exécuté dans ce genre, est au Monastère de Bethlehem, auprès Lisbonne au Portugal, tant à l'Église qu'au Cloître, ou la plupart des nervures sont de Marbre." Bethlehem is Belèm in Portugal near Lisbon. The cloister was built about 1540 in Late Gothic.

[23] They stayed three months in Reims, a year in Florence, but, on the other hand, only a very short time in Rome. Walpole became a Member of Parliament in 1741. Kenneth Clark, *The Gothic Revival*, London, 1928, New York, 1929, discusses Gray in detail on pp. 32ff. The second edition is London, 1950.

[24] Duncan C. Tovey, *The Letters of Thomas Gray*, London, 1909, I, pp. 17, 30.

[25] *Ibid.*, p. 17.

most considerable is its Cathedral, a huge pile of marble, black and white laid alternately and laboured with a Gothic niceness and delicacy in the old fashioned way."[26] Other passages of this nature could be quoted.[27] It is strange that he writes nothing more about the statues in Reims and Amiens than that they are small, but one can sense the joy of the discoverer who finds new and uncharted values. He was the first Englishman after Evelyn to admire again continental, that is, *French* and *Italian*, Gothic.

The favorite prejudice of the age, that order was lacking in Gothic, gave two brothers the idea of bringing Gothic under control and imposing upon it the missing order. BATTY (1696-1751) and THOMAS LANGLEY (ca. 1700-1751) were architects, interested in landscape architecture and in rustic architecture, about which B. Langley wrote a textbook in 1747. He was thoroughly conversant with Vitruvius and Vignola, but another side of his nature drew him to Gothic. He created five Gothic orders after the pattern of Vignola's five classical ones. His work is a record of his desire to understand Gothic and apply it in practice, but it also reveals a misconception of the style that could hardly be greater. As an example of heterogeneous stylistic compilation, this book was a forerunner of the style of King Maximilian II in Munich around 1850, as well as an attempt at a compromise reconciling Humanists and Mediaevalists by blending their architectures.[28] If art is form as the symbol of the meaning inherent in this very form,[28a] then that bastard style was indeed the artistic expression of the duality from which many a significant or insignificant man of those days suffered. A travesty, too, even an unconscious one, contains something of the artistic. It is the *homunculus* born of the marriage between Enlightenment and pre-Romanticism.

In France, the spiritual leaders—except for Soufflot—continued to be negative. Charles Louis de Secondat MONTESQUIEU (1689-1755), around 1748, affords a good example of this: "Gothic architecture seems to be very varied, but the confusion of ornaments is fatiguing because of their smallness.... A building of Gothic order is a kind of rid-

[26] *Ibid.*, p. 58.

[27] A complete survey of Gray's attitude toward art including music, painting, sculpture, and architecture is to be found in C. F. Bell, *Thomas Gray and the Fine Arts.* (Essays and Studies by Members of the English Association, xxx), Oxford, 1945, p. 50.

[28] Batty and Thomas Langley, *Ancient Architecture Restored and Improved by Rules and Proportions*, London, 1742. The second edition has the brief title which is usually cited for the work: *Gothic Architecture Improved*, 1747. More details in Clark, *op.cit.*, p. 57 n. 134. His expression "Gothic Rococo" is questionable. Langley does, however, use forms that are in part Rococo. Addison, *op.cit.*, p. 29.

[28a] See below, p. 828.

dle to the eye beholding it, and the soul is troubled, as though presented with an unintelligible poem."[29] Montesquieu was reflecting on the "Plaisirs de la varieté," and that led to this disapproval of cases where the variety was too rich.

In Italy itself, however, where no one took the trouble to reflect on Gothic, the academicians were threatened. Fra Carlo LODOLI (1690-1761) criticized classical architecture *in toto*, beginning with the ancient temples because they were translations of wooden architecture into stone. This method of building, he said, trespassed against truth and would in addition be cursed by lack of stability. The latter argument was doubtless easy to refute. Lodoli like Socrates and Jesus, left no written work, and we know of his doctrine only through his apostles.[30] He presumably said nothing about Gothic, but he seems to have been the first to think that architecture could be judged by the ethical concept of truthfulness or honesty, and to apply ethics to wood and stone. In this he was a forerunner of Pugin, Ruskin, and, in a certain sense, of Viollet-le-Duc and Semper as well. It remains to be investigated whether there was a connection running from Lodoli through Francesco MILIZIA (1725-1798), Francesco ALGAROTTI (1712-1764), and perhaps Claude Nicolas LEDOUX (1736-1806) to the Englishman, Pugin, whose father was French. In any case, the bare possibility that Pugin was influenced by Lodoli justifies the mention of this monk in a historiography of Gothic. It would only be interesting to know whether Lodoli considered Gothic bad because it, too, had been derived from architecture in wood, or whether he realized that it had originated in stone construction and nevertheless—probably—despised it.

Italy remained true to itself all the while. The Milanese Paolo FRISI (1728-1784) is its representative in this generation, though the family Fries or Friss came originally from Strasbourg. He studied mathematics and theology in Pavia, became a Barnabite, was notwithstanding strongly affected by the Enlightenment, and visited France, England, and also Vienna on his travels. In 1766 he published an essay on Gothic

[29] Charles de Secondat, baron de Le Brède et de Montesquieu, *Œuvres complètes*, Paris, 1835, p. 589. The quotation is from the uncompleted and posthumously printed essay *Sur le Goût*, written soon after 1748. "L'architecture gothique paroit très variée mais la confusion des ornements fatigue par leur petitesse. . . . Un bâtiment d'ordre gothique est un espèce d'enigme pour l'œil qui le voit, et l'âme est embarrassée comme quand on lui présente un poème obscure."

[30] Memmo, *Elementi d'architettura lodoliana, ossia l'arte del fabbricare con solidita scientifica e con eleganza non cappriciosa*, 2 vols., Zara, 1833 and 1834 (2nd ed.). On Lodoli cf. Pietro Estense Selvatico, *Sulla architettura e sulla scultura in Venezia*, 1847, p. 454. Also Julius Schlosser, *Die Kunstliteratur*, Vienna, 1924, p. 578.

that has become a great rarity.[31] I know it only in Herder's translation. Frisi begins, characteristically, with the assertion: "Straight and curved lines are the only ones that Vitruvius mentions in his work on architecture and that one sees employed by Roman and Greek architects in their temples and palaces." Vitruvius is for him, too, the architect's Bible, but he has still others of this sort, for example, Palladio, Scamozzi, and Blondel the Elder. He pronounces a number of judgments on the subject of what one may or may not build, and his reason is always that it was done thus in the good periods by good masters, but, on the other hand, was done otherwise in poor periods by poor masters. He never asked himself if his authorities did not themselves need authorization. The major portion of the treatise deals with problems of statics. On this subject he doubtless felt himself to be an expert, but here, too, errors crept in. It is, however, interesting that he, as well as the predecessors that he cites, Belidor and la Hire, was groping toward a theory of the statics of vaults and the springings of vaults. In spite of its title, the essay has little to say about Gothic itself. "Around the thirteenth century the German architects began to avail themselves of all the freedoms of the Goths and Saracens." Frisi calmly amalgamates Pseudo-Raphael's theory with that of Sir Christopher Wren.

Another example of negative judgment is that of Germain BOFFRAND (1667-1754), an influential architect and teacher of architecture. The folio-volume that Boffrand published has an introduction entitled: *Dissertation sur ce qu'on appelle le bon goût en architecture.*[32] Here also Gothic is discussed, and the seventy-eight-year-old master proves himself a loyal follower of Vasari with the exception that he equates the Druids with the Goths. It may be remembered that in 1671 Sablon had declared Chartres Cathedral to have been founded by Druids: "dediée par les anciens Druides à une Vierge qui devoit enfanter." Boffrand informs us that the Druids did not take trees (he means the trunks of trees) as a model, but chose instead their branches and leaves; thus were evolved the ramifications in the vaults. As though it were a new discovery the text continues: instead of round arches, this perfect form, the Druids built *triangle curvilignes*; instead of pursuing the idea of a *solidité raisonable* they went astray in bold and astonishing projects, "as if it were more meritorious to create works that appear to be always on the point of collapse, even though they

[31] Paolo Frisi, *Saggio sopra l'architettura gotica*, Livorno, 1766.
[32] Germain Boffrand, *Livre d'architecture . . .* , Paris, 1745.

are solid, than to build them so that they look as though they would last for ever." Nevertheless, they occasionally employed good proportions, such as are found among the ancients. Then the author indulges in unrestrained censure of Gothic sculptures: "sans goût, mal imaginées, et mal placées." The Gothic churches have been ruined by them, as well as by "des ornements de mauvais choix, et par des monstres inconnues." It must, however, be granted that these architects expended great care on the details of construction, and that their works are solid, having endured for a long time "malgré la hardiesse et la légèreté apparente."

This passage, the only one of interest for our subject, is the most uninteresting part of Boffrand's textbook: it is really a mechanical repetition of things known to every academician of his time. The one statement that is even half original explains the reason why Gothic churches have a beauty of their own despite all their faults (*ne laissent pas d'avoir leur beauté*): they are correctly proportioned as regards width and height, and all their parts are in "rapport" to the whole. Thus Boffrand silently implies that Vitruvius could also be mobilized for the defense of Gothic.

England, however, around 1750, was overwhelmed by a flood of Gothic. Gothic had become the fashion. Clark cites the following comment: ". . . our homes, our beds, our book-cases, our churches were all copied from some parts or other of our old cathedrals."[33] Then there is this description of a ball in 1752 ". . . where the room represented a wood with a grotto, extremely well expressed, and a Gothic chapel, which served as a sideboard."[34] This is the kind of thing that leaves one undecided as to whether to laugh, throw up one's hands in horror, or say sadly: here is indeed the foreshadowing of the nineteenth century. Vauxhall in London (1732), as well as Walpole's Strawberry Hill (1750) belonged to this fashion, which it is not our province to discuss.[35] One should not forget that a Chinese wave swept over English imagination at the same time as the Gothic, and it is important for the investigation of Gothic to realize that the Chinese wave ebbed away, whereas the Gothic settled and grew clear.

[33] Clark, *op.cit.*, p. 60. *The World*, March 22, 1753 (from Haferkorn, *op.cit.*, p. 125).

[34] *Ibid.*

[35] *Ibid.*, pp. 50ff. Good engravings of the exterior and interior in *The Works of Horatio Walpole Earl of Oxford*, London, 1798, II, pp. 393ff.: A Description of the Villa of Horatio Walpole at Strawberry Hill near Twickenham, Middlesex. Cf. also Paul Clemen, "Strawberry Hill und Wörlitz," in *Neue Beiträge Deutscher Forschung* (Worringer Festschrift), ed. by Erich Fidder, Königsberg, 1943, p. 37.

In the wake of the new mode garden ruins arose, made of very unsubstantial material, so that the mock ruins soon took on a very genuine ruinous appearance, and summerhouses, which transformed Gothic passion, force, and monumentality into spindly playthings. But all that did not prevent a gradual progress in the understanding of true Gothic. In 1751 Gilbert WEST (1703-1756) described in a poem the somber twilight of forest solitudes by comparing it with the light of Gothic interiors.[36]

Comments on Gothic from the first half of the eighteenth century could be cited in greater number, especially those originating in England. For the latter, reference should once more be made to Allen's book; of the countless amusing remarks and anecdotes that he has collected, one may be repeated here. George STEEVENS (1736-1800), a Shakespearean scholar who felt resentment against GOUGH, then presiding over the Society of Antiquaries, fabricated a stone inscription to the effect that Hardicanute had died as the result of drinking too much at the wedding of a Danish baron. After this stone had become the subject of much learned discussion and been dated as from the eleventh century, Steevens published the facts about his hoax in the *Evening Post*.[37] Allen remarks that today we attribute such an error to the undeveloped state of the archaeology of that day, not to the stupidity of any one individual,[38] but that then every archaeologist interested in mediaeval objects was considered a fool—at least by the Classicists. Thus the many satirical poems cited by Allen may seem to us silly, but they complete the picture by revealing the opposing side in all its overweening presumption. It must, however, be said in defense of the Classicists that they had a better scientific command of their field than the Mediaevalists did of theirs, for the activity of the latter—with the exception of Soufflot—remained on the whole amateurish. After the *Monasticon Anglicanum* of Dodsworth and Dugdale, there might have been expected a speedier increase in more scholarly stylistic studies. But even the *Entwurff Einer Historischen Architectur* by Fischer von Erlach, a folio which is in its way impressive and which represents scholarship on the "Classicistic" side, is a monument of the most naïve sort of history, if at the same time one

36 Haferkorn, *op.cit.*, p. 84.

37 Allen, *op.cit.*, II, p. 91.

38 Errors, to be sure, are not peculiar to any one age. Around 1915 the historians of art in a German Office of Public Monuments set up a counterfeit crucifix in the sacristy of a country church in such a way that their hated chief could not fail to "discover" it. The embarrassing denouement remained an official secret.

of masterly architecture. With the present state of research in the history of art in mind, including the classical, mediaeval, and modern fields, it would be easy to place both of the hostile parties of that day on the same level of ridicule, for more serious archaeology of the ancient styles did not flourish until the second half of the eighteenth century. As historians, however, we should refrain from mockery, and we ourselves cannot be careful enough in our judgments of art. To examine Allen's judgments would be very fruitful in this connection, and would not imply any lack of gratitude for the wealth of his objective results. He was, for instance, not correct in his appraisal of Rococo, siding in this matter with the Classicists; but that does not influence the value of the opinions on the style which he collected from English writers of the eighteenth century. He cites Isaac WARE (died in 1766) as an example of a classicistically-minded critic who lumped Chinoiserie, Gothic, and Rococo together, and advised any architect whose client was charmed by the mad fancies of Rococo to rely on the sound common sense of the English and say to him: this means reviving the decorations of the Goths and Vandals.[39] Even Vasari would have been astonished to hear that these barbarian hordes had also been made responsible for the elegant art of the boudoir.

Ware's warped judgment should not lead to the identification of this synthesis of Gothic and Rococo with modern stylistic parallels. He does not say that Gothic and Rococo are related styles, but merely that they are alike in value, or the lack of it, to the extent that both are bad, barbarous architecture. In those days there could be no question of stylistic comparisons, because critics were hardly capable even of giving a membrological description of the buildings. It meant much that Defoe spoke especially of portal and tower—Soufflot alone must again be excepted. With reference to the condemnation of Rococo in the same breath with Gothic, it should have been pointed out to Ware that the architect Germain Boffrand, for example, haughtily rejected Gothic, but was a master of the most refined Rococo.

On the whole, the judgments of the period from 1700 to 1750 which are favorably disposed toward Gothic reveal a persistent ignorance of the history of Gothic combined with an all too easy superficiality of observation. Instead of scholarly insight there spread an emotional love for the indigenous, more popular art as opposed to the imported doctrine of fastidious academicians.

The feud between the two parties was continued in the second half

[39] Allen, *op.cit.*, II, p. 113.

of the century. Chronologically we must begin with an article by François BLONDEL THE YOUNGER (1683-1748) in the influential *Grande Encyclopédie*,[40] in which he wrote: The Goths "destroyed the most beautiful buildings of antiquity, and architecture was reduced to such a barbarous state that the architects lost all sense of proper proportions. . . . From these abuses was developed a new manner of building, which was called Gothic, and which lasted until Charlemagne undertook to restore antiquity again." This idea goes back to Manetti (see above, page 255). Perhaps Blondel was referring to various documents from the time of Charlemagne that describe stone structures as "Gothic," meaning that they were built under the rule of the Goths in Italy, perhaps even constructed by the Goths themselves. Blondel could then conclude that buildings *after* Charlemagne were no longer "Gothic." It is, however, improbable that he knew these manuscripts, and even if he did, his confusion would not be entirely explained.

He goes on to say that the Franks, encouraged by Hugo Capet and his son Robert, became slowly active in architecture. At this point Blondel repeats Félibien's theses to the effect that building went first to the extreme of weightiness and then to the opposite extreme of slenderness, delicacy, and overornamentation, leaving the question open as to whether this taste had been imported into France from the Arabs and Moors. For the style that we today call Gothic, Blondel has no name; just as the Vandals and Goths brought the "heavy and Gothic" style from the North, so, he says, the Arabs brought the "light" style from the South. Here we have the clearest proof of the fact that for Blondel "Gothic" meant what we call "Romanesque," while our "Gothic" was designated as "Arabic."[41]

A year later Blondel expressed himself in much more detail in his great textbook. At first he explains the difference between the architecture of antiquity and that of the Middle Ages in general terms: "Gothic architecture is very different from the Greek and Roman that had preceded it; the latter simple, noble, majestic, the former laden with frivolous, poorly understood and ill-placed ornaments; there were Gothic architects who carried things to the ridiculous

[40] *Encyclopédie*, I, Paris, 1751, p. 617, s.v. Architecture. Blondel the Younger also wrote the article "Arc" (p. 593). Here he repeats what had been asserted from Manetti to Boffrand: "The pointed arch should be avoided because it is weak and makes a poor impression." Blondel's remarks on Gothic are insignificant in comparison with what he has to say in his voluminous works on modern architecture. His writings are listed in the *Universal Catalogue of Books of Art* (South Kensington Museum), London, 1870, I, p. 124.

[41] Cf. text, Appendix 25.

length of putting the capitals in place of the bases. Instead of the columns that were introduced into architecture to imitate trees, these same architects alleged that they were imitating the branches only, so that the exaggerated height of these columns was out of all proportion to their circumference, and they exerted their whole skill to erect buildings, which, although they are durable, seem to be rather astounding than subject to the rules of art. In this manner they have treated most of the churches we mentioned, some of which were constructed, nevertheless, with such *lightness* and *boldness* that one cannot help admiring them."[42] The reproach that the Gothic architects set capitals in place of bases applies to pre-Gothic buildings that Blondel includes under the heading of Gothic, for he was probably thinking of San Lorenzo in Milan, where older capitals (classical?) were actually set in as bases for two piers. Or did he allude to the South porch of Chartres Cathedral?[43]

After his general remarks Blondel considers more specific points. He differentiates between an "Architecture Gothique *ancienne*" of the sixth to the eleventh century and an "Architecture Gothique *moderne*" of the eleventh century to the time of François I; the latter he discusses on page 15 only insofar as it is a question of its derivation from the Moors or Arabs. He is obviously following Fénelon, and develops this theory in even more detail, referring to the spread of Arabic philosophy, mathematics, and medicine. The authors of works in these fields were widely read and thus Arabic architecture was extended to Europe: "as a result many churches were built in the Moorish taste, even without correcting what was more suitable for hot countries than for regions with a temperate climate." As an example of this southern, Moorish architecture he mentions Amiens. Such was the development of Wren's idea.

P. DECKER's book offers proof—if there is any need of it—for the continued existence of the forest theory.[44] He provides patterns for Gothic structures. One of them has been reproduced several times in recent literature; it represents the entrance to a garden, with the title: *Gothic Entrance to a Moat*, and is a kind of free standing Gothic triumphal arch with slender forms. It looks as though newly resur-

[42] Jean François Blondel the Younger, *Architecture françoise, ou Recueil des plans, elevations, coupes et profils des églises . . .* , Paris, 1752, I, p. 14.

[43] *Ibid.*, p. 15. Cf. the text in Appendix 26.

[44] P. Decker, *Gothic Architecture, Decorated*, London, 1759. I can find no biographical data on Decker. He seems not identical with either Paul Decker the Elder, 1677-1713, or Paul Decker the Younger, 1685-1742. Or are these engravings by the latter, published posthumously?

rected Gothic had been reduced to the point of skeletonlike emaciation. Through this portal one looks into the garden, where there is a pond and in it an island. On the island is a Gothic "arbor," a decoration for the garden, to be sure, but still practicable. This arbor is built from trees or, more properly, roots of trees; it is hardly possible to describe the shape, which is reminiscent of large coral formations. What does the whole thing signify? When one stands on the shore of this pond, like the figure in the picture that has its back turned to us, no boat can be seen. One immediately longs to be on this blissful island with its fantastic, Gothic arbor, in order there to indulge in dreams. Dreams of what? Of another island with another arbor! Romanticism is longing for longing. It is antirational, opposed to all enlightenment, a dream of "natural" Gothic. The forest myth has become a tame garden tale, and Chartres a garden arbor, in the shelter of which one may long, among other things—and perhaps quite rightly—for Chartres.

This plate 3 of the book is only one example among many. The garden arbor appears once more on a large scale in plate 12, with the title: *A Hermatic Retirement Chiefly Composed with Rude Branches and Roots of Trees* (Fig. 55). In addition, the tree theory is drastically illustrated on plate 9: *Rustic Garden Seat*, plate 10: Hermitage, and plate 11: *Summer Hermitage*. There is no point in describing these designs; one must see them in order to laugh or merely to smile. But some of the other sketches have decided charm, in spite of their comicality. On plate 6 the "Gothic order" in Langley's sense is also represented. In the copy at hand this collection of designs is bound together with an analogous one: *Chinese Architecture, Civil and Ornamental* (London, 1759). It is in part delightful and reminds one of Watteau. Chinese or Gothic, and later, at the end of the century, Egyptian garden decorations were a harmless amusement of melancholy Lords.

The fantasies of Bishop William WARBURTON (1698-1779) on the history of architecture can only partly be regarded as a progressive step in a scholarly direction.[45] Warburton distinguishes between Saxon and Norman. The "Saxon Stile" employs models from Palestine and was introduced by the Templars. It thus goes back to Greek style corrupted by Byzantine. Norman architecture, on the other hand, is descended from the Goths, after they had conquered Spain: ". . . and

[45] Bishop William Warburton (1698-1779), *Pope's Moral Essays*, 1760. I am not acquainted with the book, but found the passage quoted in full by Richard Elsam in *An Essay on Rural Architecture*, London, 1803, p. 13, where it is still regarded as a valid insight.

the genial warmth of the climate and religion of the old inhabitants had ripened their wits and inflamed their mistaken piety . . . they struck out a new species of architecture unknown to Greece and Rome, upon original principles and ideas, *much nobler* than what had given birth even to classical magnificence."[46] In spite of this veering round to a positive appraisal of Gothic—it is one of the earliest—he comes back to the forest theory. Meanwhile Walpole was contributing to the popularization of Gothic in the widest circles through his novel, *The Castle of Otranto.* The story takes place in Southern Italy, in the Middle Ages, and is full of gruesome horrors. The book had many imitations, and ever since its appearance the literary genre of the novel of horror has been called in English "the Gothic novel." Tietze says: "A flood of novels portrays the times when haunted castles, agonizing dungeons, and quiet hermits' cells seem to have been the only available lodgings."[47]

Ossian by James MACPHERSON (1736-1796) was effective in somewhat different fashion, creating vague conceptions of a noble and beautiful past of knighthood,[48] and Hurd assisted this tendency by his studies on chivalric culture.

Letters on Chivalry by Richard HURD (1719-1808) begin with the words: "The ages we call barbarous present us with many a subject of curious speculation. What, for instance, is more remarkable than the Gothic Chivalry? or, than the spirit of Romance, which took its rise from that singular situation? . . . Barbarians have their own [style], such as it is, if they are not enlightened by our reason. Shall we then condemn them unheard, or will it not be fair to let them have the telling of their own story?"[49] Ariosto, Tasso, Spenser, Milton ". . . were seduced by the barbarities of their forefathers, were even charmed by the Gothic Romances."[50] "When an architect examines a Gothic structure by Grecian rules, he finds nothing but deformity. But the Gothic architecture has its own rules, by which when it comes to be examined, it is seen to have its merit, as well as the Grecian.

46 Cf. text, Appendix 27.

47 Hans Tietze, "Wiener Gotik im 18. Jahrhundert," *Jahrbuch der K.u.K. Zentralkommission*, Vienna, 1909, p. 242.

48 James Macpherson published *Fingal* in 1761, *Temora* in 1763, and *The Works of Ossian* in 1765. He claimed to have discovered ancient Celtic fragments which he was printing in translation. This was not the case, but his poetry was unusually rich in mood, and had the greatest influence. Goethe was strongly affected by it (cf. *Werther*, 1774).

49 Richard Hurd wrote the *Letters on Chivalry* in 1762. In the London edition of 1911, pp. 79ff.

50 *Ibid.*, p. 81.

The question is not, which of the two is conducted in the simplest or truest taste; but whether there be not sense and design in both, when scrutinized by the laws on which each is projected."[51] Here, then, in the year 1762, the conviction is again affirmed that every style must be understood from within itself, every critique must be based on the innermost being of a style and not on a point of view, completely alien to it. Hurd's criticism, which is adequate to the style, comprehends—to express it in modern terminology—the artistic volition so to speak of Gothic itself. This idea appears again later in 1816 in De Laborde.

Also in the year 1762 Horace WALPOLE (1717-1797) published his *Anecdotes of Painting*.[52] Here the espousal of the cause of Gothic is even more definite and more objective: "The pointed arch, that peculiar of Gothic architecture, was certainly intended as an improvement on the circular; and the men who had not the happiness of lighting on the simplicity and proportion of the Greek orders were, however, so lucky as to strike out a thousand graces and effects magnificent yet genteel, vast yet light, venerable and picturesque. It is difficult for the noblest Grecian temple to convey half so many impressions to the mind as a cathedral does of the best Gothic taste—a proof of skill in the architects and of address in the priests who erected them. . . . I certainly do not mean . . . to make any comparison between the rational beauties of regular architecture and the unrestrained licentiousness of that which is called Gothic. Yet I am clear that the persons who executed the latter had much more knowledge of their art, more taste, more genius and more propriety than we choose to imagine. There is a magic hardiness in the execution of some of their works, which would not have sustained themselves if dictated by mere caprice."[53] Two words in this quotation may be especially stressed: "picturesque" and "magic." Clark, who, of course, discusses these remarks also, says that one would not today call Westminister Abbey "genteel." He adds, with reference to another passage where Walpole, speaking of mediaeval priests, says: ". . . they exhausted their knowledge of the passions in composing edifices, whose pomp, mechanism, vaults, tombs, painted windows, gloom, and perspectives infused such sensations of romantic devotion. . . ," that this attitude has become foreign to us. Walpole seems to imagine, continues Clark, "that a cathedral is a trap to catch converts to popery. We have

[51] *Ibid.*, p. 118.
[52] Horace Walpole, *Anecdotes of Painting in England*, Strawberry Hill, 1762-1771, 5 vols.
[53] Clark, *op.cit.*, pp. 44 and 45 (1st ed.).

long ceased to associate pointed arches and Churches of Rome, but for years this connection gave a sinister overtone to the solemn music of Gothic architecture."[54] In this Clark is not entirely right. Walpole's characterization contains a kind of theory of Gothic. For him it is picturesque, magical, and markedly religious, and in mediaeval Gothic the latter quality could mean only: Catholic. In Walpole's age of reason and enlightenment, faith and superstition were not as sharply divided as they might have been in 1928 from Clark's point of view. To many of a romantic temperament Gothic is always Catholic.

Walpole, who was as an author and especially as a letter writer always a brilliant *causeur*, and who set Strawberry Hill, with its many Gothic details, before his contemporaries in full, three-dimensional tangibility as a model for the most modern architecture, remained vague when he wrote about Gothic. For him it was an interesting, though questionable phenomenon, which could be accepted dreamily, as one would accept a fairy tale. But when we consider what all these enthusiasts actually had to say about Gothic architecture itself, we never discover more than a few characteristics—"tout est à jour," "poor taste," and so on—and still less tangible forms. Most of the writers cling to the concept of the pointed arch. Frézier, as a practical architect, speaks of Gothic vaults in very concrete terms, but without discussing their relationship to other structural members. This trend was still the popular and officially recognized one in 1762, when Walpole was writing, and it was accompanied by a split in judgment, as if one admitted the achievements of the construction and on the other hand condemned the bad taste.

This is clearly expressed by Anne Robert Jacques TURGOT (1727-1781): "L'architecture gives us an example of the mutual independence of taste and the mechanic procedures in the arts. There are no edifices of worse taste than the Gothic buildings but, nevertheless, there are no bolder ones, nor ones which demand more activity and cleverness (*lumières*) of practice in the means of execution, though these means could not be other than a succession of a multitude of trials, because the mathematical sciences were [still] in their childhood and the thrusts of the vaults and the roofs could not be calculated with precision."[55]

[54] *Ibid.*, p. 46.

[55] Anne Robert Jacques Turgot, *Discours sur l'histoire universelle*, quoted from the *Œuvres*, Paris, 1944, II, p. 666. I owe the reference to Mr. Arnold J. Toynbee. "L'architecture nous donne un example de l'indépendance réciproque du goût et des manoeuvres mécaniques dans les arts. Il n'y a point d'édifices de plus mauvais goût que les bâtiments gothiques, et il n'y en

The lack of concrete comprehension was combined with the attraction to opposite sides. Our generation is able to appreciate antique architecture as much as Gothic, taking the view that both were the expression of their time and are not models to be copied today. The men of the eighteenth century were dependent on the conventional esteem for antique art and architecture and when they dared to side also with Gothic they had a bad conscience, because, as it seems, they took their love for two different styles as a sign of indecision and had to excuse themselves. In this sense this whole pre-Romanticism is a time of transition.

A good example of a double attitude is the poet Mark AKENSIDE (1721-1770). In his youth he venerated Greek poetry and art, the outstanding task of his time seemed to him to be to "tune to Attic themes the British lyre." He despised the Middle Ages with all their monkishness and superstition. In his last years in London, on the contrary, he looked back with longing to his youth in Newcastle on Tyne and the ruins and monuments of old Monkchester. One of his friends reports that he often found him "contemplating with great earnestness the exterior of Westminister Abbey. He would frequently sit, on a fine moonlight night, on the benches of Saint James' Park gazing on the sublime structure."[56]

As late as 1788 Charles DUPATY (1746-1788) wrote the following enthusiastic sentences:

"What mass! What height! What circumference! Is this a mountain of marble that has been carved into shape? It is the cathedral.

"One enters, and at the first glance one's imagination touches the heavens; but at the second it falls, for these Gothic columns are a too feeble support.

"The Goths believed that what was grand was beautiful and that what was enormous was grand.

"What works of prose and of verse we have in the Gothic manner!

"Proportion! It is not proportion alone that makes beauty, but without it there is no beauty.

"They say that nature makes no leaps; art ought to imitate nature."[57]

---

a point de plus hardis, ni dont la construction ait demandé plus d'activité et de lumières pratiques dans les moyens d'exécution, quoique ces moyens ne pussent être que la suite d'une multitude de tâtonnements, puisque les sciences mathématiques etaient dans l'enfance, et que les poussée des voûtes et des combles ne pouvaient être calculées avec precision."

[56] Haferkorn, *op.cit.*, p. 91.

[57] Charles M. J. B. Mercier Dupaty, *Lettres sur l'Italie en 1785*, Rome (and Paris), 1788, I, p. 167 (Letter 34). Corblet, "L'Architecture du moyen-age . . . , p. 18, mistakenly refers the passage to Milan Cathedral. The letter is written from Florence:

"Quelle masse! quelle élévation! quelle circonférence! Est-ce une montagne de marbre,

This is all that he has to say about the cathedral in Florence. It is followed by an essentially more favorable opinion of the Baptistry, and that, too, is full of rhetoric. One wonders what the writings were that he calls Gothic. Was he thinking of Dante? Perhaps literary historians may be able to interpret his meaning. Not only does Dupaty's enthusiasm ring hollow beside the more solid appraisals that were then already in existence, but its weakness is evident in comparison with what Goethe had written years before on Strasbourg Cathedral.

10. Serious Judgments of the Eighteenth Century

THE repeated allusions to Jacques Germain SOUFFLOT (1713-1780) in the preceding section referred to a lecture delivered by him as early as 1741. In contrast to the way Gothic was usually regarded in the first half of the eighteenth century, his views herald a new phase of critical evaluation. All the other opinions of his generation reveal in their estimation of this style something playful, as in the adoration of ruins, or amateurish, as in the case of the antiquaries, or superficial, as in Fénelon; they betray a trace of blindness, like that of Fischer von Erlach, who apparently overlooked St. Stephen's in Vienna, although he saw it every day; or they show a certain weakness, as in the diluted Gothic of the early Gothic Revival in Walpole's style.

In the midst of this atmosphere Soufflot's attitude and above all his expert knowledge bear the impress of an extraordinarily personal achievement.[1] Born in Irancy, near Auxerre, in 1713 as the fourteenth child of a worthy magistrate, he attended the Latin School in order to prepare himself for his father's profession. He left his birthplace, however, on his own responsibility, worked in Lyons as a stonemason, and in 1731 arrived in Rome, where he earned his living as a laborer, using his free time to survey and study both ancient and modern

---

qu'on a taillée? C'est la Cathédrale. On entre, et du premier regard l'imagination touche le ciel; mais au second, elle tombe; car ces colonnes gothiques sont trop faibles pour le soutenir.

"Les Goths croyoient que le grand étoit le beau, et que l'énorme étoit le grand.

"Que nous avons d'écrits en prose et en vers, dans le genre Gothique!

"La proportion! Ce n'est pas la proportion seule qui fait le beau; mais, sans elle il n'y a point de beau.

"On dit que la nature ne fait rien par sauts; l'art doit imiter la nature."

---

[1] Jean Monval, *Soufflot, sa vie, son œuvre, son esthétique*, Paris, 1918. Further literature in Thieme-Becker.

buildings. Ability and charm, together with luck, resulted in his receiving a stipend from the Académie de France. After seven years devoted to serious study he was invited to Lyons, where he built the Hôtel-Dieu. As the architect of this building he attracted the attention of Mme. de Pompadour, who was seeking a tutor in *bon goût* for her young brother, Abel Poisson. Raised to the nobility by Louis XV, Poisson received the name of de Vandières—he was called in mockery "d'avant d'hier"—and later that of Marigny. With this favorite of the court and Cochin (1715-1790) Soufflot journeyed to Rome in 1749 for the second time, remaining there until 1751. The close friendship that developed between Marigny and Soufflot led to the latter's receiving in 1754 the commission to build the church of Ste.-Geneviève in Paris, the present Panthéon.

These brief biographical notes create the picture of an architect of French training who was inspired by the works of antiquity and the Renaissance to construct a domed edifice that can take its place beside the best examples of this type. Such works had to be his models, not those of Gothic. However, after his death (in 1780), when Ste.-Geneviève's was not yet completed, his pupil Maximilian BRÉBION (1716-1792) reported that Soufflot had had the aim of "combining the lightness of construction found in *Gothic* buildings with the purity and grandeur of *Greek* architecture."[2] His opinion of Gothic was already formed in 1741, that is to say, three years after his return from the first sojourn in Rome. He was only twenty-eight years old when he delivered in the Académie des Beaux-Arts a lecture which Monval has published for the most part verbatim.[3] This *Mémoire sur l'architecture gothique* was preserved as a manuscript in the Academy in Lyons and thus could hardly have had much influence on Soufflot's contemporaries (except Laugier). It may be assumed, however, that his views on Gothic were disseminated more widely through his conversations.

The lecture begins with the statement that most writers have thought the Goths created only bizarre and objectionable architecture. "They may have been right in many respects," but a treatise on Gothic constructions and even proportions would nevertheless be useful. François Blondel was almost the only critic to judge these favorably. Here Soufflot cites the passage from Blondel the Elder on the proportions of the façade of Milan Cathedral, and goes on to say that Gothic churches could furnish material for a very extensive book. More experience than he possesses would be necessary; however, with a prayer

[2] *Ibid.*, p. 423.

[3] *Ibid.*, pp. 424ff.

for indulgence, he submits his comparison of churches that follow the rules of antiquity with those others which he will call henceforth "nos églises." Just as Vasari felt himself to be the descendant of the Romans, so Soufflot calls the Gothic structures "*our* churches."

At this point Monval mentions the Gothic buildings that Soufflot had studied: Nôtre-Dame in Paris, Milan Cathedral, the cathedral in Lyons, St.-Nizier in the same city, St.-Maurice in Vienne, and the church of the Cordeliers in Lyons.

Equal justice is done to Classicists and Gothicists by the statement that the piers have a kind of capital almost always in poor taste but occasionally of very delicate execution. On the other hand, he admires unreservedly the galleries of Nôtre-Dame in Paris, "that offer to view, as it were, a second church, the brightness (*clarté*) of which contrasts with the darkness prevailing below; they make the church seem vaguer and higher, and cause the spectators to distinguish, as though from a distance, a thousand objects, which, now lost, now rediscovered, afford, according to the way they [the spectators] move away or approach, spectacles that are in themselves a delight."[4]

The profiles make the quadripartite ribbed vaults appear light; in many churches they create with the main ribs [*maitresses nervures*, by which are meant here perhaps the transverse arches] very ingenious compartments, for example, in St.-Nizier in Lyons—a distinctly Late Gothic structure.

On the other hand, Soufflot criticizes the façades and portals unfavorably,[5] while respecting the side views, "the great buttresses, which, though sufficiently strong to resist the thrust of the vaults, appear light because of the manner of their construction." Then, however, he ventures to assert that the modern churches, among others St.-Sulpice in Paris the Gesú in Rome, and so on, are similar to the Gothic. Thus, he says, we esteem in them, indirectly, the work of those peoples we characterize as rude and barbarous: "we have even imitated them in all points." It cannot be determined from Monval's incomplete reprint of the mansucript what Soufflot means by this. Probably he only intends

[4] *Ibid.*, p. 425: "Les tribunes de Notre-Dame de Paris sont d'une étendue considérable et produisent un effet surprenant en offrant à la vue, pour ainsi dire, une seconde église, dont la clarté contraste avec l'espèce d'obscurité qui règne dans les dessous, la fait paraître et plus vague et plus élevée, et fait distinguer aux spectateurs comme dans un lointain, mille objets qui, tantôt perdus, tantôt retrouvés, leur donnent, à mesure qu'ils s'en éloignent ou s'en approchent, des spectacles qui les ravissent à eux-mêmes." This is exactly what is meant by the term *Vielbildigkeit* (furnishing many aspects of views). Cf. below, p. 776.

[5] Soufflot's intervention with regard to the middle portal of Nôtre-Dame in Paris was motivated by this criticism, but his work was changed by Viollet-le-Duc's restoration.

to say that modern churches have not borrowed from Greek or Roman temples anything pertaining to the general arrangement of their interiors, but have, on the contrary, taken much, if not everything, from Gothic churches. In the case of St.-Sulpice one can think of the ambulatory and the buttresses, but as regards the other buildings, Gesú, S. Ignazio, S. Carlo al Corso, S. Andrea della Valle, SS. Apostoli, all in Rome, Soufflot's idea is only acceptable in a very general sense.

"When I pass to decoration I find that we imitate them there also, if not in everything, yet in much." Strangely enough, he means by decoration the arcades opening onto the aisles and chapels. "These arches are, in truth, semicircles; the piers are rectangular and are placed at right angles [frontally] to the aisles. . . ."[5a] He describes in addition the typical elements of modern churches, but stresses the fact that the entablatures fulfill the same function in the cleaning and repairing of the structures as do the Gothic galleries (*tribunes des Goths*). Galleries also occur in modern churches, in the Dome des Invalides in Paris and the Oratoire in Lyons. The windows are above the entablature, the transverse arches correspond "en quelque façon aux nervures gothiques." (p. 428)

Then he reverts to Gothic: its construction is more inventive, bolder, and more difficult even than the modern; the triforia (called here *tribunes* also), which sometimes cut across the piers at two different heights, reduce the piers to nothing, yet the latter carry the vaults, however great they may be, and in addition the often very considerable weight of the roofs. "The composition strives to create an impression of lightness, but these churches are just as stable as ours. The placing of the piers is an important element in this, for as we walk through, we never see more than one of their four sides. The Gothic pointed arches have more strength than our round arches, but they are not so graceful; with regard to the windows in severies (*lunettes*) and ribs (*nervures*) of Gothic, there are many that cannot have been easy to execute and that have a judicious shape (*coupe*) to their individual stones. The Gothic builders always knew how to direct the chief load onto the point of resistance, and this principle can be detected even in the arrangement of the stones in the interstices of the ribs. The construction of our vaults is neither so delicate nor so difficult: we likewise take care to place the weights on the strongest parts; we adorn our buildings in a grander and nobler manner, which is, however, sometimes rather heavy: our piers that carry the loads are often no more

[5a] *Ibid.*, p. 427.

massive than those of Gothic churches, but appear heavier because one necessarily sees two of their sides as one enters the churches. . . ." Soufflot adds conciliatorily that modern architects of the age of Louis XIV are not inferior to those of Gothic in correctness of execution.

In conclusion he undertakes a comparison of proportions. What he says can be summarized in a few words: Gothic interiors seem to be longer and higher than they actually are; on the other hand, St. Peter's in Rome appears smaller than it is. He means that the effect of proportions is relative, not absolute.

Soufflot differed from his contemporaries in that he discussed definite parts and characteristics of Gothic churches; with his remark about the mechanics of vaults he anticipated Viollet-le-Duc in some degree; and he appreciated Gothic vaults, just as he was perhaps the first critic to recognize and formulate the principle of diagonality in the placing of the piers as something significant of Gothic. All this is of such moment that his occasionally strange statements and his kowtowing before the Classicists cannot detract from its importance. To what extent Soufflot with his concealed flying buttresses in Ste.-Geneviève's can be considered a Gothicist does not need to be investigated here. His fundamental idea that Gothic and Renaissance must be combined can be characterized as eclectic and, indeed, as misleading, since the church of Ste.-Geneviève has nothing essentially Gothic either about its proportions or vaults. However, his inclination to unite both styles (*façons*) meant a recognition of Gothic as the equal of *architecture moderne*. In this he was not quite alone in 1741, but he excelled in depth of understanding all those who expressed themselves on the subject.

LAUGIER, like Soufflot, was born in 1713. He was a Jesuit priest (later he left the Order) and in him were inculcated the Order's twin traditions of Humanism and Mediaevalism. As an aesthetician he had a thoroughly dogmatic point of view, according to which he determined what architects might and might not do, but side by side with these outworn rules and precepts can be found other remarks of an astonishing progressiveness:[6] "I enter the church of Notre-Dame in Paris. . . . At the first glance my eyes are held, my imagination is struck by the expanse, the height, the amplitude of that vast nave; I am forced to devote a few moments to the surprise that the majestic quality of

6 P. Marc Antoine Laugier, *Essai sur l'architecture*, Paris, 1753. I quote from the second edition of 1755, p. 174. Laugier died in 1769.

the whole arouses in me. . . ."[7] Then, his academic conscience discovers countless absurdities: "but I cast the blame on the misfortune of the times. . . . Here there are many faults, but here there is also greatness. From this church I go to St. Sulpice, the most important of all the churches we have built according to the taste of ancient architecture. I am neither struck with amazement nor moved; I find the edifice far less impressive than its reputation. I see only ponderousness and masses."[8] Later he reverts to Nôtre-Dame in Paris, in order to object to the proportions. "These columns are in truth very badly proportioned; but this defect in proportion, which wounds the eye, does not increase their solidity."[9] It is very characteristic of the spirit of the age that he condemns the Gothic choir-screens, proposing in their stead iron trellises that permit a view of the high altar.

Subsequently, however, in his discussion of individual features, there occurs a passage which must be quoted in its entirety because it is important for the evaluation of Goethe's later essay. "Our forefathers [that is, the Gothic architects] excelled in the construction of towers. . . . They discovered the secret of uniting lightness and delicacy of work with elegance of forms; and avoiding equally the slender and the massive, they attained that degree of precision from which results the true beauty of these kinds of work. Nothing of this sort is comparable to the tower of Strasbourg Cathedral. This proud pyramid is a masterpiece, enchanting in its stupendous height, its exact diminution, its agreeable form, in the correctness of its proportions, in the singular refinement of the work. I do not believe that any architect ever produced anything so boldly imagined, so happily conceived, so precisely executed. There is more art and genius in this one piece of work than in all the marvels that we see elsewhere."[10] He then grows reserved

[7] "J'entre dans l'église de Notre-Dame de Paris . . . au premier coup d'œuil mes regards sont arrêtées, mon imagination est frappée par l'étendue, la hauteur, le dégagement de cette vaste nef; je suis forcé de donner quelque momens à la surprise qu'excite dans moi le majestueux de l'ensemble." (p. 174)

[8] ". . . des absurdités sans nombre: mais j'en rejette le blâme sur le malheur des temps. . . . Voilà bien des défauts, mais voilà qui est grand! De-là je passe à S. Sulpice, église la plus considérable de toutes celles que nous avons bâties dans le goût de l'Architecture antique. Je ne suis ni frappé ni saisi, je trouve l'édifice fort au-dessous de la réputation. Je ne vois que des épaisseurs et des masses." (pp. 174, 175)

[9] *Op.cit.*, p. 182. "Ces colonnes sont à la vérité très-mal proportionées; mais ce défaut de proportion qui blesse les yeux n'augmente pas leur solidité."

[10] "Nos Anciens ont excellé dans la construction des tours. . . . Ils ont trouvé le secret d'y réunir à l'élégance des formes, la légerté et la délicatesse du travail; et évitant également le grêle et le massif, ils ont atteint le point de précision, d'où résulte la vraie beauté de ces sortes d'ouvrage. Rien n'est comparable en ce genre à la tour de la Cathédrale de Strasbourg.

and academic once more, and does not recommend that towers of this type be imitated, but he points out how they differ from modern towered structures. "These [the Gothic] have almost all the boldness of grace, something grand and proud. Those have only ponderousness, harshness as their portion, no elegance, no uniqueness, no taste. This decline in a part of such an important art is absolutely humiliating. Let us endeavor to remedy it, if possible."[11]

Laugier, as a good Catholic, finds that Gothic alone has expressed the intent of the Catholic church; he is merely confused by the respect he thinks he owes to Vitruvius, Vignola, and Palladio. His rhetorical panegyric on the Strasbourg tower has been forgotten in the literature on the subject, but the memory of his blind worship of the rules, or supposed rules of antiquity has survived.[12]

Had Laugier read Wimpheling? It is certain that he knew Félibien's writings, and perhaps he was also acquainted with a work by Bohm,[13] in which the tower of Strasbourg Cathedral is called "une merveille du monde." Laugier's conception of the origin of Gothic reveals nothing new. The attractive title page of his book depicts a sylvan cottage, built with living trees (Fig. 52)—a charming illustration of Vitruvius' "wood theory."

Amadée François FRÉZIER (1682-1773) reviewed Laugier's book in 1754 in the July number of the *Mercure de France*, showing great tolerance toward Gothic but discussing in much greater detail those portions of the book that concern pilasters and Laugier's condemnation of them.

In comparison with Laugier and his halfheartedness Thomas GRAY (1716-1771) seems a convinced admirer of Gothic. After his letters of 1739 there are no actual documents referring to his studies of Gothic until the year 1754. He was writing poetry and occupying himself with mediaeval literature. Clark has given a comprehensive account of him, and it must be assumed that Gray was deepening his knowledge of English Gothic in a very intensive fashion. Of great interest to us

---

Cette superbe pyramide est un chef-d'œuvre ravissant par son élévation prodigieuse, sa diminution exacte, sa forme agréable, par la justesse des proportions, par la singulière finesse du travail. Je ne crois pas que jamais aucun Architecte ait rien produit d'aussi hardiment imaginé, d'aussi heureusement pensé, d'aussi proprement exécuté. Il y a plus d'art et de génie dans ce seul morceau, que dans tout ce que nous voyons ailleurs de plus merveilleux." (p. 200-201)

11 "Celles-ci ont presque toute la hardiesse, de la grace, quelque chose de grand et de fier. Celles-là n'ont que la pesanteur, la dureté en partage, nulle élégance, nulle singularité, nul goût. Cette décadence dans une partie de l'art si considérable est tout-à-fait humiliante. Tâchons d'y remédier, s'il est possible." (p. 202)

12 *Op.cit.*, Preface, pp. 36ff.; pp. 3, 4; p. 128 (St.-Denis), p. 280 (Gothic).

13 Bohm, *La Cathédrale de Strasbourg*, 1733.

is an essay he wrote in 1754 and showed to friends, but did not publish. Not until 1814 did the manuscript appear in print with the title *Architectura Gothica.*[14] This title is misleading. The essay deals with "the old Norman or (as Sir Christopher Wren calls it) the Saxon Architecture." In 1814 the terminology had been changed again, and Norman architecture was called "Gothic" simply because all mediaeval architecture was considered to be Gothic. Gray fixes the chronological limits of Norman architecture from 1066 to 1216, and describes the type in general, discussing in turn the round arch, the system of piers, the forms of capitals, the vaulting (or the flat ceiling, which predominated over vaulting), and ornamentation. This is the first systematic description of Romanesque. In connection with the subject of arches Gray describes the interlacing semicircular arches: ". . . rising on short columns and interlaced, so that the curve of one arch intersecting that of its neighbors, their pillars or legs stand only half the distance from each other that they otherwise would do. This, though only an ornament, might perhaps suggest the idea of building on *pointed arches*, afterwards in use, as the intersection of two round ones produces the same effect to the eye."[15]

This is a *new theory of the origin of Gothic*, for in those days, as in the time of Pseudo-Raphael or Wren, the whole of Gothic seemed to have originated with the pointed arch. The only question that needed to be answered was: whence came the pointed arch? Not from trees, and not from the Saracens, but from *intersecting round arches*—an origin put forward quite casually, but as ascribable to the imagination of Gray's ancestors. The poet was cautious enough to say: ". . . this, though only an ornament, might perhaps suggest. . . ." His theory found its adherents, but they were never very numerous and could not uproot the tree theory or dull the romantic luster of the Saracen theory.[16]

James ESSEX (1723-1749), living in Cambridge, a younger contemporary of Gray, belongs to the Gothic Revival in England. He restored Gothic buildings, was the author of some altars and Gothic churches, was praised from one side, and condemned from the other. He left notes, now in the British Museum, once single sheets, now bound together.[17] It seems impossible to guess what was their original order, if

14 Quoted from *The Works of Gray*, edited by Milford, v, London, 1843, pp. 325-332.

15 *Op.cit.*, p. 327.

16 I recall that this same theory was again invented (by Hasak?) in the last generation. Unfortunately I have not been able to locate the article in which it was propounded.

17 Donald R. Stewart, "James Essex," *The Architectural Review*, November, 1959, pp. 317ff.

there was any. He prepared a history of Gothic before Whittington and began to study the single members—plans, piers, arches, vaults, buttresses—separately, before Rickman. He recognized that the pointed arch was introduced into cross rib vaults *to reach the same height for all arches*, before Saunders did. It may be that his ideas influenced others, reaching them through oral tradition.

In 1756 there appeared a book on the Sublime and Beautiful, by Edmund BURKE (1730-1792),[18] which dominated the aesthetic thinking of the following generation, including Kant.[19] Of the innumerable ideas that resulted from Burke's system of thought, long since outmoded, two may be singled out because they became fruitful later on for the appraisal of Gothic. First, he declared "smoothness" to be an essential factor in beauty, and thus it was very natural to interpret a lack of smoothness as the reason for the traditional criticism that Gothic was not "beautiful." It could be hoped that this would be a means of circumventing the completely incalculable concept of beauty. Second, he suggested the idea of the "artificial infinite." "There are scarce any things which can become the objects of our senses, that are really and in their own nature infinite. But the eye not being able to perceive the bounds of many things, they seem to be infinite, and they produce the same effects as if they really were so. We are deceived in the like manner, if the parts of some large object are so continued to any indefinite number, that the imagination meets no check which may hinder its extending them at pleasure."[20]

In a somewhat later passage Burke says: "It is in this kind of artificial infinity, I believe, we ought to look for the cause why a rotund has such a noble effect. For in a rotund, whether it be a building or a plantation, you can no where fix a boundary; turn which way you will, the same object still seems to continue, and the imagination has no rest."[21] We today are accustomed to regard buildings such as the Roman Pantheon as textbook examples of the finite. Burke, however,

---

Cf. the article in Thieme-Becker, *Allgemeines Künstlerlexikon*. I have not yet been able to get the few writings published by the Society of Antiquarians (mentioned without exact quotation):
1. Remarks on different Modes and Stone Buildings in England.
2. Diary of a travel through Flanders and France. They may reveal his real function in the progress of scientific approach to Gothic.

18 Edmund Burke, *A Philosophical Enquiry into the Origin of Our Ideas of the Sublime and Beautiful*, London, 1756.

19 Samuel H. Monk, *The Sublime. A Study of Critical Theories in Eighteenth Century England*, New York, 1935; contains a wealth of bibliographical material.

20 Burke, edition London, 1798, p. 128 (Part II, Section VIII).

21 *Ibid.*, p. 131 (Part II, Section IX).

obviously lets his eye follow the circle again and again and can discover no end to such rotation. On the other hand, we see that he finds this "artificial infinity" also in the rows of piers in mediaeval churches. Because of his criterion of "artificial infinity" he prefers rectangular to cruciform churches. In the case of the Greek cross (with four arms of equal length) one arm hides the others: ". . . instead of a deception that makes the building more extended than it is, you are cut off from a considerable part (two-thirds) of its *actual* length. . . ."[22] The same is true, correspondingly, of the Latin cross: "Indeed there is nothing more prejudicial to the grandeur of buildings, than to abound in angles; a fault obvious in many; and owing to an inordinate thirst for variety, which, whenever it prevails, is sure to leave very little true taste."[23]

Although these observations do not at first seem very productive, they bore fruit later (cf. below, page 823). Burke does not simply condemn; he gives his reasons for what he thinks was wrong in mediaeval buildings. Certainly his theses seem to us confused. A round structure like the Pantheon is supposed to create a favorable effect because it has "artificial infinity," but a Renaissance work in the shape of a Greek cross is bad. To us the latter seems to belong typologically to the same group of forms as the Pantheon, that is, to centrally planned buildings (*Zentralbauten*).

Simultaneously, in 1759, a serious opinion was again voiced. William CHAMBERS (1726-1796) writes in his *Treatise on Civil Architecture*: "To those usually called Gothic architects we are indebted for the first considerable improvements in construction; there is a lightness in their works, an art and boldness of execution, to which the ancients never arrived: and which the moderns comprehend and imitate with difficulty. England contains many magnificent examples of this species of architecture, equally admirable for the art with which they are built, the taste and ingenuity with which they are composed."[24] In a note he says: "There is more constructive skill shown in Salisbury and other of our cathedrals than in all works of the ancients put together. The balance of the thrust of the different arches—the adjustment of thickness in the vaultings and the exceeding small ratio of the points of support in these buildings to their whole superficies—and added to these

22 *Ibid.*, p. 133.

23 *Ibid.*, p. 134.

24 William Chambers, *A Treatise on the Decorative Part of Civil Architecture*, London, 1759; 2nd ed., 1768, 3rd ed., 1791. The quotation is from the reprint published in London in 1825 by Joseph Gwilt, I, p. 128.

the consequent lightness and elegance of form which they exhibit, leave us nothing to desire in this respect."[25] Then the text continues: "One cannot refrain from wishing that the Gothic structures were more considered, better understood, and in higher estimation than they hitherto seem to have been. Would our dilettanti instead of importing the gleanings of Greece, or our antiquaries, instead of publishing loose, incoherent prints, encourage persons duly qualified to undertake a correct and elegant publication of our own cathedrals and other buildings called Gothic, before they totally fall to ruin, it would be of real service to the arts of design, preserve the remembrance of an extraordinary style of building now sinking fast into oblivion and at the same time publish to the world the riches of Britain in the splendour of her ancient structures."[26] Was Chambers unacquainted with Dugdale's work or did its engravings seem to him unsatisfactory?

The most surprising thing about this passage is that it was inserted in a treatise which offers the traditional instruction in ancient architecture, the five orders, their employment by the great Italian architects of the Renaissance, and which leans heavily on Vitruvius, Alberti, Palladio, and the like. It is a textbook with a purely Italian orientation. Chambers was widely traveled, having been even to China, and in another publication he wrote about Chinese gardens on the basis of what he had seen for himself. He had an open mind toward English Gothic—but he does not discuss it with a pedagogical view; he hopes that others will do so, and looks forward to scientific work on the subject. In this hope he was to be disappointed, for scientific literature on Gothic did not begin until after his death in 1796.

Shortly after Chambers' defense of Gothic, which showed the way to Romanticism, there appeared rather incidentally in a book written in 1763 by Thomas WARTON (1728-1790) on Spenser's *Faerie Queene* the first basic attempt at dividing the architectural history of England into periods.[27] These were as follows:

1. Saxon Style
2. Gothic Saxon, from 1200 on
3. Absolute Gothic, from 1300 to 1441
4. Ornamental Gothic, since 1441

The latter chronological limit is based on the date of King's College Chapel in Cambridge.[28]

[25] *Ibid.*

[26] *Ibid.*, p. 129.

[27] Thomas Warton, *Observations on the Faerie Queene of Spenser*, London, 1763. I quote from the edition of 1807, II, p. 208.

[28] A small monograph on King's College Chapel appeared several years later: Henry Malden,

Such a division into periods presupposes not merely the desire to apply to the vague, generalized concept of Gothic, as Gray and Walpole envisaged it, ideas of historical survey and evolutionary differentiation, but also objective knowledge and an absolute recognition of Gothic, which was no longer to be continually measured by the standards of antiquity or the Renaissance. In England, the bulwark of Northern culture, the scales were slowly tipping in favor of Gothic.

It is improbable that this change of opinion in England influenced Soufflot. From a lecture he delivered in the Academy in Lyons in 1762 it can be seen that he consistently held to his high estimation of Gothic. An architect named Le Jolivet had sent in exact survey sketches of Notre-Dame de Dijon, and Soufflot added some explanations in the Academy's meeting on December 20, 1762. The summary of this lecture reads as follows:[29] "The church of Notre-Dame in Dijon is a work of Gothic architecture, modern or Arabic, in accordance with the remarks that accompany the drawings; it was built in the thirteenth century with such stability that it has suffered no change down to the present, in spite of the lightness of the greater part of its members (*parties*), a lightness which is of a sort that many architects would call the man who should propose it as a plan for execution ignorant and foolhardy." In what follows, the edifice is pronounced a "chef deuvre [*sic*] de construction," and Le Jolivet is appointed corresponding member of the Lyons Academy in recognition of his drawings as well as his historical research on the building of the church. One hears again an echo of Soufflot's own theses when the account states that this style (*goust d'architecture*), which has quite properly been abandoned, offers no very great advantages but is exceedingly useful in showing how much material is wasted in the new churches; for most architects have believed that churches could only be built with square piers, thick walls, and buttresses, because they had not sufficiently studied Notre-Dame and other buildings of the same type in Paris, and the Royal Chapel in Versailles."

The sudden mention of the palace chapel in Versailles must be connected with the sentence in which Soufflot rejects Gothic as a style. It is not Gothic as a whole that he champions, but merely its lightness. In this same sense must be understood his praise of S. Agostino in Piacenza,

---

Chapel Clerk, *An Account of King's College Chapel in Cambridge*, 1769. The text concerns ecclesiastical history but also offers descriptions of the structure, the stained glass, etc.

29 Henry Lemonnier, *Procès-Verbaux de l'Académie Royale d'Architecture*, VII, Paris, 1922, p. 129; also Monval, *op.cit.*, p. 466.

"the architect of which still clung to the main disposition of Gothic, wishing to imitate its lightness in his construction, though his Doric columns were no less correct."[30] S. Agostino, begun in 1570, perhaps designed by Galeazzo Alessi, has absolutely no Gothic features, either in its exterior or interior.[31] Soufflot's original design for the church of Ste.-Geneviève in Paris confirms the fact that in the main he rejected square piers (like those in St.-Sulpice) and preferred slender columns (as in Nôtre-Dame), though corrected according to the canon of classical proportions. In this he approaches Laugier, or perhaps the converse is true. Laugier was likewise a member of the Academy in Lyons and probably knew Soufflot's views.

LAUGIER had written his first book on architecture in 1752; in the following years he wrote on French music, and produced several learned historical works. Then, however, he turned again to architectural aesthetics. His *Observations* of 1765 treat almost exclusively problems of classical architecture.[32] The book must be discussed here because it contains a short chapter entitled: "De la difficulté de décorer les églises gothiques." He says (page 129): ". . . not every kind of decoration suits every kind of building. The ornamentation must be adapted to the spirit and system of the architecture."[33] "Ornamentation" is to be taken here as the entire furnishing of the interior, the completion of a Gothic church. "Thence comes the great difficulty of decorating the Gothic churches. In this sort of building the massive members are generally very light and the openings infinitely multiplied. There results a *bizarrerie*, a variety of aspects, which occupy the gaze agreeably and which produce the most fascinating spectacle. To destroy this spectacle would be to annihilate the principal merit of these churches and to cause their greatest beauty to vanish."[34] But despite this remark Laugier discusses the Gothic cathedral, disregarding all the structures built into the interior: "A charming distribution, where the eye traverses so delightfully several rows of columns only to plunge finally into the chapels of the background, the stained-glass windows of which diffuse the

30 Lemonnier, *op.cit.*, p. 129.

31 Giulio Ferrari, *Piacenza*, Bergamo, 1931, p. 77; figs. pp. 69 and 82.

32 *Observations sur l'architecture par M. l'Abbé Laugier des Académies d'Angers, de Marseille et de Lyon*, The Hague, 1765.

33 *Ibid.*, p. 129: "Toute espèce de décoration ne convient pas à toute sorte d'édifices. Il faut que l'ornement soit adapté à l'esprit et au système de l'Architecture."

34 "De-là la grande difficulté de décorer les Églises gothiques. Dans ces sortes de bâtiments les massifs sont d'ordinaire fort legers et les percés multipliés à l'infini. Il en résulte une bizarrerie, une variété d'aspects, qui occupent agréablement la vue et qui produisent le spetacle le plus séduisant. Détruire ce spectacle se seroit annéantir le principal mérite de ces Églises, et faire disparoitre leur plus grande beauté."

light with uneven profusion. . . ."[35] But a criticism follows this praise: "Let us consider these same churches now with all the crazy ornaments created by the taste of the fourteenth and fifteenth centuries. A frightful rood-screen shows itself. . . ."[36] In this sense he discusses Nôtre-Dame, St.-Médéric, and St.-Germain-l'Auxerrois, all three in Paris, reiterating afterward that whoever intends to furnish or complete the interiors of Gothic churches should endeavor to comprehend them in relation to their own style: ". . . far from destroying them, he ought to try to be receptive to their effect and make the most of them."[37]

Every modern curator of monuments will agree enthusiastically, but what exactly does Laugier understand by "tirer le meilleur parti possible?"

"His endeavors ought thereafter to be confined to giving the structures a simpler, more natural, and more pleasing form, if possible. If there are obligatory (*obligés*) ornaments and if he can refine their contours, let him do so. If there are superfluous ornaments, let him remove them . . . in a word, the decorator of a Gothic church ought to rectify, improve, embellish everything where possible, be heedful, arrange, and render the edifice as worthy as he can. These principles are certain, but it is less easy than one thinks to be guided by them in practice. . . ."[38] There are many reasons why architects have introduced "Greek" forms. "One sees altar decorations where the Greek architecture contrasts badly with the order of the building. These decorations are rich and of magnificent taste, but they err in not conforming to the spirit of the thing. . . . What, then, should one do in a Gothic church that one intends to decorate? As follows: First of all, discard all the obstacles that diminish and obfuscate the variety and *bizarrerie* of its aspects. Destroy all the false ornaments with which the walls are overladen and the openings blocked. Consider the nature of the piers. See whether, either by removing or adding something, you can make them rounder until they attain a form which imitates that of columns. Prefer this form to all others. You can encrust these columns with marble or flute them in stone. You can give them bases and capitals, the profiles of which are more correct. You can

[35] "Une distribution charmante, où l'œil plonge délicieusement à travers plusiers files de colonnes dans les Chapelles en enfoncement, dont les vitreaux répandent la lumière avec profusion et inégalité; . . ." (p. 130)

[36] "Considérons présentement ces mêmes Églises avec tous les sots ornemens que le goût du 14e et du 15e siècle leur a prodigués. Un affreux jubé se présente. . . ." (p. 130)

[37] *Ibid.*, p. 135: "Loins de les détruire, il doit s'appliquer à les faire ressentir, et à en tirer le meilleur parti possible."

[38] "Son étude ensuite doit se borner à donner aux massifs s'il le peut une forme plus simple, plus naturelle et plus coulante. S'il y a des ornemens obligés et qu'il en puisse épurer les contours, qu'il le fasse. S'il y a des ornemens superflus, qu'il les retranche. . . . En un mot le décorateur doit dans une Église gothique, rectifier, soigner, embellir tout ce qui peut l'être, respecter, ménager, faire valoir l'Architecture autant qu'il peut. Ces principes sont certains. Mais il est moins aisé qu'on ne pense de s'y assujettir dans la practique. . . ." (pp. 135, 136)

replace the barbarous moldings of the ribs by well-chosen ones. You can simulate mosaics in the cells of the vaults, entwine palms, or cover the plain spots with some other ornament in good taste. If you have marble and gilding at your disposal, you can make use of it. . . ."[39]

Such is Laugier's care of monuments!

What he has to say about the remodeling of the choir of Amiens in the eighteenth century is interesting in this connection, likewise what follows on the façade of St.-Gervais in Paris: "It is absurd that the front should be in one style and the interior in another. . . . No work can be good when there is no unity of subject, no union and accord of the parts. Yes, I say boldly that if one wishes to reconstruct the portal of a Gothic church, it is absolutely necessary to reconstruct it in the Gothic style. At most one can take the liberty of correcting the forms, of improving the profiles, of carving the ornaments to conform to a better taste."[40] This is a theory of stylistic purity reminiscent of Wren (page 362), though tempered by concessions to Classicism, an aesthetics of the golden mean. Its author bows now to the right, now to the left. Gothic is, however, actually held up as a model: "Their forms in pointed arches had great advantages. Let us at least forestall the just regret that one could feel in the face of that which we have renounced. What! These men whom we pity for having lived in barbarous centuries constructed vaults that we are forced to admire; and we who flatter ourselves that we have received the torch of genius and been in the school of the god of Taste shall find it impossible to create anything approximate? . . . Let us vary the forms of our vaults, distribute thereon judiciously conceived ornaments, and we shall not have anything left

39 ". . . on voit des décorations d'Autels où l'Architecture grèque contraste mal-à-propos avec l'ordonnance du bâtiment. Ces décorations sont riches et de grand goût; mais elles pèchent, en ce qu'elles ne sont pas dans l'esprit de la chose. . . . Que faire donc dans une Église gothique que l'on propose à décorer? Le voici: Ecartez d'abord tous les obstacles qui diminuent, qui offusquent la variété et la bizarrerie de ces aspects. Détruisez tous les faux ornemens qui surchargent les massifs ou qui bouchent les percés. Considérez la nature des pilliers. Voyez si en retranchant ou en ajoutant quelque chose on peut les arrondir jusqu'à leur donner une forme qui imite celle des colonnes. Préférez cette forme à toute autre. Vous pouvez incruster ces colonnes de marbre, où les canneler en pierre. Vous pouvez leur donner des bases et des chapiteaux dont les profils soient plus corrects. Vous pouvez aux nervures des ogives substituer à des moulures barbares des moulures d'un bon choix. Vous pouvez tailler où feindre des mosaiques dans les pendentifs des voûtes, enlacer des palmes ou jetter tel autre ornement de bon goût sur les endroits lisses. Si vous avez le marbre et la dorure à discrétion, vous pouvez en faire usage. . . ." (pp. 137, 138) What Laugier means with "nervures des ogives" is not clear. Both terms mean usually the same.

40 "Il est absurde que le frontispice soit d'une façon et l'intérieur d'un autre . . . Nul ouvrage ne peut être bon s'il n'y a unité de sujet, union et accord des parties. Oui, je le dis hardiment, si l'on veut reconstruire le portail d'une Église gothique, il faut de toute nécessité le reconstruire gothiquement. On peut tout au plus se donner la liberté de rectifier les formes, de rendre les moulures plus correctes, de tailler les ornemens de meilleur goût." (p. 149)

to regret."[41] In the case of groined vaults he recommends palms along the groins (page 286).

Laugier's book must have been widely read. His fancies regarding palms were realized, and Dauthe's very charming church of St. Nicholas in Leipzig (1784) is like a direct illustration for the French treatise. But the book was also responsible for much damage in the field of conservation of monuments; progress often leaves corpses in its wake. Laugier occupies a middle position between the Englishmen, Hurd and Walpole, on the one hand, and the Germans, Winckelmann and Lessing, on the other, that is, between Mediaevalism and Humanism. At that time the Germans had not yet discovered Gothic.

Soon after Laugier's essay there appeared a book by James BENTHAM (1708-1794) on Ely, in which all the existing theories of the pointed arch were rejected. He quotes Wren, saying: ". . . but the observations of several learned travellers, who have accurately surveyed the Ancient mode of building in those parts of the world, do by no means favour that opinion, or discover the least traces of it. Indeed I have not yet met with any satisfactory account of the origin of pointed arches, when invented, or where first taken notice of."[42] Then he mentions the theory of intersecting round arches, which he knows from hearsay. Here then Gray's theory appears for the first time in technical literature. Later, still other theories followed, of an almost incredible naïveté; but one should not ignore or underestimate the tendency behind them, namely, the idea of differentiating architectural styles according to their characteristic forms. This is *one* factor in the problem of style, and it must be admitted that critics were beginning not merely to praise or blame the pointed arch, but to recognize it as a necessary member of Gothic and thus to acknowledge it.

Louis AVRIL represents another advance. This former Jesuit wrote under the pseudonym of L. May and also under the initials M. L. M.[43] His book on architecture (1774) contains detailed reflections on Gothic architecture. He rejects its derivation from the Goths (page 133) be-

41 *Ibid.*, p. 284: "Leurs formes à tiers-point avoient bien des avantages. Prévenons du moins le juste regret qu'on pourroit concevoir de ce que nous y avons renoncé. Quoi! ces hommes que nous plaignons d'avoir vécu dans des siècles de barbarie, auront construit des voûtes que nous sommes forcés d'admirer; et nous qui nous flatons d'avoir reçu le flambeau du vrai génie, d'avoir été à l'école du Dieu du goût, il nous sera impossible de rien faire d'approchant? . . . Varions les formes de nos voûtes, répandons-y de sages ornemens et nous ne laisserons rien à regretter."

42 James Bentham, *The History and Antiquities of Ely*, Norwich, 1771. In the edition of 1812, p. 37.

43 M. L. M., *Temples anciennes et modernes ou observations historiques et critiques sur les plus célèbres monumens d'Architecture grècque et gothique*, London, 1774.

cause, according to him, Gothic does not begin until the end of the tenth century. It developed from a massive style into a lighter one; in other words, Romanesque is for Avril also an early phase of Gothic (the word Romanesque was not yet in existence). In his opinion there was no progress toward harmony (as in antiquity), but architecture went from one extreme to the other.

Avril is the first to give a membrological description of Gothic. "They do not invent new forms, because it is generally enough established that sacred edifices shall have the form of a cross, but they enrich the forms and vary their distribution. The piers are set further away from each other and open great arcades; they lose some of their mass, become detached, and increase in length. Bold and light vaults conceal from view the disagreeable framework of a roof; little windows that formerly scarcely allowed the light to enter are transformed into vast windows, the painting of which contributes in emphasizing the glass. The height and width of the vaults necessitate supports for the walls that carry them, so that the former will not spread apart: therefore the exterior flying buttresses, usually simple, sometimes double. . . . These flying buttresses represent at first only something useful, the sculptures with which they were later covered, the pyramids that terminate them make of them a decoration."[44] Then follows a description of the type of façade: ". . . all the cities vied with each other to have the largest and richest church. . . . All the world knows what France possesses in the way of the most celebrated Gothic."[45] Avril next attempts to differentiate the styles of the various countries: ". . . in Germany and in the regions of the North it [the style] was more overladen with ornaments; in France and in England it was in general simpler and consequently less ponderous; in Spain it contained something of the gigantic . . . the name 'arabesque' is applied by us to the most delicate Gothic."[46] A special section of the book is devoted to

[44] "Ils n'inventent pas de nouvelles formes, parce qu'il est assez généralement établi, que les édifices sacrés auront celle d'une Croix, mais ils l'enrichissent et varient la distribution. Les pilliers s'écartent et ouvrent de grandes Arcades; ils perdent de leur masse, se délient et s'allongent. Des voûtes hardies et legères dérobent la vue d'une désagréable charpente; les petites lucarnes qui auparavant laissent à peine entrer la lumière, se changent en vastes fenêtres dont la Peinture ne tarde pas à relever les vitreaux. L'élévation et la largeur des voûtes exigent des appuis pour les murailles, qui les portent, afin que celles-ci ne s'écartent point: delà les arcs boutants extérieurs, ordinairement simples, quelquefois doubles. . . . Ces arcs boutants ne présentent d'abord que de l'utile, les Sculptures dont on les couvre ensuite, les pyramides qui les terminent en font un ornement."

[45] *Ibid.*, p. 152: ". . . tout le monde connoît ce que la France a de plus célèbre en Gothique."

[46] ". . . en Allemagne et dans les régions au Nord, il étoit plus chargé d'ornements; en France et en Angleterre il étoit en général plus simple et dés-lors moins pésant; en Espagne il tenoit du gigantesque . . . le nom d'Arabesque appliqué parmi nous au Gothique le plus delicate."

Italian Gothic (page 155). The campanile of the cathedral in Florence or of St. Mark's in Venice, says Avril, cannot be compared "with the diaphanous steeples of Strasbourg, of Chartres, of Vienna in Austria, and even of Ulm in Suabia, although the latter is still unfinished";[47] the German architects working in Italy had to adapt themselves to the Italians, materials having been an important factor.

Avril's principal passage on Gothic is entitled: "Mérite de l'Architecture Gothique." Praise and blame are mixed, but he does muster the courage to praise—in part with echoes of Laugier. The churches "present the greatest beauties together with the greatest faults; so that one cannot view them without discovering a majesty worthy of their ultimate purpose, a knowledge of the most profound aspects of the art of building, a boldness unexampled in antiquity. This lightness is derived partly, if I am not mistaken, from the fact that there is no intermediate member between the vaults and the piers. . . . The Gothic vault seems to spring from the very foot of the piers that support it; especially when the piers, imitating the Greek fluting, are composed of spindles or round shafts; pushed up perpendicularly to a certain height, they then bend over to form arcades which connect one pier with the other, the vaults of the aisles, and the *Nefs ou Ogyves* that give strength to the principal vault."[48]

The words *Nefs* and *Ogyves* are made to stand out from the text by different type. *Nefs ou Ogyves* does not make sense, and must be a typographical error. If the printer was not very familiar with architectural terms, it is possible that he took the handwritten word *clefs* to be *nefs*, especially if he was better acquainted with the word *nefs* than with *clefs*.[49] Granted that *Clefs ou Ogyves* was really the original reading, this wording would then correspond to that of the expertise

[47] ". . . avec les Clochers diaphanes de Strasbourg, de Chartres, de Vienne en Autriche et même d'Ulm en Souabe, quoique celui-ci soit resté imparfait."

[48] *Ibid.*, p. 157: the churches ". . . présentent les plus grandes beautés au milieu des plus grandes défauts; qu'on ne peut les voir sans y découvrir une majesté digne de leur destination, une science de ce que l'art de bâtir a de plus profond, une hardiesse, dont L'Antiquité ne nous fournit point d'examples. . . . Cette légèreté vient en partie, si je ne me trompe, de ce qu'entre la voûte et les pilliers il n'y a aucun corps intermédiaire. . . . La voûte Gothique parait naître du pied même des pilliers qui la portent; surtout lorsque les pilliers imitant les cannelures grecques sont composés des fuseaux ou torons, poussés perpendiculairement jusqu'à une certaine hauteur, se plient ensuite pour former les arcades, qui lient un pillier à l'autre, les voûtes des bas-côtés, et les *Nefs* ou *Ogyves* qui donnent la force à la maitresse voûte."

[49] It has been suggested to me that the original could have been *Nerfs*, not *Nefs*. It is, however, doubtful whether the word *nerfs* would also have been used for ribs, instead of *nervures*. Yet why does he talk only about the *bas-côtés*? The légèreté which he emphasizes is first of all seen in the *nef*. Perhaps one should emend: ". . . les voûtes des bas-côtés et des nefs et les clefs ou ogives. . . ."

of 1316, and "la clef qui porte la clef" would then mean: "l'ogive qui porte la clef." *Clef* and *ogive* were originally synonymous, and still are for Avril.

The text concerning these ribs is continued in a passage that forms one of the most interesting parts of the whole treatise: "Their junction is natural, and the stone presents a flexibility equal to that of the most ductile metals. The pointed arches that form rays in all directions divide the whole surface into re-entrant and salient angles; of this division into several small, symmetrically arranged parts is born that slenderness which it is difficult to give to the long vaults (*longues voûtes*) with semicircular arches such as are constructed today."[50] In conclusion these excellent remarks are followed by the abstruse advice to modern Gothicists that they should furnish the vault surfaces with sculptures—probably reliefs.

Soufflot spoke of piers, vaults, ribs and transverse arches with their profiles, of roofs, galleries, triforia, façades, portals, of proportion and frontality; Laugier talked of towers, piers, of the harmony of the style of the façades with that of the interiors; and Avril discussed, in addition to these, pointed arches and engaged shafts on piers. Beside such matters there are observations on the optical delights of spatial effects, for example, the galleries (in Soufflot) or the succession of chapels back of the piers (in Laugier). In short, definite concepts of a descriptive nature now take the place of the vague idea of Gothic, even where the aesthetic impression is the subject in question.

50 "Leur conclure est naturelle, et la pierre y présente une fléxibilité égale à celle des métaux les plus ductiles. Les Ogyves formant de toutes parts des rayons, divisent toute la surface en angles rentrans et saillans; de cette division en plusiers petites parties bien symétrisées, naît ce svelte, qu'il est difficile de donner aux longues voûtes en plein cintre telle qu'on fait aujourd'hui."

III. THE PERIOD OF THE TURN TOWARD GOTHIC

1. The Young Goethe

In April 1770 Johann Wolfgang von GOETHE (1749-1832), then twenty-one years old, came to Strasbourg. A year later the Strasbourg Lodge was dissolved; and it is one of the ironies of fate that at the same time the young poet was rousing Gothic from the dead, as far as Germany was concerned. The essay, *Von deutscher Baukunst*,[1] which he composed in Strasbourg, was published in Frankfort in 1772 after his return there. Everything said about Gothic heretofore paled beside this masterpiece of youthful excitement. If the word rhetoric is freed from its later connotations and taken in its original sense of the true art of language that intoxicates and captivates reader and listener by the skillful choice of arguments, words, and comparisons, then Goethe's essay on Strasbourg Cathedral (Fig. 57) may be called a masterpiece of the highest rhetoric. Even one who does not entirely understand it on a first reading is nevertheless carried away by enthusiasm. This effect of its "totality" may be analyzed by scholars in the field of poetics, its laws and psychological background, but here our interest is directed not toward the essay as a work of art in language and a creation of fascinating beauty but toward its content of ideas, which can be dryly summarized in a few sentences. Full of veneration, Goethe turns to the spirit of Erwin von Steinbach whom he unreflectingly takes to be the author of the cathedral. He searches for Erwin's gravestone and does not find it. But—"What need hast thou of a monument!" The whole cathedral is Erwin's monument. Italians and French—Goethe means the Classicists—scorn his work. But the poet, for his part, speaks contemptuously of Bernini's colonnades for St. Peter's in Rome. Those nations have "measured rather than felt. . . ." "For a genius principles are even more harmful than examples." Goethe rebels against classicistic rules. He addresses a certain "dear abbé," without betraying his name, criticizing his theory of the origin of architecture in four corner posts and a roof. Goethe himself confronts columns and walls as fundamentally different things or principles. "Our houses are not derived from four columns in four corners; they are derived from four walls on four sides, which stand in lieu of all columns and exclude columns entirely, and where you patch them on, they are a ponderous superfluity."

[1] J. W. Goethe, *Von Deutscher Baukunst. D. M. Erwini a Steinbach*, Frankfurt, 1772. The following year Herder printed the essay in his collection, *Von Deutscher Art und Kunst. Einige fliegende Blätter*, Hamburg, 1773. Cf. Goethe's later essays: *Dritte Wallfahrt nach Erwins Grab im Juni* 1775, Sophienausgabe, I, 37, p. 324; *Von deutscher Baukunst 1823, ibid.*, I, 49, pp. 161 and 166; *Dichtung und Wahrheit, ibid.*, I, 27, pp. 70ff., 98ff.

He relates how he was brought up with a prejudice against Gothic, doubtless a reference to his father's traditions and his own Leipzig training under Oeser. Vividly he depicts his surprise at the cathedral. The shade of Erwin von Steinbach inspires him with insight, and here he presents a somewhat vague description of what Erwin's intentions had really been, for toward the end of his stay in Strasbourg Goethe had seen the designs for the façade.[2]

This portion of the essay is followed by an outburst of anger against the type of German scholar in the field of art who, misled by envious neighbors, misjudges the merits of Gothic. "Whereas he should give thanks to God that he can loudly proclaim it German architecture, our architecture, while the Italian can boast of none of his own, still less the Frenchman." He sees beauty where others see only strength and roughness,[3] though not classical beauty. For "art is image forming, long before it is beautiful, and yet such true, great art, yes, often truer and greater than beauty itself." Anticipating much later developments in the field of study of the fine arts, he enlarges the concept of art to include the works of "savages," with their "strange traits, horrible shapes, lurid colors." This sculpture is harmonious even without proper figural proportions for "*one* emotion wrought it into a characteristic whole. . . . Characteristic art is the only true one."

The essay is concluded by a passage of incomparable poetic fervor, which one must declaim with the emphatic solemnity of a rhapsodist.

Johann Gottfried von HERDER (1744-1803) reprinted the essay in 1773 in his collection *Von deutscher Art und Kunst.* Perhaps this was the basis for the widespread view that Goethe learned from Herder to regard Gothic with such enthusiastic affirmation. But Herder added to Goethe's magnificent peroration with its poetic and rhetorical climax a note in small type which throws a douche of cold water on the reader and destroys the effect: "The following essay, which asserts almost the contrary and in the most diametrically opposite manner, has been appended here in order to give occasion perhaps to a third, more moderate one, in which data will be investigated with regard to the questions: where, when, and how did Gothic architecture actually originate? what in it answers to a nordic urge and is an exception to the rule of greater beauty, or is even perhaps a greater plan for a new kind of beauty. . . ." Then follows Frisi's essay of 1766—dry, uninspired, tedi-

2 Karl Koetschau, "Goethe und die Gotik," *Festschrift zum sechzigsten Geburtstag von Paul Clemen*, Düsseldorf, 1926, p. 461.

3 This is doubtless an allusion to Burke, who equates beauty with smoothness.

ous—translated into German by Herder. The note just quoted is strongly reminiscent of what Chambers had said in 1759 in his much read textbook.[4] Herder may have felt that it was first necessary to explore the subject itself about which Goethe was writing. In that he was right, for the attempts to answer his questions as to the when, where, and how of the origin of Gothic have persisted down to the present and have been prosecuted more and more strictly and scientifically. But Herder himself would hardly have been pleased had some one appended a similar note to one of his essays, and this act alone, so little that of a friend and also so lacking in friendly feelings toward Gothic, should suffice to refute the idea that Goethe was inspired by Herder. The latter did have a very strong influence on Goethe at that time, but with the young poet's glorification of Gothic in particular he had nothing at all to do.[5]

Lambel has made note of the passages where Herder speaks of Gothic.[6] Anyone who takes the trouble to read them all will be surprised at how empty they are and how full of prejudices against Gothic. Lambel says that Herder was already impressed by Gothic in early youth, and supports this statement by reference to an elegy. But though beautiful, this poem is, despite its emotional atmosphere and what might be called expressionistic tone, an echo of the fashionable English lyric poetry of the time, combined with all the paraphernalia of romantic notions.[7]

"Wo bin ich?—in Einsiedeleyen
find ich, fühl ich mich.
Gespenster schatteten weg—Gedankentiefen
brausen herab und ruhn!—
Da wo im Mitternachtshain auf Scheidewegen Feen wandelten—
Und Cypressen den Thau herunterrauschten auf mein entblöstes Haupt:
Um mich Gräber der Brüder, Geisterstimmen aus der Urne Schoos.
hörs; sie dumpfen herauf—St! jener Moder lispelt Antwort und schweigt
und auf sterbenden Gipfeln ewger Ulmen wandelt, hörts! der Sturm,
der von sinkenden Ritterlichen Trümmern meinen Tempel heransteigt,
in dem Gespenster den neuen Todten vor dem Altar weihen.

[4] Cf. above, p. 405.

[5] A new biography of Herder is that by F. McEachran, *The Life and Philosophy of J. G. Herder*, Oxford, 1939.

[6] Herder's collection, *Von Deutscher Art und Kunst*, has been reprinted in *Deutsche Literaturdenkmale des 18. und 19. Jahrhunderts* (ed. by Seuffert and Sauer), No. 40, Stuttgart, 1892, with a very careful philological introduction by H. Lambel. For Goethe's essay cf. pp. xxxiff.

[7] Herder's elegy can be found in the complete edition of his works by Suphan, Berlin, 1878, xxix, p. 230.

Kaum sieht Hekate selbst durch alte Fenster ihren Gelübden zu
und vom Gothisch gehörnten Thurme seufzen
Eulen ein halbes Ach!—
und mein Vater vor mir—ich schaudre, schaudernd
wach ich und um mich Nacht!—"[8]

The lines "and from the Gothic hornèd tower owls / half-sigh an ah!" can certainly not be interpreted as a testimonial to the understanding of Gothic. The adjective "hornèd" probably means a spire terminated by pinnacles, but this Gothic is no more than a means of creating mood, like the owls. Herder knew no more about Gothic than about owls. Hermitages, ghosts, midnight, parting-ways, fairies, cypresses, graves, spirit voices, urns, moldering dust, silence, ancient elms, storm, ruins, more ghosts, the dead, altars, Hecate—then Gothic and owls; it does not matter here that this series of set-pieces is really a conglomeration from the young Herder's reading. What is important is that the Gothic tower is only one feature among many, fulfilling the same function of creating a romantic mood.

The remaining passages where Herder mentions Gothic are directed *against* it. Even the phrase "Gothic grandiosity" is not used in a spirit of approbation.[9] He is speaking of the sublime style in which he tends to clothe new experiences, for example, an impression on his travels, as something monstrous in contrast to the *beautiful* style for which he strives. Here he is really the opposite of Goethe. Another passage of his travel diary is in the same spirit: "What can become of a youthful soul for whom history, art, science, and religion have been Gothically dis-

[8] (In a literal translation as follows:
Where am I?—Amid hermitages
I find, I feel myself.
Ghosts shadowed away—Abysses of thought
surge down and come to rest!—
There where in the midnight grove fairies wandered on parting-ways—
And the dew from the cypresses rustled down on my bared head:
Around me the graves of the brothers, spirit voices from the urn's womb,
Hark! They send up their hollow sound—St! the mouldering dust
whispers an answer and is silent—
and on the dying crowns of eternal elms, hark! the storm,
that mounts from the crumbling, knightly ruins to my temple,
where ghosts consecrate the newly dead before the altar.
Hecate herself can scarcely spy her votaries through the ancient windows
and from the Gothic hornèd tower owls
half-sigh an ah!—
and my father before me—I shudder, shuddering
I awake, and about me is night!—)

[9] Suphan, IV, p. 438.

torted." In deep depression and utterly pessimistic, he was referring to himself.[10]

He does not fare very well in the part of Goethe's autobiography that concerns the Strasbourg sojourn. Herder's action in publishing Goethe's article in his *Von deutscher Art und Kunst* is explained by Lambel as an expression of his sympathy for "German vigor," just as he felt his own nature akin to that of Götz von Berlichingen. His halfheartedness toward Goethe's essay is incontestably evident in the note he appended to it; and when all the evidence is summed up, nothing is left of the older assumption that through Herder Goethe's eyes were opened to Gothic architecture.[11] In the Germany of that day there was as yet no Gothic Revival. Frederick the Great had had the Nauen Gate in Potsdam built by Büsing in 1755 according to English models, and Lord Marshall Keith's good offices with regard to the project have been documented;[12] but this remained an isolated experiment, and the Gothic structure next in time, the Gothic House in the Park at Wörlitz (near Dessau), did not come into being until 1784, long after Goethe's panegyric.

Goethe could have addressed his polemical remarks also to Blondel the Younger, but he actually refers, not to Blondel, but to a "dear abbé." Koetschau says: "Beginnings of the dithyramb on German architecture go back to the Strasbourg period. Max Morris shows with good reason that they were written in Sesenheim. What little there was went with Goethe to his native city. Here, where he is a zealous collaborator on the *Frankfurter Gelehrte Anzeigen*, the polemical element enters his work. It is directed toward the *Essai sur l'architecture* by Abbé Marc Antoine Laugier and toward the aesthetic oracle of the time, J. G. Sulzer, whom he rightly turns away from the temple of his enthusiasm for other reasons also, as a pedant lacking in feeling and insight."

10 *Ibid.*, p. 456. Herder speaks of "Gothic taste" in undated early works also; cf. Suphan, XXXII, Berlin, 1899, p. 29. He means, however, the Goths as destroyers of Roman antiquity. His remarks are thus still outside the modern distinctions of Carolingian, Romanesque, and Gothic; for him "Gotischer Geschmack" refers to everything built since the destruction of Rome by Alaric. This is still the idea that had been conceived by Manetti, Ghiberti, etc. The word "Gotisch" is also used vaguely in Herder's work, *Auch eine Philosophie der Geschichte zur Bildung der Menschheit,* 1774; cf. Suphan, V, pp. 522, 534, 565. In these places he is not talking about architecture.

11 In recent times Theodor Volbehr reverted to this problem, and came likewise to a negative conclusion; cf. "Der Zwiespalt in Goethes Kunstanschauung," *Festschrift für Karl Koetschau*, Düsseldorf, 1928, p. 184.

12 The present state of this gate (1945) is no longer the original. Alfred Neumeyer has shown that the latter can still be seen on a coffee cup in the museum at Potsdam; cf. his "Die Erweckung der Gotik in der deutschen Kunst," *Repertorium für Kunstwissenschaft*, Berlin, 1928, p. 86.

It is undoubtedly correct that Goethe meant the "abbé" to be Laugier. It is also very probable that he was thinking of Sulzer when he penned certain outbursts.[13] But this does not answer the question of *who* was Goethe's guide to Gothic.

In recent times Kindermann has interpreted Goethe's essay.[14] "The art that unites wholeness and organic integrity with heroic mentality seems to Goethe essentially German." This is seen from the point of view of the Third Reich (1935). "But just on that account it is only comprehensible to 'whole souls' (and to them only intuitively), never to 'weak devotees of Taste' with an enlightened bent. Romance rationalism, from its mathematical standpoint,—as expressed, for example, in Laugier's *Essai sur l'architecture* of 1753—can never do justice to the mystery of Gothic art."[14a] Obviously Kindermann has not read Laugier at all. The latter's remarks must be repeated once more: "Rien n'est comparable en ce genre à la tour de la Cathédrale de Strasbourg. Cette superbe pyramide (page 76). . . . Il y a plus d'art et de génie dans ce seul morceau que dans tout ce que nous voyons ailleurs de plus merveilleux." It cannot be said of *this* passage that Laugier achieved merely a "conditional" appreciation of the freedom, boldness, and grandeur of Gothic cathedrals (Waetzoldt); it signifies an *unconditional recognition* despite the words "en ce genre." Laugier is unquestionably half-hearted in other places, as we have seen, and nothing that he wrote about Gothic can be compared with Goethe's fervor. But this does not alter the fact that Goethe must have read Laugier's enthusiastic words of praise for Strasbourg Cathedral before he wrote his own dithyramb.[15]

It is frequently the case that men revile the individual who has shown them the way that they would have liked to discover and go alone—a situation which may be left to the psychologists to analyze. It might be said that a Goethe needed no Laugier. It is almost certain that Goethe experienced Gothic quite directly and spontaneously as something convincing and fascinating, that in spite of the prejudices that had surrounded him, perhaps even in youthfully lively revolt against these

[13] Sulzer's *Theorie der schönen Künste*, Leipzig, 1771-1774, appeared while Goethe was working on his essay. "Gotisch nennt man nicht nur, was die Goten bauten, sondern auch die abenteuerlichen und mit tausend unnützen Zieraten überladenen Gebäude, wozu vermutlich die in Europa sich niedergelassenen Sarazenen die ersten Muster gegeben haben."

[14] *Deutsche Literatur*, ed. Kindermann, Series *Irrationalismus*, VI, Goethe, *Von deutscher Art und Kunst*, Leipzig, 1935, p. 22.

[14a] "Eben deshalb aber ist sie nur 'ganzen Seelen' (und diesen intuitiv), nicht aber aufklärerischen schwachen Geschmäklern zugänglich. Romanischer Rationalismus—wie er sich etwa in Laugiers Essay sur l'architecture, 1753, äussert,—vermag von seinem mathematischen Standpunkt niemals dem gotischen Kunstgeheimnis gerecht zu werden."

[15] Cf. below, notes 20 and 21.

prejudices, he was suddenly carried away by the immediate impression. But the fact remains that he was irritated by Laugier, this dualistic man of transition. He aimed his blows at the Classicist, only to forget to thank the Mediaevalist, in his joyous tumult of discovery. Laugier had died in 1769; he could no longer defend himself and reclaim his intellectual property. However, had he indeed put up a fight, he would possibly not have fared too well. Was his enthusiasm for Strasbourg entirely spontaneous? If he had been hunting about in Paris libraries around 1740 for books that could satisfy his interest in architecture, he must have come across Félibien, whose work had been reprinted several times and was in those days not yet outdated. Here Laugier could discover that a Classicist had singled out Strasbourg Cathedral, and the tower in particular, for enthusiastic praise. Praise is just as suggestive as blame, and we should not wish to call Laugier a plagiarist for quietly making the praise of the cathedral his own. He had been favorably disposed and now stepped forward himself as the cathedral's advocate.

But what shall we now think of Félibien? Is *he* to be credited with the phenomenal insight that we have grown accustomed to admire in Goethe? According to Kindermann Félibien would have had to be a man of heroic mentality, a "whole soul," certainly not a romance rationalist. Perhaps a Kindermann would postulate that Félibien had German ancestors, though he could have discovered another way out of this—to him—embarrassing situation. Had Félibien read Wimpheling? Nobody knows. Wimpheling was ultra-German. In his case enthusiasm for the cathedral was not as remarkable as in that of the Classicists, Félibien and Laugier, for, as we have seen (page 248), he knew neither ancient nor Renaissance architecture, but only mediaeval, indeed, only German buildings, since he had never ventured beyond the narrow confines of his fatherland. Yet he called on the Italian Aeneas Sylvius, the Renaissance Pope, as an authority.

Goethe, however, who was undoubtedly quite unconscious of having received any inspiration from Laugier, did not remain satisfied with his essay. Later he condemned it as a youthful aberration and did not want to have it reprinted in his collected works. It is common knowledge how his taste changed. In 1786, during his Italian journey, when he saw ancient architecture, he wrote: "This is indeed quite different from our conversing saints, piled one on top of the other on little consoles, in the fashion of Gothic decoration, quite different from our pipestem columns, pointed small turrets, and jagged floral ornaments; thank God

I am now rid of them forever!" Goethe joined the chorus of those who vilified Gothic.[16] Obviously he had Vasari in mind, possibly even the letter that was then still circulating under Raphael's name: "qualche figurino ranichiato et malfatto et peggio inteso per mensola a sostenere un travo"[17]—although in the passage quoted Goethe does not mean the consoles themselves. In 1788, in the *Betrachtung über die Baukunst*, he reveals still another point of view when he writes that "the greater part of so-called Gothic architecture can be explained by the woodwork[17a] with which men in the earliest times were accustomed to decorate shrines, altars, and chapels, and which, with all its curlycues (*Schnörkeln*), bars, and ledges, they later, when the power and wealth of the church increased, fastened to the exteriors of the Nordic walls, thinking thus to adorn gables and formless towers. Unhappily the Nordic decorators of churches sought to be great only in multiplied smallness." It is noteworthy that Goethe calls Gothic the "so-called" Gothic architecture. By woodwork he meant carvings. In any case this woodcarving hypothesis is not to be taken as quite the same thing as Filarete's "goldsmith theory" (Goethe could hardly have known Filarete's manuscript, then still unpublished), for by "multiplied smallness" Goethe meant that fundamental difference between ancient architecture and Gothic, which has reference to proportion. The relatively fixed proportions of the ancient orders can only be magnified as wholes. Gothic can build up the entire structure from successive parts of any desired proportions.

When he was writing his autobiography (1811) Goethe reverted to the subject of his "sin of youth," discussing it now with fatherly condescension, as though he were speaking of someone else: "If I had deigned to express these views, the value of which I will not deny, clearly and definitely in an intelligible style, the treatise *Von Deutscher Baukunst D.M. Erwini a Steinbach* would, even at the time I published it, have had a greater effect and attracted the attention of patriotic friends of art earlier; but as it was, misguided by the example of Hamann and Herder, I concealed these quite simple ideas and observa-

16 Goethe, *Italienische Reise*, letter from Venice, October 8, 1786. "Das ist freilich etwas anderes, als unsere kauzenden, auf Kragsteimlein übereinander geschichteten Heiligen der gothischen Zierweisen, etwas anders als unsere Tabakspfeifen-Säulen, spitze Thürmlein und Blumenzacken; dies bin ich nun, Gott sey Dank, auf ewig los." (The word *kauzend* is according to the Dictionary of the Brothers Grimm identical with *hockend*.) The newest edition, Hamburg 1951, contains comments by the art historian Herbert von Einem. See pp. 88, 592.

17 ". . . many small, crouching figures poorly made and still more poorly conceived as consoles to support a beam."

17a *Holzschnittwerke* is the word used here.

tions in a dust cloud of strange words and phrases, darkening the light, which had dawned, for myself and others."[18] Thus it now became Herder's fault that Goethe had written such absurd things or at least in such a poor style! What an all too human distortion of fact! Herder wrote very often in a highly unpleasant, aggressively blustering style. Goethe's polemic, on the other hand, swept the reader away by its rage. In the end we must defend the young Goethe against the old, for, after all, he wrote: "My soul was filled by a whole and great impression, which, because it consisted of a thousand harmonizing details, I could indeed taste and enjoy, but by no means comprehend or explain. They say that it is thus with the joys of Heaven. . . ." Young Goethe knew then that he was still far from "comprehending" or "explaining" Gothic; the aged Goethe had progressed further: he knew that in addition to the joys of Heaven and the joys of intuitive perception there are also those of cognition; and he lived to see the harbingers of a methodical study of Gothic. But all analysis of art presupposes that one has first experienced art as art, and been moved by it in the depths of one's soul. How deeply Laugier had been stirred is not entirely evident from his words, despite his superlatives. A god gave Goethe "the power to express" not only "what he was suffering," but also what he adored.

Quite independently of each other, both Nikolaus Pevsner[19] and Ernst Beutler[20] simultaneously discovered Goethe's debt to Laugier.

Pevsner, in collaboration with Geoffrey Grigson, has translated Goethe's essay into English and provided it with a commentary.[21] Beutler has brought together various pieces of evidence showing Goethe's acquaintance with Laugier's book. "When he returned to Frankfort from Strasbourg at the end of August 1771, Goethe consulted the books on architecture in his father's library, in order to supplement with information the great impression that the cathedral had made upon him.

[18] *Dichtung und Wahrheit*, Part 3, Book 12. In the edition of Grossherzogin Sophie, XXVIII, Weimar, 1890, p. 98.

[19] Nikolaus Pevsner, "Romantic Gothic, Scene I: Goethe and Strassburg," *The Architectural Review*, XCVIII, London, 1945, December, p. 155.

[20] Ernst Beutler, *Von Deutscher Baukunst, Goethes Hymnus auf Erwin von Steinbach, seine Entstehung und Wirkung*, Freies Deutsches Hochstift, Frankfurt a.M. (Reihe der Vorträge und Schriften, IV), Munich, 1943, pp. 31ff.

After all, the identification of Laugier with the "dear abbé" was not for the first time published by Koetschau (1926), Hermann Schmitz knew it in 1921 (*Die Gotik . . .*, pp. 183ff.) and he quotes the polemic of the architect Friedrich August Krubsacius (1718-1790) writing angrily that Goethe probably read no other book upon architecture besides Laugier. So the emphasis lies not on the identification of the abbé, rather on Laugier's estimation of the façade of Strasbourg.

[21] Another translation into English is that by Elizabeth Gilmore Holt, in *Literary Sources of Art History*, Princeton, N. J., 1947, p. 543.

The newest thing, only recently come into the house, was a German translation of the *Essai sur l'architecture* by Marc Antoine Laugier." (p. 31) Beutler surmises that Oeser had called Gothe's attention to it in 1768 in Leipzig, and that Goethe took it himself to Frankfort. In addition, his father owned Laugier's *Observations* of 1765. This makes it clear that Goethe did not merely see Laugier's books briefly and casually, but that he was able to study them at leisure. If Goethe may be supposed already to have read Laugier's *Essai* in 1768, his ingratitude would be psychologically easier to understand. For in that case there would have become established in him a readiness to appreciate the tower of the cathedral, and when he actually saw it, he might have forgotten the passage in Laugier's book, instead of making its acquaintance for the first time only in 1771.

Beutler's book goes into all the particulars of Goethe's panegyric, with unusually persuasive interpretations and very subtle stylistic analysis. He also provides an informative survey of the influence exercised by the essay. We may single out what he writes about the mathematician, Gottfried HUTH, who not only reprinted the work in his *Allgemeines Magazin für die bürgerliche Baukunst* of 1789 but also urged, with reference to it, "a history of architecture among the Germans," which should bring no joy to un-German hearts who only "in the dazzling works of the foreigner find traces of their authors' genius and energy."

Since Beutler has gone into the subsequent history of Goethe's essay in such detail, we may remind the reader of its antecedents by listing them chronologically:

1457 Aeneas Sylvius Piccolomini
1502 Wimpheling
1548 Engraving by Conrad Morant called Schweblin
1617 Osäus Schad
1647 Wenzel Hollar, engraving of 1630 and 1645
1687 Félibien
1699 Dumont
1753 Laugier
1771 Goethe

Probably there are or were still other links in this tradition of praise. An Italian leads the line, not a German.

There is no doubt that his essay of 1771 had a deep and lasting effect in Germany, but it is uncertain whether it influenced other countries. Before 1766 Claude VILLARET (1715-1766) set down some remarks on Gothic that sound like a renunciation of the prejudices of his time:

"One cannot help agreeing that in spite of ignorance of the rules, the noble simplicity, the wise distribution, and the elegance of Greek and Roman architecture, our Gothic temples offer beauties of a kind that is peculiar to them. The height, the boldness of the vaults have not been surpassed by the moderns. The ancient majesty of these sacred naves inspires a certain religious awe which seems to acquaint and imbue us with the sacredness of the mystery that is there solemnized."[22] This sounds quite different from Goethe; though it may be yet another echo of Laugier, it is at the same time an anticipation of the coming French Romanticism.

With his youthful essay Goethe introduced into the literature on Gothic the dithyrambic note, the suggestiveness of poetic language, and attained such a high level of excellence that hardly anyone who followed him on this path could equal him; at most one might mention Rodin, who likewise wrote about art as an artist. Herder's sobering footnote reminds us of the scientific requirements of clear analysis and precise concepts. At least one word that has in modern times also been employed for the understanding of Gothic was then already coined: the word picturesque. Goethe did not use it in his essay, but an excursus on its history may be justified at this point.

Those who thought only Germans were able to appreciate the Strasbourg Cathedral would have been surprised to learn that it made an impression upon a Russian. KARAMZIN (1765-1826) traveled from 1789 to 1790 through Germany, Switzerland, France, and England. His letters were published after 1797. In August 1789 he wrote in Strasbourg: "The cathedral in this town is undeniably the most majestic Gothic building, as the tower is the highest in Europe. If one enters the interior of this vast temple it is impossible to refrain from veneration and shuddering." Then he criticizes some reliefs of donkeys, monkeys, and so on, mounts the tower and describes the view below and to the mountains far away.[23]

Karamzin was the first Russian historian. His remarks are not

[22] Claude Villaret, *Histoire de France*, Paris, 1783, XI, p. 140; quoted from Corblet, *Revue de l'art chrétien*, III, 1859, p. 300. "On ne peut s'empêcher de convenir, que malgré l'ignorance où l'on était des règles, de la noble simplicité, de la sage distribution et de l'élégance de l'architecture grecque et romaine, nos temples gothiques offrent des beautés d'un genre que leur est particulier. L'élévation, la hardiesse des voûtes n'ont point été surpassées par les modernes. L'antique majesté de ces vaisseaux sacrés inspire une certaine horreur religieuse, qui semble nous avertir et nous pénétrer de la sainteté du mystère qu'on y célèbre." The work of Claude Villaret (1715-1766) was published posthumously.

[23] Tr. is from German ed. by J. Richter, Vienna, 1922, p. 150. An English tr. now exists, *Letters of a Russian Traveller*, New York, 1957.

very penetrating. Skeptics may ask whether he read the booklet of Schadaeus, if it still was on the market. Yet if he had his eyes open everywhere, why then should he need a special guide for his feeling?[24]

2. The Word Picturesque

In the sixteenth century there is one isolated occurrence of the word picturesque in Vasari's *Lives* of 1550.[1] The phrase *alla pittoresca* is used in connection with the differentiation between two types of cartoons that the painter can make for his sketches.[2] The one is composed of drawings in red or black crayon, the other is "executed in chiaroscuro on tinted sheets that produce a medium tone, and the pen makes the lineaments, that is, the inner line or the profile, and then the ink with a little water makes a sweet color, which veils and shades it (the drawing); then one heightens the lights in the drawing with a pointed brush, impregnated with gum; and this manner is very picturesque and brings out the order of the colors better."[3] Giorgio Vasari is here really thinking of drawings which we today should call picturesque in contrast to those that are merely outlined and as such approach the concept of the linear. Yet a line drawing is not necessarily linear in our sense, and Vasari, even with his second type, did not mean exclusively drawings that were picturesque in our sense of the word. Rather, the point of his differentiation is that the painter can either make drawings with crayon alone or color pen drawings with a brush. The latter blend better with the color values. "Alla pittoresca" means therefore "painted with a brush after the manner of painting," instead of drawn with crayon.

More than one hundred years passed before the word *pittoresco* again

[24] Postscript on bibliography: Goethe's praise of Gothic of 1772 is paralleled in the writings of Thomas Chatterton (1752-1770) of Bristol. Cf. Horst Oppel, "Die Entdeckung der englischen Gotik durch Chatterton," *Wandlungen Christlicher Kunst im Mittelalter*, II, Baden-Baden, 1953.

[1] For the most important lexicographical sources of *pittoresco*, *pittorescamente* cf. N. Tommaseo and E. Bellini, *Dizionario della lingua italiana*, Turin, 1861-1879; for *pitturesque*, Hatzfeld-Darmstetter-Thomas, *Dictionnaire de la langue française*, Paris, 1890-1893, and E. Littré, *Dictionnaire de la langue française*, Paris, 1869.

[2] Giorgio Vasari, *Le Vite* . . . , ed. Milanesi, I, p. 175.

[3] In the edition by Karl Frey (Munich, 1911), I, p. 111, the text reads: "Altri di chiaro et scuro si conducono su fogli tinti, che fanno un mezo, et la penna fa il lineamento, cio è il dintorno ò profilo, et l'inchiostro poi con un poco d'acqua, fa una tinta dolce, che lo vela et ombra; di poi con un pennello sottile, intinto nella biacca, stemperata con la gomma, si lumeggia il disegno; et questo modo è molto alla pittoresca et mostra più l'ordine del colorito." In the Milanesi edition, Florence, 1878, I, p. 175, with different orthography, e.g. "mezzo."

appeared. Salvator ROSA (1615-1673) wrote while traveling to Loreto: "I have now been on the way for fifteen consecutive days, and the journey is incomparably stranger and more picturesque than that from Florence, because it is a mixture of such extravagancies of the fearful and the familiar, of the flat and the precipitous [plains and mountains], so that no better feast for the eyes could be desired."[4] That Rosa uses the word picturesque is important, since in the eighteenth century the phrase "like a Salvator Rosa" was used countless times in its stead. The two expressions are synonymous. The passage just cited is not to be found in the lexicographical aids (Tommaseo-Bellini). One must, however, almost assume that even in Rosa's day the word was common in painters' circles. In the following years it occurs again several times in quick succession,[5] but by no means in the sense of modern usage, whereas Rosa means at least approximately what Gilpin, again one hundred years later, understood by "picturesque travel": a journey that stimulates one to paint and that offers motifs for landscape painting—though, of course, painting of a particular type of landscape, the "picturesque."

In 1670 the word *pittoresco* next appears in a treatise on snakes. Francesco REDI (1626-1698) was a man of versatile gifts, physician, poet, and zoologist.[6] One of his special fields was the study of snakes. In a work which reveals that he had made hundreds of experiments on animals with snake venom he discusses in detail the question of Cleopatra's suicide. He thinks she used not a live asp, but the venom collected in a box, wounding her arm with a hairpin that had been dipped in this poison. An ancient author records that a picture of Cleopatra with an asp in her hand was carried in the triumphal procession of Augustus, but that, says Redi, is merely an artistic liberty. Painters and sculptors even allow themselves the liberty of portraying her with the asp biting her breast (instead of her arm), although "Plutarch, Propertius, Orosius, Paulus Diaconus tell us that she did not let herself be bitten in the breast, but in the arm. And this picturesque license does not first appear among the moderns, but even the ancients made use of

[4] G. A. Cesareo, *Poesie e lettere edite e inedite di Salvatore Rosa*, Naples, 1892, II, p. 117, letter from Rome dated May 13, 1662; cited also by Elizabeth W. Manwaring, *Italian Landscape in Italian Painting of the Eighteenth Century*, New York, 1925. "Son stato in quindici giorni in continuo mota, et il viaggio è assai più curioso e pittoresco de cotesto di Fiorenza senza comparazione, attesochè è d'un misto cosi stravagante d'orrido e di domestico, di piano e di scosceso, che non si puo desiderar di vantaggio per lo compiacimento dell'occhio."

[5] Numerous instances in E. W. Manwaring, *Italian Landscape . . . , op. cit.*, cf. her index.

[6] Francesco Redi, *Osservazioni intorno alle vipere, scritte in una lettera al conte Lorenzo Magalotti*, Florence, 1664; *Opere di Francesco Redi*, Milan, 1811, IV, p. 165.

it. . . ."[7] Redi is so learned that he can prove this from a gem, "on which one sees engraved Cleopatra being bitten in the breast by an asp."[8] We need not investigate here whether Cleopatra poisoned herself in the arm or the breast, but must simply recognize that *licenza pittoresca* means in this passage merely what we are accustomed to call poetic license. *Pittoresco* is thus not used in our modern sense; "picturesque license" signifies here a painter's license.

It must be remembered that in the years following there were in Paris the most violent disputes about concepts that seem to be akin to the idea of the picturesque in our sense and yet are not identical with it. This is the struggle of the Rubénistes against the Poussinistes, or, if one wishes to name the leaders, of Roger DE PILES (1635-1709) against André Félibien, who was older by a generation, and Charles LE BRUN (1619-1690). It is a struggle of the younger generation against the old; in terms of contemporary slogans, of Antwerp against Bologna (Caracci), or, objectively expressed, the struggle of color versus mere drawing.[9] These main concepts are accompanied by a host of others current in the aesthetics of that time, but—unless lexicographical research has been unreliable—the word *pittoresque* never occurs in the disputes. It was still lacking in the French language. Félibien wrote a devastating criticism of Rubens; on the other hand, Roger de Piles' enthusiasm for this painter leads him to the following assertion: "The pictures [of Rubens] are more beautiful than nature itself, which seems to be but a copy of the works of this great man."[10] Today it seems to us so easy to reply that what is art in Rubens is in truth no more imitation of nature than, conversely, nature can be a weaker imitation of Rubens. But it means much that De Piles with his inversion sought to be rid of the old theory: painting is the imitation of nature (and antiquity), especially when one remembers that these conflicts took place within the Academy itself, to which Roger de Piles also belonged. It was not actually a revolution, merely a palace revolution, whereas the

7 ". . . narrano Plutarco, Properzio, Orosio, Paola Diacono, che non nel petto, ma nel braccio ella morder se fece. E questa licenza pittoresca non è sola dei moderni ma anchora gli antichi l'usano . . ."

8 ". . . nella quale scolpita si vede Cleopatra punta dall Aspido nella mammella."

9 Pierre Marcel, *La Peinture Française au début du dixhuitième siècle, 1690-1721*, Paris, 1906, pp. 55ff. Cf. also the very informative book by André Fontaine, *Les doctrines d'art en France, peintres, amateurs, critiques de Poussin et Diderot*, Paris, 1909; further, Werner Weisbach, *Französische Malerei des XVII. Jahrhunderts*, Berlin, 1932, *passim*, and Otto Grauthoff, *Barockmalerei in den romanischen Ländern*, Wildpark-Potsdam, 1928. Cf. Julius Schlosser, *Die Kunstliteratur*, Vienna, 1924, index p. 632; and Léon Mirot, *Roger de Piles*, Paris, 1924.

10 ". . . les tableaux [de Rubens] sont plus beau que la nature même, laquelle semble n'être que la copie des ouvrages de ce grand homme."

Mediaevalist trend, developing simultaneously in England, was a real revolution, though unintentional on the part of the revolutionists. The struggle of color against drawing within the framework of Classicism has affinities with the contrast that first appeared in Vasari; but the omission of the word *pittoresque* in this dispute is justifiable, if one bases its meaning on the modern sense, for however ardently color was advocated, the picturesque was not.

We meet the word *pittoresco* four more times in the seventeenth century shortly after Redi's use of it, but in none of the cases does it signify what it does today.

Daniele BARTOLI (1608-1685) says in his biography of Stanislaus Kostka: "It is all purely historical narration, not a poetic figment nor picturesque fantasy."[11]

P. Paolo SEGNERI (1623-1694) is talking about cursing, and in the course of his discussion mentions the portrayal of the gods of the winds: "In order to represent the strongest winds, the painters are accustomed to depict various puffed out faces that blow furiously. But that is their picturesque caprice. . . ."[12]

For Puccio LAMONI, *pittorescamente parlando* means approximately "in the jargon of the painters." This passage, too, has its charm. Paolo MINUCCI (1604-1664) wrote a long poem under the pseudonym of Perlone Zipoli.[13] It contains the remarkable stanza:

> "Su dadi i torsi, nobili sculture
> (Perchè in rovina il tutto il tempo mena)
> Ristaurati sono, e risarciti
> Da vere e fresche teste di banditi."[14]

Lamoni glosses the word "torsi": "He means human torsos, which in the jargon of the painters signifies the trunk alone, without head, arms, or legs, Latin *truncus*, . . ."[15] We should expect him to say that torsos

[11] Daniele Bartoli, *Vita del B. Stanislao Kostka libri due*, 2, 5. (According to Tommaseo-Bellini, vol. 4, II, p. 1986.) "Tutto è narrazione puramente istorica, non fingimento poetico nè fantasia pittoresca."

[12] P. Paolo Segneri, *Il Christiano instruito*, Florence, 1686, I, p. 8: "I pittori, per esprimere i venti piu impetuosi, sogliono figurare alcune facce gonfie, che spirano con gran furia. Ma questo è un capriccio lor pittoresco fondato a la necessità che gli stringe di rappresentar quel medesimo che non può soggiare a guardi. . . ."

[13] Paolo Minucci (Perlone Zipoli), *Malmantile racquistato*, ed. Puccio Lamoni, Florence, 1688; Canto VI, Strophe 52.

[14] Above the pedestals the torsos, the noble sculptures (since time brings all to ruins) are restored and completed by real and fresh heads of bandits.

[15] "Intende torsi d'huomini che pittorescamente parlando vuol dire in solo corpo senza testa, e braccia e come Latino truncus. . . ."

have a picturesque effect, but this is not what he means. In the history of the conservation of monuments this method of supplying torsos with the heads of decapitated bandits is certainly an instance of a seldom achieved naturalism. But *pittorescamente parlando* does not refer to the completion of the torsos, but merely to the word *torsi* itself.

In Filippo BALDINUCCI (1624-1696) the usage is no different. He describes in the driest way the proper proportions of the face—three equal parts, consisting of the portion from chin to nose, the nose itself, and finally the forehead, according to the ancient tradition of the Painters' Book from Mount Athos and Vitruvius—and so on, and then remarks: "E mancando un volto di simili proporzioni, mai potrà l'aria del medisimo essere quel segno, che si dice pittorescamente bella." That is, beauty according to the painters' language.[16]

In the eighteenth century England adopted the Italian word in 1705 in the form "picturesque"; in France it became "pittoresque" in 1712; and in Germany in 1754 "mahlerisch. [*sic*]"

It is difficult to say what "picturesque" meant when it made its first English appearance in Richard STEELE (1672-1729).[17] The young lady who is to have her portrait painted wishes to be represented as the Amazon, Thalestris, with a spear in her hand and her helmet lying on a table. In the background a dwarf is to hold a milk-white palfrey by the bridle. The painter—he is the lover in disguise—suggests the addition of a cupid who will steal the helmet as a form of disarmament. To this the young lady replies: "That circumstance may be very picturesque." Probably she means only that it is a good idea for a picture. But taken also as an allegory the notion would presumably be regarded as desirable for a painting. It is again a kind of *licenza pittoresca.*

In 1712 the word *pittoresque* appears in France. The passage in question has also escaped the lexicographers and there may well be still others awaiting discovery. It is to be found in Marcel's book. Charles Antoine COYPEL (1694-1752) says in a *Discours* of 1712 that he still remembers clearly the struggles in the Academy of a generation ago: "In this painters' war (*guerre pittoresque*) the one side raised the banner of Rubens, the other that of Poussin." In the phrase *guerre pittoresque* the adjective means clearly "among painters."[18]

[16] *Lettera di Filippo Baldinucci intorno al modo di dar proportione alle figure in pittura e scultura ora per la prima volta publicata* (da Gaetano Poggiali), Livorno, 1802 (*Opere*, II, III, Milan, 1808-1812). Baldinucci's dates are 1624(?)-1696.

[17] In Steele's play, *The Tender Husband*, 1703.

[18] P. Marcel, *op.cit.*, p. 67: "Dans cette guerre pittoresque les uns arboraient l'étendard de Rubens, les autres celui de Poussin."

Alexander POPE (1688-1744) considered "picturesque" to be of French origin. He used the word himself in 1715 in a note to the *Iliad*. Here its meaning is more or less that of "pictorial."[19]

In the *Mercure de France* of 1732 an anonymous writer described the festivities celebrating the recovery of the Duc d'Orléans and his son, Duc de Chartres, from an illness. The church, Église-des-Pères-de-l'Oratoire, was decorated; a cartouche fastened above the altar displayed an allegory of "Convalescence": ". . . the whole supported by a sham balustrade, very rich, on which one saw a Turkish carpet, embroidered in gold and picturesquely draped."[20]

In 1740 Thomas GRAY wrote from Rome, using the word picturesque in a sense that seems perfectly familiar to us: "You cannot pass along a street but you have views of some palace, or church, or square, or fountain; the most picturesque and most noble one can imagine."[21]

Only William GILPIN (1724-1804) makes any real contribution to a further development.[22] After studying at Oxford he became a clergyman. One of his first publications was a dialogue, in 1748, between two friends who converse about the beauties of the garden in Stow.[23] Here one finds the most important components of the picturesque in landscape already analyzed: variety and irregularity produce pleasure (in the eighteenth century the real goal of art). "Has not that Ruin a good effect? The Sound of the Cascade, the Shrubs half-concealing the rugged View, and those dancing Fauns and Satyrs, I assure you, raise very romantic Ideas in my Head,"[24] says Callophilos; Polyphton answers, agreeing: "Yes, indeed, I think the Ruin a great Addition to the Beauty of the Lake. There is something so costly picturesque and pleasing to the Imagination in such Objects that they are a great Addition to any Landskip. . . ."[25] Later the friends come to an "old Gothic Building," and Callophilos remarks: "As old as it looks, I assure you it is not yet finished; the Scaffolding within is not yet taken away. . . ."[26] A not yet finished ruin! This is indeed a last refinement of the picturesque!

19 Quoted by Elizabeth W. Manwaring, *Italian Landscape* . . . , p. 167.

20 ". . . le tout supporté sur une Balustrade feinte, très riche, sur laquelle on voyait un Tapis de Turquie, rehaussé d'or et drappé pittorescquement."

21 *Op.cit.*, p. 168. Letter to his mother from Rome, April 2, 1740.

22 For this and what follows cf. the unusually thorough work of William D. Templeman: *The Life and Work of William Gilpin (1724-1804) Master of the Picturesque and Vicar of Boldre* (Illinois Studies in Language and Literature, XXIV), Urbana, Ill., 1939, pp. 113ff. Both Templeman and Manwaring are of the opinion that *pittoresque* has here about the same meaning as "graphic." To me this seems inexact.

23 In great detail in Templeman, pp. 34 and 117-127.

24 Gilpin, p. 120.

25 *Ibid.*, p. 120.

26 *Ibid.*, p. 125.

Polyphton, who feels exactly as Callophilos does, finds that this new old building "performs a valuable service in the landscape."

Gilpin was himself a diligent amateur of painting, and must have had an unusually stimulating effect on his circle of acquaintances. From then on the word picturesque is used more and more frequently.[27] In 1751 Denis DIDEROT (1713-1784) included it in his *Encyclopédie*, though the two authors of the brief article understood by the word something completely different from what was later the case: ". . . A good, picturesque composition is one, the sight of which makes a great effect, following the intention and the goal that has been set. Therefore the picture must not be overloaded with figures, although there ought to be enough of them to fill the canvas. The objects must be easily distinguished. The figures ought not to mutilate each other, as when one hides half of another's head or other parts of the body, which, being proper to the subject, the painter should make visible. Finally, the groups must be well composed, the light must be judiciously distributed among them, and the local colors must not kill one another but be so disposed that there results from the whole a harmony agreeable in itself to the eye."[28] In other words, *pittoresque* is for these authors synonymous with correctly academic. It means here in general what is desirable for paintings, and thus the term revealed its weak side even in 1751. For if "picturesque" signifies what is specifically in accordance with painting, then the whole meaning of the word turns on what is declared to be painting's specific characteristic. Painting can be either classical, with local colors that do not interfere with each other, and so on, and consequently "unpicturesque"—later one said "plastic"—or it can be as Callophilos and Polyphton see the garden: "picturesque."

But the word *pittoresque* was not only applied to landscape architecture, or poetry (Pope), or street vistas in Rome (Gray, 1740), or natural landscapes, as in Friedrich von HAGEDORN (1705-1754), who, so

27 In more detail in Templeman, pp. 123ff.

28 The signature of the article, D. G., indicates Gourrier, a mathematician and physicist, and Daubenton, a doctor of medicine. "Une bonne composition pittoresque, est celle dont le coup d'oeil fait un grand effet, suivant l'intension et le but qu'il s'est proposé. Il faut pour cela que le tableau ne soit point embarassé par les figures, quoiqu'il y en ait assez pour bien remplir la toile. Il faut que les objects s'y démêlent facilement. Il ne faut pas que les figures s'estropient l'uns l'autres en se cachent réciproquement la moitié de la tête, ni d'autres parties du corps, lesquelles il convient au sujet, que le peintre fasse voir. Il faut enfin que les groupes soient bien composés, que la lumière leur soit distribuée judicieusement et que les couleurs locales loins de s'entre-tuer, soient disposées de manière qu'il résulte du tout une harmonie agréable à l'oeil par elle même." In Diderot's own writings the word *pittoresque* occurs often.

far as I can see, introduced the word *mahlerisch* [*sic*] into the German language:[29] it was also used quite generally.

VOLTAIRE (1694-1778) employs the word twice in his article, *Imagination*.[30] Both times it means approximately "descriptive" or "graphic." The epic and the ode have a greater need of *expressions pittoresques* than tragedy, presumably because tragedy is intended for the stage, where the events can actually be seen, whereas in the epic or ode they can be perceived only through the means of verbal expression. Thus the word picturesque grows vague and ambiguous, it even becomes a catchword, and from this point on there is no longer any necessity for trying to locate all the passages where it occurs.

3. The Concept of the Picturesque

IMPORTANT as it is to know the history of the word picturesque, it is even more important and interesting to see how the word gradually became associated with an appropriate concept. In 1762 Walpole, as we have seen above (page 393), called *Gothic* picturesque. In the 1760's William GILPIN (1724-1804) wrote a treatise entitled *Essay on Prints*. His friends read the manuscript, but it was not published until 1768. In 1770 he wrote a book on the landscape of the Wye,[1] and waited twelve years for its publication. Similarly, the manuscripts of his next three essays circulated for years among enthusiasts for the picturesque before they were at last printed.[2] Gilpin slowly arrived at a kind of defi-

[29] According to Jakob and Wilhelm Grimm, *Deutsches Wörterbuch*, VI, col. 1508, Leipzig, 1885. Hagedorn lived from 1708 to 1754. I do not know whether his poem, *Der Frühling*, can be dated precisely. It begins as follows:

Der mahlerische Lenz kann nichts so sinnreich bilden
Als jene Gegenden von Hainen und Gefilden.

[30] Voltaire, *Dictionnaire philosophique*, of 1764. The quotation is from the *Œuvres complètes*, Paris, 1879, XIX, p. 432: "C'est surtout dans la Poésie, que cette imagination de détail et d'expression doit régner; elle est ailleurs agréable, mais là elle est nécessaire, presque tout est image dans Homère, dans Vergile, dans Horace, sans même qu'on s'apperçoive. La tragédie demande moins d'images, moins d'expression pittoresque, de grandes métaphores, d'allégories, que le poème epique ou l'ode." (Especially in poetry this imagination in detail and expression ought to prevail; in other places it is agreeable, but here it is necessary; in Homer, Virgil, and Horace almost everything is imagery, even though one is not conscious of it. Tragedy demands fewer images, fewer picturesque expressions, great metaphors, and allegories than the epic poem or the ode.) And on page 436: "Virgile est plein de ces expressions pittoresques." Voltaire's article was also reprinted in the *Grande Encyclopédie*, 1765.

[1] *Observations on the River Wye and several Parts of South Wales . . . relative chiefly to Picturesque Beauty*, 1782.

[2] Bibliography in Manwaring, *op.cit.*

nition or analysis of the concept. One can, however, only appreciate his intellectual process if one restores the thread, here isolated, to its original texture, the general development of aesthetics in that generation. But before entering into a discussion of Gilpin's *Three Essays* we must observe the chronological sequence by interpolating a passage from François HEMSTERHUIS (1721-1790), which, though it does not contain the word picturesque, nevertheless deals with the concept.

Hemsterhuis was a popular philosopher and as such a characteristic phenomenon in the circle of the Enlighteners and Classicists. He wrote on many subjects, including sculpture. We do not need to concern ourselves here with the details of his aesthetic theory;[3] it is important to know only that he distributes his permissions and prohibitions disparately between sculpture and painting. "I recall having seen a group that represented Tereus plucking out Philomela's tongue. What an idea for sculpture! The sculptor ought not to represent anything of this kind! Painting, on the contrary, being of wider scope, can mitigate such repulsiveness by beauty in other parts of the pictures."[4] "In the group of Amphion, Dirce is charming, though bound to the horns of a bull. Let the artist be as much of a painter as he will in the expression of the action, but let him be a sculptor in order to enrich, likewise as much as possible, all the profiles, so that when the entire contour of each profile is measured one may find them all of about equal length and at the same time as short as possible."[5] This is Hemsterhuis' personal dogma, which, in mathematical terms, reduces sculpture to a maximal-minimal computation of contour lengths. He permits painting more latitude in the matter of content than sculpture; of the latter he demands the absolute exclusion of everything ugly or indecent. His theory of form makes him reluctant to recognize the existence of sculptured groups. Sculpture should represent only single figures; painting, however, may depict groups. But among the respected works of antiquity there are, embarrassingly, also groups. And this leads to an observation that was to have important consequences: "You will say that from this standpoint there is hardly any perfect large group in sculpture.

[3] François Hemsterhuis, *Lettres sur la sculpture*, 1769. In the edition, *Œuvres philosophiques*, Paris, 1792, p. 46.

[4] "Je me souviens d'avoir vu un groupe qui représentait Terée qui arrache la langue a Philomèle. Quelle idée en sculpture!"

[5] "Dans le groupe d'Amphion Dircée est charmante, quoiqu'attachée aux cornes d'un taureau. Enfin que l'artiste soit *peintre* autant qu'il veut dans l'expression de l'action, mais qu'il soit *sculpteur* pour enrichir également autant qu'il est possible tous les profiles et qu'en mesurant le contour total de chaque profil on les trouve tous à peu près d'égale longueur et de même temps aussi court qu'il est possible."

I believe that such is the case, and I venture to add that the two masterpieces of those famous Rhodians—I refer to Laocoön and Amphion—belong far more to painting than to sculpture. However, one can hardly accuse the Greeks of this fault; but one can say that our modern sculptors are too much painters, just as the Greek painters were apparently too much sculptors."[6]

The last sentence can mean for Hemsterhuis only this: in antiquity the painters were too plastic, that is, intent on concise contours; in modern times the sculptors are too "picturesque," that is, interested in the expression of an action. We shall see presently that the sentence was interpreted quite differently later on. The essential point for us is not whether Hemsterhuis was objectively and historically right, but that the picturesque is here taken as the distinguishing characteristic of a stylistic period and, though hitherto an isolated concept, is now paired with a hostile counterpart, the plastic. Disregarding the implied censure (perhaps the most important thing for Hemsterhuis, who was not loath to sit in judgment), there remains the realization that there are times when the work of the sculptor is of a plastic character and others when it is picturesque. In this generalized form Hemsterhuis' assertion lived on.

Behind this idea may be concealed the old theme of the *paragone*, the conflict of rank among the arts, which had been in actuality a dispute about social precedence between painters and sculptors. Schlosser sarcastically called this theme an academic "schoolboy's task." One may read his account of its derivation from Neoplatonic sources and its history from Cennini and Leonardo to Varchi.[7] Hemsterhuis, however, is not at all concerned with a conflict about rank, but rather with a kind of aesthetic police regulation: *Quod licet pictori, non licet sculptori.* Likewise the converse!

If, consequently, one knows what is good and bad for each art, one can tell both painter and sculptor what should or should not be done, without ranking one higher than the other. With such objectivity—within the confines of his prejudice—Hemsterhuis can now talk of good and bad epochs for each of the arts. Antiquity was good in sculpture, bad—of course, not wholly bad!—in painting, while the converse

[6] "Vous direz que sur ce pied-là il n'y a presque point de grand groupe parfait en sculpture. Je le crois, et j'ose ajouter que les deux chef-d'œuvre de ces illustres Rhodiens, je parle de Laocoon et d'Amphion, appartiennent beaucoup plus à la peinture qu'à la sculpture. D'ailleurs on ne peut guère accuser les Grecs de ce défaut; mais on peut dire que nos sculpteurs modernes sont trop peintres comme apparemment les peintres grecs étaient trop sculpteurs!"

[7] Julius Schlosser, *Die Kunstliteratur*, Vienna, 1924, p. 80 (Cennini), p. 200 (Varchi).

is true of the modern age. And though the Classicist is unaware of it, the old scheme has been shifted, for *good* meant to Petrarch the entire period of antiquity and *bad* his own time. Hemsterhuis, like Winckelmann and Lessing ignores totally the art of the whole Middle Ages, but his differentiation was bound to become significant for the understanding of Gothic, once the style was declared to be picturesque.

It was natural for Hemsterhuis to devote some thought to the Laocoön group, since Lessing had made it in 1766 the starting-point of his aesthetics, or rather his theory of art. Lessing tried to define the boundaries between poetry and painting. Painting was for him equivalent to representational arts in general; it comprised painting and sculpture quite indiscriminately. Hemsterhuis had the idea of a delimitation within image art itself, that is, between painting and sculpture. But his *aperçu*, which occurred almost at the end of his treatise, was not taken up at once by other thinkers. The years between his work of 1769 and Gilpin's *Three Essays* of 1792 offer no new ideas, while interest in the picturesque became more and more popular.[8] If research heretofore has not been misleading, this movement was confined almost entirely to England. In Germany the word *malerisch* occurs quite frequently, but the passages are nearly all of no importance for the present problem.[9] Only one, from Herder, is significant. He wrote his *Plastik* "substantially in the years from 1768 to 1770," but did not publish it until 1778. He speaks of sepulchral monuments with allegories, indulging in violent polemics against them as soon as they become a "chief work" of art. They have then no "incarnate truth"[10] but merely a juxtaposed or superimposed significance, and they can never embody this concomitant significance, "for an element of all literary and moral allegory

8 Abundant material in Manwaring, *op.cit.*, and in Christopher Hussey, *The Picturesque*, London and New York, 1927.

9 According to Grimms' Dictionary. There may be still more evidence, for the Grimms give only examples and make no attempt at completeness. In Lessing's *Emilia Galotti* there occurs the passage, II, 119: "Oder meinen Sie, Prinz, dass Raphael nicht das grösste mahlerische Genie gewesen wäre, wenn er unglücklicherweise ohne Hände wäre geboren worden?" "Mahlerisches Genie" means here, of course, "a genius of a painter." In 1776 we have Wieland, *Wintermärchen*, 2, 52: "Myrtenwäldchen und Silberquellen und graue Dunkelheiten mahlerisch versetzt mit lichten Stellen." This corresponds to what was called picturesque in England and also to the modern popular usage. In 1781 Schiller says in the *Robbers*: "Mein Auge, geübt, die mahlerischen und übermahlerischen Schönheiten der Landschaft zu entdecken, schwelgte in Betrachtung der Nähen und Fernen, der bebuschten Felsen, der sonnigen Gipfel." Goethe (cf. P. Fischer, *Goethes Wortschatz*, Leipzig, 1929) in the *Italienische Reise*, 23.3.87: "Kniep, welcher schon unterwegs die zwei malerischen Kalkgebirge umrissen . . ." and *ibid.*, 1.5.87: "weil nach so viel ausgestandenen Unbilden unseren malerischen Zwecken gar nichts entgegen kam. . . ." "Wieviel malerische Reisen mögen dergleichen Halbwahrheiten enthalten." "Malerische Reise" is presumably to be connected with Gilpin's "picturesque travel."

10 *Herders Sämtliche Werke*, VIII, ed. Suphan, p. 84, *leibhaftige Wahrheit*.

is the *group*, and this, in the strict sense of the word, sculpture does not have—'What? No groups in sculpture? And Laocoön, Niobe, the two brothers—' I know all that and more. I know that a Frenchman has just recently boasted that his nation invented a great novelty in the grouping of statues, that it was the first to group statues picturesquely, as no ancient ever did.—To group statues picturesquely? See, there is a false note already, for in the real sense of the words it is a contradiction to group statues picturesquely. Every statue is a self-contained unit and a whole: each one stands alone and self-sufficient. What the author in question censures, then, in the ancients was to them deliberate wisdom, namely, not to group, and, where a group was unavoidable, to minimize it as far as possible. For this reason Laocoön's children had to be so small. . . ."

In the commentary of Suphan's edition "a Frenchman" is glossed by the one word FALCONET (1716-1791). It is quite possible that Herder had this sculptor in mind. I have not found the passage in Falconet's collected works, though I did come across the word picturesque several times. In the nineteenth century the term was in common use, in Mme. de Staël (*Corinne*, XV, 5), Chateaubriand (*Génie du christianisme*, III, I, 8), and in others.

Gilpin's fully matured theory of the picturesque is expounded in his *Three Essays*.[11] He found a firm basis for his speculations in Burke's essay on the Sublime and Beautiful,[12] of 1757, and concluded that Picturesque should be added to these two elements as a third concept. He is conscious of making a decisive contribution toward enlarging the list of indispensable concepts.

One should not be surprised that Gilpin speaks of picturesque beauty and at the same time says that there is an essential difference between the picturesque and beauty. Burke had declared smoothness to be one of the elements of beauty; Gilpin sees in roughness, the opposite of smoothness, the chief factor of the picturesque. A structure by Palladio may in reality be as "elegant" as possible. "But if we introduce it in a picture, it immediately becomes a formal object, and ceases to please." In order to make it picturesque, that is, suitable for representation in painting: ". . . from a smooth building we must turn it into a rough

11 William Gilpin, *Three Essays: on Picturesque Beauty, on Picturesque Travel and on Sketching Landscape, to which is added a Poem on Landscape Painting*, London, 1792. The most detailed analysis of this book is given by Templeman, *op.cit.* (see above p. 433, n. 22), pp. 131-146.

12 Edmund Burke, *A Philosophical Enquiry into the origin of our Ideas of the Sublime and Beautiful*, London, 1757.

ruin. No painter who had the choice of the two objects would hesitate a moment."[13]

Templeman summarizes Gilpin's theory in three sentences: "1) Picturesque beauty is that species of beauty which appeals to the eye of a painter as suited for representation in a picture. 2) Picturesque beauty is distinguished by the quality of roughness. 3) Roughness is essential to picturesque beauty because when certain elements (execution, composition, variety, contrast, effect of light and shade and coloring) are properly pleasing in a picture they of necessity make use of rough objects."[14]

Two years later Uwedale PRICE (1747-1829) took Gilpin's book, which seemed to him too vague in its concepts, as his point of departure.[15] The picturesque is to be separated completely from the sublime and the beautiful. It is likewise independent of painting (page 49). The word is applicable to visible phenomena (page 55), not, for instance, to music. The chief elements of the picturesque are "roughness, sudden variation, joined to that of irregularity (page 61)." At this point Price contrasts Greek architecture with Gothic (page 62ff.), and thus we return to Gothic.

"A temple or a palace of Grecian architecture in its perfect entire state and with its surface and colour smooth and even, either in painting or reality, is beautiful, in ruin it is picturesque."[16] Then the effects of weathering are described, and so on.

"Gothic architecture is generally considered as more picturesque, though less beautiful, than Grecian, and, upon the same principle that a ruin is more so than a new edifice. The first thing that strikes the eye in approaching any building is the general outline against the sky (or whatever it may be opposed to) and the effect of the opening:[17] in Grecian buildings the general lines of the roof are strait, and even when varied and adorned by a dome or a pediment, the whole has a character of symmetry and regularity.

[13] Gilpin, *op.cit.*, p. 7.

[14] Templeman, *op.cit.*, p. 140.

[15] Uwedale Price, *An Essay on the Picturesque as compared with the Sublime and the Beautiful and on the use of studying Pictures, for the purpose of improving real Landscape*, London, 1794. Enlarged edition, 1796. I quote from the latter. See also Nikolaus Pevsner, "Price on Picturesque Planning," *Architectural Revue*, xcv, 1944.

[16] Price, *op.cit.*, p. 62.

[17] *Ibid.*, p. 63. The words "the effect of the opening" are explained when we read on and see that in his discussion of Gothic Price speaks of doors and windows. "The effect of the opening" means the effect of *all* openings, to which belong also the intercolumniations of the Greek temples. The thesis is correct but incomplete, for when in addition to silhouette and openings there are also present systems of supporting members, such as buttresses, etc., these are to many spectators still more striking.

"Symmetry, which in works of art particularly accords with the beautiful, is in the same degree adverse to the picturesque, and among the various causes of the superior picturesqueness of ruins, compared with entire buildings, the destruction of symmetry is by no means the least powerful.

"In Gothic buildings, the outline of the summit presents such a variety of forms of turrets and pinnacles, some open, some fretted and variously enriched, that even where there is an exact correspondence of parts, it is often disguised by an appearance of splendid confusion and irregularity. In the doors and windows of Gothic churches the pointed arch has as much variety as any regular figure can well have; the eye too is not so strongly conducted from the top of the one to that of the other, as by the parallel lines of Grecian; and every person must be struck with the extreme richness and intricacy of some of the principal windows of our cathedrals and ruined abbeys. In these last is displayed the triumph of the picturesque; and its charms to a painter's eye are often so great as to rival those of beauty itself."[18]

But Price then remarks: "I hope it will not be supposed that by admiring the picturesque circumstances of the Gothic I mean to undervalue the symmetry and beauty of Grecian buildings. . . ."[19]

If one recalls Vasari's judgment of Gothic, there is a quiet irony in the fact that the word *pittoresco* which he introduced should have developed into a weapon for the defense of Gothic. The art of antiquity is beautiful, but Gothic is picturesque. We need not criticize this point of view; it represented a transitional stage.

Gilpin died in 1804. In 1805, Richard Payne KNIGHT (1750-1824), a friend of his and of Price, published a book in which the picturesque plays a part in conformity with the interests of the period.[20] For a time, however, this popularizing of the concept progressed no further, and a satirical poem by William COMBE (1741-1823) was only an easy farce poking fun at a very seriously meant extension of the structure of aesthetic concepts.[21]

The discovery of different kinds of beauty meant exploring a more profound level of phenomena, and it was not surprising in consequence that hunting for the picturesque became a new sport in England. Combe has his Dr. Syntax refuse an invitation to hunt with the words: "Your sport, my Lord, I cannot take, / For I must go and hunt a lake. . . ."

[18] Price, *op.cit.*, pp. 63ff. [19] *Ibid.*, p. 65n.

[20] Knight, *Analytical Essay into the Principles of Taste*, 1805; cf. Manwaring, *op.cit.*, p. 198.

[21] William Combe, *Tour of Dr. Syntax, in Search of the Picturesque*, 1812. By Dr. Syntax is meant Gilpin, who was a simple schoolmaster. One must add, however, that here one of the best sides of this amiable man was ridiculed, for Gilpin, himself poor, put all the money gained from his publications into a school which he had founded in order to educate the country folk of his congregation.

What seems to be merely a concept detached from the study of the literature pertaining to Gothic was in actuality very vigorously connected with real life. Anyone who wishes to pursue this matter further should consult Allen and Hussey.[22]

4. The Concept of the Infinite

AFTER Goethe's essay on Strasbourg Cathedral the subject of Gothic remained quiescent in Germany for some time. Fifteen years passed before there was another utterance of any interest at all. Wilhelm HEINSE (1749-1803) writes in 1787 in *Ardinghello*, his novel about artists and art: "Our churches . . . are great assembly places, where often the inhabitants of the whole city are expected to spend hours on end. A solemn Gothic cathedral with its free vast, space, designed by reasonable barbarians, where the voice of the priest is turned to thunder and the congregation's chorale to an ocean storm that praises the father of the universe and strikes awe into the heart of the boldest unbeliever, while the tyrant of music, the organ, roars in like a hurricane and stirs up the deep flood, will always, for a man of unspoiled mind, shame a pretentious little concoction, even though it be patterned after the prettiest little temple of Venus by the most tasteful Athenian."[1] The organ had already pealed in Milton,[2] and it sounds not only in Gothic churches but also in Rococo churches. Heinse, however, intends to imply that thunder (of the priest), ocean storm (of the chorale), and hurricane (of the organ) belong to the "vast" space of Gothic. Even acoustic phenomena acquire grandeur through the immensity of Gothic.

Heinse's significance is to be found in his descriptions of paintings

22 Allen, *op.cit.*, especially Chapter 21, The Emergence of the Tourist, and Chapter 22, Hostile Criticism of the Natural Garden. Further, Christopher Hussey, *The Picturesque*, London and New York, 1927, *passim.*

---

1 Wilhelm Heinse, *Ardinghello und die glückseligen Inseln*, Sämmtliche Werke, ed. by Carl Schüdekopf, Leipzig, 1907, IV, p. 31.

"Unsere Kirchen . . . sind grosse Versammlungsplätze, wo oft die Einwohner der ganzen Stadt Stunden lang sich aufhalten sollen. Ein feierlicher gothischer Dom mit seinem freyen ungeheuren Raume, von vernünftigen Barbaren entworfen, wo die Stimme des Priesters Donner wird und der Choral des Volkes Meeressturm, der den Vater des Weltalls preist und den kühnsten Ungläubigen erschüttert, indes der Tyrann der Musik, die Orgel, wie ein Orkan darein rast und tiefe Fluten wälzt: wird immer das kleine Gemächt im Grossen, seys nach dem niedlichsten Venustempel von dem geschmackvollsten Athenienser bey einem Mann von unverfälschtem Sinn zu Schanden machen."

2 Milton, *Paradise Lost*, v, ll. 155ff. ". . . There let the pealing organ blow
To the full-voic'd quire below . . ."

Quoted from Haferkorn, *op.cit.*, p. 54.

and his championship of color—or his renewed championship after Roger de Piles. Like Goethe, he was later drawn into the orbit of Classicism, as represented by Winckelmann. However, we shall do justice to the solitary passage where Heinse comments on Gothic if we stress the words "a solemn Gothic cathedral with its free vast, space." Goethe had nothing to say about interior space. In Heinse we get a faint indication of a quality that was later regarded as of such importance for Gothic: its sense of infinity. This, according to Heinse, is derived from "reasonable barbarians."

The word infinite occurs in Friedrich SCHILLER (1759-1805) in quite another connection, but one which, viewed more closely, bears on the problem of Gothic in a later formulation. In the essay *On Näive and Sentimental Poetry* of 1795 we read apropos of a comparison of Homer with the type of the modern poet: "The former achieves mastery by virtue of the art of limitation, the latter by the art of the infinite." This would at first seem to apply only to poetry, but Schiller continues: "And by the very fact that the strength of the ancient artist . . . lies in limitation can be explained the great advantage maintained by the representational art of antiquity over that of more recent times. . . . A work intended for the eye can achieve perfection only in limitation; a work of the imagination can attain it also in the unlimited. For this reason the modern artist finds his superiority in ideas of little help in plastic works, for here he is obliged to *define in space* with the greatest precision the image seen by his imagination, and consequently to vie with the ancient artist in just that quality where the latter has undisputed precedence. In poetic works it is otherwise. . . . Here the more recent [poet] can surpass the ancients in that which is called in works of art *spirit* (*Geist*)."[3]

The antithesis of *Geist* and limitation is not very clearly conceived, but from the context of the whole essay it can be seen what Schiller had in mind, namely, his antithesis of naïve and sentimental art. There is still some influence from Lessing, inasmuch as Schiller is here draw-

[3] *Friedrich Schillers sämtliche Werke*, Säkularausgabe, Stuttgart and Berlin, XII, p. 190. "Jener ist mächtig durch die Kunst der Begrenzung, dieser ist es durch die Kunst des Unendlichen. Und eben daraus, dass die Stärke des alten Künstlers . . . in der Begrenzung besteht, erklärt sich der hohe Vorzug, den die bildende Kunst des Altertums über die neueren Zeiten behauptet. . . . Ein Werk für das Auge findet nur in der Begrenzung seine Vollkommenheit; ein Werk der Einbildungskraft kann sie auch durch das Unbegrenzte erreichen. In plastischen Werken hilft daher dem Neuen seine Überlegenheit in Ideen wenig, hier ist er genötigt, das Bild seiner Einbildungskraft auf das genaueste *im Raum zu bestimmen* und folglich mit dem alten Künstler gerade in derjenigen Eigenschaft zu messen, worin dieser seinen unbestrittenen Vorzug hat. In poetischen Werken ist es anders. . . . Hier kann der neuere [Dichter] den alten in dem was man in Kunstwerken *Geist* nennt, hinter sich lassen."

ing a boundary between "poetry and painting" (that is, poetry and both of the representational arts). He is not discussing architecture and therefore not thinking of Gothic. But his idea is important for the latter because it can easily be transferred to Gothic: Greek architecture achieves mastery by virtue of the art of limitation, Gothic by the art of the infinite. It cannot be proved, but this step was presumably taken with reference to Schiller's ideas. He himself might well have said reprovingly: since Gothic architecture represents the unlimited, it is inferior to that of antiquity.

The passage is of further interest because in it antiquity and modernity are now conceived of as antithetical. It might be said that Petrarch had already done this, but here the paired concepts involved are finite and infinite.

Since Newton and Leibnitz the concept of infinity had acquired a new meaning in mathematics and the natural sciences. There is still no history of it as applied to the various branches of the humanities. It may be debatable whether the interpretation of Heinse's remarks according to this point of view can be justified. In Georg FORSTER (1759-1794) the application of the idea to the Gothic interior becomes clear:[4] "Whenever I visit Cologne I always go into this magnificent temple in order to feel the thrill of the sublime. . . . The splendor of the heavenward arching choir has a majestic simplicity that transcends all imagination. Extended to an enormous length the groups of slender piers stand like the trees of a primeval forest; only at their highest tips are they split into a crown of branches that bends with its neighbor in pointed arches" (this is an inheritance from the tree theory, intended here, however, only as a figure) "and is almost beyond the range of the eye that seeks to follow them. Though the immeasurability of the universe cannot be illustrated in finite space, there is nevertheless in this bold upward soaring of piers and walls a ceaseless energy that the imagination so easily prolongs into the *illimitable*. Greek architecture is indisputably the epitome of the perfected . . . in a word, of the beautiful. Here, however . . . under arches that rest as if on nothing, are joyously poised in the air like the shady tree-top vaults of the forest—here the mind revels in the exuberance of artistic creation."[5] Greek works impress us

[4] Georg Forster, *Ansichten vom Niederrhein, etc. von 1790*. In his collected works, Leipzig, 1843, III, p. 26. On Forster cf. also W. Waetzoldt, *Deutsche Kunsthistoriker*, Leipzig, 1921, I, p. 199, and bibliography on p. 331. Further the subsequently published, very good book by Wilhelm Langewiesche, *Georg Forster . . .*, Leipzig, 1923.

[5] ". . . So oft ich Köln besuche, gehe ich immer wieder in diesen herrlichen Tempel, um den Schauer des Erhabenen zu fühlen. . . . Die Pracht des himmelan sich wölbenden Chors

as being human, Gothic, as "visions from another world." One recalls Suger, but the continuation does not sound like him: "like fairy palaces," "in order to bear witness to the creative power in man. . . ." The account ends with the regret that such a splendid building must remain unfinished.

Forster speaks of the impression of the illimitable (*das Grenzenlose*), and thinks that this is brought about by the particular proportions. It is not known whether Milner read Forster's book, but it is not very probable. However, he says the same thing a few years later and even more emphatically.

John MILNER (1752-1826) was the Catholic bishop of Castabala.[6] He is important for the theory of Gothic because he was the first to destroy Wren's Saracen theory by the very simple means of pointing out the chronology:[7] the Goths conquer Spain in 570, the Saracens appear there in the eighth century, Gothic does not originate until around 1100.

"But why need we recur to the caravansaries of Arabia or the forests of Scandinavia for a discovery the gradations of which we trace at home, in an age of improvement and magnificence, namely the twelfth century, and amongst a people who were superior in arts as well as arms to all those above mentioned, namely the Normans?"[8]

Milner condensed his ideas on the subject into three assertions: 1) All forms of Gothic are derived from the pointed arch. 2) The pointed arch was invented by chance as the product of intersecting semicircles, first in the choir of Winchester and then in 1132 in the church of St. Cross (Gray's theory, cf. above, page 403). 3) All this was discovered by the Anglo-Normans and the English. Milner's three theses have not stood the test of time, but in spite of that he can claim much merit, particularly for his recognition of the "infinite" in Gothic.

---

hat eine majestätische Einfalt, die alle Vorstellungen übertrifft. In ungeheurer Länge stehen die Gruppen schlanker Säulen da, wie die Bäume eines uralten Forstes; nur am höchsten Gipfel sind sie in eine Krone von Ästen gespalten, die sich mit ihrem Nachbar im spitzen Bogen wölbt und dem Auge das ihnen folgen will, fast unerreichbar ist. Lässt sich auch schon das *Unermessliche* des Weltalls nicht in beschränktem Raum versinnlichen, so liegt gleichwohl in diesem kühnen Emporstreben der Pfeiler und Mauern das Unaufhaltsame, welches die Einbildungskraft so leicht in das *Grenzenlose* verlängert. Die griesche Baukunst ist unstreitig der Inbegriff des Vollendeten . . . mit einem Wort des Schönen. Hier indessen . . . unter ihren Bogen, die gleichsam auf nichts ruhen, lustig schweben wie die schattenreichen Gipfelgewölbe des Waldes—hier schwelgt der Sinn im Übermuth des künstlerischen Beginnens."

[6] Cf. his biography in the *Catholic Encyclopedia*, New York, 1911, x, p. 315; also the *Dictionary of National Biography*, London, 1894.

[7] *Essays on Gothic Architecture by the Rev. T. Warton, Rev. J. Bentham, Captain Grose and the Rev. J. Milner*, London, 1800. Milner's contribution, pp. 125ff., is entitled: *On the Rise and Progress of the Pointed Arch.*

[8] *Ibid.*, p. 129.

In the introductory letter to Mr. Taylor he speaks of the traditional concepts of the sublime and the beautiful.[9] Disagreeing with Evelyn and Wren (*Parentalia*, page 297), he says that anyone who enters Yorkminster and Chapterhouse (York) or King's College (Cambridge), Windsor Chapel, Lincoln, or Winchester "is irresistibly struck with mingled impressions of awe and pleasure, which no other buildings are capable of producing."[10] This is brought about by the proportions. The sublime results precisely from that which Wren takes exception to. "But besides the *real* effect of these proportions, which were generally carried as far as they were capable of, the mind was farther impressed by an *artificial* height and length, which were the natural produce of the style employed. For the aspiring form of the pointed arches, the lofty pediments, and the tapering pinnacles with which our cathedrals are adorned, contribute perhaps still more to give an idea of height than their real elevation. In like manner, the perspective of uniform columns, ribs, and arches, repeated at equal distances, as they are seen in the isles of those fabrics, produces an *artificial infinite* in the mind of the spectator. . . ."[11]

Today we speak simply of the impression of infinity. Milner was still faithful to the terminology of Burke,[12] who meant so much to the second half of the eighteenth century. Gilpin had added to the concepts of *beauty* and *sublimity* that of the *picturesque*; now the *infinite*, which had played a minor part in Burke, entered the front rank; and these factors were so many piles driven into the morass, so that on them could be raised the structure of modern aesthetics and stylistic theory. But this aspect of the case is visible only in retrospect to the historian. For Milner and his friends the pointed arch was no doubt much more important than any talk of infinity. Since there were various forms of the pointed arch—the lancet, those corresponding to the equilateral triangle, and flatter ones—and since there were still other types of arches, the theorizers on architecture devoted their efforts to the questions of what was the origin of the pointed arches "or" Gothic, and how should the whole development be divided into separate phases. Milner himself and with him his friends fought Wren's Saracen theory on all points, with severely historical arguments and with the reports of travelers to the Orient. The publisher J. Taylor, to whom Milner's letter containing his remarks on the artificial infinite is addressed, brought out a book containing four such essays on Gothic. It would

[9] *Ibid.*, pp. xvi ff.

[10] *Ibid.*

[11] *Ibid.*, p. xvii.

[12] See above, p. 404. Milner quotes Burke.

lead too far afield to consider them individually. It should be remembered that Warton, in 1763, had divided Gothic into three periods:[13] 1) The Absolute Gothic, from 1300 on. 2) The Ornamental Gothic, beginning with King's College Chapel in Cambridge. 3) The Florid Gothic, since about 1480. Anything before 1300 is for Warton Saxon Gothic; we should say Transitional. Bentham's essay contains a survey of the entire history of English mediaeval architecture; Grose and Milner skirmish primarily against the Saracen theory.

In 1811 Milner published a treatise in which he proposed a new series of periods for Gothic:[14] three stages, called by him "orders." The first is represented by Canterbury (1175), the second by York (about 1300), the third by Henry VII's Chapel in London. Neither in Milner nor in Warton is there any animosity against Late Gothic. That can perhaps be explained by the fact that the infinite plays a part in it—but this must remain merely modern conjecture.

5. Romanticism in Germany

THE concept Romanticism belongs to the same group of auxiliary concepts of history as Middle Ages or Renaissance. It, too, implies a value judgment—for Romanticists positive, for Classicists and pseudo-Classicists negative. It, too, is both limited to a definite time in the history of ideas and extended indecisively beyond such chronological boundaries. Probably the broadest interpretation of the concept is by Ernest Antoine SEILLIÈRE (1866-1957).[1] Influenced by the preoccupation of his generation with psychologism he phrases his definition in psychological terms: "Romanticism is essentially a revolt of feeling or rather of instinct against reason."[2] At that time the doctrine of *facultés conscients* and *facultés subconscients* was introduced into psychology. Since every human being is endowed with both, and the *facultés subconscients* are to blame for Romanticism, Seillière comes to the conclusion that this phenomenon represents an eternal weakness of

[13] See above, p. 406.

[14] John Milner, *Treatise on the Ecclesiastical Architecture of England during the Middle-Ages*, London, 1811 (3rd ed., 1835). He also wrote the article on Gothic architecture in Rees' *Cyclopedia*, as well as several on the *Archaeologia* listed in the *Gentleman's Magazine* for 1826, p. 51.

---

[1] Ernest Seillière, *Le Mal Romantique, essai sur l'imperialisme irrational*, Paris, 1908.

[2] "Le romantisme est dans son essence une insurrection du sentiment ou plutôt de l'instinct contre la raison."

human nature. Historically, then, with all deference to Seillière's book, Romanticism ought really to begin with the Neanderthal Man. That idea might in the end be accepted; the difficulty is only to determine whether the *facultés conscients* are likewise so old, whether Classicism consequently begins also with the Neanderthal period. Seillière left the question open. For him Romanticism begins simply with Rousseau. How could Rousseau be forgotten? In 1778 he even used the word itself: "The shores of Lake Bienne are wilder and more romantic than those of Lake Geneva."[3] "Romantic" is in this sentence about what Salvator Rosa called *pittoresco*. But of what use is the "word"? We met it already in 1706 in Harrison's "romantik Dome," and even then it was not precisely new. According to the Oxford Dictionary it appears for the first time in Evelyn's diary.[4] Was Evelyn then for this reason the first Romanticist? An argument in favor of the idea would be that he believed in Wren's Saracen theory, but obviously this course of reasoning can lead nowhere. Seillière divided Romanticism into five "generations" of thirty-five years each. The first one extends from Rousseau to Schiller's *Robbers*, the second to about 1830, being identical with the narrower concept of historical Romanticism. Heinrich Heine, however, is assigned already to the third generation. Heine himself expressed the opinion in 1832 that Romanticism was over. In his book, *The Romantic School*, he wrote that Romanticism "was nothing but the reawakening of the poetry of the Middle Ages, as it manifested itself in songs, pictures and works of art, in art and life." But this definition represents perhaps the opposite extreme from Seillière's attitude, for it stresses only a narrower sphere of interests of Romanticism, and moreover one, historically speaking, that does not begin with the German Romanticists of about 1800 but with the "English Scholars" of 1630.

We might expect to learn from the Romanticists themselves what Romanticism is. Friedrich Schlegel revered Goethe's novel, *Wilhelm Meister*, as the climax of all poetry. This induced him to declare the novel form as such to be the highest form of poetry, ranking it consequently above drama. Since the words "Romanticism" and "*Roman*," the German word for novel, have some connection, and since the novel is a prose epic, the old differentiation between dramatic and epic poetry

[3] Jean Jacques Rousseau, *Les Rêveries du promeneur solitaire*, *Cinquième Promenade*. This book was written in 1778 during the last months of his life and was not published until 1782. "Les rives du lac de Bienne sont plus sauvages et romantiques que celles du lac de Genève. . . ."

[4] Logan Pearsall Smith, *Four Words* (*Romantic*, *Originality*, *Creative*, *Genius*) (Society for Pure English, Tract XVII), Oxford, 1926.

was then changed into the very different contrast between the dramatic and the romantic. However distorted that may be, it led Schlegel to the further assertion that the novel—because it was an absolute culmination—is really something unattainable, a goal of the unfulfilled longing of great poets. This goal can only be approached to a greater or lesser degree, and at this point Schlegel becomes somewhat more definite with regard to the idea of Romanticism: "Romantic poetry is a progressive, universal poetry." "Other types of poetry are completed . . . romantic poetry is still in process of *becoming*, indeed its real nature is that it can forever only *become*, never be completed."[5] Drama and epic, actually only *different kinds*, are for Schlegel transformed into a pair of *opposites*, which later, removed from that not very tenable connection, developed into one of the most inclusive concepts of stylistics: *Sein und Werden*, being and becoming, a polarity that Fritz STRICH (b. 1882) has restated for literary history in terms of *Vollendung und Unendlichkeit*, completion and infinity.

This stylistic factor of "becoming" touches or overlaps the field of such other qualities as imperfectibility, fragmentariness, mobility, longing as a perpetual state of being, naturalness in contrast to conventionality or artificiality, freedom in contrast to law and precept, emotion and impulse as opposed to reason. With these in mind the Romanticists chose their star witnesses: Shakespeare versus Racine, Gothic versus Antiquity, Catholicism versus Enlightenment. The Romanticists looked at the past through new eyes, though the science of history did not originate with them. They saw everything in the past romantically; in terms of Heine's definition it was longing for a better but vanished world. For architects Romanticism thus means—in brief—longing for lost Gothic.

But that again leads to an extension of the concept of Romanticism, for longing for Gothic did not begin only with William Heinrich WACKENRODER (1773-1798). Seillière extricated himself from this difficulty by conceiving the idea of pre-Romanticism. A Romanticism before Romanticism is, strictly speaking, illogical, but the term is very useful and can be justified if it is taken to mean everything that was a precursor of the ideas that came into full flower in "the" Romantic Movement. In any case, the mediaeval period as such is not yet romantic in the sense of pre-Romanticism or even of "the" Romanticism of 1800.

[5] For Schlegel, etc. cf. the basic book by Rudolf Haym, *Die Romantische Schule, Ein Beitrag zur Geschichte des deutschen Geistes*, Berlin, 1870 (3rd ed., 1914). Anyone not dismayed by a list of hundreds of titles should consult Arturo Farinelli, *Il romanticismo nel mondo latino*, 1927; further, Heinrich Lützeler, "Die Deutung der Gotik bei den Romantikern," *Wallraf-Richartz Jahrbuch*, Leipzig, 1925.

Longing for a more perfect or supposedly more perfect existence inspired Petrarch to a reawakening of antiquity. Indeed, the Romantic Movement of 1800 is a rebirth not only of Gothic but also of that for which Gothic stands. Consequently the rebirth of Gothic is only a symptom, though an unusually eloquent one, of Romanticism. Gothic had become the symbol of an attitude toward life, and its rebirth was to be the symbol of the recognition of this *Weltanschauung*. Gothic itself differs from the Romanticism of 1800 in that it attained the goal of its longing, it achieved the interpenetration of Christian faith and the reality of earthly existence. Romanticism longed for that—paradoxically—classical period of Romanticism. It felt itself too weak to bring it to life again, and the rebirth of the Middle Ages was, in Schiller's sense, sentimental. Romanticism knew the impossibility of fulfilling its longing, and resigned itself. The blue flower of Novalis, which can never be found, is the symbol of this resignation. Once it flourished. All Romanticism is permeated by sorrow for the dead beloved. Perhaps this is the real contrast to Petrarch's goal. He rejoiced in the new life of antiquity, newly awakened like the Sleeping Beauty; Romanticism, on the other hand, could never arouse the Middle Ages, and, like the ghosts that walk in pre-Romanticism, for example in Walpole, the neo-Gothic of Romanticism has almost always had something phantomlike about it.

The Romanticists themselves, however, hardly would have thought in such extreme terms. Their lives were exceedingly "lively" and they enlivened much that had become petrified in the classicistic tradition. In the strict historical sense Romanticism begins in Germany about 1797. Wackenroder,[6] ecstatic and childlike, quickened with the magic wand of his enthusiasm the subject later taken up by stronger spirits: Ludwig Tieck, August Wilhelm Schlegel and his brother Friedrich, Bernhardi, Novalis, Fichte, Schleiermacher, Schelling, and Hegel. Among the Romanticists can also be reckoned Jean Paul, Hölderlin, and Schopenhauer. All these men were to a greater or lesser degree acquainted with each other and exchanged their ideas. A number of ingenious women belonged to the group, each member of which pursued with interest the publications of the others, so that the effect of an intellectual phalanx was created. When one individual spoke he often

[6] Wilhelm H. Wackenroder, *Herzensergiessungen eines kunstliebenden Klosterbruders*, 1797; also his *Werke und Briefe*, Berlin, n.d. (after 1937), editor not named. Cf. Waetzoldt, *Deutsche Kunsthistoriker*, Leipzig, 1921, I, p. 17, and Heinrich Wölfflin, *Die Herzensergiessungen eines kunstliebenden Klosterbruders, Studien zur Literaturgeschichte Michael Bernays gewidmet*, Hamburg and Leipzig, 1893. Richard Benz, *Goethe und die Romantische Kunst*, Munich, 1940.

spoke for all. This can be said at least of the lectures delivered by AUGUST WILHELM VON SCHLEGEL (1767-1845) at the University of Berlin in 1801. Even today they impress us by their wealth and maturity of ideas, and the knowledge they display of world literature, literary history, aesthetics, and the history of art. Much that Schlegel says merely in an aside anticipates later theses. For instance, he was already considering the idea of a "history of art without names." The phenomena in the realm of art are, therefore, objectively necessary, but subjectively incidental, and from this distinction can be understood how both can exist side by side. That is, a certain work must, according to its nature, appear at some time somewhere within the whole world of art; the person of the artist is, however, merely a matter of chance. The determining factors of time and place are thus already discounted. Where and when such an intellect will enter the world cannot be foretold, nor can it be explained after its success. Whether this poet or painter is called Sophocles or Raphael or by some other name is a matter of indifference; his artistic style is the essential thing for history. His works preserve the quintessence of his inner life, his artistic personality; the outward events of his purely earthly life do not concern us. History, to be sure, tries to show the development of the artist as the result of his surroundings, the circumstances of his life, his study of his predecessors, and the like; but in all of this it must first presuppose his peculiar genius."[7]

This observation is expressed in such general terms that though it includes Gothic it makes no reference to any particular characteristics of the style. The same is true of the lectures as a whole: the remarks specifically applicable to Gothic are embedded in general aesthetic theories, and can consequently be properly understood only in connection with these theories.[8]

[7] "Die Erscheinungen im Gebiet der Kunst sind also objectiv notwendig, subjectiv aber zufällig, und aus dieser Unterscheidung begreift sich auch schon, wie beides miteinander bestehen kann. Nämlich es muss ein soches Werk, seinem Wesen nach, irgendeinmal im Ganzen der Kunstwelt zum Vorschein kommen, die Person des Künstlers aber ist dabei ganz zufällig. Hiermit sind schon die Bestimmungen der Zeit und des Ortes abgerechnet. Wo und wann ein solcher Geist in die Welt treten werde, das lässt sich nicht vorher wissen, und also auch nach dem Erfolge nicht erklären. Ob dieser Dichter oder Maler Sophokles oder Rafael oder wie sonst heissen mag, das ist gleichgültig, sein Kunststil ist für die Geschichte das Wesentliche, in seinen Werken hat er sein inneres Leben, seine künstlerische Person niedergelegt, die äusserlichen Begebenheiten seines bloss irdischen Lebens gehen uns da nichts an. Freylich sucht die Geschichte auch die Ausbildung des Künstlers durch seine Umgebung, die Umstände seines Lebens, sein Studium der Vorgänger u.s.w. zu zeigen; bei allen diesen muss sie jedoch sein eigentümliches Genie schon voraussetzen." That is the program of a "history of style without names" by Heinrich Wölfflin around 1900, in opposition to the "milieu" theory.

[8] Schlegel's lectures were not printed in full until 1884; J. Minor, *A. W. Schlegels Vorlesun-*

In the first part of his lectures Schlegel discusses the theory of art, giving an account of ancient aesthetics: Plato, Aristotle, Cicero, Dionysius of Halicarnassus, and Longinus,[8a] and then refuting the ideas of his immediate philosophical predecessors, principally Burke and Kant. On the other hand, he quotes with approval his friend, the Romanticist Friedrich W. J. SCHELLING (1775-1854), saying: ". . . if the *infinite* is given *finite representation* the result is *beauty*, in which definition the *sublime* is already comprehended, as is proper. With this I am in complete accord, except that I should like to rephrase it thus: the beautiful is a *symbolical representation of the infinite*; because then it will be at the same time clear how the infinite can become apparent in the finite. One should not consider the infinite a kind of philosophical fiction or seek it beyond the world: it surrounds us on all sides and we can never escape it; we live, move, and have our being in the infinite." From this he evolves other ideas. The infinite can only be made apparent symbolically, in images and signs. Kant spoke of a cipher language by means of which nature speaks to us *figuratively* in its *beautiful* forms. "Poetry . . . is nothing but an eternal symbolizing: we either seek an outward guise for a spiritual entity or we relate something external to an invisible center."[9] Schlegel here expresses thoughts that were not only expanded by Hegel but that have also affected the most modern developments. A formulation very similar to Schlegel's is found in August Ferdinand BERNHARDI (1770-1820), Tieck's brother-in-law. "All art is contemplation of the universe." Since contemplation is finite and the universe infinite, it follows that "art will therefore consist of representing the infinite in a limited medium, and this can only be done by means of the transformation into images and symbols."[10] It would lead too far afield to trace the lines of connection with modern investigations of the symbol. August Wilhelm Schlegel continues: "One could

---

gen über Schöne Literatur und Kunst, Stuttgart, 1884 (Deutsche Literatur-Denkmale, No. 17), I, p. 19.

[8a] Longinus was a Neoplatonist and rhetorician of the third century A.D. Cf. Pauly-Wissowa, *Real-Encyc.*, 26, 1927, p. 1400.

[9] *Op.cit.*, p. 17.

Danach ". . . ist das *Unendliche endlich dargestellt: Schönheit*, bey welcher Definition das Erhabene, wie es sich gehört, schon darunter begriffen ist. Hiermit bin ich vollkommen einverstanden, nur möchte ich den Ausdruck so bestimmen: das Schöne ist eine *symbolische* Darstellung des Unendlichen, weil alsdann zugleich klar wird, wie das Unendliche im Endlichen zur Erscheinung kommen kann. Man halte das Unendliche nicht etwa für eine philosophische Fiction, man suche es nicht jenseits der Welt: es um gibt uns überall, wir können ihm niemals entgehen, wir leben, weben und sind im Unendlichen. . . . Dichten . . . ist nichts anderes als ein ewiges Symbolisieren: Wir suchen entweder für etwas Geistiges eine äussere Hülle oder wir beziehen ein Äusseres auf ein unsichtbares Inneres."

[10] Bernhardi's remark can be found in Kindermann (see above, p. 422, n. 14).

also define art as nature that has passed through the medium of perfect mind and is transfigured and concentrated for our contemplation.... Man is in art the norm of nature." This is a conscious break with the tyranny of the theory of imitation, and points the way to the subsequent theory of Riegl's artistic volition (*Kunstwille*).

Schlegel then analyzes the concepts of manner and style, gives a classification of the arts, and discusses each in turn. From the latter part two passages are important for us. In the theory of sculpture the standard is antiquity. "Many people, to be sure, have thought to find the spirit of specifically modern sculpture in Michelangelo; I am too indirectly and incompletely acquainted with the works of this sublime spirit (*Geist*) to contradict that; but it remains very problematical whether Michelangelo's striving could ever become a general norm, whether he was not rather a private path, suited to his originality and opened solely for it; whereas in antiquity there dominates not the individual genius of this or that master, but a general artistic spirit. It is at least certain that what influence he had was very soon completely lost in manneredness. We should, however, not wonder at the inferiority of the moderns and their lack of innate strength and direction in this art. For if we were to characterize the spirit of all ancient and all modern art by subsuming it under the principle of one single kind of artistic representation, we could quite properly call the former *plastic*, the latter *picturesque*. In all their works of art the ancients reveal the purity and severe discrimination, simplicity, restriction to essentials, isolation, renunciation of material charms, which, as we have seen, are found so particularly in the nature of sculpture; modern artists seek like painting the illusion (*Schein*), the most vivid present, and accompany the main subject of their representation by *échappées de vue* into the infinite. Hemsterhuis says wittily and trenchantly: modern sculptors are too much painters, the ancient painters were, on the face of it, too much sculptors. It was natural that the intellectually dominant art had at times an inordinate influence on the other. One could in this sense also borrow terms to indicate their general character from the two chief elements of music and say that by and large ancient art was rhythmical, modern aims at harmony."[11]

Whereas Hemsterhuis himself had connected his idea with, in his opinion, the opposing requirements of the single figure and the group in sculpture, it would seem that for Schlegel all Michelangelo's lifework is a failure because it is unfortunately not plastic but merely

[11] J. Minor's ed., I, p. 156.

picturesque, and, correspondingly, whole stylistic periods are polar opposites in the sense of these concepts. Schlegel's lack of clarity with regard to the latter is apparent when he almost playfully substitutes rhythmic and harmonic for them, a reasoning based on remote analogies. Ancient rhythm in particular he called plastic, rhyme, on the other hand, is picturesque.[12] In another place, however, he says: "There are as many styles as arts: a plastic, a picturesque, a musical, a poetic . . . style all exist."[13] We should add: an architectural and a choreographic, since Schlegel counts architecture and dancing as autonomous arts. But if an individual style can be derived from each of the arts, the conceptual pair "plastic and picturesque" loses its character of polarity, each of the concepts sinking to a designation of mere otherness. Thus the yoked concepts, the "hostile brothers," created by Hemsterhuis were deprived of inner tension and antagonism even before their victorious course was well started. That does not mean that this abolition of polarity attracted much attention. Since this polarity continued to be effective down to the present, it may be pointed out that the links in the chain of the origin and transmission of the method of polar concepts are clear. FRIEDRICH VON SCHLEGEL (1772-1829) was a diligent reader of Hemsterhuis, and in his youth venerated Schiller, whose essay on Naïve and Sentimental Poetry he studied very thoroughly. August Wilhelm von Schlegel, of course, knew both authors just as well, even though in 1801, after personal recriminations, he could seldom bring himself to quote Schiller in his lectures. Hemsterhuis' essay on sculpture had already appeared in 1769, but was then reprinted in 1792 in his collected works; soon after, in 1795, came Schiller's essay, and in 1801 Schlegel's lectures. We shall see the continuation in Friedrich Schlegel, again only a few years later. One point should not be overlooked: just as in Hemsterhuis, so there is in A. W. Schlegel no talk of the Middle Ages. It is not Gothic that is picturesque, but the modern styles, that is, the Renaissance, Mannerism, the Baroque. Friedrich Schlegel was the first to assert this of Gothic also.

The second passage to be quoted here from August Wilhelm von Schlegel's lectures is that on Gothic. The section that deals with architecture is twenty-two pages long, of which about half a page is devoted to Gothic. The rest contain many generalities based on the various theories of architecture then in existence, although only Vitruvius and

12 Quoted from Fritz Strich, *Deutsche Klassik und Romantik*, Munich, 1928, p. 247 (3rd ed.).

13 Quotation from M. Pichtos, *August Wilhelm Schlegels ästhetische Ánsichten*, Diss. Berlin, 1894, p. 36.

Algarotti are mentioned by name. It is new that Schlegel classifies under architecture certain household furnishings (chair and table are his examples), and that he talks of zoomorphism, where "allusions to organic life" are involved. He speaks in considerable detail of the derivation of columns from architecture in wood, discussing it, however, as a hypothesis and accompanying it with critical and skeptical remarks. Then follows a description of the columnar orders and a disquisition on proportions, from which one sentence may be cited that sounds like an early version of the Gestalt theory: "Thus the architect has to take into account a number of relationships; it is not sufficient that he should put together parts as they ought to be proportioned in themselves and in relation to others according to certain mechanical rules, but he must observe them in their vital connection: his work must be designed according to one sole and individual idea, it must be such that *each of the parts determines all the others* and is in turn determined by them. From this it is clear that architecture, despite its character of the strictest science, is nevertheless an art, which can by no means be learned by study but only practiced in a truly inspired manner." Schlegel then discusses pediments and the like. There follow brief remarks on tables and chairs.[14] Before he takes up Gothic he concludes what has preceded in a few sentences, which I quote along with the passage itself. It is regrettable that at this point he obviously became tired of writing out all the details, and contented himself with a telegrammatic style, that is, with mere catch-words for the lecture.

"*Ancient architecture* just as perfect and unsurpassable as sculpture. The modern imitators of the ancients. At first the later monuments from periods of already debased taste known and misunderstood.—The more genuine Greek ones are only now becoming known, often very unreliably, through travelers' descriptions.—Barbarisms from the habits that still survived from the Middle Ages. Michelangelo. St. Peter's. *Gothic architecture.* The historical question of its origin. Its proper [*eigentlicher*] name. Saracens. In India. Its character falsified in Italy. In its pure state in Germany, France, England. Whether it has any artistic value at all, since it is so absolutely opposed to the Greek?—Eccentric consequence. Partial validity for one age, certain mores, especially for one religion. Origin perhaps the result of need,

[14] *Op.cit.*, p. 178. To my surprise I find that he also includes vessels for eating and drinking, as well as vases, under the heading of architecture. I, too, did this in *System der Kunstwissenschaft*, Brünn, 1938, and, as a matter of fact, with the conviction that no one heretofore had recognized the logicality of the idea. Discussions of the structure and architectonics of classical and other vessels by no means implied that they are in essence "architecture." But in any case this classification is not of first importance.

determined by a certain material. Bricks. Thin walls. Lofty and slender, pointed arches, tall windows, piers. Manifold frontons (infinity of subdivisions), countlessness its principle, as simplicity that of Greek art. Temples the primary manifestation of the latter, churches of the Gothic. Idea of a Catholic cathedral. Relation between the kind of construction and the purpose. Main altar, nave, choirs, organs, side altars, towers, bells.—Description of a portal with statues of the patriarchs, apostles, etc. The allegories therein. Walpole's remark on Gothic churches. Dante's poem considered as a Gothic cathedral."[15]

This is a liberal program. Schlegel seems to have rejected the derivation of Gothic from the Goths and offered that from the Saracens. The phrase "in India" is so strange in this connection that I had doubts as to whether the editor, Minor, deciphered the manuscript correctly.[16] It would be more natural to emend it to "in Italy." Or did Schlegel really mean here Indian architecture? Thirty years later he wrote in the *Berliner Almanach* about the increase in knowledge of India. Here he mentions Daniell's engravings, the artist in question being Thomas DANIELL (1749-1840),[17] who, with his nephew, William Daniell (1769-

[15] *Ibid.*, p. 180.

"*Antike Baukunst* ebenso vollendet und unübertrefflich als die Plastik. Die modernen Nachahmer der Alten. Zuerst die späteren Monumente aus Zeiten des schon verderbten Geschmacks kennen gelernt, missverstanden. Die ächteren griechischen lernt man erst jetzt durch Reisebeschreiber oft sehr unzuverlässig kennen. Barbarismen aus den Angewöhnungen, die man aus dem Mittelalter noch an sich hatte. Michelangelo. Peterskirche. *Gothische Baukunst.* Historische Frage über ihre Entstehung. Eigentlicher Name. Sarazenen. In Indien. Ihr Charakter in Italien verfälscht. In ihrer Reinheit in Deutschland, Frankreich, England. Ob sie überhaupt Kunstwert hat, da sie durchaus der griechischen entgegengesetzt? Exzentrische Consequenz. Partiale Gültigkeit für ein Zeitalter, gewisse Sitten, besonders eine Religion. Ursprung vielleicht aus dem Bedürfnis unter der Bedingung eines gewissen Materials. Backsteine. Dünne Mauern. Hoch und schmal. Spitzbogen, hohe Fenster, Pfeiler. Vielfältige Frontons (Unendlichkeit der Unterordnung), Zahllosigkeit ihr Prinzip wie Einfachheit der griechischen Baukunst. Tempel die Grundanschauung von dieser, Kirchen von der gothischen. Idee eines katholischen Domes. Beziehung in der Bauart auf die Bestimmung. Hauptaltar, Schiff, Chöre, Orgeln, Nebenaltäre, Thürme, Glocken. Beschreibung einer Pforte mit Bildern der Patriarchen, Apostel u.s.w. Allegorien darin. Walpoles Ausspruch über gothische Kirchen. Dantes Gedicht als gothischer Dom betrachtet."

[16] An attempt to settle the matter by reference to the manuscript itself in the Dresden archives brought the information in 1949, that it could not then be found. It was added that there was little prospect of instituting a search for it, since the director of the archives was really a bookbinder (Russian Zone). Supplement, 1950: The problem confronting us here is simply what knowledge *August Wilhelm* Schlegel could have had of Indian architecture in the year 1801—not what we know today about Mohammedan structures with pointed arches in Delhi, Agra, etc. It is improbable that Schlegel knew anything about Gothic buildings in India that were the result of the missions of the Jesuit and other orders; therefore the second question as to whether he could have supposed these works of the sixteenth and seventeenth centuries to be the models of European buildings of the twelfth to the fifteenth century should only be asked when the first question has been answered. *Friedrich* Schlegel began his studies of Sanskrit in Paris only in 1802; his book, *Über Sprache und Weisheit der Inder*, appeared in 1808.

[17] Thieme-Becker, *Alg. Lexikon der bildenden Kunstler*, VIII, p. 361. In 1831 Schlegel might have meant also the other publications of 1800 and 1810.

1837), lived for ten years in India and, together with him, published in the year 1800 the *Antiquities of India.* In 1801 Schlegel could also have known W. Hodges' book, *Views of Hindustan* (1785), and T. Maurice's *Ancient History of Hindustan* (1794), but his knowledge of the subject in general can only have been very scanty. In the short essay of 1831 he does not mention Gothic.

The phrase "eccentric consequence" means, perhaps, that he was speaking of Late Gothic, or also that Gothic is indeed eccentric but nevertheless still a consequence of ancient architecture. This would then lead quite reasonably to the sentence about the relative validity of Gothic. All the rest is clear. The (incorrect) derivation of Gothic from the use of brick as a material is new, and, in consequence, the tree theory is omitted. In its stead he set forth the Saracen theory, obviously negatively, as he would not otherwise have proposed a new one, namely that of the origin in brick. The picturesque and the infinite are lacking, unless he meant to include both under the heading "infinity of subdivisions." Only one author, Walpole, was cited; but which of his many writings was the one in question? Very typical of the "poet" in Schlegel (for he *was* also a poet) is the concluding sentence about the *Divine Comedy*. On the whole, however, this discussion of Gothic was intended to be decidedly scientific and *not* poetic. The description of Gothic is not itself very comprehensive; it is restricted first to the proportions that are indicated in the pointed arches, tall windows, and piers, second to the thinness of the walls (dissolution of the wall?), and third to the repetition of similar motifs.

The tree or forest theory that we fail to find in Schlegel appears again, somewhat transformed, in his friend, Schelling. The latter borrowed Schlegel's manuscript in 1802 and then wrote him[18] that one could sense a particularly lofty point of view in everything that he had to say on architecture. Schelling himself was completely in agreement with the criticism leveled by Schlegel against the derivation of Greek architecture from architecture in wood, but, he went on to say: "It seems to me nevertheless that there is here a higher and universal inevitability of analogy, since I hail architecture, if I may say so, as the *landscape of sculpture.*" Perhaps he meant sculptured decorative figures, but even if he considered the piers as sculpture and the cathedral as a forest, his phrase, though daring, is not merely poetical. Indeed he continues: "Gothic architecture shows nature in the raw, as yet untouched, the tree not yet deprived of its twigs and leaves; hence the disproportion of the base to

[18] Of Oct. 21, 1802; printed in Minor, *op.cit.*

the crown, the infinitely many ramifications, the wild outgrow in cloisters, vaults. . . ." But this, too, is difficult to interpret. It is not known what of Gothic works Schelling had observed. There were toward the end of the fifteenth century actual imitations of trees with truncated branches,[19] but it is much more likely that Schelling, instead of looking at Gothic buildings, built up in his imagination a Gothic that corresponded, for example, to that in Pseudo-Raphael. In 1802 and 1803 he lectured on aesthetics in Jena; the recently published manuscript gives somewhat more insight into his ideas on Gothic.[20] All of Greek architecture seems to shrink to the Doric column and, correspondingly, almost all of Gothic to the piers. His criticism is primarily directed toward the fact that Gothic does not taper its piers (or engaged shafts?) upward—from the standpoint of Gothic a harsh demand! There is, however, tapering in towers, if not in piers. He carries out the comparison of the tower of Strasbourg Cathedral to a tree. His sketch of the history of mediaeval (that is, Gothic) architecture is also strongly reminiscent of Pseudo-Raphael, but he weighs with equal seriousness the Saracen theory, only to return to Tacitus, who, as is well known, says that the Germanic people worshiped their gods beneath the trees. Thus Gothic is German, and was then transplanted to England, "where, for example, Windsor Castle was built in this style." But which of the various possibilities is correct can only be decided "on historical grounds." Instead of seeking these, he offers a new hypothesis. "There is an astonishing and striking similarity to Gothic shown by Indian architecture. . . . The architecture of the temples and pagodas is quite of the Gothic type; even in secular buildings Gothic piers and pointed turrets are not lacking. Foliage as an architectural decoration is in any case of Oriental origin. The extravagant taste of the Orientals, which everywhere avoids all limitation and aims at the unlimited, can be glimpsed unmistakably in Gothic architecture. . . . The answer to the question of how this originally Indian taste subsequently spread across Europe I must leave to the historian." Did the word India perhaps really occur in A. W. Schlegel's manuscript? Or is this Schelling's own brain child, an Indian theory of Gothic?

A few years later Friedrich von Schlegel set forth what he had to say about Gothic.[21] He traveled from Paris to Cambrai, Brussels, Lou-

19 As I see it, the prototypes for these were the glass paintings by Peter Hemmel of Andlau, after 1470. Cf. P. Frankl, *Peter Hemmel, Glasmaler von Andlau*, Berlin, Deutscher Verein für Kunstwissenschaft, 1956, p. 53.

20 F. W. J. Schelling, *Werke*, ed. by O. Weiss, III, Leipzig, 1907, pp. 231ff.

21 *Grundzüge der gothischen Baukunst; auf einer Reise durch die Niederlande, Rheingegenden,*

vain, Lièges, Aachen, Neuss, Düsseldorf, Cologne, Strasbourg, Basel, Bern, Geneva, Lyons, and back to Paris. In diary form he discusses his impressions and delivers himself of judgments. It was presumably revised subsequently for he expresses his ideas in a very well-considered sequence, only superficially connected with the stages of his journey.

What he says about the modern buildings in Paris is again an echo of Laugier, occasionally of Goethe. He regrets the restoration of the interior of Notre Dame and praises the exterior. In St.-Denis he makes cogent general remarks on the dependence of Gothic sculpture on architecture. In Cambrai he writes: "I have a great fondness for Gothic architecture. . . . It seems to me that its deeper significance . . . has not yet been in the least understood." There follows a long disquisition on the term Gothic, together with an attempt to distinguish the phases of mediaeval architectural history. It is not very easy to grasp Friedrich Schlegel's terminology at first. But he undoubtedly understands by Gothic *or* romantic architecture that of the entire mediaeval period, dividing it into two parts: the Early Christian or Grecizing, today called Romanesque; and the second florescent style, which in modern parlance we call Gothic.[22] Each stage of his journey gives rise to a different observation that is closely connected with the principal building of the place.

Once he remarks of a structure: "What especially distinguishes this building is, in addition to its character of extreme delicacy, the expression of richness, beautiful simplicity, and pure harmony." Can the reader guess to what building this judgment applies? Simplicity and harmony were usually ascribed to ancient architecture. This however, is not the Erechtheum but the City Hall in Louvain.

Of the Gothic choir of the cathedral in Aachen he says that it "is from a more recent epoch of Gothic architecture; not to be censured, yet not excellent. The many long, narrow, only slightly adorned, closely serried window arches, separated only by quite massive supports [he means the mullions and tracery], betray the style of the fourteenth century, when Gothic architecture was already in a state of decline." This is presumably the first literary evidence for the idea of the decline of Gothic in the Late Gothic period.[23] The choir was built 1350.

"The church of Neuss belongs in style to the ruder Gothic ones."

---

die Schweiz und einen Teil von Frankreich in den Jahren 1804 u. 1805 (*Friedrich Schlegels sämtl. Werke*, Vienna, 1846, VI).

22 *Op.cit.*, p. 182.

23 F. v. Schlegel saw the windows still divided into six lights. Since the restoration of 1866 the tracery has five lights. Cf. A. W. v. Schlegel's lectures, p. 451ff.

This is the converse of the preceding passage. We now call Neuss passive Transitional. Schlegel thought it represents a preliminary stage of classical Gothic. Its towers are the occasion of his discussing and rejecting the Saracen theory. This is therefore *not* the theory of Romanticism.

In Düsseldorf he made notes on the paintings in the gallery. Like his brother August Wilhelm, Friedrich calls Michelangelo a Mannerist, or "mannered," which at that time meant the same thing. Only later was the designation "father of the Baroque" applied to him, and today critics are again inclined to rate him as the father of Mannerism. As to the rest, the observations of the paintings lead to the traditional remark that classical colonnades do not belong under a Nordic sky.

In Cologne—"this ancient city is for the most part usually disliked by strangers"—Schlegel wrote down the most important things that he had to say about Gothic. He speaks in considerable detail about the cathedral, repeats Forster's comparison with "the jet of water from a mighty fountain," and stresses the fact that the decorative forms are almost all taken from the plant world. "The essence of Gothic architecture consists therefore of the profusion and infiniteness of its inner conformation, like Nature's, and the outer decoration, so rich in flowers. Hence the unwearied and unnumbered, constant repetitions of the same adornments, hence their vegetablelike quality, as in blooming plants. . . . Whereas painting must in general content itself merely with weak . . . indications of the divine, architecture, on the contrary, can . . . represent and visualize the infinite, as it were, immediately, simply through the imitation of the profusion of Nature, even without allusion to the ideas and mysteries of Christianity, which, to be sure, have had not a little influence on the origin and development of ecclesiastical architecture." This is further proof that Gothic was regarded as the symbol of Christianity *because* it represents the infinite immediately.[24] Cf. the lecture of A. W. v. Schlegel, p. 451 above.

Schlegel then discusses the origin of Gothic and the reasons for it, finding them not only in the idea of Christianity but also in the nature of the Nordic climate and the nature of the materials used, "since the inferior beauty of sandstone, compared to marble, must, with the increasing desire for beautification, of itself [inevitably or perhaps even organically] lead to forcing the art of decoration to a height that could

[24] Just as in the preceding paragraph what we call Gothic today is designated as "the second florescent style of Gothic architecture." Its first is Romanesque architecture, and Gothic implies the entire Middle Ages. But here Schlegel obviously means Gothic in our more restricted sense.

hardly be feasible in any other architectural material." But here Schlegel is talking of the Middle Ages in general, and he begins his more detailed explanation with the older style that he calls sometimes Christian-Byzantine, sometimes Grecizing, citing as examples St. Gereon and St. Aposteln. Of course he gives no structural analysis, but he describes St. Aposteln in general: western tower, form of the eastern choir, and so on, "as it were, a building composed of several artfully intertwined buildings." There follows a short digression to Hagia Sophia in Constantinople and St. Mark's in Venice, and then come general remarks on mediaeval piers and arches. The pointed arch is explained as resulting from the adaptation of the interior to the steep slope of the roof on the exterior; correspondingly, the form of the portals is derived from that of the roof (he doubtless means the Gothic decorative gables in a narrower sense). Thus Schlegel here presents a new *theory of the pointed arch*, which found no adherents. As a matter of fact, his discussion is very confused because he preserves no sharp distinction between Romanesque and Gothic styles, though he was seeking one. After the appreciation of St.-Gereon, "from the eleventh century" and also belonging "to the old Grecizing manner," comes the principal passage (page 208):

"To distinguish and characterize the two different types of Gothic architecture we may adduce the following. In the Early Christian style of building, of which St. Gereon's church in Cologne offers such a perfect archetype, the fundamental scheme of triangle and square, cross and rotunda, as well as the star-shaped hexagon and other even more numerous polygonal figures, is not merely concealed in the inner structure; but these forms manifest themselves in a . . . geometrical beauty visible in the main proportions and the highest tip of the building, thereby giving to the whole a particular *sidereal* shape, the wonderful composition of which creates a mysterious effect and is well adapted to a church in its quality of a sacred building that, as it were, ought to present us with an image of the eternal structure of the heavens on a small scale. This sidereal shape and geometrical beauty recede almost entirely in the second, florescent style of Gothic architecture, where of all those figures only the cruciform one remains in evidence and is visibly revealed; but this, too, clothed in the richest adornment and as though twined about with blossoming roses. In the conformation of piers, arches, and windows that break out in delicate tendrils like tangled branches, in the profusely foliated decoration of the ornaments, and especially in its *floral* and plantlike quality are found the essential, basic form and peculiar beauty of this style of building, the true origin and primary reason of which are to be sought in the profound German feeling for nature and in fantasy as the dominating spiritual element of that age."[25]

The "sidereal" (from *sidera*, stars) can be regarded analogously to subsequently developed concepts of the mechanical, such as crystallomorphic. Thus Schlegel creates a new pair of concepts: sidereal and vegetal. This polarity—if one may term it such—is not at all identical with plastic and picturesque. It refers also to something quite different. For Hemsterhuis and August Wilhelm Schlegel plastic connoted antiquity and picturesque, modernity. Friedrich Schlegel, on the other hand, is concerned with the two styles of the Middle Ages: Romanesque is sidereal and Gothic vegetal (he uses the words "floral" and "plant-like"). Both pairs of concepts, however, share a common tendency toward a method of describing or characterizing styles and consequently periods in the history of art by means of concepts that are *polar opposites*, a method used in the history of ideas. It must merely be added in qualification that the concepts sidereal and vegetal are not, strictly speaking, polar opposites; it is also a question what relationship these concepts bear to A. W. Schlegel's "zoomorphic." But Friedrich Schlegel's distinction is nevertheless a great step forward, for here Romanesque and Gothic are basically set apart from each other for the first time since the distinction of Blondel the younger—at least theoretically. However, Fr. Schlegel could not yet discriminate clearly among the objects themselves, but he grasped the idea. This can safely be asserted, even though he is at times not really very precise about his own concepts. For, a few pages before he introduces them, he remarks of Cologne Cathedral (page 201): "And if the whole, from

25 "Zur Unterscheidung und Charakteristik der zwei verschiedenen Gattungen der gothischen Baukunst wollen wir noch Folgendes anführen. In dem altchristlichen Baustil, von welchem die St. Gereonkirche zu Kölln ein so vollendetes Urbild darbietet, ist jenes Grundschema von Dreieck und Quadrat, Kreuz und Rotunde, sowie auch das sternförmige Sechseck und andere noch zahlreichere Vieleck-Figuren, nicht bloss in der inneren Strucktur verborgen; sondern sie treten in einer . . . geometrischen Schönheit, sichtbar an den Hauptmassen und dem höchsten Gipfel des Gebäudes hervor, und geben dem Ganzen dadurch eine eigene *siderische* Gestalt, deren wunderbare Zusammensetzung einen geheimnisvollen Eindruck macht und wohl angemessen ist für eine Kirche, als ein geheiligtes Gebäude, welches gleichsam ein Nachbild von der ewigen Structur des Himmels im kleinen darbieten soll. Diese siderische Gestalt und geometrische Schönheit tritt nun wieder ganz zurück in dem zweiten blühenden Stil der gothischen Baukunst, wo von allen jenen Figuren nur die Kreuzform in der Erscheinung bleibt und sichtbar hervortritt; aber auch diese vom reichsten Schmuck überkleidet und wie von blühenden Rosen umschlungen. Die in zarten Ranken aufschiessende Gestalt der Säulen, Bogen und Fenster, wie von verschlungenen Zweigen, der volle Blätterschmuck der Verzierungen, überhaupt aber das Blumenhafte und Gewächsähnliche bilden die wesentliche Grundform und eigentümliche Schönheit in dieser Bauart, deren wahrer Ursprung und erster Grund in dem tiefen deutschen Naturgefühl und in der Fantasie als vorherrschendem Geisteselement jenes Zeitalters zu suchen ist."

the outside, with all its countless towers and turrets, looks at a distance not unlike a forest, so the entire *growth*, when one approaches somewhat more closely, seems rather to be comparable to an immeasurable formation of *crystallized* nature." This is an unclear mixture of the vegetal and the crystalline—or sidereal. The latter as "geometrical beauty" also contains the element of regularity, lawfulness, necessity.

Schlegel ascribed the floral quality of Gothic to the profound *German* feeling for nature, although he knew something about the equally floral *French* Gothic. But national prejudice is constitutionally a part of every Romanticist, whatever his provenience.

The Rhine journey gives rise to thoughts on the architecture of castles. Schlegel says relatively little about Strasbourg, giving the most important building dates and apparently referring the date of its beginning, 1015, to the whole of the present structure; to this part of the diary is appended a brief excursus on Italian Gothic (Milan, Florence). The rest of the book is not very fruitful for Gothic. On his return to Paris, however, Schlegel finds in the library a book by an Englishman whom he does not name. "This author . . . has discovered the plantlike quality in Gothic architecture. Instead of recognizing in it a peculiar form of the beautiful as the basic idea of the florescent style of romantic architecture, he explains it all quite on material grounds as having originated in rustic cottages made of actual plaited willow withes, or from all sorts of other wickerwork and whatever other such arbitrary assumptions. . . ." Schlegel is thinking of James Hall (see below, page 481).[26]

The aesthetics of Jean Paul Friedrich Richter (1763-1825) must be mentioned in this connection only because he, too, makes use of polar concepts, though with no specific mention of Gothic.[27] Greek poetry is plastic; romantic poetry, musical (par. 16). The word musical is employed here where we should expect instead picturesque. To what extent the musical is synonymous with the picturesque in Jean Paul I have not discovered. Perhaps he meant something quite different by it. But his source, aside from August Wilhelm von Schlegel, is clearly Hemsterhuis, for he says in paragraph 22: "Let us rather ask feeling, why, for example, it calls even a particular countryside romantic. A statue is precluded from any romantic quality by virtue of its circumscribed and sharp periphery; painting already approaches

[26] James Hall, *Essay on the Origin, History and Principles of Gothic Architecture*, Edinburgh, 1797 (Transactions of the Royal Society, Edinburgh, III), new ed., 1813.

[27] Jean Paul (Friedrich Richter), *Vorschule der Aesthetik*, 1804. 2nd ed., Stuttgart and Tübingen, 1813, pp. 144ff.

it more closely in its grouping of human beings and attains it in landscapes without figures, for example, those by Claude. A Dutch garden seems merely to be a revocation of anything romantic; but an English one, which stretches out into a limitless landscape, can surround us with a romantic territory, that is, with the background for an imagination that has been allowed free scope in the beautiful."

In the remarks that follow there occurs the sentence: "The romantic is the beautiful without limitation, or the *beautiful* infinite, just as there is also a sublime one." On page 148 he mentions Indian Romanticism.

In 1803 Friedrich Schlegel was in Paris and there made the acquaintance of Sulpiz BOISSERÉE (1783-1854).[28] The latter was then twenty years old, full of enthusiasm for the rediscovery and rebirth of the Middle Ages. He and his younger brother, Melchior (1786-1851), attached themselves to Friedrich von Schlegel and became important members of the circle of German Romanticists as collectors of early German painting. After the dissolution of the monasteries in 1806 it was possible to obtain old church pictures relatively cheaply and thus to preserve them. Since 1806 Friedrich von Schlegel had been living in Cologne. In 1810 Reinhard, the French minister, brought about a connection between Sulpiz Boisserée and Goethe. The latter was at first very reserved, but was finally won over by Sulpiz's tactful and amiable behavior. In 1810 Boisserée contacted Georg MOLLER (1784-1852), the discoverer of the original designs for the façade of Cologne Cathedral, and began to make drawings of the cathedral and detailed studies of the Lodge secrets of Gothic. He reconstructed a dome over the crossing, perhaps misunderstanding Crombach's book, which he quotes on another occasion and of course, as a native of Cologne, knew well (see above, page 332ff.).

The names of all these men, the Schlegels and the others, have not been forgotten. J. C. COSTENOBLE (1769-1837), on the other hand, has fallen into oblivion. According to him,[29] architecture is a "self-forming art"—in other words, not imitative. "The chief purpose of architecture must be to arrange the building in conformity with its destination." Beauty cannot be its sole purpose. Instead of this, Costenoble talks of "true beauty," that is, *fulfillment of function*. He disapproves of picturesquely handled sketches of buildings (page 5), and his own drawings are correspondingly quite dry and schematized. A man of

[28] Ed. Firmenich Richartz, *Die Brüder Boisserée*, Jena, 1916, I.

[29] J. C. Costenoble, *Über altdeutsche Architektur und deren Ursprung*, Halle, 1812.

this tendency naturally rates the influence of climate very high. The slope of Gothic roofs is explained on this basis. The *pointed arch*, curiously enough, he derives from *construction in wood*, though only indirectly. At first roofs were formed by inclining two beams toward each other (saddle roof); this was then imitated in stone (for instance, in the dolmens) and led to the pointed arch when curves were substituted for the straight lines and the shaping and fitting of the stones invented.

Costenoble had *one* great merit: he tried to analyze the structural parts of the Gothic fabric, its *membra*, not only to present them to the pupil as types, but also to explain each one individually according to its basic principles. After the discussion of building materials and the unsuccessful attempt at a derivation of the pointed arch, he speaks of the slanting profiles, the "splay" (*Schmiegen*), of the windows, well adapted to let in light. Next he takes up doors, then mullions and tracery, vaults, bases, piers, moldings, buttresses, towers with winding staircases, oriels, gables, roofs, tower roofs, railings, and parapets. There is absolutely no recognizable system in this series; Costenoble jumps arbitrarily from one structural part to another. It is, however, the *first* attempt to discuss individual details in textbook form (1812).

In the case of vaults he makes *no* distinction between groined and ribbed vaults. The "vault with transverse arches (*Gurtengewölbe*)" concentrates the load on the four corner points. If this expression is also intended to include the groined vault, then Costenoble already knew that both forms in this respect behave alike statically. In another passage he distinguishes between projecting and nonprojecting transverse arches (that is, ribs and groins), but here his reflections are based on geometry and do not refer to statics.

In an appendix he takes issue (sometimes polemically) with other authors: Sulzer, Goethe, Blondel, Frisi, Friedrich von Schlegel.[30] Everywhere there prevails a strange, dilettantish mixture of accuracy and inaccuracy; probably the book was influential in its time.

The first history of German architecture was published by Christian Ludwig STIEGLITZ (1756-1836) in 1820. According to him, only two peoples have produced an original architecture: the Greeks the *plastic* and the Germans the *romantic*.[31] The one appeals to the reason (*Verstand*), the other "excites, with mysterious meaning, the emo-

[30] I cannot identify the author on whom he provides pages of commentary. He mentions him on page 66 merely as "an artist."

[31] Christian Ludwig Stieglitz, *Von altdeutscher Baukunst*, Leipzig, 1820, p. 20.

tions (*Gemüt*). . . . There the sensuously beautiful is resplendent, reminding us of mundane things, here the spiritual lifts the heart to heights which only faith and love can attain." He quotes Friedrich von Schlegel, and rejects the derivation of Gothic from Arabian, Indian, or Saracen forms. (Here, too, India makes a brief appearance.) His reasoning as to why Arabic-Saracen architecture has nothing to do with Gothic is very lucid. He compares them, finding them in all respects utterly different with the one exception of the pointed arch. For all its terseness his comparison is formal. Gothic has high roofs, massive towers; Arabic art, on the other hand, domes and slender minarets, and so on. Of the pointed arch he says merely (page 15): "That this is the property of the Germans and thence passed to the Arabs is not subject to any doubt." His own idea of the origin of Gothic is based—as one might say today—on the history of ideas. It is a first sketching out of a subsequently much repeated and elaborated thought. Gothic springs from the atmosphere of the age: "The romantic spirit, which at that time captured men's minds [he is speaking of the thirteenth century] and influenced their lives, which incited them to heroic and knightly deeds that inspired the poets, gave also to the imagination of the architect a nobler impulse and conjured forth a new style. This is the origin of German architecture . . . , which could, therefore, be called romantic art, since in it everything seems to be miraculous and a free play of fantasy." This is the romantic in a psychological sense, much as Seillière saw it three generations later. The question is only why it was so strong in the thirteenth century and so exclusively present in German minds that everything men undertook had inevitably to result in the romantic. Stieglitz never wearies of formulating in ever new phraseology his enthusiasm for Romanticism. "The heavenward aspiring vaults that lead the glance into the infinite, the variously intersecting transverse (?) arches (*Gurtbogen*), the sacred twilight that fills the cathedral through painted windows and is wondrously blended with the bright glitter of the gleaming colors, all this fills the soul with awe and devotion. The richly adorned altars, chapels, pulpits, monuments, the great, solemn perspectives, the striking mixture of sublimity and delicacy, all is addressed to feeling and to imagination, whence it was initially derived. Here there is more than the forest. And to fancy an origin of German architecture from the interwoven branches of trees would be to desecrate the holy spirit that inspired the artist and filled his soul with great images, that came from the heart and therefore speaks so powerfully to the heart. What can be more uplifting than to worship the divinity in the sacred structures of our pious forefathers, where everything impels us to venerate the creator, where the spirit, no longer hemmed in by low vaults, soars freely aloft, and with love and longing aspires toward the infinite." The genuine Romanticist rejects the tree theory. He sees Gothic originating not in the forest, but in the spirit and in religious emotion.

Stieglitz brings together a considerable mass of historical knowledge in his book. He discusses the well-known mediaeval buildings of Germany,[32] then some from England, France, Italy, Spain, Portugal, and Holland, ending this part of his work with the remark: "These are the Gothic churches of foreign lands in the German style. . . ." He cites Friedrich von Schlegel and the passage from Wimpheling that was quoted above on page 249. Goethe undoubtedly had seen Stieglitz' book and may have been surprised if he found his predecessor here, in Wimpheling.

In addition to the ranks of those Romanticists who admired mediaeval architecture unconditionally, there were the Classicists and a third group, definable, paradoxically, as romantic Classicists. At their head stands GOETHE. He who had once so enthusiastically absorbed the spirit of Gothic regarded the experience of Winckelmann and Rome as a turning away from Gothic and from his own youth, as his maturing. But the distinctness of the contrast faded, and the wiser and more objective Goethe became the more he was able to reconcile opposites in his heart. He followed the efforts of the Boisserée brothers with increasing sympathy, and finally even warmed to Cologne Cathedral. This change of front has been described frequently in the literature on Goethe, hence two quotations will suffice here: one from the *Elective Affinities* (1808), which is generally cited when his understanding of the peculiar atmosphere of Gothic Revival buildings is to be demonstrated, and one from the year 1810, from the time when he became acquainted with Sulpiz Boisserée.

The passage from the *Elective Affinities* is as follows: "Through the single tall window fell a solemn, many-hued light: for it was pleasingly composed of colored glass. The whole interior acquired thereby a strange tone and induced a peculiar mood. The beauty of the vaulting and of the walls was increased by the decoration of the pavement,

[32] Strasbourg, Vienna, Zürich, Cologne, Landshut, Freiburg i.B., Meissen, Magdeburg, Ulm, Erfurt, Prague, Oppenheim, Frankenberg, Xanten, Augsburg, Frankfurt a.M., Ingolstadt, Regensburg, Dinkelsbühl.

which consisted of specially shaped tiles, laid in a beautiful design and held together by a layer of poured plaster. Provision was also made for seats. Among the ecclesiastical relics had been discovered some beautifully carved choir stalls, which were now very suitably disposed about the walls. Ottilie took pleasure in the familiar parts that now appeared before her as an unfamiliar whole. She stood still, walked up and down, looked, and examined; finally she seated herself on one of the stalls, and it seemed to her, as she glanced up and around, as though she were and were not, as though she could feel and could not feel, as though all of this might vanish before her eyes, and she before herself. . . ."[33] This is related to what Suger felt, only it is more personal. At that time, even before he became connected with the Boisserée brothers, Goethe had been led back to Gothic by the architect Engelhardt. On May 14, 1810,[34] he wrote to C. F. von Reinhard, who had sent him drawings by Boisserée, or perhaps Quaglio, of Cologne Cathedral: "One cannot dictate to anyone what direction his predilection shall take and how he shall develop his innate gifts. Furthermore, everything that can make the meaning of a past age live again for us is most valuable, especially when it is accomplished in a spirit that is truly faithful to history and critical.

"Accordingly, the efforts of the young man who is responsible for the drawings before me are to be praised highly. He has gone to work very thoroughly, and I am happy to confess that the ground plan of the cathedral in Cologne, as here presented, is one of the most interesting things of an architectural nature that I have come across for a long time. The perspective sketch gives us an idea of the impracticability of such an enormous undertaking, and with astonishment and silent contemplation one sees the legend of the tower of Babel come true on the banks of the Rhine." Then follow words of praise for the reconstruction:

[33] Goethe, *Wahlverwandtschaften*, Part II, ch. 3.

"Durch das einzige hohe Fenster fiel ein ernstes buntes Licht herein: denn es war von farbigen Gläsern anmutig zusammengesetzt. Das Ganze erhielt dadurch einen fremden Ton und bereitete zu einer eigenen Stimmung. Die Schönheit des Gewölbes und der Wände ward durch die Zierde des Fussboden erhöht, der aus besonders geformten, nach einem schönen Muster gelegten, durch eine gegossene Gipsfläche verbundenen Ziegelsteinen bestand. Auch für Ruheplätze war gesorgt. Es hatten sich unter jenen kirchlichen Altertümern einige schöngeschnitzte Chorstühle vorgefunden, die nun gar schicklich an den Wänden angebracht umherstanden. Ottilie freute sich des Bekannten, ihr als ein unbekanntes Ganzes entgegentretenden Teile. Sie stand, ging hin und wieder, sah und besah; endlich setzte sie sich auf einen der Stühle, und es schien ihr, indem sie auf- und umher blickte, als wenn sie wäre und nicht wäre, als wenn sie empfände und nicht empfände, als wenn dies alles vor ihr, sie vor sich selbst entschwinden sollte. . . ."

[34] Goethe's *Briefe*, Sophienausgabe IV, vol. 21, Weimar, 1896, Letter 5994, p. 294.

". . . one would have to be very much more skilled in these things than I, if one were to dare to criticize anything about it. . . . I, too, was once interested in these matters, and likewise practiced a kind of idolatry with Strasbourg Cathedral, the façade of which I still consider, as I did formerly, to be grander than that of the cathedral in Cologne.

"To me the strangest part of all this is the German patriotism that would like to represent this obviously Saracenic plant as having sprung from its soil. Yet on the whole the epoch in which this taste in architecture spread from South to North still remains most remarkable. The whole thing seems to me like a larval or pupal stage, at which the earliest Italian artists were also held, until finally Michelangelo, when he conceived of St. Peter's, broke the chrysalis and emerged to the world as a wondrously resplendent creature.

"At the same time I do not take it amiss that our young people linger over this intermediate epoch; I even look upon this phenomenon as inevitable, and refrain from all pragmatic observations and prophecies of a universal historical nature."

In 1771 Goethe had considered Gothic pure German and had himself indulged in patriotic feelings; now he considered it Saracenic and saw in it only an inferior, preparatory stage to the Renaissance in Italy. He continues: "Mr. Boisserée has written me a very charming and intelligent letter that prejudices me in his favor as much as the drawings. I enclose a few lines for him inviting him for Michaelmas. . . ." A whole year passed before Sulpiz Boisserée visited Goethe in Weimar. Boisserée can without doubt be numbered among the Romanticists, but he belongs with equal certainty to the group of rational scholars. For this reason we shall revert to him and his visit with Goethe later when the attempts at a scientific comprehension of Gothic are to be discussed.

We possess one document from the hand of a Romantic architect of this period who is perhaps the most eminent among his German colleagues, Friedrich von SCHINKEL (1781-1841). To his design of a mausoleum for Queen Louise of Prussia in 1810 he added an explanatory text that culminates in the assertion that ancient architecture is utterly insignificant,[35] compared to Gothic, when it comes to expressing the friendly and cheerful conception of death taught by Christianity. In his long argumentation occur the following remarks: "The art of the Middle Ages proceeded from the intention of representing an immediate, spiritual idea. . . . Now the spirit became completely victorious over mass and material. . . ." In a certain sense no one,

[35] From Schinkel's *Nachlass*, ed. by Alfred, Freiherr von Wolzogen, Berlin, 1862, III, p. 153.

from Suger to Dvořak and other critics of very recent times, has surpassed this insight.

Between Goethe's ideas and Schinkel's occurred the publication of a textbook on architecture by an orthodox classicist. Surprisingly enough, important utterances on Gothic are contained in it. In his preface Alois HIRT (1759-1839) says:[36] "Little of the architectural styles of the various peoples and periods of the Middle Ages has been edited with exactitude. The monuments have only a *negative importance* for the study of architecture itself, though they do not lack charm for its historical aspects. It would be very desirable if architects paid more heed to publicizing such buildings, although the picturesqueness and the magnificence with which Murphy presented the church of Batalha in Portugal and Frick the castle of Marienburg in Prussia, after the drawings by E. Gilly, are not necessary. One pair of such splendid editions is enough." The Classicist's nerves were irritated by the picturesque quality of these reproductions, but he had nevertheless an understanding of the purely mechanical problems of Gothic.

"The higher a type of arch is the smaller is its thrust or lateral pressure; but the more the arch approaches the horizontal line the more powerful does the lateral thrust become and the stronger must the abutments be. Accordingly, the Gothic arch is the one that needs the least and the horizontal flat arch the one that needs the strongest abutments. This explains how after the decline of architecture men in the Middle Ages hit upon the high types of arches. Out of ignorance and poverty they began to erect the piers and walls of uneven, partly of very poor material, and, as a matter of fact, without proper management of the construction. They were thus forced to resort to the loftier types of arches, which exercised less thrust. In those unhappy times they built merely to satisfy a need. The feeling for beautiful forms and for a pleasing proportion had become lost in architecture as well as in the other arts. . . ."[37] Hirt is probably the first literary witness

[36] A. Hirt, *Die Baukunst nach den Grundsätzen der Alten*, Berlin, 1809, p. xii.

[37] *Op.cit.*, p. 165.

"Je höher eine Bogenart ist, desto geringer ist ihr Schub oder Seitendruck, je mehr sich aber der Bogen der wagrechten Linie nähert, desto mächtiger wird der Seitenschub und desto stärkere Widerlager sind von nöthen. Hiernach ist der gotische Bogen derjenige, welcher der geringsten und der scheitrechte, welcher der stärksten Widerlager bedarf. Dies erklärt, wie nach Verfall der Baukunst man im Mittelalter auf die hohen Bogenarten verfiel. Aus Armut und Unwissenheit fing man an, die Pfeiler und Mauern von ungleichartigen, theils von sehr schlechtem Material, und zwar ohne gehörige Besorgung der Construction aufzuführen. Man nahm also notgedrungen die Zuflucht zu den höheren Bogenarten, welche weniger Schub verursachten. Man baute in diesen unglücklichen Zeiten bloss für das Bedürfniss. Das

since Félibien to recognize that the thrust of a pointed arch is less than that of a semicircle—which of course any Gothic architect of the Middle Ages (except those in Italy) well knew—but he allows himself the sophistry of saying that just because the pointed arch is statically better it can only be employed by poor architects who can construct no adequate statical safeguard for round arches. He then gives six reasons for preferring the round arch. The sixth reads: the semicircle is more agreeable to the eye and more adaptable to beautiful decoration than any other form of arch. (The meaning of the latter part of the sentence is obscure.)

Thus Hirt's real insight is forced into the prejudiced pattern of the classicistic school. Otherwise the entire folio volume concerns only antiquity and the Renaissance.

There were still men who clung to the doctrine of the higher value of antiquity. Such a one was Arthur SCHOPENHAUER (1788-1860),[38] whose attitude toward Gothic was almost completely negative. In his chief work,[39] the dominant idea of his system leads him to the thesis that architecture is the demonstration of some of the ideas which are the lowest stages of the objectivity of the *will*: heaviness, cohesion, rigidity, hardness. We do not need to pursue here in detail the derivation of this thought from Schopenhauer's system or even to judge it critically. The thesis is simply this: in architecture the physical properties are the main thing.[40] The geometrical qualities, that is, proportion and symmetry, which are usually discussed, are not so important, "since even ruins are still beautiful. . . . Actually the struggle between heaviness and rigidity is the sole aesthetic substance of beautiful architecture."

Accordingly, consummate beauty has once and for all been achieved

---

Gefühl für schöne Formen, und für ein gefälliges Verhältnis hatte sich in der Baukunst so wie in den übrigen Künsten verloren. . . ."

38 Richard Tengler, *Schopenhauer und die Romantik* (Germanische Studien, XXIX), Berlin, 1933.

39 Arthur Schopenhauer, *Die Welt als Wille und Vorstellung*, Leipzig, 1819.

40 In this place should be mentioned Ronald Bradbury's very valuable work, "The Romantic Theories of Architecture of the Nineteenth Century in Germany, England and France (together with a brief survey of the Vitruvian School)," Diss. Columbia Univ., 1934. His subject is not identical with mine. He takes up the philosophers—Kant, Schopenhauer, Hegel, Fr. v. Fischer, Lotze—separately from the writers—Chateaubriand, Goethe, Mme. de Staël, Friedrich Schlegel, Victor Hugo, Walter Scott. This, of course, does violence to the chronology, though it is objectively justified. It is, however, incomprehensible why he pays no attention to chronology within the groups themselves. The reader who is not very careful would have the impression that Chateaubriand wrote before Goethe. Since Bradbury's aim is to give a more complete presentation of the aesthetic theories, his book should most emphatically be referred to as a supplement to the present work. He writes about Schopenhauer on pp. 46ff.

in the column and entablature of antiquity, and for reasons of climate this perfection is only possible in the South. Gothic is impaired by the northern climate. Schopenhauer also speaks briefly about the significance of light in architecture—the light of the sun, blue sky as a background, moonlight—but he does not exhaust the topic. It is in any case important that along with the element of space, which he neglects, he clearly emphasizes two other elements: *force* and *light.*

He apparently discovered afterward that Gothic had become the fashion, and so he reverted to the subject in the second volume. Some remarks must be quoted verbally.[41] "I hardly need to remind the reader that in regard to all these architectural reflections I had in mind solely the ancient style of building and not the so-called Gothic, which, of Saracenic origin, was introduced to the rest of Europe by the Goths in Spain. Perhaps the latter, too, cannot be denied a certain beauty in its way; but when it undertakes to claim equal rank with the former, that is a barbarous presumption that cannot be permitted. . . . Our pleasure in Gothic works is quite certainly based in large part on associations of ideas and on historical memories, thus on an emotion foreign to art. . . ." And now he reproaches Gothic for not having any horizontal lines or any visible load. In spite of his reluctance, however, he gradually comes closer to Gothic. He searches for a principle peculiar to it and in conformity with his emphasis on physical forces, and finds "that here the complete overcoming and vanquishing of gravity is intended to be represented. . . . Whereas in ancient art the thrusting and pushing from above downwards is just as well represented and demonstrated as that from below upwards, here the latter is decidedly predominant." But the former is after all better because it corresponds to nature; the latter is only a fiction and a delusion. "Everyone will easily be able to realize how from the fundamental idea . . . of Gothic architecture here indicated there results the mysterious and hyperphysical character that it is acknowledged to have. It arises chiefly . . . because of the fact that here the purely rational has been replaced . . . . by the arbitrary. So much that is really purposeless . . . arouses the supposition of unknown . . . purposes, that is, the mysterious appearance. On the other hand, the splendid side of Gothic churches is the interior . . . in ancient buildings the exterior is the more advantageous. . . ." He becomes apparently more and more indulgent. "But whoever now absolutely insists on regarding Gothic architecture as essential and justified may, if he

[41] Vol. II, Book 3, Ch. 35.

is at the same time fond of analogies, call it the negative pole, or even the minor key of architecture." Anyone who has some acquaintance with Schopenhauer's style, however, will realize that this is pure irony. Likewise the conclusion of the chapter preserves the same tone. One ought to spend money only on what is beautiful in itself, not for that which is valuable merely for its associations of ideas. The completion of Gothic churches seems to him "as though one intended to embalm defunct Christianity."

In his own day Schopenhauer first was ignored; only after about 1850 did he become almost the most influential philosopher. How many half-educated persons who read him took his remarks, beginning with the Saracens and Goths, as pure gold?

The aesthetic principles that Friedrich SCHLEIERMACHER (1768-1834) worked out in 1819 and made them the subject of a course of lectures at the University of Berlin remained, on the other hand, completely without influence. They were not published in full until 1893.[42] This fall into oblivion definitely did not harm the development of aesthetics. The book is trying because of the vagueness of its ideas. Schleiermacher is also rather negative toward Gothic. He stresses the fact that the Gothic church and the Gothic castle form the greatest of contrasts, representing the style of piety and that of secular life. The secular buildings, including the castles, are not such noble works of art as the cathedrals. The structures of the commercial and Hansa cities were not lifted enough above the level of immediate necessity. One certainly approaches the study of this aesthetics with the expectation that a nature so deeply religious as Schleiermacher's would have had an intuitive comprehension of Gothic, but he was generally not very sensitive to architecture.

Wilhelm Friedrich HEGEL (1770-1831) is the culmination of all romantic theories of art and aesthetics. In order to appreciate his attitude toward Gothic properly one must briefly recall how his judgment is related to his philosophical system. This is quite possible, even without assuming a knowledge of the system as a whole.[43]

In art Hegel differentiates between content and form. The content of art is the "idea," its form "the sensuous visual shaping" (*die sinn-*

[42] Friedrich Schleiermacher's *Ästhetik*, ed. by R. Odebrecht, Berlin and Leipzig, 1893. Odebrecht gives an account of the different versions and of the edition of 1842 (p. xxii ff.). The passage on Gothic is on pp. 209ff.

[43] Literature on Hegel listed in Ueberweg, *Geschichte der Philosophie*, IV, Berlin, 1913, pp. 73ff. I refer to the *Sämtliche Werke von G. W. Friedrich Hegel*, ed. by Hermann Glockner, XI-XIII. *Vorlesungen über Aesthetik*, Stuttgart, 1927.

liche, bildliche Gestaltung), in contrast to philosophy and science where the idea is manifested in the form of ratiocination and of pure mentality. "It is the function of art to bring these two sides into a free, conciliated totality."

Now Hegel postulates that the idea (although it is *per se* true in and of itself) shall not be abstract but concrete and individual, so that it may unite with the likewise concrete and individual form.[44] The level of value in art depends on the degree of inwardness and concord of fusion between idea and form. In addition there are historical stages. In the first stage the idea is still too general and indefinite and therefore does not as yet have the individuality that is requisite for the ideal (the ideal stage). In the second stage the abstract has been eradicated; idea and reality are perfectly fused. In the third stage they again become differentiated.

Each stage has a "defect" that impels it to a higher development. The defect of the first—this is obvious even from such an abbreviated exposition—is that there is developed no real congruity of form and content at all. But what can be the defect of the ideal or second stage? Here one must try to follow understandingly Hegel's paradoxical thought: mind (*Geist*) is absolute and eternal, but in classical art it becomes human and limited. Thus precisely its virtue is its defect. Whether this is comprehensible or not, the inevitable result of this virtue-defect is the third stage, where content surpasses that of the preceding stages. This content is Christianity, in which the concrete content is unity of human and divine nature. Whereas the ancient god was outside the subject, the Christian God is "self-conscious inwardness" (known by the subject). Mind is again absolute mind. The art of this stage concerns in its content the inner world of man.

Hegel postulated, therefore, *three* stages of *art*, because he made this development in three stages the fundamental principle of his whole system. It is the so-called dialectical method of thesis, antithesis, and synthesis, which results by pure logic from the structure of the conceptual world and is called dialectical because in the realm of the intellect itself it allows problems to develop as though in a dialogue. Hegel called the stages of art the *symbolical*, the *classical*, and the *romantic*. The last two he found already in existence. He was well acquainted with the writings of the Schlegel brothers, and his condescending criticism of them, instead of gratitude, is all too human.[45]

[44] *Op.cit.*, pp. 107ff.
[45] *Ibid.*, p. 99.

For the first, symbolical stage he had to search out the necessary works of art. He found them in the hitherto neglected Oriental art of the Babylonians, Indians, and Egyptians. The Schlegels had, however, just brought the Indian world closer again to the consciousness of the age[46] (Schopenhauer also, Hegel's enemy, saw in it the epitome of all wisdom), and Egypt had recently been more discovered than conquered by Napoleon. In any case, Hegel's concern with Asiatic and Egyptian art meant a magnificent expansion of the horizon of historians of art, and one should not be troubled by the fact that the introduction of these fields was based on the use of the dialectical method, with all its dubiousness, as a bridge. (In Hegelian terms this defect was the virtue or, conversely, this virtue a defect.)

It is very interesting to see how much—or how little—Hegel knew of preclassical art. All his observations, correct or not, are on a very high level, and almost everywhere new ideas are to be found. Anything new is least to be expected where he discusses antiquity; that path had been too well worn. We are interested here only in romantic art, specifically in architecture.

It is a phenomenon probably of more frequent occurrence in the history of ideas than we realize that thoughts which are subsequently to become very important stand at first on the same level with many others, before it is noted that they are more fundamental. Thus Schopenhauer had stressed the physical and optical factors in addition to the geometrical factor of symmetry, proportion, or the like, familiar from the days of Vitruvius, without, however, making any adequate impression upon his contemporaries. Hegel raised the geometrical factor, which up to that time was understood as two-dimensional, to a three-dimensional one, for he discovered the significance of "space" for the romantic stage of architecture. The terraced towers of the Babylonians, the pagodas of the Indians, the pyramids and obelisks of the Egyptians have no, or almost no, interior space. The Greek or Roman temple has an interior, but it is intended solely for the statue of the god and all artistic developments take place in the exterior architecture. Romantic architecture is an interior for the congregation, its inner part is decidedly more important than the exterior. "The *space* of the interior must not be an abstractly uniform, empty space. . . . The movement . . . of the soul in its elevation from the earthly to the *infinite*, to the other world . . . would not be architectonically ex-

[46] Cf. also the emergence of India in the work of Schelling and Stieglitz, above p. 458 and p. 466.

pressed in this empty uniformity of a rectangle."[46a] Usefulness, as is appropriate for an ordinary house, becomes here a side issue, and for this reason Hegel concludes that the strict differentiation between support and load must also be abandoned. There follows the comparison with a forest, which, however, is not to be taken as an actual prototype; then he discusses the pointed arch and the piers, and here again a thought appears for the first time: "The *pointed arch*, which seems to rise in a straight line from the pier and slowly and imperceptibly curves in order to incline toward the opposite one, presents at first the complete appearance of being nothing but the *actual continuation of the pier* itself, which forms an arch together with another one." What he means is that column and architrave are two separate things, pier and pointed arch are one single entity. He states expressly that the capitals are occasionally omitted entirely. Hegel's manner of expressing himself is not absolutely precise, since a pointed arch curves just as a semicircle does. But his meaning is intelligible, and it is not only correct but takes the first step toward tackling the stylistic analysis of Gothic from the direction of the psychological interpretation of *form*.

Hegel speaks, of course, of proportions also, and adds the remark that the piers cannot be comprehended with one glance because they soar to such lofty heights; one must follow them with the eye—upwards to God. This is related to the phraseology of Stieglitz, whose book, published in 1820, Hegel surely knew. But the other structural parts also produce this "restlessness of upward flight." He makes casual mention of the stained-glass windows "that suffuse a twilight and make the radiance of the candles shine. For here another day shall give light than the day of outward nature."

He cautiously rejects the mystic significance of numerical proportions, saying that importance was indeed attached to them in the age of Gothic, "but dim notions of the reasonable easily fasten on externalities, and these arbitrary diversions produce no higher beauty. The real spirit is to be found in something other than mystical interpretations of differences in numbers."

The description of the exterior of Gothic cathedrals and of their decoration is excellent but offers no new ideas. There is a very brief paragraph on the pre-Gothic architecture of the Middle Ages. Hegel also feels obliged to say something about secular architecture in Gothic,

[46a] Der Raum des Inneren muss nicht ein abstrakt gleicher leerer Raum sein. . . . Die Bewegung . . . des Gemüts in seiner Erhebung vom Irdischen zum Unendlichen, zum Jenseits . . . wäre in dieser leeren Gleichheit eines Vierecks architektonisch nicht ausgedrückt.

a subject that has always caused embarrassment after the discussion of the ecclesiastical—and still does so today. In conclusion he takes up landscape architecture, where all of a sudden the word picturesque occurs. "As far as actual landscape architecture is concerned we must be careful to distinguish its *picturesque* aspect from the *architectonic.*" This is a new variation of Hemsterhuis' polarity. "A large park, especially when it is furnished with little Chinese temples, Turkish mosques, Swiss chalets, bridges, hermitages, and who knows what other exotic things, claims attention for itself. . . . But this charm . . . soon vanishes, and one cannot look at such things twice, for these additions do not offer the eye anything infinite, no soul inherent is in them, and they are, moreover, only boring and annoying for conversation and discussion as one walks about." He prefers the French style of garden.[47] One might well have expected that the romantic aesthetician would have had more sympathy for romantic gardens than for classical. But Hegel's philosophy is after all one of latent contradictions.

If one wishes a thorough acquaintance with Hegel's views on Gothic, one must also consult the sections on sculpture and painting. Here this can be omitted.

He did not publish his aesthetics himself, but expounded it several times in lecture courses at the Universities of Tübingen and Berlin in the years from 1818 to 1828.[48] It is therefore impossible to connect its influence with one particular year.

In 1827 August Wilhelm von Schlegel repeated in Berlin the course of lectures delivered by him in 1801. The notes to these lectures provide a kind of substitute for the brief indications that were quoted above; they need no comment, since they add nothing new to the conception of Gothic which in the meantime had progressed. Also in other respects the lectures are said to have disappointed both their audience and, as a result, Schlegel himself. By now people already knew everything he had to say. The Berliners had meanwhile heard Hegel.

This chapter on German Romanticism can be concluded with the contributions that Heinrich HEINE (1797-1856) made to the subject of Gothic.[49] His observation that the art of antiquity is finite and therefore

[47] *Op.cit.*, p. 352.

[48] There were five lectures: the first, delivered in Heidelberg in 1818, was completely revised in 1820 for Berlin; the others followed in the years 1823, 1826, and 1828. The posthumous edition by Hotho combined them all into one.

[49] Heinrich Heine, *Die romantische Schule*, in the *Sämtliche Werke*, ed. by Elster, Leipzig and Vienna, v, 1890, pp. 217, 224, 226, published in French 1833, in German 1836.

identical with the idea of the artist is reminiscent of Hegel; from the same source would seem to come also the remark that romantic art represents the infinite and purely spiritual relationships and takes refuge in the parabolical. The latter element he discovers also in Gothic. "When we now enter an ancient cathedral, we scarcely suspect any longer the esoteric significance of its stone symbolism. Only the total impression has an immediate effect on our hearts. We feel here the lifting up of the spirit and the trampling of the flesh. The interior of the cathedral is itself a hollow cross, and we move about there inside the very instrument of martyrdom; the many-colored windows throw their red and green lights on us like drops of blood and pus; hymns for the dying fill our ears with wailing; beneath our feet gravestones and decay, and with the colossal piers the spirit strives upward, painfully tearing itself free from the body, which sinks to the ground like a tired garment. When one observes them from outside, these Gothic cathedrals, these huge structures, wrought so airily, so finely, so delicately, so transparently that they might be taken for carvings or for Brabant lace in marble: then only one really feels the power of that age which knew how to master even stone, so that it appears to be almost ghostly etherealized and this most obdurate of materials itself proclaims Christian spiritualism."[50]

If one looks back one must say that German Romanticism made an astonishingly great contribution to the understanding and evaluation of Gothic. The positive side of its achievement is not merely that it transformed the Cinderella into a princess. By means of a wealth of concepts it attempted to make the nature of Gothic clear and at the same time bring it closer to our emotions. It had a good grasp of the physiognomy of Gothic, describing it both poetically and philosophically. All the various qualities revealed by these buildings: the infinite, the romantic, the religious, the spiritual, the picturesque, the

[50] "Wenn wir jetzt in einen altem Dom treten, ahnen wir kaum mehr den esoterischen Sinn seiner steinernen Symbolik. Nur der Gesamteindruck dringt uns unmittelbar ins Gemüt. Wir fühlen hier die Erhebung des Geistes und die Zertretung des Fleisches. Das Innere des Domes selbst ist ein hohles Kreuz, und wir wandeln da im Werkzeug des Martyrtums selbst; die bunten Fenster werfen auf uns ihre roten und grünen Lichter wie Blutstropfen und Eiter; Sterbelieder umwimmern uns; unter unseren Füssen Leichensteine und Verwesung und mit den kolossalen Pfeilern strebt der Geist in die Höhe, sich schmerzlich losreissend von dem Leib, der wie müdes Gewand zu Boden sinkt. Wenn man sie von aussen erblickt diese gotischen Dome, diese ungeheuren Bauwerke, die so luftig, so fein, so zierlich, so durchsichtig gearbeitet sind, dass man sie für ausgeschnitzelt, dass man sie für Brabanter Spitzen von Marmor halten sollte: dann fühlt man erst recht die Gewalt jener Zeit, die selbst den Stein so zu bewältigen wusste, dass er fast gespenstig durchgeistigt erscheint, dass sogar diese härteste Materie den christlichen Spiritualismus ausspricht."

flowerlike, were now acknowledged. The two Schlegels attempted to say something about the objective thing itself, though very incompletely. Hegel made excellent observations, but even he, the great systematizer, did not grasp the Gothic *system*, remarking now on this, now on that. When he does speak of the whole, however, it concerns the relationship of form and idea, and other profound insights which lead away from the object itself to the sphere of abstractions, without making it clearly evident how these abstractions are connected with concrete things. Only Hirt contributed something positive and correct regarding the mechanics of the pointed arch, and only Costenoble attempted to overcome vagueness and proceed analytically. Unfortunately he was too much the dilettante and schoolmaster to produce anything really useful.[51]

6. Romanticism in England, France and Russia

Haym,[1] who was the first to write a history of the Romantic School in Germany, began with Ludwig Tieck's early works of 1790 and hardly went beyond the year 1804. Bray, writing in more recent times on French Romanticism, regarded it as beginning not before 1804 and continuing down to 1830.[2] His reason for considering 1804 the initial date is that this was when the controversy started over the threat to French literature from the popular modern melodrama, a controversy that was soon to expand into an intellectual battle of opposing principles: "La guerre entre les romantiques allemands et les classiques français," "Une querelle nationale," "France contre Allemagne." Once again German barbarians were attacking hallowed objects of culture, though this time only the unities of time and place in the French theater. Yet the roots of French Romanticism are hardly to be found

51 Postscript on bibliography, François Pariset, "Étude sur l'atelier de la Cathédrale de Strasbourg entre 1681 et 1789," *Archives Alsasiennes*, Strasbourg, Paris, 1929, p. 169; especially about the freemasons, p. 194 and about Boisserée, p. 202.

For more complete information as to what was known concerning Indian architecture at the time of Wilhelm August von Schlegel and later, the reader is referred to the two folio volumes of Louis Mathieu Langlès, *Monuments anciens et modernes de l'Hindoustan*, Paris, 1817-1821. George Wightwick's book, *The Palace of Architecture, A romance of Art and History*, London, 1840 contains (pp. 19-36) remarks concerning Indian architecture. Although popular, the book is interesting as an attempt at a universal history of architecture before Ramée and Schnaase. (This information was added by Mrs. J. Weitzmann-Fiedler.)

1 Rudolf Haym, *Die Romantische Schule, Ein Beitrag zur Geschichte des deutschen Geistes*, Berlin, 1870 (3rd ed., 1914).

2 René Bray, *Chronologie du Romantisme 1804-1830*, Paris, 1892.

here. It did, indeed, have its nationalistic side, but Chateaubriand appears first on the scene, and as far as he is concerned the roots of Romanticism are to be found in Catholicism.

Rousseau's romanticism had been of a different sort; his enthusiasm was for nature, which by no means signifies Gothic. His sole utterance on Gothic is entirely negative. "As for the contrafugues and double fugues . . . they are obviously remnants of barbarism and bad taste that only continue to exist, like the portals of our Gothic churches, in order to shame those who had the patience to make them."[3] It is, however, not our task here to write of French Romanticism in all its aspects. Only Chateaubriand, who stands at its beginning, and Victor Hugo, who wrote on Gothic a generation later, need be considered.

To define the limits of English Romanticism would be still more difficult. Here, too, only a few authors expressed themselves on the subject of Gothic, namely, Murphy, Hall, Lascelles, and Sir Walter Scott.

Of these four English worshipers of Gothic Murphy is chronologically the first. Hall comes soon after, while Scott, like Hugo, wrote a generation later. Murphy and Hall take us back to the time before the emergence of the Schlegels. It must be granted that the two English writers still had real faith in the possibility of solving the problems of Gothic by means of speculations in the traditional eighteenth-century manner. They were taken seriously in subsequent literature, and though their arguments were refuted everywhere, they were, nevertheless, still considered worthy of debate, a book by Murphy even being translated into German.[4] For us they have become merely comic figures.

James Cavanah MURPHY (1760-1814) put forward the idea that pinnacles not only look like Egyptian obelisks, but actually are derived from them historically. Since in his opinion obelisks are tombs, and in the Middle Ages people were buried in churches, the connection of thought is established. Whereas other scholars derived all of Gothic from the pointed arch, he sees both the pointed arch and everything else in Gothic as the result of the *pinnacle, or* the *tower, or* the *obelisk.*

[3] Jean Jacques Rousseau, *Œuvres complètes*, 1792, IX, "Lettres sur la musique française," p. 382: "A l'égard des contrefugues, double fugues . . . ce sont evidemment des restes de barbarie et de mauvais goût qui ne subsistent comme les portails de nos églises gothiques, que pour la honte de ceux qui ont eu la patience de les faire."

[4] James Cavanah Murphy, 1760-1814, *Introductory Discourse on the Principles of the Gothic Architecture.* This essay forms the introduction to *Plans, Elevations, Sections of Views of the Church of Batalha*, London, 1795; German translation by J. Engelhard, Darmstadt, 1813.

James HALL (1761-1832), on the other hand, has a kind of "wood theory":[5] the place of Murphy's obelisk is taken for him by any long pole—partly with, partly without leaves. To this element is added a second: the elastic willow withe—also partly with and partly without leaves. Very logically and didactically Hall combines these simple elements and inevitably arrives at Gothic, hence he deduces that such must have been the course of historical development. The chapel he built according to his method is as charming as it is touching (Fig. 54). To him the most convincing thing undoubtedly was that the curvilinear forms could be so well imitated by the willow withes.

His naïveté is all the more astonishing since he was an outstanding figure in his own field of research. He was the first to apply successfully the methods and experiments of chemistry to the reconstruction and explanation of geological processes. His trained intellect made it possible for him to invent an alluring logical method to prove a historical thesis that was pure fiction. Thus Hall's theory is more of an object of study for logicians than for historians of Gothic.

Murphy and Hall would seem to be sober men of science beside the third of these English Romanticists, Rowley LASCELLES (1775-1841). I am not acquainted with his book and must rely on Clark.[6] Lascelles reverts to the idea of the pointed arch as the embryo of all Gothic, and maintains that it was derived from the keel of Noah's Ark. He does not seem to have considered that the ark's keel might have been shaped like an ogee or keel-arch, and that consequently Early Gothic would have had to have ogee arches. Or did he think that in Noah's time arks were built with keels in the form of a pointed arch?

After the obligatory mention of these three fanciful writers we can turn again to serious authors. François René CHATEAUBRIAND (1768-1848) glorified the Catholic faith in his *Génie du Christianisme*, and in this connection wrote—and wrote beautifully—about almost all aspects of human existence. Throughout his whole work one has the feeling of being cushioned softly and warmly, encompassed by a world of kindness and beauty. A special chapter is devoted to Gothic churches.[7] Chateaubriand begins with the thesis that everything has its proper place. An Egyptian temple does not belong in Athens or a Greek

[5] James Hall, *Essay on the Origin, History, and Principles of Gothic Architecture*, Edinburgh, 1797 (Transactions of the Royal Society of Edinburgh, III), 2nd ed., 1813. For Friedrich von Schlegel's criticism see above, p. 463.

[6] Clark, *op.cit.*, p. 88. Rowley Lascelles, *The Heraldic Origin of Gothic Architecture*, 1820.

[7] François René Chateaubriand, *Génie du Christianisme*, Paris, 1801, Part 3, Bk. 1, ch. 8 (In *Œuvres complètes*, 1827, XII, pp. 322ff.).

one in Memphis or, for that matter, in Paris: "One may build very elegant, very well lighted Greek temples for the purpose of assembling the *good people* of Saint Louis and causing them to worship a *metaphysical* God, but they will always long for these Nôtre-Dame of Reims and of Paris, these basilicas, all covered with moss. . . ."[8] An edifice one has seen being constructed is not marvelous. "God is the eternal law; his origin and all that pertains to his cult ought to be lost in the night of ages."[9] The true Romanticist esteems that which is remote, unattainable, unexplorable, mysteriously obscure.

"One could not enter a Gothic church without experiencing a kind of shudder and a vague consciousness of God. One would find oneself suddenly carried back to the times when cloistered monks, after they had meditated in the forests of their monasteries, cast themselves down before the altar and praised the Lord in the calm and silence of the night. The France of the past seemed to come to life again: one thought to behold those singular costumes, that people, so different from what it is today. One was reminded of the revolution of that people, of its achievements and its works of art. The farther those times were removed from us the more magical did they seem, the more did they fill us with those thoughts that always end in reflection on the nothingness of man and the transitoriness of life.

"The Gothic order, in the midst of its barbarous proportions, always has a beauty that is peculiar to it.

"Forests were the first temples of God, and in forests men grasped their first idea of architecture. This art has had to vary according to climates. The Greeks shaped the elegant Corinthian column, with its capital of leaves, on the model of the palm. The enormous piers of the ancient Egyptian style represent the sycamore, the Oriental fig, the banana tree, and most of the gigantic trees of Africa and Asia.

"The forests of the Gauls passed in their turn into the temples of our fathers, and our oak forests have thus preserved their sacred origin. These vaults incised with leaves, these socles that support the walls and end brusquely like broken tree trunks, the coolness of the vaults, the shadows of the Sanctuary, the dark aisles, the secret passages, the low doors, all of this evokes in a Gothic church the labyrinths of the forests; it all makes us conscious of religious awe, the mysteries, and the divinity. The two lofty towers placed before the entrance to the structure overshadow the elms and the yews of the churchyard and create a picturesque effect against the azure of the sky. Now the dawning day illumines their twin heads, now they

[8] "On aura beau bâtir des temples grecs bien élégants, bien éclairés, pour rassembler le *bon peuple* de Saint Louis, et lui faire adorer un Dieu *métaphysique*, il regrettera toujours ces *Notre Dame* de Reims et de Paris, ces basiliques, toutes moussues. . . ."

[9] "Dieu est la loi éternelle, son origine et tout ce qui tient à son culte doit se perdre dans la nuit des temps."

seem to be crowned by a chaplet of clouds or augmented in a hazy atmosphere. Even the birds seem to be deceived and take them for the trees of their forests. The rooks flutter around the gables and perch on the galleries. But suddenly confused noises are emitted from the very top of these towers, driving away the startled birds. The Christian architect, not satisfied with building forests, wanted, as it were, to imitate their murmurs, and by the help of the organ and suspended bronze he has associated with the Gothic temple the noise of the winds and the thunder that rolls through the depths of the forests. The centuries, conjured up by these religious sounds, let their ancient voices be heard from the heart of the stones and sigh through the vast basilica: the Sanctuary surges with sound, like the cave of the ancient Sybil, and while the metal swings with a mighty din above your head, the subterranean vaults of death preserve an impenetrable silence beneath your feet."[10]

Of all descriptions of Gothic this is perhaps the most poetic. Goethe surpasses Chateaubriand in enthusiasm and the fire that resulted from his polemical attitude. Chateaubriand simply evokes associations, instead of describing what is to be seen. He presents the inner pictures that rise in his subjective consciousness. Much is derived from older descriptions with which we are acquainted, but nothing is meant to be taken literally; above all, the forest theory is introduced more as a comparison, not as a crude explanation, although for French readers French take the place of German forests: *forêts de Gaules.*

Chateaubriand provided a note on the phrase "sur le modèle du palmier," in which he recommends a column "qu'on pourroit appeler palmiste." This recalls Laugier.

Victor HUGO (1802-1885), a leading spirit of French Romanticism by reason of several of his works, made Gothic the basis of his novel, *Nôtre-Dame de Paris.*[11] The cathedral is the background for the romantic story of the hunchbacked bell-ringer, Quasimodo, but such is the prominence given to it that Bradbury could say: "Whereas in *Nôtre-Dame* the old cathedral sets the keynote for the plot and even modifies the characters, in Scott's novel it is the characters who by their romantic actions set the key for the architecture."[12] Bradbury's observation can well be supplemented by reading in Victor Hugo a passage that seems to be the most important one for our topic. Hugo interrupted his story in midstream and interpolated as Book III two

[10] Cf. text, Appendix 28.

[11] The novel appeared in 1831. I quote from the edition by John R. Wightman, Boston, Mass. and London, 1903.

[12] Ronald Bradbury, *The Romantic Theories of Architecture . . .*, p. 77.

chapters that are purely scholarly. The first of these describes the fabric of the cathedral, placing emphasis on everything that disfigured it at that time (1831), before the restoration. After the description of the façade we read: "This façade today lacks three important things: first the flight of eleven stairs that once raised the façade above the ground level, then the lower series of statues that occupied the niches of the three portals, and the upper series of the twenty-eight oldest kings of France that adorned the gallery of the first story, from Childebert to Philippe-Auguste, holding in their hands the imperial scepter."[13] Hugo speaks of the "sombre color of the centuries, which makes of the age of the monuments the age of their beauty."[14] Though he recognizes the positive aspect of change, he sees the negative far more strongly, especially when he comes to discuss the interior. He generalizes: "It is thus that the splendid art of the Middle Ages has been treated in almost all countries, especially in France."[15] This is a new approach to Gothic. Serious conservation of monuments and the desire for historically correct renovations become evident, an attitude essentially very different from that of Laugier, who had also, we recall, made the state of Nôtre-Dame in Paris the occasion for some remarks. Hugo enumerates three kinds of destruction: "Wrinkles and blemishes of the epidermis; these are the work of time. Accidents, brutalities, contusions, fractures; these are the work of the revolutions from Luther to Mirabeau. Mutilations, amputations, dislocations of the structure, *restorations*; these are the *Greek, Roman*, and *barbarian* work of the *professors* according to *Vitruvius and Vignola*. The magnificent art produced by the Vandals has been killed by the academies. To the centuries, to the revolutions . . . has been added the host of architects from the schools . . . substituting Louis XV chicory for Gothic lacework to the greater glory of the Parthenon."[16] Thus time changed.

[13] "Trois choses importantes manquent aujourd'hui à cette façade: d'abord le degré de onze marches qui l'exhaussait jadis audessus du sol; ensuite la série inférieure de statues qui occupait les niches des trois portails, et la série supérieure des vingt-huit plus anciens rois de France, qui garnissait la galérie du premier étage, à partir de Childebert jusqu'à Philippe-Auguste, tenant en main 'la pomme impériale.' " (p. 86).

[14] ". . . sombre couleur des siècles qui fait de la vieillesse des monuments l'âge de leur beauté." (p. 87) Notre Dame was restored in the nineteenth century by Lassus and Viollet-Le-Duc; the gallery of the kings and the sculptures of the portals have now been replaced by copies; the most famous of the gargoyles date only from this restoration. Cf. Marcel Aubert, *Notre Dame de Paris, Architecture et Sculpture*, Paris, 1928.

[15] "C'est ainsi que l'art merveilleux du moyen-âge a été traité presque en tout pays, surtout en France." (p. 87)

[16] "Rides et verrues à l'épiderme; c'est l'œuvre du temps. Voies de fait, brutalités, contusions, fractures; c'est l'œuvre des révolutions depuis Luther jusqu'à Mirabeau. Mutilations, amputations, dislocations de la membrure, *restaurations*, c'est le *travail grec*, *romain* et *barbare* des *professeurs*

Then Hugo discusses the place that Nôtre-Dame has in the development of the mediaeval architecture and says "It is an edifice of Transition." In some cases he commits mistakes, but his general historic attitude is excellent. "The great structures are works of centuries like the mountains."[17] Hugo anticipates the later method to treat each building in a monograph, although he surrounds his subject with many accessories.

Then he climbs the tower and surveys Paris "à vol d'oiseau." His description of the city is both historical and geographical. Various modern structures are mentioned, some of which are ridiculed: "The Sainte-Geneviève of M. Soufflot is certainly one of the finest Savoy cakes that has ever been made of stone."[18] The passage continues in the same sneering vein. Is Romanticism no longer on the defensive? It becomes aggressive. Soufflot, who was so fair to Gothic, might have inquired: is it now necessary to repay the shades of Filarete, Vasari, Blondel with this sort of base coin in order to appreciate Gothic?

Walter SCOTT (1771-1832) seems to have been free of such aberrations, though one would have to check over his works carefully to be quite sure. In connection with Bradbury's book, it can certainly be said that his descriptions of the Gothic castles which he chose as the setting for his stories are very graphic. Since they are painted simply as a part of the mediaeval scene, there is no place for critical judgment. Scott does not theorize. He evokes a series of vividly described characters moving against a background of Gothic architecture, as for example in Ivanhoe. In this respect he was preparing the ground for Pugin, Ruskin, and George Gilbert Scott.

"Through the mighty prose of Walter Scott the Gothic style began to spread quickly and to intrude everywhere." These words of Nicolaus GOGOL (1809-1852) give a hint of the source of his enthusiasm for Gothic. They are contained in an article written between 1833 and 1834 when he was twenty-seven years old.[19] What had he seen of genuine Gothic architecture? He mentions only briefly Milan, Cologne, and the "unfinished tower" of Strasbourg, remarking that these works are now

---

selon Vitruve et *Vignole*. Cet art magnifique que les Vandales avaient produit, les académies l'ont tué. Aux siècles, aux révolutions . . . est venue s'adjoindre la nuée des architectes d'école . . . substituant les chicorées de Louis XV aux dentelles gothiques pour la plus grande gloire du Panthéon." He means Ste-Geneviève at Paris (p. 87).

17 "Les grands édifices, comme les grandes montagnes, sont l'ouvrage des siècles." (p. 89)

18 "La Sainte-Geneviève de M. Soufflot est certainement le plus belle gâteau de Savoie qu'on ait jamais fait en pierre." (p. 97)

19 *Gogols sämmtliche Werke*, ed. by Otto Buek, Berlin, s.a., II. *Über die Architektur unserer Zeit*, pp. 315ff. I owe this information to Mrs. Josepha Weitzmann-Fiedler.

forgotten. From 1836 to 1848 he lived in Rome, but it is not clear whether it was there that he changed his attitude toward the Renaissance. In this article he wrote: "A number of inhabitants of the Byzantine Empire fled the vicious capital when it was taken by the Mohammedans and subsequently ruined the taste of the Europeans and their colossal architecture. The Byzantines had long since lost their Attic taste and had not even retained their native Byzantine taste. They brought only miserable remnants of their degenerate style to Europe." His concept of Gothic is perhaps more correct. He rejects the theory that it is derived from Arab architecture. Gothic "is sublime and all-embracing like Christianity. Here we find all united: a forest of slender piers. . . ." It would be interesting to find out what besides Scott Gogol had read about Gothic. Certainly his romantic longing made him critical of the Russian architecture of his time, and his short survey of the styles which came after Gothic testifies to the amount of his knowledge. The article, however, is one of the few expressions of admiration for Gothic to come from Russia, where Gothic did not exist. It attracted the attention of Russian readers to an architecture unknown to them. He also discusses the architecture of the Orient. "India is dotted with magnificent buildings. . . ." Again it is difficult to determine the extent of his knowledge of this architecture which he alternately praises and disparges.

Perhaps the most interesting part of the article is a long footnote in which he proposes that every city should have an avenue lined with monuments representing the entire chronicle of architectural development. Passing through a dark, heavy gate, the beholder would first encounter examples of the crude, primitive style, then those of the mighty Egyptian. He would then contemplate the beauty of the Greek, the voluptuous splendor of the Alexandrinian and Byzantine with their cupolas, the Roman with its arcades, the style of the decadence and after that the unusual splendor of the Arabian style. Next would come the rough Gothic (that is to say the Romanesque) followed by the Gothic-Arabic (?) and the pure Gothic style, the crown of art as represented by the cathedral of Cologne. It is astonishing to find that he wishes the procession to include an example of the terrible mixture of all styles under the influence of the Byzantine, the return to Greek architecture under a new guise. Finally, the avenue is to end with a gate which embraces all the elements of the latest architectural trends.

A combination of the Franzensring of Vienna and Maximiliansstrasse of Munich would produce only a partial realization of this dream of historism. For some reason, Gogol omitted Indian and Far Eastern architecture. In his volume, Fischer von Erlach was more complete in this respect.

In 1834 Gogol wrote an article about the Middle Ages. In it he describes the popes and the crusades, the veneration of women and chivalry, monarchism and the inquisition, in all of which he finds much to admire, without however being blind to the shortcomings of this culture. In attempting to give a vivid, many-sided picture of a culture, he anticipates the introduction of Schnaase and the work of various other scholars.[20]

It was Jules MICHELET (1798-1874) who became the most influential historian of this time. His history of France was published from 1833 to 1860.[21] When he came to the Gothic period, he inserted a long essay opening with a discussion of the etymology of the Latin word *ars*. Since *ars* is the opposite of *iners*, art means action like the Greek word *drama*. Because material has to endure the creative activity of man in order to receive through passion its highest form, art is analogous to generation. Art is *nature spiritualisé*. Art is the fruit of Nature, its mother, and man, its father. Art therefore possesses masculine and feminine aspects. The architecture of India, for example, has both "vastes cavernes, vulves profondes," and "pyramides que voudrait féconder le ciel."[22] From the pyramid he proceeds to the triangle and to the pointed arch which, according to Crawford, originated in India and Persia. There were pointed arches in Sicily as well and thus, "the striving of the infinite toward the infinite, in other words the universal or catholic tendency, manifests itself at both ends of the world." The Gothic church is the product of roses, tabernacles. After stating that Greece and Rome also contributed to Gothic, he explains that the word *ogive*, according to Gilbert (*Description de Nôtre-Dame de Paris*, p. 56), is derived from "*oeil ogival*" and the German word *Auge*. He then discusses briefly the meaning of Flamboyant, "flames of the heart or tears, possibly a combination of the two." Of more importance are his descriptions of Nôtre-Dame at Paris, of Reims, and St.-Denis.

Michelet anticipated the comparison between Gothic and scholasticism: "It [Gothic] subdivided and again subdivided. Its process was Aristotelian, the method of Thomas Aquinas. It became a series of syllogisms in stone, which did not attain their conclusion." Was Sem-

20 *Ibid. Über das Mittelalter*, p. 245. I owe the reference to Gogol as well as to Karmzin (p. 427) to Mrs. Josepha Weitzmann-Fiedler.

21 Jules Michelet, *Histoire de France*, I, pp. 663ff.

22 This is a forerunner of the psychoanalytical interpretations of Kaschnitz and Sterba, see below p. 748ff.

per thinking of these sentences when he coined the phrase, "steinerne Scholastik"?

Michelet found fault with the buttresses because they create the idea of an old home or of an unfinished one. "This art, questionable in its form was weak also in its social principle. The society from which it grew was too unequal and too unjust." (p. 691) Michelet was a revolutionist, he was against the Jesuits and against the Restoration of the monarchy. It is therefore understandable that in later editions he should rewrite the sections dealing with Gothic where he stated emphatically that, "l'architecture ogivale, celle qu'on dit improprement gothique, est due tout entière aux laïques, au génie mystique des maçons."[23] His attitude toward Gothic became more favorable and, having read Vitet, Viollet-le-Duc, etc., he seemed to have lost interest in India and Persia.

[23] Vol. III of the 2nd ed. (Philippe-Auguste, etc.) appendix about *Éclaircissment*. In *Œuvres Complètes*, Paris, 1900 (?), p. 306. See his criticism of the west front of Nôtre-Dame at Paris, p. 308.

IV. THE SCIENTIFIC TREND

1. The Beginning of Topographical and Membrological Study

THE achievement of Dodsworth and Dugdale and, in particular, of their illustrator, Wenzel Hollar, can only be judged properly when one realizes how long it took before a continuation of their work was forthcoming. The characteristic eighteenth century vagueness of ideas about Gothic was based not merely on the fashionable contempt with which it was regarded by admirers of Antiquity and Renaissance, but also—and far more—on the lack of a comprehensive architectural topography and of illustrations of buildings pertaining thereto. The *Monasticon Anglicanum* had appeared from 1655 to 1673. Dom Michel GERMAIN (1645-1694), one of Mabillon's most faithful collaborators, had been preparing a corresponding work on the French Benedictine monasteries, but death prevented the completion and publication of his extensive preliminary studies. Only in 1869 were about one hundred and fifty engravings published that had been intended as illustrations.[1] The first successor to Dugdale and Dodsworth, therefore, did not appear until 1727, when Browne WILLIS (1682-1760) wrote a voluminous work on the cathedrals of York, Durham, Carlisle, Chester, Man, Lichfield, Hereford, Worcester, Gloucester, and Bristol, including also an account of the churches and chapels in these ten dioceses.[2] The long title gives a survey of the book's contents: the foundings, the builders, the ancient monuments and inscriptions, endowments, sales of lands; further, the dates of the consecration of the churches, the deaths and epitaphs of the clergy, etc. It ends by calling attention to twenty drawings illustrating the ground plans and "uprights" (exterior views) of every cathedral, "newly taken to rectify the erroneous Representations of them in the *Monasticon*, and other Authors."

What Willis offers here is in principle the same thing that we expect from a modern inventory. The differences lie, of course, in the extent of historical data, for example, not just the enumeration of all the bishops but also of all precentors, and so on, and, on the other hand, in the brevity of the architectural description and the lack of any stylistic analysis. Of York Cathedral, for instance, we read that it has no cloisters, that the height of the towers can be found in the text accom-

[1] Louis Courajod, *Monasticum Gallicanum*, Paris, 1869, and shortly thereafter: Peignet-Delacourt et Léopold Delisle, *Monasticon Gallicanum*, Paris, 1871.

[2] Browne Willis, *A Survey of the Cathedrals of York . . .*, London, 1727-1742.

panying the ground plan; Willis then proceeds to give the chief dimensions of the ground plan in feet, remarks that a peal of twelve bells hangs in the South tower, and so on, that there are draughts and prospects of this church in various books, the most accurate of which being that drawn by Francis Place. "And indeed every thing of this church is so very magnificent, that it deserves a particular Representation; for Words cannot express the Beauty and Elegance of the Architecture of each Part." Willis prints all the inscriptions, and those referring to the glazier (glass painter John Petty, who died in 1508), can accordingly be found here (page 8), although there is nothing about the unusually rich stained glass itself. On the other hand, in the description of Durham some of the glass paintings are characterized at least as to their iconography (Cuthbert, St. Joseph, etc.), but not described at all or dated. If Willis' book is judged according to the standard of the history of art in its own time one will not demand more of it than it has to offer.

In 1767 a folio volume appeared on the monuments of Normandy by Andrew Coltee DUCAREL (1718-1785).[3] The book was written in English and printed in London, being dedicated to the Bishop of Carlisle, President of the Society of Antiquaries in London, who had observed as early as 1742 the contrast between the style of the Normans ("mode of architecture" means "style") and that of the Saxons of the same period in England. The author modestly gives the Bishop all the credit for the account of his travels. What interests us in the book is not the text so much as the engravings, for which Ducarel himself made the preliminary drawings. Some of them may be considered useful, others are not. The interior view of Ste-Trinité in Caen is entirely incorrect, and not merely in its proportions: Ducarel draws ribs instead of groins in the vaults of the east choir, also ribs in the side choirs, although on page 163 he says: "The church of this Abbey is a plain, neat building, both within and without, and entirely free from Gothic ornaments." Nevertheless this topography of works of art was important as the forerunner of later and better studies.

Aubin Louis MILLIN's (1759-1818) book (1790) presents rather arbitrarily a varied sequence of buildings, sepulchral monuments, Baroque sculpture, and so on, but it contains also views of Vincennes, the Abbaye de Rayaumont, Nantes, the tower of the great clock and the Palais de Justice in Rouen, and the like.[4]

[3] Andrew Coltee Ducarel, *Anglo-Norman Antiquities considered in a Tour through Part of Normandy*, London, 1767 (with 27 copperplate engravings).

[4] Aubin Louis Millin, *Antiquités nationales, un recueil de monuments . . .*, Paris, 1790-1799.

In 1799 Friedrich GILLY's (1772-1800) publication on Marienburg Castle in West Prussia appeared. The nineteen plates, very picturesquely engraved by Johann Friedrich Frick (1774-1850), are based on drawings made by Gilly in 1794.[5] They opened people's eyes to the brick Gothic of North Germany.

In view of the paucity of illustrations of mediaeval buildings, recognition of what Gothic really was could only be expected on the basis of the work done by Dugdale and Dodsworth, consequently in English-speaking territory. Here we do actually find a treatise on Gothic that is a whole generation in advance of its time, although it does not entirely deny its origin around 1800.[6] The author of this treatise, James ANDERSON (1739-1808), was also the editor of the magazine in which it appeared. Born in the vicinity of Edinburgh, he found himself obliged at the age of fifteen to take over and manage the country estates of his family. He became a specialist in all matters pertaining to agriculture, wrote on fisheries, dairies, the construction of chimneys, and the like, and edited a magazine entitled the *Bee*, which after 1799 was continued in the volumes of the *Recreations*. In these volumes, among articles on sheep raising, cheese, moths, snake bites, potatoes, and so on, can be found, in seven installments, Anderson's thoughts on Gothic, more mature than anything else written on the subject at that time. The Scottish farmers who subscribed to this journal were probably more interested in potatoes and moths than in the nature of Gothic; only very few archaeologists, on the other hand, seem to have read the magazine. Thus this article, which may be called fundamental, remained almost unknown and was then forgotten completely. Britton, Anderson's contemporary, was obviously ignorant of it.[7] It is mentioned by Loudon,[8] but apparently nowhere else.

The essay is characterized by a decided repudiation of the Greco-

5 Johann Friedrich Frick, *Das Schloss Marienburg in Preussen*, Berlin, 1799.

6 James Anderson, "Thoughts on the origin, excellencies, and defects of the Grecian and Gothic Styles of Architecture," in *Recreations in Agriculture, Natural-History, Arts and Miscellaneous Literature*, London, II, pp. 187, 280, 418; III, p. 115; IV, pp. 272, 382, 448. The second and third volumes appeared in 1800, the fourth in 1801.

7 Britton does not mention Anderson in the list he wrote in 1826 giving 66 books and essays on Gothic; cited below, p. 498.

8 John Claudius Loudon, *An Encyclopaedia of Cottage, Farm and Villa Architecture and Furniture* . . . , 1867, p. 1123. I could not consult the first edition (1830) "reprinted from the *Gardener's Magazine*" (according to the catalogue of the South Kensington Museum). It is probable that even the first printing (before 1830) contained the announcement that Dr. Anderson was the first to demonstrate to English readers the superiority of the Gothic style over the Greek. The bulky volume, which I have not studied closely, also contains a chapter on Gothic by Trotman (pp. 925ff.), which might be investigated in connection with the history of the Gothic Revival.

Roman orders and a partisanship for Gothic. The Greek order, says Anderson, was developed from architecture in wood; the proportions of the columnar intervals had to be changed when the transition was made to architecture in stone. Faith in these proportions became a kind of bigotry. The exterior colonnades were intended to afford protection from the weather, and Anderson finds their extension to walls (mock-columns), especially when used in several stories one above the other, improper, as is also the transference of the orders to interiors. After a somewhat reserved appreciation of Roman buildings, he describes the decline of ancient civilization in the wake of the bad barbarians, the survival of Christianity, and the significance of the church as the guardian of the remnants of culture during the centuries of darkness. Vaguely connected with these notions is Anderson's idea of the free-masons and their secrets (II, p. 286). He distinguishes "Old Gothic," which employs round arches adopted from Roman models, from "Modern Gothic" or "Saracenic" (II, p. 420).

At this point Anderson's originality in the treatment of his subject begins. He discusses in turn the segmental arch, the semicircular arch, and the pointed arch according to their mechanical virtues. The lateral thrust, he says, is strongest in the case of the segmental arch, weakest in the pointed arch, diminishing even more the steeper the latter becomes. The form of arch, accordingly, influences the stability of the piers. In a series of piers the contiguous arches cancel out each other's lateral thrusts, but the end of the series requires a strengthening of the corner pier. What is true of the longitudinal direction of churches applies equally to the transverse direction. But since the transverse section (in basilicas) is different from the longitudinal section, Anderson reverts to Wren's theory of pinnacles, which are no "useless ornament" but mechanically indispensable. He also discusses flying buttresses, which he calls "spandrils."

Though he does not put the determining elements of Gothic in concise order, Anderson anticipated in part Johannes Wetter's theory, discussing piers, pointed arches, and abutments as essentials of the style. In Wetter (thirty-five years later) the rib is the fourth essential element. Anderson refers to this also (II, p. 419). In the beginning the architects made wooden ceilings: "Soon, however, they would perceive that, by throwing an arch from each of these columns to that in the opposite angle diagonally across the square, these arches would meet in the centre, and thus admit of the whole of the apertures above being completely closed with stone." He uses the word rib occasionally (for example, IV, p. 452), but did not yet realize that it belongs with the other three elements (whenever classical Gothic is under discussion).

Ribs are not as important for Anderson as the pinnacles, towers, and traceried windows that he chiefly describes and evaluates, with continual sallies against antiquity and the Renaissance.

In the third volume he takes up the cruciform design of churches, and the towers over the crossing with their particular lighting "which gives to these structures a lightness that conveys the sensation of a supernatural influence which is not experienced in any of the other structures wherewith we are acquainted." (III, p. 117) In the arrangement and design of the towers, Gothic, he finds, is independent of Egyptian obelisks, Chinese pagodas, and so on, above all independent of antiquity. He praises especially the towers of Antwerp and Strasbourg; the latter he knows from Hollar's engraving (III, p. 122). He provides as an illustration a perspective view of the twin-towered church of Old Aberdeen (on the northeast coast of Scotland). The last part of the treatise turns back from this analysis of structures in their essential parts to primary questions. The Greek style is "architecture of a colonnade," the Gothic, "architecture of a church." After an interpolation to the effect that ruins of ancient colonnades are particularly "picturesque" (IV, p. 283) comes the chief dictum: ancient colonnades (orders) are not appropriate to modern buildings, and therefore Inigo Jones and Wren are to be repudiated, one need only compare St. Paul's in London with Westminster Abbey, or even better, with York and Salisbury. Reminiscent of Soufflot is Anderson's analysis of the vistas of a three-aisled basilica with massive quadratic piers and those of a Gothic church with slender membered ones (Ground plan, IV, p. 395). Finally he mentions the tree theory, concedes that the comparison is justified, remarking that vaults, too, were painted with stars and thus interpreted as the heavens, but says: "I cannot entertain a doubt that they [these resemblances] operated on the mind of the artist when these ornaments were devised." He stresses the fact that Gothic was rather the result of a long process beginning with "obscure hints corrected and matured by succeeding experience for a long period of years, somewhat after the manner described in the preceding parts of the essay. . . ." (p. 453) Here it becomes clear that Anderson considered the logic of his exposition to be a faithful copy of a logical process in the history of Gothic itself.

Anderson designates himself on the title page of his work as LL.D. (*Legum Doctor*); he was a member of scientific societies in Edinburgh, an honorary member of those in Bath, Manchester, Altringham, Newcastle, London, Dijon, St. Petersburg, Berlin, Paris, and the Philosophical Society in Philadelphia. Volume II contains his correspondence with James Anderson, a cousin of the same name in Madras and a doctor of medicine (a portrait engraving of him is to be found on page 308), who dispatched Indian plants to botanical gardens. In short, Dr. Anderson of Edinburgh was in touch with the world from Madras to Philadelphia, an extraordinary personality whose versatility was astonishing. We cannot tell, however, whether he ever set foot outside Scotland and England. Presumably his knowledge of monuments was restricted to these countries. He hardly lived to experience the beginnings of the flourishing architectural topography that he himself called for. One does justice to Anderson when one reflects that with relatively limited knowledge he was able to penetrate more deeply into the understanding of Gothic than any other scholar of the period around 1800, and that his insight was not confined merely to the analysis of the typical architectural forms but extended also to their aesthetic effect in combination, as witness his enthusiasm over the lighting of the crossing by the windows in the crossing tower.

The most productive topographer of the time was John BRITTON (1771-1857). He may be regarded primarily as the first exponent of the *topographical* method on a large scale, if not as its creator. Clark says of him that he "popularized engravings of Gothic by publishing them cheaply and in great numbers; he was no archaeologist and had no natural interest in architecture (this is clear from his autobiography, written with the egotism of a millionaire) but he had all the gifts of a newspaper owner—industry, persistency, a fine instinct for changes of fashion and perfect shamelessness in exploiting it."[9] Britton began his career as an orphan with no resources, became a writer, and made his fortune. There is as yet no study devoted solely to him; my own knowledge of his very numerous writings is restricted to individual works. Nevertheless I should like to say in his defense that he rose to his task, and his later books became in many respects increasingly more scientific.

His first topographical work is as early as 1801.[10] His *Architectural Antiquities* appeared in five volumes over a period of almost twenty

[9] Kenneth Clark, *op.cit.*, p. 94.

[10] John Britton, *The Beauties of Wiltshire*, 3 vols., 1801-1825. Again in *The Beauties of England and Wales*, xv, 1814.

years (1807-1826).[11] These consist of brief essays on individual buildings. The selection is quite arbitrary, the sequence entirely unsystematic, the importance of the various monuments very different. The very first volume of 1807 offers side by side with quite insignificant works King's College Chapel in Cambridge, with excellent drawings, which, in the case of such a building, means a great deal. But these words of praise are more applicable to the draftsman than to Britton,[12] who here first formulated the dogma of the *decline of Gothic*, at least for the English public: ". . . it is perhaps the only specimen in which the perfection and decline of what has absurdly been termed the Gothic style may be completely seen."[13] In Germany Friedrich von Schlegel had already characterized Late Gothic as decline (in the choir of the cathedral in Aachen, of 1355; cf. page 459 above).

The first division into phases had been made by Thomas WARTON (1728-1790) in 1703.[14] In the fascicle dealing with Malmesbury Britton set forth his arrangement of stylistic phases and his terminology:

1. Anglo-Saxon, 597-1066
2. Anglo-Norman, 1066-1189
3. English, 1189-1272
4. Decorated English, 1272-1461
5. Highly decorated English, 1461-1509

What comes after 1509 is "Debased English" or "Anglo-Italian," examples of which Britton often included in others of his works. (p. 3)

His text naturally required an increasing refinement of the technique of description. As an example of this some sentences from the part on King's College Chapel may be quoted: ". . . it will be seen that one direct arch is thrown across the building, from buttress to buttress, and that four other conical arches, rising one above the other, spring from the clustered capitals, and are locked by the sculptured keystone. . . . Thus the stone roof is supported by a series of double arches, concentric to the buttresses, and one arch passing through the whole; yet all mutually dependant on each other, and each contributing to support that weight of stone which is almost flat from side to side wall."[15] The

[11] The full title indicates the contents: *The Architectural Antiquities of Great Britain represented and illustrated in a series of views, elevations, plans, sections, details, of various ancient English edifices with historical and descriptive accounts of each.* I, 1807; II, 1809; III, 1812; IV, 1814; V, 1826.

[12] In this case the drawing is by the architect, Thomas Sandley, and the engraving by John Smith. Vol. I (each article has its special pagination).

[13] Britton, *op.cit.*, p. 2.

[14] Cf. above, pp. 406 and 447.

[15] Britton, *op.cit.*, I, p. 8.

description made the mention of the *ribs* unavoidable but he calls them arches, including the ridge rib.

Volume II contains equally excellent drawings of Henry VII's Chapel.

In Volume III Britton declares in the Introduction that he does not intend to proceed chronologically or present only geometric projections: ". . . the artist, amateur and the greater number of readers require variety, picturesque effect and general views."[16] In 1812, then, he was still faced with an eighteenth century public. But in Volume IV of 1814 a change has taken place, and we read in the Introduction: ". . . as the plates in the work are mostly of a miscellaneous and picturesque character, and as many architects and men of science have expressed a wish to possess a more systematic display of the rise, progress and characteristics of the ancient Architecture of England, it is my intention to publish such a work. It will consist of Plans, Elevations, Sections, details and views of various buildings and of portions of others. These will be arranged in chronological order and will comprise all the component parts of an edifice. . . ."[17] The public was demanding a more scientific approach and Britton had to conform. But systematics and a chronology could not be called into being in a hurry, and the fifth volume accordingly did not appear until 1826. This does actually contain the *first* attempt at a *coherent history* of *English* Gothic. In addition it offers an unusually careful survey of the entire literature then in existence regarding the problem of the name and origin of Gothic. Britton discusses sixty-six authors. The reader who is dissatisfied with the selection I have made from older literature and who hungers for more should turn for a supplement to this portion of Britton's work.

His first volume of 1807 is followed chronologically in 1809 by the work of George Downing WHITTINGTON (1781-1807), whose contribution to the scientific basis of architectural history was directed toward the geographical problem of the origin of Gothic.[18] He was apparently the first to rediscover the fact that Gothic originated in France, unless Sayers, whose book I do not know, anticipated him.[19] Burchard von

[16] *Ibid.*, III. Introduction p. v. On this point cf. note 57 below.

[17] *Ibid.*, IV, p. vii.

[18] George Downing Whittington, *An Historical Survey of the ecclesiastical Antiquities of France with a view to illustrating the rise and progress of Gothic Architecture in Europe*, London, 1809.

[19] Sayers, *Guide to Ely Cathedral*, 1805. In Britton, in the enumeration of the literature, we read only: "Disquisitions, etc. in which are Hints on English Architecture, 1805, concludes that the Pointed Style was introduced into England soon after the Norman Conquest and says it should be called Norman." (pp. 37, 69) Thus in Britton, *op.cit.*, V, p. xi.

Hall's phrase *opus francigenum* had not yet become recognized although his chronicle of about 1270 had been published in the eighteenth century (in 1724). The tradition had been lost, and just as Goethe regarded Gothic as German, the English thought that if it had not arisen in England it had at least first reached its peak there. Whittington traveled through France and Italy from 1802 to 1803, and subsequently composed a slim volume which, making use of source materials, relates the history of architecture from the time of Diocletian on, especially that of France. It is—after that of LeComte from 1699—the earliest architectural history for France, like that of Stieglitz for Germany a decade later. Stieglitz, however, did not know Whittington's book. The epoch-making thing about the latter is its simple reference to the date of St.-Denis, "finished in the year 1144," from which it follows that French Gothic is older than English. "All authorities concur in fixing the reign of Henry II (that is, after the year 1154) as the earliest era of the introduction into England of the mixed style of round and pointed arches which we see practised in Suger's works in France before that period."[20] Whittington rejects the early date of 1132 for St. Cross, and calls the earliest pointed arches in England those of the crypt in York, of 1171, built by Archbishop Roger, and those of the choir in Canterbury, of 1175.

In the second part of his book Whittington offers essays on St.-Germain-des-Prés, Ste.-Geneviève, St.-Denis, and Nôtre-Dame in Paris, also on the cathedral and St.-Nicaise in Reims, and the cathedral of Amiens. The pleasant little book was written by a clergyman who died at the age of twenty-six. His contemporaries paid no attention to his thesis, and a generation later several scholars disputed about priority with regard to the same discovery that Whittington had made (Didron, Mertens, and so on). Moller, Schnaase, and Dehio made casual mention of Whittington.[21] Didron claimed to be the first writer to recognize the French origin of Gothic,[22] but the articles on which he based his claim date only from 1830. He wanted to establish his priority over Fortoul (*Art en Allemagne*) and was correct in that respect, but he knew nothing of Whittington.

The latter is followed chronologically by George SAUNDERS (1762-1839), an English architect, who in 1811 with an article in the

[20] Whittington, *op.cit.*, pp. 139-140.

[21] Carl Schnaase, *Geschichte der bildenden Künste im Mittelalter*, III (V), Düsseldorf, 1856, p. 33; Georg Dehio, *Die kirchliche Baukunst des Abendlandes*, II, p. 9.

[22] Didron, "Origine et nationalité de l'architecture ogivale," *Annales archéologiques*, XVI, Paris, 1856, p. 307.

Archaeologia made an essential contribution to the deeper understanding of Gothic vault construction.[23]

He speaks first of the pointed arch, observing that it can be found in the pyramid of Giza in the form of stones inclined toward each other, and also in China, in support of which statement he refers to Barrow's *Travels in China* (1804), page 337. But he quickly puts aside this question of the origin of the pointed arch, for, he says, the *vaulting* is the essential element in the spanning of larger spaces. Thus Saunders is the initiator of the copious literature on the *construction* of mediaeval vaults.

He distinguishes four classes of "groined arches." The *first* class consists of groined vaulting, which is suitable only for small spaces. But *groins*, he says, even when constructed of cut stone in the best manner, are *the weakest part* of the vaulting: ". . . and as the builders continued to construct the groined vaulting of rubble work, when larger vaulting was desired in churches, it became necessary to fortify the weak parts. They had previously placed arched ribs in the transverse direction of the vaulting; they now added diagonal ribs under the intersections of the cross vaulting, to procure additional strength: these diagonal ribs were of cut stone, formed into mouldings, and sometimes enriched with carving. In the first application of diagonal ribs, the transverse arched ribs continued of the original plain [rectangular] form, but were afterwards moulded, to correspond the better with the diagonal ribs, as represented in Plate II, which may be considered as the second class of groined arches." (p. 3)

The terminology here is still uncertain: the four classes are all called "groined arches." As far as the actual objects are concerned, however, Saunders has very clear ideas. Turning to the curves of the arches, he says that the ribs were constructed *after* the cell of the vaulting had been built. The curve of the intersecting line of the cross vaulting "tends to the elliptical," while the diagonal rib follows a circular curve. The reason for placing ribs underneath and filling the space between the rib and the groin lines of the vault cell was to *strengthen* these lines. That can be recognized from instances in the same structure where the ribs are omitted when the reinforcement was not necessary. He cites as an example (in the Appendix C) the transept of Winchester Cathedral, of 1079-1093 (after Milner's *History of*

[23] George Saunders, *Observations on the Origin of Gothic Architecture*, delivered as a lecture in 1811, printed in *Archeologia*, London, 1814.

Winchester, 1809, II, p. 14). He makes express mention of the state of the building in 1807, saying that a restoration was intended. (p. 16)

After this incidental observation comes the main matter, familiar now to everyone who is concerned with mediaeval vaults, but first expounded to the general public by Saunders. Given a rectangular ground plan, the diagonal arches of half a circle will be higher than the longitudinal ones, and these in turn higher than the transverse arches. The means by which equal elevations of the crowns can be obtained is stilting ("having the horns of the semicircle continued downwards in perpendicular lines to the same level base as the others," p. 6). Occasionally it consisted, not of a perpendicular connection of the arch with the base, but of a continuation of the arch itself, resulting in the horseshoe arch. As examples of this form Saunders mentions Romsey, Oxford, and Winchester. Another expedient was the introduction of the *pointed arch* across the narrow side of the vault bay.

By placing a pointed arch across the wide side as well and making the diagonal rib a semicircle there was evolved the *third* class of "groined arches," "forming a work that was at once easy to execute, of great strength, and of a pleasing appearance." The introduction of the ridge rib (he dates it at the end of the thirteenth century)[24] gave rise to the *fourth* class, which required hardly any centering except that necessary for putting up the ribs.

Saunders recognized the importance of the pointed arch in the construction of vaulting, where its aesthetic significance was not called into question; the problem was transferred to a sphere of rationality. Whewell, prior to 1835, and Wiegmann, somewhat later in 1842, adopted this theory. It remained fundamentally important until the time of Gall (1915).

Although it would seem that Saunders was the first to *publish* an explanation of the pointed arch in ribbed vaults as the result of spanning different widths, he does not appear to have been the first man to acquire this insight. A brief remark by D. R. Stewart reveals that Essex had already upheld this theory.[25] "He [Essex] gave an account of the difficulties facing Norman builders in joining vaults of different width, and showed by a series of illustrations that the pointed arch was the only satisfactory solution of the problems." Essex himself wrote:

[24] The earliest ridge ribs in England are those in Lincoln Cathedral, 1192; in France there were even earlier examples (Montivillier, Lucheux).

[25] Donald R. Stewart, "James Essex," *Architectural Review*, November, 1950, p. 317, and particularly p. 320.

"This opinion of pointed arches is new." It is to be hoped that the whole section of the manuscript now in the British Museum will be published. (See above, page 502)

Along with Saunders' theory of the geometrical construction of quadripartite ribbed vaults his notions of statics have been handed down unchallenged to this day. It is still taught that the groins are the *weakest* points of a groined vault and must be strengthened by the ribs. This theory is false. The groins, being mathematical lines, do not, of course, carry, but the masonry, of which they form the visible edge, most certainly does; and these places in the severies of the vaulting are the thickest and strongest. They need no reinforcement. The true reason for the placing of ribs beneath already existing groins or for the simultaneous employment of both was a different one, a subject to which I shall revert below on page 825.

In 1811, the same year that Saunders delivered his lecture, Milner's book appeared, the most important parts of which are those concerning the concept of the Infinite (discussed above, page 445). In 1813 a book by John Sidney HAWKINS (1758-1842) was published,[26] its title suggesting a history of the origin and development of Gothic. The text, however, is disappointing. The author expounds very critically all the important theories since Wren's, but offers nothing really new, and his train of thought is very involved.

Owing to the endeavors of the English scholars in the seventeenth century and to Britton's work from about 1800 on, Gothic in England could be better surveyed from a scientific point of view than that of other countries. Only now did France begin to catch up, thanks to the lifework of Alexandre de LABORDE (1773-1842),[27] a French nobleman who was an officer, diplomat, and for a time *Directeur des ponts et chaussées de la Seine*. He was rich enough to be able to devote himself to his scholarly interests on a grand scale. He traveled through France with a staff of draughtsmen in order to make drawings of the most important monuments from antiquity on. His work appeared from 1816 to 1836 in two enormous folio volumes. The first contained almost entirely illustrations of the pre-Gothic period, chiefly Roman antiquities, but the text provided an introduction to both volumes: first a *survey* from the point of view of the *history of culture*, then a general

26 John Sidney Hawkins, *An History of the Origin and Establishment of Gothic Architecture*, London, 1813.

27 Le Comte Alexandre de Laborde, *Les monuments de la France classés chronologiquement et considérés sous le rapport des faits historiques et de l'étude des arts. Les dessins faits d'après nature par M. M. Bourgeois et Bauce. . .* , Paris, 1816, II, 1836.

description of the *styles*, and finally a discussion of individual edifices, in the form of brief *monographs* in *chronological* order, as explanatory text to the plates. As the lengthy title of the book emphasizes, the chronology of the monuments provides the clue to the sequence of the monographs, but the series is intended to be investigated in its cultural as well as its artistic aspects.

The general part dealing with the historical aspect of art is for us the most important. De Laborde distinguishes for France:

1. the Romanesque style or that with complete round arches, called indiscriminately Saxon or Lombard
2. the pointed-arch style (*style ogivique*) "inappropriately called Gothic or Arabesque"
3. the style of the Renaissance

As regards the origin of Gothic he revives the Crusader theory. These pious warriors, he says, "returned home imbued with a general spirit of reform," but it would be wrong to regard Gothic as a particular discovery (*une invention particulière*); it was developed through gradual improvements: ". . . a little more lightness, precision, elegance, and grace given to edifices then existing. . . ." (Here Félibien's influence can still be detected.)[28] De Laborde discusses the results of this refinement of Romanesque analytically, in relatively clear order. I follow his text in a free translation. (*Ogive* is for him both pointed arch and rib.)

The pointed arch is the particular mark of Gothic. Its first appearance is dated in the middle of the eleventh century, though de Laborde remarks that it was not in general use before the twelfth. Stylistic changes stem from this "heureuse innovation." The next sentence must be given literally: "They wished to imitate in stone the light wooden constructions that sprang from the walls and fell back with ornamental pendentives in the middle of the nave." It is hard to guess what he had in mind here (pendent keystones?) In any case, despite his derivation of Gothic from Romanesque churches, he believed in an influence from wooden construction. (Moller's book did not appear until two years later, in 1818.)

The second element of which de Laborde speaks is the *quadripartite*

[28] I, p. 38. ". . . un peu plus de légèreté, de précision, d'élégance, de grace, donné aux édifices alors existants. . . . On voulut imiter en pierre les charpentes légères qui s'élançaient des murs et retombaient par des pendentifs ornés au milieu de la nef. . . . L'assemblage de ces parties en fuseaux . . . semblaient des gerbes de pierre, des berceaux immenses, des tentes créés par enchantement . . . ."

vault. These vaults, he says, were employed because they create "le moins de poussée exterieur" and permit the use of lighter materials. After Wren, Félibien, Frisi, Anderson, and Hirt we meet again the point of view of mechanics, that is, that of the lateral thrust. Ease of construction was combined with practical usefulness in basilican churches, when such high proportions were involved, and to this was related the extension of the pointed arch to windows and doors as well as to all other parts of the building.

The *ground plan*—namely, the general disposition—remained unchanged, according to de Laborde: long aisles with arcades, ambulatories, and so on. He maintains that the round arch was retained in the crypts "pour leur conserver la solidité," which shows that he regarded the pointed arch as an aesthetic, not a static, refinement and "élegance." Thus, though he was approaching a mechanical interpretation of Gothic, he misunderstood the mechanics of the various types of arches, a subject which Seroux had at that time already comprehended (see below, page 509).

The *piers* are described, likewise their connection with the ribs, some metaphorical language being employed at this point: sheaves of stone consisting of immense vaults, tents, created by magic. The ribs form rays that diverge in all directions, they divide the surface of the vault by their projections and re-enterings, and give to the whole structure an aspect of elegance, grace, and boldness which astonishes and charms.

Brief mention is made of *ornaments*, as well as of *light* and *shade*.

The walls were made higher and supported by *buttresses; windows* pierced the walls up to the buttresses; and the light was tempered by stained glass, the colors of which are mysterious and the representations an enrichment of the sacred place: a combination of effects not to be found in the Greek orders, since they are too squat and massive.

The exterior he finds less satisfactory: the flying buttresses appear like scaffoldings that have not yet been removed. He lays stress upon pinnacles, verticalism, ornamentation, and figure sculpture.

Like Hurd before him (see above, page 392), he recognized that Gothic had its own peculiar value: "Gothic architecture has beauties that are proper to it. To want to judge it according to rules it did not follow would be not to compare it with itself. . . . In a word, this architecture is complete in all its parts, although it is opposed to the strict rules of the beautiful; and one can even say that it is the more perfect in its genre the more it departs from classical and regular forms."[29] This is the old distinction: though Gothic is not beautiful, it is perfect in itself (Goethe had said "characteristic").

Thus de Laborde here proposes a classification; one feels that in the sequence he gives to the analytically derived parts of the typical cathedral building there is a meaning, a *system*. Moreover he included this classificatory description along with cultural history and a chronological listing of structures, all of which made him a model later for the leading nineteenth-century German historians of art who undertook to give large surveys: Kugler and Schnaase.

In this introduction de Laborde mentions a selected number of examples (page 39): St.-Denis, les Templiers de Paris, St.-Pierre in Chartres (?), the Abbaye de Fontevrault, and so on. Then he gives the names of the most famous French architects of the thirteenth century, and goes into detail about individual buildings. He has high praise for Amiens, praise that takes us back to Romanticism again: "This church seems to be a cage with delicate compartments where the daylight streams in from all sides; it is all windows, all light, like a glass globe suspended in the atmosphere, like a baldachin that majestically covers the Holy of Holies."[30]

De Laborde's second volume (of 1836) depicts in plates 117 to 149 monuments of the Byzantine style, called by him "style byzantine ou roman," which, to judge from the objects represented, corresponds to our concept Romanesque; plates 150 to 215 present the "Monuments du Style ogivique." These are chiefly ground plans and façades of the most important cathedrals of French Gothic; there are only a few interior views (for example, Amiens), some castles, a few tombs. Among the cathedrals are found also the west and the south façade of Strasbourg. The author apologizes in the preface for offering only a very carefully chosen selection, since there are so many outstanding buildings from the eleventh century on.

The ground plans are excellent, the views of St.-Denis, Chartres, Paris, and so on, masterpieces of architectural drawing. The most

[29] *Ibid.*, I, p. 39: "L'architecture gothique a des beautés qui lui sont propres. Vouloir la juger d'après les règles qu'elle n'a pas suivies, c'est ne pas la comparant à elle-même. . . . En un mot, cette architecture est complète dans toutes ses parties, quoiqu'elle soit opposée aux règles sévères du beau; et on peut dire même qu'elle est d'autant plus parfaite dans son genre qu'elle s'éloigne davantage des formes antiques et réguliers."

[30] "Cette église semble être un cage à compartiments légers, où le jour aborde de touts côtés; elle est toute en fenêtre, toute en lumière comme un globe de verre suspendu dans l'atmosphère, comme un dais, qui couvre majestueusement le Saint-des Saints." The comparison with an altar baldachin is here to be taken figuratively. Quite recently Hans Sedlmayr used this comparison again, presumably without having read de Laborde. Sedlmayr has made, of the baldachin a basic form of Gothic, cf. below, p. 754.

beautiful of these etchings are based on drawings by Nicolas M. J. Chapuy.[31] Our eyes, sated with photographs, dwell with quiet pleasure on these portraitlike and yet personal representations. They were the best guides imaginable to the comprehension of Gothic—almost better than the accompanying texts by de Laborde himself.

Thomas RICKMAN (1776-1841), though without a doubt completely uninfluenced by de Laborde, was intellectually akin to him, inasmuch as he, too, aimed at a system of forms. All the ancestors of our modern scientific study of art began their careers in some profession other than that of the history of art. Rickman was first a doctor and apothecary, then a clerk, until in 1811 he started to concern himself with architecture as a self-taught amateur. His terminology is therefore at times unusual.[32]

As in Costenoble's case (1812), his literary style is characterized by the extreme dryness which many people confuse with scholarship. But his book of 1817, whether written with or without knowledge of Costenoble, proved to be very useful; it went through many editions and undoubtedly gave thousands of readers just what they needed: a treatise on the forms of the English mediaeval styles. Rickman distinguishes Norman Style, Early, Decorated, and Curvilinear English. Within Early English he discusses the typical forms of individual features, beginning with doors, and then, however, passing at once to windows. Arches follow, and then only come the piers, capitals, buttresses, corbeled cornices, profilings, niches, ornaments, towers, roof parapets, roofs or vaults, façades, porches, fonts, and, finally, the appearance as a whole. Ribs are mentioned casually under "Roofs."[33] Rickman gives under "General appearance" a comprehensive characterization that is typical of his romantic generation. The other two stylistic phases are treated according to exactly the same scheme: a description of what was customary in the period in question for each of the analytically isolated structural parts.

Rickman calls Gothic simply "English." He, too, took no notice

[31] Chapuy, 1790-1858, was himself an architect, but as a restorer built very little; his chief profession was that of a draughtsman and lithographer.

[32] Thomas Rickman, *An Attempt to discriminate the Styles of Architecture in England from the Conquest to the Reformation,* London, 1817. I have before me the second edition of 1819, in the preface of which Rickman says that a sketch of his ideas had appeared a few years earlier in the *Panorama of Science and Art.*

[33] On page 67 it is said of Salisbury: ". . . it has cross springers and the rib from pier to pier, but it has no rib running longitudinally or across at the point of the arches." By "cross springers" can be meant only the diagonal ribs; by "rib," the ridge rib and transverse ridge ribs. Wren also says cross springers.

of Whittington. Whereas Gothic still had no settled name, the Old Gothic or Grecizing or Old Saxon style was rechristened. The word Romanesque was proposed by William GUNN (1750-1841) in 1819; it became the accepted term after its adoption by Caumont and Pugin (in the *Quarterly Review* of 1819).[34] Gunn's book is otherwise of scarcely any interest. The later explanations of the word Romanesque always referred to Romance languages as analogous to Romanesque architecture, which is very plausible. Strangely enough, Gunn did not have this in mind: "The Italian termination *-esco*, the English and French *-esque* is occasionally allowable, thus we say pitturesco, picturesque, pictoresque, as partaking of the quality to which it refers. A modern Roman, for instance, of whatever degree, calls himself *Romano*, a distinction he disallows to an inhabitant of his native city, whom though long domiciled, yet of dubious origin, foreign extraction, or alliance, he stigmatizes by the term *Romanesco*. I consider the architecture under discussion in the same point of view."[35] Thus Romanesque was really intended originally to be just as negative a value judgment as Gothic, and the series of our stylistic designations: Romanesque, Gothic, Mannerism, Baroque, Rococo is accordingly negative down to Classicism—not to mention those of the nineteenth century. Perhaps Renaissance also belongs in this category, for the word meant in the beginning, of course, only exhumation of the seemingly dead, if one may express it so. To be sure, Renaissance itself was not regarded negatively.

Rickman's book, like Costenoble's of 1812, is a textbook. It became the ancestor of a great progeny, and even today in the French and English schools of architectural history the notion still persists that a classification of this sort must be the foundation of genuine, scientific work, indeed that it is the ultimate solution. Whatever one thinks of this method at present, it represented in the days of its inception enormous progress toward a more concrete approach to the problems of art history.

The way in which Gunn expounds the new term Romanesque makes one think that it was really he who invented it. But Gerville claims

[34] William Gunn, *An Inquiry into the Origin and Influence of Gothic Architecture*, London, 1819. There is, however, a precedent for the *word* Romanesque: it occurs in the title of a book by Col. J. J. von Wallhausen, *Romanische Kriegskunst*; cf. Thieme-Becker, s.v. Uffenbach, XXXIII, 1939, p. 538. Here, to be sure "Romanesque" or "Romanisch" is more or less equivalent to "Roman."

[35] Gunn, *op.cit.*, p. 80.

priority. He gives himself credit for its invention in a letter to Le Prevost. The matter is not entirely clear. Gerville uses the expressions *saxon* and *normand*, and then remarks: "All the world agrees that this heavy and crude architecture is the *opus romanum*, distorted or gradually debased by our rude ancestors."[36] Probably Gerville and Gunn created the new word independently of each other, each one inspired by somewhat different motives.

Rickman had confined himself to the buildings of his own country; to most scholars of that time this seemed to be a necessity. Whereas England was then sufficiently well known because of the work done from Dugdale to Britton, there was still very little familiarity with mediaeval German structures. The first attempt to offer a selection of these was made by Georg MOLLER (1784-1852).[37] This very productive architect was a pupil of Weinbrenner and imbued with his classical spirit. Moller called Gothic the child of its time and thus useless for actual modern buildings. As a historian of architecture he was interested in all German architecture of the Middle Ages, beginning with the gateway of Lorsch. The value of his works—which were praised especially by Goethe—lies in the accuracy of his drawings. He rejected picturesque representations and demanded geometrical drawings of elevations and sections. His knowledge enabled him to recognize the old elevations for the façade of Cologne Cathedral. The artist Seekatz had been commissioned to paint a transparency triumphal arch to honor the volunteers returning home to Darmstadt after the War of Liberation;[38] he found the necessary space for a studio in the attic of the inn *Zur Traube*, and here he discovered large sheets of parchment nailed to the floor and used for drying beans. He took these sheets to Moller, who had already searched for the drawings in the Cathedral Archives at Cologne and failed to find them. After the Treaty of Luneville in 1801 the archives had been divided up, the proceedings having taken place in that inn in Darmstadt. Probably none of those present had any interest in the awkward rolls. The original drawing shows the south tower. Moller set Boisserée on the track of discovering in Paris the drawing of the north tower as well. In 1818 he published

[36] M. F. Gidon, L'Invention de l'expression architecture romane par Gerville (1818)," *Bulletin de la Société d'Archéologie de Normandie*, XLII, Caen and Paris, 1935, p. 285. "Tout le monde convient que cette architecture, lourde et grossière, est l'opus romanum dénaturé ou successivement dégradé par nos rudes ancêtres." Gerville lived 1769-1853.

[37] Thieme-Becker, 1931, XXV, p. 42.

[38] Of the painters of this name mentioned in Thieme-Becker only E. Carl Seekatz, 1785-1839, Hessian court painter and lithographer, who lived in Darmstadt, can be the one in question.

both designs in the same size as the originals.[39] The reproduction that Crombach had presented was now decried as inaccurate.

From 1812 on Moller had been publishing reproductions of individual Gothic buildings according to exact measurements: in 1812 the church of St. Elisabeth in Marburg, in 1826 the Cathedral of Freiburg in Breisgau, in 1828 St. George's in Limburg on the Lahn. These were inserted in a more comprehensive series that also included the churches of Oppenheim and Gelnhausen, the Minster at Ulm, and so on.[40] The plates also reproduce a few secular buildings.

The text is dryly scientific, free from romantic emotions and fantastic theories. First of all Moller taught that one should not connect a building blindly with ancient documents. Strasbourg Cathedral serves as an example of this. There is indeed a document recording that it was built in 1015 by Bishop Wernher, but the present structure is no longer the original one: in 1815 that was a very salutary warning for many a dilettante of the history of art. Moller's anticipation of another thesis seems more surprising to us: "The forms of architecture are originally anything but arbitrary and accidental. Climate, material, and the character of the people exercise a vital effect on them." The next generation of scholars undoubtedly read Moller's brief introduction to the plates, and developed this statement in great detail.

In his historical chapters Moller indulges several times in polemics against Seroux d'Agincourt;[41] he doubts that S. Michele in Pavia dates from Langobardic times. The four pages of print devoted to the period from the eighth to the fifteenth century show how limited was Moller's knowledge of foreign architectural history. The increase in verticalism he deduces from the "increasing steepness of the roofs; consequently it was also fitting that the lower parts should be given greater height." This statement contains the correct idea that the increased pitch of the aisle roofs influenced the height of the triforia. Moller regarded the juxtaposition of round and pointed arches as inharmonious, but did not see that the German Transitional style was dependent on French Gothic. An improvement "came to pass because of the sound sense of German architects and their wish to set up something particular in place of the old." This is the only passage where romantic nationalism emerges, as the result of ignorance of the historical process.

39 Georg Moller, *Bemerkungen über die aufgefundenen Originalzeichnungen des Domes zu Köln*, Darmstadt, 1818. For the discovery of the second design, cf. p. 8.

40 A third part was added by Ernst Gladbach. Only the second (undated) edition of Moller's work was accessible to me.

41 Seroux's work appeared in 1823.

There is here (page 8) also a remark about the "simplicity and majesty of the forest groves." Moller considers the classical period of Gothic to have been the century from 1250 to 1350, but he includes in it Marburg and Cologne. After 1350 came the decline with its arbitrary flourishes. Though a Classicist, Moller asserts that Gothic is constructed better, more boldly, and more delicately than the architecture of antiquity, with less material and with the result that the buildings seem larger than they are, in contrast to St. Peter's in Rome. (One is reminded of Soufflot.)

In Chapter 4 all the older theories about the invention of Gothic are refuted, including the wood theory; Moller's own theory, however, is probably contained in the remark just quoted about the sound sense of German architects.

His work was supplemented by J. Georg BÜSCHING (1783-1829) in a travel diary from 1817,[42] in which many buildings were first introduced into the history of art. Engravings of buildings in Brandenburg, Stendal, and Tangermünde are presented, together with accounts of Havelberg, Wilsnack, Nordhausen, and others. This is no longer a "picturesque journey," but one devoted to the history of art.

The separation of the romantic trend from the rational is forced upon us in order that justice may be done to those men who wished to base their historical interests on a firm foundation of facts. It should, however, not be forgotten that both movements are simultaneous. At times it is difficult to separate them, and not merely when it comes to Büsching. The great work of NODIER, TAYLOR, and de CAILLEUX was only in part intended to serve scientific purposes;[43] its title states clearly that it is a matter of romantic and picturesque travels in old France and thus a turning back to Gilpin. The Introduction says: ". . . this journey is not a voyage of discovery, it is one of impressions." The lithographs, which grew more and more splendid as one after another of the many volumes appeared, bring the buildings closer to the heart of the non-expert by the addition of sentimental or heroic, at times even of genre-like figures, and the expert, too, takes indubitable pleasure in this humanization of lofty scholarship. One merit of the work lies in the fact that it made numerous buildings known that were not located on the main highways.

The section of Normandy to which Nodier devoted two volumes of

42 J. G. Büsching, *Reise durch einige Münster des nördlichen Deutschland im Spätjahr 1817*, Leipzig, 1819.

43 Charles Nodier, Isidore Taylor, and Alphonse de Cailleux, *Voyages pittoresques et romantiques dans l'ancienne France*, Paris, 1820-1864, 19 vols.

his work was made the subject of a study by John Sell COTMAN (1782-1842) in the same year, 1820;[44] and that year saw also the publication of Stieglitz's architectural history of Germany (see above, page 465). A year later Büsching printed his little contribution to the clarification of the concept of "Gothic."[45] He gave a detailed critical examination of the then usual designations, ending by proposing his own: for what we call Romanesque, the *Old German* style of architecture, for Gothic, the *Beautiful Old German* style. Though the book is very characteristic of its age, there is no need to go into details here. One point, however, cannot be passed over in silence: the little volume bears witness to a spirit striving for real insight and broadening its concept of what is German all the more for the very narrowness of its field of knowledge. Not only Jan van Eyck but all Holland belongs to German art, according to Büsching, while even more surprising is perhaps the annexation of England. What the English call Saxon architecture he identifies with the Continental Saxons; accordingly, English Gothic, which follows the Saxon style, is really German. This monumental aberration is, together with Moller's access of nationalism, the beginning of a long series of reflections that led to the problem, even now to some degree still unsolved, of formulating the national element in art objectively and without national vanity. To what extent German Gothic is German troubled later scholars all the more, the more evident its origin in France became.

In spite of Moller, Büsching reverted to Costenoble, whom he mentions on page 24. The Old Saxon architecture at least is derived, he says, from architecture in wood. The continuation of this thought is not very clear. The quadripartite vault is the chief form of mediaeval architecture (page 24). In speaking of Gothic he does not say in so many words that it, too, can be explained by construction in wood, but we read instead: "The dense, dark groves of oak trees arched again, turned to stone, in the naves of the churches (page 48)."[45a] This can be interpreted at will.

Monographs and attempts at presenting the architectural history of individual regions or entire linguistic territories were the preparatory stages for an all-embracing survey.

[44] J. S. Cotman, *Architectural Antiquities of Normandy*, text by D. Turner, London, 1820-1822.

[45] J. G. Büsching, *Versuch einer Einleitung in die Geschichte der altdeutschen Bauart*, Breslau, 1821.

[45a] "Die dichten, dunklen Eichenhaine wölben sich versteinert in dem Schiff der Kirchen wieder."

The first history of art to comprise all of Europe was the work of Seroux d'Agincourt. Since it did not appear until 1823, it must be listed in this chapter, although its composition goes back to the eighteenth century.

J. B. L. Georges Seroux D'AGINCOURT (1730-1814), who was descended from a family of the old nobility, became a cavalry officer in the army of Louis XV, but left the service in order to care for his younger brothers and his orphaned nephews. He occupied himself with natural sciences (botanized with J. J. Rousseau), made the acquaintance of the French artists of the period around 1770, and began at that time to take an interest in the history of art. From 1777 on he undertook journeys to England, Belgium, Holland, and parts of Germany; in 1778 he traveled to Italy, wandering, chiefly on foot, from one city to the other—Venice, Bologna, and Florence were in 1779 his principal places of study. He settled down in Rome, where he made the acquaintance of Angelika Kauffmann, and from there traveled to Naples and Sicily. Up to the time of the French Revolution he was able to collect material pertinent to a history of art without regard to money and have it prepared for publication by draughtsmen. The retrenchments that ensued after the Revolution may have delayed the completion of the work. After his death it was continued and brought out by Gence.[46]

Seroux's history of art covers the period from the fourth to the sixteenth century. His long historical introduction treats mainly of Greece and Italy in the Middle Ages. The plates present a host of objects, in small drawings and very often systematically arranged; much was made accessible here for the first time to readers with an "antiquarian" bent. The work must have had an epoch-making effect because of its coherent method. From Dodsworth and Dugdale down to Carter, the English had always dealt simply with the English mediaeval period, Athens, and Rome; now the horizon widened to include all Europe and even parts of Asia.

However admirable this accomplishment was from the point of view of the past, the modern reader will regard it critically, should he sacrifice the time to glance through a book that was already superseded in every respect even relatively soon after its appearance. This is true to a high degree of the chapter "*Règne du Systême dit Gothique.*"[47] Seroux speaks of "system" as opposed to "order"; only antiquity and

[46] J. B. L. G. Seroux d'Agincourt, *Histoire de l'art par les monuments*, Paris, 1823, 6 folio vols. with 325 plates.

[47] *Ibid.*, I, Pt. 2, p. 55.

Renaissance have orders. One should not understand the word "system" as Gothic system in the modern sense: elevation of a bay. De Laborde had already approached this concept much more closely, and we must bear in mind that Seroux's theses had already been conceived around 1780. (He quotes the book of Avril from 1774, p. 66, in the first part of volume I. See above, p. 411.)

For Seroux the *pointed arch* was of course the dominant characteristic of Gothic. Like de Laborde, he calls it *ogive*, an equivocation with the designation for the *rib* that became firmly established in the following decades, caused confusion, and was not extirpated until very late.[48] Seroux was able to date only a few buildings correctly; although he asserts several times that he is proceeding chronologically—he knew, therefore, that this was desirable—everything is jumbled together.

He located the earliest pointed arch at Subiaco, south of Rome, in the monastery Scholastica, citing the authority of a document of 847—today this structure is dated as after 1200;[49] then, however, he jumps immediately to Chiaravalle (near Ancona) and to Assisi, thence to Nôtre-Dame in Dijon, perhaps with reference to Soufflot. Only then does he speak of the great French cathedrals in the chronologically incorrect sequence Amiens, Beauvais, Chartres, Orléans, Paris, Rouen (St. Ouen), mentioning afterward several English churches. Germany is represented only by Strasbourg, Spain by Burgos, Italy by Milan, Siena, Florence, and Rome (Sta. Maria sopra Minerva). It would be unjust to discuss in detail the mistakes of this essay; perhaps it will suffice to say that he called the crossing tower of Nôtre-Dame in Dijon one of the earliest in France and England.

It should be set against Seroux's shortcomings that he refuted clearly and with historical facts the theory that Gothic was derived from the Goths. In the course of his discussion he takes up Swedish architecture to show that Gothic can also not have come from the Goths in Gotland. He likewise rejected the tree theory and finally the Saracen theory as well. By way of proof for his argument he presents numerous examples of Arabic architecture (twenty-two drawings on plate 44 and some others in scattered places). China is represented by only a few examples, also India, and the author confesses that he does not know the dates of these pointed arches.

Seroux's plates are crowded with small figures and no value is placed

[48] With regard to the history of terminology attention should be called to Seroux's remark that the pointed arch was called *arco impastrato* in Sicily.

[49] Cf. the *Enciclopedia italiana*, s.v. Subiaco.

on beauty, so that in this respect also much of the book was already far surpassed even at publication. It is pardonable that Dehio should have failed to notice that the engraving with the triangulation of S. Petronio in Bologna had already been published here (plate 46, fig. 221, reduced in width to about 5 cm). It should, however, be remembered that this first comprehensive history of European art offered thousands of reproductions and treated not merely architecture but sculpture and painting, coins, seals, and so on, as well. One must respect the lifework of a man who, almost unguided, made countless discoveries in a field still lying fallow.

Germany's mediaeval architecture was slowly being made more comprehensible in its broad outlines by Moller; but despite the descriptions of Crombach and Forster, Cologne Cathedral had, up to that time, not been properly investigated for the scholarly world. In 1823 Sulpiz BOISSERÉE published a factual description and history, together with illustrative drawings, in an awkwardly large format. In his Inventory volume Clemen has listed the older literature pertaining to the history of art that treats of Cologne Cathedral.[50] Boisserée's work is the first to do justice to the importance of the cathedral, at least for the time it was published. In 1808 GOETHE was already won back to Gothic by the architect Engelhardt, and Boisserée was able to enlist his interest also for Cologne Cathedral which he had regarded negatively up to that time. Letters written by Boisserée (1811) inform us very vividly how Goethe was in the beginning "as aristocratically unbending as possible," then gradually thawed, and on the following day became more and more sociable. On May 6, together with architect Steiner, they viewed and discussed the plans of the "neo-Greek" monastery church of Paulinzella. There were also others present (Meyer and Riemer) and by chance (?) there lay among the papers a ground plan of the Cologne towers, which suddenly monopolized all Goethe's attention. The letter of May 10, 1811, shows how Goethe relinquished his preference for Strasbourg Cathedral only after an inner struggle. There was a discussion about the differences between the two façades, and finally Goethe acknowledged the large window in Cologne as "more appropriate" to that façade and the wheel window as "more seemly" (*ziemender*) for Strasbourg.

[50] Paul Clemen, *Der Dom zu Köln,* Düsseldorf, 1937 (Die Kunstdenkmale der Rheinprovinz, VI, part III, etc.), p. 7. Quad von Kinkelbach's *Der Deutschen Nation Herrlichkeit,* 1609, should perhaps have been mentioned in the chapter on Germany in the seventeenth century, but I could not obtain the book, as was the case with a number of other things that Clemen cites without giving an account of their contents.

Goethe's reconversion to Gothic, though a purely personal event, was nevertheless symptomatic of the general change in opinion. What he was forced to recognize was Boisserée's scientific work, his "sincerity" (*Redlichkeit*).[51]

Not until 1823 was Boisserée able to begin publishing the drawings of Cologne Cathedral,[52] his last installment coming out only in 1831. The text seems to have appeared in 1823.[53] In addition to a history of the cathedral it contains a very good description with detailed investigations on triangulation. Boisserée quotes Stieglitz, Lacher (1516), and Roriczer (1486). Regarding the construction of the ground plan of the polygonal choir he refers to Vitruvius v 6 where the same method is expounded for Roman theaters. Boisserée owed his knowledge of triangulation and the method of the octagone (quadrature) to the architect Lorenz Kieskalt in Nuremberg, who in 1806 had himself been obliged to produce a "masterpiece" according to these rules. This was a living connection between lodge tradition and modern attempts to explore the mysteries of proportion. Boisserée did not understand everything, for example, he translated the word *Steinmetzengrund* by "foundation of the stonemasons' art" (instead of "ground plan"). In 1812 the Regensburg Stonemasons' Ordinance of 1459 was published for the first time by Karl C. Friedrich Krause. It may be assumed that Boisserée became acquainted with Heldmann's book after 1819.[54]

After a description of the interior and exterior of the cathedral there follows a chapter on its "vegetable" character, obviously with reference to Boisserée's friend, Friedrich von Schlegel. Boisserée goes beyond Schlegel; the vegetable ornament ceases to be ornament in the usual sense: ". . . it is seen to be not something added externally but a sprouting forth as the result of inner growth."[55] The forest theory he rejects, however, because structures from the period of the Christianizing of the Germans do not reveal any of that vegetable character; their style, he says, was introduced from Italy by the missionaries. It was "the round-arched, massive, Romanesque type of building (*Romanische Bauart*)." Vaults with pointed arches did not make their appearance until the twelfth century.

[51] The letters have been published many times; I cite from Flodoard von Biedermann's *Goethes Gespräche ohne die Gespräche mit Eckermann*, Leipzig, n.d., pp. 265ff.

[52] Sulpiz Boisserée, *Geschichte und Beschreibung des Domes von Köln*, Stuttgart, 1823.

[53] I used the first edition of the French translation, dated 1823, and the second German edition of 1842.

[54] Heldmann, *Die drei ältesten Denkmäler der deutschen Freimaurerbrüderschaft*, Aarau, 1819, p. 203.

[55] Boisserée, 2nd ed., p. 70.

At this point Boisserée finally frees his readers from the traditional narrowness of the problem: the Arabs cannot have been the creators of Gothic because they combined the pointed arch with a flat ceiling, whereas in Gothic it is combined with vaulting. "The pointed arch in and of itself is in any case of little significance, and its origin and earlier or later appearance a subordinate problem. The important thing is the application of the pointed arch as the fundamental form of a perfectly articulated, as it were organically developed system of architecture. And it was then really the Germans and their neighbors, the North French and the English, related to them through an earlier racial intermingling, by whom this architecture was *first* practiced most extensively and excellently."[56]

Nothing more is said of the English and French, nowhere does Boisserée mention Amiens as the model for Cologne, not even in the historical part where Meister Gerhard is discussed. There are, on the contrary, assertions about the "joyous, even ecstatic worship of spring among the Germans." Boisserée informs us that the "purely geometrical construction" finally coincided in many respects with "the vegetal formation," and that only the latter was specifically German—quite forgetting Reims and Amiens. The conclusion of this theory is uncommonly interesting: the causes lie in a people's habitual manner of thinking and feeling, and in this way the architecture, the "manner of building," is determined over a long period of time until finally one extraordinary spirit joins together all the dispersed elements. The *fusion* of national character and individual genius is here clearly represented as the source of the perfect work of art, "in order to quicken the dry branches and twigs as though by the breath of spring, and perfect the whole in a harmonious image."

With regard to Boisserée's glorification of the German people, fanatics about race should remember that he was of Belgian origin on his father's side and that his mother was an Italian. His education was German and he belongs intellectually to German Romanticism. In 1803 he was in Paris with his brother Melchior and their common friend, Reinhart. There he met Friedrich Schlegel, who after their return to Germany settled down with them in Cologne. Boisserée,

[56] "Der Spitzbogen an und für sich ist überhaupt von wenig Bedeutung, und dessen Entstehung und früheres oder späteres Vorkommen eine untergeordnete Frage. Es handelt sich hier von [*sic*] der Anwendung des Spitzbogens als Grundform eines vollkommen durchgebildeten, gleichsam organisch entwickelten Systems der Baukunst. Und da waren es dann wirklich die Deutschen und die mit ihnen durch frühere Stammesvermischung verwandten Nachbarn, die Nordfranzosen und Engländer, bei denen diese Baukunst zuerst am meisten und vortrefflichsten geübt wurde."

however, belongs as much to the rational trend as to the romantic: he loved Cologne Cathedral with a romantic love, but he studied it in a severely scientific way. If we recall Browne Willis, the first author mentioned in this chapter, who was also unquestionably of a scientific habit of mind, we realize that not only can a gradual progress be noted, but that Boisserée appears in addition to be specifically a scholar in the field of the history of art, in contrast to Browne Willis with his generally antiquarian tendencies.

It should not be forgotten that while Boisserée, Moller, and, in his fashion, Büsching were making German Gothic accessible, Britton was taking further steps toward the popularization of English. In 1836 he published a quarto volume on the picturesque antiquities of English cities, with seventy-nine illustrations in copperplate and woodcut and eighty-eight pages of text.[57] The illustrations were made by painters and engravers of varying quality, but everywhere the "picturesque" again predominates in order to appeal to wider circles of buyers. Anyone who knows and loves the English cities will even today turn the pages of this book with quiet pleasure. As far as the concept picturesque is concerned, an attempt to clarify that ambiguous word can be found in the Introduction. Britton says he cannot accept Gilpin's "picturesque beauty" because picturesque and beautiful are opposites; he uses, therefore, simply "picturesque." This is not a very profound means of determining what picturesque signifies, but the plates make it clear with light and shade, silhouettes, and diagonals instead of with words. Almost in every case human figures have been added to the scenes, some romantic, some amusing. The book makes one realize how severe Moller and Boisserée were in their insistence on geometrical projections.

In 1833 Boisserée reproduced in geometrical drawings as well as in more or less picturesque perspectives the churches of the lower Rhine that antedated Cologne Cathedral and from which, in his opinion, could be learned how Gothic in Germany developed in the direction of this masterpiece.[58] For each church he provided a brief text. We are somewhat amazed to see that he dates Maria im Kapitol in the seventh and eighth centuries, but we should not judge the volume by such errors. Boisserée was the first to include these churches in a history of art, and he wrote many correct things about them. That local

[57] Britton, *Picturesque Antiquities of English Cities*, London, 1830.

[58] Sulpiz Boisserée, *Denkmale der Baukunst am Niederrhein vom 7. bis zum 13. Jahrhundert*, Munich, 1933.

patriotism made him blind to French Gothic is here even more painfully evident than in the appraisal of Cologne Cathedral, but both cases reveal fundamentally the same intellectual drawing of boundaries. On the other hand we may well ask what the French archaeologists knew about German Gothic. The answer can be found in Seroux: almost nothing at all.

The Englishman, Thomas HOPE (1770-1831),[59] had by contrast quite a wide horizon. As a young man he betook himself, beginning in 1798, on journeys to Egypt, the west coast of Asia Minor, Sicily, the Peloponnese, Italy, North Africa, and Spain, then to Turkey and Syria, France, Germany, and finally back to England where he recuperated from eight years of travel and played a part in society as a collector and literary man.

The sparse drawings in his volume of plates represent chiefly buildings from Italy and the Rhineland; Gothic is almost completely lacking. But the text treats in detail of the "Pointed Style." As Hope died in 1831 his ideas are older than the little book by Wetter: they may be judged to date from the first decade of the century. By and large his description of Gothic is imbued with understanding of its system. On careful reading the same concepts can be discerned as are to be found later in Wetter: piers isolated from each other as a substitute for the wall; ribbed vaults, in connection with which he, as an Englishman, at once mentions ridge ribs; buttresses and flying buttresses; and, finally, pointed arches. He says of the latter that the vaults were provided with pointed arches in order to minimize the lateral thrust, that, furthermore, with the increasing enlargement of the windows there resulted a tendency to conform to the pointed wall arches, "and thus it was that the pointed, before only seen accidentally, and as a subordinate variety from the round arch, and neither the general foundation nor even the consequence of a peculiar new system pervading the whole structure of the edifice, now became universally and exclusively, not indeed the cause, but the consequence, of the new style of architecture."[60] He expressly refuses to recognize the pointed arch, taken by itself, as the primary form of Gothic. Like Mertens later, he believed that the nave of St.-Germain-des-Prés in Paris was completed before the death of Abbot Morard in 1014 and already possessed pointed arches; those in the Carolingian crypt of St.-Denis he considered even older (page 365). This lack of critical judgment

[59] Thomas Hope, *An Historical Essay on Architecture*, London, 1835, ed. by his son.
[60] *Ibid.*, p. 359.

allowed him to accept also Seroux's dating of Subiaco. But Hope's incorrect dates do not much affect his theory, for the pointed arch alone does not after all determine what he means by Pointed Style. He finds pointedness, its essential characteristic, everywhere—in vaults and roofs, as well as in pinnacles and ornaments. Thus Pointed Style does not mean here the pointed-arch style but a style with the quality of *pointedness*. Hope's search for the geographical origin of Gothic results in no definite conclusion. In Chapter 42 he gives a list of Gothic structures, beginning with Germany and mentioning first the choir of Aachen, then Cologne, and so on. Here he also devotes three lines to St.-Denis: "The crypt is old but handsome; nave restored by Abbot Suger, with a fine range of spreading windows: has a slight twist."[61] It is not necessary to correct the first part of this, but it may be said that it is true that the choir deviates slightly from the axis of the nave. Hope was decidedly a dilettante, in love with his subject and, in view of his inadequate knowledge, surprisingly enlightened as regards the understanding of the Gothic system. Due respect for his work, however, should not blind us to the fact that in it, too, mention of the essential elements of Gothic is so inextricably mingled with details that no clear insight could result.

The imposing list of these scholars is continued with Arcisse de CAUMONT (1801-1873).[62] He was able to utilize with fresh vigor the scholarly results of the first generation of the century, yet his achievement was of more organizational than scientific importance. In Volume IV of his *Cours d'Antiquités* (1831)[63] he wrote an introduction to the study of mediaeval architecture, prefacing it with a survey of the literature.[64] It can therefore be determined with exactitude what he owed to de Laborde and Rickman; he also knew German works, for instance, books by Stieglitz, Moller, Boisserée, and Wiebeking.[65]

In his discussion of the designations for the various styles he gives Gerville credit for the invention of the term *architecture romane* (page 39);[66] he himself used it in his earliest work.[67]

61 *Ibid.*, p. 477.

62 For Caumont's biography cf. E. de Robillard de Beaurepaire's *M. de Caumont, sa vie et ses œuvres*, Caen, 1874; also the *Bulletin Monumentale*, 1873, p. 327, and *Congrès Archéologique*, Paris, 1935, pp. 9ff.

63 Arcisse de Caumont, *Cours d'antiquités monumentales*, Paris, 1830-1841. A treatise of 1824 may be important; it was unobtainable (*Memoires de la Société des Antiquaires*).

64 Here several authors are cited whom I have not discussed.

65 The latter is cited on p. 32; I have not been able to consult Wiebeking's book of 1824.

66 Cf. above, p. 508.

67 *Essai sur l'architecture religieuse du moyen âge*, 1824.

His consideration of Gothic (in Volume IV) begins with the then unavoidable disquisition on the origin of the pointed arch, but it is superior to everything that preceded it because Caumont prints a long quotation from a letter by Lenormant (page 206), whose ideas about the divulgation of the pointed arch in the Orient are for the first time concrete.[68] Caumont comes to the conclusion that *architecture ogivale* arises from three sources: the conceptions of native (French) architects, Roman reminiscences, and Oriental taste (page 216). His ideas on the beginnings of Gothic (page 214) are partly romantic (Crusaders, religious enthusiasm) and partly rationalistic (the dilapidation of the old churches, their smallness in view of an increased population, factors of economy). The reasons for the adoption of the new style were "perhaps more complex than has been heretofore assumed."[69]

Caumont does not give a real history of Gothic but differentiates four styles: 1160-1300, 1300-1400, 1400-1480, 1480-1550, calling them simply *style ogival primitif, secondaire, tertiaire*, and *quartaire*. These apparently neutral designations do not prevent him from associating them with varying degrees of value. "In my opinion the beautiful epoch of pointed-arch architecture is the thirteenth century. From the end of the fourteenth century on there was less correctness of lines, less harmony in the whole, architecture lost height."[69a] Late Gothic is for Caumont decline again, though he describes all the stages with equal interest, pursuing Rickman's method (membrological analysis), but less pedantically.

His conception of the statics of vaults is unclear. He is of the opinion that groined vaults are subject to a sagging toward the center of the curvature—the old theory traceable to Bramante—but that ribbed vaults

[68] Charles Lenormant, 1802-1859, worked with Champollion in Egypt, taught history at the Sorbonne, and was for a time French ambassador in Athens; cf. *The Catholic Encyclopedia*, New York, 1913, IX.

[69] *Op.cit.*, VI, p. 214: "A cette époque (XIIe) beaucoup d'églises tombaient de vétusté, d'autres étaient trop petites et insuffisantes pour la population: en même temps l'enthousiasme religieux qui avait produit les croisades inspirait un zèle incroyable pour réédifier et multiplier les monuments destinés au culte." P. 215: "Les architectes qui présidaient à ce renouvellement des églises durent naturellement chercher à éviter les défauts qui avaient hâté le déperissement des anciens édifices . . . et l'on peut supposer que s'ils voulaient, en employant l'arc en tiers point, satisfaire le penchant qu'on éprouve ordinairement pour les idées et les inventions nouvelles, ils étaient aussi persuadés que cette arcade devait donner à leurs édifices plus d'élégance et de solidité."

[69a] "A mon avis la belle époque de l'architecture ogivale est le XIIIe siècle. Dès la fin du XIVe, il y eut *moins de rectitude* dans les lignes, *moins d'harmonie* dans l'ensemble, l'architecture perdit son élévation." (p. 268) By "moins de rectitude dans les lignes" he probably means Flamboyant.

are free from this fault. He does not say why the ribs should not also bend (*fléchir*) toward the center.[70] Hirt in 1809 had already had a much clearer notion of statics (see above, page 470).

Caumont's idea of the whole phenomenon of Gothic is presented as the opposite of the idea of antiquity. All through the centuries, he says, religious faith has been the foundation of architecture. The religion of the Greeks and Romans was entirely material and, it might be said, natural; it produced an architecture of proportions that never went beyond the bounds of good taste and where everything was methodical, simple, and intelligent.[71] Gothic, on the contrary, is Christian. Pious meditation transcends physical nature and exaggerates everything. "From that moment on (since the thirteenth century) everything was out of proportion with earthly ideas; the tendency toward spirituality (*esprit de spiritualité*) appeared in architecture to such a degree that the buildings are filigreed with chasing and embroideries that rival the subtleties of thought." An early emergence of the comparison between Gothic and Scholasticism can be detected here. "In ancient architecture form is everything; in Gothic both form and thought exist." "If the architecture of the ancients is *purer* as art, that of the moderns is more *touching* and *religious*."[72]

These last remarks contain no completely new ideas. For France, Caumont was the great teacher who synthesizes, clarifies, and disseminates knowledge. His main achievement was to unite all architects, archaeologists, clergymen, and the like, who were interested in the preservation of mediaeval objects, particularly those of importance to the history of art. First of all, in 1823, he called into existence the *Societé des Antiquaires de Normandie*, then he gave lectures, and

[70] *Ibid.*, VI, p. 215, n. 2: "Les voûtes cintrées sont sujettes à fléchir vers le centre de la courbure, inconvénient que ne présentent pas les voûtes en ogives. Ils trouvèrent d'ailleurs de l'économie à suivre la nouvelle méthode; on s'accorde à reconnaître qu'il serait impossible de produire autant d'effet dans un autre système, avec aussi peu de matériaux que les artistes du moyen-âge ont su le faire dans leurs constructions à ogives." (The second sentence is in the text.)

[71] *Ibid.*, IV, p. 270: "Ainsi, chez les Grecs et les Romains, la religion toute matérielle, je pourrais dire toute naturelle, a produit et devait produire une architecture basée sur des proportions qui ne dépassaient pas ce qu'on est convenue d'appeler le bon goût; l'ensemble des parties devait montrer cette grâce, cette élégante simplicité, et en même temps cette richesse que nous admirons dans les édifices des anciens, parce que l'imagination était fixée sur des choses naturelles, et que le type du vrai beau, par rapport à eux, ne sortait pas de la nature physique. La pensée, mue par une religion dont tous les dogmes étaient à la portée de l'intelligence humaine, n'avait rien d'inspiré [*sic*]; ainsi, dans l'architecture antique, tout était méthodique, simple et raisonné. Il n'en est pas de même dans l'architecture ogivale, que l'on pourrait appeler architecture chrétienne; . . ."

[72] ". . . bornons nous à poser en principe: que si l'architecture des anciens est *plus pure* comme art, celle des modernes est *plus touchante* et *plus religieuse*." (p. 272)

succeeded in establishing a firm organization for all France, a project that gained the sympathy and support of the government. From 1834 on, the various *Congrès archéologiques* met annually, each time in different cities. The reports of these congresses and the monographs in the *Bulletin Monumental*, which had been founded at the same time, became a bond uniting all research into the topography of the nations' art. Today the two series consist of about 280 volumes that form a treasury of knowledge about the French monuments of Gothic (and not only of Gothic). In his books, also in the *Abécédaire*,[73] Caumont smoothed the way for the study of secular architecture, and indeed was the first to make it possible at all for large circles. It may be said that his organization lagged behind the English Archaeological Societies of the eighteenth century, but the character of such groups had changed decidedly. It had become more serious, more critical, more specific, and knowledge of Gothic—if we think not merely of Caumont but also of the English and German endeavors—more comprehensive.

Daniel RAMÉE (1806-1887) was reared in this atmosphere. His father, himself a productive architect, seems to have educated him in his profession. When the *Commission des Monuments Historiques* had been created through Caumont's efforts, it commissioned the thirty-four-year-old Daniel Ramée in 1840 with the restoration of the cathedral of Noyon. He directed this work until 1846.[74] His intimate acquaintance with that Early Gothic church justified him in writing a characteristic of Gothic. But his interests had a wider scope. In 1843 he published a history of architecture, two little volumes,[75] which he had begun to work out in 1823. The first volume deals with Asia and the Mediterranean region up to the time of Constantine. The section on India, approximately forty-five pages long, indicates to some extent the answer to the question posed above as to what August Wilhelm von Schlegel could have known about that country in 1800. The second volume discusses the Christian architecture of the Middle Ages. Unquestionably Ramée's knowledge of the existence of buildings was more comprehensive than that of his predecessors, indeed it can be said that this is the first more or less complete architectural history of the mediaeval period, although much still remained to be done on the subject. His most important insight into Gothic can be found in the

73 A. de Caumont, *Abécédaire, un rudiment d'Archéologie, Architecture civile et militaire*, Paris, 1850. This volume treats only the secular architecture of France.

74 Charles Seymour, Jr., *Notre-Dame of Noyon. . .* , New Haven, 1939, p. 85.

75 Daniel Ramée, *Manuel de l'histoire de l'architecture chez tous les peuples et particulièrement de l'architecture en France*, Paris, 1843.

following remarks: "The *ogive* (pointed arch), the form that aspired toward heaven, was victorious. In my opinion (*selon nous*) the triumph of the pointed arch over the round was not motivated by taste or by aesthetics; I believe that this outcome was owing to the power of secular art, which, in the thirteenth century, was able to vanquish sacerdotal art. It is the influence and authority of the lay artists in society, it is the decline of the unlimited authority of the church that brought the new style into flower in Christendom." There is, says Ramée, no document to inform us about this, and thus "one must rely on the *esprit*, the character of the epoch, of which art is always the most complete *résumé* as well as the most truthful historian."[76] To this passage Ramée appends an excursus, the subject of which is cultural history. Surprisingly, he also mentions Scholasticism here, but he means the movement of the eleventh century and says that it was overcome by the universities. This "science ridicule" did damage to the arts and to the development of architecture. One must read pages 253-263 entire for the astonishing realization that Viollet-le-Duc found here ready to hand his famous explanation of Gothic as a phenomenon of intellectual history, complete with all its animosity toward the church and its veneration of the romantic spirit of chivalry: "guidée par les puissances invisibles de la religion, de l'amour, de l'honneur, du courage et de la fidelité." (p. 256).

Ramée's priority of error over Viollet-le-Duc has already been established by Rostand, though he declared not Ramée but Ludovic VITET (1802-1873) to be the father of the thesis. As early as 1831 the latter wrote in a report to the minister: "Ici des moines ou des gens d'Église; la des laïque, des francs maçon."[77] The theory, therefore, had arisen as a result of the new knowledge of the lodges (in Germany?) and is, though not entirely incorrect, nevertheless inexact. Ramée, who was working with Vitet in Noyon, followed with his account of the

[76] *Ibid.*, II, p. 253: "La victoire resta à l'ogive, à la forme qui tendait vers le ciel. Selon nous, ce n'est pas un motif de goût, d'esthétique, qui a fait triompher l'ogive sur le plein cintre; nous pensons que ce résultat est dû à la puissance de l'art séculier, qui, au treizième siècle, sut vaincre l'art sacerdotale. C'est l'influence et l'autorité des artistes laïques dans la société, c'est la décadence de l'autorité illimitée de l'Église qui a fait fleurir le nouveau style dans la chrétienté. L'esprit et le caractère de l'époque lui vinrent en aide dans son établissement, et concoururent à faire prévaloir son empire. Il est vraiment remarquable que jusqu'à présent il n'est aucune chronique, aucune charte, pas le moindre document historique écrit, qui nous atteste cette immense révolution dans l'art; il n'existe pas la plus petite phrase, qui nous fasse connaître la cause ou les motifs. Il faut donc nous adresser à l'esprit, au caractère de l'époque dont l'art est toujours le plus complet résumé ainsi que l'historien le plus véridique."

[77] André Rostand, "Viollet-Le-Duc, Historien de l'architecture française," *La Revue critique des idées et des livres*, XXIV, Paris, 1914, pp. 530ff.

subject in 1843, and then in 1845 Vitet formulated his theory himself.[78] There is no doubt that Viollet-le-Duc read both books. He propounded the enticing theory in expanded form and with convincing assurance in the first volume of his *Dictionnaire* in 1854. In 1855 Martin was already writing with rhetorical enthusiasm: "l'Ogive, art national; l'Ogive, art laïque; l'Ogive, art libre."[79] In 1856 Schnaase followed suit,[80] giving Viollet-le-Duc as his source. He believes that confidence in their own cultural accomplishments was awakened among lay persons, and they, the temporal patrons, lords, and city authorities, began to have a voice in architectural matters. They found the most talented masters and workmen among the "free, city craftsmen. Architecture, without being withdrawn from ecclesiastical influence, thus passed more and more into the hands of laymen and was inspired by the full energy and warmth of the vital force newly roused in them." Schnaase thought the free and the city craftsmen identical; Vitet had originally thought only of the lodges; and now the secular patrons were included as well. This more and more imaginative development of the theory of Gothic as *l'art laïque* is a parallel to what had been made of Wren's Saracen theory by Fénelon and Blondel the Younger. Just as they managed to declare the "most French" style Arabic, so Vitet's followers maintained that the most Catholic style was anticlerical. Of course the growing popularity of the conception was related to the increasing tendency toward emancipation from the guardianship of the church and from all metaphysics. Gothic, which that generation had learned to love, had to have the blemish of being "clerical" removed; yet these historians of architecture were very well acquainted

[78] Ludovic Vitet, *Monographie de l'Église Nôtre-Dame de Noyon*, Paris, 1845, p. 121: "Le caractère dominant de cette époque, ce n'est pas seulement le besoin de l'emancipation, c'est la tendance à la sécularisation. La société, jusque-là exclusivement monacale, aspire jouer la premiére fois à devenir laïque. La puissance temporelle de l'église, après avoir atteint son apogée, est sourdement menacée jusque dans ses fondements. La foi ne perd rien de son ardeur, mais elle aussi se sécularise pour ainsi dire . . . l'université de Paris se croit et se proclame aussi bonne catholique que l'Église; en un mot, la société laïque, en même temps qu'elle cherche à se constituer et à s'entourer de garanties vis-à-vis des pouvoirs purement temporels, s'exerce peu à peu à faire par elle-même tout ce qui était jusque-là l'apanage exclusif de la société sacerdotale." Then come arguments supporting the idea that the clergy superintended architecture in Romanesque times, and the laity in Gothic, and in this connection Vitet speaks of the *confréries masoniques*, "dont l'existence dès le 12e siècle, dans l'Ile-de-France et dans la Picardie, ne saurait être mise en doute." To be sure, he adds, their existence cannot be proved on the bank of the Rhine until around the end of the thirteenth century, but that they then appeared on a large scale is proof (*est une preuve*) that they existed long before. With such logic one can date everything two centuries back. (p. 123)

[79] Quoted after Rostand, *op.cit.*

[80] Carl Schnaase, *Geschichte der bildenden Künste im Mittelalter*, III, Düsseldorf, 1856, p. 33.

with the secular architecture of Gothic and could not be blind to the profound difference between this true *art läique* and church Gothic.

Ramée has something to say about the symbolism of geometrical figures and about the lodges, referring to books by Stieglitz and other German authors that probably offered no difficulties of language for him.[81] He was the bridge to the next group of historians of architecture. The second edition of his work, from 1860 on (the date of the volume on Gothic is 1872), reveals that he did not keep entirely abreast of the progress of research, although originally he was on the whole far in advance. What he lacked was clarity about Gothic itself, which is why, for instance, he failed to recognize in his mention of St.-Denis the significance of this work. Only in the second edition (page 883) does he say that archaeological studies have proved that Gothic originated in France and that St.-Denis is indisputably the first Gothic structure. He quotes no direct source for his statement, but mentions all the authors important in this connection. His bibliographical lists are in both editions a mine of information for the historiography of Gothic. It is of course not necessary to discuss all the books he cites, for we are interested here only in discovering the main line of development.

2. The Discovery of the Essential Members and Origin of Gothic

For the study of Gothic as we like to conceive of it today the trend toward research into topography, accompanied partly by picturesque illustrations and partly by exact geometric surveys, was undoubtedly of fundamental importance, but a deeper understanding of the subject required keen thinkers who could explore the real nature and essential characteristics of the style. The process of acquiring this insight may be said to be still continuing even now, but its beginning, or its renewed beginning (after Gervase), bears the stamp of three very diverse personalities. Wetter, Willis, and Mertens, though their merits differ, provided when taken together the basis for further development.

Little is known about Johannes WETTER (1806-1897) the man; he was an architect by profession, lived in Mainz, and as an architect

81 Ramée was born in Hamburg and seems to have grown up there.

created nothing of any importance. In his capacity as writer he produced a guide to the Cathedral in Mainz,[1] a thin pamphlet of pocket size, the price of which is duly stated: one silver groschen. This Modest little work is distinguished by two things: the description is in the nature of stylistic criticism, that is, it is based on analysis of members and comparison of forms, and secondly it states *what* Gothic is.

As an example of his description, it may be instanced that Wetter draws the pointed transverse arches of the cathedral as imposed on the ground plan (he dates them after 1191, calling them the first in Germany) and that he determines his dating after considering not only the historical information available but also such details as the corner leaves of the bases. In his experience these are found between 1160 and 1225. He also discusses the forms of the capitals, the lack of shaft rings, and even the profiles of the arches. With regard to all this his attitude is that of the monographer, such as, for example, Crombach, or, even earlier, Schadaeus, but with the difference that he writes of *forms* with the consciousness that they are tied to limited *historical* periods and therefore provide a guide to the history or, as it were, biography of the individual structure in question.

His theory of the pointed arch is still bound by tradition insofar as he refers to older pointed arches (Terracina, 1074; the cloisters of Amalfi, 1103); in a polemic against Friedrich von Schlegel, who had derived them from the steep slope of the roofs, he says that just the converse is true. He knows that pointed arches have their statical reasons, that they minimize the lateral thrust, permit the construction of thinner vault severies, and thus save material. He recognizes the practical problem of statics in the pinnacles also, which strengthen the stability of the buttresses (Wren's legacy).

Far more important, however, is his realization of the essential nature of Gothic. He expressed it in two sentences, the first of which seems somewhat long even to German readers: "The essential of the neo-Gothic system of construction lay, therefore, in the fact that the effect or tendency of the vault having been recognized as a double one (namely, vertical pressure and lateral thrust), its supports were also divided in each case into two different organs with different factors, namely, into the actual pier intended to bear the load pushing down

[1] The complete title makes a table of contents unnecessary: *Geschichte und Beschreibung des Domes zu Mainz, begleitet mit Betrachtungen über die Entwicklung des Spitzbogenstyles, das neugothische Constructionssystem in Deutschland und Frankreich und den Einfluss der lombardischen und der byzantinischen Kunst auf diese Länder. Mit einem Grundriss des Domes*, Mainz, 1835. For his other works see Appendix 29.

vertically and into the buttress intended to repel the lateral thrust (which buttress was one of two kinds: those that were merged with the actual pier in one mass but were continued beyond it up to the height of the thrusting portion of the vault; and those that, at a distance from the piers, stood about the walls of the aisles and were continued in the form of flying buttresses up to the upper part of the main vault); that, furthermore, the thrusting portion of the vault was reduced by the employment of the pointed arch, and, by dividing the vault into strong ribs with thin fields between them, its vertically bearing down weight as well as its lateral thrust were minimized, a process which, together with the division of the supports, made the attenuation of the piers possible. There resulted from this system skeletons of cut stone, soaring aloft, the wide interstices of which were in part left empty, in part closed by thin infilling of light material."[2]

It should be noted that Wetter does not talk of the infinite, the picturesque, the religious spirit, of truth, ethics, or the like, or even of the curves of the vaulting arches, as Saunders does, but of the system of construction: he comprehended Gothic as an entity, as *system*, and essentially as a constructive system. In this he goes beyond Rickman, de Laborde, and all the others. That becomes evident only when his long-winded sentence is reduced to its few fundamental ideas. That is to say, in the first sentence he talks chiefly of the *elements*, and in the second of the *result* of the stylistic change. A table will make this clear:

Pier Abutment Pointed arch Rib	are the elements; the results are	Attenuation Dissolution of the wall Verticalism Structure

[2] "Das Wesentliche des neugotischen Konstruktionssystems bestand also darin, dass man die Wirkung oder Strebung des Gewölbes als eine zweifache (nämlich senkrechten Druck und Seitenschub) erkennend auch die Stützen derselben je in zwei verschiedene Organe mit verschiedenen Faktoren teilte, nämlich in den eigentlichen Pfeiler zur Tragung der senkrecht drückenden Last und in den Strebepfeiler zur Zurückdrängung des Seitenschubes (welcher Strebepfeiler es zwei Arten gab: solche die mit dem eigentlichen Pfeiler zu einer Masse verbunden waren, aber über denselben bis zur Höhe des schiebenden Teiles des Gewölbes fortgesetzt wurden, und solche die, von den Pfeilern entfernt, um die Mauern der Seitenschiffe her standen, und in Strebebogen bis zum oberen Theile des Hauptgewölbes fortgesetzt wurden), dass man ferner den schiebenden Theile des Gewölbes durch Anwendung des Spitzbogens verminderte, und durch Zertheilung des Gewölbes in starke Rippen und dünne Zwischenfelder, dessen senkrecht drückende Last, sowie dessen Seitenschub verringerte, was verbunden mit der Zertheilung der Stützen die Verdünnung der Pfeiler möglich machte. Das Resultat dieses Systems waren hoch aufstrebende Gerippe aus Haustein, deren weite Zwischenräume theils leer blieben, theils mit dünnen Füllmassen von leichtem Material geschlossen wurden."

These ideas were also to be found in the descriptions of de Laborde, Rickman, Caumont, and Hope, amid much else, but the epochmaking feature of Wetter's two sentences is that he has picked from the confusing list of the many kinds of *membra* the four *essential* ones, emphasized their systematic connection, and related the total impression of Gothic to them. It may be inferred that the four stylistic effects are individually subordinate to the four elements, thus, structure to the rib, verticalism to the pointed arch, and so on. Wetter does not go so far as to say that one of these four elements alone, or two together, and so on, produced Gothic; it was left to his late disciples to call the rib the seed corn of the future harvest. And in any case his definition is not intended to be genetic but descriptive, and refers to the state of the matured style. Consequently it is of no importance in judging his work that flying buttresses were not evolved until around 1178,[2a] that the rib was not pointed in the beginning, and so on. In discussing the piers he says that the Gothic masters supported the transverse arches and ribs by little columns (engaged shafts). Thus he assumed an adaptation of the pier to the ribbed vault, a designing *from above downwards*, a thesis that had a long aftereffect.

He characterizes cathedral Gothic half metaphorically as soaring skeletons of stone, but remains throughout severely factual; only in a single passage does he say of the piers that they are clusters of lance-shaped or tubular columns "that shoot up like the jets or sheaves of water from spouting fountains." One is reminded here of Georg Forster and de Laborde, of vanquished Romanticism.

In Wetter's comparison of the "Lombard architecture with the neo-Gothic constructional system" (that is, of Romanesque with Gothic) there occurs the word function: "That they might be able to serve the purpose of the new system the organs were modified as to their functions and consequently also in their form. . . . New functions became necessary, therefore new organs were introduced into the organism." He paralleled this process with the development of lower to higher animal species, seeing a similar evolution from the vaulted buildings of the Romans to those of the Byzantines and the "Lombards," compared to which the Egyptian and ancient Greek architectural styles are lower orders. That, of course, is a value judgment, but one free from personal rancor or prejudice.

Wetter's objectivity made him reject the idea that Gothic originated in Germany. He cites the dates of Nôtre-Dame in Paris, "Building be-

[2a] Probably in Canterbury cathedral, in the part built by William of Sens.

gun in 1164, consecration of the altar followed in 1182," and remarks that by contrast the German churches of 1160 to 1180 were still "Lombardic, with heavy vaults, massive piers, without flying buttresses, and with small windows." Indeed, according to Wetter, German churches remained "Lombardic" even until 1225. The appearance of Gothic in Germany, he says, was so sudden that it "must have been brought in ready made from outside."

It is unexpected to find these revolutionary ideas in a little guidebook, and, what is even more astonishing, the real theory of the essential nature of Gothic is contained in two footnotes that run along for page after page beneath the text, chiefly on pages 40 to 53. Many travelers doubtless bought the guidebook, but probably few read the footnotes, and fewer still understood and appreciated them. But the new doctrine trickled through slowly to the professional people.

Robert WILLIS (1800-1878) makes quite a different impression.[3] He was born in London, studied theology in Cambridge, and in 1827 took holy orders. Theology, however, did not occupy him completely. He was interested in music and the improvement of musical instruments; his chief field was mathematics and mechanics, and he lectured on engineering, his procedure here being severely methodical. He was just as interested in architecture and its history, even inventing an apparatus for making exact copies of moldings mechanically.[4] He applied to the study of architecture his method of building up machines from their elements or of reducing them to their elements. Here he had no new principles to suggest, but everything he wrote was more intensively and clearly reasoned than what Rickman and others had contributed in this field.

In 1835, the same year as Wetter's guidebook (and the posthumous book by Hope), Willis's architectural history of the Middle Ages appeared.[5] He distinguishes between "mechanical" and "decorative" construction. Mechanical construction pertains to how the loads are *actually* supported, decorative to how they *seem* to be. With this differentiation in mind he turns to the description of the individual architectural parts. Many of his remarks are still instructive, for example, what he has to say about foliation (foils, cusps, etc.), about tracery, and about vaulting. In his discussion of piers there is one dominant pair of concepts: "continuous" and "discontinuous." As to engaged shafts, he

[3] For Robert Willis cf. the *Dictionary of National Biography*, vol. 62, New York, 1906.

[4] "Cymagraph for copying mouldings," *Engineers Journal*, July, 1842.

[5] Robert Willis, *Remarks on the Architecture of the Middle Ages, especially of Italy*, Cambridge, 1835.

differentiates face-shafts, edge-shafts, and nook-shafts, depending on whether they stand in front of the wall, on an outer edge, or in an inner corner. His geometrically trained intelligence enabled him to go beyond external description to arrive at fundamental distinctions. His book by no means treats Italy alone, but it contains a list of buildings in Italian cities with their dates. From 1832 to 1833 Willis traveled in France, Germany, and Italy, finding that Italy had been neglected up to that time. His contributions to Italian architectural history were indeed a real supplement to topography. He recognized clearly the differences between Italian and French Gothic. Seroux's dating of Subiaco he rejected (page 185).

Nevertheless Willis was indeterminate about the origin of Gothic. "With respect to the regular styles of the Gothic, England may claim the honour of inventing the Early English, the germs of which, however, are to be found in France; and I conceive the Decorated or Complete Gothic to be derived from Germany; from which country emanating, it superseded all the established styles in other countries, except Italy. The Perpendicular is our own, and heartily may we congratulate ourselves upon it, when we compare it with its sister styles in France and Germany." (page 155) As regards "Complete Gothic" he was presumably thinking of Cologne Cathedral.

In 1842 Willis returned once more to the subject of Gothic vaults in a treatise.[6] A reprint of 1910 proves that even after two generations it was not outdated. It is still unusually informative because Willis shows clearly with very simple arguments how the apparently difficult interpenetrations of the moldings by the rib imposts were actually executed and how one could locate the curvature of the individual ribs in complicated star vaults. There is also a detailed explanation of the construction and technique of the English fan vaults. Willis went far beyond Saunders and the other authors whom he mentions on the first page of his treatise.

Two books by Willis have already been cited in an earlier chapter, his philological work on *The Architectural Nomenclature of the Middle Ages* (1843) and his *Architectural History of Canterbury Cathedral* (1845). The significance of the latter lies in its being the first detailed monograph in the modern sense, with a complete analysis of all parts of the structure and reconstructions of the state of the work at various times. Willis wrote a series of similar monographs giving stylistic analy-

[6] Robert Willis, *On the Construction of the Vaults of the Middle Ages* (Transactions of the Royal Institute of British Architects, 1, Part 2), London, 1842. A reprint appeared in 1910.

ses of English Gothic cathedrals: on Herford in 1842, on Winchester and York in 1846, and so on. They were models that surpass Wetter's description of the cathedral at Mainz.

Willis' merits lie both in his extension of factual knowledge and in the strictness and clarity of his method. In spite of his religious calling he was a man of the world, in this respect a contrast to Franz Mertens; as a lecturer and a man of affable personality he influenced large circles in England, though in other countries he seems to have been for the time overlooked. Ramée at least cited Willis' book on Canterbury in the second edition of his architectural history (II, p. 1048).

Information about the life of the architect Franz MERTENS (1808-1897) can be obtained from Franz Vallentin's account of him.[7] Mertens was born in Düsseldorf and very early concentrated all his energies on research into mediaeval architecture, publishing in 1835 in the *Museum*, a journal edited by Franz Kugler, an essay that gave a very complete survey of all the literature that had hitherto appeared.[8] Soon after, he went to Paris, whence he returned in 1841 to Düsseldorf. Here he lectured on the results of his investigations in France, among other things on his discovery that Gothic had appeared for the first time in St.-Denis. He published his thesis in 1843 in Förster's *Allgemeine Bauzeitung*.[9] He calls the architecture of the Isle-de-France already Gothic from the year 1000 on, but differentiates four epochs within this Gothic, the fourth of which begins with St.-Denis (1135-1144). Of the latter he says: "With this epoch then, with this church therefore, there begins in the school of the Isle-de-France the architectural form that is generally called Gothic. It was at that time borne, as it were, by the church of St.-Denis, after having existed heretofore, to carry on the figure, only in an embryonic state. . . . If, by some exception, the school of the Isle-de-France had ended with its third epoch, its architectural style would only have been considered an abnormal kind of Romanesque; we should then overlook its organic type of structure, figuration would then remain the only measure of what was significant in vault construction, and certainly there would be no talk of a particular Gothic system. Whereas now, on the other hand, the existence of the earliest structures of the fourth epoch would suffice even by themselves alone to distinguish most emphatically their architecture as a Gothic system

[7] *Allgemeine Deutsche Biographie*, LII, Leipzig, 1906, p. 562.

[8] Franz Mertens, *Die bisherigen Studien über die Baukunst des Mittelalters*, Museum, 1835.

[9] Franz Mertens, "Paris baugeschichtlich im Mittelalter," *Förster's Allgemeine Bauzeitung*, VIII, Vienna, 1843, pp. 159ff. and 253ff. "Die französische (gothische) Baurevolution, *Förster's Allgemeine Bauzeitung*, XII, Vienna, 1847, p. 62.

from Romanesque. In all this there lies then a difference, not merely between one epoch and another but also at the same time between two more comprehensive periods in the architecture of the Isle-de-France, which may be distinguished as Romanesque and Gothic. But these names should not lead us astray; for this difference in a school that nevertheless remained one and the same despite all changes is just for that very reason by no means of the same character as the difference between Romanesque and Gothic in all the other provinces of Europe."[9a]

The interpretation of this last sentence may well remain a moot question. Near the beginning of his article Mertens says that there are natural circumstances to be taken into account, for instance, cut stone as the building material in France as opposed to brick in Germany, and, on the other hand, historical circumstances. "Those natural circumstances are also found in other provinces, particularly in Normandy, for example, without Gothic's having originated there." But it is not clear whether or not Mertens intended to express something of this sort in that doubtful sentence above.

It would be equally difficult to discern from this passage alone what he meant by the concepts *figurative* and *organic*. He himself says: "Let us first remark that the architecture which we call Romanesque contains two fundamentally different kinds of form: a figurative and an organic. These are the antithetical formations of Romanesque architecture. The first consists of the significant configuration of the structural masses and the figurative adornment of their wall surfaces by means of arches, friezes, and the like. The other is expressed in the multiple membering of the arcades and jamb shafts and in the rhythmic repetition of forms. The one is the exclusive principle of Graeco-Byzantine architecture, the chief work of which is the church of St. Sophia in Constantinople; the other is just as exclusively the principle of Gothic architecture, the acme of which is Cologne Cathedral."

What Mertens means by the word figuration only becomes clear from a passage in a work of 1850: ". . . where the former [Gothic] indulges in organic or at least quasi-organic forms, the latter [Romanesque] is intent on presenting in its formations a profuse configuration of the

9a "In alldem liegt denn ein Unterschied, nicht nur von Epoche zu Epoche, sondern zugleich auch von zwei umfassenden Perioden in der Baukunst Franziens, welche man als romanische und gotische unterscheiden mag. Nur sollten hier diese Namen nicht irreführen; denn dieser Unterschied in einer Schule, welche bei allen Veränderungen doch immer eine und dieselbe blieb, ist schon deswegen durchaus nicht des Wesens, wie der Unterschied von Romanischem und Gothischem in allen übrigen Provinzen Europas." The words "nicht des Wesens wie" could also be translated "not of the same kind."

wall surface. As the organic principle functions in the piers and buttresses of the former, so in the latter is figuration active, the picturesque shaping of the surface."[10] The antithesis "figurative: organic" thus means at the same time "picturesque: plastic," Romanesque being picturesque (two-dimensional) and Gothic, plastic (three-dimensional). (Of course Romanesque structures are also three-dimensional, but Mertens is thinking of the antithesis between wall and support, later to become so important.)

The four epochs differentiated by Mertens are briefly as follows—with *his* dates, not all of which are correct:

1. ca. 1000-1060	Chief works: St.-Germain-des-Prés; Paris (nave!), 1000; St.-Remi in Reims; the cathedral in Speyer, 1036.
2. 1060-1100	Chief works: St.-Martin des Champs, Paris, 1067; St.-Etienne, Beauvais, 1072; Nôtre-Dame in Poissy, about 1100; St.-Lucien, Beauvais, 1079; St.-Benoît-sur-Loire, 1070-1080; Ste-Trinité, Caen, 1068.
3. 1100-1135	Chief works: St.-Martin, Laon, about 1130; etc.
4. 1135-1248	Chief works: St.-Denis, about 1135-1144; Chartres, West front, 1145; cathedral in Laon, 1151; cathedral in Noyon, after 1150; St.-Germain-des-Prés, Paris, choir, 1163; cathedral in Sens, 1164; Nôtre-Dame, Paris, choir, 1163-1177.

In this same essay of 1850 there are two important observations. The first refers to the ribbed vaulting of the cathedral in Cefalù of 1130. Mertens calls it "the real connecting link in this fruitful union [of rib and pointed-arch arcades] or in this artistic coalition of the school of the Isle-de-France and the school of Palermo." (page 101)

In the other passage of interest he speaks, on page 114, of the reduction of the style as the "primary cause of the Late Gothic style," and proceeds, on page 115, to call this a decline in taste. The concept of "reduction Gothic (*Reduktionsgotik*)" appears again in Dehio, and Mertens' verdict on Late Gothic was presumably also influential down to Dehio's time.

However rich Mertens' essays are in new ideas, it seemed to him that the most important contribution was the discovery of St.-Denis as the birthplace of Gothic. Hope had maintained that the pointed arch was merely a consequence of the style, not its source; Wetter had formulated what the essential character of Gothic really was; Mertens determined where and when Gothic (in the narrower sense) appeared

[10] Franz Mertens, *Die Baukunst des Mittelalters, Geschichte der Studien über diesen Gegenstand*, Berlin, 1850, p. 22.

for the first time. All the learned research into the provenience of the pointed arch, all the fanciful speculation about its aesthetic effect and artistic significance had forthwith become obsolete, and a new epoch in the study of Gothic began.

Mertens had an almost perfect acquaintance with the older literature on the subject and was well aware of the epochmaking nature of his discovery. Whether vain or not in his motives, he had a claim to recognition, at least within professional circles, which were at that time still very narrow. To what extent he received his due is a subject for investigation. Pastor Heinrich Otte, in his *Handbuch* (the edition of 1853),[11] called Mertens, "whose contributions should not be overlooked," the man who recognized in Suger "the inventer of the Gothic manner of building," although "the spirit of the style" was "always the common product of that whole age." Otte, a faithful compiler, characterized St.-Denis, and in fact the fabric of 1137, as the oldest Germanic structure, shortly thereafter designating Cologne as the ultimate perfection of the French architectural style (Kugler had created a new confusion in stylistic terminology). But Mertens wanted to be recognized by the leaders among the critics. Kugler and Schnaase were among the auditors when he lectured in 1841. They wrote in their own works about the historical significance of St.-Denis, without mentioning Mertens,[12] who then accused them of plagiarism. Nothing, however, could be proved against these more important contemporaries who claimed to have come to their conclusions as the result of independent research. For decades Mertens fought with increasing bitterness to establish his real or fancied priority. No one seems to have supported him.

It is difficult to arrive at a fair judgment of Mertens. His works are not easy to find, while the reader is hampered in addition by their lack of clarity, and prejudiced unfavorably by the author's vanity and overestimation of the importance of his discoveries.

Four years after the appearance of his first two essays on Paris, Mertens published a third, also in the *Allgemeine Bauzeitung*, displaying great knowledge for his day but offering nothing fundamentally new.[13]

[11] Heinrich Otte, *Handbuch der kirchlichen Kunst-Archäologie des deutschen Mittelalters*, 3rd ed., 1854. I do not know the older editions. The book certainly had considerable value for scholarship in its day; in its topographical lists it is a forerunner of Lotz's *Kunsttopographie.*

[12] Neither Kugler nor Schnaase should be suspected of deliberate plagiarism. For that matter Schnaase mentioned Mertens in a note in the first edition of his *Geschichte der bildenden Künste im Mittelalter*, v (1856), saying expressly that he differs from him and that Mertens had overestimated the significance of St.-Denis for the problem of the beginning of Gothic.

[13] The article has the subtitle: "Die französische (gothische) Baurevoluzion." [*sic*] Förster's *Allgemeine Bauzeitung*, XII, Vienna, 1847, p. 62.

He assembled his accusations of a personal nature in 1858 in a little work[14] that can be of interest for us today only because in it we come across the names of men who were at that time interested in the origin of Gothic, as well as the names of those who, unfortunately for Mertens, showed no interest in it at all, namely, Napoleon III and King Frederick William. The book is a collection of letters and documents intended to throw light on the quarrel between Mertens and Kugler. Mertens' statements are for the most part so confused that it is scarcely possible to come to any objective conclusion. In a letter to Alexander von Humboldt he calls Kugler his pupil. Kugler's "plagiarism" is supposed to be contained in an essay on Cologne Cathedral. Mertens claimed that Kugler made the following admission to him in a private letter: "It is possible that my attention was indeed first drawn to this, directly or indirectly, by you; as a matter of fact I no longer know, for the general scheme and the details are, moreover, in any case based on my own studies." Mertens considered himself to have been unjustly treated by Schnaase, Olfers (a close friend of Schnaase), Quast, and Stüler, as well as by Fortoul (French Minister of Education), and Mérimée in Paris. Unfortunately Mertens' struggle for justice was complicated by financial claims, for he had no private fortune and no income. His literary projects became more and more voluminous, and he wanted corresponding advances of money. In Paris and Berlin he knocked on closed doors. He was dogmatic, ignorant of the ways of the world, and undiplomatic, so that on reading his presentation of his case one shakes one's head as at a psychological riddle. The Germans did not feel flattered to hear that their Gothic was supposed to have originated in Paris, and the French were annoyed that a German had made the discovery. Until after the time of Robert de Lasteyrie, however, they held fast to the idea that Gothic began in the Isle-de-France, not, for example, in Normandy—and that was Mertens' legacy.

His little bill of indictment is bibliographically valuable because in it all of his works are mentioned that had appeared up to that time (1858), twenty in number. There was then still to come his map of monuments, an astonishing product of his industry and his extensive knowledge of the existence of Romanesque and Gothic structures, a knowledge covering all Europe from Spain to the Baltic. The publisher Duncker stated by way of "advertisement" that the map had been

[14] Franz Mertens, *La Question de l'architecture du Moyen-Âge*, Édition de l'Auteur, Berlin, 1858. The slim volume is probably very rare. I found a copy only in the library of the Germanic Museum in Nuremberg.

drawn as early as 1840, but at that time it could not have been completed, for Duncker lists among Mertens' sources of reference Lotz's *Topographisches Lexikon für die Kunst des Mittelalters*, which was not published until 1862. The map came out in 1864 accompanied by a text entitled "The West during the Crusades."[15] Mertens here discriminates between the architectural schools in the same way as in the essay of 1850 mentioned above. In the latter he points out that the concept "school" was created by Rumohr and Waagen. Mertens undoubtedly made great contributions also to the geography of art.

His merits were exaggerated in Vallentin's warm-hearted biography because the latter assumed nothing at all useful to have been achieved before him in the field of mediaeval architecture, but even when they are reduced to their proper size they remain very great. One cannot but think sympathetically of this inwardly and outwardly lonely man. He died in 1897 at the age of eighty-nine.

Johannes Wetter died in 1897 at the age of ninety-one. We do not know whether he, too, felt injured because others were reaping the credit for his ideas. Robert Willis had died in 1875, admired and appreciated in English circles, without the thirst for fame, and satisfied by his knowledge for its own sake.

Anyone who was concerned with Gothic after it ceased to be the living expression of its age, and especially anyone who had to repair or complete Gothic structures, was obliged to acquire a clear understanding of the construction, technique, and statics of Gothic vaults. There exists—and existed—therefore a whole literature on these particular problems. Bramante is said to have written on the subject; Leonardo was interested in it. The Spanish architect Rodrigo Gil de Hontañon (ca. 1500-1577) wrote on the statics of vaults but had no clear insight into the actual distribution of forces in the vaults and their abutments.[16]

This branch of the ideas about Gothic cannot be discussed here as regards its earlier development. Willis, of whose essay (1842) mention has been made, cites the authors of the chief works: in 1568 Philibert de l'Orme, in 1624 Maturin Jousse, in 1643 Derand and also Desargues, in 1727 de la Rue, in 1738 Frézier; he also refers to Halfpenny, 1725, and to books by Nicholson that were, he said, familiar to everyone. To

[15] Franz Mertens, *Das Abendland während der Kreuzzüge. Denkmalkarte darstellend durch Zeichnung die Landgebiete der geschichtlichen Kunststyle oder die unterschiedlichen Bauschulen dieser Zeit*, Berlin, 1864. The text amounts to only 49 pages and contains two announcements of projected works by Mertens.

[16] Georg Kubler, "A Late Gothic Computation of Rib Vault Thrusts," *Gazette des Beaux-Arts*, New York, 1944, p. 135.

Willis' list should be added a work of the year 1695 by the Danzig architect Barthel Ranisch (and which I do not know). Hofstadt mentions him in his *Gothic ABC* as well as the essay by Saunders already discussed.

William WHEWELL (1794-1866) endeavored to develop Saunders' observations further.[17] He went beyond him to the extent of asserting that all changes within Gothic were a consequence of the pointed arch and thus, indirectly, of the vault, where the practical value of the pointed arch had forced itself on the attention of the builders.[18] Here the old theory of the pointed arch experiences a rebirth in the form that the pointed arch is now said to have been no accident.

Rudolph WIEGMANN (1804-1865) adopted these arguments.[19] He found that the pointed arch had already been used by the Moors in Spain, Sicily, and Egypt even before the Crusades, in the latter country as early as the eighth century. But, he says, it was employed in these buildings only on the exteriors, never in the interiors; in Germany, on the other hand, it was used in interiors and, according to Saunders and Whewell, within the vaulting structure, for logical reasons. Thus, Wiegmann continues, to Germany should be assigned the honor of being the land of origin of the pointed-arch style. This was written before the appearance of Mertens' essay on the churches of Paris. But Wiegmann knew and quoted Wetter,[20] only objecting to his assertion that the pointed arch had occurred for the first time in the cathedral of Mainz, and claiming that it had already been used earlier.[21] He attacked the datings of the French vigorously (particularly those of Ger-

[17] W. Whewell, *Architectural Notes on German Churches with notes written during an Architectural Tour in Picardy and Normandy*, Cambridge, 1830. The second edition appeared in 1835, the third unchanged in 1842 with a supplement by F. de Lassaulx, *Notes on the Churches of the Rhine.* Lassaulx was *Architekturinspektor* of Prussia.

[18] The book contains much else of interest. Whewell compares the architecture of antiquity and Gothic: "the characteristic forms of the one being horizontal, reposing, definite; of the other vertical, aspiring, indefinite." He thought that the construction of rectangular vaults with the aid of pointed arches, which Saunders had stressed, was developed more completely in Germany than in England and was "probably older in Germany."

[19] Rudolph Wiegmann, *Über den Ursprung des Spitzbogenstils. Mit einem Anhang betreffs der Bildung eines Vereins für die Geschichte der mittelalterlichen Baukunst*, Düsseldorf, 1842. This appendix reminds us that Franz Mertens was at that time interested in such efforts; he delivered lectures in Düsseldorf in 1843, and the two men were undoubtedly acquainted. Mertens was an architect, Wiegmann taught at the Düsseldorf Academy of Art. Wiegmann's book seems to be very rare. There is a copy in the Kunsthistorisches Seminar in Bonn.

[20] Wiegmann's introduction seems to have been written with Mertens in mind; it speaks of an amalgamation of Roman, Christian, and Germanic elements after a period of ferment lasting from the fifth to the tenth century.

[21] He cites the following in evidence: Memleben, 957 at the latest, Merseburg, 1015-1021, Freiburg a.U., from the same period, Basel, 1006-1019, and St. Sebald in Nuremberg, "without doubt from the same time." It is unnecessary today to discuss these wrong dates.

ville); in this connection he occasionally engaged in stylistic criticism.

The subject of vault structure then came to occupy a chapter in every book that was intended to present a history of mediaeval architecture, for example, in works by Kugler, Schnaase, later by Lübke, Dehio, and others, in works by French and English architectural historians as well as German. Acquaintance with the history of these studies is indispensable for anyone who wishes to pursue further research in this field. Investigation into the subject is by no means complete, above all if one intends to determine the historical progress of the construction of vaults. Up to now scholarship has contented itself with recognizing the various stages according to their inner logic, without being able to support its arguments by pointing to those structures in which the new solutions in question were tried for the first time, or are at least tangibly evident to us within the corpus of extant buildings.

After Wiegmann, Heinrich LEIBNITZ published a book which, in the compass of but 65 pages with but 96 illustrations to the text, provides a wealth of observations on all kinds of vaults.[22] The problems of concern to us here are treated in Chapters VI and VII (pages 29-50). Leibnitz speaks in detail of everything that pertains to the requirement of equal springings and crowns. By way of historical examples he discusses Maulbronn and Bebenhausen, and, in the Appendix, Heisterbach, Nôtre-Dame in Paris, S. Francesco in Assisi, S. Flaviano in Montefiascone, Treves, Marburg, and others. His knowledge of monuments is extensive and, as far as his subject is concerned, thorough.

Since the rib was introduced into the Romanesque quadripartite groined vault it was important to know what constructional stage the groined vault had reached at the time, especially if one took the point of view that the real reason for introducing the rib was to substitute precise forms for the unprecise groin lines. Karl MOHRMANN (1857- ?) wrote on the difficulty of achieving such precise curves by the aid of groins (in the third edition, 1889).[23] Of the older editions, I have been able to consult the first by Ungewitter in 1858, but it does not contain anything about the groin curves. In the fourth, the solutions attemped by Romanesque are juxtaposed theoretically with no reference to their absolute chronology. These solutions are represented by the four stages that are drawn in on Plate III of the *Lehrbuch*. The drawing makes it clear that in the case of a rectangular (not square) ground plan the

22 Heinrich Leibnitz, *Die Organisation der Gewölbe im christlichen Kirchenbau*, Leipzig, 1855.

23 G. Ungewitter, *Lehrbuch der gothischen Konstruktionen*, 3rd ed. by K. Mohrmann, Leipzig, 1890, pp. 10 and ff.

intersection of the barrel vaults would result in groins sinuous in space instead of ellipses; further, that with the establishment of elliptical groins, on the other hand, the longitudinal arches of the narrow side also become elliptical; that when stilted semicircles are substituted for the longitudinal arches of the narrow side the vault cell becomes conical; and finally that with the introduction of elliptical groins and pointed longitudinal arches (on the narrow side) the cell becomes a complex empirical shape. These four cases by no means exhaust all the possibilities, but they lead to some understanding of the difficulties that confronted builders before the introduction of the rib.

3. The First Great Syntheses

WAETZOLDT has described in delightful fashion the life of Franz Theodor KUGLER (1808-1858) among his circle of friends, his career as a Prussian official, as well as his varied interests and writings connected with the history of art. Gothic forced itself on his attention because he was pursuing goals related to the universal history of art; one does not have the impression that he felt especially drawn to that particular style, and therefore the man as a whole should not be judged by the following remarks. He was a friend of Jakob Burckhardt, a guarantee in itself that he stood on a high level as regards scholarship and personality.[1]

In his *Handbuch der Kunstgeschichte*, Kugler presented Wetter's chief innovation (of 1835) without naming him.[2] He gives an introductory description of the system of Gothic, which he calls Germanic architecture (in contrast to Romanesque), differentiates transverse arches and diagonal arches (ribs), and says further that the pressure of the vault is distributed to the four corner points of the vault field, thus relieving the walls, which could be thinned and much pierced by openings. He finds that from the thrust of the vault there resulted the system of buttresses, a consequence of which was verticalism, which in its turn gave rise to the pointed arch, and so on. Thus, compared to Wetter, he inverts the sequence of development. His final formulation reads as follows: "Ribbed vaults, buttresses, and pointed arches in their reciprocal relationship are therefore to be called its [the system's] pre-

[1] Wilhelm Waetzoldt, *Deutsche Kunsthistoriker*, II, Leipzig, 1924, pp. 143-172; bibliography on Kugler, p. 293.

[2] Franz Kugler, *Handbuch der Kunstgeschichte*, Stuttgart, 1842, 2nd. ed., p. 540.

eminently characteristic elements." Kugler's designation for ribbed vaults is *Gurtgewölbe*, today called *Rippengewölbe*; *Gurt* is used today only for the transverse arch.[3]

Among his various observations there is one that is very important: "In the Romanesque style the broad undersurface (intrados) of the arches always appeared as the chief feature. That is changed in the Gothic style. Here the profile acquired slanting side faces that incline toward a common point." This, in my opinion, is the difference in profiles that Gervase had in mind (see above, pp. 31 and 34). From the third edition on, the comment was omitted; its significance does not seem to have been understood.

Kugler then gives a brief—very brief—survey of the most important buildings of France, the Netherlands, Germany, etc. It is surprising that he states clearly that France was chronologically in the lead, and yet calls Gothic Germanic. According to him the Isle-de-France, Champagne, and Burgundy are the cradle of the style. The designation "Germanic Style" was rejected by scholars because Gothic has nothing to do with the ancient Germanic peoples. From the third edition on, the term used is "*Gothic* architecture," in conformity with the convention that was then sweeping everything before it. But the opinion—or prejudice—that within the French nation the Franks as Germanic descendants are responsible for the creation of Gothic persisted until the time of Dehio and after.

In 1852 Kugler published in the *Kunstblatt* several essays entitled "Fragmente zur Theorie der Kunst."[4] Among them was an essay on the Picturesque in Architecture. "The picturesque is based above all on the way in which effects of atmosphere and light are made apparent with respect to an object. The works of architecture, with their alternation of masses, of rigidly wall-like or fluidly articulated parts, of projections and depths of space, will afford manifold opportunities for the development of picturesque moments. But their relationship to the picturesque—of course aside from the tricks of chance . . . will be very different in different systems. Generally the Gothic system of architecture is considered to be preeminently the most picturesque." Kugler admits this, but expresses the reservation that Gothic is designed too

[3] *Ibid.*, p. 517; in the 2nd ed. of 1848, made by Jakob Burckhardt, on p. 542. Carl Friedrich von Rumohr introduced this designation "*Gurtgewölbe*" before Kugler, cf. his *Italienische Forschungen*, III, Berlin, 1831, p. 170. For details about Rumohr, who is not very rewarding for Gothic, see W. Waetzoldt, *op.cit.*, II, p. 164.

[4] *Kunstblatt*, 1852, No. 41. Also printed in Kugler's *Kleine Schriften und Studien zur Kunstgeschichte*, III, Stuttgart, 1854, pp. 40ff.

much in the direction of organic structure. His whole detailed argument is indecisive; he does not rightly know how he is to subsume Gothic under his concepts of the organic and the picturesque (like Mertens, see page 532). Yet his descriptions are quite in the spirit of the (subsequent) method of empathy: ". . . the consciousness of the observer ought as it were to identify itself with the life that inspires this organism, soar aloft with it, radiate out with it in the piers, curve upward with it in the vaults, and, like it, send out tendrils in the turrets and blossom forth in the flowers of the pinnacles." He sets up the ideal of this self-surrender as the proper view of Gothic, in contrast to the idea of regarding it objectively as a picture; the latter conception, he adds, affords only a conditional beauty. And in a note he tries to show that an openwork spire or Gothic buttress would never make a pure picture from any standpoint. In conclusion he declares that the element of the picturesque was most decidedly apparent in Rococo, delivering at this point in the nineteenth century one of the earliest, if not *the* earliest, positive appraisals of this style.

Earlier, on page 743, Kugler had discussed the problems of picturesque relief, anticipating many of Alois Riegl's subsequent arguments. He speaks also, like Adolf Hildebrand later,[5] of relief that projects in one layer of uniform depth. Kugler's minor works offer further insight into his step by step attempts to comprehend the essence of Gothic. To this category belongs, among others, the essay on Cologne Cathedral,[6] in which he expounds the thesis that the ground plan was evolved in France, the system in Germany; in France he found only the "beginning, as a relatively low stage of development, the noblest and purest design (*Durchbildung*) of Gothic architecture belongs exclusively to Germany." (p. 152)

The last phase of Kugler's judgment of Gothic is represented by the third volume of his *Geschichte der Baukunst*, which appeared posthumously in Stuttgart in 1859. Little need be said here about his history of the monuments themselves. He already had Schnaase's presentation at his disposal, and he arranged the material by countries, as Schnaase did, putting France first, followed by England, Germany, the Netherlands. Of course much of the work has been superseded today; but the knowledge it reveals is worthy of respect as an achievement for

[5] Kugler treats relief with reference to E. H. Toelken's *Über das Basrelief und den Unterschied der plastischen und malerischen Komposition*, Berliner Kunstblatt, 1915. Kugler took his doctor's degree in Heidelberg in 1831 under Toelken (Waetzoldt, *op.cit.*, II, p. 145).

[6] *Kleine Schriften und Studien. . .* , II, p. 123.

its time. Any consideration of the progress in the collecting of monuments and the historiography of Gothic in the strict sense would deal extensively with this book.

As far as the present topic is concerned, the history of the judgments about Gothic in their entirety, attention may be concentrated on the "Introduction," the first thirty-six pages. The first two pages are taken up by a sketch of sorts of the cultural and historical background. The chief idea is probably: "The Gothic style of building developed from the Romanesque as an isolated offshoot." Whereas its beginning, he says, was provincial, Gothic grew to European importance. Romanesque, according to him, developed "national" systems in all provinces; Gothic became the expression of that European unity which was based on the dominion of the church. There is an abundance of cultural echoes in these pages: the University of Paris, chivalry, the Albigensian Crusade, and so on.

This introduction is followed by a section entitled "The Basic Traits [*Grundzüge*] of the System," and another called "Treatment" (referring to individual forms); here the membrological description is often combined with stylistic understanding of the more profound sort. There is, however, no lack of severe criticism that occasionally becomes downright condemnation. As an example of this, the concluding sentence may be cited: "The multicolored light of the windows, instead of justifying the polychromatic procedure, seems on the contrary to make the pure and uniform effect of the architectural membering and its plastic character doubly necessary. The situation is utterly different where the membering lacks complete and refined design (*Durchbildung*). In Italian Gothic, where this is usually the case, colored decoration resulted as a natural substitute for this lack."

Kugler went so far as to add a section with the title "The Other Side of the System" (page 22), in which practically everything is criticized. One should read all six pages, for only a few phrases can be quoted here: formal schematism, delusion of organically architectural reality, barbarously tasteless manner of overloading with sculptural adornment, pleasure in clumsy and vulgar forms, and oversubtle calculation.

"The exterior, in its basic forms, was a dismembered scaffolding, the individual parts of which could not join to make an effective unit, and, with their projections and their arching masses they . . . concealed themselves and the body of the structure in constant change, affording nowhere a firm, clear picture of the total relationship, nowhere a self-contained and satisfying impression." This sentence is reminiscent of the passage from Vasari's *Lives* quoted above on page 290.

It can be seen from other remarks that Kugler knew this text. He criticizes the Gothic canopies and pinnacles, and then comments: "The point of utter insincerity reached by the Gothic exterior in its development is demonstrated in the system of decorative gables which was of such great significance for the appearance of the whole; this is a purely formal fiction, only employed for the sake of effect and having no connection with the structural or organic laws of the building. . . ." Next he criticizes the towers, making, however, an exception: "Individual works of this sort from the late period of Gothic where a more independent element reveals itself in the play of decorative fancy, somewhat like a fairy tale in character and untrammeled by strict systematic forms, do indeed attain to a physiognomy more justified in itself, especially when the total dimensions are also decreased or the whole is dissolved into individual parts, in which the decorative play can be developed with lightness and delicacy." One could almost imagine that he was thinking here of Strasbourg Cathedral and Goethe's essay, but what he says about that in his history of monuments does not support such an assumption (Kugler, pages 362ff.). He has nothing good to say about the Gothic portals, especially about the archivolts and their sculptures, "which, usually resting on canopied consoles, follow the lines of the arches and consequently, as they rise to the very peak, adopt a pendant position that becomes more and more absurd." The gargoyles he condemns with the utmost moralizing severity.

Thus he expresses himself as though under the spell of Vasari and his followers, yet he had written only a short time before (page 7): "Effulgent sublimity and uniform organization of space were the ends desired above all. The builders very consciously aimed at the mystical effect of the architectural phenomenon, which the ecstatic excitement of the spirit demanded; but the mystery was to be open to everyone." And a page further on: "Thus that mystical element is also woven into the totality of the Gothic structure. It pervades all parts of the edifice; it develops, in contrast to Romanesque, toward the light; it offers itself to view all around, and finds in the free high points its fullest and most compelling unfolding."[7]

[7] "Lichtvolle Erhabenheit und einheitliche Gliederung des Raumes wurden vor allem erstrebt. Man ging mit lebhaftem Bewusstsein auf die mystische Wirkung der baulichen Erscheinung aus, welche die schwärmerische Erregung des Geistes erforderte; aber das Myste-

Two souls, it would seem, dwelt in Kugler's breast, one classical which copied Vasari, the other romantic.

Whereas Kugler was *obliged* to concern himself with Gothic because it simply could not be avoided in view of his universally oriented scientific interests, Carl SCHNAASE (1798-1875) evidently felt an emotional kinship to the style. For details about him also Waetzoldt's essay should be consulted, for it brings out very clearly in all its complexity the personal background of his writings on the history of art.[8]

Carl Schnaase's chief profession, at least outwardly, was the law, but though he performed his duties as *Obertribunalrat* in Berlin (from 1848 on) conscientiously, in his heart he considered his chief calling to be the history of art. His interests were varied. As a student he heard Hegel lecture in Heidelberg and followed him to Berlin when the latter was called there in 1818. Courses on the history of art were in those days given in German universities only within the framework of those on aesthetics. The encyclopedic knowledge that enabled Schnaase to write his history of art in eight volumes was gained through travel and by reading all the specialized literature that was then in existence—and accessible to him. He was self-taught wherever he went beyond Hegel. Hegel used the history of art as a collection of examples for his aesthetics. Schnaase, on the contrary, used aesthetics as the basis for his history of art.

His first significant publication was in the form of travel letters,[9] and was based on notes of a journey actually undertaken in 1830, a generation after the travel letters of Friedrich von Schlegel. Schnaase's letters are composed and edited with a view to offering contributions not merely to the history of art but also to artistic theory and, characteristically, as the preface states, to the philosophy of history "which is as much empirical knowledge as *a priori* (page v)." The major part of the book treats of painting, with thoughtful essays on landscape and genre painting. The most important comments on architecture are to be found in the sixth and eighth letters. In the sixth there are general reflections on the differences of style in Italy and the northern countries. One such remark of a general nature that illustrates Schnaase's basic

---

rium sollte Jeglichem offenbar sein." "So ist auch jenes Mystische der Totalität des gothischen Baues eingewoben. Es durchdringt alle Teile des Baues; es entwickelt sich, umgekehrt als wie beim Romanismus, dem Licht entgegen; es bietet sich rings der Schau dar und findet in den freien Höhepunkten seine vollste und ergreifendste Entfaltung."

[8] W. Waetzoldt, *op.cit.*, II, pp. 70-92 and bibliography on p. 290.

[9] Carl Schnaase, *Niederländische Briefe*, Stuttgart and Tübingen, 1834. A rather bulky volume of over 500 pages.

attitude very well is: "The reasons for these differences are partly external, as, for example, the character of the material, which may be more favorable to certain forms; but equally there are also spiritual reasons that cause taste to follow a particular direction; and generally both agree in their effect, by virtue of the inner relationship between the natural features of a country and the historically molded taste ["*Sinn*"] of its people." (page 161) This sentence contains *in ovo* both Semper's "material theory" of style and Riegl's idea of the "art will" (*Kunstwollen*), and, in addition, it gives an interpretation of art on a national as well as historical basis. Since this is all merely suggested in a conglomerate whole, one point is merged indistinctly in the next, and the same vagueness also characterizes the immediately following survey of architectural styles from the Early Christian basilica to the Gothic hall church, a survey interspersed with value judgments and allusions to geographical differences and natural requirements respecting material (in the architecture of the Teutonic Knights in Prussia). Once again he asserts emphatically on page 168 that the decisive factor is not material but the "spiritual requirement." The Dutch churches are for him proof of this.

Schnaase considers it necessary to justify his terminology. He defends the designation "Gothic" against "German" and "Germanic," and uses "pre-Gothic" instead of "Romanesque," though he dropped this later in his chief work.

He makes the cathedral in Antwerp the occasion for most detailed and comprehensive aesthetic theorizing. Since this book appeared before Wetter's Cathedral Guide it may be of interest to know what Schnaase thought of Gothic at that time. His comments are dominated by observations referring to the connection between the interior and exterior appearance of a building. It is striking how much is said here about "space" long before this concept had become of central importance for any discussion of architecture (pages 196ff.). Without doubt he adopted that idea from Hegel. He considers the vertical membering to be most important for the interior or inner *space* because of "perspective." In the ancient temple, since it was principally an exterior, the horizontal dominated. "The pier system, quite aside from the cross vault, had to develop just as soon as the desire arose for an architecture in which the interior should give satisfaction. It is, therefore, not a result of the cross vault, but a preparation for it." (page 199) This is, moderately expressed, the same thought that was later put forward by Gall.

Schnaase then proceeds to a discussion of the quadripartite vault, and in particular of the ribbed vault, giving an excellent description of its spatially concentrating effect. He is also interested in the "intercolumniation," a concept that was later usually treated under the heading of proportion or occasionally also under that of rhythm. His comments range from such subjects as individual forms and their proportions to the transverse section of buildings, lighting, and comparisons with classical styles, until finally he turns to the specific forms of Antwerp Cathedral. Here his complete lack of prejudice against Late Gothic is the most striking feature. "The rows of parallel piers that separate the seven aisles present from every point of view a different picture, which continually charms the eye anew by the changing play of light on the delicate members and by the variously interlacing vaults."[9a] (page 210) He sees the flowing into each other of the forms, "so that the eye discerns no one separately, but glides gently from one to the other." (page 208) It is the anticipation of Riegel's isolation and coalescence as a pair of opposites. Schnaase quotes Friedrich von Schlegel and employs the latter's term "sidereal"—which does not otherwise occur—as a very happy designation for Romanesque exterior architecture.

Schnaase's treatise is full of anticipations, one such being the passage where he takes issue with the idea that the "antique Italian" art (he does not have the word Renaissance) had displaced Gothic. Rather, he says, did Northern architecture need the Southern, "for in both forms of degeneration [Italian Gothic and German Late Gothic] Gothic architecture was now striving toward large masses and slight adornment; it thus set tasks that contradicted its previous assumptions but that had been solved by ancient architecture."[10] (page 217) This became the foundation for certain views of Jakob Burckhardt, who read the *Niederländische Briefe* and quotes them.

With regard to the conception of Gothic in his chief work, Schnaase relies on Wetter as an authority and quotes him, at least in his discussion of Mainz Cathedral.[11] It is important in this connection that

9a "die sich mannigfaltig verschlingenden Wölbungen."

10 " . . . denn in beiden Formen der Entartung (scil. italienischer Gotik und deutscher Spätgotik) strebte die gothische Baukunst jetzt nach grossen Massen und leichtem Schmuck; sie stellte sich daher die Aufgaben, welche ihren bisherigen Voraussetzungen widersprachen, die aber in der antiken Architektur gelöst waren."

11 In Vol. IV, of the first edition (in the confusing double numeration of these volumes this is Vol. II, 2 of the section: *Geschichte der bildenden Künste im Mittelalter*), p. 103. He says that Wetter gives an essentially complete and reliable account of the historical side of Mainz Cathedral, criticizes the lack of sufficient illustrations, and makes absolutely no mention of Wetter's real merit. Another note rejects Franz Mertens' claims to priority (v, p. 31, 2nd ed).

Schnaase recognizes the principle familiar to everyone that the quadripartite vault bears only on the individual piers and not on the exterior walls as applicable to the groined vault as well as to the ribbed vault.[12] In this he follows Kugler, to whom he had dedicated the first volumes of his history of art. He imagines the development of Gothic to have been gradual, with the invention of the transverse arches coming first for reasons of safety and greater durability (he gives no further proof of this). "It was natural to apply this idea to the diagonal lines as well. The groins (*Grate, Gierungen, arrêts*) were strengthened and consequently the triangular vault cells could become thinner." This is the *statical* theory of the origin of the ribbed vault, hence of Gothic, and was derived from Saunders. It is in accordance with this that Schnaase explains the sexpartite vault (page 152) as resulting from the desire to make statical use of the intermediate piers of the alternate system, adding that only thereafter did the transition to the row of equal quadripartite vaults take place (which is historically incorrect). He goes on to say that the pointed arch helped to overcome the difficulty of achieving level crowns in the arches of the vault, and that then the vault became suitable for any ground plan, and so on (Viollet-le-Duc). The "ribwork" of the windows, that is, the tracery, is merely a result of the ribbed vault (page 155). On the whole he contrasts Romanesque and Gothic as *opposites*, Romanesque architecture being characterized by unity of the whole and repose, Gothic by the liveliness of the individual forms: in the former the rhythmic relationship is demonstrated (that is, made visible), in the latter it is a secret vital principle concealed by the exuberance of multiplicity. On page 209 he summarizes once more, stating, just as Wetter does, that the quadripartite ribbed vault, combined with pointed arches and buttresses, is the essential element of Gothic. To illustrate the appearance of the whole he quotes the familiar verses from the *Younger Titurel*.[13]

We have been obliged to point out in specific detail that Schnaase did not present an original view of these matters. His fame rests on other grounds. What de Laborde had suggested as a pattern for French architectural history Schnaase carried out for the Orient, classical antiquity, and the Middle Ages. He uses the same scheme: first an introduction dealing with cultural history, second, paradigms of style, and third, the chronological history of the buildings, here arranged according to countries. The discussion of the second point, the paradigm—or,

[12] *Ibid.*, IV, pp. 146, 148.
[13] Cf. above p. 185, n. 59.

as Schnaase calls it in the Hegelian sense, the "ideal"—of style has already been undertaken. What does the introduction devoted to cultural history contain?

In Schnaase's opinion ancient history is enacted by individual national entities, mediaeval by an aggregate of several nations. Consequently the mediaeval period is characterized by two joint evolutionary trends: the progressive development of the common spirit of the group of nations, and the strengthening and separation of the individual nations. (Later historians used instead the terms "style of the age" and "national style.") Corresponding to this duality there are, according to Schnaase, two "ideals," the cultural and the artistic. The former, which we should call a paradigm or schematic sketch of mediaeval culture, he treats from three points of view: first, that of the interaction of church and state (the idea of sinfulness, the *civitas dei*, the form of the feudal state, chivalry, monasticism, the church, the military orders); second, that of morality (Christian freedom, authority, weakness of character in the laity and clergy, hence the belief in angels and devils, divine justice despite the obvious injustices in the fate of the individual, ordeals, humility and humiliation, conventional morals of knighthood, the concept of loyalty, veneration of women, courtly love, and—somewhat incoherently—the history of costume and festivals); third, that of science, and the like. After all this "we still fail to detect traces of the spirit we recognize in art." It is this, then, that Schnaase seeks. The spirit of art, he feels, must have its foundations in culture. Where do these roots lie? "Whence this inner unity, this serenity and joyousness, which attract us in artistic productions?" And then comes the decisive answer: "It sprang from a deeper source, from an inner life. . . . One can call this attitude of mind *faith* . . . but it is not merely a matter of personal salvation, or of a world beyond, but rather of the divinely willed and guided order of the Christian world."[14]

Scholasticism, popular belief, symbolism, and encyclopedias molded, according to Schnaase, the *knowledge* and the *faith* of the age. They were full of inner conflicts, but these troubled the calm of men's minds just as little as the political-ecclesiastical conflicts. This is a somewhat too rosy picture, but Schnaase doubtless intends to say that all unrest was outweighed by the inner security, founded on faith, of the people of that time. With this point of view Schnaase attempts the solution of his problem in the history of *art*. Each of the endeavors mentioned

[14] Vol. IV of the whole, or Vol. II *Mittelalter*, 1850, p. 60, and unchanged in the second edition, 1871, p. 41.

contained an element that was needed by human beings: "the encyclopedias, the wealth of mundane material; mysticism, the idea of complete, untroubled unity; scholasticism, the law of that form by means of which variety can be reduced to unity. All these together provided, therefore, an incitement to conceive the whole; and where science could not succeed in doing this, feeling and imagination turned all the more eagerly to *art*, in order to obtain through it the fervently desired perception." (page 80) Schnaase, as has always been acknowledged, thus introduced us to mediaeval culture in a masterly way, revealed to us all its various factors, and then said: art is the result of these factors, their integration or visible synthesis. But that is not all.

In the place where he discusses Gothic in particular—the passage just quoted referred to the Middle Ages as a whole (from about 1000 to about 1500)—he provides a special introduction having to do with history of culture, and now he discovers artistic motives in culture itself: "The ideality of opinions and intentions, the noble and bold indifference to material detail . . . the pleasure in form, and the fondness for the fantastic, all these point to an artistic disposition. Even where the most arid intelligence rules, in Scholasticism, this artistic element manifests itself in satisfaction with formal truth, in emphasis on the symmetrical shape of syllogisms. We moderns incline to view art only as the imperfect copy of life; of that epoch one might say the opposite, that life was only an imperfect work of art, carried out in unfavorable materials." Yet Schnaase sees art as the crown and flower of *life*. For him poetry and architecture are related. "There is everywhere the same emotional tendency: in the soaring of the slender members and the ample span of the vaults the same boldness as in the knightly adventures, in the soft profiles the same feelings as in the lovers' laments, in the pinnacles and flying buttresses the aspiring, and in all parts the martial spirit that pervades the world of chivalry. And finally there is the same similarity in technical matters as well. . . ." Thus Schnaase, too, sees a parallel in the relationship of Gothic and Scholasticism, although he expressly denies the existence of any immediate connection between the masons' lodge and the university lecture room. "But Gothic could only come into being in an age which was accustomed to artificial systems and which, even in real life, ignored ordinary nature, creating for itself a world of opinions and customs that rested on bold assumptions and was held together by artificial means." Gothic, through its system of construction, represented the ideal element of culture as reality and simple truth. It gave expression to the most delicate impulses of the spirit of the age, it is "the richest and most vivid picture of those noble and significant times, and, with its inner consistency, has also a great aesthetic importance for all eras."

This attempt of Schnaase's to derive Gothic from the spirit of the age and demonstrate definite analogies between Gothic architecture on the one hand and chivalry, Scholasticism, and mysticism on the other has always been admired but nevertheless respectfully put aside. Why? Schnaase also adopted Viollet-le-Duc's theory, or that of Vitet and Ramée, about the influence of the laity on Gothic. His conception, however, is far more complete and on a grander scale. Viollet-le-Duc had said: ". . . ce serait peut-être tenter l'impossible." Here the seemingly impossible had been achieved by the intellectual power of one single man. Why were scholars not grateful for it? Some, were. Wilhelm Lübke, for example, adhered to Schnaase's theories in his history of architecture (1855), but, though industrious and talented, he was merely a good propagandist, not an independent thinker.

Schnaase, of course, treats the pointed arch in the course of his discussion of details of the Gothic system, and says: "The *semicircle* by reason of its inner regular cohesion still seems to be a whole and distinct from the vertical supports on which it rests. The pointed arch, on the other hand, falls into two halves that are both more closely connected with the shafts from which they rise than with each other: it is merely a moderate inclination of two vertical shafts that meet without losing their separate character." (page 107) This is absolutely correct and of fundamental importance. (Schmarsow repeated it in 1920, doubtless having forgotten Schnaase, and managed to write for fifteen pages on the subject.) But why do we accept this interpretation of the pointed arch, yet remain skeptical when soft profiles (they are by no means always soft) suggest lovers' laments, and pinnacles are martial? Is everything vertical—for instance, the Empire State Building in New York—martial? It is so tempting to combine these questions: the pinnacles have Gothic profiles; are they then martial and their profiles amorous? It is embarrassing to reproach Schnaase with such things, for one must honor him as one of the greatest of historians of art. There can be no doubt that he was aiming at something essential, and just what this was must be revealed by subsequent developments in the study of art. Thus I am for the moment relieved of the necessity of further criticism on this point. It will suffice to have pointed out that his comparison between round and pointed arches is quite differently constituted from that between pinnacles and a warlike spirit.

The third part of Schnaase's work, the listing and monographic discussion of specific buildings, was excellent for its time, but is, of course, long since out of date. It could not be more than an intermediate stage on the road to greater knowledge. But since the *spirit of the age*, the *Zeitgeist*, is treated in the introduction dealing with the cultural background, one does perhaps expect to learn something more about *national spirit*, the *Volksgeist*, as the various countries are traversed, and especially to hear what it is about French Gothic that is really French, or about German Gothic that is German. If pinnacles reveal a warlike spirit, what particular form makes them martial in a typically French way, or a German way, or is a warlike propensity independent of any national quality and always the same? No definite answers to these questions can be found in Schnaase. However, he says in the discussion of the German Transitional style (in the thirteenth century), alluding to Kugler: "If the Gothic style had really been what it has been called, the German or Germanic, it would necessarily have been understood at once in Germany, it would have been received with open arms like a brother born in foreign parts. But it was the product, not of a purely Germanic nation, but of one where Romance and Germanic peoples were commingled; it was the work of the organizing, dispersive, amalgamating talent that in mixed nations is exercised and developed in real life and through the need for union, and it bore the stamp of the artificial conditions that arise from the opposition and gradual fusion of the various groups. It partook of the same mediating and compromising character as Scholasticism and the French system of chivalry."[15] Granted that this were all true, it would merely amount to stating that Gothic unites a Germanic and, let us say, a "Latin" element, but we do not learn what it is in Gothic that is Germanic or what Latin. Schnaase goes on to say that the Germans were a national entity as the result of natural descent rather than of political cohesion, and that therefore they preferred the Romanesque style. But what is the specifically Germanic element in Romanesque?—The word *Volksgeist* proves to be a mysterious key that does not unlock the door. The conception of national spirit is an inheritance from Romanticism, specifically from Hegel, and was handed on to neo-Romanticism by Schnaase. The mysterious key has gradually acquired a venerable age, but it still cannot turn the lock.

Schnaase found a critic in Kugler, to whom he had dedicated the

[15] Vol. v (Vol. III), 1872, p. 223.

first volume of his work. The latter formulated the difference between his method and Schnaase's very clearly:[16] "I have been accustomed, and continued association with art has indeed led me more and more in this direction, to interpret the artistic phenomenon as naïvely and straightforwardly as possible, to seek the condition of its existence as much as possible in itself, and to explain its peculiarity as simply as possible on the basis of the motives nearest to hand; whereas Mr. Schnaase reduces the individual artistic phenomenon as much as possible to its general causes and conditions, eagerly traces the more refined spiritual *fluidum* of the ages, and seeks to evolve the creative process from mysterious currents of such a nature, justifying it so far as this is feasible. The one point of view owes something perhaps to that of the practical man, the other to that of the theorist. Without a doubt both have their virtues and will often be of good use to each other." Kugler means the two tendencies in the history of art, one of which considers the immanent aspect of art, the aesthetic factors, to be the essential thing, the other of which emphasizes the dependence of art on external (cultural) factors. To equate this contrast or at least difference with that between practice (as in that of the museum official and artist) and theory (as in that of the philosopher and historian) is incorrect. Yet the difference as such is very clearly personified in the spirits of these two men, and in the further development of the study of art they became the fathers of two opposing trends in Germany, trends, however, that on closer examination proved to be far less contradictory than their representatives imagined.

Schnaase himself was not exclusively a theorist; he was universally minded, and therein lay his greatness. Compared to Wetter or even Mertens, he is no student of details but a creator of the survey of a large portion of the past and a scholar with an insight into the depths, into the backgrounds of the panorama. Kugler was more modest in his aim; the relief of his history of art is less high and therefore less problematical. Schnaase's very boldness of intention, clarity of language, aloof superiority, and uniform impartiality are fascinating. One senses that he had a strong inner relationship to Gothic, yet his work encompasses all epochs down to the end of the fifteenth century. Only a monographic study could fully determine what he owes to Hegel, but Schnaase was one of those disciples who were able to create something new from their master's inspiration. He raised a

[16] Kugler, *Kleine Schriften . . .*, *op.cit.*, II, pp. 436ff., especially p. 614 (from the *Kunstblatt* of 1850).

monumentum aere perennius to his own iron patience in positive work and, even more, to his loving sensitivity to all higher human culture and his genuine piety.

4. Moralizing Aesthetics in England: The Gothic Revival

ONE manifestation of the romantic trend in the criticism of Gothic was the desire to justify the style in all respects; this was done by Pugin in a new way. Clark has called the older period of Romanticism the "Picturesque period" and the more recent one that begins with Pugin the "Ethical period."[1] Bradbury includes this group under the heading of "British moralists," comprising Pugin, the Camden Society, Ruskin, Gilbert Scott, and William Morris. The latter, however, can be passed over here. He will be discussed below, p. 686. Augustus Charles Pugin, the father (1762-1832) added to our knowledge of Gothic by making very accurate drawings. He collaborated in part with Britton and to him we owe, for example, the drawings of Ste-Trinité in Caen before Ruprich-Robert's restoration.[2] The son, Augustus Welby PUGIN (1812-1852), emulating his father, very early made drawings on his own account, for example, Rochester Castle; he also followed his father in becoming a thorough connoisseur of Gothic, but developed into an architect who applied this knowledge with dangerous facility in his practice. Clark has given an account of his life together with a very just appraisal of his accomplishments,[3] and has shown clearly that in the Houses of Parliament, built by Charles Barry from 1836 on, everything ornamental, one might say everything that is *Gothic*, was designed by Pugin. With this edifice what is called in England the Gothic Revival entered its serious phase; everything heretofore, beginning with Walpole's Strawberry Hill and continuing from Fonthill (1796) to St. Luke's in Chelsea (1819), and so on, had been mere trifling and dilettantism. But these are stages in the practical application of Gothic, whereas the developments in theory are our sole concern here.

1 Kenneth Clark, *The Gothic Revival*, London, 1928, 2nd ed., 1950, p. 150.

2 *Historical and descriptive Essays accompanying a series of engraved specimens of the architectural Antiquities of Normandy, Edited by John Britton, The subjects measured and drawn by Aug. Pugin and engraved by John and Henry Le Keux*, London, 1828.

3 Clark, *op.cit.*, pp. 152ff.

In 1863 Pugin published his *Contrasts*,[4] a work that preaches a kind of admonitory sermon by paralleling examples of buildings from the good old days with their modern counterparts. On the two views of the same city, first in the Middle Ages and then in the nineteenth century, various structures are keyed by numbers to the explanatory text below. Thus it can be seen that the beautiful Catholic churches have been replaced by the churches of the "Heretics," or have been transformed into prisons or asylums. On the site of a vanished church there is even a gasworks. That is indeed regrettable, and it should be mentioned here only incidentally that Pugin became a convert to Catholicism in 1834. No one will dispute the fact that mediaeval cities had more beauty—whatever one understands by beauty—than those of about 1836. But there is a particular type of aesthetics underlying Pugin's attitude.

The title of his second book, *The True Principles of Pointed or Christian Architecture*, is already a confession of his intention.[5] He begins with the following remarks: "The two great rules for design are these: first, that there should be no features about a building which are not necessary for convenience, construction, or propriety; second, that all ornament should consist of enrichment of the essential construction of the building."[6] One is reminded of the Vitruvian concepts of *commoditas, dispositio*, and *decor*. Pugin continues: "The construction should vary with the material employed. . . ." All his requirements are fufilled in *Gothic*, and more than this, *only* in Gothic. It is also stated here that the pinnacles are not merely adornment but serve to increase the stability of the piers by their weight.[7] "Height, or the vertical principle, emblematical of the resurrection, is the very essence of Christian architecture."[8] He says further that the splay of the window moldings is useful because more light is thereby admitted (a point also emphasized by Costenoble) and that this feature is also good for doors, piers, and arches, both for reasons of elegance and convenience. In demanding elegance as well he deviates a little from his role, but his tendency is brought out all the more clearly when he adds that elegance would not be beautiful without usefulness. He gives arguments to prove that everything can be explained on the grounds of usefulness and the nature of the materials, adducing examples for

[4] A. W. Pugin, *Contrasts, or, a Parallel between the Noble Edifices of the Middle Ages and the correspondent Buildings of the Present Day*; *showing the Present Decay of Taste*, 1836.

[5] Augustus Welby Pugin, *The True Principles of Pointed or Christian Architecture*, London, 1843 (2nd ed., 1853).

[6] *Ibid.*, p. 1. [7] *Ibid.*, p. 5. [8] *Ibid.*, p. 7.

stone, brick, metal, and wood. (It is very probable that Gottfried Semper, when he lived in London, read Pugin.) The observation that "the picturesque effect of the ancient buildings results from the ingenious methods by which the old builders overcame local and constructive difficulties,"[9] should be interpreted to mean that one should *not* try to achieve the picturesque by artificial means, "by sticking as many ins and outs, ups and downs about as possible,"[10] but that one should derive the elevation from the ground plan and the latter from the purpose of the building. The picturesque is thus for Pugin not an end in itself, but simply the expression of utilitarian aims.

To round out the picture of his theses one more statement should be quoted: "The greatest privilege possessed by man is to be allowed, while on earth, to contribute to the glory of God."[11] Gothic is *the* Christian style. The Renaissance is pagan (cf. Caumont five years earlier, page 521 above).

The tendency to emphasize utility is the same one we found more than a generation earlier in Costenoble. But now it becomes effective, in England and also elsewhere in Europe. Here the problematical side of Pugin's theory will be stressed, though with no intention of being censorious, and the question posed: what about the gasworks? Does it not partially fulfill the requirements Pugin advocates? At this point, however, it becomes clear that his theory really consists of *two* requirements. First, he speaks of, one might say, naked structure, but second, of ornament as an enrichment of the "essential construction." The gasworks is unadorned. But here condemnation of the Gothic Revival lurks in Pugin's own statements. We refer to the principle of intellectual development already touched upon earlier that the various "styles" perish as a result of their own mistakes. The rebirth of Gothic was historical; it tacitly assumed that people were still living in the Middle Ages. Moller alone contradicted this idea. Pugin remained an influence on the entire subsequent development just because he induced people to follow this false course of declaring Gothic a *rational* style and at the same time recommending it because it was supposed to represent the *irrational* Christianity that was unchanged and just as alive as in the Middle Ages.

His third publication revolves about the proposition that Gothic is Christian and that this is also true of civil architecture.[12] Pugin consequently urges the adoption of the Gothic Revival for private resi-

[9] *Ibid.*, p. 52. [10] *Ibid.* [11] *Ibid.*, p. 36.
[12] *An Apology for the Revival of Christian Architecture in England*, London, 1843.

dences also, because in England people still lived and were *housed* exactly as in the Middle Ages. Here he forgot the gasworks, which even he did not wish to see built in Gothic style. (English domestic habits always remained very conservative.)

This whole attitude had its specifically theological and ecclesiastical side. In England Catholicism no longer reigned exclusively, as in the Middle Ages, and one party of the faithful hated and feared the pope more than the devil. When these Christian "sects" sided with Gothic it was a different matter from the advocacy of the deeply committed convert Pugin. "He [Pugin] had said: To revive Gothic architecture you must also revive old forms of worship. They said [the Tractarians]: To revive old forms of worship you must revive Gothic architecture."[13] This branch of the Gothic Revival was represented by members of the Camden Society in Cambridge, who maneuvered themselves into an untenable position.

The Anglican church was at that time severely puritanical, all symbols were forbidden, and even the cross was not permitted to appear on church gables or the covers of prayerbooks. The desire to reform the ritual eventuated in the defense of Gothic. The Oxford Architectural Society concerned itself with questions that Clark has formulated, not without irony, as follows: "Can the Society advise the clergyman as to correct style and arrangement? Is a spire essential? Can a stove be placed in the vestry? Is it better for the west window to have two lights, symbolizing Christ's dual nature, or three, symbolizing the Trinity? Finally, how is it possible to raise funds?"[14] All such questions were answered dogmatically, until finally the Camden Society, having been declared papistical, disbanded. It continued to function under the name of the Ecclesiological, and pronounced the judgment that Gothic is the only truly Christian architecture, particularly the "classical" Gothic of the Decorated Style. This had further, destructive consequences for the existence of English mediaeval structures, since now churches that had a trace of that style anywhere about them were entirely adapted to it—by restoration—or, if they had none, that is, if they belonged to the Early English or Tudor styles, were torn down in order to be replaced by those in the Decorated. Clark asks whether the Camden Society did not destroy as much as Cromwell and gives the answer: "If not, it was from lack of funds, *sancta paupertas*, only true custodian of ancient buildings."

[13] Clark, *op.cit.*, p. 199. [14] *Ibid.*, p. 199.

The core of this movement was the thesis: "Good men build good buildings." The creators and advocates of the "barbarian theory" had already maintained the same principle, their meaning being, of course, quite different from that of the new barbarians. If this ethical theory of Gothic—as the Camden Society interpreted it—had been correct, the English of the period around 1840 would have had to be exceedingly bad people. But, as the proverb puts it, they were "estimable citizens but poor fiddlers." They confused ethics with aesthetics and like Pugin believed in "truth in art." This current of thought did indeed run dry, but it remains excellent subject matter for research into the course of history of ideas, in as much as such phenomena enable us to appreciate that humanity's wrong turnings constitute by far the greater part of history. All false theses live on posthumously in a ghostlike existence.

This shift from aesthetic desires to ethical obligations, so fundamental to the ideas of Pugin and the Camden Society, was continued by John RUSKIN (1819-1900), except that he is much more ingenious at creating half ethical, half aesthetic concepts. His ideas on Gothic are to be found dispersed throughout his works, beginning with the *Seven Lamps of Architecture* in 1849. The word lamp he occasionally glosses himself by "spirit." The designations for the seven illuminating forces are at first glance somewhat obscure, or at least some of them are, such as the Lamps of Sacrifice, of Power, of Life, of Memory, of Obedience. Very few readers would be likely to guess correctly the contents of these chapters. On the other hand the meaning of the Lamps of Truth and Beauty seems to be clearer. An example will indicate the direction of Ruskin's thought. In the Lamp of Truth he discusses truthfulness in life, the concept of fancy, which differs from lying (thus saving the existence of art), and deceptions in painting, poetry, and, especially, architecture. Of these latter there are three sorts:

"1st: The suggestion of a mode of structure or support, other than the true one; as in pendants of Late Gothic roofs.

2nd: The painting of surfaces to represent some other material than that of which they actually consist (as in the marbling of wood) or the deceptive representation of sculptured ornament upon them.

3rd: The use of cast or machine-made ornament of any kind."[15]

Gothic is accordingly exemplary, for: "In the vaulting of a Gothic roof it is not deceit to throw the strength into the ribs of it, and make the intermediate vault a mere shell. Such a structure would be presumed by an intelligent observer, the first time he saw such a roof. . . .

[15] John Ruskin, *The Seven Lamps of Architecture*, New York, 1849, p. 29.

If, however, the intermediate shell were made of wood instead of stone, and white-washed to look like the rest—this would of course be direct deceit, and altogether impardonable."[16] "But Gothic has itself also committed many an unforgivable offense. The most flagrant instance of barbarism that I remember (though it prevails partially in all the spires of the Netherlands) is the lantern of Saint Ouen at Rouen, where the pierced buttresses, having an ogee curve, look about as much calculated to bear a thrust as a switch of willow . . . it is one of the basest pieces of Gothic in Europe; its flamboyant traceries of the last and most degraded forms; and its entire plan and decoration resembling, and deserving little more credit than, the burnt sugar ornament of elaborate confectionery."[17] It is surprising that he is liberal enough to declare architecture in iron conceivable. "Abstractedly there appears no reason why iron should not be used as well as wood; and the time is probably near when a new system of architectural laws will be developed, adapted entirely to metallic construction. But I believe that the tendency of all present sympathy and association is to limit the idea of architecture to nonmetallic work; and that not without reason."[18] Then come arguments to prove his point, and the concession that iron may be employed as a concealed means of fastening when, for instance, statues are to be put in place, but not as "support." For in the use of iron instead of stone is the destruction of true architecture. (This would seem to contradict the foregoing prophecy.) In the following chapter (XI) the moral concepts of his criticism can be found in abundance: ". . . to be cautious how we approach the utmost limit of lawfulness; . . . the metal . . . if extravagant and frequent, derogates from the dignity of the work as well as . . . from its honesty; . . . so that it is always more honorable and it has a tendency to render the style of architecture both more masculine and more scientific to employ stone and mortar simply as such. . . ."[19] It is perfectly logical with regard to this ethical rationalism that in the above passage the word scientific is also brought into the picture, for in science there is indeed no *modus vivendi* without truth, truth is its sole enduring regulator. But in art? If one wishes to talk of truth in art it means something other than what Ruskin meant. Painting wood to look like marble is not immoral but tasteless, and without going into the whole problematical question of truth in art we may say that it is not the same thing as that with which Ruskin here reproaches Late Gothic.

[16] *Ibid.*, p. 30. [17] *Ibid.*, p. 32. [18] *Ibid.*, p. 33. [19] *Ibid.*, p. 35.

His ideas on Gothic are set forth most clearly in the chapter on the Nature of Gothic in *The Stones of Venice.*[20] This chapter falls into two very different parts, in the first of which he presents six characteristics. In Paragraph 6 he says: "I believe, then, that the characteristic or moral elements of Gothic are the following, placed in the order of their importance: 1. Savageness 2. Changefulness 3. Naturalism 4. Grotesqueness 5. Rigidity 6. Redundance." He glosses these concepts as follows: "1. Rudeness 2. Love of change 3. Love of Nature 4. Disturbed Imagination 5. Obstinacy 6. Generosity."[21] All these concepts are then discussed for many pages, or more properly, they form the point of departure for countless digressions. Only Grotesqueness is dealt with in a paragraph of eleven lines, partly because Ruskin reverts to this theme in detail when he discusses the "Grotesque Renaissance" (Vol. III, Chapter III), partly ". . . because every reader familiar with Gothic architecture must understand what I mean, and will, I believe, have no hesitation in admitting that the tendency to delight in fantastic and ludicrous, as well as in sublime images is an universal instinct of the Gothic imagination."[22] In the other cases it is not always so easy to guess what Ruskin means. He explains the concept of Savageness by means of the following example: "Our modern glass is exquisitely clear in its substance, true in its form, accurate in its cutting. We are proud of it. We ought to be ashamed of it. The old Venetian glass was muddy, inaccurate in all its forms, and clumsily cut, if at all. And the old Venetian was justly proud of it." He concludes by saying ". . . the demand for perfection is always a sign of a misunderstanding of the ends of art."[23] What he has in mind is clear and without doubt fundamentally right, but it does not apply specifically to Gothic; it is true for all styles. Ruskin wanted to point out to the neo-Gothicists how genuine Gothic differed in its effect from the modern cast-iron Gothic of English railway stations. In his explanation of Variety he observes that the Gothic "schools," that is, the local variations, are very different, "not from the mere love of change, but from practical necessities. For in one point of view Gothic is not only the best, but the *only rational* architecture, as being that

[20] In Vol. II, Ch. 6. The first edition of Vol. I, 1851, of Vols. II and III, 1853. Survey of John Ruskin's works in the edition by L. March Phillips (Everyman's Library), London and New York, 1907, p. 141.

[21] Ruskin in the fourth edition from 1886, Vol. II, p. 154. In the edition by Philipps, 1907, p. 141.

[22] *Ibid.*, II, p. 203. See III, pp. 112ff.

[23] *Ibid.*, pp. 153 and 156.

which can fit itself most easily to all services vulgar or noble."[24] Would anyone expect these remarks to come under the heading of "variety"? The recommendation of Gothic as rational was for that day a *good* recommendation: in the romantic period Gothic was championed because it was irrational, but now for the opposite reason. There is no need to discuss further these six concepts that Ruskin calls "moral or imaginative elements." They are characterized by utter vagueness and dilettantism, and in consequence attracted a wide public.

More interesting is the second part of the chapter, beginning with Paragraph 80: "There have been made lately many subtile and ingenious endeavours to base the definition of Gothic form entirely upon the roof-vaulting; endeavours which are both forced and futile: for many of the best Gothic buildings in the world have roofs of timber, which have no more connection with the main structure of the walls of the edifice than a hat has with that of the head it protects; and other Gothic buildings are merely enclosures of spaces, as ramparts and walls, or enclosures of gardens or cloisters, and have no roofs at all . . . a flat lintel from pillar to pillar is Grecian, a round arch Norman or Romanesque and a pointed arch Gothic."[25] Now he undertakes to discuss the pointed arch and establishes, surprisingly enough, a genetic connection between the pointed arch and the gable, which consists of two beams inclined toward each other—exactly as Saunders (1811) and Costenoble (1812) had done before him. Then, however, he considers the combination of arch and gable, stressing the chief types with keen insight. The comparison of classical Gothic and Late Gothic leads him to the distinction between "surfaces and lines" (Paragraph 102); his heart is with the surfaces, by which is meant that treatment of the surface by means of (foliated) ornament through which this surface is made perceptible as an integral whole. His High Gothic example is taken from Italian Gothic in Verona, his Late Gothic from Abbéville. "The one from Abbéville, though it contains much floral work of the crisp Northern kind in its finial and crockets, yet depends for all its effect on the various patterns of foliation with which its spaces are filled; and it is so cut through and through that it is hardly stronger than a piece of lace: whereas the pinnacle from Verona depends for its effect on one broad mass of shadow boldly shaped into the trefoil in its bearing arch . . . and its surface of stone is unpierced, and kept in broad light. . . ."[26] This Veronese manner

[24] *Ibid.*, p. 163. [25] *Ibid.*, p. 190. [26] *Ibid.*, p. 207.

has, moreover, the great advantage of being also more durable! Ruskin obviously recognizes the stylistic change very clearly, but is still convinced as a matter of principle that one not only *can* sit in judgment on it but *should*, and that *he* is capable of distinguishing the better from the poorer—on the basis of his particular moral code. It is pharisaism carried over into the history of art. All the artists whom he criticizes unfavorably were apparently immoral people, or at least less moral than Ruskin.

This, however, does not change the fact that Ruskin, both in love and hate, had much to say that is interesting when stripped of all partisanship. Thus his remarks on the Gothic palaces of Venice in Chapter VII and the Palace of the Doges in Chapter VIII, the latter a detailed monograph, may still be of interest even today.

But just as Ruskin rejects the new insight regarding the ribbed vault, with which we shall presently become acquainted—in whatever form he may have come to know of it—so his whole conception of the subject is two-dimensional. He does not see the significance of ribbed vaulting because he is not properly aware of the three-dimensional interior; his interest always remains fixed on the two-dimensional surfaces. His counterargument may have sounded appealing, but it is superficial (in the figurative sense). Despite Ruskin, Gothic is derived from the ribbed vault—for Reims Cathedral would of course still be Gothic even if its roof were to burn and all its vaults collapse, and, equally, many buildings are Gothic even without vaults, once, however, the vaults had given rise to Gothic.

Ruskin popularized architectural history and now people journeyed to Venice. Clark notes that a hundred years ago, when Venice was still free from tourists, picture postcards, and motorboats, a man like Gibbon could write: "Of all the towns in Italy I am the least satisfied with Venice's old and in general ill-built houses, ruined pictures, and stinking ditches dignified with the pompous denomination of canals . . . and a large square decorated with the worst architecture I ever saw."[27] One sees how inclined men are to shape their opinions according to what someone praises—and Ruskin praised in spirited and beautiful English. Is there a monument to him in Venice? The tourist industry owes him one, for Venetian Gothic was made famous by him—as well as overestimated; from the standpoint of his ethical code he ought to have kept to classical French Gothic. Ruskin instilled in the minds

[27] Quoted from Clark, *op. cit.*, p. 267.

of others at least as many bad as good ideas; in his later years he realized this, and the building of the Oxford Museum became his personal tragedy.

George Gilbert SCOTT (1839-1897) picked up Ruskin's praise of Gothic civil architecture, exploiting it in an admirably businesslike way. Ruskin lived for his ideas with priestly and aristocratic disinterestedness; Scott, on the other hand, had no scruples and was perhaps the greatest *fa presto* in architectural history—if indeed his buildings may be accounted architecture. From the year 1845 on, he erected more than 730 buildings; how many more he built in the preceding decade is not known. Thus it is understandable that he should on occasion have telegraphed his office from some railway station or other: "Why am I here?"; or that he once saw on a journey a newly built church, looked at it with interest, and asked who the architect was, only to receive the answer: "Sir Gilbert Scott."[28] *Se non è vero, è ben trovato.* I am concerned here not with Scott's 730 buildings but with his books, and in this field he was, happily, far less productive. As a matter of fact only one of his books, the *Domestic Architecture*,[29] calls for a brief discussion. It was written with reference to Pugin and Ruskin, and represents a further recommendation of Gothic within the compass of the Gothic Revival, for Scott pointed out in an eloquent and engaging style that Gothic was ideal not only for new churches but also for all other kinds of buildings, both rural and urban. He discusses its application to specific parts of houses, and the like, following the classification: windows, doors, roofs, etc., and makes a number of excellent observations that could only come from a man of such great practical experience. The most important thing in this book, however, regarding the question "What is Gothic?" is the statement that Gothic is identical as a style both in ecclesiastical and secular architecture. This is not really demonstrated by Scott, but it is in any case a very stimulating remark, since church Gothic is generally regarded as the real, if not the only form of Gothic. The more comprehensive our knowledge of church Gothic becomes the more difficult does it seem to us to include it all under one concept. This difficulty becomes immeasurable when one adds secular architecture also. Scott thus called attention to a problem that up to then had scarcely been recognized.

[28] After Clark, *op.cit.*, p. 249, who cites Lethaby as his authority.

[29] George Gilbert Scott, *Remarks on Secular and Domestic Architecture Present and Future*, London, 1857.

His later publication is more in the nature of a textbook for students,[30] presenting, with reliance on Viollet-le-Duc, the average conception of Gothic in the period around 1879.

On the whole, the line of development from Pugin to Scott is clearly defined. Pugin had already claimed Gothic as much for the construction of new dwellings as for that of churches; he had already spoken of truth. This movement extended over a period of almost exactly two decades, from Pugin's *Contrasts* in 1836 to Scott's book in 1857. It should not be called neo-Romanticism, for with its pharisaism it is a completely isolated English phenomenon and very characteristic of the England of that time. It was a cul-de-sac.

5. The Rational School in France

IN 1843 Mertens had published his theory about St.-Denis; but who read the *Allgemeine Bauzeitung*? In the course of historical study, however, many facts become so compelling that various investigators must inevitably discover them independently of each other. In 1845 Felix de VERNEILH-Pairasseau (1819-1864) claimed at least northern France generally as the birthplace of Gothic. He took issue with Boisserée, who had said the style originated either in the German territories along the Rhine or in the north of France. No, replied Verneilh, not either/or! "It was in northern France, in French France . . . that pointed-arch art slowly came into being. . . ." In a note he stresses the fact that he had written this before he learned from a book what Wetter and Hope had maintained. "Mr. Wetter thinks that this invention [of the rib] may be attributed to northern France.... Mr. Hope, on the contrary, believes that the honor of this discovery should go to western Germany, and he seeks to refute Mr. Wetter's opinion. The latter, although a German, gives the credit to France, which does not claim it, at least not up to now."[1] From then on

[30] *Lectures on the rise and development of mediaeval architecture delivered at the Royal Academy*, London, 1879.

[1] Felix de Verneilh, "Origine française de l'architecture ogival," *Annales archéologiques*, II, Paris, 1845, pp. 133 and 138 n. "C'est dans la France du Nord, dans la France française . . . que l'art ogivale a été lentement enfanté. . . ." "M. Wetter pense que cette invention (de l'ogive) doit être attribuée à la France septentrionale. . . . M. Hope, au contraire, pense que l'honneur de cette découverte revient à l'Allemagne occidentale, et il cherche à réfuter l'opinion de M. Wetter. Celui-ci, quoique Allemand, accorde cette gloire à la France que ne la réclame pas, du moins jusqu'à présent."

Verneilh asserted the claim, but confined himself to the geographical question without going into the structural system in Wetter's sense. As his source he cites Le Maistre d'Austraing (*On Tournay Cathedral*), apparently having read neither Wetter nor Hope in the original. Verneilh had a certain importance for French archaeology but does not need to be discussed further here. His note helps us to recognize the threads that in those days bound together archaeologists of various nationalities.

Verneilh is overshadowed by his contemporary, Eugène Emanuel VIOLLET-LE-DUC (1814-1879), who was so exceedingly influential as the restorer of Gothic buildings in France and as a theorist of architecture in general. His historical position can best be understood by reading Aubert's article on Romanticism and the Middle Ages.[2] Aubert brings together far more completely than was done here in the preceding chapters everything from the seventeenth century on that led to the rebirth of Gothic in France, and traces the progress of neo-Gothic itself in all fields: in Alexandre Lenoir's Museum in the Couvent des Petits-Augustins (from 1790 on), in literature, in the theater, in historical writings. We should not forget Victor Hugo's *Nôtre-Dame de Paris* and the chapter concerning his views on the conservation of monuments. It was Montalembert who in 1833 in an open letter addressed to Hugo preached a crusade against the vandalism that had set in since the Revolution.[3] Building contractors who made a practice of buying ruins and using them as stone quarries were called "*la bande noire*," and governmental and legislative measures were directed against them. Vitet, who was mentioned earlier (page 113) in another connection, was appointed *inspecteur général des monuments historiques* in 1830. He was followed by Merimée in 1833. Both were members of the Sunday Discussions at the home of the painter Étienne Jean Delécluze (1781-1863), the uncle of Viollet-le-Duc.

Family connections with art created the atmosphere for Viollet's development and at the same time the foil for his opposition, since both his father and his uncle were classicistically inclined.[4] Aubert has listed the most important architects who were then active in the restoration of monuments: Lassus, Boeswilwald, Ruprich-Robert, and others, "and at their head Viollet-le-Duc, whose restorations are titles

[2] Marcel Aubert, *Le Romantisme et le Moyen Âge*, Ch. 2 of the collection entitled *Le Romantisme et l'Art*, ed. by Edouard Herriot, Paris, 1928, p. 23.

[3] *Revue des Deux Mondes*, March, 1833.

[4] Paul Émile Gout has given a vivid account of his early development: *Viollet-le-Duc, sa vie, son œuvre, sa doctrine*, Paris, 1914.

to fame." That was still the general view in 1928; since then there has been a reversal of opinion. Here we must for the present concentrate on Viollet's theoretical writings.

His first articles appeared in Didron's journal.[5] It should be mentioned that in the same volume there was an article by his friend Jean-Baptiste LASSUS (1807-1857), who attacked the equivocation of *ogive* for both rib and pointed arch, as it was used, for example, by Caumont.[6] Clarification of terminology is always an aid in the understanding of the things themselves, as well as a help to mutual understanding in discussions. *Ogive* was restored as the term for the rib alone, in conformity with mediaeval usage.

In his first article Viollet starts out by showing why he rejects the derivation of Gothic both from the Orient and from architecture in wood, asserting that the cradle of the style was rather the Isle de France, Picardy, Champagne, and Burgundy (page 80). The pointed arch, he says, had long been known. It was used in the twelfth century for two reasons: first, because it had more solidity, and builders had learned a lesson from the collapse of so many Romanesque structures that had vaults with round arches (he took this from Caumont); second, however, because in the case of narrow (that is, not square) vault fields, it could be advantageously employed on the narrow side in order to obtain the same crown height as over the wide side, or even the same level as the intersection of the diagonals. This rather exact attention to the geometry of vaults goes back to George Saunders. Viollet-le-Duc had been in Italy for two years, from 1836 to 1837, in order to study classical architecture, but then devoted himself entirely to the study of mediaeval buildings in France. In 1840, at the age of only twenty-six, he was entrusted with the restoration of the Church of the Madeleine in Vézelay.[7] His first exact measurements were those of the vaults in the narthex, and he learned to distinguish not only groined vaults and ribbed vaults but also the various geometrically determinative parts of quadripartite vaults, an inexhaustible subject—or at least one unexhausted even today. As

[5] Viollet-le-Duc, "De la construction des edifices religieuses en France," *Annales archéologiques*, I, 1844, p. 179; II, 1845, pp. 78ff., pp. 143ff., pp. 336ff. The first section published in 1844 treats Romanesque architecture.

[6] Jean-B. Antoine Lassus, "De l'Ogive," *Annales archéologiques*, II, p. 40. Lassus restored the Ste.-Chapelle in Paris (1839 on), Nôtre-Dame in Paris (1845 on), the Cathedrals of Le Mans, Chartres, etc. Together with P. Durand he published the *Monographie de la Cathédrale de Chartres* (1842).

[7] In the same year in collaboration with Lassus he restored the Ste.-Chapelle, in 1845 Nôtre-Dame in Paris, and without Lassus in 1846 St.-Denis, in 1849 Carcassonne, etc.

regards terminology, he differentiated on the one hand *arc ogive* or *nervure* as the name for the rib, and *courbe ogive* or *tiers points* as the name for the pointed arch.[8] The narthex of the Church of the Madeleine in Vézelay has two ribbed vaults in addition to the other (fourteen) groined vaults. The nave vaults are supported by galleries, which extend to a considerable height (the so-called "*Emporenhalle*" or galleried hall).[9] The lighting was not rendered inadequate by this arrangement because the narthex has only three bays and so obtains enough light from the west window. Viollet-le-Duc concluded, therefore, that the problem of Gothic was to solve the question of vaulting the *basilica*. From then on (until even after Dehio) the thesis was handed down in the historiography of Gothic that the real subject matter of Gothic was chiefly connected with the basilica, i.e. nave with clerestory.

After discussing the *geometrical* question, Viollet-le-Duc takes up in his second article the question of *technique*, the building up of the masonry of the vaults. Romanesque vaults, he says, were poured onto a previously erected wooden shell, they consisted namely of rubble in a copious mass of mortar. When the latter had hardened, the wooden scaffolding could be removed. The author goes on to his third point, to *statics*, putting forward the thesis that the transverse arches were *elastic* and thus could yield in the case of any movement of the foundation or settling of the walls or piers, and find their new form. (This is incorrect, or is at least expressed inexactly, for the word elastic means something else; but it will be better to follow Viollet-le-Duc's doctrine here without making any criticism, since in any case we shall hear that later from Pol Abraham.) From his first thesis he then evolves the second: that the architect had to endeavor to make the vaults themselves *just as elastic* as the transverse arches. "Then, with an admirable instinct and subtlety of observation, they had the idea of substituting for their wooden centerings, which were necessary in order to build their vaults of rubble and to sustain them until the mortar had dried, centerings of stone that were to be left in place and should carry those fragile groins, the crude construction of which could not be satisfactory; then they built the long diagonal arches,

[8] Later, in the article *"Ogive"* in *Dictionnaire*, VI, *ogive* means nevertheless "pointed arch": "On donne, assez improprement, le nom d'ogive à la figure formée par deux arcs de cercle se coupant suivant angle quelconque." (The name *ogive* is given, inexactly enough, to a figure formed by two arcs of a circle that intersect at any angle.)

[9] Much that Viollet-le-Duc wrote about Vézelay has been superseded. Cf. Francis Salet, *La Madeleine de Vézelay*, Melun, 1848, pp. 59ff.

the groins called *arcs-ogives*, which carry the four triangular cells of the groined vault and make them independent of each other."[10] From then on the ribs were called in technical literature *cintres permanents* and said to "carry." Viollet-le-Duc illustrates his theory by reference to what he had observed in Vézelay. But to our very great astonishment we learn that in this early example (of about 1135) the ribs were not connected at all with the vault itself. Saunders had maintained the same thing about Winchester. Viollet-le-Duc continues: "The diagonal ribs have their extrados juxtaposed to the vault and do not form part of it. By this means the arches can move without pulling the vault with them; and equally the vault can settle without breaking the rib (*l'arêtier*) that carries it."[11] Now, therefore, both the transverse arches and ribs are elastic—according to Viollet-le-Duc—but the vault itself is still just as much of a poured vault as ever. On the one hand, the vault itself can move without influencing the ribs, on the other, the ribs, which are in no way connected with the vault, are supposed to carry! How should they carry when they are not connected with the vault? If they are only "juxtaposed" and move elastically, it must be assumed that in Viollet-le-Duc's view either the ribs slid back and forth beneath the vault (or vice versa), or even that both parts rubbed against each other as they moved. There is then the further question as to why wooden centerings were necessary for the diagonals. As long as complete wooden shells were constructed for poured vaults there was no need for diagonal centerings, or at least no absolute need, because the groin resulted from the intersection of the wooden forms. An intermediate stage of technique (by technique is understood here merely the method of setting up) must be inserted here, the primary determination of the diagonal curve by means of centerings, a thing that Viollet-le-Duc did not know about or forgot, but in any case ignored.[12]

10 "C'est alors qu'ils eurent l'idée, avec un instinct et une finesse d'observation admirable, de substituer à leurs cintres de bois, nécessaire pour bâtir leurs voûtes en moellons et pour les maintenir jusqu'à ce que les mortiers furent durcis, des cintres de pierre qui devaient rester à demeurer et porter ces arêtes fragiles dont la construction grossière ne pouvait satisfaire; c'est alors qu'ils firent ces longs arcs diagonaux, ces arêtiers appelés les arcs-ogives qui, portant les quatre triangles de la voûte d'arête, les rendirent indépendants les uns des autres." (p. 449)

11 ". . . les arcs-ogives diagonaux ont leur extrados juxtaposé à la voûte, et non point engagé. Par ce moyen, les arcs peuvent faire un mouvement sans entraîner la voûte avec eux; de même la voûte peut se fendre, sans rompre l'arêtier qui la porte." (p. 444)

12 The diagonal arches were needed for the wooden shell as soon as the older fashion of building first a semicircular barrel vault and then joining to it the two transverse cells was abandoned. This method of building the scaffolding resulted, of course, in ellipses or other curves. If the groins were to be segmental or semicircular in form, it was necessary to build

But if, after the insertion of a stage where wooden centerings were used for the *groins* (not ribs), we understand why such wooden diagonal arches were introduced at all as a technical aid, we can follow the argument that they were *later* replaced by stone ribs but we do not yet see the reason for it.

Violet-le-Duc, it seems, is of the opinion that as soon as cut stone was employed in the vault instead of poured masonry, the rib was made to interlock with the vault severy, and thus an advantage was achieved. "The four triangles of the vault, which freely rest against these diagonal arches, were already being constructed of small, regular rubble-stones, no longer laid on a wooden substructure but simply built up like a wall to a third of the vault's height; then from this point on constructed on a movable cerce, which was pushed ahead as the work advanced; because each course of stones, having been bound together and forming an arch from the diagonal rib to the wall rib or to the transverse arch, could be left to itself as soon as the last piece was set in place."[13] Viollet-le-Duc is very clear as to the technical process, that is, the actual method of labor, and also knows about the *courbe mobile* (movable cerce)! He used the latter himself in his own practice.

3. *Courbe Mobile* or Cerce (From A. Kingsley Porter, *The Construction of Lombard Vaults*, New Haven, 1911, p. 8)

Nevertheless he says that the doming of the vaults was achieved by heaping earth on the forms. Whether this tale was invented by him is not known, but it apparently makes its first appearance in literature in this place. Yet even those who do not understand the mysteries of vault construction and the techniques of vaulting, or who do not see clearly what Viollet-le-Duc means, and, finally, those who do see but are critical, must all acknowledge that a completely new way of

centerings especially for them. Formerly the diagonal curves resulted from the vault surface; now the converse was true.

[13] *Ibid.*, p. 147: "Les quatre triangles de la voûte, venant franchement s'appuyer sur ces arcs diagonaux, se construisaient déjà en petis moellons réguliers, non plus posés sur couchis, mais bâtis simplement comme un mur jusqu'au tiers de la voûte; puis à partir de ce point, maçonné sur une courbe mobile que l'on avançait à mesure que l'ouvrage se faisait; car chaque rang de moellons étant bandé, et formant un arc de l'arête diagonale au formeret, ou à l'arc doubleau, pouvait être abandonné à lui-même sitôt que le dernier morceau était posé."

looking at the problems of Gothic had been inaugurated, one that goes beyond Wetter's.

That is to say, the emphasis is no longer placed on selecting the essential elements of the "structural system" and demonstrating their aesthetic effect but on maintaining that now everything is *useful.* Thus on this point Viollet-le-Duc is just as much of a rationalist as the English moralists, Pugin, Ruskin, and Scott, however much he may differ from them in other ways.

He says Romanesque architecture is *caprice,* Gothic is *raisonné* (page 339). Every form has its practical purpose. The pinnacles are an important example of this, "which by their weight give the pier buttresses all the stability necessary to support the thrust of the flying buttresses."[14] From this thesis, traceable to Sir Christopher Wren, one would have to conclude that the flying buttresses would give way and consequently the nave vaults collapse if the pinnacles were to be removed. Paradoxically, according to this thesis, the more the piers are weighted down vertically by a superstructure, the thinner they can be made.[15] A splendid example of the utility of decorative forms is offered by the gargoyles. Whereas in modern times, as Viollet-le-Duc says reproachfully, the system for draining off rainwater is hidden, in Gothic it is not only visible but actually emphasized by ornamentation. Yet all the details are carried out with the greatest economy, one of the most convincing proofs of this being the way the stones of the weathering are shaped. One may say that Costenoble was the first to adopt this attitude, but it is hardly likely that Viollet-le-Duc knew his book, and even if he did know it, and his ideas took the same direction, he created an incomparably more perfect theory.

The following passage, typical of Viollet-le-Duc in its dry, expository style, is the most comprehensive example of this rationalism, this belief that all forms and the entire system were the result of utilitarian aims. (See text figure on p. 570 for illustration.)

"[The architects] had the idea of isolating the wall arch E from the wall H (Diagram 2) and laying between them the flagging D that forms the flooring to carry the gutter B. In this way the wall arch E transmitted the whole weight of the top onto the pier G, and the wall H, pierced by windows, carried the balustrade and the projection of the cornice. Between the transverse arch I and the flying buttress K was erected the wall FD, leaving, from F to L, an empty space serving as gallery. The pier G is

[14] ". . . qui par leur poids, donnent aux contre-forts toute la fixeté nécessaire pour maintenir la poussée des arcs-boutants."

[15] The theory that the pinnacles increase stability is also found in Pugin and Costenoble.

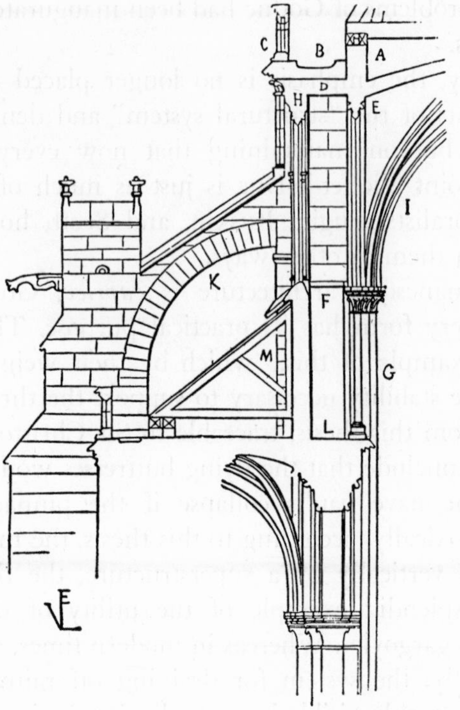

4. Gothic System from Viollet-le-Duc (*Annales Archeologique*, II, p. 348)

almost always monolithic in order to stiffen the construction at this point and to prevent a settling that could be disastrous to the lintel F; because with the principal weight bearing on the pier G, if we suppose it to be constructed in courses, it would settle more than the pier M which supports no weight and is itself relieved by the flying buttress. The lintel F would inevitably break if the pier G were to settle more than the pier M.

This charming construction, so simple and so clear, needs no commentary to be understood; it is full of sense and reason, the drawing alone makes that apparent."[16]

[16] Viollet-le-Duc, *Annales archéologiques*, II, p. 348 "[Les architects] eurent l'idée, d'isoler le formeret E du mur H, d'établir entre eux le dallage D qui forme plancher, pour recevoir le chenau B. De cette manière, le formeret E reportait bien tout le poids du comble sur la pile G, et le mur H, percé de fenêtres portait la balustrade et la saillie de la corniche. Entre l'arc-doubleau I et l'arc-boutant K était élevé le mur FD, laissant, de F en L, un espace vide servant de galerie. Presque toujours la pile G est monolithe afin de roidir la construction sur ce point, et d'éviter un tassement qui pourrait être funeste au linteau F; car le poids principal portant sur la pile G, si nous supposons qu'elle soit construite par assises, elle tassera d'avantage que la pile M, qui ne supporte aucune charge, et qui même est soulagée par l'arc-boutant. La pile G tassant plus que la pile M, le linteau F devra casser.

"Cette charmante construction, si simple, si claire, n'a pas besoin de commentaires pour être comprise; elle est pleine de sens et de raison, le dessin seul le fait voir."

Why then did Viollet-le-Duc explain "cette charmante construction"?

In the fourth article of this series he says: "L'architecture a pour but l'expression d'un besoin. . . ."[17] This is a paraphrase of what was later called *functionalism*,[18] though that term came to imply a demand that the architect should express *only* what was functional, which would of itself then, without any decoration, produce the artistic form. This is not what Viollet-le-Duc means; he has no quarrel with fantasy, with adornment, as long as fantasy is directed toward expressing function through the adornment. It must not be attached irrelevantly; it must be identical with the building's structure. With this principle Viollet-le-Duc created a new basis for the judging of Gothic.

In these articles from the year 1845 he expounded all his general principles with regard to Gothic, remaining faithful to them for his lifetime. In addition, however, he gradually amassed an astonishing wealth of specific knowledge about Gothic architecture, both ecclesiastical and secular, which he published in his nine volume *Dictionnaire raisonné*.[19] Here, however, he was not satisfied with merely pouring out studies of facts but now added a second element to his system of functionalism. The great rationalist had developed an irrational side. One might, after all, suppose that if the whole of Gothic results from statical, technical, and economic causes and from *goût* (which is already irrational), and if the elements that in Wetter were still coordinate are treated collectively under the supremacy of the idea of functionalism —a notion already suggested by Wetter—then nothing more would be left to explain. But beside or behind this idea Viollet-le-Duc now sees *esprit*. His use of this word must not always be understood in the modern sense. *Esprit* in architecture means to him that material is combined according to its nature, that the purpose of the building is fulfilled, that the procedure is economical, the execution good, and the statics satisfactory; thus *esprit* is in the first instance the same thing as functionalism. He says explicitly that these are the reasons why Gothic and not the architecture of antiquity is a model for the purposes of his time. But the word *esprit* has yet another meaning. Wood and stone can be destroyed but *esprit* lives on—that is, in the Frenchmen of 1854, specifically, one might add, in Viollet-le-Duc. Thus the programme of the *Dictionnaire* is not only to give many examples "follow-

17 *Annales archéologiques*, 1846, p. 266.

18 This is already suggested in Pugin and, less definitely, in Costenoble.

19 *Dictionnaire raisonné de l'architecture française du XIe au XVIe siècle*, Paris, 1854-1868, 10 vols. (the last vol. is merely an index).

ing a chronological order" but chiefly and above all "to make known the *raisons d'être* of these forms, the principles that have permitted them, the customs and ideas amidst which they were born. . . . But, all sympathy for this or that form of art aside, we have been struck by the complete harmony existing between the arts of the Middle Ages and the spirit of the peoples among whom they were developed."[20] He then enumerates what would really be necessary to the writing of such a history of architecture—and here occurs the remark already quoted: ". . . ce serait peut-être tenter l'impossible."[21] History of politics and the feudal system, religion, customs, and so on (that tormenting "and so on"!), in short, cultural history, such is the second element, and such are the implications of *esprit*: the history of ideas. It is Alexandre de Laborde's legacy; and it is the problem, still not satisfactorily solved, of whether the development of vaults from Romanesque form to Gothic was an internal affair of contemporary architects or whether there was another force behind it; whether, one may also say, the progress of the development was immanent or was conditioned by extraneous circumstances.

Of all the factors that in Viollet-le-Duc's opinion have influenced Gothic from the side of cultural history, that is, from without, the most important is the passing of all architectural management out of ecclesiastical into lay hands: "It is not necessary to say that this movement was held in check as long as theoretical or practical architecture remained in the hands of the religious establishments. Everything helped inevitably to arrest it: the traditions that were compulsorily followed, the severity of monastic life, the reforms attempted and achieved in the bosom of the clergy during the eleventh century and a part of the twelfth. But when architecture had passed out of the hands of the clerics into the hands of the laity, the national genius was not slow to gain the mastery; impelled to free itself of the Romanesque garment in which it was ill at ease, it stretched it until it burst, one of its first attempts being the construction of the vaults."[22] This repeats

[20] Preface, p. viii in the first edition of 1854: ". . . suivant un ordre chronologique, mais surtout et avant tout, de faire connaître les raisons dêtre de ces formes, les principes qui les ont fait admettre, les moeurs et les idées au milieu desquelles elles on pris naissance. . . . Or, toute sympathie pour telle ou telle forme de l'art mise de côté, nous avons été frappé de l'harmonie complête qui existe entre les arts du moyen-âge et l'esprit des peuples au milieu desquelles ils se sont développés."

[21] Vol. 1, Preface, p. viii (1st ed. 1858).

[22] *Dictionnaire*, 1, p. 145 (in the article "Architecture"). "Il n'est pas besoin de dire que ce mouvement fut contenu tant que l'architecture théorique ou practique resta entre les mains des établissements religieux; tout devait alors contribuer à l'ârreter: les traditions forcément suivies, la rigueur de la vie claustrale, les réformes tentées et obtenues au sein du clergé

the assumption of Vitet and Ramée that in Romanesque times all the architects were churchmen and that all churchmen were conservative and did not really have any *génie national*, whereas in Gothic times all the architects were laymen and all laymen were progressive and full of *génie national*. It is not necessary to criticize this idea further; more important is the recognition that *sociology* was for Viollet-le-Duc the key to the secret of the connection between the development of architecture and that of all other fields. Many people are inclined to see in the more limited question: "What is Gothic?" and the reply: "Gothic is functionalism" Viollet-le-Duc's rational, progressive side, and in the broader question: "How is functionalism to be explained?" and the answer: "By the *esprit des moeurs* and the *génie national* or the *Zeitgeist*" his *romantic* and, as it were, illegal side. Doubtless it had first to be established what Gothic itself was, before the question could be answered, with better success than in the older period, of why—suddenly or gradually—buildings were constructed in the Gothic style. In Viollet-le-Duc both components still stand side by side. In order to determine whether the problem of the history of *art* is to be sought only within the compass of what we can observe from the works themselves or whether we need in addition other knowledge, such as documentary sources, that can be obtained from the history of culture, from sociology, or from whatever quarter it may be, one would have to know what *art* really is: Viollet-le-Duc has not told us;[23] he probably thought everyone knew. Or did he himself not know with absolute certainty?

Two passages reveal approximately what he meant by art: "Architecture is composed of two elements, theory and practice. Theory comprises: *art* in the proper sense, the rules, inspired by taste, descended from traditions, and *science*, which can be demonstrated by unchangeable, absolute formulas. Practice is the application of theory to needs. . . ."[24] The second passage reads: "Architecture is a science; it is also an *art*, that is, the builder needs knowledge, experience, and

---

pendant le XIe siècle et une partie du XIIe. Mais quand l'architecture eut passé des mains des clercs aux mains des laïques, le génie national ne tarda pas à prendre le dessus; pressé de se dégager de l'enveloppe romane, dans laquelle il se trouvait mal à l'aise, il l'étendit jusqu'à la faire éclater; une de ses premières tentatives fut la construction des voûtes."

[23] The *Dictionnaire* contains an article "Arts" but here it is a question of the allegorical representation of the *artes liberales*.

[24] L'architecture se compose de deux éléments, la théorie et la pratique. La théorie comprend: l'art proprement dit, les règles inspirées par le goût, issues des traditions, et la science, qui peut se démontrer par des formules invariables absolues. La pratique est l'application de la théorie aux besoins. . . ." (I, p. 116) This is strongly reminiscent of Vitruvius.

natural feeling. One is born a builder; the science that one acquires can only develop the germs deposited in the brains of men destined to give to brute matter a useful function and a lasting form."[25] In other words, construction, insofar as it can be learned, is science; insofar as it is natural feeling, art. Or is the word art meant here metaphorically? No, for on the same page we read (since Viollet-le-Duc will repeat a remark endlessly): "For the architect, to construct means to employ materials according to their qualities and their own nature, with the preconceived idea of satisfying a need by the simplest and most solid means; to give the thing constructed the appearance of durability and suitable proportions that have been subjected to certain rules imposed by the senses, the power of judgment, and the instinct of man."[26] Thus art is for Viollet-le-Duc that which is produced by the light of inspiration and can never be proved, in contrast to science, which is learned and can be proved. Who can help being reminded of Vitruvius and Mignot's "ars sine scientia nihil est"? And yet Viollet-le-Duc has something quite different in mind.

His *Dictionnaire* is based on the method of classification introduced by Costenoble and Rickman, but though his series of topics is a great deal fuller, the principle of their arrangement is far less impressive than that of Rickman, who began with doors. Viollet-le-Duc began with A and followed the alphabet. He was aware that this was not very profound and remarked himself: "Perhaps our deficiencies have constrained us to give this work the form of a *dictionary*."[27] It is in keeping with his lack of really systematic power that he gradually lost interest in the rib in his ABC.

This point was taken up by his exact contemporary Joseph QUICHERAT (1814-1882), who once again discussed Caumont's improper use of the word *ogive* for both the pointed arch and the rib. In mediaeval usage only the rib may be called *ogive*.[28] Quicherat was a very clear

25 "La construction est une science; c'est aussi un art, c'est-à-dire qu'il faut au constructeur le savior, l'expérience et un sentiment naturel. On naît constructeur; la science qu'on acquiert ne peut que développer les germes déposés dans le cerveau des hommes destinés à donner un emploi utile, une forme durable à la matière brute." (IV, p. 1)

26 "Construire, pour l'architecte, c'est employer les matériaux en raison de leurs qualités et de leur nature propre avec l'idée préconcue de satisfaire à un besoin par les moyens les plus simples et les plus solides; de donner à la chose construite l'apparence de la durée, des proportions convenables soumises à certaines règles imposées par les sens, le raisonnement et l'instinct humains."

27 ". . . notre insuffisences peut-être, nous ont terminés à donner à cette ouvrage la forme d'un *Dictionnaire*." Vol. I, p. x (first edition 1858).

28 Jules Quicherat, *De l'ogive et de l'architecture ogivale*, in *Mélanges d'archéologie et d'histoire*, Paris, 1885, II, p. 74 (first published in the *Revue archéologique*, First Series, 1850, VII, p. 65; VIII, p. 145).

thinker and realized that Romanesque churches should be classified according to their vault forms,[29] but for all his clarity he committed the incomprehensible error of treating the quadripartite ribbed vault as the last of the *Romanesque* types. "The system of diagonal arches to divide the vaults between the transverse arches is, to all appearances, the most original thing that Romanesque architecture has to offer."[30] Wetter had treated the rib coordinately as one element among others, and Viollet-le-Duc did the same, except that he subsumed all the elements under the concept of functionalism. Quicherat raised the rib to first place—and yet did not realize that with it Romanesque comes to an end. In any case, he now sought for the provenience of the rib as scholars had formerly sought for that of the pointed arch. His conclusion was that the rib did not originate in Egypt or Syria or Persia but in the Occident. It was known, he says, from the year 1000 on in the Rhineland, Normandy, and the Isle-de-France; in addition it appeared as an isolated example in Brittany, namely in Ste.-Croix in Quimperlé, which he dates as 1023. St.-Martin-de-Boscherville in Normandy followed in 1059 and in the same year Senlis in the Isle-de-France; in 1069 came St.-Martin-des-Champs in Paris. Today anyone who knows anything about the beginnings of Gothic is aghast when he reads these dates. Quicherat himself soon recognized that they are all incorrect.

The accurate dating of ribbed vaults really became a burning issue when Quicherat took the last step in his considerations: "The quadripartite ribbed vault is something fundamental in mediaeval architecture. It is not exaggerating its importance to say that it is the generating element without which this architecture would not have found its laws or its physiognomy, or attained the originality that we see."[31] Now he calls the earliest ribbed vaults not those of Quimperlé, and so on, but—surprisingly—those of St.-Étienne and Ste-Trinité in Caen, withdrawing this assertion immediately, however, because the vaults of both churches are no longer the original ones. Why then did he not strike out the sentence entirely? Presumably he felt that these restored rib vaults could be regarded as copies of the originals, but

[29] *Op.cit.*, *Mélanges* . . . , II, pp. 92ff., 99ff.

[30] "Le système des arcs en croix pour diviser les voûtes entre les doubleaux, est, selon toute apparence, ce que l'architecture romane offre de plus originale."

[31] *Op.cit.*, p. 498: "La croisée d'ogives est quelque chose de fondamental dans l'architecture du moyen-âge. Ce n'est point exagérer son importance que de dire qu'elle est la pièce génératrice sans laquelle cette architecture ni aurait trouvé ses lois, ni contracté sa physionomie ni atteint à l'originalité que nous lui voyons."

that this was what he had in mind is, of course, only an assumption.

The rib was now recognized as the most important member of Gothic historically. Quicherat saw in it *la pièce génératrice.* Consequently, it could be concluded that a structure with ribs was certainly Gothic, even if it had no pointed arches, no buttresses or flying buttresses. One can now arrange the most important individual members of Gothic in the form of a genealogical tree, corresponding to the scheme already worked out for Wetter. Quicherat did not do this himself, but we may be justified in such a procedure in order to make clear what he and his school meant.

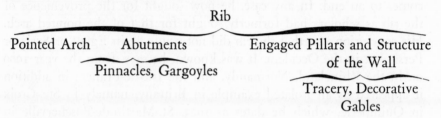

Rib

Pointed Arch — Abutments — Engaged Pillars and Structure of the Wall

Abutments: Pinnacles, Gargoyles

Engaged Pillars and Structure of the Wall: Tracery, Decorative Gables

This is not a complete synopsis, of course, but one cannot go further without imputing to Quicherat modern conceptions. In any case, the genealogical table shows how the forms that are descended from the rib inherited slenderness or thinness, and consequently contributed to verticalism. But these children or grandchildren of the rib inherited functionalism as well; and if Viollet-le-Duc's ideas are also taken into consideration, the biological metaphor can be continued: this whole family of forms was nourished by the spirit of the age, the *Zeitgeist.*

But this new genetic interpretation of Gothic further reveals clearly that the rib is *the* indispensable characteristic of Gothic in its *embryonic* stage. For *developed* cathedral Gothic it is a *necessary* but *not all-sufficient* characteristic; the others must be added to it. For the concept of Gothic as applied to the whole epoch, however, the rib is no longer an indispensable characteristic; it (the grandmother, as it were) need not appear as long as it is represented by its children, grandchildren, or great-grandchildren. This removes the objection made by Ruskin, who had not yet learned to think so genetically.

I cannot date Quicherat's new cognition exactly. The manuscript was not published until after his death, but it is possible to assign the theory itself approximately to the year 1870. In any case, it represents an expression of the general increase in evolutionary thinking, manifested in the field of artistic theory. Darwin's *Origin of Species* had appeared in 1859. Now the theory of Gothic could take its place beside strict natural science. In France, the question: "What is Gothic?" was conclusively answered, at least for a long time. We may anticipate here, and in proof of this statement quote two passages from the end of the century.

André Paul Emile LEFÈVRE-PONTALIS (1834-1904) gave a poetic formulation of Quicherat's thesis in 1894: "All Gothic art is derived from the quadripartite ribbed vault like a grain of wheat that contains the germ of a rich harvest."[32]

Auguste CHOISY (1841-1909), France's greatest authority, beside Enlart, among the followers of Viollet-le-Duc, and the man to whom we owe an insight into the vaulting technique of the Romans and Byzantines, said in 1899: "The history of Gothic construction will be that of the rib and the flying buttress."[33] "The ribbed vault is, as it were, flexible and deformable; the points of support can settle, the piers lean, it will follow their movements."[34] When an expert like Choisy said that, it is no wonder that whole generations of architects and art scholars calmly continued to live and theorize under Viollet-le-Duc's influence, although they must all have known that Gothic transverse arches, ribs, and vaults were not made of rubber. It seems even stranger to us today that all these various portions of theory were combined. To make this clear it is only necessary to go back to the two leaders of French Rationalism, Viollet-le-Duc and Quicherat.

Viollet-le-Duc works with two theories: first, in Gothic everything is functional (the assertion of the elasticity of vaults falls into this category); second, Gothic is sociologically determined. To these is added as a third Quicherat's statement that the rib is the genetic element, thus making three completely different hypotheses to explain one and the same thing. One can assume the reason to have been either that the causes of such a complex phenomenon as Gothic were actually highly complex, or that it was a matter of posing three utterly different questions. In the case of functionalism: what is the essential nature of Gothic? In that of sociology: what is the intellectual background of Gothic, its content? In that of the rib: what is the *formal*, the genetic element?

Viollet-le-Duc's fame was attacked even during his lifetime. It was

[32] Eugène Lefèvre-Pontalis, *L'Architecture religieuse dans l'ancienne diocèse de Soissons au XIe et au XIIe siècle*, Paris, 1894, I, p. 57: "Tout l'art gothique dérive de la croisée d'ogives comme un grain de blé qui contient en germe une riche moisson."

[33] Auguste Choisy, *Histoire de l'architecture*, Paris, 1899, II, p. 259: "L'histoire de la construction gothique sera celle de la nervure et de l'arc boutant."

[34] *Op.cit.*, p. 270: ". . . la voûte nervé est pour ainsi dire flexible et déformable; les points d'appui peuvent tasser, les piles se déverser, elle en suivra les mouvements."

said that his scientifically substantiated restorations of fortresses (like Carcassonne), castles (like Pierrefond), and cathedrals (like Limoges) revealed once again in embarrassing fashion the insolubility of the problem of S. Pietro in Bologna. His exact observance of stylistic detail was felt to be influenced inevitably by his imagination, while changes in the masons' method of chiseling stone resulted in ungothic surfaces. His theories, too, were rejected here and there. The aesthetician Hermann ULRICI (1806-1884), in a note,[35] called attention to the principle involved: to make technique responsible for the origin of Gothic was, he said, a proof of the invasion even of the history of art by the materialistic trend. Ulrici mentions no names, but since he could hardly have meant Semper, he must have been thinking of Viollet-le-Duc. Probably he shared his opinion with all the idealistically oriented aestheticians of his day. But Ulrici failed to see how much of the irrational is mingled with the rational in Viollet's theories, and was doubtless also unaware that his own explanation of the pointed arch as the symbolical representation of the "breaking of all selfish pride and arrogance" could not provide an acceptable substitute for the technical explanations of others, although it was certainly not materialistic.

Criticism of Viollet-le-Duc's ideas from Pol Abraham on is better reasoned and much more radical; we shall return to the subject later. But those who bow to the fashion not only of dethroning Viollet-le-Duc as an architect but also of branding him as a plagiarist with no ideas of his own, a dilettante lacking any real knowledge both of the mechanics of vaults and of history, and even a man of contemptible character forget most unjustly his historical significance.[36] As a restorer he distorted but at the same time saved many buildings; as a theoretical writer he combined his ideas with those of others into a system, and furnished for the critics who oppose him the very garland that they pluck to pieces for their own glorification.

35 Hermann Ulrici, *Abhandlungen zur Kunstgeschichte als angewandter Aesthetik*, Leipzig, 1876, p. 52; for his interpretation of the pointed arch, p. 50. Parts of the book are interesting; for example, the first chapter on ancient and Christian art, which contrasts the two types of art by means of the concepts "plastic" and "picturesque," here connected with the pair of concepts "body" and "soul." The description of the Gothic stylistic paradigm is good (Cologne Cathedral).

36 Only recently Antonia Nava has written an article: "La teoria di Viollet-le-Duc e l'architettura funzionale," *La Critica d'arte*, XXVII, Florence, 1949, pp. 59 and 230. She does not go into the question of the theory of Gothic at all; her use of the word *Romantismo* is tinged with disapproval.

6. The Idealistic Aesthetic of Form and Content in Germany

At a time when the world—in this case, Germany—was already turning away from Hegel, his aesthetic system was belatedly elaborated on a grand scale by Friedrich Theodor VISCHER (1807-1887).[1] Only historians of aesthetics still read these six volumes as a duty; for them Vischer is perhaps almost invaluable, for he represents the turning point between purely idealistic aesthetics and a more modern type. His book seems old-fashioned to the reader of today, as a glance at the table of contents will show. He begins with the metaphysics of the beautiful and then proceeds to the "simple beautiful," a section which falls—as does everything for a Hegelian—into three parts: the idea, the image, the unity of idea and image. Next he discusses the beautiful in the conflict of its phases, that is, first the sublime, second the comic, and third the return of the beautiful to itself out of the conflict of the sublime and the comic. The second volume deals with natural beauty and imagination, the third with the theory of art, and so on. The trichotomy prevails in these chapters also. The whole work is a tour de force in its mastery of enormous masses of thoughts by means of a rigid arrangement, however artificial that may be.[2]

Here only an account of the section on architecture need be given. Architecture, says Vischer, has to do with "basic relationships of inorganic nature"; it is "art's first taking possession of the objective world, it merely draws the first abstract lines through the world of matter." (paragraph 553) It elevates to beautiful form "the structure, erected of heavy material in geometrical lines according to the laws of statics, which serves man as a sheltering enclosure . . . in which process . . . *mensural seeing* is the determinative mode of the imagination." (paragraph 554) The inner soaring of the imagination demands that "gravity shall no longer be an oppressive law but must be so overcome within itself that it . . . will become capable of expressing something infinite; a transformation that gives the appearance of movement to the limit of material, of the line, and manifests itself as the rhythm of the proportions." (paragraph 557) This is intended to apply to all architecture,

[1] Friedrich Theodor Vischer, *Aesthetik oder Wissenschaft des Schönen*, Reutlingen and Leipzig, 1846-1857. The volume that deals with architecture appeared in 1852.

[2] Vischer himself gave up this schematism later in "Kritik meiner Ästhetik" (*Kritische Gänge*, New Series, Stuttgart, 1873, II, 5).

not, for instance, specifically to Gothic. We can understand it more easily if we take into consideration paragraph 561 where he refers to this remark again. "Buoyant life is injected into the relationships of weight; the motionless and silent masses now *seem* to *move*, the lines, rising, flowing horizontally, swinging in circles as they flee and find each other, appear to travel through space; indeed it is as though the ear detected sounds and reverberations caused by these motions, by means of which the tongue even of this most obdurate and unyielding of the silent arts is loosened." This is what Vischer means by the observation that the nature of architecture is the idealization of inorganic matter (a remark repeated on the same page after that earlier statement). But this Hegelian formulation would not lead one to expect the vivid feeling of the lines quoted. In fact Vischer, stimulated perhaps by Kugler, here introduced the concept of *empathy* or *Einfühlung* into aesthetics, though without as yet using the term. "The peoples present in their architectural styles the picture of the cosmos as it *appears* to them. . . . As the spirit of the Middle Ages liberates the various forces of society into harsh, thorny independence, but also into cheerful play, and nevertheless joins them in corporations and sweeps them all along in a common enthusiasm, so in the same way does it fashion an ideal image of the divine universe in its cathedrals." This is a legacy from Schnaase. "We cannot comprehend these obscure relationships . . . more definitely." He rejects the crude allegorical or symbolical explanation by means of numbers and simple geometric figures, referring explicitly to Schnaase. The rest of what he says may be passed over in order to reach the part on Gothic, for he gives a history of architecture, following Hegel in this also, though now making use of more recent research.

Of the Early Christian basilica he says among other things that the eye is perspectively guided toward the altar: "the nave appears as 'the open path to the table of the Lord' [Schnaase]; this is already an emotional trait which, alien to antiquity, now manifests itself in architecture and gives it a picturesque character." (paragraph 587) Since the picturesque is here related to perspective, we should today commonly say "optic" instead. With this should be connected the later remark from Paragraph 593 where he makes freedom turn into dependence (Hegelian) in order thus to praise and blame Gothic simultaneously. "More profoundly considered, that bold vaulting trembles on the very limit of the structural; there is to be sure not such mockery of what is lawful as there where the architectural element is treated not in a grand style but in a subjective manner with sentimental picturesqueness, in the decidedly unjustifiable fashion of mingling the style of one art in that of the other, but there is nevertheless already an approach to within a hairsbreadth of the illegitimate; the buoyant merging of the support in the supported is just on the point not of reconciling the conflict of strength and load but of obliterating it. . . ." Here then Late Gothic is censured because it is *picturesque*, to be which is really not fitting for architecture, and High Gothic, though it is not similarly criticized, is nevertheless seen by Vischer to be approaching to within a grave "hairsbreadth" of the unlawful. This is probably the most interesting passage in Vischer for our subject. His treatment of Gothic itself, in Paragraph 591 and following, is good but hardly contains anything new after Kugler and Schnaase. Worth noting is this remark: "That subjective, picturesquely perspective effect which the basilica already had, and the Romanesque church even more strongly, now finds in this inward or outward radiation [he is speaking of the interior of the Gothic choir] its no longer doubtful goal." And the picture of the course of Gothic is rounded off with a condemnation of Late Gothic, "which is unquestionably arbitrary, definitely flouts structural laws, obviously disorganizes ornamentation, and thus at bottom should really be called manner." In addition to this "lawless trifling" he discovers in it a second characteristic: a tendency "toward greater simplicity, less divided, and toward the horizontal line."

Today it seems incredible that in a history of architecture amounting to seventy-seven pages only five of these should be devoted to the entire field of *modern* architecture (beginning with the Renaissance). Vischer's attitude toward all modern styles is negative. The Italian Renaissance is, he says, uninspired imitation, it then becomes "a passionate and violent play of forms and subsequently a highly developed, feverishly emotional, luxuriant, and thoroughly intricate manner that makes a mock of all structural laws. . . ." It is clear that he by no means condemns Late Gothic alone. Renaissance, which is after all very different, receives just as little mercy, as do Baroque and Rococo. In this list of annihilating aesthetic judgments only Classicism is treated somewhat more gently. "As the violent ferment [of the French Revolution] is clarified into true humanity by virtue of the genuine absorption of the classical ideal, so now in architecture the way is prepared for the pure restoration of the Greek; modern Romanticism restores the Gothic. . . ." Thus with this brief sentence we reach neo-Gothic. Vischer, however, goes on without a pause to the Eclecticism of the nineteenth century, "which now knows, respects, and repeats all styles, and can build in any except its own." It is clear that his value judgments are also completely dependent on Hegel's, while his preoccupation with aesthetic prejudices is typical of his generation.

There seems also to be a connection between that and his condemnation of the picturesque in architecture. He had already decreed this as a matter of principle in the general part of his theory of art where he talks of "style as law of the individual arts." (paragraph 532) One speaks, according to him, of the style of an art or of a branch of an art (instead of saying simply "architecture," "church architecture") "when because of the contrast a strong light is thrown on the technical requirements that result from the intellectual conception, and this is above all the case when the conceptions or processes of one art or of one branch of art are transferred to the other. . . . Bernini treated sculpture in a picturesque way, in the sense of the worst striving for effect; the Middle Ages did this in a different and historically justifiable sense. Architectural style can occupy a place in painting justifiably or unjustifiably, as can plastic style. Conversely, architecture can be treated in plastic or picturesque style, rightly or wrongly. Thus it goes with all the arts, the methods of transference are extremely varied."[3] The subsequent discussion of the kinds of stylization does not make it clear when such stylistic transferences from one art to the other are "justifiable" and when they are not. But we can see how this subject, which had become a matter of interest from Hemsterhuis on (see above, page 436), is handed down from one critic to the other without gaining in clarity, at least for the time.

Vischer is also dependent on Hegel in that he ranges himself on the side of the aestheticians of content. The quarrel over content and form really goes back to the one-sided emphasis of Johann Friedrich HERBART (1776-1841) on the formal element. The most extensive presentation and defense of the theory that in "the beautiful" it is the "how" that counts and not the "what" was given by Robert von ZIMMERMANN

[3] ". . . wenn durch den Kontrast ein Schlaglicht auf die aus der geistigen Auffassung fliessenden technischen Bedingungen fällt, und dies geschieht vor allem, wenn die Auffassungs- und Verfahrungsweise der einen Kunst auf die andere oder des einen Kunstzweiges auf den anderen übertragen wird. . . . Bernini hat die Plastik malerisch behandelt, im Sinne der übelsten Effecthascherei, das Mittelalter hat dies in anderem und historisch berechtigtem Sinne getan. In der Malerei kann architektonischer Stil berechtigter oder unberechtigter Weise sich geltend machen, ebenso plastischer Stil. Umgekehrt kann die Architektur im plastischen oder malerischen Stil behandelt werden, mit Fug oder Unfug. So geht es durch alle Künste, die Übertragungsweisen sind äusserst mannigfaltig."

(1824-1898).[4] Laurilla has written a very good, even though incomplete, account of this dispute among learned factions.[5] It is incomplete because it does not include all the abundant literature on Renaissance studies of proportion, which, as a matter of fact, is also formalistic, yet at the same time revolves about the concept of the *idea*. But if we follow Laurilla, it would seem that the most significant thinkers, Plato, Aristotle, Plotinus, Kant, prepared the way for the posing of this problem, but that neither they nor later philosophers from Herbart and Hegel on had an even half clear notion of the concepts of form and content (or matter, substance). Gothic was not drawn into this dispute directly. Herbart's chief illustration of the principle that "the beautiful" lies only in form, in the relations of the parts, is the thorough bass of musical theory. Of course the formalists also used Greek architecture as an example. Gothic, however, was better left alone. But this dispute nonetheless formed the background for the aesthetics of Gothic also. For since the thinkers were incapable of distinguishing form and content from each other with precision, they understood by "form" not merely the mathematical and purely abstract relations of the parts, but also the parts themselves. Consequently—according to this interpretation of the concept of form—Wetter, with his reduction of Gothic to the quadripartite ribbed vault (together with the pointed arch and the buttress), belongs among the "formalists." On the other hand, Schnaase and Viollet-le-Duc were trying to fathom the idea or the content of Gothic and to interpret its "form" as the expression of this "idea" (Christianity, or, as the case may be, the divinely appointed Christian order of this world).

The convinced formalists like Robert von Zimmermann,[6] may have been soothed on the whole by the pleasant feeling of having solved all problems, at least in principle, but the situation nevertheless remained uncomfortable because the pair of concepts, form and content, could not be made to include everything that clamored for judgment. Not only did the question of ethical values thrust itself upon the attention even of pure formalists—Vischer said derisively that according to formalist theory "the beautiful" could be achieved by grouping toads at harmonious intervals—but it could also not fail to be noticed that "the

[4] Robert von Zimmermann, *Geschichte der Ästhetik*, Vienna, 1858, and *Allgemeine Ästhetik als Formwissenschaft*, Vienna, 1865.

[5] K. S. Laurila, *Ästhetische Streitfragen*, Helsinki, 1934, p. 217.

[6] I cannot, of course, go into details here. The critique by Max Diez, *Friedrich Vischer und der ästhetische Formalismus* (Festschrift der königl. Realanstalt Stuttgart), Stuttgart, 1889, is excellent in its way and dates from the time when the dispute was still a vital issue.

beautiful" was by no means identical with the totality of what was called "art." Unfavorable judgments were, of course, always being pronounced. But what were the bad works of art?—still works of *art*, even though bad. Critics did not say that Bernini's works were not *art* but that they were *bad* art. And corresponding things had actually been said with respect to Gothic from the time of Petrarch on. Now Gothic was indeed recognized, but its "form" was not that of the "beautiful."

On the other hand there was a whole series of other problems. Herbart had already said that the emotional stimulations of "the sublime, pretty, charming, graceful, dainty, decorative, grand, noble, solemn, splendid, pathetic, touching, marvelous" are different from the effect of the beautiful. Other critics, however, saw in them "modifications" of the beautiful. This is the psychological aspect of the problem. We can ask what takes place in *us* psychologically when we contemplate a Gothic structure, as well as what the *objective* cause of this effect is. Does the alternative: here form, here content likewise have anything to do with the psychological state, or does it refer merely to the object? One would suppose only the latter to be possible. But if this is not the case, then the form of *my* feeling of the splendor or the marvelousness of Chartres Cathedral is not after all identical with the form of the cathedral itself. The time was thus bound to come when the growing subject of psychology would take possession of aesthetics.

Herbart differentiated two main classes of elementary aesthetic relations: "their members are either simultaneous or successive."[7] In a cathedral—as in all architecture—all the relations are simultaneous, but we can comprehend them only successively, first the exterior, then the interior, and so on. Which relations of which parts are responsible for the "beautiful" and which for the "sublime"?

Herbart had already protested, finally, against the obliteration of the boundaries between the arts, that is, against that art "which wants to paint in poetry, compose poetry in music, and be musical in sculpture" and against the criticism "that blots out all specific differences, demanding of each art what it *cannot* accomplish and crediting none with what it *alone* can do." This is the Hemsterhuis problem, which could not easily be brought under "form and content," as the age understood these concepts.

Perhaps the whole situation is best clarified by consulting Hermann LOTZE (1819-1881).[8] His book is in three parts; the first gives a his-

[7] Robert von Zimmermann, *Geschichte der Ästhetik*, 1858, p. 782.
[8] Hermann Lotze, *Geschichte der Ästhetik in Deutschland*, Munich, 1868.

tory of general points of view (from Baumgarten, Winckelmann, and Lessing to Lotze's own time), the second a history of basic aesthetic concepts, while the third discusses the history of theories of art. Although there is overlapping of subject matter in all these three parts, the intention is clear. The first part presents the leading authorities, the second discusses the chief classes of aesthetic concepts—thus, for example, the pleasant, agreeable, beautiful, sublime, ugly, naïve, sentimental—and the third poses specific questions regarding the arts, such as are raised by the particular requirements of each art.

Consequently we find in the third part a chapter on architecture. Lotze does not intend to write an exhaustive monograph on the mediaeval styles and his treatment is rather general, but he has some good thoughts. The Romanesque and Gothic styles "seem to me to give the impression that the actually space-enclosing mass of the wall functions as a common substance, out of which the various constructive forces are crystallized at various definite points. . . . Opportunity for such formation was offered partly by the multiarticulation of the interiors, partly by the increasing employment of windows, partly by the outline of the towers; wherever the enclosing wall underwent such a change of function there was an invitation to indicate from out of its homogeneous mass, by means of external form, the forces that were gathering and straining at just that place. . . ."[9] This is based on Wetter and Viollet-le-Duc, but goes beyond them because now here, too, a *genetic* process is assumed. (Gall tried later on to interpret the whole of Gothic from this point of view.)

Lotze makes a number of concessions to the enemies of Gothic. One of its faults is: "the often disproportionate height of the towers and the lowness and narrowness of the portals, by which a misplaced symbolism pointed to Heaven and indicated the narrowness of the road to salvation."[10] He also criticizes "the by no means happy idea of the flying buttress." Verticalism, however, he defends. "Aesthetically there is no reason why the complete expression of this mood is not permissible in architecture, and why those of the Gothic monuments should be preferred that are still organized according to the fashion of the Romanesque style with a distinct emphasis on the horizontal divisions of the whole, though in a clear and pleasing way. The idea of piling story above story is in itself not artistic; . . . an unfavorable impression results from the many stories of Romanesque cathedral towers, which

[9] *Op.cit.*, p. 531.
[10] *Ibid.*, p. 533.

divide the whole mass into individual drums; the Gothic towers, on the contrary, with their masses partly extending up to the very top, partly ending independently and short of it, cause the horizontal planes to appear rightly only as by-products of an effort not intentionally directed toward them." Here again the thing itself is seen correctly and only the critical judgment distorted by prejudices. Thus it is also difficult to understand Lotze's objection to the transference of architectural forms to jewel boxes, armchairs, chalices, and the like, because, as he says, they become "many-towered and gabled miniature buildings." Filarete, on the contrary, was willing to accept Gothic only in that field. But in other respects Lotze is liberal: "That Gothic profiles are blamed for their anti-optic leanness is the result of a general diversity in tendencies of taste, and simply to set less value upon one of these than another would be a mistake of aesthetic theory." In the following passage he acknowledges the influence of the moral ideal of the age, and there is again a mixture of the theory of empathy and form-symbolism: "Characters that recognize the good almost solely in the form of justice and consistency often incline in art as well to severe, harsh, and concise forms, but equally often they indulge an unexpected preference for the melting softness to which they are in actual life utterly alien. And thus we see quite generally in music, sculpture, architecture, and poetry that ages and peoples alternate in their one-sided preferences for the dry and lean or for the rich and full, for quiet and complete motivation or for characteristic surprise, for the hard and sharply etched or for the vague and foreboding." None of these styles is exclusively "beautiful," so that another would be "unbeautiful." Lotze here calls attention to a polarity of development that was undoubtedly recognized before but never yet clearly formulated. He also differentiates distinctly (page 538) between personal and scientific judgment: "To prefer one of these fashions to the other is the indisputable right of individual taste; but aesthetic theory has no right to condemn one of them for the sake of the other."

Consequently, Lotze is able to be just to Gothic from another point of view. He concedes that the simultaneous survey of a whole (as in the Greek temple) is impressive, but remarks that "the Gothic style of building perhaps avoided this effect in order to obtain instead another of no less value." For whereas the Greeks sought lucid, harmonious seclusion, the mediaeval age strove to "erect in its cathedrals an image of the universe that was not completely comprehensible at a glance, but was inexhaustible in its succession of perspective vistas, the unity of which in relation to the whole, although it was never revealed to the eye all at once, still retained perceptual distinctness for the imagination. Once the chief aesthetic idea was placed not on the encompassing unity of a whole, divorced from the outside, but on the inner, infinite divisibility of this whole and the exceedingly many-sided interrelationship of the parts to each other, then that half-concealment of individual spaces is also justified, and a view that encompassed everything at once would be far more chilling than satisfying to the imagination thus tuned."[11] Again an aspect of the phenomenon hitherto only vaguely sensed is here recognized with absolute distinctness (see above Burke, page 405). The concept of *infinity* is joined with that of "*divisibility*" and becomes the expression of an idea that is the polar opposite of the Greek style (in its classic stage) and yet equally justified. But Lotze also expressed himself in the spirit of a future theory of form-symbolism when he recognized a particular kind of form as appropriate to Gothic and its "thus tuned imagination," namely, that of infinity and divisibility, which is the opposite of the entireness and seclusion of antiquity. That, however, was what Schnaase was seeking: the expression of the spirit of the age and of the nation by means of form.

Robert VISCHER (1847-1933) takes his place in this series,[12] specifically with reference to the work of his father, Friedrich Theodor Vischer. His dissertation, which does not relate to Gothic directly, strikes the new note of psychological aesthetics, especially that of the theory of empathy. "We can frequently make the curious observation in ourselves that a visual stimulus is often felt in a quite different portion of our bodies, in a quite different sensory sphere. When I cross a hot street in the glare of the sun and put on dark blue glasses, I always have immediately the momentary impression that my skin is cooled." Other examples are: "strident" colors, oppressive ceilings, and the like. By way of sundry intermediate considerations this leads to the concept of empathy, *Einfühlung*.

11 ". . . in seinen Domen ein Bild des Universums aufzurichten, das mit einem Blick nicht vollständig übersehbar, sondern unerschöpflich in einem Wechsel perspektivischer Durchsichten war, deren Einheit zum Ganzen, obgleich sie nie dem Blick auf einmal vorlag, dennoch für die Phantasie noch sinnliche Deutlichkeit behielt. Wo einmal der ästhetische Hauptgedanke nicht in die umfassende Einheit eines sich von aussen abschliessenden Ganzen, sondern in die innere unendliche Teilbarkeit desselben und die höchst vielseitige Beziehbarkeit der Teile aufeinander gelegt ist, da ist auch jene halbe Verdeckung der einzelnen Räume für einander gerechtfertigt und ein Anblick, der Alles auf einmal umfasste, würde die so gestimmte Phantasie noch mehr erkälten als befriedigen."

12 Robert Vischer, *Über das optische Formgefühl. Ein Beitrag zur Ästhetik*, Leipzig, 1873 (reprinted in R. Vischer, *Drei Schriften zum ästhetischen Formproblem*, Halle, 1927).

The word *Einfühlung* itself is considerably older and seems to have occurred first in Novalis: "Thus no one will comprehend nature who . . . does not, as though spontaneously, recognize and discern nature in everything everywhere, and with innate procreative joy, in intimate varied kinship with all bodies, merge himself with all natural beings through the medium of sensuous perception, feeling himself, as it were, into them."[13]

Through Theodor LIPPS (1851-1914) empathy became at the beginning of the twentieth century the ruling central concept of all psychologically oriented aesthetics. But here, too, an element corresponding to content was present: it was called association. There seems to be still no complete treatment of the development of these ideas in all their historical complexity. Association was, of course, also a psychological concept, but it can easily be seen that empathy was intended to refer to the formal aspect. This it did not do, in the sense that there could be here any real differentiation, but no one was disturbed, for it was after all no longer a question of form and content but of the psychology of feelings. And yet this was also a way of approaching the objects themselves. In order to feel oneself into them, one had in any case to look at Gothic works more exactly than when it was only a matter of trying to recognize their form and their idea.

It is difficult to find one's way through this phase of the intellectual development of the nineteenth century. Some assistance is rendered by a book by Hermann GLOCKNER (b. 1896),[14] which also contains a long and interesting study of Robert Vischer (pages 168-269). Glockner's leading concepts are rationalism and irrationalism. Analysis into form and content, he says, inevitably calls forth the question of what binds the two together. Generally form is held to be the rational element, but this notion results in confusion. Both form and content can be both rational and irrational. The essential thing is that behind both together there should be a hidden, inner life (Glockner, page 203). Friedrich Theodor Vischer sought to define this as harmony, and thence arrived at the concept of the symbol. Glockner says epigrammatically: "Aesthetics is nothing but harmonics and symbolism combined," and calls Dilthey to witness.[15] His remark, though perhaps correct, is vague.

[13] "So wird auch keiner die Natur begreifen, der . . . nicht, wie von selbst, überall die Natur an allem erkennt und unterscheidet und mit eingeborener Zeugungslust in inniger mannigfaltiger Verwandtschaft mit allen Körpern durch das Medium der Empfindung sich allen Naturen vermischt, sich gleichsam in sie hineinfühlt." Quoted in Paul Stern's *Einfühlung und Assoziation in der neueren Ästhetik* (*Beiträge zur Ästhetik*, ed. by Lipps and Werner, v), Hamburg and Leipzig, 1898, p. 3.

[14] Hermann Glockner, *Friedrich Theodor Vischer und das 19. Jahrhundert*, Berlin, 1931.

[15] Wilhelm Dilthey, *Gesammelte Schriften*, IV, p. 187.

As we have just seen, the dispute about form and content gave rise to many new concepts, the two most important being *empathy* and *symbol*. Whereas the "symbolism" of the church structure calls to mind artificial associations and pious allegories, "symbol" means, since Hegel, something that at times borders on the concept of allegory but, on the other hand, also has to do with that of empathy. Critics felt dimly that the concept symbol must be of basic importance to aesthetics, and their thoughts revolved about it without achieving any real clarity. From the time of Hegel on it acted like a magnet in the history of aesthetics, exercising a strong attraction but never actually being reached because of the manifold obstacles in the way. In the interpretation of Gothic it was not consciously employed, although of course even the hackneyed metaphor of the "forest" really signified the symbolical side: the actual form as an allusion to a particular spirituality. Johannes VOLKELT (1848-1930) has written a history of the concept "symbol" from Hegel to Fechner and his theory of association.[16]

7. The Positivistic Trend

IN THE middle years of the nineteenth century—at least in certain circles—God was once again deposed. This time it was not Reason that was placed on God's throne but merely Natural Science. A new philosophy of art was bound to arise under this new world government; its chief representatives are Semper and Taine.

Gottfried SEMPER (1803-1879)[1] set himself the task of studying the genesis of art, that is, "of tracing in detail the law and order apparent in the process of the creation and elaboration of artistic phenomena, of deriving general principles, the fundamentals of an empirical theory of art, from the data discovered." He does not wish to deal with the actual producing of a work of art by the artist or craftsman or give instruction in art, but he seeks to analyze the genesis of works of art, in other words, their "technique, insofar as this determines the law of artistic development." He protests against any imputation of wanting to give, for example, a history of art, and says expressly that his empirical theory of art or style is not an aesthetic or an abstract theory of beauty. His theory of style "conceives of beauty in a unitary way as a product or result, not as a sum or series. It seeks the constituents of form,

[16] Johannes Volkelt, *Der Symbolbegriff*, Diss., Leipzig, 1876.

[1] Biographical matter in Hans Semper, *Gottfried Semper*, Berlin, 1880.

which are not themselves form, but idea, energy, matter, and means, as it were, the preconstituents and fundamental conditions of form."[2]

That is not all too clearly expressed. But the two stout volumes of Semper's *Der Stil in den technischen Künsten* show plainly enough what his intentions were. Usually his theory is summed up in the statement that art originates from the interplay of practical purpose, material, tool, and method of production. This was not an absolutely new idea; Pugin thought along similar lines. But Semper's particular achievement lay in making "material" the basis of his theory. Each material has specific natural properties. Semper grouped all materials according to certain mechanical qualities, arriving eventually at four technical arts. First, from the mechanics of flexible but tough thread textile art is evolved; second, from soft clay that can be hardened, ceramics; third, from the properties of wood, tectonics or carpentry; and fourth, from those of cut stone, stereotomy or masonry.[3] To the notion of a development conditioned by materials is added a second, the evolutionary concept of contemporary natural science. This idea is, of course, very much older, though it was only then coming into full bloom after the appearance of Darwin's *Origin of Species* in 1859. Semper applied to artistic phenomena the principle of the economy of nature, which operates with only a few basic types, varying and combining them infinitely.

In view of these fundamental ideas, drastically summarized, we should now expect to find Semper evolving the forms of Gothic from its material. It would be interesting to read what he thought about variations in Gothic resulting from its execution in cut stone, brick, or wood, but we find nothing about this subject. The *Stil* was intended to be a work in three volumes, and it is assumed that the third of these was to be concerned with the purpose of buildings. Semper's theory is judged unjustly when it is reduced to the formula of practical purpose, material, and method of production, especially when the first of these is understood to mean something flatly useful. Evidence can be found in his other works for his ideas regarding the derivation of spatial forms from the purpose of the structure. Thus in 1853 he said: "The work of art is a result, a function of any given number of agents, Y=F (x, y, z, and so on)." F, the function, "comprises those *requirements* that are motivated by the work of art itself and are based on certain

[2] Gottfried Semper, *Der Stil in den technischen Künsten*, Munich, 1860-1863, I, p. viii.

[3] He had already published this fundamental part of his theory in 1851: *Die vier Elemente der Baukunst.*

laws of nature and of necessity that remain unchanged in all ages and under all circumstances." By this he means, as he adds explanatorily, motifs or types, for example, drinking cups. But this function that leads to standing types has reference to the "x, y, z, and so on," and the latter he arranges in three groups:

1. Materials and techniques,
2. Local, ethnological, climatic, religious, and political influences,
3. Personal influences of an individual nature, stemming from the artist or the patron.

Probably points 2 and 3 formed the programme of the unwritten third volume. His explanations of Oriental styles give an idea of his method; it derives the form of the Imperial Palace in China, the Assyrian towered structures, and the Egyptian temples from the particular "culture." The Egyptian temple, for example, began with the cage for the sacred animal. The processional routes resulted in the circumvallation, the courtyards, and so on.[4]

Prinzhorn,[5] in his dissertation on Semper, also quotes the following remarks: "In artistic creation the aspect of content is the most important and most decisive." The material and subject of all artistic endeavor is none other than man "in all his relations and connections with the external world as 1. individual (the family), 2. collective man (the state), 3. humanity (the human ideal)." Critics usually confine themselves to Semper's narrower definition: "Style is the conformity of a work of art to the history of its production."[6] It may be questioned how clear a distinction between art and style was really made here. Today, at any rate, we know that style is only one factor of art.

Semper sympathized with antiquity and did not evince much interest in Gothic. As architect he employed Gothic forms only once (in the Cholera Fountain in Dresden in 1843). His phrase about "Scholasticism in stone," however, from a footnote of his chief work, became famous: "The vain effort to enliven it [the Gothic pier] led in the fifteenth century to the architecture of tree branches which was

[4] "Über den Zusammenhang der architektonischen Systeme mit allgemeinen Kulturzuständen," Lecture, London, 1853. "Über den Ursprung einiger Architekturstile," Lecture, London, 1854. Both can be found in the *Kleine Schriften*, Berlin and Stuttgart, 1884 (ed. by his sons, Manfred and Hans Semper).

[5] Hans Prinzhorn, *Gottfried Sempers ästhetische Grundanschauung*, Stuttgart, 1909, p. 33. Cf. also Ernst Stockmeyer's *Gottfried Sempers Kunsttheorie*, Zürich and Leipzig, 1939.

[6] Semper, *Kleine Schriften*, p. 402. "Stil ist die Übereinstimmung eines Werkes der Kunst mit der Geschichte seines Werdens."

the last attempt to breathe life into that Scholasticism in stone."[7] In this context the equation of Gothic and Scholasticism must by all means be taken as a devastating criticism. Only after it had been forgotten in what connection the bon mot originated did the expression acquire a heuristic value: the parallelism of Gothic and Scholasticism was accepted dogmatically as a fact, and reasons were sought to explain this parallelism or even identity.

Semper occasionally made other remarks about Gothic,[7a] and since what he said was later seized upon—not by those of like views, but by his intellectual opposites—it must be quoted here. He is speaking of the Scandinavian churches built of wood.[8] "These churches are not structures of the central type in the Byzantine manner, they correspond rather . . . to a short basilica; but they are such [structures of central type] in the sense of a free grouping of enclosed spaces around a dominating but by no means completely subjugating main space; they are so in the sense of a pictorial principle that was carried over into the stone style, and preserved in the North. . . ." In the Romanesque style after the year 1000 awareness of this principle of buildings of the central type is, according to Semper, "dimmed," but lives on in the secular architecture of Gothic. One would expect that Gothic is in consequence picturesque, but Semper continues in a very different vein: "The picturesque grouping of masses and the lively outlines of our mediaeval cities are Old Norse Romanesque, not Gothic; the Gothic style has passed over them, and with its pointed roofs has impaired rather than embellished them. One will have difficulty in honestly conceding to those gigantic Gothic basilicas, that emerge like whales from the sea of houses, any harmony with the latter and any picturesque or even architectural *distant* effect."[9] Buildings of the central type in the region of the lower Rhine, on the other hand, reveal a conscious employment of the "picturesque-spatial-architectonic principle," and Semper sees here "in many a characteristic detail of lower Rhine-Romanesque style the direct influence of Old Norse architecture in wood; for example, the low and half-enclosed arcades (*Lauben*) or galleries of the Nordic churches, supported by wooden balusters, seem to us not an imitation of Byzantine or Roman arcaded galleries but, on the contrary, the lat-

[7] *Ibid.*, p. 475n. See also 2nd ed., 1878, p. xx: "Gothic building was the lapidary translation of the scholastic philosophy of the XII and XIII centuries."

[7a] The most comprehensive and negative criticism is to be found in the second edition in vol. I, pp. 474-478; flying buttresses are bad, stained glass windows are bad, and so on.

[8] *Ibid.*, II, p. 282 (2nd ed.).

[9] The words "the latter" (*letzterem*) refers to the sea of houses.

ter, as they occur most frequently and probably also earliest along the Rhine and in Lombardic upper Italy, seem motivated by that [namely, the Old Norse architecture in wood] . . . in other respects also the influence of a very developed and early wood architecture on stone architecture may be demonstrable."

This is the germ of the Scandinavian theory of Gothic, which took its place a generation later beside the outworn Saracen theory. It is a good illustration of the tenacity of ideas once they have been introduced that the buildings adduced by Semper as evidence for his theory are never missing later, namely, the churches of Borgund and Urnäs in Norway. Semper had never seen these buildings. His source was a book by Dahl,[10] who had been born in Norway but was living in Dresden as a teacher of landscape painting at the Academy of Art, and thus was personally known to Semper. His slender folio contains little text. The plates offer illustrations of the wooden churches of Borgund, Urnäs, Tind, and Hitterdal, including ground plans and views of interiors and exteriors. Only the church in Tind is dated, on the basis of a Runic inscription that mentions a dedication by Bishop Rainer, who was Bishop from 1180 to 1190. Semper says that Urnäs is older than Tind, and Borgund younger than Urnäs. It is not clear whether he means the series to be Urnäs, Tind, Borgund, or Urnäs, Borgund, Tind. There is also no evidence for his chronology. One can, however, say in general that these churches belong to the second half, perhaps even to the last third of the twelfth century.

According to Dahl's illustrations the church at Urnäs has (or had) a wooden barrel vaulting of segmental-arch form, resting on wooden posts with block capitals and a series of semicircular arches; that of Borgund a wooden barrel vault in a stilted semicircle; that of Hitterdal a low, flat ceiling (probably the result of remodeling). Only the door of the church at Tind with the inscription is shown. There is no relationship at all to Gothic, unless it be the slenderness of the posts. If it were only clear what is to be understood by "low, half-enclosed arcades or galleries of the Nordic churches, supported by wooden balusters"! Did Semper mean the galleries inside or the dwarf galleries outside? The latter occur in Germany (Speyer Cathedral) from 1030 on. Semper obviously assumed the churches of Urnäs, Borgund, and Tind to be quite late representatives of a far older tradition going back

[10] J. C. C. Dahl, *Denkmale einer sehr ausgebildeten Holzbaukunst aus den frühesten Jahrhunderten in den inneren Landschaften Norwegens*, Dresden, 1837. Cf. now: Andres Bugge, *Norwegian Stave Churches*, Oslo, 1953.

to before the year 1000, for, as we have seen, he says awareness of structures of the central type was dimmed after 1000, and he must therefore have believed that the pure types were older. If, however, interior galleries are meant, Semper's remark is even more obscure, for such galleries occurred in the Roman basilicas used for tribunals, for example, in the one built by Vitruvius in Fanum, not to mention even older galleried structures. But it is scarcely important to correct Semper's theses by means of historical criticism; to estimate their effect on the imagination of scholars is far more significant.

Semper continues: "The unadorned, purely functional treatment of the old Norwegian construction of church roofs . . . proves that the lining with boards now hiding them was part of the structural plan from the beginning. Norman carpentry freed itself from this upon its entrance into the Gothic system, and in fact attained its peak in the lands that became Norman, namely, Normandy, Sicily, and England."[11]

This passage is extremely interesting. Semper seems to have realized that Gothic began in Normandy and was in some way related to the tradition of wooden construction, but he was completely confused as to the true connection of events. For a proper insight a great many more penetrating studies were necessary. It must be assumed that Semper knew Viollet-le-Duc's theory,[11a] but that he was either not interested in it, because he swore by antiquity and the Renaissance, or intended to discuss it in the third volume of the *Stil*. Why this volume was never written is not known. It may perhaps be suspected that with his theory of material, as it was formulated in his book *Die vier Elemente der Baukunst* (1851), he had blocked the way to any treatment of spatial forms and their history. His comparison of cathedrals to whales was a "diminution," as least as to evaluation, analogous to Victor Hugo's malicious comparison of Renaissance domes to layer cakes. This somewhat easy, though not entirely unimaginative polemic of Semper's is unfortunately not accompanied by any really clear ideas about what he was repudiating. His "wood" and Scandinavian theory did damage later when it was seriously adopted by other scholars, likewise all too imaginative.

[11] "Die schmucklose, rein zweckliche Behandlung der alten norwegischen Kirchendach Konstruktionen . . . beweist, dass die sie jetzt versteckenden Holzschalungen von Anfang an im Plan des Baus lagen. Hiervon emanzipierte sich die normännische Zimmerei mit dem Eintritt in das gotische System, und zwar erreichte sie diese ihre Blüte in den normännischen Ländern Normandie, Sicilien, England." (*Op.cit.*, II, p. 307.)

[11a] He quotes the *Dictionnaire raisonné*, 2nd ed., I, p. 478.

His attitude toward Gothic should not prejudice us against a proper appreciation of his significant personality and real merits. The reference to Norwegian wooden churches in Semper's works represents only a fraction of his comprehensive mastery of infinite masses of research material. He enlarged the scholarly horizon geographically, ethnologically, and also chronologically by including the art of primitive and prehistoric peoples. He undoubtedly provided the stimulus for subsequent enlargements on the part of Riegl and Strzygowsky. The latter revived the Scandinavian theory; his merits and his weaknesses are similar to those of Semper. It would, however, be unjust to bring Semper down to Strzygowsky's level, for he was a far more substantial scholar.

Our chief conclusion with regard to the subject at hand is that Positivism, too, created a theory of Gothic. It is not surprising that it did not endure. Anyone who really knows how spiritual the background of Gothic actually was will never hope to be able to explain it by theories tinged with materialism.

In Hippolyte TAINE (1828-1893) Positivism takes on another guise than in Semper. The word Positivism should not be weighed too carefully here. Taine was far too fond of philosophy, literature, and history to be devoid of metaphysical interests. His belief that a work of art is conditioned by *race, milieu*, and *moment* of origin is well known. Race, as he used it, is still a modest concept, closely related to geographical zone; milieu is the sociological element, which he derived partly from Comte, partly from Viollet-le-Duc; moment is the historical situation. But these factors did not seem to Taine sufficient, and he gave *genius* its due—which was not mentioned by Semper. Taine had undoubtedly studied Viollet-le-Duc and what he said about *esprit.*

He adduces many examples in order to make his theory palatable to his pupils at the École des Beaux Arts, and thus he talks also of Gothic. He is a clever and, to a certain extent, dazzling writer, but what he says is absolutely unoriginal and shockingly superficial. His whole presentation of Gothic can be passed over in silence; it will suffice to quote only the conclusion. Although, according to Taine, Gothic is bound up with race, milieu, and historical moment, he says it lasted for centuries and dominated all Europe, but he draws no national distinctions, remarking finally: ". . . it [Gothic] set its seal not only on cathedrals and chapels but also on fortresses and palaces, the costume and dwellings of the bourgeoisie, furniture and equipment. In such wise that by its universality it expresses and testifies to the great moral crisis, at once morbid and sublime, which during the entire Middle Ages exalted and deranged the human spirit."[12]

Semper had a large public of readers who believed in technique as the sole road to salvation; Taine had a different, equally large public that hailed Positivism as a release from metaphysics. Not only did Taine achieve an assured place in the history of philosophy, whatever one may think of Positivism, but in those parts of his work that treat of painting he also said many things that were a stimulus to important contemporaries, such as Zola. To architecture, however, he had no personal reaction at all; he merely echoed others in what he felt and wrote. His inability to evaluate this style positively, which in those days indicated backwardness, and his verdict that Gothic was the symptom of a moral crisis may go to show that an adequate relationship to this style presupposes a sympathy not merely for race, milieu, and moment but also for religiosity as the real "milieu" of church Gothic. Positivism, in this case, turned into Negativism.

[12] Hippolyte Adolphe Taine, *Philosphie de l'art*, Paris, 1865, I, I, Ch. 2, Section VI, entitled: La civilisation du môyen âge et l'architecture gothique. The quotation is taken from the end of this section, which merely repeats reproaches, then already outdated, without offering anything new: ". . . elle a marqué à son empreinte, non seulement les cathédrales et les chapelles, mais les fortresses et les palais, les habits et les maisons bourgeoises, les ameublements et les équipements. En sorte que, par son universalité, elle exprime et atteste la grande crise morale, à la fois maladive et sublime, qui, pendant tout le moyen-âge, a exalté et détraqué l'esprit humain."

V. THE STUDY OF ART AS A SCIENTIFIC DISCIPLINE

1. Art for the Eye

ANYONE reading Jakob BURCKHARDT (1818-1897) for the first time is immediately fascinated by his style with its rich vocabulary, concise expression, and at times poetic imagery: the natural and seemingly spontaneous style of a man who was in fact superior in equal degree to his subject and to his public by virtue of the sureness of his judgment. The reader feels that he is face to face with the objects and that he is being helped by a master, occasionally authoritarian, occasionally one-sided in his loves and hates, but always pedagogical.

It was not Burckhardt's mission to make men better acquainted with Gothic. But even if he had said nothing on that subject, he could not be ignored here because his activity was fruitful for the whole field of the history of art and thus, indirectly, for Gothic. He did, however, make several contributions with respect to particular problems of Gothic.

One of his earliest works is the *Bilder aus Italien* in 1837 (which takes us back to the time of Pugin).[1] One should be chary of superlatives, but of all the travel literature on Italy this description is the freshest; it reproduces the immediate effect of that magic by which one is charmed upon entering Italy from middle Europe—at least when Italy was still the old Italy: "diis sacra." The nineteen-year-old author, who did not yet think of himself as a scholar, had Goethe's essay on Strasbourg still echoing in his mind, and used in part the same words: "A noble impression fills one's whole soul; it is as though . . . a joyous, buoyant feeling surrounded you, as though the spirit of the immortal master took you on his wings and bore you up to the blue heaven. And this master was a German. Though his name has been forgotten . . . his work proclaims to this very day as loudly as that of the great Erwin his enthusiasm and his power." Burckhardt, however, is not speaking of Strasbourg but of Milan Cathedral! One should read his whole account, including the scene where he surveys the city and surrounding country from the roof, hears steps on the stairs, and then watches an elderly lady lift a little boy up onto the balustrade as she says to him: " 'See, child, in the distance there, near Voghera, your grandfather fell; he was serving his emperor and was a loyal, courageous soldier.' . . . She hardly looked at anything else and turned back to the stairs. . . ." Here one really has the feeling of the country and the people. The figure

[1] Jakob Burckhardt, *Gesamtausgabe*, I, Stuttgart, 1930, p. 7.

of this heroine, "literary" as the passage is, gives warmth to the entire cold marble structure.

Of riper judgment and more coolly scientific tone is his *Kunstwerke Belgischer Städte* in 1842,[2] a book that is expressly designed to be a guidebook. It is meant to help the traveler en route find what is artistically important in the Belgian cities, and provides at the same time the necessary historical, artistic, and even aesthetic information. In the Introduction there is respectful mention of Schnaase, with whose "Letters from the Netherlands" Burckhardt does not mean, he says, to compete since his aim is a more practical one. The very first building he discusses, the Palais de Justice in Liége, is an occasion for speaking of the "last period of Gothic architecture, one sought, as is generally the case in the architecture of that time, to create effects by means of artificial intersections, but the hollow members are already very predominant, and everything that pertains to the actual decoration, bases, baldachins, and the like, is mannered." The courtyard of this building—on the Vegetable Market—"contains on opposite sides thirteen and seventeen columns with flattened pointed arches, so that the whole forms a gigantic four-sided hall, the vaults of which are industriously still ribbed, while the upper walls [above the arches] are provided with a Gothic, round-arched, blind gallery and over that with rows of windows—but the columns themselves are entirely worked in the style we Northerners very inappropriately call Renaissance." The name Renaissance, according to Burckhardt, is proper only to Italian conditions; in the North nothing that is pure Renaissance has been created. "As the particularly suitable bearer of that fantastic element in Northern architecture there appeared . . . the vegetable ornamentation. . . . Already in the last period of the fourteenth and in the fifteenth century the flowers and foliage of Gothic buildings become more and more wild, overladen, and confused." There ensues the "collapse of Gothic," the allegiance to antiquity. "The sequence showed after only a few decades what must inevitably happen to an architectural trend that wants to live on its own flowers, the ornamentation; the value and significance of all the individual members became confused, and posterity has introduced the term Rococo to describe it. A certain, more recent school also should weigh such facts well before it devotes itself to ornamentation with unhesitating confidence! . . . the whole creates a strangely picturesque effect, to which the large dimensions contribute considerably." This

2 *Op.cit.*, I, pp. 114ff.

warning to a certain, more recent school is characteristic of Burckhardt. He wants to educate and, in fact, inculcate his own aesthetic point of view, just as did Ruskin in his own fashion. How often is this admonitory and exhortative note repeated in his works!

In his description of the church of St.-Paul in Liége he criticizes French Gothic and that of the Low Countries equally because in these lands the style turned too early to the greatest possible wealth of ornament and later, going to the other extreme, carried the ribs of the vaulting down to the ground: ". . . it never found the proper mean, a beautifully membered pier with a capital for each member and a corresponding rib."[3] (page 117) Then we meet even the following: "The purest Gothic is surely always the most lasting." (page 124) We cannot help but wonder whether Burckhardt perhaps knew Pugin's *True Principles*, which had appeared in 1841. He waxes poetic again with regard to the City Hall in Louvain. "Is this really supposed to be a City Hall? Are serious, black-mantled councillors and bailiffs to gaze out of these three rows of overornate Gothic windows?—Oh no!—Come, lovely maids of Brabant with your round faces; adorn yourselves and stand at the windows to the joy of all the Netherlands." Then, however, he continues more factually: "Such wild merriment, such fantasticality, reigns in this façade from top to bottom that one would be more inclined to take the building for a dance-hall or the palace of a gay young prince than for the seat of the sober Hansa." This is unquestionably a more correct judgment than what Friedrich von Schlegel had written about it (see above, page 459).

Burckhardt's views on the development of Gothic, however, were still strangely misguided. The cathedral in Antwerp inspires him to general reflections on the flowering of the style and its second bloom. Here he confines himself chiefly to German Gothic churches, "since the French and English churches of the Gothic period are, despite all their magnificence, of hardly any importance beside the former, because they never carry out the Gothic principle with any consistency; at most, Chartres Cathedral is an exception." Kugler's Handbook did not appear until a year later, and these remarks of Burckhardt show that Wetter's knowledge had neither prevailed generally nor was able to throw light on the development of Gothic in the three chief countries. The specialists in each land knew the history of the architecture of their own coun-

[3] It may be that Lotze was referring to this passage when he repudiated a prejudiced preference for horizontalism. See above, p. 585.

try—at least tolerably well—but they were often blind to the Gothic of other nations.

Burckhardt tried to strengthen his knowledge of monuments in Germany at least, as his essay of 1843 on the pre-Gothic churches of the lower Rhine testifies.[4] Here, too, he adopts the lively tone of the travel diary interspersed with descriptions of landscapes, on the model of what his predecessors Friedrich von Schlegel and Schnaase had offered. One of the first sentences reads: "Numerous white church spires stand out most picturesquely against the slate-cliffs covered with vineyards." The word picturesque recurs several times: the triapsidal ends (St. Mary of the Capitol, and so on) "are always characterized by a great, picturesque richness" (page 292); dwarf galleries "are and remain of the greatest picturesque value as a terminating member." Of the church of the Holy Apostles in Cologne he says: ". . . like a wreath of dark flowers the sombre gallery majestically encircles the front of the apse." Even more important is the recurrence of the word Rococo. The occasion for this is furnished by St.-Gereon's, that "jewel of pre-Gothic art." "And just this splendid monument has been especially sinned against in the detail; there is manifested in it, although with moderation, an element which corresponds in modern art to the so-called Rococo." To this belongs the note: "Rococo, if one will admit the term, always originates where the real significance of the forms has been forgotten but they themselves continue to be used for the sake of effect and, indeed, mistakenly. There is consequently also a Roman Rococo, a Gothic Rococo, and so on."[5]

It was assumed that Rococo here signified what Burckhardt himself later called Baroque and we still call so today, although his explanation is better suited to what is now termed Rococo and, in a more generalized sense, Mannerism in all epochs. It is, however, not so important to decide in favor of a particular interpretation as to recognize the originality of the idea of a typical process that repeats itself over and over in the history of styles. "Gothic Rococo" is, from that point of view, a second and not very happy term for Late Gothic. But, whereas such designations as "Late Antiquity," "Late Romanesque," "Late Gothic," are in each case intended merely to signify the individual style in its later phases, the extension of the concept Rococo to all late periods implies that they have something essential in common, and this recognition was bound to suggest and at some time give rise to the idea that all peak stages of the styles also have something in common. While Wetter,

[4] *Op.cit.*, I, p. 283. [5] *Op.cit.*, p. 293; the other passage on "Rococo" in I, p. 116.

Kugler, and Viollet-le-Duc had discovered in the quadripartite ribbed vault the basic form of Gothic, there now emerged a quite different aspect of style. A structure may be Gothic, but its forms are either employed "in their real significance" or they are used merely "for the sake of their effect." In Burckhardt as in Wetter, an insight of far-reaching importance was proclaimed in a footnote.

In Italy Burckhardt continued his researches into the history of art. Ruskin's *Stones of Venice* had appeared from 1851 to 1853, opening up Venice to the English and inculcating a one-sided appreciation of Gothic and a contempt for Renaissance. Burckhardt's *Cicerone* opened up almost all of Italy to educated people in Germany and pointed the way to an understanding of the Renaissance.[6] From the point of view of the latter, Italian Gothic inevitably appeared inferior, and thus its treatment in the *Cicerone* is correspondingly cool. In the meantime (in 1848) Burckhardt had revised Kugler's Handbook for the second edition and was now as generally well versed in the history of art as the times permitted. He also adopted Kugler's designation "Germanic Style," though this was dropped from later editions of the *Cicerone*. Burckhardt's book had earlier prototypes: in addition to Ernst Förster, whom he cites in the Preface, Goethe. But the latter's *Italian Journey* is a series of letters from the journey itself, even though they are reworked, and the arrangement of the book is geographical. Burckhardt's *Cicerone*, on the contrary, is strung on a thread of chronology or biographies of artists. It is not a travel book but a history of Italian art, treating architecture, sculpture, painting, and the decorative arts in turn and in each case beginning with antiquity and continuing down to Baroque (only in later editions were the discussions of ancient art detached and united). Thus Burckhardt's work led to a presentation of the history of Italian Gothic.

"The invasion of the Germanic or Gothic architectural forms from the North was fateful to Italian art, or, if you will, unfortunate, but the latter was so only for those unskillful artists who would under any circumstances have lacked resourcefulness." (page 113) Thus Gothic was at best "fateful" and in the hands of poor architects a misfortune! Everything depends, consequently, on which architects are declared to be poor. Burckhardt's tone, like that of the Pied Piper entices his read-

[6] Jakob Burckhardt, *Der Cicerone*, Basel, 1855. I quote from the *Gesamtausgabe*, III and IV, Berlin and Leipzig, 1933, ed. by Heinrich Wölfflin, who wrote a valuable introduction giving information about the genesis of the book and about many aspects of Burckhardt's character.

ers to work their way up to the elite of those who are connoisseurs of art. Thus did Petrarch speak also.

"The first Gothic architects in Italy were Germans. It is striking and almost inexplicable that they were able so quickly and almost completely to transform according to Southern principles what they had brought with them from the North. They sacrificed the very essential, the vital principle of Northern Gothic, namely, the shaping of the church into a framework of sheer upward striving forces pressing toward development and dissolution; in exchange they adopted the Southern feeling for spaces and masses, which the Italians trained by them however manifested in a still greater degree." (page 114)

In Northern Gothic there is "too much of the organic skeletal element"; this, Burckhardt thinks, is the reason why so much remained unfinished. Italian Gothic renounces much of this organic framework, hence the flat buttresses and the omission of pinnacles, the Northern development of which "had gone infinitely far beyond the structural requirement of an abutment for the vaults." It also does not employ towers on the west fronts. Burckhardt then discusses Milan Cathedral (page 116), finding much to criticize in every part, both interior and exterior: ". . . the shape of the piers in the interior is a reminiscence of the Northern clustered shafts, but of a senseless ugliness; the bases truly barbaric; instead of capitals whole groups of statues under canopies, the sort of thing that belongs anywhere but there. . . . Milan Cathedral is an instructive example if one wants to learn to distinguish an artistic from a fantastic effect. The latter, which one can experience here undiluted, is prodigious, a transparent mountain of marble brought from the quarries of Ornavasco, splendid by day and fabulous by moonlight, on the exterior and in the interior full of sculptures and stained glass, and associated with historical memories of all kinds—a whole, the like of which cannot be found elsewhere in the world. Anyone, however, seeking an eternal content in the forms and knowing *what* designs were never carried to conclusion while Milan Cathedral was being completed at gigantic cost, will not be able to view this structure without pain." How different is the judgment of Burckhardt at fifty-seven and at nineteen!

After anticipating particular cases of the type of Milan Cathedral he then gives a more or less strictly chronological history and in part merely a list of buildings. His distribution of praise and blame is at times energetic, at times characterized by a wise reserve. Often more general thoughts are interspersed, for example, on page 124: "Tuscan architecture, in the meantime, takes a further, significant step when it transforms the clustered shafts, which it had, after all, never formed in a lively, Northern way, into quadrangular, octagonal, or round piers. The former is without question the more beautiful and the richer, but the latter form is in the present case the *truer*." This Burckhardt explains by the fact that clustered shafts are only justified in connection with ribs. We should prefer to say that the pier without engaged shafts is here more consistent. The word truer verges on both rationalism and ethics, two considerations that play a role in Burckhardt's work, though never in a narrow way as in the case of Pugin or Ruskin. He is, however, still an arbiter of taste of the old school, deciding, like Dante, who belongs in Hell and who shall go to Heaven; Purgatory is also not lacking, that indulgent way he had of meting out limited recognition to certain buildings. As an illustration of this his judgment on the cathedral in Florence may be quoted (page 127): "Anyone who approaches this building with the standard of Cologne Cathedral in mind destroys his enjoyment needlessly. There can be *a priori* no question of strict harmony in a secondary and mixed style like that of Italian Gothic, but within the given limits something peculiarly grand has been here achieved." It is as though he were patting the Florentine Cathedral benevolently on the shoulder: *ultra posse nemo obligatur*. Nevertheless, in this case he is probably right.

Yet Burckhardt's attitude toward Gothic is really not without a certain sympathy. The way he speaks when he condemns outright can be judged from the section in which he discusses Baroque. Here the word picturesque is frequently repeated, but not in a commendatory sense. In Sta. Maria in Campitelli "the forward and backward straining of the wall members is revealed with especial distinctness as a picturesque principle; variety in the lines and strong effects of shade become guiding considerations in direct contrast to all strict architecture." (page 328) As a matter of fact Burckhardt everywhere and at all times demands strict architecture or, as he had expressed it in connection with his discussion of Milan Cathedral, forms having eternal content. Hence his hatred of Bernini: "Bernini's effrontery used the bronze tabernacle of St. Peter's to advance a theory: namely, that the altar is a kind of architecture, all the individual forms of which assume motion. . . ." Because they are important for the further development of the theory of art two more examples dealing with sculpture should be mentioned. In one (IV, page 98), the subject is Bernini's draped figures: "He composes these, that is, quite according to picturesque masses and completely sacrifices their high, plastic value as a manifestation of motifs of the human body." The other is on page 100: "Affect . . . instead of mere being . . . activity at any price. . . ." One finds here and there signs that herald Wölfflin's concepts and aims.

Burckhardt came back to the subject of Gothic when he wrote his history of Renaissance architecture in 1867.[7] He still awards praise with one hand and if not blame, at least a certain restriction of praise with the other. For the fourth time he remarks on Milan Cathedral, now coining the unforgettable phrase: "Renaissance humor's votive offering at the grave of departed Gothic." (paragraph 23) The success of Gothic "was not based here [in Italy] or indeed anywhere on the merits of its decorative appearance; it was victorious as the most effective form of vaulted structure using the least possible material." But to the comparison of Gothic and Renaissance Burckhardt joins a new theory. (paragraph 30) "Gothic architecture was sheer rhythm of movement, that of the Renaissance is rhythm of masses; there the artistic content was expressed in the organism, here it lies essentially in the geometric and cubic relations. Alberti, therefore, does not appeal to sprouting forces that must be individually expressed, but to the picture produced by the structure and to the eye that observes and enjoys that picture."[8] Alberti, according to Burckhardt, thought that "the architect had first learned his columns and entablatures from the painter;—the strongest evidence for the picturesque point of view of the Early Renaissance regarding architectural forms" ("picturesque" is used here in its original sense of "from the painter's standpoint"). In Paragraph 32 we read the following: "Only a later age could recognize the Renaissance as the style of relations in space and surface, in contrast to all that had gone before. The spatial style, which the new era in architecture brings with it, is the excluding opposite of organic styles, a fact that does not prevent it from utilizing in its own fashion the forms created by the latter."

"The organic styles always have but one main type: the Greek that

[7] Jakob Burckhardt, *Geschichte der Renaissance in Italien* (Complete Works, vi), 1st ed., 1867; 2nd ed., 1878; the 3rd ed., 1904, and all subsequent ones supervised by Heinrich Holtzinger.

[8] "Die gotische Baukunst war lauter Rhythmus der Bewegung, die der Renaissance ist Rhythmus der Massen, dort sprach sich der Kunstgehalt im Organismus aus, hier liegt er wesentlich in den geometrischen und kubischen Verhältnissen. Alberti beruft sich daher nicht auf Triebkräfte, die im einzelnen ausgedrückt sein müssten, sondern auf das Bild, welches der Bau gewährt und auf das Auge, das dieses Bild betrachtet und geniesst."

of the oblong temple, the Gothic that of the many-aisled cathedral with towers in front. As soon as they turn to derivative applications of these, that is, to combinations of ground plans, they are preparing to change into spatial styles. The late Roman style is already close to this transition and develops a significant spatial beauty, which then survives to varying degrees in the Byzantine, Romanesque, and Italian Gothic styles but reaches its full height in the Renaissance." Burckhardt's successors adopted the contrast of Gothic and Renaissance as that of organic style and spatial style, but were never able to do much with it.

Schnaase reviewed Burckhardt's *History of the Renaissance.*[9] His opinion was in some respects very favorable, but Burckhardt's reference to Gothic as "sheer rhythm of movement" was criticized as "not exactly felicitous." Schnaase writes: "The word movement is used in a figurative, the word masses in a literal sense, and thus the two cannot be compared. It [Burckhardt's comparison] is also not quite correct architecturally, for 'masses' were unquestionably an essential element in the Gothic style as well, not merely (as is most obvious) in the façades and towers but also in the effect of the interiors and, actually, everywhere. And it is no less true that the Renaissance is not exclusively concerned with masses. . . . The statement, despite its absolute formulation, must be intended, therefore, in a relative sense; in Gothic the emphasis is indeed, although not exclusively, *more* on the 'rhythm of movement,' that is, on the expression of the carrying and supporting by the individual members, than on the larger spatial proportions; in the Renaissance, on the other hand, it is more on the latter than on the particular members. We approach the matter somewhat more closely in another passage where he characterizes Renaissance as the 'style of relations in space and surface' or as 'spatial style' and contrasts it not merely with Gothic but with the other styles." Schnaase goes on to say that the connection between spatial style and organic style (ancient temples, Gothic cathedrals) on the one hand and derived styles on the other is for him "completely obscure." His criticism attacked abstractions that had in fact been written down emotionally without the intention of complete clarification. Unfortunately it was not Burckhardt's nature to reply to Schnaase's critique and revise his own vague ideas.

[9] Carl Schnaase, "Die italienische Renaissance," *Zeitschrift für bildende Kunst,* Leipzig, 1867, pp. 156ff.

Dehio sought to elucidate Burckhardt's obscure remarks.[10] He thinks that the word forces should be substituted for "movement" and that then the statement: Gothic is sheer rhythm of forces; Renaissance, rhythm of masses would be accurate. But even after this correction his approval is very limited and he finally says that it would be preferable to avoid the expression "spatial style" entirely. "In Gothic, view of space [*Raumbild*] and organization go hand in hand."

As is well known, Burckhardt's *History of the Renaissance* is not a continuous history, for he thought it desirable "that in addition to the narrative history of art there should also be an exposition according to objects and categories, as it were, a second, systematic part, such as has been done for the art of classical antiquity from the time of Winckelmann on."[11] This is that systematization, the embryonic stages of which we saw for Gothic in the work of Costenoble and Rickman. Burckhardt's attempt to create a real systematics cannot be called successful. He was also not deeply enough interested in this more philosophical or logical task. But, nevertheless, his example was influential. It was felt that here a duty devolved upon the "scholarship" of art, and in this connection it should become clear that Burckhardt's course was not determined by aesthetics. He sought to approach the works of art themselves, not mere ideas or mere forms, and consequently he was searching, consciously or unconsciously, for concepts that were not aesthetic but had to do with the *scholarly* study of art (*Kunstwissenschaft*). The word sensualism has been used to characterize Burckhardt's tendency. It is unquestionably correct as long as it is not taken to mean the philosophical term but simply implies that Burckhardt stood before works of art as a sensuous man: he "saw." But that does not mean that he thought less than the aestheticians who reflected on form and content. He simply thought more of what he actually saw and sought to define it by means of new general concepts such as those of organic style and spatial style. There takes place, therefore, that shift of emphasis which has already been tentatively mentioned. In Hermann Lotze is found the old series of "aesthetic" basic principles; in Burckhardt a new series begins having reference specifically to the basic concepts of art scholarship.

In conclusion, one more thing must be said in order to do Burckhardt even half justice. His judgment is extremely individual and

10 Georg Dehio, *Die kirchliche Baukunst. . .*, 1901, II, p. 555.

11 In the Preface to the *Geschichte der Renaissance in Italien.*

one-sided, but in the course of his life it becomes more relative: he begins to esteem Baroque and his opinions in matters of taste are no longer personal but historical. That he never really condemned Gothic is probably owing to the fact that in his youth he had still beheld it through the eyes of a Romanticist.

Fiedler and Hildebrand continued and intensified Burckhardt's ability to fuse the intellectual and visual aspects of viewing a work of art into a unified attitude.

One cannot mention these two men without adding the name of Marées. Of the three friends Hans von MARÉES (1837-1887) was the oldest and without a doubt the leading spirit. We know about his theoretical views, however, only through Konrad FIEDLER (1841-1895). Hildebrand, ten years younger than Marées, took over his chief ideas and adapted them in independent fashion to his own field, sculpture. We have observations on mediaeval architecture from both Fiedler and Hildebrand. But Fiedler should not be passed over here for another reason: he inaugurated the era of *Kunstwissenschaft* as the successor to "aesthetics."

His most important ideas were formulated at once in his first treatise.[12] His aim is to get to the essential part, the nucleus, of art. ("Art" in itself does not exist, according to Fiedler, but merely "arts," and of these he considers only painting, sculpture, and, occasionally, architecture.) In order to extract this essential part he first proceeds negatively by pointing out all the things that are not important for an understanding of it. At the head of the list is the aesthetic aspect. Fiedler is the first to introduce the distinction between "aesthetic" and "artistic." Art, he says, is not identical with the pure substance of natural beauty, and he speaks of "aesthetic" rules in contrast to "artistic" rules but without defining them more precisely. Rather, he begins by stripping off all other extra-artistic sides of the work of art: first of all content (that is, such content as is not artistic, for, he says, the artistic interest begins only when the interest in content dies) and then interests pertaining to science, history, or the history of art. A description of form is also not just what he has in mind. "Knowledge of the form of a work of art is still not knowledge of the artistic significance of that form." (page 18) Architecture is particularly

[12] Konrad Fiedler, *Über die Beurteilung von Werken der bildenden Kunst*, 1876. I quote from the edition by Hermann Konnerth, *Konrad Fiedlers Schriften über die Kunst*, Munich, 1913. Cf. also H. Konnerth: "Die Gesetzlichkeit der bildenden Kunst. Eine Darlegung der Kunsttheorie Konrad Fiedlers," Diss., Berlin, 1908. See also Hans Eckstein, Konrad Fiedler, *Vom Wesen der Kunst*, Munich, 1942, especially the introduction.

subject to extra-artistic judgment (page 20). "Instead of undertaking the admittedly difficult task of determining the artistic content of an individual structure, the history of architecture . . . often chooses the easier way of making no distinction between building and architecture and of giving a history of architectural forms but not a history of the artistic quality of these forms." The consideration of works of art as results of a particular cultural life is also external since it touches only a part of them and that not the essential one. Judgments based on religion, morals, or politics he rejects, of course, as unessential—or not touching the "nucleus" of art.

All of this is now contrasted with the positive fact that, in Fiedler's opinion, there is an artistic understanding of the world which is by nature independent (that is, an unlimited, progressive process in the individual and in humanity). The specifically artistic element is bound up with *Anschauung*, by which is meant interested visual awareness. The ordinary man progresses from perception to feelings or concepts and in these perception ends for him. But in the artist it is further developed "as *Anschauung*." "Origin and existence of art are based on an immediate comprehension of the world by means of a power peculiar to the human mind. Its significance is none other than that it is a particular form in which man not only strives but in actuality is forced by his nature to make himself aware of the world." The artist does not imitate (the theory of imitation had been shaken to its foundations as far back as Goethe and the Schlegel brothers). "Artistic activity is neither slavish imitation nor arbitrary invention but a free shaping." *Gestaltung* means formation, not simply of any wild sort, but "artistic" shaping. Every human being has this capacity. The child achieves consciousness of the world by taking intellectual possession of visible and tangible phenomena. But in most cases this immediate perception becomes atrophied and the adult human being "loses the world in gaining it." Only the artist continues on that road: ". . . nothing else can be meant by artistic production but the process of bringing forth the world exclusively with respect to its visible appearance, a process taking place in and for the human consciousness." (page 55) Real artistic activity consists of the continued cultivation of perception: "the production of works of art is only an external result." And thus Fiedler finally arrives at the point of defining more clearly the actual artistic act. Perception on the part of the average man is a chaos of fragmentary, indefinite, fleeting impressions. *The artist intensifies perception* into a shaping of the *necessary*. Clarity becomes identical with necessity, and Fiedler calls this clarification of the visible "cognition" (*Erkenntnis*). We scarcely need to indulge in polemics against this rationalistic side of Fiedler's theory (although there may still be drawing masters and teachers of art who consider this confusion of art and science correct), for it is not vital to his chief tenets. The central point of his theory has been made by some into a dogma while others have not understood it at all, but it is actually simpler than first appears. One should consider what painters and sculptors really do. They create something visible, and anyone who tries to do that encounters certain difficulties, in particular the discrepancy between the model in the atelier and the blank sheet of paper on one's knees. Fiedler is thinking of this transposition with reference to Marées' practical and tragic struggles, though he fixed this transposition of nature to art one-sidedly in the mold of classical forms. But Marées' formulation remains correct: "Not the perfection of the model but the perfection of understanding makes a thing a work of art."[13] One can say that today it is no longer important how far this theory was correct; what matters is merely its splendid intention of fathoming the nature of art in a new way that was without question closer to the real process of artistic creation than all the older aesthetic theories. This way, however, was, in conformity with its age, influenced by what was then called not psychology but psychophysics; and Fiedler's dependence on the general trend toward positivism is demonstrated by the fact that he turned back to Semper when he took up architecture in more detail.

His essay on architecture[14] appeared two years after that on the judging of the representational arts. He first of all devotes some pages to polite praise of everything that research into the history of art had contributed to the knowledge of architectural history, only then to announce his thesis that such study does not lead to any genuine understanding of architecture. One must first determine, he says, what the nature of architecture is. Like Semper, he sees its highest achievement in the architecture of the Greek temple because the latter had freed form, which up to that time had still borne traces of its dependence on the demands of construction and material (he means Egypt, and so on), from these fetters, so that in Semper's words "the work of art makes

[13] In a letter from Marées to Fiedler, quoted in Fiedler's essay, *Hans von Marées*, 1889; cf. Hans Marbach: *Konrad Fiedlers Schriften über Kunst*, Leipzig, 1896, p. 452.

[14] Konrad Fiedler, *Bemerkungen über Wesen und Geschichte der Baukunst*, Deutsche Rundschau, 1878. In Konnerth's ed., II, p. 443.

one forget in perceiving it the means and the material whereby it comes into being and is effective and satisfies itself as form." Expressed in Fiedler's terminology it is a question of the spiritual appropriation of the world when the expression of the material requirements of the structure is submerged in its form: "Only when the structure has become the pure expression of form is the spiritual business of shaping concluded."[14a] But what is this pure expression of form? One understands that when one reads on: in architecture progress is the road from the shapeless to the shaped, the matter to be shaped consisting of "enclosed and covered *space*."[15] In this he follows Burckhardt. On the other hand, he defines "matter" as the requirements of the need, the properties of the material, and technical skill. In this again he follows Semper. And untiringly he rings the changes on the same thought, one which is indeed difficult to express and difficult to understand: matter and construction must vanish while form, which belongs to the spirit, remains; and that form must be found which as the pure expression of *itself* can belong to the spirit as its most peculiar creation.

The consequence of this theory is that Fiedler gives exclusive recognition to Greek temples, the merits of which do not lie, he says, in their *beauty*. No one, after all, can prescribe which qualities are indispensable if we are to call a thing beautiful! Rather: one understands Greek architecture "of the good period" (page 451) when one becomes aware of "how all lines, relations, forms have not been chosen merely for the sake of their aesthetic quality but have been so arranged with firm sureness that all memory of structural condition vanishes, and finally how the material itself, however noble it may be intrinsically, receives a covering of stucco and color in order that it may not assert itself but rather be fit to serve as the expression of something higher." This idea is connected with Semper's proof that ancient temples were totally painted.

The building seems to be removed beyond the confines of material existence and "thus seen, a Greek structure may also appear to be beautiful." This is not the usual meaning of beauty, but a higher, purely spiritual beauty.

Thus the highest goal of architecture is to provide release "from a material and limited existence to the freedom of purely spiritual expression." Is not this formula splendidly applicable to Gothic? Anyone,

14a "Erst wenn das Bauwerk der reine Ausdruck der Form geworden, ist das geistige Geschäft der Gestaltung vollendet."

15 Konnerth's ed., II, p. 443.

however, who imagines that Fiedler would have to answer this question in the affirmative has misunderstood him. Only Greek architecture of the "good period" is perfection. All derivatives—also Renaissance—are degenerate. They are not "*Gestaltung*" but combinations of constituents of form, and so on (page 458). He has something to say, of course, about the arches and vaults of the Romans (page 460) but these do not find favor. A critique of mediaeval architecture follows (page 463): Romanesque, says Fiedler, has shown signs of an independent, artistic development, the first and—until today (that is, 1878)—the last since that of the Greek temple.

From this point of view Fiedler judged Romanesque indulgently, even with relative approval. The diagonal splay of the windows, he says, brings out the strength of the walls, and the wall is likewise so treated on the exterior that its strength is apparent. "The artistic, forming mind . . . removes, as it were, a portion of the uppermost layer, as though only beneath it could one perceive the coherency of the wall." The second layer, too, was occasionally removed in order to reveal the wall in its essence, and ornament luxuriated on the edges that were left. Thus Fiedler gave an entirely new interpretation of the pilaster-strips and round-arched friezes, evaluating this layering of the wall positively as a "one in back of the other." Gothic, however, signifies "one of the strangest aberrations in the history of architecture," for its elements are derived from structural, not artistic needs. The pointed arch was, "as is well known," a means of achieving level crowns above oblong fields, "a clever idea, but an artistic subterfuge." The semicircle was mutilated into the shape of the pointed arch. The result was structural presumption: on the one hand, the structure was made as apparent as possible; on the other, the material was formed in ways that contradicted its nature (page 466).

Where now is the error? In Gothic? Or in Fiedler's theory? Fiedler was inwardly set in the classicistic mold and identified art with a *Anschauung* intensified to the point of clarity and necessity, by which he meant the Parthenon. He did not see that Amiens has its *own* clarity and its *own* necessity; he rejected the pointed arch because it is constructional, obviously thinking that he was here rejecting Viollet-le-Duc. But the latter had not said that the pointed arch *originated* because builders sought to attain level crowns. The pointed arch was already in existence and being used earlier, and was introduced into the ribbed vault for those reasons. What Fiedler objects to in the pointed arch, the constructional element, is true for the ribbed vault but not for the pointed arch when used in an arcade. But these errors are not important. Even though all his concomitant ideas are refutable the nucleus of Fiedler's theory remains: art is form,[16] and this form has its own specific cultivability. It is clear that such an approach concerns only the one half of art, but it was new to talk of form in the way Fiedler did: no longer in Herbart's or Zimmermann's sense or in the sense of an abstract codification of a definite canon of proportions which should ensure beauty, but in the sense of a clarification of "seeing."

Nine years later Fiedler presented his discovery in another long essay.[17] There is no need to discuss his theory of language, words, concepts, cognition. He makes it plain that art is something other than language, concepts, and so on. "We can test our visible possession of the world and constantly win it anew in no other way than by actual *seeing*; no other sensuous means can avail us in this, no touching, weighing, or measuring, also no sort of feeling, thinking, or cognition." (Here even cognition is excluded.) He discusses in detail the results of touching. When we call something smooth, soft, or round the *word* calls forth no tactile impression. A sculptured copy confronts us with exactly the same situation as the original in nature. The sense of sight, on the other hand, can create something new, something different: "by drawing even a clumsy outline we do for the sense of sight what we can never do for the sense of touch; we create something that represents for us the visibility of the object and we produce something new, something different from that which previously constituted our conception of sight." (page 270) This, says Fiedler, must appear to us like a deliverance. Instead of chaotic impressions art creates those that are definite, clear, regular. In consequence art can never be something generally intelligible: actually only artists understand art. But the layman can draw near to them and ascend into the pure world of the realization of being. Art gives to this elite of those understanding it a clarity in the consciousness of reality "in which nothing lives but certainty of being, unfettered by time and not subject to any concatenation of events." (page 365) Thus art becomes a timeless value. It is a second and better visibility. This emphasis on its *timelessness*, however, was no help to *historians* of art.

16 Konnerth's ed., II, p. 443. Followers of Fiedler formulated the principle: Art is shaping (*Gestaltung*). Of course! But what shaping?—Answer: artistic. One cannot advance in that fashion.

17 Konrad Fiedler, *Über den Ursprung der künstlerischen Tätigkeit*, Leipzig, 1887; in Konnerth, I, pp. 185ff.

As might be expected from the aristocratic and exclusive tone of his writings Fiedler was not a popular critic, but his theory became momentous when Adolf von HILDEBRAND (1847-1921) demonstrated it for the field of sculpture.[18] Hildebrand created a new basis for it by taking as his point of departure the statement: "Art is shaping for the eye" and investigating more closely the physiological and psychological process of seeing. The distinction between *distant* image and *near* image, his observation as a sculptor that while at work he experienced near images containing kinetic conceptions though he was really working for a distant image were all combined with his likewise practical experience of the relativity of proportions (a finger that seems strong when seen alone can appear weak if the hand is correspondingly strong), with the result that he arrived at the concept of the form of perception: the artist's business is not to copy the existential or actual form but to transform it into the perceptual form. To apprehend the image in its perceptual aspect is to see it artistically. This was a happy formulation of Fiedler's thesis. Hildebrand further observed that the artist (and in actuality every human being) "reads off" space *from front to back*, a corollary of which was the demand (Fiedler's) that one should think in terms of layers of space lying parallel and *one behind the other*. Relief as well as free standing sculpture in the round must be formed as though everything were included between two parallel sheets of glass. Enough points must lie in the front layer to determine its connection unequivocally. Accordingly, this unity of depth conception is the specific form problem of art, its consecration, and its mysterious benefaction.

At this point Hildebrand gives illustrations from architecture. "The Greek temple offers a perforated frontal layer of space. We do *not* perceive a spatial entity *before* which stand the columns which affect us, but, on the contrary, the columns help to form the spatial entity and the general depth movement progresses through them. Romanesque style likewise develops this conception of relief consistently and independently, interpreting every opening as a perforation of spatial layers situated one behind the other and revealing them by the profiling of the openings." Just what he meant by this reference to profiles is not indicated. Gothic also has profiles. Romanesque profiling differs from Gothic but Hildebrand does not say how.

18 Adolf Hildebrand, *Das Problem der Form*, Strasbourg, 1893; there are several editions. In the English translation of Max Friedrich Meyer and Robert Morris Ogden (New York, 1907, p. 36), the two terms *Daseinsform* and *Wirkungsform* are translated "actual form" and "perceptual form"—or better, "form as it is" and "form as it seems to be."

The dimension of depth, according to Hildebrand, is the disquieting, "tormenting" factor and must be rendered innocuous. Now it has two directions: from front to back and from back to front. The first of these is artistic, according to Fiedler and Hildebrand; the second inartistic. Romanesque is read off from front to back and is consequently good; Gothic, from back to front and it is consequently bad. Thus the mystery of art was now revealed; one had merely to follow the new rule. With his theory Hildebrand condemned certain tombs by Canova in which the figures stand in front of the architecture (the pyramid) in such a way that they seem to come toward us. All such "aberrations" of sculpture were now collected, including those of architecture, and condemned. For the most part the examples were taken from meretricious art, from what is called *Kitsch*, and all the blame was attributed to the principle of "from back to front," even though the faults lay elsewhere.[19] In fact, not only was Gothic damned but also Bernini and many eighteenth-century ceiling decorations, so that the one-sidedness of this standpoint inevitably became apparent. In addition there was the fact that the psychologists criticized Hildebrand's fundamental premises; his theory of vision was superseded. But one decisive thing remained: no one could any longer hesitate to acknowledge that art was actually a *problem of form*. It needed merely the concession that it is equally artistic to read off space from back to front, that is, in the Gothic manner, to neutralize the theory. It could not be a question of dictating which form was permissible, which forbidden, but rather of recognizing that these differences of form are stylistic differences and express different things. Form could not exist for its own sake but merely by virtue of its ability to express the particular meaning of the object. According to this view Robert Vischer's reflections of 1873 had already come much closer to the heart of the artistic mystery, but Hildebrand's practical experience as a sculptor in stone led to a kind of geometry of styles and therefore helped *Kunstwissenschaft* in its endeavor to become scientific. The theory about relief corresponds to the method known in the terminology of Renaissance artists as *per modo di levare*, a penetration of the stone layer by layer. The opposite method of modeling in clay was called *per modo di porre*. Thus it would seem that Hildebrand's theory was not new, though it was completely new for his generation. The *old* distinction, however, had not implied any condemnation of modeling in clay; there were simply two kinds of style.

19 Ludwig Volkmann, *Grenzen der Künste*, Dresden, 1903.

Once again critics fell into the ancient error of confusing art with value and—even more grave—of setting up as the sole artistic value that which they personally regarded as valuable. Although they were not aware of it, they had created *one* tool to use in judging styles; it was now to be hoped that the other appropriate tools would be discovered. Heinrich WÖLFFLIN (1864-1945) took the decisive step in this direction.

In his writings he did not define his attitude toward Gothic in detail, but his method had a universal character and thus was inevitably applicable to the judging of this style.

Wölfflin was at first most strongly influenced by Jakob Burckhardt, but he restricted himself even more sharply to a single portion of the history of art: to Italian, German, Flemish, and Dutch art since the Renaissance, with occasional excursions into the field of antiquity, India, and the Bamberg Apocalypse. He was not much interested in questions of attribution, technique, preservation, in short, in all that museum officials and collectors want to know. Instead he concentrated his thoughts on the conceptual mastery of the subject in the service of the history of forms or of style.

He was, in addition, attracted from the beginning by contemporary psychological doctrines. His doctoral dissertation concerns the psychological question: How is it possible for architectural forms to be the expression of something spiritual, of mood?[20] As can be seen from his quotations he had studied F. T. Vischer, Volkelt, and also Robert Vischer. He was cool toward the latter, although he himself was concerned with the theory of empathy.

Psychology and the investigation of form remained the two chief factors throughout all of Wölfflin's work. His first significant book deals with the beginnings of Roman Baroque,[21] going beyond Burckhardt's characterization of Baroque (in the *Cicerone*) by virtue of the methodical step of presenting Renaissance and Baroque as opposites, though in this a trace of value judgment can still be detected. In the lapidary sentences of the Preface he says: "The dissolution of the Renaissance is the theme of the following investigation." He seeks to recognize the symptoms of decline and "if it be possible, the law in 'degeneration' and 'caprice.' " Since he puts the words degeneration and caprice in quotation marks he no longer identifies himself completely with that

[20] Heinrich Wölfflin, "Prolegomena zu einer Psychologie der Architektur," Diss., Munich, 1886.

[21] Heinrich Wölfflin, *Renaissance und Barock*, Munich, 1888.

traditional, negative valuation of Baroque; and indeed anyone who was seeking in the spirit of the scientific trend of that time to discover a law could not abide permanently by subjective valuations. This law was the periodicity of stylistic history, a development of Burckhardt's suggestion that every style develops its Rococo. Wölfflin merely substituted Baroque for Rococo, in the sense of modern terminology. "At the last moment I dropped the plan of giving also a parallel presentation of ancient Baroque. . . . I hope soon to be able to develop this remarkable comparison in another place."[22]

It was a matter of course that the basis of his stylistic comparison should be the classification of architecture according to its members, as Burckhardt had developed it in his history of the Renaissance. But Wölfflin was no longer satisfied to pair window with window, baluster with baluster, and so on, but by comparing them he wanted to arrive at those characteristics that distinguish all forms of Renaissance jointly from all forms of Baroque. He sought to discover a "deeper stratum of concepts" and found four pairs, placing first that of "linear" and "picturesque." There is a slight similarity to what Vasari had said and all Gilpin had already known, though the formulations are now more precise. The strict architecture of the Renaissance is effective because of what it *is*, the picturesque architecture of Baroque because of what it *appears* to be ("strict" [*streng*] is here synonymous with linear). In the former, physical reality; in the latter, the impression of movement. The old style thinks in linear patterns; the succeeding picturesque style in masses: its elements are light and shade, combined with the obliteration of contour, which was the chief consideration of the linear style. Further characteristics of the picturesque style are: dissolution of regularity, oblique position in contrast to frontal position and symmetry, and, finally, the quality of limitlessness and unfathomableness. Surprisingly enough, however, Wölfflin sets this concept aside as being useless: "I confess that it does not seem to me suitable to make the concept of the picturesque fundamental."

[22] This he did, though limiting it severely to a single topic, in the essay: "Die antiken Triumphbogen in Italien," *Repertorium für Kunstwissenschaft*, XVI, 1893, pp. 11-27. At a much later date Arnold von Salis, in his book, *Die Kunst der Griechen*, Leipzig, 1919, gave a detailed treatment of ancient art from Wölfflin's point of view. Erwin Rohde in his book, *Der griechische Roman und seine Vorläufer*, Leipzig, 1876, referring to Achilles Tatius' novel Leucippe and Klitophon (around A.D. 300) writes (p. 471) about the "barocke Zierlichkeit der Schreibweise des rhetorischen Erotikers" and on page 485 he writes that the character of his style would best be described as Baroque taking this term from architecture. Certainly the father of Wölfflin, the famous Latinist had this book on his shelf and it is probable that the young Wölfflin read it. For this hint I have to thank Mr. Meyer Schapiro.

Instead, he finds three other concepts serviceable for characterizing Baroque: the grand style, mass, and movement. By grand style he meant partly the increasing of the absolute proportions of sizes, partly the simplification and unification of the composition.[23] It is not necessary to discuss these in this place for they have no direct bearing on the subject of Gothic and are mentioned here only as a first attempt on Wölfflin's part to discover concepts useful in *any* stylistic comparison. The statements comparing Renaissance and Baroque as a whole can be considered important: "Renaissance is the art of beautiful, serene being. . . . Every form appears free and whole and light. The arch rises in the purest round, the proportions are ample and pleasing, everything breathes satisfaction. . . . Baroque intends to create a different effect. It wants to grip with effective force, immediate and overwhelming. What it offers is not an even stimulation but excitement, ecstasy, intoxication. It aims at an impression of the moment, while Renaissance exercises a slower, gentler, but all the more lasting effect. One would like to dwell eternally in its precincts . . . Baroque offers no felicitous being, but a becoming, an event. . . ." The general opposites toward which Wölfflin is tending are thus *being* and *becoming*; they include the other concepts as partial notions: rest and movement, the limited and the limitless, and so on. However, Wölfflin did not raise these general opposites above the others but contented himself with the individual characteristics in order to comprehend by their aid the *essence* of the style or, as he expressed it, the *symptoms* of decline. His characterizations are intended to be objective and free from empathy.

In addition to this first task he envisaged a second: to discover the *reason* for stylistic change. He argued against Göller's theory of becoming tired of old forms, Schnaase's thesis of cultural history, and also Hegel's triadic dialectics, taking instead as his point of departure his own dissertation, in conformity with psychology. The architectural style, he says, expresses the mood of the age: ". . . to explain a style can mean only to give it its place, according to its expression, in the general history of the age, to prove that its forms say in their language nothing but what the other organs of the age express." He confines himself to what lies nearest to hand, the forms and attitudes of the human body: ". . . the place of the slender and articulated figures of Renaissance is taken by full-bodied ones, large, sluggish, with swelling mus-

[23] The concept of the *maniera grande* is a theme that can be found all through Wölfflin's works. It borders on the concept of the classical, being at times identical with it, and may be derived from certain ideas of Winckelmann. It has, of course, something in common with the notion of artistic value as found in Marées and Fiedler, but is not identical with that.

culature and billowing drapery: the Herculean." In vividly felt, concise sentences he continues: "Michelangelo has never embodied a happy existence." The same contrast can be established for poetry in Ariosto and Tasso, while in music the situation is analogous. Wölfflin's description is brilliant, but with his analogies an element of uncertainty enters into the question of the "why." It is convincingly demonstrated that the parallelism exists, but does the architectural style change *because* the feeling about bodies has changed? Perhaps this is the case. But why does the feeling about bodies change, not to mention the other factors? Where is the center from which everything is transformed and reconstituted? He gives no answer.

Five years later Hildebrand's *Problem der Form* appeared and five years after that Wölfflin's *Klassische Kunst*,[24] in which he openly proclaims himself a follower of Hildebrand's doctrine. In Wölfflin's book Early Renaissance serves as a foil to Classicism (*Klassik*), so that here also two styles—or two phases of a style—are compared. He was now concerned with a vigorous comprehension of High Renaissance "as Classicism" and consequently discusses its chief masters in the field of painting. A second part of a general nature treats the new attitude (grandeur and dignity in the object represented, in the behavior of persons), the new beauty, and the new pictorial form. Only in this last section is the formal element classified according to systematic points of view. The problem of the reasons for stylistic change can be detected everywhere, though only in the background. The book eventuates in that formal problem: "There is a conception of the history of art [he means his own in the year 1888] which sees in art merely a translation of life into pictorial language and attempts to make every style comprehensible as the expression of the dominant mood of the age. Who would deny that that is a fruitful way of looking at the question? But, after all, it leads only to a certain point, one might almost say, only to the point where art begins. Anyone who puts value only on the subject matter in works of art will manage perfectly well with this conception, but as soon as one wants to measure the objects according to *artistic* standards of value one must turn to *formal* aspects which are in themselves *without expression* and belong to a development of a purely optical nature." This is a declaration of complete allegiance to *Fiedler* and his ideal of a history of art that is a history of visualization. After further considerations

[24] Heinrich Wölfflin, *Die klassische Kunst*, Munich, 1898. In German the word for classicism is *die Klassik*. *Klassizismus* means the somewhat depraved element in antique Roman art and that from around 1800.

Wölfflin concludes by saying: "We have by no means intended this to be taken as advocating a formalistic view of art: light is indeed necessary to make a diamond sparkle." He is of the opinion that the formal aspects of Classicism cannot be derived from the temper of the age, for the general pattern of the representative characteristics of Classicism (clarification, enrichment, concentration of the parts into an inevitable unity) can recur anywhere: ". . . what distinguished Raphael from the older generation is the same thing that under quite different conditions makes a Ruysdael a Classicist among the Dutch landscape painters." Thus Wölfflin thinks that the mood of the age and the representative pattern of art are independent variables.

He persisted in this double track. His book on basic concepts begins with an introduction entitled: The Double Root of Style.[25] "Different ages produce different types of art; the character of the age is crossed with the national character. It must first be determined how many enduring characteristics a style contains before it can be pronounced a national style in the particular sense." (page 8) The one factor must be investigated by means of the psychology of form and will enlighten us as to the personal styles of individual masters, the style of a school and of a people (race); the other comprises the "modes of representation." "Not everything is possible in all ages. Each artist is confronted with particular optical possibilities by which he is bound. Seeing in itself has its history, and the discovery of these optical strata must be considered the most elementary task of the history of art." Critics of Wölfflin have always taken issue with this expression, "a history of *seeing*." It was assumed he meant that the human eye underwent physiological changes in the course of centuries. But Wölfflin was thinking in Fiedler's terms. Seeing in the physiological sense always remains constant but this form of seeing, which is common to all men and thus determines all nonartistic vision, is precisely what is *not* important in art and what must be replaced or *clarified* in art. For Fiedler this clarification was established through the norm of classicism, while Wölfflin saw instead of this norm two polar possibilities. A history of seeing is a history of *spiritual* visualization that oscillates between these poles. In later editions of his book Wölfflin changed the expression taken from Fiedler into a history of *modes of visualization: Geschichte der Sehvorstellung.*

In addition to these two factors there now emerges a further element:

[25] Heinrich Wölfflin, *Kunstgeschichtliche Grundbegriffe*, Munich, 1915.

the *artistic quality* (value). Such values are: "good," "strong," "clear." Early Renaissance did not yet "see" as well, as strongly, and as clearly as High Renaissance.

On the basis of these considerations Wölfflin distinguishes three stages in modern art: Early Renaissance, High Renaissance, and Baroque. In the first stage the insights into the perceptual form (doubtless in Hildebrand's sense) are slowly evolved; the second stage is Classicism; the third, finally, not decline, dissolution, and the like—this is Wölfflin's advanced point of view—but Classicism once more, though of an entirely different kind. It would be arbitrary, he remarks, to say that "the rosebush reaches its peak in the formation of blossoms and the apple tree in the formation of fruit." The word Classicism acquires a new meaning in this context. Not quality in the narrowest sense is meant but the *historical maturity* of the style itself. "Maturity" is here a metaphor taken from biology but applied to the *spiritual* sphere, where it signifies approximately the solution of problems immanent in an evolutionary sequence. The application of this tripartite arrangement to *Gothic* was bound to appear tempting, with Early Gothic as the preliminary stage, High Gothic as Classicism, and Late Gothic not as decline but as a second Classicism, "though of an entirely different kind." Wölfflin himself possibly expressed or alluded to this logical conclusion in his lectures.

The five pairs of concepts by means of which he sought to express the character of the "modes of representation" or the actual stylistic element are well known. He talks of the evolution

1. from the linear to the picturesque
2. from plane to recession
3. from closed form to open form (from the tectonic to the atectonic)
4. from multiple unity to unified unity
5. from absolute to relative clarity[25a]

The linear is synonymous with the plastic; the picturesque, which had been rejected as unserviceable in the book on Renaissance and Baroque, is now rehabilitated. Thus stylistic description was enriched by the addition of five pairs of concepts referring to the formal aspect of a work of art. Only the fifth is applicable to both form *and* content.

[25a] The original terms are: 1) *Das Lineare* und das Malerische. 2) Fläche und Tiefe. 3) Geschlossene Form und offene Form (Tektonisch und atektonisch). 4) Vielheit und Einheit (Vielheitliche Einheit und einheitliche Einheit). 5) Klarheit und Unklarheit (Unbedingte und Bedingte Klarheit).

Many critics thought that in this fifth conceptual pair Wölfflin was repeating what had already been said before. Though clarity is meant with reference to the formal, Wölfflin means here clarity of the objects (*des Gegenständlichen*) and this is no longer solely form but the form of something that has meaning. Wölfflin, of course, came back to the problem of the "why" of development, his last formulation being found in an essay of 1933.[26] "Human beings have probably always seen as they *wanted* to see. The picturesque style . . . has always come only when its hour had struck, that is, when it was understood. But one ought not to demand too much, after all, of the parallelism between the history of visualization and history of ideas in general, and compare incomparables; art retains its specific quality. But precisely in having here produced from the soil of pure *Anschauung* ever new forms of *Anschauung* has it been in a higher sense creative." The last sentence is entirely in harmony with Fiedler's ideas. The preceding one implies renunciation of the attempt to solve the ancient problem, with a suspicion that perhaps the question of why the history of visualization and history of ideas are parallel is wrongly posed. Perhaps the parallelism does not exist and the history of visualization is an independent thread of a special kind in the fabric of culture.

This account seeks to be neutral and not an expression of criticism. But one question must be raised: Did Wölfflin take all sides of art into consideration? Of Gothic he speaks once in passing. In that place he rejects the "morphological" element "as the style of verticalism, pointed arches, ribbed vaults, and so on." These aspects of the phenomenon, consequently, do not belong to *style*. Anyone approaching the problem from Viollet-le-Duc and Quicherat must inevitably ask whether the quadripartite ribbed vault can be neglected when style is under discussion. Or should the "morphological" element perhaps belong also to the basic concepts? Certainly it should. A historical discussion of structural members obviously does not belong in the specific history of visualization, and this limitation of the notion of art prevented the inclusion of "morphology" among the basic concepts.

Wölfflin sought to define differences in *national* styles by the same or similar concepts as for temporal styles. We shall have an opportunity of coming back to this point. He attacked many other problems but in this place only what became an indispensable prerequisite for under-

[26] Heinrich Wölfflin, *Kunstgeschichtliche Grundbegriffe, eine Revision*, Munich, 1933. (*Logos*, XX, p. 210)

standing the subsequent development of views on Gothic may be discussed.

Wölfflin's new doctrine was strongly criticized. Many shrugged their shoulders at such "formalism"; the adherents of the history of artistic personalities endeavored to obtain recognition for their great geniuses and heroes and especially for the lesser figures, talking endlessly about individuality with the watchword: "*individuum est ineffabile*"; museum officials, collectors, and dealers worried about the artistic and economic valuation of particular works of art, for the market value of all early periods seemed threatened; the historians of art were afraid of concepts in any case, and Wölfflin's were too strict for them; the philosophers in turn found them not rigorous enough; the historians also had an innate fear of concepts, which could lead, they thought, only to historical constructions and would be bound to do violence to facts; and a critic who had himself been trained in conceptual gymnastics proved that everything was wrong, writing mollifyingly in conclusion: "Wölfflin's pairs of concepts, however, should not be pronounced entirely without value,"[27] for he had himself invented something quite similar!

This placating tone is found also in other critics of Wölfflin. Schmarsow's books he put aside without comment; Wulff's essay he noted casually, remarking orally that it was commendable when a pupil tried to justify his teacher (namely Schmarsow). Only Hermann Voss' criticism did he answer.[28] His reaction to Voss' book on Late Renaissance painting is revealed in a short article. The opening sentences read: "I am optimistic enough to believe that useful ideas will in time make themselves felt by their own force, and I find it superfluous to run after everyone who is of a different opinion in order to try to gain his approbation. The main thing is that a book is read. What is true in it will take root while the erroneous part that seems to be unavoidable dies out. It is a different matter, however, when misunderstanding has taken possession of a thing, and superficiality distorted the meaning of a book. . . ." The subject of the dispute in this case was the concept of a "history of art without names." Wölfflin affirms that it never occurred to him "to transform the history of art into a history of forms of visuali-

[27] Oskar Wulff, "Kritische Erörterungen zur Prinzipienlehre der Kunstwissenschaft," *Zeitschrift für Ästhetik und allgem. Kunstwissenschaft*, Stuttgart, 1917, XII, p. 221.

[28] Heinrich Wölfflin, "In eigener Sache . . . ," *Kunstchronik und Kunstmarkt*, Leipzig, 1920, p. 397. Hermann Voss, "Künstlergeschichte oder Kunstgeschichte ohne Namen," *ibid.*, p. 435. Wölfflin, "Qui tacet consentire videtur," *ibid.*, p. 457. The first of these articles was reprinted in H. Wölfflin, *Gedanken zur Kunstgeschichte*, Basel, 1941, p. 15.

zation" and he briefly sketches his theses once again. He never implied, he says, that artistic evolution was like the independent functioning of clockwork, and he finds it quite understandable "that the narrative historians should feel distaste for such concepts, which confuse his scheme. However, the matter is not so dangerous. Who expects that on every occasion the ultimate questions as to the 'why' should be discussed?" Wölfflin did not name the critic against whom he was defending himself so condescendingly, but Hermann Voss understood that he was meant, and answered from the standpoint of history of artistic personalities. Wölfflin replied with barely one brief page. Voss had chosen as his title: History of Artists or History of Art without Names. Wölfflin replied that he saw no either/or. To Voss' characterization of Wölfflin's theory as woodcutlike the latter retorted that it was not intended to make understanding easier but to fulfill a particular task, and he implied that without his stylistic concepts scholarly research would have remained a mere collection of material.

From the standpoint of the history of Gothic one could continue to argue back and forth about this debatable question, which is not really a problem. Following the pattern set by Burckhardt, Wölfflin had an antipathy to such discussions. It is not known how many or which criticisms he read. They were probably all sent to him and he may therefore have known Croce's series of articles that Schlosser translated.[29] A generation has since passed. Croce called Wölfflin's lifework "an eclectic experiment in the historiography of the figure arts," probably the most mistaken thing that has ever been said about it. He was consequently of the opinion that the works of Walzel and Strich, which he knew only from a skeptical mention by Vossler, were superfluous; these tendencies, he said, led to a pseudo-history and were long since outdated. Not only Wölfflin would have found it hopeless to refute this criticism, for here it was a question of blindness that cannot be cured. It would have been another matter to attempt to substitute more correct ideas for Wölfflin's errors. But here a fundamental misapprehension was revealed that went much deeper than Voss' "superficiality." For the historiography of Gothic, which was untouched by these debates, an understanding of Wölfflin's trend is indispensable for it overcomes mechanistic theories and points the way to a comprehension of

[29] Benedetto Croce, "Zur Theorie und Kritik der Geschichte der bildenden Kunst," translated and with a preface by Julius Schlosser, *Wiener Jahrbuch für Kunstgeschichte*, IV (XVIII), Vienna, 1926, p. 1; specifically on Fiedler, p. 23, and on Wölfflin, p. 31. Anyone consulting this volume should read also Dagobert Frey's review of Hans Rose's new edition of Wölfflin's *Renaissance und Barock* on p. 203.

the specifically artistic element. It is a symptom of the intensity of Wölfflin's way of looking at the subject that one feels constrained within the narrowest confines of the artistic and at the same time experiences a sense of enlargement to a universalism like that of Goethe, simply because Wölfflin, as he penetrated the mystery of style, developed broad concepts. But precisely that caused offense. Thus even today the tension is still present. Talented scholars of the one type investigate such aspects of works of art as are inherently related to cultural history, others enrich our knowledge from the standpoint of monography and the history of the artists themselves, while some offer both things; but only where Wölfflin's problems are touched upon do we discover any really vital comprehension. Happily, Wölfflin was justified in his optimism to the extent that his most profound insights have long since become common property, exercising an unconscious effect even on those who criticize him.

In spite of all the critics, Wölfflin's books were read by wide circles with more enthusiasm than those of Wulff and similar thinkers. No other historian of art saw his books appear in so many editions, none experienced such triumphs as a speaker. But Wölfflin listened rather to the chorus of critics and felt himself misunderstood. It is unquestionably wrong to dispose of him as a formalist. He *was* that, but not *only* that. He was not able to solve the problem of the connection between "form and content," to use the old terminology, but he kept it alive, and within the history of style he was the first to point out a new way of improving the instruments for analyzing the specifically formal aspect of art. Leaving the formalism of Zimmermann and Fechner aside, it may be said that Fiedler merely pointed out that there was something as yet unexplored, Hildebrand offered a few new concepts while remaining one-sided in evaluating styles, but Wölfflin produced a wealth of new insights and really gave the critics something to provoke them into action. Perhaps Wölfflin's work was incomplete, perhaps it was in fact not rigorous enough. It cannot be denied, however, that it was a new road that led onward.

Although this sketch does not pretend to be an exhaustive account of Wölfflin's work and influence, it cannot be concluded without a word as to his personality. The impression created by his doctrine is inseparable from the manner of its delivery. One felt always that he dwelt with his whole being in the heights of the Classical, and was, like Burckhardt, an aristocrat for all his Swiss democracy, an unapproachable judge regarding things from a vast Olympian distance and yet possessing a surprisingly intimate knowledge of them. It has been admitted that he was unique as a pedagogue of art, as the teacher of "seeing." The most remarkable feature of his teaching was perhaps that by the model of his personal dignity and a greatness achieved by self-discipline he was able to arouse in others his own sense of the grandeur of all art. In his presence one always felt closer to the essential of life than in the workaday world.[30]

2. Riegl's Theory of the "Artistic Volition" of Gothic

WÖLFFLIN's remark quoted in the preceding chapter, "Human beings have probably always seen as they *wanted* to see," can refer only to Riegl's concept of artistic volition or *Kunstwollen*,[1] an idea that first appears in his *Stilfragen*. Alois RIEGL (1858-1905) by that time had already published more than forty writings, if all his little reviews are counted. He was six years older than Wölfflin. In the present book, however, he is discussed after Wölfflin because his first significant publication came after Wölfflin's precocious *Renaissance und Barock* (1888).

In a work of 1891 Riegl treated the subject of ancient Oriental rugs. Specialists call it a basic book. The subsequent vast increase in knowledge of specimens, far from modifying any of his fundamental ideas, merely confirmed all his conclusions. The book still had a predominantly antiquarian tendency. Riegl was an official in the Austrian Museum for Applied Arts, the Kunstgewerbemuseum, in Vienna, and had charge of the collection of textiles. Of course Semper's *Stil* was, so to speak, his daily bread. Not only did he nowhere utter any

[30] Joseph Gantner, *Schönheit und Grenzen der Klassischen Form*, Vienna, 1949, contains p. 99, "Heinrich Wölfflin, Umriss einer Biographie."

[1] For Riegl's biography see Julius Schlosser: "Die Wiener Schule der Kunstgeschichte," *Mitteilungen des österr. Inst. f. Geschichtsforschung*, Vienna, XIII, 2, 1934; cf. also Dagobert Frey in the *Jahrbuch für Kunstgeschichte*, 1923, and Wilhelm Köhler, *Mitteilungen des Instituts für Geschichtsforschung*, XXXIX, 1923.

It is difficult to translate the word *Kunstwollen* into English. The following translations have been proposed to me: art-will, artistic will, artistic volition, artistic intention, artistic aim. In his article "Style" (*Anthropology Today*, Chicago, 1953, p. 302) Meyer Schapiro gives as paraphrase: ". . . conception of art as an active creative process in which new forms arise from the artist's will to solve specially artistic problems." In German *Kunstwille* and *Kunstwollen* can be interpreted as *Wille, Kunst zu schaffen* (will to create art) but not art in general, rather art of a specific style, e.g. Romanesque or Gothic art. I shall use the phrase artistic volition, asking the reader to bear in mind the inadequacy of any translation of this word.

criticism of Semper, but he even praises him especially because he furthered reform in industrial arts around the middle of the century. Riegl does not broach the subject of artistic volition, and not merely for lack of the word. It may be noted in passing that the book includes studies in the origin and distribution of the pointed arch in Asia (Persia, and so on).[2]

Riegl's revolt against Semper, therefore, developed only after 1891. In the *Stilfragen* he begins with the distinction between "sculpture and surface."[3] Sculpture, he thinks, must be older than painting, for like Fiedler he regards the detachment of the outline from the object to be represented as a special and intellectually more difficult achievement. "That meant the discovery of the line as the element of all drawing, all painting, and indeed all two-dimensional representational art," and this step, according to Riegl, had already been taken in the Stone Age even before there was such a thing as plaiting and weaving. Consequently, Semper's theory that ornaments of a primitive kind are to be explained on the basis of a plaiting or from weaving technique is untenable. "Doubtless the technical factor also plays a part in the process described [namely, the sewing together of skins by means of sinews, resulting automatically in a zigzag line for the seam] but not nearly the dominant one that adherents of the technical and material theory of evolution would like to claim for it. The impulse was given not by technique but rather by the particular artistic volition." The primitive man who outlined the natural object to be represented simply "wanted" a copy of it and invented the necessary technique. The process is just the opposite of what the "materialistic theory" supposed (Riegl at least called it materialistic).

This concept of artistic volition later became a subject of debate.[4] Emphasis was placed on the element of will and critics discussed its psychological aspect, distinguished artistic ability from artistic volition or artistic necessity, and interpreted the concept to mean that the artist always can do what he wants to do (a suggestion that the greatest artists have always vigorously repudiated). In Riegl himself can already be found a tendency toward such speculations, which are in themselves undoubtedly of value; but what he originally intended can perhaps be understood more properly if the stress is laid on the first part of the phrase "artistic volition." Semper, who was himself

[2] Alois Riegl, *Altorientalische Teppiche*, Leipzig, 1891.

[3] Alois Riegl, *Stilfragen*, Berlin, 1893. p. 1, "Plastik und Fläche."

[4] Erwin Panofsky, "Der Begriff des Kunstwollens," *Zeitschr. f. Ästhetik u. Allgem. Kunstwissenschaft*, XIV, 1920, p. 321.

a not insignificant artist, knew that it is not enough to set out material and tools, excogitate a purpose, and then wait until the work of art automatically comes into being—wait passively, that is, and not will anything. Of course Semper *wanted* something also, but he expected too much from the technique. One must construct the corresponding phrase "*technical* volition" in order to realize that Riegl's "*artistic* volition" means that the artist wants *art* and is interested in technique only insofar as it serves to produce art. Consequently Riegl said that material, tools, and purpose are the coefficients of friction *against* which the *artistic* volition achieves its object.

He maintained that in art nothing is discovered twice. However that may be, in science it happens fairly often that the same thing is discovered twice. Riegl's artistic volition has a forerunner where one would hardly expect to find it. In 1812 Percier spoke of the change in taste in his generation, saying that Egyptian sphinxes are just as good as Greek forms. "That which gives general applicability to inventions and forms of works is neither a more proper feeling nor a more generally enlightened taste: one wants no other reason than that which makes one desire a particular cut to one's clothes or the coiffure of the day. One does not want these things because one finds them beautiful; but one finds them beautiful because one wants them; it also happens that they suddenly suffer the fate of all products of the mode."[5]

Riegl, of course, means by his *Kunstwollen* something more serious. He restored to the artist full responsibility for his work, declaring his mental activity to be the true source of art. In this original sense the concept of artistic volition is absolutely unproblematical and a most banal matter of course—for us today; but for the generation immediately following Semper it was not a matter of course, and Riegl's Copernican revolution was accordingly an achievement of grave consequence. Even today materialistic habits of thought block the way to metaphysical knowledge for countless numbers of people. But in the theory of art, at least, no one any longer believes that the mental aspects of creation are a "superstructure," an "epiphenomenon,"

[5] C. Percier and P. F. L. Fontaine, *Recueil de décoration intérieure*, Paris, 1812, pp. 11, 12. "Ce qui généralise ainsi les inventions et les formes des ouvrages, ce n'est ni un sentiment plus juste ni un goût plus généralement éclairé: on ne veut pas aucune autre raison, que celle qui fait couloir la coupe d'habit ou de coiffure du jour. On ne veut pas ces choses parcequ'on les trouve belles; mais on les trouve belles parcequ'on les veut; aussi leur arrive-t-il promptement de subir le sort de tous les produits de la mode." I am indebted to the late Mr. Emil Kaufmann (Vienna) for this reference.

or that artistic activity is the blind result of material and mechanical processes. Today many people once again acknowledge that the element of mind is *everywhere* primary. Riegl did not yet think that; he was merely interested in establishing this truth within the history and theory of art. Semper almost believed that artistic activity is determined, like the mechanics of heavenly bodies. Riegl recognized the element of free will. Artistic *volition* means no *compulsion*. (*Kunstwollen* is not *Kunstmüssen*.)

This spiritual conception of the world was not rationalism. The irrational is also spiritual. Riegl himself is a good example of this. He considered himself a positivist—which in his terminology is not the same as a materialist. By that he meant that one should adhere strictly to "given facts." Like his whole generation he had the greatest distaste and even contempt for all metaphysics, a subject considered taboo or simply absurd. He did not realize that the spiritual element was also a part of the "given facts," indeed that he himself manipulated all these facts *spiritually* by virtue of the particular spirit with which he was endowed. Even today physicists and chemists do not for the most part observe that it is their minds that create their "positive science," that they can explain everything by formulas except their own minds and the intellectual factor inherent in their formulas. Riegl, himself ostensibly a positivist, overcame "positivism" in the field of the theory of art. It is this that makes him seem irrational and paradoxical.

Riegl's concept of artistic volition can be called psychological. It underwent no appreciable change in his writings and by itself alone would indeed have been a signal to acknowledge as insufficient all explanations in the theory of Gothic that were based merely on construction and technique, but it does not exhaust Riegl's system, if one can speak of a system in his case. His basic ideas have a systematic connection although he never arranged them in strict order. They are scattered throughout his works and one must try to assemble them.[6] The significant publications lie within a short period of twelve years, from 1893 to 1905. I shall confine myself to the late works.

In the essay of 1901, *Naturwerk und Kunstwerk*, he summarizes his theory and defines his relationship to Hildebrand.[7] In the preceding development of aesthetics he distinguishes two stages: first, the idealistic

[6] Hans Sedlmayr made a very creditable attempt in the Introduction to Riegl's *Gesammelte Aufsätze*, Augsburg and Vienna, 1929 (ed. by Karl Swoboda).

[7] The essay was reprinted in the *Gesammelte Aufsätze*, the passage quoted on p. 51.

conception that saw as the goal of the *imitation of nature* an improvement, that is, a beautification of nature; second, the subsequent victory of the *idea of evolution*. However, because Semper's theory was not easily adaptable to sculpture and painting there was developed a psychological theory of "remembered images" that gradually approach pure naturalism. It was easy for Riegl to refute this theory, which was based on Wundt and Fechner, for he needed only to refer to his *Spätrömische Kunstindustrie*, published in the same year. According to the psychological theory in question Late Roman sculpture ought to have become more and more naturalistic, but the contrary is true. Where is there then any "progress"? Thus Riegl's own theory is evolved as the third stage of aesthetics. Opposing the "materialistic metaphysics" he follows the "positivistic" trend "in the broadest sense," meaning the *empirical* trend: "If one applies the principles of this trend of thought to the history of art one will have to say that artistic creation expresses itself purely as an *aesthetic impulse*: in the one case, that of the artists, to reproduce natural objects in a particular kind of way by one-sidedly intensifying some characteristics and suppressing others; in the other, that of the public, to behold these natural objects as they have been reproduced in just this way by contemporary artists. . . . The question is how a development within this artistic volition can be possible."[8] "Aesthetic impulse" is synonymous with "artistic volition"; for Fiedler, on the other hand, the artistic was distinguished from the aesthetic. We learn from this passage that artists and public always share the same artistic volition and that it is generally related to so-called stylization, "... one-sidedly intensifying some characteristics and suppressing others." The possibilities of this one-sided stylization lie between two poles, called by Riegl *haptic* and *optic*. This distinction, in conformity with the then prevailing psychophysics, had a physiological basis (as in Hildebrand also). That modern physiology and psychology analyze and explain the details of the visual process in another way makes no difference to Riegl's position, which is concerned with the objective characteristics of the natural model and its copy. It is plain that this polarity, though not exactly identical with Wölfflin's pairs of concepts, is nevertheless closely related to them. While Wöfflin's chief concepts may be assumed to have been "being" and "becoming," Riegl's are "isolation" and "connection" (*Verbundenheit*). "Natural objects reveal themselves to the *visual* perception of man as figures *isolated* yet at the same time connected with the

[8] *Ibid.*, p. 60.

universe (that is, with a practically unlimited section of it) inside an infinite whole." Art exists, accordingly, for the eye and can stylize objects either in the direction of isolation or its opposite pole, connection. This parallels Hildebrand's conception of near and distant images. Riegl's theory absorbs, as it were, Hildebrand's theory,[9] merely freeing it (as did Wölfflin) from bias toward a particular kind of stylization, so that it ceases to be a narrow-minded theory of art *pro domo* and becomes a fit instrument to measure all historical styles on a sliding scale without evaluating them. Individual works represent different levels of value, styles as such do not. There is, consequently, *no* such thing as *decline*. What was called so in the nineteenth century was simply misunderstood art, when measured by the standard of Greek art of the fifth century before Christ. Thus Riegl made the history of art more objective, that is, more scientific than it had been in the period when it was still weighed down by ideas drawn from the natural sciences. In his obituary on Riegl Dvořak relates how the former said to him: "The best historian of art is he who has no personal taste, for in the history of art the important thing is to discover the objective criteria of the historical development."[10] With such asceticism or selflessness Riegl could study all the antinaturalistic trends of art with the same impartiality as naturalistic ones, and his field became unlimited by either space or time.

Though the trend toward expressionism did not originate until after his death he understood and evaluated positively corresponding earlier historical manifestations, thus smoothing the path for the new movement itself. For historians of art, however, he opened the way to devoted absorption in all the epochs that had so long been considered artistically inferior and at best worthy of but antiquarian interest. The generation that followed him made it a point of honor to rehabilitate all despised styles and works, an interest that gradually developed into a kind of moral sport. Soon it became the badge of the *conoscente* of art to understand contemporary art also. Dvořak, Riegl's pupil, understanding the trend toward the new Expressionism, hailed it as a movement toward pure spirituality (*Geistigkeit*), and anyone who valued his reputation was able to "understand" the New Objectivity (*Neue Sachlichkeit*) and Surrealism, as they emerged upon the scene, just as well as Michelangelo and Negro sculpture. Whereas in the nineteenth century artists usually became famous only after they

[9] In the second part of the essay, *ibid.*, pp. 65ff.

[10] Max Dvořak, *Mitteilungen der K.K. Zentralkommission für Erforschung und Erhaltung der Kunst- und historischen Denkmale*, Third Series, IV, 1905, p. 262.

were dead, they were now for the most part already dead during their lifetimes, after having once been famous. In fact, people no longer had taste. But though this was perhaps no gain as far as the general public was concerned, it represented a great step forward for science. With the watchword "There is no such thing as decline," all prejudices, not merely those against Gothic as such but also even those against Late Gothic, were bound to die away.

Riegl had the intention of studying art according to its specific nature, that is, by means of such concepts as haptic, optic, and the like, and not by drawing parallels to cultural history, to investigate which is the task of the historian of culture. But, the historian of art (in this case Riegl) is much too interested in the problem to be able to wait passively until the historians of culture provide him with the necessary materials; for "all the above-mentioned nonartistic cultural areas constantly affect the history of art, the work of art (which is never without an external purpose) furnishing the outward causation, the content." Here again we meet form and content! What becomes of the sovereignty of art if content creeps in by the back door? The old ghost is back. Riegl, to be sure, thinks that investigation of content should be refined by investigation into form. "Iconography, which now . . . together with attribution of place and date, is so one-sidedly cultivated for its own sake, will only then reveal its true value for the history of art when it is posited as form and color in surface and space, in inner harmony with the manifest appearance of the work of art."[10a] Only then will it be recognized that each work "could only come into being in this and no other place" (page 64), and attributions of place and date be established intelligently and accurately; for, although artistic volition is indeed based on the idea of freedom of the will, Riegl believed with equal steadfastness in the necessity of artistic evolution, a paradox that can only be resolved if one realizes how the concepts of freedom of the will and determination are correlated and neither cancel nor exclude each other.

But since Riegl considered cultural history—the history of nonartistic, external purposes—to have an integrating effect on the history of art, he was also obliged to answer the question as to their mutual relations; and because in his opinion artist and public share the same artistic volition, he phrased the question thus: What is the "determinating"

[10a] Ges. Aufsätze, p. 64. "Die jetzt . . . neben der Orts- und Zeitbestimmung so einseitig um ihrer selbst willen gepflegte Ikonographie wird erst dann ihren wahren Wert für die Kunstgeschichte gewinnen, wenn man sie in innere Übereinstimmung mit der sinnfälligen Erscheinung des Kunstwerks als Form und Farbe in Ebene und Raum setzt. . . ."

factor? This question, he said, he could and might not answer since it was "metaphysical," but nevertheless a broader basis for the understanding of a particular type of artistic volition could be obtained. For "if we take into consideration not simply the arts but any one of the other great cultural areas of mankind—the state, religion, science—we shall come to the conclusion that in these fields also it is everywhere a matter of the relation between individual and collective unity." (page 63) Thus in society the individual element corresponds to isolation in the arts of space and the collective element to connection. The direction of *cultural* volition, *Kulturwollen* (an expression that to my knowledge does not occur in Riegl but expresses most simply what he meant and what is found in later literature based on him), has always been "in the last analysis completely identical with that of the artistic volition of the same people in the same period." Riegl uses *Weltanschauung* instead of *Kulturwollen* and concludes "that though representational art is not determined by the particular contemporaneous *Weltanschauung* it does indeed run clearly parallel to it." Only a few years later Dvořak remarked derisively of Schnaase that his combination of political and social idealism with pragmatical history of art was like a steam engine that has lost its driving belt.[11] As far as this ultimate problem of all history of art is concerned, it is not clear how Riegl can be said to have progressed beyond Schnaase. These authors regard all cultural areas as following parallel lines of development; none of these philosophers of history tells us why the paths do not go in opposite directions, cross, or deviate from each other. Riegl here capitulated on principles just as Wölfflin had done. It makes no difference whether one says that everything is simply following parallel courses or that one ought not to compare incomparables; neither statement gives any clue to the real state of affairs, not to mention the central "steam engine" postulated by Dvořak, that is, the reason or reasons for development.

What Riegl meant by a formalistically refined and deepened iconography (namely, in general terms, interpretation of content) is shown in his long treatise on Dutch group portraits.[12] Without discussing any details, one may briefly characterize this masterly work, the value of which can hardly be overestimated, by saying that it interprets the

[11] M. Dvořak, "Das Rätsel der Brüder van Eyck," *Jahrbuch der Kunstsammlungen des allerh. Kaiserhauses*, XXIV, 1903, p. 164.

[12] Alois Riegl, "Das holländische Gruppenportrait," *Jahrbuch der Kunstsammlungen. . .*, XXIII, Vienna, 1902, p. 71.

element of content psychologically by means of the concepts of will, emotion, and attention, that is to say, with reference to the persons represented in the paintings, who are objectively connected with each other by the action of the picture but who in the course of its development establish a connection with the spectator by their glances and attention. This "subjective objectivism" is one stage of a long process that ends in impressionism and parallels step by step the development of form, namely, from isolation to connection and the conquest of intermediate space (*Freiraum*). There is scarcely another treatise where the subject is imbued with such intensity. Dvořak said in his obituary that in the history of art Riegl overcame the tendency toward cultural history, aesthetical dogmatism, and historical dogmatism.

Though Riegl demonstrated the increasing subjectivation of art, the contrary was true of his own science. And this is as it should be. Every generation approached the problem of Gothic with a different philosophy of life, as Vasari, Hegel, Viollet-le-Duc, and Riegl bear witness. Gothic, however, remains objectively the same, so that criticism always results in a mixture of the truly objective element and the subjective interpretation. The objective element is only understood insofar as it *is* interpreted and, if possible, correctly, that is, objectively. Interpretation progresses from misinterpretation to better interpretation; and though many say pessimistically that the objective can never be reached, history shows an ever-increasing elimination of the subjective, to which belongs the evaluation of style as such (in pre-Romanticism and Romanticism). It is therefore always a test of any theory to see what degree and what sort of understanding it could bring to the individual work. Riegl's lecture on Salzburg, *Salzburgs Stellung in der Kunstgeschichte*, delivered in the last year of his life, offers an example by which his method may be judged.[13]

"Salzburg owes its peculiar position in the history of art . . . to a strongly marked Italian quality. . . ." Riegl considers to what extent the original Roman population might have survived down into the Middle Ages and the Baroque period, but he arrives at no positive conclusion and turns, therefore, to the architectural monuments themselves. "The most striking symptom of this tendency [namely, Italianism] is the lack of a large Gothic cathedral and indeed of any pure Gothic at all. Since Gothic is neither more nor less than the flower and perfection of the artistic development of the half or wholly Germanic

[13] Alois Riegl, *Gesammelte Aufsätze*, p. 111. The lecture was delivered in 1904 and published in 1905, the year of Riegl's death.

peoples during the Middle Ages, the indifference of the Salzburgers to Gothic proves in itself that they possessed only a very slight understanding for this flower and perfection of mediaeval Germanic art. . . . The Romanesque style is represented by the monastery church of St. Peter, the interior of which is completely Baroquified, and by the Cathedral, the predecessor of the present Baroque structure. [It is known to us through drawings.] How insignificant is St. Peter's in Salzburg compared to buildings of the same period in Germany or even France! . . . Everywhere in France, Germany, and northern Italy, from the eleventh century on, the problem of vaulting was the order of the day: Not as a technical problem, which simply did not exist, although people today have written books and undertaken large publications on the basis of this supposition; but as an aesthetic problem—as the extension of the membering to the ceiling."[14] St. Peter's has the Saxon alternate system (under the Baroque overlay); on the other hand, Riegl sees Italian (Lombardic) prototypes for the cathedral and the nave of the church of the Franciscans. There was no development of Late Romanesque in Salzburg, says Riegl, and "therefore" no Early or High Gothic either. There are no buildings in the style of the Mendicant Orders (the Franciscans adopted the Romanesque structure) and only Late Gothic is represented in Salzburg: in the choir of the church of the Franciscans by Hans of Burghausen [erroneously] called Stettheimer. This choir Riegl discusses in detail, regarding it as a unique example and an anachronistic anticipation of the picturesque (*chiaroscuro*), which does not appear in Italy until the fifteenth century. Thus for Riegl, Salzburg is, so to speak, more papal than the pope. He speaks of the consciously Baroque guidance of light, of the incompleteness of aspect, seen from the nave, so that one never sees more than sections of the choir at one time, vistas that, as in Roman Baroque, always entice the eye onward. "In such a piquant manifestation . . . this system can positively be called the forerunner of modern art." He says again that the work stands quite alone; its Late Gothic style "is in Germany parallel to the Early and High Renaissance in Italy; it signifies on the one hand an extreme intensification of the Gothic-Germanic but at the same time its disintegration and dissolution and thus the transition to a return to the Roman and Italian." The last phrase comported excellently with the lecture's main thesis: that in Salzburg the Italian element predominates. But the tendency to regard German Late Gothic as a preparation for Renaissance, or even as

[14] *Op.cit.*, p. 114. This idea appears previously in Courajod and again in Gall (1915).

identical with it, fascinated many historians of art in later times. In 1905 the idea was not new, as we shall soon see. Strangely enough, Riegl modified his opinion about the Renaissance quality of Late Gothic immediately thereafter in his discussion of St. Margaret's chapel in the cemetery of St. Peter's. He says there is created here a feeling for unified, closed interiors but ". . . the eye still follows the piers, engaged shafts, and ribs individually, as it was accustomed to do in the Middle Ages, and therefore continues to be distracted from pure appreciation of the free space in between them." (page 120) Again there is an after-effect (as in Thode's case) of Jakob Burckhardt's remarks on Italian Gothic. Thus Riegl contributed more to the investigation of the character and essence of Gothic in an indirect than in a direct way. Even if he had not expressly said so, attempts to derive Gothic from construction would now have become suspect. They follow the pattern of Semper's ideas, while the task was now to go back to the *artistic volition of Gothic*. The quadripartite ribbed vault is, from a descriptive point of view, the essential element in the inception of Gothic, and thus also genetically, if this word is taken to refer to the objective historical process. But what, psychologically speaking, was the genetic reason in the individual architect? Riegl answers: the artistic volition. And since the artistic volition is concerned with the choice between a tendency toward the pole of isolation or that toward the pole of connection, it must first be established which of the two tendencies is present in a given case. If it is that toward connection, unceasing investigation must delve deeper: Why did the individual and society as a whole turn to just this pole? Riegl has not expressed himself on that point, but the answer, from his point of view, must be: this is parallel to the artistic volition, that is, to the *Weltanschauung* of the age. Everywhere there was a tendency toward "connection." Was then the ribbed vault either "invented" or admitted because it tended in the direction of connection? Riegl did not say so, but observed instead: ". . . it extended the membering to the ceiling." Later we must see whether this road can take us further; here it will suffice to point out that Riegl touched upon the subject of Gothic only this once in all his works, but immediately injected into the debate an uncommonly fruitful idea.

Next to Wölfflin, Riegl was the greatest thinker of that generation in the field of art scholarship. Both men deepened the problems, both tended partly in the same direction, both stopped when they reached a stratum that was for them still impenetrable. It is easier to read

Wölfflin than almost any of Riegl's books and essays, for it often seems as though Riegl made things hard for himself and consequently for his readers. The two men together may be said to have cleared the way for their contemporaries and followers to a solution of problems of which older generations of art scholars were indeed aware, but which they could not approach because the instruments for research were lacking. These instruments are precise concepts and the tendency toward systematics.

VI. THE RAMIFICATIONS OF THE PROBLEMS

1. The Recognition of Late Gothic

We have seen that in 1904 Riegl's attitude toward Late Gothic was positive. He was not the first to express such a point of view; Gonse, Gurlitt, Schmarsow, and Haenel anticipated him. But whereas in Riegl's case evaluations were based on objective impartiality toward all styles, these men were inspired by quite different motives.

It should be mentioned in this connection that the versatile Ernest RENAN (1823-1892) expressed himself on the subject of Late Gothic,[1] though he referred only to the fourteenth century and already saw there a decline from thirteenth-century Gothic. His description of the latter derives essentially from the *communis opinio* current in 1862. He sees in the political history of France the reasons for the decline: "Art is largely a reflection of the society that the artist sees about him." (page 498 of the reprint) Renan, however, is more interested in depicting the "decline" of society than in discussing architecture, and in his comparison of Italian Gothic in Tuscany and Umbria with St.-Ouen in Rouen and Beauvais Cathedral (page 499) he confines himself to assigning the Italian buildings a higher rank without giving any analysis of the various architectures. Of these the Italian, he says, are as superior to the French as Petrarch is to the troubadours. Gothic perished as a result of its own faults; the Renaissance was by no means to blame. (page 501) One realizes on reading the article, which in its way is on a high level, how much of the subsequent controversy was already foreshadowed.

A generation later came Louis GONSE (1846-1921). Though he said nothing very profound about the Flamboyant style, he must be credited with having dared to champion it as early as 1890: "I could not possibly share the contempt of certain purists for this last incarnation of the art of the Middle Ages. The Flamboyant style has produced works of a lively and original character, and I for my part do not discover in it the symptoms of discouragement and fatigue that the detractors of the idea of Gothic are pleased to find there. . . . Flamboyant art had within itself more resources of warmth and life than the doctrinaire and coldly scientific art of the beginning of the fourteenth century."[2] The designation "*doctrinaire* Gothic" was later

[1] Ernest Renan, "L'art du Moyen-âge et les causes de sa décadence, *Revue des Deux Mondes*, 1862; reprinted in *Œuvres complètes*, II, Paris, 1948, p. 469.

[2] Louis Gonse, *L'art gothique*, Paris, 1890, p. 272. "Je ne saurais partager le dédain de certains puristes pour cette ultime incarnation de l'art du Moyen-Âge. Le style ogivale flamboyant a produit des œuvres d'un caractère vivace et originale, et je n'y découvre pas,

adopted by Dehio. Gonse was full of enthusiasm for everything French, and patriotism may thus have been a factor in his defense of French Late Gothic.

The real motive of Cornelius GURLITT (1850-1938) was his own Protestant belief.[3] He was an industrious scholar in the field of architectural history who never forgot his Protestant convictions and was therefore disturbed by the fact that the liberation of the individual from the papacy, inspired by Luther, had brought forth no proud fruits of church architecture. It is surely not putting a false construction on his words to say that this disappointment gave birth to his bona fide idea that Late Gothic should be interpreted as the expression of a spiritual current which later, in the ecclesiastical field and thanks to Luther's great personality, led to the Reformation. The reading of such notions into the past could only be made to seem plausible, however, by a complicated series of arguments, briefly about as follows:

The Reformation made use of Renaissance forms imported from Italy. But Renaissance does not mean the application of the forms of classical antiquity to Gothic constructions; rather (like Humanism) a revival of the classical spirit. By the latter is meant the secularization of art, which had hitherto been purely ecclesiastical. "There was developed in it a quality of purposefulness that was foreign to the Middle Ages. Art was made serviceable to man whereas it had previously been devoted only to the church; for man, ego, and individuality had been newly discovered." Gurlitt was, as we have seen, not the only one to be misled by the concept of individuality into dating the Renaissance as far back as "individualities" could be demonstrated. But purposefulness implies not merely this reorientation toward the individual but also the fact that the church building no longer exists for God but for the congregation. The Catholic, that is to say, the Gothic church had been a processional church and at the same time God's house; the Protestant church is a preacher's church and a meetinghouse for human beings. Only in these human beings themselves is the dwelling place of God to be found (when God's word is alive in them), not in the buildings. This new purpose results in the enlargement of the interior, along with the *Hallenform* that

---

pour ma part, les symptômes de découragement et de fatigue que les détracteurs de l'idée gothique se sont plu à y reconnaître. . . . L'art flamboyant avait en lui-même plus de ressources de chaleur et de vie que l'art doctrinaire et froidement scientifique du commencement du XIVe siècle."

[3] Cornelius Gurlitt, *Kunst und Künstler am Vorabend der Reformation*, Halle, 1890 (Schriften des Vereins für Reformationsgeschichte, VII).

is dependent on the position of the pulpit and the importance of the sermon. To it is also related the arrangement of the galleries. All of this is significant for the Protestant church structure *after* Luther. *Consequently*, the *tendency* toward hall-churches and the introduction of pulpits and galleries is really also Protestant even *before* Luther. Gurlitt does not say proto-Protestant, but he could have coined the word in order to express his idea briefly. All such protophenomena follow the same logical pattern: proto-Gothic, proto-Renaissance, proto-Romanticism. They always involve a complete rereading of the total in the light of a partial agreement with a new idea: *totum pro parte*, as it were. Does one need to be reminded that the *Hallenform* as such and the sermon were already in existence before Late Gothic? Otherwise one would have to let Renaissance begin with St. Francis and St. Dominic. And at this point we remember that Thode had indeed already dated Renaissance this far back. Gurlitt comes dangerously close to that neo-Romanticist. Should one call it Protestant neo-Romanticism? In Gurlitt's formulation Late Gothic is really "German Early Renaissance." (page 145) The Reformation did not supplant Gothic, "but filled it with a new spirit. In their best works Dürer, Holbein, and Cranach are characteristic of both Gothic and Reformation. The greatness of mediaeval art ended in Germany only when it became humanistic. . . . In Germany Humanism remained foreign, not until Goethe was it temporarily reconciled to the nation." (page 147) How was it possible for the German nation to commit such an error? In Late Gothic it already possessed the architectural form that corresponded to the Reformation, yet it had recourse to Italian, that is, papal Renaissance. The Protestants employed the architecture of Catholicism, which "threw itself most eagerly into the arms of Renaissance and assimilated with the greatest thoroughness its pagan element." Are then the Late Gothic churches, that is to say, the "proto-Protestant" architectures of the German Early Renaissance, perhaps also pagan? Late Gothic was surely not so! But Gurlitt says, nevertheless, that it was Renaissance, thus at least a little pagan. Yet, on the contrary, it is supposed to typify the Reformation. It must be confessed that this train of thought is unclear but it is obvious that Gurlitt intends to praise Late Gothic. The churches of that style "protest against the ostentation (*Äusserlichkeit*) of the older architectural manner, the disproportionate outlay for a house holding a relatively small number of people, the immoderate development of height that is not balanced on the ground level, these narrow halls seeming like a covered pathway to the altar, the enormous architectonic envelopes (*Hüllen*) for a narrow-chested space based on ascetic feeling." (page 130) Once again, praise of a thing is only made possible by criticism of its opposite. Riegl was the first to transcend this inability to be objective.

Nationalism was also a factor in Gurlitt's views. He spoke almost exclusively of German Late Gothic, mentioning King's College Chapel in Cambridge because it is also a single room, and regretting that there was still so little known about English architecture, as though Britton had never lived. Gurlitt's nationalism, however, remained peripheral, whereas for August SCHMARSOW (1853-1936) it became the compelling motive in his revaluation of Late Gothic.[4] On the one hand, says Schmarsow, whose opinions were narrow-mindedly modeled on French cathedrals, the Gothicist is scarcely able to recognize German Late Gothic as an artistic achievement, and maintains a conspiracy of silence about its architectural monuments, justifying his course by the assertion that the leading role had passed to painting. The connoisseur of Italian Renaissance, on the other hand, declares that Germany lagged behind Italy in the employment of classical forms and that her assimilation of them was external and awkward. "The German scholar," however, "misses in both cases any indication of the most peculiar element, the employment of the national principle." The *German core* must be sought. Critics rely on words instead of syntax, that is, wherever pointed arches and ribs are to be found they talk of Gothic; that is wrong, for the important thing is the "spatial idea." A year before, Schmarsow had delivered his lecture on the nature of architecture,[5] declaring in detail—doubtless inspired by Burckhardt's remarks on spatial styles—that space is the decisive factor in architecture, not the forms by which it is delimited. A similar view had already been expressed by the architect Lucä in an uncommonly discerning way.[6] It is hardly likely that Schmarsow knew this article, for he does not cite it. Late Gothic, then, is to be judged according to "spatial ideas." Is it essentially equal to High Gothic? If not, it represents a "document of a new volition." And "if it no longer is or purports to be Late Gothic, then according to all we have hitherto known it

[4] August Schmarsow, "Reformvorschläge zur Geschichte der deutschen Renaissance" (Berichte ü. d. Verhandlungen d. K. Sächsischen Gesellschaft der Wissenschaften zu Leipzig), Leipzig, 1899, p. 41.

[5] August Schmarsow, *Das Wesen der architektonischen Schöpfung*, Leipzig, 1893.

[6] Cf. K. Lucae's lecture, "Über die Macht des Raumes in der Baukunst," *Zeitschrift für Bauwesen*, Berlin, 1869.

must be 'Renaissance,' especially as it gives expression to a new creative principle that is foreign to the Gothic shaping of space." When this Renaissance begins cannot be decided by the expert in either Gothic or Italian Renaissance but only by "the German scholar, who is the connoisseur of the native, truly national character." Schmarsow considers that the Kreuzkirche in Schwäbisch Hall from the year 1351 marks the beginning of this "German Renaissance." He gives a still somewhat fragmentary survey of Late Gothic buildings, and remarks: ". . . what has hitherto been called Late Gothic in German architecture is in large part, indeed for the most part 'German Early Renaissance' and affords us a view of an independent development that can take its place in every respect by the side of the Italian Quattrocento as a parallel, that is to say, it not only occurs simultaneously but it also reveals a corresponding artistic character—corresponding, that is, to the nature and the past of the people on this side of the Alps." (page 55) He supports his thesis by an analysis of secular architecture, which, having sprung from the innermost heart of the Renaissance, takes precedence over religious architecture from now on and for centuries to come, including Baroque and Rococo. "The change comes in the so-called Late Gothic period. . . ." (page 60) Everything essentially as in Gurlitt! Even Arnold von Westfalen with the Meissen Castle is again a star witness (page 58). Like Gurlitt, Schmarsow appends an investigation of the picturesque element in the contemporary sculpture and painting. This national conception is, according to him, to the advantage of international art history, for now everything makes the transition to Renaissance simultaneously: Sluter is Renaissance, the brothers van Eyck are Renaissance, so is Multscher, and, in short, the entire fifteenth century in both North and South. Only in architecture does the Renaissance begin half a century earlier: in 1351.[6a]

As early as 1897 Schmarsow proposed the subject of German Late Gothic—or Renaissance—for a prize competition at the University of Leipzig, and one of his pupils was inspired to write a dissertation on it that was published at the same time as Schmarsow's essay.[7] Erich HAENEL (b. 1875) surveys the judgments that had hitherto been pronounced on Late Gothic by Schnaase, Kugler, Lübke, Dohme, Lotze (*Kunsttopographie Deutschlands*), Otte, and Göller. He himself, he remarks, is entirely in agreement with the new theory of Schmarsow

6a Today we see the beginning of German Late Gothic in the Wiesenkirche in Soest, erected 1331 (not 1351).

7 Erich Haenel, *Spätgotik und Renaissance. Ein Beitrag zur Geschichte der deutschen Architektur, vornehmlich im 15. Jahrhundert*, Stuttgart, 1899.

and Gurlitt. He, too, makes the sermon and the Mendicant Orders responsible for the Late Gothic Renaissance—or whatever one calls it. He describes in detail the essential character of High Gothic where the constructional members patiently bow to *one* master, the vaulting, which ought to remind Christians of the system of the Kingdom of God (page 106). Verticalism is not forgotten. The only new thought seems to be the suggestion that when the vault cells were painted light blue, heaven itself gazed down into the building, the roof was dematerialized, and walls and piers stood free (page 108). This Late Gothic system, he says, contains the germ of an inner transformation into the humanly natural in contrast to transcendental exaltation. "It was the reaction of healthy feeling to abnormally intensified sensibility." ". . . a clear, soberly considering consciousness demanded fixed spatial boundaries. . . . The realization that the new attitude toward the world could not make itself at home in these forms impelled the artists to stretch and strain the old system in order in some way or other to make room also for the changed feeling for space." Is this meant to apply to the attitude of 1351 (1331) or to that of 1480 or 1517?

The untenableness of Schmarsow's and Haenel's theory was demonstrated that same year in a brief essay by Georg DEHIO (1850-1932).[8] The newly proposed concept of Renaissance, he said, would include Ulm Cathedral, St. Peter's in Rome, and the Dresden Zwinger. The corresponding thing would be true for painting. Hitherto Renaissance had been taken to mean the resurrection of something ancient. "That something completely new and original like the art of the van Eycks should *also* be called Renaissance will never be accepted by anyone with sound common sense." Dehio himself had such sound common sense, but he overestimated its universality. A generation later Gurlitt and Schmarsow had innumerable followers. The misguidedness was so great that critics even equated Late Gothic reticular vaults with Renaissance coffers, failing to see that ribbed reticulations are "read off," in Hildebrand's sense, from back to front, the coffers of antiquity and Renaissance, on the contrary, from front to back. From the standpoint of membrology and relief it is a question of opposites, but without a doubt the false doctrine persists even today. Dehio scornfully reduced Schmarsow's theory to a very simple formula: "Renaissance is a spatial style, Late Gothic is a spatial style, therefore Late Gothic is Renaissance." This, he said, was not logical because not every spatial style

[8] Georg Dehio, *Über die Grenze der Renaissance gegen die Gotik*, Kunstchronik, 1899-1900, p. 272.

had to be Renaissance. He analyzed the real meaning of the "magic phrase" spatial style as used by Burckhardt, and showed that it was not applicable to Late Gothic at all. Although one must grant that up to this point Dehio was perfectly in the right against Schmarsow, his own proposal for characterizing Late Gothic seems dubious. He, too, recognizes in it a new quality, defining this as the *picturesque.* Of course, Late Gothic is picturesque—if one is willing to use the term at all—but is High Gothic *not* picturesque? We have listened to many voices proclaiming it so. Dehio thus completes the confusion over concepts by declaring that just because Late Gothic is picturesque its relationship to Renaissance must be acknowledged, for the latter is, after all, also picturesque. Wölfflin had maintained the opposite: Renaissance is linear (or plastic). Dehio proposed that Late Gothic should be called neo-Germanic, but no one adopted the term and he himself dropped the new coinage. He also failed to see, just as Schmarsow had done, that Late Gothic is completely *different* from Renaissance in its "morphology," that is to say, in the forms of its members. There is, moreover, no justification for simply overlooking the fact that while all the "kinds of forms" are *different,* Late Gothic, however, in those modes of representation taught by Wölfflin and Riegl, is not merely different but *diametrically opposite.*[9]

The positive aspect of this nationalistic movement was that Late Gothic now began to be studied, and Haenel must be credited with having been the first to assemble material somewhat more abundantly. His book could not have come to Riegl's notice, for otherwise the latter would no longer have regarded the church of the Franciscans in Salzburg as unique. But Gurlitt's attitude, partly Protestant and partly parochial *Erzgebirgisch*-Saxon, as well as Schmarsow's German nationalism, almost completely obscured the fact that there was after all a Late Gothic style also outside Germany. Consequently, this, too, had to be discovered. The revelation occurred in the course of a debate between Anthyme SAINT-PAUL (1843-1911) and Camille ENLART (1862-1927) about Flamboyant and its dependence on English Curvilinear as a result of the relations of the two countries during the Hundred Years' War.[10]

[9] Dehio alluded to the subject later in his lecture, *Krisis der Kunst des 16. Jahrhunderts,* 1913 (published in the *Gesammelte Aufsätze*).

[10] Camille Enlart, "Origine Anglaise du Style Flamboyant," *Bulletin monumentale,* 1906, p. 38. Anthyme Saint-Paul, "Les origines du gothique flamboyant en France," *ibid.,* p. 483, and Enlart's reply, p. 511. Then A. Saint-Paul again: "L'architecture française et la guerre de Cent ans," *Bulletin monumentale,* 1908, pp. 5, 269, 387. With reference to that, cf. Durand in the *Bulletin monumentale,* for 1909, p. 127, and A. Saint-Paul, *ibid.,* p. 387.

There is no reason to go into the details of this debate here. A generation later it had an interesting epilogue in a chapter of LASTEYRIE's (1849-1921) book on French Gothic.[11] Lasteyrie presents all the evidence respecting Late Gothic details in England before Flamboyant, but then insists nevertheless on the continuity of the French development from *style rayonnant* to *style flamboyant*, whereas the English went on to the Rectilinear. Nations had formerly disputed for the honor of having invented Gothic; now the dispute was repeated for the honor of having created Late Gothic. Lasteyrie always speaks of the French architects of Gothic and Late Gothic with the pronoun "*nous*." Yet this "we" of 1927 means at the same time the descendants of those who had once passionately despised Gothic. Riegl had long since transcended this nationalism that seems so childish to us today, and Lasteyrie himself was only a conservative straggler of a movement that was slowly to lead to the realization that Late Gothic is also a European phenomenon and to the recognition of its naturally national physiognomies within a supranational process.

This extension of aesthetic tolerance and its culmination in scientific neutrality must be seen in a larger connection. When the belief in exclusive standards was shaken and a new party established its creed declaring Gothic to be a model (most decisively, Pugin), efforts were at first concentrated on the Classicism within Gothic, or what was thought to be classical Gothic. We have seen that the Camden Society sought to destroy everything that was not built in Decorated style. In France after the Revolution the destruction went on indiscriminately. Victor Hugo went to the heart of the matter when he wrote that there were only two things in a building: its use and its beauty. Its use is the owner's affair, its beauty belongs to all, and it is, therefore, a violation of the law to destroy the building.[12] Destruction was finally overcome and replaced by ideas of conservationism (Commission des monuments historique, 1837), the principles of which changed with the increase in experience from generation to generatiton.

This movement in particular formed the broader frame for the recognition of Late Gothic, because a necessary condition of the preservation of monuments was a knowledge of the objects to be conserved, in other words, the creation of inventories.[13] These en-

[11] Robert de Lasteyrie, *L'architecture religieuse en France à l'époque gothique*, II, Paris, 1927, pp. 33-68.

[12] Cited according to Hans Huth, "The Evolution of Preservationism in Europe," *Journal of the American Society of Architectural Historians*, 1941, I, p. 5.

[13] The first step was taken as early as 1830 with a memorial to King Louis Philippe, written

deavors also have a history. The cataloguing of the architectural monuments of Saxony was an early undertaking by an amateur, Ludwig PUTTRICH (1783-1856), who designates himself on the title page of his book as Doctor of Laws[14] and whose knowledge of the history of art was obtained from the works of Kugler and Schnaase. Whatever the merits of his work in its own day, any really exhaustive survey could only be accomplished by the aid of state funds. The agencies of curators of monuments were gradually supplemented in all the German states by staffs of trained inventorial workers. Practical conservationists joined with the historians, and the evolution of the modern study of art history is partly to be understood from this point of view. Gurlitt himself was a cataloguer, and knowledge of many Late Gothic buildings only became available as a result of investigations in the various states and provinces.

The pace of inventorial progress varied considerably from country to country. In England the idea first emerged as early as 1737 in the work of Samuel Boyse (see above, page 380) and from Britton's time on such cataloguing remained in private hands, for the conservative English legal principles did not encourage state interference with the owners of private buildings. An inventory on the part of governmental agencies was not begun in England until 1911.[15]

In France, information about the nation's architectural monuments was collected in the two organs of the *Congrès archéologiques* and the *Bulletin monumental*, both created by Caumont in 1834. As in other countries also, the art journals accepted individual studies, but a tendency toward universality arose wherever the topographical method prevailed and scholars felt themselves obligated to obtain complete knowledge of every district.

In Germany, such activity began in Hannover about 1871 and continued in Pomerania in 1881, in the Prussian province of Saxony in 1882, and elsewhere.[16] Dvořak undertook the work for Austria;

---

by Guizot and entitled: *Inspection Générale des Monuments Historiques*. Cf. Franz Graf Wolff Metternich, *Die Denkmalpflege in Frankreich*, Berlin, 1944, p. 7. See also Charles Forbes René de Montalambert, *Du Vandalism et du Catholicism*, Paris, 1839.

14 Ludwig Puttrich, *Denkmale der Baukunst des Mittelalters in Sachsen*, Leipzig, 4 vols., 1836-1850. Cf. also his *Systematische Darstellung der Entwicklung der Baukunst in den obersächsischen Ländern*, Leipzig, 1852.

15 Royal Commission on the Ancient and Historical Monuments and Constructions of England, *An Inventory of the Historical Monuments*, . . . , from 1911 on. There is a separate-series for Wales and one for Scotland.

16 A list of all these series can be found in the first edition of Georg Dehio's *Handbuch der Deutschen Kunstdenkmäler*, which has become the cicerone for Germany.

the volumes that appeared from 1907 on made use of the experience gained by earlier enterprises and set the standard for several other series, for many of these extensive publications are still not yet brought to a conclusion. It is obvious that the history of inventorial activity—also that of Italy, Sweden, and so on—should be described connectedly. The cursory hints given here will suffice to indicate that an attitude of uniformly objective research was soon bound to become a matter of course in the work of making inventories. No one expected from the cataloguers judgments based on personal taste on individual buildings or individual styles. These men furnished the facts about the works of Late Gothic, and made it possible for others to engage in studies that might occasionally be colored by subjectivity, though they strove nevertheless for objectivity.

2. Neo-Romanticism

In the eighteenth century God had been deposed by Reason, in the nineteenth by Natural Science, but, untroubled, He continued to rule in exile, until one day He was back in His place with new devotees and new servants who called themselves neo-Romanticists. Haym's book on German Romanticism (1870) was a forerunner;[1] in 1884 came the publication of August Wilhelm von Schlegel's Berlin lectures of 1801. These books, of course, were only in part inspired by religious motives. An account of the neo-Romantic movement in all its aspects would be desirable, but here we must limit ourselves to discussing its representative in the field of art history: Henry Thode (1857-1920).

In addition to a tendency toward religiousness, an occasional aversion to clear thinking seems to be a common trait of all true Romanticists, although only the perfect union of clarity and religious feeling affords satisfactory cognition. Confusion of concepts is in Thode's case related to the relapse into obliteration of the temporal boundaries of styles. If stylistic designations were in reality nothing more than chapter headings for the convenience of the reader, the matter would not need to be taken so seriously. But such is by no means Thode's idea. He places the beginning of Renaissance in the midst of Gothic and means to indicate something by so doing. It is the chief theory that he has to offer.

[1] Rudolf Haym, *Die romantische Schule,* Berlin, 1870.

The main interest of his book centers about St. Francis,[2] one of the greatest figures of the Gothic period from the point of view of both religious and ecclesiastical history. But for Thode, Francis of Assisi marks the beginning of the Renaissance. "The Renaissance or, preferably, the new Christian art begins with the thirteenth century. . . . From Giotto to Raphael there is a coherent logical development, based on a coherent *Weltanschauung* and concept of religion." Thode's argument for this statement is "the free harmony of spatial proportions that even in the fifteenth and sixteenth centuries forms its peculiar characteristic. The Gothic form of construction merely hangs about it like a loose garment which it then suddenly casts off, around 1400, without difficulties and without regret, in order to assume instead the Greco-Roman toga." Burckhardt had already expressed himself somewhat similarly in the *Cicerone*. Thode associates this process with St. Francis because his teaching is the prerequisite for a truly Christian art: he established despised and mistreated nature in its rights as mediator between God and man. The unity of God and the world, the equality of men before God, and an immediate personal relationship to the Creator, such were, according to Thode, the fundamental tenets of St. Francis' doctrine, and he succeeded in gaining the recognition of the church for this conception, hitherto deemed heretical. The result was that the *bourgeoisie* became capable of development, and here we see in Thode the continuation of Vitet's, Ramée's, and Viollet-le-Duc's sociological theory of *architecture laïque*. The city population became a new class between the nobility and the peasantry. This is the position the Franciscans occupied between the aristocratic Cluniacs and the Cistercians (although the latter were by no means peasants but a kind of aristocratic cooperative of large landowners). On the basis of these ideas Thode developed a new understanding for the architecture of the Mendicant Orders in Italy, treating it in greater detail than Burckhardt had done in the *Cicerone*. He saw in this architecture—to some extent rightly—the prerequisite for the Pisani and for Giotto.

Thode was a forerunner; in Germany his book was at first hardly noticed and but little appreciated, while in France Paul Sabatier's book on St. Francis (1893) was greeted by a wave of enthusiasm. Gradually, however, Thode achieved recognition even in Germany, and in 1904 his book went into a second edition. It undoubtedly contributed to the winning of many hearts for St. Francis and helped

2 Henry Thode, *Franz von Assisi und die Anfänge der Kunst der Renaissance in Italien*, Berlin, 1885 (2nd ed., 1904).

to make people look at the frescoes in Assisi with piety, not merely with questions of attribution in mind. But it is equally certain that the book also tended to confuse people's ideas.

What then is Gothic? Does it cease with St. Francis? Are the "Gothic" churches of the Mendicant Orders in Italy "Renaissance"? If there is a coherent logical development from Giotto to Raphael, there ought also to be one from the church of the Franciscans in Assisi to St. Peter's in Rome. But what did the people themselves of that age think? We have traced their opinions from Petrarch to Boccaccio, Ghiberti, Pseudo-Raphael, and so on. Did they regard Italian Gothic as the immediate preparation for Renaissance? Yes, insofar as Cimabue and Giotto were meant; no, where architecture was concerned. Thode revived the false theory (of Vasari) that Giotto was Renaissance, and applied it retroactively to Gothic architecture.

Such problems are now outdated—although this particular false theory still persists here and there. All false theories ride the crest of the wave at first, only to sink and become for a long time the dogma of petty schoolmasters and many half-educated persons. Thode, however, most probably derived his theory from an excellent source, from Burckhardt's books. Schnaase had already excluded Italy, separating it from the rest of Europe and devoting to it a special volume. Burckhardt had then laid emphasis on the concepts of organic style and spatial style, and said that in Italy Gothic was not accepted as an organic style but was immediately transformed in the direction of a spatial style. He did not maintain that this Gothic was already Renaissance. That was Thode's assertion, though not quite in this caricatured form.

Unquestionably an unanswered problem became acute when Thode at first gave it a false solution. Since Quicherat it had been known that the rib was the progenitor of Gothic, though Thode, in his descriptions of the churches of the Mendicant Orders, speaks only seldom and quite casually of ribs; since Schnaase and Viollet-le-Duc it had been realized that Gothic is a reflection of the culture of the thirteenth century—including that of St. Francis; from the various handbooks it could be learned that this Gothic has a different appearance in France, England, Germany, Italy, and so on; people were fascinated by the ideas of evolution and were hearing about national spirit, race, and milieu; and yet they did not discover the proper way of judging Italian Gothic. Thode points out triumphantly that Brunelleschi, after all, built flat-ceilinged, basilicas with columns just as the Mendicant Orders did! But Brunelleschi would either have become furious, had he been told he built in the Gothic manner with the slight covering of a Roman toga, or he would perhaps have laughed heartily and said: We have not only changed our costumes, but our souls and minds as well. He might even have slipped off the toga, as St. Francis did his aristocratic clothing, but would have remarked: Behold, this is no ascetic body!

In addition to Thode's religious neo-Romanticism, this generation produced a number of other irrational and imaginative theories. The old "forest" theory had sunk to the level of a poetic metaphor in the period of real Romanticism, or, one might say, had been transfigured. But from its roots sprang a sucker, the more prosaic "wood" theory, appearing already in Costenoble who vaguely hinted that Romanesque (not Gothic) architecture originated in the wooden structures of the ancient Germanic people. Moller refuted the suggestion but Büsching returned to it. Then there appeared in Dresden the slim folio volume by Dahl, who instilled the idea in Semper. Ruprich-Robert took the thesis that Gothic was connected with wooden construction directly from Dahl, with little probability of a detour via Semper.

Victor RUPRICH-ROBERT (1820-1884), a French architect who restored and measured very exactly mediaeval structures, both Romanesque and Gothic, wrote an uncommonly important book on the mediaeval architecture of Normandy.[3] Special ornamental details reminded him of early Nordic ornamentation in Scandinavia. Despite the vagueness of this similarity he provided one chapter of his book with the very definite sounding title: *De l'influence skandinave au XIe et XIIe siècles* (page 127) and here opened vast perspectives. He calls on Viollet-le-Duc as an authority and speaks of connections with Indian art. It should be remembered that it was for Ruprich-Robert, as for Büsching, a matter of *Romanesque* style, not of Gothic. The details he has in mind are "Saxon" and the Saxons, he says, "seem to have belonged to the last emigration that left the plateaus of Northern India."[4] Saxons, Normans, Indo-Germanic people—these are all Aryans. The objects found in Celtic tombs, and so on, are North Oriental; the manuscripts that are called Saxon still have this ornamentation. But it is not merely a question of ornament! He refers to the tapestry of Queen Mathilda in Bayeux and the Nordic churches there depicted, which he identifies

[3] Ruprich-Robert, *L'Architecture normande au XIe et XIIe siècles en Normandie et en Angleterre*, Paris, 1887.

[4] ". . . paraissent appartenir à la dernière émigration partie des plateaux situés au nord de l'Inde."

with Norwegian churches,[5] namely Borgund and Urnäs. He relies on details, particularly the cubical capital, which appears in Urnäs and seems to him incontrovertible evidence of an origin in wooden construction. He returns to this matter of Scandinavian influence when he discusses the few remains of Romanesque furniture (page 227). It is true that it was at that time still quite indeterminable whether particular forms had been brought from North to South (or the converse) or even whether they had originated in Central Asia. But nevertheless Ruprich-Robert proceeded with inexcusable lack of critical judgment. He might have asked himself when the first cubical capitals had appeared outside Norway and when the Norwegian churches were built. The date of Urnäs is supposed to be somewhat earlier than that of Tind, possibly around 1170. Cubical capitals in stone, as is well known, can be found one hundred seventy years before that, witness the completely developed form in St. Michael's in Hildesheim from the year 1001.

But one may ask what that has to do with Gothic. According to present-day opinion, nothing; but it is the way to the derivation of Gothic from the wooden churches of Norway and must therefore be discussed in this book. Ruprich-Robert stated even more definitely than Büsching that Romanesque details are Germanic or Aryan, and Courajod continued this chain of thought.

From 1887 to 1896 Louis COURAJOD (1841-1896) lectured on the history of art at the École du Louvre in Paris, and after his death the lectures were published.[6] The first volume is entitled *Origines de l'art roman et gothique* but goes back into the first century after Christ, and the terminology is still somewhat reminiscent of that of the Romantic period. He remarks in one place: "the Romanesque style and the Gothic style—which are at bottom the same—" (page 458), and in this respect, therefore, nothing he says can be taken too strictly. The deeper reason for this indifference to the finer distinctions of the two styles is his idea that it was not the ribbed vault that was essential to Gothic, indeed not even the groined vault, but the *engaged shaft*,

[5] Dr. Auener in Marburg, Lahn, has kindly called my attention to the most recent study of the Nordic wooden churches: Gerda Boethius, *Hallar, tempel och stavkyrkor, studier till Kännedomen om eldre nordisk monumentalarchitektur*, I, *Den nordiske hallen, templet och starkyrkan*, Stockholm, 1913. Here, on page 69, there is a detailed discussion of the house types depicted in the Bayeux Tapestry. Cf. also André Lejard, *La Tapisserie de Bayeux. . .* Paris, 1946; further, Eric Maclagan, *The Bayeux Tapestry*, London and New York, 1943.

[6] Louis Charles Jean Courajod, *Leçons professées à l'école du Louvre publiées de H. Lemonnier et A. Michel*, Paris, 1899.

and that this was derived from the wooden construction of the "barbarians." "Barbarians" is for Courajod not a term of reproach:[7] "Without the barbarian carpentry there would probably never have been a Gothic art."[8] It is consequently understood that from the (unknown) wooden architecture of the Gauls down to Gothic everything is really the same. In this Courajod agrees with a lecture delivered by Emeric-David in 1837: "Our fathers had two methods of constructing large buildings. One was the ancient mode, the national Gallic mode; it consisted of building in wood. The other was called foreign, Roman, new, Gothic; it was the art of building in stone, in squared stone. The Goths excelled in the latter to such a degree that they were summoned—architects and workmen—to build the church of St.-Pierre-le-Vif in Rouen. Thence came the name *Gothic*."[9] A late justification of Vasari! The logic of it, however, remains incomprehensible. The Gauls built in wood, the Goths in stone. "The Goths were approximately what the Lombards still are, masons, architects, who earned their living by building. . . ," remarks E. David, in stone, to be sure (like the Romans), but in imitation of wood. Courajod says, accordingly: "How did the architects of Gothic, and before them those of Romanesque (*les romans*), conceive of the procedure of reinforcement? Is it not rather as carpentry than masonry? The wall does not count for them; their buttresses, piers, and engaged shafts *en délit* are only supports of wood translated into stone. It is a carpenter's idea adopted by masons."[10]

[7] *Ibid.*, I, p. 28: "Par le mot barbare, j'entends désigner collectivement tous les peuples en grand partie d'origine germanique qui sont passés sur le territoire gaulois du IIIe au Xe siècle."

[8] *Ibid.*, p. 443: "Sans la charpenterie barbare, il n'y aurait probablement pas eu d'art gothique."

[9] T. B. Emeric-David, "Sur la dénomination et les règles de l'architecture dite gothique," *Bulletin monumentale* v, 1839, p. 382: "Nos pères avaient deux manières de construire les grands édifices; l'une était le mode ancien, le mode national, *gallican*; il consistait à bâtir en *bois*; l'autre se nommait étranger, romain, nouveau, *gothique*; c'était l'art de bâtir de pierres, *quadris lapidibus*; les Goths excellèrent dans ce dernier genre au point qu'ils furent mandés, architectes et ouvriers, pour bâtir Saint-Pierre-le-Vif à Rouen. De la vient le nom du *gothique*." (The quotation is on p. 401.) There was an abbaye de Saint-Pierre in Rouen, later called S. Ouen. This Merovingian church of perhaps 535 is the one in question; a biography of Saint Ouen says that it was built "miro opere, quadris lapidibus, manu gothica." The appellation "le-Vif" is an error, for there was only one monastery of that name in France, namely in Sens (founded in 507, "ten times destroyed"). Cf. L. H. Cottineau, *Répertoire topo-bibliographique des abbayes et prieurés*, Macon, 1937, II, cols. 2851 and 3008. The ground plan of the destroyed church in Sens has been reproduced by Jean Hubert, *L'Art pré-roman*, Paris, 1938, pl. I. I owe the clarification of David's error to Mr. Louis Grodecki in Paris.

[10] *Op.cit.*, I, p. 582: "Comment les gothiques, et avant eux, les romans comprirent-ils les procédés de renforcement? N'est-ce pas en charpentiers plutôt qu'en maçons? Le mur ne compte pas pour eux; leurs contreforts, piles et colonettes en délit, ne sont que des étayages de bois traduits en pierre. C'est une pensée de charpentiers reprise par des maçons."

This theory is imbued throughout with a strong emphasis on the different talents of national groups. Courajod sides with the "barbarians" against antiquity. He is a Romanticist of the race theory, with all the passion that characterizes this type, as well as all the unclearness and irrationality that will not be bothered with logic and yet wants to "prove."

Thode's romanticism should not be forgotten. It was religious, but Thode was close to Richard Wagner and Chamberlain. Gobineau's books were undoubtedly known to Courajod, though he was only a fellow swimmer in the same stream, less carried away, as it were, by race than by wood. The fact that Moller had already pointed out, in controversy with Büsching, that Gothic showed development within construction in stone had long since been forgotten or was unknown in France, since both Büsching and Moller wrote German and Romanticists of race do not like to learn languages. Like Ruprich-Robert, Courajod expressly referred to the Norwegian churches (page 581) and upheld the derivation of the cubical capital from these buildings (page 583).

Jean Auguste BRUTAILS (1859-1926) took the trouble to refute the "wood" theory once more: we can, he says, trace historically the way Gothic developed within Romanesque construction in stone.[11] This, however, did not deter Strzygowski later from trying the wood track again.

Against the background of Seesselberg and Strzygowski one is inclined to judge Courajod more leniently. He did fundamental research in the dark centuries of the first millennium and presented a wealth of objects in a frame of reference that was fertile in ideas, so that his influence was felt everywhere in the following decades when efforts were made to understand the period between antiquity and the Middle Ages. He was a real scholar, a stimulating teacher, and a serious scientist in spite of his wood theory.

Friedrich SEESSELBERG (b. 1861)[12] based his theories far more consistently on the notion of race than Courajod, although the credit for having introduced racial Romanticism into the history of art belongs to neither. The idea had already emerged in Taine, and the tendency to explain all spiritual characteristics (alles Geistige) by means of

[11] Jean Auguste Brutails, *L'archéologie du Moyen-âge et ses méthodes*, Paris, 1900, pp. 76ff.

[12] Friedrich Seesselberg, *Die Früh-Mittelalterliche Kunst der Germanischen Voelker unter besonderer Berücksichtigung der Skandinavischen Kunst in Ethnologisch-Anthropologischer Begründung dargestellt*, Berlin, 1897.

race is, of course, only a practical application of positivistic thought in general to problems in the history of ideas. No exact proof, such as would be expected from an "exact" natural science, was ever adduced to show that men with particular physical characteristics, for example, blue eyes and blond hair, necessarily had to produce a particular art, for example, Gothic; but this seemed otiose since it was, of course, a question of an "empirical fact" that art was transformed whenever new races or, what was considered the same thing, new nations appeared on the scene. Most recent ethnography has another opinion about this, because it finds—empirically—the same forms among very different peoples; but in the nineteenth century scholars could not yet know that. However, they ought at least to have been able to see that the same people, for example, French or German, developed several styles one after the other.

Seesselberg finds that in the last analysis the causes of cultural processes can only be recognized "with certainty by the aid of the historical method of the study of man and the life of the race."[13] He acknowledges the obvious objection that mediaeval art was the result of the impingement of Romanesque, that is, Roman, art on Germanic racial life, but maintains that the Roman share in this process has been estimated too highly and the Germanic substratum too little. After the Napoleonic tyranny, he says, Hellenism was abandoned, men learned to feel as Germans, and the poets carried their contemporaries away with them "in an attack on the cosmopolitan citadel of clichés." (page 1) Körner, Arndt, and so on, are the poets in question, but what is meant by the "*Phrasenburg*"? "Research in Germanic linguistics and history has, with the intention of furthering national education, created truly national bibles, just as the recovered treasures of Germanic sagas of the gods and heroes, fairy tales and songs, and the splendid collections of objects of Germanic antiquity have likewise contributed an infinite amount to the intensification of national consciousness." (page 1) Seesselberg is thus consciously a follower of German Romanticism, regretting only that the surge of nationalism had abated. Especially in the "interpretation of monuments" German patriotism never reached full consciousness "because most German archaeologists persistently sought the roots of our art in the South." (page 2) All of this was later developed further by Strzygowski. Seesselberg continues: "The advance of Romanism was a concomitant

[13] *Op.cit.*, Preface, p. 2. His expression is: "*Racenleben*" (*sic*).

of Christianity. But in Germany and Scandinavia it encountered such well-developed types of indigenous national art in the pagan temple and castle buildings that it was obliged to confine its modifying influence to formalities, superficialities, and unessentials; further development of the basic architectural forms could no longer be deflected by Romanism from the national trend, just as, furthermore, the peculiar ornamentation perfected in Germanic bronzes, pottery, and carvings cannot be denied at least a fundamental influence." (page 2) The end of this sentence is a surprising qualification. Without doubt the ornamentation of the Bronze and Iron Ages, indeed the entire art of the period of the Migrations, contributed to Romanesque style not merely this or that detail but also something of its basic attitude. "The Renaissance and antiquity are also capable of being Germanicized." (page 3) Seesselberg is not exclusively an advocate of mediaeval art. "*Our* early art also . . . should therefore . . . be understood as the product of the *race*, not as the product of Christianity." (page 3) But he goes on to say: "The Roman church will, nevertheless, always be sure of the gratitude of our nation: Courageous apostles sent out from Rome staked their lives for our conversion. . . ."

As a matter of fact, Seesselberg was forced to compromise. He taught in the Department of Architecture at the Berlin Technische Hochschule, where at that time the classical columnar orders still belonged to the ABC and where the official attitude was Christian. Among other things the school had to train architects for Prussian church construction, especially for the restoration of Gothic buildings. For that reason, perhaps, Seesselberg acknowledged the merits of Christianity. But the latter, in his view, did not endow the peoples of the northern clime with any new aesthetic powers; he speaks rather of their *unalterable* racial nature (page 3). "Like the vernacular, the folksong, and folk customs, the architectural monuments were and remained, despite Christianity, creations of the primeval energy (*Urkraft*) of the folk soul." Thus, he says, one can assume that the Germanic peoples would have developed their own religion to the level of Christianity (Baldur as the Savior); the conversion to Christianity merely clothed the ancient Germanic ethical concept in new forms. At this point Seesselberg's introductory considerations culminate in the statement that is of interest to us here: "Even the idea that our art would inevitably have progressed of itself to the Gothic halls without any foreign influence is robbed of all its boldness when we reflect that the amazing, specifically Germanic wooden architecture of the Icelandic and Norwegian peoples had already traversed a very considerable distance along the way toward a style of absolute verticalism at a time when there was as yet nowhere else any thought of Gothic!" (page 4) The central feature of this whole theory is that Gothic is identified with verticalism and the latter with the character of the Germanic race. Seesselberg does not say anywhere in so many words that Gothic was derived from the Norwegian churches in wood, a conclusion that remained for his successor, Strzygowski, to draw, but he assembled all the essential elements of this thesis in such close connection that Strzygowski may well have thought that he, too, was not evincing the slightest boldness when he fused these elements. Though Seesselberg did not cite Taine, he did refer (page 141) to Gobineau, the creator of the chauvinistic theory of race.

Seesselberg's romanticism is unlike Thode's. For the latter, Gothic is Christian, Franciscan; for the former, it is Germanic despite all the admixture of Christianity. It is not difficult to say in conciliation that they are both right, so far Gothic signifies the Christian Germanic or the Germanic Christian. Each man tried to make one factor alone responsible. But neither one, and also not Ruprich-Robert, although the latter and Seesselberg were architects, paid any attention to the *vaults* and *ribs* that they should have derived from wooden architecture in order to make their theses tenable. Instead of ribs they now talk of *verticalism*, and although this element plays an *inconspicuous* role in the interiors of the Norwegian stavechurches and *none at all* in the exteriors, the *Scandinavian theory* of Gothic was here created in the geographical genealogy of Gothic, rivaling the "barbarian" and "Saracen" theories of an earlier age.

Seesselberg, however, has never been taken seriously by other historians of art, at least as regards his theory of Gothic. Hardly anyone (except Strzygowski) paid any attention to him. Only Dehio, in his superior way, seems to be alluding to him when he criticizes the derivation of architecture in stone from wooden construction.[14]

Seesselberg's ideas on "race" can be traced, directly or indirectly, to Gobineau, as is also indicated by his use of the French spelling for the term. His connection of Gothic with the Nordic race, however, probably goes back to Ruprich-Robert, Courajod (?) and presumably

14 *Die Kunst des Mittelalters*, 1904, "Internationale Wochenschrift" (*Ges. Aufsätze*, Munich and Berlin, 1914).

other authors as well, for Gobineau, it appears, knew little about Gothic and did not care for it. He mentions it only in connection with the *bourgeoisie* in Belgium and Germany, or the Hansa.[15]

Neo-Romanticism resurrected not only the "wood" theory of Gothic but also the "forest" theory itself, which is forever springing up anew.[16] In 1898 Joris Karl HUYSMANS (1848-1907) wrote: "I think it almost certain . . . that man found in the forests the so much discussed appearance of the naves and the pointed arches [ogive]. The most astonishing cathedral that Nature herself has built by making prodigal display of the pointed arches of her branches is at Jumièges. . . ." He describes very beautifully the forest there, close by the Norman ruin "that must be seen in winter, with its arched vault and all powdered with snow. . . ."[17] Why, then, did Jumièges have a flat ceiling? Why is the structure Romanesque and not Gothic? Huysmans is not thinking merely in terms of a metaphor, although even a metaphor would have been somewhat behind the times. A novel, *Der Stechlin* by Theodor FONTANE (1819-1898), had appeared only the previous year.[18] In the second chapter there is an account of three gentlemen who ride at a sharp trot as far as the avenue leading in a straight line to Stechlin Castle: "Here all three let their reins drop and rode on at a walk. Above them arched the beautiful old chestnut trees, lending to their approach something intimate and at the same time almost solemn. 'Why, this is almost like the nave of a church,' said Rex, who was riding on the left wing. 'Don't you think so, too, Czako?' 'Yes, if you like. But, pardon me, Rex, if I find the expression somewhat trivial for a ministerial assessor.' "

Advocacy of the forest theory is to be found in Huysmans' book, *La Cathédrale*,[19] a novel, that, in agreeable form, employs aesthetic theories as an accompaniment to the main theme of faith. It is not clear whether or not Huysmans knew Heinse's *Ardinghello*, but the two novels are

[15] Conte de Gobineau, *Essai sur l'inégalité des races humaines*, II, p. 475, Paris. I quote from the fourth edition (s.a.). The first edition appeared 1854 (-1884). Cf. text, Appendix 30.

[16] In 1868 Philip Veit, the painter, wrote in a book, *Über christliche Kunst*, p. 15: "Wölbungen eines Waldes, dessen Baumreihen ihre Zweige zueinander neigen." (Vaults of a forest, where the rows of trees bend their branches toward each other.)

[17] "Il est à peu près certain pour moi . . . que l'homme a trouvé dans les bois l'aspect si discuté des nefs et de l'ogive. La plus étonnante cathédrale que la nature ait, elle-même, bâtie en y prodiguant l'arc brisé de ses branches, est à Jumièges. . . . Il faut voir cela, l'hiver, avec la voûte arquée et poudrée de neige. . . ."

[18] Theodor Fontane, *Gesammelte Werke*, Series I, Vol. x, p. 16.

[19] Joris Karl Huysmans, *La Cathédrale*, Paris, 1898; in the 24th ed. of 1903, used by me, p. 63. For Huysmans' biography and a bibliography on him cf. Helen Trugdian's valuable book, *L'Esthetique de J. K. Huysmans*, Paris, 1934.

related in form. Huysmans is here less piquant than Heinse and thus far more mediaeval. His whole book is a revitalization of mediaeval symbolism, or, perhaps more properly, of allegory. Huysmans had studied the Scholastics, possibly the literature of the Camden Society as well, and by virtue of his own imagination he multiplies the number of symbols into a truly overwhelming sum. Thus one of his characters expounds the interpretation of the façade towers according to Durandus, and another according to Meliton, continuing with his own view: "One fact is certain . . . that the place for the bell-towers was never settled once and for all in the Middle Ages; one could therefore imagine new interpretations according to the spot they occupy."[20] And he interprets the crossing towers and the flèches as the aspiring of Christ's heart—for the crossing is his breast—toward God the Father in Heaven (page 122). "Consider, now, the church in all its details. Its roof is the symbol of charity that covers a multitude of sins; its slates, its tiles, are the soldiers and the knights who defend the sanctuary against the heathen who are like the storms. . . ."[21] In this connection the sources cited by Sauer should be compared.

La Cathèdrale is a great paean of praise to Chartres Cathedral. The book is in a sense a successor both to Chateaubriand's *Génie du Christianisme* and to Victor Hugo's *Nôtre-Dame,* though more scholarly than the former and less novelistic than the latter. The reader of Victor Hugo's book who was interested in the fascinating events of the novel might be willing to skip the archaeological excursuses; Huysmans' readers would like to see simple, scientific prose substituted for the dialogue form. Huysmans indulges everywhere, in fact, in descriptions evocative of mood; very pronouncedly, for example, in the description of the mass in the crypt of Chartres Cathedral.

Huysmans inveighed against Quicherat and the archaeologists who only dissect the body of the cathedrals. What he seeks is the soul (page 84). Unfortunately, modern man does not come any closer to the soul of Gothic by this road of allegory, but merely learns to know that naïve, popular play of the imagination that sees in architecture riddles for which many solutions can be found. This should not be confused, of course, with the iconography of the Middle Ages as applied to

20 "Un fait certain . . . c'est que la place des clochers n'a jamais été établie, une fois pour toute, au Moyen-Âge; l'on pourrait donc imaginer de nouvelles interprétations selon l'endroit qu'ils occupent."

21 "Considérez maintenant l'église dans ses détails; son toit est le symbole de la charité qui couvre une multitude de péchés; ses ardoises, ses tuiles, sont les soldats et les chevaliers qui défendent le sanctuaire contre les païens parodiés par les orages. . . ."

sculpture and painting, a subject already studied by Didron. The iconography of the thirteenth century was investigated on a very high plane by Mâle's book in 1898,[22] but what little he has to say about architecture in his last few pages can only be understood from the point of view of sculpture and painting.

Ten years later Huysmans applied his symbolical interpretation to Nôtre-Dame in Paris. Here all dialogue and everything novelistic has been abandoned,[23] and it is, consequently, more convenient to turn to this short treatise if one wishes to become acquainted with his views. (The other two treatises—on St.-Germain-l'Auxerrois and St.-Merry[23a] —are concerned simply with architectural history.)

The book by Josef Sauer (1872-1950) which has already been cited several times, provided somewhat later a severely scientific introduction to the symbolism of the church structure.[24] He invents no new interpretations, although, as it appears, he does not for his part entirely reject the new interpretations. So here too, we do not approach Gothic and its masters any more closely but merely that part of its public that regarded the cathedral as a book for pious analphabetes. Thus we learn exactly what we could also read in books, if we are not illiterate, for which, accordingly, we do not need art. The distinction remains, however, that sculpture and painting did actually have such allegorical content, whereas the apostles were only read into the piers since Suger, or soldiers into the slates of the roof much later. What, however, is the meaning of these piers and slates in a Gothic city hall or in other houses? No one has asked these awkward questions.

Henry ADAMS (1838-1918) was dependent on Huysmans. His book, written in an easy style for art-loving tourists (he himself uses the word "tourist"),[25] centers about Mont-Saint-Michel and Chartres. It is popular in tone and stimulating in many directions. Insofar as a certain romanticism can be detected, it is of the kind known as sentimental. The book's most important feature, however, is perhaps its emphasis on cultural history. For Adams, the *Song of Roland* is indispensable for the understanding of Mont-St.-Michel. There can, of course, be no objection to being so beautifully introduced to the spirit of this

[22] Emile Mâle, *L'art religieux du XIIIe siècle en France*, Paris, 1898.

[23] J. K. Huysmans, "La Symbolique de Nôtre-Dame de Paris" in *Trois églises et trois primitives*, Paris, 1908.

[23a] The church St.-Merry (or St.-Médéric) in Paris, built 1520-1612.

[24] Cited above, p. 213, n. 14.

[25] Henry (Brooks) Adams, *Mont-Saint-Michel and Chartres*, privately printed in 1905, published, Boston and New York, 1913. For the man himself, cf. *The Education of Henry Adams, an Autobiography*, Boston and New York, 1918.

poetry, but architectonic problems do not thereby become clearer. The same is true of Adams' (as well as Huysmans') observations on the cult of the Virgin, with which one must be acquainted in order to appreciate the sculpture and stained glass in Chartres, but it is not apparent what the cult of Mary as such has to do with the particular *architectonic* forms of Chartres. There is no need to condemn the book, which indeed hardly makes claim to be more than a long *feuilleton* on a high cultural level. Its scientific value lies more in the direction of a compilation of knowledge relating to cultural history. This opinion should not be misjudged, and the reader should note, for example, what he has to tell us about round and pointed arches: "The heavy round arch is like old cognac compared with the champagne of the pointed and fretted spire." Did Adams mean that the pointed arches of Chartres have as much to do with champagne as with the mother of God? Without a doubt, he never gave a thought to this unfortunate implication of his metaphor.

3. The Technical Theory of Gothic

The twentieth century found three different tendencies ready to hand for further work on the theory of Gothic: first, the romantic with its neoromantic variations of confessionalism, nationalism, and mystification (Adams), second, that of the German art scholarship typified by Fiedler, Wölfflin, and Riegl, which was concerned with form alone or with form and content, and third, the "morphological," which had its inception in the literature on the pointed arch and was further developed, indeed, as it seemed, perfected by the ideas of Wetter, Viollet-le-Duc, Quicherat, and Lefévre-Pontalis. For it was like a final reassurance to learn from Quicherat that the rib is the progenitor of Gothic.

But one day the question was bound to arise: and what exactly gave rise to the rib? To that there was no answer—unless it was assumed that the architect who first introduced a pair of diagonal ribs into a groined vault told himself in advance all the things that Wetter and Viollet-le-Duc later maintained: that the rib was elastic and would carry the vault cells, that everything could then be made thinner, in short, that pure Gothic would gradually be achieved. But no one dared to attribute so much intellectual profundity and prophetic insight to the first architect of ribs. In any case, it seemed like a good explanation to say that he was undoubtedly a competent engineer who anticipated the advantages of the rib, namely, that it carried and was elastic.

But what if the rib does not carry at all?

Arthur Kingsley PORTER (1883-1933) drew attention to the fact that in the ruin of Ourscamp the vault cells have collapsed while the ribs are still standing unchanged.[1] How is it possible for the cells to collapse as long as the ribs stand *and* carry them? Furthermore: in Longpont, another ruin, there are quadripartite vaults, the cells of which are still in place although the ribs have broken off.

Porter could not be satisfied with the observation that the rib does not carry. He had to ask what the purpose of the ribs was, if they are *statically* useless; and his answer is that they have a *technical* value, that is to say, for the execution of vaults. "Rib vaults therefore were invented in Lombardy as a simple device to economize wood. They were adopted by the French builders for the same purpose. The same desire to dispense with temporary wooden substructures governed the development of architecture during the entire transitional period, and eventually lead to the birth of Gothic."[2] Saving of wood resulted from the use of the "movable cerce." In this connection Porter cites Viollet-le-Duc and Choisy, but remarks that neither realized the true significance of the cerce, which lies in the fact that by its aid masons could build almost freehand from a light scaffolding, with a resulting economy of wood and working hours. The cerce freed construction from the necessity of a substructure that had only a temporary value and was expensive in proportion to its brief time of usefulness.

A consequence of Porter's understanding of the process of building by means of the cerce was that now the origin of doming was plausibly explained. Scholars had never been able to understand how these surfaces so complicated mathematically were achieved. According to Porter, they resulted automatically—without any need for the mediaeval masters to have understood them mathematically—from the cerce. The surfaces belong to the category called in geometry "nondevelopable"; they are thus neither cylindrical nor conical, but among the many nondevelopable surfaces they are also not identical with the pure spherical form. The expression "domical segment" (*Kuppelseg-*

[1] Arthur Kingsley Porter, *The Construction of Lombard and Gothic Vaults*, New Haven, 1911.
[2] *Ibid.*, p. 3.

ment) occasionally met with in technical literature is not correct.[3] Formerly the idea prevailed, probably originating in Viollet-le-Duc, that the builders first erected a complete, heavy, wooden form for an undomed quadripartite vault, then heaped earth on it, and modeled this earth according to the doming. This is entirely fantastic. The cerce was in any case cheaper and more practical than any such heaping of earth would have been.

Porter believed that ribs had been invented in Lombardy, and he therefore established a causal relationship between this discovery and the paucity of wood in that region. According to him, the rib, once discovered, governed the course of all subsequent development in the same way as that assumed by Quicherat.[4]

Economy of wood is not of any great importance in regions where wood was plentiful. Porter himself calls attention to the wooden roof timbering of the French cathedrals and quotes the passage from Abbot Suger's account where he speaks of the discovery of trees long enough for the roof of his abbey church of St.-Denis. Some support for Porter's theory could be found in Bond's assertion[5] that in the earlier Middle Ages there were as yet no sawmills, and that consequently boards were hewn to shape with an axe, with the result that each tree, whatever its circumference, produced only *one* board, everything else being waste. (See above page 14) Thick trunks were needed for the roof beams, but for the sheathing of the forms for the centering, only thin boards. Porter, however, refers to Lombardy where wood was scarce and where it was perhaps really impossible to obtain a supply of boards—if Lombardy was then already as deforested as it is today. No further research needs to be done on the latter point, however, for today most scholars would probably agree in saying that the rib did not originate in Lombardy but in heavily wooded Normandy.

The cerce was also not employed everywhere where ribbed vaults were built. When a horizontal ridge rib was introduced, as was the

[3] Gall says cautiously: "comparatively like domical segments (*Kuppelsegmente*)," *Niederrheinische und normännische Architektur*, p. 60. The cerce is a portion of a circle (arc), consequently a curve of constant curvature. But whereas in the case of a spherical surface this portion of a circle revolves about its center, it moves here along a bent axis that lies in the middle between the ribs. Its lowest point is the center of the semicircle between the feet of the two ribs, its highest the point where the ribs intersect. cf. also p. 568.

[4] The question of whether Porter's datings of Lombardic ribbed vaults are correct is not vital for the judging of his theory, but the fact cannot be passed over in silence that they are almost entirely incorrect.

[5] Francis Bond, *An Introduction to English Church Architecture*, Oxford, 1913, I, p. 288.

case in the majority of ribbed vaults in Anjou and England, doming of the cells was not the rule. But that a complete board form was used in wooded regions even with relatively small vault cells and also at a late date has been demonstrated by the miraculously preserved structure in the tower of the church in Lärbro on Gotland, Sweden, which has already been discussed above in the chapter on Suger.[6]

The chief objection to Porter's theory, however, seems to be the fact that the cerce can be used in exactly the same way in groined vaults built of masonry as in ribbed vaults. Porter knew, of course, that there were domed Romanesque groined vaults. They exist by the hundreds. How then can it be said that the cerce gives birth to the rib? There is no need of stone ribs in order to set up the cerce—wooden centerings can be used just as well, and these can be removed afterwards. And there is also no saving in wood if stone ribs are constructed, for wooden centerings are just as necessary for the stone ribs as for the groins. When the cerce is used, just as much wood is needed in either case.

The basic idea of explaining Gothic on the basis of economy in wood and scarcity of wood—as it were, a negative "forest" theory of Gothic—is absolutely unromantic, rational, and actually materialistic. Porter was still influenced by rationalism, as far as this theory is concerned, and yet it signified a further undermining of rationalistic doctrines; he maintained that the rib does not carry. Strictly speaking, he explained not the rib but merely the doming. If, however, neither the ribs nor the flying buttresses carry, what is left of Viollet-le-Duc's doctrine? And, above all, if all these forms have no practical value, why were they constructed? Had Riegl perhaps been right when he said in 1904 that the technical problem simply did not exist, but only the aesthetic one: as an extension of the membering into the ceiling? It is quite certain that Porter did not know Riegl's lecture on Salzburg; indeed, as it appears, he by no means realized fully that as a result of his technical explanation Viollet-le-Duc's theoretical structure was bound to collapse. It was a kind of time bomb that would inevitably explode when anyone who wanted to destroy Viollet-le-Duc's theory hit upon it.

Porter, however, was not completely one-sided. He writes: "That the ribs of a rib vault . . . came to assume other functions besides that of serving as a centering during the construction is not to be denied, grossly as the importance of these functions has been exaggerated by certain writers."[7]

[6] See above, p. 14.

[7] Porter, *op.cit.*, p. 16.

4. Impressionism

To IGNORE Impressionism would be to leave a gap in this account of the way Gothic has been reflected by successive temporal styles; and the omission would be all the more unfortunate since Impressionism is brilliantly represented by one of its great artists, Auguste RODIN (1840-1917). His book was published at a time when Impressionism was no longer alive, except for the few Impressionists who lived on into the new age. Rodin was born in 1840, and although he was about seventy years old when he wrote *Les Cathédrales de France*, it is filled with the enthusiasm of youth,[1] calling to life again something of the spirit of Goethe's dithyramb on Strasbourg Cathedral. It is all poetry and painting.

"... the masters of Gothic were great painters because they were great architects.—It goes without saying that we are using the word 'painter' here in its broadest and most general sense. The colors into which the painters of whom we speak dip their brushes are the very light and shade of day and the two twilights. The surfaces resulting from the great opposites that the cathedral builders had to master are not of significance solely for equilibrium and solidity, they determine in addition those deep shadows and those beautiful lights that clothe the edifice in such a magnificent garment."[2]

Rodin looks at the quadripartite vaults with the same eyes. "What elegance in these surfaces that are so simple and so strong! Thanks to them, light and shade react upon each other, producing that half-tone, the essential source of the richness of effect that we admire in these spacious structures. This effect is entirely pictorial."

He describes quite personal, momentary impressions, for example, Reims Cathedral at night.

"Distant gleams of light darken, blacken before certain columns. Obliquely they light others, feebly but regularly.

"But the depths of the choir and all the left side of the nave are plunged into thick darkness. The aspect is ghastly. Indistinct things go on in the lighted distance. . . . Each of the quadrangular spots is struck by a frightful illumination; lights flare up among the columns, which assume colossal proportions. And the interruptions, these conflicts of brightness and shadows, these four

[1] Auguste Rodin, *Les cathédrales de France; avec cent planches inedites*, Paris, 1914. With an introduction by Charles Morice. According to Marcel Tirel, *The Last Years of Rodin*, New York, 1925, p. 17 (I have only the English translation by R. Francis at hand), Rodin's travels to the cathedrals took place from about 1908 to 1910.

[2] For the original text of this and the following quotations cf. Appendix 30.

opaque columns before me, these six other lighted ones, further away, in the same line and in a diagonal direction, then the night in which I bathe and which submerges everything, make me doubtful of time and countries. There is no softness here. I have the sensation of being in a vast cave from which Apollo is about to emerge.

"I remain for a long time without being able to explain the awful vision. I no longer recognize my religion, my cathedral. Such is the dread inspired by the ancient mysteries. . . ."

Countless individual experiences are strung together as chance offered them. And how does the book end? With a section entitled *Les Moulures*:

"The molding, in its spirit, in its essence, represents and signifies the entire idea of the master builder.

"He who sees it and comprehends it, sees the whole monument.

"Its softness is that of nature itself; its life the life of the whole edifice.

"It contains the whole energy of the architect, expresses all his thought.

"Let us return to the adoration of that which it formerly imitated. It was contrived to diffuse gentle grace, power, suppleness, unity.

"Woman, the eternal model, contributes her undulating forms.

"It is not the ornament, but the molding that ought to provide a resting place for the eye. But it expresses, in profile, the character of the epoch. *Doucine* rightly is the name of the French profile.

"The moldings are sweet symphonies."

Perhaps most scholars will not find all this very useful. Yet Rodin quite definitely sensed the decisive factor and stated it explicitly: the molding—or, more properly, the profile—expresses the essential character of Gothic. It is that, in any case, to which we must finally turn.

These notes, written by Rodin around 1910 during his travels and then polished at home, were edited in 1914 by his friend, Charles MORICE (1889-1946), who provided them with an introduction of over one hundred pages in which he gives a very good anthology of French judgments on Gothic,[3] a description of French Romanesque, toward which he is very sympathetic, and a brief survey of the history of French Gothic—all written with decided literary skill and supported by a good knowledge of French technical literature hitherto published. It may be questioned whether this introduction was necessary to Rodin's text, but it is intended to provide a scholarly foundation and would be worth reading even as an independent treatise. It is, above all, a real

[3] Many of these passages could be inserted in the earlier chapters of this book.

supplement in that it discusses the relations of Monet and Pissarro, and of the Impressionists to Gothic.[4]

5. "Gothic Man"

Wilhelm WORRINGER (b. 1881) shows no interest in ribs and, indeed, hardly any at all in "morphological" details. He made a thorough study of Riegl's chief works and is therefore convinced *a priori* that the rib results from a particular *Kunstwollen.* But what is the source of this artistic volition? Worringer answers like Courajod: race. Can one say then, in abridged form, that the rib originates in race? Even the statement that the rib is created by a particular artistic volition is, after all, not entirely satisfactory. For not every type of artistic volition produces ribs, but instead —? We pause. The argument seems to go round in a circle: we try to derive the rib from artistic volition and then in turn derive artistic volition from the rib. But now to derive the rib from race would appear to be a feat of magic, and in this case there is not even a circle, for who would want to determine race on the basis of the rib? This, however, is essentially what Worringer does, not precisely with the rib but with Gothic as a whole.

Seesselberg had already said that a race has unchangeable characteristics. Albrecht HAUPT (1852-1933) also wrote on the art of the Germanic people from the point of view of the theory of race stemming from Gobineau, but did not discuss the actual Middle Ages or, above all, Gothic itself.[1] For that reason he is mentioned here only in passing. All the historians of art who are influenced by Gobineau are in danger of tying their national group down to a particular style. The thesis concerning the unchangeable characteristics of a people is useless in such indefinite form. Unquestionably certain characteristics remain constant for centuries, even, in the case of some peoples who have maintained themselves for long ages, for thousands of years—but which characteristics? Can it be concluded, therefore, that a "race" predisposed toward "Gothic" has built in the Gothic style from time immemorial

[4] Morice refers on p. LIV to Adrien Mithouard's *L'art gothique et l'art impressioniste*, giving no date. I do not know this book.

[1] Albrecht Haupt, *Die älteste Kunst, insbesondere die Baukunst der Germanen*, Leipzig, 1909; especially the chapters "die Rasse," and "Die Germanische Rasse und ihre Eigentümlichkeit in der Kunst."

and will be obliged to abide by the Gothic style to all eternity? A horrible thought for any nation that belongs to this race. Anyone who is interested in the difference between the German and the French nations, or the Spanish and the American, would find no comfort here, for all these nations build Gothic structures, even though not exclusively. The same is true of all "Germanic" peoples, including the Germans. Everyone knows that from the La Tène period to Gropius Gothic was not the only style in which people built, and consequently the "Gothic" implied by the thesis in question cannot be Gothic in the narrower historical sense but rather a secret, latent Gothic in a psychological sense. This recalls Seillière's conception of an eternal Romanticism.

In his doctoral dissertation Worringer had already sketched the basic tenets of his system,[2] and then developed it fully in his brilliant book, *Formprobleme der Gothik*.[3] Both works will be discussed together.

The subtitle of the dissertation professes adherence to psychology, in particular to stylistic psychology. The main title introduces the idea of empathic psychology, joining it, however, with "abstraction"; in the book we learn that abstraction refers to style, thus to stylistic psychology. Abstraction and empathy are here meant as opposites, as are accordingly stylistic psychology and empathic psychology as well. This terminology has been rightly criticized, especially since Worringer himself talks of empathy directed toward the abstract. He means essentially the contrast of inorganic (crystalline) and organic, and also employs the paired concepts "style" and "naturalism" (though one might again object that naturalism is also a style, even if not in the sense that Worringer has in mind). According to him, the "aesthetic" that culminates in the concept of the beautiful has been evolved in one-sided dependence on antiquity, and is applicable only to naturalism and "empathy"; it has thereby lost the ability to be just to Gothic. In support of his skepticism toward aesthetics and its separation from the theory of art, Worringer cites Fiedler (page 6 of the *Formprobleme*), although Fiedler was, after all, antagonistic toward Gothic. At any rate he wants to understand it on its own merits, an attitude already urged by Alexandre de Laborde in 1818. Worringer, however, carries out the program with a teeming wealth of ideas.

He rejects the notion of a "human being *per se*," at least for the history of art. In order to connect Gothic with the Nordic race Wor-

[2] Wilhelm Worringer, *Abstraktion und Einfühlung. Ein Beitrag zur Stilpsychologie*, Munich, 1908. English translation, London, 1953.

[3] Munich, 1912.

ringer postulates four types of human beings: the primitive, the Oriental, the classical, and the Gothic. Down to Hegel two types had sufficed, the classical and the romantic. Hegel added the Oriental because he needed three types for his thesis, antithesis, and synthesis, and because at that time art scholarship began to be aware of the Orient, by which were meant Egypt, Babylonia, Assyria, and India. As a result of Riegl's efforts the horizon had been widened to include virtually the whole globe; in any case he was as much interested in the art of Islam and of prehistoric ages as in that of antiquity. Worringer added the corresponding *fourth* type by postulating a prehistoric man; Islam he considers under the heading of "Orient." He is conscious of the hypothetical nature of his construction. His idea of Oriental man in particular is a somewhat motley abstraction, but all such concepts are supposed to be constructed only for their heuristic value and thereby justified.

Aboriginal or *primitive* man he describes as a "bewitched animal" who receives unreliable, variable "visual images" which he slowly converts into "conceptual images." Thanks to the dualism of man and environment, he lives in a constant state of metaphysical anxiety, and consequently he needs magic charms. This is, greatly abridged, the aspect relating to cultural psychology. To it corresponds, on the artistic side, flat ornamentation, consisting of severely geometrical, stylized symbols of necessity and the elimination of the element of depth. Though primitive man occasionally also models plastically and imitates the third dimension, this is not art but merely the exercise of the imitative instinct, which has always been confused with art. Worringer uses Fiedler's terms (the chaotic nature of visual images, and so on) and also Hildebrand's expression of the "tormenting" element, the fluctuation of impressions and visual perceptions in near vision (*Nahsicht*).

Classical man, on the other hand, is simply the (classical) Greek and the modern representative of the "aesthetic of the beautiful," whether as a disciple of antiquity or Renaissance or of the age of Winckelmann or Fiedler. Fear has been transformed into confident familiarity with the environment, into a "this worldly" piety in Goethe's sense. The dualism has vanished, life has become more beautiful, more joyous, but has been diminished in depth, grandeur, and dynamic force. The divine has become secularized. Correspondingly, the impulse toward abstraction (artistic will, equaling impulse) has turned into an impulse toward empathy. Everything develops into naturalism as the rhythm of the organic ("rhythm" is for Worringer almost identical with "organic") and "objectified self-enjoyment" (Lipps).

Oriental man is again closer to the primitive. (It appears, indeed, that the Oriental is older than the classical, as would be the case at least with Egypt and Buddha, 568-488 B.C., though not with Christianity, which must doubtless be regarded also as belonging to the Orient—Worringer does not say which peoples he assigns to the "Orient.") Primitive man, however, was in a state *prior* to cognition of the world, Oriental man in one *beyond* it. Dualism is felt as sublimely fated. Fear becomes adoration, resignation a religion. Art is therefore abstract, it is an expressionless line on the surface. This is the weakest point in Worringer's system. Oriental art is after all different from prehistoric, and, even within the "Orient"—Egyptian, Indian, and so on, as well as Christian—art cannot all be characterized by this same formula, indeed each of these fields individually has its own succession of styles that cannot be exhausted by the definition of the "expressionless line on the surface."

For us the chief interest of this whole construction lies in the fourth type: Gothic man. Gothic, to Worringer, is only an "academic concept." His Gothic comprises all Nordic art from the Hallstatt period to the Baroque (of the North). In the north, Renaissance was a kind of derangement. The artistic basis of Gothic is the geometrical style of all *Aryan* peoples. (Would this then be the art of primitive man?) Worringer explicitly rejects the racial Romanticism in the sense of Chamberlaine (page 29), and talks of *Germanic* development more as a matter of *convenience* because the Germanic people can stand as *pars pro toto* for that stylistic-psychological type of humanity that he has in mind. Nevertheless, he insists, just as Dehio does, that "Gothic" is only possible where there has been an admixture of Germanic "blood." The Germanic people are not the sole carriers of Gothic but a *conditio sine qua non*. Could the creation of "Gothic" art be regarded then as the surest blood test of an Aryan? Or does this naïve theory simply fall into the category of vicious circles?

For Worringer, however, this particular circle remains the prerequisite for understanding Gothic in both a broad and a narrow sense. Since "Gothic" in the "broader" sense includes Baroque, it might be expected that it could be recognized by Wölfflin's concepts as both picturesque and agitated mass or by Schmarsow's as plastic and rhythmical. But instead we are given completely new concepts. In prehistoric ornamentation of the North, in the Bronze and Iron Ages (aboriginal man is obviously restricted to the Stone Age), the line is passionately agitated, creating unrest and confusion, an intoxication and a frenzy of movement. We can experience empathy but only toward an alien, abstract world of dead lines (page 31 of the *Formprobleme*). This is the prelude to the "mathematics come alive" of "Gothic in the narrower sense." The latter is itself petrified vertical movement. Its dematerialization corresponds to the degeometrization of the line in the Iron Age. The heaviness of stone is denied in favor of purely spiritual expression. Stone and all material are spiritualized. It is not a matter of structural processes but of transcendental longing, of the thrill of eternity in the infinite, of supralogical values, not, as in antiquity, of logical ones (page 67). This "idea behind Gothic building" also explains the ribs, which Worringer declares to be decorative and *not* picturesque (pages 92 and 84). The barrel vault does not partake of any quality of activity (page 91)—by which seems to be meant that it bears down, though that is also active—the groined quadripartite vault "on the contrary" is active. The groins "give to the vault a linear mimic, corresponding to Nordic artistic volition." (At this point some scholars will perhaps think of the Roman groined vaults of the basilica of Constantine and ask whether these must be considered Nordic and as pertaining to "eternal" Gothic.) It is consequently understandable, says Worringer, that the further development of Gothic (Romanesque is, of course, also "Gothic," just as in Courajod) starts with this construction of groins. "The first step was to emphasize this linear mimic by encasing the groined arches with ribs that at first had no inner relation to the vaults and served, in addition to their purpose of support, as a reinforcement of the linear expression." Worringer here repeats Viollet-le-Duc's mistake; how can ribs that are not joined to the vault support it? Perhaps, however, he meant those ribs that are in direct contact with the vault with no intervening space. There are cases of both: in S. Ambrogio in Milan one can insert the hand between rib and vault (according to Dartein's account); in Durham, and in most Gothic cathedrals, the vault rests on the ribs. Worringer, however, says expressly that the "first step" is that the rib does not carry and the "second" that it does carry. And only then is Gothic perfected, that is to say, construction *and* mimetic or artistic expression become one identical unity. Worringer does not have a high opinion of Schmarsow's system, but the former's interpretation of the rib as mimetic expression corresponds nevertheless to Schmarsow's particular method of empathy, except that this is here regarded as the result of the permanent artistic volition of the Nordic race.

This position compels Worringer to ascribe to each race qualities that become first an inescapable destiny, and this in turn leads to contradictions. He has (in this book) absolutely no comprehension of Romanesque. He sees it not for its own sake but from the point of view of Gothic as the latter's imperfect, preliminary stage, calling Romanesque "Gothic without enthusiasm" (page 94). Nevertheless, he maintains that Romanesque is specifically *Germanic*: in Normandy and Burgundy, in Lombardy, and in Germany. Gothic, on the other hand, is *international*. The contradiction that the specifically Germanic lands created only Gothic *without* enthusiasm, whereas the French produced it *with*, must, accordingly, be explained. And Worringer provides an explanation. Namely, the Germanic man, because of his dull, chaotic urge is too ponderous for enthusiasm (page 95); the Romance man, on the other hand, can be impelled to the highest enthusiasm without losing his clarity and is therefore able to find the clear (French) formulation for the unclear, Nordic artistic volition. He creates the *system* (page 90). Only the system is French, however, not Gothic itself. Anyone is free to separate the system in Amiens from the Gothic, in order to recognize that what is left is the Germanic element. Whoever does not succeed in doing this should remember that there is in Germany a Late Gothic which may also be said to have a system, though not the French one of Amiens, and here, then, the Nordic artistic volition should appear plainly. Worringer did not perform this task. He traces the most different styles from the animal ornament of the Age of the Migrations down to the Baroque, and everywhere the differences fade before a common characteristic: the liveliness of what is dead, the uncanniness, ghostliness, spectralness, unnaturalness of this combination,—and such is the deepest meaning of the Nordic or Germanic spirit.

Worringer sought and found the eternally Gothic also in Scholasticism and Mysticism, this idea perhaps being a legacy from Hegel or from Schnaase. Nor is Semper's characterization of Gothic as Scholasticism in stone omitted. Scholasticism itself is said to have been satisfied with proving an already recognized truth afterward on grounds of reason. But this *temporal* Scholasticism is again the narrower concept—the system. There is an *eternal* Scholasticism which begins as far back as the Old Germanic riddles. As was the case there, so also in Scholasticism "the theological purpose is hardly significant in comparison with the joy in a tortuous, twisted movement of thought as such." The analogy lies only in the form. Even if Scholasticism were shown to have been interested in more than mere intellectual acrobatics, this could not disturb Worringer, since obviously the twisted movement is the decisive factor in both Scholasticism and Gothic. But of what is he thinking at this point? Of Chartres? Of Amiens? Or of St. Martin's in Landshut or the Frauenkirche in Munich? None of these buildings is twisted in its movement. Perhaps by "twisted" he means the Flamboyant Style. Or possibly the church of St. Anna in Annaberg? But even then the analogy of Gothic to Scholasticism remains a superficial suggestion as long as it is not specified more precisely; one would also like to see a more rigorous proof. Moreover, *granted* that St. Thomas Aquinas is tortuous, does he descend from Germanic stock? He is, after all, an Italian and taught in Paris. And to what race does Bonaventura belong?

The case is similar with regard to mysticism. According to Worringer this is a psychic experience whereas Scholasticism is spiritual. Mysticism is warmer, more sensuous, more personal. Worringer describes it well and has a strong feeling for the mystical element in Gothic. "As the interior is all mysticism, so the exterior is all Scholasticism." (p. 108) Inside a cathedral one does not see the system of buttresses (if it exists), and it remains a mystery how the structure continues to stand. But what if more recent theories are right and the Gothic structure is stable even without buttresses—would it then lose its quality of mysticism? On the exterior, on the other hand, the system of buttresses is clearly visible, not, however, that which it supports. Here another side of the analogy between Scholasticism and Gothic is made plain: Scholasticism is, as it were, the buttress of something invisible. But there are, after all, Gothic churches without flying buttresses: perhaps all structures before 1178 and all hall-churches. Are such Gothic buildings also mystical on the outside?

However, Worringer is undoubtedly right when he senses the mystical element in Gothic. Who would deny it? We believe it on Hegel's authority, on Schnaase's, and so on, and we also believe it on Worringer's. But he has more to maintain. Gothic mysticism is, he says, Nordic. But is it not Oriental and did not Worringer ascribe all Christianity to Oriental man? If "Gothic in the narrower sense" is Christian—and Worringer does not dispute it—why is it then not Oriental? The more one reflects on what is Oriental and what Nordic the less one is able to make sense of these concepts that on a first reading seem so stimulating and beguiling. Perhaps Worringer only posed the problem in his *Formprobleme* and did not solve it. In support of this idea it may be adduced that the first edition of the book contains reproductions that are not intended to illustrate definite passages in the text but serve merely to evoke the mood with which the author is concerned. Among them can also be found the relief of St. Peter from Moissac, a piece of sculpture from between 1120 and 1130, which even Worringer could not call Gothic "in the narrow sense." He doubtless selected this work as a representative of "Gothic in the broader sense." If, however, one handles terminology somewhat more cautiously and understands by Gothic only that in the "narrow sense," in other words, if one adheres to the "academic concept," there remains a residue of something "Nordic" which just is not merely Gothic. Worringer sought to isolate this factor, and called it, too, Gothic. Perhaps it would help somewhat if the title of the book were changed to "Problems of *Nordic* Form." This, one might say, is a legitimate task for the scientific study of art. Is *it* accomplished by Worringer? One would have to be more precise as to what is meant by "Nordic." The geographical or the ethnological aspect? The "Germanic" Valhalla in Regensburg is not Gothic. It stands in the vicinity of the Gothic cathedral of Regensburg, somewhat as the Madeleine stands in the vicinity of Nôtre-Dame in Paris. From the geographical point of view, therefore, "Nordic" means only the source of a style. The style of the Madeleine came from the Mediterranean region, that of Nôtre-Dame from the shores of the North Sea. The antique Greek style remains southern even in Paris, and the Gothic northern even in Salamanca and Cyprus; they reflect something of their place of origin. And something also of their time of origin! It is a moot question whether the Indo-Germanic "or" Aryan people began their migration in the South or in the North or in the East (in Central Asia). But what really matters is that at the time when they were creating definite styles they were living in definite geographical, namely, Nordic, regions. It is a dogma that a race has permanent spiritual qualities, a dogma that is refuted by the transformations in the history of ideas of every race. The peoples of the earth even undergo somatic transformation because of continual interminglings; a people is never stationary, only the geographical place is. Consequently, the North is today no longer inhabited by Gothic man, nor Greece by classical man. The land is overrun by peoples who change. Worringer himself is guilty of a divagation from his theory, for he points to the American skyscrapers as the only analogy to his eternal, secret Gothic, remarking that they represent the same frenzy of logic and mechanics, charged with the expression of organic life. Germanic or Nordic art has passed its peak in Europe and experiences a resurrection in a land that can scarcely any longer comprehend the old nationalistic ideas of Europe. But if one calls the Empire State Building and the skyscraper group of Rockefeller Center in New York Gothic, the concept of Gothic is being unmercifully stretched. On the basis of quantity there is perhaps more posthumous Gothic in America than original in Europe. The skyscrapers are not to be counted in this number—at most only such as have been provided by a historistic architect with pointed arches and the like. But of course Worringer does not mean these.

Twelve years after the *Formprobleme* Worringer supplemented his conception of Gothic by the thesis that Gothic, or rather this time merely cathedral Gothic, is lyrical, not monumental. Monumentality does not depend on grandeur of scale but on "inner grandeur, which presupposes elemental simplicity and macrocosmic temper of mind."[4] One thinks of Laon and Lincoln, of Albi and the Frauenkirche in Munich, and must ask in astonishment whether these churches are unmonumental and lyrical. Worringer, however, discusses the subject of brick architecture and declares that this brick style reveals an "involuntary monumentality."[5] That is a kind of perverted artistic volition. But there remains the ashlar Gothic with its "multiplication of the tiny" (a phrase of Goethe's). Worringer speaks of Adam Kraft's tabernacle in the church of St. Lorenz in Nuremberg, confessing that he cannot resist "the heretical temptation of regarding the cathedrals also as unnaturally enlarged tabernacles." The comment is reminiscent of Filarete's and Goethe's remarks, but one must ask whether historically the tabernacles, the monstrances and the like precede, or, conversely, the monumental architecture comes first before the tabernacles and the monstrances. Perhaps the most illuminating feature of this article is the admission that Worringer, in forming his concept of Gothic, did not begin with architecture but with the Gothic line, "the calligraphy of the Gothic style of drawing," "the beautifully sinuous and animated lines." It may be granted that they are lyric, not monumental, but what does that prove about the cathedrals? Since the lyric has already been mentioned in connection with Gothic and the epic with Romanesque, would it not be more justified to bring in a third genre and call

4 Worringer, "Zur Frage der gotischen Monumentalität," *Festschrift für Oskar Walzel*, Wildpark-Potsdam, 1924, pp. 211ff.

5 *Ibid.*, p. 219.

Gothic dramatic? But such a designation could only be a metaphor; the Gothic of the cathedrals is primarily architectonic. The word monumentality goes back etymologically to *monere*, "to remind," but this derivation of the word is not the decisive factor. A monument is a commemorative object. "What need hast thou of a monument, thou hast set thyself one," says Goethe when he is unable to discover Erwin's grave. It is useless to argue about words, and for Worringer "monumentality" means inner grandeur; well and good, but despite all his arguments the Gothic cathedrals have inner grandeur, nobility of spirit, they are monuments to God. This essay of Worringer's serves to remind us that monumentality is a factor inherent in many Gothic works—not in all—and that the lyric element is also a constituent of many works of Gothic architecture, sculpture, and painting—but not of all. Probably there will never be any possibility of complete agreement on this point, quite aside from the question of terminology, which is unimportant compared with the intended meaning; it will therefore not avail much to ask whether monumentality and lyricism are then absolutely irreconcilable opposites. Horace said of his *lyric* poetry: "Monumentum erigi aere perennius."

In another book Worringer answered the above objection: "If the combination of words 'Latin lyric' is in the last analysis a *contradictio in adjecto*, then the phrase 'Roman monumentality' is by the same token a tautology."[6] Monumentality is unconditionality, it is Latin; the art of the catacombs, on the other hand, is inspired by the Greek spirit. In discussing the details of this thesis, Worringer comes to Gothic. "The vibrations of what we call here the Greek cadence are by no means so entirely foreign to the Gothic. They have in common a labile and lyrically animated rhythm that places them both in similar contrast to the static quality of Roman prose. Greek and Gothic are full of music. Rome has no music. *Roma non cantat.*" (page 20)

Mention must be made of this book if ideas about Gothic are to be considered, but it confines itself, with one exception, to the realm of sculpture, painting, and ornament. The view from below of the fan vault of Peterborough is used as evidence for the connection with Celtic ornament, a good illustration of Worringer's method of declaring instances of vague kinship of form as proofs of material and biological inheritance. Yet in so doing he is well aware that such a connection of Celtic art and Late Gothic does not help his main thesis: "It is true that the entirety of the Celtic has nothing to do with the Greek; it is simply

[6] *Griechentum und Gotik, Vom Weltreich des Hellenentums*, Munich, 1928, p. 17.

a question of whether there are present in certain places possibilities of connection and influence." The Greek element is alleged to survive in Gothic, in contrast to the Latin. We learned in the past that Roman art was derived from the Greek, and we customarily view them together. Worringer tears apart this bond by applying his concept of monumentality; he is obviously struggling to find an authentic category that will make it possible to clarify conceptually the difference between Greek and Roman art. This is unquestionably a justifiable endeavor; when we learn to observe persistent or continually recurring traits of Greek character in sculpture down into Gothic and thereby liberate the master of the Reims Visitation from his historical isolation, we can listen to Worringer and follow his thought in critical agreement. But where architecture is concerned? Even if Chartres were unmonumental and lyrical, which seems to us an incomprehensible description, it would still be no Parthenon. Worringer would doubtless retort that he never said that; certainly not, but what exactly did he really say? Generations have labored to formulate correctly the problem of what Gothic is, and we have achieved considerable clarity. Paradoxical terminology, as well as adherence to Strzygowski's mishmash, does not help us advance. Gothic, says Worringer, has soft profiles (cf. Schnaase); he calls that "key minor." If we look at the forms more closely we see that there are harsh as well as soft profiles. Others have spoken of the razor sharp ribs, of the swish of fencing foils. Gothic is both hard and soft; we cannot generalize and say that it is only one of the two.

Worringer's dissertation and his *Formprobleme* went through several editions. Laymen have overestimated these works, while scholars of art have underestimated them. In France, because his books appeared in translation, it was thought that Worringer represented German scholarship. Scientific thinking must object to his formation of concepts in the minor key, but this does not preclude a feeling of respect for his intensity despite all contradictoriness. He touched a deeper layer of the problems of form than many another scholar, and we, too, must seek to delve into this layer without renouncing the task of formulating clear concepts.

Georg WEISE (1888-1957) criticized the concept of Gothic man.[7] On the other hand, HOFFMANN evolved from Gothic man the "mediaeval man," selecting Notker Labeo (ca. 952-1022) as the representative of this type. Hardly anything about Gothic can be found in Hoffmann's

[7] Georg Weise, "Das Schlagwort vom gotischen Menschen," *Neue Jahrbücher für Wissenschaft und Jugendbildung*, Leipzig and Berlin, VII, 1931, p. 404.

book,[8] which is journalistic in character and imbued with nationalism. Julius BAUM (b. 1882) has criticized Worringer seriously and with telling effect.[9]

6. Gothic as a National Phenomenon

A YEAR after Worringer's *Formprobleme*, a dissertation by Kurt GERSTENBERG (b. 1886) on German Late Gothic[1] was published. The expression *Sondergotik* in the title was intended to mean that German Late Gothic should be regarded more as a national particularism than as a late style. The French created Gothic, the Germans their *Sondergotik* or particularistic Gothic. The preface states clearly: "I was guided by the fundamental idea that every style, considered as to its expressive content, poses a problem not merely of history but also of race. For not every style can serve all peoples uniformly as an expression of their essential character, but rather, in international dissemination, every system of form must undergo far-reaching changes if it is to be of permanent value to the new bearers of art as an organ of expression. For one chapter of the history of German architecture I have tried to show the transformations that were necessary in order to Germanize an originally alien style. Eventually, this will also have to be undertaken for the other styles, with the grand ultimate goal of a history of German architecture that shall throw light on the German character of all forms."

Gerstenberg, unlike Worringer, does not extend his investigations over continents and millennia but limits himself cautiously to Late Gothic in Germany. He knew neither Worringer's book nor, it seems, his dissertation of 1908. According to Gerstenberg, Enlart's proof of the priority of English Curvilinear over Flamboyant does not get to the root of the matter but deals merely with influences, and Schmarsow along with Haenel saw only the expression of the *age*, not that of the race. This is surprising in view of Schmarsow's emphasis on the German element. Gerstenberg intends to show that the comparison of Italian Early Renaissance with German Gothic (Late Gothic) of the

[8] Paul T. Hoffmann, *Der mittelalterliche Mensch. Gesehen aus der Welt und Umwelt Notkers des Deutschen*, Leipzig, 1922 (2nd ed., 1937). He was born 1881.

[9] Julius Baum, "Der Geist der Gotik," *Kunstchronik*, New Series, XXIX, 1917-1918, col. 145.

[1] Kurt Gerstenberg, *Deutsche Sondergotik, Eine Untersuchung über das Wesen der deutschen Baukunst im späten Mittelalter*, Munich, 1913.

fifteenth century leads to a recognition of the fundamental contrast of Romance, that is, Italian, and Nordic conceptions of space. (*Raumanschauung*) He searches for this contrast and, like Wölfflin, distinguishes the mode of representation (*Darstellungsmodus*) from the expressive content (*Ausdrucksgehalt*) of the form. The theory of modes of representation is responsible for the statement that Gothic becomes increasingly picturesque the more it "declines." This is with reference to the "internationally valid stage of representation." The expressive content, on the other hand, reveals differences from the standpoint of racial psychology. "The expressive meaning of the forms is different because the bearer of art has changed." The concept of particularistic Gothic or *Sondergotik* is defined as follows on page 19: "Particularistic Gothic is the architectural style that makes free, creative use of inherited forms and, having completely emancipated itself from French tradition, develops under the domination of the specifically Germanic feeling for form chiefly in the fifteenth century, in contrast to the fourteenth century which was held in the grip of academic rigidity." A limit in time is set only for the beginning of particularistic Gothic, the date being that already given by Schmarsow: 1350. Gerstenberg leaves the end indeterminate because the "Baroque of Gothic" passes over into the Baroque—or, as one would have to say, into the "Baroque of Renaissance." In view of the distinction between expressive content and mode of representation in Wölfflin's sense, one might expect that Gerstenberg would solve the problem indicated by Worringer. In any case, we can agree with Gerstenberg up to this point.

His chapters are entitled: 1. Movement 2. Merging (*Verschleifung*) 3. Pictorialness (*Bildmässigkeit*) 4. Particularistic Gothic as a German style. Since in the third chapter the picturesqueness of Late Gothic is discussed and since this, after all, belongs to the modes of representation, it may be assumed that the first three chapters are all intended to refer to Wölffllinian modes of representation. Chapter 4, on the other hand, treats of what Gerstenberg calls the expressive content of form, and here we learn what is German about German particularistic Gothic. It is the *retardation* of tempo. German Romanesque is also slow. Slowness constitutes an essential characteristic of Germanic imaginative activity (page 109). The *irrationality* of the sudden explosion of pent-up force is German, also *desultory* (*sprunghafte*) manner. The Germanic spirit is characterized by *mood*. "One can call the Nordic conception of space intuitive because it unconcernedly accepts space in its unlimitedness and likewise seeks to give it form in works of art as the infinite and unarticulated. . . ." "The Germanic man envisages space in uninterrupted relations, the Romance man does not want to represent organic space in its irrationality but rather rational, 'comprehensible' space." (page 112) Gerstenberg identifies the Romance peoples with Renaissance and the Germanic with Late Gothic. High Gothic is a "French racial style," it is an affective style as opposed to Particularistic Gothic as a style of mood.

In the chapter on movement Gerstenberg already comments that the movement in the Late Gothic hall is slower than in the High Gothic basilica. He shows this by a comparison of the proportions of the bays, the change in the configuration of the ribs, the decrease in the vertical axis and the increase in horizontalism, the disappearance of the decorative gables, and so on. All of this is excellently observed and formulated. A further remark by Gerstenberg may also be quoted: "When one speaks of Gothic space, one actually imagines only a single space, namely the central vessel of a basilica with its upstretched slenderness." Gothic here means French High Gothic. Jantzen later said the same thing, and in connection with him we must come back to it.

What is the final achievement of Gerstenberg's dissertation? He wanted to show "the transformations that were necessary in order to Germanize an originally alien style." What he actually did show, however, was, in the main, simply the transformation of Gothic into Late Gothic, and in doing so he made very intelligent use of Wölfflin's modes of representation. What he shows to be true of German buildings in his chapters on Movement, Merging, and Pictorialness could, with certain variations, be demonstrated equally well for French, English, and Spanish Late Gothic. One can only hope to discover the specifically German element in German Late Gothic by comparing it with those parallel stylistic phases of the other nations and by separating it from the common element, namely Late Gothic. It is misleading to set up French *High* Gothic as the foil to German *Late* Gothic when one is seeking to determine the national element, for this comparison is enlightening only as to the change in the temporal style. One could just as well compare French with German *High* Gothic as French with German *Late* Gothic. But that is awkward because German High Gothic is still almost French. To try to anchor the German element to slowness, lack of self-control, and irrationality for all ages is neither demonstrable for the past nor desirable or even likely for the future. It does the Germans a disservice. But aside from that, it is not at all clear what should be done with these concepts, which, after all, characterize primarily temperament, not art and imagination, when one thinks of the great representatives of the German people. No one will find the great musicians, Mozart, for example, slow and Bach undisciplined, nor yet irrational. How Classicism of around 1800 is to be harmonized with the German character as it is here deduced from Late Gothic is incomprehensible. The conclusive fact, however, is that *no* nation can be bound down to *one* type. Thus Gerstenberg's thesis must be freed of its generalization, and then it remains to be seen whether it at least reveals the German character in the age of Late Gothic. French and English Gothic, as has been said, also retard the tempo, let alone the *duomo* of Florence, and Romanesque was "slow" everywhere. To define the really national character of the period in Germany—as well as in the other countries—simply in a purely descriptive and historical way would amount to saying approximately: "at that time" people preferred "these" forms in Germany, "those" in England. There has been, hitherto, hardly any advance over such a description. The contrast of rationally delimited, "tangible" (plastic) space and irrational-infinite (picturesque) is not adapted to exposing national or, especially, racial differences. Infinity had long since been predicated for Gothic as a whole (Förster, Milner, and so on) and Romanesque, reputedly dyed in-the-wool German (and not merely in Worringer's opinion), created rationally delimited spaces. Looked at from the other side, it must be said that irrationality and infinity are not lacking in the history of Italian style. To determine conceptually to what extent degrees of difference really do exist would be perhaps a modest beginning of the task of making the national "self" articulate.

Gerstenberg's unsuccessful efforts, however, were accompanied by a more and more penetrating understanding of Late Gothic itself, if not of its national tone, which had hitherto remained a mystery to rational science although everyone recognizes and feels it. Gerstenberg owes this deeper comprehension to Wölfflin's concepts, and performed a useful service in testing their applicability to Late Gothic. One further critical remark cannot be suppressed at this point: it was Wölfflin's example of regarding styles like Renaissance and Baroque as polar opposites that led Gerstenberg into the error of making an analogous contrast between High and Late Gothic. Perhaps this was also Wölfflin's own opinion. Gerstenberg should have asked himself if High Gothic itself was not already "picturesque." This had been asserted by others often enough to make it at least worth considering. But Gerstenberg thought that Gothic was "linear," perhaps because the thin engaged shafts and ribs of High Gothic can be metaphorically designated as lines. If, however, this is an error, if High Gothic itself is already "picturesque," then the whole problem is subject to review, and, of course, also the concepts, or at least the terms linear and picturesque which were here clearly inadequate.

Heinrich WÖLFFLIN in 1931 himself tried to determine the national difference between German and Italian art.[2] The preface has a strong undertone of skepticism against the correctness of his own thoughts. However, the reader's vague feelings are led to objective properties of those two nations, although the comparison, for example, of the *Palazzo del Consiglio* in *Padova* with the Kaufhaus in *Freiburg* (p. 24)—correct in itself—leads more to the difference between Early Renaissance and Late Gothic. The national attitude could only be touched upon, emphasizing that Italians of 1493 had used Renaissance principles more than seventy years, while Germans still adhered to Late Gothic tradition, and that the so-called German Renaissance for a long time remained faithful to "Nordic" principles in its composition before the North, so to speak, became southern. Wölfflin picked out those two buildings because they are of about the same date. Yet, as everyone knows, Europe did not progress synchronously in style in all its countries. Therefore synchronism in its strict sense affords no appropriate argument for the investigation of national differences.

Though not all Germans are slow—as Gerstenberg makes us believe—they were not only slow in accepting Italian Renaissance but, as formerly, in learning to use French Gothic. When at last they built in this style they naturally tried to continue its trend in the current style, turning to Late Gothic. The other nations did the same. Generally Late Gothic, as has been said before, could be differentiated into English, German, French and Spanish *Sondergotik*. Gerstenberg considers it the purpose of his book to show how high French Gothic had to be changed in order to be Germanized; the parallel problem would be to show how (high) French Gothic itself had to be Frenchified to become French *Sondergotik* or Flamboyant. This has to be said without malice to clarify the logic of the problem involved.

Evelyn wrote with contempt of the Henry VII Chapel. Did the English nation change when Inigo Jones built Whitehall? It is no new and no rare experience that sons deny the taste of their fathers and yet the sons remain the sons of their fathers. This is the root of the problem. Do those who write about nationality in architecture, art, poetry,

[2] Heinrich Wölfflin, *Italien und das deutsche Formgefühl*, Munich, 1931.

music—and, like Fischer von Erlach, in cooking—mean the material, biological factor, or, on the contrary, the ideas? Most of them seem to mean both sides at once, believing that always one proves the other. Therefore they have to show that although Jones accepted Renaissance, his design of Whitehall reveals secret English characteristics similar to secret ones in the Henry VII Chapel. The same problem comes up with Dürer's Renaissance or the work of the Master of Wimpfen who Germanized the *opus francigenum*, and so on *ad infinitum*. Has national character of art to be studied only insofar as nations are creating new styles or also if they are accepting, understanding, and adapting foreign creations?

In 1917 everyone knew that Gothic had been created in France. There was no need to prove it again, but Emile MÂLE (1862-1954) did so.[3] His article shows that this great scholar was well informed, though he omitted Whittington, Mertens, and Wetter, praising instead Viollet-le-Duc for the discovery of Suger's priority in St.-Denis. Certainly he is right to ridicule those German scholars who wrote that although Gothic was created in France, the architects must have been Germans or, if not Germans, they had a great percentage of German blood. Perhaps still more amusing is that Cologne Cathedral, formerly praised as a German masterpiece, suddenly became mediocre and dry, when the dependency on Amiens became known. Yet Mâle, writing as a French chauvinist about German chauvinists, was not aware that he ridiculed both at once when he concluded: "The German artist never created anything, he only copied. He did not invent any form, any ornament of his churches. . . . The German artist is the honest Meistersinger from Nuremberg, he knows all rules of art, the grammar, syntax and versification, he lacks only one small thing: le *genie*." (page 167) Mâle stopped at the end of Gothic. Perhaps he would have felt uneasy investigating how much Renaissance and Baroque architecture owed to Italian genius or the Madeleine in Paris to the Greek. Also he would have been led to the deeper part of the problem and would also have considered whether Brunelleschi, Alberti, Bramante, Palladio lacked *le genie* (of French architects of Gothic).

What is French, German, or English, in French, German, or English, art and architecture is included *implicite* in each correct description; the attempt to isolate this national factor *explicite* has never been successful up to date. It is the same with the differentiation of the single provinces of each country. Nobody will deny that there exists a Gothic particular

[3] Emile Mâle, *L'art allemand et l'art français du Moyen-Âge*, Paris, 1917, p. 109.

brand of the Isle de France, Burgundy, etc. Yet there is no connection with "blood and soil" as the same provinces created—or copied—other styles at other times. Again the explanation lies in intellectual or spiritual reasons common to those who dwell together all their lives.

There are scholars who try to solve the problems of national character of art *sine ira et studio*.[4] The history of the writings *cum ira et studio* is partly contained in the former chapters e.g. Manetti, Filarete, Vasari, Wimpheling, Goethe, Boisserée. Perhaps an American scholar—one familiar with American Gothic—could solve the problem.

7. Socialism and Gothic

John RUSKIN (1819-1900) was a supporter of Gothic revival, as was also Morris. Both men were deeply interested in the socialist movement. Yet it is not clear whether there was in their minds any real connection between Gothic and socialism. Ruskin devoted himself to the improvement of society and economy along socialist lines about 1860 after he had published all of his famous books on art. William MORRIS (1834-1896) went in for politics after 1880 when his career as architect, painter, and poet had reached its culmination. Ruskin, moreover, had not admired Gothic exclusively and Morris developed his own style along with his friends, Burne-Jones and Rossetti, in other words, with the pre-Raphaelites who took as their model the early Renaissance.

Whether Ruskin ever stated plainly that there was any connection between his admiration for Gothic and his conviction that socialism would bring about the millennium is a question which must be answered by the specialist who has read all thirty volumes of Ruskin's writings. The same also applies to Morris, though here the answer may be found more readily in the lecture entitled "Gothic Architecture."[1]

The greatest part of this lecture of 1889 is taken up with a survey of the history of architecture beginning with the barbarians, by which he probably means the Babylonians, Egyptians, etc. It follows a severe criticism of the Greek style. He talks of Greek superstition, a reproach we are more used to hearing directed against the Middle Ages. He is

[4] Dagobert Frey, *Englisches Wesen in der bildenden Kunst*, Stuttgart, 1943. This book came into my hands too late to refer to its special merit. This is true also of Nikolaus Pevsner, *The Englishness of English Art*, London, 1956.

[1] William Morris, *Gothic Architecture: A Lecture for the Arts and Crafts Exhibition Society*, London, 1893.

equally critical of "Roman pedantry." Gothic begins with the palace of the Roman emperor Diocletian (*sic*). Its first phase is Byzantine, a style which he praises highly; the second is Round Arch Gothic, also called Norman (page 30); the third, Pointed Gothic. Here he mentions the craft guilds and the implication is that Pointed Gothic is to be considered good because of the cooperative character of these guilds, but he does not develop further this line of reasoning. He praises Gothic (in the narrower sense) as "the most completely organic form of art which the world has ever seen." (page 7) There is another allusion to the social background in his statement that the Renaissance was the product of commercialism, bureaucracy, and the rule of pedants. "St. Peter in Rome and St. Paul in London were not built to be beautiful and convenient." (page 55) He returns to the Gothic and recommends it for practical modern use as being more compatible with the English climate than the Greek style; as, indeed, the only acceptable style for that age or for any other.

The idea of applying the term Gothic to as early an edifice as Diocletian's palace was outmoded in 1889 and Morris' contempt for antique architecture would have been revolutionary a century before. His quarrel with the Renaissance stems rather from his taste as an artist than from the idea that it was the product of an exploiting bourgeoisie. Ironically enough, the charming little booklet, printed in Morris' workshop, does not employ Gothic letters but antique, and the layout of the pages resembles an Italian print of the High Renaissance. One should not underrate the man, however, simply because of these all too human inconsistencies. He was genuinely interested in the preservation of Gothic monuments (Tewkesbury, Westminster Abbey) and he was a man possessed of great imagination and insight.

To return to the subject of Gothic and socialism, it is necessary to add that he, like Ruskin, hated machines. In his lecture of 1889 we find the statement that the Renaissance "turned the craftsmen into machines." Again we feel a contradiction in this attitude. Socialism did not hate machines. It simply wished to have them become the property of the working class. It was artists like Morris who hated machines because they felt that they created soulless merchandise for the masses. Ruskin opposed machines because they work against "truth" and for other pseudo-aesthetic reasons. In general, the Gothic Revival cannot be explained by socialist tendencies. We have only to think of the aristocrat Walpole and his Strawberry Hill.

What was Karl MARX's (1818-1883) opinion of Gothic? In the light of the fact that many modern writers claim that Gothic is the expression of collectivism, we would expect to find that he thought highly of it. But to our astonishment we discover that what he admired was ancient Greek art which he called, "in certain respects . . . the standard and model beyond attainment. It is well known that there have been certain periods in which the high level of artistic achievement bore no relation whatsoever to the general development of society, nor to any progress or prosperity in the material domain. Take the example of Greek society as compared with that of modern nations, or even of the society in which Shakespeare lived." From the point of view of the economic and materialistic interpretation of history invented by Marx himself, this is heresy. What is more, Marx's enthusiasm for classic art was shared by many bourgeois, even by kings and emperors, for example, Napoleon. Greek and Roman architecture were constructed by citizens who exploited slaves, the proletariat of antiquity, a class which was finally liberated through Christianity—the opium of the masses. Who can provide conclusive proof that our evaluation of an artistic style depends on our political convictions and aspirations?[2]

Though the answer would seem to be that no one can, nevertheless Wilhelm HAUSENSTEIN (b. 1882) devoted an entire book to the evaluation of art by the yardstick of socialist theories.[3] His interpretations are concerned almost exclusively with sculpture and painting, since he is mainly interested in nudes, but he also touches occasionally upon architecture. From Hegel he borrowed the idea that the stages of development are determined by thesis and antithesis, from Saint-Simon he took the notion that for society the two poles are collectivism and individualism, and that history is made up of a series of "organic" and "critical" periods. The Romanesque style is based on feudalism, a special form of individualism, while Gothic, which expresses the subordination of the individual to Christian society as a whole, is "collectivistic." Therefore—says Hausenstein—its works of art are anonymous. Yet we know many more names of artists from Gothic times than we do from the so-called individualistic era of the Romanesque style. The statement that "the whole artistic creation of cathedrals was the work of an anonymous collectivity" is misleading. Whatever the style happens to be, it is the individual architect who makes the

[2] Donald Drew Egbert and Stow Persons, *Socialism and American Life*, Princeton, 1952, I, p. 639. See the whole of Ch. 14 written by Egbert.

[3] Wilhelm Hausenstein, *Die Kunst und die Gesellschaft*, Munich, 1916.

design. He is not the laborer who prepares the ground, he does not himself execute the work of masonry, carpentry, etc., up to the last roof tile. This kind of "collectivity" on the part of his workmen cannot be used to differentiate styles of art or styles of society. It is surprising to read that only a *fabrica ecclesiae* can create convincing monuments of architecture. The Nôtre-Dame in Paris was created by two individuals, or rather by two great personalities, Bishop Sully and his anonymous architect. The same is true of St. Peter's in Rome which was created by Pope Julius II and Bramante. In both cases—as always—these men did not actually lay the stones and those who did the work "collectively" executed the idea in one instance of an "organic," in the other of a "critical" period. Was Hausenstein unaware of this obvious fact? Morris, incidentally, described Gothic as "organic."

Taste and political partisanship are a matter of personal sensibility and opinion—science is not. Hausenstein fell into the old error of judging art by its content and into the yet greater error of judging particular styles by his own prejudiced standards, praising the style of a presumably collectivistic society and condemning that of a presumably individualistic society. It is a book of propaganda, the work of a journalist, and as such belongs to some extent to the category of writings discussed in the tenth chapter of this section. It must be mentioned here, because it is one of several attempts to make use of Gothic (and art in general) for some specific purpose. For Romanticists Gothic was Catholic; for nationalists it was French (Celtic), English, or German; for practitioners functionalist; for socialists it is "collectivistic." In any case the *value* of Gothic as a style which prevailed for four hundred years of the Middle Ages cannot be judged in any such way as this. Even if it could be proved that Gothic is based on collectivism it would not follow that it is either good or bad—that is to say, good for a socialist and bad for an individualist. Yet what meaning can the concept of collectivism possibly have in the Ste-Chapelle? Is not this building less the expression of an earthly society than of the religious ideas of this society and an individual: Saint Louis?

A new and, in many respects, more serious attempt to judge art from the standpoint of socialism was elaborated by Arnold HAUSER (b. 1892).[4] The fallacies of his Hegelian thinking have been exposed with great lucidity by Gombrich.[5] The chapter dealing with Gothic opens as follows: "The art of Gothic cathedrals is an urban and bourgeois art, in

[4] Arnold Hauser, *The Social History of Art*, London, 1951.
[5] E. H. Gombrich, *Art Bulletin*, XXXV, 1953, p. 79.

contrast to the monastic and aristocratic Romanesque; urban and bourgeois in the sense that laymen took an ever-increasing part in the building of the great cathedrals, while the artistic influence of the clergy correspondingly diminished. . . ." (pages 203-204) The theory of Vitet, Viollet-le-Duc etc. is revived. The clergy and laity seem to be regarded as the representatives of individualism and collectivism respectively. We must ask then whether, in his heart, the aristocratic Abbot Suger longed for a Romanesque choir similar to that of Cluny, with which he was acquainted, and whether he was forced by his anonymous collectivistic lay architect to accept a Gothic one? Was this same compulsion the fate of the entire clergy of Gothic times? Or did the clergy also become urban and bourgeois? The Cistercians were neither urban nor bourgeois, but they accepted Gothic though of their own variety. The mendicant orders were both urban and bourgeois, yet the style which they employed differs from that of the "bourgeois" cathedral of Amiens. Again, is Amiens really bourgeois? There seems to be some confusion.

Hauser does not enter very deeply into the problems of Gothic architecture. However he touches upon the question of its origin, rejecting both the "romantic mechanism" of Viollet-le-Duc and the "aestheticism" of Riegl and Gall. Rather he believes that "so many incalculable factors entered into the creation of the rib vault as to make it simply *accidental*." By way of substantiation he quotes the statement that the rib vault "was first introduced for purely technical reasons and its artistic possibilities realized subsequently." Since I myself am the author of this sentence, written in 1923, and since a year later I again tried to explain the rib as the result of accidental factors, I am astonished to find this hypothesis accepted so long after it had been rejected by me. Quite recently, I was sharply criticized by younger scholars, who do not know that I have changed my views, for this idea of "accidental" origin. Today I am to some extent in accord with my distinguished adversaries. They may now berate Mr. Hauser for his misdemeanor, but not until they have clearly determined what they themselves mean by "accident" and "necessity." Let them leave the problem of the investigation of necessity of the universe to philosophers, that of mechanics and atoms to physicists, that of the birth of each individual architect to the biologists and concentrate upon defining "artistic necessity" or upon demonstrating the dependence of Gothic forms upon such irrational elements as economics, class struggle, etc. Once they have learned what is "chance" and what "necessity" in the creation of the system of Noyon, of Lincoln, of Chartres, of St.-Urbain in Troyes, of Prague, of Milan, of Annaberg, socialists will have more hope of tracing the pointed arch, the ogee arch, the flying buttresses, the tracery, the tiercerons, the net vaults, the profiles, the forms of capitals, and so on, to the mode of production, to class struggle, to the change from a natural economy to capitalism, and will then be able to decide what was "necessary," what "accidental."

There is no doubt that one genuine task of art history is to investigate the economic background of Gothic, as well as that of other artistic styles. But the socialist interpretation commits the error of imputing to the entire past of history the special historical background of the age in which the Communist Manifesto was written. The greatest mistake, however, is to regard works of art, architecture, poetry, and music from the point of view of their market value. Marx made many mistakes, but he felt that the materialistic interpretation of history cannot be applied to that which is based on aesthetic values. In this respect he was wiser than his followers.

However Marx's error may yet perhaps be corrected by the return of socialist society to the classic style as a kind of re-Renaissance. A short time ago we received a report about Russian architecture since 1917.[6] It was modern in the sense of Gropius and Le Corbusier until those in authority made the discovery that this style is the expression of bourgeois capitalism. The change came in 1950 when the pronouncement was made that: "all the really great works in the history of architecture are symmetrical." The new directives are to be followed also in the satellite states. In Warsaw the revolutionary proletariat received "a senatorial palazzo of the high Renaissance." The photograph shows a mixture of Palladio and Perault. While it cannot be proved, we may hazard the conjecture that this so to speak re-Revolution is based on the very personal taste of Marx which was conditioned by the aesthetics of a handful of survivors of Classicism in his day. If he had happened to be impressed by the Gothic Revival, the ukase from Moscow would perhaps have been different. But whether they would have been more or less bourgeois, nobody can say.

Meek quotes Frank Lloyd Wright who was in Moscow in 1937. The anonymous "eminent architects" with whom he spoke, "took the present situation (of grandomania of this time) with humor, and a touch of

[6] H. A. Meek, "Retreat to Moscow," *The Architectural Review*, London, March 1953, p. 143.

fatalism characteristically Russian. . . . They are men who say: Never mind—we will tear it down in ten years." When Wright observed that it would take nearly that long to finish the Palace of the Soviet, the unnamed eminent Russian architect replied: "Never mind, we may tear that down, too—even before we complete it." This was over-optimistic. While these words are interesting in that they confirm the notion that political change in Russia will come from within, in this particular case they serve to increase our doubt that socialism must necessarily build in the Renaissance style.

The leading aestheticians in Moscow will one day remember that Marx called antique art "the model beyond attainment." Those who are convinced that art and architecture is always the expression of the basic ideas of the time will claim that this goes to show that a utopian policy creates a utopian style. Historical Gothic cannot be an expression of socialist society.

8. The Trend toward History of Ideas

THE treatise of Max DVOŘAK (1874-1921) on mediaeval art is chiefly concerned with sculpture and painting[1] but in several places the subject of Gothic sacral architecture is also broached. Of course he knew Viollet-le-Duc's theory and he cites Dehio's great work, but he does not inquire about the nature and origin of the rib. He does not appear to have known Gall's book or else it seemed to him unfruitful for his own approach. Worringer's book he calls an attempt "to lift all at once the veil which had concealed from modern observers the artistic core of mediaeval art." This attempt to postulate a Gothic will to form "is an arbitrary construction which can bring many important phenomena of mediaeval art closer to our understanding but which, in view of the complicated state of affairs, is nevertheless even more fantastic than the abstract stylistic concepts of the Romanticists." Dvořak's own characterization echoes what had already been said before him, in part, also, by Worringer, but always with individual nuances, so that the two passages in his treatise where Gothic is de-

1 Max Dvořak, "Idealismus und Materialismus in der gotischen Skulptur und Malerei," Munich and Berlin, 1918 (*Historische Zeitschrift*, CXIX); reprinted in *Gesammelte Aufsätze zur Kunstgeschichte*, Munich, 1929. There also appeared a separate print, from which I quote. A complete bibliography of Dvořak's works can be found in the collected essays just cited, pp. 371ff.

scribed must really be quoted at length.[2] They are reduced here to a few essential sentences.

"Gothic architecture by no means tried to eliminate matter." It does not deny the character of stone, but stone "becomes simply and solely the expression of a unified, dominant artistic idea." "By means of a highly ingenious construction . . . two basic characteristics of the material . . . the earthbound element and . . . solidness could be overcome and matter, without complete dematerialization, be made subject to a supramaterial artistic will. . . . As though they did not stand on earth at all, the Gothic cathedrals rise above the cities in boundless verticalism, gigantic but not ponderous, dissolved in space, free growing like vegetable nature, and yet held together to the last pinnacle by an immanent order." (page 21) The last sentence recalls Friedrich von Schlegel.

The second passage supplements this characterization based on the reinterpretation of material stone. "The bounding wall disappears as an idea, that is to say, it ceases to be an aesthetic means and is replaced as far as possible by plastic bodies and intermediate space (*Freiraum*). Barriers between the inner stage that marks the limits of the earthly and the irrelevant . . . and the outside world, between the ideal and real space, have fallen." As a result the Romanesque alternate *gebundenes System* also disappears. For the Gothic cathedrals are bound only to infinite free space; "so with supernatural energy and order they grow up from the ground to vast heights, stretch out into far depths, and when they—the emanation of the materially finite in eternal boundless, universal space—, forming mighty halls, bow toward each other and join together in order to seclude the house of God . . . , like a sacred grove, from everything profane, then this delimitation no longer signifies a terminus that separates inaccessible, irreconcilable, and incomparable worlds. It is based not on opposition but on union, and what it frames, yet does not isolate, is a section of the unbounded universe. . . ." (page 21)

This is the only passage where Dvořak speaks also of Romanesque architecture; he regards it, like Cohn-Wiener,[3] as a *contrast* to Gothic. Romanesque creates fixed boundaries between the finite interior as the sanctified place for the worship of God and the profane external area of the street. Gothic, on the other hand, is a part of *infinite* space

[2] *Op.cit.*, pp. 19-21, and 58-60. In this connection cf. also p. 42 on the principle that links sculpture and painting with Gothic architecture.

[3] Cf. below, p. 775.

and also to that extent a piece of nature, like a sacred grove. The note of the forest theory is sounded faintly, but etherealized (*vergeistigt*) and related not to nature but to the infinity of the spirit.

The great value of Dvořak's treatise lies in his comprehension of the spiritual and intellectual background of Gothic rather than in his characterization of the style itself. He intended, actually, to solve the problem that Schnaase had tried to solve. The latter called the faith of the Middle Ages a belief not merely in the world beyond but also in this world as "the divinely willed and guided order of the Christian world." Dvořak's Archimedean point lies not very far removed from this. In contrast to antiquity, which produced an aesthetic-*sensuous* culture, the mediaeval period is characterized by the permeation of all circumstances of life by purely *spiritual* values and a preponderance of ethical feelings. Dvořak was thoroughly acquainted with the political and cultural history of the Middle Ages, as well as with mediaeval theology, and he could transport himself back into the spirituality of that age to such a degree that everything modern man finds alien in the Middle Ages seemed intelligible to him. His Catholic faith served him as a means to understanding, just as the idea of a permanent *Kunstwille* of the Germanic race served Worringer. The Gothic cathedrals stand patiently, defying weather and wars and allowing diverse interpretations to pass over them. It can be said at least for Dvořak's interpretation that all the Gothic architects, bishops, kings, and ordinary laymen who created the cathedrals were in reality Catholic Christians, whereas their Germanic ancestry is not always so easy to demonstrate. On the other hand, it is an exaggeration to try to explain *everything* on the grounds of Christian spirituality. Dvořak refuses to recognize "a causal relationship between the artistic phenomena and the rise of new economic, social, and religious conditions" (page 10) or to derive the former from the treatises of the theologians, but the mediaeval *Weltanschauung* underlying all branches of culture is, he says, also the basis of art. (page 11) This is undoubtedly correct and hardly very different from Schnaase, except that the penetrating exposition of the mediaeval attitude toward the world and life given by Dvořak is differently colored. Such an attitude may emphasize the common element in all areas of culture, just as in algebra the common factor is placed before the expression in brackets, but what is bracketed is nevertheless in its own way independent. Thus theology may be *Weltanschauung* "multiplied" by religion (the multiplication being meant, of course metaphorically); or, conversely, mediaeval religion itself the mediaeval *Weltanschauung* multiplied by religion. For Dvořak, then, Gothic appears, so to speak, as mediaeval *Weltanschauung* multiplied by architecture. Architecture, however, has its specific tasks. Dvořak has brilliantly developed the factor in front of the brackets, but has neither considered with the same intensity what constitutes the specific tasks of the members of a cathedral—that is, the ribs and engaged shafts—nor made it sufficiently clear what the connection is between the intellectual attitude toward the world and Gothic architecture. He said: "This art found its highest expression in gigantic church buildings . . . because these were the purest embodiment of the world institution of the Church, as it were, the symbol of the age. . . ." Not symbol "as it were," one must correct, but really a symbol! The word church itself is ambiguous: it stands first of all for the community of the saints and the faithful with the Trinity, this, in other words, is the idea of the church in its purely spiritual aspect, and, secondly, for an object built of stone. The latter church is the symbol of the first. Probably this is what Dvořak meant. But one would like to know how it is that a stone building of a particular form can be a symbol of that spiritual entity. And again Worringer can be called upon for help. Whether or not his construction is "fantastic," as Dvořak says, it does conjure up for us a unified root: "the alive-dead line as the expression of the spirit of the Germanic race." Correspondingly, there ought to be a unity existing between the mediaeval attitude toward the world and either this particular alive-dead line or whatever else may be regarded as the formula for Gothic. This unity is the mystery, it is the "artistic" element in the art of Gothic. In Dvořak, as in Worringer and Gall, the basic premise is lacking, a clear statement of what art is. Like many other writers, he assumes it to be well known. But the aestheticians and theorists of art, whose profession it was to give a definition of art, seemed to be at variance and confused, and thus it remained obscure how *Weltanschauung* is to be fused with architecture.

A brief reference to a book by Julius VON SCHLOSSER (1866-1938)[4] may be appended at this point. It is astonishing how much he offers in a very brief number of pages, but, although one feels that the author himself had complete mastery of his material, everything is regarded only from a distant perspective. Schlosser's approach to the mediaeval period and its art is related to that of Dvořak; we learn little about Gothic architecture and, in any case, nothing that had not already

[4] Julius von Schlosser, *Die Kunst des Mittelalters*, Berlin-Neubabelsberg, 1923.

been said elsewhere. This book, too, is more fruitful for sculpture and painting.

Dvořak's personal relation to the Catholic church and his love for the art of the Middle Ages as the expression of Christian spirituality can be detected very strongly in his treatise, yet his attitude remains objective. Schlosser's book is likewise colored by personal convictions, but they reveal themselves more as praise or blame for the scientific and philosophical currents of the nineteenth and twentieth centuries. In his account, the religious spirit of the Middle Ages is one factor among many others. It was not customary to make personal profession of Christianity in connection with scholarly studies in the field of art history, for an unspoken acknowledgement of the separation of church and science prevailed.

To many, therefore, it was surprising and dismaying, to others incomprehensible and annoying when Heinrich von GEYMÜLLER (1839-1909) dared to bring the matter up for discussion.[5] His book has little to say about Gothic; in its entire length of somewhat over one hundred pages so many subjects are touched upon that it would be difficult to give a brief summary of the contents. The tone is very subjective, although free from vanity and egocentricity. It is a confession of his attitude as an architect toward architecture and its styles since the time of Egypt, of his rejection of Darwinism, his recognition of the authority of the Bible, and his veneration for Renaissance. At the same time and above all, it is a confession of faith in religiosity. From an incidental remark on page 103 it is obvious that he was a Protestant, but he is not interested in Protestant ecclesiastical architecture (as Gurlitt was, for example). From other works of his we are acquainted with his doctrine that the Renaissance is a fusion of antiquity and Gothic, so that we are reminded of Soufflot. But that, also, is of minor importance compared to his efforts to comprehend and describe the relations of architecture to religion so that in these general theses Gothic is implicitly understood.[6]

Architecture, says Geymüller, is a "daughter of religion," an "independent sovereign." "Christian art is above all the art of the immortal souls of men created in the image of God." ". . . does not a sudden, blissful ardor in the heart, its pounding, convince us that we were created and destined for this higher perfection and rapturously blessed

[5] Heinrich von Geymüller, *Architektur und Religion*, Basel, 1911. The rather rare book contains brief biographical notes on p. 109 and following these a bibliography of Geymüller's writings.

[6] *Ibid.*, pp. 81ff.

beauty?" "The creation of beauty is by the grace of God . . . we can pray for it. . . ." These remarks might induce the reader to classify Geymüller as a neo-Romanticist. But for Romanticists the religious element is coordinated with many other factors, whereas for Geymüller it is fundamental. It is naïve, in Schiller's sense, not sentimental. All architecture, indeed all art, springs, according to Geymüller, from God's grace, not merely ecclesiastical or Christian art, which would, of course, include Gothic. This religious element, which is here not mysticism, does not differentiate Gothic from other styles. Only by reading between the lines is it possible to conclude that in Geymüller's opinion the essence of Gothic is the Christian religiosity of the period when out of the many Romanesque schools in the Isle-de-France one developed that attained perfection. "With the creation of the Gothic style we come to one of the most solemn and glorious moments in the history of architecture, if not of humanity." (page 60) Geymüller has something to say about the forms and form of Gothic, but nothing of this is new. He rejects Viollet-le-Duc's theory on the ground that it is a mistake to derive Gothic from logic and reason.

Geymüller's relation to the Renaissance in Italy and France and his estimation both of Gothic and of Brunelleschi as the creator of the Renaissance had led him not only to the thesis already mentioned that the Renaissance contains two indispensable elements (antiquity and Gothic) but also to the statement that the Renaissance had begun in Italy a hundred years before Brunellesco, simultaneously with Nicolo Pisano, Cimabue, and Giotto, that is to say, with Arnolfo di Cambio.[7] Instead of recognizing that Nicolo Pisano, Cimabue, and Giotto belong to Gothic, and correcting Boccaccio's error, Geymüller regarded these different artists as Renaissance in the sense of Ghiberti and Masaccio, and therefore claimed for this movement the architect Arnolfo as well. As if that were not enough, he puts the beginning of the Renaissance around 1230 with the building of the Castel del Monte for Friedrich II of Hohenstaufen. Again one is reminded of Thode. Geymüller's light on the essential nature (*Wesen*) of Gothic as an individual architectural style was negligible compared to his comprehension of its spiritual and religious roots.

The expression "essence" is ambiguous, and Geymüller does not seem to have used it. We can approach the problem more closely if we remember the significance of the rib. If we have fathomed Gey-

[7] *Friedrich II von Hohenstaufen und die Anfänge der Architektur der Renaissance in Italien,* Munich, 1908.

müller's conception of art completely, its essential nature is God himself, God as the creator of the divinely gifted artist and God, therefore, as creator (indirectly) of art. But no one will say that the essential nature of the rib is God. The rib is not even a symbol of God, but Gothic, which resulted from the rib, is a symbol of the religious spirit of the age. The tangible foreground is a symbol of the conception of God and the worship of God as it developed at that time, in the twelfth and thirteenth centuries, and its essential nature lies, therefore, in its symbolical force, its quality of being art. Lack of clarity as to the concepts "symbol" (both of meaning and form), "art," and "essential nature" led to a confusion of the concepts of style.

The opposite of Geymüller, who extended the Renaissance backward in time, was Carl NEUMANN (1860-1934), who attempted to prolong the Middle Ages (in reality Late Gothic) and thus to deny the Renaissance completely, at least in Germany and France. According to him, it was merely a local Italian phenomenon.[8] Luther is "reformed Middle Ages." This corresponds to Geymüller's contrary remark that Arnolfo was "Renaissance in Gothic garb." In Neumann's view not only are Dürer and Holbein the Younger mediaeval, but also Rembrandt, on whom Neumann was an expert, and thus also Johann Sebastian Bach. The article bubbles, flashes, and sparkles with many-sided erudition, polemics, arbitrary judgment and self-assurance; but in the end one asks: why the sound and fury? Even if Giotto, Dürer, Rembrandt, and Bach are all "mediaeval," one still wants to know what nevertheless distinguishes them individually, what *the* essential nature of *each* is. Neumann was very versatile: he was primarily a historian of politics and its source material, he was a Byzantinist, a literary historian, and a historian of art. His interests were almost as comprehensive as those of Burckhardt, about whom he wrote a book; but in comparison with Burckhardt's really Olympian superiority everything that Neumann wrote is full of convulsiveness. His criticism of the delimitation of the Middle Ages, with Friedrich II as the first modern man, Dante as a Renaissance man, the discovery of the world and of personality, is

[8] Carl Neumann, "Ende des Mittelalters?," *Deutsche Vierteljahresschrift für Literaturwissenschaft und Geistesgeschichte*, Halle, 1934, pp. 124ff. Attention should be drawn here to a comment of Wölfflin who said, thinking of Dante's position, in connection with a statement by Burckhardt: "Dilthey already rejects the idea of a separate period of 'Middle Ages'; there are only antique and modern-Christian cultural developments." Cf. the *Burckhardt-Wölfflin Briefwechsel*, ed. by Joseph Gantner, Basel, 1948, p. 38. Exactly the same division into two periods only was advocated by Karl Krumbacher in university lectures in Munich, around 1909; he said that there is only one age before Christ and one after. It is not clear why one cannot make distinctions within these two epochs.

aimed, with some slight animus, at Burckhardt, but in passing he makes hostile mention of Bode and Wölfflin as "the oracles of the age." In addition to personal resentments his theory is inspired by wounded national feeling: the "Middle Ages" are Nordic, the period is in the best sense of the word barbarian, that is to say, free of Humanism. We recall that in 1928 Worringer had distinguished sharply between Greek and Latin antiquity and had said that Greek lyricism survived in Gothic; Neumann, on the contrary, does not really speak of antiquity, of Athens and Rome, but of Humanism, consequently of Florence. Here, he says, the concept Renaissance is meaningful, and only here. Neumann's article is a good introduction to recent literature on the Late Middle Ages,[9] and is without doubt informative and stimulating. One also sees that Neumann was not alone in his opinion; he cites Troeltsch, who saw the end of mediaeval thought only in the Enlightenment of the seventeenth and eighteenth centuries. The most striking feature of all these speculations is that history of ideas is forced to make quite different periodizations according to what intellectual area and what geographically coherent group of intellectual human beings are under consideration. The contradictions only arise where an attempt is made to apply the delimitation discovered to be valid for one of the groups to all Europe generally; they immediately arise in the history of art as soon as one argues from the mistaken premise that every radical change must be felt simultaneously in architecture, painting, and sculpture. The question of the nature of the Middle Ages is not identical with that as to the nature of Gothic (and Late Gothic), although they must be related to each other. Thus the problems of the boundaries of epochs, periods, or phases, are in part illusory.

Neumann's article fails to refer to Dvořak, who in his great essay had clearly characterized the nature of Gothic both in its essential background and in architecture. Dvořak, nevertheless, was of the opinion that a history of the *Renaissance* should begin with Giotto; he made a distinction between Giotto and Masaccio, calling the former the bearer of the New Gospel and including the latter among the "Renaissance Patres," one of whom is also Brunelleschi.[10] Dvořak does not mention Gothic in this place, but it is clear that he did *not* assign

[9] He discusses books by Brandt, Haskins, Bezold, Götz, Huizinga, Stadelmann, Troeltsch, Dilthey, Taylor, Ranke, Pastor, Michelet, Walser, and, of course, the relevant passages in Burckhardt as well.

[10] Max Dvořak, *Geschichte der italienischen Kunst*, Munich, 1927. Academic lectures delivered in Vienna from 1918 to 1920, ed. by Johanna Wilde and Karl M. Swoboda.

Arnolfo to Renaissance. Since here he confined himself to Italy, he also did not discuss the classification of Nordic art, either under Gothic or under Renaissance.

A broad treatment of the mediaeval art of Italy in its intellectual and spiritual development and its relation to literature and poetry is given in Weise's excellent book which has already been mentioned.[11] It hardly deals with architecture at all and can therefore be passed over here.

This takes us back to the problems discussed in the first part of this book. Is literature and poetry the sole root of the *art* of building, or do politics, scholasticism, mysticism, and the like, also enter in? Willi DROST (b. 1892)[12] has described the polar opposition of Romanesque and Gothic very well by the concepts (not the words) "addition" and "division," and has tried to show this analysis in the development of philosophical thought. According to his view, Romanesque corresponds to "Realism," that is, to a system of thought based on ideas and general concepts (in the Platonic sense), Gothic, on the other hand, to Nominalism and Aristotelianism.[13] Hence Gothic is determined first by individualism, second by "the new consciousness of the thinking subject," and third by the "dualism in the mastery of the world of thought." To give a more detailed account, or to offer criticism, would mean investigating the history of mediaeval philosophy and asking when Nominalism began. Drost's book is important for the question of the essence of Gothic. From a different point of view, and possessing a still greater familiarity with the original writings of the Scholastics, Erwin PANOFSKY (b. 1892) returned to the relations between Gothic architecture and scholasticism.[14] An account of his ideas is given in my *Gothic Architecture* (Pelican History of Art) to be published in 1959.

It is sometimes difficult to draw the line between the history of ideas and the general history of culture. Thus the attempt of Richard HAMANN (b. 1879) to define the character of Gothic sculpture and architecture by means of the concept of courtesy as a pattern of social behavior belongs perhaps to both of these branches of historical study.[15] Referring to the sculptures of Reims Cathedral, he wrote: "Thus there

[11] Georg Weise, *Italien und die geistige Welt der Gotik*, 1939.

[12] Willi Drost, *Romanische und Gotische Baukunst, Der Wandel des mittelalterlichen Denkens und Gestaltens*, Potsdam, n.d. The book must have appeared between 1941 and 1945.

[13] Cf. above, p. 228.

[14] Erwin Panofsky, *Gothic Architecture and Scholasticism*, Latrobe, Pennsylvania, 1951.

[15] Richard Hamann, *Geschichte der Kunst von der altchristlichen Zeit bis zur Gegenwart*, Marburg, 1932. The quotations are taken from the second edition, Berlin, 1935.

arises from this proud bowing to each other (a humility that gives away, as it were, its pride) the social function of conversation, a relationship in which words and gestures carry on a cult with the other person. The accepted behavior and conversation of persons at this court creates a new virtue, born of Christianity and pride, of humility and haughtiness: courtesy." Hamann also uses this concept to interpret the rib. (page 189) "As in the portal, these bars also reach across the space with arms, with ribs that in the form of pointed arches meet transversely or diagonally, forming an espalier of arching staffs (*Stäbe*), with the function of filling the space once more with a perfect reciprocal bowing, of the same cultic form as a surging chorale, a bow that he who moves in a procession from the entrance to the choir and reaches the end of his course, now also performs. . . ." Since this interpretation is related to sociological questions, particularly to chivalric society, Hamann's approach seems to be in principle that of history of ideas, but this point of view is blended into a many-sided description of Gothic. The concept of courtesy, however, is developed chiefly with reference to French Gothic and not to that of the other countries, so that a general characterization of Gothic as a whole is not explicitly given. Gerstenberg's term, German Particularistic Gothic, which referred in the main to Late Gothic, has been so extended by Hamann in its application to German Gothic that it embraces Magdeburg and, indeed, even the Transitional style of Maulbronn, while the real German Late Gothic is almost ignored. English Gothic, to which Hamann tried to do justice despite many words of negative criticism, does not seem to arouse in him the impression of courtliness or courtesy; he says on page 346: "One senses the conqueror's will to power and domination and at the same time the private citizen's need for seclusion and rest on his return home from marauding expeditions." If the ribs in Amiens bow courteously to each other, why not those of Salisbury and Exeter? Hamann was obliged to omit much, for his book, which was intended to be a presentation of the entire history of art from the Early Christian period to the present, contained about 900 pages of text interspersed with 1,110 illustrations, and it may have been for that reason that the question of Gothic as an all-inclusive phenomenon remained unanswered. One cannot explain the earliest ribs in Durham and in Normandy by means of the concept of French courtly politeness, any more than the latest forms of stellar and reticulated vaults. But as an attempt to intepret Gothic psychologically this emphasis on the concept of courtesy makes its own contribution.

All treatments from the point of view of history of ideas, whether they deal with Gothic or other subjects, are concerned with the essential nature of the particular phenomena, with that which lies beneath the surface like a nutritive juice. The individual historians of this school look for this deeper nutrient in various intellectual areas, in religion or *Weltanschauung*, national culture in Carl Neumann's sense, poetry, metaphysics, or social behavior, but one thing is common to all of them, namely, that they divert us from the works of art themselves, only to interpret art from an extraneous perspective, thus giving rise to misinterpretations.

This does not imply a condemnation of the method of *Geisteswissenschaft*, but is merely a reflection on its limitations. In the chapter on the culture of the Gothic age something has already been said on this subject, and there will be more to come in the chapter on the nature of Gothic.[16]

9. The Studies in Rhythm, Proportion, and Harmony

SINCE August SCHMARSOW (1835-1936) evolved his theory of art largely in polemics against his younger contemporaries, Riegl and Wölfflin, it is fitting to discuss him after them.[1] His lecture on space in architecture, already mentioned, pointed the way for the period that followed.[2] Hegel and Burckhardt had already recognized that hollow space is the essential element of architecture; now, however, this idea was presented in such broad and pedantic detail that scholars of architectural aesthetics and architectural history found themselves obliged to speak not merely of piers, columns, walls, and so on, but also of the intermediate spaces.

Schmarsow did not stop with this discovery of the obvious but

[16] Otto G. von Simson, "The Birth of the Gothic," *Measure*, I, 1950, p. 275 He dismisses Wetter's Gothic "membra," the cross-ribbed vault, the pointed arch, the flying buttress, and even verticalism as "not the most important aspect of Gothic," maintaining (like Focillon) that the chief element is light. He then takes up the subject of the metaphysics of light, with particular reference to Suger whom he believes to be the architect.

By the same author: *Wirkungen des christlichen Platonismus auf die Entstehung der Gotik*, Studien und Texte zur Geistesgeschichte des Mittelalters, III, Leiden, Cologne, 1953, p. 159. Here Simson attempts to link the theories of proportion with metaphysics.

[1] Biographical material in Johannes Jahn's "August Schmarsow zum Gedächtnis," *Zeitschrift für Aesthetik und Allgemeine Kunstwissenschaft*, XXX, 1936, p. 179.

[2] August Schmarsow, *Das Wesen der architektonischen Schöpfung, Antrittsvorlesung gehalten 1893*, Leipzig, 1894.

sought to ascertain the corresponding essential element in the other arts, among which he included mimic art. His theory of art cannot be presented here in full and can, therefore, not be subjected to rigorous criticism. It led him to say that mimic art or, more properly, the mimic principle is present and fundamental in every art, consequently also in architecture. What he meant is closely connected with the concept of empathy. He assumed that we quite literally think ourselves, or should think ourselves, into the forms of architecture, and that these forms per se are merely a projection of the artist's physical sensations into his works. "Art is accordingly an attempt to react creatively to the environment."[2a] Schmarsow laid stress, therefore, on the physical structure of the human body, and established a closer relationship between each of the three dimensions of space and single arts. In this he followed Semper (*Stil*, I, Introduction). The perpendicular of height is the "dominant" of sculpture (Semper had said "authority" instead), breadth that of painting, and depth, the direction of our movement, that of architecture as a "spatial art."

To this idea was joined a second, namely, that the elementary formal principles of proportion, symmetry, and rhythm could likewise each be assigned to one of the three arts: proportion to sculpture, or to its vertical axis, symmetry to painting, or to its horizontal axis, rhythm to architecture, that is, to its axis of depth. Such systematizing is not simply superficial and arbitrary, but basically false. It imposed only a seeming order that led to wrong conclusions. Proportion does not relate merely to the vertical axis, for example, the ratio of the length of the head to that of the whole body, but equally to every ratio of a to b, thus also to horizontal lengths such as toe to foot. On the other hand, the attribution of symmetry to the axis of breadth also does not have the exclusive validity that Schmarsow claimed; in a building of the central type, each side of which is symmetrical in itself, we can regard each one singly in such a way that we relate its symmetry to the horizontal axis, yet the symmetry exists independently of this factor, and the same thing is consequently also true if we relate it to the dimension of depth in this same type of structure. Rhythm, moreover, is certainly not limited to the axis of depth and our movement; it can be found just as much in juxtaposition and superposition as in succession. But with respect to rhythm Schmarsow made of his empathy such a kind of sport or *idée fixe* that one receives the impression that all experience of architecture is a species of secret and permanent

2a ". . . eine schöpferische Auseinandersetzung mit der Umwelt."

rhythmical gymnastics. The normal attitude, on the contrary, might be conceived of as a state of complete passivity, pure receptiveness to a highly complex whole that makes an immediate effect and is slowly absorbed more deeply in us.

To this double theory that singled out one element for each art and assigned each to one of the three spatial dimensions Schmarsow added the idea of near and distant vision which he had adopted from Riegl and made fundamental to his own concepts of the plastic and picturesque. A full summary of these theories was given by Oskar Wulff, one of Schmarsow's pupils.[3] It might be thought that Schmarsow's concepts of the plastic and the picturesque would coincide with those of Wölfflin, but although he used exactly the same terminology, his conclusions were diametrically opposed to Wölfflin's. Thus Schmarsow says that Bramante, originally a painter, built "picturesquely," as, for example, in the Cancelleria;[4] Antonio da Sangallo's designs for St. Peter's he likewise calls "picturesque," also Raphael's Farnesina, and so on. Conversely, when Wölfflin says that Baroque is picturesque, Schmarsow proves that it is "plastic." The fact is that Schmarsow identified the picturesque with painting and the plastic with sculpture, whereas for Wölfflin the picturesque represented a general category, as did also the plastic. Consequently, Wölfflin distinguished within painting as a whole picturesque and nonpicturesque, that is, linear painting; and, correspondingly, in sculpture he recognized plastic and nonplastic, that is, picturesque sculpture. Schmarsow caused much confusion, but precisely in doing so he obliged people to think more clearly and use better terminology. As has already been mentioned, Wölfflin had rejected the concept picturesque in his *Renaissance und Barock* as being too complex, but then later took it up again and used it as the opposite of "linear." He could employ a vague terminology because he made his meaning clear by the manner in which he applied the terms to examples. Schmarsow, on the contrary, took the literal meaning of the word picturesque as his point of departure and identified with it everything painted. In addition, his style was rather undisciplined.

In his early book, *Barock und Rokoko* (1897), reminiscent of Wölfflin even as to title, he also attempted to enlarge upon the concept of rhythm, with the idea of comparing, or even identifying, the rhythm of prosody with that of architecture. He spoke, accordingly, of strophes

[3] Cf. p. 624, n. 27 above.

[4] August Schmarsow, *Barock und Rokoko, Eine kritische Auseinandersetzung über das Malerische in der Architektur*, Leipzig and Berlin, 1905, pp. 32 and 40. It has since been realized that the Cancelleria was not designed by Bramante.

in architecture. Not until later did he carry this theory out in detail with respect to *Gothic* churches and windows. The definition of rhythm that was lacking earlier was provided by his systematic book of 1905.[5] In conformity with his psycho-physical point of view he derives rhythm from the life process; the pulse, breathing, the human gait are all rhythmical, and even the infant sucks rhythmically (how else could it?). Schmarsow is here caught in the snare of a common error of logic. He thinks that rhythm is derived from the rhythmical life process and is an experience *a posteriori*, as though rhythm, for him, arose from the fact that he had once sucked rhythmically, that his breathing and pulse were rhythmical. Wherever and whenever we discover rhythm, it is independent of us and of any life process; it exists *a priori* and is therefore discoverable where it attracts attention. Schmarsow spent pages of wearisome detail in analyzing the human gait: left foot, arsis and thesis; right foot, arsis and thesis, and so on, without realizing that he was not deriving rhythm from walking but was observing in walking the same thing that he could observe in any rhythmic happening, because the rhythmical factor itself is already given. But our question as to what rhythm really is remains unanswered. The concept is a pillar of his system and must be read between the following lines: "Already the expression 'rhythmical' as used by Geymüller for the articulation of a vaulted bay of the interior or for a corresponding section of the façade, that is to say, for the complicated, strophelike composition of a coherent group of individual members that recurs in regular sequence or at least meets in a corresponding position its counterpart, with the interlacing of the rhyme pairs and the alternation of tempo in the sequence of members—all these characteristics of such a '*travée*,' only to be appreciated in successive perception, a *travée* that would have to consist of the simple arcade-opening below rising to the many-membered gallery arcade above and higher to the windowed clerestory area, indeed even to the vault cell and the keystone—they demand the assumption of 'movement' as an essential characteristic and no longer permit the designation of Renaissance as exclusively 'the art of beautiful, serene being,' as Wölfflin still attempted to call it." In this long, complicated sentence the phrases that refer to rhythm are: strophelike composition, recurring in regular sequence, alternation of tempo in the sequence of members, successive perception, movement. Presumably what Schmarsow meant by rhythm could be deduced from

[5] August Schmarsow, *Grundbergriffe der Kunstwissenschaft*, Leipzig and Berlin, 1905.

attentive reading and synthesis of all the passages where he mentions that quality.

Schmarsow's limitations can be attributed to the "psychologism" of his generation and thereby half excused. A true definition of rhythm presupposes that it is comprehended as something objective, not merely as something present only when the investigator "effects" it ("*vollzieht*," as Schmarsow puts it). In our opinion, rhythm is still a property of the cathedral of Paris even when the sexton has locked it for the night and not a soul remains to "effect" the rhythm. Schmarsow, however, acts as though the rhythms always are created anew only when some one arrives for mass in the morning and "effects" them. "Psychologism" looked for rhythm almost entirely in the subject and posited a permanent need for it; an undifferentiated set of impressions would be so tormenting that a man would spontaneously impose a rhythm upon them: thus, for example, a series of drops, falling, from the objective point of view, quite uniformly, would be made bearable by subjective ascription of accents. Thus man also rhythmizes work, and, in consequence, rhythm is derived—with much mental effort—from manual labor, without, however, being itself precisely defined. Again and again the truism was overlooked that one must first be acquainted with a thing before one can establish its derivation or even recognize it.

A fundamental difficulty was caused by the prejudice that rhythm was indissolubly connected with time, and that the application of the concept to space was a transference of meaning that must first be justified and excused. Schmarsow arrived at such justification by way of the concept of movement that unites time and space; because of our own spatial movement in architecture, rhythm is introduced into an otherwise atemporal art. Schmarsow misunderstood Wölfflin. When the latter thought of Renaissance as the art of "beautiful, serene being," it was quite independent of whether we stand still or move about. Serene being pertained to the object. "Psychologism" believed that it was vested in the spectator. It is, of course, equally a matter of indifference whether we stand still in a Baroque structure, move about, run, dance, or even, if it were possible, fly (one is reminded of the architect floating through the Gothic church in Moritz von Schwind's picture); for the movement, or rather the impression of movement, lies in the object, although this remains immovable. Rhythm is not a factor of time but a purely logical concept, and consequently is equally applicable both to temporal and spatial forms, occasionally also to movement as a temporal-spatial form; it is not "transferred" from time to space.

Schmarsow's pupil, Wilhelm PINDER (1878-1947), undertook to analyze the rhythm of mediaeval buildings.[6] Reduced to essentials, his dissertation may be said to center about the proposition that the wall membering of the nave creates, by its correspondence on both sides, "stopping points" (*Widerhalte*) for the depth movement. According to Pinder, the engaged shafts, therefore, had originally only *this* function. By means of such shafts groups are formed in the individual bays on the walls, thus in the plane surfaces; because of the vaulting the groups become three-dimensional in space. Rhythm here means the dividing of the axis of depth by such stopping points. In the course of architectural evolution they "rhythmize" more and more strongly and richly the depth movement from the west entrance to the choir apse, a movement that had been unbroken in the Early Christian basilica. In tracing historically the increase and variation in this process of rhythmization, Pinder never fails to take into consideration the most minute details of the buildings, describing them at length and interpreting them continually from the standpoint of Schmarsow's psychophysical gymnastics of empathy. It is plain that anyone who has the patience to read this work of Pinder's will become thoroughly acquainted with the structures, but rhythm enters into it for the most part only by implication. When Pinder analyzes the membering, rhythm is, of course, also included in the discussion, but it is not explicitly described per se. There is no lack of information as to the breadth of the piers and the intervals, and, accordingly, rhythms of piers to engaged shafts, of windows to the space between shafts, are often expressly mentioned, but if rhythm is to be considered as determinative as the title of Pinder's investigations indicates, one expects to find it expounded independently of questions of membering. Or is that perhaps impossible? To a certain extent it is. Rhythm is inherent in membering, and that is the reason why it is described by implication along with the latter, but it is not membering in itself. It is also not the stopping point itself, though it is also inherent in the stopping points. Rhythm is an elementary relation that is everywhere contained as an integral element, in every architecture; and if one knows what rhythm *itself* is, one can then talk of the rhythm of the Doric temple, of Romanesque and Gothic interiors, and can make comparative studies of rhythms. Pinder spoke also of the acceleration of the rhythm

[6] Wilhelm Pinder, *Einleitende Voruntersuchungen zu einer Rhythmik romanischer Innenräume in der Normandie*, Strasbourg, 1904; and *Zur Rhythmik romanischer Innenräume in der Normandie*, Strasbourg, 1905 (Zur Kunstgeschichte des Auslands, 24 and 26).

in Gothic. It is well known that this took place. One should try, however, to grasp *rhythm* independently of *tempo*. One and the same rhythm of 3 : 4 can be slow or fast paced, but in either case the rhythm remains constant. If the accelerated rhythm has a different effect from the retarded one, as it unquestionably does, this is then a new psychological and aesthetic problem, namely, one of tempo, and presupposes that the element of pure rhythm has already been extracted. Like Schmarsow, Pinder remained bound by "psychologism," at least in this dissertation; but he deserved credit for having concerned himself with extending the study of rhythms to Gothic.

Two other dissertations relating to rhythm are the products of Schmarsow's school. Hans Hermann RUSSACK (b. 1887) made a very useful survey of the instances where German nineteenth-century historians of art tried to define rhythm or used the word without definition.[7] From this dissertation it can be seen that the concept was, to some extent, not clearly understood by those who employed it and was, to some extent, applied by the various historians of art in differing senses. Schnaase gave no definition. Russack found that he used expressions like "rhythmic arrangement" or "rhythmic proportions," and concluded that Schnaase meant by them rhythmical alternation with recurrence; rhythm, for Schnaase, is consequently connected with time. But rhythm also means "arrangement of a whole as a well-ordered aggregate of independent parts" or "cohesion of independent, relatively equal parts in a whole." Kugler thought rhythm lay in the interrelation of spatial members.[8] He associated this idea with that of rhythmic movement, concluding that rhythm is therefore, psychologically speaking, movement that connects in temporal sequence parts juxtaposed in space; it presupposes a relationship. Burckhardt, we know, spoke of rhythm of movement and rhythm of masses. Russack quite properly remarks that just what is meant—or what in this case rhythm means—remains completely vague. Semper distinguishes simple seriation (*Reihung*), alternating seriation, and intersection by means of periodic caesuras. Intersection is supposed to foster romantic mood, having a more picturesque, musical effect, while simple or alternating seriation (eurhythmy) corresponds to "plastic beauty" (*Stil*, I, XXVIII). With Wölfflin comes the turn toward psychology. He connects rhythm of accentuation with rhythm of quantities (the distances between win-

[7] Hans Hermann Russack, *Der Begriff des Rhythmus bei den deutschen Kunsthistorikern des 19. Jahrhunderts* (Leipzig Diss.), Weida, 1910.

[8] *Ibid.*, p. 33.

dows, and so on). Dehio's terminology is nebulous. Russack also discusses Ernst Meumann's (1862-1915) and Pinder's conceptions of rhythm.

Russack did not reach a definition of his own, but he does make the statement: "Rhythm is not modified by the thing being rhythmized."[9] Since he realized that, he should have granted that it is quite immaterial whether time or space or force (accentuation) is being rhythmized. Rhythm itself is something *about* time or *about* space or *about* force. But Russack did not go into this, perhaps because in his dissertation he felt himself bound to the dogma of his very autocratic teacher, Schmarsow.

The third dissertation (counting those of Pinder and Russack) is that by Willi DROST (b. 1892),[10] who continued and deepened Russack's work. From this study we learn that in antiquity the concept of rhythm was applied solely to time; only in 1802 did Schelling speak of spatial rhythms or Herbart in 1813 of the rhythm of colors, by which he meant that one subjectively attributes to them a successiveness. Among more modern psychologists, Müller-Freienfels seems to be one of the most extreme (to judge by the quotations in Drost's book). He regards rhythm as differing according to the degree of pleasure or enjoyment. It is not quite clear whether by rhythm he intends to imply pleasant rhythm, in which case the corollary would be that unpleasant rhythm is not rhythm at all. It is to be hoped that he does not mean that! The only psychologist and historian of art who had a really objective approach to the subject of rhythm was Max DERI (b. 1878) (who, for the rest, constructed a completely uninspired, materialistic aesthetic on the basis of Mach's work).[11] Drost opposes Deri because in an objectively determined spatial rhythm, time, which is after all indispensable, would vanish; on the other hand, he praises Schmarsow who was able to combine the objective and the subjective. "Rhythm, viewed subjectively, is the rule, acknowledged objectively, the law of all play of forces in the realm of juxtaposition." What rule? What law? Drost suggests (on page 57) that rule (or regularity) is really experienced successively, lawfulness simultaneously. Nevertheless, one would still like to know what rule or what law is being invoked, since there are many.

9 *Ibid.*, p. 77.

10 Willi Drost, *Die Lehre vom Rhythmus in der heutigen Aesthetik der bildenden Künste*, Leipzig, 1919.

11 Max Deri, "Kunstpsychologische Untersuchung," *Zeitschrift für Ästhetik und Allgemeine Kunstwissenschaft*, VII, 1912 (cited according to Drost). The book edition has the title: *Versuch einer psychologischen Kunstlehre*, Stuttgart, 1912.

At that time, Schmarsow, stimulated by the dissertations of his pupils, once again expounded in detail what he understood by rhythm, specifically in Gothic.[12] Here can be found that above-mentioned description of the pointed arch, more than fifteen pages long, the substance of which had been given by Schnaase in two simple sentences. This is followed by a history of ecclesiastical Gothic in France and Germany, as well as of the exteriors of Romanesque churches to about 1250, in the course of which he often applies his idea that the architectural composition can be compared to the rhythms of strophic structure in poetry. He looks at things from many points of view, however, and by no means restricts himself to his favorite concepts.

The idea of comparing architectures with poetic strophes again raises the question of what their common element, that is, rhythm, actually is. In the case of speech-rhythms we are concerned with the combination of time-lengths of different or like nature on the one hand with accents of varying intensity on the other. The lengths or durations can be measured or prescribed exactly, if one wishes, but the relative indication long, short, long, short, or long, short, short, and so on, always suffices without exact measurements. Similarly, accents are not measured exactly but are referred to as strong or weak, with perhaps a differentiation of primary and secondary accent, that is, of stronger and weaker. It is left to the reader or certainly to the trained reciter or actor *how* long or short, *how* strongly or weakly the syllables are to be pronounced, above all to the musician how each tone is to be rendered. In architecture, on the other hand, the dimensions are exact and usually indicated unequivocally; they must not be commensurable. But these measurements differ vastly more markedly than in the strophes of poetry. It is not sufficient, therefore, to draw the comparison that in both cases there is an alternation of long and short lengths, or of degrees of stress, for the important factor is precisely the arithmetical ratio of the magnitudes of these lengths or accents.

Whereas in iambic lines the rhythm is roughly always "the same," that is to say, short/long, and so on, in architecture it can be now 1 : 2, 1 : 2, and so on, now 1 : 3, 1 : 3, or 1 : 3.5, 1 : 3.5; each time "the same" iambic rhythm is here thus a "different" one. It will not suffice, accordingly, to write it each time ⏑ –, ⏑ –, as Schmarsow did; and his attempt was silently put aside by scholars. If Gothic were

[12] August Schmarsow, *Kompositionsgesetze in der Kunst des Mittelalters*, second part of *Gotischer Kirchenbau und Aussenarchitektur des romanischen und gotischen Stils*, Bonn and Leipzig, 1920.

to be interpreted on the basis of strophic theories, the *Nibelungenlied* strophe, for example, might have been expected to suit it. But Gothic cannot be compared to any strophe. The strophelike rhythms that Schmarsow deduces could be realized equally well by Renaissance structures—again a statement to be taken with a grain of salt, for one might say, *equally badly.*

It remains to the credit of Schmarsow and Pinder that they pointed out the significance of rhythm for Gothic also. The investigation should be undertaken afresh on the basis of an exact definition of the concept of rhythm.

This question takes us back to the history of the semantic change of the word, which was already touched upon in the chapter on Vitruvius.[13] We are indeed no longer bound to one of the definitions used in antiquity, but that is of no help to us because there is today no unity with regard to a modern definition, even though a general, simple, basic conception seems to be deducible from all the various applications of the term.

The problem has been more recently treated in a Berlin dissertation by Gotthilf FLIK (b. 1901),[14] who distinguishes simple and complex rhythm. The former is "an immediate sequence of *equal* temporal or spatial intervals." (page 11) If one wishes to emphasize expressly that the members of the rhythm are to succeed each other immediately, there can be little objection made. But Flik himself calls cases of *unequal*, as well as equal intervals rhythmic. His treatise does not appear to contain a definition of complex rhythm. But rhythm ought obviously to be defined generally, regardless of whether it is simple or complex, regular or irregular, commensurable in its members or incommensurable. Flik says (page 6) that rhythm is "a sequence of several or at least two bars. . . ." Perhaps he intended to say "members," for *rhythm* as a general concept is independent of *time* or *metre.* Rhythm needs two "intervals," not two bars, since each individual bar already has rhythm if it contains at least two lengths. Flik also misuses the concept "arhythmic." A single tone or a circular line lacks rhythm, or is rhythmless; a so-called arhythmic pulse, on the other hand, is irregular in its rhythm but has a rhythm nevertheless: the *alpha privans* refers in this case to the regularity, not to the rhythm.

[13] On Schlikker's book cf. above p. 95, n. 28. Since I am confining my discussion to theories of rhythm in architecture, I shall not go into the usage of this word in Hans Kauffmann's *Albrecht Dürers rhythmische Kunst*, Leipzig, 1924, and Erwin Panofsky's article with the same title in the *Jahrbuch für Kunstwissenschaft*, Leipzig, 1926, p. 136.

[14] Gotthilf Flik, *Die Morphologie des Rhythmus*, Schramberg, 1936.

A musical example may suffice to show what the real "essence" of rhythm is. Everyone can probably call to mind Mozart's minuet from *Don Giovanni.* How do we know in what "rhythm" the tones of different pitch are to be played? The answer lies in the notes that Mozart wrote down. They indicate not only the relationships of lengths (–⏑⏑⏑⏑–⏑⏑), but also *definite* specifications for the duration of the relative lengths, *definite* distribution of stronger and weaker accents. Mozart utilized the long since developed system of musical notation in order to prescribe the relations of the magnitudes of lengths or accentuations for those notes of varying pitch that were to form the melody. If he had noted down only the tonal sequence, nothing would be known about the rhythm that he wanted to have associated with it. A different rhythm would result, namely, that of a sequence of equally long, equally accented tones of varying pitch. The rhythm lies precisely in Mozart's prescription of the "*magnitudes*." Correspondingly, the architect indicates the *magnitudes* of all spatial intervals. Whereas the composer of music indicates only approximate tonal lengths and accents and leaves the nuances to the player, the architect's spatial measures are exactly determined to the millimeter or foot and part of foot, or, in Gothic terms, by triangulation or quadrature.

Anyone wishing to undertake an investigation of the rhythm of Gothic structures must also concern himself with the subrhythms, which can hardly be comprehended analytically in their reciprocal relationships because of the wealth of engaged shafts and ribs, profiles, and so on. It may, however, be possible to measure and describe the dominant rhythms to a certain extent; this would without question lead to the elucidation of an essential factor of Gothic.[15]

Whereas the concept of rhythm is very differently defined by different authors, there is unanimity on the subject of proportion, which is generally understood to mean the relation between any two magnitudes. But this definition is too broad. The recognition that rhythm also is a relation of *magnitudes*—namely, of *coordinated* ones—forces us to limit the definition of proportion to a relation between "*subordinated*" magnitudes, for example, that between the magnitudes 2:3 "as" height and breadth "within" a rectangle, thus, such as are "subordinated" to the whole, in this case, to the figure of the rectangle.

The earlier chapters on Villard de Honnecourt and his concept of

[15] In the *System der Kunstwissenschaft*, Brünn, 1939, pp. 24ff., I gave my reasons for defining rhythm as the "relation of coordinated magnitudes" and classified it systematically among the other basic concepts. At that time I was not acquainted with Flik's dissertation.

portraiture, Magister 2 and the secret of the lodges, the expertises of Milan, Vitruvius, Roriczer, and so on, have already made us realize the significance of proportion for Gothic and Late Gothic times. In the Renaissance there was a return to the theories of antiquity where the study of proportions was related to the search for beauty, insofar as this was considered to result from specific proportions. Such studies in proportion will not be discussed here. The majority of them are restricted to the proportions of the human figure, and what the architects thought about architectural proportions can only be reconstructed tentatively from their buildings. Cesariano forms an exception. The Golden Section occasionally figures but was not obligatory. Luca PACIOLI (ca. 1445-ca. 1509) wrote a treatise about it in which he follows Euclid and discusses chiefly the regular bodies of stereometry. His theory of columns is not connected with the *sectio aurea*.[16]

In the nineteenth century Adolf ZEISING (1810-1876) devoted intensive investigations to the subject.[17] The long-winded title of his chief work, of 1854, already reveals his idea that the proportion $a:b = b:(a + b)$ prevails throughout the universe and explains its harmony. Any one interested in this branch of speculations about proportion will find here much historical material, beginning with Pythagoras. In his efforts to discover the Golden Section everywhere, Zeising occasionally exceeds the bounds of sober consideration; for example, when, on the basis of their proportions, he finds the continents of the eastern hemisphere masculine, those of the western, feminine, or when he claims that the harmonious division of the earth's axis necessarily points to the Suez Canal, and so on (page 329ff.). As far as the proportions of plants, animals, and human beings are concerned, his schemata are ideal cases from which nature is permitted to deviate somewhat, while art seeks to realize them as such. Thus he also arrives at architecture, and first of all demonstrates the existence of the Golden Section in Greek art (page 390). The proof is more difficult for Gothic art, he says, because "the whole is a complicated system of various members that hide behind, tower over, and peep through between each other, obscuring the basic distributive principle in the same measure as they multiply it." Nevertheless, he succeeds in his demonstration in the case of the ex-

[16] Constantin Winterberg, *Fra Luca Pacioli, Divina Proportione*, Vienna, 1889, Quellenschriften. . . , New Series, II.

[17] Adolf Zeising, *Neue Lehre von den Porportionen des menschlichen Körpers aus einem bisher unerkannt gebliebenen, die ganze Natur durchdringenden morphologischen Grundgesetz entwickelt und mit einer vollständigen historischen Übersicht der bisherigen Systeme begleitet*, Leipzig, 1854.

terior of the choir of Cologne Cathedral, the west front of St. Elisabeth's in Marburg, and the west tower of the Freiburg minster. A criticism of this method is unnecessary, since we shall return later to an evaluation of the principles of all such methods.

Robert BILLINGS (1813-1874) gave an amazing demonstration of the theory that in Carlisle Cathedral all the important points of ground plan and elevation are entered on a network of proportions.[18] He drew systems of intersecting or tangential circles, actually only another manner of reproducing quadrature. No one seems to have verified his data. Billings does not relate this constructional network to the method of mensuration, but sees in it a guarantee of beauty. He applies the same method to the proportions of Worcester.

Georg Gottlieb UNGEWITTER (1820-1864) called (in 1859)[19] attention to other literature on the subject since Boisserée, describing briefly the methods of Emerich HENSZLMANN (1813-1890),[20] David Ramsey HAY,[21] and Viollet-le-Duc.[22] The latter asserted in his *Dictionnaire* that in the Middle Ages the triangles that determine the chief dimensions always begin on the level of the upper edge of the bases. In his examples he draws the equilateral triangle, the "isosceles" with the *base* angle of 45 degrees, and the "Egyptian" (the base of which has four units and the altitude two and one half). The isosceles he demonstrates in the cathedral of Bourges. He censures modern Gothicists who choose their dimensions arbitrarily, and maintains that the use of the triangles results not merely in "*proportions heureuses*" but also in good statics (page 546).

Real progress in the study of proportions came from the archaeo-

18 Robert Williams Billings, *Architectural Illustrations, History and Description of Carlisle Cathedral*, London, 1840. As appendix to the above: *An Attempt to Define the Geometric Proportions of Gothic Architecture as illustrated by the Cathedrals of Carlisle and Worcester*.

19 Georg Gottlieb Ungewitter, *Lehrbuch der gotischen Construktionen*, first edition, 1859-1864, p. 609. In the fourth edition, by Mohrmann, Leipzig, 1901, this passage has been much abbreviated and provided with a skeptical note. (Karl Mohrmann, 1857-?)

20 Henszlmann's book, *Theorie des proportions appliquée dans l'architecture*, was in process of publication in 1859.

I found the book of Emerich Henszlmann in the *Bibliothèque National*. He uses the triangle consisting of the side of a cube and the diagonal of the square of the surface of this cube as the legs, and the diagonal of the whole cube as the hypotenuse. He calculated its length up to 13 decimals. (Why he chooses this kind of triangle is not clear to me.) From this figure he derives by a simple construction a series of similar figures of various sizes. He refers further to musical relations. The prospectus added by the publisher promises two more volumes (the third on Gothic architecture), but these have never been published.

21 Ungewitter's reference, *The Builder*, 1861, is incorrect. Hasak cites (cf. n. 34) D. Ramsey Hay, *Proportion or the Geometric Principle of Beauty*, 1843. Zeising, *op.cit.*, pp. 62ff., mentions another book of 1851, but this treats only human proportions.

22 Ungewitter's book seems to have appeared in fascicles; the discussion of proportions at the end of the work must refer to Viollet's *Dictionnaire*, VII, of 1864, s.v. Proportion.

logical side. August THIERSCH (1843-1916) found in taking measurements of classical buildings that specific proportions for structural parts of varying size, or for the main proportions of the whole are constant in the case of each temple.[23] This "law of similar figures," called by its admirers the "lex Thiersch," held good for Doric and Ionic temples, Renaissance structures, and even buildings by Schinkel. Thiersch wrote in the first edition of his book that this "method of similar figures" was also employed in the Middle Ages, for example in St. Elisabeth's in Marburg. In the second edition he added a drawing of the Marburg façade in which the diagonals that have been sketched in, make the recurrence of like proportions clear at a glance.[24] Thiersch knew Zeising's books, but he leaves it to us to ponder the question of why the beauty of the façade in Marburg can be demonstrated both by the method of similar figures and by Zeising's theories of the Golden Section; for each touches very different points of the elevation.

A comparison with Viollet-le-Duc's drawings suggests the idea that Thiersch was more strongly influenced by them than by Zeising. His formulations were quite different from Viollet's, and by that time it ought to have become clear that no particular species of proportions could be made responsible for the "beauty" of which Thiersch spoke, thus no specific triangles but rather the recurrence of a once chosen proportion, no matter what. Furthermore, it had likewise to be seen that both methods are related; later writers endeavored to fathom the mystery.

Thiersch's revealing essay, which appeared in 1883, had a strong effect on Heinrich Wölfflin. He, too, began to search for similar figures and found as a supplement to Thiersch's discovery that in many works of architecture the upright rectangles have the same proportion as the recumbent ones; in Doric temples, for example, the upright rectangle formed by two adjacent columnar axes has the same proportion as the recumbent rectangle of the entire front (without stylobate and pediment). Their diagonals are therefore perpendicular to each other. Burckhardt wrote the comment: "What beautiful results!"; while Thiersch, curiously enough, rejected this to us perfectly obvious con-

23 Thiersch's essay appeared in 1883 in Durm's *Handbuch der Architektur* (Stuttgart), in Part IV, Vol. I. A second edition came out in 1893. An excerpt was then inserted in the later editions of Burckhardt's *Geschichte der Renaissance* (1912).

24 This article has not been understood by some writers e.g. M. A. Texier, *Géométrie de l'architecture*, Paris, 1934, although in figure 69 he himself gives an example of "the law of similar figures" (Maison-Lafitte). (He mentions theories of Dieulafoy and of Perrot et Chipiez which are omitted in the text above; the chapter 6 on Alberti is useful, but most of the book belongs in the realm of pure imagination.)

tinuation of his theory: "I must warn against taking a path that makes the matter mathematically more complicated and is still not free from a certain arbitrariness (in the choice of the figures to be compared)."[25]

Georg DEHIO (1850-1932), who, of course, knew the *lex Thiersch*, reverted to the triangles, even to the Egyptian triangle (which Ramée had probably rediscovered). Dehio's works in this field have already been discussed; at this juncture they should be mentioned in chronological sequence in order to provide a connected survey of the development of studies on proportion. In his first treatise he drew in on the transverse sections of Gothic cathedrals equilateral triangles, one above the other.[26] There were doubts as to the accuracy of the drawings and, moreover, there was no reason to assume that the beholder ever was or would be able to sketch these triangles correctly in the air, or that they should necessarily guarantee beauty.

His second work greatly increased the number of objects investigated.[27] Despite the abundance of proofs, professional circles remained skeptical; probably not simply because they lacked confidence in the survey sketches but also because so many different "beauties" were demonstrated by this method that the concept of beauty became hazy: whether classical, Byzantine, and so on, it was always the equilateral triangle that was responsible. But at that time Dehio hit upon the right track when he vaguely hinted that it was a question of a process of transferring the measures of the drawing to the real size of the actual work, although there were no efficient yardsticks of measure available.

C. Alhard von DRACH (1839-1915) was the first to assert clearly that the method of the triangle (triangulation) was not directed toward aesthetic but toward practical goals.[28] He used both the equilateral triangle and the isosceles with the vertex angle of 45 degrees

[25] The letters exchanged on this subject by Wölfflin and Burckhardt have been published by Joseph Gantner, *Jacob Burckhardt und Heinrich Wölfflin, Briefwechsel und andere Dokumente ihrer Begegnung*, Basel, 1948, pp. 47ff. Wölfflin's essay, *Zur Lehre von den Proportionen*, is from the year 1888; it was edited by Gantner in *Heinrich Wölfflin, Kleine Schriften*, Basel, 1946, p. 48; cf. also Gantner's note, p. 248. Thiersch's critique is in the *Deutsche Bauzeitung*, 1889, p. 328.

[26] Georg Dehio, *Untersuchungen über das gleichseitige Dreieck als Norm gotischer Proportionen*, Stuttgart, 1894.

[27] *Idem*, "Ein Proportionsgesetz der antiken Baukunst und sein Nachleben im Mittelalter und in der Renaissance," Strasbourg, 1895. Relevant minor literature in the *Repertorium für Kunstwissenschaft*, XXXVIII and XXXIX.

[28] C. Alhard v. Drach, *Das Hüttengeheimnis vom gerechten Steinmetzengrund*, . . . , Marburg, 1897, p. 5. Drach employed the old phraseology; translated into modern German it would read: "vom richtigen Grundriss für Steinmetzen" (regarding the proper ground plan for stonemasons).

(that is, one quarter of 180 degrees). He calls it a $\pi/4$ triangle.[29] By drawing in other lines there is obtained a scale of decreasing sizes that are related according to geometric law.[30] Drach does not say that this method was known and employed in the Middle Ages, but he applies it to Hessian and other buildings—some Romanesque, some Gothic—and arrives at astonishing results. Among his subjects the Marburg church of St. Elisabeth again appears (page 23). He found that the Golden Section was not used anywhere there, and in any case he rejects Zeising very decidedly (page 8, note 2). He discovers instead that in the ground plan and transverse section the equilateral triangle is employed with the greatest exactness and in the façade the $\pi/4$ triangle. In the transverse section the base of the equilateral triangle is raised to the level of the sill line of the windows (below and above), and in the façade his constructional network fits the network of the actual determining lines only very loosely. Drach completely ignored the fact that Thiersch had demonstrated the "similar figures" in this façade very much more simply and convincingly. The experts who were interested in the problem could not help but be surprised that one and the same façade tolerated equally these various networks of beauty, which were in themselves so different.

Stimulated by the work of Thiersch and Drach, *Dehio* returned once more to the riddle of proportion.[31] He appended the results of his reflections to his history of Gothic. It is important that in this place he already gave a correct interpretation of the passages from the Milan expertises.[32] He wrote that "*triangulum* simply was intended to mean the equilateral triangle and *figura triangularis* the Egyptian triangle." Passages in Viollet-le-Duc's text undoubtedly were Dehio's source for the apocryphal term "Egyptian triangle." From the context it is apparent that he means the Pythagorean triangle with the sides 3:4:5 (in the preceding sentence he mentions it explicitly). He then goes back to his two earlier treatises on proportion and gives three reasons for the processes of quadrature and triangulation: first, tradition ever since the time of classical antiquity; second, technical and practical advantages; third, the aesthetic character of the equilateral triangle, as being the most manifest symbol of concentration and stability.

29 Drach thinks (p. 6) that this triangle was introduced by Albertus Magnus during the construction of the Strasbourg nave.

30 Drach described this geometric procedure on p. 6, and illustrated it in fig. 1 on his pl. III.

31 Dehio, *Die kirchliche Baukunst*, . . . , II, pp. 562ff.

32 I overlooked this fact when I wrote my article on this subject, "The Secret of the Mediaeval Masons," *Art Bulletin*, XXVII, 1945, p. 46.

With regard to the second of these reasons he says: "There can be no doubt as to the complete lack of architectural designs drawn to scale. We must believe that the Middle Ages made shift with mere sketches in planning a building. Granted this assumption, the advantage of a system of proportioning based in its chief measurements on regular geometrical figures is obvious. Once the ground plan was marked off, the normative triangle for the elevation could easily be determined on the leveled building site by moving strings. In addition, the elevations could be tested during the construction by sighting the angles."[33]

With reference to this passage Dehio quoted in a note an unusually important sentence from Drach (page 5): "If there are found in a building dimensions that are perpendicular to each other and that cannot be measured in whole numbers by the unit of measure on which the construction is based or that do not at least stand in a simple relation to each other, this is at once an indication that the proportioning of these dimensions did not result from an arithmetical basis but that the builders proceeded according to a method of geometric construction."

Part of the proportions that Dehio demonstrated by means of auxiliary lines in the illustrations on pages 593 to 599 coincide with August Thiersch's concept of "similar figures." Dehio's renewed reference to the equilateral triangles that can be entered one above the other on the transverse sections of Tournay, Amiens, and so on, is now no longer related to any (imputed) aesthetic intentions, although for Thiersch observation of the similarity of figures was based on purely aesthetic grounds. The little treatise, however, despite all its progressiveness and scholarly method, still did not get to the heart of the matter. Nevertheless, it may be regarded as a turning point in work on this subject and an introduction to the subsequent studies of other scholars.

Dehio was followed by HASAK (1856-1934), whose theory of parallel diagonals was only a modified formulation of the *lex Thiersch*. He had learned from Drach and Dehio, however, that triangulation had only been intended for mensuration, and wrote: "What has the simi-

[33] Dehio, *op.cit.*, II, p. 568. "Der völlige Mangel an nach Masstab aufgetragenen Baurissen kann nicht bezweifelt werden. Wir müssen glauben, dass das Mittelalter sich zur Vorbereitung des Baus mit blossen Skizzen beholfen hat. Unter dieser Vorraussetzung ist der Nutzen einer in den Hauptabmessungen auf regelmässige geometrische Figuren gestützten Proportionierung augenfällig. War der Grundriss abgesteckt, so konnte man auf dem geebneten Baugrund mit Leichtigkeit das für den Hochbau normative Dreieck durch Bewegung von Schnüren ermitteln. Ausserdem könnten während der Bauausführung die Höhen durch Visierung der Winkel geprüft worden sein." (The use of cords would have been not practicable; we have rather to think on Kossmann's theory.)

larity of triangles to do with beauty? Nothing."[34] Hasak drew in diagonals on the successive bays of longitudinal sections that are alike, and in so doing completely distorted the significance that Thiersch associated with his diagonals. It does not need to be proved that rectangles of equal size are also inclusively similar.

The work of Johann KNAUTH (1864-1924) was more complicated.[35] He understood by quadrature the drawing in of the triangle on the square. This triangle results when the corner points *a* and *b* of the base are joined to the middle point *m* of the upper side *cd*.[36] Knauth says that the 26° 34′ vertical angle of this triangle is also the inclination of the descending passage of the Pyramid of Cheops. Others have proved that the Golden Section plays a (hidden) role in the measurements of this pyramid.[37] It is far more important that above the entrance to the antechamber of the royal tomb chamber there is a circular boss, which, when multiplied by five, results in a measure of 63.56 cm, namely the module of the pyramid; this, in turn, when divided into twenty-five parts, results in the pyramid inch. The pyramid module (or meter) is exactly equal to a ten-millionth of the earth's axis. Still more surprising is the fact that the base square of the pyramid is equal in area to a circle having as its radius the height of the pyramid—or at least almost that. Only a thousandth of the height is lacking (squaring the circle!) The pyramid inch is identical with the English inch, or again almost so (the difference is 1/1000). The most astonishing thing of all, however, takes us back to Gothic: the uniform measure of Strasbourg Cathedral is one foot equal to 31.78 cm, thus exactly half of the pyramid meter. Knauth was the capable cathedral architect of Strasbourg who carried out important repairs of the tower foundations. He knew that the cathedral and the Pyramid of Cheops were different. Assuming that the calculations (including that of the earth's axis) are correct, what insight has been gained by this result, which Knauth called a riddle of architecture? He maintained, moreover, that the more im-

34 Max Hasak, *Der Kirchenbau . . .* (*Hdb. d. Arch.*, 2, IV, 3), 2nd ed., Leipzig, 1913, p. 28. I do not know the first edition, but assume that Hasak already declared his theses in 1903.

35 Johann Knauth, *Das Strassburger Münster und die Cheopspyramide. Rätsel der Baukunst*, Strasbourg, 1908.

36 This triangle can be constructed above all for sides, resulting in a star-shaped figure from which Knauth obtains all divisions from 2 to 10. Since Knauth's treatise is not widely known, attention should be called to illustration 16 in the article by Ueberwasser cited below, where a portion of this construction is reproduced.

37 Hermann Neikes, *Der goldene Schnitt und die Cheopspyramide*, Cologne, 1907. In the vertical triangle of the transverse section of the pyramid, half of the base line is equal to the length of the major of the diagonally rising triangular side (when this is divided according to the *sectio aurea*).

portant points of the Strasbourg ground plan and elevation were established according to the ratio of the numerical series 2:3:4:5. What need was there then for quadrature and the *sectio aurea*? Drach, on the other hand, had written in a note (page 6) that the $\pi/4$ triangle could be shown as determining the height of the springers. It is not surprising that serious scholars turned aside from this labyrinth of minute details, and yet the mystery of beauty continued to induce men to try to unveil it.

Whatever one thinks of Knauth's conclusions, it is certain that studies of measurements and proportions are closely related. HAASE (1858-1950) made a substantial contribution when, in 1911, he published an excellent historical survey of the measures of the Egyptians, Babylonians, and so on, down to the Middle Ages.[38] Less happy is his study of the proportions of Cologne Cathedral, which appeared at the same time.[39] He makes respectful mention of Knauth's method of the triangle inscribed in the square (the connection of the corners of the base with the midpoint of the opposite side) and also of the other specialists on proportions, but then he takes up the subject of the number seven and its significance in the measurements of the cathedral. The total length of the ground plan amounts to 490 feet, equaling 7 x 7 x 10, that of the nave 441 or 7 x 7 x 9, and so it goes. The seven is also repeated in the elevation. This number has often had a mystic significance, of which Haase assembles many examples. The simple explanation of the mystery has been apparent ever since Bernhard KOSSMANN's book (see above, page 66): the builders used measuring rods seven feet long. Anyone who is inclined to detect mysterious forces in numbers may say that just this choice of seven feet was the guarantee of the beauty of Cologne Cathedral. But seven feet, if one follows Haase in assuming that the foot used in Cologne was 29.5 cm, would be 2.065 m. The seven foot measuring rod was thus in this case only 6.5 cm longer than the modern two meter stick. It was equally handy. With its aid all sorts of buildings could be erected, ugly ones, beautiful ones, or plain utilitarian structures that were neither.

It is, therefore, supplementary when Haase also demonstrates the Golden Section in Cologne Cathedral. The flèche, for example, divides the roof ridge according to this proportion; in the interior the total length of the transept has a ratio equal to that of minor to major. It is of

[38] Johannes Haase, "Das Werkmass in der Tektonik der antiken Völker und seine Nachwirkung bis in die mittelalterliche Baukunst," *Zeitschrift für Geschichte der Architektur*, Heidelberg, 1912, v, p. 251; and 1913, vi, p. 129.

[39] By the same author, "Der Dom zu Köln a. Rh.," *ibid.*, v, pp. 98, 148.

no consequence that this length is measured between the engaged shafts instead of from wall to wall (154′ : 249′), for who would be sensitive to differences of less than a thousandth part? Haase rejoiced in the "peculiar, rhythmic relations of the septempartition and the Golden Section," which delighted him "as an analytical equation would a mathematician," yet he seems to have been half conscious of a doubt when he remarks: "So, then, in the course of our consideration, the vast structure of the cathedral has almost been reduced to a numerical scheme, as it were, to something invisible (page 112)." That is true of the work of most of the theoretical writers on proportions. Fiedler and Wölfflin thought that spatial art existed for the eye, from which it should follow that its value can scarcely lie in the invisible. For a time, however, the concern was not with the question of *why* certain proportions merited preference but with *whether* they were demonstrable at all.

In 1914, WITZEL (born 1883), having studied his predecessors thoroughly and investigated several new examples of Gothic, introduced in addition to Drach's $\pi/4$ triangle an analogous $\pi/5$ triangle with a vertical angle of 36 degrees.[40] It is related geometrically to the regular pentagon, thus also to the Golden Section. Witzel makes use of all these triangles, demonstrating now this one and now that in the various buildings. Though he confirms Drach's equilateral triangles in the ground plan of St. Elisabeth's in Marburg, he regards the $\pi/4$ triangle as the most suitable figure for the façade (page 29). This key figure, according to Witzel, likewise determined the west front of Cologne Cathedral. The $\pi/5$ triangle, on the other hand, prevails in the façade of Strasbourg (page 34) and that of St. Lorenz in Nuremberg (page 36). Witzel is to some extent more tolerant than his predecessors since he does not reduce Gothic to *one* of the methods of triangulation. He seems to have understood that they all served to transfer the dimensions of the drawing to true size, and he emphasizes at the same time those proportions of rational numbers that approximate the Golden Section.

Anyone who works in this field will also have to take cognizance of the studies on proportion relating to other styles. Here they can be disregarded.[41]

A book by Fredric Macody LUND (1864-1944) published in 1921, gave further impetus to the study of the problem of Gothic proportions,[42]

[40] Karl Witzel, *Untersuchungen über gotische Proportionsgesetze*, Berlin, 1914.

[41] Jay Hambidge, *Dynamic Symmetry, The Greek Vase*, New Haven, 1920; and L. D. Caskey, *Geometry of Greek Vases*, Boston, 1922.

[42] Fredric Macody Lund, *Ad Quadratum*, London, 1921.

though it is doubtful whether it can be really influential. He has investigated mediaeval and in part ancient Greek structures as well with amazing industry, but few people will have the time or patience to devote to the details. The drawings are overloaded with fine networks, which, compared to those previously in existence, seem confused, or at least confusing. The book undoubtedly contains much valuable information as to the employment of the method *ad quadratum*, if this is taken to mean also that the length of a ground plan can be divided without a remainder by whole width measures, a method formerly called quadratic schematism (Dehio). The data relating to the equilateral triangle, and so on, will also be noted by the reader with interest and, to some extent, astonishment, as an enrichment of our knowledge, and the same is true of the evidence about the use of the Golden Section in Gothic. But in the year 1921 all that was no longer new in principle. On the contrary, the increased capacity of criticism was bound to make itself felt and with it a weary skepticism.

The first short chapter entitled "Ars sine scientia nihil" can be disregarded today, for Lund translates the phrase wrongly "Art without science is nothing."[43] Some examples of Lund's innumerable other conclusions may be cited here. In his opinion, the original drawing of the west front of Cologne is wrong, and he corrects it by interweaving all at once the square, the equilateral triangle, and the *sectio aurea.* The tower of Freiburg Cathedral, with regard to which Zeising had demonstrated the Golden Section, is now constructed by Lund *ad quadratum*; that is to say, taking the complete width, including the side buttresses, as a unit and plotting it perpendicularly, one can just reach the upper edge of the balustrade above the middle window; three times takes it up (almost) to the very top (page 106). Lund makes a radical correction of Viollet-le-Duc's theses about Bourges (page 16), but to argue this point would be to lose one's way in a labyrinth. The question just what is actually gained by such research becomes urgent. There can be no doubt that Gothic architects made use of triangulation and the like, but that they excogitated networks made up of hundreds of lines in order to determine all points has not been proved and is probably indemonstrable and unlikely. So one learns that networks can subsequently be entered in on the plans of a building and is continually being astonished when everything fits, even though the networks may

[43] *Ibid.*, p. 2. He has also misunderstood the words *triangulum* and *figura triangularis.* He thinks the latter is the same as *ad quadratum*, that is to say, the triangle inscribed in the square (with an elevation equal to the side of the square), and *ad triangulum* the equilateral triangle.

differ. We have seen this before, but in Lund's case the whole procedure becomes madness with a method.

At times even the method is incomprehensible. In the case of the façade of York Cathedral (pages 20 and 94), Lund refers to the corresponding analysis of that of Cologne (page 68), but why do *part* of the diagonals in the York façade and the great circle that sets off the chief square go down into the ground? Does this measurement relate to the foundations? That would be quite possible; but then the proportions that are visible would only be compatible with those others that relate to an invisible base line if one yields to this "diagonalomania" that becomes an end in itself.

Lund's book included the question of the relationship of the methods of squares, triangles, and the Golden Section. In a work by Ernst MOESSEL (b. 1881) we find all these methods classified under the superconcept of the division of the circle, an idea already suggested in Boisserée. Moessel's book,[44] though scholarly and painstaking, is just as wearisome as Lund's; again we meet buildings that have been caught once before in a web of reticulation and are now covered with new ones—for example, the tower of Freiburg Cathedral (in I, page 87). Since to the square and the 60 degrees, 45 degrees, and $\pi/4$ triangles Moessel adds the regular pentagon, hexagon, decagon, and icosagon, all both inscribed in and circumscribed about the circle (sixteen measures in all) and since in his measurements he leaves a margin of two percent because of inaccuracies in the execution, he always arrives at a so-called fixed point.

By 1920 Moessel had already fairly completed his work and therefore could hardly have made any use of Kossmann's book, even had he known it.[45] Kossmann has previously been mentioned several times above, for with his theory of the "Great Unit of Measure" he unconsciously reverted, even in his terminology, to Stornaloco's *unitas*. From his book it was at last learned that Gothic builders employed measuring sticks; for example, the Cistercians used rods seven feet long. The Cistercians were not the only architects to use this measure, while, as the study of the Milanese records shows, other lengths, namely of eight feet or six feet, were utilized as well. This discovery was a relief after the complicated methods of Lund and Moessel. It must be clearly realized, however, that in addition to the *unitas* or the "Great Unit of Meas-

44 Ernst Moessel, *Die Proportionen in Antike und Mittelalter*, Munich, 1926.

45 B. Kossmann, *Einstens massgebende Gesetze bei der Grundrissgestaltung von Kirchenbauten* (Studien zur deutschen Kunstgeschichte, No. 231), Strasbourg, 1925.

ure" the method *ad quadratum*, as Roriczer understood it, and the *lex Thiersch* continued to be in force, and certainly also the method of the Golden Section which Gothic architects used freely in the designs of their polygonal choirs and tracery.

Once again, in 1930, Felix DURACH (b. 1893) formulated with accurate understanding the mediaeval method of measurement.[46] On page 22 he says that though the builders did indeed have units of measure, they did not reproduce them directly from the drawing but proportionally. According to Drach, they used "the possibility of varying proportionment according to mathematical laws." Durach himself continues: "The concordance between the designs and the actual construction lay in the fact that the architect employed in his drafting the same principle of proportioning that he used practically in natural size when he directed his workmen on the site."[47]

Kossmann's conclusions make it clear once and for all that the choice of proportions in the Middle Ages was motivated by practical, not aesthetic considerations. If—for practical reasons—the builders worked with equilateral triangles or other figures in order to reproduce the drafted design on the scale of the actual size, there automatically resulted from this procedure the recurrence of similar figures. In other words, the *lex Thiersch* is in mediaeval buildings only the result of triangulation, quadrature, or some other proportion used throughout the building, the purpose of which was to enlarge a sketch plan without a yardstick.

A second point is that the Great Unit served to lay out large dimensions—as, for example, was the case with Gabriel Stornaloco's *unitas*—but that Roriczer's method was used for the plotting of measures that were close together and only slightly different, as, for example, in details like pinnacles. The preference for the square, the equilateral, and the Pythagorean triangle goes back to Vitruvius and Plato (see *Art Bulletin*, 1945, page 95). In Book IX, Introduction 4, of Vitruvius, the doubling of the square is followed by the explanation of the Pythagorean triangle. As the authority for the doubling of the square Vitruvius refers to Plato, who in the *Meno* puts the demonstration in the mouth of Socrates. In the *Timaeus*, however, Plato characterized the equilateral triangle as one of the means by which God created the world. The history of these three figures, the aristo-

[46] Felix Durach, *Mittelalterliche Bauhütte und Geometrie*, Stuttgart, n.d. (ca. 1930).

[47] I did not know of this dissertation when I wrote "The Secret of the Mediaeval Masons," *Art Bulletin*, XXVII, 1945, p. 46.

crats, as it were, of planimetrics, will not be presented again here, but it should be mentioned that even in the Old Testament there is already evidence for the "Great Unit."[48]

It next became desirable to examine the credibility of the older theories. This labor was performed by Walter THOMAE (1875-1941).[49] Since most of these theoretical writers included sculpture and painting in their theses, it was not hard for Thomae to select cases that border on the ridiculous. Thus he instances the fact that Drach, in triangulating tombstones, once found himself with a corner point of his triangle on the tip of the nose of the dead man's effigy, or his dog's, and that in Moessel a "fixed point" once lay on an angel's abdomen.[50] But whereas measurements of works of sculpture or painting made after the event are in a case similar to that of the anthropologists with their skull measurements (where honest scholars admit that their exact calculations are sometimes upset by the undefinableness of the fixed points), architectural measurements really seem qualified to provide unequivocal fixed points. But very often one is at a loss even here. Thomae has called attention, moreover, to the well-known but forgotten fact that even the transverse sections of the naves of Gothic cathedrals have very different proportions, and yet no single one of these proportions can reveal the secret of beauty, since they all have their particular variety of it.

Though Thomae's work is on the whole completely negativistic, it is nevertheless very valuable because he examined all the theories in existence down to 1933 as to their exactness and because he finally undermined, if not refuted, the thesis that the beauty of mediaeval buildings is based on triangulation or related methods. In so doing, he often overshot the mark, and he lacked, above all, complete understanding of the true meaning of triangulation, although that had already been discovered by then. Only from the point of view of this practical purpose of the transference of the design to the true size of the execution can many of Thomae's objections be judged as to their validity. He takes exception, for example, to the fact that the visible transverse sections necessarily have a different proportion from the auxiliary triangles that were traced in for the axes of the piers. Today it is plain that triangulation as such cannot be criticized by maintaining

48 Ezekiel 40: 3 and 5; cf. *Art Bulletin*, 1945, p. 51 n. 21.

49 Walter Thomae, *Das Proportionenwesen in der Geschichte der gotischen Baukunst und die Frage der Triangulation*, Heidelberger Kunstgeschichtliche Abhandlungen, 13, Heidelberg, 1933.

50 *Ibid.*, p. 45.

that, as it were, the flesh-clad axes (to use Thomae's expression) had nothing to do with triangulation. Why, indeed, should they have, when the builders could plot them with simple, rational measures, meanwhile leaving themselves a free hand for the irrational measures of the visible surfaces of the space-delimiting solid forms? The extent to which the theories of triangulation deducible from the Milanese building records were applied in other architectural works is yet to be investigated. For such proposed research Thomae's book is a good mentor, warning us not to yield to our own imagination and make our own theory into a Procrustean bed for the true measures.

The most thoughtful of studies on proportion to date is the investigation by Walter UEBERWASSER (b. 1898)[51] (likewise already referred to earlier). The "right measure" is the rectangle that is formed by taking the side of the square as base and the diagonal of the same square as altitude. It was already mentioned in Vitruvius as a good proportion for a courtyard,[52] and was chosen by Schongauer as the format for his Passion series and by Dürer for the *Apocalypse*, the *Life of Mary*, and the *Great Passion*. Ueberwasser's article utilizes everything in the older studies on proportion that is tenable.[53] There are, ultimately, two main problems to be distinguished.

[51] Walter Ueberwasser, "Nach rechtem Mass," *Jahrbuch der Preussischen Kunstsammlungen*, LVI, Berlin, 1935, p. 250.

[52] Vitruvius, VI, 3, 3.

[53] Since this chapter was written a new study of mediaeval methods of measurement has been published: *Maria Velte, Die Anwendung der Quadratur und Triangulatur bei der Grund— und Aufrissgestaltung der gotischen Kirchen* (Basler Studien zur Kunstgeschichte, VIII), Basel, 1951. The proofs that the method of quadratura, and to some extent of triangulatura was used for the towers of Vienna, Strasbourg, Freiburg i. B., Basel are convincing; the theories concerning the groundplans are the same which have been advanced in earlier studies and must be reconsidered. The statements concerning Stornaloco and the cathedral of Milan are unfortunately erroneous. Nevertheless portions of the dissertation are very useful. See also Louis Hautecoeur, "Les Proportions Mathématiques et l'architecture," *Gazette des Beaux Arts*, II, 1937, p. 263. The Renaissance theories of proportion have recently been exhaustively and competently discussed in: Rudolf Wittkower, *Architectural Principles in the Age of Humanism* (Studies of the Warburg Institute, XIX), 1949. Following a list of some books on proportions omitted in the text: Odilo Wolff, *Tempelmasse*, Vienna, 1911; he believes the hexagram was used for the groundplans of Doric temples and the temple of King Solomon. The use of the hexagram is of course identical with the triangulature. Julius Haasse, *Der Dom zu Magdeburg, Eine deduktive Genese seiner Haupt- und Massverhältnisse*, Wiesbaden, 1914. Camillo Fritz Discher, *Die deutschen Bauhütten im Mittelalter und ihre Geheimnisse*, Vienna, 1932. (Both these books are unknown to me.) Karl Busch, *Raum- und Zeitgesetze deutscher Kunst*, Berlin, 1935. This is nearly worthless. Ernst Mössel, *Urformen des Raumes als Grundlagen der Formgestaltung*, Munich, 1931; a continuation of his earlier work (see above p. 723) Otto Kloeppel, *Die Marienkirche in Danzig und das Hüttengeheimnis . . .* , Danzig, 1935. He believes that *ad triangulum* and *ad quadratum* is the same because erroneously he substitutes the isosceles triangle inscribed into the square for the equilateral one. He uses for the façade of Reims Cathedral the octagon and for other façades the pentagon; e.g. also for St. Elisabeth in Marburg. His theory is full of arbitrariness. W. Juettner, *Ein Beitrag zur Geschichte der*

The *first* of these is the correlation between the practical purpose of the methods of mensuration in use during the Gothic period and their aesthetic results. The answer to this problem has already been touched upon several times: the employment of a module and of *symmetria* in Vitruvius' sense, the methods *ad quadratum* and *ad triangulum* make the transference of measures possible and are to that extent merely *practical* aids, but the congruency in proportions automatically resulting therefrom is at the same time a factor of *aesthetic* congruency—one factor, it must be emphasized, for there are others, indeed many others. This can perhaps be demonstrated most quickly and effectively by reference to the networks of beauty that many scholars trace over paintings. As a striking example of the fact that they could be and actually were used, Ueberwasser cites Erhard Schön's proportional sketch for a rider (page 270), but the network of square, inscribed circle, diagonals, and so on, is as such but a poor thing. So, also, one turns away in dissatisfaction from the reticulations that Naumann thought he could deduce for Matthis Nithard, or Hetzer for Titian.[54] No one would hang these networks of beauty on his wall. Whether Titian used such networks (in this case it is very questionable) or not, he added much that is not proportion. And so it is also with buildings. One may fish further for nets but should never lose sight of the fact that an architectural work can—for the eye—no more be reduced to mathematical proportion alone than a musical work to purely acoustical rules.

What is meant here by "aesthetic" refers to all subjective (not individually, but generally humanly subjective) transposition of perception into feeling. Our attitude can be *practical*—as in making measurements on a site, or *scientific*—as in resurveying a building, or *aesthetic*—as when we inject into the pure subjectivity of feeling the optical total impression together with all its imaginative and intellectual backgrounds, and completely humanize, indeed even personalize it. Among these feelings is one for pure harmony. Feelings are irrational,

---

Bauhütte und des Bauwesens im Mittelalter, Cologne, 1935. Partly useful. Otto von Simson, *The Gothic Cathedral*, London, 1956. He discusses proportions and connects them with the theory of music. To Simson's book an appendix by Ernst Levy is added, "On the proportions of South Tower of Chartres Cathedral." See the review of this book by Mrs. J. Weitzmann-Fiedler in the periodical of the Society of Architectural Historians, Troy, New York, 1958. Georg Lesser, *Sacred Geometry*, London, 1957.

54 Hans Heinrich Naumann, *Das Grünewald-Problem und das neuentdeckte Selbstbildnis des 20jährigen Mathis Nithart aus dem Jahre 1475*, Jena, 1930; and Theodor Hetzer, "Über Tizians Gesetzlichkeit," *Jahrbuch für Kunstwissenschaft*, Leipzig, 1928, p. 1. See also Walter Ueberwasser, *Von Mass und Macht der alten Kunst*, Strasbourg, 1933.

as is harmony. Consequently, the disharmonious is also irrational.[55] To judge objects in whole or in part according to the degree of their harmony implies the recognition and intellectual postulation of absolute harmony as the point of reference, regardless of whether it can be formulated or not. Anyone who speaks of many kinds of harmony (as we all do) means "harmoniality" *per se*. In geometry—though not in arithmetic—absolute harmony can be formulated in terms of the Golden Section. Whether and to what degree Gothic made use also of absolute harmony in its proportions is a legitimate and unavoidable question for any scholar who thinks objectively. Seen from this point of view, aesthetic empathies towards quadratures, triangulations, and so on, are focused not merely on an impression of stability, ease or unrest, longing, buoyancy, and the like, but also on that of harmony or the degree of harmony, in general, of harmoniality. A proportion can, for practical reasons, be determined according to the *unitas* and the methods related thereto, and at the same time approach absolute harmony or be deliberately far removed from it.

These considerations lead to the *second* main problem, namely, to a clarification of the question of the aesthetic element itself. We took Schmarsow as our point of departure because he emphasized especially, following Semper, the concepts of rhythm and proportion. No three-dimensional object is without proportion, and rhythm is applicable to an even wider field. Both are *relations of magnitudes* and, properly understood, *concepts of logic* as the science of the form (void of meaning or abstract form) of thinking. They are closely connected and consequently investigations into the rhythm of Gothic very often contain by implication statements about proportions and vice versa. Since we are accustomed to regard Gothic primarily from an aesthetic standpoint, aesthetic judgments and those relating specifically to harmony (generally harmoniality) insinuate themselves unnoticed into the theses.

With this in mind, one can either demand strict separation of these factors or indulgently credit scholars with not wanting to forget their real goal, the artistic comprehension of Gothic—a comprehension that always must necessarily pass through the medium of aesthetic empathy. The self-deceptions lean either toward what was called above "diagonalomania" or toward the demand for *harmony*, that is to say, in this case the *sectio aurea*, where it is a question of *harmoniality*, inten-

[55] This subject cannot be discussed in detail here; on these concepts of aesthetics cf. my *System der Kunstwissenschaft*, Brünn, 1939, pp. 436-602.

tional deviation from harmony, as, for example, in Gothic as a style. It was indeed the specifically Gothic disharmony—*its* "harmony"—that the worshipers of antiquity censured from the time of Petrarch on. From time to time Gothic may have used the proportion of the Golden Section (as in the Cathedral of Sens) or a measure approximating it.[56] It is, however, not the Golden Section that is typical of Gothic but the slender proportions that in the course of the development become in High Gothic overslender and in Late Gothic flattened and which, moreover, are different in the different national regions. These specifically Gothic proportions, which are not "golden" but could in a certain sense be called with Pacioli's term "divine," are particular determinative elements of the designs. When these "disharmonious" proportions were repeated according to the *lex Thiersch*, the concordance of these disharmonies became in a higher sense harmony.

This harmony of the disharmonious, as it might be called, is *one* factor of the *artistic* element in Gothic. If art is taken to be form as the symbol of its meaning, then the "harmony of the disharmonious" (first of all in the realm of proportions) is the expression and symbol of the Gothic spiritual and emotional worlds and of the totality of active Gothic life.

If harmony is regarded as a "concord" of different elements, an assertion that is more a hint than a definition, then at least two different members are necessary to produce it. But harmony is also attributed to single lines, and curves are said to have a more harmonious effect than straight lines. The presence in *ancient* architecture of intentional curves that deviate slightly from a straight line has been demonstrated so certainly that doubts are impossible. William Henry GOODYEAR (1846-1923) has traced the history of the discovery of the curvatures of stylobate and entablature, as well as of entasis,[57] and has also mentioned the older interpretations of these deviations. The most important and interesting one is Guido Hauck's thesis that we do not see the architectures as they would be reproduced in a geometrical

[56] The most comprehensive modern studies of the Golden Section are the following: Matila Costiescu Ghyka, *Esthetique des proportions dans la nature et dans les arts* (La Pensée contemporaine), Paris, 1927, and by the same (Rumanian) author, *Le Nombre d'Or*, Paris, 1931, 2 vols. In Vol. 1 many things that I have mentioned are discussed, for instance, Cesariano's diagram of Milan Cathedral, without noticing that the presentation differs from reality. Ghyka takes Lund and Moessel very seriously (p. 73ff.). The transverse section of the early Gothic cathedral of Sens is determined in its proportions by the Golden Section.

[57] William Henry Goodyear, *Greek Refinements: Studies in Temperamental Architecture*, New Haven, 1912.

central projection but that all long straight lines appear to be curves.[57a] On this idea was based the argument that the straight lines in the temples had to be replaced by curves so that they would give the impression of straight lines, or the contrary, that curves were made in order to strengthen their optical impression. Goodyear connected these "refinements" with the irregularities of the axial intervals in various ancient buildings, concluding that the curvatures merely served to substitute more lively forms for the rigidity of exact straight lines.

Goodyear tried to prove that there were similar refinements in *mediaeval* architecture. The irregularities that he regarded as intentional are the result of bowing because of the weight of the vaults or of settling in the foundations and the piers themselves. Every visitor to Nôtre-Dame in Paris must become aware of the deviations of the piers of the crossing from the vertical; they are equally conspicuous in many other buildings, less so in some. They were not systematically carried out, but fortuitous. Goodyear's theories were criticized by BILSON (1856-1943) and for the present one can only agree with the latter's criticism.[58]

But however incorrect Goodyear's conclusions may be with regard to the many irregularities of *mediaeval* buildings, that is, however little the deviations can be considered intentional, the existence of all these irregularities is significant in connection with the problems of proportions and harmonies. The proof of quadrature, triangulation, similar figures, the Golden Section, and whatever else there may be of this nature presupposes that the buildings themselves reveal a sufficient accuracy of execution and no intentional deviations. If, however, such should be found to be present, they must be considered in the investigation.

To this demand must be appended the comment that those harmonious curvatures of antiquity only deserve the designation "harmonious" insofar as they approximate the stereometric creation of architecture

[57a] Guido Hauck, *Subjektive Perspective und die Horizontalen Curvaturen des Dorischen Stils*, Stuttgart, 1879. Hauck lived from 1845 to 1905.

[58] John Bilson, "Amiens Cathedral and Mr. Goodyear's 'Refinements.' A Criticism," *Architectural Journal of the Royal Inst. of British Arch.*, XIII (Third Series), London, 1906, p. 397. Here Goodyear's older works are cited.

William Henry Goodyear, "Architectural Refinements, A Reply to Mr. Bilson," *ibid.*, XV, London, 1908, pp. 17-51.

John Bilson, "Amiens Cathedral and Mr. Goodyear's Refinements. A Rejoinder," *ibid.*, pp. 84-90.

Goodyear wrote once more on his theses, "The Horizontal Curves of St. John's at Chester," also in the *Architectural Journal*, XXI, London, 1914, p. 585. Here it was a question of a building in the Romanesque style.

to a living organism, which can have *its* harmony or beauty, perhaps its disharmony or possible ugliness, and never appears *dead* but always organic and *alive*. The irregularity of intercolumniations in Doric temples or of spaces between piers in mediaeval churches—which are of very frequent occurrence—belongs under the superconcept of harmoniality, for the reason that in such cases at least two members always result which are effective in their proportion even though the spectator does not recognize it until he makes measurements. These "alive" irregularities can be found by the millions in the construction of mediaeval cities and generally they are only discussed for their "picturesque" side. Undoubtedly both aspects are called into play simultaneously by the object itself; they can be judged both harmonially (with relation to harmony) and limitologically, that is to say, with relation to limits, whether these isolate or merge either part within a whole or a whole with reference to its environment.

Both factors are independently variable. One can take the Golden Section as a schematic paradigm of harmony and any rectangle of another proportion as one of "disharmony," thus, for instance, that of 1:3. Each one can be either sharply delimited or vaguely outlined, and when such harmonious or disharmonious figures are connected two by two, they can be combined both in the sense of "addition" and in that of "division."

However fundamental this reflection may be, it is for Gothic much more remarkable that by far the majority of its buildings consist of parts, each of which, having originated in a different age, is built in a somewhat different style. It is hard to choose instances of this, since one could more easily enumerate the few examples that are free from any combination of parts in various styles or from the intrusion of stylistically later detail such as tracery and so on. Such amalgamations are to the architectural historian a source of intellectual joys; his acumen can revel in analyzing the anatomy of these structures. But no one has as yet investigated the problem of why the occasionally extreme contrasts almost never cause a disharmonious effect. In the cathedral at Aachen a Late Gothic choir (1355) is joined to a Carolingian building; in Vézelay a choir in a Transitional style between Early and High Gothic is added to a Romanesque nave; and in the church of the Franciscans in Salzburg the Romanesque nave and the Late Gothic choir cooperate in creating the greatest intensification of the effect. Nor should the hall choirs in Nuremberg be forgotten, or St. Peter in Salzburg with Rococo ornament upon Romanesque cushion capitals and so on. One could go on endlessly listing examples, until finally the question arises whether buildings that are all of a piece, that is, characterized by a consistent "regularity" in the observance of a single style, are more harmonious, more beautiful, or perhaps more boring. The proof of this problem was furnished by the Gothicists of the nineteenth century who were called Purists. Comments pro and con can be found in abundance in the literature on art; a comprehensive work is lacking.

The body of literature on rhythm, proportion, and harmony already in existence shows, despite all its errors, that historians of art have recognized the necessity of a final clarification of these concepts if the history of art is to assume the character of a science.[59]

But rhythm, proportions, and harmonies or disharmonies are always present in a building at one and the same time. To discover their reciprocal relations is a task that goes beyond the studies heretofore considered. For the present, such reciprocal relations can probably be demonstrated only by practical, specific examples, for instance, in the Gothic façades.

A dissertation by Hans KUNZE (b. 1882) centers about a problem that has otherwise scarcely been recognized anywhere.[60] The characteristic type of cathedral with basilical transverse section and two-towered west façade, occasionally also with two-towered transept façades, leads to a series of individual decisions regarding the mensuration of the portals, the rose windows, and so on—decisions of which we do not become conscious because in each case we have before us a finished result. It then looks as though all these harmonizing measurements were a matter of course. But in each case they are the fruit of very complicated deliberations, and the designs for the façades were, of course, also dependent on the inner elevations of the nave or transept. The organic connection that is meant here has nothing directly to do with quadrature and triangulation; it is a matter of decisions relating to the design and preceding the determination of the precise measures. Kunze begins by observing that the towers of the façades have paired buttresses toward all four points of the compass, and that consequently the rear, that is, east, buttresses of the western towers completely or

[59] The concept of "harmoniousness" as a stylistic principle does not belong, from a systematic point of view, in the same category of concepts as rhythm and proportion; cf. *System der Kunstwissenschaft*, Brünn, 1939, pp. 70ff., or pp. 42ff.

[60] Hans Kunze, *Das Fassadenproblem der französischen Früh- und Hochgotik*, Leipzig, 1909 (Studien über Christliche Denkmäler, ed. by Johannes Ficker). I have at hand only the Strasbourg dissertation, which takes the subject down through Reims and has no illustrations.

half block an aisle window, while on the other corner of the tower a buttress is quite impossible and therefore a pier must be erected that is stronger than the other piers of the nave. These irregularities are called by Kunze "an acute dissonance." (page 4) Even if one rejects such prejudices, the fact remains that it raised problems which demanded an answer.

The whole issue is most clearly revealed in the matter of the disposition of the west rose window. "The breadth of the nave determines its diameter, and the size of this in turn establishes the height of the rose window story; that is, the latter's height depends not on the *vertical* extent of a structural member of the nave but on a *horizontal* one. The broader the middle vessel of the nave is the larger is the rose window and the higher is the story containing it; if, with the increasing verticalism of Gothic, the breadth of the nave is reduced in proportion to its height, then the rose window story also loses in importance. Each new, differently proportioned Gothic basilica thus poses new problems for the composition of the stories of the façade." Kunze sees a second difficulty in the fact that the buttresses increased the effect of the mass of the towers, with the result that the central part was diminished in aesthetic importance. (Both observations on p. 5.)

These individual troubles of the designer point the way to an understanding of the essence of Gothic from an unaccustomed and hitherto neglected side. Kunze says explicitly that the Romanesque style did not lead to such difficulties. It is not easy to comprehend fully this reciprocal dependence of all the members in Gothic; the best method of realizing it is to attempt oneself to design a Gothic façade. Anyone who lacks the necessary talent can turn to Kunze's discussions of actual façades, which no one has analyzed and intellectually mastered with such intensity and acumen as he. The wealth of subtle observations relating to structural history, which he makes incidentally, would require consideration in a history of the specialized study of Gothic. Kunze's formulation of the problem is important for the investigation of the nature of Gothic because it points to the secret of the organic connection of all the parts of a Gothic cathedral.

Behind the problems of harmony and proportion lies the feeling that they are related to religion. Fiechter, though he investigates only Greek and Byzantine buildings, at one point arrives at a general idea in quoting Plato (according to Plutarch) who used to say that God always works as a geometrician. He adds that geometrical rules are not to be taken as an instrument to insure external beauty, but to be a reflection of God's eternal harmony in human work,[61] a statement which embraces every style.

This chapter may be closed with the reference to an unusually illuminating article of the mathematician Speiser.[62] It is a mixture of rationalism and irrationalism, of reason and feeling, of seriousness and humor, of veneration and irony, touching the deepest questions of art. For those who believe that art is the product of passive inspiration he quotes an Italian author who saw in Dante "un ponderoso lavoratore" and points to a word of Jakob Burckhardt: "Be ashamed! If Raffael had only indulged in the best drinks and had appealed to his infinite feeling—what then?"

10. Modern Aberrations

THE books to be considered in this chapter could perhaps be ignored because they have contributed nothing positive to the understanding of Gothic. Each of them had his public, however, and to hear what they had to say may be instructive to some readers and amusing to others. In any case the effort must be made to do justice to their work by acknowledging whatever good may be found therein or showing why certain theories must be declared untenable.

Karl SCHEFFLER's (1869-1952) book on the "Spirit of Gothic" is a popular work. The author flutters over the meadow of artistic theories collecting nectar like a butterfly. Study of this literature gradually stimulated in him such a variety of ideas that the desire to blend them into a synthesis inevitably resulted. Since Scheffler is not a systematic thinker, he jumbled them all together like colored stones in a kaleidoscope. Many readers who lacked the time and, even more, the concentration to read original sources doubtless were delighted to trust themselves to his guidance because he provides such splendidly broad surveys. They probably had no idea how little in the book is accurate and how much false.

No complete analysis will be offered here. It will suffice, rather,

[61] Concinnitas, *Beiträge zum Problem des Klassischen*, Basel, 1944, p. 61; Ernst Fiechter, "Raumgeometrie und Flächenproportion." The sentence on p. 70 runs as follows: "So sei also nochmals gesagt, damit kein Missverständnis sich einschleiche, nicht als Instrument zur Sicherung einer äusseren Schönheit, sondern als ein Spiegelbild göttlicher Unbildlichkeit wurde Geometrie eingeordnet." (p. 70)

[62] *Ibid.*, p. 215, Andreas Speiser, "Die mathematische Betrachtung der Kunst." (p. 234)

1 Karl Scheffler, *Der Geist der Gotik*, Leipzig, 1917.

to say that by Gothic Scheffler does not mean a specifically historical stylistic phase but the opposite of classical antiquity, which he identifies with the ideal of beauty. "The idea of an absolute ideal in art has for a long time blinded our nation, and indeed our race, to the really formative element in art. The Germans have suffered especially from the theory of idealization, because they always pursue all intellectual matters to their last consequences and are thorough to the point of self-destruction."[2] The Classicistic trend, by which Scheffler seems to mean the coming of the Renaissance and Humanism to Germany in the sixteenth century, obscured the Gothic tradition. The latter was reawakened in the Romantic Movement and, with the increase in objects of study, led to the recognition that Gothic form is opposed to classical "as winter is to summer, or storm to repose, that it is a question of a world of forms that cannot be rejected critically inasmuch as under certain conditions it arose everywhere as a similar phenomenon and will always rise again."[3] Scheffler almost reverts to the original terminology of the Renaissance, which confronted "antique" with "Gothic or barbarian," only he says "Greek" instead of "antique" and, of course, drops the adjective "barbarian" since his heart is with barbarian Gothic. But what does Gothic mean? Freely copying Worringer, Scheffler jettisons the "academic" concept of Gothic. "Under the concept of Gothic have been ranged the prehistoric and the Egyptian, the Indian and the Baroque, the antique and the modern, the distant and the near." (page 22) We are here faced with the same conceptual inflation as in Worringer, though it is somewhat more concrete in the designation of all these "Gothic" styles. The "Way of Gothic" is expounded in the third chapter. It begins with the cave paintings, which are interpreted in accordance with Worringer's "Primitive Man." Then follow the art forms of the Gothic Negroes, Gothic South Americans, Gothic Bushmen, and Gothic Eskimos; next the Gothic of Egyptian art. Of the latter Scheffler writes, among other things: "A Gothic effect is created by the smooth walls of the temples, undivided even by joints, and by the pylons that, fortresslike, flank the entrance.... But then the way leads through halls of columns with horizontal entablatures, and one is surrounded by a world of forms in which the

[2] *Ibid.*, p. 13. In this sentence there is an echo of Goethe's remark that art was for a long time formative (bildend) before it became beautiful (also quoted by Scheffler on occasion), as well as the popular idea about German consistency as a fault of which they should be proud. Such combinations and compilations occur almost uninterruptedly. The extension of the concept Gothic is, of course, derived from Worringer, and that of race from the same source.

[3] *Op.cit.*, p. 21.

Greek spirit also has a large share. This Greek is likewise still Gothic, as is shown by the single column in its vertical tendency and with its massive forms, and by the monumental articulation of the moldings; but there is, nevertheless, the Greek order, the Greek balance of load and support, the sense for the logical, reasonable, and this-worldly." (page 66) If a sense for logic is Greek, then these remarks are very Gothic, assuming that Gothic is the opposite of Greek. But Scheffler continues: "Egyptian art solves the problem of being at once transcendental and mundanely representative, it is both barbaric and cultivated." (page 66) Could Scheffler's book perhaps be called Egyptian?

A section on Babylonian art follows (page 68): "There, too, Greek spirit develops on the basis of a grandiose Gothic attitude." With such a yoking of Greek and Gothic the truly Babylonian element is completely lost to view.

In the part about China Scheffler writes (page 74): ". . . the elemental has become coquettish, the urge toward the unconditional playful, the grotesque *précieux*, the hieratical graceful, and abundance refined. For thousands of years the Gothic is experienced by a whole great people as a kind of pedantic formalism, a *Zopfstil*." One should turn again to the list of polar stylistic concepts. If one is determined to make bedfellows of Chinese art and Gothic (in the sense of the "academic concept"), there are, after all, general concepts available in order to express what Scheffler presumably meant. It is surely not merely pedantic insistence on the use of a clear terminology that makes us marvel that Scheffler should have deliberately resorted to just the most primitive designation of all, one that came into use with Petrarch. Why have scholarly thinkers taken such pains for generations if a jongleur can come and offer rash notions of this sort to the general public as the ultimate truth?

After China, Scheffler takes up Europe: "If all form produced by the Gothic spirit can be called the form of suffering, then it must be observed that the European suffers differently from the Asiatic." (page 75) The idea is developed further: the one is active, the other passive. In this there is a suggestion of Worringer's "Oriental Man." We hear little about the Greeks but are told (page 77), surprisingly, that the "Fates" of the Parthenon can be called "almost a sublime Baroque" and "thus also a form from the Gothic sphere of feeling."

The progress of Gothic includes Rome. "At the beginning and end of Roman art the Gothic spirit also triumphed with a certain emphatic force. Etruscan art is quite imbued with a secret Gothic, whatever share the Greek colonial form likewise has in it externally." The "American quality of Roman architecture" (that is to say, bridges, basilicas, thermae, and so on, the Pantheon, the Colosseum) "is a manifestation of the Gothic spirit because it is the expression of a violent will" (pages 78, 79). He does not mean *Kunstwollen* as such, rather the violence of America, Rome, France, etc.

On page 81, however, there is a reference to *Kunstwollen*. It is unnecessary to go into everything, for much appears only to disappear again; the Gothic alone remains. The Early Christian mosaics inspire Scheffler to the following statement: "The general concept 'Gothic' here shrinks to its original cell: it points to the people of the Goths, whose imagination was kindled by Roman art and instructed by the last Greeks." (page 84) Can this perhaps be a reference to Riegl's *Römische Kunstindustrie*? The Goths had been made responsible for Gothic, but now the Romans and Greeks are declared to bear the blame for having seduced the Goths into Gothic paths, or at least for having prepared them to create the Early Christian mosaics.

It will be permissible to skip the section on Romanesque art; indeed, one would prefer to do the same with that on Gothic in the narrower sense. Here, on page 89, there are echoes of many theories, among them Viollet-le-Duc's thesis about Gothic as the art of laymen, a thesis that Scheffler sharpens into Protestantism, making the Catholics of the thirteenth century into Protestants, "not critical and purifying, but creative Protestants." It is as though everything had to be turned topsy-turvy. Of course the Crusades are mentioned, and, says Scheffler, "the laity, rejoicing in its self-liberation, created for itself the fertile idea of Gothic"—a Gothic that had nevertheless already been in existence since Babylon and China. "This idea is Germanic, in a narrower sense Frankish, in origin. Never would the Latin spirit, so devoted to the Greek order, have dared to express such exuberant joy in creation,"—had not Scheffler just said that Roman art was Gothic?—"never would it have been able to invent the principle of the pointed arch and apply it with such imaginative exactness, never would it have attempted these mystically deep vaulted grottoes of space, these forests of pillars, this luxuriant network of vine-like ornament, never caprice in order and order in the apparently irregular. . . ."

Perhaps these passages will suffice, although it may also interest the reader to learn that Scheffler, in discussing the Renaissance, says (page 96) "And the Doric is a form of the Gothic." Somewhat further on, the nationalistic idea appears again: "This imaginative style of a speculative self-intoxication that revels in suffering [the Baroque], this urge toward abundance, this self-expenditure, this Romantic formalism—all were necessary to the Nordic temperament." Scheffler then makes a transition to the bourgeois character of the Rococo, and finally comes to his particular field of interest, Impressionism, which is "the last form of the Gothic spirit that has hitherto been historically recognizable" (page 105). "The most revolutionary is always also the most Gothic." On the last page of the book, however, there is the conciliatory and antirevolutionary remark: "Everywhere, to be sure, the new Gothic form is also intimately linked to the Greek."

It seems as though Scheffler had a vague notion of what he had done, for on the last two pages he warns the reader against himself. "What we need are clear-cut delimitations. This admonition is placed, not without reason, at the conclusion of this book. . . ." If he had only printed this sage reflection on his first page! At the end he expresses the fear that "a general value will be given to the word 'Gothic,'" and suggests that it would be better not to use the term at all in a programmatic sense. "From the point of view of stylistic history the new will look all the less Gothic the more Gothic it is in its innermost nature. . . ." After this oracular pronouncement he demands in his last sentence: "Clarity."

In this series of literary judgments on Gothic we have included for the sake of historical objectivity many abstruse opinions on the origin of the style, for example, its derivation from Noah's Ark. We are equally obligated to discuss Scheffler's opus, which is concerned not with the origin of the pointed arch but with the myth of eternal and secret Gothic. The book should be regarded as an expression of the "feuilletonistic age," indeed as indicative of what the half-educated public around 1917 wanted to hear about Gothic; at the same time it is characteristic both of the trend in the scientific world of art historians toward the acquisition of general concepts and methods permitting "proof" of the periodicity of artistic development, and of the nationalistic trend that postulated a Nordic or Germanic or German "racial" admixture as a necessary condition of Gothic. In Scheffler, the notion of the Nordic-German race, which a few years later was termed Aryan, is enlarged to include the Babylonians, Egyptians, and Chinese.

Much that we call brilliant is paradoxical, but not everything paradoxical is brilliant![4]

On a somewhat higher plane is the book by Oswald SPENGLER (1880-1936),[5] which for a time after its appearance fascinated wide sections of the reading public. But it was without lasting influence. Today it is nearly forgotten. It presents a grandiose compilation of ideas, interesting as such and in many instances correct, but the author's own particular synthesizing ideas are false and have long since been refuted. To us it is merely important to note that a book which in the year 1917 claimed to survey the history of the world systematically and give an analytical interpretation—even if only by means of a pseudo-system—could not ignore the phenomenon of Gothic.

Spengler speaks of Gothic in three places. The first passage contrasts Greek art with Egyptian (with overtones of Alois Riegl, many of whose ideas Spengler tacitly adopted), then Gothic with Greek. The fact that Spengler traces the quadripartite ribbed vault back to Burgundy and Flanders is lost in the flood of associations. After calling the Sainte Chapelle in Paris the paradigm of Gothic, he finally contrasts Gothic with Early Christian-Byzantine art, so that in a few pages we are given a sweeping survey of the architectural history of antiquity and the Middle Ages. Since this summary of mine fails to indicate any of the specifically Spenglerian flavor of the text, it must be quoted here verbally:[6]

"The Doric column was the symbolical embodiment of the corporeally existing individual object and renounced all claim to vast and far-reaching creations. . . . Whereas the Egyptian and Faustian soul first found expression in the language of a mighty architecture, the antique soul sought to express itself in an explicit renunciation of such architecture. The expression it finally achieves is the Doric temple, which creates a merely external effect as a massive structure set in the landscape, denying the artistically quite disregarded space within it as that . . . which ought not to be there at all. . . . The exterior colonnades are vestiges of an 'interior.'

"In contrast to this, the magical and the Faustian souls raised their stone space-shapes on high as vaultings of significant interiors, the structural idea of which anticipates the spirit of two branches of mathematics, algebra

[4] There is another book by Karl Scheffler in existence: *Deutsche Baumeister*, Leipzig, 1939 (2nd ed.). The chapter on "Meister der gotischen Bauhütten," pp. 66-125, is more serious than his earlier book, but the reader may judge for himself.

[5] Oswald Spengler, *Der Untergang des Abendlandes, Umrisse einer Morphologie der Weltgeschichte*, Munich, 1917.

[6] *Op.cit.*, I, *Gestalt und Wirklichkeit*, in the 1920 edition (Munich), pp. 272ff.

and analysis. In the architectural style that radiated out from Burgundy and Flanders the quadripartite ribbed vaults with their severies and buttresses mean an actual dissolution of the enclosed space determined by sensuously perceptible delimiting surfaces. An interior is always something corporeal. But here can be felt the will to push out of it into the illimitable, a desire later evinced by the contrapuntal music that was native to these vaults. . . .

"Where polyphonic music rose to its highest possibilities, even in much later times, as in the *St. Matthew Passion*, the *Eroica*, or Wagner's *Tristan* and *Parzifal*, it became as a matter of innermost necessity *cathedrallike* and returned to its home, to the stone language of the age of the Crusades. The full force of a profoundly significant ornamentation, with its strangely frightful transformations of plant, animal, and human forms (St.-Pierre in Moissac), which denies the substance of the stone and dissolves all lines into melodies and figurations of a theme, all façades into many-voiced fugues, the bodiliness of its statues into a music of drapery-folds, had to be enlisted in order to banish the faintest trace of antique corporeality. It is just this that gives to the enormous glass windows of the cathedrals, with their colored, *translucent, and thus completely incorporeal painting* . . . their profound meaning. It is seen most clearly perhaps in the Ste-Chapelle in Paris, where the stone has almost disappeared beside the luminous glass. . . . Compare the Faustian spirit of these loftily vaulted naves, illuminated with colored light, pushing forward toward the choir, with the effect of the Arabian—in other words, Early Christian-Byzantine—domes. The dome on pendentives that apparently floats in the air above the basilica or the octagon also signifies an overcoming of the antique principle of natural gravity, as it is expressed in the relation of column and architrave. Here, too, the stone is denied. A ghostly confusing interpenetration of the forms of sphere and polygon, a ponderous mass hovering weightlessly on a ring of stone high above the ground, all tectonic lines concealed, small openings in the uppermost vault through which an uncertain light is admitted, making the spatial demarcations even more unreal—thus the masterpieces of this art, S. Vitale in Ravenna, Hagia Sophia in Constantinople, the Dome of the Rock in Jerusalem, stand before us. Instead of the Egyptian reliefs with their purely surface treatment that scrupulously avoids any foreshortening indicative of depth, instead of the stained glass of the cathedrals that draws in the world of external space, all the walls are here clothed with gleaming mosaics and arabesques in which the gold tone predominates, submerging reality in the fairy tale, uncertain light that has always been so entrancing to Nordic man in Moorish art."

The second passage is shorter but it reveals a mixture of concepts and an undisciplined use of terminology reminiscent of Scheffler;

Spengler calls Romanesque art late Arabian, this designation including the façades of the cathedrals of Burgundy and Provence—which ones? —and Strasbourg Cathedral. The term "Late Arabian," in itself an absurdity, is used here to embrace both Romanesque and Gothic as "Arab Gothic," and to the latter is added "Viking Gothic," which is thus perhaps also Late Arabian. The passage reads:

"It is true that all cultures, with the exception of the Egyptian and perhaps the Chinese, have been under the tutelage of older cultural impressions: foreign elements appear in each of the worlds of forms. The Faustian soul of Gothic, already moved to reverence by the Arabian origin of Christianity, turned to the rich treasures of Late Arabian art. The arabesques of an undeniably southern, I might say *Arabian Gothic* are spun over the façades of the cathedrals of Burgundy and Provence, dominate the language of Strasbourg Cathedral with a stone magic, and everywhere—in statues and portals, in cloth designs, carvings, metalwork, and by no means least, in the intricate figures of Scholastic thought and one of the loftiest symbols of the West, the saga of the Holy Grail—wage silent warfare with the primal Nordic feeling of a *Viking Gothic* such as prevails in the interior of Magdeburg Cathedral, the spire of the Freiburg Minster, and the mysticism of Master Eckart. More than once the pointed arch threatens to burst its restraining line and transform itself into the horseshoe arch of Moorish-Norman structures."[7]

The third passage gives a real characterization of Gothic.[8] Here the forest theory is resurrected in new guise:

"The word of God does not have the same sound beneath the vaults of Gothic cathedrals and in the monastery courts of Maulbronn and St. Gall as in the basilicas of Syria and the temples of republican Rome. In the sylvan character of the cathedrals, the mighty elevation of the nave above the side-aisles in contrast to the flat-ceilinged basilicas that were the prototype of Western church building; in the transformation of the columns, set in space as individual objects sharply defined by base and capital, into piers and composite piers that grow up out of the ground with branches and lines intertwining above their heads and losing themselves in the infinite, while an uncertain light from the gigantic windows into which the wall has been dissolved floods the whole space, can be seen the architectural realization of an attitude toward the world that found its original symbol in the great forests of the Nordic plains. And, moreover, in deciduous forests with their mysterious tangle of branches and the whisper of the endlessly stirring masses of leaves above the head of the observer, high above the earth, which the treetops strive to leave behind them as

[7] *Op.cit.*, I, p. 291. [8] *Ibid.*, p. 555.

they push upward through the trunks. One should not forget Romanesque ornament and its profound kinship with the meaning of the forests. The infinite, lonely, dusky forest has remained the secret longing of all Western forms of architecture. Consequently, as soon as the form-energy of the style becomes weary, in Late Gothic (in the Flamboyant style, in Troyes, in Prague Cathedral) as well as in the waning Baroque, the controlled, abstract language of lines dissolves again immediately into naturalistic systems of branches, tendrils, twigs, and leaves. The cypress and pine create an effect that is corporeal, Euclidian; they could never have become symbols of infinite space. The oak, beech, and linden, with fitful lights flecking their shade-filled expanses, appear bodiless, limitless, spiritual. The trunk of a cypress finds the perfect fulfillment of its vertical tendency in the clear column of its mass of needles; that of an oak seems to be an unsatisfied, restless striving upward beyond its top. In the ash the victory of the upward striving branches over the confining crown appears actually to have been achieved. It has a somewhat hazy aspect, an air of expanding freely in space, and perhaps for this reason the World Ash became one of the symbols of Nordic mythology. The rustling of the forest, a magic never experienced by any ancient poet, for it transcends the possibilities of the Apollinian feeling for nature, bears, with its secret questioning about the Whence and Whither, its merging of the momentary in the eternal, a close relationship to fate, to the feeling for history and permanence, to the Faustian, gloomily anxious orientation of the soul toward an infinitely distant future. For this reason the organ, which fills our churches with its deep and sonorous surge of sound, which has something boundless and immeasurable in its tones in contrast to the clear, firm note of the antique lyre and flute, became the instrument for Western worship. Cathedral and organ form a symbolical unity like temple and statue. The history of organ building, one of the profoundest and most moving chapters in the history of music, is a history of longing for the forest, for the language of this true temple of Western worship of the divine. From the sounds of Wolfram von Eschenbach's verses to the music of *Tristan* this longing has remained constantly fruitful. The development of orchestrated sound in the eighteenth century was unswervingly in the direction of an ever closer kinship to the sound of the organ. The word 'hovering,' meaningless with respect to things of the ancient world, is equally important in the theory of music, architecture, physics, and the dynamics of Baroque. When one stands in a tall forest of mighty trees and hears the storm raging on high, one suddenly understands the meaning of the idea of a force that moves mass."

Physics and music, literature and forest are here fashioned into a synthesis that is to represent the equivalent of Gothic. Spengler's very thinking is, as it were, polyphonic and multidimensional. Though this is not in itself a bad thing, it is questionable whether his characterization makes Gothic more understandable. Is he really talking here about Gothic? At times, doubtless. But the forest, infinity, parallels to Baroque, and Mysticism (the "merging of the momentary in the eternal") are not new points of view or new comparisons: the organ occurred back in Heinse. It is not important, however, whether or not Spengler adopted his conceptions from others; what does matter is that he stirred them all up together and breathed new life into them, but his poetic remarks were fundamentally not contributory to any concrete ideas about Gothic buildings. The mention of Prague Cathedral and Troyes, both cited as examples along with the Flamboyant style, which he calls "weary" (a notion no longer defensible in 1917), stands out from the rest of this literary phantasy on the subject of Gothic as a dilettantish misapprehension in the eyes of anyone who has a lively appreciation of these buildings as concrete entities.

Spengler's three observations on Gothic are in part inherently contradictory: Faustian "Arab Gothic" that originated in the treeless desert corresponds here to the World Ash of Nordic mythology that stems from the Germanic forests; but the domes of Byzantine architecture are also alleged to be Arabian and yet are the opposite of Faustian Gothic. It is undeniable that many of Spengler's statements ring true, but on the whole these compilations are scientifically worthless. Lack of self-discipline may be connected with the currents of relativistic philosophy and "psychologism," the so-called "philosophy of living," and the fashion for aphoristic and unsystematic thought in the late nineteenth century, so that Spengler's characterization of Gothic reflects not so much Gothic as the sipirit of subjectivism and aestheticism of the generation to which he belonged.

Also dear to the heart of this generation was the broadening of the horizon to include all lands and all ages, and the greatest world conqueror within the history of art was Josef STRZYGOWSKI (1862-1941). It is not my task to discuss the exceedingly complicated ramifications of his misguided theses; only his ideas on Gothic are important for this book. To this subject he devoted a chapter in the second volume of his work on Armenian architecture,[9] or at least a title that reads "Armenia and the origin of the Nordic church form (Gothic)." One paragraph has a special heading: "The origin of the ribbed vault."

I have already given a strictly objective critique of this derivation of the quadripartite ribbed vault from Armenia in a previous article.

[9] Josef Strzygowski, *Die Baukunst der Armenier und Europa*, Vienna, 1919.

Here I can only repeat that Strzygowski proved the existence of "ribs" in Armenia, that is, transverse arches he calls ribs, and also the existence of vaults, but *never* that of a *single* quadripartite ribbed vault.[9a]

In 1924 Strzygowski published an essay that began with a violent philippic against me. I read it expectantly, convinced that now at last proof of the Armenian ribbed vaults would be forthcoming. But without devoting a single word to Armenia, he let it drop, and all Asia as well, only to declare that he had discovered the origin of Gothic in Europe. "It was inexcusable with regard to the architecture of the Middle Ages not to ask first what attitude (*Baugesinnung*) of architecture the church found current when it set out to conquer the North." If Strzygowski himself called it inexcusable, was I then not in the right? But he thought otherwise.

The European conception of architecture before 1050, says Strzygowski, was one of wooden structures. One must try to understand this basic idea in all seriousness. It becomes clear from the final section of a book by Strzygowski's pupil Heinrich GLÜCK (1889-1930),[10] and we shall do best to follow his argument first. Reduced to its briefest compass, it is that the inadequate, chronological, *linear* method of investigation, which, for example, seeks to establish an unbroken sequence of intermediate links between Roman and Gothic vaulting, should be replaced by a *stratified*—that is to say, not linear (temporal) but two-dimensional—spatial, or *geographical* type. This geographical stratum is folk art, which spreads over wide areas and is something "temporally lasting." Folk art is like a tree that bears blossoms in various places. It is wrong to try to derive one from the other according to the sequence of their flowering, for they can only be understood with reference to the tree itself; one must, therefore, study both the tree trunk and root.

Applied to Gothic this means that it is wrong to explain it on the basis of other earlier vaulted styles—but at this point one encounters a difficulty since Glück himself definitely regards Gothic as having been derived from vaulted construction. Consequently, one must now turn from him to Strzygowski, who provides a clear example of his method in his essay on European Art.[11] He poses questions about the

9a "Herkunft und Wesen der Gotik," in *W. Timmling, Kunstgeschichte und Kunstwissenschaft*, Leipzig, 1923, p. 11ff.

10 Heinrich Glück, *Der Ursprung des römischen und abendländischen Wölbungsbaus*, Vienna, 1933 (completed in 1927, but published posthumously), pp. 341ff.

11 Josef Strzygowski, *Der Norden in der bildenden Kunst Westeuropas, Heidnisches und Christliches um das Jahr 1000 unter Mitwirkung von Bruno Brehm, Ernst Klebel, Friedrich Wimmer, Johannes Schwieger*, Vienna, 1926, p. 143; "Die Europäische Kunst," specifically,

folk art of Europe around 1050: How can it be discovered? What do we know about building with wood before 1050?

According to Strzygowski there are in Europe three areas of wooden construction: the Eastern sphere, the Western sphere, and that of the North Sea; and, corresponding to these, three different types of such building: block construction, half-timbering, and mast construction ("mast construction" or *Mastbau* is a new term for the older "stave construction"). This sounds very clear.

Though the first two strata of block construction and half-timbering are here unimportant for what comes later, that is, the derivation of Gothic, they illustrate the license Strzygowski allows himself in his method. For the temporal proof of block construction in the *Eastern* sphere *before* 1050 comes from churches of the *last* centuries, and the geographical locale of the buildings includes Armenia, the Ukraine, Croatia, Bohemia, Dalmatia, and Spain. Eastern Europe means, as seems to be indicated by a sentence about Spain, the Visigothic world. Thus the geographical stratum must be understood from the ethnological point of view. Not only is Strzygowski's chronology meaningless but his geography as well. The Eastern sphere shifts.

The *Western* sphere, that is to say, the region of half-timbering, "extends over the whole *South*, beginning with England [*sic*] Northern France and spreading through all Western and Southern Europe and across the territories of the former Islamic empires to India." A *West* European example is Katznase in *East* Prussia, others are located in Norway, and one, Saloinen, lies in Sweden. Whereas the block construction of Eastern Europe leads to the dome, "half-timbered construction developed to maturity that idea of an ordered sequence of bays and transverse arches which distinguishes West European architecture of the finest period in a broad stratum and sets it apart from all the other artistic currents of the earth." (Half-timbered work has "bays" only as long as the compartments or panels between the posts have not been filled in, that is to say, during its construction—at least in my experience.) There are cruciform churches of half-timbered construction that have a wooden quadripartite vault in the crossing; these typical examples of the *Western* sphere are in part situated in Finland and date from the seventeenth century (this, according to Strzygowski, represents the period before 1050). The *Western* sphere stretches from England to India but includes all of *Southern* Europe; it is almost

p. 161. At the end of the volume, on p. 271, there is an essay by Johannes Schwieger, "Der Begriff Norden."

identical with the *Eastern* sphere, though the latter, strangely enough, does not extend to India. (On page 47 we read that Iran is Nordic.) Since Strzygowski must undoubtedly have learned in school what is meant by West, East, and so on, he must have meant his terms to imply something different from what is understood by geographers or sea captains. But the "Western sphere" is not defined ethnographically. What does it mean? It is to be feared that the answer is: nothing at all.

The *Northern* sphere or North Sea region comprises England and Scandinavia (which had already been assigned to the Western sphere). From there the Normans bring their native Nordic fashion of building up the Seine. Now the ethnographical significance of the word "North" is clearer: it means the Normans.

Gol in Norway, after Seesselberg's drawing, serves as an example of the mast church. To some extent Strzygowski revived Seesselberg's theories. It is not a case of plagiarism, for the re-creation is rather to be explained according to Glück's theory as a new blossom on the old stem, which one might here call romantic popular science.

Gol has "masts." But these consist of three superimposed units that are separated by horizontal boards. Some of the verticals in the upper story are moved out of position sideways with respect to the lower story, so that they do not even form a continuous line. There is not the slightest similarity to Gothic. Ribbed vaults are no more to be found here than in Armenia, indeed there are no vaults at all but instead open roof trusses. It is a purely wooden architecture. There are no pointed arches, no buttresses, no chalice capitals, no ornamental gables, and so on. The membering of the exterior is distinctly horizontal. Strzygowski's doctrine is, to use Worringer's expression, a Nordic riddle. The dating of the churches that are still extant is uncertain, but that makes no difference to this method.[12] In any case they are *after* 1050.

Strzygowski had a predecessor in Courajod, among others, inasmuch as the latter advocated the derivation of Gothic from *wooden* construction—although from the Celtic, not the Scandinavian. Brutails countered this theory with the statement that Gothic was entirely a development within architecture in *stone* and that construction in wood had definitely been relegated to second place by about 1100. It may be remembered that Friedrich von Schlegel had already rejected the "willow withe theory" of James Hall in favor of a derivation from

[12] Strzygowski writes in *Early Christian Art in Northern Europe*, New York and London, 1928, p. 134, that the Norwegian "stave church" in Torpe is first mentioned in 1310, but that it was contemporaneous with Gol, "thus about 1200." By that time Laon and Nôtre-Dame in Paris were almost completed, and Chartres under construction!

Romanesque. Thus on this point Strzygowski was more romantic than the Romanticists. Gall had spoken of a "thought-form." Strzygowski said (page 54) that verticalism originated in mast construction: "Gall could have taken this thought-form as his point of departure." But even at best Strzygowski could have derived only verticalism by this means, not Gothic and its vaults. Gall called Jumièges proto-Gothic; accordingly, the mast churches of Gol, Borgund, and so on, would be proto-proto-Gothic. But if Jumièges is not Gothic at all but merely "proto," then Gol, Borgund, and the rest are also only "proto-proto." Again: not everything vertical is Gothic and not everything Gothic is vertical.

But there remains the other thesis, Strzygowski's fundamental idea, that the art of the ruling classes is dependent on folk art and folk art on blood and soil. This is a thesis of popular or folk science, a dogma. The science of the ruling classes, as it were, must test it just as medical science tests the ideas of quackery. This difficult task cannot be undertaken here. Possibly it is correct to say that the people of the Northern countries have verticalism in their blood, but how can such an empirical *a priori* ever be susceptible of proof? Perhaps the Normans brought the vertical elements to Jumièges. Their horizontal ships, like all sailing ships, had vertical masts. Why then does horizontalism prevail in England? Gothic remains Nordic even where it emphasizes the horizontal line. Can we not study folk art, the art of wooden construction, with full appreciation of its worth, without burdening it with the obligation of being the father of Gothic? Or its grandfather?

Porter had explained Gothic on the basis of lack of wood; Strzygowski explains it on that of a superfluity of the same commodity. Strzygowski's geographical-ethnographical method is also determined by natural science or rather by materialistic physiology, where it is, after all, a matter of intellectual and spiritual problems. Natural science, to be sure, would probably insist on greater precision in the employment of the points of the compass, and will call Strzygowski's thesis only a hypothesis. The chain is clearly recognizable: Büsching, Dahl, Semper, Courajod, Seesselberg, Strzygowski. What a strange figure Semper cuts in this group of Romanticists! It is interesting to speculate on who will be the next to join it, but perhaps—only perhaps!—Strzygowski and Seesselberg with their modernized forest-wood-barbarian theory will succeed in causing this dry branch to break off once and for all. It is barbaric in the pejorative sense.

Heinrich Glück's book must be taken far more seriously than Strzygowski's historical method beyond space and time, though here, too, everything is so jumbled together—antiquity, folk art, Islam, Gothic—that I shall not attempt to give an account of it. Attention should merely be called to his remarks on the architecture of the Visigoths.[13]

Another member of Strzygowski's circle is Ernst DIEZ (b. 1878), who wrote an essay entitled "Oriental Gothic."[14] The pointed arch, he says, originated in India, along with the gesture of folding the hands in prayer, which was introduced to Christianity under Pope Nicholas I (858-867): "*jumeis manibus, digitis compressis, compositis palmis.*" The hands so folded would form a pointed arch. (Again one seems to have been transported back to the days when the pointed arch was supposed to be derived from Noah's Ark.) "Does it need to be proved by documentary evidence that the countless series of pointed arches from Pamir to England symbolize prayer to the divinity and therefore became the uniform expression of the transcendental *Weltanschauung* of the Indo-European race?" Most people will answer: no. Diez says (page 170) that Romanesque is an Early Gothic. Is then the pointed arch not essential to Gothic at all? Did people in Romanesque times arrange their hands in round arches when they folded them in prayer? The answer must be in the negative, for Pope Nicholas I was already praying in the pointed arch way. But why, in spite of this, was the architecture of his time Carolingian instead of Gothic?

Diez has not revealed how he would manage to derive the ogee arch as well as the countercurved arch (*Vorhangbogen*) from praying hands. But here another theory comes to our aid—the science of psychoanalysis,[15] which is now so much in vogue. Richard STERBA (b. 1898) has discovered the psychoanalytical background of Gothic. The arch, he says, originated in the barrel vault, which "represents in its round vaulting an obvious substitution for the womb. . . . The arch can be regarded as the product of an inhibitory impulse, of an attempt at release from the compulsive reminiscence of the primal intra-uterine situation." This is followed by remarks about Roman and Romanesque arches, and finally the Gothic arch is discussed. "The arch now rears upward, slender and quickly spanned by the eye. . . ." This signifies freedom from the feminine, a tendency toward the masculine, and so on. And now comes the climax: because the pointed arch still retains a vestige of femininity (see Sterba's argument for this on page 364),

[13] *Op.cit.*, p. 169.

[14] *Josef Strzygowski zum 60. Geburtstag*, Vienna, 1923, p. 168.

[15] Richard Sterba, "Zur Analyse der Gotik," *Imago*, x, 1924, p. 361. (In the same volume an essay by H. Kuhnen, "Psychoanalyse und Baukunst," p. 347.)

Gothic "added an ogee peak to the pointed arch. The innovation can be interpreted as an attempt to transfer pleasurable zones to a higher level. . . ."

In his discussion of the Gothic pier Sterba also tries to show that here, too, it is a question of the suppression of the mother-element. He then takes up the subject of towers. Paired towers symbolize the legs of the mother. (Why do these legs point vertically to heaven?) Single towers, as in the minster at Frieburg in Breisgau, are a doublet of the cathedral itself, thus again wombs. But then, says Sterba, there are also cases where one tower has remained unfinished, as in Strasbourg: "and in consequence the completed tower reveals all the more clearly what it was intended to express. As an individual, sharply erect object it already partakes in this age of phallic significance." (page 367) Sterba recognizes a "tendency toward masculinization" in Gothic. But what is Gothic, then? Masculine, feminine, or hermaphroditic? It is surprising that Sterba has overlooked in his interpretation the prohibition against towers issued by various monastic orders. He should have asked himself whether the Freiburg Minster ought not rather to have been crowned with a factory chimney and whether that would have been more Gothic or merely more masculine.

The usefulness of psychoanalysis in medical practice is not the point at issue here; Sterba's interpretation of Gothic is pseudo-science and, to put it baldly, nonsense. Gothic has nothing to do with hysteria, neuroses, or the libido; architecture is neither masculine nor feminine. Sterba has only a very vague knowledge of the history of Gothic, and one can merely make the friendly suggestion that he stick to his own last.

Sterba, however, has an ally in Guido KASCHNITZ-WEINBERG (b. 1890), though he does not apply his interpretations to the Gothic.[16] Kaschnitz persuades the reader that all Greek architecture is based on the phallic cult introduced into the region of the Mediterranean by Nordic, Indo-Germanic tribes, and that Roman architecture is the expression of the aboriginal population who worshiped the mother earth in subterranean grottos, meaning the womb, the tomb as well as heaven, because the whole world is a grotto. Primitive religions mixed the ideas of breeding, birth and death with those of the creative and destructive powers of nature. Primitive art and architecture therefore employed sexual symbols to represent fertility. It may be that phallic forms were trans-

[16] Guido Freiherr von Kaschnitz-Weinberg, *Die mittelmeerischen Grundlagen der antiken Kunst*, Frankfurt a.M., 1944.

formed into piers and columns; it may be, on the contrary, that these forms were created and developed independently and that some people were reminded of the older meaning of older forms. Kaschnitz believes that there was a direct derivation. Even if we grant that the later *forms* developed from earlier ones, it is a mistake to suggest that the *younger forms* retain the *old meaning*. It is an error to regard the metaphors of primitive cultures as equations eternally valid for all later cultures. Although Kaschnitz does not state in so many words that the porticus of the Pantheon in Rome is masculine, the interior feminine, this is the inevitable conclusion in the light of his application of primitives modes of thought to those of more developed thinking. These conclusions are inadmissible and Sterba's interpretations of the Gothic are even more so. Mediaeval people in their churches were reminded of the Holy City, not of the maternal womb. They were more interested in their future life after death than in their prenatal existence as embryos. While it may be true that primitive people have always existed who are in need of psychoanalytic treatment, yet neither the architect of the Pantheon nor that of the Cologne Cathedral were primitive men. If certain scholars insist on interpretations in the manner of Kaschnitz and Sterba, they will at least have to concede that the Pantheon is a Roman womb and the Cologne Cathedral a Gothic one. It is difficult to take such theories seriously, and one cannot resist the temptation to ask how one is supposed to interpret the Statue of Liberty in the harbor of New York, or that of Bavaria in Munich. Both statues are hollow and can be entered. Are they therefore Roman—following Kaschnitz—or Gothic—following Sterba? If every statue is masculine, being a substitute for a column, are the Karyathides of the Erechtheum masculine and at the same time Roman? The absurdities to which all this leads are obvious.

This selection of modern interpretations of Gothic that reveal so little about Gothic and so much about our own age can be continued in a different direction. Whether Gothic is masculine or feminine is a matter of indifference to those who see in it chiefly the German element.

Anyone seeking the solution to the problem of what is specifically German will turn eagerly to a book by Richard BENZ (b. 1884).[17] It contains four essays dating from 1915 to 1927. Its character is fairly uniformly that of emotion and confused thinking. The opening sentences are as follows: "Renaissance and Gothic are comprehensive concepts of a cultural nature and almost generally accepted. They are

[17] Richard Benz, *Renaissance und Gotik, Grundfragen deutscher Art und Kunst,* Jena, 1928.

antithetical concepts which apparently exclude each other but are nevertheless foreordained to be jointly subsumed under a third, higher concept, not yet recognized as a comprehensive and universally valid cultural concept, that of music." Hitherto Gothic and Renaissance were understood as *styles*, and music as one of the *arts* that could be characterized by either Renaissance or Gothic styles. It might be assumed that the concept of music is meant here metaphorically as musical style. But Benz continues: "One can set forth the interchangeable paradoxes that the spirit of the Renaissance has assumed Gothic form only in music; that the spirit of Gothic has survived in modern times under the forms of Renaissance only as music—and in so saying one will have defined the whole extent of the problematic question of German character since the sixteenth century." But what is this—Gothic—music? "It begins at the point where Gothic ended: Bach's Gothic, sublimated and completely thought through, so greatly surpassing even the freest creations of the Middle Ages in intellectual breadth and freedom, is nevertheless in the sphere of music only, as it were, the Romanesque period of a still relatively dogmatic tradition. . . ." (page 23) On page 116 Benz discusses Gothic itself, but casually and without saying anything new. Many things are touched upon that have only a vague connection with the subject, and in the end the reader asks himself what German character and art are really supposed to be. Are they Bach, Mozart or Johann Strauss, etc.? Are they Gothic spirit in Renaissance forms? What does one learn from such a book about the real nature of Renaissance and Gothic? The title, after all, promises enlightenment.

No one can be criticized for smiling at Scheffler's Gothic Semites in Babylonia, Strzygowski's conflict with the points of the compass, or the theories of Diez, Sterba, and Benz; but it should also not be forgotten that these absurdities were meant seriously and given serious consideration. Such authors have an appallingly large public, and if one were to classify humanity, just as it is, according to types, the type of the intellectual tightrope walker should not be overlooked. To watch such *artistes* at fairs or in the circus is a fearful pleasure, but in science it is merely fearful and no pleasure at all. The intellectual tightrope performer will inevitably plunge from his rope—intellectually, but he lives on to be admired by a troop of grown-up children.

There are other authors whom one cannot but respect in spite of their errors. From this point of view a book by Heinrich G. LEMPERTZ (b. 1879) should be judged. It has been killed by a conspiracy of silence, nor would an all too rigorous critique redound to its advantage.[18] With happy instinct Lempertz rejects Worringer and Scheffler, following Dvořak's path, though the latter's essay was unknown to him when he conceived his work. Like Dvořak he puts the idea of Christianity or, more precisely, Christian dualism, in central place. By this he means that Christianity has two principles and, correspondingly, Gothic also. The first of these is that all things are shaped corporeally in space; the second, that they are animated by an inner form-determining energy. That is true. But can it not be said of any style in any age? As far as the first factor is concerned, Lempertz acknowledges influences from classical antiquity, yet Gothic does not seek classical beauty but "beauty of the heart and the recognition of God in nature." (page 10) With regard to the second factor he distinguishes, on the basis of one passage in the text, four stages: the earth together with plants, animals, human beings, God. These are the essential characteristics and are supplemented by "secondary qualities." A perusal of the book will, of course, indicate the significance of all this, but a more detailed account of it would still not help anyone who wants to know what the nature of Gothic actually is. Lempertz does, indeed, have much to say about the plastic element, and remarks (doubtless influenced by Gall) "that the transformation of the wall was due not to structural and scholastic, but to aesthetic and artistic causes"; but here, too, one must ask whether other styles are not also "plastic," if one insists on using this term for the wall membering.

Lempertz's terminology is in any case doubtful, sometimes even shocking. He calls the Rhenish Transitional style the first phase of deliberate Gothic form (as Boisserée once did), St. Elisabeth's in Marburg Early Gothic, and, what is even worse, Nôtre-Dame-la-Grande in Poitiers also Early Gothic, thus placing the latter church in the same stylistic category as Marburg, perhaps because pointed arches occur in the façade. How can such methods be expected to reveal the essential nature of Gothic? At that particular time indifference toward concepts of style and stylistic designations had become prevalent because the problem seemed insoluble. Lempertz had a sincere desire to discover the "nature" (*Wesen*) of Gothic, but from the very beginning he confused Gothic with non-Gothic. He is also a victim of the contemporary indifference toward exact concepts in general, and since that was a contributory source of all modern research in the history of art, one sentence of his book may be cited as an example: "Thus adornment and

[18] Heinrich G. Lempertz, *Wesen der Gotik*, Leipzig, 1926.

form became far more intimately connected than in the preceding phase." Is there adornment that is not intimately connected with form? Or did Lempertz mean to speak of ornamental form and contrast it with structural form or something similar? Was he clear in his own mind about what adornment, ornament, decoration are?

There are still other examples or modern aberrations in art scholarship, but this selection will suffice. The question of just what the "essential nature" of Gothic is, still remains to be answered.

After studying these vagaries of recent times one might ask whether much that has been said about Gothic ever since Petrarch, Vasari, and others, does not, from a more comprehensive point of view, also belong under the heading of aberrations. Such is certainly the case; but those older thinkers did not have at their disposal the knowledge and insights that had already been won for the writers who have been mentioned in this chapter. He who wishes to teach is obligated first to learn, and one should also take pains to think clearly when one intends to say something both new and valuable.

In a recent sensational book about Gothic Hans SEDLMAYR (b. 1896) presented many new thoughts, which, unfortunately, are, to a large extent, not valuable. He accepts up to a certain point the attitude of the Romanticists without specifying whom he means. He praises Kugler (page 13), which is surprising as Kugler was so critical of Gothic (see above page 542). Still more surprising is the statement that from then on the understanding of Gothic became continually worse. Schnaase was already "a step behind." (page 15) Wölfflin's concepts and Riegl's categories were quite inadequate for describing the specific mediaeval phenomena. Somewhat more successful were the attempts of Schmarsow and Pinder. Viollet-le-Duc and Gall were entirely wrong. He also mentions me in this list of misguided scholars. "The abstract history of style overlooks the concrete artistic phenomena of the cathedral. It lacks a technology, a phenomenology, and an iconology of the cathedral. Not only does it not succeed in bringing us closer to an understanding of the cathedral, but in the end—working as it does with inappropriate abstract concepts—it destroys the inner unity of the cathedral which is evident to every man of artistic feeling. For Paul Frankl the cathedral from the beginning of the thirteenth century is a hybrid structure, half Romanesque, half Gothic, which does not become a stylistic unit until 1250."[19] I never wrote or thought such nonsense.[20]

[19] Hans Sedlmayr, *Die Entstehung der Kathedrale*, Zürich, 1950, p. 19.

[20] See the article: "Die Rolle der Ästhetik in der Methode der Geisteswissenschaften," *Zeit-*

Yet Sedlmayr believes that, except for himself no one since Kugler has seen the "concrete artistic phenomena." What are his new ideas?

"The elements of the interior of the cathedral are not supporting walls and ceiling, but baldachins with filling walls." (pages 44-50) The term baldachin was introduced by Sedlmayr years ago to call attention to the connection of the supports with their (flat or curved) ceiling.[21] If the ceiling is carried by the walls and the columns stand independently in front of the walls he does not call the system a baldachin. He is differentiating between columns in front of the wall and those in the wall. In the first case the primary element is the wall and the ceiling is added, in the second the primary element is the baldachin (supports and ceiling taken as an inseparable unit) and the walls seem to be filled in. This second form is the essential element of mediaeval architecture, or one of them.

The walls in Gothic (and this is not new) are dissolved, they "create lattices." (page 51) He then follows Jantzen's theory of the "diaphane structure," which, surprisingly enough, he does not include among the abstract concepts of style. Correcting Dvořak he says that the cathedrals are "hermetically closed" because the stained glass creates "luminous walls. . . . It is senseless to talk about windows." Dvořak, like all the others since Milner who have felt that Gothic space is infinite, was also quite aware that the "windows" are hermetically closed. What they were trying to say was that in spite of this the interior seems infinite. It is much the same as when the valves of the entrance doors of Nôtre-Dame in Paris are locked late in the evening; the profile of the door case still creates the fluid connection between interior and exterior, and *aesthetically* the two are connected whether the doors are actually open or closed. The same is true of the windows—if we are allowed to talk here of windows.

It remains a question as to how Sedlmayr classifies the lower interiors of the western towers of Chartres Cathedral from his standpoint of style. Is the "baldachin" the primary element here and the walls filled

schrift für Ästhetik und allg. Kw., 1927, p. 51. I do not feel obliged to cling today to the very same opinions which I expressed thirty-one years ago, and I have not had the opportunity of reporting to scholars of art history every time I changed my mind. My earlier views concerning mediaeval sculpture still seem quite clear to me however. One factor, the relief of the folds has been investigated just recently: Fritz Kämpfer, "Das Faltenprofil der mittelalterlichen Plastik," *Wissenschaftliche Zeitschrift der F.S. Universität*, Jena, 1952, p. 107. Perhaps Sedlmayr will take exception to this sort of analysis and to the fact that the geometric factor is studied separately from that of stance (*Körperponderation*) and light, etc.

[21] H. Sedlmayr, "Das erste mittelalterliche Architectur-system," *Kunstwissenschaftliche Forschungen*, II, Berlin, 1933, pp. 25ff.

in between the corner shafts? In the period around 1140, of course, there was no lattice filling. Other people call this interior Gothic because it has a rib vault, but in Sedlmayr's thinking, apparently, the ribs are negligible.

The structure (*Gefüge*) of the filling lattices—if they are present—is determined by the principle of the "overlapping form." (page 55) As an example he cites the windows—if we may use this term—of St.-Denis (nave). "Overlapping form" is a term introduced in the article mentioned above. It means an arch which overlaps two or more smaller ones. Sedlmayr shows that in antiquity arches were always placed in juxtaposition, whereas in the Middle Ages they are set as a group into a larger one. He asserted that concepts like "addition" and "subdivision" cannot be used to describe differences of form as he discovered in the case of the baldachins, and that this would also apply to such differences as he found between the antique structures and the overlapping arches. Yet both forms are *types*. Types consist of specific arrangements of members and hence, from the point of view of membrology, they can be Byzantine, Romanesque, Gothic, etc. Types and members are independently variable. A type may also vary in the relation of the parts to the whole. The two types of juxtaposition and subordination shown in Sedlmayr's article in a diagram are clearly opposites in the sense of addition (totality) and subdivision or interpenetration (partiality). If we turn from these abstract schemes and look at the three-dimensional realizations, we find that both can be treated in both ways. It all depends on the forms of the members and their profiles. Therefore we find Romanesque as well as Gothic "baldachins" (if we wish to use this word). While Sedlmayr professes to despise such abstract concepts as addition and subdivision, he nevertheless uses them unconsciously.

"The interior floats (*schwebt*)." (page 59) "However in the preclassic phase as seen in the cathedrals of Laon and Paris . . . there is a break between the zone of the columns and all the parts above them. Here the first floor looks massive, earthly. The columns have stout Romanesque proportions which are not to be found elsewhere in the edifice. . . . Upon this socle-zone the baldachin architecture is built. Above the massive piers they . . . float." (pages 59f.) This statement is surprising. Does Sedlmayr regard the cathedrals of Laon and Paris "as hybrid structures, half Romanesque, half Gothic"? Is he destroying their "inner unity which is evident to every man of artistic feeling"? Certainly not! Laon and Paris are still very much intact in spite of his criticism. He is merely analyzing them, leaving the task of dismembering them to the military. Every scholar analyzes and Sedlmayr is no exception. What is missing in his analysis is an explanation of why the lower parts of those cathedrals should be called Romanesque? Because the proportions are stout? What is Romanesque? What is Gothic? When can a cathedral be said to be wholly Gothic, when only partially so? These questions cannot be settled by decree or by a majority vote, but only by a method of analysis which employs abstract concepts. Scholars are not afraid of abstract analysis. Sedlmayr wants to be a scholar, but he shrinks from analysis. His own analyses do not go far enough.

The supports of the "baldachins" of High Gothic cathedrals—the piers and shafts—"do not grow up from below, they let themselves down from above. They are, so to speak, aerial roots." (page 60) Sedlmayr means that it is not only strange for us to hear that the *sursum corda* comes *down* from the keystones, but that all Gothic seems strange to modern man. It was not strange to Goethe. Is there any mediaevalist today who finds Gothic strange? "Probably only in Gothic architecture is it possible for an edifice to be enlarged downward—as was sometimes the case when the floor was opened up and the threads of the shafts continued downward." (page 61) What this means remains a mystery.[22] The façades are formed of "layers one behind the other" (page 63) so that the higher ones seem to float. According to Hildebrand, it would be more correct to say one *in front of* the other. The pinnacles are also baldachins. (page 66) This is correct. The thin layers containing the Gothic gables, he calls *Splitterflächen* (page 66), a word which can be translated as splinters. In his discussion of the flying buttresses, he emphasizes the oblique views: "but one should not speak in terms of picturelike vistas (*bildmässige Durchsichten*) or of picturesque sectors (*malerische Ausschnitte*)." (page 71) Why not admit that diagonality begins with the first ribs? In the so-called wheel windows or roses the columns are both upside down and distorted. (page 79) The cathedral, in reality, is composed only of stone and glass, yet other materials are implied in its structure. (page 84) Here, following the poet Albrecht, he calls the stained glass precious stones and mentions the use of gilding. "In some places, as in the gilded rose windows, what is obviously suggested is gold, at others, a kind of transfigured and sublimated stone." (page 84) It would, however, be wrong to say that the cathedral belies its character as a monument of stone. "It pre-

[22] He may mean the side aisles of the Rouen Cathedral and those of Eu. Yet here it is not the whole edifice which is enlarged downward and the widening does not continue beneath the floor.

serves it completely, but idealizes it. . . ." (page 85) These remarks lead to a discussion of the grail temple in the younger Titurel which bears out Sedlmayr's entire interpretation, including the character of the baldachin and the fact that shafts let themselves downward. "For the time from 1220 to 1230, however, certain reservations must be made." (page 91) We would like to have these reservations specified, for example, for Amiens.

The cathedral is an *Abbild* of the Holy City. (page 95) Translated into English *Abbild* means portrait, copy, illustration, representation in a picture. It has never before been applied to architecture. Sedlmayr is certainly aware that architecture and painting (ikon) are two different things, and yet he applies the same word to both, mixing architecture with painting and sculpture and all three at times with poetry. All of them are "*Abbildungen*," illustrations of an "abstract" idea which he calls "concrete." "To be informed of the symbolic illustrative (*abbildenden*) meaning of the cathedral is not merely the concern of the historian of ideas or of the theologian . . . it is absolutely essential for anyone who wishes to see these structures concretely. Their forms suddenly reveal themselves in a new light and become quite clear to us the moment we grasp this meaning (*Darstellungssinn*)." (page 135) On page 18 he says that the abstract history of style "always overlooks the concrete." For Sedlmayr, it is not the building which is concrete—this is new—but such symbolical ideas as that of the Holy City. The number eight, for example, signifies perfection or the state of blessedness (*Seligkeit*) because the octave (in the musical scale) returns to the tonic. (page 158) Thanks to the studies of such men as Sauer, we are now acquainted with hundreds of examples of mediaeval symbolism. Does Sedlmayr seriously believe that we can understand the octagonal upper part of a tower, an octagonal canopy, etc. only if we recall that some people in the Middle Ages who were better acquainted with literature and theology than with architecture, connected the octagon with the blessed state? He even expects us to interpret half octagons in this way. Are the people who have never read Sauer incapable of understanding Gothic choirs? Yet Sauer says that there were a great many interpretations of the number eight, that it might, for instance, represent the eight persons who were saved in Noah's Ark. And what of choirs constructed in the form of half decagons, etc.? Must we always count the corners and then thumb through Sauer's book? Is this the way to see an artistic creation as a whole rather than to "tear it to pieces."

Nobody will deny that every Catholic church symbolizes the Holy

City. Sauer claims that the symbolism can be traced back to Jerome and that it applies to every new church—whatever its style—which is consecrated. There is a difference between saying it symbolizes, it represents, and it "depicts." Why not keep the old words, why create new abstract concepts which are incorrect? We know that ceilings since antiquity have been painted to represent heaven.[23] In German *Himmel* means both sky and heaven. Tiepolo's sky in the Würzburg castle is not supposed to suggest heaven, rather Olympus. Many Baroque vaults in churches represent the sky and symbolize heaven. Gothic vaults are sometimes studded with stars and in such cases they are meant to symbolize heaven, as for example those in the temple of the grail (see above p. 181). But Gothic vaults have *ribs*, while the sky, of course, does not, nor do the Holy City of St. John, Byzantine, Romanesque, Baroque and Rococo churches, nor those constructed in the classical style of around 1800. And yet they are all Holy Cities. Ribs interfere with paintings except those which have stars and flowers (Paradise?). What was the symbolic meaning of ribs? Sauer does not give any interpretation. Is it impossible for us to understand ribs without reference to something else?

Similar questions arise in connection with the oculus windows. They "depict" (*bilden ab*) the wheel of fortune. This is a well-known fact and is borne out by the surrounding sculptures. In other cases they symbolize the sun, the king, Christ. (page 145) In wheel windows, as we were told before, the columns were simply topsy-turvy, and this became a permanent characteristic of circles with tracery (starting with the western rose of Reims). In late Gothic the filling becomes flamboyant. How is the development to be explained if we must always start with the symbolic meaning of the sun and Christ? How is the change of the tracery affecting the meaning? There is another difficulty. In the *Metrical Life of St. Hugh*, we read that the two round windows in the transept of Lincoln Cathedral are symbolically explained as *oculi*, as eyes. Today in Lincoln one still talks of the Bishop's eye and the Dean's eye. The Bishop's eye looks to the South "ut vivet," the Dean's eye looks to the North "ne pereat." South is the Holy Ghost, North the Devil. Sedlmayr probably would take the same North window to mean Christ; yet it is the eye of the poor Dean seeing Hell. The Western *oculus* does not belong to a special personality but it sees itself the *candelabra coeli* and the *tenebras Lethes*. So it could be meant as the

[23] Karl Lehmann, "The Dome of Heaven," *Art Bulletin*, XXVII, 1945, p. 1.

setting Sun. This leads to the question whether North *oculi* could ever mean the Sun?[24]

Since the study of style leads to a formulation of abstract schemes for Early, High, and Late Gothic and also for the historical phenomenon of Gothic as a whole, Sedlmayr accuses it of setting up "standards of stylistic purity based upon theoretical abstractions." (page 1330) Sedlmayr does not seem to be aware that it is possible to work out an abstract scheme and at the same time to enjoy, admire, and love the hundreds of actual Gothic churches which do not possess this pure style, and may even contain many discordant elements. It is sheer malice to identify theoretical methods with the practical purifications of the nineteenth century. Today these are universally condemned and Sedlmayr is by no means alone in his opinion. What is most astonishing about his outburst is that he himself has and employs a standard of pure Gothic which is either Amiens or Cologne. Laon and Paris, as we were told, are still partly Romanesque and after Cologne—roughly speaking—there were no pure cathedrals. This is an old prejudice. Durand stated that the decadence has already begun in the choir of Amiens. Sedlmayr does not consider English Gothic as equal in value to the French. He has little to say about Late Gothic and he even refers slightingly to the fourteenth century as "doctrinaire" (a word borrowed from Dehio who took it from Gonse). The rest of Sedlmayr's new ideas may better be omitted here. The best criticism of them is to be found in *The Times Literary Supplement*, January 4, 1952. (The name of the writer is not given.)

It is to be admitted that such a bulky volume contains also some good ideas, they may be new or old; in general it is incomprehensible why a scholar who formerly wrote some excellent books suddenly lost all common sense: up is down, abstract is concrete, he scores analysis and analyses, he fights abstract concepts and creates new ones, he confounds architecture with painting, partly with poetry. Of all aberrations quoted in this chapter this is the most amazing. The others are at least amusing; this one, on the contrary, is disappointing and depressing for everyone who wants to increase his understanding of Gothic.

24 James Francis Dímrock, *Metrical Life of St. Hugh, Bishop of Lincoln*, Lincoln, 1860, p. 36. Folke Nordström from Upsala kindly called my attention to this passage. Here it may be noted that at the top of the window in Sens with the story of the Good Samaritan in the cathedral in Sens from ca. 1210 a town is painted with the inscription: The Second Jerusalem. See Lucien Bégule, *La Cathédrale de Sens*, Lyons, 1929, p. 52.

VII. CONCENTRATION ON ESSENTIAL PRINCIPLES

1. The Theory Concerning the Structure of the Wall

Ernst GALL (1888-1958) summed up the advantages of the ribbed vault in four statements:[1]

1. The ribs strengthen the weakest points of the quadripartite vault.
2. They permit a thinning of the cells, thus also of the piers or, as the case may be, walls.
3. They make it possible to adapt the quadripartite vault to any ground plan.
4. Finally, they bring about a saving in wood and make it possible for the vault cells to be filled in freehand.

The fourth item is taken from Porter's book (of 1911), the second and third from Wetter, while the first can be found in Dehio but made its original appearance in Saunders (1811). As far as the first item is concerned, it must be repeated that the weakest points are not to be taken as meaning the groins. The groin, this mathematically thin curve, cannot carry the load of the vault (see above on page 500); it is a question, rather, of the thickness of the vault behind the groin, where the intersection of the cells makes the vault thicker than, for example, in the crowns of the cells. If one reckons on this full thickness behind the groin, such places cannot be called the weakest but may be claimed to be the strongest, and it remains to be considered how much they themselves are statically strengthened when ribs are placed below them. It will be assumed that these places have become stronger since that carrying thickness is increased in the diagonals by means of ribs. If the rib has a spur and thereby partially penetrates the vault, the spur is then, from the mechanical standpoint, a part of the actual vault masonry. This is not really carried by the projecting part of the rib; if it is thick enough it carries itself. But this principle of the mechanics of vaults is not of decisive importance for the theory proposed by Gall. In any case, he was already firmly convinced by reason of his three other points that the rib offered several advantages. But, he asks, did it owe its *origin* to these advantages?

Gall quotes (page 30) a passage from Quicherat: "The subsequent transformations in the architecture of the churches were a consequence

[1] Ernst Gall, *Niederrheinische und normännische Architektur im Zeitalter der Frühgotik*, I, Berlin, 1915 (Vol. II has not appeared), p. 30.

of this convenient fractionization of the vaults. Experience having shown that it permitted a considerable attenuation of the body of the building between the piers [*massifs*] on which the thrusts were concentrated, the architects, tempted by such a great advantage, had no other aim than to push this lightness to its utmost limit. The uninterrupted progress that they achieved in this matter (each one outdoing the work of his predecessors by some new reduction) led them in a short time to bring about the emergence of the slender Gothic construction from the heavy and dark Romanesque nave."[2] Gall remarks quite rightly that it is incomprehensible how one can claim to explain Gothic only by reason of the fact that the builders were "tempted" by a structural advantage into creating ribs, and he counters this with his own theory: ". . . the idea of membering the wall organically and for this purpose transforming it into a veritable framework is beyond a doubt older than the employment of ribbed vaults on French soil. For this reason the latter appear in an entirely different light; they are no longer the cause but the means, and the history of their development is brought out of the mysterious darkness of chance into the bright light of artistic necessity." In other words, the older structural principle, that of the dissection of the wall into active supports and passive filling, led inevitably, upon the introduction of vaulting, to the fractionizing of these vaults also into carrying ribs and passive filling (the cells). Only ribbed vaults corresponded to such wall memberings. The rib is thus a result of the membering of the wall. Gall repeats what Courajod had said (he cites him polemically in another connection)—and for that matter what had already been expressed in Pinder's books (on rhythm)—but was the first to center interest on this observation.

Whereas in Quicherat's opinion the *rib* was the most important element and historically primary, Gall thought the *pier* the most important element and historically primary. According to Quicherat, the rib, once in existence, brings about the membering of the wall; according to Gall, the membering of the wall, once in existence, brings about the membering of the quadripartite vault by means of the rib. And here

[2] *Ibid.*, from Quicherat, *Mélanges d'archéologie et d'histoire*, II, Paris, 1886, p. 499: "Les transformations ultérieures de l'architecture des églises furent la conséquence de ce commode fractionnement des voûtes. L'expérience ayant montré qu'il permettait d'atténuer considérablement le corps de l'édifice entre les massifs sur lesquels s'exercaient les poussées, les architectes, séduits par un si grand avantage, n'eurent plus d'autre visée que de pousser l'allègement à son dernier terme. Les progrès continus qu'ils accomplirent sur cette donnée (chacun renchérissant par quelque réduction nouvelle sur l'œuvre de ses devanciers) les amnèrent en peu de temps à faire sortir du lourd et sombre vaisseau roman la svelte construction gothique."

Gall repeats what Riegl had said; it was, of course, not possible for him to have known the lecture on Salzburg, which was not published until 1929. Quicherat did not yet command Gall's historical knowledge, which was built up on the basis of Bilson's article. Gall's thesis seems compelling, therefore, in contrast to Quicherat's, because historically the membering of the wall in Normandy is older than the rib. Thus the rib appeared to have been explained by Gall as a result of the wall membering. Both Quicherat's and Gall's theses say the same thing insofar as they characterize Gothic as structure. The difference between them lies in the question of the priority of the two elements: rib and pier. One can express it by the formula that according to Quicherat Gothic—that is, Gothic structure—originated at the top and moved downward, whereas according to Gall it began at the bottom and moved upward.

But if wall membering and rib are to be explained as the result of structural arrangement, the concept of *structure* becomes of primary importance. It is for Gall of the same importance as function was for Viollet-le-Duc, or the transcendentally enhanced expressiveness of the line for Worringer. Lefèvre-Pontalis thought, from the evolutionary point of view, that in the nucleus "rib" was contained the germinative *force* of "function"; Gall thought, from the same point of view, that the germinative *force* of "structure" was contained in the nucleus "wall membering."

He therefore began his investigation by expounding his idea of structure: ". . . an enclosed space with completely unmembered walls has seemed crude to all ages. Only by applying a definite principle of articulation does any type of building activity succeed in creating a higher art form, which is distinguished from a merely utilitarian building simply by virtue of this element."[3] Lotze had remarked of Romanesque and Gothic jointly that the space-enclosing wall acts as a general substance out of which the various structural forces are crystallized (cf. above, page 585). In this connection one must remember the psychologist Meumann who said about the same thing, only with this difference: that he suggested as the reason for the crystallization the impulse to enliven uniformity by means of rhythm. Whether this is entirely correct (quite aside from the concept of rhythm, which Gall does not employ) need not be considered in this place. The difficulty seems to be that Gall means by the concept of structure something that is not

[3] Gall, *op.cit.*, p. 6.

characteristic of Gothic alone but that represents a possibility of form that exists *a priori* and can occur in many styles, hence has appeared and will yet do so. There is Doric structure and Romanesque structure, and thus also, among others, Gothic structure. French High Gothic is undoubtedly structure. But though the structural element is indeed a necessary characteristic of this style, it is not all-sufficient, since there exists also un-Gothic structure. Gothic, moreover, is by no means always structure.[4] What, then, is "Gothic" in that *Gothic* structure?

The concept of structure belongs among the fundamental concepts of style. In Viollet-le-Duc's terminology it is concealed in the word construction. The difference between the two concepts is that by *construction* Viollet-le-Duc meant (rationally) *real* carrying and being carried, whereas Gall thinks only of the *aesthetic impression* of active carrying and passive filling. The inadequacy of Gall's theory, however, lies not only in the concept of structure but in the lack of several other concepts.

The first objection must be that the wall membering of the engaged shafts in the Romanesque buildings of Normandy was *frontal* in position. Consequently it is indeed reasonable to say that the idea of structure suffices to explain the transverse arch that connects the pier with its *frontal* vis-à-vis; but in order to connect the pier with its *diagonally* opposite, the structural principle must be supplemented by that of *diagonality*. In Romanesque everything is disposed according to the dictates of strict frontality, that being one of its basic principles; it did have *structure*, but *not* diagonal structure. As a result of the introduction of the rib into the groined vault the structure is given a diagonal direction, and this is an infraction of the hitherto inviolable principle of frontality. The groin, to be sure, had already run diagonally, but there is a difference between groin and rib. This is the second objection to Gall's theory, and here lies *the* distinction between Romanesque and Gothic, a point to which I shall have to return. (See below page 820) Frontality and diagonality are, like structure and texture, "fundamental concepts" (*Grundbegriffe*). But we also cannot define Gothic by employing *two* or *three* fundamental concepts instead of only one.

The difficulty Gall encountered in finding a suitable stylistic designation for Norman wall membering shows that the concept of structure is inadequate. The rib is "Gothic," its father is supposed to be the wall

[4] Gall does not speak of Late Gothic, which is not "structure." There is also, then, a Gothic without structure, but this objection is not at all necessary here in order to show the incorrectness of Gall's idea.

membering. And what is the wall membering? Gall would obviously have liked most to call it, too, Gothic—but he calls its proto-Gothic.

The expression "proto-Gothic" is a half truth, indeed a contradiction in itself. The emphasis unquestionably does not lie on the "proto," for not everything that precedes Gothic historically is to be designated "proto-Gothic." Only what is *Gothic before* Gothic is proto-Gothic. One is painfully reminded of Worringer's secret, latent Gothic or crypto-Gothic. Gall's intelligence is, however, immune to the danger of such an extension of the concept, but he, too, sought to expand it without becoming aware that historical stylistic concepts tear when stretched. Structure and diagonality are general, abstract concepts. Gothic is not; it is a concrete, historically limited process. The wall membering Gall has in mind can only be either Romanesque or Gothic. A building, taken as a whole, can *still* be Romanesque and yet *at the same time* have parts that are Gothic. Thus the rib, according to Quicherat's conception of it (though not his terminology), is actually Gothic and with it the whole ribbed vault, whereas in those early cases where the flat ceiling (or the open roof truss) of a Romanesque church was replaced by Gothic vaulting the old substructure remained what it was, that is to say, Romanesque. Anyone accustomed to thinking logically will insist that *Romanesque* wall membering is and remains *Romanesque*. It does not become Gothic, or even "proto-Gothic," because of a subsequent Gothic vaulting. What has just been observed should not be confused with the designation for the building as a whole. If a structure is still Romanesque and contains in part Gothic forms, it is called a building of the *Transitional* style. Gall, from his point of view, rejected the concept of Transitional style, introducing that of proto-Gothic not exactly instead of it but still as a compromise. But only the building as a whole becomes a "transition"; its parts are not transitional, rather some are Romanesque, others Gothic. One and the same structural member (*membrum*) cannot simultaneously be Romanesque *and* Gothic. Thus it is, for example, with St.-Étienne in Caen; the wall membering remained *Romanesque* even *after* the original ribbed vaulting (renewed in the seventeenth century). Jantzen also recognizes the logic of this.[5]

The concept of proto-Gothic refers at the same time to the *verticalism* of Norman wall membering. Here the logic is the same as in the case of the engaged shafts. There is a Romanesque verticalism and a Gothic verticalism. Again let us emphasize: not everything vertical is Gothic

[5] Cf. below, p. 787.

and not everything Gothic is vertical. It is really almost too easy to adduce examples of Gothic buildings possessing the quality of horizontalism. Anyone regarding verticalism as a necessary and indispensable characteristic of Gothic is discomfited by buildings of English Gothic and then maintains that English Gothic is not Gothic. But, in analogy to what has been said about wall membering, it may be observed that verticalism is an abstract concept and Gothic a historical concept; we can determine Gothic only empirically. But behind the error of calling the Romanesque wall membering of the Norman buildings Gothic—or proto-Gothic—because they contain the element of verticalism lurks the failure to recognize clearly what distinguishes Romanesque from Gothic wall members. It is most certainly not a matter of proportion. One can elongate a Romanesque wall membering upward at will; one can, for example, redesign St.-Saturnin in Toulouse so that the transverse section has the proportion of the choir of Beauvais; but one does not achieve Gothic by this procedure, even though St.-Saturnin also has extensive wall penetration. Both verticalism and structure are variables, independent of the styles of Romanesque and Gothic. French classical Gothic has structure and verticalism, but French classical Gothic is only *one phase* and *one* school of Gothic, and we cannot define or evaluate Gothic simply according to it.

Gall seems to have realized that however important knowledge of the chronological priority of the wall membering may be (Courajod, Pinder), the rib is not adequately characterized thereby. He says somewhat casually,[6] that "the ribs are employed for the sake of their decorative or rather plastically articulating function." Worringer, too, said that they were decorative. Unfortunately, Gall did not define these concepts, but the context reveals what they mean.[7] "Decorative" is here the same thing that Viollet-le-Duc has in mind in his discussion of Vézelay, which Gall follows in this matter: "The only two vaults of the porch possessing ribs could do without them, for they are nothing but a decoration and do not actually carry the fillings of rubble-stones."[8] "Decorative" is thus for Gall as for Viollet-le-Duc "merely decorative," in contrast to "both decorative and carrying." By "plastic" or "plasti-

[6] Gall, *op.cit.*, p. 44.

[7] Gall writes on p. 5 of the Rhenish architecture of the twelfth century (referring to the apses of the Church of the Apostles in Cologne): "Basically, the architectural attitude is here entirely unplastic and its treatment rather in the direction of the two-dimensionally decorative."

[8] "Les deux seules voûtes de ce porche possédant des arrêtiers pourraient s'en passer: ceux-ci ne sont qu'une décoration et ne portent réellement pas les remplissages en moellons." *Dictionnaire*, IV, p. 33.

cally articulating" Gall means simply three-dimensional. There is, however, the following objection: one can touch the wall, it is two-dimensional; the engaged shaft not only can be touched but grasped, it is three-dimensional. (The wall as a whole is, of course, also three-dimensional, but its surface is only two-dimensional.) Correspondingly, the vault cell in its whole mass is three-dimensional, but what we see of it, the surface, is only two-dimensional, and the *groin* is indeed merely a one-dimensional line. The *rib*, on the other hand, is *three-dimensional* or "plastic." This term, as we have seen, is also used as the polar opposite of "picturesque" (from the time of A. W. Schlegel), but Gall does not mean that here. Thus "decorative and plastic" must be taken as implying approximately a noncarrying, three-dimensional decorative member. If all Gothic is composed of such members, it is hard to see how this formula can indicate the difference between Gothic and many other styles. The column orders of Renaissance and Baroque are likewise characterized in their interiors and exteriors by decorative and plastic structure. We naturally understand what Gall means because we know the buildings to which he refers or have at hand reproductions of them. But his words and concepts do not express with precision what he really wants to say. We also know what a rib is, but why the rib is Gothic is not explained by its quality of being plastic and decorative. Why is it not suitable in Renaissance buildings, the memberings of which are also plastic and decorative, or in Baroque structures?[9] Why, then, one must ask repeatedly, is the rib Gothic? It is, after all, understandable that Romanesque wall membering should mistakenly be termed proto-Gothic because it supposedly produced the Gothic rib; but it is absolutely incomprehensible that the rib should be called Gothic because of the fact that the wall membering is supposed to have been proto-Gothic. And one can find no other reason in Gall's book. Thus consideration of this problem becomes focused on the question: what distinguishes Gothic from Romanesque?

Confusion regarding this stylistic difference is also displayed by Gall's opinion on Lombardic ribbed vaults. Porter had considered them older than those of Normandy but for Gall that question does not exist since he thinks the rib was invented—or "discovered"[10]—independently in

9 The rib, as is well known, is present in Baroque architecture, but why is it regarded there as a foreign element? In any case, Gall is concerned only with the problem of ribs in Gothic, the latter in the sense of a chronologically limited epoch of the Middle Ages.

10 Even in his second book, *Die Gotische Baukunst in Frankreich und Deutschland* (1925), he wrote on p. 29 in the note: ". . . but Porter's assertions (scil. as to dates) are quite untrustworthy, even though I am convinced that the Lombardic ribbed vaults were not influenced by France."

each country (he is opposed to speaking here of an "invention"). The Lombardic ribbed vaults differ greatly from the Norman, their ribs having a transverse section with a rectangular profile, and the planes of the cells a different curvature. It is a question of two completely separate schools or styles of architecture. At the time when Quicherat's doctrine that the rib produced Gothic was considered correct, scholars should have been surprised that the Lombardic ribs did not produce a Gothic from the top downward. According to Gall's theory they must now wonder why Gothic ribs did not arise in Lombardy from below upward, out of the "proto-Gothic" wall membering that was likewise present there. The Lombardic ribs are certainly also plastic, perhaps also decorative, but are they also Gothic? Gall merely says that the Lombardic structures are in a quite different style from the Norman; he does not say what style. If one were to fill this gap by saying that they are Romanesque—and S. Ambrogio in Milan is, after all, generally regarded as Romanesque—it looks as though Gall considered the combination "Romanesque rib" permissible, although he does not use it. Worringer does actually speak of "Romanesque ribs." There was no need to go into this matter above; it seems to be a contradiction in terms.

Gall thought that the (Romanesque?) ribs found in Lombardy were *not* decorative, that is to say presumably, not exclusively decorative; rather, they had both a static and a technical purpose. They helped, he said, to carry the heavy load that pressed in part also against the walls, and they were a means, as was maintained by Porter's thesis, of economizing on the wooden sheathing.[11] The weight of these vaults, and their domical form, which bore on the side walls, did not permit of any dissolution of the wall. Consequently, in Gall's view, the rib was not an *artistic* necessity in Lombardy. It is perhaps the most fundamental point of Gall's argument when he claims that by means of his explanation of the origin of the rib and the continuation of the principle of wall membering up into the vault the history of the development of ribbed vaults is "brought out of the mysterious darkness of chance into the bright light of artistic necessity." He thus—it may be repeated—entirely shares the standpoint of Riegl's thesis: art can only be understood artistically, from the point of view of the artistic will. According to this theory it does not seem to matter whether the rib carries or not, for in either case its artistic function is only to look as though it carried.

[11] Cf. p. 664, n. 1. I shall come back to the statics of steeply curved vaults in connection with Pol Abraham's theory.

But Gall has more to say, namely, that the introduction of the rib in Normandy was not chance but an artistic necessity. What is meant by chance and necessity is an exciting subject for debate by physicists and metaphysicians, but here it is a question of *artistic* chance and *artistic* necessity. Gall can only have meant that the unknown architect who created the first quadripartite ribbed vault was not obeying the dictates of a mere inspiration but the *compulsion* of the wall membering that he found in existence and approved. Hence the introduction of the rib in Normandy was an artistic necessity. But in Lombardy, on the other hand? Was it there an artistic chance? No, but neither was it an artistic necessity. What was it then? It was, says Gall, not artistic at all but merely static. This is baffling. In S. Ambrogio there were engaged shafts, and the ribs of the (original) vaults do not really carry. Why did not these ribs lead to a Gothic style? Gall says rightly that the real *Italian* Gothic is not derived from these Lombardic ribbed vaults but from *French* models. Thus Gothic, according to him, was imported into Italy but the rib had already arisen there autochthonously as a technical-statical structural member. That need not be discussed here, for it is indeed quite immaterial to the understanding of the nature of a thing to know how it originated, and important to know only what it *is*. The troublesomeness of the discussion about how the rib originated shows, after all, that the reason for its origin cannot be made the criterion of how it actually works, of what its function is, whether artistic or aesthetic. We must ask: However it originated, as a continuation of the engaged shafts or because of technical and statical causes, what is its function—to use Fiedler's expression—for the eye? What do we see in S. Ambrogio in Milan? What do we see, on the contrary, in Amiens? Has Gall made that clear? His conception of Gothic is revealed by the following connected sentence: "Gothic is . . . the expression of an artistic will that is directed toward so articulating the containing walls of a space that all its parts, distinctly separate as carrying or filling bodies, shall be united in an organism in which the structurally effective forces appear to be concentrated on the vertically soaring members." (p. 78) This emphasizes once more that Gothic is structure and verticalism, and thus the same as proto-Gothic. The latter, however, is not Gothic, according to the general view, but Romanesque. Consequently, Gothic is not *merely* structure and not *always* verticalism—and we owe it to Gall's book, so distinguished by painstaking and intensely zealous scholarship, that this formulation has been made possible as a basis for further considerations. It marks as significant an epoch in the history of the judgments on Gothic as Johannes Wetter's definition eighty years previously.

An important supplement to Gall's study is given in two articles by BONY.[12] He too begins with the interpretation of the vertical members which subdivide the walls of the nave: they had the function to strengthen the wall supporting the heavy roof. It cannot be denied that static and at the same time economic considerations were involved together with aesthetic. Bony is very illuminating in showing the development from the thin to the bulky wall (*mur mince* and *mur épais*) and in explaining the evolution of the triforia. Yet his whole argument remains bound to Romanesque buildings except his remark that "the *mur épais* killed the *muralité*," that is, the character of the wall. He calls this "a taste already gothic"; one is tempted to talk of "une experience pregothique." (page 162) This leads to the conclusion that the (Romanesque) formation of the walls is another part of origin of Gothic beside that of the development of the rib vault. He does not say that the rib is the son, so to speak, of the wall membering; he rather sees two separate factors which finally were combined in an organic unit. The concept pregothique is the same as Gall's "protogothic." The objection, therefore, is in both cases the same; it is not a pedantic quarrel over words, but rather the recognition that the profile is the decisive factor in changing the Romanesque membering of the wall into Gothic and in adjusting them in this way to the rib vault. Of course the investigations of Gall and Bony present a deep understanding of the *Romanesque* type of "structure" which afterwards was translated into the Gothic language, a process which perhaps began in St.-Denis and is apparent in Noyon.

2. Stylistic Polarities

THE tendency to create pairs of antithetical concepts had appeared in Hemsterhuis merely as a clever mode of expression. It was adopted by Schiller, however, as well as by the brothers Schlegel, and has continued to flourish down to the present. Such attempts only became really fruitful when Wölfflin connected such paired concepts with

[12] Jean Bony, "La technique Normande du mur épais à l'époque romane," *Bulletin Monumentale*, XCVIII, 1939, p. 189. Bony was born in 1908.

Burckhardt's *aperçu* about the ever-recurring "Rococo." As a result of the idea of periodicity, the paired concepts took on the function of revealing, behind the confusing abundance of stylistic changes, general principles of form that make it possible to recognize *two* "styles" as phases of *one* "style" of a *general* nature. Wölfflin carried this out for Renaissance and Baroque. Baroque had, of course, been regarded long before that as a continuation of Renaissance, but was held to be merely the degeneration of one and the same style. Now the value judgment was discarded (or at first moderated), and a new aim resulted, namely to demonstrate that this change from the style of *being* to a style of *becoming* was a typical historical process. All force of thought was so concentrated on this transmutation that historians of art nearly forgot what binds Renaissance and Baroque together: the so-called morphological element. The next generation of scholars sought to organize the entire history of art according to the pattern of "Renaissance and Baroque," that is to say, to show evidence of periodicity, but displayed almost no interest in what differentiates the various stylistic groups. In order to understand the application of polar concepts to the paired styles of Romanesque and Gothic, it may be helpful to arrange concepts of this sort in chronological order (first only to 1914). Although, strictly speaking, it does not belong here, we shall begin with that of Humanism which still echoes in the remark Hemsterhuis makes about antiquity and modernity, a remark that implies the creation of the concept "Middle Ages."

From Petrarch to Vasari		ancient	barbarian, Gothic
1757	Burke	—	artificial infinite
1769	Hemsterhuis	*trop sculpteur*	*trop peintre*
	Herder	sense of touch	sense of sight
		plastic	picturesque
1790	Forster	—	infinite
1792	Gilpin	smoothness	picturesqueness
1795	Schiller	naive	sentimental
		limitation	spirit
1800	Milner	—	artificial infinite (Burke)
ca. 1800	F. v. Schlegel	classical	romantic
1801	A. W. v. Schlegel	plastic	picturesque
		rhythmic	harmonic
1804	Jean Paul	plastic	musical
1805	F. v. Schlegel	sidereal	vegetal
		crystalline	vegetal

1820	Stieglitz	plastic	romantic
		earthly, sensuous beauty	spirit and faith
1818-1830	Hegel	1. symbolical 2. classical	3. romantic and infinite
		1. symbolical 2. architectonic	3. picturesque
1830	Whewell	definite	indefinite
1831	Caumont	*plus pure*	*plus touchant*
			plus religieux
1835	Willis	discontinuous	continuous
1836	Pugin	pagan	Christian
1843	Burckhardt	(classical)	rococo
		organic style	spatial style
		rhythm of masses (Renaissance)	rhythm of movement (Gothic)
1850	Mertens	figurative	organic
1870	Nietzsche	Apollonian	Dionysian
1888	Wölfflin	delineatory (linear)	picturesque
		contour	mass
		repose	movement
		being	becoming
1881-1896	Courajod	antique	barbarian (like Boccaccio, etc.)
1893	Hildebrand	near image (*Nahbild*)	distant image (*Fernbild*)
		reading off from front to back	reading off from back to front
1897	Schmarsow	picturesque (Renaissance)	plastic (Baroque)
ca. 1900	Riegl	near vision (*Nahsicht*)	distant vision (*Fernsicht*)
		tactile or haptic	optic (like Herder)
		isolated	interconnected
		objective	subjective
1908	Worringer	empathy	abstraction
		antique	Germanic
1909	Cohn-Wiener	1. tectonic, objective	3. directionless
		2. having uniform movement	
1912	Worringer	French—affect	German—mood
		Gothic—linear	Late Gothic—picturesque
1912	Gerstenberg	rational	irrational
1914	Wölfflin	1. linear	picturesque
		2. plane	recessional
		3. closed	open
		4. multiplicity	unity
		5. absolutely clear	relatively clear

This list shows what varied use was made of more or less antithetical concepts in order to characterize intellectual movements, cultures, or styles. As far as the understanding of Gothic was concerned, this tendency was fruitful for drawing contrasts now between antiquity and Middle Ages, now between Gothic and Late Gothic, and finally also between Romanesque and Gothic. In this connection Gervase should not be forgotten, whose characterization of the old and new choirs of Canterbury was based on the logical opposition of surface-emphasis and depth-emphasis, isolation and interconnection, thus anticipating Wölfflin's and Riegl's concepts as well as their application to the comparison of Romanesque and Gothic.

In 1909 Ernst COHN-WIENER (1882-1941) made the first attempt to view Gothic within the larger general frame of a stylistic history of all ages.[1] The two popular little books treat not only the representational arts (sculpture and painting), as the title implies, but architecture as well. Riegl's artistic volition and Wölfflin's stylistic concepts are Cohn-Wiener's foundation. He has understanding for Romanesque and recognizes the structural and therefore surface-emphasizing nature of its members, as well as their objectivity. (*Sachlichkeit*) In characterizing Early and High Gothic he also follows Viollet-le-Duc, but in the dissolution of the wall he sees the opposite of Romanesque. In contrast to the strict objectivity of Romanesque, Gothic, he says, is more "decorative and picturesque"—at least in its accessories (reliquaries and the like). Late Gothic, finally, is completely picturesque and creating recession. He postulates a periodicity: "The Late Gothic style forms a uniform complex of phenomena, and the dissolution of the Late Gothic altar as to composition is as completely in harmony with the star vaults above it and the strong play of light and shade in its carved figures as the spatial extent of the Arch of Titus is with the feeling for space in its friezes." (page 120) The parallelism in the development of ancient and mediaeval architecture lies in a sequence of three chief stages for each: "first, the tectonic stylistic form; second, that which reveals unified motion; and third, that which moves without direction" (by the latter is meant equal movement in all directions).[1a] For antiquity his examples are the Doric temple, the altar of Zeus in Pergamum, and the round temple in Baalbek; for the Middle Ages, the church of St. Michael in Hildesheim, Strasbourg

[1] Ernst Cohn-Wiener, *Die Entwicklungsgeschichte der Stile in der bildenden Kunst*, Leipzig and Berlin, 1909 (2nd ed. 1917). Cf. Dvořak's favorable review of Cohn-Wiener's two volumes, *Kunstgeschichtliche Anzeigen*, Vienna, 1910.

[1a] "Die tektonische, die einheitlich bewegte und die richtungslos bewegte Stilform."

Cathedral, and the latter's St. Lawrence Portal. Here, then, Romanesque and Gothic are recognized as being contrasting styles. Cohn-Wiener, however, was only able to present this idea sketchily in the narrow compass of his popular little book.

Taking as my point of departure Wölfflin's paired concepts in the form in which they appeared in his earlier works, I myself sought to arrive at more precise concepts.[2] Although at that time I was chiefly interested in modern architecture (since the Renaissance), I tried to proceed in a way abstract enough to permit these concepts to be used *a priori* for any sort of style independently of particular historical details. In actuality, given Wölfflin's opposites of being and becoming and, on the other hand, Riegl's contrasting isolation and interconnection, everything had already been done. Greater incisiveness seemed possible if one were to formulate this contrast separately for the various aspects of the phenomenon: between the crystalline, isolated being and the organic, interconnected becoming. These aspects are in architecture space, force, and light (an analysis that had already emerged in the writings of Hegel and Schopenhauer), and to these I added purpose. Purpose has long been considered a special factor in architectural theory (ever since Vitruvius), and it also played a great role in the debates about "form and content," since purpose was indeed regarded as really the "content" of architecture. I realized much later that it is not logically defensible to place purpose on the same level as the other three factors or "elements." But at that time this objection did not trouble me and I arrived at the following pairs of concepts:

for the spatial form	addition	subdivision (penetration)
for the corporeal form	jet of force	stream of force
for the light form	single view (*Einbildigheit*)	multi-view (*Vielbildigheit*)
for the purposive form	freedom of purposive attitude (*Freiheit der Zweckgesinnung*)	determination of purposive attitude (*Gebundenheit der Zweckgesinnung*)

Using these concepts, I attempted to describe the development from Renaissance to Baroque, Rococo, and Classicism. At the same time I promised an analogous treatment for the mediaeval styles though

[2] Paul Frankl, *Die Entwicklungsphasen der neueren Baukunst*, Berlin and Leipzig, 1914. The word classicism is used here according to its use in the German language for the style around 1800 and buildings derived from the classical style.

this has not yet materialized. I made only an initial attempt when I employed the concepts of addition, jet of force, and concentration into one view in my discussion of Romanesque architecture.[3] Furthermore, I sought to establish this method of stylistic comparison in an essay in the following way.[4] The interior aspect of the choir of St.-Benoît-sur-Loire is one of a number of entirely individual spaces that are sharply isolated from each other; especially the clear separation of the vaulting—barrel vaults in the side aisles, and barrel vaults and terminating half dome of the apse in the nave—creates the impression that each part is a self-contained, detachable whole, just as the ambulatory and the chapels are isolated spaces. From the outside, correspondingly, one recognizes each spatial division as an independent unit and regards the roofs as independent pieces. Their horizontal drip moldings are just as separating as the springing lines of the vaults in the interior. Nowhere does one thing merge into another, it all remains a strict—*additive*—juxtaposition and superposition. A Gothic choir like that of Amiens is in every way the opposite. The ribbed vaults of the choir and apse are the interpenetration of a vertical tendency rising from the lower space and a horizontal one in the vaulting zone, and everywhere the eye is thereby led from the interior to the exterior (and conversely). In St.-Benoît-sur-Loire the chapels were separated from each other by considerable intervals of space so that there was room between them for a window opening from the ambulatory. The Romanesque ambulatory is thus directly visible on the exterior. In Amiens, on the other hand, the chapels are arranged in close sequence and the ambulatory consequently becomes entirely a part of the interior; it is, as it were, sucked into the interior. It is therefore not visible on the Gothic exterior because it is concealed by the series of chapels. These themselves are half hidden among the buttresses rising beyond and above them, so that the chapels appear to be a *division* of the radial interstices of the buttressing system. The part of the exterior space coming above them is, however, not exterior space in the same sense that must be applied to that above the chapel roofs of St.-Benoît. For these interstices of the system of buttresses still belong to the cathedral itself and the exterior space seeps into

[3] *Die frühmittelalterliche und romanische Baukunst* (Handbuch der Kunstwissenschaft), Neubabelsberg, 1926 (written from about 1920 on).

[4] *Der Beginn der Gotik und das allgemeine Problem des Stilbeginnes. Festschrift für Heinrich Wölfflin*, Munich, 1924.

the cathedral everywhere, as it were, like fog. The boundary is not as clear as in pure Romanesque where the space flows off smoothly on the outside. One can extend this analysis in the same way to all the other parts of the cathedral. In St.-Benoît the crossing emerges dominant from the whole in the shape of a tower. Amiens has only a flèche (*Dachreiter*); the crossing is pressed into line with the general contour, and, though its presence can indeed be detected from the outside, it cannot be seen directly. The demarcations of the cornices, which in Romanesque are so uninterruptedly clear and beneath which the buttresses stop, are destroyed in Gothic or at least devaluated by the gables that cut across them and—themselves a species of roofs—cause the lower space to rise, for the eye, into their roof space, creating in consequence a penetration where Romanesque would demand isolation (addition). Romanesque treats each part as an independent whole, even though it may be a "*sub-whole*" (*Unterganzes*); Gothic treats each part as a *fragment* of the whole, it loses its individuality in favor of a higher wholeness that *logically* (descriptively) appears to be primary. For it is not a question of analyzing the psychological impression to determine whether the observer imagines that in Romanesque the whole came into being through a gradual shoving together of parts or in Gothic existed first of all *as* a whole, namely, in its exterior contour, into which afterwards the interior contours (crossing, ambulatory) were fitted; but rather one of recognizing that the finished work, as it confronts us, has in Romanesque an *additive*, in Gothic a *divisive effect.* I have always meant these concepts to be taken in a *descriptive*, not genetic, sense.

To illustrate contrasting treatments of the corporeal form one may choose the nave interiors of the church of the Madeleine in Vézelay and the cathedral of Amiens. In the former church one can easily trace the lines of the composition and note how each part is built up above the other in strict structure and how everywhere support and load are differentiated, whereas in Gothic there is a tendency to make the structure seem like a vertically rising stream of force. At that time I was not able to determine precisely how this effect is created.

The light-form contains several factors; here I shall merely record that among other things I called it as seen by the beholder, *frontal* in Romanesque, *diagonal* in Gothic.[5] The cathedral's central axis runs

[5] The factors of the light-form itself: degree of brightness, color, reflection (brilliance and dimness), as well as the space-light-form (perspective, etc.), are discussed in detail in *System der Kunstwissenschaft*, pp. 228, 243.

from west to east, those of its bays from north to south. Romanesque piers are placed with their own axes parallel to this axial system. In High Gothic, on the contrary, the pier axes are in a diagonal position (turned 45 degrees), and this diagonality is felt everywhere—in the ribs, the flying buttresses, the profiles—as was stressed long ago (since the time of Costenoble).

With regard to what in 1914 I had called purposive form (*Zweckform*) I could only suggest that the leading men of the Romanesque period stood side by side, socially and politically, as autonomous individuals, as barons—whether in friendship or enmity; the ideal of Gothic, however, was the fusion of all into a unity where the individual becomes a fragment and feels himself a part of the Kingdom of God on earth as represented by the Church. It seemed to me that the parallel tendencies of the four elements formed the style. Because the tendency was now in the direction of creating everywhere the idea of the *totality* of the individual, now that of his *partiality*, I called Romanesque the style of totality and Gothic the style of partiality. And, like Dvořak, I saw in the cathedral as a whole a partiality of the universe, a portion of the Infinite with which the interior is linked. The idea here implied was one Riegl had characterized by isolation and interconnection, and was also related to the contrasting terms of finite and infinite—without being identical with them—and I believed I had reduced these always vaguely felt effects to objective, mathematically comprehensible properties of the buildings.

Such a sharp separation of the two styles could only be demonstrated by choosing examples from classical Romanesque and classical Gothic. The concepts have the value of *coordinates*. They are theoretical constructions, imaginary pure cases, according to which the actual historical works of art can be adjudged to incline either to the pole of totality or to that of partiality. There seemed to me, consequently, to be no difficulty about speaking of a Transitional style. Style is not merely the *pure* case but also the *mixed*. Verticalism, therefore, regarded as proportion, does not mean an indispensable characteristic of Gothic—even though no one would deny that verticalism is a characteristic of the cathedrals of Amiens and Beauvais or that classical Gothic is obviously linked historically to verticalism—but there is another reason for the fact that the same proportions in Romanesque do not create the same impression of verticalism and also that even slightly elongated proportions of Gothic structures seem more vertical than many more elongated ones of Romanesque. I did not go into this matter then.

Gall's theory could certainly have been corrected from that point of view.

In the same essay I also touched upon the subject of secular architecture and presented the hypothesis I then held regarding the origin of the rib, a hypothesis that I soon after (ca. 1927) recognized as incorrect.

The theory of Gothic that I advocated at that time and expounded in lectures at the University of Halle has been held fast in its essentials in a book by Richard KRAUTHEIMER (b. 1897).[6] With this as a basis he examined the architecture of the German churches of the Mendicant Orders in an independent way. His attitude toward this hitherto rather negatively regarded branch of Gothic was positive but free from Thode's romanticism. A wealth of concrete, detailed research is here combined with an attempt to present a unifying view of a great complex of works.

Ernst Gall, of course, resisted Strzygowski's friendly enticement to derive the "Norman thought-form" from Scandinavia; in 1925 he published a work on the history of Gothic of which unfortunately only the first volume has as yet appeared.[7] His conception of Gothic has changed in only one respect: he now sees Gothic against the background of Romanesque. "In Cluny, part after part of the building felt as an individual member, the whole a well-organized mosaic of clearly defined bodies of space, subordinated to the dominating mass of the altar space and as though added on from the outside; in Reims, shaping from the interior of the space outward, a conformation to which nothing could be added without almost completely destroying the idea engendered by a unified conception." By the phrases "added on from the outside" and "shaping from the interior outward" is meant what I had called "additive" and "divided." Gall combined that with Alberti's famous dictum, which certainly does not correspond to *my* distinction between addition and subdivision. Alberti's assertion that in a work of art nothing can be taken away or added without destroying the harmony refers simply to harmony. And that is possible in both an additive and a divisive style, both in Cluny and in Reims.

Gall says (page 17): "In contrast to St.-Étienne [in Caen] we have here [in the façade of Laon] the composition of picturesquely connected memberings and the verticalism of vigorously agitated form—

[6] Richard Krautheimer, *Die Kirchen der Bettelorden in Deutschland*, Cologne, 1925 (on p. 3 can be found the reference to my lectures at the University of Halle from 1921 to 1922).

[7] Ernst Gall, *Die gotische Baukunst in Frankreich und Deutschand*, I, Leipzig, 1925.

all characteristics of a decided late style." Gall has in mind here what I have called, following Wölfflin, the style of becoming. Of the ambulatory of St.-Denis he remarks: "Whereas formerly one section of space stood out boldly against the other, the chapels freed themselves individually from the enclosed ambulatory, and seams were everywhere to be felt, now the picturesque charm of interpenetrating spatial boundaries that lose themselves in darkness is sought and depth gradually achieved in the cumulative effect of shallowly curved chapel walls." Again, one page further on: "The architects of the eleventh century composed their churches by treating each portion of space by itself, setting it off from its neighbor as clearly as possible. . . ." And on page 52: ". . . for the ambition [of the twelfth century] was directed toward unification and synthesis, and above all toward the inclusion of the side aisles and chapels in the total spatial effect, the picturesque appearance of which was sought with especial fondness particularly in the second half of the twelfth century." Gall thus supplemented the conception of Gothic he had had in 1915 by incorporating in it the thesis that Gothic is a style of becoming. But he retained Wölfflin's terminology and called Gothic *picturesque*, at the same time employing the word "plastic" for the wall membering of Norman churches of the eleventh century. He says there in summary: "Thus here, too, plastically formed, soaring bodies instead of unmembered surface." Gothic is now, according to Gall, at once plastic and picturesque. But to him this is not really contradictory for in his terminology plastic means merely three-dimensional and not "plastic" in the sense of the opposite of "picturesque."

A lecture by Rudolf KAUTZSCH (1866-1945) of the year 1927[8] was influenced by the conceptions of Gall and von Lücken:[9] he calls the organization of the wall into a framework of members Gothic or at least "incipient Gothic." But he was obviously troubled by the existence of a classicizing tendency in Burgundian architecture, and sought to resolve this paradox of an incipient Gothic and a classical disposition.

The characteristics on which he bases his description of the structural skeleton are not new. 1) The increasing height makes the interior difficult to apprehend and irrational, whereas the breadth remains apprehensible and rational. The building seems to grow by its own energy. The coherence of the terrestrial world seems to be nullified

[8] Rudolf Kautzsch, *Werdende Gotik und Antike in der burgundischen Baukunst des 12. Jahrhunderts. Vorträge der Bibliothek Warburg*, Leipzig and Berlin, 1927, pp. 331ff.

[9] G. von Lücken, *Die Anfänge der Burgundischen Schule*, Basel, 1920.

and the whole obeys apparently supranatural laws. 2) Hence abolition of the definite spatial form: it becomes infinite. The space is *intentionally* incomprehensible and irrational. 3) The building is oriented toward the altar, as Hegel and Schnaase had already maintained.

He then says that this irrational height is already to be found in Cluny, and formulates the following antithesis (page 343): There are ages that recognize reality and those to which reality means nothing, "to which the voices and visions of inward experience are much more important than anything this poor world can offer them." There are echoes of a number of antitheses, for example, those of Worringer as well as those of Jung (extroverted and introverted attitudes). "A disposition toward both possibilities is present in all ages and in all peoples. But which disposition is permitted to develop depends on the general spiritual situation of the particular age or people. In the Middle Ages the individual is so intimately connected with the spiritual movement of his age and his environment that the two dispositions can only find expression in the fluctuation of a longer lasting current that dominates more extensive areas. The closer we come to modern times the faster does the tempo of the fluctuation become."

This solves the problem for Kautzsch: even in the Middle Ages there existed the current that recognized reality, was sensible to its beauty, and at the same time thought rationally. Hence an antique character is possible or plausible in incipient Gothic.

A detailed criticism of this solution of the problem does not seem to be necessary here. At that time I entered into a polemical exchange of articles with Kautzsch, and though these were written in connection with other general problems, they partially relieve me of the task of further discussion here.[10] When I now reread these articles I recognize clearly the fundamental confusions both in Kautzsch's observations and my own. Thus my final answer to his thesis will be contained only in what I shall have to say at the end of this book. But though in some respects my views may have diverged even more from those of Kautzsch, I have, on the other hand, come closer to his way of thinking on certain points. I, too, acknowledge the existence of two currents in the same period. The desire to define styles exactly led to the practice of identifying each age with a single style, whereas in actuality there is always a main current and at least one—perhaps sometimes several—undercurrents.

[10] *Kritische Berichte zur kunstgeschichtlichen Literatur*, 1927-28.

Nevertheless, Kautzsch misunderstood Burgundian architecture. It is in reality a style of totality like antiquity to which it inclined; it is High Romanesque, *not* "incipient Gothic." Since I have already gone into this matter with respect to Gall, there is no need to take it up again.

Kautzsch was an unusually conscientious scholar and his conscientiousness was perhaps the source of his reluctance to employ precise concepts. His book on the *Romanesque* churches of Alsace gave us the important information about the oldest ribs in the German language area.[11] Are now these cross ribbed vaults *Gothic* within otherwise *Romanesque* buildings? We have at hand Dehio's term "passive transitional style" to describe this piecemeal transformation. But Kautzsch expresses himself somewhat differently. In discussing the choir of Murbach he says (page 76) that "thanks to the short engaged shafts the vaults seem to float high overhead, the abundance of light pouring into the space from the six windows dissolves it, makes it vague, unearthly, transfigured. We do indeed feel distinctly that effects are here achieved which we are accustomed to expect from Gothic. But anyone with any perceptiveness who has gazed from the naves of Alpirsbach or Schaffhausen into the crossing and the choir has also realized that in these Cluniac churches there lives a secret Gothic, a quite different spirit from that of the earth-bound spaces of Rosheim and Gebweiler."

The polar opposition is here expressed by the words "earth-bound" and "unearthly." Kautzsch had the impression of a "*secret Gothic*" in Alpirsbach and Schaffhausen. With regard to the Gothic quality of the choir of Murbach he makes the lighting and the proportion (1 : 2.25), in addition to the ribs, responsible for what he would like to call secret Gothic, putting such a high value on light and proportion that wherever they are present he speaks of secret Gothic, even though ribs or other Gothic characteristics are lacking. In connection with Ruskin's objections the point has already been made that there is such a thing as Gothic *without* ribs, but only after other Gothic forms had been developed from Gothic *with* ribs. Similarly, it must be admitted that light plays a great role in Gothic. Who does not know that today? Yet not, after all, light in general but specifically Gothic light. Thus also the steepness of proportion is per se by no means Gothic, not even secretly Gothic.

[11] Rudolf Kautzsch, *Romanische Kirchen im Elsass*, Freiburg i.B., 1927. A revision appeared under the title: *Der Romanische Kirchenbau im Elsass*, Freiburg i.B., 1944.

There is a very profound reason for Kautzsch's sincere struggles. He let himself be guided by the subjective impression he received, and such impressions unquestionably do and must provide the initial impulse for the thinking of every historian of art. But just the kind of thinking that is stimulated by impressions demands rigorous analysis and consequently strict abstraction, if one is to discuss such abstract factors as proportion, verticalism (in this case), treatment of light, or abundance of light. Kautzsch was too quick to identify his impressions of closeness to earth and remoteness from earth with Romanesque and Gothic. Moreover, anyone who might be inclined to be impressed by unearthliness in Alpirsbach and Schaffhausen should not blind himself to the fact that these buildings are both absolutely pure examples of Romanesque—except for some Gothic additions in Alpirsbach. In Romanesque style the interiors simply vary in character. A discussion of this whole complex of problems would lead very far afield, but it may perhaps be said in metaphorical language that the Heavenly Jerusalem can be built in different manners: a Romanesque heavenly Jerusalem is just as heavenly as a Gothic; one is "total," the other "partial." That leads to the paradoxical thesis that Rosheim and Gebweiler are earthbound heavens while Alpirsbach and Schaffhausen (for Kautzsch) are heavens remote from earth. Such paradoxical manner of expression casts light on the confusion that ensues when analysis and abstraction are not carried far enough. This last remark should not be interpreted as pedantic superciliousness. The problem of the essence of Gothic remains a task common to all historians of art, and often enough even erroneous or half-correct investigations can be of help. One could agree with Kautzsch if instead of Alpirsbach and Schaffhausen he had chosen, for example, Chartres and Reims as the opposites of the impressions roused by Rosheim and Gebweiler. But in that case the secret Gothic which was for him the important thing would be changed into a Gothic no longer secret.

In a short bibliographical report Hans JANTZEN (b. 1880) expressed his opinion of various theories about Gothic, including those of Rave, Krautheimer, Gall, and myself.[12] He denies that Gothic is picturesque, without, however, *defining* "picturesque." He also rejects the idea that St.-Étienne in Caen is Gothic (Gall). His conception of Gothic

[12] Hans Jantzen, *Zur Beurteilung der gotischen Architektur als Raumkunst*, Kritische Berichte zur kunstgeschichtlichen Literatur, vol. for 1927, p. 12. As far as his criticism concerns me, I have learned from it that one cannot express oneself precisely enough not to be misunderstood. But it seems to me unfruitful to go back to specific misapprehensions, more fruitful to study Jantzen's own theory closely.

is geographically and historically limited:[13] when he speaks of Gothic he means the Northern French churches of the twelfth and thirteenth centuries.

Furthermore the spatial boundary of Gothic does not mean to him the limit determined by the contour of the transverse section, thus including the side aisles and their outer walls, but merely "the delimitation of the central nave, and, as a matter of fact, this in its entire length, including the end of the choir . . . as far as the analysis of the spatial delimitation is concerned it is consequently first of all a question of the high nave wall." This was also Gerstenberg's view. Previous interpretations—first, dissection into purely carrying and purely filling organs; second, a conception analogous to our own organism (according to Wölfflin's *Prolegomena* and *Renaissance and Baroque*); third, arrangement according to principles of rhythmical membering, as in Schmarsow's theory—could not reveal "the structure of the spatial boundary" as specifically *Gothic.* Jantzen finds this specifically Gothic element in a quality of the composition that he calls "*diaphanous structure.*"

Diaphanous structure is not synonymous with penetration or dissolution of the wall in the usual sense. There is also a Romanesque penetration that can be carried to a considerable extent. "But this has a fundamentally different character from the diaphanous structure of the Gothic spatial boundary. In Romanesque the decisive conception of the wall always remains that of a coherent mass of masonry expanding in width. Even in the case of the greatest possible piercing, for instance in the broad openings of arcades, the round arch first of all assumes the function of emphasizing the masses and the continuity of the wall in closest conjunction with the basic frontality of all members."[14] In diaphanous structure the case is different: here is expressed basically "the relation of the (corporeally and plastically formed) wall to the portions of space lying behind it as a *relation*

[13] The same "Über den gotischen Kirchenraum," *Freiburger Wissenschaftliche Gesellschaft*, Freiburg i.B., 1928. Reprinted under the same title together with other articles, Berlin, 1951.

[14] "Die diaphane Struktur ist nicht gleichbedeutend mit 'Durchbrechung' oder 'Auflösung' der Hochschiffwand im üblichen Sinne. Auch die Romanik kennt eine sehr weitgehende Durchbrechung der Raumgrenze des Mittelschiffs. Aber diese hat grundsätzlich andern Charakter als die diaphane Struktur der gotischen Raumgrenze. In der Romanik bleibt immer entscheidend die Auffassung der Wand als einer zusammenhängenden, in der Breite sich entfaltenden Mauermasse. [Here he points to the illustration showing St.-Étienne in Nevers.] Auch bei grösstmöglicher Durchbrechung, etwa bei beiden Arkadenöffnungen, übernimmt zunächst schon der Rundbogen die Funktion der Betonung der Mauer- oder Wandkontinuität in engster Verbindung mit der prinzipiellen 'Frontalität' aller Glieder."

between body and background, that is to say, the wall as the delimitation of the entire body of the nave is not conceivable without the ground of space from which it derives its effective value. The spatial ground is revealed as an optical zone that is, as it were, placed behind the wall. . . ." (The distinction between "pattern and ground" was introduced into the theory of art by Riegl.)

Although on first reading these words I said to myself that here was—excellently formulated—exactly what I also meant, Jantzen declares that this is absolutely not the case. That is to say, it is not the case as far as the Gothic of the twelfth and thirteenth centuries is concerned. "Spatial coalescence" (*Raumverschmelzung*) (a term which he uses to refer to my concept of spatial division and spatial penetration) becomes "without doubt the goal for the later Gothic of the fourteenth century"; the spatial boundary is then moved to the outer walls of the side aisles. The amount of wall penetration is not the decisive factor in this process. In Gothic the penetrations are in part filled in again, that is, latticed by the insertion of columns, for example, into the openings of the galleries. Jantzen qualifies this somewhat in a note by admitting that such columns also occur in the openings of Romanesque galleries, for example in Mont-Saint-Michel. "But these memberings do not produce the effect of a latticework." What is it, then, that "conduces to diaphaneity as an interspersion of the wall with ground space"?

The first of the favoring factors discussed by Jantzen is light. The Romanesque churches are gloomy and so are also the Gothic, for example, Chartres, but they have colored light. The side aisles are darker than the nave when the entrance of light is basilical.

The second factor is the round support as the carrying member in the arcade story, since it permits the side aisles to show through (diaphaneity) as "ground."

Third: the triforium is diaphanous structure in its purest form.

The fourth factor is the dissolution of the window zone into two shells.

Accordingly, the entire spatial delimitation of the nave becomes "a plastically relieflike, membered lattice that is underlaid at various levels of depth with an optically dark ground or a ground of colored light."

Jantzen then discusses several examples of diaphanous structure, concluding with the remark that he has analyzed the Gothic spatial boundary only according to a *formal* principle. The last sentence of the book, which follows immediately, must be quoted verbally: "An investigation, however, that seeks to interpret the principle of 'diaphaneity' as the result of the cultic process itself would need to be entitled: Space as Symbol of Spacelessness." Gothic has never been more concisely and at the same time more profoundly defined than in these words.

Jantzen emphasizes the quality that characterizes the space-*light*-form of Gothic, as Gall had emphasized its space-*force*-form. Both are contained in Gothic: first, structure as a pattern on an optical ground (a dark ground or one of colored light); second, structure as force combined with verticalism. But neither is sufficient to characterize High Gothic; one must supplement them by what Jantzen calls spatial coalescence, that is to say, what Gall antiquatedly terms "picturesque." The word structure refers to the *dynamic* form of the bodies, the word diaphanous to the *light*-form. It is as surprising as a *deus ex machina* when Jantzen suddenly talks of *space*—as symbol of the spaceless. But diaphaneity is obviously not possible without a certain spatial form. If by diaphaneity it is only meant to imply that one can and should look through openings from *one* space into a *second* behind it, then St.-Étienne in Caen, which Jantzen (in contrast to Gall), rightly terms Romanesque structure is also diaphanous, or, for example, St.-Saturnin in Toulouse. But of course he does *not* mean that! In what, then, does the difference between Romanesque and Gothic diaphaneity lie? Jantzen well realizes, naturally, that a Romanesque gallery opening, even though columns may have been set into it as in Mont-Saint-Michel or Nevers, and so on, creates a different effect from a Gothic one like that in Nôtre-Dame in Paris. If he quite correctly assumes that the round support is responsible for the merging of central nave and side aisle in the arcades, why does not the column of the Romanesque gallery opening likewise produce spatial coalescence (in my sense) or diaphanous structure in Jantzen's sense? He has not explained that. I had already presented what seemed to me the solution to this problem in the Wölfflin Festschrift, though only sketchily: "The arches of the arcade lose their separating function, since Gothic profiling appears in place of the broad intrados." This, *the profiling*, seems to be the deciding factor, a matter that will be discussed later in detail. Jantzen views the side aisles in the cathedrals of the thirteenth century only as dark backgrounds. The Ste.-Chapelle has no side aisles and is nevertheless diaphanous in structure even without them. Every side aisle of a High Gothic cathedral is just as Gothic as the nave that belongs with it. Every one-aisled choir of a Gothic church is Gothic, though very often not diaphanous. Even though war or an earthquake were to destroy one of these cathedrals except for a side aisle or even a bay of this side aisle, that part would still be Gothic; every capital would be Gothic, every portion of a rib, and so on. Of course it is correct to say that the view from the west entrance toward the choir, the view that follows the longitudinal axis of the nave, is (just as in the Early Christian basilicas) the *chief* view (Hegel, Schnaase). But when one asks what Gothic is, one is not asking what the chief view is but what stylistic quality is common to *all parts* of the edifice as well as to the whole. When in ruined buildings pieces of tracery or a capital or a rib lie about on the ground, they are all Gothic without displaying diaphanous structure. However, they are so formed that in the proper place they must produce diaphanous structure. What is this Gothic form? The answer will be found in the chapter on the aesthetic function of the cross ribbed vault (see below, pages 819ff.).

But when one asks what Gothic is, the question includes that as to the character of Early, High, *and* Late Gothic. Whether Late Gothic was the unconscious goal of the development may be questionable or still in need of proof, but in any case Late Gothic is *also* Gothic, not something totally different from High Gothic. Otherwise we (including Jantzen) could not call both Gothic. But Jantzen has pointed out with unusual acuteness the particular characteristics of High Gothic and his analysis serves as a warning not to judge High Gothic negatively by the standard of Late Gothic. This would be just as wrong, indeed, as the converse, the negative evaluation of Late Gothic according to the standard of High Gothic. One ought also to be able to evaluate Early Gothic positively and to understand it from the point of view of history of ideas, hence "artistically."

Perhaps what Jantzen means to imply by the term "diaphanous structure of French High Gothic" would really become clear if he told us what the corresponding conceptual formulation would be for Late Gothic. Diaphanous structure belongs in the series of polar stylistic concepts even though its opposite (that is to say, diaphanous texture) is not expressed. Jantzen means *Gothic* diaphanous structure in contrast to *Romanesque*, and he has not said explicitly what—in this case as everywhere in general—the difference or even contrast is between Romanesque and Gothic. And yet with his allusion to the background of history of ideas he must have had in mind not merely a *difference* but a *contrast*. Where, then, does Late Gothic belong in Jantzen's unexpressed system of concepts?

His theory of Gothic is in part *concretely* descriptive inasmuch as he is concerned with the real interplay of the membra, in part aesthetically interpretative, and at times, therefore, *psychologically* descriptive. It is this that we need. Why then is his theory not entirely satisfactory? Because it is incomplete. Gothic is not always diaphanous structure, it can also be diaphanous texture and is then all the more Gothic. It is not only diaphanous structure or texture, that is to say, force-light-form, but it is also spatial form, and also meaning (and, as everyone knows, still other things, for example, technique). First Jantzen speaks of the Gothic *form*, then of the most profound *meaning* of Gothic, thus touching on the question of "form as symbol." He has not explained how form can become a symbol, as though this were a matter of course, and he ought to state clearly what is meant by "symbol"—or at least what it is *here*. It is impossible to arrive at *complete* understanding when the concepts are not fully represented and when they are left without a systematic connection. Random concepts can be a source of witty *aperçus* but not of exhaustive insight.

The difference between the methods of history of culture and history of ideas was expounded by Dagobert FREY (b. 1883) at the beginning of his book.[15] The former method seeks to explain the development of art by means of *outward* conditions (geographical, political, economic), the latter by means of *inward* conditions, of *intellectual* and *spiritual* forces. For Dvořak this method meant the reduction of mediaeval art to spirituality as the *meaning* of Christianity; for Frey it signifies the *form* of spirituality itself. "The basis of an history of ideas is an evolutionary history of the human power of imaginative conception. . . . The first basic question is how the environment appears to the minds of the men of a definite evolutionary period, or how the perceptive and recollective notion is reflected in the reproduced form, how the way of conceiving of things determines the entire thinking of an age."[16] By "conceiving of things" is meant the equivalent of the *form* of imaginative conception which is different from the *content* of conception: many contents can assume the same form. Such psychic forms are *succession* and *simultaneity*. While walking along and glancing about, we can perceive space as a temporal succession of one thing after the other as well as all at once as a juxtaposition. According to Frey the former way of looking at things is the *spiritual* presupposition of Gothic, the latter that of Renaissance. It would

[15] Dagobert Frey, *Gotik und Renaissance*, Augsburg, 1929.
[16] *Op.cit.*, p. xxvii.

perhaps be more accurate to speak here of *psychic* presupposition. Without quibbling over words it may nevertheless be remarked that Jantzen's attitude could rather be called that of history of ideas inasmuch as he wants to go back to the central idea of the cult. From Frey's point of view one would not ask about the central idea of the cult as content but about the particular forms that this central idea assumed in the course of the cult's development. The possibilities of polar form in successive and simultaneous conception seem to belong to *psychology*;[17] the cult itself, however, belongs in the realm of the spirit (which is here differentiated from the soul or psyche).

However that may be, Frey has mastered an astonishing wealth of material by this method, and his treatment has contributed much to the investigation of what the different cultural areas have in common stylistically, "the common denominator of the epoch," to use one of Wölfflin's expressions. Various sorts of spatial representation, including Renaissance perspective, cartography, the representational arts and architecture, poetry and music, and so on, are analyzed in a uniform way. One receives a distorted impression of the book as a whole when of all its contents only Gothic is singled out for attention, but here we may and indeed must confine ourselves to this section.

Frey compares Romanesque and Gothic in detail (page 68ff.), chiefly from the standpoint of differences in their statics. He describes the Gothic vault as an "organically connected structure, a labile system, that is only kept in a state of equilibrium by the interaction of pressures," in contrast to the Romanesque, which because of its mortar is a uniform mass. (Whether this distinction is a radical *contrast* was called into question by the work of Sabouret and Abraham; it is undoubtedly a *difference*.) In Frey's opinion the differentiation of the wall by means of engaged shafts does not necessarily follow from the invention of the rib, for both are traceable to the same conception of a kinetic process. He is more or less in agreement with Gall and considers the rib to have been prefigured by the Romanesque engaged shaft. Frey's formulation is more cautious than Gall's. He describes

[17] The concepts of the successive and the simultaneous play a considerable part in the psychology of Wilhelm Wundt. (*Grundriss der Psychologie*, 1896, *passim*) Related to this polarity is the contrast between the coexistent and the consecutive, which obtrudes itself again and again in Lessing's *Laokoon*. It there refers to the difference between painting and poetry, and in Ch. 18 is formulated as an analogy to the difference between space and time. I have discussed the deceptive factor in the differentiation between spatial arts and temporal arts on p. 501 of the *System der Kunstwissenschaft*. Time, as well as space, is an integrating element of architecture; consequently Frey is justified in regarding it from the standpoint of both possibilities of succession and simultaneity.

the steps in the development of Gothic, the oblique position of the capitals of the rib shafts, and so on, the transformation of the whole structure "into a system of independent lines of force and light, in contrast to which the surfaces of the wall represent a neutral background of space like the patterned backgrounds in miniature painting." The wall, which has become a background of space, is pierced through in its depth. Here, too, Frey follows Gall in principle though he makes many observations of his own. Only Late Gothic achieves full penetration. Frey already adheres to the view that the development of the *style* from High to Late Gothic is in an ascending line. Since he belongs to the "Viennese school" this is not surprising; it is an idea that flourished naturally in the atmosphere of Riegl's traditions. It is simply necessary to distinguish between increase in value in an *aesthetic* sense and consistent maturing or perfecting in a *stylistic* one.

The novel element in Frey's judgment of Gothic is to be found in the following remark: ". . . We must read off a work of Gothic architecture just as successively as a Gothic picture. We follow the rows of piers, the obliquely receding cornices, the galleries and triforia, into the depth and experience the shaping of the space as a temporal process; we look up along the clustered pillars and shafts [Forster and Hegel had already emphasized this] and as we follow the vertical lines the space grows. . . . The Gothic building, in the conception proper to it, is not something accomplished, something finished and complete, something at rest in itself, *not rigid being*, but something always rising anew, something inwardly unfinished and in process of completion, a thing in motion, an eternal *becoming*."[17a] This harmonizes perfectly with my conception of Gothic that goes back to Wölfflin's terminology. But there is a difference. Frey concurs with me only in the objective judgment that Gothic is a style of becoming; the reason he gives for his opinion, however, is the psychology of the artist and his age: Gothic is a style of becoming *because* the age lived in the form of successive conception.

One can accept this but must immediately ask why men thought in

[17a] *Op.cit.*, p. 75. "Eine gotische Architektur müssen wir ebenso subzessive ablesen wie ein gotisches Bild. Wir folgen den Pfeilerreihen, den Kaffgesimsen, den Emporen und Triforien in die Tiefe und erleben die Bildung des Raumes als einen zeitlichen Vorgang, wir blicken an den Pfeilerbündeln und den Diensten hinauf, und indem wir den vertikalen Linien folgen, wächst der Raum vor unseren Blicken empor, um sich in unschätzbarer Höhe über uns zu schliessen. Wie in der Malerei wird die Abfolge der Wahrnehmungseindrücke, der genetische Vorgang des Vorstellungsprozesses von dem Betrachtenden auf das Objekt übertragen. Das gotische Bauwerk ist in der ihr gemässen Vorstellung nicht etwas Gewordenes, ein abgeschlossenes Fertiges, etwas in sich Ruhendes, nicht starres Sein, sondern etwas immer neu Entstehendes, etwas innerlich Unvollendetes, ein Bewegtes, ein ewiges Werden."

this form. Did the conceptional form develop spontaneously, so that the particular content—Jantzen's central idea of the cult, for example—was, as it were, poured into it, or was it the content that created its forms? The latter case would be not psychology but the science of ideas. In spite of Frey's recourse to the successive form of conception there is no avoiding this last question. *Why* were ribs constructed? Frey does not mention Quicherat. But even if one sides with Courajod and Gall in stressing the fact that the engaged shafts came first chronologically, that they were continued into the vaulting, or that their structural character was continued, there still remains the question why. Was it merely because the walls had first been treated as structure? Is this reason enough? Frey thinks that *space* and *time* were not yet logically differentiated in Gothic (page 88) and that in their inseparable union can be found the explanation for its characteristic movement. This is a profound thought. But one runs aground if one formulates the question in these terms: Were the ribs built (or, even earlier, the engaged shafts) because space and time were not yet logically differentiated. Nor in the age of Romanesque, were space and time treated as separate categories.

Two more points should be considered. Frey holds that High Gothic "ought to be seen frontally, axially, like Renaissance" and that only Late Gothic produced vistas and oblique views (page 77). This is not in accordance with the facts. Diagonality is created everywhere in Gothic: above all, even in Early Gothic in the ribs, but equally in High Gothic in the oblique position of the piers and pinnacles, the very turning of the *abaci* on the engaged shafts carrying the transverse arches, in the sloping lines of the buttresses, and so on. As to the second point, Frey is of the opinion that rhythm is a matter of leaps; proportion, he says, can only be understood spatially, rhythm in the passage of time (page 80). "The gaze, hurrying on into the depth, leaps over from one pier to the other, from one vertical to the other, while the rhythm may be faster or slower, more or less strongly marked, regular or changeable." This idea is worked out in more detail and presented as a contrast to Renaissance. Probably many people associate rhythm with a leaping motion. Leaping *is* itself not rhythm but *has* rhythm. If Frey means to say that *Gothic has* a leaping rhythm he is making a genuine contribution to the characterization of the style.

These authors, Gall (1925), Jantzen, Frey, and in a certain sense Kautzsch also, belong to the group of those who sought for polar opposites as a means of drawing distinctions in stylistic history. Gall adopted, though not the words, my concepts of totality and partiality derived from Wölfflin; Jantzen's diaphanous structure is contrasted as a Gothic feature with Romanesque structure, which he does not define precisely, as well as, presumably, with diaphanous texture; Frey bases his theory on the psychological contrasts of successive and simultaneous perception; and Kautzsch sees beside Gothic an antique undercurrent that exercises an effect at the same time. All these polar stylistic concepts tend toward a periodization of the history of art. The list given above on page 773, however, which extends to 1914, consists almost entirely of the various attempts that were made to find polar concepts without as yet so generalizing their validity that they could serve to characterize recurring and "necessarily" recurring qualities of successive periods.

This generalization emerged in Burckhardt's footnote already quoted.[18] Wölfflin spoke of "antique Baroque" and in 1901 Dehio followed suit with the statement that "every architectural style has Baroque as its last phase."[19] Like Burckhardt, whose note he did not know when he wrote, he speaks of the fact that every style reaches a point in its modifications where it utilizes "inherited forms that have been taken out of their system, indeed often even opposed to their real meaning, to create free effects." What Dehio designated as Baroque (as a generic term, namely, as an ever-recurring stylistic modification) has been called since 1919 by Werner WEISBACH (1873-1953) *Mannerism.* "Mannerism is found where forms that originally and in their pristine manifestations possess a distinct meaning and expressive value are carried to the extreme and distorted, so that they appear affected, artificial, hollow, stale, and degenerate."[20] Although Weisbach means here by Mannerism an ever recurring stylistic type, he also uses the general term for its historically unique realization in Italy in the sixteenth century. He confines himself at first to the painting of this period, but a few years later the concept was extended to architecture (Panofsky) and here, too, we have the equivocation of the historically unique phenomenon of Mannerism and the unhistoric idea of a stylistic potentiality existing *a priori.*[18a] This latter "Mannerism" of a general kind was by its very nature bound to be claimed for use in attempts at periodization, and thus there resulted the

[18] Cf. p. 602 n. 5 above. [18a] Erwin Panofsky, quoted above, p. 293, n. 14.

[19] Dehio, *Die kirchliche Baukunst. . .*, II, p. 190.

[20] Werner Weisbach, "Der Manierismus," *Zeitschrift für bildende Kunst*, New Series, XXX, Leipzig, 1919, p. 161. As a key to the relevant literature and also for its own sake, attention should be called to Richard Zürcher's *Stilprobleme der italienischen Baukunst des Cinquecento*, Basel, 1947. Werner Weisbach's *Manierismus in mittelalterlicher Kunst*, Basel, 1942, does not treat architecture.

search for Mannerism within Gothic. In this process of stylistic research according to the tenets of the philosophy of history Dehio's remark is still unclear, for it remains an open question whether his concept Baroque does not here correspond to the later developed one of Mannerism. This question is of decisive importance in judging Late Gothic. Even if both the historically unique and the unhistoric, "general" Mannerism are purged of any trace of a negative evaluation, it is not a matter of indifference whether one draws a parallel between Late Gothic and the Baroque of the seventeenth century or the Mannerism of the sixteenth.

Mannerism as an unhistoric, stylistic potentiality, indeed even Mannerism as a unique stylistic phase of Renaissance (Late Renaissance), spoiled the theoretical edifices that were based on stylistic pairs, for now a third style had to be accommodated. In the list given above systems based on three or four members, can already be found, but they are all unsatisfactory. Nevertheless, a number of thinkers among historians of art have endeavored to construct systems of periodization into which history could be fitted. These were always systems where the chief concepts were intended to differentiate both larger epochs and within them, as a model on a smaller scale, the subdivision into individual phases. Mention should be made of Hauttmann, Coellen, Ligetti, Lehel, Kraus, and Gramm.[21] Not all of them included Gothic in their systems. Lehel,[22] however, did. He distinguishes three chief epochs: A) the primitive age, B) classical antiquity, C) the Baroque modern age; each epoch is analogously divided into a, b, and c. The modern age, which is as a whole "Baroque," extends from 900 [*sic*] to the present (or at least to 1929); it is divided into a) the primitive modern age (Romanesque), b) the classical modern age (Gothic), and c) the Baroque modern age (Renaissance). Lehel proclaims that Gothic is classical and Renaissance is Baroque! This is, as it were, a Mannerism of logic, but such aberrations caused by the tendency to transform history into a soulless mechanism should not blind us to the originally correct inference that there can be some common factor even in styles that look extremely different when taken as a whole.

In order to obtain a clear insight into this matter and, above all, in order to be able to judge the position of Late Gothic in history, one

[21] In detail in my article: "F. Adama van Scheltema, Die Kunst unserer Vorzeit," *Kritische Berichte*, VI, 3 and 4, Leipzig, 1936.

[22] Franz Lehel, *Fortschreitende Entwicklung, Versuch einer reinen Kunstmorphologie*, Munich, 1929 (translated from the Hungarian).

should have recourse to the most comprehensive attempt at periodization that exists, that of Fritz Adama van SCHELTEMA (b. 1884). He obtained his stylistic concepts from the field of prehistoric art.[23] The prehistorians have received this philosophical penetration of their field of research by analysis of form coolly; their hearts are moved more by detailed studies than by clarity and range of vision. Many historians of art, on the other hand, concern themselves little or not at all with the art of prehistoric times, and thus Scheltema's uncommonly clarifying book has not attracted sufficient notice. Since then he has investigated the entire history of art from the standpoint of his concepts.[24] The term cultural morphology in the title indicates that it is a question of a close linking of art history with history of ideas, a union in which the spiritual element is much more comprehensively represented than in other attempts of this nature. In the brief discussion of Gothic, tendencies of the age, such as courtly love and the like, are placed more in the foreground than architecture, which later came into its own in *Die Kunst des Mittelalters* (Stuttgart, 1953). Neither does the even shorter section on Late Gothic reveal van Scheltema's opinion of it as an architectural style. But according to his three-part scheme of periodization Late Gothic is the C period of the Middle Ages and it, in turn, is divided into three stylistic phases. In such a brief presentation van Scheltema could not take up in detail the differentiation of these three phases of Late Gothic, nor does he give any chronological delimitations; but one can see from the table on page 188 that all "periods" have three "phases" each, the structures of which are repeated on a subordinate level. It can be concluded from this that Late Gothic as the C period of the Middle Ages corresponds on the one hand to the C period of the prehistoric age (Germanic Iron Age) and on the other to the C period of the modern age that is called "late modern age" and extends from the Enlightenment to the present. Mannerism is to be found in the A period of the modern age (Renaissance) as the third stylistic *phase*. If one hunts in the table for the corresponding *phases* designated by c, one finds the end phase of Germanic animal

[23] Frederick Adama van Scheltema, *Die Altnordische Kunst, Grundprobleme vorhistorischer Kunstentwicklung*, Berlin, 1923.

[24] A brief summary of van Scheltema's life work can be found in his *Die geistige Mitte, Umrisse einer abendländischen Kulturmorphologie*, Munich, 1947. This was a temporary substitute for a manuscript of six volumes, the publication of which has hitherto been delayed by the war and its consequences. Up to now two of these volumes have been published: *Die Kunst der Vorzeit*, Stuttgart, 1950; and *Die Kunst des Mittelalters*, 1953. The latter contains an important contribution to the ideas about Gothic. Unfortunately there was no opportunity to include in this book a report adequate to its rank.

ornamentation, the end phase of Late Gothic, and in the modern age firstly the "Mannerism of the Late Renaissance," secondly the Rococo, and thirdly "the modern style" which as a whole, beginning with the Realism of the nineteenth century, is "Mannerism" and in turn falls into three subdivisions, the last of these being the "late modern style" or Expressionism, thus a Mannerism to the second power. What we learn from this is that van Scheltema does not parallel *all* of Late Gothic with Mannerism and Rococo but merely its last phase.

A critical appraisal of this conception is unavoidable here but it must be confined to matters of principle. The question may be set aside as to how the three-part scheme harmonizes with the originally basic polarity or two-part arrangement. On the other hand, it seems more fruitful to separate Mannerism from the stylistic category that was meant by the polar contrast of "Renaissance and Baroque." Burckhardt, as has already been said, originally implied by the word Rococo not what we today call Baroque but what we call Mannerism. To recapitulate: His Rococo is produced "where the real significance of the forms has been forgotten and they themselves continue to be used for the sake of the effect and, indeed, mistakenly," a criterion that is the same as Weisbach's definition of Mannerism. The Mannerism of the sixteenth century, therefore, *cannot* be expressed by the polar contrast of Renaissance and Baroque or, in general terms, the unhistoric "Manneristic" element by the concepts of totality and partiality; this "Manneristic" element has, logically analyzed, a different root. Totality and partiality refer to the nature of the *delimitations* (line and spot, discontinuity and continuity, and so on); Mannerism, on the other hand, refers to the weakened connection between form and its content. Neither is Mannerism logically identical with disharmony, although it usually includes disharmony of meaning even where it offers a relative harmony of form.[25]

In these concise sentences is contained the thesis that history—be it of art or culture or ideas—cannot be organized by means of polar concepts *alone*, but that polar concepts *also* are necessary if history, which is per se a continuous chronological chain and at the same time a geographical network as well—thus a continuous chain of networks—is to be meaningfully organized. For this purpose one needs, in all, the five

25 This was tentatively worked out in more detail in the *System der Kunstwissenschaft*, p. 1005. In some respects I have progressed beyond the arguments there presented: "The 'Crazy' Vaults of Lincoln Cathedral," *Art Bulletin*, XXXV, 1953. There I proposed the term Akyrism as a substitute for the general term Mannerism.

categories of stylistic principles which have already been mentioned several times: membrism, which concerns the members (as meaning and form); "general Mannerism" (akyrism), which refers to the type stemming from the (neighborly) composition of these members; regularism as the degree of regularity of the members themselves and of their grouping; limitism as the treatment of delimitations according to the poles of whole and part (of meaning and form simultaneously); and, finally, harmonism with its central point of reference in pure harmony.[26]

All these concepts, the results of the entire preceding development, are only points of reference and together form a system of reference for the appraisal of actual history. None of the five individual coordinates is sufficient by itself for the organization of history; all five must be applied simultaneously. It remains anyone's prerogative to subdivide history according to pragmatic criteria, for example, according to centuries or generations, or according to kings and the dates of their reigns. At times this procedure may be sensible. But only an arrangement that begins with the things themselves can be truly meaningful in the history of art and of artistic styles. Van Scheltema is right when he calls the opponents of the philosophically oriented stylistic investigations of Wölfflin and Riegl blind to the real problems.

It would seem that many circles of scholars consider the craze for discovering historical laws and constructing periodizations specifically German. The tendency, however, need not be wrong on that account. It is not right to reject this intellectual labor together with its fruits because of the fact that history is complex, for it does make one contribution toward the achievement of an understanding of the history of art and consequently also of Gothic and Late Gothic. It is, moreover, also an error to accuse the representatives of this trend of being one-sided; except for a few extremists none of those who worked at such constructions spoke exclusively of this one factor. They felt moved to discipline their thinking and repudiated vague, irresponsible rambling. They believe that they are performing work which is scientifically just as indispensable as that of collecting, classifying, and dating, for a chain of properly dated buildings is still far from being a history.

26 This terminology differs to some extent from that in the *System* and is perhaps preferable. If the conceptual pairs of the realization of the stylistic type and the intentional deviation therefrom and, on the other hand, harmony and disharmony should come to be regarded as polar opposites, they still remain variables independent of each other as well as of the contrast between totality and partiality. That is to say, Gothic is a style of becoming in contrast to Romanesque, but both can be either harmonious or disharmonious and both evolve types or deviations from these types.

"Facts" are of course the necessary foundation, but without interpretation, without adequate understanding, they are but a desert waste—quite aside from the consideration that the facts of yesterday and today are sometimes by no means the facts of tomorrow.[27]

3. Problems connected with the Rib

AFTER the studies of Whewell, Wiegmann, Leibnitz and Mohrmann, Rudolf KÖMSTEDT (b. 1887) was responsible for the first enlargement of our knowledge of the geometric construction of cross-ribbed vaults.[1] He discussed in particular the type commonly used in Anjou and Westphalia, those pointed-arched, very steeply rising vaults that begin at the springing as cross vaults (with a groin angle of more than 180 degrees) and turn into domed vaults (with a hollow angle of less than 180 degrees). Here the function of the rib is the usual one for the lower part of the quadripartite vault, namely to produce a neat or regular curve, but for the upper part its task is to correct the so-called flattening of the groin by means of the clearly projecting, three-dimensional, and precisely drawn lines of the rib's form.

By far the most complete survey of mediaeval vaulting systems was given by Clarence WARD (b. 1884);[2] this applies both to his information

[27] Postscript on bibliography: Otto Förster, "Von Speyer bis Chartres," *Neue Beiträge deutscher Forschung* (Worringer Festschrift, published by Erich Fidder) Königsberg Pr., 1943, p. 106, rejects the traditional concept of the antithesis of two fictions, of two so-called styles (quoting W. Pinder to support his argument) and substitutes for it the "apparently obvious statement that what is involved is a realization." Unfortunately, since all "so-called styles" are realizations, the question arises as to how they are to be distinguished from one another and which "realizations" belong to a given historical type. It is a fight against windmills. Förster attacks concepts in general and continues to make use of them. How could he avoid doing so? For example, he uses the antonyms picturesque and linear, but without giving a clear definition. In a new publication: *Grundformen deutscher Kunst*, Cologne, 1952, the theme is resumed. In a chapter entitled "Style," he talks about the "Barockzeit" (p. 220) and the "Rokokotheater" (p. 221). Styles? Or so-called Styles?

C. L. V. Meeks, "Picturesque Eclecticism," *Art Bulletin*, XXXII, 1950, p. 226. This most interesting study of the architecture of the nineteenth century discusses the concept of the Picturesque in connection with other concepts and refers to several books and articles which escaped my attention. As analogies to Wölfflin's five principles of the Baroque he quotes from different authors of the nineteenth century: 1) roughness (savageness, ruggedness), 2) movement, 3) irregularity, 4) variety, 5) intricacy (unclearness). From Jacques Barzun, *Romanticism and the Modern Ego*, New York, 1943, he quotes a set of six concepts as characteristics of romantic art: drama, strife, contrast, color, richness, variety. Many of these authors have snatched up their concepts, without aiming at systematic order.

[1] Rudolf Kömstedt, *Die Entwicklung des Gewölbebaues in den mittelalterlichen Kirchen Westfalens*, Strasbourg, 1914.

[2] Clarence Ward, *Mediaeval Church Vaulting*, Princeton, 1915.

about vault types in their relation to the various parts of the church interior—nave, aisles, ambulatories, chapels, and so on—and to his data about the structures themselves in France and England as well as other countries.

But our knowledge of the geometry of vaults is not definitive. Future investigations will have to continue the trend represented excellently by John BILSON and Charles Herbert MOORE (1840-1930), the endeavor to make exact measurements of all the extant Romanesque and Gothic cross vaults and thus transform our hitherto relative conception of chronology into an absolute one—as far as this is attainable.

Modern scholarship has been more interested in the statics of ribbed vaults than in their geometry, especially with regard to the question of whether the rib carries.

The first doubts about Viollet-le-Duc's theory appear to have been raised by Jean August BRUTAILS (1859-1926), at least he criticized as early as the year 1900[3] the assumption that the system of buttressing served a useful purpose. In 1904 Riegl grandly pushed the whole problem aside.[4] In 1906 Bond observed that the flying buttresses remained standing even when the vaults had collapsed.[5] Porter's objections of 1911 followed.[6] He was of the opinion that the value of the rib as a carrying member had been "grossly exaggerated" for there were ruins where the ribs had broken off and yet the vaults held (as quoted above on page 666). In 1915 Gall wrote that the early ribs were curved in the form of a segmental arch and thus had scarcely any statical value but that later the secret of their usefulness was discovered and the ribs consequently became *also* statically useful; he really saw in them, however, more the "decorative" factor.

Alfred HAMLIN (1855-1926), whose uncommonly lucid arguments have been rather overlooked, had doubts of a much more general nature.[7] At first he tried to define Gothic, criticizing the few attempts that had already been made (by Russell Sturgis, Bond, and others). After remarking that the styles called Gothic are descended from the common source of Romanesque and possess certain general traits, he proceeds to list the typical members. Even though he does not touch upon the really "formal" characteristics, it is nevertheless very much to his credit

[3] Jean Auguste Brutails, *L'archéologie du Moyen-Âge et ses méthodes*, Paris, 1900, p. 157.

[4] Cf. above, p. 636.

[5] Cf. above, p. 664.

[6] Porter also talks of "logic," but this is meant with regard to economy of centering.

[7] A. D. F. Hamlin, "Gothic Architecture and its Critics," *Architectural Record*, XXXIX, 1916, pp. 338ff., 419ff.; XL, p. 97; XLI, p. 3.

that he includes the starting-point, namely Romanesque, in his definition, which is not concerned with technical or statical qualities. He criticizes Viollet-le-Duc: "The leitmotif of Viollet-le-Duc's discussions on French Gothic is the word and idea of *logique*."[8] He finds it incredible that such great works of art should be supposed to have been inspired by cold logic. The structural lines, he says, may indicate the logic of the construction, but the details encompassed by these structural lines cannot be explained by logic. He admires the *Dictionnaire raisonné*—like everyone else—but "it takes the French cathedrals to pieces."

His chief criticism is directed against the statical interpretation of the flying buttresses and pinnacles. The former merely transmit the load, they do not oppose the counterload (page 109). The latter, the pinnacles, are much too light to be really able to paralyze the thrust of the flying buttresses and the vaults, they have an "imaginary value." The thrust of the flying buttresses against the clerestory wall is indeed minimal—especially when they are supported at this point by a pier or a column. Really statically effective is the external buttress (rising along the aisles). The situation in the ruin of Melrose can be explained in that way. Some people committed the error of assuming that the flying buttress pushed against the vault, whereas it pushes only against the outer buttress. If, therefore, the vault should collapse, there is no reason for the flying buttress to overthrow the wall. The vertical buttress simply remains standing, together with the arch, which now presses on the piers with its own weight only, no longer with that of the vault.

But Hamlin continues inexorably. The engaged shafts are unnecessary; they only *appear* to carry (page 110); consoles would suffice and have often done so. They are "aesthetic logic" in contrast to structural logic and also to scientific logic. Aesthetic logic is, to be sure, a *contradictio in adjecto* but an uncommonly happy paradox. Everyone understands immediately what is meant. Hamlin lists under the heading of this "logic" "the gables, lofty spires, openwork gables, wall traceries, niches, and tabernacles having no function in the structural framework." One ought not first to derive Gothic from structure and then try to eliminate from it everything that is not structure.

Hamlin therefore approves of Late Gothic buildings unreservedly. He quotes Ralph Adams CRAM (1863-1942) to the effect that whatever

[8] Hamlin, *op.cit.*, XL, p. 101.

they may lack of the shining and divine serenity of the thirteenth century, they nevertheless belong among the loveliest works of human hands, and discusses the point in some detail. His conclusion is: "Architecture is, after all, not all science; it is preeminently an art in which imagination and the love of pure beauty of form have their place."[9] This is directed against Viollet-le-Duc, and at a later date Marcel AUBERT (b. 1884) said something similar. What seems so much a matter of course became clearer and clearer, namely that architecture is made up of construction *and* imagination and does not consist merely of one of them. It was, however, easier to acknowledge this fact than to determine conceptually the relationship of the two factors.

The fresh ruins of the First World War afforded a sad opportunity of examining the actual statical conditions. Roger GILMAN (b. 1874) studied principally Reims and Soissons.[10] The result of his unprejudiced and very conscientious investigation was surprising, for the ruins showed that the ribs were in some cases noncarrying and, on the other hand, in many other cases carrying. Consequently Viollet-le-Duc's theory seems to be neither refuted nor proved. Gilman, too, does not regard the flying buttresses as having the function of exercising a thrust against the vault: transmission of the load rather than equilibrium, he says, is what we recognize as the truth of this matter (page 65). This approximates Hamlin's opinion that the statically important structural member is the outer pier buttress (rising outside of the aisle). It must be so stable that it will not collapse outward when the thrust of the vault is transmitted to it. Gilman reflected in general on just what is "logical" in Gothic and concluded that neither the enormous height of the French cathedrals nor the dissolution of the wall and stained glass can be called logical. To erect a solid wall of cut stone would have cost far less in France because building material could be had abundantly and cheaply. Dehio had already written on occasion that the treatment of the stone in Gothic cathedrals cost far more time and consequently money than simple masonry (as in Romanesque buildings). After considering many aspects of the subject Gilman, too, came to the conclusion that Gothic is indeed strikingly logical in its construction but not *merely* logical, and he remarked that it sometimes happens that such a principle (of logic) is transformed in spirit from a means to an end in itself.

9 *Ibid.*, XL, p. 113.

10 Roger Gilman, "The Theory of Gothic Architecture and the Effect of Shellfire at Rheims and Soissons," *American Journal of Archaeology*, XXIV, 1920, p. 37.

Despite this article Viollet-le-Duc continued to be regarded with approval, and years passed without any particular excitement over the aspersions cast on the value of the ribs. A more serious attack was not made until 1928.[11]

Victor SABOURET (1851-[?]) seems to have read neither Porter's book nor Gall's. As an engineer he arrived independently at the conviction that the rib does not carry.[12] His article contains a reference to typical cracks in cross vaults which give a better insight into the actual mechanical processes than had hitherto been enjoyed.[13]

It is a familiar fact that in the case of a semicircular arch the lower part of the arch acts, from the standpoint of mechanics, like a continuation of the pier. The arch can be built up to about 30 degrees without being supported; the stones do not slide off because they are held in position partly by friction, partly by the chemically adhesive power of the mortar after it has hardened. In a completed semicircular arch the distribution of force is such that the upper part of the arch lying between the two pieces that can still be accounted as pertaining to the pier tends by its weight to force the lower parts asunder. If the foundations give up or the piers are too weak, the lower parts of the arch move apart and the result is a crack at a height of about 30 degrees. The middle part of the arch then breaks also, namely in the crown; and here, too, a crack results. The two side cracks are visible from inside, but the crack in the crown can only be seen from the outside, above the vault. All this is true of every transverse arch, which is of course simply a barrel vault with a relatively very short longitudinal axis. It is equally true of a barrel vault of any desired length of longitudinal axis.

If a masonry barrel vault is provided with transverse arches, they carry themselves like any arch and like any transverse section of the barrel vaulting that lies between two transverse arches. The transverse arches do not carry the barrel vault when this consists of stone.[14] They only make the vault unnecessarily heavier, if we judge from the standpoint of purely mechanical function. In the nave of Durham Cathedral transverse arches are present *between* each pair of cross vaults but omitted *within* the pair. Thus, according to Sabouret, transverse arches

[11] Victor Sabouret, "Les voûtes d'arêtes nervurées," *Le Génie Civil*, Paris, 1928, p. 205.

[12] *Idem*, "L'évolution de la voûte romane du milieu du XIe siècle au début du XIIIe," *Le Génie civil*, Paris, 1934, p. 240.

[13] Leonardo da Vinci had already made some observations about cracks in vaults, cf. J. P. Richter, *op.cit.*, II, pp. 77ff.

[14] The transverse arches would carry if the barrel vaulting were made by laying on wooden boards, but here we are talking about stone, smaller than the distances between the transverse arches.

are, wherever placed, merely "decorative," that is to say, not mechanically or statically required.

Cross vaults consist of several portions of barrel vaults. In these portions, the severies, one can call every arch (parallel to the wall, for example) self-carrying, just as in every barrel vault. Accordingly, a cell of the cross vault with a straight, horizontal crown transmits no weight to the longitudinal wall (when all the individual courses of stone in the cell lie horizontal). Since the walls settle differently from the mass of the vault cell, cracks often result in the vault along the wall or, more properly, not *in* the vault but *between* cell and wall—further proof that here no weight is carried over from the vault to the wall, for no pressure can be carried across a gap. Where a separate arch was built against the wall (formeret) the rational reason may have been, among other things, that the builders wanted to cover up the expected crack from the very beginning, but the wall rib (longitudinal rib) is not statically necessary, it is "decorative." This theory was already held by BRUTAILS (1859-1926), who spoke of *couvre-joint.*

Statically, the rib is likewise superfluous: there are cases where it has come away from the vault as a result of settling, so that there is a gap between it and the vault. Sabouret also discusses the vaults that were subjected to bombardment in the First World War, finding in them further proofs of his thesis that the rib is statically just as unnecessary as the transverse arch and the wall arch.

If Viollet-le-Duc's theory is thereby nullified, why were ribs nevertheless built? Sabouret says: "The rib was really born in the Romanesque period on the day when the transverse arches of a continuous barrel vault were created. The transverse arch obviously contributed no reinforcement to such a vault but it justified the rising of the high engaged shafts from the ground by uniting them and giving them the appearance of useful organs."[15] The transverse arch is thus only a consequence of the wall shaft. A similar assertion is made with regard to the rib: "But it soon became evident that the rising of the vertical lines could be still better justified by adding to the transverse arch the ribs on the groins. In an architecture of cut stone, which draws all its decoration from the strengthening of the great lines and their profiling, a molded projection could not be refused to a line as important as that

[15] In the article of 1928, p. 209: "La nervure est vraiment née pendant la période romane, le jour où on a créé le doubleau d'un berceau continu. Le doubleau n'apportait manifestement aucun renforcement à une telle voûte, mais il justifiait l'ascension des hautes colonettes, parties du sol, en les réunissant et leur donnant ainsi l'apparence d'organes utiles."

of the vault groin."[16] This statement made in 1934 is almost the same as what Gall had already said in 1915.

The transverse arches suffice to "justify" the frontal engaged shafts; for *that* purpose ribs are no longer necessary. Nevertheless Sabouret says of the ribs that those frontal transverse arches also justify the engaged shafts subsequently, obviously the rib shafts, and that they are, moreover, a consequence of the stylistic principle as a whole. This principle he characterizes as the strengthening of the dominant lines, which is *structure* in Gall's terminology and in that commonly used. The rib is thus not, as Viollet-le-Duc thought, *real* structure but rather "decorative" structure and a result of other, previously introduced decorative structure, namely the shafts carrying the transverse arches and these arches themselves.

Just this latter point is problematical. Does it suffice to say that the structure of Romanesque called forth the structure of Gothic? Both are, of course, structure. But how can a *new* style be produced by the rib, if they are both the same? Here I see a crack in the theory (as it were, *une fissure de Sabouret lui-même*).

As with Gall, one must say: Both are structure, but not *merely* structure. It does not suffice to say that the structure of Romanesque demanded the structure of Gothic. One would first have to explain how the *frontal* structure of Romanesque called forth the *diagonal* structure of Gothic, and if that proved impossible supplement the statement by saying that the desire for absolutely consistent structure was so strong that the destruction of frontality, one of the most important and basic principles of Romanesque, was accepted as a necessary consequence. But why was diagonality now made the stylistic principle of the subsequent development? We shall return to this point.

In the same year as Sabouret's essay there appeared a book, in a rather popular style, written by René SCHNEIDER (b. 1869-1938).[17] He gives a description of Gothic that makes use of all Viollet-le-Duc's concepts and assertions and sees antiquity and Gothic as opposites: "The Greek temple was an architecture of sheer stability and repose. The Gothic church is a system of forces in motion. The stone lives. The perpetual duel between opposing forces that takes place in the heart of the stone results in a lasting immobility; but it is the opposite of inertia. And one must

16 *Ibid.* "Mais il devint vite évident qu'on justifierait encore mieux l'ascension des lignes verticales, en ajoutant au doubleau les nervures des arêtiers. Dans une architecture de pierre taillée, qui tire toute sa décoration du renforcement des grandes lignes et de leur mouluration, on ne pouvait refuser une saillie profilée à une ligne aussi importante que celle de l'arêtier."

17 René Schneider, *L'art français des origines à la fin du XIIe siècle*, Paris, 1928.

admire this beautiful audacity that places the supports on view on the outside and derives mighty effects from so doing. This is without doubt one of the most profound differences between the art of the Middle Ages and that of antiquity. Building in stone, our masters think like carpenters, sons of the barbarians! To throw an arch of stone across the void like a wooden beam . . . that was a defiance of all traditions."[18] Schneider serves up the barbarian and wood theory again; he has obviously read Courajod and forgets that the Greeks also once used wood (*ces barbares*?). This passage has been quoted here only because it goes back to Viollet-le-Duc's theory of the flying buttress and because Schneider insinuates, rather unexpectedly in this popular account, a doubt as to the usefulness of the flying buttress: "After all, the flying buttress is not an absolutely necessary and constant result of the ribbed vault. The churches of the South, the Saintes Chapelles, dispense with it. . . . Is the flying buttress so necessary even in the great monuments with side aisles? If it fell, would the walls collapse under the pressure of the vault, bringing about total ruin? If this is a vain fear, if Gothic art has there created a superfluous organ, then we must revise all our ideas about its delicate sense of necessity and its rational logic."[19] "But one day it occurs to an anonymous stonemason to throw from one pier of a bay to the other two intersecting ribs. Immediately the thrust of the whole is transmitted and localized at the ends where they rest. . . . Immediately the consequences are derived from the principle with a rigorous logic. Always our logic!"[20]

In 1934 Victor Sabouret published a second article, chiefly concerned with Romanesque buildings, which contributed nothing new to the theory of Gothic. From it we learn, however, that Pol ABRAHAM (b. 1883) had deposited his thesis in the École du Louvre in 1923. He thus arrived independently of Gall and Sabouret, the latter of whom he cites in detail, at the conclusion that the rib does not carry. Since he men-

[18] *Ibid.*, p. 107: "En construisant en pierre, nos maîtres pensent en charpentiers, fils des barbares! Lancer sur le vide . . . un arc de pierre comme un poutre de soutien . . . c'était un défi à toutes les traditions."

[19] *Ibid.*, p. 109: "Du reste, l'arc-boutant n'est pas une conséquence absolument nécessaire et constante de la voûte ogivale. Les églises du midi, les saintes-chapelles, s'en dispensent. . . . Même aux grands monuments à bas-côtés l'arc boutant est-il si nécessaire? S'il tombait, les murs se renverseraient-ils sous la poussée de la voûte, entraînant la ruine totale? Si cette crainte est vaine, si l'art gothique a créé là un organe superflu, c'est qu'il faut réviser toutes nos idées sur son sens délicat de la nécessité et sa logique rationelle."

[20] *Ibid.*, p. 106: "Mais voici qu'un jour un maçon anonyme s'avise de lancer d'un pilier à l'autre, sur une travée deux nervures qui se croisent. Immédiatement la poussée de l'ensemble est transmise et localisé aux extrémités où elles retombent. . . . Immédiatement les conséquences dérivent du principe avec une logique rigoureuse. Toujours notre logique!"

tions neither Porter nor Gall, even in 1934 he did not know their works on the subject.[21] But Abraham goes further than other writers when he criticizes and in his opinion demolishes Viollet-le-Duc's system as a whole and in detail by means of the appartus of mathematics and mechanics. Was Viollet-le-Duc not an architect? Is not every architect who builds vaults that do not collapse an authority, a mathematician, an expert in mechanics? And especially Viollet-le-Duc for whom Gothic itself was a science! No, says Abraham: "It is almost from one end to the other a romanticized mechanics. Romanticized science is moreover a subjective attitude. This is not the place to investigate . . . the circumstances that led him to adopt that strange thesis which reduces the most lyric architecture, that of Beauvais for example, to the level of the narrowest utilitarianism. This venture (*gageure*) can be explained above all on psychological grounds: a magnificent pride, the presentiment that the 'École' would bring him no glory, a sort of suppressed Romanticism, an ashamed Romanticism. Viollet-le-Duc, who had no originality as far as the plastic was concerned and who revealed a sad poverty of artistic imagination, aside from the *pastiche*, too intelligent not to sense his weakness, found his way in a pure construction of the intellect, paradoxical yet prophetic, that of an architecture which, though subject to the narrowest material necessities, nevertheless creates therefrom the very substance of beauty. An admirable idea, powerful and fertile, and one from which the international architecture of the twentieth century has in large measure resulted. But also a combative attitude, a war machine against the Academie in the struggle where he was to figure as the hero of national and modern art opposed to the moribund Graeco-Roman tradition."[22]

This suggests a new aspect to consider in our endeavor to present a history of Gothic theory. Of course, we may ask how the attitudes of

[21] Pol Abraham, *Viollet-le-Duc et le rationalisme médiéval*, Paris, 1934.

[22] *Op.cit.*, p. 102: "Cest à peu près, d'un bout à l'autre, de la mécanique romancée. Science romancée est aussi attitude subjective. Ce n'est pas le lieu de rechercher ici . . . les circumstances qui l'amenèrent à adopter cette thèse étrange, qui ravale l'architecture la plus lyrique, celle de Beauvais par exemple, à l'utilitarisme le plus étroit. Cette gageure s'explique avant tout par des raisons psychologiques: un orgueil magnifique, le pressentiment que 'l'École' ne lui apporterait pas la gloire, une sorte de romantisme refoulé, de romantisme honteux. Viollet-le-Duc qui n'eut pas d'originalité plastique et dont l'imagination artistique était, en dehors du pastiche, d'une attristante pauvreté, trop intelligent pour ne pas sentir sa faiblesse, trouva sa voie dans une pure construction de l'esprit, paradoxale mais prophétique, celle d'une architecture qui, soumise aux plus étroites nécessités matérielles, en ferait, cependant, la substance même de la beauté. Admirable idée, puissante et féconde, et dont l'architecture internationale du XXe siècle est, en grande partie, sortie. Mais, aussi, attitude de combat, machine de guerre, contre l'Académie, dans la lutte où il fera figure de héros de l'art national et moderne contre la tradition gréco-romaine moribonde."

Vasari, Goethe, and others look to the psychologist, but actually it is not a question of the persons but of their theories. In the case of Viollet-le-Duc, Abraham is perhaps not entirely wrong. Nevertheless one should be chary of calling every mistake made in matters of mechanics "science romancée." Perhaps Abraham also was mistaken. Who today has any particular interest in defending Viollet-le-Duc, not to speak of his theory? In no sense, however, is it romanticism, but, as Abraham himself says elsewhere, rationalism. And rationalism and romanticism are not the same thing.[23]

According to Abraham's criticism, the transverse arch neither carries the barrel vault nor the rib the cross vault nor the engaged shafts the transverse arches and ribs. Everyone should be urged to make a thorough study of this presentation of the mechanics of vaults. The action of the effective forces in the vaults is made very vivid by Abraham's reference to the path taken by a ball that, left to itself, rolls down on the exterior of the vault. It does not roll to the wall, of course, but in accordance with the theory that every section parallel to the wall results in a barrel vault which carries itself, along the curve of the section. The ball always rolls in the direction of the strongest curvature and, reaching the hollow line above the groin, rolls on in this channel to the pier.

Abraham demonstrates that even strongly domed vaults exercise no thrust against the wall. His figure 16 shows the path taken by the rolling ball that lands on the part of the vault which, mechanically speaking, still belongs to the pier, without reaching the wall. He likewise refutes Viollet-le-Duc's other thesis. Flying buttresses can never cancel the thrust of the vaults; pinnacles cannot by their weight make the pier more resistant to forces pressing sideways. Abraham cites historical examples to show that neither flying buttresses nor pinnacles were necessary. Many a French cathedral had none and acquired them only when restored by Viollet-le-Duc. Historians of art may thus always be skeptical with regard to French pinnacles. Completely untenable, according to Abraham, appears to be what Viollet-le-Duc said about elasticity. By elasticity is understood the property of certain materials to stretch when pulled or to bend when pressed but to resume their original shape (spatial form) when pull or pressure ceases. There can be no question of this in constructions of stone. Vaults twist out of shape and

[23] Abraham says *Mécanique romançée, science romançée*. The correct translation is "romanticized." Although the meanings of the French and English words are not absolutely identical, the underlying sense is the same.

then come to a standstill, only to move again when subjected to new shifting of forces, and so on. This results in fissures. But the vault never has the tendency to return to its original form.

Thus the result of this investigation is that the interpretation of the mechanical relations in Gothic vaults is actually different from what Viollet-le-Duc had taught. For anyone who follows Abraham's reasoning the *entire* system of the greatest theoretician of Gothic is destroyed. Architectural forms are consequently to be interpreted not from the *structural* but from the *decorative* point of view. We shall revert to this subject.

But Abraham's brilliant refutation of Viollet-le-Duc was immediately doused with cold water. H. MASSON,[24] an engineer in the tradition of Choisy, criticized Abraham's basic thesis in the calmest and most objective way. Abraham's theory that in a barrel vault every cross section carries itself and the transverse arch also carries itself, is essentially correct. But the cohesion of the mortar does bind these parallel cross sections. Of course, if no transverse arches are present, they cannot carry. But if they are present, they carry the neighboring portions of the barrel vault to some extent. Likewise, a barrel vault needs no terminating walls on the narrow sides, as everyone knows, but the surprising discovery has been made that if very strong transverse arches are placed at both ends, the walls of the long sides can be left out. This modern construction reminiscent of feats of magic is called *voûtes autoporteuses*. Now since the ribs can be considered as like the transverse arches, it appears that the rib is statically not so completely useless after all. It is scarcely necessary to go into further detail, which anyone can get by reading Masson. The result is, as in the case of Gilman, a partial rehabilitation of Viollet-le-Duc. He was not always right and not always wrong, so much seems to be established. But just where he was right and where wrong seems to be still fairly unclear. And the same thing can be said, correspondingly, of Abraham's essay.

These debates unquestionably robbed of their feeling of security those who had built on the basis of Viollet-le-Duc's system and, accordingly, the official spokesmen for the old tradition in France, Aubert and Focillon, took up the cudgels.

Marcel Aubert just happened to be on the point of composing a long article on the early ribbed vaults when Abraham made his attack. Since he was apparently able to consult the manuscript or the proofs,

[24] H. Masson, "Le rationalisme dans l'architecture du moyen-âge." *Bulletin monumentale*, Paris, 1935.

he was in a position to take issue with the new situation. The second part of his essay (page 203) investigates "le rôle de la voûte d'ogives" and after mature reflection and with full knowledge of the actual buildings he arrived at the following conclusion:[25]

"The role of the cross ribbed vaults, as the masters of the works in the Isle de France understood them, is thus double.

"First, the cross ribbing facilitates the erection of the vault and gives a certain security to the builder during the settling and hardening of the mortar.

"Then it reinforces the vault on its weak points along the groins and in the crown area, and this all the more when the cells are constructed lightly or of material that is mediocre in quality.

"Strongly supported by the pier buttresses, then by the flying buttresses, it provided the architects of the Middle Ages with a solution to the problem of vaulting, which they had hitherto not succeeded in solving."[26]

He describes how this construction of the architects of the Isle de France conquered the world although nowhere did a like audacity of building manifest itself; then turning to the other side of the phenomenon, he continues: "I add that the ribbed vault has a decorative value also. It heightens the impression of the upward surge produced by these high, narrow naves where the verticals predominate, prolonging under the vaults the ascending lines of the long delicate shafts that, attached to the piers and the walls, mount toward heaven; and it is thus in harmony with the dream that the Gothic architects pursued even to the point of imprudence, as for example in Beauvais."[27]

Ribbed vaults, then, have in addition to their technical, statical advantages still others. Like Gall and Sabouret, Aubert stresses the fact that they are a continuation of the verticals, and there is an inner connection between this and that upward soaring called by Dvořak ***sursum***

[25] Marcel Aubert, "Les plus anciennes croisées d'ogives. . . ," *Bulletin monumentale*, 1934, pp. 1 and 137ff. See in the same volume Abraham's article, pp. 69ff.

[26] *Ibid.*, p. 234: "Le rôle de la croisée d'ogives, tel que l'ont compris les maîtres d'oeuvre de l'Ile-de-France est donc double.

Elle facilite d'abord le montage de la voûte et donne une sécurité certaine au constructeur pendant le tassement et la prise des mortiers.

Elle renforce ensuite la voûte sur ces points faibles le long des arêtes et sur le plan des sommets, et celà d'autant plus que les compartiments sont construits légèrement ou en matériaux de qualité médiocre.

Fortement contrebutée par les murs-boutants, puis les arcs-boutants, elle apporte aux architectes du moyen-âge la solution du problème du voûtement qu'ils n'avaient encore pu résoudre."

[27] *Ibid.*: "J'ajoute que la croisée d'ogives a aussi une valeur décorative. Elle augmente l'impression l'élancement qui se dégage de ces nefs hautes et étroites où dominent les verticales, en prolongeant sous les voûtes les lignes ascendantes des longues et fines colonettes qui, accrochées aux piles et aux murs, filent vers le ciel, et elle répond ainsi au rêve que poursuivaient jusqu'à l'imprudence, à Beauvais par exemple, les architectes gothiques."

corda. Aubert says finally: "In that I recognize the mark of genius in these masters of the Middle Ages who transformed the processes of the mason into the elements of beauty: architecture is not pure construction, it is also an art."[28] For Riegl Gothic was *only* art, for Aubert (as for Viollet-le-Duc) it is *also* art. Aubert obviously means to warn: Do not lose sight of the chief thing!

The ideas of Gerhard ROSENBERG (b. 1912) are based entirely on Viollet-le-Duc, though he is more progressive in that he has a command of modern knowledge of the mechanics of vaults.[29] Although he cites much out-of-the-way literature he does not seem to have heard anything about the whole new debate. Anyone wishing to delve more deeply into the mechanics of vaults should, therefore, note this essay, but it does not further the elucidation of the problem as it pertains specifically to art history.

Henri FOCILLON (1881-1943) continued the fight on Viollet-le-Duc's side but without calling the opposing party entirely wrong. He asks: "What is the true function of the rib? Does it carry? Does it support, does it relieve the vault? . . ."[30] He lumps all the previous questions together, the thesis of the mere *couvre-joint*, of the "valeur purement plastique," and so on: "The rib is (for the opponents of Viollet-le-Duc's thesis) a plastic element having also the purpose of suggesting an illusory structure."[31] Focillon here says the same thing that was remarked above in objection to Porter's theory, namely that if the rib is useful during construction the same is true also of the wooden centerings, which are in any case necessary in the construction of these same ribs. Why then *cintres permanents* of stone if they do not carry? But Focillon thinks the rib is found at the point of greatest pressure; its spur has a contributory effect since it is of better, harder material and can be constructed in a pure line before the cells are filled in with masonry. He differentiates the various stages of construction. The mediaeval architect thought much as Viollet-le-Duc did. But—and now comes the chief point—he did not merely *think*. Architecture is visible,

[28] "En cela, je retrouve la marque du génie de ces maîtres du moyen-âge qui transforment en éléments de beauté des procédés de maçons: l'architecture n'est pas construction pure, elle est aussi un art."

[29] Gerhard Rosenberg, "The Functional Aspect of the Gothic Style. . . ," *Journal of the Royal Institute of British Architects,* XLIII, 1936, pp. 273ff. and 364ff.

[30] Henri Focillon, *Art d'occident. Le Moyen-âge romain et gothique,* Paris, 1938, p. 143. "Quelle est la vraie fonction de l'ogive? Est-elle portante? Soutient-elle, soulage-t-elle la voûte? . . ."

[31] "L'ogive est (pour les adversaires de la thèse de Viollet-le-Duc) un élément plastique ayant aussi pour but de suggérer une structure illusoire." (p. 144)

it has light and shade. "To fail to appreciate the plastic elements—and even the effects of the illusion—would be to commit as grave an error as to describe an edifice according to its plan alone. The rib is of a *constructive, structural*, and *optical* value."[32] Focillon remarks here rather casually that a *purer line* could be constructed by means of the rib. It is convincing that this desire for the pure line as opposed to the imprecise one of the groins was the real reason for the introduction of the rib.

Focillon did not enter into a discussion of the details of this debate. And, for that matter, how could historians of art be expected to reveal the mysteries of statics and technics? We can get a clearer picture of the present state of the problem by formulating a few groups of questions after we have come to the realization that the ribs and, like them, the other structural members of Gothic, have both a purely practical (nonartistic) and an aesthetic (or even artistic) aspect. The former is called abbreviatedly and inexactly the constructive, the latter, also inexactly, the decorative. Let us turn to the former.

1. What did the architects of Gothic think about the "constructive" aspect of the ribbed vaults? We have only one single piece of evidence for that, the expertise of Chartres from the year 1316, where it is said that the four transverse arches that help to *carry the vault* are good and strong and that the four ribs that *carry* the keystone are good and strong. This proves that the masters of 1316, who knew something about the matter if anyone did, believed that the *transverse arches carried*; one *can* interpret the passage to mean that they also believed that the *ribs* carried. The latter point is not so absolutely certain.

2. What actually takes place in the vaults? The Gothic masters built on the basis of their progressing experiments. Their knowledge of mechanics and mathematics was not sufficient to explain what actually happens in the vaults and their supports. Can we do that today? The differences of opinion among the various writers on the subject can only make us very skeptical. Today we know more than Viollet-le-Duc knew but we have lost all certainty of judgment. The historian of art who has learned enough mechanics and mathematics to be able to read this branch of the literature intelligently is nevertheless not qualified to decide whether the rib carries, or sometimes carries, and when. He can, however, collect the material and pass it on to the physicist. The

[32] *Op.cit.*, p. 147: "Méconnaître la part des données plastiques—et même des effets d'illusion—serait commettre une erreur aussi grave que de définir un édifice d'après son seul plan. L'ogive est valeur *constructive, structural* et *optique*."

student who hears for the first time what a cross vault is rejoices when he has happily comprehended that it is a penetration of two half cylinders. Anyone who then continues to concern himself with cross vaults for the next fifty years discovers that there are very different cross vaults even among the groined vaults and certainly among the ribbed vaults. He finds, furthermore, that things become more and more complicated the more he goes into them. A ribbed vault is constructed in two stages. First the ribs are erected and, when they have set, the cells. But in the case of the latter one can proceed in different ways. Assuming that the movable arch form (cerce) is used, the builder is still free to lay the stones parallel to the line of the crown or diagonally. And the statics always differs according to this position of the stones, the material of the rib, of the cells, and the mortar. For the mortar one even needs a chemist as well! But what concern is all this of ours? Certainly it is interesting, but we should do better to wait until the physicists have agreed among themselves.

3. In the meantime we can turn our attention to the second aspect of the ribbed vault, that called "decorative." And therewith we come back to Abraham. If the whole complicated apparatus is unnecessary from a rational point of view, what is its significance *aesthetically*? Abraham answers that all those structural members—ribs, transverse arches, engaged shafts—have the function "of creating a plastic illusion." And how is the rib to be explained? "There is obviously a discord, there is a rupture in the edifice between the vertical parts and the vaults. The transverse arch will be a first means of continuing in the vaults the stability of the pier, of having good and precise work, rich stonework from the ground level to the top of the building. But if the transverse arch suffices to regularize the barrel vault, it is insufficient for the groined vault and much more so for the dome. The diagonal arches will therefore satisfy one or the other of these two cases. With their help not only the groined vaults and the domes but also the intermediate vaults between these types . . . can become as stable in aspect as the piers themselves: the stonework of the whole building will have become homogeneous in appearance."[33]

[33] "Il y a désaccord évident, il y a rupture, dans l'édifice, entre les parties verticales et les voûtes. Le doubleau sera un premier moyen de prolonger dans la voûte la fermeté de la pile, d'avoir du travail bien fait et précis, de la maçonnerie riche de la base au faîte de l'édifice. Mais si le doubleau suffit à régulariser le berceau, il est insuffisant pour la voûte d'arêtes et bien plus encore pour la coupole. Les arcs diagonaux vont alors satisfaire à l'un ou l'autre de ces deux cas. Par leur moyen, non seulement les voûtes d'arêtes et les coupoles, mais ces voûtes intermédiaires entre ces deux types . . . pourront être aussi fermes dans leur aspect

That is essentially the same as what Sabouret said or what Gall had already said. To Abraham the chief term for the positive explanation of Gothic is "l'illusion d'une structure." But does not Romanesque also produce an illusion of structure? Yes! But that of *another* structure. It is the old, so frequent error of confusing two things because one gives them both the same name. The important point now is to say what this otherness is. That has become the precise question after the long series of opinions from Petrarch to Abraham.

Abraham, it seems, sensed this and almost answered the question. He contrasts St.-Lazare of Autun (1120) with the nave of St.-Denis (1231).

"In St.-Lazare of Autun the lines discerned by the eye are geometrical lines formed by the intersection of two surfaces of considerable extent and differently lighted: two vertical planes for the edges of the piers, vertical planes and cylinders for the edges of the arcades, and clumsy surfaces for the groined vaults.

"In St.-Denis the lines observed by the eye are the engaged shafts themselves, the ribs themselves, and also the moldings of the arcades. The play of lines and of materialized lines has been substituted for the simple play of surfaces. The revolution is especially profound in the vault and constitutes truly the great novelty of Gothic."[34]

Abraham has thus said that the difference between Romanesque and Gothic is *not* that Romanesque offers no illusion of structure whereas Gothic does, *but* that the *profiling* is different. What is this difference?

Abraham chose a Burgundian example with pilasterlike members in the nave because that intensified the contrast to Gothic. But a nave with round engaged shafts throughout as, for example, in St.-Étienne in Nevers, is just as Romanesque as Autun. And if one grants that, then St.-Étienne in Caen in its original state is just as Romanesque as Autun. Why are the engaged shafts throughout St.-Étienne in Nevers and St.-

---

que les piles elles-mêmes: la maçonnerie de toute la bâtisse sera devenue, dans son aspect, homogène." (p. 110)

[34] "A Saint-Lazare d'Autun les lignes discernées par l'oeil sont des lignes géometriques formées par l'intersection de deux surfaces d'étendue notable et diversement éclairées: deux plans verticaux pour les arêtes des piles, des plans verticaux et des cylindres pour les arêtes des arcades et des surfaces gauches pour celles des voûtes d'arêtes.

A Saint-Denis, les lignes que l'oeil réalise sont les colonettes elles-mêmes, les nervures elles-mêmes et aussi les moulures des arcades. Le jeu des lignes et des lignes matérialisées s'est substitué au simple jeu des surfaces. La révolution est surtout profonde dans la voûte et constitue véritablement la grande nouveauté gothique." (p. 111)

Étienne in Caen Romanesque, those in St.-Denis, on the other hand, Gothic?

Wilhelm RAVE (b. 1893)[35] seems to have been ignorant of all the literature since Gall and to have discovered the problem of the rib for himself. First he inveighs against Dehio and corrects him in detail; then he discusses pointed arches, the rib, and the system of abutments from the standpoint of statics. As far as the pointed arch is concerned, his conclusion is "that the pointed arch, which is always cited first as the characteristic mark of the style and is also almost exclusively used in wall openings and groinings, loses much of its supremacy in the construction of the Gothic vault and does not play the role here in our statical investigation that one would at first expect."(p. 197) This judgment, of course, does not apply to the significance of the pointed arch for the geometrical construction.

Of the rib he says: "We have already seen that the statical function of the rib in the completed vault is no longer worth mentioning. One could even remove the underlying ribs entirely, as the wooden centerings were also taken away again after the completion of the vaults. And one could chisel off the external parts of the inlaid ribs without causing any noticeable diminution of stability. *They are all, at bottom, decorative ribs.* Consequently there is no point in making 'ethical' distinctions between genuine, carrying ribs and false, decorative ones."

In the same year, 1939, Focillon, together with friends and pupils, published a collection of articles on the problems of the "ogive."[36] How should the word ogive be translated here? In the third article ogive is understood to be the pointed arch, as it was formerly in Caumont's view; in the other articles it is used for both transverse arch and rib, in all their various possibilities. We recall that especially in the eighteenth century and in the nineteenth down to Wetter scholars sought to discover what was the origin of the pointed arch. Since this is important for Gothic, the question was entirely legitimate; but finally it had to be recognized that there were many pointed arches that did not give rise to a style, particularly not to that which we today call Gothic.

[35] Wilhelm Rave, "Über die Statik mittelalterlicher Gewölbe," *Deutsche Kunst und Denkmalpflege*, XLI, 1939, p. 193.

[36] "Le problème de l'ogive." *Recherche*, No. 1, Paris, 1939. This first number of the journal *Recherche* contains six essays: 1) Henri Focillon, "Le problème de l'ogive." 2) Pol Abraham, "Les données plastiques et fonctionnelles du problème de l'ogive." 3) Walter H. Godfrey, "L'arc ogival, raison esthétique plutôt que nécessité fonctionnelle." 4) Eli Lambert, "La croisée d'ogives et l'architecture islamique." 5) Jurgis Baltrusaitis, "La croisée d'ogives dans l'architecture transcaucasienne." 6) Marcel Aubert, "Origine et développement de la voûte sur croisée d'ogives."

Moller's sarcastic remark that even Euclid knew the pointed arch can be supplemented by a reference to the intersecting circles in the ornamentation of prehistoric art. After Wetter the question could only read: when and where was the pointed arch connected with the quadripartite ribbed vault? Wetter did not yet know that the earliest ribs were not pointed at all but semicircular or even in the form of a segmental arch. The architect Bilson was the first to localize historically the introduction of a pointed arch into the vault: transverse arches in the nave of Durham around 1130;[37] pointed treatment of the ribs, which was what Wetter really had in mind, followed later. For the age after Wetter the question was not "Where did the first *pointed arch* occur?" but "When and where did the first *pointed rib* occur?"

From this there follows the next question, as it seems: "Where did the first rib appear?" Since the authors of the articles in *Recherche* call all kinds of arches in vaults ogives, there opens out before them a wide field, including Armenia where the rudimentary stages of the rib can be found. Again it may be said that since the rib is an important member for Gothic, one must regard the search for its antecedents as legitimate. But the logical situation is similar to that in the case of the pointed arch. As far as the problem of Gothic is concerned the question is not: "Where do ribs occur?" but "Where were ribs joined with quadripartite vaults?" or, as Focillon expresses it more generally, with "*voûtes à pénétration*."

Inasmuch as these essays have to do with the antecedents of the Gothic ribs and thus prove the existence of un-Gothic "ribs" they should be gratefully received. One must simply avoid any confusion of terms and never lose sight of the ambiguities. In the German language—at least in recent literature on the history of art—*Gurt* means (in three-aisled churches) the transverse arch from a pier to its opposite in the nave or from a pier to the wall in the aisle; *Rippe* or "rib," on the other hand, is the diagonal arch and in the later development also the horizontal stone member in the crown of the vault (*Scheitelrippe*, ridge rib, *lierne*), as well as an arch or portion of an arch in reticular and star vaults. The English language even today often uses "rib" for "transverse arch," while the German gets into difficulties when in developed Gothic the transverse arches receive the same profile as the ribs. Despite all this it is clear that both arches acquire their significance partly through their *position* in the general disposition of the building,

[37] Ernst Gall, *Niederrheinische. . .* , p. 41.

partly through their connection with different kinds of ceiling. In the first case we distinguish frontal and diagonal arches, calling the former transverse arches, the latter ribs; in the second case we speak of diaphragmic arches (*Schwibbogen*) when the arch is walled vertically up to the flat ceiling (Haouran, and so on), or of ribs when the arch is placed below a domical vault (half-dome in apses), domed vault, or quadripartite vault, always, however, diagonally. Only in the case of domes is this terminology precarious, because they may contain both frontal and diagonal arches simultaneously, which we then call either all transverse arches or all ribs. In the case of the narthex of the church of the Holy Apostles in Ani (Armenia) the diaphragmic carry portions of flat ceilings but in the middle field between the two pairs of diaphragmic arches there is a dome that rises on the horizontals of the enclosing masonry (cf. the illustration in the article by Baltrusaitis, page 77); here, too, one ought *not* to call the diaphragmic arches ogives.

Whether or not there is agreement on terminology, the fact remains that from none of the forms that are called ogives in these articles did *Gothic* ogives result, that is to say, ribs, which called forth that consistent transformation and adaptation of the rest of the forms of the building, the results of which we term Gothic. Only the combination of the rib, in other words the diagonal arch, with the groined quadripartite vault gave rise to Gothic. It may be said that the tranverse arches in the tower halls of Bayeux, in the midst of the region where we surmise that the earliest Gothic ribbed vaults originated, must have suggested to the architects the idea of applying arches within vaulting, and these suggestive transverse arches are descended from other transverse arches that can be traced back to Armenia. But this concentration on filiation obscures the problem.

What is meant by this last statement can easily be made clear. Wetter's formula contains four elements. One does not speak of the pier, buttresses, certainly not of flying buttresses, when the beginnings of Gothic are being sought, because the system of abutments was introduced only relatively late. But the first element that Wetter lists is the pier. No one has yet asked where the pier came from. Scholars were interested only in discovering when the Romanesque pier developed into a Gothic one and what, then, distinguishes a Gothic from a non-Gothic pier. To search for the antecedents of the rib by extending the meaning of the word and accordingly the territory as well is as much an obfuscation of the problem as though one were to ask about the origin of the pier. In both cases it is a question of the epithet Gothic; we seek the *Gothic* rib, the *Gothic* pier, just as we do the *Gothic* quadripartite vault, and so on. We learn what Gothic is by studying those buildings that are classically Gothic. From the standpoint of methodology Wetter was right in deriving his formulation from classical Gothic. Our task now is to demonstrate the stages of the process that began with primitive experiments and led to the classical peak and beyond. For the accomplishment of this task the studies of Bilson and Gall (in his first publication of 1915) are still of primary importance.

The articles in *Recherche* are not merely concerned with these questions. Focillon in particular tried to see all aspects of the phenomenon, the geometrical, mechanical, plastic, and optical (page 20), and it is in allusion to Fiedler and Wölfflin that he says: "Even though it is not a revolutionary novelty to think that architecture was made for the eye (*pour la vue*) and that its 'optical' data, which are neither purely a matter of taste nor vague caprice, belonging to the history of forms, illumine the history of the spirit, it is well to recall it sometimes to mind."[38] Thus in the efforts to explain the rib the notion emerges over and over again that it always carries "for the eye"; that it is interesting for the architect who builds it or the engineer who judges it according to its mechanics to know whether it *really* carries; but that for the architect who creates its design or who beholds it as an architect, that is to say, as an *artist in building*, the other aspect (one might say the appearance, the illusion) is the only important one. Both "appearance" and "illusion" are dubious terms; applied to art they create the impression that it is being accused of deception, and from this point of view, from the ethical side, can be explained both Viollet-le-Duc's endeavor to prove the actuality of the carrying and other functions and the exaggeration of Fiedler, Wölfflin, and his adherents, who emphasized the aspect of "seen-ness" so strongly that almost everything else is forgotten. One ought to invert Aubert's dictum (which goes back to Viollet-le-Duc): architecture is not only art, it is also "construction," which here must be understood to include statics, mechanics, and economic planning.

But in that classical pronouncement Focillon went even further, asserting that the optical data "qui ne sont ni pur goût, ni vague caprice" —which means about the same thing as Wölfflin's "not everything is possible in all ages"—belong not merely to the history of forms but also to the history of ideas.

[38] *Recherche*, p. 27: "Si ce n'est pas une nouveauté révolutionaire de penser que l'architecture est faite pour la vue et que ses données 'optiques,' qui ne sont ni de pur goût ni de vague caprice, appartenant à l'histoire des formes, éclairent l'histoire de l'esprit, il est bon de le rappeler quelquefois."

Whatever degree of clarity the thought of generations appears to have achieved with regard to this subject, there nevertheless remains that unclearness resulting from the alternatives of "structural" and "decorative." All writers seem to assume that everyone understands what is meant by "decorative." But one need only ask: Is the rib an adornment, *decor*? Foliage on a capital, statues on a portal are adornment, but the rib? If the rib is adornment one arrives at the point of calling transverse arches and pier shafts that also, as, for example, Sabouret did. There is then no longer any stopping place. Are the bases simply adornment, and so on? What is there in a cathedral that is not adornment? Is it perhaps not an adornment in its entirety, a decoration of the city and the landscape? One scholar may answer yes to all these questions, the other no. But then they should both define what they mean by adornment; it is even more imperative to go beyond the conceptual level of mere adornment, and to say what ornament and what decoration ought to signify.[39] Not the choice of terms is important but the meaning that one wishes to have associated with them.

The meaning of the word decorative as used by the authors just considered is made clear enough, even without more detailed investigation, by their repeated references to *illusion*. That is already implied in Hamlin's "aesthetic logic." The aesthetic impression blots out any real or supposed knowledge of the mechanics of forces. The rib bends—but only apparently, for, statically speaking, it does not bend. Apparently the rib rises and the engaged shaft and the pier rise, but statically they bear down, and one need pulleys to raise the individual stones slowly and set them in place. And so one could go on arguing. Most authors who have said the rib was decorative used the word as a synonym for illusionary.

From this it follows that the master of Gothic who was responsible for the production and durability of its stylistic monuments had to test the stones for stability and be thoroughly acquainted with their mechanical (statical) behavior. That task he had in common with the masters of all the other styles; what he wanted as a *Gothic* builder, however, was the creation of the aesthetic impression of a rising and streaming of forces and spaces, the bending of the ribs, and so on. It remains an inescapable duty of the builder, the technician, the architect as *ingeniere*, to know structural mechanics so that his work will not collapse; but the art historian, who wants to understand the architect as

39 All three concepts of adornment (*Schmuck*), ornament, and decoration are defined, as I understand them, in the *System der Kunstwissenschaft*, p. 356, etc. See its Index.

artist, comes back to Fiedler's formula: Art exists for the eye. This does not mean that he should be blind to the work of art as a mechanical object but that he *dare* not be blind to that which for art is the essential.

The whole dispute about the physical question of whether the rib does or does not carry thus tends to culminate in the psychological-aesthetic question of what it is "for the eye."

4. The Aesthetic and Stylistic Function of the Cross-ribbed Vault

RODIN said of the molding: "It contains the whole energy of the architect, expresses all his thought." His sketches represent not merely "moldings" but also all types of profiles. There are cross sections of piers, of arcade arches, of ribs; he occasionally draws them in his perspective sketches as we see them in the joints of the courses of stone and the radial stones of the arches.

What was done by Rodin, the impressionistic sculptor, is exactly what we find in countless travel sketches drawn by architects from the time of Villard de Honnecourt on. Every historian of art who is concerned with Gothic makes a note of the profiles, for they, together with ground plan and photographs, enable him to reconstruct the entire building in his memory. These sketches of profiles repeat what the architectural designer specified and, especially in Gothic, had to specify. Bonaventura, for example, determined in Milan the profile according to which the piers were to be constructed, and in so doing left a decisive mark on the whole building. The profile is not the sole deciding factor; everyone knows that it is also important how many piers one builds, what the intervals are, and what the elevations, but even these rhythms and proportions by no means exhaust all the possibilities. The profiles, however, are particularly important for the impression created on the beholder. Neither the casual traveler nor the faithful believer who goes every Sunday to the same Gothic or non-Gothic church pays any attention to the profiles, but these determine the impression such persons receive all at once and without analyzing it, synthetically. Just as the architect-designer must decide each time which profile to draw, so the architectural historian must observe the form of the profile attentively when he analyzes the synthetic impression. He then finds that there are Romanesque profiles and Gothic profiles, and that these are essentially different from each other.[1]

This difference is in its ultimate effect the same as that between Romanesque groined vaults and Gothic ribbed vaults. It is best to orient oneself first by the simplest theoretical examples, cross vaults above a square ground plan with horizontal barrel vaults for the cells, in the one case with *groins,* in the other with *ribs.* In both cases spatial penetrations are indicated and in both cases half ellipses result at the points of intersection. But in the groined vault the cells lying opposite each other form mathematically direct horizontal continuations without separation; to the eye the groined vault is poised above the four corner piers as a unit, it remains horizontal in position. The ribbed vault changes this character into its opposite; the ribs destroy the horizontal character and produce a vertical reorientation.[2] For the ribs are *arches* and any arch, be it that of an arcade or a door or a window, is inconceivable and invisible without the plane (in these instances the vertically upright plane) in which it is situated. An opening in the wall is not conceivable unless we first think of the wall as a whole and then as opened, as pierced. A wire bent in the shape of a semicircle and hanging free in the air creates the idea of the vertical plane in which it is located. This is also true of a half ellipse, and consequently the elliptical groin of the simple (Roman) groined vault also implies a vertical plane. But only *one*—mathematically thin—plane. Every arch in a wall or a transverse arch stretching from pier to pier, on the other hand, creates not only *one* plane but *two* parallel planes corresponding to its *thickness*; it creates a vertical *layer* of space. In a Romanesque nave each transverse arch creates such a narrow, vertical layer of space between two bays, and whether the beholder is conscious of it or not it is recognized as the spatial boundary *between* the bays when one walks through them or even when one stands still and simply looks. When one walks through, one can say to oneself: I am going from the first bay into the second by crossing the separating spatial layer of the transverse arch. If the transverse arch is carried down to the ground by means of its supports, the architecture exercises an irresistible compulsion to do this. Our counting of the bays is also based on these separating spaces.

[1] Frederick Apthorp Paley, *A Manual of Gothic Mouldings,* 4th ed. enlarged by W. M. Fawcett, London, 1877.

[2] That holds not merely for the ribs, here theoretically assumed, but also for the early segmental-arch ribs and the semicircular ribs. The introduction of the pointed arch into the rib intensifies the verticalism of its vertical plane that is characteristic of every rib.

Since *every* arch exercises this function of creating a vertical layer of space, the same is also true of the rib; it no longer permits the undisturbed continuation of one cell into its opposite but divides the cells by means of the vertical lamellae of space that can be restricted to the vault area but are, however, continued downward as soon as engaged shafts are placed beneath the ribs and the rib arch together with its rib shafts becomes a diagonally placed archway between two piers that are diagonally opposite each other.

Willis coined the term archway[3] for this unit of two supports, vaulted and connected by an arch. It is fitting to turn back to him also because his second chapter is entitled: "On Mechanical and Decorative Construction." He defines the former as *actual* construction, the latter as *apparent* construction. Using Willis' term we may say: because the ribbed vault has two intersecting "archways" there are created in every vaulting compartment two intersecting, diagonally situated, vertical layers of space. We no longer have a vault that is, as it were, all of a piece, but one consisting of *four* separate cells incapable of independent existence. The vault is "divided," separated into interdependent fragments of space. This is indeed the core of what we call Gothic in its *initial stage*: the rib substitutes for the Romanesque groined vault with its additive effect the divisive Gothic. (The Romanesque quadripartite vault, although a penetrative form, is placed above the lower space additively.)

The terms addition and division, for which better expressions have not yet been found, have led to misunderstandings because they were taken *arithmetically*. Subtraction in arithmetic is the opposite of addition, for subtraction means a real taking away. *Geometrical* division, on the other hand, is not a taking away, for the parts remain, as, for instance, when one draws the diagonal or both diagonals in a square; the figure is divided without anything's being subtracted. It is this *geometrical subdivision* that is meant by division of space as the opposite of *geometrical addition*. For in the case of geometrical addition it is, correspondingly, also not a question of the arithmetical calculation or calculability of the sum; one does not calculate the area of two bays of Romanesque buildings when one makes a statement about their geometrical addition but simply establishes the fact that both bays, although "parts" of the nave, are nevertheless not "parts" in the same sense as in Gothic buildings. In each case they are parts, but their characters as

[3] In the book by Willis cited above (p. 529, n. 5).

such are very different, even diametrically opposite. In the first case the parts are "subwholes" that preserve their independence within the "superwhole" to use the terms of Gestalt psychology.[4] In the second case they are fragments without independence. In the first case they are *also* parts, in the second *only* parts. And again the meaning of the word division is not that one should calculate arithmetically what part of the whole this fragment is, as, for example, when there are ten bays, a tenth of the nave, but that one should recognize the geometrical fact that the nave is the descriptively prescribed primary whole and the bays the result of descriptively secondary division.

The word descriptive means here that the process is not "genetic." The genesis of a rectangle consisting of two equal squares can be imagined as a process either of joining a second square to a given one or, on the other hand (in a sketch of the Old Sacristy in Florence), of first giving the outline of the rectangle and then creating the two squares by drawing the appropriate middle line. That led to the idea that the figure could be called both added and subdivided. This would be correct if the concepts were meant genetically, but the phenomenon that is here concealed—and which is fundamental in far greater spheres than the differentiation of Romanesque and Gothic—must be understood and descriptively defined as such. The question is not how the figure is *produced* but of what it *consists*.[5] However one imagines that the figure of the rectangle with its middle line has come into being, it can be differentiated, for example, from a figure that consists of a

[4] The terms *Unterganzes* and *Oberganzes* have been coined by Max Wertheimer in his Gestalt-psychology, he has used them orally since about 1900.

[5] These concepts of addition and division have been criticized by Edgar Wind in his article: "Zur Systematik der künstlerischen Probleme" (*Zeitschrift für Ästhetik und allgemeine Kunstwissenschaft*, XVIII, Stuttgart, 1925, p. 485). He realized that these concepts are not to be taken arithmetically, but rather that they apply to the putting together of single pieces and to the creating of parts by dividing a whole geometric figure. He also understood that they have a meaning quite different from that of geometrical principles, and that even the polarity of the concepts is based on aesthetic empathy. Yet he said: "Whether in an acute triangle I draw the altitude, thus dividing it into two right-angled triangles, or whether I start with these two right-angled triangles and put them together so that they form an acute triangle, the configuration remains the same." This nobody will deny, but it is beside the point. *Aesthetically* this acute triangle with its altitude will always be "divided" because the base which the altitude touches at its lower end has an angle of 180 degrees, while that at the apex of the triangle and at the upper end of the altitude is less than that. The outline remains constant regardless of the altitude and the main triangle remains *one* divided in two. If on the contrary one were to put the two right-angled triangles together in such a way that their position was altered, the outline of this configuration would be broken by an angle of less than 180 degrees (namely 90) and both triangles would inevitably give the impression of being and remaining *two* separate units added one to the other. These remarks represent only a small portion of Wind's general comments which cannot be discussed here.

larger and a smaller square, like the ground plan of the Old Sacristy of San Lorenzo in Florence by Brunelleschi. The difference between these two composite figures is geometrically determined by the re-entering angles within the common outline. Seen from within these angles are 270 degrees (three right angles), from without 90 degrees. In the case of a junction of two equal squares, on the other hand, the angle at the place where the corner points coincide is 180 degrees.

This is an unambiguous geometrical differentiation. From a purely *geometrical* point of view the figures are *different* but not opposites. *Aesthetically*, however, they are not merely different but also *opposites.* For when the angle is 180 degrees, we have the aesthetic *feeling* that the total contour of the rectangle is primary (constitutionally, not genetically!). The outline of the "whole" is unaffected by the interior division and the interior division is thus aesthetically secondary. When, on the other hand, the angle is greater than 180 degrees, we have the feeling that the total contour of the "octagon" of Brunelleschi's sacristy (which has six salient and two re-entrant corners) is secondary (constitutionally, not genetically!). In this case, therefore, we do not speak of an "octagon" at all. Each of the two squares seems to preserve its own original square outline; and now it is this outline of the "part," of the subwhole, that persists unaffected, although the juxtaposition has created a new total contour. The word unaffected indicates an *aesthetic* empathy with respect to the geometrical figures. We endow them with life and ascribe to them the power of feeling independent, respectively dependent. The geometrical characteristic of the angular magnitude (of 180 degrees, or of less than 180 degrees in contrast to that of more than 180 degrees) refers to the determination now of the lack of a re-entering angle, now of the presence of one. Because in the case of these spatial forms an exact angular measurement is possible, we are in a position to use the geometrical formulation for an exact, *rational* differentiation of aesthetic phenomena. The aesthetic interpretation of the figures, however, remains itself *irrational.* We project ourselves into these squares. The squares themselves are merely geometrical figures, but the aesthetically vivified squares have become human, psychical, personal, and as such their existence seems to be now independent, now interdependent; because *these* characteristics are opposites, we speak of *polarity.* What lies behind such terminology is *our* self-estimation either as isolated, sovereign persons or as persons reciprocally linked to others. Either we have only our own contour (figuratively speaking) or we are embraced by a larger, common contour, be it that of family, city, state, universe. The aesthetically vivified squares become form symbols of the meaning of independence and, on the other hand, of dependence and "absolute dependence" in Schleiermacher's sense, including everything that echoes or can echo in these words. It is our feelings of independence (totality) and interdependence (partiality) that find their form symbols in the styles. They are the psychologically primary element.

What can be learned from the paradigmatic figures that have been reduced to lines remains valid when for these one-dimensional lines three-dimensional bodies are substituted: walls, piers, arches, and so on. The rectangle consisting of two squares, which in the linear figure can only be looked upon as division of space, becomes, when a sequence of two bays, either additive or divisive (thus either Romanesque or Gothic) according to the form of the piers and the transverse arches. Instead of the intermediate point of the linear sketch of two square bays we have in a Romanesque pier a rectangular wall member with two re-entering corners in plan, or—from a three-dimensional standpoint—re-entering vertical edges; the corresponding thing holds for the Romanesque transverse arch. The Gothic pier, the more "Gothic" it becomes, does indeed produce *one* re-entering corner, but because of the change from the rectangular form of Romanesque to the triangular forms of Gothic profiles there is a gliding back and forth on the part of the two bays; they have become spatially a unit. The French Gothic architects shaped the bases as half octagons and turned the abacus of the capitals in such a way that one point falls in the middle between two bays. The English Gothicists were even more consistent and gave the bases and abaci round shapes (semicircles or larger sectors) which precluded re-entering angles as such. The entire development of Gothic is essentially a transformation of Romanesque into a style of partiality by means of various solutions of the problem of divesting the profiles of their additive character, so that the spaces, though they do have boundaries, nevertheless glide past them.

To follow this process in detail is only possible in a circumstantial history of Gothic.[6] Of the rib it can be said that as an arch it is "apparent structure" in a cross vault and at the same time "divisive." It should not be called adornment, it is not *decorative,* nor is it "*decorative* structure," but it is—what else could it be—*architectonic.* It is a structural member, a work of creative imagination. But every structural member

[6] This is the aim of my *History of Gothic,* which is now in the press for the Pelican History of Art. It will be published in 1960.

and every building as a whole are simultaneously useful works dependent on technique, statics, economic planning. Thus with regard to the rib there also come into play the factors of construction, durability, economy. They interest the man who commissions the work, the architect, the stonemason, the carpenter who builds the scaffoldings, and they also interest the historian of art, though not as problems of art.

What does interest us is the significance of the rib—that it is diagonally divisive because of its profile (which is called, inexactly, plastic)—and the resulting symbolical significance of this form, realized by way of aesthetic empathy, for the idea of the dependence of the part upon the whole. We shall return to this latter point in the next chapter.

It should be added here that the rib presumably originated because of the unprecise groin curves that were obtained as a result of the intersection of the wooden planking, for the intersection produced curves of double flexure and the weight of the stones embedded in mortar pressed the wooden sheathing out of shape. If the builders began instead with *centerings for the groins themselves*, there was a better prospect of obtaining *precise lines*. The radical solution was the *stone rib*, that is to say, the *transference* of the transverse arch to the place of the groin. Inasmuch as the transverse arches were a preliminary to this process it is a legitimate task to be on the look-out for transverse arches in barrel vaults (Bayeux, etc.) and domes and half domes in apses. But whereas these never produced a Gothic, the ribbed cross vaults were the beginning of Gothic—even in their initial stage when the ribs were segmental arches (because the builders wanted to approach the form of the ellipse).

The ribbed quadripartite vault destroyed the unity of the Romanesque style, which was based (among other things) on frontality and addition. Faced with the question of whether the cross rib should therefore be abandoned, the generation of around 1090 in Durham and Normandy decided in the negative because the aesthetic advantage of clean lines could be achieved in no other way. The retention of the rib meant that everything else had to be *adapted* to it, and just that process is the history of Gothic as an architectural style.

But despite its aesthetic advantage of replacing the ugly, depressed lines of the groins by means of regular curves, the rib would not have been retained had it not been in complete harmony with the spirit of the age. Diagonality and spatial subdivision were welcome because they were symbols of the union of fragmentary parts and men were themselves tending to adopt this attitude toward life. The rib is an "architectonic" structural member—only later did it become "decorative," in the reticular, star, and fan vaults; it is spatial, optical, and an expression of a force. It is all of these things at one and the same time, and immediately or soon after its introduction proved itself to be useful for and during the process of building. Insofar as it also corresponded to the spirit of the age it was still more: it was the symbol of that new spirit. This brings us to the question of the essence, not merely of the rib, but of Gothic in general.

5. The Essence of Gothic

ALMOST everyone who has ever reflected and written about Gothic has tried to fathom its "essence." In order to clarify the concept of essence it is helpful to distinguish it from that of the "essential." When surgeons differentiate between essential and inessential parts within the human body they mean what is necessary or unnecessary for the continued existence of the patient. But they do not thereby define the essence of man. An arm can be amputated, it is not necessary to life, but for a violinist it is essential since the essence of the violinist ceases with the amputation. The essence of the musician in this violinist, on the other hand, survives. The search for the essence always takes us from the external to the inward. Those who try to discover the essence of man and go beyond the sphere of social functions come finally to a closed door on which is written: the essence of man can only be understood *sub specie aeternitatis*, the essence of man is the significance that he has for God. Many will be dissatisfied with this decision, for instead of an answer they are given a signpost pointing to the unfathomable.

Is it thus with all attempts to define essence? Must we also be resigned to failure in our efforts to answer the question as to the essence of Gothic? There are obviously stages within the concept of essence. Wetter put his finger on what was essential to High Gothic, the four *membra*: pier, pointed arch, ribbed vault, and buttresses; but he did not thereby touch the essence of Gothic. Closer to the solution came Ramée, Vitet, Viollet-le-Duc, Schnaase, with their tendency to investigate the cultural-historical background that corresponded to those structures consisting of piers, pointed arches, ribs, and buttresses or, from another point of view, that demanded and produced those Gothic structures. But the essence of Gothic is not simply that background, it must be sought within Gothic itself. The essence of Gothic is, in a few words, that cultural and intellectual background insofar as it entered into the building and was absorbed by it; it is the interpenetration, the saturation, of the form of the building by the meaning of the culture.

The concept of purpose is a special case of the supreme concept of all: *meaning*. Essence also is a special case of meaning. With utilitarian objects the purpose is at the same time the essence of the thing, as long as the purpose holds. A castle has the purpose of protection, defense, attack, compulsion, domination. Its essence is thus recognized, unless one wants to go back to the social organization of feudalism that underlies the entire complex of all the mediaeval castles of a country. If this changes radically or vanishes, the castles (in this mediaeval form) become useless, they perish with their purpose. Their essence remains.

The church building is also an object of use; its purpose is the disposition of the place of the cultic act. Its essence is thereby defined, again with the reservation: unless one wants to go back to the social organization of the Catholic church that underlies the entire complex of all the mediaeval churches of Europe. The churches are different from the castles in that they remained purposeful and usable even though the Protestant rite was introduced into them. The thought of the iconoclasts serves to remind us of how much was thereby rendered "useless." But here, too, the essence endured. A church altar painting that escaped the iconoclasts, found its way to a junk shop, and ended in a museum has lost its purpose, but its essence is eternal—comprehensible even in the junk shop *sub specie aeternitatis*. The same thing holds true of a church that its profaned as a stable, salt depot, and so on. Its purpose has shifted but its essence endures.

In the light of these reflections, let us return to Gothic, turn from the castle to the *Gothic* castle and from the church to the *Gothic* church! Their "Gothicness" relates to the spirit of feudalism, or the spirit of the mediaeval Catholic church. But spirit is here only another expression for essence. The essence of Gothic is the intellectual and spiritual factor inherent in it, its eternal content. This essence, if we now confine ourselves to church Gothic, is the sustaining basic idea of Christianity in the age of Gothic and this same essence is the basic impulse in the shaping of the church buildings.

Iconographists, cultural historians, and historians of ideas have long since stressed the difference between God the Lord and God the Son of Man. In Romanesque sculpture God appears as the stern judge, the Lord and Ruler at the Last Judgment, the Crucified One, unmarked by suffering, who actively wills His lot. In Gothic sculpture He appears as the mild, all-pitying, and all-loving One, the God suffering on the Cross as the Son of God who in humility submits to His lot or feels Himself forsaken. On Romanesque crucifixes Jesus stands upright and alive; nailed to his cross, he is independent. On Gothic crosses he droops in weakness or death; he is dependent. In each case these adjectives are used in their literal sense. They are the same words we use when we try to make the concepts of totality and partiality intelligible. The God of Romanesque, though he may be called Jesus, is nevertheless God the Father, he has still something of the Jehovah of the Old Testament about him; the God of Gothic is Jesus. Is then the essence of Gothic the same as the essence of that Jesus who lived in the hearts of the monks and nuns and all pious folk of the twelfth and thirteenth centuries and gradually changed in the two centuries that followed? No. This thesis would express only half the truth: the meaning. The essence of church Gothic is the form of the churches of the twelfth and thirteenth centuries *as* the symbol of Jesus. This formulation is very general. The idea that was associated with Jesus changed in every generation and acquired a different significance in the case of cathedral churches, orders with varying rules, chapels of kings and princes, city churches, and so on. The form, on the other hand, not only changed as this idea did, but was also not absolutely determinable for each nuance: various forms were tried in one and the same generation. But this general formulation indicates that it is the essence of Gothic to be *art*, thus to be a form symbol for the meaning of Jesus, an immediately intelligible symbol for anyone who understands the language of forms and has, moreover, sufficient knowledge of the meaning of the idea of Jesus. We have two factors that are fused together, not a sum in addition: form plus meaning, but both simultaneously.

Applied very strictly, the analysis can go even further. What was here designated as meaning already has its spiritual and intellectual form and what was called form, the Gothicness of the building, has its spiritual and intellectual meaning. For instance: the form of the meaning "Jesus" is in our case the form of the ritual, with its dogma, its prayers, and so on; the meaning of the Gothic forms lies in the spaces and bodies, in the piers and arches, the vaults and profiles and so on. Each of them has its *own* meaning and together they have that of the whole church *qua* church (as the architectural historian usually regards it when he studies it). It is only this double-sided analysis of the liturgy as a deliberately shaped course of meaningful, sacred actions and the church building as the meaningfully formed scene of these actions that leads to complete understanding of their interpenetration.

Such knowledge of the "ecclesiastical" significance of the church building could never be totally forgotten. Yet in the days of Darwinism, positivism, materialism, Marxism, atheism, scholars were inclined to talk about *esprit laïque*, construction, economy of materials, especially the saving of wood, about logic or the lack of it, statics, empathy, masculinity and femininity, the expression of the race, the spirit of the Celts or the Germanic peoples or the barbarians (as a term of praise), about the qualities of the intoxicating, the successive, about the secret of the lodges, the forms of the structural members—but not on any account about God. But there were always men who had the courage to touch the core of Gothic. Gurlitt was such a convinced Protestant that he anticipated the spirit of the Reformation in Late Gothic, thus showing himself to be more denominational than religious. Thode grasped the essence of Gothic but he isolated the Franciscan trend from its context and called it Renaissance, an even greater aberration than Gurlitt's. Sauer, and like him other strictly orthodox Catholic scholars, unquestionably realized what the essence of Gothic was, but to them this insight was a matter of course and not a problem that needed many words for its elucidation. Geymüller, though a Protestant, comprehended the essence of Gothic in its whole depth and sought to bear witness to it. But one expects more clarity, more impersonal objectivity in the scientific attitude. The essence of Gothic as an eternal content and a form discovered once and for all is an eternal idea, utterly removed from any subjective taste or subjective belief. Subjective inner affinity may make the approach easier, but the realm of science is objective knowledge.

All search for the *essence* of Gothic relates to "the form as symbol of its meaning." This schematic formula becomes of inestimable richness once one describes Gothic form, on the one hand, and, on the other, seeks and recognizes the Gothic meaning in the liturgy, poetry, theology, and metaphysics, becoming finally aware of the interaction between Gothic *form* and Gothic *meaning*, between partiality of *form* and partiality of *meaning*. For Gothic the individual is a fragment of the universe. But that is by no means all: this partiality of meaning manifests itself within the framework of a quite definite, individual world of concepts and ideas that is historically *unique* and must be studied for itself, apprehended, and lovingly comprehended. But that is still not enough: this Gothic form as the symbol of its Gothic meaning is constantly in flux, it is not merely historically unique but it has its own history. The essence of Gothic has come into existence, developed, spread over whole nations, and merged with the essence of various lands and peoples. The essence of Gothic can be deduced even from the first rib, though it can be understood better in the French cathedrals of the thirteenth century and then also in the English, German, and so on. It is best of all when one is acquainted with the whole course of its development and diffusion, that is, with the *history* of Gothic, if not in all, at least in its "essential" masterpieces.

Whoever, then desires to formulate the essence of Gothic in concepts and words must above all things free himself from the erroneous notion that Gothic is an absolutely fixed thing identical, for example, with those schematic drawings of the system of the Gothic cathedral that appear in textbooks as an aid to beginners. One remains a beginner if one is satisfied with this or merely goes on to speculate whether Gothic without verticalism or Gothic with wooden roof timbering or Gothic garden walls (Ruskin), and so on, are really Gothic. Gothic is a process. It is a unique, historical process. It runs its appointed course. Just as human individuals remain themselves even though their knowledge and abilities, their relations with others, their points of view change; and a man at twenty, at fifty, at seventy, is always the same person though he has become different and sometimes very different, so, too, the individual Gothic master can change and after him his journeyman and pupil when he has become a master and has to carry on the work of his predecessor. But as long as he does not introduce or adopt a completely different style—Renaissance—he continues "Gothic," which is always the same and is always changing.

What remains is the essence. What changes and is either clarified, intensified, perfected or obfuscated, deformed, watered down, is this essence of Gothic. Both the meaning and the form of this essence are partiality; that means that each part is a fragment of a whole which itself tends to be only a fragment of infinity. Here the results of the preceding chapter on the explanation of the rib should be applied.

Partiality is the essence of many another style and consequently the essence of Gothic is not exhausted by this one word. It is a characteristic of the essence of Gothic that this partiality came to dominate church building in its earliest stage of Romanesque. Gothic originated during the development of Romanesque—in Durham and in Normandy; in many regions Romanesque developed into High and Late Romanesque, so that in these areas Gothic did not set in until after Late Romanesque. Gothic may have adopted types from contemporaneous buildings in the Romanesque style but it translated them from the totality of Romanesque buildings into the partiality of the new conviction that the believer is only a fragment, absolutely dependent on a higher being. The Romanesque types of spatial forms—basilican churches and hall churches and so on—of corporeal forms—piers, arches, and the like—and of light forms were translated into partiality, but when the Romanesque vault was translated into Gothic it remained a vault. These structural parts, these specific "members," belong with other elements, to the essence of church architecture. The battlements belonged to the essence of castle architecture, city walls, and city gates, but not to the essence of church architecture (although they also occurred there). Battlements, too, could be translated into the language of Gothic, and anyone who seeks and finds the essentially Gothic element in Gothic battlements, aside from their purpose of defense, will again encounter partiality, expressed in the profiling.

The essence of Gothic can thus also be described as the principle of partiality applied to the historically existing Romanesque church architecture from about 1093 on, and this essence was endowed with the creative power to produce new forms that were in harmony with itself, that gradually freed it from everything Romanesque and "total," eventually revealing it in all its purity and unfolding it to itself. Gothic itself awoke, grew up, and became conscious.

One can describe this essence by means of five concepts: partiality, membrology, type, degree of regularity, harmoniality, but this method remains abstract. Thus one reverts to the recognition that the changing, self-realizing essence of Gothic, this essence that slowly "finds itself," is comprehensible by patiently accompanying the process in its real history.[1]

Understanding of the essence of Gothic, seen from its *formal* aspect, appeared about 1180 in Gervase, the monk of Canterbury. The literature of the lodges, beginning with Villard de Honnecourt, was concerned with problems of mensuration. The Scholastics sought to approach from the side of meaning, from theology and ethics, from the realm of what was much later called aesthetics. Modern aesthetics of the nineteenth century, reverting at first to this confusion of ethics with aesthetics, then freed itself and found the way to the work of art as a visible object. In the wake of this change of direction there originated those conceptual tools that, although meant to apply to concrete works and themselves the results of highly personal experiences, were abstract. Our present concepts are connected with the intellectual lifework of

[1] See p. 797.

Wölfflin. But here the tension between abstract concepts and reality became so acute that, whatever the concepts that were worked out, their relation to history was bound to become the central problem.

This contemporary situation can perhaps be understood most clearly with the help of an often quoted statement by Wölfflin.[2] In several places in his works Wölfflin repeated the remark that "not everything is possible in all ages." The word possible has here the meaning of "realizable." But in everyday language as well as in philosophy possible means also approximately the same thing as facultative, that is, available *a priori*, independent of whether it is realized or not. What Wölfflin called the linear element is a "possibility" independent of time and country, and the picturesque is likewise another simultaneous and ubiquitous "possibility." These two possibilities are abstract ideas, and Wölfflin's statement was intended to imply that these two ever-present possibilities are not always possible. The paradox is easy to resolve because, as has been said, the word "possible" has the two different meanings of abstractly possible and concretely possible.

It would be ungrateful to quarrel with Wölfflin over this point; it was simply the historical necessity that he intended his abstract concepts to be historical ones, conditioned by time and place and accordingly not realizable everywhere and in every age. But the latent dilemma of his brilliant thought lay in this tension between abstract concepts and concrete processes.

Two steps are requisite and necessary to resolve this tension. One must endeavor to discover all the abstract concepts that aid the intellectual mastery of the history of art and must use them as coordinates in order to understand it more deeply and judge it better.

Wölfflin worked out only *some* concepts, and others, which already existed, he suppressed as of minor importance, for example, the element of the membrological. It is a trite statement that Gothic has pointed arches, yet it should neither be overlooked nor passed over in silence. Thanks to Wölfflin it is possible to understand the quadripartite ribbed vault as "depth-emphasizing" (diagonal) but before one can do that, one must see the quadripartite ribbed vault itself, name it, and recognize it as an integral part of Gothic. Thus one can and must reflect further. Since in this place a tracing of all the necessary concepts would indeed be possible, as it were, but is impracticable, a table containing a supplement and generalization of Wölfflin's concepts must suffice:

[2] Heinrich Wölfflin, *Kunstgeschichtliche Grundbegriffe. Das Problem der Stilentwicklung in der neueren Kunst*, Munich, 1915. Last sentence of the Preface.

Wölfflin's historical concepts	*Abstract concepts*
Not everything is (concretely) possible in all ages.	Everything is (abstractly) possible in all ages.
	1. *Membra* (pointed arch, rib, and so on)
	2. Type (basilica, transept, and so on)
	3. *Ordo* (regularity—irregularity)
4. Closed—open	4. *Limes* (totality—partiality)
1. Linear—picturesque	
2. Plane-Recession	
3. Multiple unity—unified unity	
	5. Harmony—disharmony

In this table Wölfflin's conceptual pairs are rearranged, and the fifth, absolute clarity and relative clarity (or clarity and unclearness), is omitted, a liberty that makes it easier to compare both sides of the table.

The concept of the classical with which Wölfflin struggled again and again is not identical with any one of his five basic concepts, for in his view there is a classicism both of the linear and the picturesque, and so on. On close examination it must be said that he did not develop his fifth concept of clarity for architecture with complete lucidity, but, after he has discussed the first four pairs of concepts with relation to their share in the creation either of clarity or its opposite, he writes: "In this we are not saying anything new; it was only a matter of combining remarks made earlier under the heading of objective distinctness. In every chapter the Baroque concept meant a kind of obscuration." By the phrase "objective" distinctness is meant the *meaning* that the building or part of a building manifests. Wölfflin speaks further of "clarity of the object." This turning from the *form* to the object itself, to the *meaning* of the object, forces us to distinguish between the theory of form (morphology) and the theory of meaning (noology). Anyone who carries this reasoning to its conclusion will arrive within noology at exactly the same basic concepts of membrism, typism, and so on, and Wölfflin's fifth conceptual pair of objective clarity and objective obscuration will then fall under the limitology of the meaningful, that is, under the concepts of totality and partiality of meaning.

This parallelism of the two series of basic concepts lifts the veil from the supposed mystery of the parallelism of artistic development and cultural development, inasmuch as the form of styles is a symbol of the meaning of the particular culture. However, it also draws a veil across the other mystery: that often the two are not identical and that there are artists who live outside their age—which may be taken with a grain of salt.

Historians, and especially art historians, who want to keep a free hand for their thoughts, refuse to accept a complete series of abstract concepts. But let there be no misunderstanding! The five abstract concepts with which the essence of Gothic, as of every other style, can be described are *style* concepts. The possibilities of an individual building are not exhausted when one calls it Gothic, for that designation covers "merely" the essence of its style. It is anyone's privilege to search for a sixth basic concept of *style*, but in such a search for *all* concepts the seeker will have to resign himself to the *deductive* method. Though one can indeed gather up such concepts, one can never be sure that one has garnered them all. One is, however, able to arrive at deduction only after a long course of empiricism.

In order to describe the individual work (not the styles) one needs the concepts of *magnitudes*: scale, rhythm, proportion, which can be applied to every spatial structure. *Gothic* is *Gothic*, whether on the smallest or the largest scale, in a reliquary or Cologne Cathedral; it has rhythms of widely varying nature; and it can appear in the slenderest verticalism or in comfortably spread proportions. Thus the criteria-hungry scholar can find many concepts besides the problem of style as grist for his intellectual mill and can rejoice in his freedom. One of these concepts is that of *quality*. There are Gothic buildings of very different quality. Anyone talking of quality must realize either that he does not mean the style at all—for even those who with Vasari would deny Gothic all quality do not deny its Gothicity—or is speaking of precisely the quality of the style, and then he must ask himself whether he means its aesthetic or its artistic aspect, that is, either the fineness of the execution of all factors down to the grade of the stone, the manner of dressing its surfaces, the treatment of the joints, and so on, or the *symbolizing power of the form* to express the meaning.

This brings us to the second step. Once all the abstract concepts are assembled—it remains an open question whether we have them all today—they are logical tools for those historians who want more than just a mass of chronologically arranged and geographically determined factors. History is concrete, unique, and infinitely complicated; it is really infinite, for it is a network of human aspirations, conflicts, and tragedies. The Milan expertises, by affording us in one individual case a glimpse of the all too human aspects of the buildings of great cathedrals—and even then only a fragmentary glimpse—serve to remind us that the cathedrals which stand silent and unaffected by the judgments of the different generations that look up to them in awe were created by individual men or groups of men, and that a bishop or abbot doubtless differed with his architect and the differences were ultimately resolved. Nothing of all that has been handed down in any detail by tradition, but the abstract concepts make it possible for us to formulate the correct questions: what was the dispute about and what motivated the agreement from which resulted the historical monument?

It is a misuse of abstract stylistic concepts to turn them into historical laws. The network of actual history can only be reconstructed by uncovering the real facts. But anyone who wants to understand this network needs the abstract concepts as coordinates. The concepts are absolute, or at least intended to be absolute; the relative can be understood as such only when it is measured by their absoluteness.

Gothic had its essence, both as to form and meaning; it was the inevitable form for the meaning of the age, the so-called *Zeitgeist*, that is, the common process of the many-sided spiritual activity in the particular generation. To attempt to describe the essence of history itself (aside from art) by means of stylistic concepts presupposes that it, too, has style, cultural style. Necessity in the course of cultural styles is a most profound problem. Again and again one comes back to this mystery. To fathom it completely would be perhaps to paralyze ourselves forever through self-knowledge. But the fear that we shall reach this point can be postponed.

Why then these difficult considerations? Because we want to know the history of Gothic and this history takes on different shapes according to whether one is merely seeking for a jumble of interesting facts or trying for a real understanding. If one wants to understand history one cannot avoid the question of what the essence of that Gothic is, the history of which we hope to understand. The historical picture will change according to our understanding of the essence of Gothic. The closer we come to an accurate insight into the essence of Gothic the better are we prepared to reconstruct also an accurate history of Gothic. The more accurate our abstract concepts, our coordinates, become the more easily can we recognize the essence of Gothic, the simpler does it become to describe this essence, and the nearer do we come to an understanding of the concrete history of Gothic.

This history of Gothic belongs to cultural as well as architectural history. The picture of a churchman and an architect sitting down together at one table, whenever a church was to be built, in order to make sketches, consider them, correct them, and then submit them to the judgment of other members of the chapter or the citizenry or the aristocracy provides the clue to the specific connecting links between two intellectual areas of Gothic. This brings us back, in a different manner, to what has already been discussed above. The human beings concerned, as members of society, are the mysterious agencies that absorb from all cultural areas whatever are the latest ideas and then, after a process of inner assimilation, give them forth again. These concrete situations are sometimes made more vivid for us by names, sometimes by more detailed accounts. But always we need those abstract coordinating concepts in order to understand the concrete buildings, the works, that outlasted those persons, to understand them accurately, despite our changed culture, and if possible in the same way that the builders themselves understood them.

The theory of the essence of Gothic that has been here presented is the outgrowth of the steps that went before. The Romanticists taught us to look at Gothic positively; in addition to the older concepts of the picturesque, the sublime, the infinite, they introduced the pregnant one of the romantic. Hegel led the way to a clearer distinction between form and content and also to emphasis on the factor of space. The idealistic aesthetic of Hegel's followers was supplemented by the pure description of Wetter and his continuers, Viollet-le-Duc, and so on. Wölfflin brought about the change to a psychological aesthetic and the development of polar stylistic opposites. Riegl progressed to the recognition of the objective equality of all styles as the particular symbols of the contemporary culture; he explained art as nevertheless autonomous. His ideas on *artistic* volition were succeeded by those on artistic *volition.* However much was also contributed to an understanding of Gothic by the trend toward history of ideas, the efforts to define the national factor, and all the other theories, the development tended toward a synthesis of all fruitful individual theories. Scholars learned both to comprehend Gothic descriptively and to understand it psychologically in the sense of aesthetic empathy; beyond that, Drost came to recognize the aesthetically experienced form as the symbol of the meaning of this very form and therefore to realize the unity of the process of mutual interaction between the art and the (non-artistic) culture of

Gothic;[3] and finally, scholars learned to follow Gothic in its historical dynamism as a development both of architectural and of cultural style.

This retrospective summary explains why it was necessary in this book to include many theories that were not intended to apply specifically to Gothic, since they have led indirectly to that deeper understanding of Gothic and to a more satisfying conceptual mastery of the tasks of art history and art scholarship in general.

However many attempts have been made to describe Gothic, they are all merely steps. Anyone who undertakes a new one must realize that his attempt will also be merely *one* step. For science is also a stream. Neither the conception of the essential nature of Gothic nor the investigation of individual works has been brought to completion. The history of opinions about Gothic from Suger, 1145, to the present ought to put everyone in a cautious mood, for no generation has ever suspected what was yet to be thought and discovered about Gothic. We, too, cannot foresee what is still to come.

This should not make anyone lose heart or, above all, become a relativist. Gothic is an objective phenomenon. We have seen that it could be judged falsely, that there were and still are eccentric thinkers who talked nonsense about it, that there were scholars who honestly believed they had discovered the truth about it, that many scholars found parts of the truth, but that Gothic remains what it was and is, while our attempts to reach its core from one side after the other gradually leads us closer and closer to the truth.

Relativists like to cite the saying of Heraclitus that one cannot step twice into the same river. That is a witty remark but it should not be misused. Anyone who steps twice into the Danube does step each time into different water, but always into the same river. The Danube is the channel that endures—even though it may itself change in many respects. Gothic is just such a spiritual channel. The historian steps into this stream and his duty and tendency lead him to swim on with the water always in the same stream. He notices that the water undergoes changes, that one part evaporates, new water flows in from side branches or is supplied by rain; he observes that this water changes color, grows broader or deeper, that finally part of it trickles away and part of it merges with another stream, the stream of history in which we ourselves stand and then swim on. The recognition that Gothic changes implies an admission that though it is a process it is never-

[3] Willi Drost, *Form als Symbol*, Dritter Kongress für Aesthetik und allgemeine Kunstwissenschaft, Stuttgart, 1927, p. 254.

theless something enduring, something coherent, and was a spiritual, organic growth, a historical entity, which we seek to understand as we do all human past because we admire it, to use Geymüller's words, as one of the most solemn and splendid moments in the history of mankind.

APPENDICES

Appendix 1a

Abbot Suger, *De Consecratione*, 1144

Lecoy, *Œuvres complêtes de Suger*, Paris, 1867, p. 224. (Panofsky, *Abbot Suger on the Abbot Church of St.-Denis and Its Art Treasures*, Princeton, 1946, p. 98.)

Communicatio siquidem cum fratribus nostris bene devotis consilio, quorum *cor ardens erat de Jesu dum loqueretur eis in via*, (Luc. XXIV) hoc Deo inspirante deliberando elegimus, ut propter eam quam divina operatio, sicut veneranda scripta testantur, propria et manuali extensione ecclesiae consecrationi antiquae imposuit benedictionem, ipsis sacratis lapidibus tanquam reliquiis deferremus, illam quae tanta exigente necessitate novitas inchoaretur, longitudinis et latitudinis pulchritudine inniteremur nobilitare. Consulte siquidem decretum est illam altiori inaequalem, quae super apsidem sanctorum dominorum nostrorum corpora retinentem operiebat, removeri voltam usque ad superficiem criptae cui adhaerebat; ut eadem cripta superioritatem sui accedentibus per utrosque gradus pro pavimento offerret, et in eminentiori loco Sanctorum lecticas auro et preciosis gemmis adornatas adventantium obtutibus designaret. Provisum est etiam sagaciter ut superioribus columnis et arcubus mediis, qui in inferioribus in cripta fundatis superponerentur, geometricis et aritmeticis instrumentis medium antiquae testudinis ecclesiae augmenti novi aequaretur, nec minus antiquarum quantitas alarum novarum quantitati adaptaretur; excepto illo urbano et approbato in circuito oratoriorum incremento, quo tota clarrissimarum* vitrearum luce mirabili et continua interiorem perlustrante pulchritudinem eniteret.

* After the publication of his book on Suger, Panofsky changed the word *sacratissimarum* to *clarissimarum*. Cf. Erwin Panofsky, "Postlogium Sugerianum," *The Art Bulletin*, XXIX, 1947, p. 119.

Appendix 1b

Abbot Suger, *De Consecratione*, 1144

Lecoy, *Œuvres complètes de Suger*, p. 227. (Panofsky, *Abbot Suger*, p. 104.)

Medium quippe duodecim Apostolorum exponentes numerum, secundario vero totidem alarum columnae Prophetarum numerum significantes, altum repente subrigebant aedificium, juxta Apostolum, spiritualiter aedificantem: "*Jam non estis*," inquit, "*hospites et advenae; sed estis cives sanctorum et domestici Dei, superaedificati super fundamentum Apostolorum et Prophetarum, ipso summo angulari lapide Christo Jesu*, qui utrumque conjungit parietem, *in quo omnis aedificatio*, sive spiritualis, sive materialis, *crescit in templum sanctum in Domino*." (Eph. 2:19)

Appendix 1c

Abbot Suger, *De Consecratione*, 1144

Lecoy, *Œuvres complètes de Suger*, p. 230. (Panofsky, *Abbot Suger*, p. 108.)

Nec illud etiam silere dignum duximus, quod dum praefatum novi augmenti opus capitellis et arcubus superioribus† ad altitudinis cacumen

† Panofsky interpreted the words *arcus superiores* as meaning the vaults of the central nave of the choir in contrast to those of the side aisles. I suggest that Suger meant the wall arches of the central nave in contrast to all arches lying below them. *Altitudinis cacumen* would then mean the dripping line of the roof.

producerctur, cum necdum principales arcus singulariter voluti voltarum cumulo cohaererent, terribilis et pene intolerabilis obnubilatione nubium, inundatione imbrium, impetu validissimo ventorum subito tempestatis exorta est procella; quae usque adeo invaluit, ut non solum validas domos, sed etiam lapideas turres et ligneas tristegas concusserit. Ea tempestate, quadam die, anniversario gloriosi Dagoberti regis, cum venerabilis Carnotensis episcopus Gaufredus missas gratiarum pro anima ejusdem in conventu ad altare principale festive celebraret, tantus oppositorum ventorum impetus praefatos arcus nullo suffultos podio, nullis renitentes suffragiis impingebat, ut miserabiliter tremuli, et quasi hinc et inde fluctuantes subito pestiferam minarentur ruinam. Quorum quidem operturarumque impulsionem cum episcopus expavesceret, saepe manum benedictionis in ea parte extendebat, et bracchium sancti senis Simeonis signando instanter opponebat, ut manifeste nulla sui constantia, sed sola Dei pietate et Sanctorum merito ruinam evadere appareret. Sicque cum multis in locis firmissimis, ut putabatur, aedificiis multa ruinarum incommoda intulisset, virtute repulsa divina titubantibus in alto solis et recentibus arcubus nihil proferre praevaluit incommodi.

Appendix 2

Abbot Suger, *De Administratione* 1145

Lecoy, *Œuvres complêtes de Suger*, p. 198. (Panofsky, *Abbot Suger*, p. 62.)

Omnis, inquam, *lapis preciosus operimentum tuum, sardius, topazius, jaspis, crisolitus, onix et berillus, saphirus, carbunculus et smaragdus.** De quorum numero, praeter solum carbunculum, nullum deesse, imo copiosissima abundare, gemmarum proprietatem cognoscentibus cum summa ammiratione claret. Unde, cum ex dilectione decoris domus Dei aliquando multicolor gemmarum speciositas ab extrinsecis me curis devocaret, sanctarum etiam diversitatem virtutum de materialibus ad immaterialia transferendo, honesta meditatio insistere persuaderet, videor videre me quasi sub aliqua extranea orbis terrarum plaga, quae nec tota sit in terrarum faece nec tota in coeli puritate demorari, ab hac etiam inferiori ad illam superiorem anagogico more Deo donante posse transferri. Conferre consuevi cum Hierosolymitanis et gratantissime addiscere, quibus Constantinopolitanae patuerant gazae et Sanctae Sophiae ornamenta, utrum ad comparationem illorum haec aliquid valere deberent. Qui cum haec majora faterentur, visum est nobis quod timore Francorum ammiranda quae antea audieramus caute reposita essent; ne stultorum aliquorum impetuosa rapacitate, Graecorum et Latinorum ascita familiaritas in seditionem et bellorum scandala subito moveretur.

* The words in italics are a quotation from Ezek. 28:13.

Appendix 3a

Gervase, *Chronica*, after 1174

William Stubbs, *The Historical Works of Gervase of Canterbury*, 1, London, 1879, p. 19.

Coepit, ut longe ante praedixi, novo operi necessaria praeparare et vetera destruere. In istis primus annus completus est. Sequenti anno, id est, post festum Sancti Bertini, ante hiemem quatuor pilarios erexit, id est, utrinque duos; peracta hieme duos apposuit, ut hinc et inde tres essent in ordine: super quos et murum exteriorem alarum, arcus et fornicem decenter composuit, id est, tres claves utrimque. Clavem pro toto pono ciborio, eo quod clavis in medio posita partes undecunque venientes claudere et confirmare videtur. In istis annus secundus completus est. Anno tertio duos utrimque pilarios apposuit, quorum duos extremos in circuitu columpnis marmoreis decoravit, et quia in eis chorus et cruces convenire debuerunt, principales esse constituit. In quibus appositis clavibus et fornice facta, a turre majore usque ad pilarios praedictos, id est, usque ad crucem, triforium inferius multis intexuit columpnis marmoreis. Super quod triforium aliud quoque ex alia materia et fenestras superiores aptavit. Deinde fornicis magnae tres claves, a turre scilicet usque ad cruces. Quae omnia nobis et omnibus ea videntibus incomparabilia et laude dignissima videbantur. De hoc ergo tam glorioso principio hilares effecti et futurae consummationis bonam spem concipientes, consummationem operis ardentis animi desiderio accelerare curavimus. In istis igitur annus tertius completus est, et quartus sumpsit initium. In cujus aestate a cruce incipiens, decem pilarios erexit, scilicet utrinque quinque. Quorum duos primos marmoreis ornans columpnis contra alios duos principales fecit. Super hos decem arcus et fornices posuit. Peractis autem utrisque triforiis et superioribus fenestris, cum machinas ad fornicem magnam volvendam in anni quinti initio praeparasset, repente ruptis trabibus sub pedibus ejus et inter lapides et ligna simul cum ipso ruentibus, in terram corruit, a capitellis fornicis superioris altitudine, videlicet, pedum quinquaginta. Qui ex ictibus lignorum et lapidum acriter diverberatus, sibi et operi inutilis effectus est, nullusque alius praeter ipsum solum in aliquo laesus est. In solum magistrum vel Dei vindicta, vel diaboli desaevit invidia. Magister itaque sic laesus et sub cura medicorum ob spem salutis recuperandae aliquandiu lecto decumbens, spe fraudatus convalescere non potuit; veruntamen quia hiems instabat, et fornicem superiorem consummari oportebat, cuidam monacho industrio et ingenioso qui cementariis praefuit opus consummandum commendavit, unde multa invidia et exercitatio malitiae habita est, eo quod ipse, cum esset juvenis, potentioribus et ditioribus prudentior videretur. Magister tamen in lecto recubans, quid prius, quid posterius fieri debuit ordinavit. Factum est itaque ciborium inter quatuor pilarios principales; in cujus ciborii clavem videntur quodammodo chorus et cruces convenire. Duo quoque ciboria hinc et inde ante hiemem facta sunt. Pluviae autem fortiter insistentes plura fieri non permiserunt. In istis annus quartus completus est, et quintus sumpsit initium. Eodem anno, scilicet quarto, facta est ecclipsis solis, octavo idus Septembris, hora quasi sexta, ante casum magistri. Sentiens itaque praefatus magister nulla se medicorum arte vel industria posse convalescere, operi renuntiavit, et mari transito in Franciam ad sua remeavit. Successit autem huic in curam operis alius quidam Willelmus nomine, Anglus natione, parvus quidem corpore, sed in diversis operibus subtilis valde et probus. Hic in anni quinti aestate crucem utramque, australem scilicet et aquilonalem, consummavit, et ciborium quod desuper magnum altare est volvit, quod ne fieret praeterito anno, cum omnia parata essent, pluviae impedierunt. Praeterea ex parte orientali ad incrementum ecclesiae fundamentum fecit, eo quod capella Sancti Thomae ibidem ex novo fieri debuit. Hic ergo locus ei provisus est, capella scilicet Sanctae Trinitatis, ubi primam missam celebravit, ubi lacrimis et orationibus incumbere consuevit, sub cujus cripta per tot annos sepultus fuit, ubi Deus per ejus merita multa fecit miracula, ubi pauperes et divites, reges et principes eum venerati sunt, unde exivit sonus laudis ejus in totum orbem terrarum. Coepit igitur magister Willelmus causa fundamenti monachorum cimiterium fodere, unde compulsus est multorum sanctorum monachorum ossa effodere. Quae diligenter in unam collecta reposita sunt in fossa grandi, in angulo illo qui e est inter capellam et domum infirmorum ad meridiem. Facto itaque muri exterioris fundamento firmissimo ex lapide et cemento, murum etiam criptae usque ad bases fenestrarum erexit. In istis annus quintus completus est, et sextus sumpsit initium. Vere autem ejusdem, id est, sexti anni post incendium intrante et tempore operandi instante, desiderio cordis accensi chorum praeparare curaverunt monachi, ut ad proximum Pascha introire possent. Videns autem magister monachorum desiderium viriliter institit, ut voluntati conventus satisfaceret. Murum igitur qui chorum circuit et presbiterium cum summa festinatione construxit. Altaria quoque tria presbiterii erexit. Locum requietionis Sancti Dunstani et Sancti Aelfegi sollicite praeparavit. Paries quoque ligneus ad secludendas tempestates ex parte orientis per transversum inter pilarios penultimos positus est, tres vitreas continens fenestras. Chorum itaque, cum summo labore et festinatione nimia utcunque vix tamen praeparatum, vigilia Paschae cum novo igne intrare voluerunt. Sed quia omnia quae fieri oportebat illo die sabbati, propter solennitatem sancti diei ad plenum ut decebat fieri non valebant, necesse fuit ut sancti patres et patroni nostri, Sanctus videlicet Dunstanus et Sanctus Aelfegus, coexules monachorum, ante diem illum in novum transferrentur chorum.

Appendix 3b

Gervase, *Chronica*, after 1174

William Stubbs, *Historical Works of Gervase*, I, p. 27.

Dictum est in superioribus quod post combustionem illam vetera fere omnia chori diruta sunt, et in quandam augustioris formae transierunt novitatem. Nunc autem quae sit operis utriusque differentia dicendum est. Pilariorum igitur tam veterum quam novorum una forma est, una grossitudo, sed longitudo dissimilis. Elongati sunt enim pilarii novi longitudine pedum fere duodecim. In capitellis veteribus opus erat planum, in novis sculptura subtilis. Ibi in chori ambitu pilarii viginti duo, hic autem viginti octo. Ibi arcus et caetera omnia plana, utpote sculpta secure et non scisello, hic in omnibus fere sculptura idonea. Ibi columpna nulla marmorea, hic innumerae. Ibi in circuitu extra chorum fornices planae, hic arcuatae sunt et clavatae. Ibi murus super pilarios directus cruces a choro sequestrabat, hic vero nullo interstitio cruces a choro divisae in unam clavem quae in medio fornicis magnae constitit, quae quatuor pilariis principalibus innititur, convenire videntur. Ibi caelum ligneum egregia pictura decoratum, hic fornix ex lapide et tofo levi decenter composita est. Ibi triforium unum, hic duo in choro, et in ala ecclesiae tertium. Quae omnia visu melius quam auditu intelligere volenti patebunt. Hoc tamen sciendum est quod novum opus altius est veteri quantum superiores fenestrae tam corporis chori quam laterum ejus a tabulatu marmoreo in altum porriguntur. Ne autem futuris temporibus cuiquam veniat in dubium, qua de causa tanta chori latitudo quae est juxta turrim tantum in capite ecclesiae coarctetur, causas dicere non inutile duxi. Quarum una est, quod duae turres, Sancti Anselmi videlicet et Sancti Andreae, in utroque latere ecclesiae antiquitus positae, latitudinem chori in directum ad lineam non permiserunt procedere. Alia causa est, quod capellam Sancti Thomae. . . .

Appendix 4

The Expertise of Chartres, 1316

Congrès Archéologique de Chartres. Paris, 1901, I. Rapport des experts, pp. 312-315. Anno Domini M°CCC° decimo sexto, die Jovis post festum Nativitatis Beate Marie Virginis Sancte, fuit relacio defectuum ecclesie per magistros ad visitandum dictos defectus deputatos per capitulum in modum infra scriptum:

Seigneurs, nous vous disons que les IIII ars qui aident à porter les voutes sunt bons et fors, et les pilliers qui portent les ars bons, et la clef qui porte la clef bonne et fort; et ne convenrra oter de vostre vouste plus de la moitié, là où l'an verra que mestier sera. Et avons regardé que l'eschaufaut movra d'audesus de l'enmerllement des verriesres; et de cel eschaufaut se aidera on à covrir vostre lesteril et les gens qui iront par dessous, et s'en aidera l'an à faire les autres eschaufaus à faire en la vouste, ce que l'an verra qu'il convendra à faire et mestier sera.

Vez ci les déffauz qui sont en l'iglise Nostre Dame de Chartres, veuz par mestre Pierre Chielle, mestre de l'euvre de Paris, par maistre Nicolas de Chaumes, mestre de l'euvre de Nostre Sire le Roy, et par maistre Jaques de Lonc- Jumel, mestre charpentier et juré de Paris, en la présence mestre Jean de Reate, chanoine de Chartres, originaire d'Italie, maistre Simon Daguon, mestre de l'euvre, mestre Simon, le charpentier, et meistre Berthaust, jurez de ladite euvre, dou comandement au déen.

Prumierement, nous avons veu la vouste de la croez: il i faut bien amendement, et qui ne li metra briefment, il y porroit avoir grant peril.

Item, nous avons veu les arz bouteréz qui espaulent les voustes: ils faillent bien à jointeer et recercher, et qui ne le fera briefment, il y porra bien avoir grant domage. . . .

Page 318: Item, nous avons regardé, pour le profit de l'iglise, que le premier eschaufaut mouvra de desus l'en(s)mellement des verrieres, pour faire la voste de la croez.

Appendix 5 (See postscript on p. 873.)

Expertises for Milan, 1391-1400

Annali della fabbrica del Duomo di Milano, I, Milan, 1877, p. 224.

In the original each of the ten questions is followed by answers.

1. Se il lavoro incominciato da maestro Giovanni Mignoto intorno alle vôlte e alle crociere incominciate sui capitelli sia solido?

2. Se sia bello e lodevole?

3. Se è più bello e più solido il lavoro come era stato incominciato prima, oppure questo intrapreso da maestro Giovanni Mignoto?

4. Quale si farà con minore spesa del primo o del secondo, e se tale spesa sarà molto eccessiva?

5. Se in questo secondo progetto si potranno adoperare le pietre della stessa ampiezza e qualità come nel primo, e se saranno necessarie di una ampiezza maggiore?

6. Qual numero di pietre poste in opera giusta il progetto già incominciato si dovrebbe rimuovere facendo il secondo?

7. Se sequendo la forma del secondo progetto si muterebbero soltanto per questa opera le precendenti disposizioni circa la maggiore altezza o larghezza della chiesa, od in qualche sua forma sostanziale?

The answers fill up more than five pages. The answers to question 2 are:

Marco da Carona: Rispondo che è bello, ma che per tuttavia non è lodevole.

Antonio da Paderno: Rispondo che è bello ma non lodevole, perchè non è lodevole ciò che è fuori delle regole.

Onofrio de Serina: Rispondo che è bello, e diverebbe ancora più bello, se si avesse a mutare la forma, ma in entrambi i modi non è adattato nè sufficiente pel mosaico che vi si deve fare al di sopra, giacchè il primo è lodevole pel detto mosaico, e le pietre da sovrapporsi non devono essere levigate al disopra dei capitelli.

Porolo da Calco: Rispondo che non è nè bello nè lodevole, giacchè se da detto Giovanni Mignoto e da Giovanni Alcherio si asserisce che in Parigi vi siano molti archi fatti a somiglianza di questo, progettato da maestro Giovanni, la nostra chiesa non richiede cose vecchie ma nuove, e questo non è degli archi più belli. Gli sembra però che sarebbe molto più elegante se fatto a norma del disegno da farsi.

Lorenzo Donato: Dico che è più bello dell'altro.

Giovanni Alcherio: È bellissimo e lodevolissimo.

Guidolo della Croce: Sono certo che non si potrebbe farlo nè più bello nè piu lodevole, e che detto Mignoto è un verso maestro di geometria, giacchè trovo che i suoi progetti sono consimili a quelli di quell'eccellentissimo maestro Enrico, che altre volte abbiamo avuto qui, come se ci fosse stato mandato da Dio, e che avremmo ancora se non lo avessimo espulso.

Giulano Scrosato: È bello e lodevole.

Galetto: È solido, bello e lodevole.

Simone da Cavagnera: Dicho che sono bellentissime e laudabile, e che se de' tenire ognia modo perchè siano fatte, perchè la nostra giexia habia tuto so drito in ogni cossa.

Appendix 6

Expertises for Gerona, 1417

Eugenio Llaguno y Amirola y Juan Agustin Céan-Bermudez, *Noticias de los arquitectos y Architectura de España desde su restauracion*, I, Madrid, 1829, pp. 261-275.

P. 262: Interrogatorio. En nombre de Dios nuestro Señor y de la Vírgen nuestra Señora Santa María deben ser preguntados los maestros obreros y canteros, llamados para la direccion de la obra de la catedral del Gerona por los interrogatorios siguientes:

1. Si la obra de la dicha iglesia catedral de una nave empezada antiguamente mas arriba se podrá continuar con designio de quedar segura y sin riesgo.

2. Supuesto que no pueda continuarse dicha obra de una nave con seguridad, ó que no se quiera continuar, si la obra de tres naves, seguida despues, es céngrua, suficiente, y tal que merezca proseguirse; ó por el contrario, si debe cesar, ó mudar de forma; y en este caso hasta qué altura debe seguir, y se especificará todo de manera que no pueda errarse.

3. Qué forma ó continuacion de las dichas obras será la mas compatible

y la mas proporcionada á la cabeza de la dicha iglesia, que está ya comenzada, hecha y acabada.

Los maestros y canteros, antes de ser preguntados sobre estos artículos, han de hacer su juramento; y despues de haber dado sua declaraciones, el Sr. obispo de Gerona y el honorable cabildo elegirán dos de los dichos maestros para que formen una traza o diseño, por la que se habrá de continuar la obra. Todo lo extenderá despues el secretario del cabildo en una pública.

[Then follow the answers of eleven architects. *Ibid.*, p. 272]

Guillermus Boffiy magister operis sedis dictae ecclesiae Gerundensis simili juramento à se corporaliter praestito super primo articulo dictormu articulorum interrogatus, dixit et deposuit.

1. Que la obra de una nave de la iglesia de Gerona, empezada mas arriba, se puede hacer y continuar muy bien; y que si se continúa será firme y segura sin duda alguna, y que lo zócalos, y los otros que se hagan come ellos, son y serán buenos y firmes para sostener la dicha obra de una nave. Añade, que es verdad que los dichos zócalos, aunque no fuesen tan robustos, serian suficientes para mantener la dicha obra de una nave, pues tienen un tercio mas de anchura y de lo que necesitan; por lo que son mas fuertes y no ofrecen peligro alguno.

2. Que la obra de tres naves de la misma iglesia no merece ser continuada en comparacion de la de una nave, porque de la de tres se seguirian grandes deformidades, grandes gastos, y nunca seria tan buena como la de una nave.

3. Que sin comparacion la obra de una nave es mas conforme á la cabeza de la iglesia, ya empezada y hecha, y que no lo seria la obra de tres naves. Y que si se continúa la de una nave tendrá tan grandes ventajas y tan grandes luces, que será una cosa muy hermosa y notable.

P. 273: . . . in unum concordes deliberaverunt sub Navi una prossequi magnum opus antiquum Gerundensis ecclesiae praelibatis rationibus quae sequuntur: . . . tum quia etiam multo majori claritate fulgebit quod est laetius et jucundum: tum quia vitabuntur expensae, nam ad prosequendum alterum operum praedictorum modo quo stare videntur opus navis unius molto minori praetio, quam opus trium navium, et in breviori tempore poterit consumari.

Appendix 7

The Laws of King Rothari, 634

Ludovicus Antonius Muratori, *Rerum italicarum scriptores*, I, pars secunda, Milan, 1725, p. 25.

Art. 143: Si Magister Comacinus, cum collegis suis, domum ad restaurandum, vel fabricandum super se placito finito de mercede susceperit, et contigerit aliquem per ipsam domum aut materiam, aut lapide lapso mori, aut quodlibet damnum fieri, non requiratur domino, cujus domus fuerit, nisi Magister Comacinus cum consortibus suis ipsum homicidium aut damnum componat, qui, postquam fabulam firmatam de mercede pro suo lucro susciperit, non immerito sustinet damnum. (If a Magister Comacinus and his colleagues have agreed in a signed contract involving monetary compensation to repair or to build a house and it happens that someone is killed by this house or by any of the building materials [destined for it] or by a falling stone, or if any other damage occurs, the man who owns the house shall not be held liable, but it is the Magister Comacinus and his partners who must make restitution for the manslaughter or damage. It is not unfair that he should pay the damages since he has signed for his own advantage a contract involving monetary compensation.)

Art. 145: Si quis Magistrum Comacinum unum aut plures rogaverit, aut conduxerit ad operam dictandum, aut solatium diurnum praestandum inter suos servos ad domum aut casam faciendam, et contigerit per ipsam casam, aliquem ex ipsis Comacinis mori non requiratur ab ipso, cuius casa est. Nam si cadens arbor, aut lapis ex ipsa fabrica, et occiderit aliquem extraneum, aut quodlibet damnum fecerit, non reputetur culpa Magistro, sed ille, qui conduxit, ipsum damnum sustineat. (If someone has asked or engaged a Magister Comacinus or several [Magisters] to superintend a job or to pay wages by the day to his employees to construct a building or house, and if it happens that one of these Comacini is killed by this house, the owner of the house shall not be held responsible. If, however, a falling beam or stone from this building kills an outsider or causes any sort of damage, the Magister shall not be held responsible, but the damages shall be paid by the person who engaged him [the Magister].)

Appendix 8

Réglemens sur les Arts et Métiers de Paris, 1258

Georges Bernhard Depping, *Réglemens sur les Arts et Métiers de Paris, rédigés au XIII Siècle et connus sous le nom du Livre des Métiers d'Étienne Boileau* (Collection de Documents inédits . . . , Première Série, XXXI) Paris, 1837, p. 107. Des Maçons, des Tailleurs de pierre, des Plastriers et des Morteliers.

Il puet estre maçon à Paris qui veut, pour tant que il sache le mestier, et qu'il oevre as us et aus coustumes du mestier, qui tel sunt:

Nus ne puet avoir en leur mestier que j aprentis, et se il a aprentis, il ne le puet prendre à mains de vj ans de service; mès à plus de service le puet-il bien prendre et à argent, se avoir le puet. Et se il le prenoit à mains de vj anz, il est à XX s. de par. d'amende, a paier à la chapèle monseign.

Saint-Blesve [Blaise], se ce n'estoient ses filz tant seulement nez de loial mariage.

Li maçon pueent bien prendre j autre aprentiz si tost come li autre aura acompli v ans, à quelque terme que il eust le premier aprentis prins.

Li Rois qui ore est, cui Diex doinst bone vie,[1] a doné la mestrise des maçons à mestre Guill. de Saint-Patu, tant come il li plaira. Lequel mestre Guill^{e}. jura à Paris es loges du Palès pardevant dit que il le mestier desus dit garderoit bien et loiaument à son pooir ausi pour le poure come pour le riche, et pour le foible come pour le fort, tant come il plairoit au Roy que il gardast le mestier devant dit. Et puis celui mestre Guill^{e}. fist la forme du serement devant dit pardevant le prevost de Paris en Chastelet.

Li morteliers et li plastrier sons de la meisme condicion et du meisme establisemens des maçons en toutes choses.

Li mestre qui garde le mestier des maçons, des morteliers et des plastriers de Paris de par le Roy, puet avoir ij aprentis tant seulement en la manière desus dite, et se il en avoit plus des aprentis, il amenderoit en la manière desus devisée.

Les maçons, les morteliers et les plastiers puent avoir tant aides et vallès à leur mestier come il leur plaist, pour tant que il ne monstrent à nul de eus nul point de leur mestier.

Tuit li maçon, tuit li mortelier, tuit li plastrier doivent jurer seur sains que il le mestier devant dit garderont et feront bien et loiaument, chascun endroit soi, et que se il scevent que nul il mesprengne en aucune chose, qu'il ne face selonc les us et les coustumes del mestier devant dit, que il le feront à savoir au mestre toutes fois que il le sauront, et par leur serement.

Li mestres à cui li aprentis ait fet et par accompli son terme, doit venir pardevant le mestre du mestier, et tesmoigner que son aprentis a feit son terme bien loiaument: et lors li mestres qui garde le mestier doit fère jurer à l'aprentis seur sains que il se contendra au us et as coustumes du mestier bien et léaument.

Nus ne puet ouvrer el mestier devant diz, puis none sonnée à Nostredame en charnage, et en quaresme au sémedi, puis que vespres soient chantées à Notre Dame, se ce n'est à une arche ou à un degré fermer, ou à une huisserie faire fermant assise seur rue. Et se aucun ouvroit puis les eures devant dites, fors es ouvraignes desus devisées ou à besoing, il paieroit iiij den. d'amende au mestre qui garde le mestier, et en puet prendre li mestre les ostieuz à celui qui seroit reprins par l'amende.

Li mortelier et li plastrier sont en la juridiction au mestre qui garde le mestier devant dit de par le Roy.

Se uns plastiers envoioit plastre pour metre en oevre chiés aucun hom, li maçon qui oevre à celui à cui en envoit le plastre, doit prendre garde

[1] King Louis IX, 1226-1270.

par son serement que la mesure del plastre soit bone et loiax; et se il en est en soupeçon de la mesure, il doit le plastre mesurer ou faire mesurer devant lui. Et se il treuve que la mesure ne soit bone, li plastrier en paiera v s. d'amende; c'est à savoir à la chapèle Saint-Bleive [Blaise] devant dite ij s., au mestre qui garde le mestier ij s., et a celui, qui le plastre aura mesuré xij den. Et cil à qui le plastre aura esté livré, rabastera de chascune asnée [charge d'un âne] que il aura eue en cèle ouvrage autant come on aura trouvé en cèle qu'il aura esté mesurée de rechief; mes j sac tant seulement ne puet-on pas mesurer.

Nus ne puet estre plastrier à Paris se il ne paie v s. de paris. au mestre qui garde le mestier de par le Roy; et quant il a paié les v s., il doit jurer seur sains que il ne metra rien avec le plastre fors du plastre et que il liverra bone mesure et loial.

Se li plastrier met avec son plastre autre chose que il ne doive, il est a v s. d'amende, à paier au mestre, toutes les fois qu'il en est reprins. Et se li plastriers en est coustumiers, ne ne s'en voille amender ne chastoier, li mestres li puet deffendre le mestier; et se li plastrier ne veut lessier le mestier pour le mestre, le mestre le doit faire savoir au prevost de Paris, et li prevoz doit celui plastrier faire forjurer le mestier devant dit.

Li mortelier doivent jurer devant le mestre du mestier, et devant, autres preudeshomes du mestier, qu'il ne feront nul mortier fors que de bon liois[2] et se il le feit d'autre pierre, ou le mortiers est de liois et est perciez au faire, il doit estre despeciez, et le doit amender au mestre du mestier de iiij den.

Li mortelier ne pueent prendre leur aprentis à mains de vj ans de service et cent s. de Paris pour euz aprendre.

Le mestre du mestier a la petite joustice et les amendes des maçons, des plastriers et des morteliers, et de leur aydes et de leur aprentis, tant come il plera au Roy, si come des entrepresures de leurs mestiers, et de bateures sanz sanc, et de clameur, hors mise la clameur de propriété.

Se aucun des mestiers devant diz et adjornés devant le mestre qui garde le mestier, se il est defaillans, il est à iiij den. d'amende à paier au mestre; et se il vient à son jour, et il cognoît, il doit gagier; et se il ne paie dedenz les nuiz, il est à iiij den. d'amende a paier au mestre; et se il nie, et il a tort, il est a iiij den a paier au mestre.

Le mestre qui garde le mestier ne puet lever que une amende de une querèle; et se cil qui l'amende a faite est si eroides,[3] et si foz que il ne voille obéir au commendement le mestre, ou s'amende paier, le mestre li puet deffendre le mestier.

Se aucun du mestier devant dit a cui le mestier soit deffenduz de par le mestre, ovre puis la deffense le mestre, le mestre li puet oster ses ostiz,[4] et tenir-les tant que il soit paié de s'amande; et se cil li voloit efforcier,[5]

[2] A sort of stone. [3] Derived from *irratus*. [4] Outils. [5] Resister avec violence.

le mestre le devroit faire savoir au prevost de Paris, et le prevost de Paris li devroit abatre la force.

Les maçon et les plastriers doivent le gueit et la taille et les autres redevances que li autre bourgois de Paris doivent au Roy.

Li mortelliers sont quite du gueit, et tout tailleur de pierre, très le tans Charles Martel, si come li preudome l'en oï[6] dire de père à fil.

Le mestre qui garde le mestier de par lou Roy est quite du gueit pour le service que il li feit de garder son mestier.

Cil qui ont lx ans passé, ne cil à qui sa fame gist, tant come èle gé, ne doivent point de gueit; mès il doivent faire savoir à celi qui le gueit garde de par le Roi.

Appendix 9

Rules for the Guild in Siena, 1292 (?)

Guglielmo della Valle, *Lettere senesi sopra le Belle Arti*, vol. 1, Venice, 1782, p. 280. Nell'Archivio dell'Opera, al Numero 1344.

In nomine Domini Amen. Ad honorem Dei et Beatae Virginis Mariae et Potestatis Populi et Vigintiquatuor Senensium et ad honorem et bonum statum Magistrorum Lapidum Senensium et eorum Dominorum qui erunt in futurum. Haec est voluntas Magistrorum Lapidum infrascriptorum videlicet quod in publica convocatione Magistrorum vel majoris partis debeant eligi tres Rectores et unus Camarlengus qui debeant durare et stare in eorum Signoria per sex menses et non plus et quilibet ex Dominis debeat habere pro suo feudo X Sol. et Camarlengus habeat V Sol. et ante finem eorum termini per unum mensem debeant Eligi similiter alios tres Rectores et unum Camarlengum et sic de singulis sex mensibus et in VI menses donec dicta societas duraverit, et hoc modo debeant eligi scilicet quod fiant brevia et mittantur simul de quibus tres sint scripta et debeant ire ad capiendum eos LXI Magistri. XXI de terzerio Civitatis et XX de Valle Sancti Martini et XX de Camullia et quicunque dicta Brevia scripta caperent ipsi debeant eligere Rectores et Camerarium et XIII Consiliarios V. de Cevitate IIII. de Valle Santi Martini et IIII. de Camullia.

Item quod dicti Consiliarij nec aliquis eorum possint sive possit cambiari nec aliquis alius in loco ipsorum vel ipsius mitti nisi esset infirmus vel extra Civitatem Senarum (a). [Footnote]

Item quod quicunque fuerit Rector vel Camerarius, vel Consiliarius deinde ad III. annos non possit habere in dicta Arte aliquam Signoriam.

Item quod Rectores et Camerarius nec aliquis eorum non possit pro comune dictae artis aliquas expensas facere sine consilio omnium Magistrorum vel majoris partis.

Item quod si quis Magister habuerit cum aliquo ex Magistris dictae

[6] l'ont oui.

Artis aliquam litem vel brigam possit unusquisque coram eorum Rectoribus ducere Indices et Notarium et Advocatos ad dicendum eorum jura et ad audiendum eos.

Item quod si quis Magister foretaneus intraverit in dicta Arte Magister dictae Artis ipsum debeant Sociare.

Item quod Camerarius teneatur XV. diebus ante finem sui termini reddere rationem de lucris acquisitis et expensis in publica convocatione et superfluum distribuere inter Magistros pro parte (a).

Haec petunt mitti et statui in Brevi Magistrorum Senensium cum emendabitur.

a) Il Tizio all'anno 1292. dice, che in questo tempo furono volgarizzati gli statuti *Statuta materna lingua edita sunt ad ambiguitates tollendas, etc.*

Forse questi non furono volgarizzati; perche quasi tutti gli Scultori essendo anche Pittori, si reggevano con gli Statuti Pittorieri, contenti di qualche piccola aggiunta.

This footnote "a" is added by Valle.

Appendix 10

York Minster Mason's Ordinances, 1370

Douglas Knoop and G. P. Jones, *The Mediaeval Mason*, Manchester, 1933, p. 248, contains original text. For the following rendering in modern English I am indebted to Professor David Coffin of Princeton University.

"It is ordained by the Chapter of the church of Saint Peter of York that all the masons who shall work at the works of the same church of Saint Peter, shall, from Michaelmas day until the first Sunday of Lent, be each day at morning at their work, in the lodge, that is ordained to the masons at work within the close beside the aforesaid church, as early as they may skillfully see by daylight in order to work; and they shall stand there truly working at their work all the day after, as long as they may skillfully see to work, if it be all workday: otherwise until high noon be struck by the clock, when holyday falls at noon, except within the aforesaid time between Michaelmas and Lent; and at all other time of the year they may dine before noon, if they wish, and also eat at noon where they like, so they shall not remain away from their works in the aforesaid lodge no time of the year at dinner time except so short a time that no skillful man shall find fault in their remaining away; and in time of meat at noon they shall, at no time of the year remain away from the lodges, nor from their aforesaid work, over the space of the time of an hour, and after noon they may drink in the lodge: and for their drinking time between Michaelmas and Lent they shall not cease nor leave their work exceeding the time of half a mile away: and from the first Sunday of Lent until Michaelmas they shall be in the aforesaid lodge at their work at sunrise, and stand there truly and busily working upon the aforesaid work of the church all the day, until there is no more space than time of a mile away before the sunset, if it be workday; otherwise until time of noon, as it is said before, except they shall, between the first Sunday of Lent and Michaelmas, dine and eat as is said before, and sleep and drink after noon in the aforesaid lodge; and they shall not cease nor leave their work during sleeping time exceeding the time of a mile away, nor in drinking time after noon, exceeding the time of a mile away. And they shall not sleep after noon no time but between Saint Elenmes and Lammes; and if any man remain away from the lodge and from the aforesaid work, or make default any time of the year against this aforesaid ordinance, he shall be chastised with abating of his payment, at the decision and direction of the master mason; and all their times and hours shall be revealed by a bell ordained therefore. And, also, it is ordained that no mason shall be received at work, to the work of the aforesaid church, but he be first proved a week or more upon his working well; and after he is found sufficient at his work, be received of the common assent of the master and the keepers of the work, and of the master mason, and swear upon the book that he shall truly and busily at his power, without any manner of deception, pretence, or deceit hold and keep holy all the points of this aforesaid ordinance, in all things that touch or may touch him, from the time that he is received to the aforesaid work as long as he shall remain mason hired at work at the aforesaid work of the church of Saint Peter, and not go away from that aforesaid work unless the masters give him leave to part from that aforesaid work: and whosoever comes against this ordinance and breaks it against the will of the aforesaid Chapter has he God's curse and Saint Peter's."

Appendix 11

Niavis, ca. 1460-1514

A. D. Richter, *Umständliche aus zuverlässigen Nachrichten zusammengetragene Chronika der . . . Stadt Chemnitz nebst beygefügten Urkunden*, Zittau and Leipzig, 1767, I. Theil. Das 6. Kapitel, p. 72. For the copy of this text, not easily available, I am indebted to Professor Herbert Koch in Halle a.S. It is useful to reproduce the whole passage both for a full understanding of the sentence on the brightness of late Gothic and for the specific vivacity.

Paulus Niavis, den ich schon mehrmal angeführt, lobet erstlich in seinem Idiomate, das er pro Religiosis, ohne Benennung des Jahres und des Ortes, drucken lassen, Cap. 2, das damalige Klosterbier, wenn er sagt: certe optima est cerevisia, nam omnino substantiosa est, servat tenuitatem mediocrem, nam potius bibo, quam Kempnicensem; und alsdenn erzehlet er folgende Umstände von diesem Kloster: Es wäre nemlich bey dem Kloster ein schöner Lustgarten, darinnen viele wohlriechende und medicinische Kräuter gepflanzet wären, auch wäre auf diesem Kloster ein schöner Brunnen, und das Wasser springe auf der einen Seite aus einem Löwenkopfe, auf der anderen Seite aus einem Menschenkopfe. (per os leonis et hominis). Es stünde auch in dem Kloster, im Gange, (in ambitu) ein Krucifix mit einem krummen oder schiefen Maule, (os eius incurvatum) von Holze, das soll einer in dem Hussitenkriege, da die Hussiten in das Kloster eingefallen, und alles darinnen verwüstet, ausgespottet haben, der von Stund an ein krummes offenstehendes Maul behalten, und stumm geworden wäre. Er sagt ferner von der damalas noch alten Klosterkirche, dass es ein starkes, aber altväterisches Gebäude, und dass sie nicht lichte gewesen, weil man vorhin gemeynet, es trüge vieles zur Andacht bey, dass eine Kirche nicht so gar lichte wäre; fit enim, spricht er, saepe in seculo, ubi ecclesias habent prorsus lucidas, ut dediti homines libidini, quum inspiciunt amantes, plus cupidini operam dent, quam orationibus. Den Bach bey der Schlossmühle lobet er als fischreich; die Wälder um das Schloss herum, darinnen der Abt zu seinem Vergnügen gejaget, reich an Widpret. Ferner sagt er, dass die Mönche aus dem Schlosse eine Badstube gehabt, darin sie alle 14 Tage einmal gebadet. Das Schloss wäre mit einer grossen Scheune, Ställen für Kühe, Pferde, Schweine, und Gebäuden für das Gesinde zur Wohnung versehen, und würden viele Pfaue gehalten, und zwar wegen des Ungeziefers, (quia vermes auferunt) desgleichen sehr viele Hüner, denn die Mönche speiseten wenig Fleisch, aber viele Eyer. Auch wäre auf dem Schlosse eine Trinkstube, und es wohneten in den Gebäuden, wo die Trinkstube darinnen wäre, zugleich viele Handwerksleute vor das Kloster, als Schuster, Schneider, und andere. Wann ein Mönch in das Kloster verlangte aufgenommen zu werden, so musste er zu drey verschiedenen malen darum anhalten. Denn so spricht, in diesem angeführten sermone Pauli Niavis, ein Mönch zu einem Ankömmling: neminem accipimus nisi fecerit idem ter petitiones. Cap. III. Locut. secunda sagt dieser Paulus Niavis durch die Personen, die er redend einführet, dass, wenn einer verlangt hätte, ein Mönch auf diesem Kloster zu werden: so habe zu solcher Aufnahme erst der Abt sein Votum gegeben, hernach, wenn diess erfolget, so wäre auch das Capitul darum gefragt worden, dass ein jeder sein Votum geben sollen, ob sie den neuen Ankömmling zu einem Mönch annehmen wollten, und habe der Prior bey beyden, sowohl bey dem Abte, als dem Capitul, solche Anfrage und den Vortrag thun müssen. . . . Anbey vermut ich, dass der jetzige grosse Schlossteich entweder ein neues Werk, oder doch damals noch nicht so gross, und die Pleisse zu der Zeit noch nicht mitten drinne, wie jetzo, gewesen sey. Denn dieser Paulus Niavis sagt in eben diesem Idiomate de Religiosis Cap. I, Locut., 1 dass man sich von oben herab vor dem Kloster, an dem Anschauen dieses unten bey dem Kloster vorbeyfliessenden Baches der Pleisse vergnügen können.

The last sentence is a literary counterpart to the painted landscapes of the same time.

Adam Daniel Richter was director of the College (Gymnasium) in Zittau in Saxonia and member of several associations of scholars.

APPENDIX 12

Giovanni Boccaccio, ca. 1469

Il Decameron, 49 Novelle commentate da Attilio Momigliani, 2nd ed., Milan, 1936, p. 260.

(VI, 5). E l'altro, il cui nome fu Giotto, ebbe uno ingegno di tanta eccellenzia, che niuna cosa dà la natura, madre di tutte le cose e operatrice, col continuo girar de' cieli, che egli con lo stile e con la penna o col penello non dipignesse sì simile a quella, che non simile, anzi più tosto dessa paresse; in tanto che molte volte nelle cose da lui fatte si truova che il visivo senso degli uomoni vi prese errore, quello credendo esser vero che era dipinto. E per ciò, avendo egli quella arte ritornata in luce, che molti secoli sotto gli error d'alcuni, che più a dilettar gli occhi degl'ignoranti che a compiacere allo'ntelleto de'savj dipignendo, era stata sepulta, meritamente una delle luci della fiorentina gloria dir si puote; e tanto più, quanto con maggiore umiltà, maestro degli altri in ciò vivendo, quella acquistò sempre rifiutando d'esser chiamato maestro.

APPENDIX 13

Filippo Villani, ca. 1400

Liber de civitatis Florentiae famosis civibus, ed. G. Camillo Galletti, Florence, 1847, p. 35.

Mihi quoque fas sit hoc loco, irridentium pace dixerim, egregios pictores Florentinos inserere, qui artem exanguem et pene extinctam suscitaverunt.

Inter quos primus Iohannes, cui cognomento Cimabue nomen fuit, antiquatam picturam, et Naturae similitudine, pictorum inscitia pueriliter discrepantem, coepit ad Naturae similitudinem, quasi lascivam et vagantem longius, arte et ingenio revocare. Constat siquidem ante hunc Grecam, Latinamque picturam per multa secula subcrassae (im)peritiae ministerio iacuisse, ut plane ostentunt figurae et imagines, quae in tabulis atque parietibus cernuntur sanctorum ecclesias adornare.

Cf. Julius Schlosser, *Geschichtsquellen . . . op.cit.*, p. 370, also his "Lorenzo Ghibertis Denkwürdigkeiten," Vienna, 1910, in *Kunsthistorisches Jahrbuch der K.K. Zentralkommission . . .* IV, Vienna, 1910, and his article "Gotik" from 1910, reprinted in *Präludien*, Berlin, 1927, p. 270, finally his *Kunstliteratur*, Vienna, 1924, p. 41.

APPENDIX 14

Aeneas Silvius Piccolomini (Pius II), 1457

Aeneas Silvius, *Germania*, 1457, ed. Friedrich Heininger, Leipzig, 1926, Ch. 3, p. 5.

Argentina vero tantus splendor, tantum decus, ut non ab re id nomen eiinditum fuerit. Quae similitudinem Venetiarum exhibet, multiplicibus divisa canalibus, quae naves in omnes ferme plateas vehunt: Eo salubrior atque amoenior, quod Venetias salsae et grave olentes, Argentinam et dulces et perspicuae percurrunt aquae. Hinc Rheni bracchio, inde tribus aliis fluminibus urbem intrantibus et triplicem murorum ordinem ambeuntibus. Ecclesia pontificalis, cui monasterio nomen est, secto lapide magnifice constructa in amplissimam fabricam assurexit, duabus ornata turibus, quarum altera, quae perfecta est, mirabile opus, caput inter nubila condit. Sunt et alia sanctorum delubra et monachorum coenobia et amplitudine et ornatu splendidissima. Praetorium excellens et civium et sacerdotum aedes, quas nec reges incoluisse pigerit.

Page 7: In Franconia supra Moenum iacet Francfordia, inter inferiores et superiores Teutones commune emporium, et urbs quamvis magna ex parte lignea pluribus tamen palatiis ornata lapideis, in quibus et reges haud indigne recipiantur, templa vero deo sacra et secto lapide superbissima visuntur. Et pons saxeus mirae longitudinis partem urbis trans Moenum minorem maiori coninungit. Hic et praetorium nobile, in quo saepe principes electores conveniunt de rebus acturi communibus et hic, cum vacat imperium, caesarem eligunt. . . .

Noricum oppidum flumine Pegnisia intersectum, nam hodie Franconibus datur, praeterire non possumus. Dic, rogamus, nam hinc uxorem duxisti castissimam aeque amoenitas, ac pulchram: Quaenam facies huius urbis, quis splendor, quae deliciae, quis cultus, quae forma regiminis, quid illic ad civitatem omnium ex parte perfectam, desiderare quispiam potuerit! Quis venientibus Franconia inferiori et procul spectantibus eius urbis adspectus, quae maiestas, quod decus ab extra visentibus, quis intus nitor platearum, quae domonum munditiae! Quid sancti Sebaldi templo magnificentius, quid splendidius divi Laurentii delubro! Quid arce regia vel superbius vel munitius, quid fossa, quid moenibus illustrius? Quot ibi civium aedes invenias regibus dignas! Cuperent tam egregie Scotorum reges quam mediocres Nurimbergae cives habitare.

Appendix 15a

Jacob Wimpheling, 1501

Epitoma rerum Germanicarum usque ad nostra tempora, cap. 67. (Quoted also in A. Horawitz, "Kunstgeschichtliche Miscellen aus deutschen Historikern," *Zeitschrift für bildende Kunst*, Leipzig, 1873, I, p. 26.)

In Architectura Germani excellentissimi sunt, quorum aedificia Aeneas Sylvius mirari se potuisse, scribit, non commentare. Sunt meo, inquit, judicio Theutonici mirabiles mathematici, omnesque gentes in Architectura superant. Hoc homo Italus de Germanis testatur, nec falsa loquutus est, quod ut caetera aedificia, (quae passim in Germania magnificentissime extructa sunt) ommittam, Argentinense Templum et turris in aedificata abunde demonstrant. Hac una structura nihil in universo orbe contenderim esse preciosius, nihil excellentius. Quis satis mirari, satis laudare potest Argentinensium turrim, quae caelatura statuis simulachris, variarumque rerum effigie omnis Europae aedificia facile excellit. cujus altitudo excedit numerum CCCC et XV cubitorum. Miraculum est, tantem molem in tam altum attolli potuisse, quid si isti a laudatis Autoribus laudati artifices reviviscerent, Scopa, Phidias, Ctesiphon, Archimedes, profecto in Architectura disciplina se victos esse a nostris, vel palam faterentur, atque hoc opus Dianae Ephesiae templo, et Pyramidibus Aegypticis, atque his omnibus quae inter septem spectacula numerantur, longe anteferrent.

Appendix 15b

Jacob Wimpheling, 1501

Epitoma rerum Germanicarum, cap. 68. De Pictura et Plastica.

Nostrates quoque pictores esse praestantissimos, vel ipsa experientia (quae rerum magistra est) apertissime docet. Icones Israelis Alemanni per universam Europam desiderantur, habenturque a pictoribus in summo precio. Quid de Martino Schon Colmariensi dicam, qui in hac arte fuit tam eximius, ut ejus depictae tabulae in Italiam, Hispanias, in Galliam, in Britanniam, et alia mundi loca abductae sint. Extant Colmariae, in templo Divi Martini, et Sancti Franscisci, praetera Sletstadii apud Praedicatores in ara, quae Divo Sebastino (sic)sacra est, imagines hujus manu depictae, ad quas effingendas exprimendasque pictores ipsi certatim confluunt, et si bonis artificibus et pictoribus fides adhibenda est, nihil elegantius, nihil amabilius, a quoquam depingi reddique poterit. Ejus discipulus Albertus Durer et ipse Alemanus hac tempestate excellentissimus est, et Nurnbergae imgines absolutissimas depingit, quae mercatoribus in Italiam transportarentur, et illic a probatissimis pictoribus non minus probantur, quam Parrhasii aut Apellis tabulae. Jonnes Hirtz Argentinensis non est ommittendus, qui dum in humanis esset, apud pictores omnes in magna fuit veneratione, cujus in pictura peritiam clarissimae ac speciosissimae imagines tum alibi, tum Argentinae in natali solo depictae testantur. In Plastica (hoc est figulina arte, quae ex terra similitudines itidem fingit) Germani praestantes sunt, quod ipsa figulina vasa, et plurima vasorum fictilium genera, quae modo humanae vitae usui sunt, iudicant et demonstrant. Hic sunt, quos vel Corebus Atheniensis, figulinae artis inventor, admirari possit et laudare.

Appendix 16

Lorenzo Ghiberti, ca. 1450

Commentarii. Text following Julius Schlosser, *Lorenzo Ghiberti Denkwürdigkeiten*, Berlin, 1912, p. 35.

Adunche al tempo di Constantino imperadore et di Siluestro papa sormontò su la fede christiana. Ebbe la ydolatria grandissima persecutione in modo tale, tutte le statue et le picture furon disfatte et lacerate di tanta nobilità et anticha et perfetta dignità et così si consumaron colle statue et picture et uilumi et commentarij et liniamenti et regole dauano amaestramento a tanta et egregia et gentile arte. Et poi leuare uia ogni anticho costume di ydolatria constituirono i templi tutti essere bianchi. In questo tempo ordinorono grandissima pena a chi facesse alcuna statua o alcuna pictura et cosi finì l'arte statuaria et la pictura et ogni doctrina che in essa fosse fatta. Finita che fu l'arte stettero e templi bianchi circa d'anni 600. Cominciorono i Greci debilissimamente l'arte della pictura et con molta roçeza produssero in essa; tanto quanto gl'antichi furon periti, tanto erano in questa età grossi et roçi. Dalla edificatione di Roma furono olimpie 382.

It follows the anecdote how Cimabue discovered the young Giotto when he drew a sheep and continues: "Giotto . . . fu discepolo di Cimabue, tenea la maniera greca, in quella maniera ebbe in Etruria grandissima fame." The maniera greca, according to Ghiberti, lasted from Charles the Great up to Cimabue.

Appendix 17

Antonio Averlino Filarete, 1464

Wolfgang von Oettinger, *Antonio Averlino Filarete's Traktat über die Baukunst usw.*, Vienna, 1890 (*Quellenschriften für Kunstgeschichte usw.* N.F. III), p. 428.

Do, per nostra fê, Signore, perchè, credete uoi, che questa scientia sia uenuta così meno, e che si sia così intralasciata l'usanza anticha, poich'ell'era così bella? Dirouelo, Signiore. Egli è stato per questo. Chè come le lettere mancorono in Ytalia, cioè che s'ingrossorono nel dire e nel latino, ê uenne una grossezza, che se non fusse da cinquanta o forse da sessanta anni in qua, che si sono asottigliati et isuegliati gl'ingegni. Egli era, come ò detto una grossa cosa; e così è stata questa arte; che per le ruine d'Italia, che sono state, e per le guerre di questi barbari, che più uolte l'anno disolata e sogiogata. Poi è accaduto, che pure oltramonti è uenuto molte usance e loro riti; e perchè di questi grandi hedifitij non si faceuano, per cagione che Ytalia era pouera, gl'huomini ancora non si exercitauano troppo in simili cose. E non essendo gli huomini exercitati, non si assottigliauano di sapere, e così le scienze di queste cose si perdono. Et uenuto poi, quando per Ytalia s'è uoluto fare alcuno hedificio, sono ricorsi quegli, che anno uoluto far fare, a orefici e dipintori, e questi muratori, i quali, benchè appartenga in parte al loro exercitio, pure è molta differentia. E che anno dato quegli modi, che anno saputo e che è paruto a loro, secondo i loro lauori moderni. Gli orefici fanno loro a quella somilitudine e forma de'tabernacoli e de'turibili da dare incenso; et a quella somilitudine e forma fatti i dificij perchè a quegli lauori paiano begli; et anche più si confanno ne'loro lauori, che non fanno ne'dificij. E questo huso e modo anno auuto, come ò detto, da tramontani, cioè da Todeschi e da Francesi; e per queste cagioni si sono perdute.

Appendix 18

François Rabelais, 1533

Œuvres de François Rabelais, ed. Abel Lefranc . . . , III, Paris, 1922, p. 102. Le temps éstoit encores tenebreux et setant l'infelicite et la calamite des Gothz, qui avoient mis a destruction toute bonne literature; mais, par la bonté divine, la lumière et dignité a este de mon eage rendue es (aux) lettres, e y voy tel amendement que de present a difficulte seroys je receu en la premiere classe des petitz grimaulx (écoliers des classas élémentaires) qui en mon eage virile estoys non a tord reputé les plus scavant dudict siecle.

Lefranc, the editor, adds in his commentary: Chez tous les humanistes du temps de Rabelais, ce mot (Goths) tend à devenir synonym de barbares et à désigner les gens et les oeuvres du moyen-âge en général.

Another passage of similar tendency follows in Rabelais p. 119. The first edition of Pantagruel is from 1533, the first from Gargantua from 1535. The third book was published 1546, the fourth 1548-1552.

Appendix 19

Giorgio Vasari, 1550

Le vite, ed. Gaetano Milanesi, I, Florence, 1878, p. 137.

Ècci un'altra specie di lavori che si chiamano tedeschi, i quali sono di ornamenti e di proporzione molto differenti dagli antichi e dai moderni. Nè oggi s'usano per gli eccellenti, ma son fuggiti da loro come mostruosi e barbari, dimenticando ogni lor cosa di ordine; che più tosto confusione o disordine si può chiamare, avendo fatto nelle lor fabbriche, che son tante che hanno ammorbato il mondo le porte ornate di colonne sottili ed attorte a uso di vite, le quali non possono aver forza a reggere il peso di che leggerezza si sia. E così, per tutte le facce ed altri loro ornamenti, facevano una maledizione di tabernacolini l'un sopra l'altro, con tante piramidi e punte e foglie, che, non ch'elle possano stare, pare impossibile ch' elle si possano reggere; ed hanno più il modo da parer fatte di carta, che di pietro o di marmi. Ed in queste opere facevano tanti risalti, rotture, mensoline e viticci, che sproporzionavano quelle opere che facevano; e spesso con mettere cosa sopra cosa, andavano in tanta altezza, che la fine d'una porta toccava loro il tetto. Questa maniera fu trovata dai Goti, che, per aver ruinate le fabbriche antiche e morti gli architetti per le guerre, fecero dopo coloro che rimasero le fabbriche di questa maniera: le quali girarono le volte con quarti acuti, e riempierono tutta Italia di questa maledizione di fabbriche, che per non averne a far più s'è dismesso ogni modo loro. Iddio scampi ogni paese dal venir tal pensiero ed ordine di lavori; che, per essere eglino talmente difformi alla bellezza delle fabbriche nostre, meritano che non se ne favelli più che questo. E però passiamo a dire delle volte.

Appendix 20

Philibert de L'Orme, 1567

Architecture, Paris, 1568, 2nd ed., p. 107 and Rouen, 1648, p. 107.

Les maistres maçons de ce royaume, et aussi d'autres pays, ont accoustumé de faire les voutes des eglises esquelles y a grande espace (comme sont grandes sales) auec vne croisée qu'ils appellent croisées d'ogiues. Aucuns y vsent de liernes, formerets et tiercerons, auec leurs doubleaux, et plusieurs autres sortes de branches, lesquelles ils mettent dans les voutes: les vnes en forme de soufflet, qui sont formes rondes, et rampent pour rencontrer les branches. Telles choses sont difficiles à conduire, principalement quand on y veult faire vn pendentif par dessus qui soit de pierre de taille, et s'accomode iustement sur les branches ou arcs de pierre, qui sont tous d'vne mesme grosseur, et correspondants aux moulures des croisées d'ogiues, liernes, formerets, et autres. Ces façons de voutes ont esté trouuées fort belles, et s'en voit de bien executées et mises en oeuure en divers lieux de ce royaume, et signamment en ceste ville de Paris, comme aussi en plusieurs autres. Auiourd'huy ceux qui ont quelque cognoissance de la vraye Architecture, ne suiuent plus ceste façon de voute, appelée entre les ouuriers, La *mode Françoise*, la quelle veritablement ie ne veux despriser, ains plutost confesser qu'on y a faict et pratiqué de [*sic*] fort bon traicts et difficiles. Mais pour autant que telle façon requiert grande boutée, c'est à dire grande force pour seruir de poulser et faire les arcs-boutans, afin de tenir l'oeuure serrée, ainsi qu'on le voit aux grandes eglises: pource est il que sur la fin de ce present chapitre pour mieux faire entendre et cognoistre mon dire, ie descriray vne voulte auec sa montée, telle que vous la pourrez voir soubs la forme d'vn quarré parfaict, autant large d'vn costé que d'autres, ou vous remarquerez la croisée d'ogiues, ainsi appelée des maistres maçons, qui n'est autre chose que l'arc ou branche allant diametralement ou diagonalement (selon diuerses situations de la figure) d'vn angle à l'autre, comme vous le voyez aux deux lignes marquées B, qui monstrent ladite croisée d'ogiues.

Appendix 21

Fernando de la Torre Farfan, 1671

Fiestas de la Iglesia metropolitana y patriarcal de Sevilla, Seville, 1671, p. 11.

Grandezza del Templo es la Fabrica deste Ilustre Edificio Incomparable anunque Antigua, y Veneracion Admirable de las Naciones que el Gran Comercio desta Ciudad awastra desde lo mas Remoto del Orbe, aun despues de aver visto los Milagros Esparcidos en la Hermosura de Italia, y Abrewiados en la Soberania de Roma.

In Arquitectura es Gotica, o por ser la mas Excelente en aquella Edad, o porque se reputaria por la de Mayor Sufrimiento como Obra que se criava para sufrir el Peso Continuado de los Siglos, y mantener en ellos el Cetro de la Mayestad assegurado en las Calunas de su Fortaleza. Tal se venera en el Archiuvo desta Iglesia el Arcuerdo de aquellos Insignes Capitulares, que con Santo Diclamen dexaron las Suyas para labrarle a Dios tan coudigua Casa. De donde procede, que la Grande Techumbre por la parte de a fuera vaya formando Places y Calles espaciosas, formadas de los muchos Arcos, que coronan el Edificio para la Seguridad, y Finneza, ayudando a leuantar su Hermosura la Variedad continua de Remates, y Capiteles dividos en bellos Obeliscos, y corpulentos Piramides cuya Labor llaman Cresteria y cuya Pintura non cabe en la Descripcion, y solo puede examinarla la Comprehension de la Vista; Aunque no se escusa el dezir, que quien sube a tantearlo Curioso, siempre buelve Confuso; Y ordinariamente los que van a buscar Diversion suelen hallar Laberintos.

Appendix 22

Roland Fréart de Chambray, 1707

John Evelyn published an English translation: A Parallel of Ancient Architecture with Modern in a Collection of ten Principal Authors who have written upon Five Orders . . . to which is added an "Account of Architects, in an Historical and Etymological Explanation of certain Terms particularly affected by Architects. With Leon Baptista Alberti's Treatise of Statues." London, 1664. The second edition of this translation, published after Evelyn's death (1707) contains the following passage on page 9, not contained in the first edition.

To Enlarge on the several Heads of *Civil Architecture* (of which there are very many) would be to Extend this Discourse to a length not so proportionable to that which is design'd: Let it then Suffice to take Notice, That it is the Ancient *Greek* and *Roman Architecture* only, which is here Intended, as most entirely answering all those Perfections requir'd in a Faultless and Accomplish'd Building; such, as for so many Ages were *so* Renowned and Reputed, by the Universal Suffrages of the Civiliz'd World, and would doubtless have still subsisted, and made good their

Claim, and what is Recorded of them; had not the *Goths, Vandals* and other Barbarous Nations, Subverted and Demolish'd them, together with that Glorious *Empire* where those stately and pompous Monuments stood; Introducing in their stead, a certain Fantastical and Licencious manner of Building, which we have since call'd *Modern* (or *Gothic* rather) Congestions of Heavy, Dark, Melancholy and *Monkish Piles*, without any just Proportion, Use or Beauty, compar'd with the truly *Ancient*: So as when we meet with the Greatest Industry, and expensive *Carving*, full of *Fret* and lamentable *Imagery*; sparing neither Pains nor Cost; a Judicious Spectator is rather Distracted and quite Confounded, than touch'd with that Admiration, which results from the true and just *Symmetrie*, regular Proportion, Union and Disposition; Great and Noble manner, which those *August* and Glorious Fabrics of the *Ancients* still Produce.

It was after the Irruption, and Swarmes of those Truculent People from the North; the Moors and Arabs from the South and East, over-running the Civiliz'd World; that wherever they fix'd themselves, they soon began to Debauch this Noble and Useful Art; when instead of those Beautiful *Orders*, so Majestical and Proper for their Stations, becoming Variety and other Ornamental Accessories; they set up those Slender and Misquine *Pillars*, or rather bundles of *Staves*, and other incongruous Props, to support incumbert Weights, and pondrous Arched Roofs, without *Entablature*; and tho' not without great Industry (as M. D'Avilier well observes) nor altogether Naked of Gaudy *Sculpture*, trite and busy Carvings; 'tis such as rather Gluts the Eye, than Gratifies and Pleases it with any reasonable Satisfaction: For Proof of this (without Travelling far abroad) I dare Report my self to any Man of Judgment, and that has the least Taste of Order and Magnificence; If after he has look'd a while upon *King Henry* the VIIth's *Chappel* at *Westminster*; Gaz'd on its sharp *Angles*, *Jetties*, Narrow Lights, lame *Statues, Lace* and other *Cut-work* and *Crinkle Crankle*; and shall then turn his Eyes on the *Banqueting-House* built at White-Hall by *Inego Jones* after the Ancient manner; or on what his *Majesties* present *Surveyor* Sir *Christopher Wren* has lately advanc'd at St. *Paul's*; and consider what a Glorious Object the disign'd *Cupola, Portico, Colonads* and other (yet Unfinish'd) Parts, will then present the Beholder: Or compare the *Schools* and *Library* at *Oxford* with the *Theatre* there; or what he has lately Built at *Trinity College* in *Cambridge*, and since all these at *Greenwich* and other Places (by which time our *Home-Traveller*, will begin to have a just *Idea* of the *Ancient* and *Modern Architecture*) I say, let him well consider, and compare them judiciously, without Partiality and Prejudice; and then Pronounce, which of the two *Manners* strikes the Understanding as well as the Eye with the more Majesty, and solemn Greatness; tho' in so much a Plainer and

Simple Dress, Conforme to the Respective Orders and *Entablature*; and accordingly determine, to whom the Preference is due: Not as we said, that there is not something of solid, and *Odly* Artificial too, after a sort: But then the Universal and unreasonable Thickness of the Walls, Clumsy Buttresses, Towers, sharp pointed Arches, Doors and other Apertures, without Proportion; Non-Sense Insertions of various Marbles impertinently plac'd; Turrets, and Pinacles thick set with *Munkies* and *Chimeares* (and abundance of buisy Work and other Incongruities) dissipate, and break the Angels of the Sight, and so Confound it, that one cannot consider it with any Steadiness, where to begin or end; taking off from that Noble *Aier* and *Grandure*, Bold and Graceful manner, which the *Ancient* had so well, and judiciously Establish'd: But, in this sort have they, and their Followers ever since fill'd, not all *Europe* alone, but *Asia* and *Africa* besides, with Mountains of Stone, Vast, and Gygantic Buildings indeed; but not Worthy the Name of *Architecture*: Witness (besides frequent Erections in these Kingdoms, Inferior to none for their utmost Performances) what are yet standing at *Westminster, Canterbury, Salisbury, Peterborow, Ely, Wells, Beverly, Lincoln, Gloucester, York, Durham* and other *Cathedrals* and *Minsters*: What a *Utrecht*, Harlem, *Antwerp, Strasburg, Basil*, in the lower and upper *Germany*: At *Amiens, Paris, Roan, Tours, Lyons* etc. in *France*; at *Milan, Venice, Florence*, nay in *Rome* herself: In Spain, at *Burges* and *Seville*, with what the *Moors* have left in Athambrant, Granada. The *Santa Sophia* at *Constantinople*; That of the *Temple* of the *Sepulchre* at *Jerusalem* (at the Decadence at least of the Art.) The *Zerifs* Palace at *Marocco*, etc. besides the innumerable *Monasteries* and Gloomy *Cells*, built in all these Places by the *Christians, Greeks, Latines, Armenians, Moors*, and others since the Ruin of the Empire; and compare (almost numberless as they are) with *One* St. *Peter's* at *Rome* only, which, with the rest of those venerable *Churches*, Superb and Stately *Palaces* there and at *Naples, Florence, Genoa, Escurial, Paris, Amsterdam*, etc. were yet all but sorry Buildings, till *Bramante, Raphael, Mich. Angelo, Palladio*, (*Bernini*) and other *Heroes* and Masters of our *Parallel*, Recover'd and even Raised this *Art* to Life again, and Restor'd her to her Pristine Splendor and Magnificence, after so tedious and dismal a Night of Ignorance and Superstition, in which *Architecture* had lain Buried in Rubbish, and sadly deform'd for so many Ages: The same may likewise be affirm'd of all those other *Arts* attendant upon her, *Sculpture* and *Painting* especially, and in deed of *Letters*, and all good Learning too, which had about this time their *Resuscitation* also; In a Word, and after all that has been said of *Architecture* Ancient, or Modern; 'tis not we see enough to Build for *Strength* alone (for those *Gothic* Piles we find stand their Ground, and the *Pyramids* of *Aegypt* have out-lasted all that Art and Labour have to shew) or indeed for bare Accommodation only, without due *Proportion, Order* and *Beauty*, and those other *Agreements*, and genuine *Characters* of a Perfect, and Consummate Building; and therefore an *Art* not so easily attain'd by every Pretender, nor in Truth at all; without a more than ordinary *Disposition*, accompanied with Judgement, Industry and Application; due Instruction, and Rules of Art Subservient to it. Thus Accomplish'd, an *Architect* is perfectly qualified to answer all the *Transcendences* of this Noble *Art*, which is to Build *Handsomly, Solidly* and *Usefully*.

Appendix 23

Christopher Wren, 1668

James Elmes, *Memoirs of the Life and Works of Sir Christopher Wren*, London, 1823, p. 255. A report of Christopher Wren on the Cathedral of Salisbury.

The whole pile is large and magnificent and may be justly accounted one of the best patterns of architecture in the age where-in it was built. The figure of the church is a cross, upon the intersection of which stands a tower and spire of stone, as high from the foundation as the whole length of the *navis*, or body of the church; and it is founded only upon the four pillars and arches of the intersection. Between the steeple and the east is another crossing of the *navis*, which on the westside only wants its aisles; all other sides of the main body and the crosses are supported on pillars with aisles annexed, and buttressed without the aisles, from whence arise bows, or flying buttresses, to the walls of the *navis*, which are concealed within the timber roof of the aisles. The roof is almost as sharp as an equilateral triangle. . . . The whole church is vaulted with chalk between arches and cross springers only, after the ancienter manner without orbs and tracery, excepting under the tower, where the springers divide, and represent a wider sort of tracery. And this appears to me to have been later work, and to be done by some other hand than that of the first architect, whose judgment I must justly commend for many things beyond what I find in divers Gothic fabrics of later date; which, though more elaborated with nice and small works, yet want the natural beauty which arises from the proportions of the first dimensions. . . . The windows are not too great, nor yet the light obstructed with many mullions and transoms of tracery work, which was the ill-fashion of the next following age: our artist knew better, that nothing could add beauty to the light; he trusted to a stately and rich plainness, that his marble shafts gave to his work: I cannot call them pillars, because they are so small and slender, and generally bear nothing, but are only added for ornament to the outside of the great pillars, and decently fastened with brass.

(There follows an enumeration of the errors.)

The document is important in its terminology. For example, he calls the double curved arches in the crossing "tracery." Still more interesting is the fact that he calls late Gothic "more elaborate with nice and small works" yet wanting the "natural beauty." By this he means the proportions of classical style.

Appendix 24

François de Salignac de la Motte Fénélon, 1714

Œuvres de Fénélon, Lettre sur les occupations de l'Académie Française, addressée a M. Dacier, pp. 157ff. The title of the last chapter is: Sur les anciens et les plus modernes, p. 238.

P. 259. Il est naturel que les modernes, qui on beaucoup d'élégance et de tours ingénieux, se flattent de surpasser les anciens, qui n'ont que la simple nature. Mais je demande la permission de faire ici une espèce d'apologue. Les inventeurs de l'architecture qu'on nomme *gothique*, et qui est, dit-on, celle des Arabes, crurent sans doute avoir surpassé les architectes grecs. Un édifice grec n'a aucun ornement qui ne serve qu'a orner l'ouvrage; les pièces necessaires pour le soutenir ou pour le mettre à couvert, comme les colonnes et la corniche, se tournent seulement en grâce par leur proportions: tout est simple, tout est mesuré, tout est borné à l'usage; on n'y voit ni hardiesse ni caprice qui impose aux yeux; les proportions sont si justes, que rien ne paroît fort grand, quoique tout le soit; tout es borné a contenter la vraie raison. Au contraire, l'architecte gothique élève sur des piliers tres-minces une voûte immense qui monte jusqu'aux nues; on croit que tout va tomber, mais tout dure pendant bien des siècles; tout est plein de fenêtres, de roses et de pointes; la pierre semble découpée comme du carton; tout est à jour, tout est en l'air. N'est-il pas naturel que les premiers architectes gothiques se soient flattés d'avoir surpassé, par leur vain raffinement, la simplicité grecque? Changez seulement les noms, mettez les poètes et les orateurs en la place des architectes: Lucain devait naturellement croire qu'il étoit plus grand que Vergile; Sénèque le tragique pouvoit s'imaginer qu'il brilloit bien plus que Sophocle; le Tasse a pu espérer de laisser derrière lui Virgile et Homère. Ces auteurs se seroient trompés en pensant ainsi: les plus excellens auteurs de nos jours doivent craindre de se tromper de même.

Appendix 25

François de Salignac de la Motte Fénélon, 1718

Dialogue sur l'Éloquence en général et sur celle de la chaire en particulier, Paris, 1718, pp. 156ff.

A: Connoissez-vous l'Architecture de nos vielles Églises qu'on nomme Gothique?

B: Oui, je la connois, on la trouve partout.

A: N'avez-vous pas remarqué ces roses, ses points, ces petits ornemens coupez et sans dessein suivi, enfin tous ces colifichets dont elle est pleine. Voilà en Architecture ce que les anthithèses et les autres jeux de mots sont dans l'Éloquence. L'Architecture Grecque est bien plus simple, elle n'admet que des ornemens majestueux et naturels, on n'y voit rien que de grand, de proportionné, de mis en sa place. Cette Architecture qu'on apelle Gothique, nous est venues des Arabes; ces sortes d'esprits étant fort vifs et n'ayant ni régle ni culture, ne pouvaient manquer de se jetter dans de fausses subtilitez. De-là vint ce mauvais goût en toutes choses. Ils ont été sophistes en raisonnemens, amateurs de colifichets en Architecture, et inventeurs de pointes en Poësie et en Éloquence. Tous cela est du même génie.

B: Cela est fort plaisant. Selon vous un Sermon plein d'antithèses et d' autres semblable ornemens est fait comme une Église batie à la Gothique.

A: Ouy, c'est précisement cela.

Appendix 26a

François Blondel the Younger, 1751, article *Architecture*.

Diderot, *Encyclopedie*, I, Paris, 1751, p. 617.

Ensuite Alexandre Sévère soûtint encore par son amour pour les arts l'architecture: mais il ne put empêcher qu'elle ne fût entraînée dans la chûte de l'empire d'Occident, et quelle ne tombât dans un oubli dont elle ne put se relever de plusieurs siecles, pendant l'espace desquels les Visigots detruisirent les plus beaux monuments de l'antiquité, et où l'architecture se trouva réduite a une telle barbarie, que ceux qui la professoient, négligerent entierement la justesse des proportions, la convenance et la correction du dessein, dans lesquels consiste tout le mérite de cet art.

De cet abus se forma une nouvelle maniere de bâtir que l'on nomme *gothique*, et qui a subsisté jusqu'à ce que Charlemagne entreprit de rétablir l'ancienne. Alors la France s'y applica avec quelque succès, encouragée par Hugues Capet, qui avoit aussi beau coup de goût pour cette science. Robert son fils, qui lui succéda, eut les mêmes inclinations; de sorte que par degrés l'architecture, en changeant de face, donna dans un excès opposé en devenant trop légere; les architectes de ces tems-là faisant consister les beautés de leur architecture dans une délicatesse et une profusion d'ornemens jusq'alors inconnus: excès dans lequel ils tomberent sans doute par opposition à la gothique qui les avoit précédés, ou par le goût qu'ils reçûrent des Arabes et des Maures, qui apportèrent ce genre en France des pays méridionaux; comme les Vandales et les Goths avoient apporté du pays du nord le goût pesant et gothique.

Appendix 26b

François Blondel the Younger, 1752

Architecture Françoise, I. The passage on the *chapiteaux à la place des bases* in which he differentiates between an *architecture gothique ancienne* from the sixth to the eleventh century and an *architecture moderne* from the eleventh century to François I is on p. 14 and is followed on p. 15 by the judgment upon this second style.

La seconde Architecture Gothique nommée moderne, a duré environ depuis le onzième siècle jusque vers le régne de François premier, et elle a une origine bien différente, suivant le sentiment de quelque-uns qui l'attribuent aux Maures ou aux Arabes, qui ont eu dans leur Architecture le même goût que dans leur Poësie, l'une et l'autre étant aussi chargées d'ornemens superflus qu' éloignées du naturel; ceux-ci n'ayant cherché à se distinguer des Goths que par l'excessive hardiesse de l'élévation de leurs monumens, aussi bien que par l'abondance, la finesse et la bizarrerie de leur ornemens. Pour convenir de cette vérité, il ne faut que consulter ceux qui ont vû ou donné les descriptions des Mosquées et des Cathédrales d'Espagne bâties par les Maures; et l'on verra que c'est de la région de ces peuples que cette Architecture a passé en Europe. En effet les Lettres fleurirent chez les Arabes dans le tems que leur Empire etoit le plus puissant, et ils cultiverent la Philosophie, les Mathématiques et la Médicine: leur example ranima l'amour des sciences dans les pays qu'ils avoient conquis aux environs de l'Espagne; on lut leurs Auteurs, leur Philosophie se répandit dans l'Europe, et l'Architecture Arabe avec elle; ensuite l'on bâtit beaucoup d'Églises dans le goût Moresque, sans corriger même ce qui convenoit plutôt à des pays chauds qu'à des régions tempérées. Cette manière a duré jusque vers la fin du quinzième siècle, et c'est dans l'espace de ce temps que l'on a édifié en 1220 l'Eglise Cathédrale d'Amiens. . . .

Appendix 27

William Warburton, 1760

Richard Elsam, *An Essay on Rural Architecture*, London, 1803, p. 13. Quotation from Warburton, *Pope's Moral Essays*, 1760.

Our Gothic ancestors had juster and manlier notions of magnificence on Greek and Roman ideas, than these mimics of taste, who profess to study only classic elegance; and because the thing does honour to the genius of those barbarians, I shall endeavour to explain it. All our ancient churches are called, without distinction, Gothic, but erroneously: they are of two sorts; the one built in the Saxon times, the other in the Norman. Several cathedrals, and collegiate churches of the first sort are yet remaining, either in whole or in part; of which this was the original;

when the Saxon kings became Christians, their piety (which was the piety of the times) consisted chiefly in building churches at home, and performing pilgrimages abroad, especially to the Holy Land; and these spiritual exercises assisted and supported one another; for the most venerable, as well as the most elegant models of religious edifices, were then in Palestine. From these the Saxon builders took the whole of their ideas, as may be seen by comparing the drawings which travelers have given us of the churches yet standing in that country, with the Saxon remains of what we find at home, and particularly in that sameness of style in the latter religious edifices of the knights templars (professedly built upon the model of the church of the Holy Sepulchre, at Jerusalem) with the earlier remains of our Saxon edifices. Now the architecture of the Holy Land was Grecian, but greatly fallen from its ancient elegance. Our Saxon performance was indeed a bad copy of it; and as much inferior to the works of St. Helene and Justinian, as theirs were to the Grecian models they had followed; yet still the footsteps of ancient art appeared in the circular arches, the entire columns, the division of the entablature into a sort of architrave, frieze, corniche, and a solidity equally diffused over the whole mass. This by way of distinction, I would call the Saxon architecture. But our Norman works had a very different original. When the Goths had conquered Spain, and the genial warmth of the climate, and the religion of the old inhabitants, had ripened their wits and inflamed their mistaken piety (both kept in exercise by the neighbourhood of the Saracens, through emulation of their service, and aversion to their superstition), they struck out a new species of architecture, unknown to Greece and Rome, upon original principles and ideas, much nobler than what had given birth even to classical magnificence.

For this northern people having been accustomed, during the gloom of paganism, to worship the Deity in groves (a practice common to all nations), when their new religion required covered edifices, they ingeniously projected to make them resemble groves as nearly as the distance of architecture would permit, at once indulging their old prejudices, and providing for their present conveniences, by a cool receptacle in a sultry climate; and with what skill and success they executed the project, by the assistance of Saracen architecture, whose exotic style of building very luckily suited their purpose, appears from hence, that no attentive observer ever viewed a regular avenue of well-grown trees, intermixing their branches over head, but it presently put him in mind of the long visto through the Gothic cathedral; or even entered one of the larger and more elegant edifices of this kind, but it presented to his imagination an avenue of trees; and this alone is what can be truly called the Gothic style of building. Under this idea of so extraordinary a species of architecture, all the irregular transgression against art, all the monstrous offences against nature, disappear; every thing has its reason, every thing is in order, and an harmonious whole arises from the studious application of means proper and proportioned to the end. For, could the arches be otherwise than pointed, when the workmen were to imitate that curve which branches of two opposite trees make by their insertion with one another, or could the columns be otherways than split into distinct shafts, when they were to represent the stems of a clump of trees growing close together? On the same principles they formed the spreading ramification of the stone-work in the windows, and the stained glass in the interstices, the one to represent the branches, and the other the leaves, of an opening grove, and both concurred to preserve that gloomy light which inspires religious reverence and dread. Lastly, we see the reason of their studied aversion to apparent solidity in these stupendous masses, deemed so absurd by men accustomed to the apparent, as well as real strength of Grecian architecture. Had it been only a wanton exercise of the artist's skill to show he could give real strength without the appearance of any, we might, indeed, admire his superior science; but we must needs condemn his ill judgment. But when one considers that this surprising lightness was necessary to complete the execution of his idea of a sylvan place of worship, one cannot sufficiently admire the ingenuity of the contrivance. This too, will account for the contrary qualities in what I call the Saxon architecture. These artists copied, as has been said, from the churches of the Holy Land, which were built on the models of the Grecian architecture, but corrupted by prevailing barbarism; and still further depraved by a religious idea. The first places of Christian worship were sepulchres and subterraneous caverns, low and heavy from necessity. When Christianity became the religion of the state, and sumptuous temples began to be erected, they yet, in regard to the first pious ages, preserved the massive style, made still more venerable by the church of the Holy Sepulchre, where this style was, on a double account, followed and aggravated.

Appendix 28

Francois René Chateaubriand, 1801

Génie du Christianism, Paris, 1801, Troisieme partie, Chapitre VIII.

On ne pouvoit entrer dans une église gothique sans éprouver une sorte de frisonnement et un sentiment vague de la Divinité. On se trouvoit tout-à-coup reporté à ces temps où des cénobites après avoir médité dans les bois de leur monastères, se venoient prosterner à l'autel, et chanter les louanges du Seigneur dans le calme et le silence de la nuit. L'ancienne France sembloit revivre: on croyoit voir ces costumes singuliers, ce peuple si différent de ce qu'il est aujourd'hui; on se rappeloit et les révolutions de ce peuple, et ses travaux et ses arts. Plus ces temps étaient éloignés de nous, plus ils nous paraissaient magiques, plus ils nous remplissaient de ces pensées qui finissent toujours par une réflexion sur le néant de l'homme et la rapidité de la vie.

L'ordre gothique, au milieu de ces proportions barbares, a toutefois une beauté qui lui est particulière.

Les forêts ont été les premiers temples de la Divinité, et les hommes ont pris dans les forêts la première idée de l'architecture. Cet art a donc dû varier selon les climats. Les Grecs ont tourné l'élégante colonne corinthienne, avec son chapiteau de feuilles sur le modèle du palmier. Les enormes piliers du vieux style égyptien représentent le sycomore, le figuier oriental, le bananier et la plupart des arbres gigantesques de l'Afrique et de l'Asie.

Les forêts des Gaules ont passé à leur tour dans les temples de nos pères, et nos bois de chênes ont ainsi maintenu leur origine sacrée. Ces voûtes ciselées en feuillages, ces jambages qui appuient les murs et finissent brusquement comme des troncs brisés, la fraîcheur des voûtes, les ténèbres du sanctuaire, les ailes obscures, les passages secrets, les portes abaissées, tout retrace les labyrinthes des bois dans l'église gothique; tout en fait sentir la religieuse horreur, les mystères et la Divinité. Les deux tours hautaines, plantées à l'entrée de l'édifice, surmontent les ormes et les ifs du cimetière, et font un effet pittoresque sur l'azur du ciel. Tantôt le jour naissant illumine leurs têtes jumelles; tantôt elles paroissent couronnées d'un chapiteau de nuages, ou grossies dans une atmosphère vaporeuse. Les oiseaux eux-mêmes semblent s'y méprendre, et les adopter pour les arbres de leurs forêts: des corneilles voltigent autour de leurs faites et se perchent sur leurs galeries. Mais tout-à coup des rumeurs confuses s'échappent de la cime de ces tours et en chassent les oiseaux effrayés. L'architecte chrétien, non content, à bâtir des forêts, a voulu, pour ainsi dire, en imiter les murmures; et, au moyen de l'orgue et du bronze suspendu, il a attaché au temple gothique jusqu'au bruit des vents et des tonnerres, qui roulent dans la profondeur des bois. Les siècles évoqués par ces sons religieux, font sortir leurs antique voix du sein des pierres, et soupirent dans la vaste basilique: le sanctuaire mugit comme l'antre de l'ancienne Sibylle; et tandis que l'airain se balance avec fracas sur votre tête, les souterrains voûtés de la mort se taisent profondement sous vos pieds.

Appendix 29

Johannes Wetter, 1835

The importance of Wetter to the present subject justifies the inclusion of a few biographical notes.

His father, Augustin Wetter (1765-1838), was municipal architect in Mainz, his mother's maiden name was Wolf. Johannes was the eldest of eight children (parish register of the Catholic church of St. Emmeran in Mainz). In the death roll he is entered as living on his private income and unmarried. In H. E. Scriba's *Lexikon der Schriftsteller des Gross-*

herzogtums Hessen, Darmstadt, 1843, there is just this single sentence: "Johann, born 1795 in Mainz, was a pupil at the French Lycée in this town, devoted his life to architecture and resided in his native town." His life seems to have been a quiet one. His writings up to 1843 are enumerated in Scriba's book, a list of the rest can be found in the catalogue of the municipal library in Mainz.

The early writings deal with the architecture of theaters in Germany, the art of printing, the paintings of the dome at Mainz and the guide to the cathedral mentioned in the text (page 526). The publications after 1843 are as follows:

"Conrad Henlif or Henekis, Buchdrucker and Buchhändler zu Mainz, der Geschäftsgenosse Peter Schöffers," *Zeitschrift des Vereins zur Erforschung der rheinischen Geschichte und Altertümer in Mainz*, I; *Der Mythos vom Atlas und seine neueren Deutungen, eine mythologische Forschung*, Mainz, 1858.

"Die Kirche zum heil. Geist in Mainz, ein Denkmal der Baukunst in romanischen Styl, lombardischer Art, aus der Mitte des dreizehnten Jahrhunderts," *Zeitschrift des Vereins*, II, 1859.

Appendix 30a

Auguste Rodin, 1914

Les Cathédrales de France, Paris, 1914, p. 2.

Et comme toute application rationnelle d'un principe juste a d'heureuses conséquences dans tous les domaines, au delà des prévisions immediates du savant et de l'artisan, les Gothiques furent de grands peintres parce qu'ils étaient de grands architectes.—Il va de soi que nous prenons ici le mot peintre dans un sens vaste et général. Les couleurs dans lesquelles les peintres dont nous parlons trempent leurs pinceaux sont la lumière et l'ombre même du jour et des deux crépuscules. Les plans, obtenus par les grandes oppositions que devaient rechercher les constructeurs des Cathédrales, n'ont pas seulement un intérêst d'équilibre et de solidité; ils déterminent en outre ces ombres profondes et ces belles lumières qui font a l'édifice un si magnifique vêtement.

P. 3: Ainsi des vastes plans engendrés, dans les monuments gothiques, par la rencontre des arcs diagonaux qui constituent la croisée d'ogives. Quelle élégance dans ces plans si simples et si forts! Grâce a eux l'ombre et la lumière réagissent l'une sur l'autre, produisant cette demi-teinte, principe de la richesse d'effect que nous admirons dans ces amples architectures. Cet effet est tout pictural.

Appendix 30b

Auguste Rodin, 1914

Les Cathédrales de France, p. 97.

Reims. La Cathédrale La Nuit

Des lueurs lointaines rembrunissent, noircissent devant certaines colonnes. Elles en éclairent d'autres de biais, faiblement mais régulièrement.

Mais le fond du choeur et toute la partie gauche de la nef sont plongés dans des ténèbres épaisses. L'effet est horrible à cause de l'indécision des choses dans le lointain éclairé. . . . Tout un espace carré est frappé d'un éclairage formidable; des lumières flambent entre les colonnes qui prennent des proportions colossales. Et les interruptions, ces conflits de clartés et d'ombres, ces quatre colonnes opaques devant moi, ces six autres éclairées plus loin, sur la même ligne et en biais, puis la nuit où je baigne et qui submerge tout, me font douter du temps et des pays. Il n'y a pas de douceur. J'ai la sensation d'être dans un antre immense d'où va se lever Apollon.

Je reste bien longtemps sans pouvoir définir l'horrible vision. Je ne reconnais plus ma religion, ma cathédrale. C'est l'horreur des mystères antiques. . . .

Appendix 30c

Auguste Rodin, 1914

Les Cathédrales de France, p. 159.

Les Moulures

La moulure, dans son esprit, dans son essence, représente, signifie toute la pensée du maitre d'oeuvre.

Qui la voit et la comprend voit le monument.

Sa douceur est celle de la nature elle-même; sa vie la vie de tout l'édifice. Elle contient toute la force de l'architecte, elle exprime toute sa pensée.

Revenons a l'adoration de ce qu'elle a copié autrefois. Elle s'est ingéniée a répandre la grâce douce, la puissance, la souplesse, l'unité.

La femme, éternel modèle, donne ses formes onduleuses.

Ce n'est pas l'ornement, c'est la moulure qui doit être le repos des yeux. Mais elle exprime, en coupe, le caractère de l'époque.—Doucine est bien le nom de la moulure française.

Les moulures se suivent dans l'ordre, les contours lancés se développent comme des mouvements qui parfois se détournent de leur ligne initiale, les nuances se chargent de l'expression locale.

La Renaissance a fait passer la chair adorée de la femme et sa tendresse dans la moulure, dans l'ornement, dans toute l'architecture, cette musique de chair. . . .

Les moulures sont des symphonies douces.

Appendix 31

Conte de Gobineau, 1854

Essai sur l'inégalité des races humaines, II, Paris, 1854, p. 475. The quotation is from the 4th ed. n.d.

Ne méprisant ni les sciences ni les arts, s'associant d'une facon grossière mais active au goût de la noblesse pour la poésie narrative, elles avaient peu conscience de la beauté, et leur intelligence essentiellement attachée à des conquêtes pratiques n'offre guère les côtés brillants du génie italien à ses différentes époques. Cependant l'architecture ogivale leur dut ses plus beaux monuments. Les églises et les hôtels de ville des Flandres et de l'Allemagne occidentale montrent encore que ce fut la forme favorite et particulièrement bien comprise de l'art dans ces régions; cette forme semble avoir correspondu directement à la nature intime de leur génie, qui ne s'en écarta guère sans perdre son originalité.

POSTSCRIPT TO APPENDIX 5

Annali della fabbrica del Duomo di Milano, I, Milan, 1877, p. 209.

Item dicit quod quatuor turres sunt incoeptae pro sustinendo tiburium dictae ecclesiae et non adsunt piloni nec aliud fundamentum habiles pro sustinendo dictas turres, imo si ecclesia esset facta in toto illico cum dictis turribus infalibiliter rueret, super iis vero quod certe per passiones factae sunt per aliquos ygnorantes allegantes quod voltae acutae sunt plus fortes et cum minori onere quam voltae retondae, et plus super aliis propositum est ad voluntatem, quam per viam virtutis; et quod est deterius oppositum est quod scientia geometriae non debet in eis locum habere eo quia scientia est unum et ars est aliud. Dictus magister Johannes dicit quod ars sine scientia nihil est, et quod sive voltae sint acutae sive retondae non habendo fundamentum bonum nihil sunt, et nihilominus quamvis sint acutae habent maximum onus et pondus.

Item dicunt quod turres quos dixerunt sibi velle facere dicunt pluribus rationibus et causis, videlicet, primo pro retificando praedictam ecclesiam et croxieram quod respondent ad quatrangulum secundum ordinem geometriae; alia vero pro fortitudine et pulchritudine tiborii, videlicet quasi per istum exemplum in paradixo Dominus Deus sedet in medio troni, circha tronum sunt quatuor evangelistae secundum Apocalissim, et istae sunt rationes quare sunt incoeptae. Et quamvis non sint fundati duo piloni pro qualibet sacrastia incipiendo super terram, ecclesia est tamen fortis bene istis rationibus, quia reprexae super quibus dicti duo piloni et praedictae reprexae sunt de magnis lapidibus et inclavatis cum clavibus ferri sicut dictum est supra cum aliis capitulis, et quod pondus dictis tribus turribus ponderat ubique super suum quadrum, et erunt aedificatae recte et fortiter, sed rectum non potest cadere; unde dicunt qod fortes per se et ergo dabunt fortitudinem tiburio, quia clausus est in medio illarum, turrium unde dicta ecclesia bene fortis est.

3. .... Item dicunt et respondent in eodem capitulo quod ubi dicit quod scientia geometrica non debet in iis locum habere, dicunt suprascripti quod si hoc testante videlicet per regulam geometriae Aristotulus dixit hominis

autem motus secundum locum quem vocamus lationem, aut reclusus aut circularis aut ex eis mixtus. Item idem dixit alibi omne corpus perfectum est in tribus et motus ipsius et dictae ecclesiae ascendit ad trangulum ut jam declaratum fuit per alios inzignerios, unde dicunt quod omnia sunt per rectam lineam, aut per sextum, ergo concluditur qod quae facta sunt, sunt facta per geometriam et per practicam, quia ipse dixit quod scientia sine arte nihil est; de arte autem jam respnsum est in aliis capitulis.

Index

BY DR. JOSEPHA WEITZMANN-FIEDLER

PERSONS

PLACES

SUBJECTS

PLATES

1. St.-Denis, Ambulatory, 1140-1144 (photo: Franceschi)

2. Lärbro, Gothic Scaffold in the Tower, ca. 1330 (photo: Hahnloser)

3. Canterbury Cathedral, Choir seen from East Transept, after 1174
(photo: Marburg)

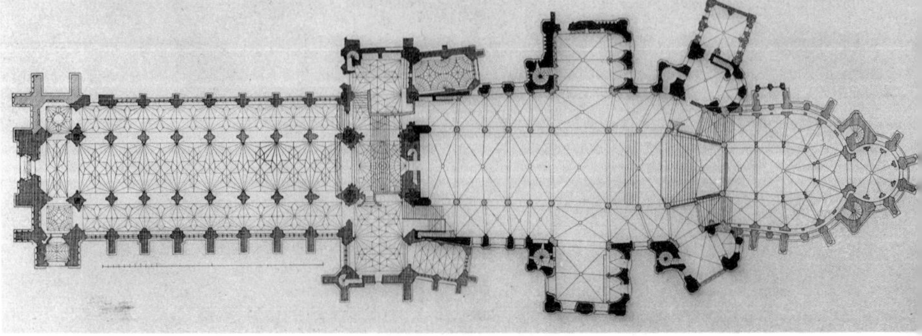

4. Canterbury Cathedral, Ground Plan, after 1174

5. Gerona Cathedral, 1416 (photo: Mas)

6. Chartres Cathedral, Crossing seen from South Transept 1194-ca. 1210; Vault renewed 1316 (photo: Hamann)

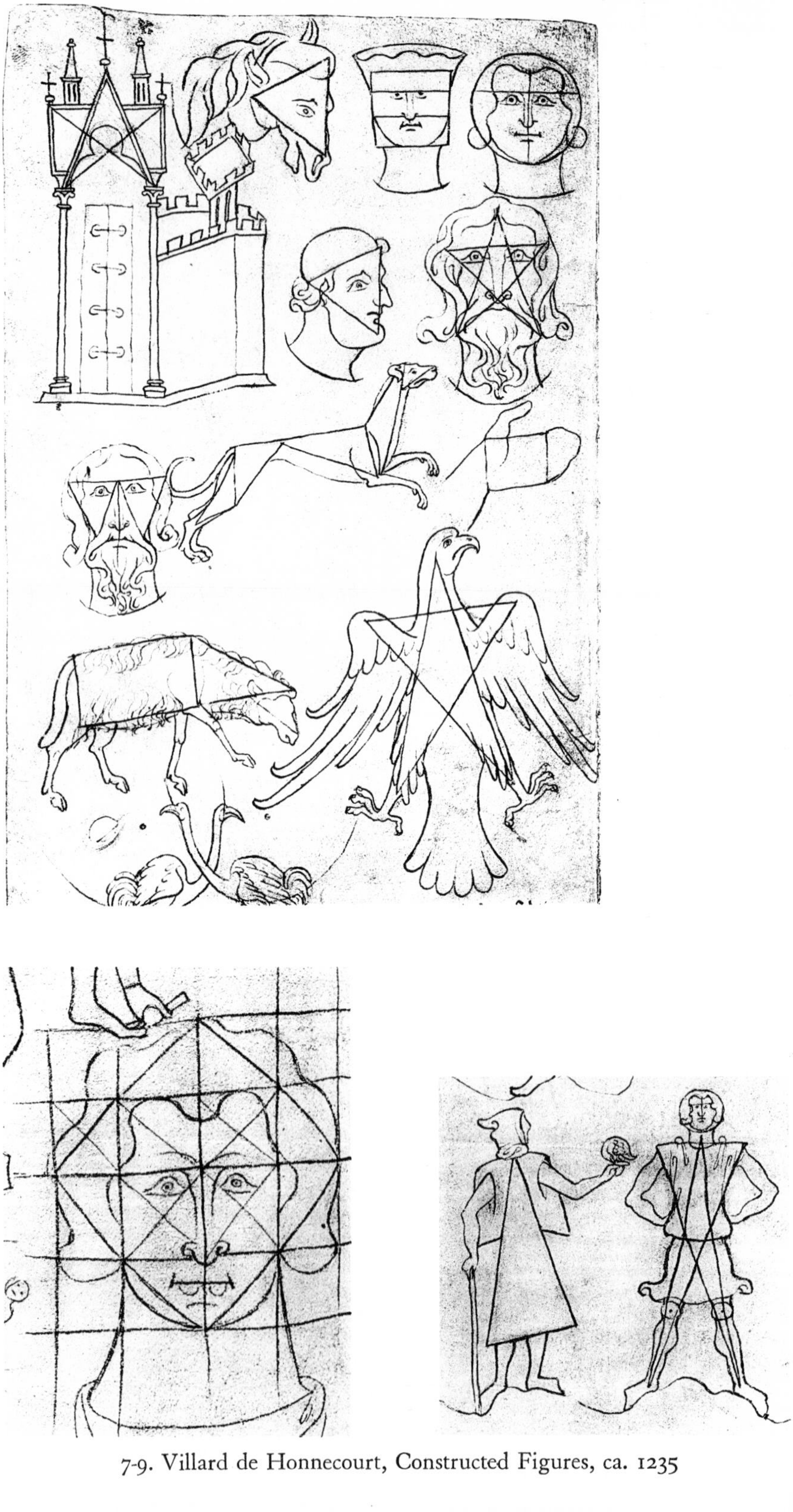

7-9. Villard de Honnecourt, Constructed Figures, ca. 1235

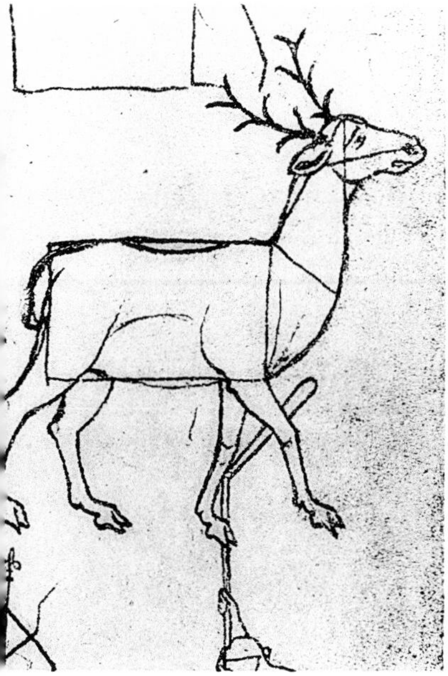

Villard de Honnecourt, Constructed Stag, ca. 1235

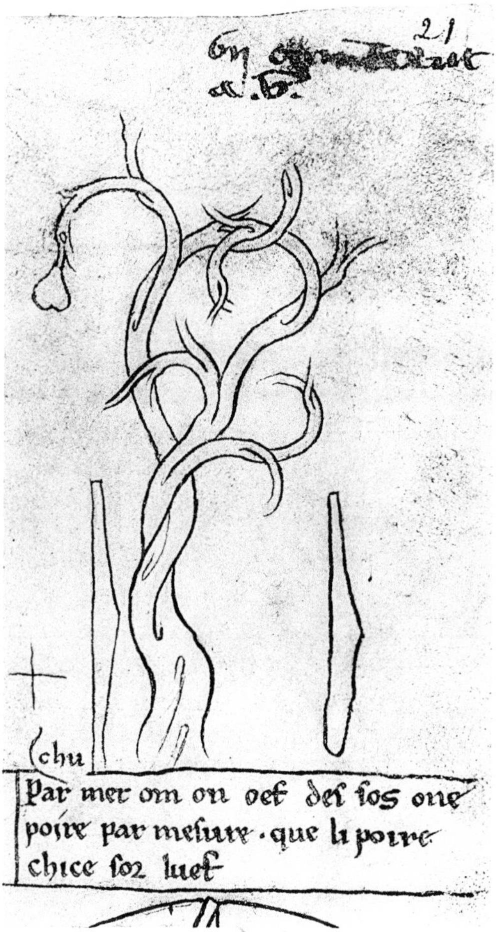
chu
Par mer om on oef del fos one
poire par mesure · que li poire
chice sor luef

11. Villard de Honnecourt, Demonstration of Vertical Projection of a Point, ca. 1235

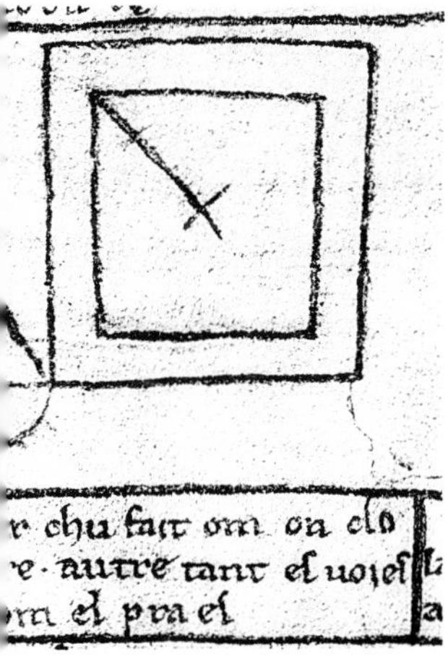

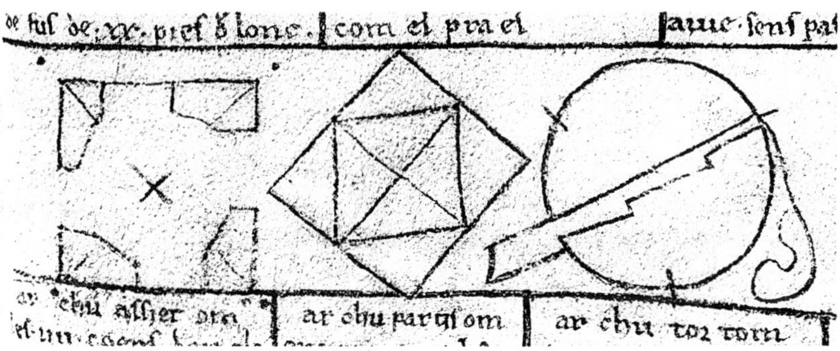

12-13. Magister 2. Quadrature, ca. 1260

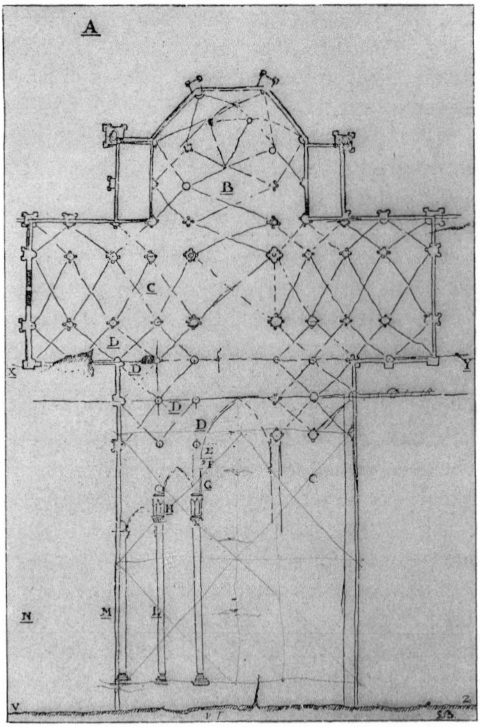

14. Antonio di Vicenzo, Sketch of Ground Plan of Milan Cathedral, 1390

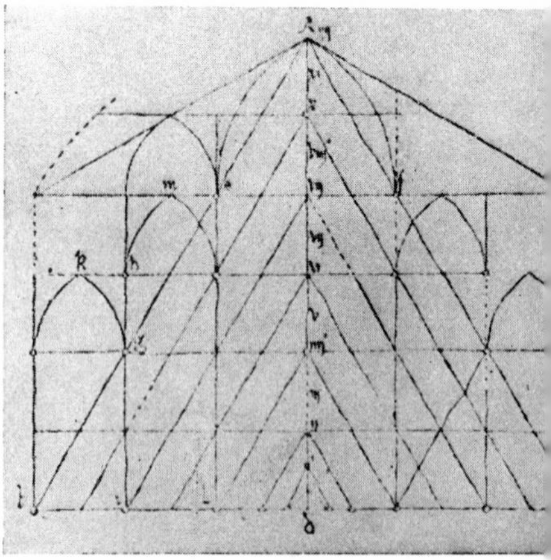

15. Stornaloco, Proposal for the Cro Section of Milan Cathedral, 1391

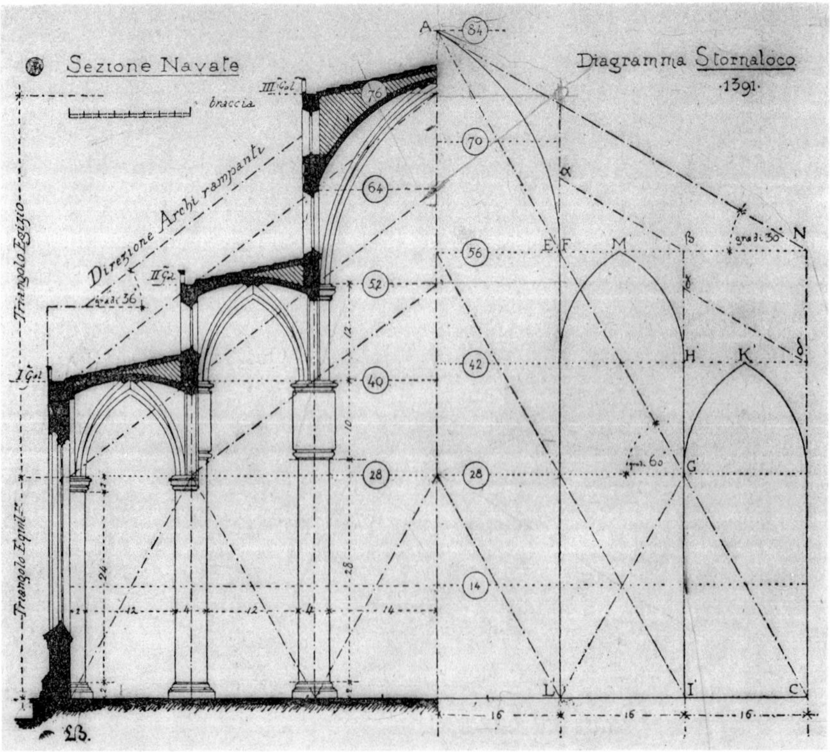

16. Proportions of Milan Cathedral as Proposed by the Session, May 1, 1392; and by Stornaloco, 1391

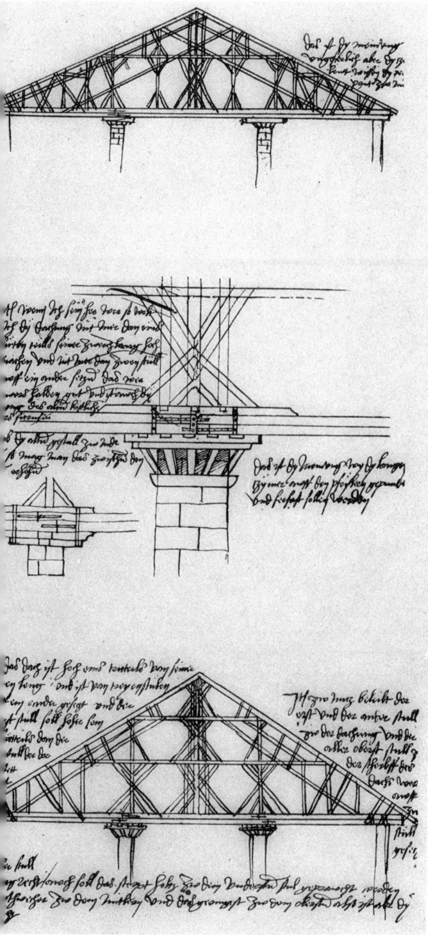

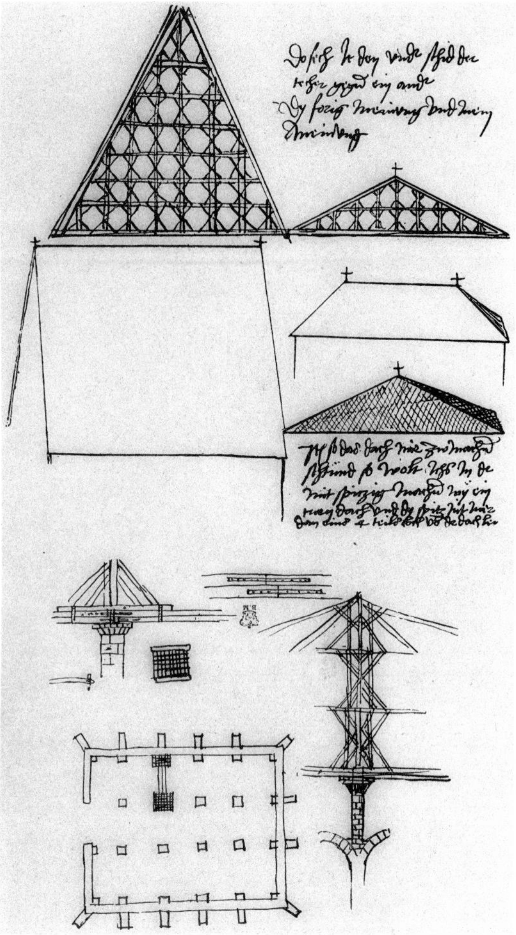

17-18. Albrecht Dürer, Construction of a Roof, Left and Right Halves
London, British Museum, MS III, fols. 45, 147

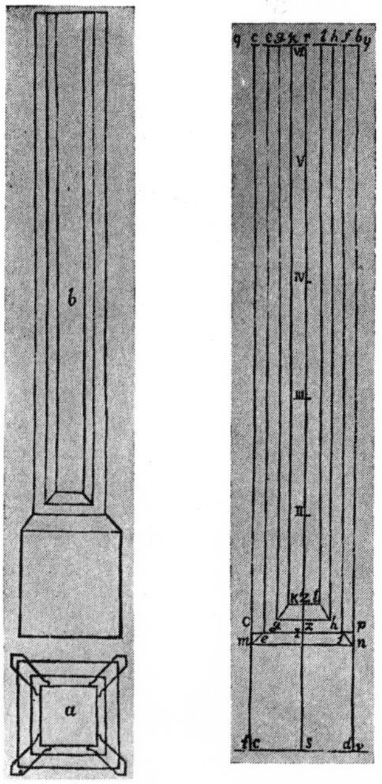

19. Konrad Roritzer, Construction of a Pinnacle, 1486

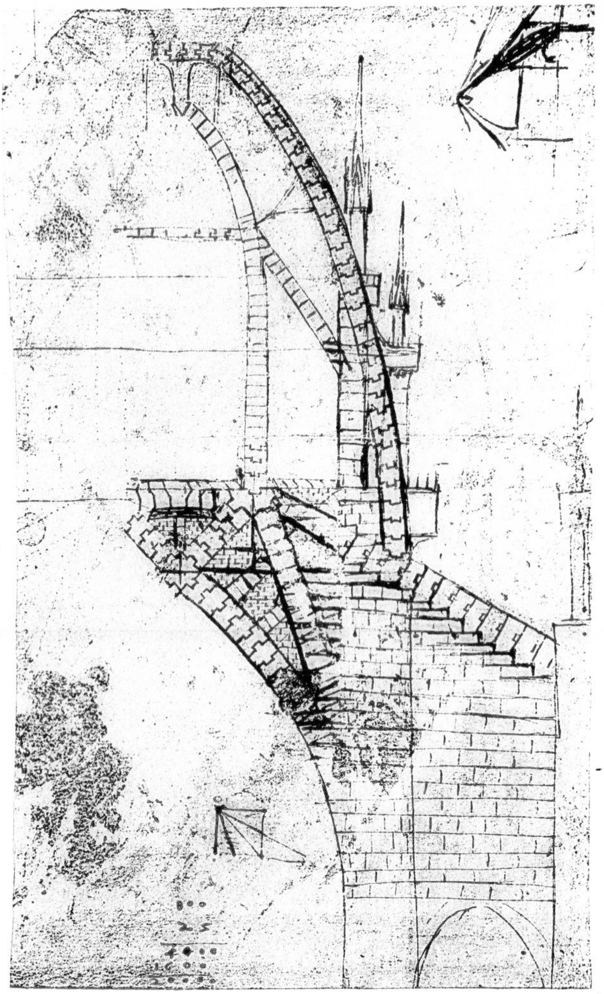

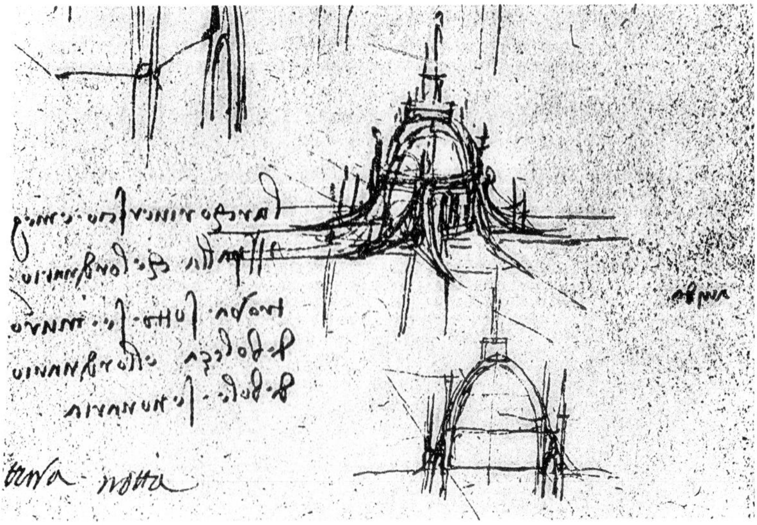

20-21. Leonardo da Vinci, Sketches for the Tiburio of Milan Cathedral, ca. 1460. Cod. Atl. 310a and MS Trivulzio 8a

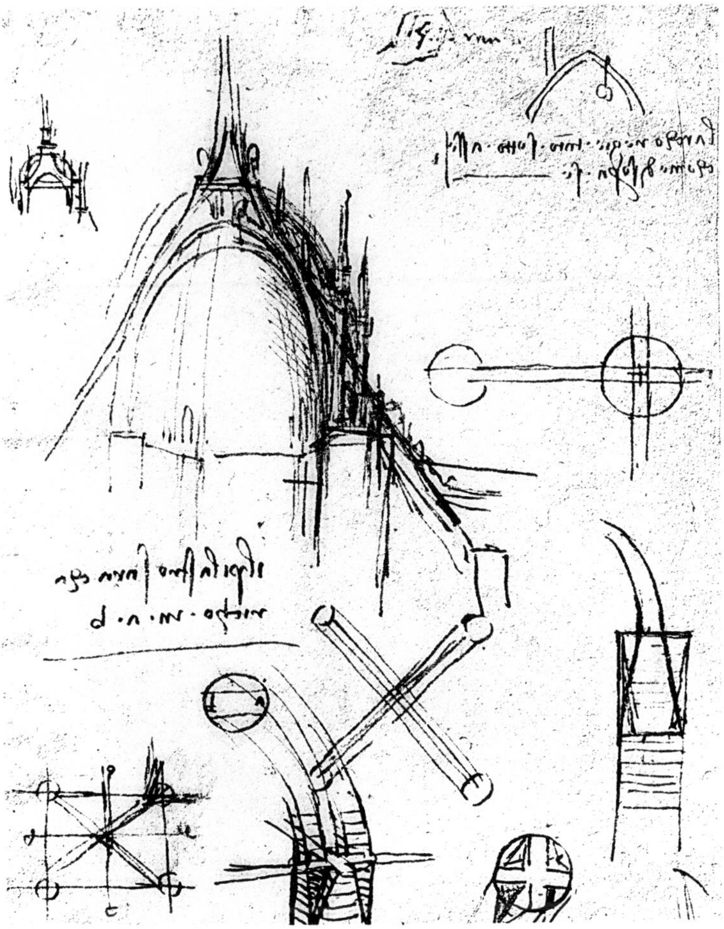

22. Leonardo da Vinci, Sketches for the Tiburio of Milan Cathedral, ca. 1460. MS Trivulzio 22b

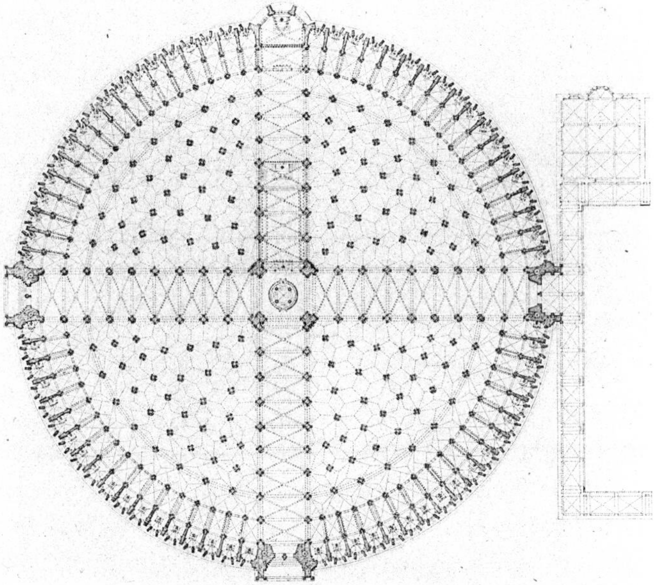

23. Reconstruction of the Temple of the Grail according to Sulpice Boisserée, 1835

24. View of Monte Serrado near Barcelona (photo: Mas)

25. Raphael, *City of Hell*, ca. 1500-1502
(architectural detail), Paris, Louvre

26. Raphael, *La Belle Jardinière*, ca. 1505-1507 (architectural detail) Paris, Louvre

27. Raphael, *Holy Family with the Lamb*, ca. 1500 (architectural detail), ca. 1500. Madrid, Prado

28. Raphael, *The Dream of Scipio*, ca. 1500 (architectural detail)
London, National Gallery

29. Raphael, *Madonna in the Meadow*, ca. 1505 (architectural detail)
Vienna, Kunsthistorisches Museum

30. Raphael, *Terranuova Madonna*, ca. 1505 (architectural detail)
Berlin, Dahlem

31. Raphael, *Canigiani Holy Family*, ca. 1507 (architectural detail)
Munich, Ältere Pinakothek

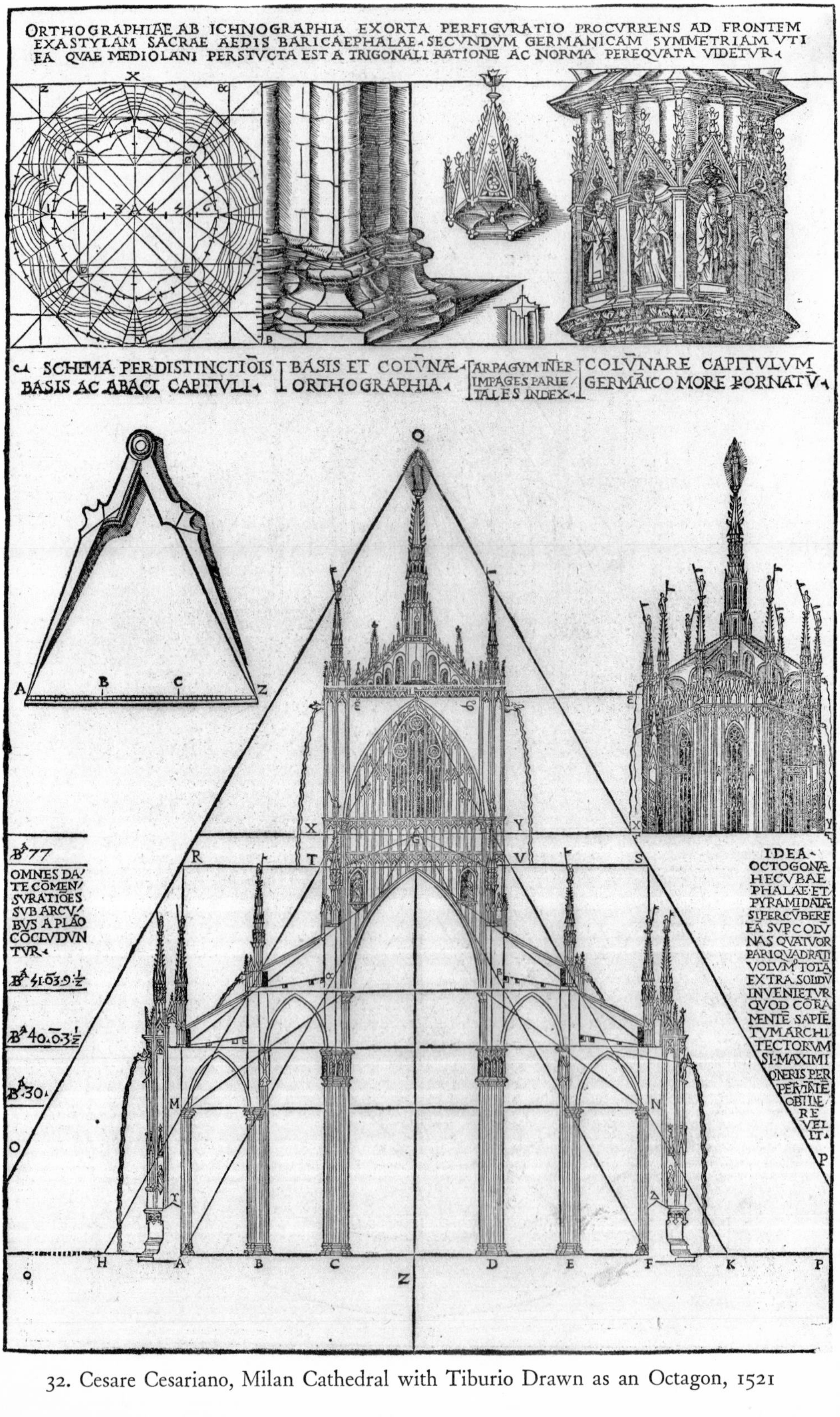
ORTHOGRAPHIAE AB ICHNOGRAPHIA EXORTA PERFIGVRATIO PROCVRRENS AD FRONTEM
EXASTYLAM SACRAE AEDIS BARICAEPHALAE. SECVNDVM GERMANICAM SYMMETRIAM VTI
EA QVAE MEDIOLANI PERSTVCTA EST A TRIGONALI RATIONE AC NORMA PEREQVATA VIDETVR.
SCHEMA PERDISTINCTIŌIS BASIS AC ABACI CAPITVLI.
BASIS ET COLVNÆ ORTHOGRAPHIA.
ARPAGYM INĒR IMPAGES PARIETALES INDEX.
COLVNARE CAPITVLVM GERMĀICO MORE ĒORNATV.
OMNES DATE CŌMENSVRATIŌES SVB ARCVBVS A PLĀO COCLVDVNTVR.
IDEA OCTOGONÆ HECVBAE PHALAE ET PYRAMIDATÆ SIPERCVBERE EA SVP COLVNAS QVATVOR PARI QVADRATI VOLVMĒ TOTA EXTRA SOLIDV INVENIETVR QVOD CORĀ MENTE SAPIĒTVM ARCHITECTORVM SI MAXIMI ONERIS PERPETVITATE OBTINERE VELIT.

32. Cesare Cesariano, Milan Cathedral with Tiburio Drawn as an Octagon, 1521

33. Albrecht Dürer, *Annunciation*, 1526. Chantilly

34. Sebastiano Serlio, *Scena Comica*, 1547

35. Sebastiano Serlio, *Scena Tragica*, 1547

36. Sebastiano Serlio, *Scena Satyrica*, 1547

37. Baldassare Peruzzi, Design for the Stage, 1521

38-39. Baldassare Peruzzi, Designs for S. Petronio. Bologna, 1521

40. Giulio Romano, Design for S. Petronio. Bologna, 1546

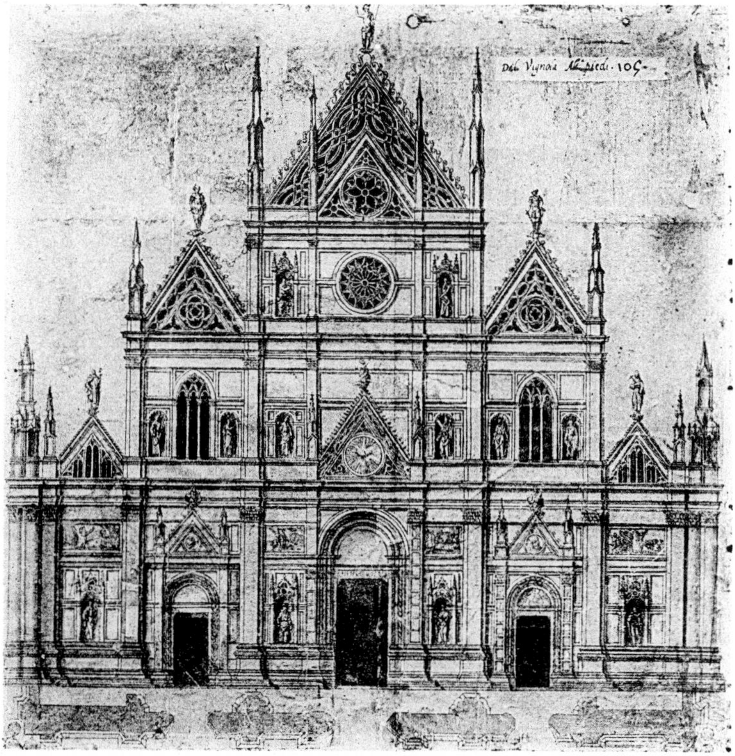

41. Giacomo Barozzi Vignola, Design for S. Petronio
Bologna, 1543-1546

42. Domenico Tibaldi, Design for S. Petronio, Bologna, 1546

43. Francesco Terribilia, Design for S. Petronio. Bologna, 1580

44. Albrecht Dürer, Architectural Sketches, 1277v, ca. 1495
Berlin, Kupferstichkabinet

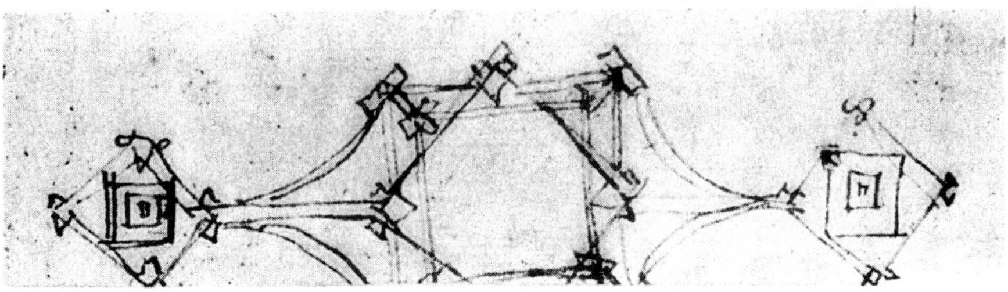

45. Albrecht Dürer, Ground Plan. Veste Coburg, T38, ca. 1492

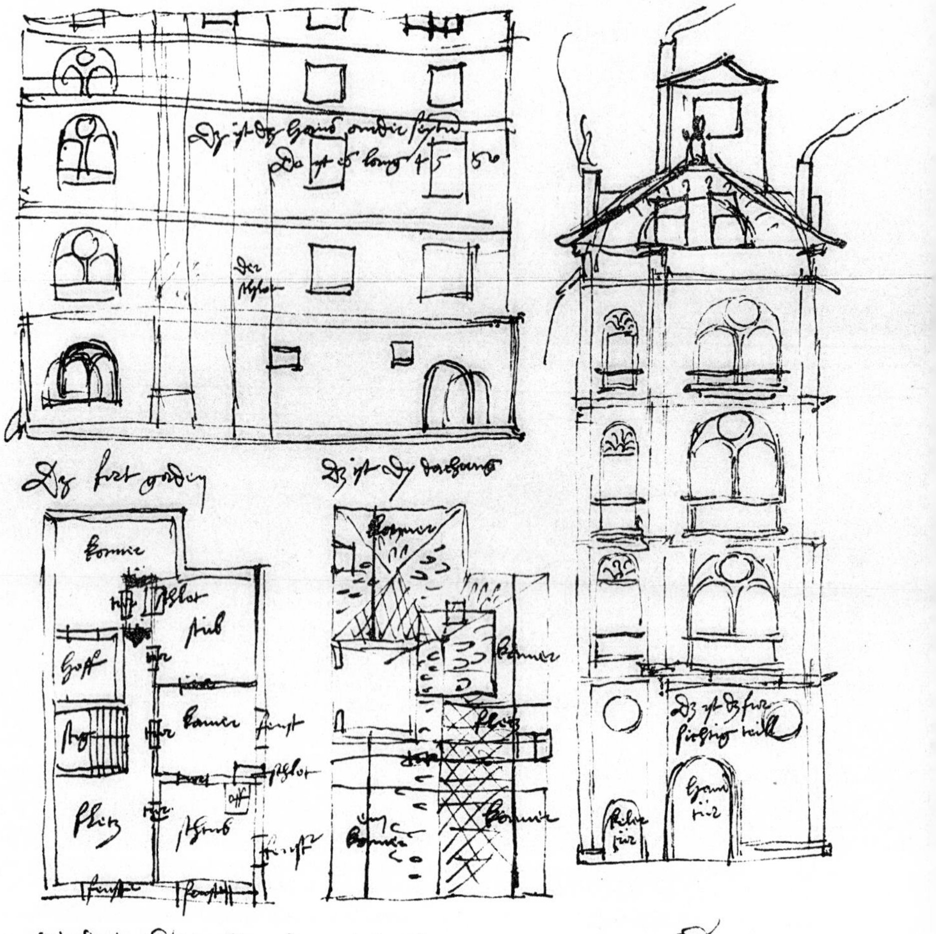

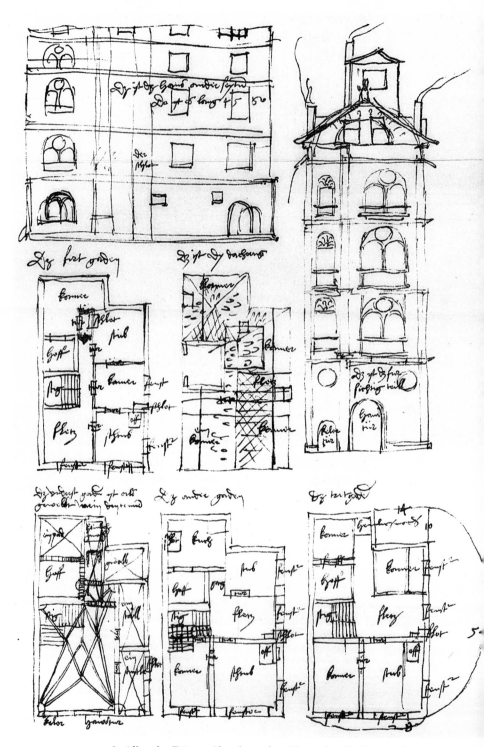

46. Albrecht Dürer, Sketches of a House in Venice, 1506
London, British Museum, MS II, fol. 167

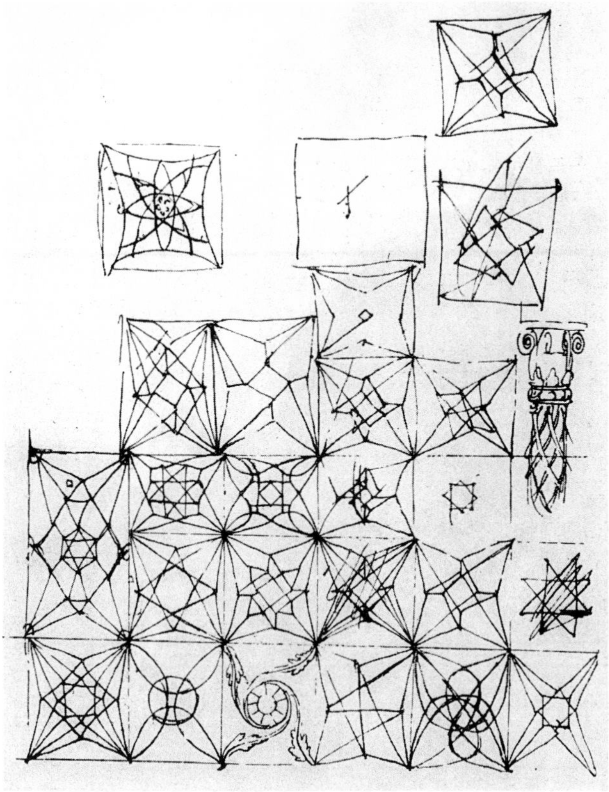

47. Albrecht Dürer, Sketches of Star Vaults
London, British Museum, MS II, fol. 167v

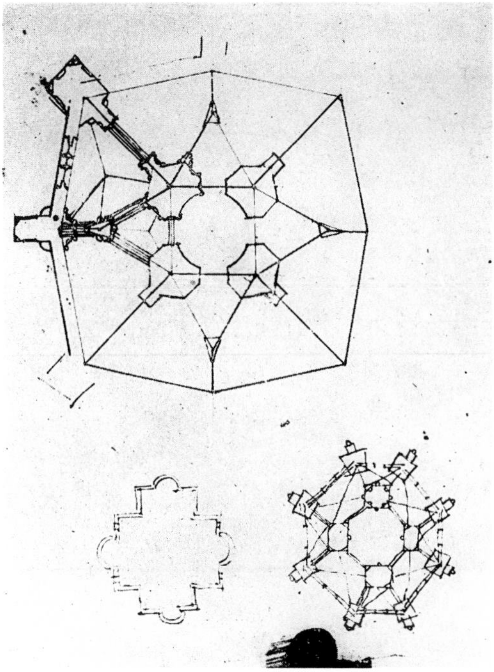

48. Albrecht Dürer, Ground Plan. London,
British Museum, MS Sloan 5229, fol. 171r

49. Wendel Dietterlin, Architectural Fantasy from *Architectura*, 1598, pl. 202

50. Wendel Dietterlin, Architectural Fantasy from *Architectura*, 1598, pl. 24

W. Hollar fecit 1645
TVRRIS ET ÆDES ECCLESIÆ CATHEDRALIS ARGENTINENSIS.
à Wenceslao Hollar Bohemo, primo ad vivum delineata, et aquæ forti æri insculpta, A°. 1630. denuoq facta Antverpiæ, A°. 1645.

51. Wenzel Hollar, Strasbourg Cathedral from the North, 1645

52. Frontispiece to *Essai sur l'architecture*, 1752
by Marc Antoine Laugier

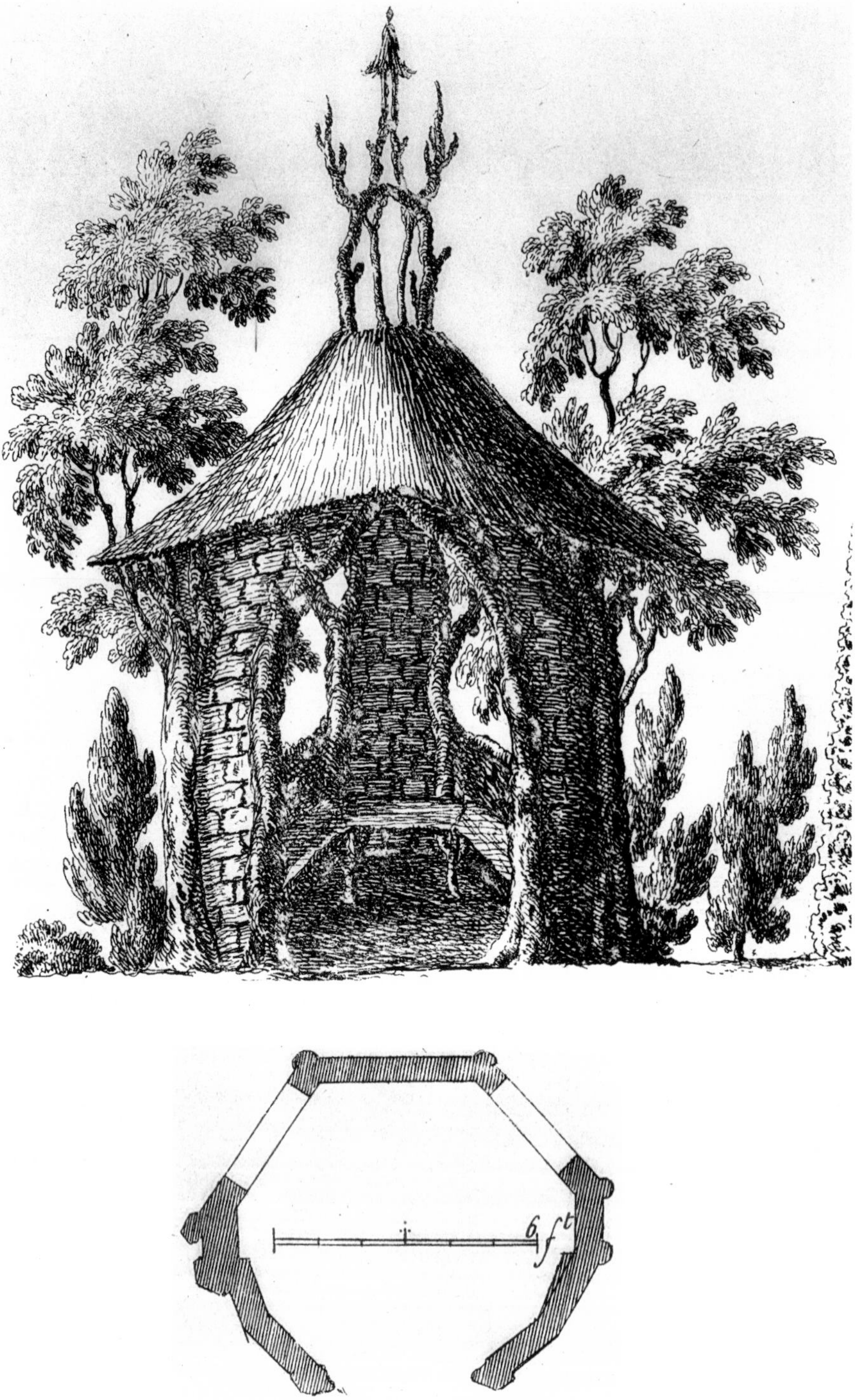

53. Paul Decker, Gothic Arbor, 1759

54. Frontispiece to *Essay on the Origin, History, and Principles of Gothic Architecture* by James Hall, London, 1813

'VRRIS ALTIOR TEMPLI ARGENTORA-ENSIS, MIRABILE OPVS, CAPVT INTER NVBILA CONDENS, SE-ptem mundi mirabilibus, octauo loco adiungitur. In superiore parte turris, ubi est initium Galeæ & fastigii turris, leguntur hæc Christianissima Axiomata, per circulum turris lapidibus incisa.

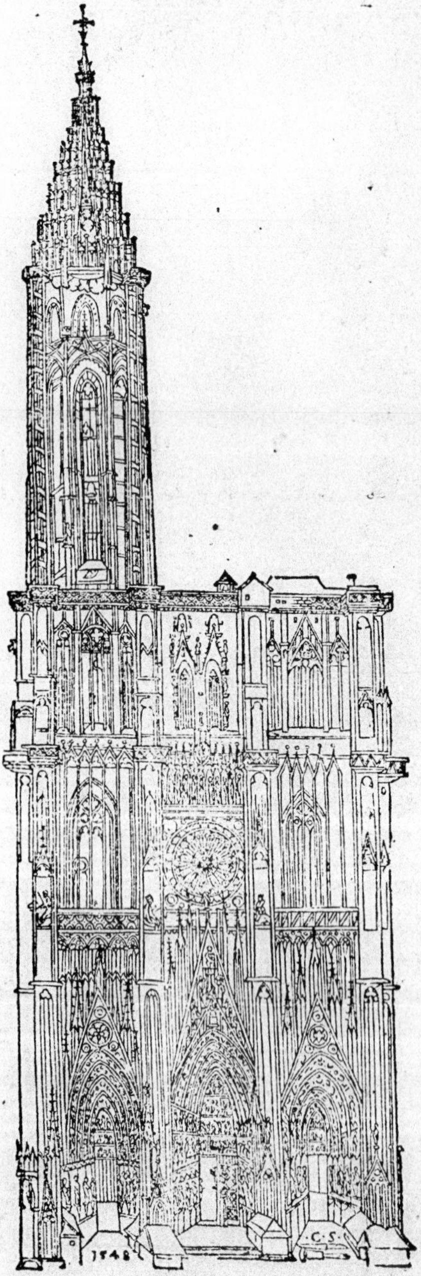

Ad Orientem.

Christus glorificat. *Christus cunctis donat.*

Ad Septentrionem.

Christus coronat. *Christus & superat.*

Ad Occidentem.

Christus rex triumphat. *Christus semper regnat.*

Ad Meridiem.

Christus & imperat. *Christus nos renouat.*

Das acht wunder der Welt der Münsterthurn zů Straßburg.

ANno/1015. hat Berengarius der erst/ Bischoff zů Straßburg/ das fundament legen lassen.

ANno/ 1277. vnder Bischoff Conraden von Liechtenberg hat Erckwin võ Steinbach die Thürn angefangen zů bauwen/ vnd biß auff die vier schnecken bracht/ biß man zalt 1384.

DAs vberig biß vnder die Kron/ haben die lobwirdigen Junckherrn von Prag außgemacht.

ANno/ 1548. hats Conrad Morant von Basel/ Burger zů Straßburg dem lieben Vatterland zů lob/ vnnd allen werckmeistern Teütscher Nation zů besonderm wolgefallen/ abconterfät.

Mit R. K. Ma. freiheit auff acht jar/ nit nach zů trucken/ bey peen zehen marck lötigs Golds

55. Conrad Morant, Strasbourg Cathedral, 1548

56. Façade of Strasbourg Cathedral (photo: Hamann)

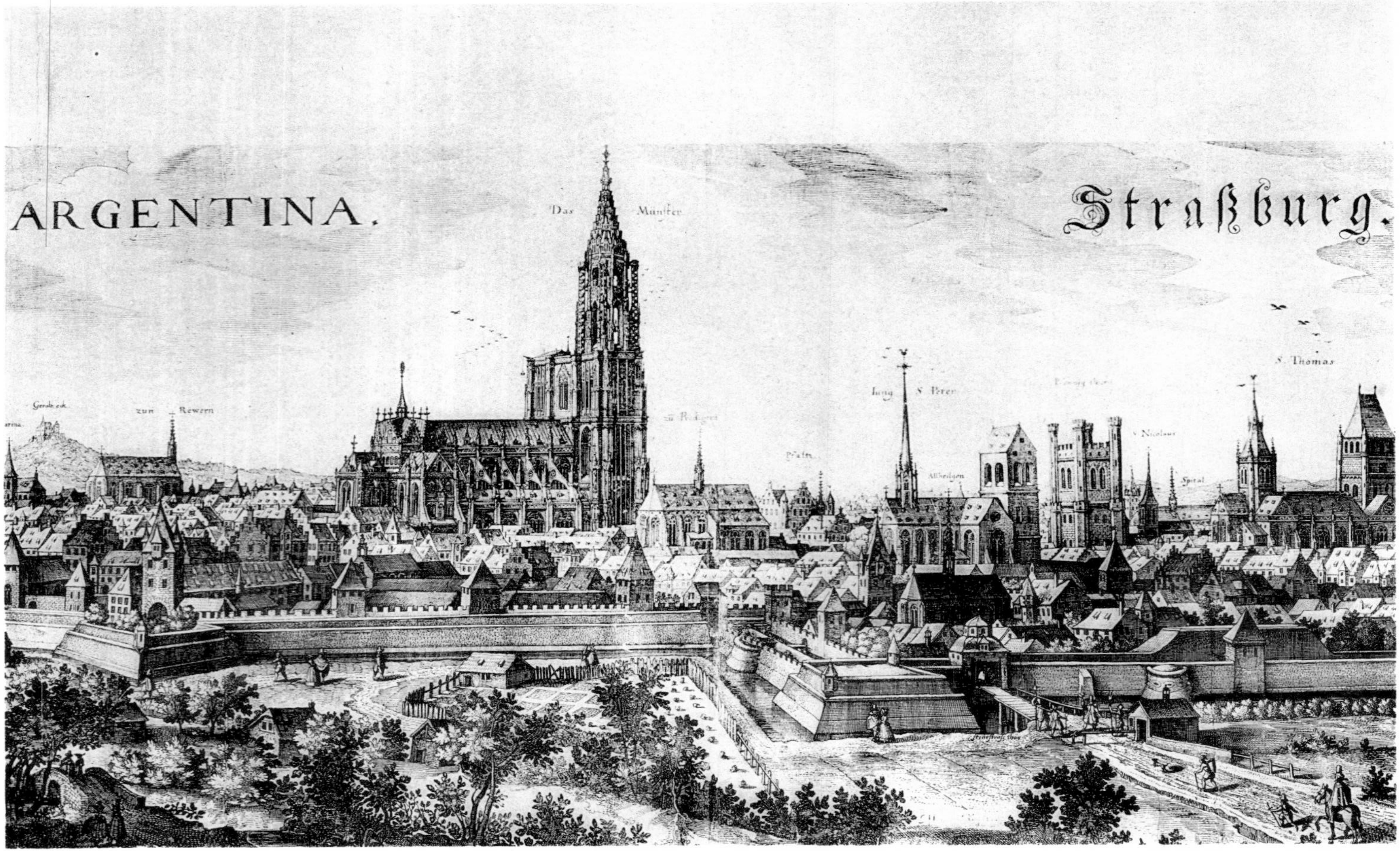

57. Matthias Merian, Strasbourg, 1548

8.75